			House			
Winner's Electoral College Vote %	Winner's Popular Vote %	Congress	Majority Party	Minority Party	Party	ʲity Party
**	No popular vote	1st	38 Admin †	26 Opp	17 Admin	9 Opp
		2nd	37 Fed ††	33 Dem-R	16 Fed	13 Dem-R
**	No popular vote	3rd	57 Dem-R	48 Fed	17 Fed	13 Dem-R
		4th	54 Fed	52 Dem-R	19 Fed	13 Dem-R
**	No popular vote	5th	58 Fed	48 Dem-R	20 Fed	12 Dem-R
		6th	64 Fed	42 Dem-R	19 Fed	13 Dem-R
HR**	No popular vote	7th	69 Dem-R	36 Fed	18 Dem-R	13 Fed
		8th	402 Dem-R	39 Fed	25 Dem-R	9 Fed
92.0	No popular vote	9th	116 Dem-R	25 Fed	27 Dem-R	7 Fed
		10th	118 Dem-R	24 Fed	28 Dem-R	6 Fed
69.7		11th	94 Dem-R	48 Fed	28 Dem-R	6 Fed
		12th	108 Dem-R	36 Fed	30 Dem-R	6 Fed
59.0	No popular vote	13th	112 Dem-R	68 Fed	27 Dem-R	9 Fed
		14th	117 Dem-R	65 Fed	25 Dem-R	11 Fed
84.3	No popular vote	15th	141 Dem-R	42 Fed	34 Dem-R	10 Fed
		16th	156 Dem-R	27 Fed	35 Dem-R	7 Fed
99.5	No popular vote	17th	158 Dem-R	25 Fed	44 Dem-R	4 Fed
		18th	187 Dem-R	26 Fed	44 Dem-R	4 Fed
HR	39.1 †††	19th	105 Admin	97 Dem-J	26 Admin	20 Dem-J
		20th	119 Dem-J	94 Admin	28 Dem-J	20 Admin
68.2	56.0	21st	139 Dem	74 Nat R	26 Dem	22 Nat R
		22nd	141 Dem	58 Nat R	25 Dem	21 Nat R
76.6	54.5	23rd	147 Dem	53 AntiMas	20 Dem	20 Nat R
		24th	145 Dem	98 Whig	27 Dem	25 Whig
57.8	50.9	25th	108 Dem	107 Whig	30 Dem	18 Whig
		26th	124 Dem	118 Whig	28 Dem	22 Whig
79.6	52.9					
–	52.9	27th	133 Whig	102 Dem	28 Whig	22 Dem
		28th	142 Dem	79 Whig	28 Whig	25 Dem
61.8	49.6	29th	143 Dem	77 Whig	31 Dem	25 Whig
		30th	115 Whig	108 Dem	36 Dem	21 Whig
56.2	47.3	31st	112 Dem	109 Whig	35 Dem	25 Whig
–	–	32nd	140 Dem	88 Whig	35 Dem	24 Whig
85.8	50.9	33rd	159 Dem	71 Whig	38 Dem	22 Whig
		34th	108 Rep	83 Dem	40 Dem	15 Rep
58.8	45.6	35th	118 Dem	92 Rep	36 Dem	20 Rep
		36th	114 Rep	92 Dem	36 Dem	26 Rep
59.4	39.8	37th	105 Rep	43 Dem	31 Rep	10 Dem
		38th	102 Rep	75 Dem	36 Rep	9 Dem
91.0	55.2					
–	–	39th	149 Union	42 Dem	42 Union	10 Dem
		40th	143 Rep	49 Dem	42 Rep	11 Dem
72.8	52.7	41st	149 Rep	63 Dem	56 Rep	11 Dem
		42nd	134 Rep	104 Dem	52 Rep	17 Dem
81.9	55.6	43rd	194 Rep	92 Dem	49 Rep	19 Dem
		44th	169 Rep	109 Dem	45 Rep	29 Dem
50.1	47.9 †††	45th	153 Dem	140 Rep	39 Rep	36 Dem
		46th	149 Dem	130 Rep	42 Dem	33 Rep
58.0	48.3	47th	147 Rep	135 Dem	37 Rep	37 Dem
–	–	48th	197 Dem	118 Rep	38 Rep	36 Dem
54.6	48.5	49th	183 Dem	140 Rep	43 Rep	34 Dem
		50th	169 Dem	152 Rep	39 Rep	37 Dem

Source for election data: Svend Peterson, *A Statistical History of American Presidential Elections*. New York: Frederick Ungar Publishing, 1963. Updates: Richard Scammon, *America Votes* 19. Washington D.C.: Congressional Quarterly, 1991; *Congressional Quarterly Weekly Report*, Nov. 7, 1992, p. 3552.

Abbreviations:

Admin = Administration supporters
AntiMas = Anti-Masonic
Dem = Democratic
Dem-R = Democratic-Republican
Fed = Federalist

Dem-J = Jacksonian Democrats
Nat R = National Republican
Opp = Opponents of administration
Rep = Republican
Union = Unionist

UNDERSTANDING AMERICAN GOVERNMENT, ALTERNATE EDITION

TWELFTH EDITION

Understanding
American Government
ALTERNATE EDITION

SUSAN WELCH
The Pennsylvania State University

JOHN GRUHL
University of Nebraska–Lincoln

JOHN COMER
University of Nebraska–Lincoln

SUSAN M. RIGDON
University of Illinois at Urbana–Champaign

WADSWORTH
CENGAGE Learning™

Australia • Brazil • Japan • Korea • Mexico • Singapore • Spain • United Kingdom • United States

Understanding American Government, Alternate Edition

Susan Welch, John Gruhl, John Comer, Susan M. Rigdon

Sponsoring Acquisitions Editor: Edwin Hill

Development Editor: Rebecca Green

Assistant Editor: Kate MacLean

Editorial Assistant: Matthew DiGangi

Associate Development Manager: Caitlin Holroyd

Marketing Manager: Amy Whitaker

Marketing Communications Manager: Heather Baxley

Senior Content Project Manager: Josh Allen

Art Director: Linda Helcher

Print Buyer: Rebecca Cross

Permissions Editor: Margaret Chamberlain-Gaston

Production Service: The Book Company

Photo Researcher: Katharine S. Cebik

Internal designer: Mike Stratton

Cover illustration: © Paul Giovanopoulos

Compositor: Graphic World, Inc.

For product information and technology assistance, contact us at **Cengage Learning Customer & Sales Support, 1-800-354-9706**

For permission to use material from this text or product, submit all requests online at **www.cengage.com/permissions**.

Further permissions questions can be emailed to **permissionrequest@cengage.com**.

Library of Congress Control Number: 2008943013

Student Edition:
ISBN-13: 978-0-495-56839-1
ISBN-10: 0-495-56839-2

Alternate Edition:
ISBN-13: 978-0-495-56840-7
ISBN-10: 0-495-56840-6

Wadsworth
20 Channel Center Street
Boston, MA 02210
USA

Cengage Learning products are represented in Canada by Nelson Education, Ltd.

For your course and learning solutions, visit **www.cengage.com**.

Purchase any of our products at your local college store or at our preferred online store **www.ichapters.com**.

Printed in Canada
1 2 3 4 5 6 7 13 12 11 10 09

BRIEF CONTENTS

CONTENTS

PART TWO

Links between People and Government

PART THREE

Institutions

PART FOUR

Civil Liberties and Rights

Martin Luther King once said that the civil rights movement would not just change the lives of black people, but it would change the soul of America. The tears of joy shed by millions of people, black and white alike, on November 4 revealed that America has changed profoundly. Older African Americans who during their lifetimes had seen friends and neighbors murdered because they fought to integrate public facilities or claim the right to vote, or simply failed to pay adequate deference to whites; middle-aged African Americans who have seen much progress in race relations in the United States but never believed they would live to see a black president; young people of all races who were inspired by a new voice and face in American politics; and the white Americans who believed, as did both Martin Luther King and Barack Obama, that there are millions of white Americans who believe in equality: all of these groups and more celebrated the victory of Barack Hussein Obama. The acknowledgment by President George W. Bush, John McCain, and many other Republicans that this was an historic step forward for America added to the feeling of change.

But of course, this election may not have changed as much as we think. Racism and conflict have not disappeared. Millions of voters were bitterly disappointed by the election outcome because they had different views of the direction the country should take. Moreover, the essential nature of American politics is not going to change. And President-elect Obama cannot possibly live up to all the expectations and hopes of his supporters. In other words, the election of America's first black president does not eradicate the serious problems that our country faces nor the divisions over what the remedies should be.

Obama was not successful because Americans simply decided it was time to have a black president. Rather, his election was a result of his own well-organized and technologically savvy campaign launched in what was widely seen to be a Democratic year. His organization focused on mobilizing new voters and keeping in frequent touch with them through technology. Through the same technology, he motivated millions to give time and money.

But all that might not have been successful if it had not been a Democratic year. That is, political scientists argue that the election outcome can usually be predicted far in advance of the election by a few things: the state of the economy, the popularity of the incumbent, and the number of terms the incumbent party has served (voters like change). The unpopularity of President Bush and a slowing economy, which took a nosedive in October, set the stage for the Obama campaign's ability to persuade voters that this young senator was the best choice.

Despite the historic and unprecedented election, which included the first woman who was able to win millions of votes and many primaries, and the Republican party's first female vice-presidential candidate, we hope students reading this book will come to understand that much about politics is predictable and rooted in the larger principles of government and political culture. We want to convey to students, whether they are taking this course as an elective or a requirement, why it is important for every American to understand how our government functions. We hope they find that it is also an interesting and often exciting subject that has relevance to almost every aspect of their lives.

We believe an introductory course succeeds if most students develop an understanding of the major concepts of our form of government, an interest in learning more about politics, and an ability to analyze political issues and evaluate the news. Students should come out of an introductory course with a firm grounding in the essential "nuts and bolts" of American government, but it is also crucial that they understand the political environment in which government functions. We offer the essentials of American government, but we also want the student to understand why (and sometimes how) these important features have evolved, their impact on individual citizens' relationship with government, and why they are sometimes controversial and worth learning about. For example, we prefer that students leave the course remembering why government tries to regulate corporations, how it does so, and the political factors that lead to stronger or weaker regulations rather than memorizing specific regulatory acts. The latter will change or soon be forgotten, but understanding the "whys" will help the student understand the issues long after the course is over.

We have also tried to interest students by describing and discussing the impact of various features of government. For example, students who do not understand why learning about voter registration laws is important may "see the light" when they understand the link between such laws and low voter turnout.

Therefore, a particular emphasis throughout the book is on the *impact* of government: how individual features of government affect its responsiveness to different groups (in Lasswell's terms, "Who gets what and why?"). We realize that nothing in American politics is simple; rarely does one feature of government produce, by itself, a clear outcome. Nevertheless, we think that students will be more willing to learn about government if they see a relationship between how government operates and the impact it has on them as American citizens.

We also focus on *responsiveness* of government. In a democracy, we assume government is responsive to the citizens, primarily through elections. But some of the constitutional features of our government, the systems of checks and balances, make it, by design, less than responsive. And other features of contemporary politics in this incredibly diverse country also limit responsiveness.

We hope a greater understanding of and appreciation for American government may encourage those not already engaged in civic and political activities to become more active citizens. Though students did vote at a higher rate in 2004 and 2008 than they have in decades, a 2006 survey by the National Constitution Center found that more teenagers could identify the Three Stooges (59 percent) than could name the three branches of government, six times as many knew the hometown of Bart Simpson than knew where Abraham Lincoln came from, and not even 2 percent could correctly identify James Madison.

The Organization and Contents of the Book

Although the basic organization of American government books is fairly standard, our text has a unique chapter on money and politics. Other features include a civil rights chapter that integrates a thorough treatment of constitutional issues concerning minorities and women, a discussion of the civil rights and women's rights movements, and contemporary research on the political status of these groups. We include in this chapter the special legal problems of Hispanics and Native Americans.

This alternate edition is for instructors who prefer not to use any of the policy chapters. The book stands as a whole without them because many policy examples are integrated into the rest of the text.

The organization of the book is straightforward. After material on democracy, the Constitution, and federalism, the book covers linkages, including money and politics, then institutions. Civil liberties and rights are treated after the chapter on the judiciary.

But the book is flexible enough that instructors can modify the order of the chapters. Some instructors will prefer to cover institutions before process. Others may prefer to discuss civil liberties and rights when discussing the Constitution.

Changes in the Twelfth Edition

The historic 2008 presidential election and the issues leading up to it provide new examples and areas of inquiry for those interested in American government. The plummeting of presidential popularity, the continuing war in Iraq, and the seeming freefall of the economy all set the stage for intensely fought primary elections in both parties and for a general election campaign that engaged a higher level of interest than in recent elections. The 2008 elections, including the outcome, are covered in several chapters, although the book went to press before President-elect Obama had taken office.

The text of every chapter has been substantially revised. We have comprehensively revised, rewritten, and reorganized Chapter 6 on interest groups. Though streamlined, it includes expanded coverage of why people join interest groups, the influence of the Christian Right, and the role of lobbyists in the 2008 election campaign. Chapter 7, on political parties, has also undergone a major revision in this edition. In addition to a reorganization, we address in more detail the party affiliations of Asian Americans. Chapter 2 includes a new treatment of the Founders' religious views and their impact on the Constitution; and in Chapter 8 the Electoral College and its strategic implications are given a revised interpretation. These are just a few examples of the constant updating and rethinking that has gone into the text.

Throughout, we have also replaced photos and cartoons to complement the new material and to give students a chance to learn through graphic as well as textual material. As always, we have updated the judiciary, civil liberties, and civil rights chapters to incorporate new Supreme Court decisions. Expanded treatment of gay rights appears in the chapters on interest groups and civil rights. The book has been updated throughout to reflect new public policy developments.

New Features

"**Talking Points**," short descriptions of a situation that lead students to consider a major feature of government, open each chapter. For example, in Chapter 14, the perspective of the photographer who took the photos that received worldwide publicity provides new insight into the violations committed at Abu Ghraib by American soldiers and their leaders. In Chapter 9, on money and politics, Talking Points focus on Barack Obama's decision to reject public funding for his presidential campaign and the impact that has on our campaign finance regulatory system.

Behind the Scenes boxes are also new. These boxes focus on an aspect of politics not likely to be widely publicized, but which have interest to students and importance to the institution or process discussed. For example, in Chapter 4, "Public Opinion," the impact on getting accurate results in surveys of a new generation of potential survey respondents who have cell phones but not land lines is explored. A Behind the Scenes box, "The Rope Line," in Chapter 8, "Elections," uses examples from the 2008 campaign to describe the rare spontaneous interchanges between candidates and their supporters on the rope lines following stump speeches and other campaign events. Anti-Semitism on the Supreme Court in the early twentieth century is the subject of a Behind the Scenes feature in the judiciary chapter (Chapter 13).

Ethical Dilemmas boxes describe situations that pose ethical issues and ask students to decide whether the behavior is ethical. For example, Chapter 3, which deals with federalism, focuses on the ethical dilemmas of using lotteries and other state-authorized forms of gambling to raise revenue. The chapter on Congress (Chapter 10) describes a situation in which members of Congress have a direct financial interest in companies or industries that their committees regulate. The national archivist, caught between professional obligations to make historical documents available to the public and the administration's wish to classify tens of thousands of historical documents, many of which had already been made public, is the subject of the ethical dilemmas feature in Chapter 12 on the bureaucracy.

Constitution icons, ⭐, appear when the text of the Constitution is referred to, making it easy to reference the document in the appendix and to see how the Constitution deals with the topic at hand. The purpose of this is to call students' attention to the ways in which this founding document shapes our institutions and processes.

Democracy? questions ask students to consider how democratic a particular process or institution is. This feature is intended to alert students to the fact that democracy is not a simple concept and that our Constitution and our practices include both democratic and undemocratic features.

Key names have been added to the key terms at the end of the chapter.

We are delighted to have the opportunity to write this twelfth edition and to improve the text further in ways suggested by our students and readers. We have been extremely pleased by the reaction of instructors and students to our first eleven editions. We were especially gratified to have won three times the American Government Textbook Award from the Women's Caucus for Political Science of the American Political Science Association.

Additional Special Features

Student interest and analytic abilities grow when confronted with a clash of views about important issues. Today there is much discussion about how to stimulate the critical-thinking abilities of students. Beginning with the first edition, our text has provided features especially designed to do this by involving students in the controversies—and excitement—of American politics.

In addition to the new features described above, this edition contains the following features continued from earlier editions.

Government Responsiveness

These boxes bring the book's central theme into sharper focus in each chapter. We examine who the government is responding to and why, or why not, on issues including immigration policy, gridlock in Congress, science policy, presidential powers, and conflict in the Middle East, for example.

American Diversity

In many chapters, **American Diversity** boxes illustrate the impact of the social and economic diversity of the American population on political life. These boxes help students understand how a variety of backgrounds and attitudes shape views of politics and positions on issues.

Boxes

In each chapter, other boxes highlighting interesting aspects of American politics draw students into the material. Many illustrate how government and politics really work in a particular situation—how a corporation lobbies for government benefits, how a seemingly powerless group is able to organize for political action, and how political polls are done. Others highlight features of government that may be of particular interest to students, such as how teen pregnancies and abortions affect the abortion debate.

Key Terms

Key terms and names are boldfaced within the text and listed at the end of each chapter and in the glossary.

Supplements for Instructors

For details, please contact your Cengage representative or visit www.cengage.com/tlc/.

PowerLecture DVD with JoinIn™ for Understanding American Government

ISBN-10: 0495570141 / ISBN-13: 9780495570141

Featuring interactive PowerPoint® lectures and much more, PowerLecture is a one-stop lecture and class preparation tool that makes it easy for you to assemble, edit, publish, and present custom lectures for your course. The Power-Point lectures bring together text-specific outlines; audio and video clips from historic to current events (including from our 2008 ABC® video collection); new animated learning modules illustrating key concepts; tables, statistical charts, and graphs; and photos from the book as well as outside sources. In addition, you can add your own materials—culminating in a powerful, personalized, media-enhanced presentation. The disk also includes:

- A Test Bank in Microsoft® Word® and ExamView® computerized testing that offers a large array of well-crafted multiple-choice and essay questions, along with their answers and page references.

- An Instructor's Manual that includes learning objectives, chapter outlines, discussion questions, suggestions for stimulating class activities and projects, tips on integrating media into your class (including step-by-step instructions on how to create your own podcasts), suggested readings and Web resources, and a section specially designed to help teaching assistants and adjunct instructors.

- JoinIn™, which offers book-specific "clicker" questions that test and track student comprehension of key concepts. "Political Polling" questions simulate voting, engage students, foster dialogue on group behaviors and values, and add personal relevance; the results can be compared to national data, leading to lively discussions. "Visual Literacy" questions are tied to images from the book and add useful pedagogical tools and high-interest feedback during your lecture. Save the data from students' responses all semester—track their progress and show them how political science works by incorporating this exciting new tool into your classroom.

- The Resource Integration Guide, which outlines the rich collection of resources available to instructors and students within the chapter-by-chapter framework of the book, suggesting how and when each supplement can be used to optimize learning.

Political Theatre 2.0 DVD

ISBN-10: 0495793604 / ISBN-13: 9780495793601

Bring politics home to students with Political Theatre 2.0. This is the second edition of this DVD series and contains video and audio clips drawn from key political events of the last 75 years: presidential speeches, campaign ads, debates, news reports, national convention coverage, demonstrations, speeches by civil rights leaders, and more.

JoinIn on Turning Point for Political Theatre

ISBN-10: 0495095508 / ISBN-13: 9780495095507

For even more interaction, combine Political Theatre with the innovative teaching tool of a classroom response system through JoinIn™. Poll your students with questions created for you or create your own questions. Built within the Microsoft PowerPoint software, it's easy to integrate into your current lectures in conjunction with the "clicker" hardware of your choice.

ABC® News Videos for American Government 2010 DVD

ISBN-10: 0495573094 / ISBN-13: 9780495573098

This collection of three- to six-minute video clips on relevant political issues serves as a great lecture or discussion launcher. It has been updated to include coverage of the Democratic and Republican National Conventions. These clips are available on DVD and include: Primary 2008—Three States Dominate; Mitt Romney—The Role of Religion in the Race for the Presidency; The Ailing Economy Rescue Plan; Joe Biden on CIA Interrogation Techniques and Iran Report; and many more.

Supplements for Instructors and Students

Understanding American Government Alternate Edition Resource Center with InfoTrac® College Edition Instant Access Code

ISBN-10: 0495570885/ISBN-13: 9780495570882

The Resource Center for *Understanding American Government* offers a variety of rich online learning resources designed to enhance the student experience. These resources include podcasts, quizzes, sixteen new simulations, animated learning modules, Internet activities, self-assessments, videos, an Associated Press newsfeed, and links to Election 2008 information and analysis. All resources are correlated with key chapter learning concepts, and users can browse or search for content in a variety of ways. More than a collection of ancillary learning materials, however, the *Understanding American Government* Resource Center also features important content and community tools that extend the education experience, including tools for instructors to author their own content, content-sharing features, blogs (online journals) available for each registered user, and a built-in messaging center for class communications. We provide separate options for the delivery of an e-book.

WebTutor™ on WebCT

ISBN-10: 0495570834 / ISBN-13: 9780495570837

WebTutor™ on Blackboard

ISBN-10: 0495570818 / ISBN-13: 9780495570813

Rich with content for your American government course, this Web-based teaching and learning tool includes course management, study/mastery, and communication tools. Instructors can use WebTutor™ to provide virtual office hours, post the class syllabus, and track student progress with WebTutor's quizzing material. For students, WebTutor™ offers real-time access to interactive online tutorials and simulations, practice quizzes, and Web links—all correlated to *Understanding American Government*.

Companion Website for *Understanding American Government*

www.cengage.com/politicalscience/welch/uag12e

Students will find open access to Learning Objectives, Quizzes, Chapter Glossaries, Flash Cards, Crossword Puzzles, and Internet activities, all correlated by chapter. Instructors also have access to the Instructor's Manual and PowerPoint presentations.

Election 2008: An American Government Supplement

ISBN-10: 0495567485 / ISBN-13: 9780495567486

American government concepts come alive with this election booklet, which covers the 2008 presidential, congressional, and gubernatorial races and outcomes.

The Handbook of Selected Court Cases

ISBN: ISBN-10: 0495127744 / ISBN-13: 9780495127741

This handbook includes more than thirty Supreme Court cases addressing American government topics discussed in the textbook.

The Handbook of Selected Legislation and Other Documents

ISBN-10: 0495127825 / ISBN-13: 9780495127826

This handbook features excerpts from laws passed by the U.S. Congress that have had a significant impact on American politics.

Acknowledgments

We would like to thank the many people who have aided and sustained us during the lengthy course of this project.

We first want to thank Michael Steinman, our original coauthor and original primary author of Chapters 1, 11, and 12, who helped plan this book and continued his coauthorship for several editions. The shape of the book still reflects his insights and efforts. Then, we thank Margery Ambrosius and Jan Vermeer for their intellectual contributions to this book through their coauthorship in previous editions. Our current and former University of Nebraska and Penn State colleagues have been most tolerant and helpful. We thank them all. In particular, we appreciate the assistance of Philip Dyer, David Forsythe, John Hibbing, Robert Miewald, John Peters, David Rapkin, and Beth Thiess-Morse, who provided us with data, bibliographic information, and other insights that we have used here. Susan Welch's Penn State colleagues Ron Filippelli and Ray Lombra have been a source of encouragement, support, and many interesting political insights.

We are also grateful to the many other readers of our manuscript and earlier editions of the book, as listed here. Without their assistance the book would have been less accurate, less complete, and less lively. And thanks, too, to those instructors who have used the book and relayed their comments and suggestions to us. Our students at the University of Nebraska have also provided invaluable reactions to previous editions.

Our editors at Wadsworth Publishing also deserve our thanks. Clark Baxter was a continual source of encouragement and optimism from the beginning of the first edition through the beginning of the ninth edition. Carolyn Merrill and Edwin Hill have been able replacements for this new edition. Special thanks go to our terrific production team of Gary Kliewer, our conscientious and careful production manager, and Kate Cebik, our tireless and creative photo researcher. They were always willing to do a little more.

REVIEWERS OF THE NEW EDITION

Russell Benjamin, *Northeastern Illinois University*

Michael D. Cobb, *North California State University*

Rebecca Deen, *University of Texas at Arlington*

Dennis Driggers, *California State University–Fresno*

Lois Duke-Whitaker, *Georgia Southern University*

Dennis Falcon, *Cerritos Community College*

Kenneth W. Moffett, *Southern Illinois University*

Peter Parker, *Truman State University*

Bernard Rowan, *Chicago State University*

Rorie Solberg, *Oregon State University*

Ronnie Tucker, *Shippensburg University*

Paul Vayer, *Brevard Community College–Cocoa*

REVIEWERS OF PREVIOUS EDITONS

Alan Abramowitz, *State University of New York at Stony Brook;* Larry Adams, *Baruch College–City University of New York;* Danny M. Adkison, *Oklahoma State University;* James Alt, *Harvard University;* Margery Marzahn Ambrosius, *Kansas State University;* Kevin Bailey, *North Harris Community College;* Bethany Barratt, *Roosevelt University;* Kennette M. Benedict, *Northwestern University;* James Benze, *Washington and Jefferson College;* Melinda K. Blade, *Academy of Our Lady of Peace;* Timothy Bledsoe, *Wayne State University;* Jon Bond, *Texas A&M University;* Paul R. Brace, *New York University;* Joseph V. Brogan, *La Salle University;* James R. Brown Jr., *Central Washington University;* Kent M. Brudney, *Cuesta Community College;* Chalmers Brumbaugh, *Elon College;* Alan D. Buckley, *Santa Monica College;* Richard G. Buckner Jr., *Santa Fe Community College;* Ronald Busch, *Cleveland State University;* Bert C. Buzan, *California State University–Fullerton;* Carl D. Cavalli, *Memphis State University;* Stefanie Chambers, *Trinity College;* Richard A. Champagne, *University of Wisconsin, Madison;* Mark A. Cichock, *University of Texas at Arlington;* Michael Connelly, *Southwestern Oklahoma State University;* Gary Copeland, *University of Oklahoma;* George H. Cox Jr., *Georgia Southern College;* Paige Cubbison, *Miami-Dade University;* Landon Curry, *Southwest Texas State University;* Jack DeSario, *Case Western Reserve University;* Robert E. DiClerico, *West Virginia University;* Ernest A. Dover Jr., *Midwestern State University;* Georgia Duerst-Lahti, *Beloit College;* David V. Edwards, *University of Texas at Austin;* Ann H. Elder, *Illinois State University;* Ghassan E. El-Eid, *Butler University;* C. Lawrence Evans, *College of William and Mary;* Rhodell J. Fields, *St. Petersburg College;* Robert Glen Findley, *Odessa College;* Murray Fischel, *Kent State University;* Bobbe Fitzhugh, *Eastern Wyoming College;* Jeff Fox, *Catawba College;* Stephen I. Frank, *St. Cloud State University;* Marianne Fraser, *University of Utah;* Jarvis Gamble, *Owens Community College;* Sonia R. Garcia, *St. Mary's University;* David Garrison, *Collin County Community College;* Phillip L. Gianos, *California State University–Fullerton;* Doris A. Graber, *University of Illinois–Chicago;* Michael Graham, *San Francisco State University;* Ruth M. Grubel, *University of Wisconsin–Whitewater;* Stefan D. Haag, *Austin Community College;* Larry M. Hall, *Belmont University;* Edward Hapham, *University of Texas–Dallas;* Peter O. Haslund, *Santa Barbara City College;* Richard P. Heil, *Fort Hays State University;* Peggy Heilig, *University of Illinois at Urbana;* Craig Hendricks, *Long Beach City College;* Marjorie Hershey, *Indiana University;* Kay Hofer, *Southwest Texas State University;* Samuel B. Hoff, *Delaware State College;* Robert D. Holsworth, *Virginia Commonwealth University;*

Jesse C. Horton, *San Antonio College;* Gerald Houseman, *Indiana University;* Timothy Howard, *North Harris College;* Peter G. Howse, *American River College;* David W. Hunt, *Triton College;* Bernard-Thompson Ikegwuoha, *Green River Community College;* Pamela Imperato, *University of North Dakota;* Jerald Johnson, *University of Vermont;* Loch Johnson, *University of Georgia;* Terri Johnson, *University of Wisconsin–Green Bay;* Evan M. Jones, *St. Cloud State University;* Joseph F. Jozwiak Jr., *Texas A&M University–Kingsville;* Matt Kerbel, *Villanova University;* Marshall R. King, *Maryville College;* Orma Lindford, *Kansas State University;* Peter J. Longo, *University of Nebraska–Kearney;* Roger C. Lowery, *University of North Carolina–Wilmington;* H. R. Mahood, *Memphis State University;* Kenneth M. Mash, *East Stroudsburg University;* Alan C. Melchior, *Florida International University;* A. Nick Minton, *University of Massachusetts–Lowell;* Matthew Moen, *University of Maine;* Michael K. Moore, *University of Texas at Arlington;* Michael Nelson, *Vanderbilt University;* Bruce Nesmith, *Coe College;* Walter Noelke, *Angelo State University;* Thomas Payette, *Henry Ford Community College;* Theodore B. Pedeliski, *University of North Dakota;* Jerry Perkins, *Texas Tech University;* Toni Phillips, *University of Arkansas;* C. Herman Pritchett, *University of California–Santa Barbara;* Charles Prysby, *University of North Carolina–Greensboro;* Sandra L. Quinn-Musgrove, *Our Lady of the Lake University;* Donald R. Ranish, *Antelope Valley Community College;* Catherine C. Reese, *Arkansas State University;* Linda Richter, *Kansas State University;* Jerry Sandvick, *North Hennepin Community College;* James Richard Sauder, *University of New Mexico;* Eleanor A. Schwab, *South Dakota State University;* K. L. Scott, *University of Central Florida;* Earl Sheridan, *University of North Carolina–Wilmington;* Edward Sidlow, *Northwestern University;* Cynthia Slaughter, *Angelo State University;* John Squibb, *Lincolnland Community College;* Glen Sussman, *Old Dominion University;* M. H. Tajalli-Tehrani, *Southwest Texas State University;* Kristine A. Thompson, *Moorehead State University;* R. Mark Tiller, *Austin Community College;* Gordon J. Tolle, *South Dakota State University;* Susan Tolleson-Rinehart, *Texas Tech University;* Bernadyne Weatherford, *Rowan College of New Jersey;* Richard Unruh, *Fresno Pacific College;* Jay Van Bruggen, *Clarion University of Pennsylvania;* David Van Heemst, *Olivet Nazarene University;* Kenny Whitby, *University of South Carolina;* Donald C. Williams, *Western New England College;* James Matthew Wilson, *Southern Methodist University;* John H. Wilson Jr., *Itawamba Community College;* Clifford J. Wirth, *University of New Hampshire;* Ann Wynia, *North Hennepin Community College;* Alex H. Xiao, *Sacramento City College;* and Mary D. Young, *Southwestern Michigan College.*

ABOUT THE AUTHORS

SUSAN WELCH received her A.B. and Ph.D. degrees from the University of Illinois at Urbana-Champaign. She is currently Dean of the College of Liberal Arts and Professor of Political Science at The Pennsylvania State University. Her teaching and research areas include legislatures, state and urban politics, and women and minorities in politics. She has edited the *American Politics Quarterly*.

JOHN GRUHL, a Professor of Political Science, received his A.B. from DePauw University in Greencastle, Indiana, and his Ph.D. from the University of California at Santa Barbara. Since joining the University of Nebraska faculty in 1976, he has taught and researched in the areas of judicial process, criminal justice, and civil rights and liberties. He has won University of Nebraska campus-wide and system-wide distinguished teaching awards and has become a charter member of the University's Academy of Distinguished Teachers.

JOHN COMER is a Professor of Political Science at the University of Nebraska. He received his A.B. in political science from Miami University of Ohio in 1965 and his Ph.D. from the Ohio State University in 1971. His teaching and research focus on interest groups, public opinion, voting behavior, and political parties.

SUSAN RIGDON received A.B. and Ph.D. degrees in political science from the University of Illinois in 1966 and 1971. She has taught American government at several institutions in the United States and China and has other teaching and research interests in comparative government, poverty and development, and culture and politics. She is a Research Associate in Anthropology at the University of Illinois at Urbana-Champaign.

Why is *Understanding American Government* the right book for you?

An emphasis on the IMPACT and RESPONSIVENESS of government . . .

- This theme is woven throughout the book, and each chapter ends with a summary examination of whether government is responsive to the topic at hand. See, for example, Chapter 4's conclusion, *Is Government Responsive to Public Opinion?* on page 99.
- *Government Responsiveness* boxes examine who the government is responding to and why, or why not. See:
  - *Immigration: The States Step In*, p. 68
  - *Party Government and Legislative Gridlock*, p. 289
  - *From Imperial to Diminished Presidency?*, p. 328
  - *Science and Politics in the Bush Administration*, p. 367
  - *Wall Street or Main Street?* , p. 502
  - *The GI Bill of Rights*, p. 542
  - *Ideals and National Interest in Middle East Policy*, p. 578

The leader in DIVERSITY coverage . . .

- The book emphasizes the significance of our ethnic, religious, and economic diversity in the shaping and implementation of American government, as well as in our historic and future challenges. This important premise is first introduced as the framework for Chapter 1: *The American People* starting on page 1.
- The treatment of women, racial and ethnic minorities, and other marginalized groups is the best on the market. See, for example, the well respected chapters on *Civil Liberties* starting on page 403 and *Civil Rights* starting on page 446.
- *Understanding American Government* is a three-time winner of the American Government Textbook Award for the Best Treatment of Women in Politics, by the Women's Caucus for Political Science.
- Lively *American Diversity* boxes illustrate the impact of the American population's social diversity on politics. See:
  - *Identity in the Age of DNA*, p. 10
  - *Founding Mothers*, p. 22
  - *Political Culture and Federalism*, p. 56
  - *The Marriage Rights of Gays and Lesbian as a Moral Issue*, p. 80
  - *Color and the Clicker*, p. 132
  - *The Origin of Gay and Lesbian Rights Groups*, p. 148
  - *Organizing Protest: The Montgomery Bus Boycott*, p. 160
  - *The Changing Asian American Voter*, p. 186
  - *Blacks and Hispanics in Office*, p. 196
  - *Women in Office*, p. 200
  - *Racism and Sexism in the 2008 Campaign*, p. 224
  - *Men and Women Target Different Candidates*, p. 241
  - *Congress Is Not a Cross Section of America*, p. 270
  - *Women and Minorities in the Civil Service*, p. 360
  - *Do Women Judges Make a Difference?* , p. 384
  - *Anti-Semitism on the Bench*, p. 395
  - *Black Masters*, p. 450

CURRENCY and respected SCHOLARSHIP . . .

- The text, citations, and photo program have been thoroughly updated to include current events through the 2008 election results, cutting-edge research, and the latest scholarship. See Chapter 8: *Elections* starting on page 192 as just one example.
- A unique chapter on *Money and Politics* focuses on laws that regulate how money can influence politics, the role and impact of money in elections, and examines conflicts of interest on the part of decision makers in Congress and the executive branch. See Chapter 9 starting on page 234.

Encourages CRITICAL THINKING and an EVALUATIVE, NUANCED VIEW of American government . . .

- *Ethical Dilemmas* boxes pose challenging situations in politics and ask readers to consider the ethical ramifications of the actions in question. See:
  - *George Washington and His Slaves*, p. 38
  - *Should States Rely on Gambling for Revenue?*, p. 71
  - *Is It Ethical to Leak?*, p. 113
  - *Interest Groups Respond to 9/11*, p. 146
  - *Regulating Mortgages*, p. 285
  - *Trading Favors*, p. 336
  - *To Declassify or Not*, p. 353
  - *Neutral Competence in Intelligence Gathering*, p. 365
  - *A Valentine from Guantanamo Bay*, p. 439
  - *Choice for Men?*, p. 486

	• *Democracy?* questions appear periodically within the narrative and ask readers to consider whether a particular process or institution being discussed is democratic or not. Students become alert to the fact that democracy is not a simple concept and that our Constitution and our practices include both democratic and undemocratic features. See pages 134 and 319 for two examples.
ENGAGING writing and features spark students' interest and give them a BEHIND THE SCENES look at American government . . .	• Over 40 new *Behind the Scenes* boxes give readers a fascinating glimpse into interesting and important aspects of politics not widely publicized. See *An Accidental Classic* on page 53, *The Rope Line* on page 209, and *Hidden Costs of War* on page 510 for a few examples.
An ACCLAIMED PHOTOGRAPHY & ILLUSTRATIONS program . . .	• With over 370 carefully chosen photographs, cartoons, and figures—an average of 20 per chapter—the subject matter comes alive for students. Instructors praise the authors' use of candid, powerful images to reinforce important concepts, relay America's rich diversity, address difficult issues in our country's history and present political landscape, and maintain interest in the topic. Flip through the book, and the photo program will quickly draw you in.

The American People

1

Talking Points

Barack Obama built a campaign strategy around a story of political identity, presenting himself, with a white mother from Kansas and black father from Kenya, as a kind of quintessential crossover, bridge-building, hyphenated American. His search was a journey millions of Americans have taken over the past thirty years as they studied family history and emerged with more clearly defined ethnic and racial identities and in some cases new political allegiances.

However, in the earliest days of our nation, it was taken for granted that creating a *nonhyphenated* American identity was essential for shaping a nation out of a loose confederation of competing states populated by immigrants from English, German, French, and Spanish-speaking countries. At least one in five colonists had remained loyal to Britain during the Revolutionary War; some were driven from the country but many remained. The founding generation of politicians believed people would have to be carefully taught how to be American, learning a common language in public schools from books with common content and dictionaries whose vocabulary and spellings would be distinctly American. They saw a need for a new civic literature, including hagiographies of the Founders that would make them into something more than mortal men and thus focal points of a national identity.

By the late nineteenth century, in another peak period of immigration, leaders were still calling for the thorough "Americanization" of new arrivals. We "must see that the crucible turns our people out as Americans, of American nationality," Theodore Roosevelt argued, "and not as dwellers in a polyglot boarding house." An immigration-friendly politician, Roosevelt said the "hand of welcome" would be extended to all, but only if they threw off old ideas and became Americanized "in every way."[1] Any naturalized citizen who did throw off Old World habits and mores would then stand on level ground with any other American, including those descended from the Pilgrims. It was "a base outrage," Roosevelt said, for any voter "to oppose a man because of his religion or birthplace;" but at the same time he argued that no politician should ever compete for any vote by appeal to the voter's national origins.

Nevertheless, in the 1970s, after viewing the TV series *Roots*, inspired by Alex Haley's book of the same name, millions of Americans went in search of their ancestors and it became increasingly common for people to assume a hyphenated identity, that is, to identify themselves both by citizenship and family heritage. Today the hyphen has been dropped, but many of us cling to two-, three-, and even four-part identities as African, Chinese, Cuban, Irish, Arab, Mexican or—fill in the blank—Americans. This distinguishes contemporary Americans from earlier generations of immigrants, as well as Americans who had already been here for generations who are unlikely to call themselves German-, Anglo-, Spanish-, Dutch-, or Swedish Americans, though proud of their heritage. If asked, they may well have responded as Theodore Roosevelt, the descendant of Dutch immigrants, did when he declared himself an "American-American."[2]

"Actually, I prefer the term Arctic-American."

Americans take pride in their form of government but express ambivalence toward the political process. We cherish the Declaration of Independence and the Constitution and love the symbols of democracy. We visit Washington, D.C. to marvel at the Washington Monument, the Jefferson and Lincoln memorials, the Capitol, and the White House. We show these symbols of our democracy to our children, hoping they will learn to revere them too.

But at the same time that we point with pride to the documents and symbols of American democracy, we often seem unwilling to accept the realities of democratic practice or to spend the time it takes to familiarize ourselves with candidates and issues.[3] We are impatient with the slow pace at which government deals with the nation's problems. We refer to debates over issues as quarrels or bickering; we call compromises "selling out;" we too readily label conflict as mere self-interest and tag interest groups and political parties as *special* interests. In other words, we love the concept of democracy but hate the rough-and-tumble, the give-and-take, and the conflict of democracy in action.[4]

An era without "politics as usual," without conflict and debate and without partisanship and ideology, isn't going to happen. People differ over values and goals as well as the means to reach them. "Things get disagreeable because people disagree."[5] That's why we have politics.

Yet, despite the conflict in our political life, Americans are members of one community. We are parties to a single legal contract, the Constitution, and are all equally subject to the protections and obligations of a common set of laws. We also share an economic system, and our perception of how well we are doing financially is linked to our confidence in government.

Government is the instrument for forging one interest out of many, and **politics** is a means through which indi-vidual and group interests compete to shape government's impact on society's problems and goals. The term *politics* can encompass a much wider spectrum than actions directed toward government policy, but in this text we are concerned with politics as it affects competition for and performance in government office and efforts to influence policy made by government officials.

In their attempts to shape policy, individuals and groups compete and sometimes join together through political parties and many other extragovernmental organizations. Government's role is to mediate among them, resolve conflicting points of view, and formulate policies that represent a collective view. Thus politics is essential to the art of governing. This is why more than two thousand years ago **Aristotle** wrote that politics is the most noble endeavor in which people can engage, partly because it helps individuals know themselves and partly because it forces individuals to relate to others. Through political participation, he argued, individuals pursue their own needs and interests, but they must also consider the needs of other citizens. In other words, it is through politics that we learn to balance our own needs and interests against the good of the political community as a whole.

Today, Americans are less inclined to share Aristotle's conception of politics than they are the cynical view of novelist Gore Vidal: "Who collects what money from whom in order to spend on what is all there is to politics."[6] Yet the ideals of the Founders and the beliefs in democracy that we claim to cherish are about far more than who collects what to spend where.

This chapter begins the discussion by profiling the American people, identifying the political values we share, and describing how they are expressed in our form of government. It also briefly describes how democracy, when practiced by people who are ethnically, economically, and religiously diverse and scattered across a vast and varied landscape, is destined to be characterized as much by competition and conflict as by cooperation and community.

A Demographic Profile

When the poet Walt Whitman wrote, "Here is not merely a nation but a teeming Nation of nations," he said a lot about our country and its politics.[7] It is a cliché, yet true, that the United States is a land of immigrants, peopled by individuals from all over the world. Americans are a conglomeration of religions, races, ethnicities, cultural traditions, and socioeconomic groups—what one historian calls "a collision of histories."[8]

Our diversity was foreshadowed by the word *America*. The continent was named by a German mapmaker "working in a French college, who intended to honor an Italian explorer (Amerigo Vespucci) sailing under the Portuguese flag."[9]

Immigrants crowd a New York City neighborhood in 1890.

Immigration and Ethnic Diversity

Long before Europeans arrived, the population of North America was characterized by cultural diversity. Anthropologists are still debating the timing and points of origin of the first inhabitants, but many probably arrived by crossing a land bridge from Asia thousands of years ago, and others may have entered South America by sea and migrated north. Although sometimes characterized by a single term such as *Indians* or *Native Americans*, the first immigrants went on to found many different civilizations. Their nations were competitive and at times at war, and their differences were substantial enough to doom eighteenth-century efforts to form pan-Indian alliances against European colonization.[10] Today, the U.S. Census Bureau recognizes 562 different tribes, many fewer than 300 years ago, but still suggestive of the wide array of cultures that predated European settlement.

The umbrella term *European* is itself somewhat deceptive in that European settlers emigrated from countries that not only differed linguistically, religiously, and politically but also had often been at war with one another. Migrants carried some of these conflicts with them to America.

Because the colonies were ruled from England, and its language and culture were dominant, we tend to think of early Americans as Anglos and Protestants. But the earliest European settlers of the southeastern and southwestern territories were more likely to be Roman Catholics from France and Spain than Anglo-Protestants. In fact much of what are now Arizona, New Mexico, California, and Texas was populated by Mexican Catholics of mixed Spanish and Indian descent. Over time, Germany, a distinctly non-Anglo country and one evenly split between Catholics and Protestants, provided more immigrants to America than England.

By preference, or to avoid discrimination by earlier-arriving or more dominant settlers, immigrants often self-segregated into territories (Puritans in Massachusetts, Quakers in Pennsylvania and Rhode Island, Catholics in Maryland), which later became states. These different beliefs and traditions contributed to the rise of distinctive local cultures and to the varying character of state governments and politics.

BEHIND THE SCENES
THE TORCH PASSES

In 1882 a group of New Yorkers organized an art exhibit to raise money to pay for the erection of "Liberty Enlightening the World," the monumental sculpture France had gifted to the United States. One of the organizers asked a prominent New York writer to compose "some verses appropriate to the occasion."[1] Working only from photographs of the statue, which was yet to be shipped from France, **Emma Lazarus** wrote, "The New Colossus," which included these now famous words: "…give me your tired, your poor, your huddled masses yearning to breathe free, the wretched refuse of your teeming shore. Send these, the homeless, tempest tossed to me, I lift my lamp beside the golden door!"

Until Lazarus wrote those lines, neither the statue's donors nor its American recipients thought the Statue of Liberty had anything to do with immigration. Rather, it stood for the triumph of the republican form of government over monarchy. The woman with the torch symbolized the Enlightenment philosophy which had so influenced both American and French revolutionaries, and served as a reminder of how the pursuit of enlightenment through reason and science could bring liberty to the world.

Why did Lazarus, whose family had been in America since at least the mid-1700s, who mingled with the families of America's literary aristocracy—Ralph Waldo Emerson, Nathaniel Hawthorn, James Russell Lowell, and Henry James—and who had shown no prior interest in immigration, want to redefine the statue's meaning? Lazarus was a secular Jew who just recently had been drawn into the cause of resettling Jewish immigrants fleeing pogroms in Russia and eastern Europe. Her shock on learning about the conditions driving them from their home countries broadened her interest in all refugees entering the United States and she believed erection of the statue in New York's harbor could be used to draw public attention to their plight.

Lazarus's poem *was* read at the fund-raiser despite the divergence of her views from those of the statue's benefactors and even though no one wanted to hear the lines about "wretched refuse." But it was then put aside and virtually forgotten. Lazarus died several years later, at 38, still a celebrated literary figure, but "The New Colossus" was little mentioned in obituaries. In 1903, in a service commemorating the twenty-fifth anniversary of her death, the poem was engraved on a plaque, deposited inside the statue's base, then once again ignored.

But with the rise of fascism in Germany, Italy, and Spain in the 1930s, a new round of refugees began streaming toward America. The country began to celebrate itself as a land of immigrants and "The New Colossus" plaque was moved nearer the statue's entrance. Alfred Hitchcock's wartime film, *Sabateur*, ended with the heroine reciting the Lazarus poem while standing in the statue's crown. By the post-war years, Americans were beginning to see the statue as Lazarus had: not as the symbol of liberty through reason, but as "The Mother of Exiles" lighting the way for all who were fleeing oppressive political or economic conditions. (That might have been little solace to Lazarus had she known that most European Jews had been denied entry before and during World War II.)

[1] This account is based on Esther Schor, *Emma Lazarus* (New York: Schocken Books, 2006), 189–256.

Like Europeans, Africans, too, came from a huge continent that encompassed many languages, cultures, and religions. Even though the European slave trade was concentrated in coastal areas of West Africa, the men and women forcibly removed to the Americas did not share a common tradition. But their experience in the American colonies united most in a common condition as noncitizens lacking all political and economic rights.

After the Revolution and the formation of the United States, the new government began to articulate an immigration policy, removing it from the hands of state governments. Ever since, there have been disagreements over the standards for regulating admission. Congress began restricting immigration in 1798, when, through the Alien Act, it gave the president power to deport people he deemed "dangerous to the peace and safety" of the country. And the time required for "free white citizens" to become naturalized citizens was extended from two, to five, and then to fourteen years. An 1807 law prohibited the migration or "importation" of people for purposes of slavery.

But the ethnic and racial composition of the American population broadened in the mid- to late-nineteenth century as new waves of settlers came from southern and eastern Europe, China, and Japan, as well as Ireland and Germany. They included large numbers of Roman, Eastern, and Russian Orthodox Catholics; Jews; and some Buddhists until the 1882 Exclusionary Act prohibited further immigration from China (See the "Behind the Scenes" box.) A 1907 agreement with Japan restricted Japanese entries to the Hawaiian Islands. But immigration continued at high levels into the twentieth century before peaking in the decade 1905–1914, when more than 10 million immigrants entered the country.

| Figure 1 | Immigration Reached an All-Time High in the 1990s |

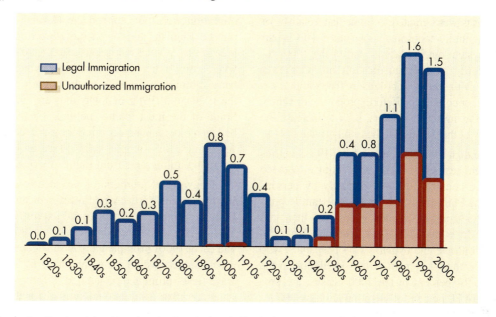

Note: Unauthorized migration is net; legal immigration is arrivals only. Totals shown are rounded.
SOURCE: Jeffrey Passel and D'Vera Cohn, U.S. Population Projections: 2005–2050, Pew Research Center: Washington, D.C. (February 11, 2008), 85. pewhispanic.org/files/reports/85.pdf

This surge led to efforts to slow the number of admissions. Between the 1920s and 1960s, immigration was open mainly to the European countries represented in the American population at the time of the 1910 census, thereby favoring British, German, and northern Europeans and penalizing southern and eastern Europeans and those from other continents. Laws passed through the end of World War II added new categories of people prohibited entry, including anarchists and revolutionaries, members of communist parties, and others deemed undesirable.

Not all immigrants who came stayed. In addition to deportations, about 30 percent of those who arrived between 1900 and 1990 returned voluntarily to their home countries. For a few years during the Great Depression of the 1930s, more people left the United States than entered.[11]

In 1965 the civil rights movement led to the end of the nationality restrictions on immigration that had been in place since the 1920s. With the removal of the old quota system, the door opened to people of every race, religion, and nationality.

People in some political categories have been given preferential treatment. During the Cold War, for example, virtually everyone fleeing a communist country, including several million Cubans, Russians, Eastern Europeans, Vietnamese, Cambodians, and Laotians, were allowed in. Thousands of Chinese students were granted permanent residency under an amnesty following the 1989 Tiananmen Square massacre in Beijing.

Rivaling the surge in legal immigration in the 1990s are the millions of people who have arrived without papers since 2000, most of whom entered the country by crossing the Mexican border into the southwestern United States. (See Figure 1.)

In 2008, nearly 12 million undocumented people were living in the United States. Until immigration enforcement was stepped up during the 2008 election season, the number of people entering the country illegally each year was almost equal to the number granted legal entry. Even with stepped-up border control about a half million people enter the country illegally each year.

When permanent residents become citizens—and one-third of all Americans who are foreign-born *are* naturalized U.S. citizens—all immediate members of their families living

| Figure 2 | Immigrants as a Percentage of the American Population |

The number of immigrants relative to our population peaked in the 1890s and 1910s, but the percentage today is nearly that level if illegal immigrants are included.
SOURCE: Time, Inc., October 30, 2006, 45.

outside the United States automatically qualify for residency visas. In 2007, for example, almost 65 percent of all permanent residency visas were granted to immediate relatives of new citizens or to family-sponsored applicants.[12] This is part of a preference system put in place as part of the 1960s reforms; it gives priority to family reunification and, in far fewer numbers, to those with specific job skills in, for example, science, engineering, or computers. Reform proposals, driven by corporate needs for high-tech workers, seek to increase the job skills category at the expense of the family category.

In 2007 more than 1 million people from 193 countries were granted legal residency. More were born in Mexico than in any other country, followed distantly by persons born in China, the Philippines, and India. The family preference system for granting residency ensures, then that current trends in the ethnic diversification of the American population will continue and explains why Hispanics, who accounted for less than 7 percent of the population in the 1990 census and 14 percent in the 2000 census, are projected to be almost 30 percent of the population by 2050 if current trends persist.[13] (Figure 3)

Immigration and Political Cleavage

Antiforeign, or nativist, sentiments have been common throughout our history. Some native-born Americans have feared economic competition from newcomers or have perceived non-English-speaking people or anyone with different traditions and religious practices as cultural threats. A wave of Germans arriving in Pennsylvania in the 1750s had Benjamin Franklin complaining about the use of bilingual street signs in Philadelphia and warning that if German immigration were not stopped the German language would replace English, and "even our government will become precarious."[14] Such sentiments usually are most pronounced when immigration levels are high, which is why strong nativist sentiments influenced the politics of the mid-1800s, the 1920s, the 1990s, and why they are again a force today. Some of the most intense political cleavages have arisen between older and newer immigrants. Over half of Hispanic Americans, for example, believe that the United States has too many immigrants from Latin America.[15]

The wave of immigration produced by Ireland's potato famine in the 1840s created a fever of anti-Irish and anti-Catholic sentiment, which found expression in the Know-Nothing Party. The anti-immigrant wave in the late 1800s and early 1900s prompted a reaction against big-city political machines, which were supported by immigrants. This wave also prompted concerted efforts to establish the American flag as a national symbol for the diverse immigrants.[16] Public schools started flying the flag in 1890; the Pledge of Allegiance was adopted in 1892; and people started saluting the flag in 1898.[17]

Patriotic fervor during World War I produced hostility toward Americans of German ancestry, and the Russian Revolution led to the Red Scare of the 1920s and the deportation of many Russian and Eastern European immigrants. During World War II, Japanese Americans were targeted as potential collaborators with Japan, had their property confiscated, and were imprisoned in camps under military guard (discussed further in Chapter 14).

Figure 3 | **Changes in the Race and Ethnicity of Americans, 1960–2005**

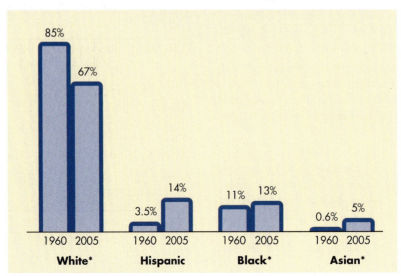

SOURCE: Jeffrey Passel and D'Vera Cohn, U.S. Population Projections: 2005-2050, *Pew Research Center: Washington, D.C.*, (February 11), 2008, 85. pewhispanic.org/files/reports/85.pdf.

Nativist sentiment flared when the waves of immigrants arrived on the shores of America in the 1800s. This illustration depicts Irish and German immigrants, symbolized by whiskey and beer barrels, stealing a ballot box.

Although each generation of immigrants has faced resentment from preceding generations, each has contributed to the building of America. Early European immigrants settled the eastern seaboard and pushed west to open the frontier. Africans' slave labor helped build the South's economy. Germans and Scandinavians developed the Midwest into an agricultural heartland, and free blacks and Irish, Italian, Polish, and Russian newcomers provided labor for America's industrial revolution and turned many cities into huge metropolises. Chinese immigrants helped build the transcontinental railroad linking East and West, and Japanese and Hispanics were instrumental in making California our top food producer. More recently, young Chinese and Indian immigrants have figured prominently in high-tech industries, and older Indian immigrants dominate the motel business in the United States. All immigrant groups have gone on from their initial roles to play a fuller part in American life.

Religious Diversity

Voltaire, the great French philosopher, once wrote that a nation with one church will have oppression; with two, civil war; with a hundred, freedom.[18] We know that many of our earliest settlers—French Huguenots, German Anabaptists, British Methodists, Catholics, and Quakers—came here to escape religious intolerance in Europe. Nevertheless, few who emigrated to the Americas expected to live in an areligious state. Once here, however, many found it necessary to establish separate communities to ensure freedom for their form of religious practice. New Jersey, Pennsylvania, and Maryland were conceived and established as "plantations of religion" that gave state protection to specific religious groups.[19] Rhode Island was founded by the religious dissident Roger Williams, who, after being expelled from the

Puritan society in Massachusetts, bought land from the Narragansett Indians and founded a colony for other religious outcasts.[20]

With independence, the United States disassociated itself not just from the government of England, but from its state religion, the Church of England (or Anglican church), which was, and is still today, headed by the monarch. Some at the Constitutional Convention wanted to name the Episcopalian church, the newly independent Anglican church in the United States, as the state religion, but most knew that in a country of wide religious diversity, a Constitution with such a provision would never be ratified. But six of the thirteen original states did establish an official religion, and some levied a religious tax, leaving it to individual taxpayers to designate which church would receive their tithes. State religions were not disestablished in Connecticut, Massachusetts, or New Jersey until the nineteenth century, and even then, some courts considered Christian teachings an integral part of common law.[21]

Despite the diversity in religious practice, instruction and textbooks in public schools drew much of their content from the Protestant Bible. School officials maintained that instruction was "nonsectarian," but their reluctance to remove blatantly anti-Catholic material led to the creation of Catholic church-run schools, which remain today a major alternative to public schools. Occasionally, religious differences led to violence, as in Philadelphia's Bible riots of 1843, when Protestants burned down a Catholic school and thirteen people were killed.[22] The Philadelphia church burnings targeted only Irish Catholic churches, not those of the older American German Catholic population.

The Know-Nothing Party won popularity during this period by spreading fear of a Catholic takeover. Catholic-Protestant conflict lasted well into the twentieth century, could be intense, and sometimes trumped ethnicity. In the small farm community of Carroll, Iowa, for example, German and other Protestants joined forces against allied German and Irish Catholics, passing "puritan Sunday" laws that prohibited Catholic church dances, singing parties, and serving alcohol on the Sabbath.[23]

These anecdotes from the distant past are a reminder that being all white and all Christian did not spare communities from exclusionary or repressive assimilationist tactics or violence against those of a different ancestry or church affiliation. Claims that our political unity is being undermined by ethnic and religious diversity are hardly new.

America's religious profile is changing along with its ethnic makeup. This is not simply a function of immigration; Americans are becoming as religiously changeable as they are geographically mobile. A 2007 survey found that 25 percent of American adults had left the faith they were raised in and that 44 percent of all adults had made some shift in religious affiliation. Although nearly 80 percent still identify as Christians, they are split among dozens of sects and denominations, and the once dominant Protestants are

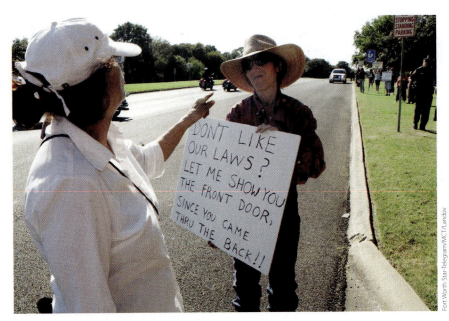

Two Anglo women in Irving, Texas, debate the city's efforts to identify and deport illegal aliens.

now barely half of the population. Sixteen percent of Americans claim no religious affiliation, and most of the remainder are adherents of other major religious traditions: Jews, Muslims, Hindus, and Buddhists.[24] (See Table 1.) To some observers, these figures represent the potential for social fragmentation; but a proliferation of religious affiliations may both bolster liberty and serve as its measure.

Economic and Demographic Diversity

Diversity involves more than differences in national origin, race, and religious affiliation. Where people settle, what they do for a living, how much they earn, when they were born, and how long they have been here are all potential bases for political difference, and over time these factors are probably more important than religion or country of origin.

Although racial and ethnic cleavages have garnered much of the attention throughout our history, economic diversity is at least as important. We may think of America as a land of opportunity, but most people who are born poor in the United States stay poor. Opportunities knock harder and more often for those who are born into the upper and middle classes. And although our society is not as class conscious as many others, our personal economic situations play an important part in shaping our views toward politics and our role in the process. Most people who are poor, for example, do not vote, but those who do vote tend to vote Democratic. Most affluent Americans do vote, and they vote in larger numbers for Republicans than for Democrats. Economic inequality continues to grow as a flashpoint for political conflict as the gap between the lowest and highest income groups in America has grown from 35-fold to 75-fold over the past thirty years.[25]

Regional and residential differences can also be important, especially since they often intertwine with economic

interests. Farmers in California and the Midwest, for example, are more likely than city dwellers to be supportive of farm subsidy legislation. City dwellers may be far more enthusiastic about federal laws creating national parks or wilderness areas than the Western ranchers who use the land to graze their livestock. The classic and most costly example of regional conflict in our history was the division between South and North over the right of southern states to secede from the Union in order to maintain a regional economic system rooted in slavery. Although in that case economic and political disparities led to the bloodiest conflict in our history, regional diversity usually results in no more than political difference and economic competition. However, in the face of growing income inequality and the residential segregation of gated communities, there is the danger that residential separation will lead to the political indifference of the well-off to the needs of poor neighborhoods.

Age differences, too, can affect political orientation. The needs and interests of older citizens are substantially different from those of young adults. The United States, like Canada and Western Europe, has an aging population; although mitigated by higher birth rates among newer immigrants, about one in eight Americans was sixty-five or older in 2008. Their interest groups are among the most powerful in the country and in the 2008 presidential election they formed 23 percent of the electorate, compared to 18 percent for the under-thirties.. This fact has made economic security and health care for senior citizens high-priority policy issues, even while the number of children living in poverty is increasing.

Diversity and Identity Politics

Why, when the American population has always been so heterogeneous, does diversity seem to have so much more meaning in contemporary political life? One reason is that although

Table 1 | Religious Affiliations of Americans

Major Religious Traditions in the U.S. Among all adults . . .%		
Christian		**78.4**
Protestant	51.3	
Evangelical churches		*26.3*
Mainline churches		*18.1*
Hist. black churches		*6.9*
Catholic	23.9	
Mormon	1.7	
Jehovah's Witness	0.7	
Greek Orthodox	<0.3	
Russian Orthodox	<0.3	
Other Christian	0.3	
Other Religions		**4.7**
Jewish	1.7	
Reform		*0.7*
Conservative		*0.5*
Orthodox		*<0.3*
Other		*0.3*
Buddhist	0.7	
Zen Buddhist		*<0.3*
Theravada Buddhist		*<0.3*
Tibetan Buddhist		*<0.3*
Other		*0.3*
Muslim*	0.6	
Sunni		*0.3*
Shia		*<0.3*
Other		*<0.3*
Hindu	0.4	
Other faiths	1.5	
Unitarians and other liberal faiths		*0.7*
New Age		*0.4*
Native American rel.		*<0.3*
Unaffiliated		**16.1**
includes Atheists, Anostics, and	1.6	
Religious unaffiliated	2.4	
Don't Know/Refused		**0.8**
		100

Due to rounding, figures may not add to 100 and nested figures may not add to the subtotal indicated.

*From "Muslim Americans: Middle Class and Mostly Mainstream," Pew Research Center, 2007

SOURCE: Pew Research Center, February 26, 2008

society was diverse in the early decades of the Republic, the political spectrum was narrow, and the majority of citizens were excluded from participation. Those granted full rights of participation varied from state to state, but two groups— women and African American men, with the exception of a small number of free black men living in the North—were comprehensively shut out after the ratification of the Constitution. (So were some white men who did not own property or, for a brief time, did not belong to an established church).

Diversity's scope for expression has been greatly broadened through the slow expansion of the electorate and the opening up of the political system. The voting and politically active public has become steadily more heterogeneous since the 1920s. Later, the federal government's adoption of race, gender, and ethnic preference programs, beginning in the Nixon administration, and the wave of immigration from Asia and Latin America in the 1980s and 1990s, have also increased the importance of diversity in American politics.

As government adopted affirmative action policies to compensate for historical discrimination (see Chapter 15), an individual's race, gender, or ethnicity took on added political importance. The use of such factors to influence the division of public resources has given rise to **identity politics**. This is the practice of organizing on the basis of one's ethnic or racial identity, sex, or sexual orientation to compete for public resources and to influence public policy.[26]

Paradoxically, identity politics has intensified during a period in which racial and ethnic boundaries are beginning to blur (see the box "Identity in the Age of DNA"). DNA testing has shown how problematic the concept of race is when used as a census category in the United States. The ways we group by ethnicity or cultural heritage are just as slippery.

American Indians reflect the tug of identity politics in recent decades. Their once apparently dwindling population is now burgeoning. Their numbers began increasing with the Indian rights movement in the 1960s, as more people with Indian ancestry felt new pride and reclaimed their heritage. The environmental movement in the 1970s prompted others to view earlier Indians as good stewards of the land and wildlife. The enactment of affirmative action programs and the growth of the gambling industry on reservation land undoubtedly attracted still others. As a result, each census from 1970 through 2000 has found more Americans identifying themselves as Indians. This includes persons who have full Indian ancestry and those who have only partial or distant (or even imagined) Indian ancestry, who did not choose to identify themselves as Indians in earlier decades. According to the census, the population of Indians has more than quadrupled since 1960, a population increase that cannot be explained by birth and death records.[27] Today some federally recognized tribes are authorized to issue a Certificate of Degree of Indian Blood, or "white card," that certifies the carrier has a specified Indian "blood quantum" in order to be eligible for certain benefits.[28] Despite their common usage, many of the identity categories are simplistic. Hispanic is a census catchall term for Mexicans, Puerto Ricans, Cubans, and others with national origins in Central and South America and the Caribbean. Americans of Spanish ancestry tend to reject the Hispanic label altogether as a means of self-identification, and more than 40 percent of Hispanics would choose a racial category other than what is offered on the census, most often identifying with their country of national origin.[29] These are culturally and linguistically distinct groups of people, very mixed racially, and with different legal status within the United States: All people born in Puerto Rico are citizens by birth, for example, and Cuban immigrants enter the country under rules that do not apply to other Hispanics seeking entry.

Hispanic residential patterns also vary by country of origin. Mexican Americans are heavily concentrated in California and the Southwest, though there are significant populations in Illinois and increasing numbers in other parts of the Midwest and South. Puerto Ricans tend to live in New York, New Jersey, Boston, Chicago, and other large cities in the Northeast. Cubans are heavily concentrated in South Florida. The "African" census category could apply to an African American whose ancestors have been in the United States since the seventeenth century, or to first-generation Americans who emigrated after laws restricting immigration from Africa were lifted in the 1960s. Since that change, more Africans have come to the United States than were brought here against their will during all the years of slavery.[30] The arrival of people who share some African ancestry but who came from many different countries and cultures has complicated group identity by race. In 2007, 47 percent of African Americans either believed blacks were not a single race or were not sure.[31]

Asian Americans are also a heterogeneous group. Those who have been here longest include the Japanese, Chinese, and those from the Philippines. Newer groups include Viet-

american diversity | Identity in the Age of DNA

Since the first census in 1790, Americans have been counted by race. Nineteenth-century laws that segregated blacks prompted people to try to figure out which persons were black and which ones were white. For precision, the **United States Census** developed multiracial categories for those of mixed black and white, terming them *mulatto* or even categorizing further into *quadroon* or *octoroon* for those with one-fourth or one-eighth African American ancestry.

The census also classified Asians as Chinese or Japanese, then in the early twentieth century, Filipino, Korean, and Hindu (confusing religion with race) appeared. Mexicans, who had been counted as white, in 1930 were labeled as a race, but the category was dropped after a protest by the Mexican government.[1] After the U.S. Census Bureau dropped the mulatto categories, those of mixed white and other ancestry were usu-

ally counted as "other," at the discretion of the census taker.[2]

It was not until the 1980 census that an individual's ethnicity and race were determined entirely by self-classification. In the 1990 census, the choice was limited to one of four racial groups: black, white, American Indian or Native Alaskan, Asian or Pacific Islander. In addition to selecting a racial group, one could claim Hispanic/Latino ethnic heritage.

As a result of immigration and interracial marriage, many Americans complained that they couldn't choose a single category, they were multiracial. For example, former general and Secretary of State Colin Powell, a first-generation American whom President Clinton often held up as a model for affirmative action, is another prominent example. Born to immigrants from Jamaica, his maternal grandparents were Scots, and on petitioning in 2004, he was issued a Scots heraldic crest.[3] So the 2000 census offered five racial

categories and allowed every individual to check as many boxes as applicable.

While such a system may have made better sense to golf pro Tiger Woods, who describes himself as a "Cablinasian," a person of white, African, American Indian, and Asian ancestry, only 2.4 percent of Americans checked multiple boxes and thereby identified themselves as multiracial, far below the actual percentage of Americans who are multiracial. Many Hispanics are mixed race, and by some estimates, three-fourths of African Americans are too.[4]

That notions of "race"—African, Caucasian, Native American, or Asian— reflect common or social usage rather than scientifically determined biological differences, but it has become ever more clear with advances in genetic research. Now, the commercial availability of DNA testing has brought a new twist to racial and ethnic self-identification by providing a scientific basis for denamese and Cambodians from Southeast Asia, many of whom fled their countries after the Vietnam War; those from the Indian subcontinent of South Asia; native Hawaiians; and many others with very different cultures and histories. The population of Asian Americans is found disproportionately on the West Coast, Hawaii, the larger cities of the East Coast, and Chicago.

Similar variance can be found in religious categories. No one today would suggest that "Christian," as an unmodified category, is a predictor of political views or voting behavior, but this is also true for "Muslim." American Muslims are among the most diverse in the Islamic world. Twenty percent are native-born African Americans, one-quarter have Arab ancestry, eighteen percent are South Asian, while the remainder have come from Iran, Europe, Africa, and other regions.[32]

The decidedly mixed ancestry of Americans is steadily becoming more complex through intermarriage. So much racial and ethnic mixing occurs that by the 1990 census,

one hundred million Americans could name no specific ancestry, or they reported multiple ancestries.[33] At some point in our history at least forty states had laws preventing marriage between men and women of different races, but by the 2000 census more than 5 percent of marriages were mixed-race couples. Today, 22 percent of all Americans say they have at least one relative in a mixed marriage.[34]

Political Culture

In recent years, *diversity* has become a political catchword and has been raised to the level of a civic virtue. Yet our national motto is *E Pluribus Unum* ("Out of Many, One"), referring to the union of many states and the molding of one people from many traditions. There is a popular saying that Americans are people of many cultures united by a single idea. But what is that single idea, and is it, however fundamental, sufficient to form a political culture? A **political**

termining one's ancestry. The results have surprised many Americans. In a 2007 Public Broadcasting System series, the noted African American scholar, Henry Louis Gates, led nine prominent African Americans through a search for their ancestors, including DNA tests.[5] Gates himself was amazed to find out that 50 percent of his genetic heritage was European, including an Ashkenazi (Jewish) woman. Others, too, were surprised that their ancestors included Asians, American Indians, and, of course, whites. Students in a race and ethnicity class at The Pennsylvania State University, who can have their DNA tested as part of a class, often discover mixed-race ancestry they knew nothing about.

DNA testing of racial classifications has practical applications. "Naturally when you're applying to college you're looking at how your genetic status might help you," said a man who had adopted twin boys whose skin was a tannish color. DNA testing showed his sons, whose biological parents were "white," were 9 percent Native American and 11 percent northern African. The father said he learned the results too

late for the admissions process but thought it might help get financial aid.[6]

Mixed-race ancestry revealed by DNA testing could have implications for federal policies if it affects how people report race on census forms. Laws guaranteeing equal access and representation have meant, in practice, that the racial or ethnic composition of the population affects who is admitted to universities, how the boundaries of legislative districts are drawn, whether school districts need to submit desegregation plans, and whether minorities are adequately represented among workers hired on federally funded projects and among business owners receiving federal contracts.

What percentage of genetic inheritance does one have to have to claim identity as a minority? And what counts most in qualifying for a preference program—one's genes or one's culture and life experience? Diversity programs were designed to right historical discrimination. If a person was unaware of minority ancestry, never experienced the culture, and was never subject to dis-

crimination targeting the minority, can genes alone define group membership? Those who say genetic heritage is not enough fear that the tests could undermine programs meant to compensate those who in fact have been denied opportunity because of their race or ethnicity.

DNA testing may force us to re-think the categorization of people by race and ethnicity in an increasingly multiracial/multiethnic society. Almost half of both black and white respondents to a poll said that the U.S. Census, like Canada's, should not collect information on race at all.[7]

[1] Background material drawn from Kenneth Prewitt, "Does Ethno-Racial Classification have a Place in Policy Making?" *Public Affairs Report* 44, Spring 2003 (www .igs.berkeley.edu/publications/par/spring2003/ classification .htm).
[2] Campbell J. Gibson and Emily Lennon, "Historical Census Statistics on the Foreign-Born Population of the United States: 1850–1990," Census Bureau, Population Division Working Paper, no.29 (February 1999), p. 9.
[3] The Scotsman Website (thescottsman. scotsman.com/index .cfm?id 535722004).
[4] "Politics of Identity Resurface with Census," *Champaign-Urbana News-Gazette*, March 25, 2001, B8.
[5] *African American Lives*, a multi-part documentary broadcast on PBS in 2007–2008, and hosted by Henry Louis Gates.
[6] Amy Harmon, "The DNA Age: Seeking Ancestry in DNA Ties Uncovered by Tests," *The New York Times*, April 12, 2006.
[7] Tom Morganthau, "What Color Is Black?" *Newsweek*, February 13, 1995, 64.

The National Museum of the American Indian on the Washington Mall reflects identity politics. Native Americans lobbied for the museum, consulted on its design, and here participated in opening ceremonies.

culture is a shared body of values and beliefs that shapes perception and attitudes toward politics and government and in turn influences political behavior.

The Significance of Political Culture

For their stability and vitality, governments rely on the support of citizens: their identification with the country and its method of governing and their adoption of the political values and behavior necessary to sustain the system. Without this support, government is ineffective or placed in the position of attempting to gain obedience through force or coercion.

In a democracy, sharing a political culture does not mean that citizens must agree on specific issues or even on the government's role in dealing with the country's problems. Democracy embraces conflict and competition just as it requires cooperation and a sense of community. A basic function of government is to establish the rules under which interests can compete. Thus, the essence of political culture is not agreement on issues but on fundamental principles and on a common perception of the *rights* and *obligations* of citizenship and the rules for participating in the political process. These shared values reduce the strains produced by our differences and allow us to compete intensely on some issues while cooperating on others.

Learning Political Culture

Whether the newly created United States of America came about by "design of Providence," was a "lucky accident," or was the result of the Founders' skill in shaping a workable Constitution, it faced a problem common to all political systems: how to create a national identity among the citizenry.[35] Although American society has often been characterized as a melting pot, it has been a slow melt, and it has not happened by luck or accident. The Founders spoke of a united country, a people with common ancestry, a shared language, the same religion, and a commitment to the same political principles. From what you have read earlier in this chapter, you know this view was in some part wishful thinking. One of the most significant challenges to establishing a national political culture was the division of Americans among sovereign states. It is easy to forget that not long ago, people's identity as Virginians or Pennsylvanians was much more important to them than being American. And it was not until the Civil War, under the influence of Abraham Lincoln's powerful reference at Gettysburg to the "unfinished work" of preserving the Union that Americans began referring to the United States with the singular *is* rather than the plural *are*.[36]

Most of the Founders believed that an educated citizenry was essential to the survival of the new republic, and advocates of public education such as Daniel Webster and **Thomas Jefferson** argued that only educated citizens would be able to understand public issues, elect virtuous leaders, and "sustain the delicate balance between liberty and order in the new political system."[37] As the public school system emerged, increasing emphasis was placed on the "training of citizens in patriotism, political knowledge and public affairs."[38] Although schools were then (as they are now) under local control, there was some common content in civic education around the country. By the mid-twentieth century, most elementary school children were studying current events in their *Weekly Reader* and beginning each day by reciting the Pledge of Allegiance to the flag. Many high school students are required to pass an exam on the U.S. Constitution, and perhaps their state's constitution as well, to graduate. However, civics is not one of the subject areas in which students must show proficiency under the new federal system of mandatory testing, and there is evidence that it is being increasingly neglected in favor of math, science, and English, courses that *are* subject to proficiency standards.[39]

The mass media emerged as another important agent (discussed in Chapters 4 and 5). Newspapers, magazines, radio, and then television also provide information on the workings of government and the rules of the game. Television, especially, provides shared experiences to viewers.

Today, one of the most controversial issues in the debate over what is required to sustain a political culture is whether all citizens should speak a common language. But the Founders took it for granted that English would be the national language, and **Noah Webster's** 1783 textbook promoting "a new national language to be spelled and pronounced differently from British English" was one of the first attempts to create an American national identity.[40] Webster, a Connecticut schoolteacher, wanted British textbooks banned from the classroom, saying that the wiping out of old world maxims had to begin in infancy: "Let the first word he lisps be Washington."[41] In 1828 Webster published the *Dictionary of American English*—a dictionary "suited to the needs of the American people"—because, he argued, Americans could never accept the British definitions of senate, congress, assembly, and courts.[42] Another objective was to standardize the multitude of dialects, some

mutually unintelligible, spoken by Americans of the time.[43] Today the United States has fewer spoken dialects than any other of the world's largest countries, a considerable accomplishment given the diversity of our collective heritage and strong regional cultures.

Webster's belief that a single language was essential to developing a common political culture has been an abiding issue in American politics. But when new states were carved from French and Spanish-speaking territories through the Louisiana Purchase and the Mexican-American War, there was official acceptance of bilingualism. It was not until after the Civil War, when new emphasis was place on one nation rather than many states, that state laws and local policies embracing bilingualism were erased from the books. New assimilationist policies also attempted to stamp out dozens of Native American languages by enrolling Indian children in English-speaking schools. Fear of German-speaking immigrants in the early part of the twentieth century led Iowa to pass a law requiring all groups of two or more people to speak in English, even when using the telephone.[44] In the current era, when most immigration has come from non-English-speaking countries and some urban school districts teach in a hundred or more languages, thirty states have passed laws establishing English as the official language.

CAN YOU PASS THE TEST TO BECOME A CITIZEN?

The civics test required for those seeking to become naturalized citizens includes 100 questions. Here are 10. For the answers and the rest of the questions, see www.uscis.gov.

1. How many amendments does the Constitution have?
2. What stops **one** branch of government from becoming too powerful?
3. The House of Representatives has how many voting members?
4. There are four amendments to the Constitution about who can vote. Describe **one** of them.
5. What are **two** rights only for United States citizens?
6. The Federalist Papers supported the passage of the U.S. Constitution. Name **one** of the writers.
7. What territory did the United States buy from France in 1803?
8. Who was president during World War I?
9. Name **one** U.S. territory.
10. Why does the flag have thirteen stripes?

This woman from Yemen is one of 600 immigrants sworn in as new citizens in Detroit.

© Jim West/The Image Works

And proof of minimal competency in English is part of the civics test given to those applying for U.S. citizenship. (See box "Can You Pass the Test to become a Citizen?")

The Core Values

Our "nation of nations" is crosscut with cultural, political, and economic cleavages, but despite our sometimes overwhelming diversity, most Americans do share some basic goals and values. The words Americans use to characterize their form of government are less likely to come from the Constitution than from the second paragraph of the Declaration of Independence: "We hold these Truths to be self-evident, that all Men are created equal, that they are endowed by the Creator with certain unalienable Rights, that among these are Life, Liberty, and the Pursuit of Happiness."

From these words we can infer the basic assumptions, or core beliefs, on which the American system was founded: universal truths that can be known and acted on, equality before the law, belief in a higher power that transcends human law, and rights that are entitlements at birth and therefore can be neither granted nor taken away by government. The fundamental concept is liberty, especially the freedom to pursue one's livelihood and other personal goals that lead to a "happy" life.

The Declaration was primarily a political argument for separation from Great Britain, so it was concerned with the basic principles and philosophy of government.[45] Later, the Constitution reinforced the Declaration's emphasis on equality while specifying other core principles of American democracy: majority rule exercised through elected representatives and minority rights (a reference to political and religious minorities, not to racial and ethnic minorities). The Declaration is all principle; the Constitution is, of necessity, founded on political compromise.

Here we look briefly at each of the core principles of our political culture. Chapter 2 provides a more detailed description of how they are expressed in the Constitution.

Individual Liberty

Our belief in individual liberty has roots in the Judeo-Christian belief that every individual is equal and has worth before God. It has also been shaped by the works of the English philosophers **Thomas Hobbes** and **John Locke.** Briefly, they wrote that individuals give up some of their rights to government in return for creation of a society governed by laws in which they would be protected from one another. Individuals then use their remaining liberties to pursue their individually defined visions of the good life. There was a difference between Hobbes and Locke on what price individuals paid for surrendering some of their liberty to government. Hobbes believed the surrender of rights was near absolute once the people put themselves under government protection, and the curtailment of freedom was justified by the selfish, greedy nature of human beings.[46] Locke did not share this dark view of the need for unlimited government. He believed that in creating government individuals were entering into a voluntary covenant with one another (the "whole people"), that their surrender of rights was limited, and that the government created was subject to alteration or dissolution if it did not fulfill its purpose of protecting individual liberty.[47] He articulated the concept of **natural rights,** which are inherent, so they exist as soon as people are born; unalienable, so they cannot be taken away by rules; and self-evident, so they can be known to all.[48]

Hobbes's dark view of human nature was certainly shared to some degree by many Founders and is reflected in the institutional arrangements of our federal constitution. But it was Locke's concept of limited government operating according to written law that had greatest sway over the writers of our state and federal constitutions.

Influenced by these ideas, and reflecting the long tradition of individual rights in British law, early Americans emphasized individual liberty over other goals of government, and later Americans have reinforced this emphasis. ⭐ Thus liberty is clearly reflected in both the Bill of Rights adopted by the Founders and in court rulings articulated by later generations of judges. Liberty is also reflected in the way we talk. Most Americans speak of "the government," that is, a government in opposition to the people, rather than "our government."[49]

"If you hold those truths to be so self-evident, how come you keep harping on them?"

Assimilation can take awhile. These children of Asian immigrants—from Taiwan, India, the Philippines, Bangladesh, and Korea—have grown up in America but feel, one said, "like the hyphen" in Asian-American—that is, between Asian and American.

Such individualistic values have molded popular expectations. Immigrants often came and still come to America to be their own bosses. Living in a society with a clear commitment to individual liberty can be exciting and liberating. The other side of this coin is that we are also at liberty to fail and accept the consequences. And people who are limited by prejudice or poverty are given less help by government in overcoming these problems than people are given in other countries, which put more emphasis on the community as a whole rather than on the individual.[50]

The commitment to liberty is not absolute, however. Some restrictions are imposed on individual rights for the good of the community. For example, local zoning laws may restrict the liberty of one person to build a gas station in a residential neighborhood out of consideration for the neighborhood's residents and the value of their property. But our emphasis on individual liberty means that for better or worse—actually, for better *and* worse, there are fewer restrictions than in other countries where different values prevail.

A lively debate in recent decades has been sparked by those who believe that individual liberty has been overemphasized at the expense of community interests. Advocates of this position believe that our fixation on individual rights has led to a declining sense of community and a general lack of civility. They advocate revitalizing the concept of citizenship, including the responsibilities to participate in public life and "the qualities of character that self-government requires."[51] They call their program *communitarianism* and claim that it is much closer to the Founders' republican conception of freedom than is the modern liberal celebration of the unencumbered individual.

Political Equality

The Judeo-Christian belief that all people are equal in the eyes of God led logically to other types of equality, such as **political equality.** The ancient Greek emphasis on the opportunity and responsibility of all citizens to participate in ruling their city-states also contributed to our notion of political equality. Thus, the Declaration of Independence proclaims that "all Men are created equal." This does not mean that all people are born with equal talents or abilities. It means that all citizens are born with equal standing before government and are entitled to equal rights.

In the early years of our country, however, as in the ancient Greek city-states, full rights of citizenship were conferred only on those thought to have the intellectual and moral judgment to act in the public interest. In both Greece and the United States, such thinking denied political rights to slaves, who were believed incapable of independent judgment, and to women, whose knowledge was seen as limited to the private or domestic sphere. This left a deep tension between the religious view that sees each individual as equal before God and the secular concept of differential political rights. Over time, this conflict was resolved in favor of the inherent worth of every individual and hence the political equality of all. The conscious closing of this gap was noted by Lyndon Johnson when signing the 1964 Civil Rights Act into law: "those who are equal before God shall now also be equal in the polling places, in the classrooms, in the factories . . . ."[52]

Long before the Civil Rights Act was passed, most Americans considered themselves relatively equal politically and socially, if not economically. At minimum, Americans tend to believe that they are *inherently* equal, even when

"We can't come to an agreement about how to fix your car, Mr. Simons. Sometimes that's the way things happen in a democracy."

equality cannot be realized in the political arena. **Alexis de Tocqueville,** a perceptive Frenchman who traveled through the United States in the 1830s, observed that Americans felt more equal to one another than Europeans did. He attributed this feeling to the absence of a hereditary monarchy and aristocracy in this country. Americans did not look up to royalty and aristocrats as their "betters" the way Europeans did.[53]

Popular Sovereignty

A belief in political equality leads to **popular sovereignty,** or rule by the people. President **Abraham Lincoln** expressed this concept when he spoke of "government of the people, by the people, and for the people." If individuals are equal, no one person or small group has the right to rule others. Instead, the people collectively rule themselves.

Popular sovereignty, then, led to our form of government, a **democracy.** The word *democracy,* derived from the Greek, means "authority of the people." If all political authority resides in the people, then the people have the right to govern themselves. Of course, this entails a government by the many rather than by the few (aristocracy or oligarchy or theocracy) or by just one (monarchy or dictatorship).

Majority Rule

If political authority rests in the people collectively, and if all people are equal, then the majority should rule. That is, when there are disagreements over policies, majorities rather than minorities should decide. If individuals are equal, then policies should be determined according to the desires of the greater number. Otherwise, some individuals, the minority, would have more authority than others.

Majority rule helps provide the support necessary for a government. Those in the minority go along because they accept this principle and expect to be in the majority on other issues or at other times. (It helps if everyone wins some of the time.[54]) The minority also go along because they expect those in the majority to respect their basic rights. If these expectations are not fulfilled, the minority is less likely to accept majority rule and to tolerate majority decisions. Thus majority rule normally entails minority rights.

Minority Rights

The Founders were concerned about the rights of political and religious minorities. As a result of the expansion of individual rights in the twentieth century, Americans today are concerned about the rights of racial, ethnic, and sexual minorities as well.

Although **minority rights** are necessary to preserve majority rule in the long run, the two concepts clash with each other on a daily basis. For a democratic government, it's a delicate balance, and a constant struggle, to find an appropriate accommodation between majority rule and minority rights. Because the majority has more power, it tends to flex its muscles at the expense of the minority. The most egregious example has been the enslavement, segregation, and discrimination directed at African Americans, but other examples occur every day in our society. The idea that everyone loses when minority rights are trampled is a lesson that does not stay learned.

DEMOCRACY?

Throughout the text, we will be raising questions about democracy, and the compatibility of aspects of our government and our beliefs with it. Let's start with a tough one: are minority rights compatible with majority rule?

Economic Rights

The American Revolution was triggered by what the colonists saw as unfair taxation and other economic burdens placed on them by the British Parliament. To a certain extent, Americans fought the Revolution to be left alone to pursue their livelihoods and to ensure that they would not have to give up any part of their wealth without their consent.

Economic freedom, specifically the **right to own property,** is an adjunct to our concepts of individual liberty and natural rights. Locke considered this right an important natural right. According to Locke, when people work the land, clearing it and planting it, they mix their labor with it. This work makes the land their property. Although Americans had gotten the land through theft from the Indians and through luck from their ancestors (who had gotten it for little or nothing by royal grants in colonial times), in this view, the important thing is what they do with their land. Some inevitably accumulate more property and create more wealth than others. Yet, Locke believed that property rights would lead to greater productivity for society.[55]

Just as tension exists between individual liberty and the good of all, and between majority rule and minority rights, tension also exists between the political equality the Declaration of Independence avows and the property rights the Constitution protects (the latter will be discussed in Chapter 2). In reality, people who amass more wealth than others also exert more power over government.

The ancient Greeks, and some Founders such as Thomas Jefferson, feared that democracy could not tolerate extremes of wealth and poverty. They thought that a wealthy minority, out of arrogance, and an impoverished minority, out of desperation, would seek their own improvement and disregard the public interest. Most Founders worried less about this. They thought they could create a government that would protect individual diversity, including economic disparity, and still survive.

But the pursuit of political equality in a real world of great economic inequities has led government to a much greater role in regulating economic activity than the Founders anticipated. When we discuss antitrust laws and unfair business practices and when we discuss welfare, health care, and Social Security policies, we're implicitly debating whether government should reduce inequalities of wealth.

DEMOCRACY?

Can democracy function well when there are extreme differences in wealth and income? Why or why not?

We can see that democratic principles sometimes contradict each other. Americans have struggled for more than two centuries to reconcile practice with democratic aims and to perfect a system of government that was revolutionary for its time. We will see these contradictions many times in this book as we explore how government actually works.

The American Citizen

Supreme Court Justice Louis Brandeis once said, "The most important office in a democracy is the office of citizen."[56] That democratic principles come alive only when

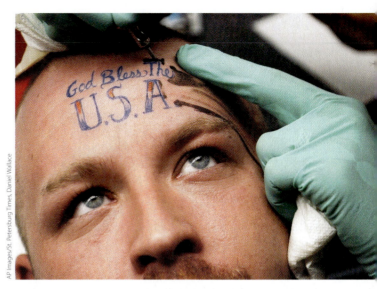

AP Images/St. Petersburg Times, Daniel Wallace

Americans, such as this man in St. Petersburg, Florida, are very patriotic, but many don't participate in our democracy.

people participate in government is a commonly held view. This raises two basic questions: how do rules for participation affect the level of participation, and how willing and prepared to participate is the average citizen?

One fundamental given that sets limits on citizen participation is that our form of government is an **indirect democracy**, also known as a **republic**. Citizens do not pass laws or make policy; they select policy makers to make decisions for them. It is members of Congress, not individual citizens, who vote most bills into law. These officials are not rulers or independent agents, but representatives of the people who draw their authority from a constitution sanctioned by the people.

This contrasts with a **direct democracy**, in which citizens vote on most issues and legislate for themselves. In the United States, forms of direct democracy exist only at the state and local levels. The best example is the town meeting, which has been the form of governance of many New England towns for over 350 years. Although town meetings today are often attended by relatively small numbers of citizens, they still offer one of the few opportunities people have to govern themselves directly. Citizens attending town meetings make their own decisions (for example, whether to put parking meters on the main street) and elect officers to enforce them (such as the police chief and city clerk).

Another form of direct democracy, the initiative, allows proposed legislation that has been initiated by members of the public (either individuals or interest groups) to be placed on a statewide election ballot if enough voters sign petitions supporting the proposal. If an initiative receives a majority of votes, it can, under some state constitutions, become law, allowing citizens to legislate directly. (More information on the initiative can be found in Chapter 3.)

As with many provisions in the U.S. Constitution, there are different ways to interpret what the Founders intended in choosing the republican form of government. Some people emphasize the impracticality of a direct democracy for any but a small citizenry, such as a town or a city-state. How could people from thirteen states meet to legislate for the country as a whole? Or how could so many individuals ever reach the compromises reflected in the final wording of most legislation? In this interpretation, the Founders never considered direct democracy because it was impracticable. Other interpreters of the Founders' intentions place more emphasis on the fear of popular rule, and there is no doubt that some Founders thought of direct democracy as something closer to mob rule. Specific provisions in the Constitution, such as those for suffrage, which was deferred to the states, and selection of government officials, allowing only House members to be directly elected, suggest that fear of direct democracy was a significant, if not primary, reason for selection of the republican form.

Given that the republican form of government does delegate decision-making authority to a limited group of officials, what must citizens contribute to the political process to make our government function democratically? The Founders did not leave many instructions for citizens. Obviously, they expected that some of the citizens ruled eligible by their states would vote, expected that some would stand for office, and expected that most would come to the defense of the country in emergencies (although service was not compulsory). We can also deduce that they expected that the small part of the electorate who voted would need to spend some time becoming acquainted with issues, which explains the Founders' support for education. Beyond that, however, little was said.

Political Participation

If you rented one of the classic movies about American government, you would likely see a story about a handful of idealistic elected officials who, with backing from the mass of equally idealistic citizens, triumph over complacent, jaded, or corrupt politicians. These stories reflect what is sometimes called our *self-belief*, our belief in the efficacy of our system of government and our fitness to govern ourselves. If our political process worked the way moviemakers, philosophers, and model builders think it should—and many Americans think it does—the majority of the public would be well informed, would discuss public affairs regularly, would let public officials know what they think, and would vote. In other words, most citizens would be committed to learning about and participating in government. And if you were to read most American government textbooks written before World War II, that is how the functioning of our democracy would have been described.

However, as more rigorous methods were applied to polling and survey studies, researchers discovered that far fewer citizens take advantage of their democratic rights than old theories and models predicted. For example, voting is the easiest way to participate in politics and the least costly in terms of time and energy. Yet slightly more than half of all eligible Americans vote in presidential elections, far fewer in non-presidential-year elections, and fewer still in local elections. Even in 2008, in what was hyped as one of the most exciting elections of the modern era, just over 61 percent of those eligible turned out to vote. Instead of being motivated to participate in politics as in a model democracy, most Americans are little involved. Only a tiny minority are activists who take full advantage of opportunities to participate. In fact, one-fifth of the electorate do nothing political at all; they do not even discuss politics.[57] Chapter 7 discusses the issue of participation in more detail.

Conclusion: Is Government Responsive?

This book is organized around the theme of government responsiveness. How responsive are government officials and policies to popular demands? The conclusion of each chapter will try to answer this question as it applies to whichever aspect of American government is covered in that chapter. (This will be more evident in the remaining chapters than in this introductory chapter.) In this first chapter, we have looked at the people's relation to and responsibility for government. So perhaps it is fair to ask ourselves how we measure up as citizens.

Americans love the idea that the average person has a say in government. Voting is the basic way, and the easiest way, to do so, yet barely half of us vote in presidential elections, far fewer in congressional and local elections.

Even after 9/11, when Americans were expressing a more favorable view of government, there was no increase in political participation. There was flag waving and a proliferation of flag magnets on cars, and there was vocal support for our troops abroad, but these actions don't make the country a democracy.

Many Americans practice "couch potato politics," refusing to accept the responsibilities of national citizenship.[58] In fact, a majority of Americans think it is possible to be patriotic without getting involved in political or civic life.[59]

Why do these Americans like their government on paper but dislike participating in it? Are they too busy to be bothered? Or has government failed? Are its laws and policies not what the people want? Are people turned off because the media emphasize the negative side of government? Are people alienated because some individuals and groups wield disproportionate power? Are average citizens actually shut out of the process? Or is the problem really the fault of citizens and not government at all? When asked, "What's wrong with government?" most Americans typically cite elected officials, political parties, the media, and special interests. Rarely do they blame the voters, or the public in general.

Dropping out of the political process because we think it is futile or controlled by special interests is like cutting off our noses to spite our faces. Throughout this book we'll see that government *is* responsive, but to people and groups who participate in politics. The old adage "the squeaky wheel gets the grease" applies to government as well as to other things.

Americans often say, "It's all politics." *Of course it is!* Diverse people and groups have different views about what the government should do. In a democracy, they're free to express their views and to influence their officials and insti-

tutions to adopt them. If we all agreed, there would be no need for debate, bargaining, compromise, or delays. So debates about issues and conflicts over elections are political. They reflect the competition and diverse views inherent in a democracy.

Ignoring politics and the institutions that represent the people to government, such as political parties and interest groups, would not eliminate politics. Neither would muzzling political parties and interest groups. Rather, it would eliminate the most effective way yet developed for the public to influence government's decisions.

Key Terms

politics
identity politics
United States Census
natural rights
political equality
popular sovereignty
democracy
minority rights
right to own property
indirect democracy
republic
direct democracy
political culture

Key Names

Aristotle
Emma Lazarus
Noah Webster
Thomas Jefferson
Thomas Hobbes
John Locke
Alexis de Tocqueville
Abraham Lincoln

Please visit our companion website at www.cengage.com/politicalscience/welch/uag12e or use CengageNOW for additional resources dealing with this chapter.

Despite his religious views, George Washington was pictured ascending to heaven. Soon after their deaths, the Founders were venerated by the people.

The Constitution

2

Talking Points

Today some politicians and church leaders tell Americans that the Founders were devout Christians who built the country on religious principles. Although some settlers did come to America for religious reasons and some colonies were established as religious bastions, the views of the most prominent Founders, including Benjamin Franklin, George Washington, Thomas Jefferson, and James Madison, were closer to deism than to Christianity.[1]

The Founders were products of the **Enlightenment**, also called the "Age of Reason," an intellectual force throughout Europe in the 1600s and 1700s. In this era, learned men rejected traditional religious, political, and social notions in favor of rational thought and scientific observation. They became more skeptical, more doubting of received "wisdom" passed down from prior generations and established institutions such as the church.

Deism reflected the spirit of the age. Deists believed in a Supreme Being who created the world but who didn't play an active role in day-to-day life. They believed that Jesus Christ was a great philosopher but not a divine figure (not the Son of God). They rejected most Christian doctrine, including biblical revelations and the existence of Hell, and criticized the Christian church and clergy.[2]

Although these prominent Founders were aware of the people's expectations that as leaders seeking or holding office they display the Christian faith in their church affiliation and public statements—you have probably read quotations illustrating this—their private beliefs differed significantly.[3]

George Washington, while acknowledging that conventional religion may be useful for lower classes and for the troops in the army, modeled his life on Roman philosophers and leaders rather than on Christian teachings.[4] He shied away from public pronouncements and made no private comments in his voluminous correspondence in support of the Christian faith. He felt obligated to join the Anglican (Episcopalian) Church, but he went infrequently and always left before communion. When the pastor rebuked him for setting a bad example by leaving, he stopped attending. He didn't keep the Sabbath. According to a contemporary, "card-playing and wine-drinking were the business of his parties, and he had more of such company on Sundays than on any other day."[5] On his deathbed, he didn't call for a minister, as many people did, and he didn't offer any prayers or indicate any expectation of eternal life.

Thomas Jefferson was more outspoken, calling Christianity "our particular superstition."[6] With a razor, he cut out all references to miracles or revelations in his Bible, and he urged his nephew to subject the New Testament to the same scrutiny he would give other ancient histories.

After Jefferson, James Madison was the most vocal proponent of separation of church and state. He warned against proclaiming Christianity our national religion, believing that religion was a divisive rather than unifying force. As he got older, Madison apparently became agnostic.[7]

Of the six most prominent Founders, only John Adams and Alexander Hamilton could be considered Christian.[8] Yet even they rejected some Christian doctrine. Consequently, it's not surprising that the Constitution is a secular document. It doesn't mention "God," "Creator," "Providence," or "divine."[9] It doesn't claim to be a compact between the people and God (or, like some monarchies, between the rulers and God); rather, it's a compact among the people, as the Preamble underscores—"We the people. . . ."

Early settlers came to America for different reasons. Some came to escape religious persecution, others to establish their own religious orthodoxy. Some came to avoid debtors' prison, others to get rich. Some came to flee the closed society of the Old World, others to make money for their families or employers in that world. Some came as free persons, others as indentured servants or slaves. Few came to practice self-government. Yet the desire for self-government was evident from the beginning.[10] The settlers who arrived in Jamestown in 1607 established the first representative assembly in America. The Pilgrims, who reached Plymouth in 1620, drew up the Mayflower Compact in which they vowed to "solemnly & mutually in the presence of God, and one of another, covenant and combine our selves together into a civill body politick." They pledged to establish laws for "the generall good of the colonie" and in return promised "all due submission and obedience."[11]

During the next century and a half, the colonies adopted constitutions and elected representative assemblies. Of course, the colonies lived under British rule; they had to accept the appointment of royal governors and the presence of British troops. But a vast ocean separated the two continents. At such distance, Britain could not wield the control it might at closer reach. It had to grant the colonies a measure of autonomy, which they used to practice the beginnings of self-government.

These early efforts toward self-government led to conflict with the mother government. In 1774, the colonies established the Continental Congress to coordinate their actions. Within months, the conflict reached flash point, and

american diversity | Founding Mothers

Charles Francis Adams, a grandson of President John Adams and Abigail Adams, declared in 1840, "The heroism of the females of the Revolution has gone from memory with the generation that witnessed it, and nothing, absolutely nothing remains upon the ear of the young of the present day."[1] That statement remains true today; in the volumes written about the revolutionary and Constitution-making era, much is said of the "Founding Fathers" but little about the "Founding Mothers." Although no women were delegates to the Constitutional Convention, in various ways—besides birthing and rearing the children and maintaining the homes—women contributed significantly to the founding of the country. Many contributed directly to the political ferment of the time. Their political role during the revolutionary and Constitution-making era was probably greater than it would be again for a century.

Before the Revolutionary War, women were active in encouraging opposition to British rule. Groups of women, some formed as the "Daughters of Liberty," organized resistance to British taxes by leading boycotts of British goods such as cloth and tea; they made their own cloth, hosting spinning bees, and their own drinks from native herbs and flowers.

A few women were political pamphleteers, helping increase public sentiment for independence. One of those pamphlet writers, Mercy Otis Warren, from Boston, was thought to be the first person to urge the Massachusetts delegates to the Continental Congress to vote for separation from Britain.[2] She also wrote poems advocating independence and plays satirizing British officials and sympathizers among the colonists (although the plays could only be read, not staged, because Puritan Boston forbade theater). Through-

out the period before and after the Revolution, Warren shared her political ideas in personal correspondence with leading statesmen of the time, such as John Adams and Thomas Jefferson. Later, she wrote a three-volume history of the American Revolution.

When the Declaration of Independence was drafted, the printer—a publisher in Maryland named Mary Katherine Goddard—printed her own name at the bottom of the Declaration in support of the signers who were in hiding from the British.

Because the Continental Army lacked money to pay, feed, and clothe the troops, women raised funds, canvassing door to door, and also made clothes for the soldiers. One group of women in Philadelphia made 2200 shirts.

During the Revolutionary War, many women followed their husbands into battle. As part of the

the Congress urged the colonies to form their own governments. In 1776, the Congress adopted the Declaration of Independence.

After six years of war, the Americans accepted the British surrender. At the time it seemed they had met their biggest test. Yet they would find fomenting a revolution easier than fashioning a government and drafting a declaration of independence easier than crafting a constitution.

The Articles of Confederation

Even before the war ended, the Continental Congress passed a constitution, and in 1781 the states ratified it. This first constitution, the **Articles of Confederation**, formed a

"league of friendship" among the states. As a confederation, it allowed each state to retain its "sovereignty" and "independence." That is, it made the states supreme over the national government.

Under the Articles, American elites became dissatisfied with their governments. They disparaged the weakness of the national government and feared the democracy of the state governments.

National Government Weakness

The Articles of Confederation established a Congress, but they limited the powers that Congress could exercise, and they provided no executive or judicial branch. The Articles

American army, most filled traditional women's roles as cooks, seamstresses, and nurses, but there are reports of women swabbing cannons with water to cool them and firing cannons when their husbands were wounded. After Margaret Corbin's husband was killed, she manned his artillery piece and was wounded three times. Later she received pay as a disabled soldier, including the ration for rum or whiskey. (Many years later she was reburied at West Point.) Some women disguised themselves as men (this was before a military bureaucracy mandated preenlistment physicals) and fought in battle. One wrapped tight bandages around her breasts and served three years and survived two wounds. Fellow soldiers thought she was a young man slow to grow a beard.[3] Still other women fought to defend their homes using hatchets, farm implements, and pots of boiling lye in addition to muskets.

Women also served as spies. When British soldiers commandeered one house for their quarters, the mother asked if she and her children could remain. One

This English political cartoon satirizes a gathering of leading women of North Carolina who drew up a resolution to boycott taxed English goods.

night she overheard the officers plotting a surprise attack on Washington's camp, and she sneaked out of town to warn the camp. A sixteen-year-old girl rode forty miles to warn a militia of another pending attack.[4]

Women were so prominent in the war that British general Lord Cornwallis said, "We may destroy all the men in America, and we shall

still have all we can do to defeat the women."[5]

Following independence, a few women continued an active political role. Mercy Otis Warren campaigned against the proposed Constitution because she felt it was not democratic enough. Abigail Adams called for new laws, unlike English laws which gave all power to husbands, that would provide some equality between husbands and wives. She also called for formal education for girls.

Yet independence did not bring an improvement in the political rights of women. It would be another century before the rights of women would become a full-fledged part of our national political agenda.

[1]Quoted in Linda Grant De Pauw and Conover Hunt, *Remember the Ladies* (New York: Viking, 1976), 9.
[2]Alice Felt Tyler, *Freedom's Ferment* (New York: Harper & Row), 1962.
[3]Cokie Roberts, *Founding Mothers* (New York: HarperCollins, 2004), 79–82.
[4]Mrs. Betsey Loring also made a heroic contribution to the cause by keeping a British general so "lustily occupied" in Philadelphia that he failed to move his troops to Valley Forge, where he could have destroyed the Continental Army. Alas, her motive was not patriotism; she sought a position in the British army for her husband. Roberts, *Founding Mothers*, xviii.
[5]Ibid., xix.

© Bettmann/Corbis

Although the Articles of Confederation gave the national government authority to print money, the states circulated their own currencies as well.

reflected the colonial experience under the British government. The leaders feared a central government with a powerful legislature or a powerful executive like a king. They thought such a government would be too strong and too distant to guarantee individual liberty.

Furthermore, the Articles reflected a lack of national identity among the people. Most did not yet view themselves as Americans. As Edmund Randolph remarked, "I am not really an American, I am a Virginian."[12] Consequently, the leaders established a very decentralized government that left most authority to the states.

The Articles satisfied many people. Most Americans worked small farms, and although many of them sank into debt during the depression that followed the war, they felt they could get their own state government to help them. They realized they could not influence a distant central government as readily.

But the Articles frustrated the bankers, merchants, manufacturers, and others in the upper classes who envisioned a great commercial empire replacing the agricultural society that existed in the late eighteenth century. More

than local trade, they wanted national and even international trade. For this they needed uniform laws, stable money, sound credit, and enforceable debt collection. They needed a strong central government that could protect them against debtors and against state governments sympathetic to debtors. The Articles provided neither the foreign security nor the domestic climate necessary to nourish these requisites of a commercial empire.

After the war, the army disbanded, leaving the country vulnerable to hostile forces surrounding it. Britain maintained outposts with troops in the Northwest Territory (the Midwest today), in violation of the peace treaty, and an army in Canada. Spain, which had occupied Florida and California for a long time and had claimed the Mississippi River valley as a result of a treaty before the war, posed a threat. Barbary pirates from North Africa seized American ships and sailors. (See box "The Black Flag on the High Seas.")

Congress could not raise an army, because it could not draft individuals directly, or finance an army, because it could not tax individuals directly. Instead, it had to ask the states for soldiers and money. The states, however, were not always sympathetic to the problems of the distant government. And although Congress could make treaties with foreign countries, the states made (and broke) treaties independently of Congress. Without the ability to establish a credible army or negotiate a binding treaty, the government could not get the British troops to leave American soil or the Spanish government to permit navigation on the Mississippi River.[13]

In addition to an inability to confront foreign threats, the Articles demonstrated an inability to cope with domestic crises. The country bore a heavy war debt that brought the government close to bankruptcy. Because Congress could not tax individuals directly, it could not shore up the shaky government. The states competed with each other for commercial advantage. As independent governments, they imposed tariffs on goods from other states. The tariffs slowed business growth.

In short, the government under the Articles of Confederation seemed too decentralized to ensure either peace or prosperity. The Articles, one leader concluded, gave Congress the privilege of asking for everything while reserving to each state the prerogative of granting nothing.[14] A similar situation exists today in the United Nations, which must rely on the goodwill of member countries to furnish troops for its peace-keeping forces and dues for its operating expenses.[15]

State Government Democracy

State constitutions adopted during the American Revolution made the state legislatures more representative than the colonial legislatures had been. Most state legislatures also be-

THE BLACK FLAG ON THE HIGH SEAS

Americans faced attacks from pirates as well as threats from foreign powers. As many as a hundred merchant ships sailed from American ports to Mediterranean cities each year, bringing salted fish, flour, sugar, and lumber and returning with figs, lemons, oranges, olive oil, and opium. Barbary pirates from North Africa—Tripoli (now Libya), Tunis (Tunisia), Algeria, and Morocco—preyed upon ships in the Mediterranean Sea, seizing sailors, holding them for ransom or pressing them into slavery, and extorting money from shippers and governments.[1] Historians estimate that a million Europeans and Americans were kidnapped or enslaved by these pirates in the seventeenth and eighteenth centuries.

Although American ships were protected by the British navy (and by the British government's willingness to pay tribute) during colonial times, they were not shielded after independence. The weakness of the government under the Articles of Confederation left the ships' crews to fend for themselves. The marauding pirates were a nasty rebuke not only to American merchants' desire for international trade but also to our citizens' belief in free trade on the seas, without acts of violence or demands for payments.

The conflict was mostly over riches—the Barbary states used piracy to finance their governments—but it also reflected religious conflict. The Barbary states were Muslim, and although their societies would not be called fundamentalist or Islamist today—in fact, they treated their Jewish residents better than most European societies did at the time—their leaders told American officials that the Koran gave them the right to enslave infidels.[2]

The piracy would not cease until the new government under the Constitution created a strong navy and fought the Barbary Wars (1801–1805)—the first deployment of the American military overseas.[3]

[1] Other pirates patrolled the Caribbean, with some operating out of New Orleans.
[2] Previously, European states had held Muslim slaves.
[3] This led to the line in the Marines Corps anthem "to the shores of Tripoli."

SOURCES: Christopher Hitchens, "Black Flag," *New York Times Book Review*, August 21, 2005, 7–8; Max Boot, *The Savage Wars of Peace* (New York: Basic Books, 2002), 3–29.

---

gan to hold elections every year. The result was heightened interest among candidates and turnover among legislators. In the eyes of national leaders, there was much pandering to voters and horse trading by politicians as various factions vied for control. The process seemed up for grabs. According to the Vermont Council of Censors, laws were "altered—realtered—made better—made worse; and kept in such a fluctuating position that persons in civil commission scarce know what is law."[16] In short, state governments were experiencing more democracy than any other governments in the world at the time. National leaders, stunned by the changes in the few years since the Revolution, considered this development an "excess of democracy."

These leaders, most of whom were wealthy and many of whom were creditors, pointed to the laws passed in some states that relieved debtors of some of their obligations. The farmers in debt pressed the legislatures for relief that would slow or shrink the payments owed to their creditors, and some legislatures granted such relief.

These laws worried the leaders, and **Shays's Rebellion** in western Massachusetts in 1786 and 1787 frightened them. Boston merchants who had loaned Massachusetts money during the war insisted on being repaid in full so they could trade with foreign merchants. The state levied steep taxes that many farmers could not pay during the hard times. The law authorized foreclosure—sale of the farmers' property to recover unpaid taxes—and jail for the debtors. The law essentially transferred wealth from the farmers to the merchants. The Massachusetts government wasn't as sympathetic to debtors as some other states were. The farmers protested the legislature's refusal to grant any relief from the law. Bands of farmers blocked entrances to court-houses where judges were scheduled to hear cases calling for foreclosure and jail. Led by Daniel Shays, some marched to the Springfield arsenal to seize weapons. Although they were defeated by the militia, their sympathizers were victorious in the next election.

Both the revolt and the legislature's change in policy scared the wealthy. To them it raised the specter of mob rule. Nathaniel Gorham, the president of the Continental Congress and a prominent merchant, wrote Prince Henry of Prussia, announcing "the failure of our free institutions" and asking whether the prince would agree to become king of America (the prince declined).[17] Just months after the uprising, Congress approved a convention for "the sole and express purpose of revising the Articles of Confederation."

To a significant extent, then, the debate at the time reflected a conflict between two competing visions of the future American political economy—agricultural or commercial.[18] Most leaders espoused the latter, and the combination of national problems and state problems prompted them to push for a new government.[19]

The Constitution
The Constitutional Convention
The Setting

The **Constitutional Convention** convened in Philadelphia, then the country's largest city, in 1787. State legislatures sent fifty-five delegates. They met at the Pennsylvania State House—now Independence Hall—in the same room where many of them had signed the Declaration of Independence eleven years earlier. Delegates came from every state except Rhode Island, whose farmers and debtors feared that the convention would weaken states' powers to relieve debtors of their debts.

All of the delegates were men (see the box "Founding Mothers"). They were distinguished by their education, experience, and enlightenment. **Benjamin Franklin**, of Pennsylvania, was the best-known American in the world. He had been a printer, scientist, and diplomat. At eighty-one, he was the oldest delegate. **George Washington**, of Virginia, was the most respected American in the country. As the commander of the revolutionary army, he was a national hero. He was chosen to preside over the convention. The presence of men like Franklin and Washington gave the convention legitimacy.

The delegates quickly determined that the Articles of Confederation were beyond repair. Rather than revise them, as instructed by Congress, the delegates decided to draft a new constitution.[20]

The Predicament

The delegates came to the convention because they thought their government was too weak, yet the Americans had fought the Revolution because they chafed under a government that was too strong. "The nation lived in a nearly constant alternation of fears that it would cease being a nation altogether or become too much of one."[21] People feared both anarchy and tyranny.

This predicament was made clear by the diversity of opinions among the leaders. At one extreme was Patrick Henry, of Virginia, who had been a firebrand of the Revolution. He feared that the government would become too strong, perhaps even become a monarchy, in reaction to the problems with the Articles. He said he "smelt a rat" and did not attend the convention. At the other extreme was Alexander Hamilton, of New York, who had been an aide to General Washington during the war and had seen the government's inability to supply and pay its own troops. Ever since, he had called for a stronger national government and had even suggested a monarchy. He did attend the convention but, finding little agreement with his proposals, participated infrequently.

In between was **James Madison**, of Virginia. The debate revolved around his plan. Throughout the convention, Madison was "up to his ears in politics, advising, persuading, softening the harsh word, playing down this difficulty and exaggerating that, engaging in debate, harsh controversy, polemics, and sly maneuver."[22] In the end, his views more than anyone else's would prevail, and he would become known as the Father of the Constitution.[23]

Consensus

Despite disagreements, the delegates did see eye to eye on the most fundamental issues. They agreed that the government should be a **republic**—a form of government that derives its power from the people and whose officials are accountable to the people. The term more specifically refers

---

BEHIND THE SCENES
SMALL BUT SAVVY

James Madison was described as "no bigger than half a piece of soap."[1] Though small and frail, timid and self-conscious as a speaker, he was nonetheless an intelligent and savvy politician.

He operated behind the scenes to organize the Constitutional Convention and to secure George Washington's attendance. Washington was in retirement at his plantation at Mount Vernon and had not planned to attend the convention. Because his presence would lend the convention more legitimacy, Madison notified other delegates that Washington would attend—without asking Washington first. After Madison created the expectation that he would attend, Washington reluctantly agreed to do so.[2]

Before the convention, Madison, who had studied other countries' governments, concluded that the Articles of Confederation should be replaced rather than reformed. He realized that he would have more influence if he had a plan to offer the delegates, who were disenchanted with the Articles but uncertain what to substitute. Madison secretly drafted a plan for a new constitution, a sharp departure from the Articles. Ultimately, his plan would set the agenda for the convention and lay the foundation for the Constitution.

[1] Quoted in Gary Wasserman, *Politics in Action* (Boston: Houghton Mifflin, 2006), 5.
[2] Fred Barbash, "James Madison: A Man for the '80s," *Washington Post National Weekly Edition*, March 30, 1987, 23.

to an indirect democracy in which the people vote for at least some of the officials who represent them.[24]

They also agreed that the national government should be stronger than under the Articles and that it should have three separate branches—legislative, executive, and judicial—to exercise the three functions of government—making, administering, and judging the laws. They thought that both the legislative and executive branches should be strong.

⭐ When we refer to constitutional provisions, we'll call attention to them with this icon, and we'll also provide the location in the Constitution (unless the paragraph already indicates the location). The composition and authority of the legislative branch is addressed in Article I, that of the executive branch in Article II, and that of the judicial branch in Article III.

Conflict

Although there was considerable agreement over the fundamental principles and elemental structure of the new government, the delegates quarreled about the specific provisions concerning representation, slavery, trade, and taxation.

Representation Sharp conflict was expressed between delegates from large states and those from small states over representation. Large states sought a strong government that they could control; small states feared a strong government that could control them.

When the convention began, the Virginia Plan, drafted by Madison, was introduced. According to this plan, the legislature would be divided into two houses, with representation based on population in each. But delegates from the small states calculated that the three largest states would have a majority of the representatives and could dominate the legislature.

These delegates countered with the New Jersey Plan. According to this plan, the legislature would consist of one house, with representation by states, which would have one vote each. This was exactly the same as the structure of Congress under the Articles, also designed to prevent the largest states from dominating the legislature.

James Wilson, of Pennsylvania, asked for whom they were forming a government—"for men, or for the imaginary beings called states?"[25] But delegates from the small states would not budge. Some threatened to leave the government and align themselves with a European country instead.[26]

The convention deadlocked, and some delegates left for home. George Washington wrote that he almost despaired of the likelihood of reaching any agreement. To ease tensions, Benjamin Franklin suggested that the delegates begin each day with a prayer, but they could not agree on this either; Alexander Hamilton insisted that they did not need "foreign aid."

Faced with the possibility that the convention would disband without a constitution, the delegates, after weeks of frustrating debate, compromised. Delegates from Connecticut and other states proposed a plan in which the legislature, Congress, would have two houses. In one, the **House of Representatives**, representation would be based on population, and members would be elected by voters. In the other, the **Senate**, representation would be by states, and members would be selected by state legislatures. Presumably, the large states would dominate the former, the small states the latter (see the box "Is the Senate Democratic?"). The delegates narrowly approved this **Great Compromis**e, or Connecticut Compromise.[27] The compromise has been called "great" because it not only resolved this critical issue but paved the way for resolution of other issues.

This decision began a pattern that continues to this day. When officials face implacable differences, they try to compromise, but the process is not easy. It is an apt choice of words to say that officials "hammer out" a compromise; it is not a coincidence that we use *hammer* rather than a softer metaphor.

Slavery In addition to conflict between large states and small states over representation, conflict emerged between northern states and southern states over slavery, trade, and taxation.

With representation in one house based on population, the delegates had to decide how to apportion the seats. They agreed that Indians would not count as part of the population but differed about slaves. Delegates from the South, where slaves made up one-third of the population, wanted slaves to count fully in order to boost the number of southern representatives. Although slaves had not been counted at all under the Articles or under any state constitution, southerners argued that their use of slaves produced wealth that benefited the entire nation. Delegates from the North, where most states had outlawed slavery or at least the slave trade after the Revolution, did not want slaves to count at all. Gouverneur Morris, of Pennsylvania, said the southerners' position

> comes to this: that the inhabitant of Georgia and South Carolina who goes to the coast of Africa, and in defiance of the most sacred laws of humanity tears away his fellow creatures from their dearest connections and damns them to the most cruel bondages, shall have more votes in a government instituted for the protection of the rights of mankind than the citizen of Pennsylvania or New Jersey who views with a laudable horror so nefarious a practice.[28]

Others pointed out that slaves were not considered persons when it came to rights such as voting. Nevertheless, southerners asserted that they would not support the constitution if slaves were not counted at least partially. In the **Three-Fifths Compromise**, the delegates agreed that three-fifths of the slaves would be counted in apportioning the seats.

IS THE SENATE DEMOCRATIC?

After slavery was abolished and the right to vote was extended to racial minorities and women, the equal representation of states in the Senate is perhaps the most undemocratic aspect left in the Constitution.[1]

Because each state gets two senators regardless of its population, small or sparsely populated rural states enjoy disproportionate representation relative to their size. California, the most populous state, and Wyoming, the least populous state, have equal representation, although California has seventy times more people. Therefore, voters in California have one-seventieth as much representation, or power, in the Senate as voters in Wyoming have. (See Figure 2.1.)

The equal representation of states in the Senate is not the result of some grand theory of government. As explained in the text, it was a major concession to the small states to maintain their allegiance to the country and to obtain their support for the Constitution. At that time, people identified more closely with their state than with the nation as a whole. Today, our mass society, mass media, and transportation networks weaken these ties and strengthen our sense of national identity.

Do the people in small states have special needs to protect that would justify their greater representation? The Constitution, including the Bill of Rights and later amendments, guarantees fundamental rights. Federal laws and court decisions preserve various rights. Federalism, which splits power between the national government and the state governments, provides states with more authority than they would have in nonfederal systems. Do the people in small states have additional needs to protect beyond these? If so, what are they? And are these needs greater than the needs of other people who do not get extra representation, such as the people who are disabled or the people who have been the victims of widespread discrimination, such as African Americans or Native Americans, just to name a few groups?

What if a similar rationale were applied to African Americans? If the 12 percent of Americans who are black had as many senators representing them as the 12 percent of Americans who live in our smallest states have representing them, the Senate would include forty-four black senators. Would this seem fair?

Yet even if most Americans decide that the equal representation in the Senate is unfair and undemocratic, it is unlikely they could change it. The Constitution stipulates, "No state, without its consent, shall be deprived of its equal suffrage in the Senate."[2] Furthermore, Article 5, which addresses amendments, limits amendments in two categories. The provision regarding the importation of slaves could not be amended until 1808, and the provision regarding the representation in

Figure 1

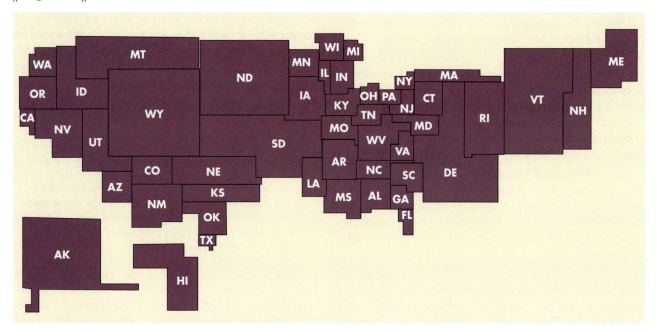

The size of each state in this map reflects the relative power of its citizens in the Senate.
SOURCE: Michael Lind, "75 Stars," Mother Jones (January–February 1998), p. 130. Reprinted with permission.

the Senate cannot be amended ever.

Some constitutional scholars suggest that an amendment repealing this provision could be adopted first and an amendment altering the representation itself could be adopted

next. Other scholars think the courts would not tolerate this obvious sabotage of the Founders' intentions.[3] Regardless, it is a moot point, because amendment of the Constitution requires ratification by three-fourths of the states. Just thirteen states can block an amend-

ment favored by the rest of the country. The thirteen smallest states, with only 5 percent of the nation's population, thus can thwart the wishes of the thirty-seven largest states, with 95 percent of the nation's people. Does this seem democratic?

[1] Most information in this box is from Robert A. Dahl, *How Democratic Is the American Constitution?* (New Haven, Conn.: Yale University Press, 2001).
[2] This provision is reinforced by Article 4, which stipulates that "no . . . state shall be formed by the junction of two or more states, or parts of states, without the consent of . . . the states concerned." Therefore, small states cannot be forced to combine as a way to reduce their representation.
[3] J. W. Peltason, *Corwin and Peltason's Understanding the Constitution,* 9th ed. (New York: Holt, Rinehart and Winston, 1982), 113. For a creative alternative, see Michael Lind, "75 Stars," *Mother Jones* (January–February 1998), 44–49.

Art. I, Sec. 2 This compromise expanded the political power of the people who were oppressing the slaves. The votes of southern whites became worth more than those of northerners in electing members to the House of Representatives and also in electing presidents (because the number of presidential electors for each state was based on the number of members in Congress from the state). By 1860, nine of the fifteen presidents, including all five who served two terms, were slave owners.[29] Ultimately, twelve presidents were slave owners.

Southerners pushed through two other provisions addressing slavery. One forbade Congress from banning the importation of slaves before 1808; another required free states to return escaped slaves to their owners in slave states. In these provisions, southerners won most of what they wanted; even the provision permitting Congress to ban the importation of slaves in 1808 was little limitation because by then planters would have enough slaves to fulfill their needs by natural population increases. In return, northerners, who represented shippers, got authority for Congress to regulate commerce by a simple majority rather than a two-thirds majority. Thus northerners conceded these provisions, which reinforced slavery, to benefit shippers.[30]

Art. I, Sec. 9 Yet the framers were embarrassed by
Art. IV, Sec. 2 the hypocrisy of claiming to have been
Art. I, Sec. 8 enslaved by the British while allowing enslavement of African Americans. Their embarrassment is reflected in their language. The three provisions reinforcing slavery never mention "slavery" or "slaves"; one gingerly refers to "free persons" and "other persons."

Slavery was the most divisive issue at the convention. As Madison noted, "The real difference of interests lay, not between the large and small, but between the northern and southern states. The institution of slavery and its consequences formed the line of discrimination."[31] The unwillingness to tackle the slavery issue more directly has been called the "Greatest Compromise" by one political scien-

tist.[32] But an attempt to abolish slavery would have caused the five southern states to refuse to ratify the Constitution.

Trade and Taxation

Art. I, Sec. 9 Slavery also underlay a compromise on trade and taxation. With a manufacturing economy, northerners sought protection for their businesses. In particular, they wanted a tax on manufactured products imported from Britain. Without a tax, British goods would be cheaper than northern products; with a tax, northern products would be more competitive—but prices for northern and southern consumers would be higher. With an agricultural economy, southerners sought free trade for their plantations. They wanted a guarantee that no tax would be levied on agricultural commodities exported to Britain. Such a tax would make their commodities less competitive and, they worried, amount to an indirect tax on slavery—the labor responsible for the crops. The delegates resolved these issues by allowing Congress to tax imported goods but not exported ones.

After seventeen weeks of debate, thirty-nine of the original fifty-five delegates signed the Constitution on September 17, 1787. Some delegates had left when they saw the direction the convention was taking, and three others refused to sign, feeling that the Constitution gave too much authority to the national government. Most of the rest were not entirely happy with the result (even Madison, who was most responsible for the content of the document, was despondent that his plan for a national legislature was compromised by having one house with representation by states), but they thought it was the best they could do.

Features of the Constitution

Years later, however, a British prime minister said the American Constitution was "the most wonderful work ever struck off at a given time by the brain and purpose of man."[33] To see why it was unique, we'll examine its major features.

© Bettmann/Corbis

This plan of a slave ship shows the overcrowding that led to inhumane conditions, rampant disease, and high mortality.

A Republic

The Founders distinguished between a democracy and a republic. For them, a *democracy* meant a **direct democracy**, which permits citizens to vote on most issues, and a *republic* meant an **indirect democracy**, which allows citizens to vote for their representatives, who make governmental policies.

DEMOCRACY?

What are the implications—for our elections, officials, and laws—of having an indirect democracy rather than a direct democracy?

Although many small towns in New England used (and some still use) a direct democracy, the Founders opposed a direct democracy for the whole country. Some city-states of ancient Greece and medieval Europe had a direct democracy but could not sustain it. A large country, the Founders thought, would have even less ability to do so because people could not be brought together in one place to debate and vote. Moreover, the Founders believed that people could not withstand the passions of the moment, so they would be swayed by a demagogue to take unwise action. Eventually, democracy would collapse into tyranny.

⭐ Art. I, Sec. 2 & 3 The Founders favored a republic
Art. II, Sec. 1 because they believed that the government should be based on the consent of the people and that the people should have some voice in choosing their officials. So the Founders provided that the people would elect representatives to the House. They also provided

that the state legislators, themselves elected by the people, would select their state's senators as well as their state's electors for the Electoral College, which chooses the president. In this way, the people would have a voice but one partially filtered through their presumably wiser representatives.

The Founders' views reflect their ambivalence about the people. Rationally, they believed in popular sovereignty, but emotionally, they feared the concept. New England clergyman Jeremy Belknap voiced their ambivalence when he declared, "Let it stand as a principle that government originates from the people; but let the people be taught . . . that they are not able to govern themselves."[34]

The Founders would have been aghast at the proliferation of such experiments in direct democracy as initiatives, referenda, and recall elections in many states. The **initiative** process allows citizens and interest groups to collect signatures on petitions and place a proposal on the ballot. If enough voters favor the proposal, it becomes law.[35] The **referendum** process allows the legislature to place a proposal on the ballot. **Recall elections** enable voters to remove officials from office before their terms expire.

The Founders considered a democracy radical and a republic only slightly less radical. Because they believed that the country could not maintain a democracy, they worried that it might not be able to maintain a republic either. It is said that when the Constitutional Convention ended, Benjamin Franklin was approached by a woman who asked, "Well, Doctor, what have we got, a republic or a monarchy?" Franklin responded, "A republic, Madam, if you can keep it."

Fragmentation of Power

Other countries assumed that a government must have a concentration of power to be strong enough to govern. However, when the Founders made our national government more powerful than it had been under the Articles of Confederation, they feared that they also had made it more capable of oppression, so they fragmented its power.

The Founders believed that people are selfish, always coveting more property, and that leaders always lust after more power. They assumed that this aspect of human nature is unchangeable. Madison speculated, "If men were angels, no government would be necessary." "Alas," he added, "men are not angels." Therefore, "in framing a government which is to be administered by men over men, the great difficulty lies in this: you must first enable the government to control the governed; and in the next place oblige it to control itself."[36] The Founders decided that the way to oblige the government to control itself was to structure it so as to prevent any one leader, group of leaders, or factions of people from exercising power over more than a small part of it. Thus the Founders fragmented government's power. This is reflected in three concepts they built into the structure of government—federalism, separation of powers, and checks and balances. (The Founders' views are conveyed in the *Federalist Papers*, especially in Nos. 10 and 51, which are included in the Appendix of this text.)

Federalism The first division of power was between the national government and the state governments. This division of power is called **federalism**.[37] The U.S. government under the Articles of Confederation had been confederal (as the Confederacy of southern states during the Civil War would also be); that is, the state governments wielded most authority. The national government exercised only the powers given it by the state governments. At the other extreme, most foreign governments had been unitary; the central government wielded all authority.[38]

The Founders, who had had unhappy experiences with a confederal system (their own government under the Articles) and a unitary system (the British government during colonial times), wanted to avoid both types. Instead, they sought a strong national government but reasonably strong state governments as well. They invented a federal system as a compromise between the confederal and unitary systems.

They saw federalism as a way to provide sufficient power for the government to function while checking excessive power that could lead to tyranny. They worried about the **"mischiefs of factions"**—groups seeking something for themselves without regard for the rights of others or the well-being of all.[39] According to Madison, factions could be controlled through federalism.[40] A faction might dominate one state but would be less able to dominate many states. (Nevertheless, we should note that federalism is not necessary for a democratic government. Some unitary governments, such as those of Britain and Sweden, are among the most democratic in the world today.)

The Constitution delegates some powers to the national government and reserves other powers for the state governments. Authority over foreign affairs—to make treaties, repel attacks, and declare war—is given to the national government. Authority to print and coin money and to regulate interstate commerce was also given to the national government, and authority to tax was given to both levels.

Art. I, Sec. 8 These provisions ensured a stronger
Art. 6 national government in foreign and domestic matters than under the Articles.[41] In addition, the Constitution's **supremacy clause** declares that the Constitution is the supreme law of the land and that any laws and treaties made "in pursuance thereof" also are the supreme law of the land whenever they conflict with state laws or actions. But authority over many other matters, including broad authority to provide for the welfare of the people, was given to the state governments. The **Tenth Amendment**, which reflects the general understanding of the time, stipulates that the powers not delegated to the national government are reserved for the states. So this guarantee ensured reasonably strong state governments as well.[42]

Yet the Constitution's language is so general and so succinct that it is very ambiguous. This made the document acceptable both to advocates of a strong national government and supporters of strong state governments, but it also made the document flexible so it could be interpreted as later generations desired or critical challenges required. The language could support either nation-centered federalism, which underscores the power of the nation in the arrangement, or state-centered federalism, which emphasizes the power of the states. (These concepts will be explored further in Chapter 3.)

Separation of powers The second division of power was within the national government. The power to make, administer, and judge the laws was split into three branches—legislative, executive, and judicial (see Figure 2.2). In the legislative branch, the power was split further into two houses. This **separation of powers** contrasts with the parliamentary systems in most developed democracies, in which the legislature is supreme. In parliamentary systems, both executive and judicial officials are drawn from the legislature and are responsible to it. There is no separation of powers.

Art. II, Sec. 2 To reinforce the separation of powers,
Art. III, Sec. 1 officials of the three branches were chosen by different means. Representatives were elected by the people (at that time mostly white men who owned property), senators were selected by the state legislatures, and the president was selected by the Electoral College, whose members were selected by the states. Only federal judges were chosen by officials in the other branches. They were

nominated by the president and confirmed by the Senate. Once appointed, however, they were allowed to serve for "good behavior"—essentially for life—so they had much independence. (Since the Constitution was written, the Seventeenth Amendment has provided for election of senators by the people, and the state legislatures have provided for election of members of the Electoral College by the people.)

Officials of the branches were also chosen at different times. Representatives were given a two-year term, senators a six-year term (with one-third of them up for reelection every two years), and the president a four-year term. These staggered terms would make it less likely that temporary passions in society would bring about a massive switch of officials or policies.

The Senate was designed to act as a conservative brake on the House, due to senators' selection by state legislatures and their longer terms. Upon his return, Thomas Jefferson, who was in France during the Constitutional Convention, met with George Washington over breakfast. Jefferson protested the establishment of a legislature with two houses. Washington supposedly asked, "Why did you pour that coffee into your saucer?" "To cool it," Jefferson replied. Similarly, Washington explained, "We pour legislation into the senatorial saucer to cool it."[43]

Separation of powers creates the opportunity for **divided government**. Rather than one political party controlling both elected branches, one party might win the presidency while the other party wins a majority of seats in one or both houses of Congress. Divided government has been common throughout the nation's history. Since the emergence of the Democratic and Republican party system (1856), it has occurred as a result of two of every five elections.[44] Since World War II, it has been the dominant mode of government.[45] In this way, American voters have added another element to Madison's concept of separation of powers.

DEMOCRACY?

What implications from divided government would you expect? How might divided government affect the ability to pass laws? The need to foster compromise?

Checks and balances To further prevent concentration of power, the Founders built in **checks and balances** (see Figure 3). Madison suggested that "the great security against a gradual concentration of the several powers in the same department consists in giving those who administer each department the necessary constitutional means and personal motives to resist encroachments by the others. . . . *Ambition must be made to counteract ambition.*"[46] To that end, each branch was given some authority over the others. If one branch abuses its power, the others can use their checks to thwart it.

Art. I, Sec. 7   Thus rather than a simple system of separation of powers, ours is a complex, even contradictory, system of both separation of powers and checks and balances. The principle of separation of powers gives each branch its own sphere of authority, but the system of checks and balances allows each branch to intrude into the spheres of the other branches. For example, due to separation of powers, Congress makes the laws; but due to checks and balances, the president can veto them and the courts can rule them unconstitutional. In these ways, all three branches are involved in legislating. One political scientist calls ours "a government of separated institutions competing for shared powers."[47]

With federalism, separation of powers, and checks and balances, the Founders expected conflict. They invited the several parts of government to struggle against each other and to limit any one part's ability to dominate the rest. The Founders hoped for "balanced government." The national and state governments would represent different interests, as would the branches within the national government. The House would represent the "common" people and the large states; the Senate, the wealthy people and the small states; the president, all the people; and the Supreme Court, the Constitution. Although each part would struggle for more power, it could not accumulate enough to dominate the others. Eventually, it would have to compromise and accept policies that would reflect the interest of all of the parts and their constituencies.

Undemocratic Features

The Founders left undemocratic features in the Constitution that later generations would have to deal with.[48] They denied some Americans the right to participate in their government and some Americans equal treatment by their government.

The Constitution did not forbid slavery. It did not allow Congress to halt the slave trade for over two decades. The Three-Fifths Compromise actually institutionalized slavery and increased the political power of slaveholders.

Furthermore, the Constitution did not guarantee the right to vote, allowing states to exclude African Americans, Native Americans, other minorities, and women. For some years, states also excluded white men who didn't own property and those who weren't members of the established church from voting. The Founders created the Electoral College to prevent the people from choosing the president. Even with the advent of popular election of the electors, the Electoral College still allows the election of a candidate who did not receive the most popular votes. The Founders

Figure 2 | Separation of Powers

Branch:	Legislative Congress		Executive Presidency	Judicial Federal Courts
	House	Senate	President	Judges
Officials chosen by:	People	People, (originally, state legislatures)	Electoral College, whose members are chosen by the people (originally, by state legislatures)	President, with advice and consent of Senate
For term of:	2 years	6 years	4 years	Life
To represent primarily:	Common people	Wealthy people	All people	Constitution
	Large states	Small states		

Separation of powers, as envisioned by the Founders, means not only that government functions are to be performed by different branches but also that officials of these branches are to be chosen by different people, for different terms, and to represent different constituencies.

stipulated that state legislatures would choose the senators to prevent the people from choosing them. By giving each state two seats in the Senate, the Founders gave disproportionate power to the people who happen to live in small states (as explained in the box "Is the Senate Democratic?").

The Founders included these features partly because of their need to compromise and partly because of their view that the people could not be trusted. The people were seen as an unruly mob threatening stable, orderly government. As later history would show, however, the Founders exaggerated the dangers of popular majorities. When Americans became more egalitarian in the decades following the adoption of the Constitution, they demanded a greater role for the average person. One political scientist concluded that if the Constitution had been written in 1820 instead of 1787, it would have been a very different, and more democratic, document.[49]

Motives of the Founders

To understand the Constitution better, it is useful to consider the motives of the Founders. Were they selfless patriots, sharing their wisdom and experience? Or were they selfish property owners, protecting their interests? Let's consider the philosophical ideas, political experience, and economic interests that influenced the Founders.

Philosophical Ideas

The Founders were well-educated intellectuals who incorporated philosophical ideas into the Constitution. At a time when the average person did not dream of going to college, a majority of the Founders graduated from college. As learned men, they shared a common library of writers and philosophers.

The Founders, reflecting the ideals of the Enlightenment, studied past governments to determine why the governments had failed in the hope that they could apply these lessons to the present. From all accounts, they engaged in a level of debate that was rare in politics, citing philosophers ranging from the ancient Greeks to the modern British and French.

The writings of **John Locke**, as explained in Chapter 1, underlay many of the ideas of the Founders. In addition to his views on natural rights and property rights, the Founders endorsed Locke's views about the relationship between the people and their government. Locke maintained that the people come together to form a government through a **social contract**—an implied agreement between the people and their government—that establishes a **limited government**, strong enough to protect their rights but not so strong as to threaten these rights. This government should not act without the consent of the governed.[50]

The views of **Charles de Montesquieu**, an eighteenth-century French philosopher, also influenced the debate at

Figure 3 || Checks and Balances

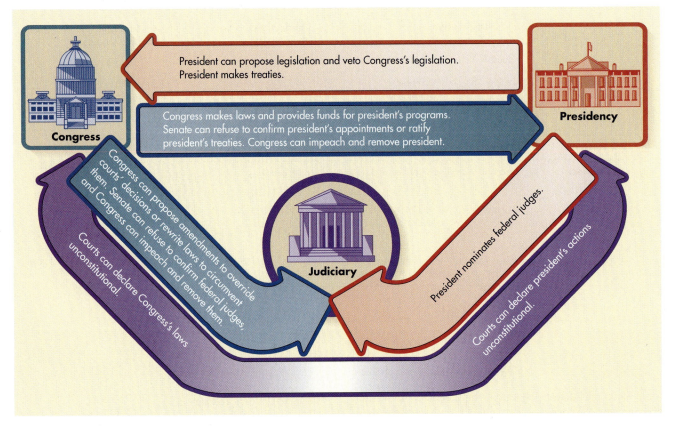

President can propose legislation and veto Congress's legislation. President makes treaties.

Congress makes laws and provides funds for president's programs. Senate can refuse to confirm president's appointments or ratify president's treaties. Congress can impeach and remove president.

Congress

Presidency

Judiciary

Congress can propose amendments to override courts' decisions or rewrite laws to circumvent them. Senate can refuse to confirm federal judges, and Congress can impeach and remove them.

Courts can declare Congress's laws unconstitutional.

President nominates federal judges.

Courts can declare president's actions unconstitutional.

Most of the major checks and balances among the three branches are explicit in the Constitution, although some are not. For example, the courts' power to declare congressional laws or presidential actions unconstitutional—their power of "judicial review"—is not mentioned.

the convention and the provisions of the Constitution. Although others had suggested separation of powers before, Montesquieu refined the concept and added that of checks and balances. The Founders cited him more than any other thinker.[51] (Presumably, they cited him more than Locke because by this time Locke's views had so permeated American society that the Founders considered them just "common sense."[52])

The principles of mechanics formulated by **Isaac Newton**, a late seventeenth- and early eighteenth-century English mathematician, also pervaded the provisions of the Constitution. Newton viewed nature as a machine, with different parts having different functions and balancing each other. Newton's principle of action and reaction is manifested in the Founders' system of checks and balances. Both the natural environment and the constitutional structure were viewed as self-regulating systems.[53]

Political Experience

Although the Founders were intellectuals, they were also experienced and practical politicians who had "to operate with great delicacy and skill in a political cosmos full of enemies."[54]

The Founders brought extensive experience to the convention. Eight had signed the Declaration of Independence, and thirty-nine had served in Congress. Seven had been governors, and many had held other state offices. Some had helped write their state constitutions. The framers drew on this experience. For example, although they cited Montesquieu in discussing separation of powers, they also referred to the experience of colonial and state governments that already had some separation of powers.[55]

As practical politicians, "no matter what their private dreams might be, they had to take home an acceptable package and defend it—and their own political futures—against predictable attack."[56] So, they compromised the difficult issues and ducked the stickiest ones. Ultimately, they pieced together a document that allowed each delegate to return home and announce that his state had won something.

Economic Interests

At the same time, the Founders represented an elite that sought to protect its property from the masses. The delegates to the convention included prosperous planters, manufacturers, shippers, and lawyers. About one-third were slave owners. Most came from families of prominence and married into other families of prominence. Not all were wealthy, but most were at least well-to-do. Only one, a delegate from Georgia, was a yeoman farmer like most men in the country. In short, "this was a convention of the well-bred, the well-fed, the well-read, and the well-wed."[57]

The Founders championed the right to property. The promise of land and even riches had enticed many immigrants to come to America.[58] A desire for freedom from arbitrary taxes and trade restrictions had spurred some colonists to fight in the Revolution.[59] And the inability of the government under the Articles of Confederation to provide a healthy economy had prompted the Founders to convene the Constitutional Convention. They apparently agreed with Madison that "the first object of government" is to protect property.[60] They worried that a democratic government, responding to popular pressures, might appropriate their property or impose high taxes to help less wealthy people. They wanted a government that could resist such populism.

Yet the Founders' emphasis on property was not as elitist as it might seem. Land was plentiful, and with westward expansion, more would be available. Already most men were middle-class farmers who owned some property. Even those who owned no property could foresee the day when they would, so most wanted to protect property.

The Founders diverged from the farmers in their vision to create a national commercial economy in place of the small-scale agricultural economy. Toward this end, the Founders desired to protect other property, such as wealth and credit, in addition to land.[61] So the delegates included provisions to protect commerce, including imports and exports, contracts, and debts, and provisions to regulate currency, bankruptcy, and taxes.[62] (See the box "Constitutional Provisions Protecting Property.")

Political scientists and historians have debated which of these three influences on the Founders—philosophical, political, or economic—was most important. Actually, the influences are difficult to separate because they reinforce each other; the framers' ideas, political experience, and economic interests all point to the same sort of constitution.[63]

Ratification of the Constitution

Ratification was uncertain. Many people opposed the Constitution, and a lively campaign against it appeared in newspapers, pamphlets, and mass meetings.

Knowing opponents would charge the framers with setting up a national government to dominate the state governments; those who supported the Constitution ingeniously adopted the name **Federalists** to emphasize a real division of power between the national and state governments. They dubbed their opponents **Anti-Federalists** to imply that their opponents did not want a division of power between the governments.

The Anti-Federalists faulted the Constitution for lacking a bill of rights. The framers had not included one because most states already had one in their constitutions. The framers also thought that fragmenting power would prevent any branch from becoming strong enough to deny individual rights. Yet critics demanded provisions protecting various rights, and the Federalists promised to propose amendments guaranteeing these rights as soon as the government began.

The Anti-Federalists also criticized the Constitution for other reasons. Localists at heart, they were wary of entrusting power to officials far away. They worried that the central government would accumulate too much power and the presidency would become a monarchy or Congress an aristocracy. One delegate to the Massachusetts convention blasted the Federalists:

> These lawyers, and men of learning and moneyed men, that talk so finely, and gloss over matters so smoothly, to make us poor illiterate people swallow down the pill, expect to get into Congress themselves; they expect to . . . get all the power and all the money into their own hands, and then they will swallow up all us little folks . . . just as the whale swallowed up Jonah![64]

But the Anti-Federalists had no alternative plan. They were divided, with some wanting to amend the Articles of Confederation and others wanting to reject both the Articles and the Constitution in favor of some yet undetermined form of government. Their lack of unity on an alternative was instrumental in their inability to win support.[65]

"Religious freedom is my immediate goal, but my long-range plan is to go into real estate."

take up arms, or go into exile. They continued, as before, to be full and free citizens, but now living in a new republic."[66]

Changing the Constitution

The framers expected their document to last; Madison wrote, "We have framed a constitution that will probably be still around when there are 196 million people."[67] Yet, because the framers realized it would need some changes, they drafted a Constitution that can be changed either formally by amendment or informally by judicial interpretation or political practice. In doing so, they left a legacy for later governments. "The example of changing a Constitution, by assembling the wise men of the state, instead of assembling armies," Jefferson noted, "will be worth as much to the world as the former examples we had given them."[68]

Within six months, nine states ratified the new Constitution, and the new government, with George Washington as president, began in 1788. Within one year, the four remaining states approved the Constitution.

Although this process might seem unremarkable today, this marked the first time that a nation had proposed a new government and then asked the people to approve or reject it. And the process occurred with little violence or coercion. As a constitutional historian observed, "The losers were not jailed, hanged, or politically disabled. They did not boycott,

By Constitutional Amendment

That the Articles of Confederation could be amended only by a unanimous vote of the states posed an almost insurmountable barrier to any change at all. The framers of the Constitution made sure that this experience would not repeat itself. Yet they did not make amendment easy; the procedures, though not requiring unanimity, do require widespread agreement. More than nine thousand amendments have been proposed in Congress, but only twenty-seven (including the ten in the Bill of Rights) have been adopted.[69]

CONSTITUTIONAL PROVISIONS PROTECTING PROPERTY

Numerous constitutional provisions, some obvious and others not, were designed to protect property:

Provision	Effect
For the House of Representatives, "the Electors [voters] in each State shall have the Qualifications requisite for Electors of the most numerous Branch of the State Legislature."	Allows states to set property qualifications to vote.
"The Congress shall have Power . . . To coin Money."	Centralizes currency.
"No State shall . . . emit bills of credit."	Prevents states from printing paper money.
"Congress shall have Power . . . To establish uniform Laws on the subject of Bankruptcies."	Prevents states from relieving debtors of the obligation to pay.
"The Congress shall have Power . . . To regulate Commerce . . . among the several States."	Centralizes commerce regulation and thereby establishes a national economy.
"No State shall . . . pass any . . . Law impairing the Obligation of Contracts."	Prevents states from relieving debtors of the obligation to pay and thereby establishes stable business arrangements.
"The United States shall guarantee to every State [protection] against domestic Violence."	Protects states from debtor uprisings.
"The Congress shall have Power . . . To provide for calling forth the Militia to execute the Laws of the Union, suppress insurrections."	Protects creditors from debtor uprisings.

Procedures The procedures for amendment entail action by both the national government and the state governments. Amendments can be proposed either by a two-thirds vote of both houses of Congress or by a national convention called by Congress at the request of two-thirds of the state legislatures. Congress then specifies which way amendments must be ratified—either by three-fourths of the state legislatures or by ratifying conventions in three-fourths of the states. Among these avenues, the usual route has been proposal by Congress and ratification by state legislatures.

⭐Art. V *Amendments* In the first Congress under the Constitution, the Federalists fulfilled their promise to support a bill of rights. Madison drafted twelve amendments, Congress proposed them, and the states ratified ten of them in 1791. This **Bill of Rights** includes freedom of conviction and expression—religion, speech, press, and assembly (First Amendment). It also includes numerous rights for those accused of crimes—protection against unreasonable searches and seizures (Fourth), protection against compulsory self-incrimination (Fifth), guarantee of due process of law (Fifth), the right to counsel and a jury trial in criminal cases (Sixth), and protection against excessive bail and fines and against cruel and unusual punishment (Eighth). (These will be covered fully in Chapter 14.) It also includes a right to a jury trial in civil cases (Seventh).

Two amendments in the Bill of Rights grew out of the colonial experience with Great Britain—the right to bear arms to form a militia (Second) and the right not to have soldiers quartered in homes during peacetime (Third). The Bill of Rights also includes two general amendments—a statement allowing for additional rights beyond the ones in the first eight amendments (Ninth) and a statement reserving powers to the states that are not given to the national government (Tenth).

Among the other seventeen amendments to the Constitution, the strongest theme is the expansion of citizenship rights:[70]

- Abolition of slavery (Thirteenth, 1865)

- Equal protection, due process of law (Fourteenth, 1868)

- Right of black men to vote (Fifteenth, 1870)

- Direct election of senators (Seventeenth, 1913)

- Right of women to vote (Nineteenth, 1920)

Authorities empty barrels of beer after the Eighteenth Amendment, which prohibited alcohol, was adopted in 1919. The Twenty-first Amendment repealed the Eighteenth in 1933.

Library of Congress #LC-US262-123257

- Right of District of Columbia residents to vote in presidential elections (Twenty-third, 1960)

- Abolition of poll tax in federal elections (Twenty-fourth, 1964)

- Right of persons eighteen and older to vote (Twenty-sixth, 1971)

In recent decades, two amendments proposed by Congress were not ratified by the states. One would have provided equal rights for women (discussed in Chapter 15), and the other would have given congressional representation to the District of Columbia as though it were a state.

Although the Constitution expressly provides for change by amendment, its ambiguity about some subjects and silence about others virtually guarantees change by interpretation and practice as well.

By Judicial Interpretation

If there is disagreement about what the Constitution means, who is to interpret it? Although the Constitution does not say, the judicial branch has taken on this role. To decide disputes before them, the courts must determine what the relevant provisions of the Constitution mean. By saying that the provisions mean one thing rather than another, the courts can, in effect, change the Constitution. Woodrow Wilson called the Supreme Court "a constitutional convention in continuous session." The Court has interpreted the Constitution in ways that bring about the same results as new amendments. (Chapters 13, 14, and 15 provide many examples.)

ethical dilemmas | George Washington and His Slaves

George Washington inherited ten slaves and died with 123.[1]

Washington was the third son of a family with a medium-sized plantation, so he didn't inherit enough land to establish himself as a planter. Instead, he became a surveyor. Eventually, while deep in debt, he married Martha Custis, a rich widow. Then he was able to buy land and also to buy and sell slaves.

As a planter, Washington had a zeal for efficiency. He was the first to breed mules and the first to compost manure in America. He rotated crops and transformed marshland into meadows. He expected his slaves to work hard, and he required husbands to live near the fields where they toiled and wives and children to live near other fields where they toiled.[2]

Though not as harsh or brutal as some slave owners, Washington did have his slaves whipped upon occasion. He also threatened to sell them or to ship them to the West Indies, where slaves were worked to death in sugarcane fields. And when Washington needed teeth for his dentures, he had teeth from his slaves pulled and inserted into his dentures. (He did pay his slaves for their teeth, as wealthy Europeans paid poor people at the time.)[3]

Washington's views toward slavery began to change during the Revolutionary War. At first, Washington and fellow generals refused to accept any blacks in the Continental Army. As the war dragged on and white sympathy for the war waned, however, he needed more soldiers and recruited free blacks to the ranks.[4] By the end of the war, black soldiers made up a quarter of the army. Washington was impressed by their loyalty and bravery.

Soon after the Constitutional Convention, Washington expressed "regret" over slavery, which he now found repugnant. When he was elected president, he considered freeing his slaves before taking office. When he was serving as president, he again considered freeing his slaves. If he had done so, either before or during his presidency, he would have set a precedent for future presidents. Three of the next four presidents were also slave owners. But he did not free his slaves then because his wife and relatives opposed doing so, and he feared losing the support of southern members of Congress. In fact, he signed the Fugitive Slave Act, which created a process for reclaiming escaped slaves, and when one slave escaped from his family's household, at his wife's insistence he tried to get the slave back.

For the most part, Washington kept his desire to free his slaves secret, as he struggled with the moral dilemma—not a moral dilemma today, of course, but a difficult choice for some owners at the time. Washington's conscience wrestled with his loyalty to his wife and other relatives and with the prevailing views all around him. Yet, foreseeing that slavery would tear the country apart, he told a visiting Englishman that "nothing but the rooting out of slavery can perpetuate the existence of our union."[5] He confided to his secretary of state that if the union did break up he would side with the North.[6]

In the last year of his life, Washington had a dream that he believed foretold his death, which prompted him to write his will. Concerned about posterity's judgment as well as slavery's immorality, he instructed his heirs to free his slaves upon his wife's death, except for the children, who were to be taught to read and write so they could support themselves. The children were to be freed at age 25. Washington evidently feared resistance from his relatives, so he elaborated upon these instructions for three pages, using more direct and forceful language than in the rest of his will.

The provision that his adult slaves be freed upon his wife's death made Martha fear that they might kill her, so she freed them within a year of her husband's death.

Although he could not bring himself to do so sooner, Washington resolved his moral struggle in his last year. No other prominent Founder freed his slaves, and none planned to educate them.[7]

---

[1] The information for this box is drawn from Henry Wiencek, *An Imperfect God: George Washington, His Slaves, and the Creation of America* (New York: Farrar, Straus and Giroux, 2003).
[2] For most slaves, there was no official recognition of their "marriage," but many slaves were considered, by themselves, other slaves, and their owners, as husband and wife.
[3] Wiencek, *An Imperfect God*, 112. Other historians confirm Washington's efforts to use slaves' teeth. Philip Morgan, "'To Get Quit of Negroes': George Washington and Slavery," www.ucd.ie/amerstud/archives/Morgan.htm; James C. Rees, "George Washington: Some Personal Facts," www.srmason-sj.org/council/journal/feb99/REES.HTM. Apparently the procedure wasn't successful. Contrary to legend, Washington didn't have wooden teeth. However, he did use cows' teeth and ivory tusks, filed down to fit his mouth.
[4] Washington's decision may also have been affected by the British decision to promise freedom for any slaves who fled their plantations and joined the British army. Some of Washington's own slaves joined the British side.
[5] Wiencek, *An Imperfect God*, 352.
[6] Ibid., 362, citing Julian P. Boyd, et al., eds., *The Papers of Thomas Jefferson*, 30 vols. (Princeton, N.J.: Princeton University Press, 1950–),28: 568, "Notes of a Conversation with Edmund Randolph." Washington made this comment in a conversation with his secretary of state, Edmund Randolph, who reported it to Jefferson.
[7] Wiencek, *An Imperfect God*, 5.

By Political Practice

Political practice has accounted for some very important changes. These include the rise of political parties and the demise of the Electoral College as an independent body. They also include the development of the cabinet to advise the president and the development of the committee system to operate the two houses of Congress. (Chapters 7, 8, and 10 explain these changes.)

The Founders would be surprised to learn that only seventeen amendments, aside from the Bill of Rights, have been adopted in over two hundred years. In part this is due to their wisdom, but in part it is due to changes in judicial interpretation and political practice, which have combined to create a "living Constitution."

Evolution of the Constitution

The Constitution has evolved since the Founding. This section will introduce the major conceptual changes, which have given us a quite different constitution than the one the Founders drafted.

Early Conflicts

The country faced secessionist threats almost immediately after its creation—by southern states when the Federalists (under John Adams) were in power and then by New England states when the Jeffersonians (under Thomas Jefferson) were in power. These threats were averted, but frequent conflicts between the nation and the states arose.

Supreme Court Rulings

The Supreme Court became the principal arbiter of the Constitution and soon faced questions about national supremacy. **John Marshall**, chief justice of the United States from 1801 to 1835, was a Federalist, a firm believer in a strong national government, and the decisions of his Court supported this view.

The Marshall Court established the legal bases for the supremacy of national authority over the states. Among the Marshall Court's most important rulings was **McCulloch v. Maryland** in 1819.[71] The case grew out of a dispute over the establishment of a national bank. The bank was unpopular because it competed with smaller banks operating under state laws and because some of its branches engaged in reckless and even fraudulent practices. When the government of Maryland levied a tax on the currency issued by the branch in Baltimore, the bank's constitutionality was called into question and a case was brought before the Court. The claim was that Congress, by establishing a national bank, infringed on the states' authority.

Marshall's ruling upheld the establishment of the bank and struck down the tax by the state. "[T]he power to tax involves the power to destroy," Marshall wrote, and the states shouldn't have the power to destroy the bank, because the bank was "necessary and proper" to carry out Congress's powers to collect taxes, borrow money, regulate commerce, and raise an army. Marshall maintained that if the goal of the legislation is legitimate, "all means which are appropriate, which are plainly adapted to that end, which are not prohibited, but consistent with the letter and spirit of the Constitution, are constitutional."

Art. I, 8 Marshall interpreted "necessary" quite loosely. The bank was not essential, but it was useful. This interpretation of the **necessary and proper clause** allowed Congress, and thus the national government, to wield much more authority than the Constitution appeared to grant. This interpretation recognized the existence of **implied powers**—ones implicit in the explicit powers specifically cited—for the national government. It meant that Congress can legislate in almost any area it wishes. Thus the Marshall Court embraced nation-centered federalism. By laying the foundation for a strong national government for our rapidly expanding nation, *McCulloch* would become one of the two most important rulings of the Marshall Court and indeed of the Supreme Court ever. (The other was *Marbury* v. *Madison*, which will be covered in Chapter 13.)

DEMOCRACY?

What might be the implications for democracy of a broad interpretation of the necessary and proper clause and a recognition of implied powers?

Conflicts between the nation and the states continued, and debates over slavery exacerbated them. These conflicts led to southern states' efforts to secede from the Union and to the Civil War.

The Civil War and Reconstruction

The Civil War, from 1861 through 1865, and Reconstruction, from the end of the war through 1876, constituted a "second American Revolution."[72] After the bloodletting and scorched earth, more than six hundred thousand soldiers lay in graves—one of every seven men between the ages of fifteen and thirty—and parts of the South lay in waste. The North's victory preserved the Union, but it did far more than this. It also altered the Constitution—in the minds of the people and in formal amendments to the document.

Although the North's leader, President **Abraham Lincoln**, a Republican, held views that would be considered racist today (he believed that black people were inherently

This view of the remains of Richmond, Virginia, conveys the destruction of the Civil War.

Library of Congress #LC-B811-3241

forced in the parts of the Confederate states where the Union army was not in control. Thus, as a legal document, the proclamation was problematic. However, as a symbolic measure, it was successful. The proclamation made clear that the war was no longer just to preserve the Union, but to abolish slavery as well. It captured people's imagination, and when slaves heard about it, many left their plantations and some joined the Union army. The desertion sowed confusion in the South and denied a reliable labor force to the region.

The Gettysburg Address

President Lincoln's **Gettysburg Address** set the tone for new interpretations of the Constitution.[76] The battle at Gettysburg, Pennsylvania, in 1863 was a Union victory and the turning point in the Civil War. Lincoln was invited to deliver "a few appropriate remarks" during the dedication of the battlefield where many had fallen. Lincoln was not the main speaker, and his speech was not long. The main speaker took two hours, recounting the battle and reciting the names of the generals and even some of their soldiers; Lincoln took two minutes to give a 268-word speech. (He spoke so briefly that the photographer, with his clumsy equipment and its slow exposure, failed to get a single photograph.) Lincoln used the occasion to advance his ideal of equality.

He began: "Four score and seven [eighty-seven] years ago our fathers brought forth on this continent a new nation, conceived in liberty and dedicated to the proposition that all men are created equal." Here Lincoln referred not to the Constitution of 1787 but to the Declaration of Independence of 1776. For Lincoln, the Constitution had abandoned the principle of equality that the Declaration had promised. He sought to resurrect this principle. Lincoln did not mention slavery or the Emancipation Proclamation, which were divisive. A shrewd politician, he wanted people to focus on the Declaration, which was revered.

Lincoln concluded by addressing "the great task remaining before us . . . that we here highly resolve that these dead shall not have died in vain, that this nation, under God, shall have a new birth of freedom, and that government of the people, by the people, for the people shall not perish from the earth." This phrase, which Lincoln made famous, was borrowed from a speaker at an antislavery convention.[77] It depicted a government elected by all the people, to

inferior and that they should emigrate from the United States),[73] he despised slavery because it deprived persons of their unalienable rights to life, liberty, and the pursuit of happiness promised by the Declaration of Independence. But efforts to abolish slavery were constrained by the political climate, and Lincoln was a practical politician. Before the war, he was willing to allow slavery in the southern states as long as the Union was preserved. But one year into the war, he found this goal too limited.[74] Abolitionist sentiment was spreading in the North, providing Lincoln the opportunity to lead efforts to abolish slavery as well as preserve the Union.[75] In the process, he helped reinvent America.

The Emancipation Proclamation

The **Emancipation Proclamation** offered the promise of redefining the Constitution. President Lincoln announced the proclamation in September 1862 and ordered it to take effect in January 1863. The document proclaimed that the slaves "shall be . . . forever free" in the Confederate states where the Union army was not in control. Its language limited its sweep, for it exempted those parts of the Confederate states where the Union army was in control and also the slave states that remained loyal to the Union (Delaware, Kentucky, Maryland, and Missouri). And despite its language, it could not be en-serve all the people.[78] Lincoln's conclusion reinforced his introduction—both emphasized equality.

Although his speech was brief, Lincoln used the word *nation* five times, including the phrase "a new nation." His purpose was not to encourage support for the Union, but to urge people to think of the nation as a whole, its identity now forged in a bloody war of brother against brother, rather than as simply a collection of individual states with their own interests.[79]

Thus the president essentially added the Declaration's promise of equality to the Constitution, and he substituted his vision of a unified nation for the Founders' precarious arrangement of a balance of power between the nation and the states. According to one historian, "He performed one of the most daring acts of open-air sleight-of-hand ever witnessed by the unsuspecting. . . . The crowd departed with a new thing in its ideological luggage, that new constitution Lincoln had substituted for the one they brought with them."[80]

The Gettysburg Address was heard by an audience of perhaps fifteen thousand, but its language was spread through word of mouth and newspapers and eventually by politicians and teachers. It was read, repeated, and sometimes memorized by generations of schoolchildren. Although some critics at the time perceived what Lincoln was attempting—the *Chicago Times* quoted the Constitution to the president and charged him with betraying the document he swore to uphold—most citizens came to accept Lincoln's addition. His speech, which has been called "the best political address" in the country's history, thus became "the secular prayer of the postbellum American Republic."[81] (The speech is reprinted in the appendix.)

The Reconstruction Amendments

If the Gettysburg Address became the preamble of the new constitution, the **Reconstruction Amendments** became its body. These three amendments, adopted from 1865 through 1870, began to implement the promise of equality and the vision of a unified nation rather than a collection of individual states.

The Thirteenth Amendment abolished slavery, essentially constitutionalizing the Emancipation Proclamation.

The Fourteenth Amendment declared that all persons born or naturalized in the United States are citizens, overturning the Supreme Court's ruling before the Civil War that blacks, whether slave or free, could not be citizens.[82] The Fourteenth Amendment also included the equal protection clause, which requires states to treat persons equally, and the due process clause, which requires states to treat persons fairly. The equal protection clause would become the primary legal means to end discrimination, and the due process clause would become the primary legal means to give persons the full benefit of the Bill of Rights.[83] (This amendment and these clauses will be examined further in Chapters 14 and 15.) This amendment, one legal scholar

observes, was "a revolutionary change. The states were no longer the autonomous sovereigns that they thought they were when they claimed the right of secession. They were now, in fact, servants of their people. [They] existed to guarantee due process and equal justice for all."[84]

The Fifteenth Amendment extended the right to vote to blacks. Because women could not vote at the time, the amendment essentially provided the right to vote to black men. (This amendment will be addressed further in Chapters 8 and 15.)

As important as the substantive content of these amendments was a procedural provision authorizing Congress to enforce them. ("Congress shall have power to enforce this article by appropriate legislation.") That is, the amendments gave Congress broad power, beyond that granted in the original Constitution, to pass new laws to implement the amendments. Consequently, the federal government would come to oversee and even intervene in the policies of state and local governments to make sure that these governments did not disregard the guarantees of the amendments. These amendments thus marked the start of a trend of federalizing the Constitution by increasing the power of Congress.[85] Five later amendments also would include this provision.

DEMOCRACY?

How does this provision have similar implications for democracy as the Supreme Court's interpretation of the necessary and proper clause in the *McCulloch* v. *Maryland* case?

During Reconstruction, the Union army occupied the South and enforced the amendments and congressional laws implementing them. But southern whites resisted, and eventually northern whites grew weary of the struggle. At the same time, there was a desire for healing between the two regions and lingering feelings for continuity with the past. In 1876, the two national political parties, the Democrats and the Republicans, struck a deal to withdraw the Union army and to allow the southern states to govern themselves again. The entrenched attitudes of southern whites prompted them to establish segregation and discrimination in place of slavery, thus preventing blacks from enjoying their new rights. As a result, the new constitution stressing equality and powers of the national government to enforce equality, as envisioned by Lincoln, would not really come into being until the 1950s and 1960s, when the civil rights movement, Supreme Court rulings, presidential initiatives, and congressional acts would converge to give effect to the ideal of racial equality. (These developments will be examined fully in Chapter 15.) In the meantime, the new constitution would lie, in our collective consciousness, as an unfulfilled promise, occasionally emerging to foster greater equality.[86]

DEMOCRACY?

Consider the vast implications for democracy of the Civil War, Emancipation Proclamation, Gettysburg Address, and Reconstruction amendments.

During the industrialization and urbanization that followed the Civil War, the national government continued to extend its reach and expand its power, but more significant changes would occur during the Great Depression.

The Great Depression and the New Deal

In the 1928 election, Herbert Hoover, the Republican candidate who would become the next president, predicted, "We shall soon, with the help of God, be in sight of the day when poverty will be banished from this nation."[87] One year later the Great Depression began when the stock market crashed. Wealthy people lost their investments, and business activity declined. Ordinary people lost their jobs, with a quarter of them becoming unemployed. Many people lost their savings when the banks collapsed. Unlike today, there was no systematic program of relief—no unemployment compensation, no food stamps, no welfare. Cities and states, which had provided aid to the poor, were overwhelmed; they didn't have the funds or organizations to cope with the increasing needs. Private charities didn't have enough resources to assume the burden. So, millions of Americans were hungry and homeless, and many of them were hopeless. Their suffering and dislocation threatened the political stability of the country.

In the 1920s, the economy and stock market were booming. Herbert Hoover capitalized on the country's prosperity in the 1928 election.

President Hoover, expecting the economy to right itself, resisted aggressive action and as a result lost his bid for reelection to **Franklin Roosevelt**, a Democrat, in 1932. President Roosevelt immediately initiated an ambitious program, heralded as "a new deal for the American people," to stimulate the economy and help the people who were suffering. Within his first hundred days, Congress had passed numerous proposals to regulate the activities of business and labor and establish a national welfare system. FDR's program and his administration came to be known as the **New Deal**.

This era also altered the Constitution—not by formal amendments, but through judicial rulings and political practice. In the process, it changed the minds of the people.[88] As a result, we replaced our small, limited government, as envisioned by the Founders, with a big, activist government.

Judicial Rulings

In the late nineteenth and early twentieth centuries, a laissez-faire economic philosophy was popular in this country and was reflected in governmental policies. According to this philosophy, government should not interfere in the economy (*laissez-faire* means "leave it alone" in French). Although government could *aid* businesses, it should not *regulate* them.[89] People who believed this philosophy thought it would create a robust and efficient economy. Indeed, industrialization produced an array of new products for consumers and an increase in personal wealth for owners, but it also led to negative consequences for employees, who were forced to labor in harsh, even dangerous, conditions for long hours and little pay.

For decades, when Congress and state legislatures passed laws regulating child labor, maximum hours of work, and minimum wages for work, the Supreme Court usually followed the traditional philosophy and declared the laws unconstitutional. After Roosevelt took office and Congress passed the laws implementing his recovery program, the Court's majority often declared these laws unconstitutional as well. The impasse reached a climax in 1935 and 1936 when the Court invalidated twelve laws—the core of FDR's program. The Court's resistance made clear that the New Deal reforms were not simply fine-tuning governmental policy toward the economy, but were overhauling the long-standing policy.[90] In response to the Court's resistance, members of Congress introduced thirty-nine constitutional amendments to reverse the Court's rulings.

After Roosevelt was resoundingly reelected in 1936, intense pressure from the president, Congress, and the public prompted two justices who had voted against government regulation of business to switch sides and vote for such regulation in 1937. The switch allowed the government to extend its reach far beyond what was thought permissible just a few years before.

During the Depression, many people who lost their job lost their ability to put food on the table. Breadlines and soup kitchens were common. Here the unemployed wait for coffee and doughnuts at one of fifty-two relief kitchens in New York City in 1934.

AP/Wide World Photos (Los Angeles: Clymer Publications, 1974) Reprinted by permission.

These transformative rulings created a "constitutional revolution."[91] They took the place of formal amendments to the Constitution, which were no longer necessary once the Court acquiesced to the policies of the president and Congress. As a result, government could regulate businesses when the public believed that regulation would be beneficial.

Political Practice

Before the Depression, Washington, D.C. had been "a sleepy southern town," in the eyes of reporters.[92] When Roosevelt took office, he was uncertain exactly what to do, but he was willing to experiment. Roosevelt's personality and ambitious ideas attracted hundreds of thousands of people to the capital, some simply relieved to find a job, but others excited to work for the government. These reformers brought new ideas, even radical ideas for the time, that would receive consideration in the depths of the Depression. As federal efforts to provide relief and regulation spread throughout the country, many other people got jobs in federal offices outside Washington.

Within six years of Roosevelt's taking office, the number of federal workers in the District of Columbia had more than doubled,[93] the number of federal workers in the country had almost doubled, and the size of the federal budget had almost doubled.[94] In the process, the scope of the federal government had expanded considerably. In short, the country got big government and activist government in less than a decade. These changes were so dramatic that one political scientist has said they created a "second American republic."[95]

Roosevelt's exuberance and experimentation had given people hope. As the country gradually pulled out of the Depression (though the country would not fully recover until the economic activity generated by World War II provided the final boost), people gave Roosevelt credit, electing him to an unprecedented four terms and returning Democrats to Congress to support him.[96]

Ever since, Americans, albeit to different degrees, have expected the government to tackle society's problems. While sometimes mouthing the language of the Founders—for example, Thomas Jefferson's assertion, "That government is best which governs least"—they have generally accepted the reality of the government that was expanded during the Depression.[97]

DEMOCRACY?

What implications would these changes during the Depression have, not simply for the size of our government, but for the nature of our democracy?

The changes during the Depression would lay the foundation for the government of the 1960s, which would promote the equality advanced during the Civil War. Without a powerful government pushing for change, the entrenched attitudes supporting segregation and discrimination would not have been overcome.

A Combination of Constitutions

As a result of President Lincoln and the Radical Republicans in the 1860s and 1870s and President Roosevelt and the New Deal Democrats in the 1930s and 1940s, our government is very different from the one the Founders bequeathed us.[98] Later generations of Americans made the eighteenth-century Constitution work in the nineteenth century, and then they made it work in the twentieth century—by remaking that Constitution. Changes in the nineteenth century added the concept of equality and elevated the national government over the state governments. Changes in the twentieth century transformed a relatively small, limited government into a very large, activist government.

The original Constitution and the remade Constitution reflect competing visions. Should we emphasize liberty or equality? Should we demand that individuals solve their own problems or ask government to help them? Americans have not reconciled these visions. Sometimes we cling to the Founders' Constitution; other times we embrace the post–Civil War and post-Depression Constitution. In political debates, politicians, commentators, or citizens take positions without articulating, perhaps without even realizing, that these positions hark back to the Founders' Constitution, whereas opponents espouse views that rely on the post–Civil War and post-Depression Constitution. Although, of course, we have only one Constitution on paper, we have two constitutions coexisting, sometimes uneasily, in our minds and in government policies.[99] As a consequence of our history, then, we actually have a combination of constitutions.

Conclusion: Does the Constitution Make the Government Responsive?

The Constitution established a government that has survived for over two centuries. Although the United States is considered a relatively young country, it has one of the oldest constitutions in the world. As a result, the United States has the oldest democracy, oldest republic, and oldest federal system in the world.[100]

In the Constitution, the Founders set forth a mechanism to govern a vast territory and to provide for majority rule while allowing minority rights. This government has enabled more people to live in liberty and in prosperity than the people of any nation before or since.[101] Americans have been grateful, venerating the Founders and embracing the Constitution as a secular Bible. Citizens consult it for guidance and cite it for support at the same time they debate the meaning of its provisions.

Despite its status as a political icon, however, the Constitution has been copied by few countries.[102] Although provisions of the Bill of Rights, such as freedom of speech, and of the Fourteenth Amendment, such as the equal protection clause, have been adopted by other countries,[103] the structure of our government has been less popular. Among the twenty-two democratic countries that have remained stable since 1950,[104] only five others have a federal system with significant power at the state level, only three others have a bicameral legislature with significant power in both houses, and only four others have one house with equal representation for the states regardless of their population. No others have a presidential system, and only two others have a judicial system that exercises judicial review of national legislation.[105] Our Constitution and governmental structure are seen more as a reflection of historical factors and political compromises than as a desirable form of government.

The Founders did leave important problems unresolved for succeeding generations. Most notable was slavery and the treatment of African Americans. Also troublesome was the uncertain relationship between the nation and the states. As we have seen, later Americans would have to tackle these problems, and in the process they, too, would contribute to the Constitution. Succeeding generations remade the Constitution most noticeably in the wake of the Civil War and the Great Depression, and they remade it more than many Americans realize.

Despite the major changes brought about by the Civil War and the Great Depression, and all the changes brought about by other events at other times, the basic structure of government and the underlying fragmentation of power in the Constitution remain. The combination of federalism, separation of powers, and checks and balances, along with the unique method for choosing the president, make our government perhaps "the most intricate ever devised."[106] It is also perhaps "the most opaque . . . , confusing, and difficult to understand."[107]

The structure of government and fragmentation of power make it difficult for citizens to hold their leaders accountable. If you disapprove of some policy, whom do you hold accountable in the next election—the president, the Senate, the House of Representatives, the unelected judges, or the state governments? Usually there is divided responsibility, resulting in less accountability.

Of course, the Founders sought a government that would be responsive to the people only to a limited extent. The Constitution created a republic, which granted the people the right to elect some representatives who would make their laws. In this way, the people had more say in government than the people in other countries at the time. Yet the Constitution was expected to filter the public's passions and purify their selfish desires. Thus the original

Constitution allowed citizens to vote only for members of the House of Representatives—not for members of the Senate or the president. Furthermore, it fragmented power, so a single group could not control the entire government. Amendments to the Constitution that have expanded opportunities for citizens to participate in government have done little to modify the structure of government or its fragmentation of power.

This configuration has prevented many abuses of power, although it has not always worked. During the Vietnam War and the Iraq War, for example, one branch—the presidency—exercised vast power whereas the others acquiesced.

This configuration has also provided the opportunity for one branch to pick up the slack when the others became sluggish. The overlapping of powers ensured by checks and balances allows every branch to act on virtually every issue it wants to. In the 1950s, President Eisenhower and Congress were reluctant to push for civil rights, but the Supreme Court did so by declaring segregation unconstitutional.

But the system's very advantage has become its primary disadvantage. In their efforts to fragment power so that no branch could accumulate too much, the Founders divided power to the point where the branches sometimes cannot wield enough. In their efforts to build a government that requires a national majority to act, they built one that allows a small minority to block action.

This problem has become increasingly acute as society has become increasingly complex. Like a mechanical device that operates only when all of its parts function in harmony, the system moves only when there is consensus or compromise. Consensus is rare in a large, heterogeneous society; compromise is common, but it requires more time as well as the realization by competing interests that they cannot achieve much without engaging in it.

At best, the system moves inefficiently and incrementally; at worst, it moves hardly at all. The Constitution has established a government that is slow to respond to change. "By intent," one political scientist noted, "the U.S. government works within a set of limits designed to prevent it from working too well."[108] Therefore, the system tends to preserve the status quo and to respond to the groups that benefit from the status quo.

Although the changes made in the wake of the Depression brought us big, activist government, they did not negate all of our historical aversion to such government. We still have a more limited government than other advanced industrialized countries. Contrary to what many Americans believe, our taxes are lower and governmental policies in numerous areas, such as health care, welfare, and transportation, are less ambitious.[109] This, of course, limits our ability to address our problems.

Yet some political scientists believe the American people actually prefer a system that is hard to move. Because the people are suspicious of government, they may be reluctant to let one party dominate it and use it to advance that party's policies. In surveys, many people—a quarter to a third of those polled—say they think it is good for one party to control the presidency and the other to control Congress.[110] In presidential and congressional elections, more than a quarter of the voters split their ticket between the two parties.[111] As a result, from 1969 through 2000, opposing parties controlled the executive branch and both houses of the legislative branch for all but six years. Divided government has been less common after 2000. From 2001 to 2006, the Republicans controlled the presidency and both houses of Congress (except for one year, when a Republican senator defected and gave the Democrats a temporary majority in the Senate). In 2008, the Democrats captured the presidency and both houses of Congress.

Such divided government reinforces the fragmentation of power in a way that makes it difficult, if not impossible, for citizens to pin responsibility on particular officials and parties for the decisions and policies of government. "If no individual or institution possesses the authority to act without the consent of everybody else in the room, then nobody is ever at fault if anything goes wrong. Congress can blame the president, the president can blame the Congress or the Supreme Court, the Supreme Court can blame the Mexicans or the weather in Ohio."[112] If citizens cannot determine who is responsible for what, they cannot hold those individuals accountable and make them responsive.

Key Terms

Enlightenment

deism

Articles of Confederation

Shays's Rebellion

Constitutional Convention

republic

House of Representatives

Senate

Great Compromise

Three-Fifths Compromise

direct democracy

indirect democracy

initiative

referendum

recall elections

federalism

"mischiefs of factions"

supremacy clause

Tenth Amendment

separation of powers

divided government

checks and balances

social contract

limited government

Federalists

Anti-Federalists

Bill of Rights

McCulloch v. *Maryland*

necessary and proper clause

implied powers

Emancipation Proclamation

Gettysburg Address

Reconstruction Amendments

New Deal

Key Names

Benjamin Franklin

George Washington

James Madison

John Locke

Charles de Montesquieu

Isaac Newton

John Marshall

Abraham Lincoln

Franklin Roosevelt

Please visit our companion website at www.cengage.com/politicalscience/welch/uag12e or use CengageNOW for additional resources dealing with this chapter.

Crowded and polluted freeways have prompted California to set higher standards for carbon emissions than Congress has established. In this tug-of-war between the federal government and a state government, the Bush administration refused to let the state set higher standards.

Federalism

3

Talking Points

Many states want to set higher standards for carbon emissions from trucks and cars than those set by Congress or federal agencies. Any state whose clean air laws predated the Clean Air Act of 1970 can petition for a waiver from federal rules so that it might set its own standards. California's Governor Arnold Schwartzenegger did petition for such a waiver after the Calilfornia state legislature passed new auto emission standards. If granted by the EPA, the waiver would have allowed California to implement stricter emissions standards for cars and trucks than those set by the federal government. And if California were allowed to do this, other states were waiting to follow in its footsteps.

The EPA denied California's petition in 2008, but with a Catch-22 kind of logic. For seven years the Bush administration had been denying that climate change was being driven by human behavior and the use of fossil fuels. Yet in rejecting California's petition, EPA administrator Stephen Johnson said that global warming was undeniable, that "manmade emissions are largely responsible," and that they are likely to have "devastating consequences" if not contained by federal regulation. It was the

first admission by the Bush administration that national regulations were needed to deal with global warming.[1] However, the EPA admitted to the scope of the problem only to deny California's right to set stricter controls on emissions and to reject a state-by-state response.

Given that climate change does not affect a single state but the nation as a whole, the EPA ruled, it was best dealt with by national rather than state regulation. However, no new rules have been set by the federal government to contain global warming and the EPA has supplied no explanations on how it will carry out court-ordered regulation of carbon emissions. The states were left with the will but no way to go beyond the federally set standards for fuel emissions.

Tension between the federal government and the states is endemic in a federal system. During the George W. Bush administration, a good deal of the friction between Washington and state capitals came from the federal government's *refusal* to regulate, as in the case of fuel emissions. The "states rights" position so often advocated by conservatives to limit federal action was rejected when states proposed policies more liberal than those supported by the Bush administration.

The victory of the Union over secessionist states in the Civil War (1861–1865) established that the Union was indivisible and that the states could not nullify federal law or the Constitution. The war settled little else about the federal relationship, but war, economic crises, and the varying political philosophies of presidents, members of Congress, and Supreme Court justices have all contributed to our transformation from a small agrarian to a large, complex nation and inevitably to changes in the way our federal system functions. In just over two hundred years, the national government grew from a few hundred people with relatively limited impact on the residents of thirteen small states to a government employing several millions, affecting the daily lives of more than three hundred million people in fifty states and billions of people beyond our borders.

Americans disagree about just how big and how strong our national government should be. Nevertheless, because of the sheer size and complexity of our country, its role in world affairs, and our expanded expectations of government, we live in a nation with a strong central government. One indication of how dominant the national government has become in the public consciousness is the conflation of *federal* with *national*. It is a confusing but now common usage to say *federal government* when referring to the national government.

Chapter 2 explained much of the Founders' reasoning in choosing federalism, how they provided for it in the Constitution, and how the Marshall Court set the government on its course toward nation-centered federalism with its ruling in *McCulloch* v. *Maryland*. In this chapter, we look in greater detail at the politics behind the choice of federalism, how the distribution of power between Washington and the states has changed over time through territorial expansion, national crises, and the political philosophies of presidents, governors, and legislators as well as federal court rulings. In describing the everyday workings of federalism we identify sources of cooperation and conflict in the division of powers. Finally, we look at the role of the people in the federal relationship.

Federal and Unitary Systems
Federal Systems

The term **federalism** describes a system in which power is constitutionally divided between a central government and subnational or local governments. In the United States, the subnational governments are the states. All federal systems are not alike: Germany, Belgium, Canada, India, Brazil, and Mexico, for example, vary greatly in their basic economic and political characteristics. They are similar only in that

Federalism may not seem like a scintillating topic, but we did fight a civil war over it.

each has a written constitution allocating some powers to the national and some to the subnational governments.

In American federalism, both levels of government receive their grants of power from a higher authority, the will of the people (popular sovereignty) as expressed in the Constitution. In other words, federalism divides something—sovereignty—that is theoretically indivisible. This is the source of some of the conflict over jurisdiction that inevitably arises between levels of government. Making arrangements even more complex, the powers granted to each level are not necessarily exclusive. Both national and state governments have the power to tax, regulate, and provide benefits. And because each level of government is sovereign in its own right, neither can dissolve the other.

In contrast, in a **confederal system**, the central government has only those powers given to it by the subnational governments; it cannot act directly on citizens, and it can be dissolved by the states that created it. (See Figure 1 below.) The first American government, established by the Articles of Confederation, was a confederal system in which all sovereignty was vested in the states. The national government was the creation of the states—not the people—and it existed only at the pleasure of the states. Like the first government of the United States, the United Nations is an example of a confederal system. The lack of central authority in such systems makes them basically unworkable as governmental arrangements for modern nations.

Unitary Systems

In contrast to federalism, the national government in a **unitary system** creates subnational governments and gives them only those powers it wants them to have. Thus the national government is supreme. In Britain, for example, the national government can give or take away any power previously delegated to the subnational governments, and it can even abolish them, as it did with some city governments in the 1980s. In unitary Sweden, the national parliament abolished 90 percent of its local governments between 1952 and 1975.

At least one delegate to the Constitutional Convention proposed abolishing the states to create a unitary system, but few took this option seriously.[2] However each of the fifty states is unitary with respect to its local governments. Cities, counties, townships, and school districts can be altered or even eliminated by state governments. Yet every state is (and is required to be by the U.S. Constitution) a republic—that is, a representative democracy.

Unitary systems can be democratic or authoritarian. Some unitary systems are among the most democratic in the world (Britain and Sweden); others are authoritarian (Egypt and China). Likewise, federal systems can be democratic, such as Canada, Australia, Germany, or India, or authoritarian, like the Congo, the former Soviet Union, and the former Yugoslavia.

| **Figure 1** | Confederal, Unitary, and Federal Systems

The arrows indicate the flow of power and authority. The arrow on the right indicates a central government both created and elected by the people, by the people. In democratic unitary systems, the people elect representatives to the central as well as local governments.

It is misleading simply to classify federal systems as decentralized and unitary systems as centralized. All modern governments have to delegate some power because a central government, even in a unitary system, cannot run every local service or deal directly with every local problem. In Great Britain, for example, a good deal of local autonomy has devolved onto assemblies in Scotland, Wales, and Northern Ireland. And despite constitutional stipulations, the division of power in federal systems is not static. In the United States the competition among governmental units to shape and implement policy is never-ending and the balance of power is constantly shifting, often issue by issue.

Contemporary Federal Systems

Except for a few loosely organized leagues of states, there were no federal governments before the United States was created. Yet by the 1960s, as much as half the world's territory was governed by federalism.[3] Some new nations created after World War II chose federalism because they, like the American colonies, were trying to unite diverse states or territories into a single country. Federal systems are often ethnically, linguistically, religiously, or racially diverse, though not always. In 2005, Iraqis wrote a constitution with a federal division of power among Arab Shia and Sunni Muslims and the mostly Muslim but non-Arab Kurds to get the bitterly divided factions to accept the new government. Agreeing to divide power among levels of government may be the only way to unite people who have strong motivation to live apart.

The power-sharing arrangements in federal governments often do not work, and many have failed. In the Iraq case, it remains to be seen if federal arrangements will work. In some cases, there are not enough shared values to hold a nation together. Muslims left predominantly Hindu India to create Pakistan, and the Bengali people split from Pakistan to create Bangladesh. Sometimes too much power has been invested in the central government, and sometimes too little. Federal systems that were not created by popular will are likely to fail when the authoritarian center collapses. Yugoslavia, the Soviet Union, and Czechoslovakia ceased to exist, and their constituent republics became independent countries. There have been failed secessionist movements in Nigeria, Canada, Mexico, the United States, and many other federalist nations. Unions have been kept together by military force, by political compromise, and by granting greater local autonomy. The ethnically French, Catholic population of Quebec (the Quebecois) tried unsuccessfully for fifty years to separate from British, Protestant-dominated Canada. But the province was given greater autonomy, and in 2006 the prime minister proposed that the seven million Quebecois be recognized as a nation within the Canadian union. Canada's prime minister must be bilingual but the Queen of England, who is also head of the Church of England, remains Canada's head of state.

The United States faced secessionist threats almost immediately after its creation—by southern states when the Federalists (under John Adams) were in power and by New England states when the anti-federalists (under Jefferson) were in power. Secession was averted, in part because of the fear of external threats, but mainly by key political leaders' commitment to make the Union work. Of course, more than seventy years after the Constitution was adopted, the southern states did secede, instigating our Civil War (1861–1865).

DEMOCRACY?

If the U.S. population becomes more geographically segregated along ethnic, religious, or racial lines as it continues to grow, will its survival as a federal republic be threatened?

Choosing Federalism: The Political Context

As Chapter 2 made clear, the Founders of the United States did not choose federalism as an ideal form of government or as a principle in itself. The few historical examples suggested little to recommend it as a form appropriate to the American situation. The Founders had to write from scratch a document that would accommodate the political reality of their loose compact of states. But it was necessary to find a compromise that could satisfy those who thought only a strong central government could work and those who thought the Union could be preserved only if the individual state governments retained most of the authority they had under the Articles of Confederation. The Founders proposed a dual form of government, a hybrid to be created by mixing the *national* form with a strong central government favored by some delegates and the *confederal*, or league of states, form favored by others. In arguing for its ratification, James Madison defended the Constitution in just this way, saying it would create a government that was partly national and partly federal.[4] Although today we refer to the government in Washington as the "federal" government, the Founders referred to the government they created by the type of democracy it was—a republic. The word *federal* does not appear in the Constitution.

The Fear Factor

Given the tenuous ties that often exist between political entities agreeing to unite under a single government, one scholar argues that federal systems "more than any other kind of government benefit from written constitutions." Because they "originate in particular bargains struck at a particular time for a particular purpose, written constitutions are useful, even necessary records, of the terms of the bargain."[5]

In the public debates arguing for ratification of the Constitution and in those arguing just as vehemently against it there was one dominant theme: fear.[6] The Federalists were afraid of another confederal arrangement and believed a new constitution had to create a central government strong enough to maintain the Union and protect it against external threats. The anti-federalists feared that, having just overthrown the British crown, they would be establishing another abusive central government if they ratified the Constitution. For them perhaps nothing raised the red flag higher than the Supremacy Clause, which they thought would emasculate state legislatures.

From every point on the political spectrum people found something to fear in the proposed new government: some feared because there were no written guarantees for individual liberties, others feared that too much power was left with the state governments, but still others feared the opposite, that too many powers were invested in the national government—to tax, borrow money, keep a standing army, and make treaties. Each branch of government raised its own set of fears: that the six-year term for senators would create

a political class or aristocracy, that the executive would be too weakened by the power of impeachment, that an independent judiciary would have too much power, and that the judiciary would not have enough independence. And there were the people to fear as well: as described in Chapter 2, many of the Founders were wary of direct democracy and the "passionate tendencies" of the masses. Federalism was the scarcely tried form of government chosen to assuage these fears, and that meant those making the case for ratification had to convince the public that the Constitution was creating a national government that could and would do *only* what needed to be done at the center, leaving state sovereignty intact.

Perhaps the benefit of the federal arrangement for the American colonies can be best understood by the adage "politics is the art of the possible." The division of powers made the Union possible. It allowed states their differences, ceded control over local affairs, and in the process protected against both an abusive central government and the tyranny of factions. But having reached agreement on a division of powers with great difficulty, the Founders left

Behind The Scenes

An Accidental Classic

Collected in a single volume as *The Federalist*, the eighty-five essays **James Madison, Alexander Hamilton,** and **John Jay** wrote in support of ratification of the Constitution have been described by contemporary scholars as "by far the greatest book on politics ever written in America."[1]

The "book," of course, was not a book in any conventional sense, but a collection of papers written by three men in a hurry, trying to hold together a tenuous union of thirteen states. In fact, the three men listed as coauthors were single authors working alone; they did not coordinate their work or collaborate to try to bring coherency to their arguments or writing style before publishing their es-

says. One authority on the papers says, "there is no evidence that one writer's work was ever revised on the advice of the others," even though the men's views—especially those of Madison and Hamilton, who between them wrote all but five of the essays— were known to conflict. Madison himself said that none of the authors could be expected to answer for the ideas of the other two.[2]

Under pressure from the short timeline for ratification, the three men wrote and published an average of a thousand words a day. They wrote so much so quickly that they borrowed heavily from their own earlier writings. Madison's landmark *Federalist* 10 (see Appendix) was taken almost entirely

from a letter he had written to Thomas Jefferson a month earlier. Other of his essays were drawn from research notes he prepared prior to the Constitutional Convention.

The Federalist essays were only one of twenty-four series of articles written to argue for or against ratification and it is not known how widely they were read or how many minds they swayed. Many scholars believe at best the essays may have influenced a few undecided voters in crucial ratification contests.[3] Yet they came to be regarded as one of the most "coherent Treaties on the basic principles of political theory" ever written. So many constitutional scholars have cited them as evidence of the intent of the Founders,

and so many federal court rulings have referenced them that, as for the Bible and the works of Shakespeare, a concordance was developed.[4] Nevertheless the divergent views of the authors are so apparent—John Adams said they read like "rival dissertations"—that the writings are said to suffer from a split personality.[5] In this sense, they are a true reflection of the competing arguments on how the Founders divided power among the nation, the states, and the people, and why, to this day, the country still suffers from a split personality.

[1] Bernard Bailyn, *The Federalist Papers* (Washington D.C.: Library of Congress, 1998).
[2] Ibid.
[3] Roy P. Fairfield, ed. *The Federalist Papers* (New York: Anchor Books, 1961), x–xi.
[4] Bailyn, 10–11.
[5] Ibid, 8.

James Madison.

© The Granger Collection, New York

vague the details of how the nation-state relationship would work. The Constitution did not specify the individual or institution that would resolve disputes over state and federal jurisdictions, but the federal courts assumed that role during the tenure of Chief Justice Marshall. (See the "Behind the Scenes" box on page 53 and also Chapter 13.)

Dueling Federalisms

Once ratified, the Constitution was evidence of a bargain between Federalists and anti-federalists, but that was no guarantee that each side would interpret the terms of the document in the same way. It was immediately clear that they had not even resolved their disagreement over who had been the original parties to this social contract. Those who saw the Constitution as written by representatives of the people and ratified by the people were inclined to view the national government as the supreme power in the federal relationship. Alexander Hamilton clearly articulated this view of **nation-centered federalism** in the *Federalist Papers*. This interpretation acknowledges that the Constitution grants many powers to the states, recognizes that they existed before the Union, and agrees that states are sovereign in the sense that they cannot be dissolved by the national government. But the nation-centered view is that the national government's sovereignty is supreme and its ultimate responsibility is to preserve the Union and ensure its indivisibility.[7] In support of their argument they cited the **Supremacy Clause,** the very wording so feared by anti-federalists.

Art. VI, Sec. 1

The clause says that treaties, the Constitution, and "laws made in pursuance thereof" are to be the supreme law of the land whenever they come into conflict with state laws or state actions. It also stipulates that when there is a difference of opinion as to whether state actions are in conflict with the Constitution or federal law, the matter is to be decided at the national level.[8] Nation-centered federalism (also called centralized federalism) was the view used by northerners to justify a war to prevent the southern states from seceding in 1861.

Opponents of the Hamiltonian interpretation, including many from the South, argued that because the Constitution recognized the states' existence as sovereign entities before the creation of the Union, the form our system was to take was **state-centered federalism,** giving precedence to state sovereignty over that of the national government or the Union. They believed the Tenth Amendment ⭐ limited congressional powers to those specifically mentioned in Article I and that this view was reinforced by Madison's words in *Federalist Paper* 45: "The powers delegated . . . to the federal government are few and defined. Those which are to remain in the state governments are numerous and indefinite." In this view, any attempt by Congress to go beyond these explicitly listed powers violated state authority.

In justifying their secession from the Union, southerners held to the extreme version of state-centered federalism: that the Constitution had been written by representatives of the states, not the people. In their view, if the states had created the Union, they could dissolve it.

DEMOCRACY?

Would there be any implications for the democratic nature of our government if the states rather than the people were determined to be the original contractors of the Union?

The Constitution can also be interpreted as having created a government in which the division of power leaves neither level dominant over the other. In this view—**dual federalism**—the Constitution created a system in which the national government and the states each have separate grants of power, with each supreme in its own sphere. In this interpretation of the division of powers, sovereignty is not just divided but divided in such a way as to leave both levels of government essentially equal. The differences between levels derive from their separate jurisdictions, not from inequality of power. Madison's description in *Federalist Paper* 39 of the government created by the Constitution as a hybrid of national and federal forms provides one basis for this interpretation.

Over the years, the dominant interpretations of power sharing in our form of federalism have shifted among the nation-centered, state-centered, and dual views. Overall, there has been a general trend away from state-centered and

toward nation-centered federalism, but significant shorter-term
shifts have occurred back toward
the states.

Describing our form of government as centralized federalism
indicates where the preponderance
of power lies; it does not suggest
that at any time there is a national
consensus on where it does or
should lie. For decades after the
Civil War, for example, the states
that had remained in the Union
were much more likely to accept
the authority of the center to apply
uniform rules to the states than
were those states that had joined
the Confederacy. (See Chapters 8
and 15.) State governments were
able to refuse enforcement of basic constitutional guarantees on
civil rights and liberties in large
part because there was no national
will to force compliance. But it
was also recognition of the tenuous bargain struck by the Founders on the division of powers.
Having fought our deadliest war
over secession, the deal made in
the postwar (Reconstruction) years
restoring full powers to the secessionist states reflected that
the primary concern continued to lie with keeping the
Union intact. But the Union can also falter if too much
value is placed on accommodation of state or regional preferences, especially if the differences among the states become more important than their commitment to common
principles.

The constitutional provisions protecting the rights and
individuality of the states were meant to accommodate
what is sometimes called our "psychology of localism."[9]
(See the American Diversity box "Political Culture and
Federalism.") Although we are now a more mobile and a
more nation-oriented people than we were in the eighteenth
and nineteenth centuries, with communication and transportation links that bind us together, we retain enough local
allegiance and commitment to individualism to tilt our federal system toward decentralization and fragmentation. Indeed, federalism creates separate power centers, and keeping them separate becomes an interest of those holding that
power.[10] In part, federalism is *intended* to do this, but if
taken too far, it can prevent coherence and unity. Even
when there is need for national policy—whether on energy,
the environment, health care, or defense spending—
members of Congress may still base their votes primarily
on local interests (see Chapter 10).

American Stock/Getty Images

As the country grew, our government grew too. Washington sent soldiers, surveyors, road builders, and mail carriers to accommodate the needs of settlers. Here wagon trains head west in 1890.

The Evolution of Federalism

The first fifty years under the new constitution were characterized by the growth of nation-centered federalism in legal
doctrine, by small-scale state and national government in
practice, and by the beginning of intergovernmental cooperation. In the administration of George Washington the
federal government had only one thousand employees, and
this number had increased to only thirty-three thousand by
the presidency of James Buchanan seventy years later. Little revenue was raised by any level of government; most of
the funding for the national government came from import-
export and excise taxes. State governments, too, were small
and had limited functions. There were only a few federal-
state cooperative activities. For example, the federal government gave land to the states to support education and
participated in joint federal-state-private ventures, such as
canal-building projects initiated by the states.

In this section we look at how territorial expansion, war,
and economic crises required a greater exercise of power
at the national level—raising armies, regulating trade
and interstate commerce, and building infrastructure, for
example—which in turn demanded an expansion of taxation authority and a larger bureaucracy. We also look at the
roles of the federal courts and Congress in shaping the division of powers.

american diversity | Political Culture And Federalism

When we refer to the Midwest, the Southwest, New England, or the Deep South, certain images still come to mind, not just of geographical areas but of lifestyles, partisan preferences, ideology, and local economies. Our nicknames—Bible Belt, Lala Land, the Corn, Sun, and Rust belts—reflect this. Individual states have developed sufficiently different political styles and attitudes that campaign strategists would never design the same electoral strategy for a candidate in New York as they would for one in Idaho. For the same reason, candidates for national office change the points of emphasis in their stump speeches as they move from state to state.

States want to be different from one another. Each has its own constitution, flag, motto, and symbols of state, not to mention its very own official state bird and flower. Each state is basically a political actor competing for a share of the nation's resources. Just as individuals organize around identity issues, states compete with one another on the basis of their distinctive profiles.

In Chapter 1 we defined political culture as a shared body of values and beliefs that shapes perceptions and attitudes toward politics and government and that influences behavior. For much of the twentieth century, the United States was said to have three geographically based political subcultures—three distinctive ways of looking at and participating in politics.[1] The tendency of people in New England and the upper Midwest to view politics as a way of improving life and to believe in their obligation to participate was labeled a *moralistic* political culture. In the *individualistic* political culture, said to be typical of the industrial Midwest and the East,

the ultimate objective of politics was not to create a better life for all, but to get benefits for oneself and one's group. In the *traditionalistic* political culture, associated with the states of the Deep South, politics was seen not as a way to further the public good but as a way to maintain the status quo, and little value was placed on participation. Today, traces of these patterns remain, but much has changed.

The Deep South, for example, having been the site of intense political mobilization during the modern civil rights movement, is now a center of significant grassroots activity, especially among religious conservatives. The out-migration of African Americans during the decades of segregation has been reversed, with a significant impact on electoral politics in the region.

The transformation of the United States from an industry- and agriculture-based economy to a high-tech and service economy also has had an inevitable impact on regional political cultures. The mobility of the American population makes it less likely that people will have political orientations as strongly rooted in a state or regional identity as in earlier decades. Every year, about one in seven Americans move, one-third of those from one state to another.[2] At the extreme, only 25 percent of Nevadans were born in Nevada, for example. Mass media, especially television and the Internet; franchises and chains bringing the same products to all parts of the country; and transportation systems that can carry us across the nation in a few hours have all had a leveling effect on some of our regional differences.

Yet the country is just as diverse as ever; indeed, it is ethnically and

racially more diverse. Patterns of dispersion of African Americans, Hispanics, and Asians, and the clusters of immigrants settling by country of origin in a handful of states and big cities, contribute to the retention of regional differences and distinctive state profiles. In New Mexico, 44 percent of the population is of Hispanic origin, compared with just over 1 percent in Maine. In Mississippi, African Americans make up over 37 percent of the population; in Vermont, 0.6 percent. Minorities, collectively, now form the majority of the population in four states, including Texas. In Florida, almost as many people are over age sixty-five (19.5 percent of the population) as are under eighteen (21 percent), but in Utah, young people outnumber senior citizens more than 3 to 1. In Mississippi, annual per capita income is only 54 percent of what it is in Connecticut ($32,938 versus $50,941).[3]

These disparities make for different politics in the states. The priorities of older people (health care, for instance) are different from those of younger people (financial aid for education, for example). In states with larger numbers of Hispanics and African Americans, civil rights issues are more salient than in states with predominantly white populations. Southern Baptists, who comprise 11 percent of all American Christians, live predominantly in southern states and vote overwhelmingly Republican. Jewish Americans, who tend to be more liberal and vote Democratic, are concentrated in a handful of states, including New York, Florida, and California. And Mississippi, West Virginia, and Arkansas, whose citizens are poorer than those in the rest of the country, face greater demands for services and have correspondingly fewer resources to provide them.

Although state and regional differences have not been homogenized, the three old archetypes have morphed into the two more comprehensive categories now familiar to everyone as red states and blue states. Another scheme labels them retro (red) and metro (blue), but the basic distinction is between conservative and liberal policies and lifestyles.[4] The politically conservative/moralistic/red/retro label is now attached to the South, Plains states, lower Midwest, and near West. The liberal/nontraditional/ blue/metro state label lumps together the Northeast, upper Midwest, northwestern coastal states, and California.

In fact, the division of states into such broad categories masks the diversity within the two groups and is misleading in suggesting a consonance of lifestyles and political orientation within them. The divorce rate in the Bible Belt states is 50 percent higher than the national average, whereas the nation's lowest divorce rate is in Massachusetts, the bluest of blue states.[5] The wealthiest states are all in the blue column and the poorest in the red column, which means that the citizens of conservative states who are most likely to oppose social welfare policies and government programs receive substantially more per capita in government benefits than they pay in taxes.[6]

State boundaries do still mean something beyond identifying the place where you register to vote. In policy areas as diverse as economic development, taxation, welfare, and regulation of personal morality, states vary widely. (See Figure below.) Nevada is the only state in the nation where prostitution is legal; Utah the only state where polygamy has been tolerated (even though illegal). South Dakota passed a law banning abortions that would never make it through the Massachusetts legislature, whereas Massachusetts and Vermont passed laws allowing same-sex marriages that would never have been passed in South Dakota. Federalism, even with a strong national government, provides sufficient autonomy for states to adopt and maintain policies consistent with their own political cultures.

[1] Daniel Elazar, *American Federalism: A View from the States*, 3rd ed. (New York: Harper & Row, 1984).
[2] U.S. Census Bureau, *Statistical Abstract of the United States, 2006* (Washington, D.C.: Government Printing Office, 2005), tab. 30, p. 36.
[3] All figures in this paragraph from *Statistical Abstract of the United States, 2008*, tabs. 17, 18, and 684, pp. 22, 23, 453.
[4] John Sperling, et al., *The Great Divide: Retro vs. Metro America* (Sausalito, CA: PoliPoint Press, 2004).
[5] Jim Holt, "States' Rights Left?" *New York Times Magazine*, November 21, 2004, 27.
[6] Sperling, *The Great Divide*, 34.

Political Culture is Reflected in States' Policies

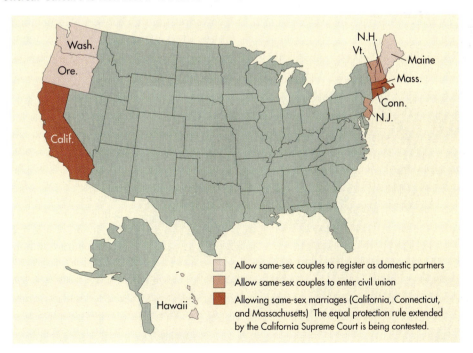

Allow same-sex couples to register as domestic partners

Allow same-sex couples to enter civil union

Allowing same-sex marriages (California, Connecticut, and Massachusetts) The equal protection rule extended by the California Supreme Court is being contested.

States tend to have a more liberal or more conservative political culture, which is reflected in their policies, whether for moral or other issues.

SOURCE: Pew Forum. Pewforum.org/docs/?DocID=287]

Growth of Government and the Exercise of Power

Government has grown because, as society changes, new problems emerge and people demand that government respond to them. Government has also grown because emergencies such as wars and depressions occur, and those in power see the need for a bigger government to cope with them. Presidents come to office with some idea of how they will use the powers of office—whether they will be maximalists or minimalists, or something in between. But a president's theoretical view of the power of the federal government can be superseded by events. How presidents respond to needs arising from war, social movements, economic crises, or natural disasters can lead to changes in the division of power, whether intended or not intended.

Thomas Jefferson called his election a revolution, abolished all internal taxes, and set about making government as small, simple, and informal as possible. He tried to keep the United States out of war in Europe and closed down ports and foreign trade, but he soon found he needed federal policing to enforce his policy.[11] And despite his support for small government and state-centered federalism, Jefferson bought the Louisiana territories from Spain. His expansionist vision instantly changed the country from a small coastal nation to a vast continental empire in which his idea of a small agrarian republic would no longer be possible.

Abraham Lincoln, who was as loath as Jefferson to interfere with states' rights when it came to slavery, had no doubts about denying states the right to secede from the Union nor about using his role as a wartime commander in chief to assume extraordinary powers in domestic policy. The Civil War's outcome reaffirmed the Supremacy Clause and the indivisibility of the republic and guaranteed that there would be only one national government in the continental United States. Northerners saw their Civil War victory as a severe blow to state-centered federalism, but southerners continued to see the Union, in which they were forcibly retained, as one governed by a state-centered form of federalism.

By the time **Theodore Roosevelt** (1901–1909) assumed the presidency, agrarian America was being replaced by a rapidly urbanizing and industrializing society. Living and working conditions for many city dwellers were appalling. Adults and children who moved into the cities often took jobs in sweatshops— factories where they worked long hours in unsafe conditions for low pay. Roosevelt's presidency was a time of tremendous government activism. He saw his office as a "bully pulpit" from which to advocate for the improvement of working conditions, environmental protection, and the regulation of big business, especially its corrupting influence on state legislatures and the U.S. Senate, which was then still elected by the legislatures. These years saw a flood of new legislation and regulatory activity as Roosevelt's concept of government as advocate for the average citizen changed the direction and purpose of government at the outset of the twentieth century.

During this period, the revenues of both the national and state governments grew. The new revenue for the federal government came through a tax on personal income, a tax Congress had power to levy only after the **Sixteenth Amendment** to the Constitution was ratified in 1913. ⭐ The power to tax individual income established a direct power relationship between Washington and the people and also slowly expanded the reach of the federal government by providing fiscal support for many new activities. Some states also adopted income taxes and many states and localities levied gasoline and cigarette taxes and raised property taxes. Federal support for state programs also grew through land and cash grants given by the federal government to the states.[12] By the late 1920s, however, the federal government still provided few direct services to individuals. States and localities were clearly the dominant partner in providing most services, from health and sanitation to police and fire protection.

As Teddy Roosevelt had expanded the federal government's role in order to curb the negative consequences of economic expansion on the individual and the environment, **Franklin Delano Roosevelt** (FDR; 1933–1945) expanded government power at all levels to mitigate the effects of the Great Depression, the worst economic crisis the

The industrialization of the late 1800s and early 1900s led to extensive child labor and harsh working conditions. These boys toil in an Indiana glass factory in 1908.

Theodore (Teddy) Roosevelt rode into the presidency determined to use government to improve working conditions, eliminate business corruption, and preserve national resources.

country had experienced. When the stock market crashed in 1929, wealthy people became poor overnight. In the depths of the Depression, one-fourth of the workforce was unemployed, and banks failed daily. Unlike today, there was no systematic national program of relief for the unemployed—no unemployment compensation, no food stamps, no welfare, nothing to help put food on the table and pay the rent. Millions of Americans were hungry, homeless, and hopeless. States and localities, which had the responsibility for providing relief to the poor, were overwhelmed; they did not have the funds or organizational resources to cope with the millions needing help. And private charities did not have enough resources to assume the burden. FDR's predecessor, Herbert Hoover, had taken a minimalist approach, and by the time FDR came to office the dislocation and suffering of millions of Americans threatened the political stability of the country.

During his first two terms, FDR formulated and Congress passed a program called the **New Deal.** Its purpose was to stimulate economic recovery and aid those who were unemployed, hungry, and in ill health. New Deal legislation regulated many activities of business and labor, set up a welfare system, and began large-scale federal-state

cooperation in funding and administering programs through federal grants-in-aid. In the FDR years, grants-in-aid provided federal money to states (and occasionally to local governments) to initiate programs that targeted categories of needy people—the aged poor or the unemployed, for example. Overall government spending grew, and, as Figure 2 indicates, the federal share of spending for domestic needs (exclusive of military spending) nearly tripled, from 17 percent in 1929, before the New Deal, to 47 percent in 1939. The states' share of overall government spending stayed constant. Local governments' share of public spending dropped by half, and yet in absolute terms increased dramatically, given the huge increase in total public sector spending. Some of that increase was from federal grants-in-aid to fund unemployment compensation, emergency welfare, and distribution of farm surpluses to the needy and for free school lunches, among other programs.

New regulations on banks and working conditions, federal redistributive programs designed to protect the poor (Aid to Dependent Children), and social insurance for the elderly poor, retired, and disabled (Social Security) were other New Deal policies that directly affected everyday life. Overall, the New Deal brought a dramatic change in the relationship between the national government and its citizens, making government more personal both because of its greater involvement in daily life and because of the closer, more interdependent relationship between the president and the people.

World War II also stimulated the growth of the national government during this era. FDR, a former assistant secretary of the navy who was well versed in defense policy, relished his role as commander in chief. He assumed—as Lincoln had during the Civil War—extraordinary powers to meet the emergencies of wartime, including price controls, rationing, and the suspension of some civil liberties (in fact, all civil liberties for Japanese Americans). Spending on armaments and the military gave a tremendous boost to the economy, and defense spending has remained an important element of many states' economies ever since.

By the 1950s, some public officials had become uneasy about the growing size of the federal government and its involvement in so many state and local programs. But the Cold War created a host of new demands for spending on national security—expansion of intelligence operations, a bigger, better equipped military with forward bases around the world, and development of a whole new arsenal of unconventional weaponry. President **Dwight D. Eisenhower** (1953–1961), a Republican politically inclined toward small government, had been a career military officer and leader of the Allied Forces in World War II. He went along with increased spending on many new federal programs, ranging from the massively expensive interstate highway program to college programs in science, engineering, and languages. All of these, especially interstate highway construction, were driven by defense planning and competition with the Soviet Union.

Thirty-two years after his cousin Teddy became president, Franklin D. Roosevelt (FDR) used his unbridled confidence and public support for his New Deal to greatly expand the role of the federal government.

Spending on grants to the states to implement these new programs nearly tripled during Eisenhower's administration. Even while accepting the United States' expanded role in world affairs, Eisenhower warned about the impact of military expenditures on the economy and the dangers to democracy of a growing military-industrial complex.

The size of government spiked again during the tenure of **Lyndon Baines Johnson** (1963–1969), a Texas Democrat and experienced legislator whose concept of federalism was born in the New Deal era. This time the cause was growing pressure from the movements for social justice and racial equality. Johnson's presidency coincided with the peak activism of the modern civil rights movement, whose struggle for political equality was brought into every home by television. As Americans watched protestors being beaten or attacked by police dogs, Johnson, like Eisenhower before him, had to call up, or threaten to nationalize, state militia to force state and local officials to comply with federal law. At the same time, the mass media were making the country aware of the high levels of poverty and hunger in the United States. When the movement for greater economic justice joined forces with the civil rights movement, and when passive civil disobedience tactics were supplanted by riots, looting, and fires in some northern cities, there was concern that the United States might be approaching the dangerous levels of civil unrest that developed during the Great Depression.

Johnson responded to these problems by pushing through Congress voting rights legislation and a massive package of social welfare proposals. These so-called Great Society proposals increased the scope of government and changed the nation-state relationship in two important ways. To implement Great Society programs, the federal government began funding, through expansion of the grants-in-aid initiated during the Great Depression, work in domains that were formerly state and local preserves—law enforcement, urban mass transit, public education, and fire protection. But the grants came with increasingly burdensome regulations that stipulated how and for what the grants were to be used. With a tripling of aid to fund new programs, state and local governments became increasingly dependent on federal funding.[13]

Second, with federal voting rights guarantees in place, state governments no longer had the power to pass laws that denied the vote to, or restricted political participation by, African Americans. This profoundly changed the power relationship between Washington and state governments, especially those in the Deep South, because it gave federal law enforcement officials, including the FBI and the Justice Department, a strong role in monitoring state voting procedures to see that they conformed to federal guidelines. Eventually, these reforms also changed the distribution of power in state governments. (See Chapter 8.)

These cases illustrate that, during most of the two hundred plus years of American history, presidential leadership, especially in periods of domestic and foreign crises, led to the growth of the federal government. But many of these presidents, especially Jefferson, Lincoln, and Eisenhower, did not run as candidates advocating big government or expansion of the power of Washington at the expense of the states. Even FDR ran on a balanced budget platform. The bigger-than-life personalities of the Roosevelts and Lyndon Johnson surely affected their concepts of government activism; one can imagine them looking for problems for

Figure 2 | **Share of Nonmilitary Spending by the Federal, State, and Local Governments before and after the Passage of New Deal Legislation**

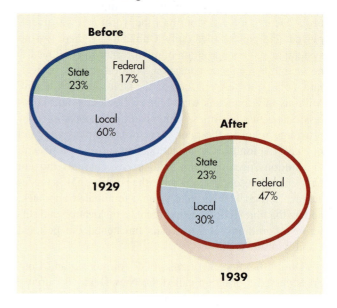

SOURCE: Advisory Committee on Intergovernmental Relations, Significant Features of Fiscal Federalism (Washington, D.C.: Government Printing Office, 1979), 7.

government to solve. But Teddy Roosevelt did not create exploitative labor practices or corrupt state legislatures, any more than FDR created the Great Depression or started World War II or Lyndon Johnson the problems of inequality in American society. The expansion of federal power during their tenures occurred when their proclivity for activism came up against situations crying out for government response. Except for Theodore Roosevelt's support for ending the election of U.S. senators by state legislatures and Lyndon Johnson's fight to abolish the right of states to effectively nullify constitutionally guaranteed civil rights, these presidents did not attempt to curb the powers of state government.

Role of the Federal Courts

Such was the gulf between those who thought they were creating an indivisible Union and those who thought they were writing a contract between states that the Constitution might never have been ratified if it had contained specifics on the practice of federalism. Ultimately, it is the Supreme Court that decides where the lines are drawn between what is state and what is federal authority. There have been many Court rulings on the division of power between Washington and the states since the Marshall Court's ruling in *McCulloch* v. *Maryland* (Chapter 2), but like presidents, the federal courts swing between support for nation- and state-centered federalism, depending on the judicial philosophies of the justices.

Before the Civil War, in the years of small government, the Supreme Court overturned only two congressional and sixty state laws. But beginning in the 1880s, as Congress took a larger role in regulating business and the economy, a conservative Supreme Court used the dual federalism doctrine to rule unconstitutional many federal attempts to regulate. But this proved to be more of a probusiness bias than a dual federalist view. When state governments, spurred by the same revelations of unsafe and degrading conditions that led Congress to act, passed laws against child labor and to protect workers, the federal courts often ruled that they, too, had overstepped their powers. From 1874 to 1937, the Supreme Court found fifty federal and four hundred state laws unconstitutional, including some of FDR's key New Deal legislation.[14] After FDR was elected to a second term and had a chance to replace conservative justices, the Court looked on his legislative program more sympathetically. (See Chapter 13 for more on the Court and the New Deal.)

The Court decisions approving New Deal legislation were, in a sense, a return to the nation-centered federalism of **John Marshall**'s day. But although the Supreme Court upheld much of the New Deal, it also approved more sweeping *state* regulations of business and labor than had the less activist pre–New Deal Court. Thus the change in Court philosophy did not enlarge the federal role at the expense of the powers of the states; *it enlarged the powers of both state and federal government.* In doing so, the Court was responding to the public's preference for government

The WPA (Works Progress Administration) was part of President Franklin Roosevelt's effort to put the unemployed back to work constructing government buildings, sidewalks, and streets during the Depression.

to play a larger role in helping people cope with the crises stemming from the Great Depression.

In the 1960s and early 1970s, during the height of the civil rights and women's movements, the federal courts struck down many state laws that restricted voting rights, criminal defendants' rights, and women's economic and educational opportunities. But since the 1990s, a federal court system dominated by Republican appointees has been reversing that trend by constricting Congress's power to overturn state laws.

In the past two decades, the rulings of the Supreme Court have shown a trend toward empowering the states at the expense of the national government. In 1992, the Court handed down the first of several key decisions that restrict Congress's ability to impose rules and regulations on state governments and prevent litigants from bypassing state courts to seek remedies in federal courts. In a 1995 decision, the Court ruled for the first time since the New Deal that Congress had exceeded its authority to regulate interstate commerce, and in the following eight years it "overturned all or parts of thirty-three federal statutes, ten of them on the grounds that Congress had exceeded its authority either to regulate interstate commerce or to enforce the constitutional guarantees of due process and equal protection."[15]

Once the thinking of the Court's majority was known, dozens of other federalism suits were filed by those who wanted to limit Congress's ability to extend federal laws to state jurisdictions. These suits have been successful in preventing some disabled people from suing their employers in

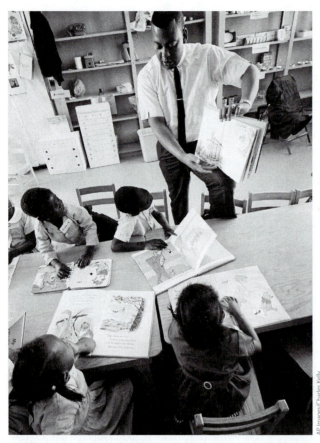

AP Images/Charles Kelly

President Lyndon Johnson's Great Society programs addressed the plight of the poor and underprivileged, such as the students in this classroom in Mississippi.

state courts for alleged violations of their civil rights as guaranteed under the Americans with Disabilities Act. The limitation placed on such suits by the Court has been summarized as "rights without remedies," or one that permits Congress to confer rights on citizens but not to tell the states how to enforce them. The four dissenting justices in those rulings said that decisions giving states immunity from federal rules are the "result of a fundamentally flawed understanding of the role of the states within the federal system" and that they intend to go on dissenting in all cases where this principle of state immunity is applied by the Court's majority.[16]

The Court's decision to overrule the Florida courts and intervene in the Florida vote count during the 2000 presidential election to give the election to George W. Bush is some evidence that their rulings have been animated more by conservative principles than dual federalism. After all, elections, whether for national, state, or local office, are the jurisdiction of the states, not the federal government. This assertion of federal power came during a high tide of Court rulings in defense of states' rights.

Other exceptions to the Court's rulings in favor of states' rights also suggest that conservative principles rather than just states rights are driving the Court's decisions. The Court has been willing to allow Congress to overturn state

laws on what might be classified as conservative values issues, such as its refusal to uphold state or local laws on medical use of marijuana or gun control laws that are stronger than those passed by Congress. In a departure from this trend the Court did rule in 2006 that Congress could not use federal antidrug laws to overturn an Oregon "right to die" law that allows doctors to administer, at the request of terminally ill patients, lethal doses of drugs. But it is too early to know how the current Court will ultimately come down on the issue of state- versus nation-centered federalism.

Role of Congress

Only the president and vice president have a national constituency; the power of all other elected officials is based in the states and localities. It behooves members of Congress, though federal officials, to cater to the localities; in fact, the Constitution invests them with this responsibility by giving each a specific geographic area to represent. And this is exactly what they do. Most members of the U.S. House and Senate spend far more time pursuing the interests of their districts and states than they do in defining and pursuing the national interest.

Depending on its composition at any given time, Congress is more, or less, sympathetic to nation-centered federalism. The tremendous growth of government during FDR's first three terms brought a backlash from Republicans and Southern Democrats who wanted to swing the locus of power away from the center and back to the states. Similarly, the growth in social welfare programs during the Johnson era eventually led to the Reagan-Republican smaller-government rebellion in the 1980s and 1990s and a reemphasis on states' rights. Nevertheless, since the end of segregationist governments in southern states, Congress has had few advocates of pure state-centered federalism.

Although willing to delegate authority to state governments for administration of the biggest, costliest social insurance programs, Congress continues to supersede the states in rule making whenever state laws are in conflict with its will. In recent years, bills have been introduced to supplant state laws on drunk driving with a national standard, allow property owners to bypass state courts and go directly to federal courts to protest local zoning laws, and to override state laws on late-term abortions, medical use of marijuana, and assisted suicides.[17] In 2006, Congress, at the behest of lobbyists for the food industry and money lenders, was considering one bill that would supplant all state food safety regulations that are more protective than federal standards and another that would override state laws that block access to consumer credit ratings.

Both Democrats and Republicans have repeatedly used congressional authority to regulate interstate commerce to prevent state governments from taxing e-commerce and other Internet activity, a prohibition that states claim has cost them billions in lost revenue.[18] Even after states negotiated interstate tax collection agreements and lobbied hard for lifting the ban, Congress continued to renew it, even during periods of huge budget deficits.

One member of Congress said of his colleagues that they "don't really believe in states' rights; they believe in deciding the issue at whatever level of government they think will do it their way. They want to be Thomas Jefferson on Monday, Wednesday, and Friday and Alexander Hamilton on Tuesday and Thursday and Saturday."[19]

It is important to remember that although the federal relationship has changed significantly with the growth of government and through the exercise of executive powers and court rulings, the constitutional provisions defining the relationship between the national and state governments remain as written, except in the area of human and civil rights. By deferring voting rights to the states, the Founders essentially gave them the right to disenfranchise whomever they chose. By constitutional amendment, this power is gone from the states forever.

 Amendments 13-15, 19, 24 and 26.

Power Sharing in American Federalism

Although few people argue that the states could do a better job than Washington providing for the national defense, there is sharp disagreement over which level of government can make other policies more efficiently and effectively. States are not bureaucracy free. However, state officials are often more aware of how national problems like access to health care, climate change, and shortcomings in K–12 education affect local populations. States are also under more pressure to act to solve them. Governing units below the state level—counties, townships, cities, school and park districts, for example—often believe they are better equipped to legislate for local areas than state government.

The relations between Washington and the states and localities are a mixture of cooperation and conflict. One expert calls it "competitive federalism" because states and the federal government are competing for leadership of the nation's domestic policy.[20] But given the large number of governments in the United States (see Table 1), cooperation in carrying out the day-to-day work of government is essential. In this section, we look at the main points of cooperation and conflict in the everyday practice of federalism. Special attention is paid to the flow of tax revenues between Washington and the states and the conflict over fiscal issues.

Cooperative Federalism

The term **cooperative federalism** describes the day-to-day joint activities and continuing cooperation among federal, state, and local officials in carrying out the business of government: distributing payments to farmers, providing welfare services, planning highways, organizing centers for the elderly, and carrying out all the functions that the national and state governments jointly fund and organize. It also refers to informal cooperation in locating criminals, tracking down the source of contagious diseases, and many other activities.

One example of informal but intensive cooperation is the Centers for Disease Control and Prevention in Atlanta, which helps state and local governments meet health emergencies and prevent the spread of contagious diseases, such as the bird flu virus. National and state police and other crime-fighting agencies share data on crimes and criminals. The federal government and the states also jointly regulate in many areas, including occupational safety and the environment. Today, state agencies are responsible for 90 percent of all environmental enforcement actions.[21] And since the 2001 terrorist attacks, there has been increased reliance on state resources to help with national defense, especially through training programs for first responders and use of state militia (National Guard) to supplement regular army troops in combat zones abroad.

The National Guard often figures in one of the best-known areas of state-federal cooperation—disaster relief. Destruction caused by a hurricane, flood, tornado, or earthquake may be so severe and widespread that the resources of the affected states and localities are overwhelmed. The governor can ask the president to declare the stricken counties a federal disaster area or the president can declare a national emergency without a formal request for assistance from local officials.

The principal agency for coordinating relief efforts is the Federal Emergency Management Agency (FEMA). The agency was created in 1979 to cope with the effects of a nuclear attack, but before 9/11 it was called on mainly to provide financial help, temporary shelters, and other emergency aid to areas struck by natural disasters. Created for one purpose and diverted to another, the agency got off to a rough start and it has had a mixed record ever since. The collaboration of FEMA and other federal agencies with city and state offices after the September 11 attacks, with the help of nonprofits and volunteers from around the country, resulted in one of the most remarkable intergovernmental responses to disaster the country had ever seen. In the first nine months, federal, state, local, and nonprofit agencies cleared debris, repaired the damaged roads and sidewalks in the vicinity of the World Trade Center, and provided crisis counseling and a ferry service into Manhattan to replace the subway stations destroyed by the collapse of the towers. The Trade Center site was cleaned up six months ahead of schedule at one-tenth of the estimated cost.

But FEMA was not a priority of the Bush administration. FEMA fell into disarray as the administration filled leadership positions with political cronies and left many positions unfilled. So, when Hurricane Katrina hit southern Mississippi and Louisiana in 2005, there was barely a hint

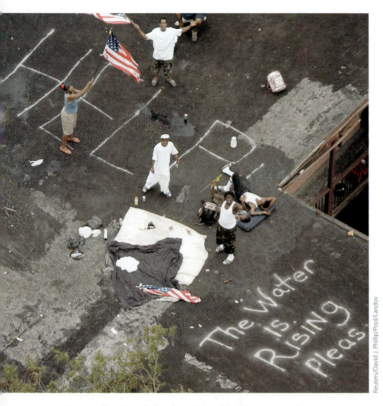

During disasters, federal, state, and local rescue and recovery agencies are supposed to join forces to aid victims and organize the cleanup. Coordination failed badly when Hurricane Katrina hit Louisiana and Mississippi in 2005. In New Orleans, some residents climbed to their roofs, where they waited for days to be rescued or given water and food.

of the federal-state cooperation that made the post-9/11 recovery so remarkable. Over a million people in Mississippi and Louisiana were left homeless; 100,000 New Orleaners were stranded in the city, most in the poorest neighborhoods; almost eighteen hundred died, and hundreds went missing. Bodies floated in the flooded streets with no one to recover them, and thousands were trapped in their homes or on rooftops for days waiting for rescue, without food, water, or electricity, and in some cases, medications. Half of its citizens still had not returned to New Orleans by 2008.

With a leadership vacuum at the national level, and first responders disabled or unable to communicate with one another, a profusion of public and private agencies responded on their own with little coordination of effort. It took several days just to assign the military responsibility for distribution of food and water. FEMA's successes and failures are lessons in the fundamental need for effective communication and clear chains of command among federal, state, and local agencies during emergencies.

Another important area of cooperation is in the management of federally owned land—military bases, weapons facilities, national parks, and wilderness areas. The federal government holds almost 27 percent of all land within the United States, the majority in western states. In those states (Nevada, Idaho, Utah, Alaska, and Oregon) where half or

more of the land is federally owned, state governments often do not have the control they would like to have over the state's natural resources, and cooperation can turn to competition and even conflict. Usually the friction is over economic exploitation of resources in park land, but sometimes states object to activities they believe put their populations at risk—radioactivity from weapons production or the testing and storage of nuclear waste. Nevada has been fighting the federal government in the courts for years to stop preparation of a national nuclear waste storage center just ninety miles from Las Vegas. One former governor even threatened to stand in front of any train carrying nuclear waste into the state.

Governors must work closely with the president and congress on fiscal matters because a substantial portion of state spending is paid for with tax dollars returned by Washington. This is often a source of conflict, as discussed in the next section, but the indirect financial boost states get in the form of deductions for individual taxpayers is not. When reporting income to the Internal Revenue Service, residents of all states are allowed to deduct the amount of income, real estate, and personal property taxes they paid to their states and localities. By lowering the amount of tax paid to Washington, every year hundreds of billions of dollars are left in consumer pockets to be spent in the states and stimulate local economies.

Shared administration of the programs funded by the nearly half-trillion in tax dollars returned annually to the states to provide federally mandated services is marked by both cooperation and competition—competition because most states want as few strings as possible placed on how grants-in-aid are spent. It is worth noting, however, that despite imposing some inefficiencies, the performance standards and regulations attached to the grants have increased the professionalism of state and local bureaucrats.

Devolution

The amount of control the president and Congress are willing to cede to the states in administering federal programs is an important indicator of the degree of federal-state cooperation. **Devolution** is the assignment of policy making or implementation powers from higher levels of government to lower levels. The amount of devolution changes over time, as we illustrate with examples from five administrations.

Washington shares with the states the power to determine how, and on what, grants-in-aid are spent. Remember that **grants-in-aid** are the tax revenues the federal government returns to states to help pay for essential services provided by state and local governments—mass transit, community development, social welfare, and unemployment compensation, for example. (See Figure 3.) Around 30 percent of all state and local spending is funded from grants-in-aid.[22]

Figure 3 | What Does the Federal Government Give the States Money to Do?

In billions of dollars

2009 (est.)

Eighty-four percent of the estimated $476 billion the federal government is sending back to the states in 2009 is for programs in these areas.

SOURCE: *Budget of the United States, Fiscal Year 2009, "Historical Tables"* (Washington, D.C.: Government Printing Office, 2008), tab. 12.2, p. 240.

Presidents and Congress want to achieve administrative efficiency while carrying out their policy and political goals when they send money to the states to administer. They may also have ideological goals. In his Great Society programs, for example, Lyndon Johnson increased the number of grants that went directly to localities, bypassing states, be-cause he believed rural-influenced state legislatures would be less responsive to the needs of the inner cities. Johnson's policies were results oriented, not ideological.

When Republican **Richard Nixon** (1969–1974) came into office, he wanted to make government "more effective as well as more efficient." Nixon took a managerial approach to streamlining the cumbersome structure created by the profusion of Great Society programs. He saw a messy bureaucratic problem and an overconcentration of decision making at the federal level, and he tried to find a solution through more efficient management.[23] He did this by consolidating grants-in-aid into block grants, leaving it to the states and localities to determine how to fund programs in these functional areas. This greater leeway gave local officials more opportunity to target projects to local needs, and it streamlined the process at the federal level.

In contrast to Nixon's managerial approach, the new federalism of Republican **Ronald Reagan** (1981–1989) had a more ideological purpose, which he made clear in his first inaugural address: "Government is not the solution to our problems," he said. "Government is the problem." Thus Reagan wanted to reduce the power and influence of Washington rather than to improve intergovernmental management. His new federalism was rooted not so much in state-centered or dual federalism as it was in his opposition to government in general.[24] This approach—cutting federal spending on local and state programs to downsize government at all levels—contrasts with Nixon's approach, in which making government more efficient and effective was an end in itself.

Although Reagan had an ideological commitment to smaller government, he had no significant programmatic approach to achieve it, and he was often more preoccupied with the Cold War than with his domestic programs. In fact, the size and expenditures of the federal government grew during his administration, and states gained few new powers.

Democrat **Bill Clinton** (1993–2001) came to office with an ex-governor's wary view of Washington and a commitment to working in partnership with the states. Reforming state-federal relations had been a special interest when, as governor, he chaired both the National Governors Association and a reform group within the Democratic Party. A native of a southern state (Arkansas) where the states' rights tradition held sway, Clinton claimed to be a supporter of states' rights except in the area of civil rights policy. But he was not an advocate of state-centered federalism or smaller government for its own sake. He was committed to the idea (earlier articulated by Justice Louis Brandeis) of the **"states as laboratories"**— that is, as places for policy experimentation. He used the phrase frequently, wrote it into executive orders, and eventually based his welfare, health care, and education policies around it.[25] From 1994 through the end of his administration, both Clinton and congressional Republicans supported policies that delegated more powers to the states. But the Republican-controlled Congress favored devolution because it was ideologically opposed to central government in domestic policy, whereas Clinton's federalism policies, like Nixon's, were primarily geared toward making government more efficient.

George W. Bush (2001–2009), like Clinton, came to the presidency from the governorship of a southern state (Texas), but unlike Clinton, Bush openly advocated returning power to the states. Clinton had favored delegating rule implementation to state agencies, but he insisted on the right of federal agencies to set national standards, such as for clean air and water and consumer and worker safety, as well as to intervene in states to defend voting rights. Within months of taking office, Bush reversed Clinton-imposed regulatory standards for arsenic levels in water, pollutants in the air, and health and safety in the workplace. In addition, he issued a new order making it harder for federal officials to overrule state decisions, including in the area of voting rights. The *rhetorical* position of the Bush administration on the nation-state division of power in domestic policy might be best summarized by a close adviser's description of an ideal government as one "cut 'down to the size where we can drown it in the bathtub'."[26]

However, the Bush administration ended up sending mixed signals on state-centered federalism. Offsetting his advocacy of devolution in domestic policy making was an expansive view of presidential powers. His support for expanding the role of the states in making and implementing welfare policy was countered by his intervention in public education to impose mandatory national testing on local school systems. He resisted governors' demands that the distribution of electric power should be regulated at the state, not the national, level and he butted heads with governors many times in the area of business and environmental regulation. When a dozen states tried to adopt stronger regulatory standards for fuel efficiency and clean air than those set by the federal government, his administration fought them in court. (See "Talking Points.")

In exchange for being delegated greater responsibility for administering federal social welfare programs, states also demanded far greater control over who is eligible and what kind of services will be provided. Governors of some states demanded and received **superwaivers,** exemptions from federally set standards for eligibility and benefits provided to clients enrolled in federal health care and welfare programs. This gives governors and state bureaucrats maximum flexibility in deciding who is eligible for a federal health care or welfare program, what services will be provided, and the size of benefit to those enrolled. For years, standards for eligibility and types of services offered had been tightly controlled at the federal level. But in 2007 when governors in some states tried to broaden coverage of health programs to children in middle-

income groups, the Bush administration, an otherwise strong supporter of superwaivers, refused their petitions on the grounds that public programs would be providing services that private insurers could offer.

As should be clear by now, rule-making and administrative authority delegated by the center can be taken back, whether by the same administration that granted it or by its successors. This is where the divergence of views occurs among contemporary supporters of devolution. Advocates of state-centered and dual federalism believe that with devolution Washington has only surrendered powers that by right belong to the states, whereas the nonideological supporters of devolution see it as a practical measure to bring more efficiency to policy making and implementation. And even presidents who support states' rights sometimes yank back powers from the states when they articulate policies in conflict with the current administration.

Money and Conflict in the Federal Relationship

A great deal of money flows between Washington and the states and it is often a source of conflict. Unlike the president, most governors are required by law to have balanced budgets. Therefore, the financial burdens on states from unfunded federal mandates are especially controversial. **Unfunded mandates** are laws or regulations the federal government imposes on the states without sufficient funding to implement them. Implementation of federal environmental regulations alone, for which the states now bear the greatest burden, imposes heavy costs. Other federal laws order states and localities to make alterations to public buildings, sidewalks, and transportation facilities to ensure that they are accessible to people with disabilities. States are also required to educate the children of illegal immigrants and to pay for emergency health care for them, as well as to pay for increased law enforcement costs due to failure of federal authorities to control border crossings.

These costs have become so staggering in the states with the highest numbers of illegal residents that some governors have sued the federal government for reimbursement. (See the Government Responsiveness Box "Immigration: The States Step In" on page 68.)

In the 1990s, the financial burden of unfunded mandates led state and local officials to join together to mount a national campaign to restrict their use. Congress passed a bill reforming procedures under which unfunded or underfunded mandates, especially regulatory mandates, are sent to the states, but it stopped short of prohibiting them. The federal government is required to provide information on the costs of implementing laws and rules before Congress or an executive branch agency, such as the Environmental Protection Agency, can adopt them. And federal agencies are required to consult with states and localities before imposing mandates and to adopt regulations that impose the smallest burden for implementation.[27] The National Conference of State Legislatures maintains a Mandate Monitor page at its website to track the costs federal laws are imposing on the states. According to the NCSL, as of 2007, the federal government had imposed at least $100 billion more in obligations on the states than it had provided funds for.[28]

But unfunded mandates roll on under Democrats and Republicans alike: George W. Bush's "No Child Left Behind" program imposed a testing and reporting regime on states and local school districts, and new rules for state Homeland Security departments require spending on an array of new law enforcement and disaster preparation functions. States have also had to fund many of the secondary costs of having their state militia troops called up for national service. Since the first Gulf War, presidents have nationalized hundreds of thousands of state troops to serve abroad; Guard units from the fifty states have provided more than one-third of all troops who have served in the Iraq War. The federal government pays and equips them while they are under U.S. command, but the states have had to pay for social services and other assistance to the families of the wounded and dead. In addition, the states are left without the full complement of troops and equipment to deal with state emergencies such as forest fires and floods. A survey of the states' Homeland Security directors found that more than half of all states were less prepared for emergencies than before because of the demands being made on their National Guard troops by the federal government.[29]

Congress also mandated state involvement in the counterterrorism effort by passing the Real ID law in 2005. The law gave states two years to put in place standards for issuing drivers' licenses and other identity cards that will ensure that those in the country illegally cannot obtain legal means of identification. States claimed their (unreimbursed) start-up and ongoing administrative costs would be so great that they petitioned for time extensions, saying they may need up to ten years to implement it. Several states have made no attempt to implement the law, and Montana legislators said they never will.[30]

Governing in the States

Collectively, state and local governments account for over 87 percent of all civilian governmental employees, and their joint revenues were just over 10 percent of GDP in 2007, compared with almost 20 percent for the federal government.[31] State and local spending accounted for almost 36 percent of all governmental spending (closer to 45 percent when federal grants are added to states' internal sources).[32] State government is no small operation. Voters in the fifty states elect about 7400 representatives and senators to their state legislatures who, in turn, pass more than forty thousand laws each year that reflect the policy preferences of each state's citizens.[33] These laws, combined with those passed by local governments, affect many aspects of our daily life: the quality of public schools; tuition at public universities; maintenance of roads and bridges; terms for registering to vote or getting a driver's license; sales, property, municipal, and recycling tax rates and part of what you pay in income and excise taxes; conditions under which you can be married or divorced or gain child custody; police and fire protection; licensing of doctors and lawyers; choosing water and electricity suppliers; regulating cable; writing building codes and zoning laws; creating and maintaining parks and recreational facilities; and enforcing environmental and business regulations. In addition, state courts handle 95 percent of all litigation. It is also important to remember that governors are the chief executive officers of their states and they like to run their own shows. And, at any given time, a number of them are trying to burnish their records for a run for the presidency.

In this section, we look at the scope of state government today and discuss cooperation and competition both among states and between states and local units of government.

States as Power Centers

State activism has been on the increase since the partisan infighting and gridlock of the 1990s made it impossible for Congress to reach consensus on many major issues. The states experimented with charter schools and vouchers for private schools, rolled back affirmative action and bilingual programs, looked at new ways to try to teach religion in schools, and adopted a variety of crime laws, such as mandatory sentencing, three-strike laws, and victims' compensation. Fifteen states have adopted term limits for elected officials, and a few have passed tax caps and their own campaign-financing laws. Some placed restrictions on gay rights, whereas others passed laws strengthening those rights, granting health benefits to gay partners. A few states recognized the right to same-sex marriages. After gaining control over welfare during the Clinton years, the states experimented with many different job-training and work programs.[34]

Throughout the second Bush administration, while the president and Congress were preoccupied with the wars in

government responsiveness

Immigration: The States Step In

The Constitution unequivocally puts the regulation and enforcement of immigration and rules for naturalization in the hands of the federal government. Art. 1, Sec. 8. But it is governors and local officials, not the president or Congress, who have to deal with the day-to-day problems of unregulated immigration. This is especially true for border states, where governors and mayors deal daily with migrant deaths from heat exhaustion and dehydration, human smugglers (*coyotes*), drug trafficking, business owners complaining of labor shortages, and demands for more schools and access to health care providers.

States can legislate who is eligible for public health benefits, but federal law does not allow hospitals to turn away emergency cases. Federal law also mandates that children be educated, without respect to their immigration status. One federal court has ruled that a pregnant woman in the country cannot be deported because her fetus is already a citizen. These decisions are beyond the jurisdiction of governors, mayors, and state legislatures. But states and localities must obey federal rulings and find a way to pay for compliance, or for that portion of costs that federal grants do not cover. Therefore, when the federal government fails to enforce immigration law or to reform it in ways that respond to both national and local needs, the states are left holding the bag. This puts great pressure on governors and local officials to act in lieu of the federal government.

One of the border states hardest hit by the lack of border enforcement is Arizona. By August 2005, crossings along Arizona's 372-mile border with Mexico had reached an unmanageable half-million people per year. The foot crossings had local ranchers and some environmentalists up in arms because of property, livestock, and environmental damage, while the Arizona Homeland Security department was worried that terrorists could be among those crossing over. People entering the country with no papers, little money, and no transport caused a spike in certain crimes, especially car thefts. The Arizona Corrections system housed more than 4000 undocumented workers.[1] Border posses were forming, and some local law enforcement officers, not empowered to enforce federal laws, were looking for any kind of local statute, such as trespassing or loitering laws, to detain people who were in the state illegally. Arizona's Governor, Janet Napolitano, and Governor Bill Richardson in neighboring New Mexico declared states of emergency.[2]

Napolitano had come into office and remained an immigration-friendly governor who favored reforming federal laws, creating a guest worker program, and finding a way to resolve the status of those who had entered the country illegally or who had come in on visas and overstayed them. But her hand had been forced, she said, by federal inaction: "ranchers are at their wits' end…both federal governments [Mexico and the United States] let us down—there doesn't seem to be any sense of urgency." Gov. Richardson also called the state of emergency he declared in New Mexico "an act of desperation."[3] The vigilante action along the border and the millions protesting in the streets for legal status, Napolitano said, "was a cry from the country saying we want an immigration system that works and can be enforced."[4]

Governors across the nation shared this sense of urgency. State lawmakers introduced hundreds of immigration bills in the first half of 2006; Colorado empowered its attorney general to sue the federal government if it did not take action to enforce immigration laws.[5] And in faraway Pennsylvania, the town of Hazelton, in what would become an emblematic test case, passed ordinances that would allow the suspension of business licenses of any employer who hired workers without residency papers and another making it illegal for a landlord to rent to an undocumented resident. Hazelton's mayor had begun his term with a sanguine view of the immigrants settling in his town to work in nearby factories, but when the number of undocumented workers reached 10 percent of the town's population, budgetary pressures increased and locals began accusing new arrivals of an increase in violent crimes. So, like Napolitano in Arizona, the mayor acted. The ordinances' constitutionality was immediately challenged in federal courts on the grounds that they preempted federal immigration law and as such were violations of the Supremacy Clause.

In 2007, Napolitano found herself signing a similar law for Arizona, knowing it, too, would face a court challenge. But two years had passed since the state of emergency. She had asked Bush to send the National Guard to patrol the border, which he eventually did, but in numbers too small to matter. She had tried reminding Washington that border security was the responsibility of the federal government and that forcing state agencies to take it on was a de facto unfunded mandate because of the large costs states would incur in training new personnel to take on immigration-enforcement duties.[6] She had signed a bill giving local police more enforcement authority and she billed the U.S. Department of Justice for $217 million to cover the costs of incarcerating illegal immigrants who had committed crimes.[7] Nothing worked.

By 2007, 9 percent of Arizona's residents were in the country illegally and it had supplanted Nevada as the fastest-growing state in the country. Arrests were running at over 1400 per day; and that year almost 200 died trying to cross the desert, with hundreds more in need of rescue. Arizona needed funds to build at least one new school each year to keep pace with new enrollments. So once again Napolitano reluctantly signed a bill increasing local enforcement of federal law, this one, like Hazelton's, to revoke or suspend the business license of any employer who hired undocumented workers. In signing the law Napolitano was just doing what she had to do said one of the coauthors of the 1986 immigration reform law that provided amnesty to those in the country illegally. He said she is a political leader who "wants to make sure she's not left on the wrong side of this cresting wave."[8]

Unlike the ruling in Pennsylvania striking down Hazelton's city ordinances, the federal district court in Arizona upheld the state statute. Drawing on a 1976 Supreme Court ruling, the judge said the states are

Illegal immigrants trek across Arizona's desert.

not prohibited from passing laws to enforce immigration law if they are consistent with federal law. In addition he cited wording in the 1986 immigration law that provided an exemption allowing states to restrict licensing.[9] Hazelton's ordinance had tried to regulate housing, an area, unlike business licensing, not dealt with by federal immigration law; the Pennsylvania judge also ruled the ordinances violated due process for employers, landlords, and immigrants.

Over 1500 bills, dealing with everything from border enforcement and human trafficking, access to social services, and issuance of identity cards and driver's licenses, were introduced in states legislatures in 2007. Forty-six states passed 240 bills, triple the number in 2006.[10] Almost all of these will face court challenges. Knowing

the burden states and localities were carrying and that some of the new legislation may be preempting federal law, Washington again failed to act in 2007, paralyzed by the upcoming presidential election in which the major parties were defining their differences in part over immigration policy.

[1] Janet Napolitano, "Message of the Week," August 17, 2005, 1, azgovernor.gov/dms/.
[2] Randal C. Archibold, "Arizona County Uses New Law to Look for Illegal Immigrants," New York Times, May 10, 2006, A19.
[3] Ralph Blumenthal, "Citing Violence, 2 Border States Declare a Crisis," New York Times, August 17, 2005, A14.
[4] John M. Broder, "Governors of Border States Have Hope, and Questions," New York Times, May 17, 2006, 1.
[5] Katie Kelley, "A Deal in Colorado on Benefits for Illegal Immigrants," New York Times, July 12, 2006, 18. Data from the National Conference of State Legislators.
[6] Paul Davenport, "Napolitano Calls Summit on Immigration Law," June 8, 2005, www.azcentral.com.
[7] Napolitano, "Message of the Week," August 17, 2005, 1.
[8] Former Rep. Romano L. Mazzoli (D.-Ky.) quoted in Michael Sandler, "Immigration: From the Capitol to the Courts," Congressional Quarterly Weekly, December 10, 2007, 3648.
[9] Ibid., 3647.
[10] National Conference of State Legislatures data, released February 26, 2008, www.ncsl.org/programs/immig/2007/immigrationfinal.htm.

Iraq and Afghanistan, huge budget deficits, and then a recession, state activism continued to expand. Four states established centers for stem cell research after the Bush administration refused to fund such work on religious grounds. As federal regulations were rolled back or went unenforced, the states began reregulating, especially in the areas of consumer and worker safety. Some state legislatures outlawed predatory lending.[35] Thirty-four states enacted some form of equal-pay legislation, and seventeen states raised the minimum wage above the national level. States adopted "clean car" standards, setting more stringent air quality standards than those set by the EPA. The mayors of 132 cities in thirty-five states signed on to the Kyoto protocols on global warming rejected by the Bush administration. And unhappy with Washington's inaction on illegal immigration, local law enforcement officials around the country started using local ordinances (e.g., trespassing, loitering) to detain illegal immigrants in their towns.

With no legislative initiative from the federal level and health care costs skyrocketing, governors began experimenting with their own health insurance programs. Illinois established a program that covers all children, and Massachusetts became the first state to adopt a mandatory universal coverage plan. Other states followed because health care consumes an increasing part of state budgets. Such moves have supporters among some reformers in Congress who believe the political odds are against finding a uniform national solution to health care problems. They advocate the states-as-experimental-laboratories approach, postponing formulation of national legislation while allowing each state to first try what works for its particular demographic and economic conditions.[36]

Some scholars of federalism argue that the United States has become too large to govern from the center; they say that Madison's arguments about the advantages of size for protecting against the mischiefs of faction were made when the country had only four million people and no longer apply to a country of several hundred millions. Now they say we should pay more attention to Madison's concern about the capacity of well-financed elites at the center of a large nation to capture a "widely dispersed population."[37]

Governors seem to be worried less about the power of big interest groups to sway local electorates than about Washington tying their hands at the very time it is unwilling to solve the problems that are debilitating state and local government. Governor Arnold Schwarzenegger (R-Calif.) made the case for his state's unwillingness to wait on Washington to come to grips with climate change or rising heath care costs, saying California has the resources to solve its own problems: "We are the modern equivalent of the ancient city-states of Athens and Sparta. We have the economic strength…the population and the technological force of a nation-state."[38]

Interest groups sense a power shift away from Washington and many have begun directing their lobbying efforts at the states. Some of the largest groups have lobbying operations in all fifty states.

Both liberals and conservatives are focusing on the states. Liberals, believing they are unlikely to win on issues fought in federal courts that are now dominated by Republican appointees or to get legislation passed in a closely divided Congress, have redirected their efforts to the state level. Conservatives pursuing a Christian-values agenda, who find attempts to gain congressional passage of bills or constitutional amendments failing because of opposition from Democrats and moderate Republicans, have also turned to state legislatures and ballot initiatives. One lobbyist for Christian conservatives said, "It is on the state level where most family issues are decided."[39]

This continues the pattern of the past seventy years, with the fulcrum of change or reform shifting back and forth between Washington and the state capitals. When states could not or would not respond to calls for government action, Americans have turned to Washington. But when a consensus is reached that Washington is not responding to public or interest group demands, or not running programs effectively, people turn to the states. As one cynic has put it, for those times when "we have wrecked one level of government, the Founding Fathers had the foresight to provide a spare."[40]

States and Localities as Interest Groups

Lobbying is a crucial part of the relationship between the states and the federal government. The importance of federal money to state and local budgets, the imposition of unfunded mandates, conflict over federal administration of state lands, and the need for coordination between federal and state bureaucracies led to the creation of interstate organizations such as the National Conference of State Legislatures (NCSL), the National League of Cities, and the American Public Welfare Association. These groups lobby for favorable legislation for states and localities and work with federal agencies to ensure that new regulations are implemented in a way that is acceptable to the states. Most of these organizations have multimillion-dollar budgets and employ sizable staffs. Many individual states and cities have their own Washington lobbyists, some very successful. Between 2001 and 2006, one lobbyist representing forty-four state agencies and local governments in Florida persuaded Congress to earmark $173 million for projects sought by his clients. For every dollar Floridians paid the lobbyist, they got $18 in federal spending in return.[41]

But why should states form interest groups or hire lobbyists when they are all represented by their elected representatives in the House and Senate? The members of a state's congressional delegation may belong to different parties than state leaders, or they may not agree with state leaders—as, for example, when Congress waived state sales taxes on e-commerce strongly favored by most state leaders. Or a state may have an urban majority, whereas its congressional delegation is closer in views to rural and suburban residents. But mainly states hire lobbyists because there is a lot of money at stake.

The Assembly on Federal Issues, the group that coordinates the lobbying of the National Conference of State Legislatures, monitors bills under consideration by every major committee in Congress. The group looks especially for any new provisions that would undercut state laws, have an impact on state revenue, or tie the hands of state officials in some policy area. For example, some states are concerned about the free-trade agreements Congress has approved. Many states are big exporters, and laws exempting foreign nations from paying import taxes could affect the competitiveness of a state's businesses and revenues. So states lobby in large part to maintain maximum control over their legislative, regulatory, and taxing authority.

The National Governors Association (NGA) and regional governors' associations exist primarily to facilitate cooperation and exchange of information among state governments, but they also lobby Washington. In 2006, the NGA wrote President Bush stating its opposition to the Department of Defense's plans to redefine the role of the National Guard in national defense planning. All fifty governors signed the letter.[42] The Western Governors Association also has pressured the government to take action on illegal immigration and the price of gasoline.

Relations between the States

Dealing with Washington is not the only intergovernmental relations problem that the states face. State governments must also work with one another, and the measure of cooperation and conflict in these relations is similar to that between Washington and the states.

★ **Article 4, Sect. 1** The U.S. Constitution laid down some of the ground rules governing interstate relationships. One important provision is the **full faith and credit clause,** which requires states to recognize contracts made in other states. The Constitution also provides that if a fugitive from justice flees from one state to another, the suspect, once captured, will be extradited (sent back) to the state with jurisdiction.

ethical dilemmas | Should States Rely on Gambling for Revenue?

Most states are required by their constitutions to have a balanced budget, so when they face budget shortfalls, as 29 states will in 2009, governors are left with little choice but to cut spending, find new sources of revenue, or use up the reserves in their rainy day funds.[1] Cuts in social spending are hard to justify at a time when higher unemployment combined with rising health care and fuel costs leave lower-income citizens in greater need than ever of government-supported programs.

Over the past two decades many states have turned to gambling as a reliable source of new revenue, especially to lotteries as a way to help fund public schools. But lottery-ticket buyers are dis-proportionately low-income, which means that many states are trying to raise revenue from their poorest citizens, including states like Illinois, which already has a regressive income tax. During the 2008 economic crunch, four states even tried to increase ticket sales by offering free gas fill-ups instead of cash prizes.[2]

Casinos provide another source of state revenue; there are more than 500 state-licensed casinos. Like state lotteries, some casinos are essentially state-sanctioned monopolies, and because they make huge profits, the states' cut can be substantial. However an estimated one-third or more of those profits are earned from the 2.4 percent of patrons who are problem or compulsive gamblers and whose lives are often ruined by their addiction.[3] And, overall, gamblers do not beat the house; if they did, casinos would not be such high-profit enterprises.

Is it ethical for states to raise revenue from gambling by licensing lotteries and casinos knowing that much of the revenue will come from lower-income people or from those with gambling addictions? Is it ethical even if that money will help fund schools and social programs?

[1] Elizabeth C. McNichol and Iris Lav, "29 States Face Total Budget Shortfall of at Least $48 Billion in 2009," Center for Budget and Policy Priorities, June 9, 2008 (www.cbpp.org/1-15-08sfp.htm) .
[2] Carmen Gentile, "Lottery Adds to Prizes: Now Gas as Well as Cash," New York Times, July 8, 2008, A13.
[3] Christopher Caldwell, "Bad Bet," New York Times Magazine, April 13, 2008, 13–14.

Normally, meeting full faith and credit requirements is rather routine. However, politics vary from state to state, and occasionally for one state to honor the laws of another can be controversial. A historical example is the Fugitive Slave Act, which required the authorities in every state to return escaped slaves to their owners. Abolitionists (those favoring the abolition of slavery) living in free states were loath to return escaped slaves to their owners yet were bound to do so by the Constitution.

More recently, marriage contracts have become an issue. Some opponents to gay marriage have argued that under the full faith and credit rule, a gay marriage contracted in one state would have to be recognized by every state. When Vermont became the first state to register same-sex unions, it set off a controversy in other states worried about having to extend to gay partners the same legal status and rights (health, retirement, and inheritance benefits) as they do to married heterosexual couples. In response, Congress passed the Defense of Marriage Act, which gave every state the right not to recognize same-sex marriages conducted in other states. But after a few states began issuing marriage licenses to gay couples, officials in states that did not want to honor these contracts appealed to the Bush administration to support an amendment to the U.S. Constitution that would define marriage as a contract between a man and a woman. To resolve some of the interstate conflict, the Massachusetts Supreme Court, which does recognize same-sex marriages, ruled that out-of-state same-sex couples cannot be married in Massachusetts if their home states make such unions illegal.

Cooperation between states is encouraged by the fact that all governors have to deal with a set of common problems, such as resource management, education, fostering economic growth, taxation, crime, and prison systems. In addition, they all have to manage a relationship with Washington. These common interests prompted the formation of the NGA and its regional counterparts.

Most state-to-state interaction is informal and voluntary; state officials consult with and borrow ideas from one another. Sometimes states enter into formal agreements, called *interstate compacts,* to deal with a shared problem—operating a port or allocating water from a river basin, for example. A common type of agreement between states is to exempt citizens from neighboring states who have taken up temporary residence from paying local income taxes. As energy demand and costs rose in 2006, fourteen states formed a new pact to cooperate in regulating electric power. And tired of waiting for Washington to act on greenhouse gases, governors have entered into regional pacts to limit carbon emissions. The governors of Utah, California, and Montana even appeared in a nationally televised ad saying the governors were acting on climate change and now it was Congress's turn.[43]

Along with the cooperation there has always been rivalry among the states, due to cultural, political, and regional differences and because they compete for private investment and for aid from the federal government. Changing economic patterns and an overall loss of economic competitiveness by the United States in the world market have stimulated vigorous competition among the states to attract new businesses and jobs. Governors market their states to prospective new businesses by touting lower taxes, a better climate, a more skilled or better educated workforce, and less government regulation than other states competing for the same business. Most states are willing to give tax subsidies and other financial incentives to companies willing to relocate. Critics believe that these offers erode a state's tax base and have little impact on most business relocation decisions, and there is some evidence to support that view.[44] Nevertheless, without offering tax breaks or deferments or other subsidies, most states feel at a competitive disadvantage in recruiting new businesses.

Success in competing for new investment requires states to pay close attention to their human capital as well. At least forty million Americans are on the move every year. States, especially those with aging populations, are trying to increase their populations with programs like Michigan's Cool Cities Initiative, aimed at keeping their own youth in the state and attracting young professionals. The competition between states for the "creative class" of "technically savvy" under thirty-fives has been called a "hipness battle," as cities hype amenities (jazz and rock concerts, street cafes, "greenness," for example) to prove their "coolness."[45] Increasing the share of young professionals in its demographic makes a state more attractive to investors, and the new pool of young adults also means more children, schools, and growth in general.

Access to water is one of the most common areas of state cooperation and conflict. One certain prerequisite for business and population growth is an ample water supply. Maintaining or increasing water flow into and out of states is a high-priority issue, especially for states that do not have large bodies of water within their boundaries. How much water should New York State officials agree to take from upstate farmers for urban dwellers or for use in New Jersey and Connecticut? The waters of the Upper Colorado are shared by four states and those of the Lower Colorado by three others. Rural residents of Colorado constantly struggle to keep ever more water from being channeled from the Colorado River to meet the needs of fast-growing metropolitan areas in these other states. As drought crippled Atlanta in 2007, Georgia engaged Tennessee, Alabama, and Florida in disputes over boundaries and water rights. These are the everyday issues that governors and other state officials are continuously negotiating.

As the federal government continues to devolve responsibilities to the states, and as federal aid has grown as a percentage of state spending, competition among states to get ever larger shares of that aid has increased. Thirty-four states use "contingency fee" consultants whose job is to get as much money as possible from Washington to cover state Medicaid outlays. Because the consultants get a share of the money they bring in, they have every incentive to find any way within the law to claim additional payments to the states that employ them.[46]

States with high-ranking members in their congressional delegations usually fare better than others in the share of federal tax dollars returned to their home districts. And smaller states at times find common interest in voting as a bloc in the Senate to prevent the largest states from getting a share of aid in proportion to their population or need. An egregious case was the allocation of homeland security funding, which found the more populous and higher-risk states such as New York outvoted by smaller states in attempts to win funding proportionate to their larger populations and greater chance of attack.[47] It took several years of publicity about irrelevant equipment purchases by small rural states and municipalities to reallocate funding closer to security priorities.

State-Local Relations

The relationship of states to their localities—counties, cities, and special districts—is another important feature of contemporary federalism. All but 51 of 87,476 government units in the United States are local governments (see Table 1). These relationships are defined by state constitutions; they are not dealt with in the federal Constitution. Although states cannot be altered or dissolved by the national government, localities can be eliminated or altered by their states. Yet some of the same problems that affect national-state relations also affect state-local relations. City and county officials often wish for more authority and fewer mandates from the state capitol. Some state constitutions grant **home rule** to local governments, giving them considerable autonomy in such matters as setting tax rates, regulating land use, and choosing their form of local government. Cities of different sizes may have different degrees of autonomy, depending on the state. And in some states, counties are given the power to create levels of government below them. In Illinois, for example, each county can decide whether to establish township governments or do without them.

Thirty-six states must also maintain working relationships with the tribal governments of Native Americans. Although local units of government may be altered or abolished by the state, tribal land is sovereign territory under treaty agreements with the United States government. States have no authority to govern these areas and must negotiate any conflict over tax and environmental issues and land or other resource use with tribal councils.[48]

The People in the Federal Relationship

One of the most important elements in the federal relationship is the people. In a system with power divided among levels of government and responsibilities divided among thousands of governmental units, where do the people fit? How do they elect and communicate with all these officials and get them to be responsive? There is also the matter of individual liberty and the constant struggle to keep government at all levels from encroaching on the rights guaranteed by the Bill of Rights, including those general rights reserved by the Tenth Amendment.

It is often claimed that people feel closer to their state than to the national government. At the state level, the argument goes, government and its decision makers are nearby and more accessible to the voters, more likely to have a sense of their public mood, and consequently more responsive to their specific preferences. This is important because economic conditions and political culture vary from state to state, resulting in different policy preferences. Moreover, local officials may have a better grasp of local conditions and therefore be better situated to shape policy to fit these preferences. Are state governments more responsive to the people? State governments are undeniably smaller than the national government. Yet, 42 percent of all Americans live in states with more than ten million residents—hardly small units. At the other end of the spectrum, eight states have populations under a million. If the basic premise about size and distance were correct, then people would be even closer to local government than to state government. But smaller does not make for greater familiarity; the average person is not better informed about state and local government than national officials. Most local candidates and officeholders get far less media exposure than national candidates, partly

Table 1	Number of Government Units in the United States

Part of the reason that intergovernmental relations in the United States are so complex is that there are so many units of government. Though the number of school districts has decreased dramatically since World War II and the number of townships has declined slowly, the number of "special districts" created for a single purpose—such as parks, airports, or flood control management—continues to grow.

Year	States	Counties	Municipalities	Townships and Towns	School Districts	Special
1942	48	3,050	16,220	18,919	108,579	8,299
2007†	50	3,033	19,429	16,519	13,501	37,381

* Includes natural resource, fire protection, housing, and community development districts.
† The Census Bureau takes a count of governmental units every five years, in years ending in 2 and 7.
SOURCE: U.S. Census Bureau, http://www.census.gov/govs/cog/GovOrgTab03ss.html.

because there are so many of them. And voter turnout rates for local and state elections suggest that there is less interest in state and local than in national government.

There are also layers of local government, some with taxing authority, such as townships, special districts, or planning agencies, that Americans know little about. And although most Americans know about school districts and city councils, voter turnout is much lower in elections for those bodies than for state and federal offices, and public knowledge about most of these officials is also low.

There is no evidence that state and local officials are more ethical and more trusted by the people in their states. Lobbyists working in state capitals are at least as powerful as those working in Washington. Twenty-eight percent of state legislators who filed financial disclosure statements in 2004 sat on committees that regulated one of the entities in which they had a financial interest; 18 percent had ties to organizations that lobbied their state government. In most states these ties are far more hidden that those between federal legislators and lobbyists because the press does not cover most state legislatures as intensely as the national press covers Congress.[49]

One indication that Americans do not believe that state and local governments are especially responsive to them is how frequently they resort to the use of the **ballot initiative.** This is a means for placing policy questions on state ballots and having them decided directly by voters. In the 24 states that permit initiatives, interest groups use them to bypass not only Congress but state legislatures. Doing an end run around their state and local elected representatives, over the past fifteen years voters have approved initiatives that have killed state laws on affirmative action, sanctioned medical use of marijuana, imposed limits on campaign spending and contributions, expanded casino gambling, and given adopted children the right to know the names of their biological parents. About one-third of ballot initiatives in the 2006 elections became law, whereas only a tiny percentage of bills submitted to legislatures get passed into law.[50]

California remains the champion of legislating by ballot, putting so many measures before voters that one newspaper called it "government by referendum," and asked why California hadn't had a proposition against propositions.[51] Trying to legislate in this way can be both confusing and dangerous. One year, California's citizens had to wade through a 222-page pamphlet outlining ballot choices. In San Francisco, facing a ballot with more than one hundred items, voters passed one proposition for public financing of campaigns while simultaneously passing another measure outlawing it.[52] In 2006, voters in Arizona passed a strong anti-immigration initiative while elsewhere on the ballot they reelected officials who opposed the initiative.

Initiatives *can* achieve substantive change, however, and put power in the hands of the public. Thirty years ago, for example, Californians used a ballot initiative to create the California Coastal Commission, a twelve-member panel that monitors use of the state's 1100-mile coast by developers, local government, and private homeowners alike, with the power to kill construction and other projects. It has been called the single most powerful land-use authority in the United States.[53]

Whether binding or not, ballot initiatives continue to appear on everything from the Iraq War to prescription drug plans, tax cuts, gay marriage, and election reforms. In 2006, Maine voters were asked to exercise a "people's veto" by voting to overturn civil rights protections for homosexuals passed by the legislature. In Michigan the same year voters prohibited the use of affirmative action in public institutions, while in South Dakota a measure failed that would have punished judges whose decisions the public did not approve. But initiatives are not a simple or clear reflection of local views. Big interests influence voting on ballot measures, with huge sums of money flowing into states from outside organizations to support or defeat them. In 2008, when as many 138 initiatives may make it on to state ballots, interest groups for or against gay marriage, abortion, stem cell research, affirmative action, and physician-assisted suicide used state votes on these issues to force presidential candidates to take a stand.

DEMOCRACY?

What problems do the abilities of well-financed national campaigns to defeat or to pass state ballot initiatives present for Madison's explanation of federalism as the way to constrain the "mischiefs of faction" in a large country?

Still, some see the move toward greater state autonomy and more direct democracy as taking us nearer to the Founders' ideal of a government closer to the people. But the increasing use of grassroots initiatives is *not* a move toward the kind of government the Founders envisioned. The Founders established a system of checks on popular passions.[54] Indeed, the Founders feared policy making getting too close to the people and government being too responsive to popular demands. They saw the potential for overheating the political process through too much direct democracy, which is why they chose an indirect or republican form of democracy and a federal division of power. The challenge is how to keep a balance in these divisions sufficient to prevent a tyranny of factions while maintaining a sense of national unity and purpose.

Conclusion: Does Federalism Make Government More Responsive?

As federalism was designed and is practiced in the United States, the locus of power is never fixed. The sometimes clear, sometimes ambiguous, division of power has meant that the struggle between the center and the lower levels of government to change the balance is constant. The competition is built into our form of government as a check on the overconcentration of power at any one level. Whenever events or presidential leadership tip the balance of power in the federal relationship too far toward Washington, there is movement to reset the balance.

After years of a big-government president such as Teddy Roosevelt, a party may nominate a string of small-government candidates (Taft, Harding, Coolidge, and Hoover). Conversely, if Washington is too slow to act when a federal response is needed, the people may elect an activist president (FDR) to replace a more passive one (Hoover).

Our history suggests that most people are pragmatic, favoring policies that work by whichever level of government can make them work. In the 1990s when the public consensus was that Washington was not running welfare programs effectively, much of the responsibility was passed to the states; when state and local governments were judged to be failing at running public schools, Washington stepped in. And so it has gone for decades.

It is foolish to pretend to know how the Founders might deal with our complex federal system. However, it is reasonable to assume that, as astute politicians, they would have known that the government they had created would have to evolve along with population, territorial growth, and social and economic change. Still, they probably did not foresee a national government that would surpass the states in power and scope of action in domestic policy. Yet one of the paradoxes of our system is that as the national government has gained extraordinary power, so have the states and localities. All levels of government are stronger than in the eighteenth century. Federal power *and* state power have grown hand in hand. It is also paradoxical that although Americans have supported the continuous growth

and expansion of the country, they have continued to believe that there is something more true or sacred about small and local government. At the same time, many Americans think government at every level is not sufficiently responsive, as indicated by the frequent use of ballot initiatives to bypass both national and local legislators.

Today, across the United States, our belief in democracy, equality, and the rule of law binds us together. But to say that Alabama is more like New York than it used to be is certainly not to say they are alike. Our federal system helps us accommodate regional differences by allowing both state and federal governments a role in policy making.

Is such a complex system responsive? It is very responsive in that groups and individuals whose demands are rejected at one level of government can go to another level. The federal system creates multiple points of access, each with power to satisfy political demands by making policy that was rejected at another level.

In polls conducted in the months immediately following the 2001 terrorist attacks, Americans viewed government more favorably, but by 2006 most Americans said that government is almost always wasteful and inefficient. Trust in the federal government had fallen to about half of what it was in 2001.[55] It fell even further during the last year of George W. Bush's administration, but during all those years the public's positive view of state and local government barely changed.[56] In some ways, that should make the Founders happy: there must be enough confidence in government for it to function and the Union to hold, yet there must be enough suspicion of government to prevent the abuse of power.

Key Terms

federalism
confederal system
unitary system
nation-centered federalism
Supremacy Clause
state-centered federalism
dual federalism
Sixteenth Amendment
New Deal
cooperative federalism
devolution
grants-in-aid
states as laboratories
superwaiver
unfunded mandates
full faith and credit clause

home rule
ballot initiative

Key Names

James Madison
Alexander Hamilton
John Jay
John Marshall
Thomas Jefferson
Abraham Lincoln
Theodore Roosevelt
Franklin D. Roosevelt
Lyndon B. Johnson
Richard Nixon
Ronald Reagan
William J. Clinton
George W. Bush

Please visit our companion website at www.cengage.com/politicalscience/welch/uag12e or use CengageNOW for additional resources dealing with this chapter.

Supporters of Barack Obama cheer during a rally at Rhode Island College.

Public Opinion

4

Talking Points

The 2008 election mobilized hundreds of thousands of new voters who registered and voted. These new voters included many young people who had never been interested in politics before but were inspired by one of the candidates, especially by Barack Obama. Pollsters estimated that the number of young primary voters had tripled since 2004.[1] As a result, the proportion of the electorate in early primaries and caucuses made up of voters less than 30 years old increased by 5%.[2] In most primaries and caucuses, the youth vote went heavily for Obama.

This picture of an active and engaged young electorate contrasts sharply with the past behavior of young Americans. In general, young people have been the least informed and least involved segment of the electorate. A 2006 survey found that although 59 percent of teenagers could name the Three Stooges, only 41 percent could identify the three branches of the U.S. government. Seventy-four percent knew where Bart Simpson lives, but only twelve percent knew where Abraham Lincoln had lived. And only 2 percent knew that James Madison was

the principal author of the U. S. Constitution and fourth president of the nation.[3]

But, at least in 2008, this pattern changed. Although young people are still less likely than older adults to get their information from newspapers and television news, millions are consulting the Internet, listening to speeches on You Tube, and networking on Facebook and MySpace. By the midpoint of the primary campaign, Barack Obama had about one million "friends," Hillary Clinton 330,000, and John McCain 140,000.[4] Forty percent of young voters claimed to have watched political ads, interviews, debates, or speeches on line. When Barack Obama gave an important speech on race relations and his association with his pastor, 3.4 million people, many of them young voters, watched it on YouTube.

Although there is no evidence that young people have surpassed older ones in their political knowledge and sophistication—older adults also were galvanized by the 2008 election—the spurt in participation and information seeking by young adults can only be a positive for our political system.

Public opinion is often contradictory. The public is hostile toward political leaders for failing to respond to the public's needs yet, at the same time, complains that leaders simply follow the latest polls. Many are angry with the government. They do not trust it; they think it is too big and spends too much money. Yet they like the services it provides, and very few are willing to cut spending to eliminate services or programs that benefit them.

This chapter explores public opinion to better understand these contradictions. It describes how public opinion is formed and measured, assesses how informed and knowledgeable the public is with respect to public affairs, discusses the role of ideology in American politics, treats divisions within the population over some important issues, and concludes with an assessment of the extent to which government is responsive to public opinion.

Nature of Public Opinion

Public opinion can be defined as the collection of individual opinions about issues or objects of general interest—that is, those that concern a significant number of people. It can be either positive or negative, that is, for or against something. This is the direction of public opinion. On any

particular issue or with respect to a public official or candidate for public office, some people are positive, others negative.

Intensity reflects the strength of public opinion. The public may have weak feelings about something or feel strongly about it. Intense opinions often drive behavior. Many people now oppose the invasion of Iraq, for example, but only the most intense write a letter to their senator or representative or take to the streets to protest the war. Public opinion is not very intense on most issues. A small minority may feel intensely about an issue, but a majority rarely does.

DEMOCRACY?

In a democracy, should public officials be more responsive to a minority of citizens with very strong feelings about an issue or to the majority with less intense feelings?

Opinions also vary in stability. Some are constantly changing, whereas others never do. Stable opinions are often intense and grounded in a great deal of information—some of it accurate, some inaccurate. Feelings of attachment to political parties tend to be stable, while opinions about candidates and public officials, particularly high-profile ones like the president, fluctuate in response to

| Figure 1 || George W. Bush's Approval Ratings Peaked after 9/11, Then Declined

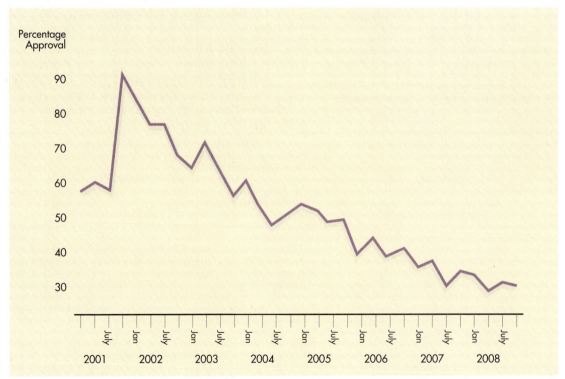

SOURCE: From the Gallup polls, reported in http://www.presidency.ucsb.edu/data/popularity.php

changing events and circumstances. President George W. Bush began his presidency with a 60 percent job approval rating. This rose to 90 percent shortly after 9/11 and then dropped steadily to 30 percent in 2007 and remained at that level through the last year of his presidency. (See Figure 1.)

Formation of Public Opinion

People learn and develop opinions about government and politics through the process of **political socialization.** As in other spheres, individuals learn about politics by being exposed to new information supplied or filtered through parents, peers, schools, the media, political leaders, and the community. These **agents of political socialization** introduce each new generation to the rights and responsibilities of citizenship (see Chapter 1) as well as shape opinions and positions toward officeholders and political issues. Individuals, particularly adults, also learn about politics and develop opinions through personal experiences.

Political learning begins at an early age and continues throughout life. In young children, learning is influenced by reasoning capacity and expectations.[5] The greater the child's intellect and the demands placed upon the child, the more and faster the child is likely to learn.

Preschoolers are unable to distinguish political from nonpolitical objects. Some are unable to separate political figures from cartoon characters, and some confuse religion with politics. A significant number of five- and six-year-olds report that the president takes his orders from God.[6] By first grade, these confusions are resolved and children begin to see government as separate and unique.[7]

However, the inability to understand abstract concepts or complex institutions means the conception of government is limited. Most identify government with the president.[8] Children at a very early age recognize him. In a 2002 study, 97 percent of a group of fourth graders were able to identify the president by name,[9] a proportion that has stayed constant for several decades.[10] Many, no doubt, see him on TV and understand that he is the leader of the nation. Experiences with parents and other adults give children a basis for understanding their relationship with authority figures like the president with whom they have no contact.[11] Feelings children have toward parents are generalized to the president. Studies in the 1950s found children describing the president as good and helpful;[12] many saw him as more powerful than he really is.[13] A more recent study notes children are considerably less likely to evaluate the president as good.[14] At the same time, they are likely to describe the president as benevolent. The difference may reflect the greater capacity of children today to draw a distinction between the institutional presidency and the individual who occupies the office.

Older children are introduced to political ideas and political institutions in school and through the media. Their concept of government includes Congress, the act of voting, and ideas such as freedom and democracy. The positive view of government reflected in feelings toward the president gives way to more complex and realistic images. The process can be accelerated by political events and the reaction of others to them. Children were much less positive toward the president and government in the 1970s than in the 1960s. The Watergate scandal in 1973 lowered both adults' and children's evaluations of the president.[15] The Clinton sexual scandals and the impeachment proceedings of 1998, however, had no impact on adult evaluations of the president and government, and presumably none on children. The approval ratings of the president reached record levels, and confidence in the executive branch remained unchanged from the year before.[16] Even when scandal lowers children's evaluations of government, the effect may not last. The negative feelings of children during Watergate diminished as they aged.[17]

In adolescence, political understanding expands still further. Children discuss politics with family and friends. By the middle teens, positions on issues develop.[18] Some fifteen- and sixteen-year-olds develop opinions that resemble those of adults. Although they begin to recognize faults in the system, they still believe the United States is the best country in the world. They rate the country low in limiting violence and fostering political morality but high in providing educational opportunities, a good standard of living, and science and technology.[19] For most, the positive feelings toward government learned earlier are reinforced.

In adulthood, opinions about specific personalities and policies develop, and political activity becomes more serious. Although most Americans revere the country and do not want to change the system, they tend to be cynical and distrustful of political leaders. Some of this negative feeling grows out of Americans' dislike of conflict and partisanship in politics.[20] Some of it, no doubt, flows from the perception that government is inefficient and can't deal with the nation's problems. Some is caused by media coverage, which not only highlights conflict but often exaggerates it. At the same time, the media are committed to and supportive of the American system.[21] Americans may get angry at their government, but, except for the Civil War, that has never boiled over to the point of mass violence directed toward political institutions or leaders.

Critical comments about government and political leaders sharply declined after 9/11, but the drop was short-lived. Most Americans felt gratitude toward the brave souls—many of whom lost their lives—who courageously rushed to aid those attacked. Yet, except for people who were called to serve in the armed forces or who were able to volunteer to help in the World Trade Center cleanup, Americans were not asked to translate these positive feelings into action. Though commentators on 9/11 and immediately afterward predicted that nothing would ever be the same, for most Americans life did return to normal quickly and with it, skepticism toward government.

american diversity | The Marriage Rights of Gays and Lesbians as a Moral Issue

Any issue may have a moral element, but some issues are primarily moral and these issues have the greatest potential to divide the public. Slavery almost destroyed the nation. In the first decades of the twentieth century, prohibition—banning the sale of alcoholic beverages—was a controversial, if less contentious, moral issue.

Abortion emerged as a moral issue in the 1970s and remains so today. Although Americans are highly supportive of abortion when the health and safety of the mother is on the line, they are quite divided when the issue is simply ending an unwanted pregnancy.

In the 1990s, the rights of gays and lesbians became a visible moral issue. As gays and lesbians increasingly came out of the closet and organized for social and political change, they became more visible. Seven of ten Americans say they know someone who is gay or lesbian. With more acquaintance and interaction has come more acceptance. Americans increasingly have been willing to extend rights to homosexuals. Thus a majority of the public endorses equal rights in the workplace and accepts the legality of homosexual relations between consenting adults.

Public support for allowing homosexual couples to form civil unions and enjoy rights similar to those of married couples has also increased. In 1996, about one-third favored such unions; today, from 50 to 60 percent do (depending upon how the question is phrased).

However, public support for same-sex marriages is much lower. Only 37 percent of the public favors same-sex marriages. To many Americans, the concept of civil unions reflects equal rights, while the concept of marriage entails religious beliefs and traditions. Therefore, more people view same-sex marriage as a moral issue.

Yet the trend toward greater tolerance of homosexuality is likely to continue because younger generations are more accepting of it than are older generations. Younger generations are less opposed to homosexual marriages. Although a majority of people over sixty-five oppose same-sex marriages, only one-fourth of people between eighteen and thirty-four do. Thus as older generations pass from the scene, public opinion, and then public policy, are likely to change.

Sources: Gallup Poll, May 15, 2003; "Same Sex Marriage and Civil Unions," Religious Tolerance.org; "Gays getting more acceptance as they're more open, polls says," *Lincoln-Journal Star*, (April 11, 2004). See also "Status of Gay Marriages and Civil Unions," report prepared from Gallup and other national polling data on Ontario Consultants on Religious Tolerance, www.religioustolerance.org/home_polls5.htm, and Scott S. Greenberger, "One Year Later, Nation Divided on Gay Marriage," *Boston Globe* (Mary 15, 2005): A1.

Agents of Political Socialization

It is the agents of political socialization—principally the family and schools—that are responsible for ensuring that each new generation of Americans resembles those generations that have come before.

Family

While recent research suggests that each of us is born with a predilection toward political traits and points of view,[22] children's identification with a political party is strongly shaped by the family, particularly because of its strong emotional ties and exclusive control during the early years.[23]

The family influences opinions in several ways. Parents share their opinions directly with children, who often adopt them. They say or do things that children imitate. Children overhear parents' comments about the political parties and adopt them as their own. Children also transfer feelings toward parents to political objects. When children harbor negative feelings toward their parents, they are more likely to be negative toward the president.[24]

The family also shapes the personality of the child. A child who is encouraged to speak up at home is likely to do so in public. Children also inherit their social and economic position from their parents, which influences not only how they view themselves but also how they view the world and how the world views them. A child from a wealthy family begins with advantages and opportunities that a child from a poor family can only dream about.

Children are more likely to reflect their parents' views when these views are clearly communicated and important. Parents often, if unintentionally, convey how they feel about political parties during election campaigns and children pick it up, although other opinions are less likely to be communicated to children. Seventy percent of high school seniors, for example, were able to correctly identify their parents' political party, but no more than 36 percent could identify their parents' opinion on other issues.[25]

However, even where parental influence is strong, it is not immutable. As young adults leave their parents' circle, agreement declines between their opinions and party allegiances and those of their parents. New agents and experiences come into play.[26] Even among younger children, parental influence may not be as strong as in the past. Parents no longer have exclusive control during a child's preschool years, and the number of households with both parents working or with a single parent who works means less contact with parents. Other entities can be expected to fill this void. Today, schools often play a larger role in children's lives than in the past. While parental influence may be declining, whether or not one is raised in the traditional two-parent family or one with a single parent has little or no impact on important political opinions and political behavior.[27]

School

A child of our acquaintance who came to the United States at the age of five could not speak English and did not know the name of his new country. After a few months of kindergarten, he knew that George Washington and Abraham Lincoln were good presidents, he was able to recount stories of the Pilgrims, he could draw the flag, and he felt strongly that the United States was the best country in the

This boy, at a white supremacist rally, likely was socialized in these views by his parents.

© Robin Nelson/Black Star

world. This child illustrates the importance of the school in political socialization and how values and symbols of government are explicitly taught in American schools, as they are in schools in every nation.[28]

Although we do not understand exactly which aspects of formal schooling influence political opinions, there is little doubt that education and years of formal schooling—the skills it provides and experiences it represents—make a difference. People who have more education are more interested in and knowledgeable about politics.[29] They are also more likely to participate in politics and to be politically tolerant.[30] Yet education does not seem to lead to a greater appreciation of the real workings of democracy, that is, a form of government where disagreements are typically resolved through bargaining and compromise.[31] Education does not prepare citizens for how democracy works in practice, or to recognize that disagreement is fundamental to democratic processes, or to build positive feelings toward these processes.

How do the schools influence the political opinions of children? Schools promote patriotic rituals. They often begin each day with the Pledge of Allegiance and include patriotic songs and programs in many activities. In the lower grades, children celebrate national holidays such as Presidents' Day and Thanksgiving and learn the history and symbols associated with them. Involvement in such activities fosters love and respect of country. In the upper grades, mock elections, conventions, and student government introduce students to the operation of government. School clubs operate with democratic procedures and reinforce the concepts of voting and majority rule. The state of Illinois let the state's elementary school children vote to select the official state animal, fish, and tree, conveying the message that voting is the way issues are decided.

Textbooks often foster commitment to government and the status quo. Those used in elementary grades emphasize compliance with authority and the need to be a "good" citizen. Even textbooks in advanced grades present idealized versions of the way government works and exaggerate the role of citizens in holding public officials accountable and in shaping public policy. Textbooks are less likely, however, to emphasize the need for citizens to uphold democratic values such as participating in politics and tolerating others' views. Nor do they help students understand that conflicts and differences of opinion are inevitable in a large and diverse society and that the role of politics is to address and resolve these disagreements.

The number of civics courses taken in high school improves students' knowledge of government and politics and fosters beliefs that government pays attention to people and that elections are important in holding government responsible. Courses during the senior year are particularly important. Seniors are ready to make the transition to adulthood and thus government and politics may be more meaningful to them.[32]

Reading habits and language skills are also important to democratic citizenship. Those who spend time reading are more likely to reflect attributes of democratic citizenship—including knowledge of public affairs, interest in politics, and tolerance—than those who do not.[33] Proficiency with language is important, too, as language is the mechanism for communicating and assessing information and evaluating new ideas and arguments.[34] Teachers as role models also contribute in significant ways. Perceptions that school administrators and teachers are fair are linked with expressions of trust toward other people.[35]

In sum, the major impact of schooling from kindergarten through high school seems to be that it creates "good" citizens—citizens who accept political authority and the institutions of government and who limit their political activities to the conventional and routine, such as voting in elections. In this way, elementary and secondary education serves government and the status quo in ways that the dominant interests in society prefer. Schools are not particularly effective, however, at fostering political participation and commitment to democratic values. Nor do they provide students with the skills to critically assess social, political, and economic structures that are at the root of the nation's problems or strategies for dealing with injustice and effecting political change.[36] In this regard, the failure of schools is often attributed to the "hidden curriculum."[37] Schools are not democratic institutions where students are encouraged to participate in a meaningful way. Indeed, most schools foster a climate averse to controversy. Such an environment is unlikely to produce active and engaged citizens.

DEMOCRACY?

Thomas Jefferson once wrote: "What signify a few lives lost in a century or two? The tree of liberty must from time to time be refreshed with the blood of patriots and tyrants. It is its natural manure." Is this view more or less supportive of democracy than the alternative of socializing each generation to the existing political authority and routine ways of political participation?

The college experience often broadens students' perspectives and leads to greater understanding of the world around them. They become more open and tolerant, less rigid and bound by tradition. Most students go to college to get a better job, make more money, prepare for a specific career, broaden their knowledge of the world, or learn about things that interest them. Some attend because their parents insist or because everyone else is going. Few go to college seeking to become more tolerant, but this is often the result. College students are more open and tolerant than the population as a whole, and the longer they are in college, the more open and tolerant they become—seniors more so than freshmen, and graduate students more so than undergraduates.[38]

Some recent commentators argue that college professors indoctrinate students and even suggest that state legislatures should investigate such "indoctrination."[39] Several states have introduced legislation to prevent faculty from sharing their views on controversial issues. None of these proposals, however, has passed. College and university faculty do have a predominantly liberal orientation. One study reports 72 percent identify themselves as liberal, 15 percent conservative. (Liberalism and conservatism are discussed on pages 92-94). Another reports 5 percent identifying themselves as far left, with 47 percent liberal. The same study finds 18 percent labeling themselves conservative, with less than 1 percent far right.[40]

But does this mean that college faculty are brainwashing their students? A 2006 study found 48 percent of those between the ages of 18 and 25 identifying with the Democratic party, while only 35 percent were Republican, the lowest number since 1987. Those under 26 voted Democratic in the 2006 midterm elections by 58 to 37 percent. However, in the early 1990s, when college faculty were just as liberal, Republican identification in this age group was 55 percent.[41]

Other evidence also suggests it is unlikely that professors indoctrinate their students. At the height of the Vietnam War (1968–1971), students were more likely to identify themselves as liberal than students before or after the war.[42] During the same period, the outlook of college faculty changed very little, and while faculty strongly opposed air strikes in Afghanistan following 9/11, 79 percent of college students supported the war.[43] While there is no doubt that college faculty are more liberal than the general public in their political orientations, it is unlikely that students reflect this. At large universities, where the largest percentage of students attend, the environment is sufficiently diverse to reinforce many points of view. Arts and sciences faculty may be liberal, but it is likely that engineering and business faculty are not. Moreover, it is college that provides students with the self-confidence and independence that enable them to resist indoctrination.[44]

College freshmen look much like the population as a whole, liberal on some issues but conservative on others. They are liberal in wanting the government to do more to control the sale of handguns, provide national health care to cover everyone's medical costs, and guarantee homosexuals the right to marry and in believing that racial discrimination remains a problem. They are conservative in attitudes about crime: majorities wish to retain the death penalty and believe that the courts show too much concern for the rights of criminals. Small majorities are pro-choice and support taxing the rich more (see Table1). Freshmen attending black colleges are more liberal than freshmen in general with respect to controlling handguns and national health care, but more conservative with respect to the legal rights of same-sex couples, laws prohibiting homosexual relations, and abortion. During the past several years, freshmen have become slightly more liberal in their opinions and in identifying themselves as liberal; however, a plurality identify themselves as moderate or middle of the road.[45]

The most distinctive characteristic of college freshmen in recent years has been their low interest in politics,[46] although this is changing. Since 2001, there has been a slight increase, but the 30 percent who report frequently talking about politics in 2007 is far less than the high of 60 percent in 1968, during the Vietnam era.[47]

Peers

In many instances, peers simply reinforce the opinions of the family or school. When there is a conflict between peer and parental socialization, peers sometimes win, but only on issues of special relevance to youth. Peers have the most influence when the peer group is attractive to the individual and when the individual spends time with the group. With growing numbers of single-parent families and working parents, parental influence may be diminishing and friends and associates may be taking on greater importance than adults.

Mass Media

The primary effect of the media on children is to increase their information about politics. The primary effect on adults is to influence what they think about—that is, the issues, events, and personalities they pay attention to.[48] The media also influence opinions about issues and individuals; in recent years, the media have reflected a high degree of cynicism and negativism toward political leaders. Research shows that changes in public opinion tend to follow sentiments expressed by television news commentators.[49] The impact of the media is explored in more detail in Chapter 5.

Adult Socialization

Not all political socialization occurs in the pre-adult years. Opinions develop and change throughout life as one experiences new and different things. Marriage, divorce, unemployment, a new job, or a move to a new location can affect political opinions.[50]

Economic, political, and social events have the potential to change the way Americans think about politics. Many hard hit by the Great Depression were drawn to politics to seek help. Most, voting for the first time, cast their ballot for the Democrats in 1932 and continued to vote Democratic throughout their lifetimes. World War II and the attack on Pearl Harbor shaped the opinions of a generation of Americans. The Vietnam War moved many college students to the streets in protest, whereas others moved to Canada to avoid the draft. In contrast, in the short term the terrorist attacks on the Pentagon and the World Trade Center pushed the public closer to government, although the impact soon dissipated (see the box "The Short-Term Impact of 9/11 on Public Opinion," p. 85).[51]

The unpopular war in Iraq may, however, shape young Americans in a more lasting way. Elections in 2006 and 2008 indicated a rise in Democratic party affiliation among this age group, perhaps brought about by the war and general unpopularity of the Bush administration when this generation came of age.

Table 1	Opinions of College Freshmen in 2007		
		All Colleges	**Black Colleges**
The federal government should do more to control the sale of handguns.		76%	84%
A national health care plan is needed to cover everyone's medical costs.		75%	84%
Same-sex couples should have the right to legal marital status.		64%	49%
Wealthy people should pay a larger share of taxes than they do now.		58%	59%
Abortion should be legal.		57%	52%
There is too much concern in the courts for the rights of criminals.		56%	44%
Affirmative action in college admissions should be abolished		48%	29%
Marijuana should be legalized.		38%	38%
Federal military spending should be increased.		31%	32%
The death penalty should be abolished.		35%	46%
It is important to have laws prohibiting homosexual relationships.		24%	35%
Racial discrimination is no longer a major problem in America.		20%	12%

The percentages are those agreeing strongly or somewhat with the statement.
SOURCE: John H. Pryor, Sylvia Hurtado, Jessica Sharkness, and William Korn, *American Freshman: National Norms For Fall 2007* (Los Angeles, Calif.: Higher Education Research Institute, 2007), pp. 37–38., February 3, 2006.

Televised images of the abuse of Iraqi prisoners by American jailers at the Abu Ghraib prison outside Baghdad influenced public opinion in the Middle East as well as in the United States.

Impact of Political Socialization

Each new generation of Americans is socialized to a large extent by the one preceding it, and so in many ways each new generation will look and act much like the one that came before. In this sense, political socialization represents a stabilizing and conserving influence. Typically, it leads to support for and compliance with government and the social order. Although many disagree with particular government policies, few question the basic structure of government.

Measuring Public Opinion

Pollsters measure public opinion by asking individuals to answer questions in a survey or poll. Of course, other techniques are used to measure opinion, and before scientific polls these techniques were all that were available. Elected officials consider the opinions of people who talk to them or write or e-mail them; journalists gauge public opinion by talking selectively to individuals; letters written to newspaper editors or newspaper editorials are a measure of public opinion. Protests and demonstrations also reflect public opinion. All of these techniques provide an incomplete picture, however. Letters or messages to public officials and newspapers are more likely to come from people with extreme opinions[52] or from those with writing skills—that is, people with more education. Editorial opinion is even less likely to provide an accurate picture of public opinion because most newspaper publishers tend to be conservative, and this point of view is often reflected in their editorials.

In most presidential elections in the twentieth century, newspapers favored the Republican candidate by about three to one.[53] The exception to this was in 2004 when more newspapers endorsed John Kerry over George W. Bush by a small margin.[54]

Polls are the best measure of public opinion, but they are not perfect. The mere fact of conducting a poll runs the risk of creating public sentiment rather than allowing public opinion to reveal itself. Rather than focus on what the public is concerned about, polls concentrate on what pollsters and their sponsors are most interested in. For this reason, many issues of public importance may never become the subjects of a poll. In spite of this and other problems, polling remains the only accurate way to assess what the nation as a whole thinks about political issues and public officials.

Early Polling Efforts

The first attempts to measure popular sentiments on a large scale were the **straw polls** (or unscientific polls) developed by newspapers in the nineteenth century.[55] In 1824, the *Harrisburg Pennsylvanian*, in perhaps the first poll to assess preferences for candidates, sent reporters to check on support for the four presidential contenders that year. The paper reported that Andrew Jackson was the popular choice over John Quincy Adams, Henry Clay, and William H. Crawford. Jackson did receive the most popular votes, but John Quincy Adams was elected president after the contest was decided by the House of Representatives. Toward the

THE SHORT-TERM IMPACT OF 9/11 ON PUBLIC OPINION

Although the Great Depression had a long-lasting impact on American public opinion, and the Japanese attack on Pearl Harbor changed Americans' views of their role in the world, the traumatic attacks of 9/11 influenced public opinion intensely but only briefly.

Before the terrorist attacks, some Americans took government for granted and considered it unimportant and irrelevant to their lives. The booming economy and surging stock market during the 1990s led to complacency. A steady stream of negative commentary about the government, emanating from the media and those politicians who found it useful to their careers or causes, led to cynicism toward the government.

But the devastation and the flames of 9/11 had an immediate impact on Americans' attitudes. From the ashes of the World Trade Center and the Pentagon sprang a feeling of patriotism, national unity, and a willingness to help others and see the nation through a difficult crisis. Suddenly government was a positive force. More than 80 percent, compared with just 50 percent the year before, had a favorable view of the national government, and trust in government nearly doubled following the attacks.[1] The public standing of the president and Congress similarly spiked, as government seemed necessary again. As someone remarked, "the only persons going up the stairs of the World Trade Center while everyone else was going down were government officials"—police officers, firefighters, and emergency personnel. "The events brought home the fact that the government does important work."[2]

But these attitudes were short-lived. Perhaps they would have been longer lasting if the nation had been called upon to sacrifice as it had been in World War II, when gas, oil, and some foodstuffs were rationed and Americans were urged to plant "victory gardens" to feed their families. Instead, the president and Republicans in Congress used 9/11 to push a partisan agenda—tax cuts for the rich, a war in Iraq, and a great increase in presidential power. The president didn't urge the nation to use less energy to check our growing dependence on foreign oil, which increases our vulnerability to instability and turmoil in the Middle East. Nor did he call on the nation to support higher taxes to pay for the wars in Afghanistan and Iraq. The president's advice to Americans was, "Live your lives, hug your children."[3] When the president was asked how Americans could help, he suggested, "Go shopping" (to stimulate the economy). Thus the president called for no sacrifices and asked for no help. Even though millions of Americans were prepared to offer a helping hand, he essentially told them to act as if nothing had happened. In doing so, he may have limited the impact of 9/11 on public opinion, as Americans turned back to their private lives.

[1] Alexander Stille, "Suddenly, Americans Trust Uncle Sam," *New York Times,* November 3, 2001, online article.
[2] "Public Opinion Six Months Later," PewResearch Center for the People and the Press, news release, March 7, 2002.
[3] Benjamin Wallace-Wells, "Mourning Has Broken," *Washington Monthly,* October 2003, 16–18.

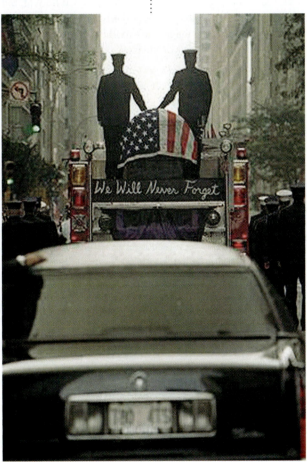

New York City firefighters march in a memorial parade for the victims of 9/11.

Bieman Linsley/Aurora/for *Time*

end of the nineteenth century, the *New York Herald* regularly tried to forecast election outcomes in local, state, and national races. During presidential election years, the paper collected estimates from reporters and political leaders across the country and predicted the Electoral College vote by state.

Straw polls are still employed today. Some newspapers have interviewers ask adults at shopping malls and other locations about their voting preferences. Several television networks run Internet polls about serious and trivial issues. CNN asks viewers of its early evening news show to register their opinions on different issues and reports the results before the broadcast ends. Major events often trigger media polls. After each presidential debate, national media invite people to cast a vote via the Web on who won. Preferences are electronically recorded and tabulated. Straw polls are unscientific because there is no way to ensure that the sample of individuals giving opinions is representative of the larger population. If these polls are unrepresentative, they are unlikely to reflect public opinion accurately.

The famed *Literary Digest* poll is a good example of an unrepresentative poll. The magazine conducted polls of presidential preferences between 1916 and 1936. As many as eighteen million ballots were mailed out to persons drawn from telephone directories and automobile registration lists. Although the purpose was less to measure public opinion than to boost subscriptions, the *Literary Digest* did predict the winners in 1924, 1928, and 1932. In 1936, however, the magazine predicted Alfred Landon would win, but Franklin D. Roosevelt won by a landslide. The erroneous prediction ended the magazine's polling, and in 1938 the *Literary Digest* went out of business.

Why did the *Literary Digest* miss in 1936? The sample was biased. Working-class and poor people, the people most likely to vote for Roosevelt, the Democrat, did not own telephones and automobiles in the depths of the Great Depression.[56] Since the sample was drawn from telephone directories and auto registration lists, Roosevelt voters were significantly underrepresented. Today we know that unrepresentative samples lead to erroneous conclusions, but in spite of that, data from such samples are still regarded as valid as data from samples that are representative. For example, a recent study reported a very high rate of drinking and unprotected sex engaged in by college women on spring break. Although the report claimed the data were from a random sample, it included only women who volunteered to answer questions and 25 percent of the group never took a spring break trip.[57] Such a "sample" is hardly representative of college women in the United States.

Emergence of Scientific Polling

Scientific polling began after World War I, inspired by the new field of marketing research. After the war, demand for consumer goods rose, and American businesses, no longer engaged in the production of war materials, turned to satisfying consumer demand. Businesses used marketing research to identify what consumers wanted and, perhaps more important, how products should be packaged so consumers would buy them. The American Tobacco Company, for example, changed from a green to a white package during World War II because it found that a white package was more attractive to women smokers.[58]

The application of mathematical principles of probability was also important to the development of scientific polling. To determine the frequency of defects in manufactured products, inspectors made estimates on the basis of a few randomly selected items, called a **sample**. It was a simple matter to extend the practice to individuals and draw conclusions regarding a large population based on findings from a smaller, randomly selected sample.

In the early 1930s, **George Gallup** and several others, using probability-based sampling techniques, began polling opinions on a wide scale. In 1936, Gallup predicted that the *Literary Digest* would be wrong and that Roosevelt would be reelected with 55.7 percent of the vote. Gallup's accurate prediction of the outcome lent credibility to probability-based polls, even though he underestimated Roosevelt's actual vote. In time, Gallup Polls would become a feature of American politics and probability-based polls the standard for those wanting to know what the public thinks.

Increasingly, government used polls. In 1940, Roosevelt became the first president to use polls on a regular basis, employing a social scientist to measure trends in public opinion about the war in Europe.

Use of Polls

Many major American universities have a unit that performs survey research, and there are hundreds of commercial marketing research firms, private pollsters, and newspaper polls. For politicians, polls have almost become what the Oracle of Delphi was to the ancient Greeks and Merlin was to King Arthur—a source of divine wisdom. During a budget debate between President Clinton and congressional Republicans, Republicans used polls that told them promising to "put the government on a diet" would be popular in the upcoming 1996 election. Polls led Clinton to counter by accusing the Republicans of trying to cut Medicare. When the media wanted to make sense of the debate, they conducted more polls.[59]

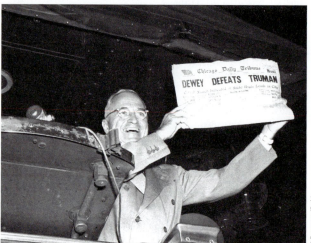

Harry Truman exults in incorrect headlines, based on faulty polls and early returns, the morning after he won the 1948 election.

Use by Politicians

Beginning in the 1960s, presidents increasingly turned to polls to assess the public's thinking on issues.[60] President Clinton took the use of polls to a new high. He spent more on polling than all previous administrations combined and tested every significant policy idea and the language with which to promote it.[61] Weekly polls shaped his centrist message, leading to his reelection in 1996. If polls showed a position to be popular, Clinton was likely to adopt it as his own. He embraced welfare reform, a Republican idea opposed by Democrats in Congress and liberals in his administration, partly because it was popular.[62] A White House poll in 1997 suggested that Americans preferred using the budget surplus to bolster Social Security rather than administer a Republican-preferred tax cut. In his State of the Union address, he called on Congress to "save Social Security first." Clinton even used polls to select a vacation spot.[63] Rather than vacation on Martha's Vineyard and play golf, Clinton went hiking in the Rockies instead, having been told by a consultant that golf was a Republican sport and that the voters he needed to win were campers.

Of course, Clinton did not always adopt positions because they were popular. He bucked public opinion and many leaders of his own party in his support for NAFTA (the North American Free Trade Agreement) and was again out of step with public opinion in his support for a multibillion-dollar bailout when the Mexican peso collapsed. He also defied public opinion in sending troops to Bosnia. To his surprise, his standing in the polls rose.[64]

George W. Bush expressed disdain for the polling done by the Clinton White House. Yet, his administration also made extensive use of polls, but in a different way.[65] Along with its polling, the Bush administration mastered the use of **crafted talk**, which enabled him to cater to the views of the right-wing Republican base—while appearing to remain in the middle.[66] Thus, whereas Clinton relied on polls to identify policies with broad public support, Bush relied on them to package—some might say camouflage—policies favored by his conservative base so these policies would appear more attractive to mainstream voters.[67] For example, Bush proposed partial privatization of Social Security. But his pollsters learned that the word *privatization* scared the public by implying that the government would no longer guarantee a lifetime income, as Social Security does. Instead, the president opted to use such terms as *retirement security, personal accounts, choice,* and *opportunity*—without changing the substance of his proposal.

The president also proposed the elimination of the inheritance tax, which is triggered when wealthy people die and leave their estates to their heirs. Traditionally this tax was called the "estate tax" because it was imposed on people with large estates. But the president and congressional Republicans called it the "death tax" to convey the notion that it was imposed on people when they die—that is, on everyone. In fact, it is imposed on just the wealthiest

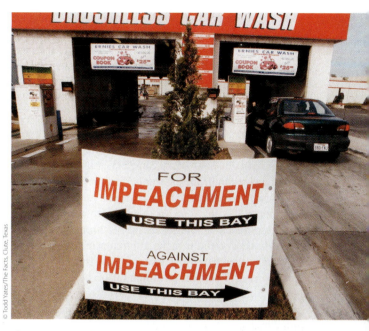

© Todd Yates/The Facts, Clute, Texas

This gimmick may have attracted customers, but it was not a scientific way to measure public opinion about President Clinton's impeachment.

1–2 percent. Yet the phrase *death tax* was a rhetorical success, persuading a majority of middle-class Americans to favor its elimination even though it would never affect them. Poll findings encouraged the administration to describe President Bush's energy plan as "balanced" and "comprehensive" and as one that relies on "modern" methods to prevent environmental damage. The findings also prompted officials to call his proposal to give parents vouchers that would enable them to send their children to private schools "school choice" or "opportunity scholarships" rather than "school vouchers" or "aid to private schools."

DEMOCRACY?

What are the implications for democracy if politicians rely heavily on public opinion polls to govern the nation?

In addition to polls, focus groups also help politicians find language to which the public reacts well. **Focus groups** are small groups of men and women brought together to share their reactions to candidates or policies. A focus group is not a scientific poll, and the participants might not be a cross-section of the population, but the process allows political consultants to explore participants' feelings in depth. The consultants search for the language, whether positive toward their side or negative toward the other side, that produces the desired effect on the participants. This language then can be used to discuss issues and can be incorporated in speeches or commercials. The same process is employed by market researchers to develop strategies to sell commercial products.

Many private pollsters work for one party or candidate. Although they undoubtedly wish to collect accurate data for their clients, their goal is to present their client in the most favorable light.[68] They may sometimes manipulate the wording of questions to benefit their client. The results, when publicized, give the impression that the public thinks something that, in fact, it does not.

Push polls are an egregious example of misuse of polling. A pollster for Jones asks whether the person called supports John Jones or Mary Smith or is undecided in an upcoming election. If the answer is Smith or undecided, the voter is asked a hypothetical question that leaves a negative impression. "If you were told that Smith drives a high-powered sports car at dangerous speeds through residential neighborhoods, would it make a difference in your vote?" The voter is then asked her preference again. The pollster hopes the level of support for Smith falls. The goal is to see whether certain "information" can "push" voters away from a candidate or a neutral opinion and toward the candidate favored by those doing the poll.[69]

Learning the weaknesses of the opposition has always been a part of politics, but push polls seek to manipulate opinion, and they often distort the facts, including candidates' records. In the 2008 Republican presidential contest in Iowa, a third-party group supporting Mike Huckabee used push polling techniques to attack Huckabee's opponents. If a voter said she supported McCain, for example, the pollster pointed out that he opposed a constitutional amendment to ban gay marriage; if the voter supported Rudy Giuliani, he was told that Giuliani was pro-abortion and in favor of civil unions for same-sex couples.[70]

An even more vicious tactic is to pump thousands of calls into a district or state under the guise of conducting a poll but with the intent of spreading false information about a candidate. Senator John McCain (R-Ariz.) accused the George W. Bush campaign of spreading false information in the guise of a poll in the 2000 South Carolina primary when both were seeking the Republican presidential nomination. Rumors were spread that McCain had become mentally unstable as a result of his imprisonment by the North Vietnamese in the Vietnam War and had fathered an illegitimate black child (in fact, he and his wife had adopted a child). This phony poll halted McCain's momentum, which had been surging until this primary. Both the push poll and the phony poll are violations of polling ethics and corruptions of the political process.

Use by Media

Along with polling by candidates, polls by news organizations have also increased. **Tracking polls**, in which a small number of people are polled on successive evenings throughout a campaign in order to assess changes in the level of voter support, began in 1988 and exploded in 2000.

BEHIND THE SCENES

DOUBTING THE HOLOCAUST?

A major problem for pollsters is designing questions that accurately measure opinions. Do you agree that it's not the case that a few words don't make a lot of difference in a poll question? You do, don't you? Questions with a double negative are difficult to understand. Results from such questions are unreliable. Poorly worded questions can confuse respondents and cause pollsters to draw the wrong conclusions.

The point was illustrated in a poll to discover the proportion of Americans who doubt that the Holocaust happened. The survey asked the following question: "As you know, the term Holocaust usually refers to the killing of millions of Jews in Nazi death camps during World War II. Does it seem possible or does it seem impossible to you that the Nazi extermination of the Jews never happened?" The results: 22 percent said it was possible that the Holocaust never happened; another 12 percent were not sure. The conclusion: About one-third of the country either doubted that the

Holocaust occurred or were uncertain.

Since no reputable historian denies that the Holocaust happened, this "finding" was shocking. Commentators reflected on how the public could be so ill-informed regarding a major event, not just of the twentieth century, but of recorded history.

But the wording of the question was the culprit. Another version asked, "Does it seem possible to you that the Nazi extermination of Jews never happened, or do you feel certain that it happened?"

This time only 1 percent said it was possible that the Holocaust never happened. Eight percent were unsure, and 90 percent were certain that it happened.

Why the difference? A study of thirteen polls, with estimates of Holocaust doubters ranging from 1 to 46 percent, found that high estimates resulted from confusing language.

SOURCE: Richard Morin, "From Confusing Questions, Confusing Answers," *Washington Post National Weekly Edition*, July 18, 1994, 37.

Virtually every TV news network features daily tracking polls in presidential campaigns.[71] The polls monitor the movement of candidates during the campaign, who is gaining and who is falling behind. This "horse race" element makes a good story and attracts viewers. Polling on the horse race and related coverage during presidential campaigns has started earlier and earlier, in some cases before the nominees are decided. They are also regular features during presidential primaries.

The ease of conducting polls explains, in part, their increasing use. Pollsters can conduct a poll at a moment's notice and have results within hours. This ease often leads to abuse. On clearly defined issues where the public has thought about something carefully and holds strong views, such as the vote in an election taking place in a few days, a well-designed poll can provide an accurate picture of the public's views. However, polls taken well in advance of the election are flawed simply because voters have not made up their minds. Early polls tend to measure how well the public knows various candidates rather than specific opinions about them. Poll results reflecting support for candidates seeking office for the first time, or in primary elections, often jump up and down simply because voters do not know much about the candidates.

Even when issues are well defined and opinions are fairly stable, it is increasingly difficult to obtain a sample that provides a representative picture of public opinion. Many respondents refuse to be interviewed[72] either because they don't want to be bothered or because they fear they'll be asked to buy something or contribute money to a cause. Response rates for telephone surveys have also decreased because of extensive cell phone use and call-screening technologies that allow potential respondents to avoid calls altogether.[73] (See Behind the Scenes Box "Cell Phones and Surveys" on page 90.)

Nonrespondents, those who refuse to be polled or cannot be reached, are an increasing proportion of those called and can be as high as 80 percent. Pollsters are concerned that those who do respond reflect the views of stay-at-homes who are too bored, too infirm, or too lonely to hang up rather than the views of Americans as a whole.[74] However, those who participate in these national polls differ little from those who do not, at least on issues that matter to pollsters.[75]

Other problems make it difficult for pollsters to get an accurate reading of public opinion. For example, there is the tendency of some respondents to express an opinion when they don't have one. No one wants to appear uninformed. Some respondents volunteer an answer even though they know little or nothing about a subject. The problem is getting worse as pollsters increasingly probe topics on which the public has no opinion and on which there is little reason to believe it should. For example, pollsters asked citizens whether the levies in New Orleans were strong enough to hold back the surge of a major hurricane and

whether the U.S. military has enough troops on the ground in Iraq to win the war.

Polls taken a few days before an election asking about vote choice, on the other hand, tend to be quite accurate. All eight of the election-eve polls in the 1996 presidential election predicted the winner, and the average error was very small.[76] In 2000, the Democratic and Republican candidates each received 48 percent of the vote, with Gore a half million votes ahead. The election proved too close to call, but all election-eve polls predicted the candidates' totals within each poll's margin of error. The polls taken the day before the 2004 election also were quite accurate, despite the closeness of the election. The average of fourteen major newspaper and network commercial polls had Kerry at 47.4 percent and Bush at 48.9 percent. The actual vote was 48 percent to 51 percent.[77]

In the 1980s, some white voters were reluctant to indicate that they intended to vote against the black candidate and falsely reported that they intended to vote for that candidate. It was first identified in the 1982 California gubernatorial election where Tom Bradley, an African American candidate, was defeated despite pre-election polls showing him leading the white candidate. For that reason, this discrepancy is often called the **Bradley effect**. Later in the decade, Doug Wilder, another African American, was elected governor of Virginia by a much smaller margin than polls had predicted.[78]

Most pollsters believe that the Bradley effect is no longer a factor in elections. In the 2008 primaries, for example, Obama's actual vote totals were close, sometimes larger and sometimes smaller, than the last pre-election polls. The one exception was in New Hampshire, where Obama had a significant lead then lost in a close race to Hillary Clinton. However, most pollsters think that differences was mostly a result of a late surge by Clinton rather than a Bradley effect.

Election-day **exit polls** are ubiquitous and controversial features of media coverage. Before election day, the networks identify key precincts around the nation. On election day, as voters leave these precincts, pollsters ask them how they voted. Their responses, coupled with early returns and an analysis of how these precincts voted in past elections, are used to project the winner in the current election. When enough precincts in a state have been analyzed, the networks "call" the state for the winner. Since the 1960s, television networks have used exit polls to project the winners before all of the votes have been counted. To reduce costs, the networks jointly contract with one polling service, so they all receive the same data, and usually they all project the same winner about the same time. Because of fierce competition among the networks, however, each tries to beat the others, even if only by minutes.

Usually the exit polls have been accurate, but not always. At 7:50 P.M. on election night in 2000, the networks declared Democratic candidate Al Gore the winner in

BEHIND THE SCENES
CELL PHONES AND SURVEYS

Most household surveys rely on phone contact with respondents. Respondents are chosen through a process of random dialing from a list of area codes chosen to represent geographic units in communities, counties, or states. But as more and more homes replace landlines with cell phones, surveying becomes more difficult. Accurate sampling is more difficult with cell phones because they are not geographically based and they are usually connected to an individual, not a household. Moreover, cell phone users often have to pay for the minutes they use, diminishing their enthusiasm for talking to a pollster.

These problems are increasing because cell phone–only households have increased from 3 percent to 16 percent since 2003, and the proportion is predicted to approach 25 percent by 2009. And, cell phone–only households are not a random sample of the population; they are younger and more likely to be male, poor, and in urban areas.[1] Thus the people in these groups are less likely to be included in surveys. Despite this problem, survey researchers so far have not found large differences in attitudes between cell phone respondents and landline respondents.

But the researchers anticipate significant differences between these respondents in the future, so they continue to work on ways to include cell phone users in their samples to make sure that, as cell phone–only use grows, this segment of the population will be adequately sampled.

[1] Megan Thee, "Cellphones Challenge Poll Sampling," *New York Times* (December 7, 2007), www.nytimes.com/2007/12/07/us/07polling.html?scp=3&sq=Megan+Thee&st=nyt Source: Ibid.

Florida. Because the election was very close and Florida had many electoral votes, it was already clear that whoever won this state probably would win the election. About 9:30 P.M., the polling service that conducted the exit polls notified the networks to pull back. Florida was "too close to call." At 2:15 A.M. the next morning, the networks declared Republican candidate George W. Bush the winner in Florida, and thus the next president of the United States, with 271 electoral votes, just 1 more than needed. They flashed their prepared graphics with a beaming Bush. But as more ballots were counted, Bush's lead in Florida eroded. About 3:30 A.M., the networks again pulled back. Florida again was "too close to call." Despite Dan Rather's assertion that if CBS called a state, "you can put it in the bank," the networks botched their calls two times in one night.

What happened? The election in Florida, as well as nationwide, was extremely close and the polling sample was too small to reveal the winner in such a close election. (The networks, which had been taken over by corporations such as General Electric, for whom accurately predicting the election outcome was not seen as important, slashed costs so much that the polling service couldn't sample enough precincts.[79]) Those polled were not representative of those who voted.[80]

In addition to the small sample, other problems compromised exit poll results. Some absentee ballots cast before the election were not counted. In one large county, because of a confusing ballot layout, many voters thought they were voting for Gore but really had voted for a third-party candidate. Voters leaving the polls did not realize this

and told pollsters they voted for Gore. Others simply refused to be interviewed. Conservative voters especially, those likely to vote for Bush, were less likely to grant an interview.[81]

The wrong calls were not merely an embarrassment to the networks. Because the networks initially called Florida for Gore ten minutes before polling places in the state's western panhandle closed, it is possible that a few Republicans on their way to vote might have turned around and gone home. Because the networks later called Florida for Bush, proclaiming him the "forty-third president," it is likely that many people around the country considered Bush the legitimate winner even when the networks eventually decided that the election was too close to call. Once the election was over and the two sides struggled to make their case regarding who was elected president, the fact that the networks declared Bush the winner made it appear that Gore was trying to take the presidency away from him.

Although the networks vowed to fix the polls, more problems popped up during the 2004 election. Exit polls showed John Kerry beating George Bush by a substantial margin. An aide took the president aside to tell him that he was going to lose. Of course, he did not. It is difficult to know just what happened. The pollsters may have oversampled Kerry voters or undersampled Bush voters by accident. An alternative explanation is that the actual votes may have been tampered with. Postelection investigations showed some fraud, though not enough to change any state's election results. However, the peculiar, and difficult-to-explain, finding is that the difference in the Democratic vote between the exit polls and the final tally was greatest in swing states, in areas with electronic voting machines, and in states with Republican governors.[82]

Even accurate and reliable polls can affect politics in a negative way. Poor standing in the polls may discourage otherwise viable candidates from entering a race, leaving the field to others who have less chance of winning or who lack the skills necessary to govern effectively. In 2000, several potential Republican candidates passed up the presidential race when early polls suggested that George W. Bush was the odds-on favorite to win the Republican nomination. And, in an unprecedented move, in 2002 Senator Robert Torricelli (D-N.J.) withdrew from his reelection race just thirty-six days before the election when polls showed that he could not win (he had been censured by the Senate for unethical conduct).

Additionally, polls can have a negative effect on political campaigns. Prior to polling, the purpose of campaigns was to reveal the candidates' views on the issues and their solutions to the pressing problems of the day. Instead, polls find out what the voters want, and the candidates then adopt positions and develop images to suit the voters. Too often, they follow the voters rather than lead them. They consider this strategy safer than trying to educate the public about complex problems or new solutions. Former senator Daniel Patrick Moynihan (D-N.Y.) decried politicians' addiction to poll results: "We've lost our sense of ideas that we stand by, principles that are important to us," he said.[83]

Poll results also influence fund-raising, and without money, a candidate cannot mount an effective campaign. Donors, especially large ones, give money to candidates who have a chance of winning. Candidates and would-be candidates with low poll numbers find it hard to raise the money that could give their candidacy visibility and raise their standing in the polls. Governor Tom Vilsack (D-Iowa) entered the race for the 2008 presidential election and withdrew just two months later. Never getting more than a couple of percentage points in the polls, he was unable to raise the necessary funds to be competitive.

It is possible that the sheer number of polls may lead everyone to take them less seriously. Still, it is unlikely that ambitious politicians bent on winning will abandon something that may help them win.

In spite of problems and abuses, polls still provide a valuable service to the nation. If direct democracy, like the New England town meeting, is the ideal, the use of public opinion polls is about as close as the modern state is likely to get to it. Polls help interpret the meaning of elections. When voters cast their ballots for one candidate over another, all anyone knows for sure is that a majority preferred one candidate. Polls can help reveal what elections mean in terms of policy preferences and thus help make the government more responsive to voters. Republicans claimed their victory in the 1994 congressional elections was an indication that voters supported the party's Contract with Amer-

"Is 'oblivious' the same as' undecided'?"

ica, a series of policies the party vowed to enact if it won a majority in the House. Polls showed that most Americans had never heard of it.

Knowledge and Information

Asking citizens their opinions on matters of public policy, candidates for public office, and the operation and institutions of government presumes they possess sufficient knowledge and information to form opinions and that expressions of opinion reflect real preferences. But many Americans are ignorant and misinformed regarding many aspects of government.

Nearly one-third of Americans do not know the name of the vice president, a proportion that has been constant for the past 20 years.[84] Only one-fourth can name their two senators,[85] and only one-third can name their U.S. representative.[86] Almost half can recognize the Speaker of the House, Nancy Pelosi, many more than could name her predecessor.[87] It is likely that the attention given to her status as the first woman speaker drew public attention. A mere 15 percent knew her counterpart, Harry Reid, Majority Leader in the Senate.[88] Generally speaking, more people can identify sports and entertainment personalities than major political figures.[89]

Most of the public doesn't have a factual knowledge about policy either. For example, two-thirds are unaware that the United States has a trade deficit and that more civilians than soldiers have died in Iraq.[90] Slightly more than one-half can correctly name the number of American military casualties in the Iraq war. Only a small percentage can identify a single piece of legislation passed by Congress.[91]

Misperception regarding government policies is widespread. Although polls showed Americans in favor of reducing the size of the federal government, most have no idea whether the size of government is growing or shrinking.[92] Most Americans feel that the country spends too much on foreign aid and think we should cut its amount, but one-half estimate foreign aid to be about fifteen times greater than it is. Asked what an appropriate spending level would be, the average answer is eight times more than the country spends.[93] In one poll, nearly half of the public had an opinion on a fictional and nonexistent law, the "Public Affairs Act." Fearing to admit that they had never heard of it, people gave an opinion anyway, just as they would for real policies they had never heard of.[94]

Although Americans revere the Constitution and see it as a blueprint for democracy, many do not know what is in it. One-third think it establishes English as the country's official language, and one-sixth think it establishes America as a Christian nation. One-fourth can't name a single First Amendment right (freedom to assemble and petition government, freedom to practice any religion, freedom of speech, and freedom for the press), and only 6 percent can name all four.[95] Perhaps more disturbing, while levels of education have increased significantly over the years, levels of knowledge regarding politics have not changed much since the 1940s.[96]

Despite these levels of ignorance, some argue that average citizens know what they need to know to make sound political judgments.[97] Most citizens take an active interest in politics and pay attention when they have a personal stake. Eighty percent know that Congress passed a law requiring employers to provide family leave following the birth of a child or in an emergency. When times are bad, voters do tune in to government more. With the war in Iraq and a shaky economy, six in ten Americans reported giving the 2004 presidential election a lot of thought as early as February, much earlier than in 2000.[98] And, as more and more Americans grew concerned over the direction of the nation, turnout in the 2008 primaries soared, with many states setting new records and voters reporting greater interest in the campaign than before.

The average American may not know details of government, but most have strong opinions they rely on, opinions about whether things are going well or not.[99] At the same time, lack of knowledge is an impediment to holding government accountable and responsible to the people. Those who are less politically knowledgeable find it difficult to sort through the claims and counterclaims of politicians. Some support candidates and policies that work against their self-interest. By their lack of information, they are asking to be manipulated, and they are.[100]

Politicians often contribute to citizen ignorance and misperception. They often avoid discussing issues, especially controversial ones, or worse, mislead by trumpeting suspect or false information. Even after no weapons of mass destruction were found in Iraq, eight out of ten Americans continued to believe Iraq had them.[101] Nearly one-half responded that Saddam Hussein was directly involved in carrying out the 9/11 attacks with no evidence supporting such a link.[102] The Bush administration had encouraged these views, orchestrating officials' comments to assert explicitly that Iraq had weapons of mass destruction and to suggest implicitly that Iraq was linked to al-Qaeda. Even when their charges were shown to be false, the administration was reluctant to correct the record.[103]

It is hard work to stay informed. It takes time and energy. With work and family, average men and women have little time for politics. But failure to stay informed means that politicians can often ignore what the public wants.

DEMOCRACY?

Can a political system be a democracy when most citizens lack basic knowledge about what their government does?

Ideology

Average Americans hold opinions on a variety of different issues. These opinions may be consistent with each other and reflect a broader framework or worldview, what scholars call an **ideology**, or they may be inconsistent and unrelated. One might, for example, express support for government assistance to farmers hit by hard times but oppose it for out-of-work steelworkers whose jobs have been outsourced to foreign countries.

Most Americans lack an ideological worldview; that is, they do not have a consistent and coherent set of opinions on political issues. Nor are they consistent in evaluations of candidates for public office or political parties. Yet the major contemporary ideologies, liberalism and conservatism, are useful in thinking about public opinion and understanding the institutions of American politics and political and social conflicts in society. Liberalism is sometimes identi-

"When I was young I was progressive liberal. Later on I became a fiscal conservative. Now I'm basically a crotchety tightwad."

fied by the label *left* or *left wing* and conservatism by the label *right* or *right wing*. These terms date from the French National Assembly of the early nineteenth century when liberal parties occupied the left side of the chamber and conservative parties occupied the right.

Modern liberalism, used in the American political context, embodies the notion that government can be a positive and constructive force in society, responsible for assisting individuals, businesses, and communities in dealing with social and economic problems. Franklin Roosevelt and the Democrats' New Deal policies of the 1930s were enacted to relieve the economic hardships of the Great Depression and limit the harsh consequences of an unrestrained free market economy through government regulation and control. Central to liberalism is the belief that government has a responsibility to make life better for average men and women. A more recent manifestation of liberalism has been support for civil rights to promote equality of opportunity for racial minorities and women.

While liberalism endorses government action to bring about social equality and ease the hardships of economic distress, it opposes government intrusion into personal matters such as abortion and contraception, the so-called **social issues**. Keeping government out of the bedroom is sometimes a rallying cry for liberals. Liberalism is also identified with opposition to government invasions of privacy, such as monitoring phone calls, reading material, and Internet activity.

Modern conservatism generally encompasses the notion that individuals and communities are better off without government assistance and that economic activity should be free from government interference. Central to conservatism is the belief that the free market should be allowed to function unencumbered by government rules and regulations, and individuals, rather than the government, are responsible for their own economic well-being. Short of harming others,

individuals should be allowed to do as they please, succeeding or failing without government stepping in to hold them back or push them forward. Consistent with this view, the apparatus and role of government is necessarily small, and where there is a need for government, it is best if it is at the state or local rather than the more distant federal level.

While conservatism subscribes to the idea of an unfettered free market economy, this principle has been abandoned in practice throughout the nation's history, as conservatives have unapologetically promoted commercial and business interests and favored occupational groups such as farmers with large subsidies and other government benefits. It has been observed that American liberals as well as conservatives are rhetorically conservative but "operationally" liberal. Americans talk about small government and low taxes, but they remain quite attached to the services that government provides.[104]

As liberalism has its contradictions, so does conservatism. Opposed to government interference in most everything else, many conservatives endorse the heavy hand of government when it comes to sexual behavior and its consequences. Many conservatives favor severe restrictions on abortion, some favor limiting the availability of contraceptive devices, and most oppose giving homosexuals the right to marry or even enter into civil unions. Some conservatives also favor government action to monitor personal phone calls, restrict political activity, and abolish some rights of defendants in time of war. Again, the Bush administration and the Republican congressional majority after 9/11 put in place policies to monitor certain personal communications, obtain information on individual's book purchases and library checkouts, and to restrict the rights of those accused of sympathy toward terrorist organizations.

However, not all conservatives agree with these policies. Many traditional "small-government" conservatives

---

Figure 2 ‖ **Liberals and Conservatives Differ on Spending for Safety Net and Environmental Issues**

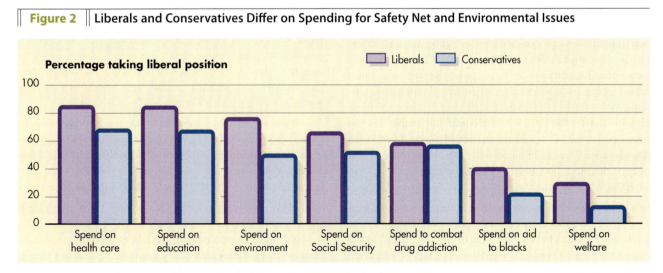

The proportions are those who want to increase spending on each area.
SOURCE: General Social Survey, 2002 (Ns = 602 to 1301).

are appalled at these invasions of privacy, whether political or sexual, and many oppose what they label George W. Bush's big-government conservatism. One commentator dubbed him the "nanny-in-chief" of the "nanny state."[105]

These broad descriptions capture the core ideas of liberalism and conservatism, but individual politicians, the Democratic and Republican parties, and most Americans reflect them imperfectly. Though liberalism and conservatism are not political parties, the Democratic Party has a much higher proportion of liberals than does the Republican party, and the reverse is true for conservatives. There is, of course, a broad consensus between liberals and conservatives that government has some role in making people's lives better, but that consensus often breaks down when specifics are addressed.

Most Americans tend to be conservative on some matters and liberal on others. A little more than a third identify themselves as conservative, and a little more than a fourth identify themselves as liberal. However, more—about 40 percent—identify themselves as **moderate**, or middle of the road, neither liberal nor conservative.[106] Because moderates are the swing group, not only in voting but also in building support for policies, public officials will typically move to the middle or even incorporate ideas from those of different ideologies in order to garner majority support for their ideas. President Bill Clinton endorsed a major overhaul of the nation's welfare program, limiting government assistance to families in need, typically considered a conservative position. President George W. Bush, while governing mostly from the right, confounded some conservatives by proposing an expansion of the Medicare program to include a drug benefit for seniors, usually considered a liberal position.

Public Opinion in Red States and Blue States

Liberalism and conservatism not only find expression in partisan differences but also reflect geographical differences. Ideological divisions have strong historical roots stemming from differences between northerners and southerners going back to the time of America's founding. The Civil War (1861–1865) was a stark manifestation of these divisions. After the Civil War and continuing to this day, the more conservative agrarians in the Midwest have often found themselves in alliance with the southern agrarians against the more liberal urbanites in the East.

In the parlance of today's media, the conflict is referred to as the **red states** versus the **blue states** (an updated version of the conflict between the "gray" and "blue" in the Civil War). Others have labeled the divide the "retro" states versus the "metro" ones. The red and blue labels stem from the maps employed on election night by the TV networks in 2000 and 2004 that colored those states that voted Republican for president in red and those that voted Democratic in

blue. Figure 3 illustrates how most people in each state voted in 2000 and 2004. Presented this way, it appears that the nation is divided, with majorities in New England, the upper Midwest, and the West Coast supporting the Democrats, and most voters in the South, the Border and Plains states, and the Rocky Mountain West supporting the Republicans. The red states comprise most of the landmass of the United States but are more rural and sparsely populated than the blue states, which include many of the metropolitan centers.

Red versus blue provides an interesting story line for journalists and pundits. It reduces the election outcome to a simple and intriguing explanation and one that is easily grasped by average Americans. Conservative red America has been described as religious, moralistic, patriotic, white, masculine, and less educated. Liberal blue America has been depicted as secular, relativistic, internationalist, multicultural, feminine, and college educated. Reds are seen as supporting guns, the death penalty, and the Iraq War; blues as supporting abortion and the environment. According to the stereotypes, in red America Saturday's pastime is NASCAR; Sunday's is church. In blue America, Saturday is for the farmer's market, and Sunday is for reading the *New York Times*.[107]

There are differences between red states and blue states. Religion is one difference. The red states encompass the **Bible belt**, a broad area of the country where most people identify with a religion and evangelical Protestants are common. This area comprises most of the South and parts of Kansas and Missouri. In contrast, the West Coast and parts of the Southwest are much more secular. Forty-four percent of those living in red states identify themselves as born-again Christians; only 26 percent in blue states do. Many fewer people in the blue states identify with any religious organization. These religious differences are significant, because in recent national elections, born-again Christians and regular church attendees have been more likely to vote Republican than those with weaker religious faith. After the 2004 election, a map circulated on the Internet, identifying the states that supported Kerry as one country—the "United States of Canada," as though they had seceded and joined Canada—and the states that supported Bush as another country—"Jesusland."

Other differences also reflect more conservative values in the red states. For example, in red states, women are less active in politics, less likely to hold political office, have lower incomes, and are less likely to be managers and professionals than in the blue states. Red states impose more restrictions on abortion and incorporate more abstinence education in sex education classes (see Table 2).

Red states are more hostile to labor unions, so they have adopted laws that enable many companies to avoid unionizing their workforce. Wal-Mart, which began in Arkansas and then spread through the South, does everything in its power to keep its workers from forming or joining unions.

| Figure 3 | Party Strength Displays Geographic Patterns |

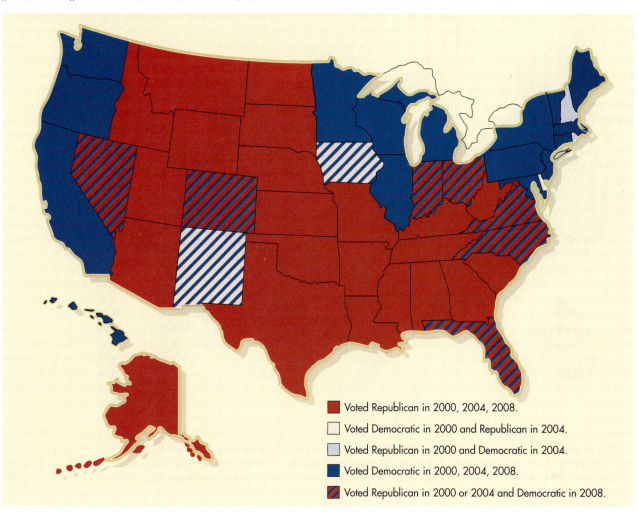

Voted Republican in 2000, 2004, 2008.

Voted Democratic in 2000 and Republican in 2004.

Voted Republican in 2000 and Democratic in 2004.

Voted Democratic in 2000, 2004, 2008.

Voted Republican in 2000 or 2004 and Democratic in 2008.

In contrast, blue states are more hospitable to labor unions. Cities such as New York, Chicago, and San Francisco are union bastions.[108]

For the 2004 election, the stereotypes were on full display. During the spring primaries, a conservative interest group ran a commercial opposing the candidacy of Howard Dean, Vermont's governor, who was running for the Democratic nomination for president. In the commercial, average people advised Dean to "take his tax-hiking, government-expanding, latte-drinking, sushi-eating, Volvo-driving, *New York Times*-reading, body-piercing, Hollywood-loving, left-wing freak show back to Vermont, where it belongs." During the fall campaign, John Kerry, the Democratic nominee from "Taxachusetts," was derided for his ability to speak French.

Based on such differences, in the aftermath of the 2004 election, one commentator declared that "the red states get redder, the blue states get bluer, and the political map of the United States takes on the coloration of the Civil War."[109] One adviser to President Bush commented, "You've got 80 percent to 90 percent of the country that look at each other

like they are on separate planets."[110] Conservatives sneer at blue staters for being chardonnay-sipping elitists out of touch with average people, while liberals deride red staters for being beer-guzzling, gun-toting rednecks. However, these stereotypes are exaggerated and lack historical context. (See Figure 4 and page 226 for a 2008 electoral map.)

In each category there is a mix of values and opinions, as then Senator Barack Obama (D-Ill.) so eloquently stated at the 2004 Democratic National Convention. "We worship an awesome God in the blue states, and we don't like federal agents poking around our libraries in the red states. We coach Little League in the blue states and have gay friends in the red states. There are patriots who opposed the war in Iraq and patriots who supported it. We are one people, all of us pledging allegiance to the Stars and Stripes, all of us defending the United States of America." Indeed, polling data confirm a mix of opinions and reveal surprisingly little difference between red and blue. Citizens in red states are only slightly more conservative than those in blue states. And as Figure 5 shows, majorities in red states are usually on the same side of various issues as majorities in blue states.

Figure 4 ║ **Most States are Purple**

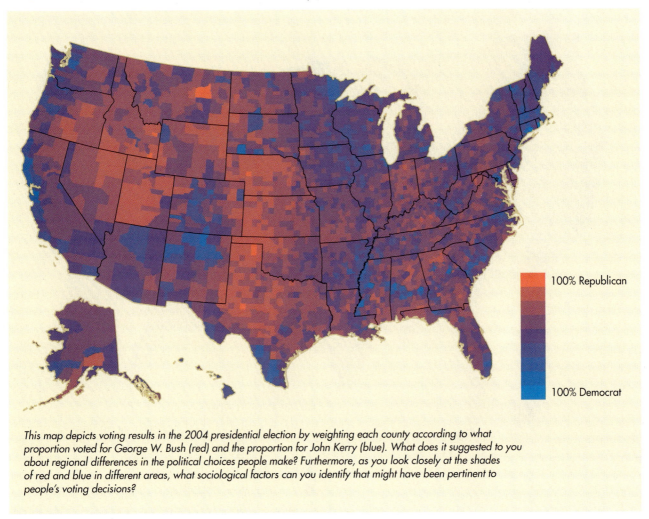

This map depicts voting results in the 2004 presidential election by weighting each county according to what proportion voted for George W. Bush (red) and the proportion for John Kerry (blue). What does it suggested to you about regional differences in the political choices people make? Furthermore, as you look closely at the shades of red and blue in different areas, what sociological factors can you identify that might have been pertinent to people's voting decisions?

Despite all the talk about red states and blue states, most states are purple—a combination. This map shades each county according to the way its residents voted in the 2004 presidential election. If they voted heavily Republican, the county is brighter red; if they voted heavily Democratic, the county is deeper blue.

SOURCE: Conceived by Robert Vanderbei, Princeton University, based on national election results and U.S. census data.

And although many in the media, based on exit polls, pointed to "moral values" as the reason for George W. Bush's victory in 2004, further analysis revealed that moral values were no more likely to be mentioned as a reason for voting Republican than in either of the two previous elections. When voters identified their main concerns in the election, they were much more likely to mention war and terrorism than moral values. Among those who did cite moral values, one-fourth to one-third voted for Kerry. The relative absence of clear-cut divisions appears even in personal contexts. When unmarried Americans were asked whether they would be "open to marrying someone who held significantly different political views" from their own, 57 percent said they would.[111]

Like other simple story lines about politics, the characterizations of the states contain some truth but are exaggerated. They apply to a minority of the populations in the red and blue states. They apply most clearly to political activists and political junkies—the people who are the most involved and most interested in politics. These partisans in both parties are sharply divided, and increasingly so.[112] The characterizations apply more and more to elected officials, who themselves are increasingly polarized.[113] Most are nominated in primaries, and primaries are dominated by the more extreme members of their parties. Only a minority of the public votes in primary elections, and these are the most partisan voters. (Until 2008, primary turnout was typically about 15 percent, though the 2008 turnout exceeded that). Republican candidates have to appease conservatives in their party, whereas Democratic candidates have to appease liberals in their party. Moreover, with little competition in most congressional districts, the more extreme and polarized views are not effectively challenged.

Bettmann/Corbis from John Sperling, The Great Divide.

Long before the media coined the terms "red states" and "blue states," differences in values and culture were evident between rural and urban America. One issue in the 1920s, as in the twenty-first century, was evolution. When Tennessee (and fourteen other states) banned the teaching of evolution or other theories challenging Divine creation, John Scopes, a biology teacher, tested the law. Clarence Darrow, a Chicago lawyer, defended Scopes, while William Jennings Bryan, the Nebraska senator and Democratic presidential candidate, testified for the state of Tennessee against the idea of evolution. In this photo, Darrow is appropriately on the left and Bryan on the right.

The media also contribute to the sense that the nation is divided. The media frame issues as debates and elections as contests between two sharply opposing sides. With the proliferation of cable TV channels, talk radio shows, and Internet blogs, the public can tune in those voices, and only those voices, with which they agree. This prompts the media to enlist the personalities who are extreme in their positions and hostile to the opposition. In contrast, in the early decades of television, there were only three national networks, which sought high ratings by not targeting their newscasts toward any one segment of the audience.

With political activists and public officials generally representing the more extreme views of their party, and the media usually emphasizing those views and characterizing opposing views as un-American, it is not surprising that our political debate has become more polarized despite the fact that the average American is not extreme in either direction.

DEMOCRACY?

What are the implications for democracy when citizens or elites are widely divided over the direction that public policy should take?

Public Opinion Toward Race

Public opinion has influenced, as well as responded to, the progress of the African American struggle for equality. Polls extending as far back as the 1940s show white Amer-

ica increasingly opposed to segregation and discrimination, at least in principle.[114] In fact, the change might be characterized as revolutionary. Whereas only one-third of whites accepted the idea of black and white children going to the same schools in 1942, in the 1980s more than 90 percent approved. Today nearly everyone approves. Over 80 percent respond that they have no objection to sending their children to schools where more than half of the students are black. Nearly two-thirds say they would not object to schools where most of the students are black. The percentage of people believing that whites have a right to keep African Americans out of their neighborhoods has been cut in half since 1963.[115] Thirty-eight percent of whites were against laws forbidding interracial marriage in 1963; 85 percent were opposed in 1996.[116] Before Barack Obama became a candidate, most Americans said that they would vote for a black candidate for president. His success in the Democratic primaries in many mostly white states indicated that many racial barriers have indeed fallen.

Public opinion can change because individuals change or because older individuals with one set of opinions are replaced by a new generation with a different set of opinions. Changes in whites' racial opinions through the 1960s occurred for both reasons. Older whites with more stereotyped views of blacks were replaced by a younger generation who were more tolerant. At the same time, the civil

Table 2	State Laws Affecting Reproductive and Homosexual Rights

An analysis of twenty-five categories of state laws affecting reproductive and homosexual rights, ranging from laws restricting contraception and abortion to laws recognizing same-sex partnerships, found sharp differences among the states. The states with the most restrictive laws were all red states, and the states with the most permissive laws were almost all blue states. (New Mexico was the exception, although it voted Democratic in 2000 and nearly did so again in 2004.)

Most Restrictive States	Most Permissive States
Ohio and South Dakota (tied for most restrictive)	New York and New Mexico (tied for most permissive)
Indiana	New Jersey
North Dakota	Washington
Oklahoma	California
Mississippi	Vermont
Kentucky	Massachusetts
Utah	New Hampshire
Nebraska	Connecticut
Missouri	Hawaii

SOURCE: Analysis conducted by the National Gay and Lesbian Task Force and two pro-choice groups—Ipas and the SisterSong Women of Color Reproductive Health Collective. David Crary, "In Gay, Reproductive Rights Rankings, S. Dakota, Ohio Last," Lincoln Journal Star, June 1, 2006, 4A.

rights movement prompted many Americans to reconsider their views on race. (See Figure 6.)

Since the 1970s, most changes have occurred because of the replacement of older, more prejudiced whites with younger, less prejudiced ones. Differences in socialization between those born in the 1920s and 1930s and those born in the 1950s and 1960s have led to much greater support for racial integration. More change can be expected in the future as today's teens age and replace older Americans. For example, a majority of white adults believe the reason that blacks lag behind whites in jobs, education, and income is because they fail to take advantage of opportunities available to all, whereas a large plurality of white teens believe discrimination by whites is responsible.[117]

Although white Americans accept integration, they have been much slower to accept government initiatives to achieve it. For example, racially segregated schools often are in poor central-city areas and offer inferior education, but busing to achieve racial balance in schools has never had much appeal for whites. Only about one-third would support it.

Why is there a discrepancy between the increasing majorities of whites who support integration and the majorities who believe that government should not make special efforts to help minorities? In some cases, unwillingness on the part of whites to endorse government initiatives to end segregation reflects racist sentiments.[118] Although only 10 percent of white Americans respond that differences in jobs, housing, and income between whites and blacks are the result of biological differences,[119] 43 percent cling to the racist belief that it is lack of motivation and will power on the part of blacks.[120] Thus anywhere from 10 to 40 percent of white Americans harbor racist beliefs in spite of

their willingness to accept blacks, live in integrated neighborhoods, and have their children attend integrated schools.

However, some whites oppose government help for blacks on principle. They object to being told what to do by government or feel government assistance for blacks is discrimination against whites. For some, government help violates their sense that individuals have a responsibility to provide for themselves.

Another reason that some white Americans are reluctant to accept government intervention is that many do not

---

Figure 5 | **Red- and Blue-State Voters Have Similar Opinions on Many Controversial Issues**

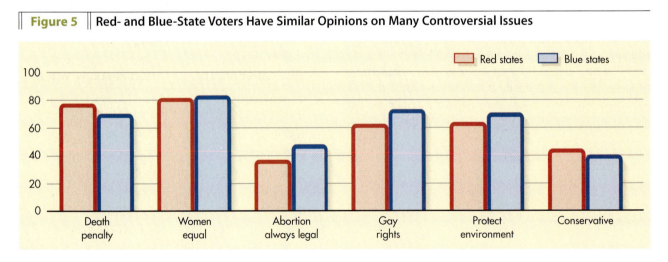

These are proportions of voters who (1) favor the death penalty; (2) believe in an equal women's role; (3) believe abortion should be legal under all conditions; (4) oppose discrimination against gays and lesbians; (5) believe we should do whatever it takes to protect the environment; and (6) see themselves as conservative.
SOURCE: 2002 Pew National Survey reported in Fiorina, 2005. The American Prospect, February 2005. © Tom Tomorrow.

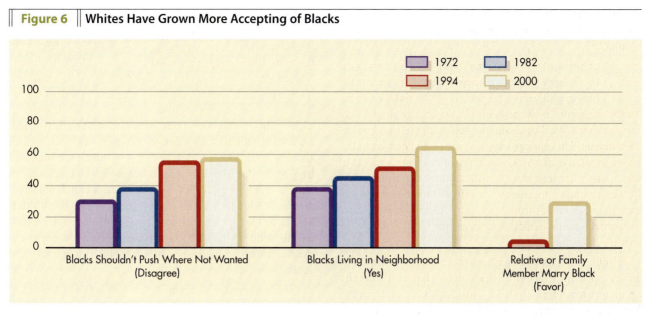

Figure 6 **Whites Have Grown More Accepting of Blacks**

Source: General Social Survey, Selected Years (Ns range from 1130 in 1990 to 2070 in 2000). Data from whites only.

see the need. African Americans and white Americans live in very different perceptual worlds. Anywhere from 40 to 60 percent of whites believe that the average African American is as well or better off than the average white American in schooling, job, income, and health care.[121] This is a direct contradiction to the reality that blacks lag behind whites on virtually every social and economic indicator. But misperceptions such as these lead many whites to reject any government effort to equalize the social and economic standing of the races. Whites who more accurately recognize the plight of black Americans are more likely to accept the government's role in providing equal education for black and white children and ensuring that blacks are treated equally by courts and police.[122]

Blacks, not unexpectedly, see things differently. A majority view themselves trailing whites in education, income, jobs, and health care, and of course this is the reality.[123] A majority of black men see the economic system stacked against them, but a significant proportion also believe that the problems facing black men result partly from what they have failed to do rather than what white people have done to blacks.[124] While 80 percent are optimistic about their personal future, only 30 percent report things are getting better for black men as a group.[125] Like whites, African Americans have become somewhat less supportive of government initiatives to improve their lots. In 1964, 92 percent thought the federal government should ensure blacks fair treatment in jobs; by 1996, only 64 percent did. Support for government assistance in school integration has also declined. Some blacks fear that government initiatives will only antagonize whites. Others fear that black children will suffer if they are in a climate where they are an unwanted minority. Still others believe government is ineffective in

bringing about an end to discrimination.

The candidacy of Barack Obama reflects both promise and problems in achieving equality in America. Obama's successes in winning Democratic primaries in many states, including those with few African Americans, suggest that Americans have come a long way. But the racism experienced by his campaign workers in many parts of the country, and the fact that in some areas a significant proportion of whites still say that race was a factor in their vote, indicate that we have a distance to travel.

Conclusion: Is Government Responsive to Public Opinion?

In a democracy, government should be responsive to the wishes of the people. Those wishes, collectively, comprise public opinion. But is government responsive?

The most direct way to assess whether public policy is responsive to public opinion is to compare changes in policy with changes in opinion. One study compared responses to policy questions in several hundred public opinion surveys conducted over a forty-five-year period. On more than 300 items, public opinion had changed. And when opinions changed, policies also changed more than two-thirds of the time. The policy changes matched the opinion changes especially when the opinion changes were large and stable (and when the opinion changes moved in a liberal direction). The researchers concluded that the policy changes may have caused the opinion changes about half of the time. However, the opinion changes probably caused the policy changes, or they both affected each other, the rest of the time. On important issues, when changes in public opinion were clear-cut, policy usually became consistent with opinion.[126]

Yet policy isn't as consistent with opinion now as it used to be. Twenty years ago congressional laws reflected public opinion polls about 60 percent of the time; more recently, the figure is 40 percent.[127] This change may reflect the growing polarization among public officials and political activists. This change may also reflect the gerrymandering of legislative districts, which provides most members of the House of Representatives with a safe seat—either safely Republican and conservative or safely Democratic and liberal. Representatives from those districts don't have to cater to centrist opinion in their district as much as they did in the past.[128]

Public officials also pay attention to the intensity of public opinion. Elected officials may support a minority opinion that is intensely held. President Bush continued to push tax cuts, whereas a majority of Americans preferred that their tax dollars be used to reduce the deficit or fund social programs.[129] The president was responding to his core constituency that strongly favors tax cuts. A minority with intense feelings was more likely to make financial contributions, provide campaign help, and ultimately vote for a candidate who does what they want or against a candidate who does the opposite than was a majority with weaker feelings.

There are other reasons why public policy may not reflect public opinion. Interest groups, political parties, and public officials' own preferences influence policy, and they may not agree with public opinion. Before the 2006 election, for example, Republicans held solid majorities in both the House and Senate. After newly elected and reelected members were seated in January 2007, the Democrats controlled both houses. Polls showed that large majorities of the public voted for the Democrats because they thought we should not be in Iraq. Though public opinion was heavily in favor in 2003 when we invaded Iraq, by 2006 majorities blamed the Republicans for getting us into the war and then mismanaging it. Newly elected Democrats pledged to reflect their constituents' attitudes and get us out of the war, which was rapidly becoming a quagmire. Yet, just a few weeks after the new Democratic congress was sworn in in January 2007, the president decided to send more troops to Iraq, to escalate the war—in the administration parlance, to have a "surge" of troops. Though Democrats protested, there was little they could do, short of cutting off all funding. This illustrates that though government can be responsive to public opinion, responsiveness is not always in the short term and sometimes happens only after months and years.

Some observers worry that political activists and interest groups manipulate public opinion through the increasingly intrusive media, which distort the issues and blind the public to its own self-interest. Even when public opinion accurately reflects the public's real attitudes, this opinion is not sacred. Public officials do not have to follow public opinion. The course of action favored by a majority may not be the best course. The Founders didn't want public opinion necessarily to become public policy. They established a federal system with separation of powers and checks and balances to ensure that the majority, in the heat of the moment, cannot work its will easily. In our system, therefore, we should not expect public policy always and instantaneously to match public opinion. However, the fact that governmental policy usually reflects majority opinion, especially when that opinion is large and stable, does indicate that the government generally is responsive.

Key Terms

public opinion

political socialization

agents of political socialization

straw polls

sample

crafted talk

focus groups

push polls

Bradley effect

tracking polls

exit polls

ideology

liberalism, liberals

social issues

conservatism, conservatives

moderates

red states

blue states

Bible belt

Key Names

George Gallup

Photographers follow a spacecraft atop a rocket on its way to Pluto.

News Media

5

Talking Points

Men and women pay attention to different media. Women are more likely to turn on television news, whether a national network (ABC, CBS, or NBC) or a local station. They are more likely to watch both the morning and nightly newscasts. Men are more likely to switch on a cable network (CNN, Fox, or MSNBC), and they are more likely to check the Internet for news or listen to radio talk shows for commentary and news.[1]

Among more serious sources of news, men are more likely to read newspapers and newsmagazines (*Newsweek* or *Time*), though women are equally likely to follow the detailed newscasts of National Public Radio (NPR), which is the only "hard-news" source whose audience is about half female.[2]

More significantly, men and women pay attention to different stories in the media. Men tend to favor sports stories and "hard news" examining government and politics. Women tend to prefer entertainment, lifestyle, health, safety, and religion stories. They like "soft news" that has a human interest angle.[3] They follow crime news more closely.[4]

Men pay more attention to international affairs, while women pay more attention to the weather. Forty percent of men, compared with 27 percent of women, followed articles about the tension between the United States and Iran. During the same time, 40 percent of women, compared with 25 percent of men, followed articles about devastating tornadoes within the United States.[5]

These media habits suggest that men are more interested in politics than women. Indeed, 42 percent of men, compared with 34 percent of women, told pollsters they are "very interested" in government and public affairs. Sixty percent of women, compared with 54 percent of men, said they are only "somewhat interested."[6]

Because men are more interested in politics, they are more likely to discuss politics than women are. According to one survey, 31 percent of men, compared with 20 percent of women, said they discussed national politics nearly every day; and 22 percent of men, compared with 16 percent of women, said they discussed local politics nearly every day.[7]

Social scientists are uncertain why this gender gap exists. Some believe it may be due to the small number of female governmental officials.[8] (Chapter 8 will address another gender gap—in elections.)

A *medium* transmits something. The mass media—which include newspapers, magazines, books, radio, television, movies, records, and the Internet—transmit communications to masses of people.

Although the media don't constitute a branch of government or even an organization established to influence government, such as a political party or an interest group, they have an impact on government. In addition to providing entertainment, the media provide information about government and politics. This chapter focuses on the news media—those media that deliver the news about government and politics.

The Media State

The media have developed and flourished to an extent the Founders could not have envisioned. As one political scientist noted, the media have become "pervasive . . . and atmospheric, an element of the air we breathe."[9] Without exaggeration, another observer concluded, "Ancient Sparta was a military state. John Calvin's Geneva was a religious state. Mid–nineteenth-century England was Europe's first industrial state, and the contemporary United States is the world's first media state."[10]

Americans spend more time being exposed to the media than anything else. In a year, according to one calculation, the average full-time worker puts in 1824 hours on the job, 2737 hours in bed, and 3256 hours exposed to the media (almost 9 hours a day).[11] Ninety-eight percent of American homes have a radio, and the same percentage have a television. For years, more homes had a television than had a toilet.[12] Almost 20 percent of children younger than two have a television in their bedroom; more than 40 percent of children between four and six do; and almost 70 percent of older children do. A third of children younger than six live in homes where the television is left on all or most of the time.[13] The average child (from eight years old on) or adult watches television 3 hours a day.[14] By the time the average child graduates from high school, he or she has spent more time in front of the tube than in class.[15] By the time the average American dies, he or she has spent one-and-a-half years just watching television commercials.[16]

With the evolution in digital technology, such as the Internet, companies are working "to weave media and electronic communication into nearly every waking moment of our lives."[17] Already, kids and young adults expose themselves to multiple media simultaneously. One study found that eight- to eighteen-year-olds on average pack in 8½ hours of media in 6½ hours of time. A third of them pay attention to more than one medium "most of the time," usually music or television while using the computer.[18]

And the young aren't just consumers of the news; they're also conduits, sending links to stories and videos to their friends and the members of their social networking websites such as Facebook and MySpace. They're using the technology of the media as people traditionally have used word-of-mouth.[19]

As Internet use has shot up, it has cut into family time more than anything else. Although the average Internet user spends 30 minutes less time watching television than before, he or she spends 70 minutes less time interacting with family members than before.[20]

The rest of this section will examine three continuing trends in journalism: the shifting dominance of various media, the increasing concentration of the media, and the increasing atomization of the media.

Dominance of the Media

American newspapers originated in colonial times, and political magazines appeared in the 1800s, but there were no "mass media" until the advent of broadcasting. Radio, which became popular in the 1920s, and television, which became popular in the 1950s, reached people who could not or would not read. Television especially became so central and influential in American life that one scholar speculated that the second half of the twentieth century will go down in history as "the age of television."[21]

As television became popular, newspapers waned. People didn't need their headlines anymore, and many people didn't want their in-depth coverage either. Papers struggled for readers and advertisers. Since 1970, the percentage of regular readers has declined, and the percentage of young adult regular readers has declined the most.[22] Newspapers have become the least preferred source of news for young

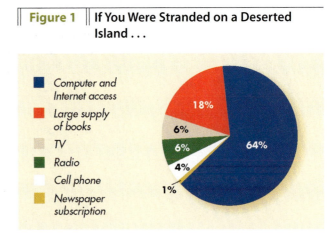

Figure 1 | **If You Were Stranded on a Deserted Island . . .**

- Computer and Internet access
- Large supply of books
- TV
- Radio
- Cell phone
- Newspaper subscription

64%
18%
6%
6%
4%
1%

and could take only one of the following with you, which would you take?
SOURCE: Asked of 1000 households with Internet access. IPSOS Insight U.S. Express Omnibus, August 2004, cited in "Primary Sources," Atlantic Monthly, *January–February, 2005, 54.*

people. Only 19 percent of Americans between eighteen and thirty-four say they read a daily newspaper. The average age of regular newspaper readers is fifty-five.[23] As a result, more than three hundred daily newspapers have folded.[24] A majority of the survivors have shrunk, cutting reporters and reducing pages, to save money.[25]

For several decades the evening newscasts of the major networks—ABC, CBS, and NBC—replaced newspapers as the dominant medium for coverage of politics. However, as cable television, talk radio, and the Internet became available, the audience for the networks' evening newscasts has declined. Since the mid-1990s, the percentage of regular viewers has dropped from 60 percent to 34 percent.[26]

These trends will likely continue. Newspapers will lose more readers while television, especially the traditional networks, will lose its dominance and the Internet will gain new users (see Figure 1).[27]

Today, different media appeal to different groups. Seniors read newspapers and watch the major networks' evening newscasts, whereas young adults are more likely to surf the Web (see Table 1). The cable networks attract the least educated, and news magazines, political magazines, and the Internet attract the most educated. Conservatives tend to watch Fox television and listen to talk radio, whereas liberals tend to watch the Public Broadcasting System (PBS) and listen to National Public Radio (NPR).[28] Conservatives and liberals both scan the Web but favor different sites (see Table 2).

Concentration of the Media

Journalism is a big business, and it has become a bigger business in recent decades. First, small media organizations owned by local families or local companies were taken over by chains (owning multiple newspapers, radio stations, or television stations) or conglomerates (owning multiple newspapers, radio stations, and television stations). Then large media organizations were taken over by chains or conglomerates. Finally, chains and conglomerates were bought out by larger chains and conglomerates.

| Table 1 | News Consumption by Age |

Percentages who say they regularly learn something about the presidential campaign from . . .

	18-29 years	30-49 years	50 and more years	Gap between youngest and oldest
Local TV news	25%	39%	50%	−25%
Sunday network political shows	4	12	21	−17
Nightly network newscasts	24	28	40	−16
Daily newspaper	25	26	38	−13
Public TV newscasts	6	12	14	−8
Morning network shows	18	21	25	−7
Religious radio	5	8	12	−7
Cable network newscasts	35	36	41	−6
National Public Radio (NPR)	13	19	19	−6
Cable network talk shows	12	11	18	−6
News magazines	8	9	13	−5
Talk radio	12	16	17	−5
TV magazine shows	21	19	25	−4
C-SPAN	6	9	9	−3
"Lou Dobbs Tonight"	7	5	8	−1
Late night talk shows	10	8	9	+1
TV comedy shows	12	7	6	+6
Internet	42	26	15	+27

Source: Princeton Survey Research Associates International for Pew Research Center for the People and the Press, *Social Networking and Online Videos Take Off: Internet's Broader Role in Campaign 2008*, www.pewinternet.org/pdfs/Pew_MediaSources_jan08.pdf. Based on a nationwide sample of 1430 adults (18 and older) interviewed on land lines and cell phones, December 19-30, 2007.

Table 2 | News Consumption by Democrats and Republicans

(Percentages who use these media daily)

	Democrats	Republicans
Local Newspapers	48%	44%
Local Television News	63	53
Nightly Network News	43	25
Morning Network News	35	24
Cable Network News	35	37
Public Television News	33	26
Public Radio News	23	14
Radio Talk Shows	17	25
Internet Websites	18	29

Results are based on interviews with 1,010 adults, December 11–14, 2006, by the Gallup Poll. Reported in Lydia Saad, "Local TV is No. 1 Source of News for Americans," Gallup News Service, January, 5, 2007, and with additional data provided to the authors.

Seven huge companies—Time Warner, Viacom, News Corporation, Sony, General Electric, Bertelsmann, and Disney—form the top tier of media conglomerates. Time Warner, the largest, has over eighty thousand employees and $30 billion in annual revenues. It boasts 50 percent of the online business, 20 percent of the cable television business, 18 percent of the movie business, and 16 percent of the record business in the country. It also has 160 magazines, five publishing houses, and "Looney Tunes" cartoons.[29] Twenty other companies, which are major players in one or two media, form a second tier of media conglomerates.[30]

The seven huge companies are linked to each other, owning parts of each other and engaging in ventures with each other. These arrangements reduce their competition, lower their risks, increase their profits, and at the same time erect high barriers for any upstarts that try to challenge their dominance.[31]

Their goal is to control the information and entertainment markets of the future. Each conglomerate wants to offer the entire range of media—television stations, radio stations, newspapers, magazines, books, movies, records, and computer services. Each conglomerate seeks to become the sole source of your news and entertainment.

Already, an early expectation for the Internet—that it would provide unlimited diversity and offer an alternative to established media—is being dashed as powerful conglomerates are racing to swallow their competitors and influence the government to adopt policies that will lock in their advantage.[32]

This trend toward concentration of the media is certain to continue. It will provide much more convenience, at somewhat more cost, for consumers.

DEMOCRACY?

Consider the implications of this trend not for consumers, but for citizens in a democracy who rely on the media to inform them about their government and officials.

This trend already makes some problems apparent. The news comes from fewer sources than it used to. Although there are tens of thousands of media entities in the United States, the numbers are misleading. Chains and conglomerates own the television stations with most of the viewers, the radio stations with most of the listeners, and the newspapers and magazines with most of the readers.[33] One media analyst, referring to these chains and conglomerates, observed, "Two dozen profit-driven companies, owned and managed by billionaires operating in barely competitive markets, account for nearly the entirety of the U.S. media culture."[34]

Just ten companies publish the newspapers that reach 51 percent of the readers.[35] Six companies broadcast to 42 percent of the radio audience, and five companies broadcast to 75 percent of the television audience.[36] Six companies have more than 80 percent of the cable television market. Four companies sell almost 90 percent of all music recordings, and six companies earn more than 90 percent of all film revenues.[37] One company controls over 70 percent of live music concerts in the country.[38]

Moreover, just one wire service—the Associated Press (AP)—supplies the international and national news for most newspapers. Only four television networks—ABC, CBS, NBC, and CNN—furnish the news for most television stations.

With fewer sources of news, there is a narrower range of views—less of a marketplace of ideas—than is healthy for a democracy. Instead, a small number of powerful people provide information and opinion—essentially, define reality—for the rest of the people.

These chains and conglomerates have begun to exercise their power through political activism and censorship. During the Iraq War, Clear Channel Communications, the largest radio chain with over twelve hundred stations nationwide, organized pro-war rallies in seven cities.[39] Cumulus Media, the second-largest radio chain, halted airplay of Dixie Chicks songs on its country stations after a member of the band criticized President Bush.[40] Comcast, the largest cable company, and CNN, owned by Time Warner, rejected peace groups' attempts to buy time for antiwar ads.[41] Sinclair Broadcast Group, the largest television chain with sixty-two stations, forbade its ABC affiliates from airing *Nightline* the night Ted Koppel read the names of military personnel killed in Iraq. The company said the show would "undermine" the war effort.[42] Two weeks before the presidential election, the company ordered its stations to broadcast a film in prime time accusing John Kerry of betraying American prisoners when he returned from Vietnam and testified against the war.[43] (The company modified this directive after intense criticism prompted some advertisers to pull their commercials, some viewers to threaten a boycott, some shareholders to vow a revolt, and its stock plummeted.) These instances, although relatively minor in themselves, are ominous signs for the future. It would be naive not to expect more attempts by media chains and conglomerates to flex their muscles.

In addition, the chains and conglomerates have exercised self-censorship when news coverage has threatened corporate interests. ABC killed a story that Disney, its owner, followed employment practices that allowed the hiring of convicted pedophiles at its parks.[44] NBC broadcast a report about defective bolts used in airplanes and bridges built by GE, its owner, and by other companies, but the references to GE were removed. When the president of NBC News complained about the removal and corporate interference in their newscasts, the boss of GE poked a finger in his chest and shouted, "You work for GE!"[45]

Another problem resulting from concentration of the media is financial pressure to reduce the quality of news coverage. News organizations are expected to match other divisions in their corporations and generate sizable profits each year. Corporate officers feel the heat from Wall Street analysts and major stockholders, who are more concerned with the value of the stock than the quality of the journalism. As a result, costs are cut—some reporters are let go, while others are shifted from time-consuming in-depth or investigative reporting to more superficial stories.[46] A reporter for a midsize newspaper in Illinois admitted, "If a story needs a real investment of time and money, we don't do it anymore." He lamented, "Who the hell cares about corruption in city government, anyway?"[47]

A decline in local news is a common casualty of the media's concentration. A veteran reporter for the *Baltimore Sun* noted that the number of staffers on his paper was shrunk from 500 to 300, and "in a city where half the adult black males are unemployed, where the unions have been busted, and crime and poverty have overwhelmed one neighborhood after the next, the daily newspaper no longer maintains a poverty beat or a labor beat. The city courthouse went uncovered for almost a year…. The last time a reporter was assigned to monitor [the] burgeoning prison system, I was a kid working the night desk."[48] The executives of the company that runs the paper live in Chicago.

When a train derailed in Minot, North Dakota, and released over 200,000 gallons of ammonia, authorities tried to notify residents to avoid the area and to stay indoors. But when police called the six local commercial radio stations, nobody answered. The stations were all owned and programmed by Clear Channel, based in San Antonio, Texas.[49] By the next day, three hundred people had been hospitalized, and pets and livestock had been killed.[50]

Atomization of the Media

Despite the increasing concentration of the media, a contrary trend—an atomization of the media—has also developed in recent decades. Whereas concentration has led to a national media, atomization has fragmented the influence of the national media. The major newspapers and broadcast networks have lost their dominance, and other media, some not even considered news organizations, have played a significant role in politics.

This trend is partly the result of technological changes, particularly the development of cable television and the Internet. Cable television, with a multiplicity of channels, can offer more specialization in programming. It can provide **narrowcasting** to appeal to small segments of the audience in contrast to major networks' **broadcasting** to appeal to the overall audience. For example, C-SPAN covers Congress on three channels and, unlike the networks, lingers on member speeches and committee hearings. Other national cable networks cater to blacks and Hispanics.[51] A cable system in Los Angeles and New York caters to Jews. A cable channel in California broadcasts in Chinese, one in Hawaii broadcasts in Japanese, and one in Connecticut and Massachusetts broadcasts in Portuguese. Stations in New York also provide programs in Greek, Hindi, Korean, and Russian. (And it's worth noting that at least Spanish-language newscasts in Los Angeles offer fuller coverage of state and local politics—with more sources from more perspectives and persistent demands for adequate explanations from public officials—than the mainstream newscasts in the city do.)[52]

Cable television can also offer 24-hour news, as CNN, Fox, and MSNBC do.

The Internet, which is a combination of a research library, a news source, and a debating forum as well as an entertainment medium, hosts numerous news sites. Major newspapers post their articles before the papers themselves are delivered. Online "magazines" also address politics. Self-styled "journalists" hawk their "news" as well. Matt Drudge

A newsstand in Brooklyn, New York, sells sixteen Russian-language newspapers to area immigrants.

offers political gossip on his own website, the Drudge Report, which originated in his one-bedroom apartment.[53]

The trend toward atomization of the media is also partly the result of the populist backlash against government officials and established journalists, perceived as "Washington insiders," that has characterized American politics since the 1980s. This populism is reflected in the popularity of radio talk shows. Many stations have such programs, and many people tune in.[54] Their numbers make talk radio a force in politics. The middle-class audience acts as a national jury in governmental controversies about which the average person has an opinion.

The populist backlash also is reflected in the increasing attention paid to fringe media by the public. In the 1992 presidential campaign, the *Star*, a supermarket tabloid, published allegations by Gennifer Flowers, a former nightclub singer, that she had had a twelve-year affair with Bill Clinton while he was governor of Arkansas. Flowers also appeared on *A Current Affair*, a syndicated television show, rated Clinton as a lover on a scale from 1 to 10, and sang "Stand by Your Man." Thus Flowers did not need to take her story to the major media; she got the tabloid media to tell it and pay her for it ($150,000 from the *Star* and $25,000 from *A Current Affair*).[55]

During the impeachment of President Clinton, Larry Flynt, the publisher of *Hustler* magazine, was offended by what he considered to be the hypocrisy of the president's adversaries. He offered to pay for information about any affairs that Republican leaders had. Ultimately, he published an article about an affair involving the Speaker of the House designate, Robert Livingston (R-La.). Although the article appeared only in his magazine, the revelation received publicity in other media and caused Livingston to resign.

Because the public pays attention to the fringe media more than it used to, politicians have begun to use these media. Instead of announcing their candidacy at a press conference, as politicians traditionally have, some have announced their candidacy on television talk shows. During the campaign, they have appeared on other television shows. Bill Clinton played the saxophone on the *Arsenio Hall Show,* and George W. Bush kissed the host on the *Oprah Winfrey Show.* John McCain played a minor role as a wedding guest in the movie *Wedding Crashers.* In the 2008 campaign, Hillary Clinton performed a skit on *Saturday Night Live,* and Barack and Michelle Obama cooked on *Rachel Ray.* Candidates swapped jokes with Jay Leno and David Letterman—and prayed they wouldn't look silly.

All this blurs the line between politics and entertainment. When Senator Bill Bradley (D-N.J.), campaigning for the Democratic nomination for president, appeared at a Houston radio station, he expected to discuss his new book. Instead, the disc jockeys had two women disrobe from the waist up to report his reaction.[56]

Politicians have to be good sports, because people who pay little attention to political news do pay attention to these shows. Almost a third of adults said they get political information from late-night comedy shows; over a third of those under thirty said they get more information from these shows than from any other source.[57] So it may not be a joke when Letterman proclaims, "The road to the White House goes through me!" (though Letterman himself may be out of date, as young viewers pay more attention to Jon Stewart and Stephen Colbert than to Leno and Letterman).

Because of the expanding role of fringe media, mainstream journalists envision a shrinking role for themselves. They no longer monopolize the market of political information; they no longer control the gates through which such information must pass.

This trend toward atomization of the media has significant implications beyond its impact on the established media and their professional journalists. Although this trend makes the news more accessible to more people, it also makes the news less factual and less analytical.

The proliferation of news outlets and the availability of newscasts around the clock create intense competition for news stories. The media have more time or space to fill than information to fill it. So they feel pressure to find new stories or identify new angles of old stories. In addition, they use talk shows that blend news, opinion, gossip, rumor, and speculation, because these shows are cheap to produce and, if the hosts and guests are provocative, entertaining for viewers. The media can fill their time and attract an audience. But the result is a commingling of facts and nonfacts. Then these facts and nonfacts are repeated by other organizations seeking to make sure that they are not left behind. In the rush to broadcast and publish, the media put less emphasis on assessing the accuracy of the content they disseminate than they used to. The "great new sin," a veteran reporter observed, is not being inaccurate but being boring.[58]

Interest groups exploit the competition among the media and aggravate the problem. In the 2004 presidential campaign, the "Swift Boat Veterans for Truth" ran a TV commercial charging that John Kerry had not deserved his medals from the Vietnam War. The "facts" alleged in the commercial apparently were false[59], and the commercial originally was run in only a few cities, but it had a whopping impact on the election. Its metamorphosis from a local ad to dominant news story illustrates how news often is disseminated today. The ad and the charges against John Kerry were first publicized by conservative bloggers who made no attempt to discern the truth of the charges by seeking official records or interviewing people who were actually there. Talk radio, dominated by conservatives, picked up the story. Radio commentators, whose staple is opinions about opinions, had no interest in discerning the truth of the charges either. Then Fox News, the generally Republican television network, publicized the ad, prompting MSNBC and CNN to do so too. Meanwhile, Bush contributors donated more money so the ad could be run nationally and frequently. Eventually, the mainstream media felt obligated to address it as well. Thus the dishonest commercial became the major story of the campaign for a month and a major factor in the outcome of the election.[60] (Even so, if Kerry had responded more effectively, he might have defused its impact.)

The fringe media also aggravate the problem. Their goal is entertainment and their audience is politically unsophisticated, so these media are less careful about the accuracy of the information they disseminate. Some pay for stories, pos-

Foreign-language media aren't new in America. Benjamin Franklin published a German-language newspaper to cater to the influx of German immigrants in his time.

sibly encouraging people to lie for the money; many sensationalize stories, possibly distorting the truth. Although the mainstream media are also commercial enterprises subject to the pressures of the marketplace, they have a tradition to uphold. Reporters at major newspapers and broadcast networks often speak of their responsibility to follow journalistic standards, whereas members of the fringe media sometimes reflect the views of radio talk show host Don Imus, who asserted, "The news isn't sacred to me. It's entertainment . . . designed to revel in the agony of others."[61]

The Internet aggravates the problem even more. Any person with a computer and a phone line can create an independent web log—a **blog**—to convey his or her information or views worldwide. Blogs are an alternative to mainstream journalism, allowing citizen journalists to compete with media giants. Unlike "the sober, neutral drudges of the establishment press, the bloggers are class clowns and crusaders, satirists and scolds."[62] Some attract thousands or even hundreds of thousands of visitors per day. The most popular political blog—Daily Kos—has 600,000 readers each day, which is more than all but a handful of newspapers.[63]

About two hundred American soldiers in Iraq kept blogs (until the military cracked down), describing *their* war. "Sergeant Lizzie" described the result of a roadside bomb under her Humvee:

I started to scream bloody murder, and one of the other females on the convoy came over, grabbed my hand and started to calm me down. She held onto me, allowing me to place my leg on her shoulder as it was hanging free. . . . I thought that my face had been blown off, so I made the remark that I wouldn't be pretty again LOL. Of course the medics all rushed with reassurance which was quite amusing

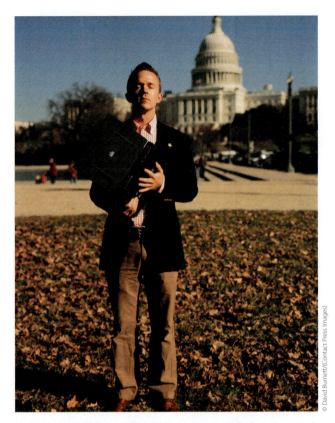

On his blog, Lane Hudson posted amorous e-mails from Rep. Mark Foley (R-Fla.) to a male congressional page. The mainstream media picked up the story, and five days later Foley resigned from Congress. "My heart stopped," Hudson said. "I thought, Oh my God, what have I gotten myself into?"

as I know what I look like now and I don't even want to think about what I looked like then.[61]

Similar to talk radio, blogs can act like "a lens, focusing attention on an issue until it catches fire."[65] Senate Majority Leader Trent Lott (R-Miss.), at a one-hundredth birthday party for Senator Strom Thurmond (R-S.C.) in 2002, made a remark seeming to praise Thurmond's past advocacy of racial segregation. Although the mainstream media ignored the remark, the blogs kept it alive until other media addressed it. Two weeks later, Lott resigned his leadership position.

Yet some blogs push pure hokum—for example, that the U.S. government, rather than al-Qaeda, destroyed the World Trade Center; that a cruise missile, rather than a hijacked jet, hit the Pentagon; and that United Flight 93 was shot down by an Air Force fighter, rather than forced down by its own passengers. And some bloggers are partisan operatives who have been trained to engage in "guerrilla Internet activism" while presenting themselves as average people.[66] Their fealty to the truth may be far less than their passion for the cause.

In 2004 a blogger "exposed" Barack Obama as a "Muslim who has concealed his religion." In fact, Obama has long been a Protestant. But the charge circulated through the blogosphere, and by the beginning of the 2008 primary campaign half as many people believed Obama is a Muslim as believed he is a Protestant (and two-thirds of all Americans admit to being prejudiced against Muslims).[67] Another blogger claimed, also falsely, that Obama was educated at an Islamist madrassah (an Islamic school that teaches fundamentalist religious doctrine) as a child in Indonesia. Political sophisticates may roll their eyes when they hear such accusations, but many folks believe that they are true or at least might be true. An elderly voter in a small town spoke for others when he said he didn't know which biography to believe—the one reported in the mainstream media or the one seen on the Internet and heard at his neighbor's house, at the grocery store, and at his son's auto shop.[68]

Professional journalists, who may have spent years understanding the subjects of their stories, disdain the amateurs who blog. The journalists complain that the bloggers normally offer only opinion, rarely news, especially not in-depth reporting.[69] A *New York Times* editor said they just "recycle and chew on the news."[70] The journalists also point out that the bloggers don't have editors or fact checkers—the layers of "review, revision, and correction" that mainstream media have.[71] The bloggers counter that their readers serve as fact checkers. Thus the blogs have a self-correcting mechanism. Moreover, the mainstream media's own record, as evidenced by its coverage of the run-up to the Iraq war, undermines its claims of accuracy and objectivity (as will be seen later in this chapter). Indeed, the blogs have corrected inaccuracies in the mainstream media's coverage. When CBS News displayed a letter relating to the National Guard service of President George W. Bush, bloggers with knowledge of old typewriters identified the letter as a fake.

DEMOCRACY?

What are the implications for a democracy when the media are dominated by professional journalists, with their fact checkers and editors? What are the implications when the media are more numerous, with fringe media and citizen journalists? Which situation do you think better enables citizens to distinguish the blarney from the gospel truth when candidates and officials speak?

In sum, two opposite trends—concentration of the media and atomization of the media—are occurring. The key question is how much control the media conglomerates will exercise and how much news and how many views will emerge through other outlets. Financial pressures are bearing down, and powerful corporations are competing to dominate the media business. At the same time, the Internet is wresting control from news organizations. Indeed, the Internet is transforming the relationship between news producers and news consumers. A participatory medium, the Internet allows consumers not only to forward news to friends but to produce "news" as well. An undergraduate at Temple University produced the "Obama Girl" music video

© David Burnett/(Contact Press Images)

that was downloaded and forwarded millions of times. Suggesting that Obama was young and exciting but also shallow, the video may have helped and hurt the candidate simultaneously. Regardless, it was created and circulated independent of Obama's campaign and of news organizations as well. It came from the bottom up rather than from the top down. In the future, then, the huge conglomerates may dominate more than they do now, while independent voices from the Internet will break through on matters that have a human interest angle.

Relationship between the Media and Politicians

"Politicians live—and sometimes die—by the press. The press lives by politicians," according to a former presidential aide. "This relationship is at the center of our national life."[72]

Although this relationship was not always so close—President Herbert Hoover once refused to tell a reporter whether he enjoyed a baseball game he attended[73]—politicians and journalists now realize that they need each other. Politicians need journalists to reach the public and to receive feedback from the public. They scan the major newspapers in the morning and the network newscasts in the evening. President Lyndon Johnson watched three network newscasts on three televisions simultaneously. (Presidents Ronald Reagan, who read mostly the comics, and George W. Bush, who read mostly the sports section, were exceptions to the rule.)[74] In turn, journalists need politicians to cover government. They seek a steady stream of fresh information to fill their news columns and newscasts.

The close relationship between the media and politicians is both a **symbiotic relationship**, meaning they use each other for their mutual advantage, and an **adversarial relationship**, meaning they fight each other.

Symbiotic Relationship

President Johnson told individual reporters, "You help me, and I'll help make you a big man in your profession." He gave exclusive interviews and, in return, expected favorable coverage.

Reporters get information from politicians in various ways. Some reporters are assigned to monitor beats. The Washington beats include the White House, Congress, the Supreme Court, the State Department, the Defense Department, and some other departments and agencies. Other reporters are assigned to cover specialized subjects, such as economics, energy issues, and environmental problems, which are addressed by multiple departments or agencies.

The government has press secretaries and public information officers who provide reporters with ideas and information for stories. The number of these officials is significant; one year the Defense Department employed almost fifteen hundred people just to handle press relations.[75] The Department of Homeland Security has an entertainment liaison office to provide information to help moviemakers and, at the same time, persuade moviemakers to portray the department positively.[76]

The government supplies reporters with a variety of news sources, including copies of speeches, summaries of committee meetings, news releases, and news briefings about current events. Officials also grant interviews, hold press conferences, and stage "media events." The vast majority of reporters rely on these sources rather than engage in more difficult and time-consuming investigative reporting.

Interviews

Interviews show the symbiotic nature of the relationship between reporters and politicians. During the early months of the Reagan presidency, *Washington Post* writer William Greider had a series of eighteen off-the-record meetings with budget director David Stockman. Greider recounted:

> Stockman and I were participating in a fairly routine transaction of Washington, a form of submerged communication which takes place regularly between selected members of the press and the highest officials of government. Our mutual motivation, despite our different interests, was crassly self-serving. It did not need to be spelled out between us. I would use him and he would use me. . . . I had established a valuable peephole on the inner policy debates of the new administration. And the young budget director had established a valuable connection with an important newspaper. I would get a jump on the unfolding strategies and decisions. He would be able to prod and influence the focus of our coverage, to communicate his views and positions under the cover of our "off the record" arrangement, to make known harsh assessments that a public official would not dare to voice in the more formal setting of a press conference, speech, or "on the record" interview.[77]

In 2004, when the "Green Zone," the American compound in Baghdad, was coming under attack, Dan Senor, the American spokesperson, was asked about the increasing violence. "Off the record: Paris is burning," he answered. "On the record: Security and stability are returning to Iraq."[78]

Leaks

Interviews can result in **leaks**—disclosures of information that officials want to keep secret. Others in the administration, the bureaucracy, or Congress use leaks for various reasons.

Officials in the administration might leak information about a potential policy—float a trial balloon—and then gauge the reaction to it without committing themselves in case it is shot down. As a result of bureaucratic infighting, officials might leak to prod the president or high-ranking official into taking some action[79] or to prevent the president or high-ranking official from taking some action. When President George W. Bush decided to appoint a Clinton administration attorney to be an antiterrorism adviser, Vice President Cheney's office leaked information to discredit the attorney and block the appointment.[80] (The attempt failed.)

Officials might leak to force public debates on matters that would otherwise be addressed behind closed doors. After Congress investigated the intelligence failures leading up to the terrorist attacks on September 11, 2001, someone leaked the information that the National Security Agency—the ultrasecret agency that engages in electronic surveillance around the world—had intercepted al-Qaeda messages on September 10 saying "Tomorrow is zero day" and "The match begins tomorrow" but had not translated the messages from Arabic until September 12.

Officials might leak to shift blame for mistakes or problems. When the Iraqi insurgency cast doubt upon our presumed victory in the Iraq War, officials apparently from the State Department leaked information suggesting that the Pentagon had rushed the country into war. Then officials apparently from the Pentagon leaked information claiming that the CIA had exaggerated the intelligence about Iraq's nuclear weapons program. Then officials apparently from the CIA leaked information indicating that the administration had distorted the intelligence about Iraq's weapons of mass destruction. Each group tried to absolve itself of the blame as the war turned sour.

Officials might leak to hurt an adversary. Diplomat Joseph Wilson was sent to Niger, which exports uranium, to investigate the possibility that Iraq had sought a type of uranium used in nuclear weapons. Wilson found no evidence to support the claim. Yet President Bush included the claim as a fact in his next State of the Union address, and others in the administration repeated it to persuade the public to support a war against Iraq. Breaking his silence, Wilson wrote an article in the *New York Times* maintaining that the administration had "twisted" the intelligence to "exaggerate" the threat. In retaliation, officials in the White House leaked the identity of Wilson's wife, Valerie Plame, who had worked for the CIA as an undercover spy.[81] Unmasking Plame effectively ended her career as a spy and jeopardized the operations she had established and contacts she had made in foreign countries.[82]

Officials might leak embarrassing information to help an ally or protect themselves. By leaking this information at a particular time or in a particular way, they can minimize the damage it would otherwise cause. So, officials leak embarrassing information during holidays or weekends, when the news receives less attention. They leak to small- or medium-size newspapers rather than to the *New York Times* or the *Washington Post* because these influential papers dislike giving prominent play to stories broken by less prestigious papers.[83] After President George H. W. Bush nominated Clarence Thomas to the Supreme Court, an official in the Bush administration leaked the fact that Thomas had experimented with marijuana in college. The official's purpose was to inoculate Thomas from the greater controversy that could have occurred if the press had discovered and revealed this fact closer to the confirmation vote.[84]

After diplomat Joseph Wilson (right) challenged an administration claim that Iraq had sought uranium for nuclear weapons, administration officials leaked the identity of his wife, Valerie Plame (left), who had been a CIA undercover agent.

© Carol Joynt/Getty Images

Despite the common belief that leaks are from low-level employees of the opposite party, most are from high-ranking officials of the president's party. "The ship of state," one experienced reporter noted, "is the only kind of ship that leaks mainly from the top."[81] During the Vietnam War, President Johnson himself ordered an aide to leak the charge that steel companies were "profiteering" from the war. After an executive complained, Johnson assured him that "if I find out some damn fool aide did it, I'll fire the sonuvabitch!"[86] During the Iraq War, President Bush authorized an aide to leak classified information to counter mounting criticism about the administration's use of intelligence before the war.

Presidents as far back as George Washington have been enraged by leaks. Reagan said he was "up to my keister" in leaks, and Nixon established a "plumbers" unit to wiretap aides and plug leaks once they learned who was responsible. George W. Bush, embarrassed about leaks revealing that the CIA operated secret prisons in foreign countries and the National Security Agency (NSA) wiretapped American citizens who made phone calls to foreign countries, launched the most extensive crackdown since Nixon. FBI investigations and CIA polygraph tests targeted government employees considered possible sources for the reports, and the Justice Department warned media organizations of prosecution, under a 1917 statute, for revealing secret information.[87]

Leaks may serve the public by disclosing information that otherwise would not be available, but leaks would serve the public better if reporters explained the leakers' motives so the public could understand the bureaucratic or ideological conflict driving the story. Yet reporters are wary of antagonizing the leakers—their sources—for fear of not getting a story next time.

Leaks often enable reporters to break stories before their competitors can report them. Competition for these **scoops** is intense. During the 2004 presidential campaign, CBS showed a letter regarding George W. Bush's National Guard service. In its zeal for a scoop, CBS aired the story before verifying the authenticity of the letter.[88] It turned out that the letter had been forged and the network had been snookered, which proved highly embarrassing to CBS and costly to Dan Rather, who lost his anchor position.

Press Conferences

Press conferences also show the symbiotic nature of the relationship between reporters and politicians. Theodore Roosevelt, who was the first president to cultivate close ties to correspondents, started the **presidential press conference** by answering questions from reporters while being shaved.[89] Franklin Roosevelt, who was detested by newspaper publishers, realized that the press conference could help him reach the public. He held frequent informal sessions around his desk and provided a steady stream of news, which editors felt obligated to publish. This news publicized his policies at the same time that editors were ranting against them. John Kennedy saw that the press conference could help him reach the public more directly if he allowed the networks to televise it live.[90] Then editors couldn't filter his remarks.

As a result, presidents and their aides transformed the conference into a carefully orchestrated media show. Now an administration schedules a conference when it wants to convey a message. Aides identify potential questions, and the president rehearses appropriate answers. (Former press secretaries brag that they predicted at least 90 percent of the questions asked—and often the reporters who asked them.[91]) During the conference, the president calls on the reporters he wants. Although he cannot ignore those from the major news organizations, he can call on others whom he expects will lob soft questions. The George W. Bush administration even gave press credentials to a Republican operative posing as a real reporter so he would ask the questions the president wanted to answer.[92]

ethical dilemmas | Is It Ethical to Leak?

If you were a member of the administration, would it be ethical to leak secret (though not classified) information to the media? Ever? In what situations?

Would it be ethical to leak to spur a public debate on an important issue? To correct the public's misconceptions about the administration's policy? To advance your favored policy among the various proposals put forth?

Would it be ethical to leak to protect the president or another official? To shift blame from yourself or your office? To discredit a proposal or embarrass a person from the opposing party?

If you don't think it would be ethical to leak, would you nevertheless do it if it helped you keep your job? Would you also do it if it helped you maintain your reputation or authority in the administration?

Beaming the conference to the nation results in less news than having a casual exchange around the president's desk, which used to reveal his thinking about policies and decisions. Appearing in millions of homes, the president cannot be as open and cannot allow himself to make a gaffe in front of the huge audience.

The transformation of the conference frustrates reporters and prompts them to act as prosecutors. As one press secretary observed, they play a game of "I gotcha."[93] Still, reporters value the conference. Editors consider the president's remarks news, so the conference helps reporters do their job. It also gives them a chance to bask in the limelight.

Media Events

"Media events" also show the symbiotic nature of the relationship between reporters and politicians. Staged for television, these events usually pair a photo opportunity with a speech to convey a strong impression of a politician's position on an issue.

The **photo opportunity** (often simply called a *photo op*) frames the politician against a backdrop that symbol-izes the points the politician is trying to make. Photo ops for economic issues might use factories—bustling to represent success or abandoned to represent failure. Presidential candidates in 2008 appeared at Google headquarters, which represents technological advancement, to identify themselves with the future. The strategy is the same as that for advertisements of merchandise: Combine the product (the politician) with the symbols in the hope that the potential buyers (the voters) will link the two.[94]

In the run-up to the 2004 presidential election, employees of the Homeland Security Department were instructed to provide one homeland security photo op a month as a way to link President Bush with 9/11 and the war on terrorism.[95]

Photo ops can be misleading. To persuade people that President Bush's tax cuts, which were designed primarily to benefit wealthy taxpayers, would help working Americans, the Speaker of the House, Dennis Hastert (R-Ill.), asked well-heeled lobbyists who favored the tax cuts to dress as construction workers and appear in photo ops featuring "a sea of hard hats" and signs proclaiming "Tax Relief for Everyone." The lobbyists were urged to participate: "WE DO NEED BODIES—they must be DRESSED DOWN, appear to be REAL WORKER types, etc."[96]

"What do you want to know, boys?" President Franklin Roosevelt holds a casual press conference in 1935.

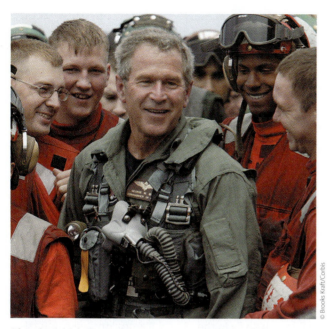

After the initial phase of the Iraq War in May 2003, President Bush used the opportunity for a dramatic photo op designed for his reelection campaign. Landing a navy jet on an aircraft carrier off the California coast, he swaggered across the deck, sporting a flight suit and backslapping the sailors. Standing under a banner that proclaimed "Mission Accomplished," he (prematurely) announced the end of major combat in Iraq.

After Saddam Hussein's regime was overthrown during the Iraq War, his statue was pulled down by a crowd of joyous Iraqis in a spontaneous celebration. Or so it appeared. The incident convinced many Americans that the Iraqis were grateful for our presence. In reality, the incident was staged as a photo op by the American military. The statue, which was attached to a cable, was pulled down by a tank, and the Iraqis, who were transported to the square for the cameras, numbered only 30 to 40. A video that was taken from a distance revealed a more accurate version than the close-up that was shown on television screens.[97]

The speech at a media event is not a classical oration or even a cogent address with a beginning, middle, and end. It is an informal talk that emphasizes a few key words or phrases or sentences—almost slogans, because television editors allot time only for a short **sound bite.** And the amount of time is less and less. In 1968, the average sound bite of a presidential contender on the evening news was about 42 seconds, but in 1988 it was under 10 seconds, and since then has dropped to less than 8 seconds.[98]

Speechwriters plan accordingly. "A lot of writers figure out how they are going to get the part they want onto television," a former presidential aide explained. "They think of a news lead and write around it. And if the television lights don't go on as the speaker is approaching that news lead, he skips a few paragraphs and waits until they are lit to read the key part."[99] This approach doesn't produce coherent speeches, but the people watching on television won't know, and the few watching in person don't matter because they are just props.

Singer Elvis Presley met with President Richard Nixon in the White House in 1970. Presley, whose popularity was waning as the Beatles were dominating pop stardom, asked the administration to appoint him "federal agent at-large" in the war on drugs. Nixon, whose popularity was lagging among the young, thought that an association with Presley would boost his image in the eyes of these voters. The result was this strange meeting and photo op. Yet by this time, neither man had much cachet to lend the other.

BEHIND THE SCENES
PHOTO OPS IN THE 2008 CAMPAIGN

To show that they were regular "guys," Hillary Clinton downed a shot of whiskey, followed by a chaser of beer, in a working-class bar in Indiana, as reporters noted that she didn't flinch when the liquor hit her throat; and Barack Obama bowled in a working-class bowling alley in Pennsylvania. While Clinton, who was raised in an upper-middle-class suburb, mastered the act, Obama, who was raised by a single mother on food stamps, failed to portray himself as working class. He wore a shirt and tie and bowled pathetically (scoring 37 in 7 frames). He would have been better off not bowling at all. And reporters noted that he took "delicate" sips, rather than "big swigs," from his can of beer.[1]

To highlight his status as a war hero and burnish his credentials for foreign policy experience, John McCain frequently surrounded himself with other war vets or national security figures.

Perhaps the most intriguing use of photos ops was the Obama campaign's staging of the people who appeared behind the candidate when he made speeches. His campaign tried to downplay his race out of fear of alienating those white voters still uncomfortable with the prospect of a black president. (Of course, Obama is half white and half black, but he is perceived as black by many people.) Although the crowds who attended Obama's speeches and many volunteers who knocked on people's doors in the South Carolina primary were disproportionately black, the cameras showed a "sea of white faces nodding approvingly or cheering wildly behind Obama." Campaign workers had ushered photogenic white families to seats on the speaker's platform in the cameras' eye and had ushered most black supporters to seats in the audience out of the cameras' eye.[2]

In the Pennsylvania primary, Obama campaigned heavily in the Philadelphia suburbs before adoring white supporters, but lightly in the city itself, where the crowds would have been mostly black. The campaign worried about the state's high number of blue-collar workers reluctant to vote for a black candidate. Showing Obama surrounded by enthusiastic whites would help defuse that concern; showing him surrounded by enthusiastic blacks would exacerbate it.

In response, the Clinton campaign placed young people and African Americans, two groups heavily in favor of Obama, immediately behind Hillary. Clinton had strong support among old people and blue-collar whites and sought more support from young people and African Americans. Both campaigns were appealing to television viewers who were undecided.

After the nomination was decided, Obama campaign workers moved two Muslim women in headscarves out of camera range at a rally, due to the Internet accusations that Obama is a secret Muslim.

[1] Maureen Dowd, "This Bud's For You," *New York Times*, May 4, 2008, WK13.
[2] Jim Hoagland, "Candidates on Message," *Washington Post National Weekly Edition*, February 25–March 2, 2008, 5.

Perhaps more than any other source of news, media events illustrate the reliance of politicians on television and of television on politicians.

DEMOCRACY?

The head of CBS News said, "I'd like just once to have the courage to go on the air and say that such and such a candidate went to six cities today to stage six media events, none of which had anything to do with governing America."[1] Do you agree, or do you think that these media events are beneficial for the voters in a democracy today?

[1] David Halberstam, "How Television Failed the American Voter," *Parade*, January 11, 1981, 8.

Adversarial Relationship

Although the relationship between the media and politicians is symbiotic in some ways, it is adversarial in others. Since George Washington's administration, when conflicts developed between Federalists and Jeffersonians, the media have attacked politicians and politicians have attacked the media. During John Adams's administration, Federalists passed the Sedition Act of 1798, which prohibited much criticism of the government. Federalist officials used the act to imprison Jeffersonian editors. Later, President Andrew Jackson proposed a law to allow the government to shut down "incendiary" newspapers. Even now, a former press secretary commented, "there are very few politicians who do not cherish privately the notion that there should be some regulation of the news."[100]

The adversarial relationship stems from a fundamental difference in perspectives. Politicians use the media to persuade the public to accept their proposals, so they want the media to act as conduits, conveying their messages directly to the public. But journalists see themselves not as conduits for the politicians but as servants of the people in a democracy. They examine policies and question officials so the people can learn more about them. According to one correspondent, "My job is not to say here's the church social with the apple pie, isn't it beautiful?"[101] The media disseminate additional information, even contradictory information, which usually ensures that the administration's proposals receive public scrutiny and generate public debate.

Inevitably, politicians fall short of their goals, and many blame the media for their failures. They confuse the message and the messenger, like Russian Tsar Peter the Great, who, when notified in 1700 that his army had lost a battle, promptly ordered the messenger strangled. When President Kennedy became upset by the *New York Times*'s coverage of Vietnam, he asked the paper to transfer its correspondent from Vietnam. (The *Times* refused.) When President Nixon became angry at major newspapers and networks, he had Vice President Spiro Agnew lash out at them. He also ordered the Department of Justice to investigate some for possible antitrust violations and the Internal Revenue Service to audit some for possible income tax violations. When aides to President George W. Bush read a *Washington Post* article questioning the truthfulness of the president's statements, they suggested that the reporter be removed from the White House beat. (The *Post* refused.[102])

However, it would be incorrect to think that the relationship between the media and politicians is usually adversarial. Normally, it is symbiotic. Although journalists like to think of themselves as adversaries who stand up to politicians, most of them rely on politicians most of the time.[103]

Yet the relationship has become more adversarial since the Vietnam War and the Watergate scandal fueled cynicism about government's performance and officials' honesty.[104]

Many reporters, according to the editor of the *Des Moines Register*, "began to feel that no journalism is worth doing unless it unseats the mighty."[105] New reporters especially began to feel this way. Senator Alan Simpson (R-Wyo.) asked the daughter of old friends what she planned to do after graduating from journalism school. "I'm going to be one of the hunters," she replied. When he asked, "What are you going to hunt?" she answered, "People like you!"[106]

In response, politicians, fearing that they will say something that will be used against them, have restricted reporters' access. In turn, reporters, worrying that they will not get the information they need to do their job, have complained that politicians are not accessible. During the George W. Bush presidency, one lamented, "The idea of a truly open press conference, an unscripted political debate, a leisurely and open . . . conversation between political leaders, or even a one-on-one interview between a member of the press and an undefended politician had become almost quaint in conception."[107] (See the box "He Wasn't a Straight Shooter.")

At the same time, politicians have become more sophisticated in their efforts to **spin** the media—to portray themselves and their programs in the most favorable light, regardless of the facts, and to shade the truth. Politicians' spin prompts reporters to become more cynical. "They don't explicitly argue or analyze what they dislike in a political program but instead sound sneering and supercilious about the whole idea of politics."[108] Reporters' cynicism then prompts politicians to escalate their efforts to spin the media, which prompts reporters to escalate their comments that politicians are insincere or dishonest. And so the cycle continues.

After Vice President Al Gore announced his candidacy for president in 2000 from his family's farm in Carthage, Tennessee, ABC correspondent Diane Sawyer conducted an interview reflecting these dynamics. She began, "Are you really a country boy?" He replied, "I grew up in two places. I grew up in Washington, D.C. [as the son of a senator from Tennessee], and I grew up here. My summers were here. Christmas was here." Sawyer taunted Gore, "You mucked pigpens?" Gore answered, "I cleaned out the pigpens . . . and raised cattle and planted and plowed and harvested and took in hay." Sawyer, not satisfied, challenged Gore in an attempt to show that he was a hypocrite: "I have a test for you. Ready for a pop quiz? . . . How many plants of tobacco can you have per acre? . . .What is brucellosis? . . . What are cattle prices roughly now? . . . When a fence sepa-

Washington Post reporters Carl Bernstein (left) and Bob Woodward uncovered the Watergate scandal.

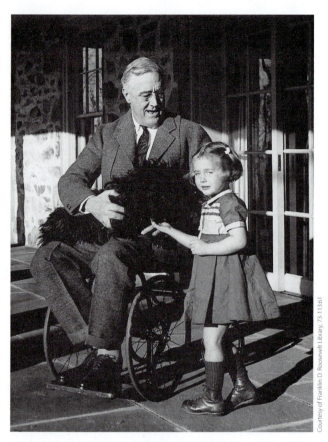

Courtesy of Franklin D. Roosevelt Library, 73-11361

Due to polio, Franklin Roosevelt spent much of his life in a wheelchair, but journalists didn't photograph him in it. A friend snapped this rare picture. Journalists were reluctant to photograph or write about officials' afflictions or behaviors until the Watergate scandal ushered in a new era of more personal coverage.

rates two farms, how can you tell which farm owns the fence?" By announcing from his family's farm, Gore was trying to convey his rural roots; by interviewing him in this manner, Sawyer was trying to question his sincerity.[109]

The increasingly adversarial relationship is also due to other factors mentioned earlier in the chapter. There are so many media, with so much space to fill, that they have a voracious appetite for news and a strong incentive to compete against each other for something "new." As a result, they often magnify trivial things. And because the fringe media now play a more prominent role, and because their stories eventually appear in the mainstream media, all media pay more attention to politicians' personal shortcomings with sex, drugs, and alcohol and raise more questions about politicians' "character" than they ever used to.[110] In 1977, one of every two hundred stories on network newscasts was about a purported scandal; by 1997 (*before* the Monica Lewinsky affair was revealed), one of every seven stories was.[111]

After 9/11, reporters were sensitive to, and even intimidated by, the public's fear and anger stemming from the terrorist attacks and its vocal support for the Iraq War. Consequently, reporters relaxed their stance. But they became

more adversarial again when the American victory evaporated during the Iraqi insurgency.

Yet the apparent toughness usually is "a toughness of demeanor" rather than a toughness of substantive journalism.[112] Reporters exhibit tough attitudes rather than conduct thorough investigations and careful analyses. In fact, few engage in investigative journalism.[113]

Even seven years after 9/11, there has been remarkably little investigation of important questions: Why didn't the administration heed repeated warnings of the pending attack? If they discounted the warnings, why did top officials go to unusual lengths to protect themselves? After 9/11, why was Osama bin Laden allowed to escape from Afghanistan, and why were al-Qaeda fighters airlifted out of Afghanistan? What arrangements—a deal?—were made with Pakistan?[114]

Before hurricane Katrina, reporters failed to notice that the Federal Emergency Management Administration (FEMA) was headed by political hacks rather than by officials experienced in disaster response. Nor did reporters question why a study found that employees' morale at FEMA was lower than that at any other federal agency.[115]

Relationship between the Media and the President

Franklin Roosevelt created the model that most contemporary presidents use to communicate with the public. Newspaper publishers, who were conservative businessmen, opposed the president and his policies. In fact, a correspondent recalled, "The publishers didn't just disagree with the New Deal. They hated it. The reporters, who liked it, had to write as though they hated it too."[116] Recognizing that he wouldn't receive favorable coverage, Roosevelt realized that he would have to reach the public another way. He used press conferences to provide a steady stream of news about his policies. He also used radio talks, which he called **fireside chats**, to advocate his policies and reassure his listeners in the throes of the Depression. He had a fine voice and a superb ability to speak informally—he talked about his family, even his dog. He drew such an audience that he was offered as much airtime as he wanted (though he was shrewd enough to realize that too much would result in overexposure). This tactic enabled him to avoid the filters of reporters and editors and to take his case directly to the people.[117]

In addition, Roosevelt was the first president to seek systematic feedback from the people. He used public opinion polls to gauge people's views toward his policies. Thus for him, communication was a two-way process—to the people and from the people.

Ronald Reagan refined the model. As a young man, Reagan idolized Roosevelt, even developing an imitation with an appropriate accent and a cigarette holder.[118] As

HE WASN'T A STRAIGHT SHOOTER

When Vice President Cheney accidentally shot a fellow hunter on a Texas ranch, neither he nor his staff nor the White House reported it to the press. The next day, the ranch's owner reported it to the local newspaper. Despite the media's demands for statements or interviews, the vice president refused to respond for four more days. Eventually, he agreed to an interview with Republican-friendly Fox news.[1]

Comedians had a field day using the vice president as a punch line. Jay Leno on *The Tonight Show with Jay Leno*: "I'm surprised Dick Cheney loves to hunt so much. The five times the government tried to give him a gun, he got a deferment." Jimmy Kimmel on *Jimmy Kimmel Live*: "Kind of a sad study out today that single women over the age of 35 are more likely to be shot by the vice president than find a husband."

Why all the jokes? Why such media clamor? This incident resembles previous incidents in which the media seemed to make a mountain out of a molehill. Vice President Dan Quayle, appearing in a grade-school class for a photo op, misspelled the word "potato." President Jimmy Carter, fishing in Georgia, shooed away a swamp rabbit approaching his boat and gnashing its teeth. This led to stories about the "killer rabbit." Although these incidents them- selves were truly minor, they reflected shortcom- ings already perceived by reporters and people. The Quayle incident reflected doubts about the "Veep's" smarts, and the Carter inci- dent reflected conclusions about the administration's haplessness.[2] These spon- taneous and comprehen- sible incidents brought "all the abstractions together into one concrete image."[3]

Although Vice President Cheney's reluctance to re- port and acknowledge the shooting may have been due simply to his personal anguish, the merciless jokes reflected the journal- ists' beliefs that the vice president, and administra- tion foreign policies for which he was a driving force, were secretive, ar- rogant, and even incom- petent. So the incident—a poor decision, which led to an unfortunate result, which was not acknowl- edged until the outcry became too great—stands in for aspects of the war on terrorism and the war in Iraq. And it represents the journalists' feelings that the vice president, though a good shot, wasn't a straight shooter.[4]

[1] Vice President Cheney's standard contract for public appearances stipulated that the temper- ature be set at 68 degrees; an array of diet so- das be available; and any televisions be pre- tuned to Fox News. *Wait, Wait, Don't Tell Me,* NPR, March 25, 2006.
[2] Mark Z. Barabak, "Political Blunders Crumble Careers," *Lincoln Journal Star,* February 20, 2006, A7.
[3] Psychologist Anthony Pratkanis, quoted in ibid.
[4] Even when Cheney eventually addressed the issue, he was reluctant to tell the truth. He said he was thirty yards away when he fired, but the injuries to his friend were more serious than they likely would have been from this distance. Jacob Weisberg, *The Bush Tragedy* (New York: Random House, 2008), 179.

president, Reagan duplicated Roosevelt's success in using the media. Although Reagan's command of the facts about his proposals and government programs was uncertain, his ability to convey his broad themes was uncanny. Reporters dubbed him the "Great Communicator."

As Roosevelt used radio, Reagan used television. By the time he reached the White House, after a career as an actor in movies and television, Reagan had mastered the art of speaking and performing in front of live audiences and on camera.[119] Tall, handsome, and poised, he knew exactly how to use an inflection, a gesture, or a tilt of his head to keep all eyes and ears focused on him. His speeches and even his casual comments were highly effective.

His aides knew how to make his appearances especially impressive. The administration knew that the media would cover the president extensively to fill their news columns and newscasts. An aide explained the strategy: "The media, while they won't admit it, are not in the news business; they're in entertainment. We tried to create the most enter- taining, visually attractive scene to fill that box [the TV screen], so that the networks would have to use it."[120]

Aides sent advance agents days or weeks ahead of the president to prepare the "stage" for media events—the spe- cific location, backdrops, lighting, and sound equipment. A trip to Korea was designed to show "the commander in chief on the front line against communism." An advance man went to the demilitarized zone separating North and South Korea and negotiated with the Army and Secret Ser- vice for the most photogenic setting. He demanded that the president be allowed to use the most exposed bunker, which meant that the army had to erect telephone poles and string thirty thousand yards of camouflage netting to hide Reagan from North Korean sharpshooters. The advance man also demanded that the Army build camera platforms on a hill that remained exposed but offered the most dramatic angle to film Reagan surrounded by sandbags. Although the Se- cret Service wanted sandbags up to Reagan's neck, the ad- vance man insisted that they be no more than four inches above his navel so viewers would get a clear picture of the president wearing his flak jacket and demonstrating "Amer- ican strength and resolve."[121]

The Reagan administration also developed the tech- nique of highlighting a single theme with a single message for every day and every week to emphasize whatever pro- posal the president was pushing at the time. The administra- tion then arranged the president's appearances and offered

News photo of President Reagan in Korea, staged to reflect "American strength and resolve."

the media information that would reinforce the message. Aides strictly controlled the president. They determined "the line of the day" and instructed him what to say. They also instructed him not to answer reporters' questions about other matters. They didn't want other remarks to overshadow the message of the day. The strategy was to set the agenda rather than letting the media set it.[122]

By alternately using and avoiding the media, President Reagan's administration managed the news more than any previous administration.

Bush Administration

The **George W. Bush** administration emulated the Reagan administration in trying to manage the news by alternately using and avoiding the media.

Aides established a message for every day and e-mailed talking points to administration officials, instructing them to address these points. The president voiced the message at his appearances, where backdrops bearing the message printed as a slogan reinforced it. Administration officials who were contacted by the press repeated it. All were expected to "stay on message."

Otherwise, access to the president and White House officials was strictly limited. The president was made available for speeches to friendly audiences or for interviews with friendly reporters. Press conferences were rarely scheduled. Bush held far fewer conferences than other modern presidents.[123] Reporters who displeased the administration were punished by losing their access.[124] When veteran reporter Helen Thomas of the Associated Press displeased the president, he refused to answer her questions at press conferences for three years.[125] As a result of this

process, according to President Reagan's communications aide, the Bush administration was "the most disciplined White House in history."[126]

When the president attended a meeting in Ireland, an Irish reporter who had submitted questions in advance, as was required for interviews with Bush, was dissatisfied when the president answered in generalities. She interrupted him and pressed him for more specific answers. Her behavior was so unusual that it became a news story. Unlike most American reporters, she didn't worry about future access to the White House.

The administration's communications strategy also entailed a very active and well-financed public relations machine. The administration contracted with public relations firms and advertising agencies to produce pseudo news reports, purporting to be actual news stories, which portrayed the administration as vigilant and compassionate.[127] These were distributed to television stations around the country, which integrated them into their newscasts. To viewers, they appeared to be news rather than propaganda. In a 2½-year period, seven cabinet departments spent $1.6 billion on 343 public relations contracts for news releases and other services.[128] The administration even paid some real reporters to say positive things about the administration's policies.

President Bush was not comfortable in front of television cameras. Initially, he shunned the role of "communicator in chief." When aides scheduled public appearances, he bristled.[129] When he gave formal speeches or made informal remarks, he often looked awkward and sounded inarticulate. Reporters observed that he was "perhaps the least confident public performer of the modern presidency."[130] An aide to the previous president commented, "In the Clinton administration, we worried the president would open his zipper, and in the Bush administration, they worry the president will open his mouth."[131] As governor of Texas, Bush had worked behind the scenes and evidently expected to do the same as president.

The terrorist attacks thrust Bush into the public role he had avoided. Although he failed to return to the White House on September 11 to reassure Americans from the Oval Office,[132] later he visited the site of the World Trade Center and galvanized public support when he picked up a bullhorn and talked to the workers. Gradually, he grew into his new role, appearing more comfortable on the national stage. Converting "grief to anger to action,"[133] he rallied the public behind the war on terrorism and the war in Afghanistan.

Bush's strength was to speak to moral clarity. The terrorist attacks allowed Bush to talk in these terms. But September 11 was "one of history's rare unnuanced days," a presidential adviser admitted.[134] On other issues, where there was less moral clarity, such as the clash between Israelis and Palestinians, Bush was less effective. His black-and-white view of the world and his "poverty of language"[135] made it difficult for him to convey any nuances

BEHIND THE SCENES
"INDEPENDENT" MILITARY ANALYSTS

Before and during the Iraq War, the television networks featured many military analysts who addressed the military strategy and the likely success of the war. These analysts were retired, high-ranking officers, who were presented as independent experts. Unbeknownst to the viewers or apparently even to the networks, however, these analysts were a part of the Bush administration's efforts to generate favorable coverage for its policies in Iraq.

Before the war, the Pentagon assembled the group of retired officers. Before and during the war, the group gathered for periodic briefings. The ex-officers met with Secretary of Defense Donald Rumsfeld at least eighteen times and with senior officials in the Pentagon dozens of other times. They were trained to echo the administration's talking points, and they were instructed not to reveal their connections to the Pentagon. The administration's goal was to disseminate political propaganda under the guise of independent analysis.

The analysts' positive comments often contradicted professional reporters' negative assessments, after the apparent victory turned into a long quagmire, and led to the public's complaints that the mainstream media were ignoring "the good news" in Iraq.

The administration expressed satisfaction with the results of its program. On some days, an official observed, "We were able to click on every single station and every one of our folks were up there delivering our message. You'd look at them and say, 'This is working.'"

Eventually, some analysts recognized a huge gap between what they were told to say and what was happening on the ground. One commentator did remark that the United States is "not on a good glide path right now." Then he was dropped from the list of ex-officers recommended to the networks. Others were too fearful to reflect any doubts or pessimism. "There was no way I was going to go down that road and get completely torn apart," a former Green Beret said. "You're talking about fighting a huge machine."

The ex-officers were reluctant to disregard instructions especially because most were employed by military contractors—private companies that sell weapons systems to the government—after leaving the military. At the time they were speaking to the public, on behalf of the administration, they were working for companies that were seeking contracts from the administration. Any who might have been inclined to voice concerns were reluctant to do so for fear of costing their companies lucrative contracts. A retired lieutenant colonel said he worried that "some four-star could call up and say, 'Kill that contract.'" So instead they dispensed false information about our progress in the war.

After these revelations, the program was suspended by the Pentagon.

Source: David Barstow, "Behind Analysts, Pentagon's Hidden Hand," *New York Times*, April 20, 2008, Y1. All quotes from p. 26. This program was still in operation when this article appeared.

News Channels Using Military Officers as Analysts Who Parrot Pentagon Line

...AND NOW WE TURN TO OUR MILITARY ANALYST, GENERAL GEORGE ARMSTRONG CUSTER (RETIRED)...

CABLE NEWS

UH... THINGS ARE GOING WELL...

DANZIGER
NYTS/CWS Apr 22 08 (3575)

Danziger, CartoonArts International-NY Times Syndicate

in his comments. (He in fact told one senator, "I don't do nuance."[136])

Bush's speechwriters were quite effective in communicating with his supporters. The speeches incorporated religious language that appealed to evangelical Christians.[137] In addition to references to *evil* and *evildoers*, there were terms, such as *work of mercy* and *wonder-working power*, that were recognized by the devout. When the president announced the invasion of Afghanistan, his speech included allusions to Revelation, Isaiah, Job, Matthew, and Jeremiah.[138] (The president, however, did spur a backlash in the United States and abroad when he called the war on terrorism a *crusade*, thus linking it to the Crusades by European Christians against Eastern Muslims in the Middle Ages.)

Although his formal speeches were good, Bush tended to stumble when he spoke without a script. At times he forgot his train of thought, made up words, and left listeners bewildered.[139] But his lack of polish didn't seem to hurt him in the polls, at least until his policies became unpopular. He talked like many men, in his tone and simple words—even the belligerence in his voice—and thus related well to many voters. Sounding like a frontier sheriff in the Wild West, he declared that Osama bin Laden was "wanted, dead or alive." When Iraqi insurgents began to use roadside bombs against American soldiers, Bush threatened, "Bring 'em on." While some people were appalled by such comments, others liked the swagger in his delivery and the confidence in his gestures (at least until the war turned into a quagmire). One observer called Bush "a master of the American vernacular, that form of expression which eschews slickness and makes a virtue of the speaker's limitations."[140]

Relationship between the Media and Congress

Members of Congress also use the media but have less impact. They hire their own full-time press secretaries, who churn out press releases, distribute television tapes, and arrange interviews with reporters.[141] The Senate and House of Representatives provide recording studios for members and allow television cameras into committee rooms and C-SPAN into the chambers. Yet members still have trouble attracting the media's eye. One president can be the subject of the media's focus, but 535 members of Congress cannot. Only a handful of powerful (or, occasionally, colorful) members receive coverage from the national media. Other members get attention from their home-state or district media, but those from large urban areas with numerous representatives get little publicity or scrutiny even there.[142]

Congressional committees also use the media to influence public opinion. During the Whitewater hearings, President Clinton talked with a Republican senator on the investigating committee. "They were impugning Hillary," he recalled, "and I asked this guy, 'Do you really think my wife and I did anything wrong in this Whitewater thing?' He just started laughing. He said, 'Of course you didn't do anything wrong. That's not the point. The point of this is to make people think you did something wrong.' "[143]

Relationship between the Media and the Supreme Court

Unlike presidents and members of Congress, justices of the Supreme Court shun the media. They rarely talk to reporters, and they also forbid their law clerks from talking to the press. They try to convey the impression that they aren't engaged in politics and therefore shouldn't answer reporters' questions or concern themselves with public opinion.

As a result, the media don't cover the Supreme Court nearly as much as the presidency or Congress. Few newspapers have a full-time Court reporter; no newsmagazines or television networks do. In one recent year, only twenty-seven reporters had Court press credentials, whereas an estimated seventeen hundred reporters had White House press credentials.[144]

When the media do cover the Supreme Court, they focus on the Court's rulings.[145] They seldom investigate or peer behind the Court's curtains. They often ignore even relevant concerns, such as questions about the justices' health. Most reporters on this beat, called "Washington's most deferential press corps,"[146] reject the role of watchdog. Consequently, the justices are shielded from both the legitimate investigation and the excessive scrutiny that officials in the other branches are subjected to.

Relationship between the Media and the Military

During wartime, the military has tried to control media coverage to avoid the negative reports and the disturbing photographs that typified the last years of the Vietnam War.[147] For the Afghanistan War, the Bush administration bought the exclusive rights to the photographic images from all private satellites so that news organizations would be unable to use any. Thus American taxpayers paid private companies more than $2 million per month to prevent themselves from seeing what was happening.[148] The military also kept the journalists far away from the fighting.

For the Iraq War, the military tried a new approach, embedding the journalists into fighting units. Hundreds of journalists ate, slept, and traveled with the soldiers and were allowed to report live. They were prohibited from revealing sensitive information and from having anonymous interviews, which would allow the soldiers to make critical comments.

The military's goals were to appease the news organizations and at the same time use them to show the technological prowess of our military and the heroic exploits of our fighters. The news organizations would also report human interest stories about individual soldiers. According to an official, it was "important for the public to be invested in this emotionally and personally."[149] Studies show that the arrangement worked exactly as the military expected. The embedded reporters, compared with the less numerous independent reporters, covered the war form the military's perspective—the soldiers' viewpoint—focusing on threats to American troops rather than on casualties among Iraqi civilians or consequences for Iraqi society.[150]

The military was so anxious for uplifting coverage that when Pat Tillman, the Arizona Cardinals defensive back who volunteered for the army after 9/11, was killed by friendly fire, the army refused to reveal the cause of death to the public or even to his parents for over a month. Instead, it issued a false press release exaggerating his actions. As its most famous volunteer, Tillman was used as an heroic poster boy.[151]

Bias of the Media

Every night, Walter Cronkite, former anchor for *CBS Evening News,* signed off, "And that's the way it is," implying that the network held a huge mirror to the world and returned a perfect reflection to its viewers, without selection or distortion. But the media do not hold a mirror. They hold a searchlight that seeks and illuminates some things instead of others.[152]

From all the events that occur in the world every day, the media can report only a handful as the news of the day. Even the fat *New York Times,* whose motto is "All the News

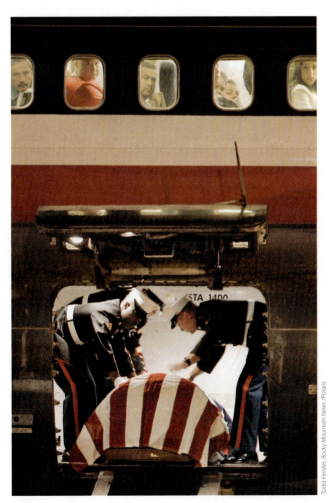

The Bush administration tried to prevent journalists from photographing coffins returning from the Iraq War, usually flying the coffins to military bases in the middle of the night. But a journalist observed this coffin coming home to Reno, Nevada.

Todd Heisler, Rocky Mountain News / Polaris

That's Fit to Print," cannot include all the news. The media must decide what events are newsworthy. They must decide where to report these—on the front page or at the top of the newscast, or in a less prominent position. Then they must decide how to report them.

When the Wright brothers invited reporters to Kitty Hawk, North Carolina, to observe the first airplane flight in 1903, none considered it newsworthy enough to cover. After the historic flight, only seven American newspapers reported the flight, and only two reported it on their front page.[153]

In making these decisions, it would be natural for journalists' attitudes to affect their coverage. As one reporter acknowledged, he writes "from what he hears and sees and how he filters it through the lens of his own experience. No reporter is a robot."[154]

Political Bias

Historically, the press was politically biased. The first papers, which were established by political parties, parroted the party line. Even the independent papers that succeeded them advocated one side or the other. The attitudes of publishers, editors, and reporters seeped—sometimes flooded—into their prose.

But the papers gradually abandoned their ardor for editorializing and adopted the **practice of objectivity** to attract and retain as many readers as possible. This means that in news stories (not in editorials or columns) they try to present the facts rather than their opinions. When the facts are in dispute, they try to present the positions of both sides. They are reluctant to evaluate these positions. Even when one side makes a false or misleading assertion, they are hesitant to notify their readers. Instead, they rely upon the other side to do so. They hope that their readers can discern which is accurate.

Although most mainstream media today follow the practice of objectivity, the public still thinks the press is biased. Many people think the press is "out to get" the groups they identify with. Executives believe the press is out to get businesses, and laborers believe it is out to get unions. Conservatives believe the press is biased against conservatives, and liberals believe it is biased against liberals. Republicans believe the press is biased against Republicans, and Democrats believe it is biased against Democrats.[155] For many people, the press is a scapegoat, "a secular devil for our times."[156]

Indeed, the public is more critical today, when most media at least attempt to be objective, than in the past, when the media did not even pretend to be. Back then, citizens could subscribe to whichever local paper reflected their own biases. Now, as local newspapers and television stations have given way to national newspapers and networks, and as independently owned newspapers and television stations have given way to large chains and conglomerates, people have less opportunity to follow only media that reflect their views. People with strong views are disappointed with today's more balanced coverage. So partisans on both sides criticize the same media for being biased—though in opposite directions.

To assess the presence and the direction of **political bias**, it is necessary to examine the differences in coverage by the advocacy media and the mainstream media, the differences in coverage of elections and issues, and the differences in coverage of domestic policies and international policies.

Bias in the Advocacy Media

Some media don't try to be neutral. Advocacy media intentionally tilt one way or the other and seek an audience of people who share their views. Advocacy media can be found at both ends of the political spectrum, though far more are conservative than liberal.

Because conservatives perceived a liberal bias in the mainstream media, they established their own media in the 1980s and 1990s. This vocal complex includes newspapers, such as the *Washington Times*, the *New York Post*, and the *Wall Street Journal* (just its editorial page—not its news pages), various magazines, numerous radio and television talk shows, and Internet websites, plus a network of columnists, commentators, and think tanks. These conservative journalists see themselves as part of an ideological movement, as members of the same team, rather than as objective journalists.

These conservative journalists contrast with the mainstream journalists who don't see themselves as part of an ideological team. In fact, the mainstream journalists who are liberal have made a point of criticizing liberals and Democrats as a way of demonstrating their independence and impartiality. During the years in which conservatives established their own media, mainstream journalists offered relentless criticism of Bill Clinton and snide portrayals of Al Gore and John Kerry.[157]

The role of conservative journalists in talk radio has been especially powerful. The expansion of talk radio began in the 1980s when the daytime television audience was mostly female and the daytime radio audience was mostly male, and a gender gap emerged in political preferences, with men becoming more conservative and women remaining more liberal. In this decade, a backlash against feminism and affirmative action developed among middle-class and lower-middle-class whites, especially among those who were men. During these years, a few large chains, with conservative owners, bought out many stations. They decided to capture these conservative male listeners and convey their own political views at the same time, so they adopted a talk radio format with conservative hosts.[158]

Today, more than thirteen hundred talk stations fill the airwaves, and more than a fifth of American adults consider talk radio their primary source for news.[159] The vast majority of talk shows are hosted by conservative commentators,[160] such as Rush Limbaugh, Sean Hannity, Bill O'Reilly, G. Gordon Liddy,[161] Oliver North, and numerous others. The Republican National Committee, in fact, has a Radio Services Department that provides talking points to these hosts every day so that they will reinforce the Republican message.[162] According to one analysis, 91 percent of the talk on the 257 news/talk stations owned by the top five chains was conservative; only 9 percent was liberal.[163]

The impact of talk radio was apparent concerning the immigration issue in 2007. President Bush and congressional Democrats agreed on a bill, which had broad public support, but the compromise bill was denounced by talk show hosts because it wasn't punitive enough toward illegal immigrants. The hosts rallied their listeners, who pressured their representatives to kill the bill.[164]

The conservative advocacy media also include the Fox News Channel. Fox is the first major network to *narrowcast*—intentionally appeal to a narrow segment of

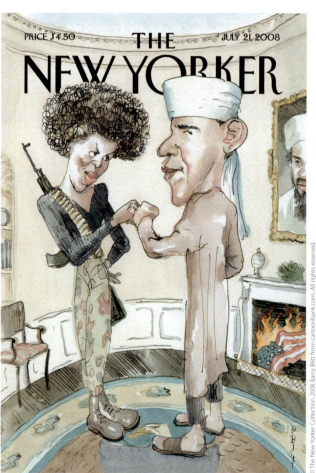

After Internet sites and Fox News questioned Obama's Christianity and his patriotism, a cartoonist depicted Barack and Michelle Obama as radical Muslims bent on destroying America. Through exaggeration, the cartoonist lampooned the false accusations. Some Obama supporters, however, thought the cartoon reinforced the damning perceptions many Americans held.

the entire audience—rather than broadcast.[165] Owned by a conservative media mogul and operated by a former Republican consultant, Fox appeals to conservatives disenchanted with the mainstream media.[166] It presents a skewed lineup of commentators and guests, featuring prominent conservatives with strong personalities paired with relatively unknown liberals with relatively weak personalities. Fox also follows the talking points from the Republican National Committee. After years of critical coverage of President Clinton, Fox offered fawning coverage of President Bush (criticizing him only after the failures in the Iraq War became obvious).

Throughout its programming, the network blurs the distinction between news and commentary. For instance, when reporting on a proposal by President Bush to cut taxes, the network ran a line along the bottom of the screen urging, "Cut 'em already."[167] When reporting on Swiss protesters against the Iraq War, an anchor referred to the demonstrators as "hundreds of knuckleheads." Another referred to France, which opposed the war, as a member of the "axis of weasels." The network then ran that phrase along the bottom of the screen when reporting about France. Fox aired relentlessly upbeat coverage of the Iraq War. Its correspondents were urged to downplay American casualties. (A memo from a senior executive instructed: "Do not fall into the easy trap of mourning the loss of U.S. lives.") They were also told to refer to Marine snipers as "sharpshooters," because the word *snipers* has a negative connotation. And all along, the network questioned the patriotism of liberals and critics of the war.[168] When apparent progress in the war deteriorated, Fox scaled back its coverage rather than report the failures of the war.[169] Not until numerous conservatives began to criticize the war did Fox air critical views.

Fox launched a crusade against what it labeled the "War on Christmas" in 2005, criticizing businesses and individuals who wished folks "Happy Holidays" instead of "Merry Christmas." It broadcast fifty-eight segments in one five-day period.[170]

During the presidential campaign in 2004, Fox repeatedly called for President Bush's reelection. In 2008, the network questioned Obama's patriotism and compared the candidate to Karl Marx—the communist theorist who called religion the "opiate" of the people.[171] Fox also compared Obama to Adolph Hitler; to Joseph Stalin—the murderous Soviet leader; to Chairman Mao—the ruthless Chinese leader; and to the Iraqi insurgents. Just before the election, Fox broadcast a "documentary" citing wild accusations, from unreliable sources, about Obama's radicalism. When Barack and Michelle Obama bumped fists, Fox's E.D. Hill speculated that the gesture could be a "terrorist fist jab."

A former Fox correspondent said it was common to hear producers remind them, "We have to feed the core"—that is, their conservative viewers.[172] Yet the network retains a veneer of neutrality. It claims to be "fair and balanced" and "spin free." The marketing strategy is to attract viewers by offering them conservative commentary but with the reassurance that this commentary is truth rather than opinion.

MSNBC has taken tentative steps to attract liberal viewers, airing nightly programs with two outspoken liberal commentators.[173]

The conservative media also include Christian radio networks, television organizations, and more than thirteen hundred radio and television stations.[174] These media address political issues as well as spiritual matters.

Although liberals have as many magazines and Internet websites, the only advocacy media they dominate are documentary films.[175] For example, Michael Moore's films, such as *Fahrenheit 9/11* and *Sicko*, also offer a combination of facts, opinions, and speculation, though from the left rather than from the right.

Bias in the Mainstream Media

Although the advocacy media are far more slanted, allegations of bias are leveled against the mainstream media far more often. Conservative groups and commentators, especially, claim that these media are biased toward liberal candidates and policies.[176]

Journalists for the mainstream media are not very representative of the public. They are disproportionately college-educated white males from the upper middle class. They are disproportionately urban and secular, rather than rural and religious, and they are disproportionately Democrats or independents leaning to the Democrats, rather than Republicans or independents leaning to the Republicans. Likewise, they are disproportionately liberals rather than conservatives.[177]

Journalists who work for the most influential organizations—large newspapers, wire services, newsmagazines, and radio and television networks—are more likely to be Democrats and liberals than those who work for less prominent organizations—small newspapers and radio and television stations.[178] Journalists in the most influential organizations are more likely than the public to support the liberal position on issues. At the same time, they support capitalism and do not think that our institutions "need overhaul."[179] Thus they are not extremely liberal.

Focusing on journalists' backgrounds and attitudes assumes that these color journalists' coverage. But several factors mitigate the effect of these traits. Most journalists chose their profession not because of a commitment to an ideology—according to veteran columnist David Broder, "There just isn't enough ideology in the average reporter to fill a thimble"[180]—but because of the opportunity to rub elbows with powerful people and be close to exciting events. "Each day brings new stories, new dramas in which journalists participate vicariously."[181] As a result, most journalists "care more about the politics of an issue than about the issue itself,"[182] so they are less likely to express their views about the issue. In addition, mainstream organizations pressure journalists to muffle their views because of a conviction that it is professional to do so and also a desire to avoid the headaches that could arise otherwise—debates among their staffers, complaints from their audience, perhaps even complaints from the White House or Congress.[183] Some organizations fear public perceptions of reporters' bias so much that they restrict reporters' private lives, forbidding any political activity, even outside the office and on their own time.[184]

For these reasons, mainstream media don't exhibit nearly as much political bias toward candidates or policies as would be expected from journalists' backgrounds and attitudes.

To measure bias, researchers use a technique called content analysis. They scrutinize newspaper and television stories to determine whether there was an unequal amount of coverage, unequal use of favorable or unfavorable statements, or unequal use of a positive or negative tone. They consider insinuating verbs ("he conceded" rather than "he said") and pejorative adjectives ("her weak response" rather than "her response"), and for television stories, they evaluate the announcers' nonverbal communication—voice inflection, eye movement, and body language.

Bias in Elections

Researchers have examined media coverage of presidential campaigns the most and have found relatively little bias. The media typically gave the two major candidates equal attention, and they usually avoided any favorable or unfavorable statements in their news stories. They typically provided diverse views in editorials and columns, with some commentary slanting one way and other commentary slanting the opposite way. The authors of a study examining forty-six newspapers concluded that American newspapers are "fairly neutral."[185] Other studies have reached similar conclusions about various media.[186] An analysis of the data from fifty-nine studies found no significant bias in newspapers, a little (pro-Republican) bias in newsmagazines, and a little (pro-Democratic) bias on television networks.[187]

The first studies of the 2008 campaign, examining media coverage during the summer, found that the major television networks gave Obama more time than McCain. However, the networks criticized Obama more often than McCain. Although most statements in the stories were neutral, among the statements that weren't neutral, 28 percent were positive and 72 percent were negative toward Obama. Toward McCain, 43 percent were positive and 57 percent were negative.[188] This pattern reversed as the campaign continued in the fall.

Overall, there is less bias than the public believes or the candidates feel. When candidates complain, they are usually objecting to bad news or are trying to manipulate the media. The strategy is to put reporters on the defensive so that they will go easier on the candidate or harder on the opponent in the future, just as sports coaches "work the refs" over officiating calls.

Yet the way in which the media cover campaigns can have different implications for different candidates. The media report the facts that one candidate is leading while the other is trailing, that one campaign is surging while the other is slipping. "We all respond like Pavlov's dogs to polls," an experienced correspondent explained.[189] This coverage has positive implications for those who are leading or surging—swaying undecided voters, galvanizing campaign workers, and attracting financial contributions—and negative implications for those who are trailing or slipping. Such coverage does not benefit one party over the other party in election after election, but it can benefit one party's candidate over the other party's candidate in a particular election.[190] People who support the losers consider such reporting biased. Journalists, however, consider it simply a reflection of reality.

Another habitual practice has different implications for different candidates. The press pays more attention to minor things that are easy to report—and easy to ridicule—than to substantive issues that are difficult to explain.[191] Hence the voluminous coverage about President Clinton's sexual affairs. Although reporters are willing to criticize or even ridicule candidates about minor matters, they are usually reluctant to challenge them on substantive issues. Doing so would require more knowledge about substantive policies or more nerve to draw conclusions about these policies than most reporters have.

Likewise, when covering presidential debates, the press pays more attention to style and tactics than to substantive issues—more attention to how something was said than to what was said.[192] Reporters act more like theater critics than helpful guides to confused voters. These practices don't reflect bias by reporters as much as they reflect superficiality in reporting.

There are two exceptions to the generalization that overt political bias in elections is minimal. First, the media usually give short shrift to third-party candidates.[193] Ralph Nader, who first ran for president in 2000, was well known and held views partly shared by numerous voters, but he received scant coverage. When he held enthusiastic rallies on college campuses and in large coliseums, the national media virtually ignored them. Only when the election between Gore and Bush tightened and it appeared that Nader might be a spoiler did the national media pay attention. Then they focused on his potential as a spoiler rather than on his views that had attracted the crowds.[194]

Second, newspapers traditionally print editorials and columns that express opinions. In editorials before elections, papers endorse candidates. Most owners are Republican, and many influence the editorials. Since the first survey in 1932, more papers have endorsed the Republican presidential candidate, except in the elections of 1964, 1992, 2004, and 2008, when Obama received 287 and McCain only 159 endorsements.[195]

In columns, writers offer their own opinions. Although most newspapers provide a mix of columnists, the majority are conservative, according to a study of 96 percent of the country's English-language daily newspapers.[196] Sixty percent of the papers print more conservative than liberal columnists, while 20 percent print more liberal than conservative columnists, and 20 percent print an equal number. Evidently the Republican owners want their paper's columns, like their paper's editorials, to reflect their conservative views.

Bias against All Candidates and Officials

Some critics charge that a general bias exists against all candidates and officials—a negative undercurrent in reporting about government, regardless of who or what is covered. President Nixon's first vice president, Spiro Agnew, called journalists "nattering nabobs of negativism." Critics believe that this bias increased after the Vietnam War and the Watergate scandal made reporters more cynical.

There is considerable validity to this charge. Analyses of newspapers, magazines, and television networks show that the overwhelming majority of stories about government and politicians are neutral.[197] However, the rest are more often negative than positive.[198]

Emphasizing the negative distorts what candidates say. In the 1996 presidential campaign, 85 percent of the candidates' comments made a positive case for the candidates, but 85 percent of the media's coverage dwelled on the negative attacks by the candidates.[199]

Emphasizing the negative also distorts what officials do. The *Washington Post* reported that Senator Robert Byrd (D-W.Va.) got the National Park Service to fund a project for his state, including the renovation of a train station—for his "personal pork barrel." "Why did the National Park Service spend $2.5 million turning a railroad station into a visitor center for a town with a population of eight?" The compelling reason—Senator Robert C. Byrd, "who glides past on Amtrak's Cardinal Limited from time to time, head-

ing to and from his home in Sophia, a few miles south." But Byrd did not ride that train, and that train did not go to that town. Moreover, the Interior Department recommended the project; it was not "slipped" into other legislation "unwanted," as the article claimed. When the reporter was questioned, he replied with disgust, "Look, everyone knows that this is the way the world works in Washington. What's the big deal?" Indeed, this is the way things work in Washington sometimes, but apparently not this time. This article, which prompted editorials in newspapers across the country, reinforced readers' cynicism.[200]

Emphasizing the negative conveys the impression that the individuals involved are unworthy of the office they seek or the one they hold. It ultimately conveys the impression that the political process itself is contemptible.[201]

Bias toward Issues

The relative lack of bias in the coverage of elections (except for the negative tone against all candidates) doesn't necessarily mean there is the same lack of bias in the coverage of issues. Because elections are highly visible and candidates are very sensitive about the coverage, the media take more care to be neutral for elections than for issues.

Domestic issues Empirical studies of the coverage of several domestic issues, including abortion, school busing, and nuclear power, indicate a tilt toward the liberal positions.[202] Anecdotal reports of the coverage of other domestic issues, such as gay rights, gun control, capital punishment, the environment, and homelessness, also suggest some bias toward the left.[203]

At the same time, the media exaggerate crimes, drugs, and other urban pathologies that stereotype African Americans and, to a lesser extent, Hispanics.[204] In this respect, they don't reflect a bias toward the left.

Popular television programs, movies, and records often promote social ideas or trends characterized as liberal, such as diversity, multiculturalism, acceptance of racial minorities, acceptance of casual sex, and disparagement of traditional religion. Conservative Christians, especially, feel that their beliefs are under daily attack by the "liberal media." (However, television programs and movies also glorify violence and guns—and since 9/11, torture of suspected terrorists[205]—which don't reflect liberal values. Moreover, television programs and movies rarely have their female characters choose an abortion when they face an unwanted pregnancy.[206]) These programs might have as much or even more effect on individuals' views than the news does. But this chapter focuses on the news media, not the entertainment media, which are beyond the scope of this text.

Although debates about bias revolve around liberalism and conservatism, perhaps the question actually should be reframed: does the coverage of domestic issues reflect class bias? An examination of the debate over the North American Free Trade Agreement (NAFTA), drafted to ease trade

"But, what if we're attacked in the press?"

between American and Canadian and Mexican companies, showed more emphasis on the benefits of free trade than on the loss of jobs from the treaty. Thus the media reflected the views of businesses over those of workers.[207]

Analysts now suggest that for domestic issues the most significant bias is not liberal or conservative but upper-middle class over working class.[208] This bias usually favors the liberal positions on social issues and the conservative, or business, positions on economic issues.[209] This bias closely reflects the suburban origins and the college education and social class of most journalists. Most journalists are "unlikely to have any idea what it means to go without health insurance, to be unable to locate affordable housing, to have their children in underfunded and dilapidated schools, to have relatives in prison or on the front lines of the military, [or] to face the threat of severe poverty."[210] Thus, "media bias in our country is not to the left or to the right, but to the top."[211]

Foreign issues   The bias in the coverage of foreign issues is quite different from that of domestic issues. The mainstream media toe the government line, at least until it becomes obvious that the official policy isn't working.[212] This is often the conservative position.[213]

During the Cold War, this meant harsh attacks on not only the Soviet Union but also on leftist Latin American regimes.[214] During the Persian Gulf War, this meant jingoistic coverage and unquestioning acceptance of administration claims.[215] Even during the Vietnam War, which is often cited as an example of harsh criticism of governmental policies, the media in fact offered blindly positive coverage for many years and then relatively restrained criticism near the end of the war.[216]

This bias, reflecting governmental policy, was apparent after the 2001 terrorist attacks. The media not only quoted the president and other officials extensively, as would be expected, but they also adopted the mindset and language of administration officials. An analysis of the editorials of twenty metropolitan newspapers showed that they echoed the president's rhetoric, magnifying our feelings of fear and portraying a conflict between values decreed by God and evil perpetrated by the terrorists and their supporters. Like the president, the newspapers emphasized urgent action over debate and national unity over dissent.[217] The television networks also followed the administration, featuring patriotic logos and melodramatic music.

Some media went further. Two newspapers fired columnists who criticized the president's delayed return to the Capitol on September 11, and cable systems yanked *Politically Incorrect*, whose host Bill Maher questioned the president's use of the word *cowardly* to refer to the terrorists.[218] CNN's head warned the staff, "If you get on the wrong side of public opinion, you are going to get into trouble."[219] The patriotic fervor diminished media coverage and therefore public awareness of important matters, such as Arab opinion, the conflict between the Israelis and the Palestinians, and the disagreements among the countries fighting terrorism.[220]

This bias was also evident in coverage of the Iraq War. In the run-up to the war, the sources cited in television news were overwhelmingly prowar—according to one study, 71 percent were prowar, whereas only 3 percent were antiwar[221]—and the pundits appearing on television talk shows were heavily prowar as well. Although there were snippets of doubt and clips of protests on television newscasts, there was no substantive debate.[222]

The media conveyed, without examination, officials' assertions that there was a link between Saddam Hussein and 9/11. They also conveyed, without examination, officials' assertions that Iraq possessed weapons of mass destruction—biological, chemical, and nuclear weapons. For many people, these became primary justifications for the war. (See the box "What You Watch Affects What You Believe"). Yet no evidence of either claim has been found (at least as of fall, 2008).

During the war, the networks used special music, graphics, and promotions to dramatize American patriotism and evoke viewers' emotions. Fox and MSNBC used the administration's moniker for the war, "Operation Iraqi Freedom," and most networks used the administration's term *coalition forces,* thus endorsing the administration's claim that there was a broad coalition. (In fact, the war was fought by troops from the United States, with some troops from Great Britain, fewer troops from South Korea, Italy, and Poland, and token representation from other countries.) CNN, with audiences around the globe, used two news teams to cover the war. One team, beamed to the United States, was overtly prowar; the other team, beamed to the rest of the world, was more neutral.[223] And, for good measure, MSNBC removed Phil Donohue from his afternoon show out of fear that his liberal sensibilities would offend conservative viewers during wartime.[224]

Throughout the war, the American media, compared with European and Middle Eastern media, sanitized the combat. They were slow to report negative news[225] and reluctant to depict the blood and gore—the reality of war—in both words and pictures of both Americans and Iraqis.[226] For example, the media reported that U.S. bombers were "softening up" Iraqi defenses. The Air Force commander was amused by the phrase. "We're not softening them up," he said. "We're killing them."[227] When the behavior by American soldiers at Baghdad's Abu Ghraib prison was disclosed, the worst abuses weren't covered by many news organizations.[228] The media sanitized the coverage because "the dirty little secret of much war 'news' is that much of the audience wants to entrance itself into emotional surrender, and news officials want to elicit precisely that surrender."[229] The media didn't offer grimmer reports and starker photographs until the insurgency and the lack of real security in Iraq became apparent.

WHAT YOU WATCH AFFECTS WHAT YOU BELIEVE

A majority of Americans have had serious misperceptions about important questions relating to the Iraq War, according to a study based on a series of seven polls spanning nine months. Respondents were asked whether world public opinion favored the United States going to war, whether there was clear evidence that Saddam Hussein was working with al-Qaeda, and whether weapons of mass destruction were found during the war. (Responses to the second and third questions are shown in Figure 2.) Respondents were asked what their primary source of news is and how often they watch, listen to, or read this source.

Respondents' misperceptions varied according to the media they followed. Those who watched Fox had the most misperceptions, whereas those who watched public television or listened to public radio had the fewest.[1] The misperceptions were not due to people's paying little attention to the news. Just the opposite: those who watched Fox more often had more misperceptions than those who watched it less often.

The results not only suggest biased or superficial coverage by some media more than others, but the results also have policy implications. Respondents' misperceptions were related to their support for the war. Those with the most misperceptions expressed the most support for the war.

Remarkably, as late as 2006, 50 percent of all Americans still believed that Iraq had weapons of mass destruction right before the war.[2]

| Figure 2 | Misperceptions and Their Origins |

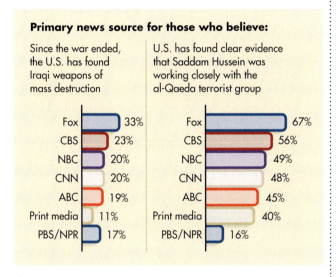

Primary news source for those who believe:

Since the war ended, the U.S. has found Iraqi weapons of mass destruction		U.S. has found clear evidence that Saddam Hussein was working closely with the al-Qaeda terrorist group	
Fox	33%	Fox	67%
CBS	23%	CBS	56%
NBC	20%	NBC	49%
CNN	20%	CNN	48%
ABC	19%	ABC	45%
Print media	11%	Print media	40%
PBS/NPR	17%	PBS/NPR	16%

SOURCE: Program on International Policy at the University of Maryland and Knowledge Networks. Poll of 3334 adults, conducted January–September 2003, with a margin of error of 1.7 percent (www.knowledgenetworks.com/ganp).

[1]Researchers tried to control for the possibility that people presort themselves according to ideology by comparing the same demographic groups for each source and also by comparing similar political groups—for example, they compared people who planned to vote for Bush in 2004 and watched Fox with people who planned to vote for Bush but followed other media.

[2]Charles J. Hanley, "Half of Americans Still Believe WMD Claims, Polls Show," *Lincoln Journal Star,* August 9, 2006, 1A.

For some time, the media were cowed by the power of the administration as well as by the demands of the public. Officials insinuated that any criticism, even questioning, by reporters was unpatriotic. Officials also issued veiled threats to reporters. The White House press secretary remarked, "People had better watch what they say."[230] Another official ominously warned a reporter that his name was on "a list," presumably of disloyal journalists who would be watched and, perhaps, dealt with.[231] The administration also threatened to deny access to reporters who displeased officials. This would mean no interviews, no tips or leaks, no invitations to special events, and no seats on the plane for presidential trips. Because access is all important, this would make it difficult for reporters to do their jobs. The result was a chilling effect on reporters, editors, and executives.[232] So most media, including supposedly "liberal newspapers" such as the *New York Times* and the *Washington Post*, were little more than stenographers, writing down and passing on administration statements without serious questioning. In the run-up to the war, the *Post* had 140 front-page articles making the administration's case for the war and only a handful questioning the administration's claims.[233] Later, the *Post* acknowledged that its reporting before the war and early in the war was "strikingly one-sided at times."[234] (Ironically, Comedy Central's fake newscasts left a more accurate impression than the major networks' newscasts did.)[235]

As the aftermath of the invasion revealed serious flaws in U.S. policy, many media became more critical. The *Times* apologized for its lack of scrutiny and skepticism of administration claims.[236] Its apology prompted a letter to the editor that could have been sent to most American news organizations:

I've followed all the stories and the "spin" to create a case for war from the beginning. . . . As a university student, I sat through it and asked questions as cabinet members made their case for war. In the sixteen months leading up to my activation to fight in Iraq as a tank platoon commander, I felt that this spin was an effort to find a magic button of support with the citizenry. . . .

So off I went, to lead my men on this quest. We fought and died holding up the soldiers' end of the democratic bargain. I lived with many of the young men fighting and dying who had such blind faith in our system of government. They felt it was just right to do what we were doing, even though many of them could not explain or justify why.

So on this Memorial Day weekend, as I sit and think about what I've done, the people who have been hurt, the future of this ongoing tragedy, I come to this conclusion: Shame on you.[237]

The mainstream media reflect the government line on foreign policy because they rely on government officials as their sources for most news.[238] They fear losing access to these officials. This means that their stories will bear officials' imprint. It also means that their stories will revolve around debates among officials—what "he said" versus what "she said." When there is little dissent within the government, as in the run-up to the Iraq War, there is little coverage of opposing views by the media, even if there are alternative views in our society.[239] Journalists seem flummoxed when they can't frame an issue as a debate between opposing groups of officials.

When the media try to investigate government policies rather than simply repeat what they've been told by government officials, reporters can face a real struggle. See the box "Prying Loose Those Documents."

Perceptions of Bias

We've seen that in the mainstream media there is minimal bias in favor of particular candidates or parties in elections, and there is some liberal bias in the coverage of social issues, some conservative bias in the coverage of economic issues, and often conservative bias in the coverage of foreign policy. Overall, however, there is far less political bias than many people believe. In particular, there is far less liberal bias than many conservatives believe.[240] Why do so many people perceive so much bias?

As noted earlier, there is some negative bias against all candidates and officials. People sense this bias against the candidates or officials on their side but don't see it against the candidates or officials on the other side. In addition, people hear aides to the candidates or officials complain about the media without realizing that the aides are simply "working the refs" rather than sincerely lodging a complaint.[241] Also, people hear the steady drumbeat from interest groups and talk shows that the media are biased against their side. Eventually, they come to believe it. They don't realize that the leaders of interest groups and hosts of talk shows are just trying to get people riled up so they will join

BEHIND THE SCENES
PRYING LOOSE THOSE DOCUMENTS

To uncover the information about retired officers who served as military analysts for television networks, described in the box "'Independent' Military Analysts" earlier in the chapter, the *New York Times* reporter filed a request for the information under the Freedom of Information Act (which will be described in Chapter 12), as the law allows. He asked for expedited handling, as the law also allows. His request was denied. He appealed, but four months later his appeal was denied. He continued to ask for the information, and two months later he received a small portion of what he requested. After more letters and phone calls, he received a larger portion but with many long passages blacked out. These passages didn't include national security secrets, and he pressed for the complete transcripts. The Pentagon continued to stonewall, so the *Times* sued. In federal court, the Pentagon agreed to a series of deadlines to turn over the information, but as the weeks went by it missed the deadlines and pleaded for more extensions. In a hearing, the judge lost patience and accused the officials of playing "cute." Threatening them with contempt citations (which can result in fines or even jail), he stated, "I am not used to having to do this five or six times." By now, two years had elapsed since the reporter requested the information and almost six months had passed since the judge ordered the administration to turn over the information. The threat of contempt citations, however, prompted the Pentagon to hand over more pages, although the officials still withheld some pages, and the lawsuit continued.

This is one reason why the media do little investigative reporting. Most news organizations could not or at least would not devote the time and money—lawsuits are especially costly. Government officials recognize these constraints and refuse to disclose the information, even when the law obligates them to do so. They hope to discourage all but the most persistent and best financed news organizations.

Source: Clark Hoyt, "Information That Doesn't Come Freely," *New York Times*, May 11, 2008, WK 12.

the group, make a contribution, subscribe to a magazine, or listen to the show. One influential conservative downplayed liberal bias in an interview but at the same time was claiming liberal bias in subscription pitches for his magazine.[242]

Karl Rove, top aide to President Bush, also dismissed the idea of liberal bias in the media.[243] Given the coverage of Clinton's presidency, especially the Whitewater investigation and the impeachment effort, or Bush's presidency, especially after the terrorist attacks and during the first years of the Iraq War, it's hard to insist that the media demonstrate an overall liberal bias.[244]

Yet many conservatives assume the existence of liberal bias. Studies show that strong partisans with strong views perceive more bias than average people.[245] When strong partisans on opposite sides evaluate the same stories in the same media, both groups see bias against their side, even when the stories are balanced.[246] Certain that their side is correct, they consider coverage that is actually balanced as slanted because it gives their opponents more credence than their opponents deserve. And although these partisans say that biased coverage will not affect them, they fear it will affect others who are less aware or astute.[247] When strong partisans evaluate coverage that is clearly biased toward their side, they see no bias or less bias than average people do.[248] They consider this coverage fair, because in their eyes it reports the "truth."

Even if people's perceptions are inaccurate reflections of media coverage, their perceptions determine which newscasts they will watch. As a result of conservatives' criticism over the years, some mainstream media have become cowed. CNN has ordered producers to include more conservatives than liberals in their stories.[249] During the 2004 presidential campaign, CBS twice postponed a documentary on the faulty intelligence about Iraq's purported weapons of mass destruction. The network said that it would show the documentary after the election, when the network couldn't be accused of trying to affect the election's outcome.[250]

Commercial Bias

Although the public dwells on charges of political bias, **commercial bias** is far more pervasive and important in understanding media coverage of politics. As Ted Koppel, former anchor of ABC's *Nightline*, notes, "The accusation that [the] news has a political agenda misses the point. Right now, the main agenda is to give the people what they want. It is not partisanship but profitability that shapes what you see."[251]

Reasons for Commercial Bias

Traditionally, the mainstream media believed they had a "public trust" to meet journalistic standards and provide important news. Newspapers made less money than other businesses, and television news divisions lost money every year. When *60 Minutes* first aired, the head of CBS told the creator of the show, "Make us proud."[252] The show became a hit, and in its first decade it made so much profit—more than the Chrysler Corporation did during the same years[253]—that the executives started telling the producers, "Make us money!"[254] At the same time, television newscasts became more popular and even profitable. This transformation of the news from an economic backwater to a profit stream has had a huge impact on the major media.

As private businesses, American media, except for public broadcasting, are run for a profit. The larger their audience, the more they can charge for their advertising. An increase or decrease of 1 percent in the ratings of a television news program in New York City, for example, can mean a difference of $5 million in advertising for the year.[255] NBC's news division generates 40 to 50 percent of NBC's overall profit, with its entertainment and sports divisions dividing the rest.[256] Local stations' news programs also provide 40 to 50 percent of the stations' overall profit.[257]

With chains and conglomerates taking over most media, the pressure to make a large profit has escalated. In the 1970s, big-city newspapers expected to make a 7 or 8 percent profit; today, chains and conglomerates expect these papers to make a 20 to 30 percent profit.[258] Corporate executives worry that financial analysts will consider their companies a poor investment and mutual fund managers will refuse to buy or keep their stock if their earnings fall below those available "from investments anywhere else in the financial universe, from a shirt factory in Thailand to the latest Internet start-up."[259]

The pressure to make a profit and the need to attract an audience shape the media's presentation of the news and lead to commercial bias. Sometimes this means that the media deliberately print or broadcast what their advertisers want. CBS bowed to demands by Procter & Gamble that it drop episodes of *Family Law* dealing with gun ownership, capital punishment, interfaith marriage, and abortion.[260] Sometimes the media censor themselves. In 2004, VH1 and MTV pulled clips of, and refused to run ads for, the documentary *Super Size Me*, which shows what happened to a guy who ate every meal at McDonald's for a month. They feared losing advertising from fast-food restaurants.[261]

Usually, though, commercial bias means that the media print or broadcast what the public wants, which is to say what the public finds entertaining. (See box "Color and the Clicker.") This creates a "conflict between being an honest reporter and being a member of show business," a network correspondent confessed, "and that conflict is with me every day."[262] When Dan Rather was asked why CBS devoted time to the demolition of O. J. Simpson's house two years after his trial, Rather answered, "Fear. . . . The fear that if we don't do it, somebody else will, and when they do it, they will get a few more readers, a few more listeners, a few more viewers than we do. The result is the 'Hollywoodization of the news.'"[263]

american diversity | Color and the Clicker

Television news features African Americans in "lights-and-sirens" stories about crimes and drugs and in other stories about urban pathologies, such as single parenthood, that reinforce negative stereotypes.[1] However, television news shuns African Americans in other contexts—not just in the newscasts that focus on government officials but also in the newsmagazines, such as *Dateline, 20/20, 60 Minutes,* and *48 Hours,* that air human dramas.[2]

A network staff member lamented, "Can't we do a story about day-care centers and have a black day-care owner . . . ? Why can't they

be regular, normal people doing regular, normal things that aren't just associated with their ethnic backgrounds? It makes me sick."[3]

A producer working on a story about a mental disability was searching for a family who had a child with that disability. "I found a great, great upper-middle-class family in Miami, but they were black. I was told . . . : 'Find another family.'" Many network staff members have had similar experiences.

"It's a subtle thing," said one. "A story involving blacks takes longer to get approved. And if it is approved, chances are that it will sit on the shelf a long time before

it gets on the air. No one ever says anything. The message gets through."

Sometimes it's not so subtle. Staffers were told by executives that a particular story was "not a good story for us" or that it would "not have broad appeal in the Midwest and in the South." Instead, they were told to feature "families with lots of blond-haired, blue-eyed children."[4]

One reporter observed, "They whisper it, like cancer: 'Is she white?'"

"'Yeah, she's white.'"

"'Are you sure?'"

The dilemma is most marked for television. Many people who watch news on television are not interested in politics; a majority, in fact, say that newscasts devote too much time to politics.[264] Some watch newscasts because they were watching another program before the news, others because they were planning to watch another program after the news. Networks feel pressure "to hook them and keep them."[265] Therefore, networks try to make the everyday world of news seem as exciting as the make-believe world depicted in their entertainment programs. One network instructed its staff, "Every news story should, without any sacrifice of probity or responsibility, display the attributes of fiction, of drama. It should have structure and conflict, problem and denouement, rising action and falling action, a beginning, a middle, and an end."[266] As one executive says, television news is "**infotainment**."[267]

Consequences of Commercial Bias

The media's commercial bias has important consequences. One is to sensationalize the news. The anthrax infections that occurred after the terrorist attacks in 2001 deserved our full attention, but the media would not let up. Even after the initial flurry of reports, they ran one overwrought piece after another. *Time* magazine featured families who bought gas masks. The *Washington Post* wrote that America is "on the verge" of "public hysteria."[268] In fact, few people panicked. In polls, large majorities expressed concern but not

fear. Yet the media realized that generating fear would force people to pay attention to the news.

Another consequence of commercial bias is to feature human interest over serious news. In 2005, the three main television networks devoted a total of 84 minutes to Michael Jackson's trial for child molesting but only 18 minutes to the massive genocide in Darfur, Sudan.[269] In 2006, *Time* magazine paid a reported $4 million for photos of Brad Pitt and Angelina Jolie's baby but let go two top-notch investigative reporters because the magazine couldn't afford them any longer.[270]

In 2007, according to a search of news sources, 985 articles included the words "Britney" and "underwear."[271]

The media's tendencies to sensationalize the news and to feature human interest over serious news lead to greater emphasis on scandal, sex, and crime. During President Clinton's terms, the media provided saturation coverage of the Whitewater scandal[272] and various other scandals, although a succession of special prosecutors could find nothing more damning than that the president lied about having sexual relations with a White House intern named Monica Lewinsky.[273]

The media plunged into the affair with abandon.[274] The *Los Angeles Times* assigned twenty-six reporters to examine Lewinsky's life, interviewing babysitters and kindergarten classmates.[275] The networks even interviewed one person who had eaten lunch with her three years earlier. The public

"'Well, it says they are from Slovakian descent; I'm assuming.'"

"'Well, go out and check.'"

A producer on an evening newscast, working on a health series, found a story about a doctor who encouraged women to get mammograms. The doctor hauled her equipment to beauty parlors where she could test the women conveniently. But when the executive producer saw the piece, he exclaimed, "You didn't tell me that the doctor was black . . . that the people were black!" And he spiked the story.

This pattern is pervasive. A senior executive at a major network confessed, "It's our dirty little secret."

The reason? Research shows the demographic makeup of the audience for every program, and minute-by-minute ratings reveal which stories attract and keep an audience. Many middle-class whites don't want to watch stories about either lower-class people or racial minorities. When such stories come on, these viewers click to another channel. The networks, under pressure to boast the most viewers to generate the most profits for their corporate owners, cater to the tastes of middle-class whites—the largest segment of the audience.

What appears to be racial bias by the networks is actually commercial bias, just as we have seen that what appears to be political bias by the media is usually commercial bias. But the commercial bias here has racial implications, just as the commercial bias elsewhere has political implications.

As a result, television news, which could forge understanding between the races by showing sympathetic people of all colors facing common challenges, makes little effort to do so. Instead, it accepts the subtle racism of those white viewers who won't watch the same story if it portrays black folks rather than white folks.

[1] Jeff Cohen, "Racial Tension," *Brill's Content*, October 1999, 54.
[2] The record of *60 Minutes* is not as bad as the others, perhaps because *60 Minutes* is the only one without prime-time competition. Robert Schmidt, "Airing Race," *Brill's Content*, October 2000, 145.
[3] Av Westin, "The Color of Rating," *Brill's Content*, April 2001, 84. Quotations are from this article, unless otherwise noted.
[4] Schmidt, "Airing Race," 114–115.

was offered breathless reports about phone sex, the president's cigar as a sex toy, and the intern's dress with a semen stain. There was tittering about the "distinguishing characteristics" of the president's genitals—and speculation about how these would be proved or disproved in court.

Although the national media cover crime extensively, the local media cover it even more fully. Local television news is, in Ralph Nader's words, "something that jerks your head up every ten seconds, whether that is shootings, robberies, sports showdowns, or dramatic weather forecasts."[276] Media consultants advise local stations how to attract the largest audience and make the most money for their chain or conglomerate.[277] The saying "If it bleeds, it leads" expresses, tongue in cheek, many stations' programming philosophy. Thus crime coverage fills one-third of local newscasts.[278] A week before one presidential election, local stations in Columbus, Ohio, devoted more than twice as much time to various crimes than to the election, although the outcome in the state, and in the nation, was in doubt.[279] One station, however, did find time for an undercover investigation of a topless car wash.

A jaded reporter put it bluntly: "It doesn't matter what kind of swill you set in front of the public. As long as it's got enough sex and violence in it, they'll slurp it up."[280] (Even so, American stations don't go as far as the Bulgarian program *The Naked Truth*, which had women disrobe as they read the news.)

Another consequence of commercial bias is to highlight conflict. Stories about conflict provide drama. Reporters, one admits, are "fight promoters" rather than consensus builders.[281] So reporters frame issues as struggles between opposite camps. After the murderous rampage at Columbine High School in Littleton, Colorado, the media posed the question, Was the incident caused by the availability of guns in our society *or* by the glorification of violence in the media? In this moronic debate, the media prodded people to choose sides, as though the cause had to be one *or* the other rather than a combination of the two or something else entirely.

Sometimes this practice is taken to the extreme. Some stories about Holocaust survivors include bizarre statements by Holocaust deniers claiming that the Nazis didn't have a plan to exterminate European Jews or that Hitler wasn't aware of the effort or that the Germans didn't kill many Jews. The stories present these absurd statements as though they constitute an opposing opinion entitled to a public hearing.[282] With their fixation on controversy, the media allow themselves to be manipulated by ignorant or unscrupulous people. In the process, they promote confusion among those people who don't know any better.

In highlighting conflict, the media frame issues as though they have two—only two—sides, which are polar opposites. As one reporter admits, "the middle ground, the sensible center, is dismissed as too squishy, too dull, too likely to send the audience channel surfing."[283]

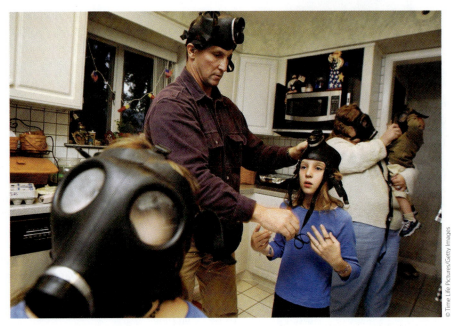

The media frenzy over anthrax prompted some families, like this one in Chicago, to buy gas masks.

DEMOCRACY?

In highlighting conflict and framing issues as though they are debates between two polar opposites, the media polarize the public. What are the implications for a democracy? What are the consequences for the efforts by politicians and parties to find common ground? To forge compromises?

Another consequence of commercial bias is to use a **game orientation** in reporting about competing candidates, officials, or parties.[284] The assumption is that politics is a game and politicians, whether candidates campaigning for election or officials performing in office, are the players. The corollary to the assumption is that the players are self-centered and self-interested. They are seeking victory for themselves and defeat for their opponents, and they are relatively unconcerned about the consequences of their proposals or of government's policies. With this orientation, reporters spotlight politicians' strategies and tactics, and they slight the substance and impact of politicians' proposals and policies.

The game orientation appeals to journalists because it generates human interest. It offers new story lines as new information comes to light, much like a board game where "chance" cards inject unexpected scenarios and alter the players' moves and the game's outcomes. This orientation also appeals to journalists because it is easy and relatively free from charges of partisan or ideological bias. (Stories emphasize which contestants are winning, not which ones should win or what consequences might result.) If journalists seriously examined policies and proposals instead of using the game orientation, they would be less able to offer human interest and would be more vulnerable to charges of bias.

The game orientation attracts an audience, but it breeds more cynicism. It creates the impression that politics is just a game, not an essential activity for a democratic society; that politicians are just the players, not our representatives; that politicians act just in their self-interest, not in the public interest; and that politicians' goal is just to beat others, not to make good public policy.

For elections, the game orientation results in what is called **horse race coverage**, with "front-runners," "dark horses," and "also-rans." Although the race was a staple of journalism even in the nineteenth century,[285] the proportion of election coverage focusing on the race has increased in recent decades.[286]

Today, horse race coverage dominates election reporting. As much as two-thirds of the reporting by newspapers, television networks, and websites features the horse race, and much of the remaining reporting features the candidates' strategies. Far less reporting examines the candidates' positions or proposals.[287]

The quintessential feature of horse race coverage—reporting of candidates' poll standings—has increased greatly. Not only do the media report the results of polls taken by commercial organizations but they also conduct polls themselves.[288] Nowadays, coverage of polls takes more space than coverage of candidates' speeches, and it usually appears as the lead or next-to-lead story.[289]

Even after elections, the game orientation continues. When President Clinton proposed a plan to overhaul the welfare system, all major newspapers focused on the political implications for his reelection; few even explained the plan, let alone its substantive implications.[290]

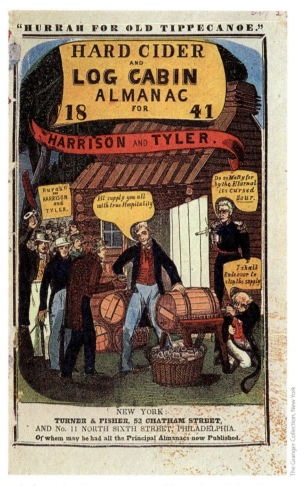

Long before television cameras, candidates shaped their image. In 1840, William Henry Harrison campaigned as the log cabin and hard cider candidate—a common man—even though his father was a wealthy planter, a Virginia governor, and a signer of the Declaration of Independence. To underscore his purported origins, Harrison gave Indian war whoops at rallies.

DEMOCRACY?

What are the consequences of the game orientation and horse race coverage for our elections? Do you think that these practices generate more interest and participation in the campaign? Or do you think that they leave the voters less informed and able to cast knowledgeable votes?

Commercial bias in the media leads to additional consequences for television specifically. One is to emphasize events, or those parts of events, that have visual interest. The networks have people whose job it is to evaluate all film for visual appeal. Producers seek the events that promise the most action, camera operators shoot the parts of the events with the most action, and editors select the portions of the film with the most action.[291] Television thus focuses on disasters and protests far more than their occurrence justifies, and it displays the interesting surface rather than the underlying substance of these events—for example, the protest rather than the cause of the anger.

Another consequence of commercial bias for television is to cover the news very briefly. A half-hour newscast has only 19 minutes without commercials. In that time, the networks broadcast only a third as many words as the *New York Times* prints on its front page alone. Although cable television has ample time, it follows this format, too, endlessly repeating the same stories without adding new information.[292]

Television stories are short—about 1 minute each—because the networks think viewers' attention spans are short. Indeed, a survey found that a majority of eighteen- to thirty-four-year-olds with remote controls typically watch more than one show at one time.[293] Therefore, the networks don't allow leaders or experts to explain their thoughts about events or policies. Instead, the networks take sound bites to illustrate what was said. Although their correspondents try to explain the events or policies, they have little time to do so.

A network correspondent was asked what went through his mind when he signed off each night. "Good night, dear viewer," he said. "I only hope you read the *New York Times* in the morning."[294]

When the chairman of the board of one network, in conversation with a former Reagan aide, asked what the networks could do to provide more responsible reporting, the aide answered, "Easy, . . . just eliminate ratings for news. You claim that news is not the same as entertainment. So why do you need ratings?" The chairman sighed, "Well, that's our big money-maker, the news."[295] The networks use ratings to show potential advertisers how many people watch the news and whether their audience is greater than their competitors'. A former executive concluded, "Because television can make so much money doing its worst, it often can't afford to do its best."[296]

Overall, commercial bias in the media results in no coverage or superficial coverage of many important stories. This, more than any political bias, makes it difficult for citizens, particularly those who rely on television, to become well informed. During the year before the September 11 terrorist attacks, al-Qaeda was mentioned only once on the networks' evening newscasts.[297] However, seven months before the airplane hijackings, a report predicting a "catastrophic attack" was issued by a government commission. A statement warning that Osama bin Laden's network was the "most immediate and serious threat" facing the country was made by the CIA director at a Senate hearing. Their dire predictions generated little interest among the media. Following the terrorist attacks and during the first years of the Iraq War, the media paid more attention to foreign affairs. In recent years, however, the media have scaled back their coverage of foreign affairs, despite two wars—in Iraq and in Afghanistan—the globalization of our economy, and our dependence on foreign oil. A survey of newspaper editors in 2008 found that almost two-thirds of their papers publish less international news than they did three years before.[298] In the first half of 2008, CBS News devoted just

8 minutes to the war in Afghanistan, though the war was deteriorating and more Americans were dying there than in Iraq during these months. The chief foreign correspondent for CBS, who finds it difficult to get her stories on the air, remarked, "If I were to watch the news that you hear . . . in the United States, I would just blow my brains out because it would drive me nuts."[299]

DEMOCRACY?

This chapter is premised on the assumption that it's important for citizens in a democracy, which entails self-government, to be informed about candidates and issues before voting. Is this assumption, which comes from classical democratic theory, correct in a mass society with different educational levels and individual interests? People aren't required to understand architecture before entering a building or aeronautics before flying in a plane or technology before using a computer. Should they be expected to understand, say, the politics of the Middle East before casting a vote? Should they be informed? Why or why not?

Conclusion: Are the Media Responsive?

To make a profit, the media have to be responsive to the people. They present the news they think the people want. Because they believe the majority desire entertainment, or at least diversion, rather than education, they structure the news toward this goal.[300] For the majority who want entertainment, national and local television and radio provide it. For the minority who want education, the better newspapers and magazines provide it. Public radio, with its morning and evening newscasts, and public television, with its nightly newscast, also provide quality coverage. In addition, Internet websites provide news on demand. The media offer something for everyone.

When officials or citizens get upset with the media, they pointedly ask, "Who elected you?" Journalists reply that the people—their readers or listeners or viewers—"elected" them by paying attention to their news columns or newscasts.

To say that the media are responsive, however, is not to say that they perform well. Giving the people what they want most is not necessarily serving the country best. "This business of giving people what they want is a dope pusher's argument," says a former president of NBC News. "News is something people don't know they're interested in until they hear about it. The job of a journalist is to take what's important and make it interesting."[301] Instead, most media offer superficial coverage of complex events, which leaves the public unable to understand these events and ultimately unable to force the government to be responsive.

Even though the media give the people what they want, the people criticize the media. Almost two-thirds tell pollsters that the media "don't get the facts straight."[302] Actually, the media usually do get the facts straight, but the nature of their reporting leads to this belief. The practice of objectivity—repeating what he said versus what she said without evaluating the truth of either—passes along false and misleading statements and confuses people rather than enlightens them.[303]

Other media practices also alienate the people from their government. The negative bias against all candidates and officials undermines them directly, and the game orientation undermines them subtly. The emphasis on conflict, though intriguing the public, polarizes and alienates the public.

The result of these practices may be to foster **media malaise** among the public.[304] This is a feeling of cynicism and distrust, perhaps even despair, toward government and officials. Indeed, according to a survey, the public is even more cynical than journalists themselves. Seventy-seven percent of the public gave government officials a low rating for honesty and ethics, whereas only 40 percent of the journalists did.[305] Most of the public believed that politicians could "never" be trusted to do the right thing. Yet the journalists saw the American political process as "a flawed but basically decent means of reconciling different points of view and solving collective problems."[306] They apparently report in a more cynical fashion than they actually feel because of the conventions of contemporary journalism. But the public, though deploring these practices, evidently sees them as reflections of reality. Thus cynical coverage by the press leads to even more cynical attitudes in the citizenry.[307]

The cynical attitudes have important implications for politics. They likely reduce satisfaction with candidates and officials and reduce turnout in elections. At the same time, they probably increase votes for "outsiders" who present themselves as "nonpoliticians."

In short, one writer observes, "the press, which in the long run cannot survive if people lose interest in politics, is acting as if its purpose was to guarantee that people are repelled by public life."[308]

The media's problems are compounded by a declining interest in politics and a decreasing number of people who read newspapers or watch newscasts (greater than the increasing number of people who search the Web for news). Although the public is better educated now than in the 1960s, it is less likely to follow the news and less able to answer questions about the government.[309] People under thirty-five especially reflect these trends. To retain their shrinking audience, many newspapers and newscasts have revamped their formats to replace hard news with soft features. If this process continues, it will have disturbing implications. Citizens who are not aware of the news or who do not understand it cannot fulfill their role in a democracy.

The problem is circular, as one political scientist points out:

> Because most members of the public know and care relatively little about government, they neither seek nor understand high-quality political reporting and analysis. With limited demand for first-rate journalism, most news organizations cannot afford to supply it, and because they do not supply it, most Americans have no practical source of the information necessary to become politically sophisticated.[310]

Individual journalists are aware of the shortcomings of contemporary journalism but pessimistic about their ability to improve the coverage. Because of commercial pressures, newsrooms across the country are experiencing low morale.[311]

Nevertheless, we should not lose sight of the fact that the American media, despite their shortcomings, provide very fast and relatively accurate reports of events. They also probe wrongdoing in society. Thus, they serve as a check on government in many situations. As a former government official noted, "Think how much chicanery dies on the drawing board when someone says, 'We'd better not do that; what if the press finds out?' "[312]

Key Terms

narrowcasting

broadcasting

blog

symbiotic relationship

adversarial relationship

leaks

scoops

presidential press conference

photo opportunity

sound bite

spin

fireside chats

practice of objectivity

political bias

commercial bias

infotainment

game orientation

horse race coverage

media malaise

Key Names

Franklin Roosevelt

Ronald Reagan

George W. Bush

Please visit our companion website at www.cengage.com/politicalscience/welch/uag12e or use CengageNOW for additional resources dealing with this chapter.

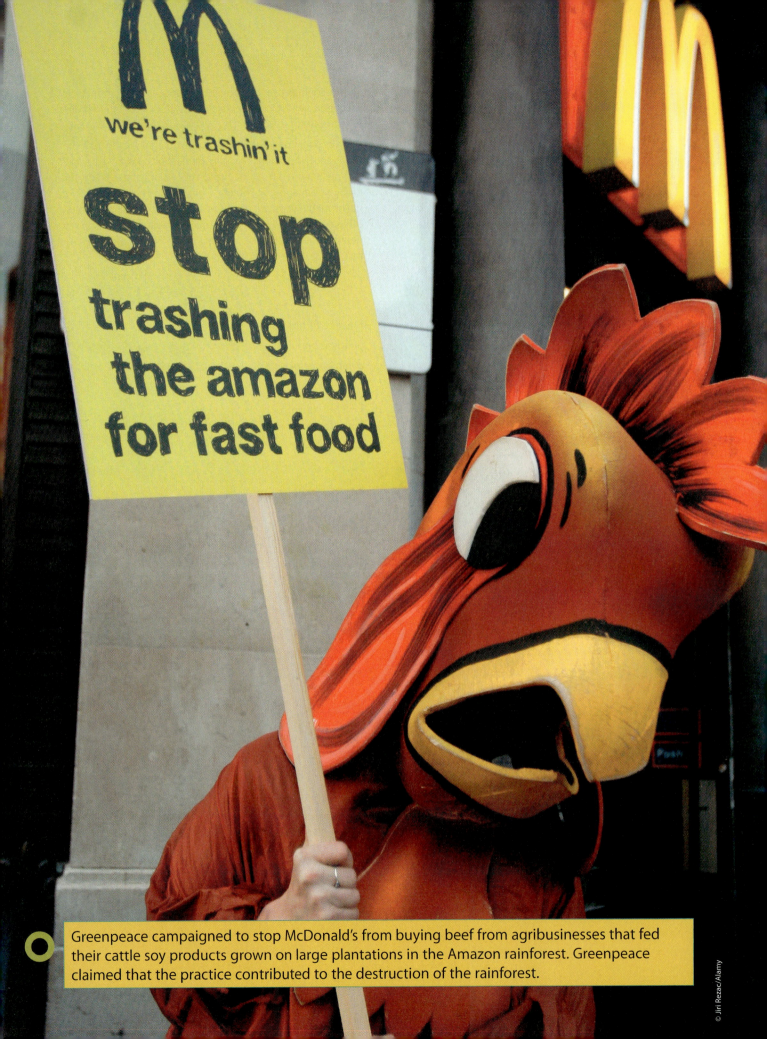

we're trashin' it

stop trashing the amazon for fast food

Greenpeace campaigned to stop McDonald's from buying beef from agribusinesses that fed their cattle soy products grown on large plantations in the Amazon rainforest. Greenpeace claimed that the practice contributed to the destruction of the rainforest.

Interest Groups

chapter 6

Talking Points

In Darfur, the western region of Sudan, a genocidal war has resulted in the death of two hundred thousand people, the raping or branding of tens of thousands of women and girls, and the displacement of two and a half million residents.[1] Many countries have called on the United Nations (UN) to dispatch forces to bring about an end to the racial, ethnic, and religious conflict, but the People's Republic of China has blocked action, apparently because of its considerable economic interests in the North African country. China, whose demand for oil is escalating, imports oil from Sudan and exports products, including weapons, to Sudan.[2]

To break the diplomatic stalemate and bring relief to the people of Darfur, Dream for Darfur, a Washington-based interest group with a staff of four, and with actress Mia Farrow as its public voice, spearheaded a movement in spring 2008 to pressure the Chinese government to change its position. As hosts of the 2008 Summer Olympic Games, the government hoped to show the world an image of a peaceful and progressive country. Government officials didn't want negative publicity swirling around the Games.

While some human rights groups pushed for an Olympic boycott, because of the government's policy toward Darfur or its policy toward Tibet, Dream for Darfur opposed a boycott. Rather, the group wanted to use the Games to pressure the government to change its policy. The strategy was to shine a spotlight on the policy before and during the Games.

The group adopted the slogan "Genocide Olympics," which it used in its press releases and emblazoned on members' T-shirts when they demonstrated at the Chinese Embassy in Washington.

The group urged corporate sponsors of the Olympics to express their concern to Chinese officials. Then the group graded the corporations on their response (www.dreamfordarfur.org/storage/dreamdarfur/documents/section_i_report_card_jj_revised.pdf). Adidas and Kodak received a B+ for writing the UN and allowing their letters to be made public. Johnson and Johnson and McDonalds received a C+ for taking private action, while other firms, including Microsoft, received a D or an F. The International Olympic Committee, which organized the Olympics, itself got a failing grade for "shirking the messy and difficult business of genocide."[3] Then the group demonstrated against some firms that received low grades, such as Coca-Cola, General Electric, Swatch, and Volkswagen. And it launched a *Turn Off/Tune In* campaign, asking television viewers to turn off any commercial broadcast by a failing corporation and tune in to a broadcast featuring Mia Farrow live from the Darfur refugee camps.

The group also asked prominent individuals who were helping to stage the Olympics to withdraw. Film maker Steven Spielberg did withdraw as a creative consultant for the opening ceremonies. Speilberg, director of the award-winning film *Schindler's List*, which portrayed the courage of a man who protected Polish Jews against the Nazis, said, "my conscience will not allow me to continue business as usual."[4]

Although a senior Chinese diplomat acknowledged that the Chinese government "will persuade [the Sudanese government] in a direct way to work with the international community and be more cooperative,"[5] Dream for Darfur's campaign didn't appear to have much effect. Although a group like Dream for Darfur can gain publicity for a cause, it is very difficult in the short term to change the actions of its own government, let alone a foreign government.

In the United States, everything from fruits to nuts is organized. From apple growers to filbert producers, nearly every interest has an organization to represent it. These organizations touch nearly every aspect of our lives; members of the American College of Obstetrics and Gynecology bring us into the world, and members of the National Funeral Directors Association usher us out.

Organizations that try to achieve their goals with government assistance are **interest groups.** Fruit and nut growers want government subsidies and protection from imported products; doctors want a rational system for reimbursement of health care costs; and funeral directors want to limit government regulation and oversight.

The effort of an interest group to influence government decisions is called **lobbying.** Lobbying may involve direct contact between a **lobbyist**—or consultant or lawyer, as they prefer to be called—and a government official, or it may involve indirect action, such as attempts to sway public opinion, which in turn influences government officials.

People organize and lobby to promote their interests and enhance their influence. "The modern government," one lobbyist observed, "is huge, pervasive, intrusive into everybody's life. If you just let things take their course and don't get involved in the game, you get trampled on."[6]

The Founders feared the harmful effects of interest groups, which they called "factions." The Founders, however, didn't attempt to limit the opportunity of people to organize and speak out. When the Bill of Rights ⭐ was adopted, the First Amendment protected the right to speak, assemble, and petition the government. James Madison's answer to the **"mischiefs of faction"** was fragmenting government through federalism, separation of powers, and checks and balances (as explained in Chapters 2 and 3). These elements of the Constitution make it difficult for a single group or small part of society to dominate or constantly prevail.

However, Americans today complain about interest groups, calling them "special interests" and insisting that Washington caters to them while ignoring the interests of average men and women. Some analysts agree that the constitutional checks don't prevent "special interests" from manipulating government contrary to the interests of the majority or the society as a whole.[7]

Do interest groups undermine the interests of average men and women? Or, do they enhance their influence, making government more responsive to them by providing a way to participate in the political process? These questions are explored in this chapter.

Formation of Interest Groups

America is a nation of joiners. As early as the 1830s, the Frenchman **Alexis de Tocqueville**, who traveled throughout the country, saw the tendency of Americans to form and join groups: "In no country in the world has the principle of association been more successfully used or applied to a greater multitude of objects than in America."[8] Even now, Americans are more likely than citizens of other countries to belong to groups.[9]

Why Interest Groups Form

Groups organize in the United States for a number of reasons. The freedom to speak, assemble, and petition government, guaranteed in the **First Amendment** ⭐, facilitates group formation. Without such freedom, only groups favored by government or those willing to risk punishment for speaking out against government would exist. The federal structure of government, with the national government, fifty state governments and thousands of local governments, also facilitates group formation. All have significant authority, so groups develop at each level to influence them. Groups also organize because the United States, compared with most countries, is racially, ethnically, and religiously diverse. This diversity gives rise to varying interests and conflicting views on public issues and consequently to groups representing them.[10]

In addition to these features, which distinguish the United States from other countries, groups form here and elsewhere because of social changes, economic pressures,

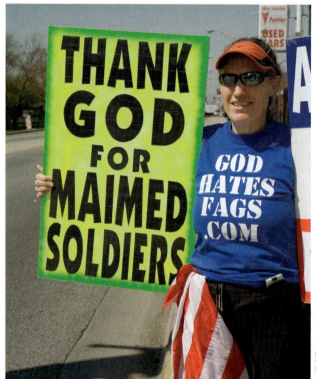

The First Amendment protects interest group speech, even repulsive speech such as this message from a church in Topeka, Kansas, whose members believe that God is punishing Americans for tolerating homosexual behavior.

and technological developments. When these disturb the status quo, groups form to cope with or benefit from the disturbances. These historical changes come in waves, so the formation of groups occurs in waves too, surging at some times, stable at other times.[11]

Social changes and economic pressures often lead to these surges. In the decades before the Civil War, debates over slavery led to the formation of abolitionist groups and, in response, to proslavery groups. In the decades after the Civil War, rapid industrialization led to the formation of trade unions and business associations. The greatest surge in group formation occurred between 1900 and 1920. Stimulated by the shocks of industrialization, urbanization, and immigration, the United States Chamber of Commerce, American Farm Bureau Federation, National Association for the Advancement of Colored People (NAACP), and countless others formed.[12]

Another great surge occurred in the 1960s and 1970s. The civil rights and antiwar movements created new groups, and their success spurred others representing racial minorities, women, consumers, the poor, the elderly, and the environment. Then the number of business groups surged in reaction to the success of consumer and environmental groups pushing government to regulate business.[13] In the two decades, the number of groups increased by 60 percent, and the number sending lobbyists to Washington doubled.[14]

Technological changes also accelerate group formation. In the 1960s and 1970s, computer-generated direct mail made it easier to recruit members and raise money. In the 1990s, the spread of personal computers and the growth of the Internet facilitated communication among people with an endless variety of narrow interests. The Internet is particularly useful for those wishing to organize citizen groups on a low budget.[15] It is also useful for groups outside the mainstream who wish to operate anonymously.

Through history, there's a pattern of action and reaction. When government passes a law, people who are adversely affected organize to get it changed.[16] In 1890, Yosemite National Park was established to preserve a spectacular stretch of the Sierra Nevada mountains in California. Cattle ranchers, who wanted the land for grazing, proposed that the park be reduced by half. This prompted preservationists to form the **Sierra Club,** today a major environmental group, to block the ranchers' proposal, which it did. This pattern of action and reaction leads to a continuous expansion of the number of interest groups.

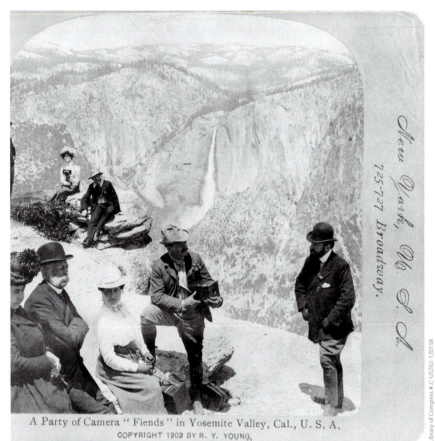

A Party of Camera " Fiends " in Yosemite Valley, Cal., U. S, A, COPYRIGHT 1902 BY R. Y. YOUNG,

Preservationists formed the Sierra Club to protect Yosemite National Park. After the park was created in 1890, cattle ranchers sought to reduce it by half.

DEMOCRACY?

Should the rights of individuals to form or join interest groups be restricted in a democracy? Should the right of interest groups to lobby be restricted?

Why People Join

Although individuals can enhance their political influence by joining an interest group, many groups find it difficult to attract new members as well as keep the members they have. Some people lack a sense of **political efficacy**—the belief that they can make a difference. Instead, they feel that "I'm just one person. What can I do?" Even the people who possess a sense of political efficacy may not join because they're unwilling to bear the costs, such as the dues or their time and effort. They assume that the group will succeed without them, so they let others do the work. But they still expect to share the benefits if the group reaches its goal.[17] For example, if a group prods the government to reduce water pollution in a local river or lake, everyone who uses the river or lake, not just the members of the group, will share the benefits of cleaner water. This is called the **free-rider problem.**[18] Why should individuals join the group if they don't have to?

To overcome this natural human resistance, groups offer a variety of benefits—psychological, social, and economic—to attract members. Groups offer the psychological satisfaction that comes from doing good. So they emphasize the worthiness of their cause and exaggerate the harm that will occur if their cause doesn't prevail. Groups also offer the social sense of belonging that comes from joining fellow citizens who share similar interests. They host meetings, dinners, and other activities to create feelings of solidarity among members. The National Rifle Association (**NRA**), which lobbies against gun control, provides safety and training classes for new shooters and sponsors competitions for the entire family. Groups also offer economic benefits. The American Association of Retired Persons (**AARP**) provides discounted drugs; health, home, and auto insurance; a motor club; a travel service; investment counseling; and several magazines. These services lure members and generate millions for the organization.

Some people join groups because they are coerced. In a majority of states, lawyers are required to join the bar association, and employees in certain trades are required to join the labor union.

Which People Join

Although America is a nation of joiners, many don't take advantage of the opportunity to join interest groups. Some are more inclined to do so than others. Those with more education and income are much more likely to belong. They are more interested in the news and government policies. They can afford membership dues, and they have the free time or flexible schedules that allow them to take part and the intellectual ability and social skills that enhance their participation. They also appear more attractive to many groups, and therefore are more apt to be recruited.

Men are somewhat more likely to join than women, and whites are somewhat more likely to join than blacks.[19] The elderly and middle-aged participate at higher rates than the young.

Have People Stopped Joining?

A widely publicized book, *Bowling Alone,* documents the decline in group membership in recent decades.[20] A variety of organizations, from labor unions to churches, PTAs, and bowling leagues, have experienced a decline.

More families are headed by a single parent or by two parents who work outside the home. Women's lives especially have changed over the past generation, with most women now in the paid workforce while still carrying the largest share of household and child-raising activities.

Women used to be the backbone of many local educational, religious, civic, and political groups, but they have far less time and energy to devote to these volunteer activities today than women did in the 1950s and 1960s. The entrance of women into the workforce also means that many men do more around the house and with their children than their fathers did. This too decreases the time and energy available for organized groups.

At the same time, technology, from television to computers, has enabled us to create little islands of our own at our homes; we don't need to join others for entertainment. Figuratively speaking, we still bowl, but we bowl alone.

DEMOCRACY?

What implications does the decline in traditional face-to-face groups have for democracy? Consider the roles that interest groups play in representing people, fostering discussions, fashioning compromises, and forging relationships and trust among citizens. Also consider the ways that interest groups conduct their meetings, elect their officers, and decide their positions on issues. How do these procedures reinforce democracy?

However, at the same time that formal membership in interest groups has decreased, membership in issue advocacy groups is increasing.[21] These groups solicit "members" who "join" by donating money—writing an occasional check to support the organization's leaders and activities.[22] These **checkbook members** contribute to the cause but don't interact, face to face, as members of the group. But, through the Internet, these members sometimes can communicate with each other. Interest groups have websites that provide information about the group and its causes, and some provide podcasts and streamed video. Many also host a forum for members to offer comments and suggestions and carry on "discussions" with others. In these ways, involved members can feel a part of the group beyond simply sending their checks. However, technology doesn't yet offer an effective way to reach workable compromises on difficult issues. Moreover, web discussions can be abusive and divisive because anonymity loosens restraints on behavior. If you don't have to interact on a personal basis with others, you don't have the same incentive to compromise or even to agree to disagree.

Types of Interest Groups

Interest groups come in various sizes and configurations. Some have large memberships, such as the American Federation of Labor–Congress of Industrial Organizations (AFL-CIO), a labor union with 9 million members. Others have small memberships, such as the Mushroom Growers Association with only 14. Some have no members at all. Corporations, which act as interest groups when they lobby government,[23] have managers and stockholders but no members.

Some interest groups are formally organized, with elected or appointed leaders, dues-paying members, regular meetings, and established bylaws. Others are loose-knit, with no leaders and few rules.

Thus, interest groups can be distinguished according to their membership and their organizational structure. They can also be distinguished by their goals, as explained below.

Private Interest Groups

Private interest groups seek economic benefits for their members or clients. Examples include business, labor, and agriculture groups.

Business

Business organizations are the most numerous and among the most powerful interest groups in Washington (see Figure 1). Much of politics is essentially the interaction between business and government.[24] Businesses seek to maximize profit, whereas government, at least sometimes, works to protect workers and consumers from the unfettered effects of profit-seeking businesses through regulation of employees' wages and working conditions, product safety, and monopolistic practices.

Today, however, there is less confrontation between business and government than in the past. The Republican Party has long favored business, and since the 1990s the Democratic Party, anxious to compete for campaign contributions, has often favored business too.[25] In a capitalist economy,

---

| **Figure 1** | **Contemporary Interest Groups** |

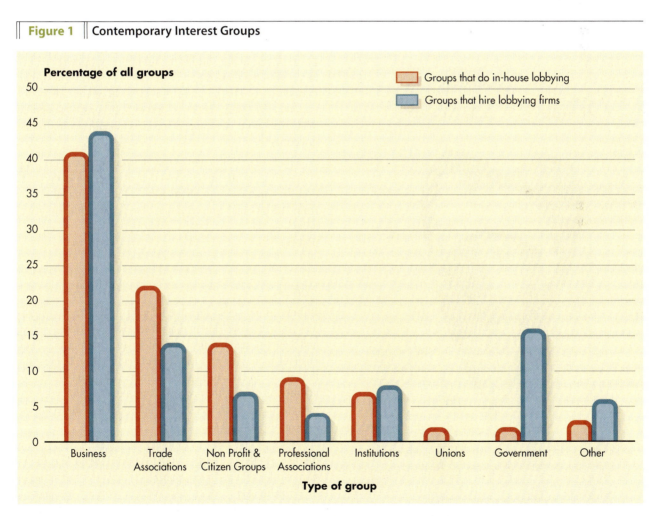

Business interests dominate the modern interest group system. This graph categorizes 2810 groups that maintain an office in Washington, D.C., and 6601 groups that lobby there.

NOTE: Data are based on filing reports with the government. Those identified as hiring lobbying firms represent only those with no in-house lobbyists.

SOURCE: Frank R. Baumgartner and Beth L. Leech, "Interest Niches and Policy Bandwagons: Patterns of Interest Group Involvement in National Politics." Journal of Politics 63 (November, 2001): 1191–1213.

there are powerful incentives and pressures for politicians of all political persuasions to accede to, rather than antagonize, business, which is so important to the nation's economic success.[26] If the economy falters, politicians get blamed. So business usually does well regardless of which party occupies the White House or dominates Congress.

Lobbying by the pharmaceutical industry, one of the most powerful in Washington, illustrates the influence of business. Well financed, the industry spends over $100 million a year in lobbying activities and campaign contributions, with the aim of reducing government regulation of drugs and preventing government bargaining for low prices for the drugs used by those elderly enrolled in government prescription drug programs.

The industry employs lobbyists in more than 130 lobbying and law firms, totaling 3000 lobbyists, a third of whom are former federal officials who served as members or staffers in Congress or as bureaucrats in government agencies involved in health care.[27] Bristol-Myers Squibb alone retains 15 firms with 57 lobbyists.

This postcard commemorates the death of a seventeen-year-old woman murdered while striking for recognition of her union, an eight-hour day, and extra pay for overtime and holidays.

Until the Democratic takeover of Congress in 2006, the industry supported Republican candidates and officeholders two to one.[28] In 2007, the industry split its contributions equally between the parties in an effort to purchase the sympathy of, and access to, Democrats while maintaining the support of Republicans.[29] Former Republican Representative Billy Tauzin, now president of the Pharmaceutical Research and Manufacturers of America (PhRMA), says the Democratic takeover means that "we just have more friends than we used to have. We are trying to find more."[30] The industry recruited Democratic lobbyists to represent it partly to prevent adversaries from hiring them instead.

The pharmaceutical industry did very well during George W. Bush's presidency. A big victory came with passage of the Medicare prescription drug bill, which subsidizes prescription drugs for senior citizens.[31] The industry and health maintenance organizations spent an estimated $14 million lobbying for the bill. The law not only guarantees huge sales for the companies but it includes some restrictions that enhance their profits. It forbids the government from negotiating with drug companies for lower prices, and it forbids the reimporting of drugs manufactured in the United States but sold overseas for less than they do here. The program provides billions in profits for the industry. (See the box "Interest Groups Respond to 9/11" for more coverage of business efforts to lobby the government.)

Given their political clout, it is no surprise that the drug companies are the most profitable of the largest corporations in America, with about $200 billion in annual profits from "take-home" prescriptions (that is, not counting drugs administered in hospitals, doctors' offices, or nursing homes).[32]

Labor

Labor unions seek agreements with businesses and policies from the government that protect workers' jobs, wages, and benefits and ensure the safety of workplaces. They channel money to political candidates, chiefly Democrats, though far less than businesses funnel to Republicans. In addition to money, they rely on their membership to distribute campaign literature, man phone banks, and canvass door-to-door to get out the vote.

Winning the right to unionize was a bitter struggle in the late 1800s and early 1900s. Before federal legislation gave workers the right to organize, companies often brought in strikebreakers—men and women willing to cross a picket line of striking workers and work for whatever the company would pay. Striking workers were often attacked by police or thugs hired by owners. Many large companies had a more potent arsenal than local police forces. In these confrontations, hundreds or thousands of workers were killed, but brutal incidents shocked the nation and led to the legislation that guaranteed the right to organize.

However, after unions boosted workers' standard of living in the 1950s and 1960s, they came to seem less important. And as manufacturing jobs, which had been the backbone of union strength, dwindled in the 1970s, union membership declined. From 35 percent of the workforce in 1955, their membership dropped to 20 percent in 1983 and to only 13 percent today (see Figure 2).[33] With the decline in membership came a decline in political clout.[34]

Because of strong antiunion sentiment in parts of the United States, particularly in the South and Southwest, 84 percent of union members are located in just twelve states.[35] This concentration limits their ability to influence the national government. Members of Congress generally reflect their constituents' opinions but are less sensitive to any groups located in other states.

Although unions have gained new members by organizing teachers and government workers, they have not had the political power to overcome the antiunion efforts of businesses. Although such acts are illegal, they are rarely prosecuted and even then barely penalized. In just five years during the 1990s, 125,000 employees lost their jobs for supporting a union.[36]

Unions have charged Wal-Mart with preventing its workers from organizing to boost wages and improve benefits. (Most Wal-Mart employees don't make minimum wage and don't have health insurance.) When meat cutters at a Wal-Mart in Texas organized, executives shut down the meat counters in the Wal-Marts throughout Texas and five neighboring states. When employees at a Wal-Mart in Canada organized, executives closed the store.[37] As the largest private employer in the United States, Wal-Mart sets the standard for large retailers. To compete with Wal-Mart, they also keep workers' wages and benefits low and obstruct workers' right to unionize.[38] Unions have established two interest groups—Wake Up Wal-Mart and Wal-Mart Watch—to publicize company policies and to propose state and local laws that make it more difficult for the company to open new stores.[39]

Unions have also been hurt by global competition and government's unwillingness to protect American workers threatened by this competition. Fearful of losing their job or putting their employer at a disadvantage in a competitive market, workers are reluctant to strike. Without the threat of a strike, there is little reason to heed workers' demands.

| Figure 2 | Union Membership in the United States |

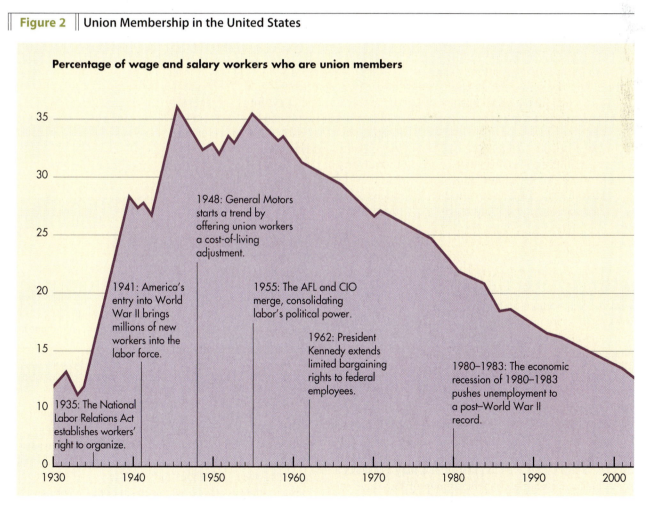

SOURCE: *U.S. Census Bureau,* Statistical Abstract of the United States, *online at www.census.gov/prod/www/statistical-abstract-02.html.*

ethical dilemmas | Interest Groups Respond to 9/11

We like to think that in a time of national crisis, all of us would pull together. But the efforts of interest groups to secure benefits from government don't necessarily stop because of a national tragedy. Instead, groups can refocus their lobbying efforts to take advantage of the situation.

In the wake of September 11, 2001, scores of lobbyists pleading for special interests repackaged their demands in patriotic wrapping. As television commentator Bill Moyers observed, "It didn't take long for wartime opportunists—the mercenaries of Washington, the lobbyists, lawyers, and political fundraisers—to crawl out of their offices on K Street to grab what they can for their clients."[1]

It began with the nation's airline industry. By September 22, the government had given the airlines billions of dollars in cash and loans to compensate for the drop in air travel, a bailout so large that it exceeded the combined value of the major airlines: United, American, Delta, Northwest, US Airways, America West, and Continental.[2]

With virtually no debate, Congress approved the measure for an industry in which several carriers were near bankruptcy before 9/11 (and less than three years later, two carriers would be bankrupt again). One small carrier, Midway Airlines, which had declared bankruptcy in August 2001, nonetheless got an $11 million bailout.[3] And, of course, the American taxpayers received no ownership in the airlines for their huge investment.

The airlines' success prompted the manufacturers of small airplanes; the operators of small airports, flight schools, and skydiving companies; and even Alaska bush pilots whose business wasn't affected by the attacks to seek their own government handout.

Others followed the airlines' strategy. Steel companies, arguing that their product is essential to national security, lobbied for subsidies as well as restrictions on imports of less costly foreign steel. Although one or two steel mills could provide all the steel needed for defense,[4] the president approved restrictions on imports at a

big cost to U.S. taxpayers. (The restrictions had to be lifted after the World Trade Organization declared that they violated free-trade agreements.)

The Agricultural Act of 2001, which authorized $167 billion in farm subsidies, was retitled the Farm Security Act of 2001. The National Taxpayers Union marketed a capital gains tax cut as a national security initiative.

Ethanol producers asked for more subsidies to reduce the nation's dependence on foreign oil. Manufacturers of traffic signs proposed more spending on highway safety, arguing that traffic-routing devices would help motorists flee cities faster and safer during future terrorist attacks. The American Bus Association, representing a thousand private companies providing intercity bus service, lobbied for $400 million to improve bus security and safety.

Not to be outdone, bison producers also bellied up to the trough because, as they put it, fear of terrorism drove patrons away

---

The decline of unions has led to lowered wages—directly because strong unions gain higher wages for their workers and indirectly because higher wages for their workers pressure nonunion employers to pay higher wages to nonunion workers as well. The decline in unions has also blunted the liberal thrust of American politics because unions lobby not only for workers' rights but for other progressive policies, such as government-funded health care.

In an effort to expand membership in recent years, unions have reached out to low-wage service workers, such as hotel maids and nursing home employees, and to some non-blue-collar workers, such as computer specialists in Silicon Valley[40] (and even to graduate teaching assistants at some major universities—another group of low-wage service workers!).[41] Nonetheless, labor still lags far behind business in ability to influence government.

Agriculture

Agricultural organizations are important in agricultural policy making. Large groups address general farm policy, and hundreds of commodity organizations promote particular products. Commodities such as cattle, milk, tobacco, cotton, and wool all have lobbies. Large agribusiness firms such as Cargill and Archer-Daniels-Midland also have lobbies in Washington.

Because American agriculture is dominated by agribusiness and large corporate farms, agriculture groups are dominated by these interests today. Although lobbyists invoke the small farmer and the family farm in their public appeals—they talk about the need to "save" the family farmer—they ask Congress for subsidies that go primarily to large corporate enterprises. Government spends more than $20 billion subsidizing crop production, or in some situafrom the fancy restaurants that serve bison steaks and burgers.

And the American Shore and Beach Preservation Association sought additional funds to maintain public beaches because "America needs to make a major commitment to its energy and water infrastructure, both for security and economic reasons."[5]

None of these groups was asking for anything different from what it had sought before 9/11. But 9/11 offered an opportunity to make a stronger argument for their requests. One lobbyist expressed what many others were thinking: "What happened was a tragedy certainly, but there are opportunities. We're in business. This is not a charity."[6] A member of Congress captured the view of lobbyists and lawmakers: "It's an open grab bag, so let's grab."[7]

Unlike some previous wars, the administration did not call for any sacrifices from the public or business. So it is not surprising that interest groups behaved as they did. In the absence of leadership defining a shared sacrifice or a

"Pardon me, but could you tell us where the public trough is?"

national interest, groups decided to continue pursuing their special interests.

[1] Bill Hogan, "Star-Spangled Lobbyists," *Mother Jones*, March–April 2002, 59–63.
[2] Alan Guebert, "Lugar's Proposal Calls Groups' Bluff," *Lincoln Journal-Star*, October 21, 2001.
[3] Sally B. Donnelly, "Largesse for a Defunct Airline," *Time*, December 17, 2001, 14.
[4] Hogan, "Star-Spangled Lobbyists."
[5] Ibid.
[6] David E. Rosenbaum, "Since Sept. 11 Lobbyists Use New Pitches for Old Pleas," *New York Times*, December 31, 2001, B1.
[7] Hogan, "Star-Spangled Lobbyists."

tions nonproduction, and most of this money goes to the largest and wealthiest—usually the corporate—farms.[42]

Public Interest Groups

While nearly all groups, even private groups that seek their own financial gain, think of themselves as pursuing the "public" interest, **public interest groups** are those that work for a cause that extends beyond the members of the group. Amnesty International lobbies for the rights of political prisoners around the world even though its members aren't prisoners. The National Taxpayers Union lobbies for reduced taxes; although its members would receive lower taxes if it succeeds, other taxpayers would too.

The term *public interest* doesn't mean that a majority of the public favors the goals of these groups or that their goals are good for all or even most people. Both pro-choice and pro-life groups in the abortion debate are public interest groups, even though members of each side don't believe for a minute that members of the other are working in the public interest.

Public interest groups increased dramatically during the 1960s and 1970s.[43] The various groups founded by Ralph Nader and committed to the safety of consumer products reflect this trend. Today there are 2500 public interest groups with 40 million members.[44]

Multiple-Issue Groups

Public interest groups can be classified as multiple- or single-issue groups. Multiple-issue groups address a range of issues.

Racial and ethnic groups   Organizations promoting the interests of racial and ethnic minorities are multiple-issue groups because they address a variety of issues of concern to racial and ethnic minorities. Chapter 15 discusses these organizations and their role in the civil rights movement.

Women's groups   Groups advocating women's equality range from large, mass-based organizations interested in a number of issues to smaller ones focused on a few. The National Organization for Women (**NOW**), the largest and most prominent, has 250,000 members and chapters in each state.[45] It lobbies at the national, state, and local levels in a number of policy areas, including reproductive freedom and economic rights. NOW's success spurred the creation of smaller, conservative groups such as the Independent Women's Forum, which opposes government programs to achieve gender equality.[46]   EMILY's List—*EMILY* stands for Early Money Is Like Yeast (it makes the "dough" rise)—recruits, trains, and funds pro-choice Democratic women to run for public office. The National Federation of Republican Women helps Republican women get elected.

Gay and lesbian groups   Organizations promoting the interests of gays and lesbians fight for equal rights and more recently for same-sex marriage. The Lambda Defense Fund represents gay and lesbian students who have been discriminated against or harassed in school, and it educates teachers, administrators, and legislators about the challenges encountered by these students. (The box "The Origin of Gay and Lesbian Rights Groups" and Chapter 14 discuss these organizations.)

american diversity | The Origin of Gay and Lesbian Rights Groups

In the 1950s, homosexuals usually kept their sexual orientation private. When their orientation did receive public attention, homosexuals were characterized as deviates and subjected to humiliation. They were often fired (as they still can be in many places).

Consequently, gays and lesbians, especially those who hung out together, were vulnerable to blackmail and police harassment. Following a raid on a gay bar in 1954, a Miami newspaper headlined its story "Perverts Seized in Bar Raid." A decade later, New York's liquor authority declared that a meeting of three or more homosexuals in a bar was reason enough for the bar to lose its license.[1] Through the 1960s, police entrapment of homosexuals, with plainclothes officers patronizing gay bars and waiting for a proposition, was common.

The first national group organized to speak for homosexuals was the Mattachine Society, founded in 1950 to raise political consciousness among gays and to fight the persecution of gays that came with the anti-Communist blacklisting in that decade.[2] But the Mattachine Society had branches in only a few cities, and the organization declined when it was revealed that some of its leaders were Communists.

The modern gay rights movement began when police raided a seedy bar, the Stonewall, in New York's Greenwich Village, in 1969. Rumored to be owned by the Mafia, the bar operated without a liquor license and served as a dope hangout. It was a popular meeting place for a diverse group of gay men, "including drag queens, hippies, street people, and uptown boys slumming."[3] That summer the city's police were cracking down on illegal bars, especially those frequented by gay men, Latinos, and blacks. Several gay bars had already been raided without incident before the Stonewall, but each raid heightened the anger and desperation in the gay community.

A small police unit entered the Stonewall at 3 a.m. The employees were arrested for selling liquor without a license, and the customers were asked to leave. When a police van arrived to take away the arrested employees, the crowd grew hostile and began to throw things—first coins, then cans and bottles, and then larger items. The police took refuge in the club, but the increasingly angry crowd pressed to break in, and the police drew their weapons. Soon lighter fluid and a match were thrown inside the building and a fire started, although casualties were averted when police reinforcements arrived. The crowd, feeling empowered by its attempt to fight back, moved down the street shouting "gay power" and celebrating newfound strength and solidarity.

Religious groups Many religious denominations have organizations representing their interests in Washington. Protestant groups are found on the left and right as well as in the middle and speak out on a wide range of issues. Catholic groups have long been active in the antiabortion and antinuclear movements and have recently become outspoken on the immigration issue. Jewish groups have long supported liberal causes and stressed Israel's security. Muslim groups lobby for Palestinian rights and favorable policies toward Muslim countries. In the aftermath of 9/11, they have taken up the cause of fair treatment for American Muslims.[47]

Evangelical Protestant denominations—the **Christian right** (sometimes called the "religious right" to encompass conservative Jewish groups as well)—have been the most potent religious force in American politics.[48] They came together as a movement to protest the Internal Revenue Service's removal of tax-exempt status for Bob Jones University in North Carolina due to racial discrimination.[49] After this foray into national politics, the Christian right became intensely involved in the hot-button issues of abortion and homosexuality and the related issues of divorce, birth control, and women's rights. The movement opposes the teaching of evolution and restrictions on religious symbols and practices in public schools and buildings. In general, it wants government's laws and policies to be based on Christian principles and to be acknowledged as such. It pushes its agenda through religious schools; religious media, including newspapers, magazines, radio, and television; and thousands of politically mobilized churches.[50]

After the unrest ended, gays' sense of injustice and pride from the protests were transformed into an organization, the Gay Liberation Front. Its founders were determined to use radical means to fight discrimination against homosexuals. Not long after, moderate gays and lesbians broke from the Gay Liberation Front to form the Gay Activist Alliance. Later, other groups evolved that used mainstream politics and legal challenges to support the cause. By the early 1970s, gay pride parades, usually held in late June to commemorate the anniversary of the Stonewall raid, were common in major cities.

Changes in the status of homosexuals soon followed. In 1973, the American Psychiatric Association removed homosexuality from its list of mental disorders. In the 1980s, the AIDS tragedy focused media attention on the gay community and brought public awareness to the discrimination issue. Entertainers and celebrities who acknowledged their homosexuality, including some who suffered from AIDS, raised public consciousness. As more homosexuals "came out of the closet," they received more support from straight people.

[1] Robert Amsel, "Back to Our Future? A Walk on the Wild Side of Stonewall," www.gayastrology.com/stonewall.shtml (excerpted from *Advocate*, September 19, 1987).
[2] The source for much of this discussion is Eric Marcus, *Making History: The Struggle for Gay and Lesbian Equal Rights, 1945–1990* (New York: HarperCollins, 1992); see also Jeffrey Schmalz, "Gay Politics Goes Mainstream," *New York Times Magazine*, October 11, 1992, 18ff.
[3] Amsel, "Back to Our Future?"

"We're not doing anything for Gay Pride this year. We're here, we're queer, we're used to it."

The Christian Coalition, a prominent group within the Christian right, was established in the 1980s by television evangelist Pat Robertson, who sought the Republican presidential nomination in 1988.[51] The coalition is heavily involved in politics and closely linked to the Republican Party. In the early 1990s, its members were a majority in many Republican state and local party organizations.[52]

The Christian right urged the resignation or impeachment of President Clinton after his affair with Monica Lewinsky was revealed.[53] The movement helped deliver the presidential nomination to George W. Bush in 2000 by mobilizing its followers against Bush's rival, Senator John McCain (R-Ariz.). Then it helped deliver the presidential election to Bush in 2000 and again in 2004. With the election of Bush, the Christian right gained visibility and power in the highest reaches of government. Their leaders, emboldened by having conservative Republicans in control of all three branches of the federal government, flexed their muscles.

But the harder they pushed, the greater the backlash from moderate Americans.[54] Since the 2004 election, the power of the religious right has waned. Robertson and fellow television preacher Jerry Falwell, founder of the now defunct Moral Majority, didn't help their cause by making outrageous statements (for which they later apologized). Falwell proclaimed that AIDS reflected "the wrath of a just God against homosexuals"[55] and that the 9/11 attacks reflected God's judgment of "the pagans, and the abortionists, and the feminists, and the gays and lesbians."[56]

The resistance was especially evident in 2005 after the strident attempts to use Terri Schiavo's case as a rallying cry. Schiavo, who was forty-one years old, had been in a persistent vegetative state for fifteen years. She was kept alive by a feeding tube. Her husband petitioned to remove the tube, but her parents resisted. After nineteen Florida courts heard the case, and all three levels of the federal courts, including the Supreme Court, refused to intervene, the result was a court order to disconnect the tube. Conservative Christian groups, seeing a connection to their pro-life movement, made the case a cause celebre, pressuring Florida officials and then Congress to intervene and overturn the court rulings. Congress urged federal courts to hear the case, and President Bush interrupted a break at his ranch to return to the capital to sign the bill. The courts, however, rejected the plea. So did 70 percent of the public.[57] In an effort to rally the movement, religious and Republican leaders alienated moderate Americans.

Some in the movement have become disillusioned because political activity has produced so little. Although their support has helped the Republicans control the presidency or Congress for much of the past quarter century, their electoral successes haven't led to many policy achievements. Gay marriage has been defeated at the ballot box in many states, but the idea of gay rights and a tolerance of gay lifestyles have become more accepted throughout the country. The movement hasn't succeeded in eliminating abortion, reinstating school prayers, or reshaping school curricula to teach creationism or intelligent design along with evolution. Some evangelical Christians, who comprised the majority of the religious right, feel used by the Republican party—useful as loyal foot soldiers when it's time to march to the polls, but ignored when the GOP's bigwigs set the party's agenda and priorities.[58]

At the same time, some evangelicals have edged to the left. Now a majority express more interest in protecting the environment, alleviating poverty, tackling HIV/AIDS, and promoting human rights and less interest in addressing abortion and homosexuality than in the past. A third even say that Christian political activism has hurt Christianity.[59]

Moderate and liberal religious groups have also called for more attention to the plight of the poor.[60] These groups put greater weight on the Christian message of helping the less fortunate than on the social issues that have been so important to the religious right.[61]

Environmental groups   Earth Day 1970 marked the beginning of the environmental movement in the United States. Spurred by an oil spill in California, a "teach-in" on college campuses became a day of environmental awareness for millions of Americans nationwide. A minority movement in the 1970s, the environmental lobby today is large and active, and its values are supported by most Americans.[62]

Some environmental groups, such as the Sierra Club, National Audubon Society, and Natural Resources Defense Council, have permanent offices in Washington staffed with skilled professionals.[63] Other groups, such as Greenpeace, Earth First!, and Sea Shepherds, which seek a green cultural revolution, shun conventional lobbying in favor of confrontation. They are less willing to compromise with businesses and polluters.

Environmental groups were on the defensive during the administration of George W. Bush. Conservative Republicans often opposed environmental regulations, arguing that businesses should be allowed to regulate themselves. In response to the demands of its business allies, the administration rolled back environmental regulations adopted by the Clinton administration.[64] But heightened public concern about global climate change and the rising price of oil have given environmental groups more influence.

Single-Issue Groups

Public interest groups include single-issue groups as well as multiple-issue groups. **Single-issue groups** are distinguished by their intense concern for a single issue. Their zeal makes these groups reluctant to compromise.

The National Rifle Association (NRA) is an example. Its members are passionate in their opposition to gun control. They live in every congressional district, and they can be mobilized to contact their representatives in Congress. Although a majority of Americans have supported gun control for many years, the NRA has prevented Congress from passing most gun control proposals. And it has prevented the Treasury Department's Bureau of Alcohol, Tobacco, and Firearms from strictly enforcing the gun control laws that are on the books.[65]

The NRA campaigned for the election of George W. Bush, with a high-ranking official boasting that a Bush win would mean direct access to the Oval Office.[66] Indeed, the Bush administration was a close ally. Reversing sixty years of government policy, the administration adopted the position that the Second Amendment protects a right for individuals to keep and bear arms rather than the right of government to arm a militia to maintain domestic security.[67] (The Supreme Court, with Bush's appointees providing the votes to form a majority, agreed with the administration in 2008.[68]) The administration and congressional allies of the NRA also blocked the renewal of the ban on assault weapons and semiautomatic rifles.

The NRA has been so successful that some politicians, especially in "red" states, which are inclined to support gun control measures, have concluded that the risks to their election or reelection are so great and the probability of passing gun control measures is so small that it's prudent to go along with the NRA. It was an indication of the NRA's influence that after the Virginia Tech shootings in 2007 there were few calls in Congress for new gun control laws.

Yet the NRA may be shifting its focus. In recent years, the organization has become increasingly worried about the shrinking wildlife habitat available for hunting and fishing, as continued development near big cities has transformed fields and streams and as the Bush administration's energy policies have opened more federal land for oil and gas drilling. Some members now consider the dwindling habitat a greater threat to hunting and fishing than gun control legislation, and they have pressured leaders to address this concern.[69]

The **pro-life** and **pro-choice groups** in the abortion debate are other examples of single-issue groups. Pro-life groups, such as the National Right to Life Committee, want a constitutional amendment banning all abortions. Because this is unlikely, they have pushed for federal and state laws restricting the availability of abortions, such as laws requiring waiting periods and parental notification or consent for minors. In some states they have pushed for extra-stringent building codes or staffing requirements for clinics. The goal is to make abortions more difficult for the woman, the doctor, and the clinic.[70] Like the Christian right, from which it draws members, the pro-life movement is closely allied with the Republican Party. In 2004, it got the Republican-controlled Congress to forbid the late-term abortions ("intact dilation and extraction") called "partial birth abortions" by the movement and the media.

Pro-choice groups, such as the National Abortion Rights Action League (NARAL) and Planned Parenthood, want to maintain a woman's right to choose. (Often identified with abortion rights, Planned Parenthood also advocates for access to birth control, sex education in schools, and quality reproductive health care for women.) These groups are closely allied with the Democratic Party.

Single-issue groups have increased in recent decades, alarming some observers and many politicians. When groups form around highly emotional issues and refuse to compromise, politicians can't deal with them as they deal with other groups, so the issues continue to boil,[71] consuming the time and energy of politicians at the expense of issues that many consider more important. On the other hand, single-issue groups have always been part of politics,[72] and they may represent interests that aren't represented by multiple-issue groups. Fears about single-issue groups may result from the groups' heavy media coverage, their exaggerated claims of influence, and, for some, their confrontational tactics.

DEMOCRACY?

Do you think that multiple-issue groups or single-issue groups pose a greater threat to American democracy? Or neither?

PACs and 527s

Political action committees (**PACs**), which raise and donate money to election campaigns, and **"527 organizations,"** which raise and spend money on political advertising (both explained further in Chapter 8), are specialized interest groups in modern American politics. Most large interest groups and corporations have a PAC, and an increasing number of groups have formed a 527 organization.

"If you still want to belong to an organization dedicated to killing Americans, there's always the tobacco lobby."

Both PACs and 527s are authorized by federal law regulating the flow of money to political candidates and the use of money for political advertising. Both have leaders, who articulate the group's views and decide how to spend the group's funds, and checkbook members who decide whether the group's views merit their donations.

PACs can be affiliated with private or public interest groups. 527s also can be private or public interest groups, though most are public interest groups.

Strategies of Interest Groups

Interest groups use several strategies to influence public policy. These include initiating action, blocking action, and influencing key appointments.

Initiating Action

Interest groups initiate governmental action that will help them. They lobby Congress to pass new laws, and because the president is involved and influential in this process, they lobby the administration to push these bills. After the terrorist attacks and the anthrax scare, there was concern that terrorists might use smallpox in future attacks. The government decided to stockpile smallpox vaccine. The pharmaceutical industry lobbied Congress for a law that would grant drug companies immunity in case the vaccine, which can have serious side effects, caused illness or death.[73] As the bill worked its way through Congress, one drug company, Eli Lilly, got the bill's sponsors to sneak in a provision that would grant immunity for another drug made by the company that was unrelated to the smallpox vaccine or to potential terrorist attacks. The provision was removed from the bill only when it was noticed by a few senators at the last minute.

Groups also lobby the administration to adopt new policies that don't require congressional action. When it was uncertain whether the United States would use economic sanctions or military attacks against Iraq in 1991, defense contractors lobbied the first Bush administration for war because they could sell more weapons to the government and see how the weapons performed on the battlefield. The National Wooden Pallet and Container Association, which represents companies that make pallets used to transport supplies, and the Composite Can and Tube Institute, which represents companies that make cardboard containers and the tubes around which toilet paper and paper towels are wrapped, also lobbied the administration for war, because the government would buy more pallets and cardboard containers, toilet paper, and paper towels.

Groups also lobby the White House to increase or decrease the enforcement of federal laws. As the head of the executive branch, the president is responsible for executing the laws. But in practice the president has discretion. Sometimes the laws are ambiguous, so they can be interpreted one way or another. Sometimes an agency lacks enough trained personnel to enforce all the laws it's responsible for, so it has to choose which ones to emphasize. In response to a group's pressure, the president may enhance or reduce an agency's capacity to enforce the laws through budgetary shifts or bureaucratic reorganizations.[74]

Groups also lobby the bureaucracy to adopt new rules. Congress passes relatively general laws, and it delegates authority to the bureaucratic agencies with expertise in the subject matter to adopt specific rules to implement the laws. These rules can be more important to the individuals or companies affected by them then the laws themselves. When the Federal Aviation Administration (FAA), which regulates air travel, banned firearms from airplanes in the 1960s, the NRA persuaded it to allow knives. This policy was still in effect on 9/11.

Thus, bureaucrats, like members of Congress, are targets of lobbying. Enron CEO Ken Lay telephoned Curtis Hébert, appointed by President George W. Bush to head the Federal Energy Commission (FEC), to tell him that Enron would support him in his new job if he changed his views on electricity deregulation.[75] (Enron was urging deregulation.)

Businesses also lobby government agencies to obtain **government contracts**—orders to purchase goods or services. Businesses are anxious to sell everything government wants to buy, whether big or small. Halliburton got lucrative no-bid contracts to supply services to troops in Iraq (so lucrative that the company was charging the government $100 for each 15-pound bag of laundry its workers put in washing machines and $45 for each case of soda);[76] other companies got contracts to provide private soldiers for security details in Iraq. Companies that make playing cards vie for government contracts for the decks distributed as souvenirs to people who fly on "Air Force One"—the president's plane. These special cards are embossed with the presidential seal.

Blocking Action

Interest groups also work to block governmental action that will harm them, so they do the reverse of what groups do to initiate action. They lobby Congress not to pass proposed bills and the administration not to push these bills. They lobby the administration not to adopt new policies under consideration. They also lobby the administration not to increase or decrease the enforcement of federal laws that affect them. They lobby the bureaucracy not to adopt new rules under consideration. After 9/11, the FAA finally banned knives from airplanes, but airlines lobbied against the change, asking how first-class passengers could eat their steak without a knife. If these efforts fail, groups might file lawsuits either to delay the harmful action or to scuttle it altogether if the courts declare it illegal or unconstitutional.

Of the two strategies—initiating action or blocking action—interest groups resort to, and succeed with, the latter more often. In our system of federalism, separation of powers, and checks and balances, power is fragmented and government is decentralized. Initiating action may require a group to clear each level—federal and state. At the federal level alone, initiating action may require a group to clear each part of each branch—at the legislature, to win favorable decisions from multiple committees and both houses of Congress; at the executive, to win favorable decisions from the president and his advisers and from multiple agencies in the bureaucracy; and at the judiciary, to win favorable decisions from several levels of the courts. Groups that want to change a law or policy have to persuade officials at every step in the process. Groups that wish to maintain a law or policy only have to persuade officials at one point, any point, in the process. The American system, which was designed to prevent hasty action by individuals or groups, favors the status quo.

DEMOCRACY?

What are the implications for democracy of the bias toward the status quo in our governmental system?

Whether a group is interested in changing or preserving the status quo, the struggle to influence government can be

---

BEHIND THE SCENES

FROM THE SENATE TO A LOBBYING FIRM

Each "senator" cited in this cartoon is actually a former senator who became a lobbyist after losing reelection to, or retiring from, the Senate.

	Last year in the Senate
Bob Torricelli (D-N.J.)	2002
Rod Grams (R-Minn.)	2000
Tom Daschle (D-S.D.)	2004
Slade Gorton (R-Wash.)	2000
Asa Hutchinson (R-Ark.)	2002
David Durenberger (R-Minn.)	1994
Bob Packwood (R-Ore.)	1995
Bennett Johnston (D-La.)	1996
Jake Garn (R-Ut.)	1992
Zell Miller (D-Ga.)	2003
John Breaux (D-La.)	2004
Al D'Amato (R-N.Y.)	1998
Dan Coats (R-Ind.)	1998
Jim Talent (R-Mo.)	2006

ongoing. For example, environmental groups persuaded the Clinton administration to impose more stringent efficiency standards for air conditioners to conserve energy. Then air conditioner manufacturers got the Bush administration to scale back these standards to save money in manufacturing costs. (More stringent standards require more expensive technology.) Then a federal court ruled that the Bush administration violated a law when it scaled back the standards. We can be sure that both sides will continue to press their case as technology improves and as attitudes toward energy use and global warming evolve.

Influencing Appointments

To shape government policy and accomplish their goals indirectly, interest groups also try to influence important appointments. The president nominates and the Senate confirms appointees to high positions in the executive branch and judges to the federal courts. Having a friend or ally in a key position can help secure a group's goals.

The auto industry opposed several of President Clinton's nominees to head the National Highway Traffic Safety Administration, fearing that they were more concerned with safety and consumers than they were with the auto manufacturers. The pharmaceutical industry vetoed Dr. Alastair Wood, a drug safety expert who was under consideration by President George W. Bush to chair the Food and Drug Administration (FDA). Drug company CEOs complained that Wood was "too aggressive on drug safety issues."[77]

Increasingly, interest groups have tried to influence presidential appointments of federal judges, as will be discussed in Chapter 13.

In pursuing these strategies—initiating action, blocking action, or influencing appointments—like-minded groups may join in a **coalition.** For example, amusement parks, lawn and garden centers, Kingsford Charcoal, and 7-Eleven stores joined the Daylight Saving Time Coalition to lobby Congress to extend daylight saving time. All wanted additional evening daylight hours for the users of their services and products: amusement parks so visitors have more time to play; lawn and garden centers so homeowners have more time to work in their yards; Kingsford so picnickers have more time for barbecues; and 7-Eleven so drivers have more time to stop for a snack while it is still daylight.

Tactics of Interest Groups

To implement their strategies, interest groups rely on a variety of tactics. Some try to influence policy makers directly, whereas others try to mold public opinion and influence policy makers indirectly.

Direct Lobbying Techniques

Direct lobbying entails individual contacts between lobbyists and officials. Thirty-two thousand lobbyists are registered in Washington.[78] Some are salaried employees of the groups they represent; others are contract lobbyists—"hired guns" who represent any individual or group willing to pay for their service. Contract lobbyists include the numerous lawyers affiliated with the city's prestigious law firms.

Gaining access is the first and essential step in direct lobbying. As busy people, public officials are protected by their receptionists and aides whose job is to shield them from those who would take their time.

Because former members of Congress, congressional staffers, White House aides, and federal bureaucrats already have contacts with current officials and knowledge about current policies, they are recruited as lobbyists once they leave public service. An official with the Securities and Exchange Commission (SEC), which regulates the stock market, hoped to capitalize on "Washington's revolving-door tradition whereby high-ranking federal officials move into high-paying private industry jobs." With his contacts and knowledge, he expected "to springboard to at least a $300,000 salary" with a lobbying firm when he left the SEC.[79] Representative Billy Tauzin (R-La.), who steered the Bush administration's Medicare drug bill through the House, was rewarded by the pharmaceutical industry with a job as the head of the pharmaceutical lobby—at a salary of 2 million dollars a year.[80]

In addition to contacts and knowledge, former members of Congress have access to the House and Senate dining rooms and chambers, where no one but members and former members is allowed. They can buttonhole current members just before a vote. When they first came to Washington, most planned to return home after serving in Congress, but the longer they experienced the highly charged atmosphere of the most political city in the country, the harder it got to return home—and the more valuable they became to the myriad interests that lobby in Washington. So they decided to remain as lobbyists. Since 1998, more than 250 members of Congress and 275 aides to the president have registered as lobbyists.[81] When Bob Dole (R-Kan.) resigned from the Senate to run for president in 1996, he said he'd have no place to go but back to his hometown of Russell, Kansas, if he lost the election. Instead, he joined a lobbying firm as a "rainmaker," a prominent person who can attract clients who will bring millions of dollars to the firm.[82] (See box "From the Senate to a Lobbying Firm.")

Usually both Democrats and Republicans are recruited as lobbyists, so firms have access to both parties. This practice ensures that lobbying firms maintain access when control of government shifts from one party to the other.

When the Republicans controlled Congress in the 1990s, however, they pressured the firms to employ only Republicans as their lobbyists. And then they pressured the lobbyists to make campaign contributions only to Republican office-holders and candidates. The goal was to deprive the Democratic Party of the funds necessary to remain competitive. The plan was dubbed the "K Street strategy" after the K Street corridor, home to lobbyists representing the nation's largest business corporations and trade associations.

House Republican leader Tom DeLay (R-Tex.) compiled a list of the four hundred largest contributors to the parties. Their lobbyists were summoned to his office, one by one, and shown their name in either the "friendly" (Republican) or "unfriendly" (Democratic) column, depending upon which party's candidates they had contributed to. DeLay told them, "If you want to play in our revolution, you have to live by our rules." Friendly lobbyists were invited to help write legislation affecting their clients. So, chemical industry lobbyists helped decide hazardous waste regulations, oil company lobbyists helped determine energy policies, and defense contractors helped write weapons contracts.[83]

An old adage states, "Power corrupts and absolute power corrupts absolutely."[84] The Republicans' control of government and their aggressive efforts to maintain control led to corruption, forcing some members of Congress to resign and sending some lobbyists to prison. The spectacle contributed to the Democratic takeover of Congress in 2006. As a result of new Democratic majorities in Congress, the lobbying firms scurried to hire more Democratic lobbyists.[85] (See box "From a Lobbying Firm to the White House?")

Contacting Officials

Lobbyists pay a visit or make a call to officials. Lobbyists don't need to contact every legislator. Rather, they contact key legislators—party leaders and the members who sit on the committees with jurisdiction over the subject of the lobbyists' concern—and the professional staffers serving those committees.[86]

Successful lobbying is based on friendship. As a former chair of one House committee observed, "The most effective lobbyists here are the ones you don't think of as lobbyists." Referring to a prominent Washington lobbyist, he said, "I don't think of him as a lobbyist. He's almost a constituent, or a friend." Senator Barbara Boxer (D-Cal.), referring to the same gentleman, described him as "a lovely, wonderful guy. In the whole time I've known him, he's never asked me to vote for anything." She joked that he's almost "a member of the family."[87]

BEHIND THE SCENES
FROM A LOBBYING FIRM TO THE WHITE HOUSE?

John McCain, Arizona senator and Republican candidate for president in 2008, has long spoken out against the influence of lobbyists and "special interests" in Washington.[1] However, when he assembled a team for his run to the White House, he called on lobbyists to staff key positions in his campaign. Although the campaigns of Barack Obama and Hillary Clinton, like the campaigns of past candidates, also were aided by lobbyists, McCain put lobbyists in charge.

McCain's campaign manager was a lobbyist for several telecommunications companies, and his top fundraiser was a lobbyist for an airline, a telecommunications company, and the trade association representing the pharmaceutical companies before joining the campaign. Other key advisors lobbied for General Motors, United Technologies, and Wall Street investment bank JPMorgan. Some of McCain's advisors continued to lobby for their clients during their "spare time" from the campaign.

When reporters questioned the campaign about lobbyists, one responded, "I do not lobby McCain, and if an issue comes up that involves a client, I tell him and stay out of the discussion."[2] McCain defended his associations, stressing that his friendship with lobbyists does not influence his judgment on issues.[3]

McCain's use of lobbyists illustrates the way of Washington. As members of Congress become lobbyists, so lobbyists become aides in presidential campaigns and, if successful, in the administration. Many Washingtonians alternate between lobbying, when their party is out of power, and joining the administration when their party is back in power.

[1] Information drawn from Michael D. Shear and Jeffrey H. Birnbaum, "Who's Advising McCain," *Washington Post National Weekly Edition* (March 3–9, 2008), 13; Michael D. Shear and Matthew Mosk, "The Appearance of Hypocrisy," *Washington Post National Weekly Edition*, March 17–23, 2008, 14.
[2] Shear and Birnbaum, op. cit.
[3] And he issued guidelines for the lobbyists working on his campaign. Barry Meier, "In McCain Campaign, A Lobbying Labyrinth," *New York Times*, May 25, 2008, 14.

Providing Expertise

When lobbyists contact officials, they might provide expertise that officials lack. Lobbyists make sure that they fully understand their client's business and the industry in which it operates. Consequently, lobbyists are an invaluable source of information for members of Congress and aides in the White House, who tend to be generalists rather than experts about policies. Officials rely on lobbyists to educate them. When Congress considered standards for high-definition TV in the 1990s, a representative of the Information Technology Association of America referred to "pixels." A member of Congress spoke up, "I'm trying to stay with you here, but one of the first times I ever took a ride on an airplane was when I came to Washington to take this seat, and I remember looking out the window and thought part of the wing was falling off when we landed because the flaps came up."[88]

Lobbyists often draft legislation. A legislator may ask a lobbyist known to be an expert in an area to draft a bill, or a lobbyist may draft a bill and ask a legislator thought to be sympathetic to the cause to introduce the bill in Congress. (See box "For American Business, It's the Bottom Line.")

Giving Money

Lobbyists also give money, in the form of campaign contributions, to candidates for office and incumbents running for reelection. To give money, groups, including businesses and unions, set up PACs, which channel contributions to parties and candidates.

Lobbyists give to those with whom they agree and those who are likely to be elected or reelected. The money greases the skids; it ensures access. A longtime financial backer of Ronald Reagan said that having a dialogue with a politician is fine, "but with a little money they hear you better."[89] A Democrat commented, "Who do members of Congress see? They'll certainly see the one who gives the money. It's hard to say no to someone who gives you $5000."[90]

Consequently, interest groups often give to candidates they disagree with. Despite its liberal reputation, the entertainment industry donated more money to Republican candidates (59 percent) than to Democratic candidates (41 percent) in the 2006 congressional elections. Hollywood studios even donated to conservative Republicans who sat on committees with jurisdiction over issues, such as intellectual property rights, important to the industry.[91] With the Republicans in the majority at the time, Hollywood moguls were guided by their business interests rather than their ideological views.

So far, this discussion presumes that the groups freely decide whether to contribute their money. However, once the parties and candidates got used to receiving contributions, and as they faced escalating costs for television advertising, they began to pressure the groups to make contributions, as Republican leader Tom Delay did when he told lobbyists they had "to pay to play"—that is, to contribute if they wanted to influence congressional bills or obtain government contracts.

BEHIND THE SCENES
FOR AMERICAN BUSINESS, IT'S THE BOTTOM LINE

Following 9/11, political leaders turned their attention to thwarting another terrorist attack. One line of defense was to prevent terrorists from hijacking airplanes; another was to prevent them from entering the country. But just as troubling to some officials was our lack of port security. Ships bring seven million cargo containers to U.S. seaports each year. The containers are loaded onto trucks and transported to locations throughout the county. Only a fraction of the containers are ever inspected. Security consultants worry that a container could hold a "dirty bomb" (a radiological device) and that the lack of inspections poses a risk to people who live near the ports.

Wal-Mart, as America's largest retailer and importer,[1] dominates the Retail Industry Leaders Association, which lobbies on behalf of retailers. The association opposes increased inspections and cargo fees that would finance them, calling such measures "ill-advised and onerous."[2] More inspections, whether in foreign ports where the containers are loaded or in American ports where the containers are delivered, would entail new fees, longer delays, and therefore higher costs for importers, who would have to pass these costs on to their consumers, who might look elsewhere for bargains. So the association, spurred by Wal-Mart, has worked behind the scenes to counter the calls for more inspections. Wal-Mart rose to the top with a mantra to cut costs—in its operations and to its consumers—in every way possible. The company is reluctant to relax this strategy, even for port security.

[1] Jeffrey Goldberg, "Selling Wal-Mart: Can the Company Co-opt Liberals?" *New Yorker*, April 2, 2007, www.newyorker.com/reporting/2007/04/02/070402fa_fact_goldberg
[2] William Finnegan, "Watching the Waterfront," *New Yorker*, June 19, 2006, 61.

Lobbyists come in all shapes, sizes, and... species. This "dolphin" is trying to raise awareness of an effort in Congress to remove a provision of the Marine Mammal Protection Act restricting commercial fishing practices that entangle dolphins and whales in mammoth nets.

Thus leverage is exercised in both directions. The groups give money to the parties and candidates as a way to influence current and future officials, and the parties and candidates demand money from the groups as a way to finance their campaigns. With only some exaggeration, one might say that the groups are practicing a legalized form of bribery and the parties and candidates are practicing a legalized form of extortion.

DEMOCRACY?

What are the implications of this pattern of legalized "bribery" and "extortion" for democracy?

Litigating in Court

Although interest groups do not lobby judges the way they do legislators and bureaucrats, some do use litigation to persuade courts to rule for their side in disputes over policies and laws. The groups may file a lawsuit, represent a defendant facing criminal prosecution, or submit a brief—written arguments—in favor of one side in a case.

Although most groups don't use litigation, some use it as their primary tactic, particularly those that lack influence with the legislative and executive branches. Litigation was a successful strategy for civil rights organizations. Throughout the first half of the twentieth century, when Congress and presidents were unsympathetic to the rights of black Americans, the National Association for the Advancement of Colored People (NAACP) fought segregation in the courts. Litigation has been the usual strategy of civil liberties groups, especially the American Civil Liberties Union (ACLU). (These groups' efforts are covered in Chapters 14 and 15.)

Environmental groups use litigation to challenge governmental policies. In local communities, environmental groups file lawsuits against new developments that threaten environmental damage. They hope to block the projects or, at least, delay the projects, so the costs will increase and the developers will have an incentive to make modifications. Then the developers may be more willing to make concessions in the future without the threat of a lawsuit.

Indirect Lobbying Techniques: Going Public

Traditionally, lobbyists limited themselves to direct lobbying, but increasingly, they have turned to indirect lobbying, known as **going public**.[92] This technique includes mobilizing their supporters and molding public opinion. The goal is to get people to contact officials or to get them to vote in elections. By working through the public, groups lobby indirectly.

Mobilizing Supporters

Groups mobilize their members and supporters—**the grass roots**—through direct mail, e-mail, websites, and faxes. To insure a response, groups often exaggerate their opponents' views or strength or the dire consequences that could result if supporters don't heed the call. Such communications are "about scaring the hell out of people."[93]

The NRA is especially adept at mobilizing its members. It can generate thousands of letters, e-mails, or calls to members of Congress within days. The calls from irate members led one senator to remark, "I'd rather be a deer in hunting season than run afoul of the NRA crowd."[94] At rallies in 2000, NRA president Charlton Heston called the presidential election "the most important since the Civil War." If Gore won, he asserted, his Supreme Court will "hammer your gun rights into oblivion." Members turned out in droves, and that turnout was credited in moving West Virginia, a traditionally Democratic state, to the Republican column.

Messages don't always succeed, especially if they don't reflect a broad base. Senator Tom Harkin (D-Iowa) received hundreds of letters opposing his antitobacco position, though from only one part of his state. Then he learned that all the letters came from employees of a Kraft food plant, owned by tobacco company RJ Reynolds.[95]

To be effective, the messages should appear spontaneous and sincere. Groups often provide sample letters to aid their members, but these aren't as convincing as those written in a member's own words. Postcards with preprinted messages aren't very convincing either. With the Internet, groups are using online petitions. Although these aren't as effective as individual communications, a huge number of signatures may have an impact. MoveOn.org, a liberal group with an e-mail list of nearly 2 million, can with the click of a mouse send hundreds of thousands of messages hurtling toward Washington.[96] (See box below)

Molding Public Opinion

Groups try to mold public opinion through commercials on television and radio and ads in newspapers and magazines. Groups also stage media events, including photo ops, to attract media coverage.

BEHIND THE SCENES

MOVEON.ORG: WHERE DID THEY COME FROM, AND WHAT ARE THEY UP TO?

MoveOn.org burst upon the American political scene in 1998 when congressional Republicans launched the impeachment of President Clinton. Husband and wife, Wes Boyd and Joan Blakes, opposed the impeachment. Instead, they urged Congress to censure the president and then "move on." From their home in Berkeley, California, they started the website MoveOn.org. Their postings struck a responsive chord among liberal Democrats angered by the impeachment drive and the political circus surrounding it.

MoveOn surged during the presidency of George W. Bush, especially after the war in Iraq began. The organization vehemently opposed the war and sharply criticized President Bush and Vice President Cheney for initiating it. But the organization also targeted congressional Democrats for going along. In fact, the organization reflected a broader insurgency against the party's establishment. MoveOn, like other liberal websites, spurned conservative Democrats and liberal Democrats who were considered too timid almost as much as it criticized the Bush administration.

The sites, like MoveOn, that cater to the people who are called the **"netroots"**—that is, the grass roots mobilized by political websites—represent those citizens who are impatient with their party's organization and leaders. Netroots are also active on the Republican side, though they were less prominent during the Bush years.

MoveOn sends members e-mails about various affronts and outrages in the news, and it solicits donations for commercials to broadcast on television. It offers interactive opportunities, such as contests for members to create political commercials. Then the organization asks its members to choose the commercials to air.

MoveOn boasts 3.3 million members ready to rally for a liberal cause. The membership includes twenty-somethings and middle-agers, with most in their forties and fifties. Contrary to expectations, they don't reside primarily in the liberal citadels on the east and west coasts. Many live in the suburbs and rural areas of the Midwest. Through MoveOn, they find a connection to liberal causes they don't find in their communities. For liberals who live in "red" states where Democrats are few and far between and where the local and state Democratic Party is moribund, the MoveOn community is just a click away.

Source: Matt Bai, "Profiting from Pummeling," *New York Times Weekly Review,* August 23, 2007, 1, 14.

The founders of MoveOn.org, Wes Boyd and Joan Blakes, run the organization from their Berkeley, California home.

Framing an issue—causing people to view it one way rather than another—can be crucial in winning public support. Business groups pushing "tort reform," which would limit the money that courts can award to individuals injured in auto accidents, air disasters, unsuccessful surgeries, and other mishaps, focus on notorious cases in which the victims have gotten huge awards relative to their injuries, such as the grandmother who spilled McDonald's coffee onto her lap and was awarded $2.9 million for her burns. (But, like many awards, this one was dramatically reduced by the judge (to $840,000) and then further reduced through secret negotiations between the litigants to avoid an appeal.) These groups hope to convince the public that "tort reform" is overdue and necessary to ensure that American businesses will remain competitive or, in malpractice cases, to ensure that American doctors will continue to practice medicine.[97] Lawyer groups that oppose "tort reform" instead focus on the poor victims seriously injured and left penniless by the careless behavior of big corporations or rich doctors.[98] These groups frame the debate as the little guy versus the big bully.

In their zeal to shape public opinion, groups occasionally fabricate information. Although there's a cardinal rule that lobbyists should not mislead officials because they would never be trusted again, there's no comparable rule against misleading the public. ExxonMobil, which opposes government efforts to reduce global warming, has tried to discredit the science of global warming. Although the scientific opinion on the existence of global warming is nearly unanimous, Exxon Mobil, according to one calculation, gave $16 million to forty-three groups between 1998 and 2005 to mislead the public into believing that the science is inconclusive and that the scientists are in disagreement.[99] The corporation assumed that it wasn't necessary to persuade people that there's no global warming; it was necessary only to convince them that the issue isn't resolved, so difficult steps to counter it don't have to be taken yet.[100]

Engaging in Protest   If groups are excluded from the political process or if they simply lack the money necessary to influence the process, they can turn to protest. In 2006, the House of Representatives passed a strict bill that would have led to more deportations of illegal aliens and more denials of social services to these aliens. The bill also would have subjected anyone who helped them to five years in prison. Legal immigrants worried because many Latino families include both legal and illegal immigrants. The bill would have split these families, deporting some members while sending their relatives to prison for helping them. Latino organizations launched massive demonstrations to show Americans how valuable immigrants are. They proclaimed a "Day Without Immigrants," urging workers to leave construction sites and restaurants undermanned, hotel rooms uncleaned, and crops unattended and to march in the streets. They asked students to leave classrooms and join them. Thousands flooded the streets of American cities and generated awareness of the issue, which is the first step in a long struggle.

The civil rights movement is the best example of a successful protest in twentieth-century America. By demonstrating against legalized segregation, black and some white protestors called attention to the discrepancy between the American values of democracy and equality and the inferior status of blacks in the South. The protestors also called attention to the contrast between their own peaceful behavior and the police and vigilante brutality unleashed against them. In marches, sit-ins, and other demonstrations, the protestors practiced **civil disobedience**— intentionally but peacefully

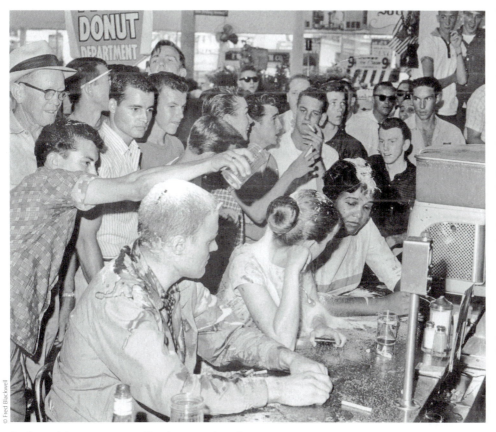

Students sit-in at a segregated lunch counter in Jackson, Mississippi, during the civil rights era.

© Fred Blackwell

Actress Mia Farrow calls public attention to the genocide in Darfur, Sudan. The group Dream for Darfur used the phrase "Genocide Olympics" to pressure the Chinese government to alter its policies toward Sudan.

violating laws and getting arrested, so they could challenge the laws in court. (See the box "Organizing Protest: The Montgomery Bus Boycott.")

Some environmental groups, such as Greenpeace, also practice civil disobedience. The organization got its start in 1971 when environmental and peace activists sent two boats to Amchitka Island (near Alaska) to protest a U.S. underground nuclear weapons test. In other protests, members placed themselves in the path of a harpoon to protect endangered whales and parachuted over coal-powered plants to protest acid rain. The goal was to generate eye-catching publicity and energize the public.

Sometimes protest leads to hostility against, rather than sympathy for, the protesters. Antiwar demonstrations by college students in the 1960s and 1970s angered not only government officials, who targeted the leaders for harassment, but also ordinary citizens, including many who opposed the war. They were more antiprotest than antiwar.

american diversity | Organizing Protest: The Montgomery Bus Boycott

The 1955 Montgomery, Alabama, bus boycott was the first successful civil rights protest, and it brought its twenty-six-year-old leader, Dr. **Martin Luther King, Jr.,** to national prominence.

Montgomery, like most southern cities, required blacks to sit in the back of public buses, reserving the seats in the front for whites. Between the two was a "no-man's-land" where blacks could sit if there were no whites. If whites boarded the bus and needed the seats, however, blacks had to move to the back.

One afternoon, **Rosa Parks,** a seamstress at a department store and a leader in the local NAACP, got on the bus to go home. The bus was crowded, and when a white man boarded, the driver called on the four blacks in "no-man's-land" to move to the back. Three moved, but Parks, tired from a long day and tired of the racial injustice, refused. Under a law that

gave him the authority to enforce segregation, the driver arrested her.

That evening, a group of women professors at Alabama State College, a black college in Montgomery, led by Jo Ann Robinson, drafted a letter calling on their brothers and sisters to stay off the buses on Monday. Although fearful for their jobs and concerned that the state would cut funding to the college if it became known that they had used state facilities to produce the letter, they worked through the night, making thirty-five thousand copies of the letter to distribute to the city's black residents.

The following day, black leaders agreed to the boycott, and on Sunday, black ministers encouraged their members to support the boycott. On Monday, 90 percent of black workers walked, shared rides in private cars, or took black-owned taxis. The boycott inspired

confidence and pride in the black community. Hundreds of blacks jammed the courthouse, as nervous police looked on, to make sure that Rosa Parks was safely released after being convicted.

At a mass rally later that evening, Martin Luther King, Jr., cried out, "There comes a time when people get tired of being trampled over by the iron feet of oppression." Noting that the right to protest is the glory of American democracy, King appealed to the strong religious faith of the crowd: "If we are wrong, God Almighty is wrong. . . . If we are wrong, Jesus of Nazareth was merely a utopian dreamer. . . . If we are wrong, justice is a lie." These words established King as a charismatic leader of the civil rights movement.

Due to its initial success, the boycott was extended. Each successive day was a trial for the residents and their leaders. Thousands had to find a way to get to work,

Protest demands skill from the leaders and sacrifices from the followers. Continued participation, essential to real success, robs activists of a normal life. They can face jail, physical harm, or even death, and they need discipline to refrain from violence, even when they are targeted for violence.

Once protest groups find sympathetic officials willing to listen, they often shift to an inside strategy, working with those in power rather than against them. They switch from demonstrations to conventional lobbying techniques.

Success of Interest Groups

Politics is not a game of chance in which luck determines the winners and losers. Some groups are more successful than others because of their resources and goals.

Resources

Money is important for success. Groups with money can establish and operate an organization, hire experienced lobbyists, and make campaign donations. They can also mold public opinion through television commercials and in other ways. Groups with money, such as business groups, have a tremendous advantage in our political system.

Size—number of members—might substitute for money, especially if members can be mobilized. AARP has 35 million members, senior citizens who focus on Social Security and health care and who vote in high numbers. (They pay dues, so AARP has a thick bankroll along with its huge membership.) The number of members relative to the number of potential members in a group can also be important. The American Medical Association (AMA) enrolled 70 percent or more of the nation's doctors for years,

Rosa Parks is fingerprinted in Montgomery, Alabama, after her arrest for refusing to give up her seat on the bus to a white man. Her refusal triggered a boycott of city buses that became the first successful civil disobedience in the civil rights movement and made Parks a hero to black and white Americans alike.

and leaders struggled to keep a massive carpool going. But each night's rally boosted morale for the next day's boycott. The rallies became prayer services, as the black community prayed for strength to keep on walking, for courage to remain nonviolent, and for divine guidance for their oppressors.

The city bus line was losing money. City leaders urged more whites to ride the buses to make up lost revenue, but few did. Black leaders, recognizing that the boycott could not continue forever, agreed to end it if the rules for "no-man's land" were relaxed. In response, city leaders concluded that they were on the verge of breaking the boycott, and they rejected the offer. Police officers began to harass carpoolers and issue bogus tickets for trumped-up violations.

City leaders issued an ultimatum—settle or face arrest. A white grand jury indicted more than 100 boycott leaders for the alleged crime of organizing the protest. In the spirit of nonviolence, the leaders, including King, surrendered.

The decision to arrest the leaders proved to be the turning point of the boycott. The white editor of the local paper said it was "the dumbest act that has ever been done in Montgomery." With the mass arrests, the boycott finally

received national attention. Reporters from all over the world streamed into Montgomery to cover the story. The boycott became a national event, and its leader, Martin Luther King, Jr., became a national figure.

A year later, the U.S. Supreme Court declared Alabama's local and state laws mandating segregation on buses unconstitutional. Only after the city complied with the Court's order did the boycott end.

When Rosa Parks died at the age of ninety-two in 2005, she was lauded as one of the key figures in the civil rights movement. Fifty thousand people filed through the U.S. Capitol Rotunda, where she lay in state, the first woman and second African American to be honored in this way. Thousands attended her funeral, and thousands more lined the streets to witness her casket pulled by a horse-drawn carriage to the cemetery.

SOURCES: Taylor Branch, *Parting the Waters: America in the King Years* (New York: Simon & Schuster, 1988), chs. 4 and 5; Juan Williams, *Eyes on the Prize* (New York: Viking, 1987).

AP/Wide World Photos

and it enjoyed a lot of clout. As its percentage of American doctors declined, its influence declined as well.

Cohesion and intensity might substitute for money and size. Public interest groups, especially single-issue groups such as pro-choice and pro-life groups, have cohesive and intense members who can be mobilized to contact officials, write letters to the editor, persuade their friends, and vote.

Groups that marshal the greatest resources are the most likely to influence government. They may even overcome the majority view, as reflected in public opinion polls. Supporters of gun control have long had public opinion on their side, but their main group, the National Council to Control Handguns, has less money, fewer members, and less cohesion and intensity among its members than the NRA can boast. As a result, the NRA has triumphed over public opinion for decades.

Goals

Groups that promote change, especially sweeping change, usually are less successful than groups that work to preserve the status quo. In our system of federalism, separation of powers, and checks and balances, groups promoting change must persuade numerous officials in multiple institutions; groups opposing change may have to persuade only one key official, or perhaps several important officials, in just a single institution. Thus it is more difficult to produce government action than to prevent such action.

When President Bill Clinton proposed a major health care reform, medical, dental, hospital, and insurance associations and companies voiced their opposition. Different groups opposed different aspects of the proposal, and they came together to fight it. The plan became the most heavily lobbied initiative in history.[101] The plan's scope, along with the opponents' power, ensured the plan's defeat. Although health care costs continue to spiral out of control, significant reform may require a crisis, or at least the perception of one, to overcome the resistance of the groups affected by it.

On the other hand, Clinton's welfare reform, which was a major revision of an entrenched policy, was adopted. It set work requirements for welfare recipients, who are the poorest and least politically active Americans. They don't have strong interest groups representing them, so they weren't able to block the requirements.

Groups that seek narrow benefits for themselves are usually more successful than those that seek broad policy changes for the entire society. If the proposals are complex, the media are less likely to call attention to them and the public is less likely to be aware of them. Virtually everyone is aware of hot-button issues such as abortion and capital punishment, but relatively few are aware of technical provisions that regulate or tax businesses. The accountancy profession opposed regulations that would make the financial status of corporations more transparent in the 1990s. Few

people, except for executives in the corporations and auditing firms, were aware of the financial implications until Enron collapsed with the complicity of auditing firm Arthur Andersen.

The tax code is riddled with exemptions for industries and corporations that slipped through Congress without raising an eyebrow.[102] Some beneficiaries aren't identified by their name. One provision exempts Phillips Petroleum, identified in the law not by its name but as a "corporation incorporated on June 13, 1917, which has its principal place of business in Bartlesville, Oklahoma."[103] A member of Congress from a district with three national bakeries succeeded in inserting a provision into a tax bill that simply deleted "bakery drivers" from the list of occupations treated as employees.[104] The drivers, although hired by the bakeries, would be defined as self-employed rather than as bakery employees. This meant that the bakeries wouldn't have to pay Social Security, Medicare, or unemployment taxes on their drivers. Instead, their drivers would have to pay extra Social Security and Medicare taxes themselves. This ripoff was removed only when a congressional staffer noticed and publicized it.

DEMOCRACY?

Does it seem that interest groups enhance or detract from democracy?

Conclusion: Do Interest Groups Make Government More Responsive?

In an indirect democracy, as in the United States, citizens elect representatives to pass laws and make policies for them. However, elections usually focus only on a few issues or on the candidates' personalities. They aren't referendums on all the issues that citizens want government to address. Furthermore, elections infrequently occur, and many citizens don't vote. So, elections don't reflect citizen's views on many issues. To supplement the ballot box in our political system, interest groups play an important role. They offer citizens the opportunity to join with others, and they monitor government action and make their views known to public officials.

By joining and paying dues or making contributions to a group, citizens essentially hire private representatives—the groups' leaders—to act on their behalf much as citizens elect public officials to do so. Most citizens can't monitor the actions of the president, 535 members of Congress organized into almost 200 committees and subcommittees, and more than 100 bureaucratic agencies. And most citizens can't communicate their views to these officials, committees, and agencies. But interest groups can.

The theory that groups represent citizens and compete for the attention of and influence over government is called **pluralism**. There are thousands of groups representing the interests of millions of Americans. According to the theory, groups compete with each other for favorable treatment by the government, much as businesses compete with other businesses to sell their products and services. From this spirited competition in the political marketplace, policies are adopted that reflect the interests of the groups. Occasionally, some groups win while others lose, but usually the groups compromise, with each winning part of what it sought. Thus, according to the theory, our government is responsive to the people, because the people are represented by the groups in this competition.

However, although many people do join groups—more people than in other countries—some people don't join groups, so these people aren't represented by groups, or at least by many groups or strong groups. People with the least education and the least income are the least likely to join groups. Therefore, groups don't represent, or don't adequately represent, the poor, the working class (except for those in unions), and the politically disinterested. Instead, they disproportionately represent the well-to-do and their businesses. A political scientist's observation from 1960 remains valid today: "The flaw in the pluralist heaven is that the angelic chorus sings with an upper class accent."[105]

The middle class can wield power, through its sheer numbers, when it is very aware of and interested in an issue. And sometimes middle-class concerns do benefit working-class people as well. The middle-class members of AARP protect the interests of the elderly in general.

The rapid proliferation and expanded power of interest groups in recent decades has led to what some political scientists call **hyperpluralism.** According to this view, there are so many groups with so many supporters and resources, and government authority is so decentralized, that it is difficult to find common ground to forge solutions to problems. The groups pull the government in too many directions, and they wield a de facto veto over proposals they dislike. The result is gridlock. The Clinton White House had to work with 1100 interest groups on its health care proposal, and it couldn't find an acceptable solution in this political thicket.[106] Modern technology abets the tendency toward gridlock. At congressional hearings on tax reform, lobbyists used cell phones to start an avalanche of protests by phone and fax the moment anyone mentioned something their clients opposed.[107]

In this climate, the groups make government responsive to their members, but their efforts prevent government from solving critical problems, even when a majority of citizens

Consumer advocate Ralph Nader testifies against dangerous automobiles in 1968.

want government to address these problems. So, ironically, as the groups are making government responsive to their members, they are rendering it unresponsive to the rest of society.

Both pluralism and hyperpluralism are important for understanding American politics, but they cannot explain all of what happens. Consider the successes of **Ralph Nader,** the son of Lebanese immigrants and a crusader for average Americans against the giants of corporate America. Nader spearheaded an array of interest groups, including Public Citizen, that attracted young professionals (dubbed "Nader's Raiders") and fought for safer products and a healthier environment. More than any other person, Nader is responsible for seat belts, air bags, padded dashboards, steering columns that won't impale drivers, and fuel tanks that won't explode upon collision. Because of Nader, drinking water, baby food, and dental X-rays are all safer. Infant pajamas are less likely to catch fire.

To a significant extent, Nader is also responsible for the creation of important government agencies—the Environmental Protection Agency (EPA); the Consumer Product Safety Commission (CPSC), which tries to ensure safe products; and the Occupational Safety and Health Administration (OSHA), which tries to ensure safe workplaces. Nader deserves credit for the Freedom of Information Act, which exposes government actions and ensures greater accountability.[108] His work is a testament to how much concerned and active citizens, working through interest groups, can do, even when they are up against powerful opponents.

Key Terms

interest groups

lobbying

lobbyist

"mischiefs of faction"

First Amendment

political efficacy

free-rider problem

checkbook members

private interest groups

labor unions

public interest groups

Christian right

single-issue groups

pro-life groups

pro-choice groups

527 organizations

political action committees (PACs)

government contracts

coalitions

gaining access

going public

the grass roots

"netroots"

civil disobedience

pluralism

hyperpluralism

Key Names

Alexis de Tocqueville

Sierra Club

NRA

AARP

NOW

Martin Luther King, Jr.

Rosa Parks

Ralph Nader

Please visit our companion website at www.cengage.com/politicalscience/ welch/uag12e or use CengageNOW for additional resources dealing with this chapter.

Our party preference is partly determined by our geographic location. Even without the flag, we might predict that these folks in rural North Carolina prefer the Republican Party.

Political Parties

chapter

7

Talking Points

Sometimes "new" politics clash with old politics. In Pennsylvania, a key primary state, the idealism of the Obama campaign for the Democratic nomination collided with the gritty political traditions of Philadelphia. In that city, candidates typically deliver "street money" to the local party organizations, a tradition dating from the heyday of big-city machines. A few days before the election, local party operatives hand out $20, $50, and $100 bills to foot soldiers whose job it is to work the neighborhoods on election day to make sure a candidate's supporters get to the polls.[1]

Philadelphia, home to Independence Hall, is also home to an old-style political machine, a shadow of its former self, but still functioning as it did 100 years ago. In those days, political campaigns were labor-intensive. To get out the vote required thousands of party workers. Most were drawn from the ranks of government employees who owed their job to the party.

With the party no longer in control of government jobs, in Philadelphia the money to pay party workers on election day comes from "street money" provided by the candidates. Philadelphia's ward leaders argue plausibly that paying someone $100 for an honest day's effort working for the party is probably more democratic than the millions used for high-priced consultants and pollsters who are now a staple of virtually all campaigns. Of course, not all street money goes where it is supposed to. Some gets siphoned off into "back-porch money." It's not enough to build a house, but it may be enough to add a new porch.

The word on the street was that "Obama won't pay." Doling out an estimated $500 thousand to party workers ran counter to his call for a change in the way Washington does business. He and his managers thought that if he paid the money, he would look like any other politician. But if he refused, it might cost him votes. Obama indicated that he objected to paying people to support his candidacy, though he had no qualms with spending millions on pollsters, media consultants, and television ads. And of course, like paying a pollster to take a poll, paying the street money to those who would be getting the voters to the polls would in fact be paying for fourteen hours of hard work.

Obama stuck to his principles. He didn't fork over any street money. He took little risk, however. His support among the black voters, who comprised 44 percent of Philadelphia's population and more than three-quarters of its Democratic electorate, favored him overwhelmingly. And, his primary opponent, Hillary Clinton, did not provide street money either. Both were saved by the party. Tapping its own coffers, the local organization provided $100 in street money to each worker on election day.

But Obama's principles on the topic of street money were soon overcome by pragmatism. Pennsylvania is a key state in the fall presidential election and Philadelphia, with its 800,000 Democrats, is the largest city in Pennsylvania, by far. In the general election, which was expected to be very close in Pennsylvania, he decided to provide street money after all.

James Madison, the "Father of the Constitution," warned against the "mischief of factions," which today would include interest groups and political parties. George Washington, the "Father of the Country," cautioned against the "baneful" effects of parties and called them the people's worst enemies. Years later, however, a respected political scientist, E. E. Schattschneider, claimed that "political parties created democracy and that democracy was impossible without them."[2]

The public reflects these contradictory views. Americans, especially young adults, are cynical about parties and believe the country would be better off without them. People complain that politics is too **partisan**—that candidates and officeholders make decisions based on party affiliation rather than what is best for the country. People say they're tired of "partisan bickering," as though the parties argue over nothing, like little children. Many believe that the parties create conflict where none exists. Despite these views, however, most people identify with one of the parties, and many vote solely on the basis of party affiliation.

This chapter examines American political parties to see why they persist—indeed, why they are important—despite the criticism they face. It begins with an overview of American political parties.

Characteristics of American Parties

Political parties consist of three interrelated components: (1) citizens who consider themselves members of the party, (2) officeholders who are elected or appointed in the name of the party, and (3) activists who run the party organization at the national, state, and local levels (see Figure 1).[3]

The American party system is unusual among Western democracies, which can be seen when examining its distinguishing characteristics.

Two Major Parties

The American party system is a **two-party system**. Only two parties—the **Democratic Party** and the **Republican Party**—have a realistic chance to win the presidency or

---

║ Figure 1 ║ The Three Components of Political Parties

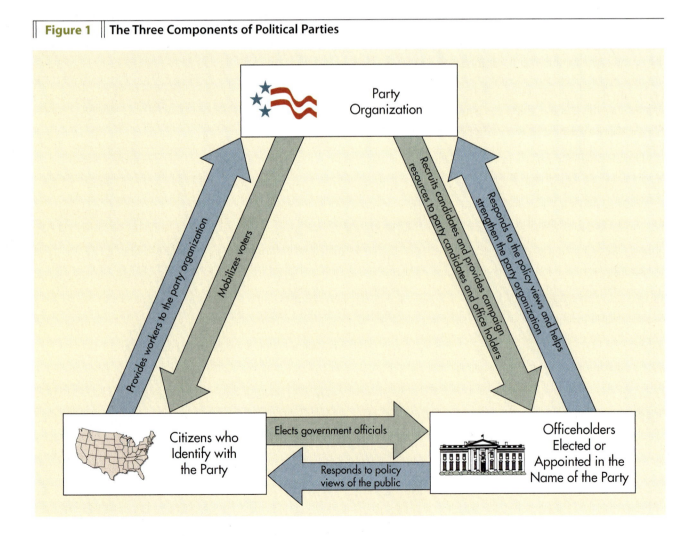

most seats in Congress. (Occasionally an independent wins a seat; today a socialist—Senator Bernie Sanders (Vt.)—holds a seat.)

Two-party systems are rare. In Western Europe, **multiparty systems** are the rule. Italy has nine national parties and several regional ones; Germany has five national parties. Great Britain, although predominantly a two-party system, has several significant minor parties. Multiparty systems are also found in Canada, which has three parties, and Israel, which has more than twenty.

Why two parties in the United States? The most common explanation is that American elections, with **single-member districts** and a **winner-take-all provision**, favor two parties.[4] These features mean that only one individual—the one who receives the most votes—is elected from a district. Although these features seem natural, even inevitable, to Americans, they contrast with **proportional representation** (PR), which is found in multiparty systems. PR systems employ multimember districts, where more than one individual is elected. In most, voters cast a ballot for a party slate, with each party receiving a percentage of seats equal to the percentage of votes it received in the district.[5] (There is no winner-take-all provision.) Consequently, representation in the national legislature is roughly proportional to the popular vote each party receives nationwide.

In single-member-district, winner-take-all elections, only the major parties are likely to win a legislative seat. In PR elections, even a modest showing—15 percent or less—may win a legislative seat, enabling a small party to have a voice and a base to attract more supporters in the next election. The prospect of winning some seats even with a modest showing encourages and sustains minor parties.

Minor Parties

Although the American party system disadvantages minor parties, also called "third parties," they do exist. Most, such as the Prohibition Party (since the 1860s), which opposes the sale of alcoholic beverages, and the Communist Party USA (since the 1920s), which proposes the adoption of communism, receive little notice and few votes. But some, such as the Progressive Party in the late 1800s and early 1900s, have had a major impact on American politics by setting a new agenda to which the major parties had to respond.

Some minor parties, chiefly in the twentieth century, are nothing more than an individual candidate seeking the presidency and those working in the campaign. In 1968, Alabama's segregationist governor, George Wallace, split from the Democratic Party to run for president as the candidate of the American Independent Party. In 1992, Texas businessman Ross Perot decided to run for president. His willingness to use his personal fortune to fund an expensive campaign made him a viable alternative to the major-party candidates. He received 19 percent of the vote, an extraor-

dinary showing for a minor-party candidate, but his candidacy didn't influence the outcome, as he siphoned votes from both major-party candidates. However, his campaign did push the issue of the budget deficit to the top of the national agenda.

Consumer advocate **Ralph Nader** ran in 2000 and 2004. In 2000, he was the nominee of the Green Party, an offshoot of the antinuclear and environmental movements. He claimed that the major parties were simply pawns of corporate America, and he called for more checks on big business. In 2000, he received just 3 percent of the vote nationwide, but his total included 97,000 votes in Florida. Because most Nader voters preferred Al Gore over George W. Bush, many of their votes would have gone to Gore if Nader hadn't been on the ballot. In the tight election, Nader's votes were enough to deny Gore a victory in the state and, consequently, in the Electoral College.[6] (Of course, in such a close election, other factors affected the outcome as well.)

In 2004, Bush donors helped finance Nader's campaign in an attempt to pull votes from Democratic candidate John Kerry,[7] but this time Nader received less than 1 percent of the vote and didn't affect the outcome in any state.

Despite Nader's impact as spoiler, third parties must overcome substantial barriers to have an impact. Most Americans feel long-standing loyalty to one of the major parties. They also recognize that minor-party candidates can't win, and thus don't want to "waste their vote" or, worse, help their least-preferred candidate, as Nader's Florida voters helped Bush. Because minor-party candidates can't win, they have difficulty raising funds to mount an effective campaign or attracting media coverage to get their message out.[8] Although sometimes more than half of Americans tell pollsters that they would vote for a minor or third party, few ever do.

Historically, minor parties have done well only when the country faces social or economic challenges that the major parties fail to address. Should a minor party attract voters with an appealing idea, the major parties are likely to adopt it as their own, diminishing the appeal of the minor party. After Perot made the budget deficit a national issue, the incoming Clinton administration made the deficit its chief economic priority, and the reason for supporting Perot disappeared.

Moderate Parties

The American party system features ideologically moderate political parties. In a two-party system, both parties are "big tents" with diverse members. To win, especially the presidency, the parties have to attract many voters. Unlike in a multiparty system, where parties can gain legislative seats without winning a majority in any district, American parties can't focus their campaigns on one or a few segments of the electorate. If they want to win, they must appeal to most of the electorate, so they must choose pragmatism over ideol-

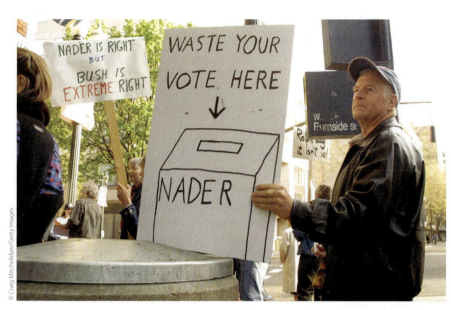

Minor parties have trouble gaining traction because representatives of the major parties remind voters that candidates of the minor parties can't win.

public opinion supported Clinton and he won reelection. In his second term, Republican congressional leaders impeached the president. Again, public opinion supported Clinton and he survived.

Following the 2000 election and the 9/11 attacks, Republicans again pushed a conservative agenda for both foreign and domestic policies. Although the agenda seemed out of step with Americans' views toward domestic policies, Americans' fears of terrorism and their sense that the Republicans could better confront that challenge led to Republican victories in the 2002 congressional election and to Bush's reelection in 2004. It wasn't until 2006, when terrorist threats appeared to have receded, that voters elected Democratic majorities to Congress.

ogy. Most voters cluster toward the middle, rather than at the extremes (see Figure 2), so parties pitch their campaigns toward the middle, at least in nationwide contests.

The Democrats are a center-left party, and the Republicans are a center-right party. To win the presidency, the parties usually nominate moderate candidates or ones who appear moderate. When they nominate a candidate at their extreme—a Democrat on the left or a Republican on the right—the candidate typically moves toward the center during the campaign. After he became the likely Republican nominee, John McCain disassociated himself from unpopular conservative policies on energy and the environment. And Barack Obama antagonized his liberal supporters by moving to the right on issues such as religion and gun control. Both were trying to appeal to moderate voters.

Of course, words in the campaign do not always predict actions once elected. George W. Bush called himself a "compassionate conservative" in the 2000 election in an effort to signal to moderate voters that he was actually a moderate (but couldn't say so without alienating conservative voters). However, once elected, he pursued quite conservative policies consistent with the conservative base that dominated the Republican Party at the time.

Although the parties aim for the center in national elections, both have members and supportive interest groups—left of center in the Democratic Party and right of center in the Republican Party—tugging them toward their extreme. In recent decades, this tendency has been stronger in the Republican Party, as conservatives wrested control of the party's state and local organizations and the party's congressional leadership from moderates. In an effort to discredit President Clinton, Republican congressional leaders shut down the government over a budget dispute. However,

Fragmented Parties

American political parties are also fragmented. That is, their power is dispersed among their components. Their party organizations and party officials at the national, state, and local levels; their government officeholders in the executive, legislative, and judicial branches; and their voters throughout the country aren't all unified through either a tight structure or a common program. They're relatively independent of each other. This independence reflects the nature of American government itself, which disperses power through federalism, separation of powers, and checks and balances.

Fragmentation makes it difficult for party leaders to fashion a coherent and consistent program and persuade their officeholders to accept it. Although presidents usually get support from their party members in Congress,[9] some party members go their own way. To get reelected, they need only the votes of their constituents—not the approval of the president or party leaders. When President Clinton proposed an increase in gas taxes to reduce the deficit, Sen. Herbert Kohl (D-Wisc.) told him the increase could be no more than 4.3 cents per gallon. Clinton had to accept Kohl's figure because the bill's outcome was in doubt and the senator's vote was important. When President Bush proposed immigration reform, conservative Republicans rebelled and refused to pass the bill.

Party Organization

Party organization—the professionals and activists who staff the party apparatus at each level—reflects the fragmentation of the parties. The organization isn't a hierarchi-

Figure 2 ‖ **Where the Voters Are**

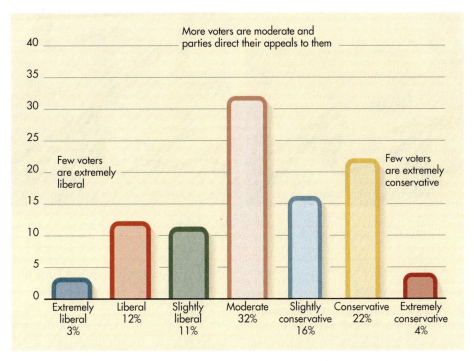

The labels indicate how the voters characterize themselves today. In recent years, more have characterized themselves as conservative than as liberal, but most have characterized themselves as moderate. Thus, the parties usually aim their campaigns at the middle.
SOURCE: *Data from General Social Survey, 2004.*

cal, top-down structure like the military, in which the higher-ups issue commands that are followed by the underlings. The national party organization doesn't dictate policies to the state and local levels or impose penalties on these levels. Party organization is layered, with each layer linked to, but independent of, the others.

National Party Organizations The **national party chair** heads the national party organization, called the **national committee**. The chair is appointed by the president or, for the opposition party, by its national committee. The chair raises money and speaks out on behalf of the party. The national committees rarely meet, although they do choose the site of the party's national convention and determine the formula for calculating each state's number of delegates.

Both parties also have House and Senate campaign committees, which raise money, recruit candidates, and develop strategy for upcoming campaigns.[10] Representative Rahm Emanuel (D-Ill.) headed the Democratic Congressional Campaign Committee in 2006. A former ballet prodigy, he was charged with producing a House Democratic majority for the first time in twelve years. Hyperactive and ruthless—he was nicknamed "Rahmbo"—Emanuel recruited centrist candidates for conservative districts, such as retired NFL quarterback Heath Shuler of North Carolina. Shuler resisted Emmanuel's pleas to run, insisting that he wanted to spend time with his family. Emmanuel persisted, calling him five times a day.[11] Reported Schuler, "He calls

one morning: 'Heath, I'm taking my kids to school,' then he just hangs up. At 11:30, he calls and says, 'I'm leaving my office to eat lunch with my kids.' Then, 'Heath, it's 3:30, and I'm walking into school.'"[12] Shuler finally relented— and won his election—and Emanuel delivered a majority for the Democrats.

State and Local Party Organizations State and local party organizations have chairs and committees to direct party activities at these levels. Some communities have strong party organizations made up of volunteers who recruit candidates to run and citizens to work the precincts and man the telephones. In other communities, the parties are so weak that they have little organization at all. In most communities, any citizen who wants to become active in the party needs only to show up at party meetings and be prepared to work.

Having described some features of American political parties, we'll turn to history to see how the parties originated and developed and to see what roles they play in the American political system.

The Rise of American Parties

The Founders dreaded the prospect of political parties, fearing that rival parties, seeking to win favors for themselves at the expense of the common good, would undermine the

Democratic officials recruited traditional, masculine men to run for Congress in more conservative districts and states in 2006. The winners included (left) sheriff Brad Ellsworth (Ind.), in the House, and farmer John Tester (Mont.) in the Senate.

new nation and its fledgling government.[13] They hoped, unrealistically, to govern by consensus.

Because of the Founders' misgivings, the Constitution doesn't mention political parties. Nevertheless, the Constitution created a government in which parties, or something like them, were inevitable. With popular election as the mechanism for selecting political leaders, an agency for organizing and mobilizing the supporters of competing candidates became necessary.

Birth of Parties

With George Washington's unanimous election to the presidency in 1788, it appeared that the nation could be governed by consensus. But differences soon emerged. **Alexander Hamilton**, Washington's secretary of the treasury, favored a strong national government. He and his supporters in Congress, who called themselves **Federalists**, were opposed by **Thomas Jefferson**, Washington's secretary of state, who feared a strong central government. The conflict led Jefferson to challenge John Adams for the presidency in 1796. Jefferson lost but saw the value of organization. He recruited political operatives in each state, and they established newspapers to get his message out, thus creating the first American political party. Backed by his new party, the **Jeffersonians**, he won the presidency in 1800.

Before Jefferson left office, most members of Congress—more than 90 percent—were either Jeffersonians (later called Jeffersonian Republicans) or Federalists and consistently voted in support of their party's positions.[14]

Development of Mass Parties

Andrew Jackson introduced the idea of a political party with a large following among rank-and-file voters. Running for president in 1828, he reached out to the masses. His appeals drew five times more voters to the polls than in 1824. Jackson's opponents deplored his approach, calling him a "barbarian" and his campaign "the howl of raving democracy."[15]

Like Jefferson, Jackson saw the strength of American democracy in the common person. His administration encouraged participation in government. Property ownership as a qualification for voting was lifted in most states where it still existed,[16] extending the franchise to almost all white men. Members of the Electoral College were elected by the people rather than selected by state legislatures. National party conventions, with representatives from every state and locality, were established to nominate presidential candidates.[17]

With the enhanced participation fostered by these reforms, the idea of a political party with a mass following took root in American politics. Reflecting this era's emphasis on the common person, historians refer to the spirit of **Jacksonian democracy**. Due to the reforms and population increases, the electorate continued to expand, doubling by 1840.[18]

Golden Age of Mass Parties

Parties reached their high point after the Civil War. Party leaders controlled nominations for public offices through political machines. Party organizations mobilized voters during election campaigns. Voting rates reached their highest levels in American history.

Political Machines

Local parties created **political machines**, powerful organizations that could deliver the vote. Known as "urban machines" because they were found in America's largest cities, they flourished in the late nineteenth and early twentieth centuries, and some lasted until the middle of the twentieth century.

The machines were hierarchical organizations, unlike today's parties. A city was divided into small neighborhoods called precincts, and the precincts were grouped into larger neighborhoods called wards. Party operatives were designated as "precinct captains" and "ward heelers." Their job was to know their constituents, tend to their needs, and then get their votes for the party's candidates on election day. The head of the machine was a boss, who often served as mayor and who directed the organization and ran city government to maintain his power and control the government for his party. (See the box "A Day in the Life of a Machine Politician.")

The machines relied on the votes of the poor and working class, many of whom had recently immigrated from Europe. Although most accounts of machine politics are negative, dwelling on corruption, the machines provided valuable services for their constituents.

Providing Welfare   The machines served as an informal welfare system for poor people during an era before government had any formal welfare system. The party provided food, clothing, or housing for people in need.

Party workers were an early "Welcome Wagon" for new immigrants, meeting them on the dock as they came off the ship and helping them settle into their new community in this strange country.

Longtime member of Congress Tip O'Neill (D-Mass.) told the story of Boston mayor James Curley, a leader of the city's Democratic organization in the early twentieth century. As winter approached, Curley called Filene's, a local department store, and told the owner he needed five thousand sweaters. When the owner balked, Curley reminded

him that it was time to reassess Filene's property for tax purposes, a none-too-subtle threat that its taxes would go up if the sweaters weren't delivered. So, the sweaters were delivered and distributed to poor people in the city.[19]

It is highly unlikely that altruism had anything to do with such assistance. Party machines were motivated principally by self-interest. They did favors to get votes in return. As New York City's boss George Washington Plunkitt said, "If a family is burned out, I don't ask whether they are Republicans or Democrats. . . . I just get quarters for them, buy clothes for them if their clothes were burned up and fix them up 'til they get things runnin' again. It's philanthropy, but it's politics too—mighty good politics. Who can tell me how many votes one of these fires brings me?"[20]

Providing Jobs   The machines also served as an informal employment agency. The machines controlled government jobs, operating a **patronage system.**[21] During this era, virtually all government jobs, from the mayor's top aide to street sweepers, went to political appointees. When one party captured control of city government, city workers who supported the losing party were fired and new workers who supported the winning party were hired in their place. "To the victor belong the spoils," the saying went. So the patronage system came to be known as the **spoils system.**

The practice began with the presidency of Andrew Jackson, whose supporters were western frontiersman rather than eastern businessmen. Jackson wanted common people to get a share of government jobs. In adopting the practice, machines provided jobs to some middle-class people and to many poor people and new immigrants. By

In 1828, opponents of Andrew Jackson called him a jackass (left). Political cartoonists and journalists began to use the donkey to symbolize Jackson and the Democratic Party. In the 1870s, cartoonist Thomas Nast popularized the donkey as a symbol of the party and originated the elephant as a symbol of the Republican Party. His 1874 cartoon (right) showed the Democratic donkey dressed as a lion frightening the other animals of the jungle, including the Republican elephant.

A DAY IN THE LIFE OF A MACHINE POLITICIAN

George Washington Plunkitt was a ward leader in the infamous Tammany Hall machine, the Democratic Party organization that governed New York City for seven decades in the late nineteenth and early twentieth centuries. Although Plunkitt was on the city payroll, he did not have a free ride. The demands of his job were exhausting. Providing social services to his constituents, he had opportunities to build support for the party.

Entries from Plunkitt's diary illustrate the typical tasks he faced each day.

- **2:00 A.M.** Aroused from sleep by a bartender who asked me to go to the police station and bail out a saloon keeper who had been arrested for violating the excise law. Furnished bail and returned to bed at three o'clock.

- **6:00 A.M.** Awakened by fire engines. Hastened to the scene of the fire . . . found several tenants who had been burned out, took them to a hotel, supplied them with clothes, fed them, and arranged temporary quarters for them.

- **8:30 A.M.** Went to the police court to secure the discharge of six "drunks," my constituents, by a timely word to the judge. Paid the fines of two.

- **9:00 A.M.** Appeared in the municipal district court to direct one of my district captains to act as counsel for a widow about to be dispossessed. . . . Paid the rent of a poor family and gave them a dollar for food.

- **11:00 A.M.** At home again. "Fixed" the troubles of four men waiting for me: one discharged by the Metropolitan Railway for neglect of duty; another wanted a job on the road; the third on the subway; and the fourth was looking for work with a gas company.

- **3:00 P.M.** Attended the funeral of an Italian. Hurried back for the funeral of a Hebrew constituent. Went conspicuously to the front both in the Catholic church and the synagogue.

- **7:00 P.M.** Went to district headquarters to preside over a meeting of election district captains, submitted lists of all the voters in their districts and told who were in need, who were in trouble, who might be won over [to Tammany] and how.

- **8:00 P.M.** Went to a church fair. Took chances on everything, bought ice cream for the young girls and the children, kissed the little ones, flattered their mothers, and took the fathers out for something down at the corner.

- **9:00 P.M.** At the clubhouse again. Spent $10 for a church excursion. Bought tickets for a baseball game. Listened to the complaints of a dozen pushcart peddlers who said they were being persecuted by the police. Promised to go to police headquarters in the morning and see about it.

- **10:30 P.M.** Attended a Hebrew wedding reception and dance. Had previously sent a handsome wedding present to the bride.

- **12:00 A.M.** In bed.

Source: Alistair Cooke, *Alistair Cooke's America* (New York: Knopf, 1973), 290–291; adapted from William L. Riordon, *Plunkitt of Tammany Hall* (New York Dutton, 1963), 91–93.

George Washington Plunkitt holds forth in his unofficial office, a boot-black stand at the New York County Court House.

1900, New York City's machine controlled 60,000 city jobs. In the 1960s and 1970s, Chicago's mayor, Richard Daley, one of the last of the big-city bosses, controlled 35,000 city jobs and, indirectly through public contracts, 10,000 private ones.[22]

Recipients of welfare and jobs from the party were not only grateful but indebted to the party. Fearful of losing their jobs, they provided an army of workers for campaigns, going door-to-door, and, if necessary, taking residents to the polls to cast their votes for the party.

Turnout in elections was sky-high in the era of machine politics. In the 1896 presidential election, party workers managed to get 90 percent of eligible voters (outside the South) to the polls, an astonishing number when many voters lived in isolated rural areas and used horses and buggies for transportation.[23]

Engaging in Corruption   Although the machines provided undeniable benefits, they also engaged in undeniable corruption (as the story about the sweaters illustrates). Bribes and kickbacks were common. Payoffs were necessary for businesses to get government contracts. Widespread corruption eventually produced a backlash against the machines, and the middle class, which was less dependent on the machines, pressured state legislators to enact reforms that led to their demise.

DEMOCRACY?

Does it seem that the parties in this era made government more democratic or less democratic than the parties of today do?

Functions of Parties

When political parties were at the height of their power, they performed important functions for society. When we speak of institutions performing "functions," we mean that institutions do things that society finds useful. These things become their functions. The parties' primary function, then as now, was to get their candidates elected, but to do that, they had to perform other political and social functions that society also found useful. We've already seen that the parties provided welfare and jobs to many people.

The parties recruited candidates for public office from among individuals who were active in the parties. Most started with low-level jobs and worked their way up. (The boss of New York City's machine began by delivering coal to poor people in the winter.) Once the workers had proven themselves, party leaders would consider them for elective office. The party controlled nominations at the local level (city council and mayor), state level (state legislature and governor), and national level (Congress and the president). These nominations weren't open contests in which any aspiring citizen could compete; they were awarded to those who had proven themselves and demonstrated their loyalty. Without the party's blessing, no candidate could secure the nomination nor hope to win the election.

After parties nominated their candidates, the parties ran political campaigns. They mapped strategy, raised funds, and recruited workers. In the 1896 election, party workers brought 750,000 persons from all over the United States to the Ohio home of Republican candidate, William McKinley, who greeted visitors on his front porch.[24]

Parties also provided information about politics through party newspapers. While one-sided, the newspapers helped party supporters learn about politics and government and recognize their stake in politics.[25] After gaining people's allegiance by providing welfare, jobs, and political infor-

mation, the parties were in position to mobilize their supporters on election day.

If successful, especially over consecutive elections, a party could control government. Its elected officials could enact the party's policies. In this way, the party made government responsive to the needs and demands of average citizens.

Thus, the value of political parties in a democracy was to give average people political power. As individuals, ordinary people were powerless. But as members of a political party, they were powerful. Collectively, they could wield power that only corporations or wealthy individuals otherwise could exercise.

So, parties at that time benefited society and in the process strengthened themselves by performing functions that made them indispensable to society. What, however, would happen if parties could no longer perform these functions? We will return to this question shortly.

The Decline of Parties

Although many Americans think that political parties are too powerful today, they are in fact far less powerful than they were in the late nineteenth and early twentieth centuries.

Progressive Reforms

American political parties began to lose power with the advent of the **Progressive movement**, which morphed into a third party, the Progressive Party, in the early 1900s. Middle-class Americans concerned with the corruption of big-city machines fueled the movement, which sought to wrest control from the machines and from the immigrants and poor people they served. The movement championed numerous reforms that reduced corruption but also seriously weakened the power of political parties.

Election reforms including voter registration, the secret ballot, and primary elections brought the golden age of political parties to an end. **Voter registration**, which required voters to register their name and address before an election, made it difficult for parties to stuff ballot boxes with fraudulent votes. (Parties could no longer urge their workers to "vote early and vote often.") The **secret ballot** prevented party workers stationed at the polls from knowing how citizens actually voted. This reduced the incidence of corruption because parties did not know who to reward or who to punish for their votes.

Primary elections were more devastating to the parties. These elections, held several weeks or months before the general election, allowed voters rather than party leaders to decide who would be the party's nominees. Party's leaders could no longer reward the most loyal or effective workers with nominations. Thus, they could not demand allegiance to the party and its policies once a candidate was elected.

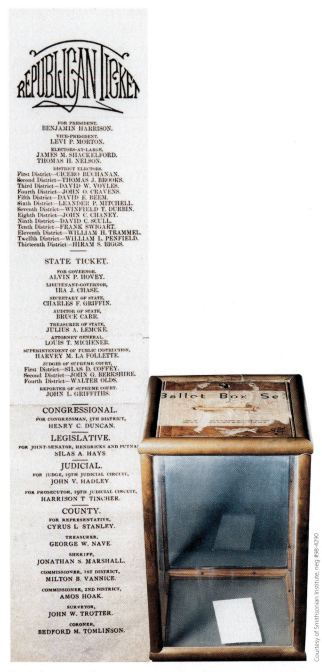

Courtesy of Smithsonian Institute, neg #98-4290

Until the 1890s, there was no pretense of secrecy in voting. Each party's ballot was a different color. Voters chose their party's ballot, like this Republican ballot for the 1888 election in Indiana, and placed it in a clear, glass-sided ballot box.

Primary elections, perhaps more than any other reform, undermined the strength and influence of political parties.

Another Progressive reform, the **merit system**, allocated government jobs on the basis of competence rather than allegiance to the party. Once established, merit systems were expanded to cover more and more jobs. Eventually, the merit systems at the local, state, and national levels replaced the patronage systems for all but a small number of jobs—the top aides to the president, governor, and mayor.

Although the Progressive Party never captured the presidency, it became the most influential third party in American history. Its ideas were enacted into law throughout the country, consequently weakening party organizations.

Impact of the Great Depression

During the Great Depression (starting in 1929), the federal government established welfare programs for the needy and the elderly—basic welfare, now known as Temporary Assistance, and Social Security. In later decades, it added food stamps, Medicaid (health care for poor people), and Medicare (health care for the elderly and others on Social Security). In addition, it provided unemployment compensation to those temporarily out of work.

Because these benefits are available from the government, citizens don't have to rely on political parties to provide them. Thus, government welfare programs, along with government merit systems, severed the links between political parties and many people. No longer the source of welfare and jobs, political parties had less of a hold on the votes of lower- and middle-class Americans.

For the most part, the changes pushed by the Progressives and wrought by the Depression were desirable. Government's welfare programs reached everyone in need, not just those supportive of the political party in power, and merit systems promoted the idea of capable government employees rather than partisan hacks. Although party appointees weren't necessarily incompetent, because party leaders had an incentive to appoint party workers who would reflect well on the party, political appointments did result in incompetent workers performing some jobs. (The downside of staffing government jobs with inexperienced political cronies rather than experienced competent managers was evident when hurricane Katrina hit the Gulf Coast. The political appointees of the Bush administration heading the Federal Emergency Management Administration (FEMA) were ill prepared to deal with the crisis. Their incompetence cost many Americans their lives.)

Rise of Independent Media

The parties also lost their monopoly over political information. Independent newspapers providing a broader and less partisan perspective took the place of party newspapers, and radio and television gained a mass audience, exposing individuals to several news sources. Thus, the monopoly that political parties enjoyed in disseminating political information ended. With parties no longer controlling the information reaching their supporters, people made up their own minds how to vote.

Diminution of Campaign Role

The parties don't even perform their core functions of nominating candidates and running campaigns as they used to.

Party officials no longer determine their nominee for president; party voters in primary elections do. In 1976, Democratic officials were reluctant to endorse Jimmy Carter, who was relatively inexperienced, but Democratic voters in the primaries liked his decency. Carter received enough support from them that the party had to nominate him. Although he won the general election (thus vindicating the voters in the primaries), he was unable to govern effectively (thus vindicating party officials). Consequently, in 1980 he lost his reelection bid.

Party voters in primary elections choose the nominees. The parties still hold their conventions, but the conventions merely ratify the choices of the voters and rally public support for the ticket.

Parties aren't the driving force behind campaigns either. Although candidates receive money, advice and workers from local, state, and national party organizations, most rely on their own campaign teams. Modern media elections require extensive expertise. Candidates for major offices need specialists in polling; fund-raising; and advertising, including experts to design and produce the ads, others to buy TV time and newspaper space for the ads, and others to generate direct mail. Now candidates also need specialists to design and maintain web pages and blogs. They need campaign managers and speechwriters. Some use speech and drama coaches to help them speak, gesture, and move effectively.

This talent is expensive. The 2008 presidential primary candidates spent, collectively, nearly $1 billion. The parties help foot the bills, but they can't afford much of these costs, so the candidates turn to wealthy individuals and interest groups for most of the costs. If elected, the candidates may feel more beholden to their contributors than to the party.

Thus, interest groups play a big role in funding campaigns. As the parties have lost power, interest groups have gained it. Picture a teeter-totter with political parties on one end and interest groups on the other. As the power of political parties has gone down, the power of interest groups has gone up.

For these reasons, elected officials are more independent of their party, and less obligated to follow its platform, than they used to be. Therefore, the parties aren't able to control the government as they used to.

Erosion of Popular Support

Because parties aren't as important as they once were, people, understandably, aren't as attached to them as they once were. **Dealignment** refers to the lessening of citizens' attachment to the parties;[26] it is apparent in several ways.

Increase in Independents

One way is the increase in the proportion of citizens calling themselves **independents** rather than Democrats or Republicans. The proportion has risen from less than 15 percent in 1960 to more than 40 percent in 2000.[27] Younger Americans in particular are more likely to consider themselves independent, which means that the electorate is more likely to become even more independent over time. Although the number of independents is higher now than in the 1960s, the increase in independents may have peaked in the late 1970s and slightly reversed.[28]

Increase in Split Ticket Voting

Another way is the increase in **split-ticket voting**, which is voting for a member of one party for one office and a member of another party for a different office—for example, voting for the Republican presidential candidate but a Democratic House candidate. Voters who split their ticket are not voting on the basis of partisanship, but something else such as the personalities of the candidates or the issues in the campaign. Ticket splitting is more common today than in the 1950s (see Figure 3).[29]

Disinterest in Parties

Americans are also less interested in political parties. As an indication, increasing numbers of Americans say there is nothing they like or dislike about either the Democrats or the Republicans.[30] Parties aren't engaging voters, because they aren't seen as relevant.[31]

DEMOCRACY?

What are the consequences for democracy of the loss of interest in, and support for, the parties? Consider the impact on voting and other forms of political participation.

Figure 3 | Support for Parties

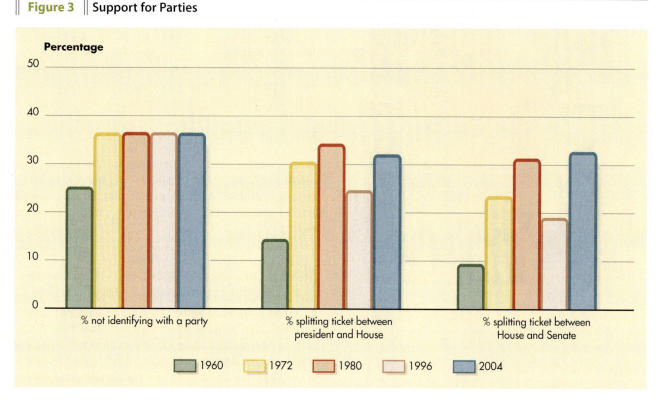

SOURCE: National Election Studies, Center for Political Studies, University of Michigan, 1960–2004 www.umich.edu/nes.

The Resurgence of American Parties

American political parties are resilient. Having emerged early in the nation's history in spite of the Founders' strong reservations, they continue to thrive despite significant public antipathy. In recent decades, parties have adjusted to the changing political landscape by raising substantial amounts of money and bolstering their organizations with professional and specialized staffers and linking with political consultants. Although they are weaker today than a century ago, they still play a very important role in American politics.

Information

Parties continue to provide information to supporters, now through direct mail, radio and television advertising, and the Internet. During election campaigns, party supporters may receive direct mail, e-mails, and phone calls from national, state, and local party organizations and congressional campaign committees extolling the merits of the party's candidates and soliciting contributions for them.

Nominations and Campaigns

Although the parties no longer control the nominations, they do continue to recruit candidates, encouraging individuals to run and providing them with campaign services and financial support. They host workshops on topics such as fund-raising and dealing with the media, and sometimes offer the services of specialized consultants.

Governing

Political parties continue to dominate Congress. The majority party in each house organizes and runs its chamber. It selects the presiding officers, who set the agenda, deciding which issues are debated and which are voted upon. The majority also designates the chairs of the committees and subcommittees and controls the committees and subcommittees.

Members of Congress usually vote with other members of their party, and members of the president's party usually follow his lead. Partisan voting in Congress has increased dramatically since the 1970s.[32] During the Bush presidency, House Republicans voted together 90 percent of the time, and the Democrats voted together about 85 percent of the time (on issues over which the parties opposed each other). (See Figure 4.)

Figure 4 | Party Unity in the House of Representatives is High

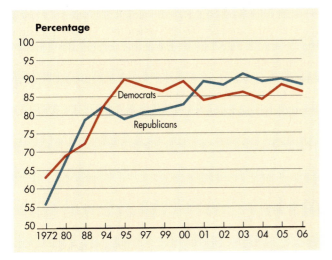

SOURCE: CQ Weekly, *January 3, 2004, 48.*

Before the 1980s, congressional Democrats included many southern moderates and conservatives, who sometimes voted with the Republicans, and congressional Republicans included some northern moderates and liberals, who sometimes voted with the Democrats. Thus, party voting was less prevalent. Since then, southern conservatives have gravitated to the Republican Party, and northern liberals have moved to the Democratic Party (as we'll explain in the next section). Thus, both parties in Congress have become more ideologically consistent.[33]

Party voting in the past fifteen years also reflects the election of conservative Republican members of Congress during the Clinton administration and the election of George W. Bush in 2000 and 2004. Determined to capitalize on their control of the White House and Congress and later on the swell of public support for the president following 9/11, the Republican leaders in Congress pushed a very conservative agenda. With the aid of talk radio, Fox News, and conservative interest groups, Republican leaders pressured the remaining moderate Republicans to go along. If they didn't, they were dubbed "RINOs"—Republicans in name only.[34]

Facing intense heat, the moderates wilted, rationalizing their capitulation by saying that the voters need to see that the party could govern the country.[35] At the same time, Democrats, traditionally less united than Republicans, came together in an attempt to check the very conservative policies of the Republicans. These dynamics led to more partisan voting in Congress.

Party-line voting is likely to remain high as long as each party has a distinct vision of where it wishes to take the country. However, a president committed to building bridges across party lines and a minority party willing to work with him might lessen party voting.

Most Americans deplore partisan wrangling, but clear partisan divisions do help voters recognize the differences between the parties and also help them hold elected officials accountable for their policies. Thus these divisions, which reflect the reality that people don't agree on how to solve the difficult and complex problems facing the country, increase the likelihood of popular control of government.

For example, consider the war in Iraq. The Republican Party's position is to continue it indefinitely, withdrawing only very slowly while trying to ensure that Iraq becomes a democracy. The Democratic Party's position is to establish a timetable for withdrawal. Voting for a Republican candidate means registering an opinion for continuation of the war. Should the Republicans win control of government, the war is likely to continue for some time. The Democrats, should they win, are likely to end the war sooner. The clear distinction between the parties appears to enable voters to choose between them on this issue. In reality, a policy-based choice between the parties is complicated, if not impossible, because not every member of each party has the same view. Moreover, voters typically are interested in more than one issue. They may agree with a party on one, but disagree with it on another.

Despite the increase in partisan voting, the American party system falls short of what political scientists call **responsible party government**. Such government would require that political parties take clear and opposing positions on major issues, that voters understand these differences and vote on this basis, and that officeholders once elected enact the party's positions into law. Some European democracies come close to this ideal. In Britain, members of Parliament vote with the party on major issues, and should they defect—a rare occurrence—they risk being expelled from the party.

In the United States, separation of powers makes responsible party government unlikely. One party may control the presidency, while the other may hold a majority in one or both houses of Congress. When government is divided, voters are unable to fix responsibility for its policies and actions.

Most Americans, who hold individualistic rather than communitarian values, would abhor the lockstep discipline of responsible party government. Yet our free-wheeling system, in which our elected representatives may disregard their party's positions, means that voters don't know how their representatives voted on most matters, so the voters can't hold their representatives accountable for bad policies.

Party Realignments

Although we have two competitive parties, at any given time the two parties aren't evenly matched. Usually one is dominant, winning the presidency and Congress in election after election. Eventually, some major event, such as a war or a depression, destabilizes voters' party allegiance and triggers a massive movement of voters from one party to the other party, which then becomes the dominant party. The process by which one party loses many supporters to the other party is referred to as a **realignment**.

These upheavals—revolutions without bloodshed—have occurred about every 32 to 36 years. Since the party system was established, there have been three major realignments—during the Civil War in the 1860s, the depression in the 1890s,[36] and the Great Depression in the 1930s.[37] There have also been minor realignments limited to certain geographical regions or demographic groups. (See Figure 5.)

Major Realignment in the 1930's

The realignment of the 1930s set the stage for the politics of recent decades. The Republicans had dominated since the realignment of the 1890s. When the Great Depression rocked the country, those hit hardest, such as the poor, working men and women, recent immigrants, and black Americans, who had favored Abraham Lincoln's party since the Civil War, turned to the Democrats. In 1932, **Franklin D. Roosevelt** (FDR) was elected president and

| Figure 5 | Evolution of Political Parties in the United States

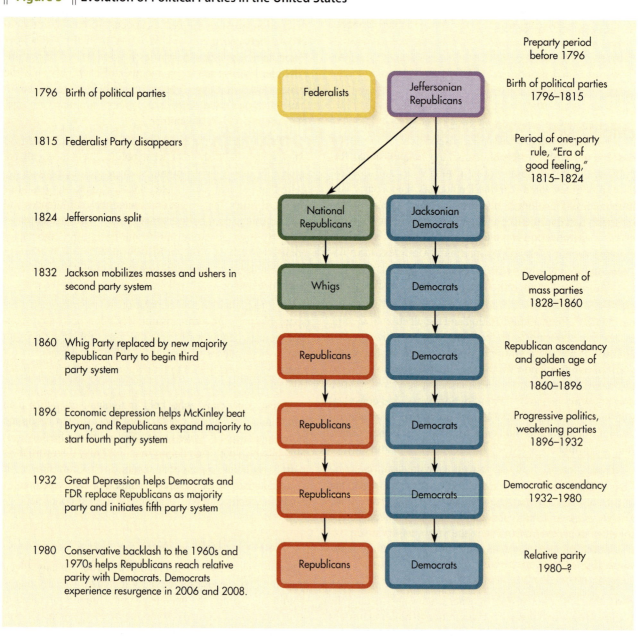

Democratic majorities were sent to Congress. The election started a major realignment, from Republicans to Democrats, and marked a new era. First-time voters and many supporters of the Republicans in previous elections turned to the Democrats for answers to the economic crisis. Democrats would control the presidency for the next twenty years, electing FDR to an unprecedented four terms, and would control at least one house of Congress until 1954.

Roosevelt's **New Deal coalition**, composed of city dwellers, blue-collar workers, Catholic and Jewish immigrants, blacks, and southerners, was a potent political force, but it was an uneasy alliance—conservative, rural, white southerners committed to racial segregation and liberal, urban, black and white northerners. After FDR's death in 1945, the coalition began to fray. With the party's support for civil rights beginning in 1948, which alienated white southerners, and U.S. involvement in the Vietnam War, which split the party in 1968, the coalition continued to erode. Even though the party would continue to dominate Congress until 1994, it would win the presidency only three times after Lyndon Johnson's victory in 1964.[38]

According to the historical pattern, a new realignment occurs about every 32 to 36 years. Thus there should have been another realignment during the 1960s. With the Democratic Party in disarray in 1968 and 1972, Republican Richard Nixon was elected. Nixon's landslide victory in 1972 seemed to confirm a realignment, but his Watergate scandal, forcing him to resign in 1974, tarnished the Republicans' reputation and delayed or diminished the anticipated realignment. The Democrats continued to control Congress and Democrat Jimmy Carter won the presidency in 1976.

Minor Realignment in Recent Decades

A conservative backlash arose by the decade's end. In 1980, Republican Ronald Reagan was elected president (over Carter) and reelected in 1984 in a landslide. His vice president, George H. W. Bush, was elected president in 1988. Although Democrat Bill Clinton was elected president in 1992 and 1996, Republicans gained control of both houses of Congress in 1994, the first time in four decades.

Clearly, the Democrats were no longer the dominant party, but neither were the Republicans. There had been enough realignment to dethrone the Democrats but not enough to enthrone the Republicans. A minor realignment limited to certain geographical regions and demographic groups established a rough equality between the parties. Some blocs of voters had shifted to the Republicans, while others had shifted to the Democrats, with a net gain for the Republicans.

The minor realignment included southern whites, northern blue-collar workers, white-collar professionals, and regular churchgoers.

Southern Whites

In the 1960s, the combination of the civil rights movement and the federal government's efforts to eliminate racial segregation caused many southern whites to leave their long-time home in the Democratic Party. Their move to the Republican Party was the most monumental switch in this minor realignment.

White southerners' unhappiness with the Democratic Party had a long history. After World War II, Democratic President Harry Truman, who took office upon Roosevelt's death, integrated the Armed Forces. In a bid for election in his own right in 1948, Truman and the Democrats included a civil rights plank in the party's platform. The move prompted Strom Thurmond, Democratic governor of South Carolina, to walk out of the party's nominating convention and form a breakaway party, the States' Rights Party, better known as the Dixiecrats. Thurmond ran for president as a minor-party candidate against Truman and carried four southern states. Although the Dixiecrats returned to the fold for a short while, southern discomfort with the party grew in the 1950s when northern Democrats again proposed civil rights legislation. Many white southerners left the party and joined the fledgling Republican Party in the South.

The exodus gained momentum when Democratic president **Lyndon Johnson** pushed, and the Democratic Congress passed, the landmark Civil Rights Act of 1964. The legislation, also supported by many Republicans, gave African Americans the right to patronize private businesses open to the public, such as restaurants, hotels, and theaters. The bill was strenuously opposed throughout the white South and by southern Democrats in Congress because it undermined traditional white supremacy. Upon signing the bill, Johnson commented that it would deliver the South to the Republicans for "the next fifty years."[39]

It didn't take long for his prediction to come true. **Barry Goldwater**, the Republican presidential nominee running against Johnson in 1964, denounced the act as an affront to "**states' rights**." While Goldwater himself seemed not to have a racial motive and believed in states' rights in other areas too, Republicans used his opposition to appeal to southern segregationists.[40] With a wink and a nod, "states' rights" became code for letting the South maintain segregation. Goldwater carried five states in the Deep South, more than any Republican since the New Deal.

In his bid for the presidency in 1968, **Richard Nixon** consciously pursued a **southern strategy** to lure disaffected southern whites from the Democratic Party. He promised "to change the direction" of the Supreme Court, which had ordered desegregation of the public schools, and to appoint southern judges to the Court. Appealing to white voters, he used racial code words such as "states' rights," "law and order," and "welfare." This sent a clear message that the states should be allowed to handle their racial matters as they saw fit; the states should be allowed to control black demonstrators, rioters, and criminals better than the courts were permitting them to; and the states should be allowed to crack down on welfare cheats, who were African American. After taping a campaign commercial stressing "law and order in the schools," he said to his aides, "Yep, this hits it right on the nose. . . . It's all about law and order and the damn Negro–Puerto Rican groups out there."[41]

In 1980, Ronald Reagan followed Nixon's lead. He opened his presidential campaign with a "states' rights" speech in Philadelphia, Mississippi, where three civil rights workers had been brutally murdered by local citizens with assistance from law enforcement officers, one of the most notorious crimes of the civil rights era (see Chapter 15). Reagan also referred to "welfare queens," a thinly veiled reference to black women presumably living the high life on welfare.

George H. W. Bush, campaigning against Democratic nominee Michael Dukakis in 1988, ran a television commercial featuring a black felon, Willie Horton, whom Dukakis, as the governor of Massachusetts and following the policy of the state, had granted a weekend furlough. While on furlough, Horton raped a white woman. The link between black criminals and Democratic candidates evidently was a deliberate strategy, and a new iteration of the southern strategy. The commercial was so powerful that when people were asked after the election what they recalled about the campaign, they mentioned "Bush, Dukakis, and Willie Horton."[42]

Although hardly concealed, the racial strategy of the Republican Party was implemented carefully and cautiously, with code words that stated one thing but meant something else. Candidates and party officials rarely, if ever, praised segregation or used racial epithets, as politicians of both parties had in earlier generations. Whenever confronted about their racial strategy, Republicans claimed that their statements were not racist.

However, in an unguarded moment celebrating the 100th birthday in 2002 of Strom Thurmond, who formed the Dixiecrats and later joined fellow southerners who switched to the Republican party, Trent Lott, a Mississippi Republican and Senate majority leader, disregarded these norms. He declared that his state was proud to have voted for Thurmond in 1948. He added, "And if the rest of the country had followed our lead, we wouldn't have had all these problems over the years either." For his lapse, Lott apologized, but the public condemnation, including a rebuke by President Bush, forced him to resign his position as majority leader.

The shift of white southerners to the Republican party doesn't mean that all or even most are racist. What is clear, however, is that since 1964 the Republicans have used a

Arizona Senator Barry Goldwater captured the Republican nomination for president in 1964. His nomination reflected the ascendancy of the conservatives in the party. Moderate and liberal Republicans worried that his defense of "extremism" would alienate many Americans. In response, his supporters at a Republican women's convention wore smiling masks to ease these concerns.

Strom Thurmond broke with the Democratic Party to run for president in 1948 on the Dixiecrat segregation ticket. Later he became a Republican. In 2002, President Bush and Senate leader and fellow Republican Trent Lott (center) congratulate him on his 100th birthday.

conservative and sometimes implicitly racist approach to race-related issues to build their dominance in the region, just as Democrats did for generations before them.

Although racial attitudes were the early driving force behind the shift of southern whites, their conservative views on other issues, ranging from foreign policy to gun control to matters of faith, made the Republican Party a congenial place for them.

The southern strategy proved highly successful for the Republican Party. The South went from a solidly Democratic region to a reliably Republican one. Since 1968, the Republicans have carried the South in every presidential election except 1976, when the Democrats nominated former Georgia governor Jimmy Carter. Even then, a majority of southern whites voted for the Republican, Gerald Ford. Since 1994, Republicans have garnered a majority of southern white votes for their congressional, state, and local candidates as well. At the same time, southern blacks have become the mainstay of the southern Democratic Party.[43]

The shift of conservative southern whites to the Republican Party not only makes the South more Republican but it also makes the Republican Party more conservative. The southern Republican members of Congress are more conservative than the southern Democratic members they replaced, and they are more conservative than many Republican members in the North. They push the party to the right, and the departure of southern Democrats from the Democratic Party makes that party more liberal. Thus, the transformation of the South has made the parties more ideological and led to greater polarization and less cooperation between the parties in Congress.

Northern Blue-Collar Workers

Blue-collar workers, the second- and third-generation sons and daughters of European immigrants, especially from Catholic countries such as Ireland and Italy, were at the heart of the New Deal coalition.[44] But when southern whites left the Democratic Party in the latter part of the twentieth century, some northern blue-collar workers did too.[45]

With the New Deal's success and the 1950s' and 1960s' booming economy, blue-collar workers enjoyed the economic security that allowed them to consider other issues. As the Democratic Party turned from bread-and-butter issues to civil rights, the Vietnam War, and women's equality—issues that motivated the upper middle class more than the lower middle class—some blue-collar workers abandoned the party. Although liberal on economic issues, they were conservative on social issues and on foreign policies. Many were drawn to the Republicans' emphasis on "traditional" values.

Reagan captured most of these voters in 1980 and 1984. However, as the economy turned sour in the 1990s, some returned to their partisan roots and voted for Clinton. "In 2000, 2004, and 2008, majorities of blue collar workers continued to support the Democrats. Thus, the movement of blue collar workers to the Republicans was temporary, though it did contribute to Democratic defeats in the Reagan years."

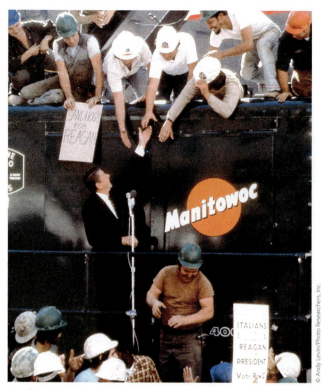

The Republican Party has tried to pull blue-collar workers away from their traditional home in the Democratic Party. As president, Ronald Reagan was especially effective in luring these voters.

White-Collar Professionals

From the Depression through the 1980s, more affluent, better-educated, white-collar workers voted Republican. However, as blue-collar workers flirted with the Republican Party, white-collar professionals, especially teachers, lawyers, doctors, and scientists, found the Democratic Party more attractive. (Most business executives remained in the Republican Party.)

In general, professionals rejected the uncompromising and intolerant approach of the Republican core on social issues. They tend to be supportive of abortion rights and take a "live and let live" approach to homosexuality.[46] While the Democratic Party's embrace of the civil rights, environmental, and women's movements turned off blue-collar workers, professionals were drawn to the party because of it. White-collar professionals also have more liberal attitudes toward foreign policies than blue-collar workers have. (Student demonstrators, many of whom would become professionals, infuriated the "hard hats" by protesting against the Vietnam War.) In recent elections, the Democrats have fared very well in affluent communities populated by white-collar professionals.[47]

Regular Churchgoers

Catholic and Jewish immigrants were also a significant part of Roosevelt's New Deal coalition. Since the Depression, Catholics and Jews tended to be Democrats, while Protes-

tants tended to be Republicans. As economic issues gave way to social issues in the 1980s, differences in the party affiliation of Protestants, Catholics, and Jews declined.

A new religious cleavage has emerged between those who are very religious and those who are not. Weekly churchgoers congregate in the Republican Party and less religious people connect with the Democratic Party. Church attendance now is more correlated with party affiliation than either income or education is.[48] Because there are more weekly churchgoers than non-churchgoers, the shift has benefited Republicans. That shift may be temporary, as the number of non-churchgoers is growing faster than regular churchgoers. Among people 18 to 25 years old, 20 percent report no religious affiliation, up from 11 percent in the late 1980s.[49]

The Supreme Court's abortion ruling in 1973 was a catalyst prompting conservative Christians who deplored the sexual revolution and the secular drift of modern America to become politically active. They formed pro-life groups that coalesced into the Christian right. Eventually, the Christian right became one of the strongest forces in the Republican Party. Former senator John Danforth (R-Mo.), himself a minister, observed that his party had been transformed "into the political arm of conservative Christians."[50]

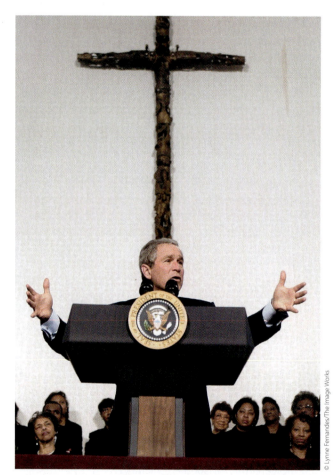

Republicans have allied themselves with conservative Christians, especially churchgoing Protestant Evangelicals. George W. Bush spoke their language.

BEHIND THE SCENES
GIVE ME THAT OLD TIME RELIGION

Prior to a campaign rally in Minnesota during the spring presidential primaries, one of the candidates seeking his party's nomination joined hands with his campaign staff and prayed.[1] The practice had become something of a ritual from the first days in Iowa. Probably Mike Huckebee? Maybe Mitt Romney? Could it be John McCain? Actually, it was Barack Obama. Obama, a Christian, is more open about his faith their either John Kerry, the 2004 Democratic nominee, or Al Gore, the 2000 nominee.

Kerry's opponent, George W. Bush did more religious outreach in 2004 than any campaign in history. In Florida alone, the party employed a leader for Evangelical outreach who appointed a dozen regional coordinators and designated outreach chairs in each of the state's 67 counties. Republican county chairs recruited dozens of volunteers to contact and register their Evangelical friends and neighbors. The Kerry campaign, in contrast, hired one inexperienced staff aide and an intern to oversee religious outreach. His reluctance to fight for the religious vote may have cost him the election.

On the campaign trail, John Edwards, Kerry's running mate, carried a copy of *The Purpose Driven Life*, a popular devotional book by Evangelical author and megachurch pastor Rick Warren. Edwards read the book daily like tens of millions of other Americans, but voters never learned about this. Republican strategists, on the other hand, trumpeted the fact that Bush started every morning with readings from a popular book of Evangelical essays.

And when Terry McAuliffe, then chair of the Democratic National Committee, was introduced to Warren during the campaign, McAuliffe with a smile stuck out his hand, "Nice to meet you Rick and what do you do."[2]

In battleground Ohio, Democratic Catholic activists approached the campaign about canvassing Catholic churches in Columbus to appeal to Catholic voters. To their amazement, they were told, "We don't do white churches."[3]

When Kerry finally did get around to sharing something of his faith and values a week before the election, it wasn't at a Catholic university in Ohio as planned, but because of staff concerns about an abortion protest, it was in a senior center in Florida. Kerry lost the Catholic vote in Ohio 44 percent to 55 percent, and the state by 118,000 votes.

In contrast, Obama advised the party to reach out to religious voters and empowered Evangelicals in his campaign. Instead of avoiding Catholic voters, the campaign initiated discussions about abortion. Instead of silencing pro-life supporters, he encouraged Democrats to show tolerance and respect. And Obama is on a first-name basis with Rick Warren.

[1] Amy Sullivan, "Finding their Faith," *Time*, February 25, 2008, 38–39.
[2] Ibid.
[3] Ibid.

The Current Party System

In this minor realignment, the net result is a gain for the GOP, because the southern whites, northern blue-collar workers, and regular churchgoers who left the Democratic Party far outnumber the white-collar professionals who left the Republican Party. This minor realignment has created a rough parity between the two parties. Neither party dominates. A major realignment that would have put the Republicans on top has not occurred.

A major realignment is not likely to occur now. In the early 2000s, with the patriotic fervor following the 9/11 attacks, back-to-back elections of President Bush and Republican majorities in Congress, the party had an extraordinary opportunity to solidify and expand its gains. Karl Rove, the president's top political adviser, worked mightily to achieve his goal of a permanent realignment. But the party overreached, adopting policies to benefit its core constituencies rather than the nation as a whole. Tax cuts went to the wealthiest Americans and big business. Energy, environmental, and consumer regulations were rolled back. Religious conservatives were courted with heated rhetoric about gay marriage and abortion. Most damaging, the administration pursued an aggressive foreign policy, using the "war on terrorism" to launch a preemptive attack on Iraq. As the war dragged on and deficits from tax cuts, war spending, and new entitlements soared, the popularity of the president and the party plummeted, allowing the Democrats to win control of both houses of Congress by small margins in 2006.

When we look to the future, we see a cloudy crystal ball. In 2008, voters were highly energized and partisan. Hundreds of thousands of voters registered for the first time, and turnout in the election was higher than for many years. The vast majority of the new voters were Democrats, and many counties across the nation switched from Republican to Democratic in their allegiances. Although this might suggest a realignment changing the balance of power to Democratic dominance again. It is far too soon to predict that. The party's success in governing will determine whether the Democratic resurgence in 2006 and 2008 is only temporary.

Party Identification

Party identification is the psychological link that individuals feel toward a party. Unlike European parties, which have official members who pay dues and sign pledges accepting party principles, American parties have no formal members. You are a Democrat or a Republican if you see yourself as one.

Almost two-thirds of Americans identify with a party. In 2008, about 35 percent of Americans identified themselves as Democrats, 30 percent as Republicans, and the rest as independents.[52]

We like to think that we're rational individuals exercising free will when we adopt a party, but that isn't the case for most people. Party identification typically is determined by our parents' party affiliation; our sexual, racial, ethnic, and religious characteristics; and various geographic factors.

The previous section has explained the party identification of some groups that have realigned, but we'll recapitulate those groups and address other groups so you'll have a complete picture of party identification today.

Parents' Party Affiliation

Party identification usually develops through the process of political socialization, explained in Chapter 4. Parents pass down political views, including party identification, to their children. If both parents identify with the same party, their children are likely to identify with that party. If the parents identify with different parties, their children get mixed signals and may identify with either party or be independent. If both parents are uninterested in politics, their children may ignore or reject both parties.

While the party identification of one's parents is the most important determinant of party identification, other factors in life can reinforce or weaken it.

Sexual, Racial, Ethnic, and Religious Characteristics

The two genders and some racial groups, ethnic groups, and religious groups favor a particular party, so if you belong to one of these groups, it's likely that you'll favor the same party.

From the time women earned the right to vote through most of the twentieth century, men and women voted simi-

larly. In the 1980s, however, a **gender gap** emerged. During this conservative era, more men moved to the right than women did. Men liked Reagan's muscular foreign policies and his probusiness views.[53] Women preferred the Democrats' social policies, using government to cushion life's hardships and to regulate business's impact on its employees and on the environment. Women also rejected aggressive foreign policies, including military action and military spending. (The gap isn't due to abortion views. Men's and women's views are similar.) The gap is most marked for working women and unmarried women. These women are more likely to be Democrats. Men and stay-at-home moms are more likely to be Republicans.[54]

The greater tolerance of the Democratic Party to alternative lifestyles is a strong incentive for homosexuals to identify with that party. Republican opposition to same-sex marriage and civil unions has resulted in large numbers of gays and lesbians identifying themselves as Democrats.

Racial minorities tend to be Democrats. African Americans cast a higher percentage of their votes for Democratic candidates than any other group. They have never left the New Deal coalition because the Democrats have championed civil rights and economic policies favorable to working people.

Latinos are not a monolithic group; their political preferences vary by their country of origin and that of their parents. Cuban Americans in South Florida have been staunch Republicans, though some generational differences are beginning to emerge. Puerto Rican, Mexican, and Latin Americans tend to be Democrats, though to a lesser extent than African Americans. In recent elections, Asian Americans have also supported Democratic candidates. (See box, "The Changing Asian American Voter.")

Although some Latinos and Asians have lived in the United States for generations, especially Latinos in the Southwest who predated the arrival of Anglos in the East, many are immigrants or from families of recent immigrants. As relative newcomers, their party identification isn't as fixed as other Americans' identification is. Both parties are vying for their loyalty, especially for Latinos' loyalty, because they are the fastest-growing population group in the United States.

The Republicans are concerned that they will not remain a competitive party without the support of significant numbers of Latino voters. The Bush administration made a concerted effort to woo them. The president gave his weekly radio address in Spanish, appointed a Hispanic as White House counsel and then attorney general, and proposed immigration reform that would allow illegal immigrants in the United States for a long time to work toward citizenship rather than be deported. His immigration proposal, however, was rejected by Republicans in Congress.

Most Jews remain Democrats, but Catholics waver between the parties, giving a slight majority to Bush in 2004, but to Gore in 2000. As with Protestants, regular churchgo-

american diversity | The Changing Asian American Voter

Though Chinese first came to this country in the early nineteenth century, and the first Asian Americans were elected to Congress in 1962, it is only in the past two decades that Asian Americans have become a political force nationally. In the past few presidential elections, candidates have sought their votes.

Unlike other racial and ethnic groups, whose political allegiances have been relatively constant during the past two decades, Asian Americans have made an interesting shift. The figure shows that the proportion of Asian Americans voting Democratic in the last four presidential elections has risen sharply.

Given that the same principles govern the party allegiances of Asian Americans as any other group, that is, that party allegiances through time tend to be stable, why do we see such a rapid change in allegiance? In the case of Asian Americans, the composition of the population has changed rapidly with immigration. What formerly was a small part of the American population, and dominated largely by Japanese Americans and to a smaller extent Chinese Americans, is now a growing segment of the population. More than ten million Asian Americans live in communities all over the United States. To the existing Japanese and Chinese American population have come Koreans, Vietnamese, Indians, Filipinos, to name only the largest groups who have arrived since 1980.

These abrupt changes in the composition of the population brought about new ways of thinking and generational shifts. This is similar to how other seismic historical events, such as the New Deal or the civil rights movement, shaped the party loyalties of other generations of Americans.

Asian Americans Increasingly Support Democratic Presidential Candidates

The figures are the percentage of votes cast by Asian Americans for the Democratic presidential candidates in 1992 through 2004.
SOURCE: CNN Exit Polls.

ing Catholics favor the Republicans; less religious Catholics favor the Democrats.

Socioeconomic Characteristics

Individuals' education, occupation, and income, which indicate their social class, also influence their party identification. Historically, the parties split clearly along class lines, with the upper classes being Republicans and the lower classes being Democrats. However, the pattern has blurred in recent decades because of the emergence of social issues, such as abortion, gay rights, and gun control. The upper class itself still prefers the Republicans, and the lower class itself strongly prefers the Democrats. But educational and occupational characteristics have created exceptions to the historical pattern.

Individuals with graduate degrees (beyond undergraduate school) have gravitated to the Democrats. They are part of the minor realignment that has occurred in recent decades. In addition, white-collar workers in the public sector—government and education—are mostly Democrats. On the other hand, white-collar workers in the private sector remain disproportionately Republicans.

Geographic Factors

Party identification is also influenced by residence. Both region of the country and whether a community is urban, suburban, exurban, or rural are related to party identification.

The Great Plains and the Rocky Mountain West traditionally have been Republican bastions. The South, in the minor realignment of recent decades, has become another Republican region. The Northeast and the West Coast are mostly Democratic regions. These patterns give rise to red and blue states, discussed in Chapter 4.

Big cities are strong Democratic locales, and small towns and rural areas tend to have large Republican majorities. Suburbs lie in between. Some resemble the stereotypical suburb, spotted with posh homes owned by business executives, and they are mostly Republican. Others, located on the fringe of the city itself, are mostly Democratic. Exurbs, which are the rapidly growing areas just beyond the suburbs, are heavily Republican.

Now consider the last three categories addressed previously—sexual, racial, ethnic, and religious characteristics; socioeconomic characteristics; and geographic factors. These characteristics and factors themselves don't make people Democrats or Republicans. Residing on the coast doesn't make one a Democrat any more than residing in the heartland makes one a Republican. Rather, each of these characteristics represents a set of experiences or a network of family, friends, and neighbors at home or of colleagues at work that leads individuals to identify with one party rather than another. Black Americans, for example, have a history of economic hardship and pervasive discrimination, which prompted them to become Democrats in the twentieth century. Thus individuals are surrounded by others who reinforce their party affiliation.

Changes in Party Identification

Party affiliation usually remains constant through an individual's life. However, one's party identification can change if the country experiences a major economic, political, or social upheaval. The Great Depression was a catalyst for some people, prompting numerous Republicans to become Democrats. The civil rights movement and the Vietnam War were catalysts for other people, prompting numerous Democrats to become Republicans and some Republicans to become Democrats (as we've seen).

Individuals who come into the electorate at a particular time are shaped by the partisan environment that prevails. For example, most voters who first voted in the 1930s supported Roosevelt and became Democrats, (and most of them still are Democrats). Many voters who first voted in 1980 supported Reagan and became Republicans. Voters who came of age during the Clinton and George W. Bush administrations increasingly became Democrats. For a glimpse of partisan differences from one generation to the next, see Figure 6.

One's party identification can also change if one's social status changes—for example, getting a college degree, especially a graduate degree; pursuing a professional career; and moving to a different place. Such changes provide new experiences and more exposure to different people, which can lead to new political views and party identification.

In the next chapter, we'll see that party identification is one factor—an important factor, but only one factor—that determines how people vote.

DEMOCRACY?

In what ways do parties make American government more democratic?

Conclusion: Do Political Parties Make Government More Responsive?

Although the Founders initially opposed the idea of political parties, some eventually turned to parties when they realized that there was no consensus to govern the country. Then, as now, there were sharp differences among the people. To prevail, political leaders recognized that they needed a following of loyal supporters to elect the candidates and adopt the policies they favored. Parties arose, and continue, primarily as vehicles to organize people to win elections.

But parties not only serve the needs of politicians, they also serve the needs of citizens. The party label next to a candidate's name on the ballot provides an important piece of information, especially for citizens who have little knowledge regarding a candidate's stand on issues. Even citizens who pay attention to politics can be confused when deciding which candidate is best for them because campaigns do not always illuminate the differences between the candidates or their stands on complex issues. Indeed, sometimes campaigns obscure them. So voters can use party labels as cues. Because the parties and their candidates have a history of taking positions and casting votes on issues, knowing a candidate's party provides a general understanding of the candidate's positions. Thus parties ease the tasks of citizens and increase the probability that they will make decisions that serve their interests.

By attracting and aggregating millions of people, the parties help average Americans influence government officials and policies. The parties give ordinary people political power they would not have otherwise. Without the parties, only wealthy people or celebrities would have the money or

Figure 6 | Party Affiliation by Generation

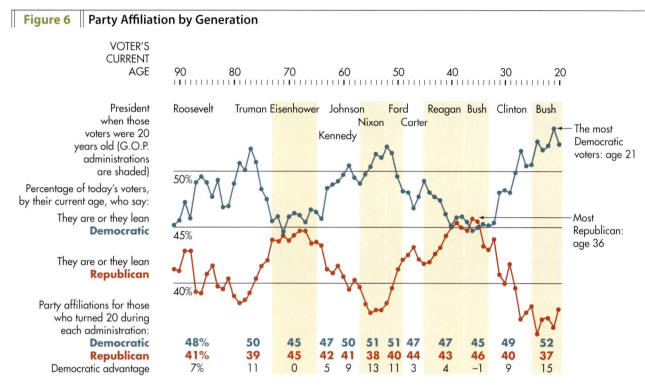

Some new voters are affected by the political atmosphere that prevails when they come of age, and most continue to vote for the same party as they grow older. Those who came of age during the Depression, World War II, the Vietnam War, or the Watergate scandal were very likely to become Democrats. Those who came of age during the Eisenhower or Reagan years were less likely to do so. Those casting their first votes in recent years have been the most Democratic, and least Republican, voters of any generation.

prominence to wield any clout. Thus the major contribution of parties to democracy is to make government more responsive to citizens.

The parties also provide a counterweight to interest groups. Although interest groups represent people, and large interest groups represent many people, they represent a narrower range of people—those with a particular interest—than parties do. Each of the parties—the two "big tents"—tries to attract a majority of the people. When the parties succeed, they can check the influence of special interests.

There is no doubt that parties are weaker than they were a century ago. However, they have halted their decline and have, in fact, experienced a resurgence. All three party components—members, officeholders, and party organizations—show signs of reinvigoration. The number of people claiming party allegiance has grown slightly, while the number claiming to be independent and casting a split ticket has decreased slightly. Partisan voting in Congress has increased markedly. Party organizations, particularly at the national level, have become much stronger and taken on new roles to help their candidates.

These changes have come at a time when conservatives, in response to what they see as the liberalism and secular-

ism of the 1960s and 1970s and the influence of these trends ever since, have launched aggressive attempts to redirect government policy. In doing so, the conservatives have made the Republican Party more cohesive and forced the Democratic Party to become more cohesive as well in order to defend its values against Republican initiatives. Once these cultural struggles subside, will the two parties be able to maintain the vigor they display today?

American citizens, especially young adults, are cynical toward parties. Yet parties serve important functions. Without parties, voters would face a bewildering array of candidates. They would be at the mercy of campaign consultants, big donors, special interests, and the media. Without parties, conflicts over how to use the nation's limited resources—what politics is about—would still exist, but narrower interests would have greater influence, and average men and women would have less.

The dean of American political scientists recently concluded that "we can be pretty sure that a country wholly without competitive parties is a country without democracy."[55] Although the existence of competitive parties is no guarantee that average men and women will prevail, they would most assuredly fail without parties.

Key Terms

partisan

political parties

two-party system

Democratic Party

Republican Party

multiparty systems

single-member districts

winner-take-all provision

proportional representation

national party chair

national committee

Federalists

Jeffersonians

Jacksonian democracy

political machines

patronage system

spoils system

Progressive movement

voter registration

secret ballot

primary elections

merit systems

dealignment

independents

split-ticket voting

responsible party government

realignment

New Deal coalition

"states' rights"

southern strategy

party identification

gender gap

Key Names

Ralph Nader

Alexander Hamilton

Thomas Jefferson

Andrew Jackson

Franklin D. Roosevelt

Lyndon Johnson

Barry Goldwater

Richard Nixon

Please visit our companion website at www.cengage.com/politicalscience/welch/uag12e or use CengageNOW for additional resources dealing with this chapter.

John McCain's last-minute choice of Sarah Palin as his vice presidental running mate surprised and energized the Republican Party and its conservative base.

Brooks Kraft/Corbis

Elections

8

Talking Points

Because of the geographic mobility and economic circumstances that allow most Americans to move around more than previously, Americans are much more likely than in previous generations to live among others of similar economic statuses and cultural beliefs. For example, although in 1970 people with college degrees were fairly evenly spread across cities, today college graduates cluster in particular areas.[1] And, in turn, those areas are booming, while other areas decline. Young people are leaving some areas and congregating in others.

Because cultural differences influence political choices, this "**Big Sort**" has had dramatic political consequences. As the author of the book by that name illustrates, before 1980, only about a third of voters lived in counties where one or the other presidential candidate won by a landslide (at least 20 points). In 2004, nearly half of the voters did.

That sorting, in turn, has consequences for democracy. Communities of like-minded individuals can become homogeneous and even extreme in their political attitudes because there is not a diversity of opinions generated by individuals of widely different circumstances. Central cities are overwhelmingly Democratic while many suburbs and small towns are overwhelmingly Republican.

Each community can act boldly based on its relatively homogeneous constituency; some communities pass end-the-war resolutions while others pass those supporting the president, for example. The representatives they send to Congress are, however, more extreme than if the community was moderate and diverse. Consequently, Congress becomes more polarized and dysfunctional as communities become more homogeneous and able to act.

Americans have fought and died in wars to preserve the rights of citizens to choose their leaders through democratic elections. Some have even died here at home trying to exercise these rights. Despite this, most Americans take these important rights for granted; about half do not bother to vote even in presidential elections, and fewer still participate in other ways.

Moreover, the process by which we choose our leaders, especially the president, has been sharply criticized in recent years. Critics charge that election campaigns are meaningless and offer little information to the voters, that candidates pander to the most ill-informed and mean-spirited citizens, and that public relations and campaign spending, not positions on issues or strength of character, determine the winners. Then in 2000, and again in 2004, it also became apparent that some voters' votes were not counted even when they went to the polls, largely due to defects in the election process itself.

In this chapter, we analyze why voting is important to a democracy and why, despite its importance, so few do it. Then we examine political campaigns and elections to see how they affect the kinds of leaders and policies we have. We will see that the lack of participation by many reinforces the government's responsiveness to those who do participate, especially those who are well organized.

The American Electorate

During the more than two centuries since the Constitution was written, two important developments have altered the right to vote, termed **suffrage**. First, suffrage gradually was extended to include almost all citizens aged eighteen or over. This expansion occurred largely through federal action: constitutional amendments, congressional acts, and Supreme Court decisions. Second, recently, serious issues of lack of access to the ballot have arisen. These limitations are largely being imposed by several states under the guise of ensuring that only eligible voters vote.

Early Limits on Voting Rights

Although the Declaration of Independence states that "all men are created equal," at the time of the Constitution and shortly thereafter the central political right of voting was denied to most Americans. States decided who would be granted suffrage. In some, only an estimated 10 percent of the white males could vote, whereas in others 80 percent could.[2]

Controversial property qualifications for voting existed in many states. Some argued that only those with an economic stake in society should have a say in political life. But critics of the property requirement repeated a story of Tom Paine's:

You require that a man shall have $60 worth of property, or he shall not vote. Very well . . . here is a man who today owns a jackass, and the jackass is worth $60.

Today the man is a voter and he goes to the polls and deposits his vote. Tomorrow the jackass dies. The next day the man comes to vote without his jackass and he cannot vote at all. Now tell me, which was the voter, the man or the jackass?[3]

Because the Constitution gave states the power to regulate suffrage, ⭐ the elimination of property requirements was a gradual process. By the 1820s, most were gone, although some lingered to midcentury.

In some states, religious tests also were applied. A voter had to be a member of the "established" church or could not be a member of certain religions (such as Roman Catholicism or Judaism). However, religious tests disappeared even more quickly than property qualifications.

By the time of the Civil War, state action had expanded the rights of white men. However, neither slaves, Indians, nor free southern blacks could vote, although northern blacks could in a few states.[4] Women's voting rights were confined to local elections in a few states.[5]

Blacks and the Right to Vote

The Civil War began the long, slow, and often violent process of expanding the rights of blacks to full citizenship. Between 1865 and 1870, three amendments were passed to give political rights to former slaves and other blacks. One, the Fifteenth Amendment, ⭐ prohibited the denial of voting rights on the basis of race and thus gave the right to vote to black men.

For a short time following the ratification of this amendment, a northern military presence in the South and close monitoring of southern politics enabled blacks to vote and hold office in the South, where 90 percent of all blacks lived. During this **Reconstruction** period, two southern blacks were elected to the Senate and fourteen were elected to the House of Representatives between 1869 and 1876. One state, South Carolina, even had a black majority in its legislature. In most places, however, blacks did not dominate politics or even receive a proportional share of offices; whites saw blacks' political activities as a threat to their own dominance. White southerners began to prevent blacks from voting through intimidation that ranged from mob violence and lynchings to economic sanctions against blacks who attempted to vote.

Northerners tolerated these methods, both violent and nonviolent. The northern public and political leaders had lost interest in the fate of blacks or had simply grown tired of the struggle. In 1876, a compromise ended Reconstruction. In the wake of the disputed 1876 presidential election, southern Democrats agreed to support Republican Rutherford B. Hayes for president in return for an end to the

RADICAL MEMBERS

OF THE FIRST LEGISLATURE AFTER THE WAR

SOUTH CAROLINA

Dusenberry	Mayes	Demars	Rivers	Miteford	Smith	Swails
McKinlay	Jillson	Brodie	Duncan	White	Pettengill	Perrin
Dickson	Lomax	Hayes	BOOZER	Barton	Hyde	James
Wilder	Jackson	Cain	Smythe	Boston	Lee	Johnston
Hoyt	Thomas	Maxwell	Wright	Shrewsbury	Simonds	Wimbush
Randolph	Webb	Martin	MOSES	Mickey	Chesnut	Hayes
Harris	Bozeman	Cook	Sancho	Henderson	McDaniel	Farr
	Tomlinson	Miller	Sanders	Hewell	Williams	Meade
	Wright *		Nuckles	Hayne	Gardiner	Thompson
				Mobley		Rainey
				Hudson		
				Nash		
				Carmand		

* Afterwards associate Justice of the Supreme Court of the State

7578 G.

Library of Congress

Blacks comprised a majority of the population in South Carolina in 1866 and elected a black majority to the state legislature. The black legislators worked for civil rights, black male suffrage, and state constitutional reform. *Radical* was the name given to Republicans at that time.

northern military presence in the South and a hands-off policy toward activities there. By the end of the nineteenth century, blacks were effectively disfranchised in all of the South. The last southern black member of Congress served to 1901. Another would not be elected until 1972.

Southern constitutions and laws legitimized the loss of black voting rights. **Literacy tests** were often required, supposedly to make sure voters could read and write and thus evaluate political information. Most blacks, who had been denied education, were illiterate. Many whites also were illiterate, but fewer were barred from voting. Local election registrars exercised nearly complete discretion in deciding who had to take the test and how to administer and evaluate it. Educated blacks often were asked for legal interpretations of obscure constitutional provisions, which few could provide.

Some laws had exemptions that whites were allowed to take advantage of. An "understanding clause" exempted those who could not read and write but who could explain sections of the federal or state constitution to the satisfaction of the examiner, and a "good moral character clause" exempted those with such character. Again, local election registrars exercised discretion in deciding who understood the Constitution and who had good character. Finally, the

grandfather clause exempted those whose grandfathers had the right to vote before 1867—that is, before blacks could legally vote in the South.

The **poll tax** also deprived blacks of voting rights. The tax, though only a couple of dollars, was often a sizable portion of working people's monthly income. In some states, individuals had to pay not only for the present election but also for every past election in which they were eligible to vote but did not.

In the **white primary**, where party nominees were chosen, blacks were barred from voting. Because the Democrats always won the general elections, the real contests were in the Democratic primaries. The states justified excluding blacks on the grounds that political parties were private rather than government organizations and thus could discriminate just as private clubs or individuals could.

Less formal means were also used to exclude blacks from voting. Registrars often closed their offices when blacks tried to register, or whites threatened blacks with the loss of jobs or housing if they tried to vote. Polling places were sometimes located far from black neighborhoods or were moved at the last minute without notifying potential voters. If these means failed, whites threatened or practiced violence. In one election in Mobile, Alabama, whites wheeled a cannon to a polling place and aimed it at about 1000 blacks lined up to vote.

The treatment of blacks by the southern establishment was summarized on the floor of the Senate by South Carolina Senator Benjamin ("Pitchfork Ben") Tillman, who served from 1895 to 1918. As he put it, "We took the government away. We stuffed ballot boxes. We shot them. We are not ashamed of it."[6]

Over time, the Supreme Court and Congress outlawed the "legal" barriers to black voting in the South. The Court invalidated the grandfather clause in 1915 and the white primary in 1944. Through the ⭐ Twenty-fourth Amendment, Congress abolished the poll tax for federal elections in 1964, and the Court invalidated the tax for state elections in 1966.[7] But threats of physical violence and economic reprisals still kept most southern blacks from voting. Although many blacks in the urban areas of the rim South (such as Florida, North Carolina, Tennessee, and Texas) could and did vote, those in the rural South and most in the Deep South could not; in 1960, black voter registration ranged from 5 to 40 percent in southern states.[8] (See the box titled "Blacks and Hispanics in Office.")

The Voting Rights Act and Redistricting

Despite our shameful history of depriving African Americans the right to vote, today black voting rates approach those of whites. In the Deep South, much of this dramatic change was

american diversity | Blacks and Hispanics in Office

Before the Voting Rights Act (VRA) in 1965, few African Americans held major public office. Only a handful were members of Congress, and few were state legislators, mayors of major cities, or other important political officers. Following the VRA, southern blacks began to have the political clout to elect members of their own race to office for the first time, and northern blacks began to increase their influence, winning races in districts where blacks were not always majorities. Progress, slow to be sure, has occurred; in 1970, there were only 179 blacks holding state and national legislative seats; by 2001, the number had more than tripled, to 633. Only two African Americans have won a governor's seat in modern times, Virginia's Douglas Wilder and, in 2006, Massachusetts' Deval Patrick. In 2004, with blacks as candidates of both major parties in Illinois, Barack Obama (D-Ill.) won to become the only African American member of the U.S. Senate and only the third to hold a Senate seat in the modern era.

Richard Hatcher, who became mayor of Gary, Indiana, in 1968, was the first African American mayor of a major U.S. city. By 2007, more than 500 African Americans served as black mayors in northern and southern cities, nearly 50 of them in cities of 50,000 and more and many in communities where blacks are far less than half the population.[1] Nationally, the number of black officeholders has increased from an estimated 1200 in 1969 to more than 9400 in 2002. Although this is far from proportional representation, it is a dramatic increase.

Hispanics, too, have improved their representation in political office. From a total of little more than 3000 Hispanic public officials in 1985, their numbers by 2007 had grown to more than 5100, including 270 elected to state and national office.[2] Hispanic officials are more geographically concentrated than African American ones, with about 60 percent in California or Texas.

In sum, though progress has been slow, African Americans and Hispanics, like other ethnic groups, have achieved political power through elections. The election of Barack Obama is, of course, the most visible manifestation of that success. In his remarkable campaign, Obama won support from millions of whites, Asian Americans, and Hispanics as well as more than 90 percent of African Americans. Obama largely avoided the issue of race in his campaign, and likewise, millions of voters chose him for reasons other than race.

[1] These data are from the Joint Center for Political and Economic Studies.
[2] These data are from the website of the National Association of Latino Elected Officials.
SOURCE: *Statistical Abstract of the United States 2003* (Washington, D.C.: Government Printing Office, 2001), tabs. 408 and 417; website of the National Council of Black Mayors, Inc., www.blackmayors.org.

---

brought about by the 1965 passage of the **Voting Rights Act (VRA)**, which made it illegal to interfere with anyone's right to vote. The act abolished the use of literacy tests, and, most important, it sent federal voter registrars into counties where less than 50 percent of the voting-age population (black and white) was registered. The premise of this requirement was that if so few had registered, there must be serious barriers to registration. Registrars were sent to all of Alabama, Mississippi, South Carolina, and Louisiana, substantial parts of North Carolina, and scattered counties in six other states.[9] Any changes in election procedures had to be approved by the Department of Justice or the U.S. District Court for the District of Columbia. States or counties had to show a clean record of not discriminating for ten years before they could escape this supervision. Those who sought to deter blacks from voting through intimidation now had to face the force of the federal government.

Though black registration had been increasing in the rim South due to voter registration and education projects, the impact of the VRA in the Deep South was dramatic.[10]

Within a year after federal registrars were sent, hundreds of thousands of southern blacks were registered, radically changing the nature of southern politics. In the most extreme case, Mississippi registration of blacks zoomed from 7 to 41 percent. In Alabama, the black electorate doubled in four years. Due to these increases, not only have dozens of blacks been elected but white politicians must now court black voters to get elected. Even the late George Wallace, the segregationist Alabama governor who had opposed the civil rights movement in the 1960s, eagerly sought black votes in the 1970s and 1980s.

The VRA was renewed and expanded in 1970, 1975, 1982, and again in 2006, despite some grumbling by white Republican conservatives about the continuing federal scrutiny of voting rights in the South. It now covers more states and other minorities, such as Hispanics, Asians, Native Americans, and Inuits (called Eskimos in the past), and thus serves as a basic protection for minority voting rights. For example, states must provide bilingual ballots in counties in which 5 percent or more of the population does not speak English.

Blacks line up to vote in Peachtree, Alabama, after enactment of the Voting Rights Act of 1965.

The VRA dramatically changed the face of the electorate in the South and then later in other parts of the nation. Given the success of the VRA and faced with an expanded black electorate, some white officials in areas of large black populations used new means to diminish the political clout of African Americans. Their technique was **gerrymandering**. Through devices that political scientists call "**cracking, stacking, and packing**," districts were drawn to minimize black representation, depending on the size and configuration of the black and white populations. *Cracking* divides significant, concentrated black populations into two or more districts so that none will have a black majority; *stacking* combines a large black population with an even greater white population; and *packing* puts a huge black population into one district rather than two, where blacks might otherwise approach a majority in each.

Initially, the Supreme Court was reluctant to find these practices illegal without specific proof that their intent was to discriminate against black voters.[11] But in 1982, congressional revision of the VRA required states with large minority populations to draw boundaries in ways to increase the probabilities that minorities will win seats. The focus of the voting rights legislation then turned from protecting the right of suffrage to trying to ensure that voting rights result in the election of African American and other minority officeholders. With this new statute as an indication of congressional intent, the Court then did strike down districting in North Carolina as inappropriately diluting black voting power.[12]

After the 1990 census, eleven new **majority-minority districts** were created for blacks and six for Hispanics. Partly as a result of this redistricting, blacks and Hispanics dramatically increased their congressional representation. Blacks were elected to Congress for the first time since Reconstruction in Alabama, Florida, North Carolina, South Carolina, and Virginia. Hispanics were elected for the first time ever in Illinois and New Jersey.[13] However, after this post-1990 redistricting, which used extensive gerrymandering to create the majority-minority districts, some white voters challenged their legality. In a series of cases, the Supreme Court then ruled that racial gerrymandering, the drawing of district lines specifically to concentrate racial minorities to try to ensure the election of minority representatives, is as constitutionally suspect as the drawing of district lines to diffuse minority electoral strength.[14] Despite the consequent redrawing of several majority-minority districts after the 1994 election, the African American incumbents were still able to win reelection in 1996 and after.

Creating majority-minority districts has affected the partisan composition of some southern states. Black voters were redistricted from solid Democratic districts to create new majority black districts. This left their old districts with Republican majorities and helped Republicans get their first victories in eighteen congressional districts in the 1994 elections.

Women and the Right to Vote

When property ownership defined the right to vote, women property owners could vote in some places. When property requirements were removed, suffrage came to be seen as a male right only. Women's right to vote was reintroduced in the 1820s in Tennessee school board elections.[15] From that

Women's contributions to the war effort during World War I helped lead to the ratification of the women's suffrage amendment in 1920. Here Broadway chorus women train as Home Guards during the war.

time on, women had the vote in some places, usually only at the local level or for particular kinds of elections.

The national movement for women's suffrage did not gain momentum until after the Civil War. Before and during that war, many women helped lead the campaign to abolish slavery and establish full political rights for blacks. When black men got the right to vote after the Civil War, some women saw the paradox in their working to enfranchise these men when they themselves lacked the right to vote. Led by Susan B. Anthony, Elizabeth Cady Stanton, and others, they lobbied Congress and the state legislatures for voting rights for women.

The first suffrage bill was introduced in Congress in 1868 and each year thereafter until 1893. Most members were strong in their condemnation of women as potential voters. One senator claimed that if women could hold political views different from their husbands, it would make "every home a hell on earth."[16]

When Wyoming applied to join the Union in 1889, it had already granted women the right to vote. Congress initially tried to bar Wyoming from the Union for that reason, but then relented when the Wyoming territorial legislature declared, "We will remain out of the Union one hundred years rather than come in without the women." Still, by 1910, women had complete suffrage rights in only four western states.

Powerful interests opposed suffrage for women. Liquor interests feared that women voters would press for prohibition because many women had been active in the temperance (antiliquor) movement. Other businesses feared that suffrage would lead to reforms to improve working conditions for women and children. Southern whites feared that it would lead to voting by black women and then by black men. Political bosses feared that women would favor political reform. The Catholic Church opposed it as contrary to the proper role of women. According to some people, suffrage was a revolt against nature. Pregnant women might lose their babies, nursing mothers their milk, and women might grow beards or be raped at the polls (then frequently located in saloons or barber shops).[17] Others argued less hysterically that women should be protected from the unsavory practices of politics and should confine themselves to their traditional duties.

About 1910, however, the women's suffrage movement was reenergized, in part by ideas and tactics borrowed from the British women's suffrage movement. A new generation of leaders, including Alice Paul and Carrie Chapman Catt, began to lobby more vigorously, reach out to the working class, and engage in protest marches and picketing, all new features of American politics. Eight more western and prairie states granted suffrage to women between 1911 and 1917 and others granted the right to vote in presidential elections. [18]

In 1917, the National Women's Party organized around-the-clock picketing of the White House; their arrest and subsequent torture through beatings and forced feedings embarrassed the administration and won the movement some support. These incidents, plus contributions by women to the war effort during World War I, led to the adoption of the Nineteenth Amendment ⭐ guaranteeing women the right to vote in 1920. Although only 37 percent of eligible women voted in the 1920 presidential election, as the habit of voting spread, women's voting rates equaled those of men. (See the box "Women in Office.")

Young People and the Right to Vote

Federal constitutional and legislative changes extended the franchise to young adults. Before 1971, almost all states required a voting age of nineteen or more. The service of eighteen-year-olds in the Vietnam War brought protests that if these men were old enough to die for their country, they were old enough to vote. Yielding to these arguments and to the general recognition that young people were better educated than in the past, Congress adopted and the states ratified the Twenty-sixth Amendment ⭐ giving eighteen-year-olds the right to vote. As we will see, however, young people are a lot less likely to vote than other groups.

Felons and the Right to Vote

The restriction of felons' voting rights is an exception to the general liberalization of the right to vote. (Felons are those convicted of serious crimes.) Most states bar convicted felons from voting while in prison or on probation, but four states, including Florida and three other southern states with large black populations,[19] bar felons from voting forever. In some states, these laws stem from Reconstruction-era policies targeted to reduce the voting power of blacks. Since 2004, three states have reinstituted voting rights to felons after they serve their time.

Nationally, more than 5 million people are prevented from voting by felony convictions, including one in seven black men (in Alabama, one in three black men are barred).[20] Nationally, 40 percent of those barred from voting are black.[21] Analyses of the impacts of these laws suggest they have had a significant effect in putting conservative Republicans in office in states with large black populations.[22]

Some might argue that we should not worry about the voting rights of felons. Loss of voting rights might be seen as part of their punishment. However, most felons barred from voting have served their time and returned to society. Many times they were convicted as young people and have been law-abiding citizens for years or even decades since. Moreover, this particular punishment does not really seem to fit the crime.

In sum, only convicted felons, the mentally incapable, noncitizens, and those not meeting minimal residence requirements are legally barred from voting now. Voting has become an essential right of citizenship, except for felons, rather than a privilege just for those qualified by birth or property.

Electoral Reform and New Threats to Voting Rights

In recent elections, new threats to voting rights, especially voting rights of African Americans, have occurred. The most widely publicized problems were in the 2000 and 2004 elections. Months after the 2000 presidential election that saw Al Gore win the popular vote but George W. Bush win the electoral vote and the presidency, half of the electorate thought that the outcome was unfair or downright crooked. (See "The 2000 Election: A Perfect Storm" on p. 228.) Many African Americans, who believed they were systematically disfranchised by the way the election was run in Florida, were especially outraged. One of ten votes in largely African American precincts in Florida were thrown out as invalid, compared with one of thirty-seven in white precincts, significantly reducing the Democratic vote and changing the outcome of the presidential election.[23]

Voter Reform Legislation

The 2000 election revealed a number of problems with our electoral system. (The problems had existed for a long time, but in a close election they become more crucial.) Many areas had voting equipment that not only was old but also did not work well, resulting in many votes not being counted. Many states also had unclear laws governing procedures for recounts and challenges to voter eligibility.

To deal with some of these issues, Congress passed electoral reform legislation in 2002. This new legislation offered states funding to buy new, modern voting equipment; mandated statewide registration lists; and required states to train poll workers, post a list of voters' rights in each polling place, keep up-to-date computerized lists of voters, and allow voters whose names do not appear on the precinct lists to cast a provisional ballot, which can be accepted or challenged later.

This legislation did bring about some positive changes. Though most of the money to purchase the machines was not provided by the federal government, many areas did buy new electronic machines that work like ATMs, responding to touches on the screen.[24] And many states en-

Election campaigns in the nineteenth century featured more hoopla, which spurred tremendous turnout. This illustration shows the 1840 Whig gimmick—party members rolled a huge ball from town to town—that prompted the phrase "keep the ball rolling."

Courtesy of the Smithsonian Institute

american diversity | Women in Office

Hillary Clinton is probably the most highly visible woman officeholder in the United States, but even before women were given the right to vote nationally, they held political office. Women officeholders in colonial America were rare but not unknown. In 1715, for example, the Pennsylvania Assembly appointed a woman as tax collector.[1]

Elizabeth Cady Stanton, probably the first woman candidate for Congress, received twenty-four votes when she ran in 1866.[2] It was not until 1916 that the first woman member of Congress, **Jeannette Rankin** (R-Mont.), was actually

elected. In 1872, Victoria Claflin Woodhull ran for president on the Equal Rights Party ticket teamed with abolitionist Frederick Douglass for vice president.

More than 100,000 women now hold elective office, but many of these offices are minor. Inroads by women into major national offices have been slow. Vice presidential candidate Sarah Palin brought excitement to the Republican ticket in 2008, but like vice presidential candidate **Geraldine Ferraro** in 1984, was not successful in her bid to be the first woman in that office. In recent years, women have only

gradually increased their membership in Congress. Women have continued to gain seats and, after 2006, numbered about 16 percent of both the House and Senate. More than two-thirds of the women in each house are Democrats.[3] Nancy Pelosi (D-Calif.), as the first woman (and Italian American) Speaker of the House, is now third in the line of presidential succession.

Real progress has also been made in state and local governments. Women hold 12 percent of the governorships (Democrats) and 28 percent of the lieutenant gover-

acted new standards for counts and recounts. However, these changes brought new problems. Most technical experts, and many others, are fearful that some of the new electronic machines are open to fraud. One information-security expert argues that one particular system was "so deficient in security it could be compromised by a bright teenager intent on hacking an election."[25] The reason is that in most of the new machines there is no paper backup. Your vote for *X* could be counted as a vote for *Y* and you would never know it. Various studies have shown the ability to tamper with machines takes only a minute, and in some machines it can be done wirelessly. To deal with this potential for fraud, thirty-two states have now required paper backup for all electronic machines. Nearly one-third of the states have also required mandatory random audits of the paper records.[26]

The requirement to have computerized, up-to-date lists of voters has also had unintended negative effects. States are purging registration lists, ostensibly to keep them up-to-date but sometimes to reduce the number of voters of the party not in control of the state's election machinery (in most states, elections are controlled by the office of the Secretary of State or some similar statewide office whose head is elected). Though states have a legitimate interest in making sure that voter lists reflect current voters and their addresses, sometimes purging reflects less high-minded motives. This tactic is used to disfranchise lower-income and minority voters or to reduce the other party's voters.[27] Sometimes private companies are hired to purge voter lists

and are paid according to how many they purge. Florida, in trying to update its voter lists, purged 22,000 black voters (largely Democratic) from the voter registration lists, but only 61 Hispanics (who, in Florida, are more likely than blacks to be Republicans). Florida officials claimed this partisan purge was accidental, though others disagreed.[28]

Voter Turnout

Paradoxically, as the *right* to vote has expanded, the proportion of eligible citizens *actually* voting has contracted.

Political Activism in the Nineteenth Century

In 1896, an estimated 750,000 people—5 percent of all voters—took train excursions to visit presidential candidate William McKinley at his Ohio home during the campaign.[29] This amazing figure is but one indication of the high level of intense political interest and activity in the late nineteenth century.

In those days, politics was an active, not a spectator, sport. People voted at high rates, as much as 80 percent in the 1840 presidential election,[30] and they were very partisan. They thought Independents were corrupt and ready to sell their votes to the highest bidder. In colonial America, voters usually voted just by voice. By the mid-nineteenth norships. They comprise about 16 percent of mayors of medium and large cities.

In 1969, only 4 percent of the state legislators were women; today, 23 percent are. However, the rates of increase have slowed in recent years, with only a 2 percent growth in the past decade.[4] The proportion ranges widely, from not quite 9 percent in South Carolina to more than 30 percent in Arizona, Colorado, Hawaii, Maine, Maryland, Minnesota, New Hampshire, Oregon, Vermont, and Washington. Women are also making inroads in local political offices.[5]

Does it make a difference in terms of policy to have women officeholders rather than men? Behavioral studies of women members of Congress and other legislative bodies indicate that they are, on the whole, more liberal than men.[6] Women tend to give issues relating to women, children, and the family higher priority than do male legislators.[7] Across numerous industrialized democracies, legislatures with more women were more likely to adopt family leave legislation.[8] Women are also less likely to be involved in corrupt activities.

As more and more women are getting graduate and professional education and working outside the home, and as the public increases its support for women in politics, the trend toward more women in public office will continue.

[1] Joseph J. Kelley, *Pennsylvania: The Colonial Years* (Garden City, N.Y.: Doubleday, 1980), 143.
[2] Elisabeth Griffin, *In Her Own Right* (New York: Oxford University Press, 1983).
[3] Data are from Center for the American Woman and Politics, National Information Bank on Women in Public Office, Rutgers University, www.rci.rutgers.edu/cawp/pdf/elective.pdf.
[4] Kira Sanbonmatsu, *Democrats, Republicans, and the Politics of Women's Place* (Ann Arbor: University of Michigan Press, 2002).
[5] Data are from the Center for American Women and Politics, Rutgers University, 2006, www.cawp.rutgers.edu/Facts.html#leg.
[6] Susan Welch, "Are Women More Liberal Than Men in the U.S. Congress?" *Legislative Studies Quarterly* 10 (1985), 125–134.
[7] Sue Thomas and Susan Welch, "The Impact of Gender on Activities and Priorities of State Legislators," *Western Political Quarterly* 44 (1991), 445–456; Miki Caul Kittilson, "Representing Women: The Adoption of Family Leave in Comparative Perspective," *Journal of Politics* 70 (April 2008), 323–334.
[8] Miki Caul Kittilson, "Representing Women: The Adoption of Family Leave in Comparative Perspective, *Journal of Politics* 70 (April 2008), 323–334.

century, most states used paper ballots. Elaborate and well-organized parties printed and distributed the ballots. Voters, after being coached by party leaders, simply dropped their party's ballot into the box. **Split-ticket voting**—that is, voting for candidates from different parties for different offices—and secrecy in making one's choice were impossible.[31]

Progressive Reforms

The **Progressive reforms** of the late nineteenth and early twentieth centuries brought radical changes to election politics. Progressive reformers, largely professional and upper middle class, sought to eliminate corruption from politics and voting. But they also meant to eliminate the influence of the lower classes, many of them recent immigrants. These two goals went hand in hand because the lower classes were seen as the cause of corruption in politics.

The Progressive movement was responsible for several reforms: primary elections, voter registration laws, secret ballots, nonpartisan ballots (without party labels), and the denial of voting rights for aliens, which removed a major constituency of the urban party machines. The movement also introduced the merit system for public employment to reduce favoritism and payoffs in hiring.

The reforms, adopted by some states at the end of the nineteenth century and by others much later, were largely effective in cleaning up politics. But the reformers also achieved, to a very large extent, their goal of eliminating the lower classes from politics. Taking away most of the reason for the existence of the political parties—choosing candidates and printing and distributing ballots—caused the party organization to decline, which, in turn, produced a decline in political interest and activity on the part of the electorate. Without strong parties to mobilize voters, only the most interested and motivated participated. The new restrictions on voting meant that voters had to invest more time, energy, and thought in voting. They had to think about the election months in advance and travel to city hall to register. As a consequence, politics began to be a spectator activity. Voter turnout declined sharply after the turn of the century.

Turnout figures from the nineteenth century are not entirely reliable and not exactly comparable with today's figures. In the days before voter registration, many aliens could vote, and some people voted twice. In some instances, more people voted in a state election than lived there! Nevertheless, it is generally agreed that turnout was very high in the nineteenth century and that it has diminished substantially; it dropped from more than 77 percent from 1840 to 1896 to 54 percent in the 1920 to 1932 era, when the Progressive reforms were largely in place. During the New Deal era, when the Democratic Party mobilized new groups of voters, turnout rose again, but it has never achieved the same levels as in the nineteenth century.

Modern campaigns have their own ephemera, but the products, such as these 2008 condoms, are usually generated by private businesses rather than by political parties.

Recent Turnout

Between 1964 and 2000, turnout in presidential elections slowly declined, from 62 percent to 52 percent. However, in 2004, that proportion increased significantly, to 58 percent.[32] And in 2008, voters seemed more energized than in years. In state after state, the turnout in the winter and spring primaries far exceeded previous turnout. (Figure 1 illustrates this for a few states.) More than 3 million new voters registered and voted in the primaries.[33]

The increase in turnout was especially pronounced in the Democratic primaries. Senator **Barack Obama** sparked the enthusiasm of hundreds of thousands of new voters, many of them young, and they registered and voted in huge numbers. Voters under the age of thirty increased from 9 percent of Democratic primary voters in 2004 to nearly 15 percent in 2008. But many older citizens turned out too. **Hillary Clinton** energized tens of thousands of working-class voters, especially women, to register and vote. And tens of thousands of African American voters, especially young people, registered and voted for the first time too, excited by the candidacy of Barack Obama. The turnouts in almost every primary state moved into the 30 to 40 percent range, hardly numbers to brag about, but far exceeding the usual dismal primary turnout. (See Figure 1.)

Although nations count their turnouts differently, it is clear that Americans vote in much lower proportions than citizens of other Western democracies. Only Switzerland, which has allowed women to vote just since 1971, approximates our low turnout levels. Within the United States,

turnout varies greatly among the states. In the 2004 presidential election, for example, 77 percent of Minnesota's citizens voted, but only 46 percent of Hawaii's did.[34] Turnout tends to be lower in the South and higher in the northern Plains and Mountain states.[35]

Not only are voting rates low but even fewer participate actively in political campaigns. For example, in a recent year, about one-quarter of the population said that they worked for a party or candidate. About an equal proportion claimed that they contributed money to a party or a candidate. Smaller proportions attended political meetings or actually belonged to a political club. Unlike voting, rates of participation in campaigns have not declined over the past twenty years. This suggests that people are about as political as they always have been, but that something about elections themselves has decreased voter turnout. Indeed, more people give money to candidates and parties than they used to, probably because, unlike twenty years ago, candidates and parties now use mass mailings and the Internet to solicit funds from supporters.[36] Hundreds of thousands of potential donors can be reached in a very short time. The candidates are getting very good at using the Internet to raise funds, and Obama, especially, in 2008 was a pathbreaker. We will discuss this further in the next chapter.

Who Votes?

There are vast differences in voting habits among different groups of people.

| Figure 1 | 2008 Presidential Primaries Stimulated Significantly Increased Turnout (% turnout of eligible voters) |

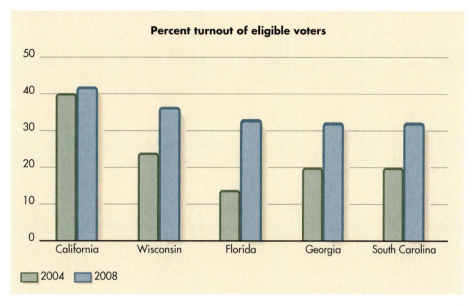

SOURCE: Michael McDonald://elections.gmu.edu/Voter_Turnout_2008_Primaries.htm; http://elections
.gmu.edu/Voter_Turnout_2004_Primaries.htm

Socioeconomic Class

Voting is related to education, income, and occupation—that is, to socioeconomic class. Those who are more educated, have more money, and have higher-status jobs vote more often. If you are a college graduate, the chances are about 70 percent that you will vote; if you have less than a high school education, the chances are less than half that.[37] Differences between higher- and lower-income people are also quite large and growing. Although voting among all groups of Americans has declined in the past forty years, the proportion of college-educated persons who participated fell by less than 10 percent, while that of high school–educated persons dropped by nearly 20 percent. Education apparently is linked to voting because those with more years of education are more interested in, and knowledgeable about, politics.

Differences between voting rates of those in the middle and upper classes are much wider in the United States than elsewhere and wider today than in nineteenth-century America.[38] Something unique about the contemporary American political system inhibits voting participation of all citizens, but particularly those whose income and educational levels are below the average.

Just as there is a strong class basis to voting, there is also a strong class basis for participation in campaign activities.[39] Those with more education and income are more likely to participate. Those with some college education actually increased their participation over the past twenty years, whereas those with less than a high school education decreased theirs. Thus, the class bias in participation, as in voting alone, has increased.[40]

Age

Voting is also much more common among older people than younger people. Young people are volunteering in their communities in record numbers,[41] so why the low voting rates? Young people's initial tendency to vote is positively influenced by their parents' education and political engagement and by their own high school experiences and that of going on to college. Later in life, getting married, establishing a stable residence, and becoming active in the community are important to continuing their voting habits.[42] Thus, low turnouts may reflect many who grew up in homes where there was a low interest in government and the news; they did not learn that politics are important.[43] Then, too, like many of their elders, some young people cannot discern significant differences between the two major political parties, or they believe that candidates do not address issues of primary concern to young people. Low voter turnout is also a product of the high degree of mobility of young adults; they change their residences frequently and do not have time or do not take time to figure out how and where to register. Many young people are preoccupied with major life changes—leaving home, going to college, beginning their first full-time job, getting married, and starting a family.

The 2008 campaign generated tremendous political interest and enthusiasm among many young voters who had never been engaged in politics before. When asked whether they were paying attention to the campaign, fully 74 percent of those under 30 said "yes," compared to only 42 percent in 2004, and a meager 13 percent in 2000.[44] Still, the turnout of young people was lower than that of their elders. And, it remains to be seen if the enthusiasm sparked in this election carries over to future ones or is a brief flurry of interest sparked by particular candidates.

Participation in Other Activities

In other kinds of political participation, even taking education into account, men usually participate slightly more than women, whites somewhat more than blacks, older people more than younger people, and southerners more than northerners. But these differences change over time. Young people participated more than their elders, and blacks more than whites, during the late 1960s and early 1970s.[45] The civil rights and anti–Vietnam War movements drew many young and black people into political activity.

Why Turnout Is Low

In addition to class and age, there are other personal and institutional reasons why more Americans, especially low-income and young Americans, do not vote. These include

Third-party or nonmainstream candidates, such as Rep. Ron Paul (R-Tex.) in 2008, stimulate interest among some voters. Although Paul didn't get many votes in the primaries, he did raise lots of money and was a pacesetter among the Republican candidates in his effective use of the Internet.

citizens' attitudes, lack of social rootedness, failures of political parties to mobilize voters, lack of strong labor unions, state barriers to registration and voting, partisan efforts to deter voting, and in the case of legislative elections, noncompetitive districts.

Attitudinal Explanations

Some explanations for not voting lie with voters' attitudes.

Voter Satisfaction?   For example, one reason sometimes given for low rates of voter turnout is that nonvoters are satisfied; failing to vote is a passive form of consent to what government is doing.[46] This argument falls flat. Voter turnout has decreased in an era when public trust in government has decreased, not increased. Moreover, if staying at home on Election Day were an indication of satisfaction, one would expect turnout to be lower among the well off, not among the working class and the poor.

Negative Attitudes toward Politics   General attitudes about politics offer a more likely explanation. Significant proportions of nonvoters, when asked why they did not vote, say they are disgusted with politics.[47] In explaining low turnout, analysts often point to the hateful advertising, attacks on other candidates, candidates who do not tell the truth about their positions, incessant polling, and lack of thoughtful media coverage.[48]

These analyses surely contain some grains of truth, but how many? There is little evidence that negative campaigning has increased over time while voter turnout has declined.[49] And, after all, people who are most likely to pay attention to the media, watch the ads, hear about the polls, and follow the campaigns are the most likely to vote, not the least. It is possible that the increasingly media-oriented campaigns have decreased overall turnout during the past generation (and we will have more to say about these campaigns later in the chapter). In fact, turnout is inversely related to media spending; the more the candidates spend, the lower the turnout. But negative advertising does not affect turnout much, if at all,[50] and negative advertising and other media attention cannot explain the class bias in nonvoting.

In addition to the *quality* of the campaigns, some people think turnout has declined because our elections are so frequent, campaigns last so long, and so many offices are contested that the public becomes bored, confused, or cynical.[51] At the presidential level, the sheer quantity of coverage, much of it focused repetitively on "who's winning," may simply bore people. At the local level, voters elect so many officeholders, all the way down to weed and mosquito control commissioners, that many have no idea for whom or what they are voting. This proliferation of elective offices, thought by some to promote democracy and popular control, may promote only voter confusion and alienation. The problem is compounded because elections for different offices are held at different times. For example, most states have decided to hold elections for governor in nonpresidential election years because they think this will focus more attention on the governor's race. However, in fact, this decision reduces both turnout in the presidential election and even more significantly reduces the turnout in these gubernatorial elections.[52] Primary elections also affect turnout. One estimate is that holding primary campaigns diminishes the general election turnout by 5 percent.[53]

By contrast, in Britain the time between calling an election (by the current government) and the actual election is only a month. On May 9, 2001, Prime Minister Tony Blair called the election, and on June 7, 2001, it was held. All campaigning was done during that time. There were no primaries. Moreover, as in most other parliamentary democracies, British citizens vote only for their representative in Parliament and (at one other time) for their local representative. Voters are not faced with choices for a myriad of offices they barely recognize.

Voting as a Rational Calculation of Costs and Benefits

A more general attitudinal explanation for nonvoting is that it may also be the result of a rational calculation of the costs and benefits of voting. When 35 percent of Americans think voting on *American Idol* is more important than voting for the president, obviously many voters do not think that the stakes in elections are great.[54]

Economist Anthony Downs argued that people vote when they believe the perceived benefits of voting are greater than the costs.[55] If a voter sees a difference between the parties or candidates and favors one party's position over the other, that voter has a reason to vote and can expect some benefit from doing so. For that reason, people who are highly partisan vote more than those less attached to a party, and people with a strong sense of political efficacy, the belief they can influence government, vote more than others.

Voters who see no difference between the candidates or parties, however, may believe that voting is not worth the effort it takes and that it is more rational to abstain. In fact, 40 percent of nonvoters in 1990 gave only the excuse that they were "too busy," suggesting a large degree of apathy.[56] Others think that their vote does not matter. Perhaps misled by the continual public opinion polling and the widely publicized results, some may believe they don't need to vote.

Nevertheless, many people will vote even if they think there is no difference between the candidates because they have a sense of civic duty, a belief that their responsibilities as citizens include voting. In fact, more voters give this as an explanation for voting than any other reason, including the opportunity to influence policy.[57]

Downs assumes that the costs of voting are minimal, but, in reality, for many people the time, expense of time off from work or transportation costs, and possible embarrassment of trying to register are greater than the perceived benefits of voting. This is especially true for lower-income people who perceive that neither party is attentive to their interests. Moreover, they are especially vulnerable to a climate where voters are being challenged at the polls over their right to vote. The frequency, length, and media orientation of campaigns may lower the perceived benefits of voting for people of all incomes by trivializing the election and emphasizing the negative.

Lack of Social Rootedness

Turnout is low partially because of what one analyst has called lack of "social rootedness."[58] Middle age, marriage, and residential stability lead to rootedness in one's community. Americans move around, marry late, and get divorced more than those in other nations. Mobility alone may reduce voting by as much as 9 percent. However, American turnout is still low, even taking into account these factors.

Americans living abroad, whether in the armed forces or for private reasons, have special barriers to registering and voting. In a bizarre development, in 2004, the Pentagon discouraged citizens living abroad from voting by shutting down a state-of-the-art website designed to make it easy for those citizens to register and obtain ballots.[59]

Failures of Parties to Mobilize Voters

Voter turnout in the United States may not increase substantially until one of the political parties works to mobilize the traditional nonvoters through policies that appeal to them. For example, Roosevelt's New Deal mobilized thousands of new voters. If voters believe they have a reason to vote, then their calculation of the benefits of voting increases relative to the costs.

Traditionally, political parties did mobilize voters to turn out. In the 1980s and 1990s, however, the parties spent more time raising funds than mobilizing voters.[60] The failure of parties to mobilize voters is another reason for low voter turnout, especially among the working class and poor. Because of their low income, a majority of nonvoters are Democrats. If mobilized, they would probably vote for Democrats, but not to the degree many Republicans fear. In many elections, the preferences of nonvoters have simply reflected the preferences of voters.[61]

In 2004, and even more in 2008, parties and their candidates returned to their traditional mobilization function, and consequently, voting increased. The parties, and in the 2008 primaries, the candidates, emphasized registering voters and getting them to the polls. Both parties have used increasingly sophisticated technology to link information about each party supporter with neighborhood information. Each party communicated with its core supporters via e-mail and frequently urged them to register and vote.

Both parties have developed sophisticated databases recording individuals' residential location, gender, education, race, homeowner status, and many other variables. They gather data not just from public sources such as voter registration rolls and driver's license registrations but also from consumer data from stores ranging from book vendors to auto dealerships. So, for example, we know that Republicans are more likely to drink bourbon and Democrats gin, Democrats buy Volvos and Republicans Fords and Chevys.[62] Parties increasingly use sophisticated polls to develop profiles of characteristics of voters likely to support them. Then, they can use census and other neighborhood data to target areas on which to focus their get-out-the-vote drives. The Republicans have led in their sophistication in these databases that cross-reference political and personal information.

Republicans are more likely to oppose legislation making it easier for members of the general electorate to vote, because they already do an excellent job mobilizing their own supporters.[63] States with the highest turnout tend to have active and liberal Democratic parties, giving voters a choice and thus a motive to vote.

Decline of Strong Labor Unions

Working-class citizens are much less likely to vote than white-collar and professional workers. Yet, among working people, union members are much more likely to vote than are others. Unions inform their members about the stakes of the election and then work to get their members and their families to the polls. Just as parties can increase the perceived benefits of voting by educating voters about the consequences of election choices, so too do unions among their membership. As labor union strength has declined, here and elsewhere, voting turnout has decreased.[64] Despite recent declines in labor strength in other nations too, most other democracies have much stronger labor unions than the United States and consequently higher rates of turnout among blue-collar workers.

State Barriers to Registration and Voting

States can raise or lower the costs of voting to individual citizens by making it easy or hard to register and to vote.

Barriers to Registration Many people do not vote because they have not registered to vote. Most other democracies have nonpersonal systems of voter registration. That is, the state or parties are responsible for registering voters. Voter registrars go door-to-door to register voters, or voters are registered automatically when they pay taxes or receive public services. Usually, these registrar offices are nonpartisan and consider it their duty to register voters. Consequently, almost everyone is registered to vote.

The United States is unique in putting the responsibility for registering on the individual citizen. Moreover, registration is handled at the state level, usually by agencies controlled by one party or another. These conditions are a major impediment to voting. Only about 70 percent of U.S.

citizens are registered.[65] Difficult registration procedures have a special impact on low-income Americans, who were 17 percent less likely to vote in states with difficult registration procedures than in other states.[66]

Given that states are laboratories—some things are tried in one state, other approaches tried in another—we know that some registration procedures encourage people to register and vote and others do not. One estimate is that voter turnout would be 9 percent higher if all states' procedures were similar to those of states that try to facilitate voter registration.[67] Procedures that work to increase voter registration include registration periods lasting up to Election Day (most states require registration at least twenty-five days before the election),[68] registration offices located in neighborhoods rather than just one central county office, registration by mail, registration offices open at convenient hours, and a policy of not purging voters from the registration lists who fail to vote.

In other jurisdictions, voter registrars do not provide these options, and some actually try to hinder groups working to increase registration. Some states do not allow volunteers to register voters outside the registration office.[69] Florida passed a law imposing fines of $250 for every voter registration form filed more than ten days after it is collected, even if a hurricane passes through in the meantime, and a fine of $5000 for every form that is not submitted. The Florida League of Voters, which has conducted nonpartisan voter registration drives for nearly seventy years, is suing to block the new rules, saying that its entire budget could be put at risk if a natural disaster or car accident or another such event delayed submission of forms.[70]

To increase registration, a national law—the **motor voter law**—allows people to register at public offices, such as the Department of Motor Vehicles and welfare offices.[71] The law led to the greatest expansion of voter registration in American history; 5 million new voters registered,[72] but it has not increased actual turnout.[73]

Barriers to Voting Some states work to facilitate voting turnout of those already registered while others do not. For example, some states do not provide sample ballots or publicize where voters should go to vote, whereas other states mail sample ballots and information about where to vote to registered voters. Some states have limiting polling hours; others open the polls very early and keep them open until 9 p.m. or later so that voters can vote before or after work. About half the states, including most of those west of the Mississippi, allow voters to vote with absentee ballots, even if they are not planning to be absent from their homes on Election Day. Absentee balloting makes voting something that can be done at the voter's convenience. One observer remarked, "The concept of Election Day is history. Now it's just the final day to vote."[74] Though this is clearly an overstatement, almost all Oregon voters vote before Election Day, perhaps a harbinger of the future for other states.[75] To reach these early voters, parties must begin television advertising and flyer mailing much earlier. Providing information, extended polling hours, or absentee ballots has a positive impact on voting rates, particularly for those who have less education or who are younger.[76]

Other states make it harder to vote. The states with the highest barriers to voting tend to be states with the largest minority populations. Some estimates are that one out of four Ohio voters in 2004 experienced problems on voting day, including having to go to more than one polling place, having to wait more than twenty minutes to vote, or leaving the polls before voting. Nearly half of Ohio's African American population experienced one of those problems.[77] African Americans were also more likely to be asked for identification and to feel intimidated at the polls.

Many states are considering requiring identification at the polls, a change that could result in fewer low-income people voting.

Partisan Efforts to Discourage Voting

Sometimes, political parties try to raise the costs of voting for the other party's likely voters in hopes of deterring their votes. In the 2004 election, there were many instances of partisan attempts to deter registration and voting. Most of the examples that have come to light have been Republican efforts to deter Democrats, although undoubtedly there are reverse examples. In Nevada, the Republican National Committee employed a private company to register voters; it discarded those forms filled out by Democrats. In Wisconsin, Republicans tried to challenge thousands of registrants in heavily Democratic Milwaukee, and in one county in Ohio, some voters received an advisory on fake Board of Elections letterhead warning them that if they registered through the Kerry campaign or the NAACP they couldn't vote.[78]

Noncompetitive Districts

In most states, legislatures draw the boundaries for congressional districts and state legislative districts, so districts are normally drawn to benefit the party in control of the legislature. A district whose boundaries are devised to maximize the political advantage of a party or a racial or ethnic group is known as a gerrymander (for more on gerrymanders, see Chapter 10). A gerrymander not only can ensure that one party dominates in a particular district, which is the point of the gerrymander, but as a side effect it reduces voter turnout.

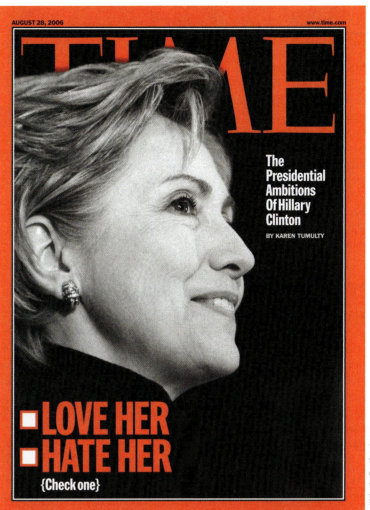

AUGUST 28, 2006   www.time.com

The Presidential Ambitions Of Hillary Clinton

BY KAREN TUMULTY

■ **LOVE HER**
■ **HATE HER**
{Check one}

Diana Walker/for *Time*/Getty Images

As Hillary Clinton embarked on a campaign for the Democratic nomination for president, *Time* magazine ran a cover story that generated more mail than any other cover story that year. In fact, the mail was seven times greater than the mail prompted by the runner-up story about the Dixie Chicks. The response revealed the strong pro or con feelings Clinton sparked.

The scarcity reduces accountability to the voters, because legislators are safe from being challenged, and it deters voters from voting. With the candidate from the dominant party sure to win, the benefits of voting are greatly diminished. In 2006 congressional races, voter turnout in districts won by a landslide (defined as 80 percent and more) was only 60 percent that of races where the margin was 20 percent or less. There are huge differences among states in their turnout; in that election, the average margin in Massachusetts was 75 percent, while in neighboring New Hampshire, it was 5 percent. Millions more might vote in off-year elections if they were more competitive. The best way to ensure that is to take redistricting out of the hands of the legislature and put it in the hands of a nonpartisan or bipartisan group, which has been done successfully in Iowa and Washington.[79]

Presidential Nominating Campaigns

Many Americans believe in the Horatio Alger myth, which states that with hard work anyone can achieve great success. This myth has its parallel in politics, where it is sometimes said that any child can grow up to be president. In fact, only a few run for that office, and even fewer are elected. Most people have little chance of being president: they are unknown to the public; they do not have the financial resources or contacts to raise the money needed for a national campaign; they are the wrong race or gender; they have jobs they could not leave to run a serious campaign; and their friends would probably ridicule them for even thinking of such a thing. [80]

Who Runs for President and Why?

Most candidates for president are senators or governors.[81] In recent decades, governors (**George W. Bush, Bill Clinton, Ronald Reagan**, and Jimmy Carter) have been more successful than senators (George McGovern, Robert Dole, and **John Kerry**), but the 2008 election returned a senator to the White House, the first since Richard Nixon. Vice presidents also frequently run, but until George H. W. Bush's victory in 1988, they were not successful in the twentieth century.

Why do candidates run? An obvious reason is to gain the power and prestige of the presidency. But they may have other goals as well, such as to gain support for a particular policy or set of ideas. Ronald Reagan, for example, clearly wanted to be president in part to spread his conser-

vative ideology. Ron Paul (R-Tex.) ran in 2008 to promote his libertarian ideas (libertarians combine a conservative disdain for government regulation of the economy with liberal distain of big government regulation of personal behavior into an ideology that favors very little government action at all). Sometimes candidates run for the presidency to be considered for the vice presidency, probably viewing it as an eventual stepping-stone to the presidency. But only occasionally—as when John Kerry picked **John Edwards**—do presidential candidates choose one of their defeated opponents to run as a vice presidential candidate.

How a Candidate Wins the Nomination

The nominating process is crucial in deciding who eventually gets elected. Boss Tweed once said, "I don't care who does the electing, so long as I get to do the nominating."[82] American presidential candidates are nominated through a process that includes the general public, the financial supporters of each party, and other party leaders.

Over time, voters and fundraisers have gained more power at the expense of party leaders. Presidential candidates try to win a majority of delegates at their party's national nominating convention in the summer preceding the November election. Delegates to those conventions are elected in state caucuses, conventions, and primaries. Candidates must campaign to win the support of those who attend caucuses and conventions and of primary voters.

Normally, candidates formally announce their candidacies in the year preceding the presidential election year. Their aim is to persist and survive the long primary and

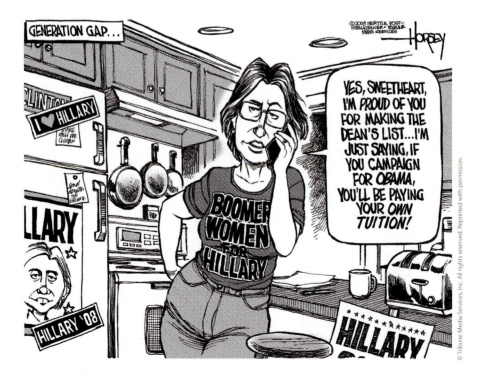

BEHIND THE SCENES
THE ROPE LINE

Though presidential campaigns are conducted primarily through the media, candidates do make personal appearances in towns and cities across the United States. And usually, after a speech or event, the candidate will stay for a few minutes—or longer—to shake hands and speak briefly with some of those who came to see him or her. This ritual takes place at "the rope line," now usually a metal barrier separating the candidate and the surging crowd.

At the rope line, a member of the public might shake a candidate's hand, give her a memento (a coin, rabbit's foot, book, photograph, or any number of other odd items), ask to have a photo taken with the candidate (usually with a cell phone camera), get an autograph, give the candidate advice about a policy or even about getting enough sleep, or tell the candidate of a personal problem—all in a few seconds. Sometimes these brief encounters are reflected in later speeches, where the candidate will mention a person, sometimes by name, who told of a harrowing

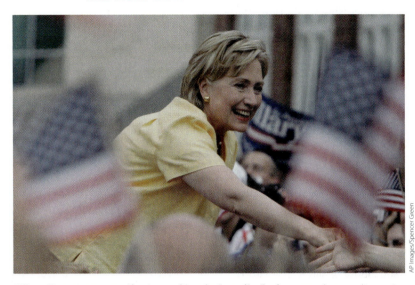

Hillary Clinton was very effective working the "rope line" at her campaign stops.

personal story that could be alleviated or avoided with better government policies or procedures.

The rope line offers a relatively spontaneous moment in what are usually very tightly controlled appearances. "I got to smell him, and it was awesome," said one Obama fan, caught between him and another woman trying to hug him.[1] "I can't believe she picked me out of a crowd," said a Clinton supporter, after she gave him a bottle of water and signed a photograph for him.[2] (The reporter noted that the man had fainted in front of her, so he was easy to pick out.)

Observers reported that Obama is not much of a hugger or hand-shaker and does "about 20 voter touches per 30 seconds…." He rarely signs autographs on the spot.[3] Hillary Clinton is "a rope lining dynamo," charging into the crowd, spending more time with supporters, signing autographs on everything from T-shirts to Krispy Kreme boxes, and like her husband, seeming to enjoy the experience. On the other hand, John McCain, reported an observer, "invites respectful distance." His war injuries make it difficult for him to reach out with his arms.

"His approach is dutiful, like a Boy Scout mowing a lawn."[4]

Of course, the secret service does not like rope lines. They are unpredictable as people press in on the candidate. One man on a Hillary Clinton rope line reported that he was asked to take off his respirator mask, but was "allowed to keep his goggles and blue rubber gloves on." (He wanted to talk about the chemical industry.)[5]

[1] Mark Leibovich, "Where to Catch the Sights, Sound and Smell of a Campaign," *New York Times*, May 24, 2008, www.nytimes .com/2008/05/24/us/politics/24rope.html.
[2] Ibid.
[3] Ibid.
[4] Ibid.
[5] Ibid.

caucus season that begins in January of election year and continues until only one candidate is left. Candidates use a number of methods to maximize their chances of survival. They carefully choose the primaries and caucuses where they will devote their resources. Candidates must be successful in enough primaries so they are seen as national, not regional, candidates, but they cannot possibly devote time and resources to every primary or caucus. Especially important are the early events—the Iowa caucus and the New Hampshire primary—and the larger state primaries.

Caucus and primary strategies played a big role in the 2008 elections. On the Republican side, former New York City mayor Rudolph (Rudy) Giuliani decided that since he probably wouldn't win the early primaries and caucuses in rural states, he would save his money and focus on the Florida primary, held three weeks and six primary and caucus events after the Iowa caucus. (Florida Republicans include many former New Yorkers.) He failed to foresee that by not campaigning in those first six states, he would get very little media attention while the frontrunners were building name recognition and a track record of success. Consequently, when the Florida primary was held, he finished third, and a few days later quit the race.

Fred Thompson, another Republican and an actor who had starred in *Law and Order*, also misjudged the dynamics of the primary and caucus season. Commentators and party activists were thrilled by the idea that he might run; some saw him as the new Reagan. But rather than getting organized, he apparently relished the positive attention he was getting without campaigning. He delayed his formal announcement and active campaign until September, 2007. Although this date was well before the Iowa caucus in early January, the other Republican candidates had been campaigning and building name recognition during most of 2007. By September, they had already held nine televised debates, for example. Observers joked that Thompson's campaign peaked the day before he announced. He fizzled when actual primary and caucus voting occurred and withdrew after the first few events in January.

On the Democratic side, Senator Hillary Clinton and her campaign made a huge strategic error by not paying much attention to the caucus states. In those contests, most of them early in the primary season, victory goes to the best organized, and the Obama organization focused early on organizing in the caucus states. Obama won all but one of them, many by lopsided margins. Even though the caucuses have tiny turnouts (typically 1 to 5 percent of registered voters, though Iowa with 16 percent was an exception), their electoral votes added up and gave Obama a small lead by the end of February that was impossible for Clinton to overcome, despite the fact she won most of the large state primaries and had a string of other successes in March, April, and May.

Candidates also attempt to raise substantial amounts of money early. A large war chest can mark a candidate as unbeatable. George W. Bush started strong in the 2000 primaries because he had raised millions more than all his opponents combined. Barack Obama's fundraising success gave him a large advantage in the 2008 primary campaign.

Candidates also try to find the position, slogan, or idea that will appeal to the most voters. In 1984, Ronald Reagan presented himself as the candidate embodying traditional America. As one of his staff aides wrote in a campaign memo, "Paint RR as the personification of all that is right with, or heroized by, America."[83] Barack Obama was the candidate for "change," rallying his supporters around the slogan "it's our time" to change the country. **John McCain**'s campaign did not have a simple slogan, but he capitalized on his reputation as an independent "maverick" and his war hero

credentials. Hillary Clinton took too long to find a theme that resonated. Her early emphasis on experience sent a mixed message because much of the public was fed up with Washington and many people already had strong feelings about her from her days as first lady. Later in the campaign she combined the "ready on day 1" theme with a strong populist message of fighting for the underdogs, a message that resonated with many women and blue-collar workers especially.

To compete successfully, candidates also need considerable media coverage. They must convince reporters that they are serious candidates with a real chance of winning. Journalists and candidates establish expectations for how well each candidate should do based on poll results, the quality of a candidate's campaign organization, the amount of money and time spent in the campaign, and the political complexion of the state. (Sometimes these journalists and campaign pros are jokingly called "the expectorate".[84]) If a candidate performs below expectations, this may be seen by the press as a weakness. Even if a candidate wins, the victory may be interpreted as a loss if it's by a narrower margin than anticipated. On the other hand, a strong showing when expectations are low can give a boost to a candidate's campaign. Consequently, candidates try to lower media expectations. Bill Clinton finished second in the New Hampshire primary in 1992, but because the top vote-getter (Paul E. Tsongas) was from neighboring Massachusetts, Clinton's second-place finish was considered a victory. Coming from far behind, he pronounced himself "the comeback kid," a designation that became the story of the primary.

In 2008, McCain was counted out before the primaries even started because his campaign was disorganized and he lagged far behind his rivals in raising funds. And he finished fourth in the Iowa caucuses. Yet, a personal style that went over well in town meeting settings, his national visibility, and the deficits of his opponents led to victories in early primaries. His major opponent, Mitt Romney, withdrew in early February.

Mike Huckabee surprised most observers by winning the Iowa caucuses. A Baptist minister, he won enthusiastic support among many of the Republicans' religious conservative-base voters. Yet, while he won some later Southern primaries and stayed in the race until early March, he was not able to broaden his base beyond the religious right. Thus, a surprise early victory does not automatically mean success.

On the Democratic side, after being the dominant frontrunner before the first caucus and primary, Hillary Clinton finished below expectations in the Iowa caucus, finishing third. She then turned around and surprised the "expectorate" by winning the following week in New Hampshire, thus setting the stage for the long, back-and-forth Democratic primary. Nonetheless, continuing to run behind because of her poor caucus showing, she was increasingly called on to leave the race by the press and Obama operatives, implicitly challenging her right to continue to compete.

The Republicans are looking for the next Ronald Reagan who can unify the party and win over the voters. In the Air Force One Pavilion at the Reagan Presidential Library, ten Republican candidates debate during the 2008 primaries.

In sum, the primary season is a game among the media, the candidates, and the voters, with the candidates trying to raise voter enthusiasm and lower media expectations simultaneously.

The common wisdom about presidential primaries is that the key ingredient is "momentum." That is, a candidate needs to win early, or at least do better than expected, to gain momentum, and then keep winning to maintain momentum. The "expectorate" needs to pronounce him a winner. In 1976, Jimmy Carter, then an unknown governor from Georgia, won the Iowa caucuses, which attracted tremendous media attention and, in turn, led to further primary wins and eventually the nomination. John Kerry, by winning Iowa and then New Hampshire in the 2004 Democratic primaries, gained so much momentum that he knocked the other candidates out of the race very quickly, in what was originally billed as a tightly contested race. In 2008, however, on both the Republican and Democratic side, the momentum seemed to shift back and forth.

Candidates must avoid making a big mistake or, worse yet, being caught covering up a mistake or untruth. Gary Hart's 1988 candidacy collapsed when the media discovered that his marriage did not prevent him from having an affair with other women. He compounded the damage by lying. This incident raised questions about his character and honesty. In contrast, during the primary campaign, Clinton admitted his marriage was not perfect. (The Monica Lewinsky scandal occurred after he was in the White House and was already a popular president.)

Incumbent presidents seeking renomination do not have the same problems as their challengers. Incumbents usually have token or no opposition in the primaries. No incumbent who sought renomination was denied it in the twentieth century.

In addition to these general strategies, candidates must deal specifically with the particular demands of caucuses, conventions, and primaries.

Presidential Caucuses and Conventions

Some states employ caucuses and conventions to select delegates to attend presidential nominating conventions. A caucus is a neighborhood meeting of party members. They discuss the candidates and then vote for their preference. These results are then added across the state. A convention, on the other hand, is usually a statewide event. Delegates to the convention are elected at the local level by party voters.

The Iowa caucuses, except for their timing and newsworthiness, are similar to those in other states. Iowa, as the first state to hold its caucuses, normally gets the most attention. Thousands of representatives of the media cover these caucuses, which have gained importance beyond what one would normally expect for a small state. Although only a handful of delegates to the national convention are at stake, a win with the nation's political pros watching can establish a candidate as a serious contender and attract further media attention and financial donations necessary to continue the campaign.

Presidential Primaries

Delegates to presidential nominating conventions are also selected in direct primaries, sometimes called **presidential preference primaries**. In these elections, governed by state laws and national party rules, voters indicate a preference for a presidential candidate, or they vote for the delegates committed to a candidate, or both. (In states where voters merely indicate their preference, the delegates are actually selected in conventions or caucuses and the primaries are called "beauty contests" because they are meaningless in terms of winning delegates, though they can be important in showing popular support.) Like other primaries, presidential primaries can be open (to all voters) or closed (to non-party members).

Through the 1960s, presidential preference primaries usually played an insignificant role in presidential nominations because only a handful of states employed primaries to select delegates. Thus Vice President **Hubert Humphrey** gained the Democratic Party's nomination in 1968 without winning a single primary. A majority of the delegates to the Democratic convention were selected through party caucuses and state conventions, where party leaders supportive of Humphrey had considerable influence. Humphrey's nomination severely divided the Democratic Party. Many constituencies within the party, particularly those opposed to the Vietnam War, charged that the nomination was controlled by party elites out of touch with rank-and-file Democrats.

Delegate Selection Reform

In response, the Democratic Party changed delegate selection procedures to make delegates more representative of Democratic voters. One change established quotas for blacks, women, and young people to reflect the groups' percentages in each state's population. These reforms significantly increased minority and female convention representation and, quite unexpectedly, made the primary the preferred method of nomination. Criteria of openness and representativeness could be more easily satisfied through primary selection. In recent years, more than 70 percent of the Democratic delegates have been chosen in primaries. The Democrats have replaced quotas for minorities with guidelines urging minority involvement in party affairs. However, the quota remains that half the delegates must be women.

The Republican Party has not felt as much pressure to reform its delegate selection procedures, but Republicans have tried to eliminate discrimination and increase participation in the selection process.

Reforming the Nomination Process

Each election year political observers discuss changing the presidential nomination process. They correctly complain that primaries weaken political parties by removing the decision from party officials and that primaries have very low, unrepresentative turnouts. Caucuses empower the party elite but are a barrier to broad participation and are even more unrepresentative than primaries.

The Caucuses

The caucus system came under attack in 2008, especially by Clinton supporters. Although it was the Clinton organization's fault that they did not pay close attention to the rules that gave caucuses significant power, it is also true that, as they alleged, caucuses favor individuals who have a good deal of flexible time, such as independent professionals. They do not empower working-class people. The reason is that to participate in a caucus, you must devote several hours. Thus, those with child care responsibilities, who are out of town, who are ill or disabled, or who have inflexible work schedules are disfranchised.

Moreover, the small number of participants means that caucuses can be very unrepresentative of the overall primary electorate. In 2008, in the four states that had both primaries and caucuses, Obama won the caucuses by margins from 5 to 34 percent greater than the popular vote and thus piled up huge delegate margins. (In three of the four states, the primaries were only "beauty contests"; the vote didn't count in the delegate selection.) On the Republican side, McCain did very poorly in the caucuses because of his organizational problems, yet was able to win most of the big primaries, which, because of the Republican's method of delegate allocation, he converted into large numbers of delegates.

The Primaries

The primary electorate, often in the 25 to 35 percent range, is much larger than caucus participants but significantly smaller than that in the general election. Primary voters include the citizens who are most interested in politics and tend to hold more extreme views than other people. Thus Democratic primaries have a disproportionate number of liberals, and Republican primaries have a disproportionate number of conservatives. These primary voters pull the Democratic candidates further to the left and the Republican candidates further to the right than the candidates might choose to position themselves or than the electorate as a whole might want the candidates to position themselves.

Moreover, until 2008, the system gave disproportionate influence to two small states, Iowa and New Hampshire, that come first in the process. Voters in most other states did not get to see most candidates; they had already been weeded out by the time the April, May, and June primaries occurred. There are some advantages to having the small states go first,[85] particularly that the campaigns in small states can be personal and relatively inexpensive compared to the costs of the big media markets in large states. But in 2008, the system changed. Legislators in the larger states moved to get their states into the early action. The Iowa caucus and then the New Hampshire primary remained first, but a month later twenty-two states, including many large states, held primaries. This new lineup put a much bigger premium on having money and gaining support early, since only media buys allowed candidates to be visible in so many large states simultaneously.

Rearranging the schedule does not address the central problem of primaries, removing power from political parties. Many people are glad that we no longer have the "smoke-filled rooms" where party bosses chose the nominees. Nevertheless, the primary system has weakened political parties, and the small primary electorate is unrepresentative of the general public, though it is more representative than the caucuses. It is possible that primary voters are less representative of the public than the party bosses who met in smoke-filled rooms. Certainly they know less about the nominees than the party bosses did. But the days when party leaders could anoint the nominees are probably gone forever.

Another issue with primaries is how the votes are counted. The Republicans operated with a winner-take-all system, that is, the candidate winning the most votes wins all the delegates in the state. This is analogous to the electoral college system for determining the general election winner. The Democrats, on the other hand, split each state's delegates according to the proportion of votes they received in the primary or caucus. Thus, a 51 percent victory for John McCain gave him all the state's delegates; a similar victory for Barack Obama gave him only 51 percent. Several commentators have pointed out that had the Democrats operated under the Republican rules, Hillary Clinton would be the nominee.

DEMOCRACY?

Can we know whether caucuses or primaries are more representative of the party? Of the general electorate? Which is more democratic, primaries or caucuses?

The National Conventions

Once selected, delegates attend their party's national nominating convention in the summer before the November election. Changes in party rules have reduced the convention's role from an arena where powerful party leaders came together and determined the party's nominee to a body that ratifies a choice based on the outcome of the primaries and caucuses. That is, the conventions now routinely nominate whichever candidate wins the most primaries.

In the "old" days, often many ballots were necessary before a winner emerged. In 1924, it took the Democrats 103 ballots to nominate John W. Davis. Now nominees are selected on the first ballot. Sometimes commentators predict a close nomination race, which would force the deci-

sion to be made at the convention, but this hasn't happened since the primaries have been used extensively. Instead, the national party conventions served other purposes: to endorse the nominee and his choice for vice president, to construct a party platform, to whip up enthusiasm for the ticket among party loyalists, and to present the party favorably to the national viewing audience. Thus even without choosing the nominee, the national conventions give meaning to the notion of a national party.

After the reforms of 1972, convention delegates have become a more diverse group, especially on the Democratic side. In 2004, 50 percent of the Democratic and 43 percent of the Republican delegates were women; 18 percent of the Democratic and 6 percent of the Republican delegates were black. (Only 2 percent of Republican voters are black and 28 percent of Democratic voters are.) Similarly, Democratic delegates are much more likely to be Latino and very slightly more likely to be Asian than are Republican delegates.[86] Compared to the population, delegates to national

---

Figure 2 | National Convention Delegates Are More Ideologically Extreme Than Rank-and-File Members

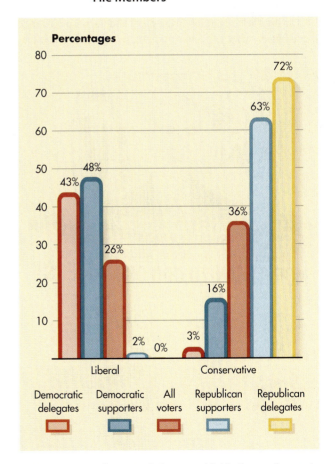

SOURCE: Data are from 2008 Delegate and Public Surveys Reported in the New York Times, September 1, 2008, graphics8.nytimes.com/packages/pdf/politics/20080901-poll.pdf?scp=5&sq=delegate%20survey&st=cse.

party conventions are well educated and well off financially. Delegates also tend to be more ideologically extreme than each party's rank and file. Democratic delegates are more liberal and Republican delegates more conservative than their party's supporters and the public in general.

The Activities of the Convention

National party conventions are full of color and portray at least a semblance of excitement. They are a montage of balloons, placards, and demonstrations. Candidates and their lieutenants scurry around in search of uncommitted delegates. Behind-the-scenes negotiators try to work out differences among factions of the party. Journalists are everywhere, covering everything from the trivial to the momentous. The keynote address reviews the party's glorious past, speaks to a promising future, and levels attacks, usually relatively gentle, at the opposition. Each candidate is placed in nomination by a party notable who reviews the candidate's background and experience. The roll call of the states ratifies the party's choice, and on the last night delegates cheer the acceptance speeches of the presidential and vice presidential nominees. Those who contested the nomination often join the nominees on the platform at the end in a display of party unity.

During the convention, each party endorses a platform, a statement of what it plans to do dressed up in flowery lan-

guage about how it is the only possible choice for patriotic Americans. Although platforms are filled with platitudes, they do have some substance. Most of the platforms contain pledges of proposed future actions, and most of those pledges are fulfilled.[87] Platforms do provide observant voters with information about what the party will do if elected.

Finally, the conventions close with the acceptance speeches of the presidential and vice presidential nominees, which are the highlights for most viewers.

Overall, the function of the conventions might best be summarized by the comment, "Conventions are now like bar mitzvahs. They are rites of passage. But rites of passage are very important in society. The guy is changing from a politician and a candidate to one of the two people who are going to be president for sure; it gives them a certain majesty."[88]

The Media and the Convention

With the beginning of radio coverage in 1924 and television coverage in 1940, the conventions have become media events. In 2004, there were six times as many media representatives as delegates at the conventions.[89] The parties try to put on a show they hope will attract voters to their candidates, controlling who speaks and when. Polls usually show the party's candidate doing better during and after the party's convention, called the "convention bounce," though the effect does not last long.

When there are deep divisions in the party, it may be impossible to prevent them from surfacing at the convention during prime time. This has not happened for many years, since the classic 1968 Democratic Convention. It was filled with conflict—conflict inside the convention between the supporters of Hubert Humphrey and opponents of the Johnson policies on the Vietnam War and conflict outside the convention on the streets of Chicago between antiwar demonstrators and the Chicago police. Television covered both events, associating the division in the convention with the turmoil outside, and dimmed Humphrey's chances of winning the election.

Because subsequent conventions have been predictable, with few controversial issues, the major networks are no longer showing them "gavel to gavel," leaving that coverage to public television or specialty cable networks such as CNN and C-SPAN. The major networks showed only a few prime-time events of each 2008 national convention: the keynote speech and an occasional speech by a party luminary, such as ailing Ted Kennedy at the Democratic convention and several of the defeated presidential candidates at the Republican one. The vice presidential and presidential nominees' acceptance speeches were also given extensive coverage. In 2008, coverage of the Democratic convention focused on whether Clinton supporters would rally round Obama and focused extensively on speeches by Hillary Clinton and Bill Clinton. At the Republican convention the focus was on the contro-

In the 1950s, at the dawn of the television age, Democratic Party leaders instruct their delegates how to behave on camera.

Courtesy of the Smithsonian Institute

When Barack Obama was nominated as the Democratic Party's candidate for president, he gave his acceptance speech in a football stadium rather than in the convention hall. Seventy-eight thousand supporters packed the Denver Broncos' stadium.

versies swirling around John McCain's surprise pick of Sarah Palin, governor of Alaska, as his vice presidential nominee. This limited coverage is the logical outcome of the successful attempt of party leaders to control the conventions. Still, even if there's no controversy, the media's talking heads will work hard to create conflict and excitement.

Selecting a Vice Presidential Nominee

In modern times, selection of a vice presidential candidate is done by the party's presidential nominee and then merely ratified at the convention, although in 1956, Democratic presidential nominee Adlai Stevenson broke with tradition and left the decision to the convention. In earlier years, party bosses chose the running mate. When Rutherford B. Hayes (1877–1881) first got word that William Wheeler was to be his running mate, Hayes responded, "I'm ashamed to say: Who is Wheeler?"[90]

Presidential candidates usually select a vice presidential nominee who can balance the ticket. What exactly does "balance" mean? A careful analysis of vice presidential choices of both parties since 1940 revealed that presidential candidates tend to balance the ticket in terms of age—choosing a running mate from a different age cohort, as John Kerry did with John Edwards.[91] Those with little Washington experience usually balance the ticket by choosing a Washington insider as a running mate (as, in 1992, outsider Clinton did by choosing Gore and as, in 2000, outsider George W. Bush did by choosing Dick Cheney).

Although common wisdom also suggests that presidential candidates balance the ticket in terms of region (for example, **John F. Kennedy** from Massachusetts chose Texan **Lyndon Johnson** in 1960) or ideology (for example, the more liberal Michael Dukakis chose the more conservative Lloyd Bentsen in 1988), this happens only occasionally.[92] In 2004, both presidential candidates had running mates whose ideologies were similar to their own.

Gender traditionally has not been part of a ticket-balancing effort, but since Walter Mondale's historic choice of Geraldine Ferraro in 1984, women are sometimes among those given consideration. Much discussion of both parties' tickets in 2008 swirled around the issue of whether a woman would be asked to join the ticket. Though Barack Obama passed over Hillary Clinton as his choice in favor of Senator Joe Biden (Del.), John McCain did choose Sarah Palin (Alaska). His primary aim may have been to woo disaffected Clinton supporters, but the major impact was to rally the religious right to his ticket. Palin, a conservative Republican, energized the Republican base and gave the ticket new excitement.

Presidential candidates believe that choosing a vice presidential candidate from a large state will help win that state in the November election.[93] In fact, this is not true; the added advantage of a vice presidential candidate in his or her home state is less than 1 percent, and the bigger the state, the less the advantage.[94] About one-third of the vice presidential candidates since 1960, including John Edwards, did not even carry their home state.[95] Bush and Kerry in 2004 and Obama and McCain in 2008 ignored the large-state

When Bill Clinton selected Al Gore as his running mate in 1992, he chose someone who was from the same generation and region and who had the same ideology (moderate liberal). Although Gore, unlike Clinton, was a Washington insider, observers were surprised that there wasn't more effort to balance the ticket. Yet the two couples (including Hillary Clinton and Tipper Gore) developed a chemistry that energized their campaign.

potential in choosing their running mates. In fact, Dick Cheney, Sarah Palin, and Joe Biden came from the nation's smallest states, with three Electoral College votes each.

Do vice presidential choices affect the election outcome? In most cases, no, although Kennedy's selection of Johnson probably enabled him to carry the state of Texas in the tight 1960 race. Without Texas, Kennedy would have lost. In recent years, presidential candidates have been more attentive to the possible contributions a vice president would make after being elected. Other than that, as one commentator quipped, "... picking a running mate is ... like picking a pet. How much time are you planning to spend with the little fellow? How much exercise will he be getting on an average day? On the one extreme, you have the William Wheeler model (Rutherford B. Hayes's vice president. There's the living room, go find a corner and sleep in it). On the other end, there's the Cheney version in which the pet takes over the checkbook, diversifies the family investment portfolio and starts strafing the neighbor's cat."[96]

Third-Party and Independent Nominees

Independent and third-party candidates are part of every presidential campaign. Most of the candidates are invisible to all except the most avid political devotee. It's not easy for independents to get on the ballot; state laws control access to the ballot, and state lawmakers are Republicans or Democrats. But in recent elections, strong independents have emerged with some frequency, including Ross Perot in 1992 and 1996, and Ralph Nader in 2000. The Nader candidacy probably cost **Al Gore** the election by taking some liberal votes away from him in closely fought states.

The General Election Campaign

We take it for granted that the election campaign is what determines who wins, and it does have a modest effect.[97] But consider this: only twice since 1952 has the candidate who was ahead in the polls in July, before the national conventions, lost the election. Those years were 1988 when Dukakis led and 2000 when Al Gore led (and since Gore won the popular vote, perhaps his case is only a partial exception to the rule).[98] This suggests that although campaigns can make a difference, a lot of other factors determine who is elected.

Campaign Organization

Staffing the campaign organization is crucial, not only hiring talented people but also getting those with considerable national campaign experience and a variety of perspectives. The candidate's own personal organization is only one part of the overall campaign organization. The national party organization and state parties also have some responsibilities, including the very important functions of registering potential party voters and getting them to the polls, as well as trying to make sure that the presidential candidate's local appearances will help the party's congressional and state candidates. Party organizations are also crucial in raising funds after the conventions, when direct fundraising by candidates is no longer legal if the candidate accepts public funding.

Campaign Strategies

In developing a strategy, candidates seek to do three things: mobilize those who are already loyal to them and their party, persuade independent voters that they are the best candidate, and try to convert the opposition. Most candidates emphasize mobilizing their own voters; relatively little effort is actually spent on converting the opposition. Democrats have to work harder at mobilizing their voters than do Republicans because Democratic voters often do not vote.

Most partisans vote for their party's candidate, so the job there is to mobilize them. Both parties must try to persuade independent voters, who are swing voters and can determine the outcome; even though true independents are only about 10 percent of the electorate. (Most of those who say they are independent lean strongly to one party or another; for example, in 2004, among white voters, 88 percent of those who claimed to be independent but "leaning Democratic" voted for Kerry, and 87 percent of their Republican-leaning independent counterparts voted for Bush.)

The crucial strategic question is where to allocate resources of time and money: where to campaign, where to buy media time and how much to buy, and where to spend money helping local organizations. Success in raising money is also one of the keys to a successful political campaign. We will discuss this more fully in the next chapter.

Allocating Resources among States

Candidates must always remember that they have to win a majority of the Electoral College vote (see "The Electoral College" section later in this chapter). The most populous states, with the largest number of electoral votes, are vital. However, compared to thirty years ago, more states are now "safe," as we described earlier in discussing the Big Sort. So candidates focus their resources on a decreasing number of so-called **battleground states**, or **swing states**, where the results are in doubt. That includes not just the large states of Ohio, Pennsylvania, and Florida, but medium-sized states such as Wisconsin and Iowa and even smaller states such as New Mexico with its five electoral votes and New Hampshire with its four.

Thus in the 2004 presidential campaign, there was little advertising or activity in several of the largest states—California, Illinois, New York, and Texas—because the first three were considered sure Kerry states and the last a sure Bush state. But on the other hand, the swing states received massive attention. For example, President Bush visited Pennsylvania eighteen times during the campaign, and Senator Kerry visited it twenty-two times. Ohio was John Kerry's most frequent stop (with twenty-six visits), and it was second for George W. Bush (with seventeen visits). "More money was spent on television advertising in Florida … than in 45 states and the District of Columbia combined. More than half of all campaign resources were dedicated to just three states—Florida, Ohio, and Pennsylvania."[99]

In focusing on swing states, candidates are attempting to expand their existing bases of support. Most of the Rocky Mountain states have been solidly Republican in their presidential loyalties. Republicans must build on this base and their strength in the South by carrying some of the large eastern or midwestern industrial states to win.

Democrats had a strategic problem given the near-solid Rocky Mountain and Southern Republican bloc. Between the end of Reconstruction (in 1877) and 1948, the South was solidly Democratic. Since 1976, the Democrats had consistently lost the South, as we discussed in Chapter 6. President Clinton proved that Democrats could win without most of the South, although he did win three southern states in each election. (This strategy was also used successfully by the Republicans between the 1870s and the 1920s, when they were able to capture the White House regularly without ever winning a southern state.)

In 2008, McCain struggled to win states that Bush had won in 2004, and in the end lost nine of them. During the last week or so of the campaign, he spent most of his time and campaign advertising in Florida and Ohio, which had supported Bush, and Pennsylvania, where Kerry won, but in a tight race. McCain still lost those. Obama campaigned hard and won not only these states but also others where he had a good organization, such as Iowa and Wisconsin, and he brought some Southern (Virginia and North Carolina) and mountain states (Nevada and Colorado) into the Democratic fold for the first time in decades.[100]

Creating Images

Largely through the media, candidates try to create a favorable image and portray the opponent in an unfavorable way. In 2000, George W. Bush used his warm personality to establish a positive image despite the concerns many voters had about his abilities. Voters were comfortable with Gore's abilities but had reservations about his personality. After eight years of Clinton's evasions and lies about personal issues, Gore's exaggerations may have seemed too much like those of Clinton. In 2004, Bush tried to define himself as a resolute war leader and define Kerry as a "flip-flopper" with no principled positions. Kerry, in turn, painted Bush as an arrogant person unwilling to listen to criticisms or admit failures. McCain portrayed Obama as a celebrity, out of touch with ordinary people, while Obama challenged

In 2000 many people told pollsters that they voted for George Bush over Al Gore because they liked his personality. In one survey, the voters said that they would rather have a beer with Bush.

McCain's ability to relate to ordinary people given his wealth.

Issues can also be the basis for an appeal to voters. Democrats traditionally have used the "pocketbook" issues, arguing that economic times are better with Democratic presidents. In 2004, though, the Iraq War and the war on terrorism were the predominant issues of the campaign. Although Kerry sought to turn attention to domestic issues, the campaign was fought largely on the issue of who would be the stronger leader in a dangerous world. And the results indicated that those voters concerned about this issue voted strongly for Bush.

By 2006, though, the unpopular war turned the war issue to a plus for Democrats. In 2008, the McCain campaign tried to again turn that issue to the Republicans' advantage, arguing that Obama was an untried leader and that, as McCain argued, Obama would rather win an election than the war. Republican surrogates even cast doubt on Obama's patriotism, while far-right ideologues tried to make an issue out of Obama's middle name, Hussein.

Given the problematic state of the economy, high gas prices, and the slumping housing market, the Democrats, tried to fight the 2008 campaign on economic issues. It was likely that Obama's success or failure would depend to a large extent on his success in focusing the campaign on economic issues rather than on personality or foreign policy.

Issue appeals are usually general, and often candidates do not offer a clear-cut choice even on the most important controversies of the time. For example, the 1968 presidential election offered voters little choice on Vietnam policy, because the positions of candidates Nixon and Humphrey appeared very similar.[101] Voters who wanted to end the war by withdrawing or others who wanted to escalate the war had no real choice between the candidates. In 2008, the situation was somewhat clearer, with Obama pushing for a timetable for withdrawal, while McCain argued for staying until we win.

Ideally, the major campaign themes and strategies have been put into place by the end of the summer, but themes and strategies are revised and updated on a daily, sometimes hourly, basis as the campaign progresses. Decisions are made not only by the candidate and the campaign manager but also by a staff of key advisers that includes media experts and pollsters. Sophisticated polling techniques are used to produce daily reports on shifts in public opinion across the nation and in particular regions. Campaign trips are modified or scratched as the candidate's organization sees new opportunities. And media events can be planned to complement the paid advertising the candidate runs.

Campaign Communication

Candidates use multiple ways of communicating with their supporters and with the millions of swing voters who might vote either way. Campaign advertising, appearances on television, candidate debates, mass mailings, and many forms of electronic communication are all part of campaign communication. They inform, they help set the campaign agenda, and they help persuade voters.[102]

Media Advertising

Paid advertisements allow candidates to focus on points most favorable to their cause or to portray their opponents in the most negative light. In 2004, the presidential candidates and associated groups spent more than $1 billion on advertising in an attempt to sway public opinion.[103] Most advertising is done through television, although radio and the Internet also reach significant audiences.[104] Television ads were first used in the 1952 campaign. One, linking the

Democratic Truman administration to the unpopular Korean War, showed two soldiers in combat talking about the futility of war. Then one of the soldiers is hit and dies. The other one exposes himself to the enemy and is also killed. The announcer's voice says, "Vote Republican."[105] Today's ads are shorter and less melodramatic but still appeal to emotions. The 1984 Reagan commercials hearkened back to an idyllic past before the turmoil of the 1960s and 1970s and proclaimed American greatness again. Their cheerful tag line was "It's morning in America."[106] (Many historic ads are available for viewing online at www.movingimage.us.)

There is both an art and a science to campaign ads. Most political ads are quite short, thirty or sixty seconds in length. Campaigns are sophisticated in placing ads. Selection of television shows and media markets is important. For example, in 2004, President Bush ran many of his ads on crime shows such as *Law and Order* and *NYPD Blue* because he thought there would be an audience of conservative men sympathetic to Republican appeals watching those shows. The Kerry campaign ran more ads on shows catering to women, such as *Judge Judy* and *Oprah*, and to younger and older men, such as the *Late Show with David Letterman*.[107] Kerry also advertised more on shows with African American stars. Both campaigns spent a lot to advertise on morning news shows and popular daytime shows such as *Dr. Phil*.[108] Both campaigns focused on the battleground states and wasted little of their advertising budget on states already thought to be sure for one candidate.[109] But within the battleground states, the Bush campaign focused more on the rural and exurban (outer suburban) areas than did the Kerry campaign.

Campaigns also have to decide what combination to run of positive ads, touting their own programs; negative ads, attacking their opponents; and response ads, responding to opponents' charges. Negative ads were more prominent in the 2004 election than in the recent past. The Bush campaign ran far more negative ads than the Kerry campaign.[110] This high level of negativity is unusual for an incumbent but probably reflected his low approval ratings. Strong front-runners tend to stay positive.[111] The 2004 election was so close that both sides made liberal use of negative ads. However, many ads were run not by the candidates themselves, but by independent advocacy groups.

Negative ads do provide some helpful information about issues, supplementing media news coverage, which focuses heavily on personalities, conflicts, and the "horse race" aspect of campaigns.[112] Many, though not all, negative ads contain a grain of truth. Kerry did vote for numerous tax increases, but not as many as the Republicans charged. Hundreds of thousands of jobs were lost during the Bush administration, but not as many as the Democrats claimed.

However, some negative ads are simply false. Among the most discussed negative ads in 2004 were those of the Swift Boat Veterans for Truth. The group attacked Kerry's war record. (Kerry, as a young naval lieutenant, commanded a "swift boat" in the Vietnam War and won medals for heroism as well as for his wounds.) The Swift Boat Veterans did not serve with Kerry, and several were angry with him for opposing the war after returning from Vietnam. The Kerry campaign was slow to respond to these August ads and lost ground in the polls during this period despite the fact that independent reexaminations of the record found nothing to substantiate the Swift Boat Veterans' ad claims. The Swift Boat ads were so effective that reporters coined a new verb—"to swift boat"—meaning to produce a commercial that is dishonest but plausible to viewers.

Negative ads, some true, some false, tend to reinforce viewers' previous beliefs. So, if you believed that Kerry wouldn't be a strong leader, or that Democrats wouldn't stand up to foreign threats, you would be more likely to believe the Swift Boat ads that questioned Kerry's Vietnam service and implicitly draw these damning conclusions. Campaign advisers think that negative ads are very effective, even though most people say they do not like them.[113] One adviser said, "People won't pay any attention [to positive ads]. Better to knock your opponent's head off."[114] Polls do show that negative ads can have a dramatic short-term effect on a candidate's standing. The Swift Boat commercials suggest that negative ads, even if false, can have a long-term effect as well.

Some observers speculate that negative ads increase voter cynicism and thus depress turnout, but there is little evidence of this effect. In fact, negative ads may activate the supporters of the attacker while depressing the turnout of the person being attacked.[115] However, there is evidence that Republicans and independents find negative ads more believable than Democrats do, perhaps because Republicans and independents are more cynical about politics and government to begin with.

Technology allows the opposition candidate's ads to be evaluated continuously and new ads prepared immediately to counter attacks that might be having an impact. After the Swift Boat fiasco, Kerry began responding to other negative ads. One day in October, the Kerry campaign learned that President Bush had just charged that Kerry would "weaken America and make the world more dangerous." Within three hours, the Kerry campaign had made an ad accusing Bush of "desperately attacking" Kerry. By late afternoon, the script and video were sent to reporters.[116] The Bush campaign had a similar instant-response operation.

Other checks do exist on negative campaigns.[117] One check is the press, which could point out errors of fact. In recent campaigns, the press has tried to do this. In 2004 and again in 2008, fact-checkers were more active, and many papers ran critiques of the truthfulness of ads (and the statements in debates). In the process, however, the press often simply gave more attention to the negative messages.[118] Another check is the voters, who might become outraged. But although the voters complain, campaign research shows that negative ads often influence the voters, perhaps even the same ones who complain.

"In the end, he decided to go negative."

Historians tell us that negative campaigning is as American as apple pie. When Thomas Jefferson faced John Adams in 1796, a Federalist editorial prophesied that if Jefferson were elected, "[m]urder, robbery, rape, adultery and incest will be openly taught and practiced."[119] When Andrew Jackson ran for president in 1832, his mother was called a prostitute, his father a mulatto (someone of mixed races, black and white), his wife a profligate woman, and himself a bigamist.[120] A British observer of American elections in 1888 described them as a "tempest of invective and calumny . . . imagine all the accusations brought against all the candidates for the 670 seats in the English Parliament concentrated on one man, and read . . . daily for three months."[121]

Television Appearances and Media Events

Campaigns are expensive because they rely so heavily on the media to get the candidate's message to the voters. As one observer argued, "Today's presidential campaign is essentially a mass-media campaign. It is not that the mass media entirely determine what happens. . . . [b]ut it is no exaggeration to say that, for the large majority of voters, the campaign has little reality apart from the media version."[122]

Increasingly, candidates are getting free publicity by appearing on various television shows. In earlier elections, candidates appeared only on "serious" shows, such as the Sunday morning talk shows where candidates would be interviewed by one or more members of the press. Now it is increasingly common for candidates to appear in more informal, sometimes humorous, settings such as late-night talk shows or comedy shows. The candidates hope to use these settings to show voters that they are approachable and down-to-earth. It also gives candidates a chance to poke fun at their own foibles and thus possibly defuse opponents' attacks.

National television appearances might be the only sight that voters in a majority of states ever get of the candidates.

Given the increasing sophistication of the campaigns, most television and radio ads never appear in states that are solid for one candidate or another. Although voters in battleground states might consider it a blessing to not face an onslaught of campaign ads, voters in other states may feel less connected to the campaign.

Candidates spend most of their time going from media market to media market, hoping to get both national and local coverage.[123] Vice presidential candidates often appear in the smaller media markets, while the presidential contenders hit the major metro areas. They stage media events with photo opportunities in front of enthusiastic crowds and patriotic or other positive symbols.

Televised Debates

Candidates also use televised debates as part of their media campaigns. In 1960, Kennedy challenged Nixon to debate during their presidential campaigns. Nixon did not want to debate because as vice president he was already known and ahead in the polls. He remembered his first election to the House of Representatives when he challenged the incumbent to debate and, on the basis of his performance, won the election. Afterward he said the incumbent was a "damn fool" to debate. Nevertheless Nixon did agree to debate, and when the two contenders squared off, presidential debates were televised to millions of homes across the country for the first time.

Nixon dutifully answered reporters' questions and rebutted Kennedy's assertions. But Kennedy came to project an image. He sought to demonstrate his vigor, to compensate for his youth and inexperience. He also sought to contrast his attractive appearance and personality with Nixon's. So he quickly answered reporters' specific questions and then directly addressed viewers about his general goals. Kennedy's strategy worked. He appealed to people and convinced them that his youth and inexperience would not pose problems. While Kennedy remained calm, Nixon became nervous, smiling at inappropriate moments, with his eyes darting back and forth and beads of sweat rolling down his face, which had a five-o'clock shadow that projected a somewhat sinister look.

According to public opinion polls, people who saw the debates thought that Kennedy performed better in three of the four. (The only debate in which they thought Nixon performed better was the one in which the candidates were not in the same studio side-by-side. They were in separate cities, and with this arrangement Nixon was less nervous.) Yet people who heard the debates on radio did not think Kennedy performed as well. They were not influenced by the visual contrast between the candidates or the Kennedy strategy of looking directly into the camera. Clearly, television made the difference.

No more presidential debates were held for sixteen years. The candidates who were ahead did not want to risk

Before television, candidates made personal appearances. But for many years, personal appearances and speeches were considered beneath the dignity of the presidential office. William Jennings Bryan was the first presidential candidate to break this tradition. In 1896, he traveled more than 18,000 miles and gave more than 600 speeches. One observer complained that he was "begging for the presidency as a tramp might beg for a pie." Although Bryan lost the election to William McKinley, his approach became the standard. This photo illustrates how the term **stump speech**, used to refer to candidates' boilerplate campaign speeches, may have developed.

their lead. But in 1976, President Ford decided to debate Carter, and in 1980, President Carter decided to debate Reagan. Both incumbents were in trouble, and they thought they needed to debate to win. Although President Reagan was far ahead in 1984, he decided to debate Mondale because he did not want to seem afraid. By agreeing to debate, he solidified the precedent begun anew in 1976.

In 2000, the media's low expectations for Bush's performance, coupled with his congenial, personal style, helped him hold his own or even win the debates in the view of many, even though the debates revealed his limited grasp of issues and misstatements of facts. Gore's mannerisms seemed stiff and overbearing. And the press, which is far more inclined to evaluate the debates as theater performances than as policy discussions, addressed Gore's body language more than Bush's grasp of issues and misstatements of facts.

Because candidates have different strengths, each campaign wants a debate format that builds on its candidate's strengths. The "debate about debates" has become as predictable a part of campaigns as the debates themselves. Representatives of candidates debate the number of debates, the formats, the topics to be covered, the size of the audience, even the size and shape of the podia. The 2004 debates were governed by a thirty-two-page set of rules agreed to by the candidates' representatives.

In 2004, those negotiating for Bush argued that the first debate should be about foreign policy, ostensibly Bush's strength. He thought he could easily show Kerry to have an uncertain grasp and a vacillating policy. Instead, Kerry looked assured and confident and attacked Bush's foreign policy mistakes throughout the debate. When cameras focused on Bush listening to Kerry, he looked surly and angry at being attacked. And when Bush responded, he wasn't able to offer a coherent defense of his policies. Consequently, although Kerry had been trailing in the polls before the debate, his performance in this debate narrowed the gap.

Bush was not used to direct criticism of his policies. Within the White House, criticism was not welcomed, and on the campaign trail, Bush usually spoke only to hand-picked Republican supporters, whose tough questions tended to be about whether he liked broccoli or what he felt about his legacy.[124] Thus he did not have much recent experience facing criticism nor with presenting a serious counterargument to it. The ridicule and dismissiveness that he used in his campaign stump speeches did not work well when faced with a real-life opponent making real-life arguments on stage. The president prepared more for the second and third debates and looked more confident and pleasant.[125]

A newer feature of debates is that in recent primary campaigns, various groups have sponsored debates among primary candidates. The results of these debates tend to be minimal, especially when, as in the 2008 race, there are a lot of candidates. A debate among seven or ten candidates allows for even less direct exchange than a debate between two candidates. However, these debates are a way for the people who are paying attention to the election to learn more about the candidates.

e-Campaigning

Candidates are increasingly relying on electronic communication to keep supporters informed about the campaign and the issues, to raise money, and to solicit volunteer activity. This includes websites, e-mail, blogs, YouTube, text messaging, and the use of the social networking sites like MySpace, Facebook, and Friendster.

All the leading candidates for the presidency in 2008 had active websites. All candidates use e-mail to communicate with hundreds of thousands of people, making them feel like insiders and encouraging their continued support and allegiance. These e-mail messages supplement the use of direct postal mailings, which are more expensive and less responsive to breaking events. An e-mail can be prepared and sent in a few hours and can be linked to a website or streamed video.

Barack Obama has been a leader in using the Internet to attract supporters and keep them engaged. Obama's Facebook site showed more than 1.2 million supporters, and his website links to Flickr, where supporters can view continu-

Families all across the country gathered in front of their TVs to watch the first televised presidential debates in 1960, featuring Senator John F. Kennedy and Vice President Richard Nixon.

ally posted photos of the candidate and his events; Twitter, where supporters can follow postings and videos on his daily events; Black Planet, AsianAve, Faithbase, EONs, Glee, MiGente, MyBatanga, LinkedIn, and DNC Party-Builder, social networking sites for African Americans, Asian Americans, religious believers, baby boomers, gays and lesbians, Latinos, Latinos again, business professionals, and Democrats.

The Republican candidates, with the exception of Ron Paul, were not as effective in using the networking capacities of the Internet. For example, even in summer 2008, the McCain website offered places for supporters to sign up and keep in contact but did not offer links to networking sites. Thus, it is not surprising that the McCain Facebook address had less than 200,000 supporters.

YouTube is increasingly used as a campaign tool. Of course, it can be a negative, because a candidate's dumb statements or actions, if captured on camera, live on forever in cyberspace and are easily retrievable with YouTube. George Allen (R-Va.), during his campaign for reelection to the Senate in 2006, called an Indian American "macacca." This exchange was videotaped by someone in the crowd and posted on YouTube. There it was replayed to another 100,000 people and picked up by the major media and replayed on television. This no doubt contributed to his narrow defeat for reelection.[126] In 2008, Barack Obama was under attack when a video of a sermon by his preacher, including the phrase "God damn America," was posted on the Internet, played millions of times, and became the subject

of intense journalistic and blogosphere discussion. Eventually, Obama repudiated the minister and left the church.

But YouTube can also be a tremendous asset to a campaign. For example, Obama recorded a brief response to George Bush's 2008 State of the Union address. Though the media gave it little attention, it had more than 1 million hits on YouTube, and more than 500 blog sites linked to it.[127] Other candidates, too, link their video, whether policy statements, interesting events, or campaign ads, to YouTube, where millions of Internet users have access to them and can share their reactions and spread the word through blog sites.

Blogs also have become a campaign tool. Candidates and their supporters can air their views and attack opponents through blogs; a few prominent ones are read by millions.[128] Although talk radio is dominated by conservative Republicans, the most popular political blogs are those on the liberal side.

These e-strategies only work because more people than before are using the Internet as a source of news. In fact, by spring 2008, nearly half of Americans said they look online for news about the campaign or get e-mails about it. Seventeen percent claimed to look for campaign news online on a daily basis. As to be expected, younger people are more likely to use the net as a news source—half of those under 50 look online for news compared to only 15 percent of those over 65. Similarly, less educated and lower-income people are less likely, by a considerable margin, to go online. However, there are few racial differences in using the net for political news.[129]

BEHIND THE SCENES
BLOGS AND THE BIG SORT

Political blogs are a new way to keep track of politics. About one-third of individuals claim to read blogs, and of those about half read political blogs. One survey identified 476 political blogs, though that probably only scratches the surface.

Most blogs are read by only a few people, perhaps friends and acquaintances of the blogger. On the other hand, blogs such as the Huffington Post and Daily Kos (both on the left) and the Drudge report (on the right) are read by millions. Some nonpartisan blogs are widely read too, such as RealClearPolitics, which posts articles and information from many ideological perspectives.

As we would expect, blog readers are more likely to be educated and highly interested in politics (not just marginally interested). They are likely to be strong Democrats and individuals who consider themselves liberal or very liberal rather than moderate or conservative, though very conservative individuals also read blogs more than those with more moderate positions. Thus, though fewer Republicans than Democrats are bloggers, those that do blog are disproportionately very conservative. Consistent with the "Big Sort" models of the American electorate, blog readers tend to read the blogs that

are consistent with their political views. More than 94 percent of blog readers read only blogs from one side of the spectrum, and only 6 percent read blogs from both sides. With few exceptions, only liberals read the Daily Kos and only conservatives the Drudge report, for example.

Television news also has a polarized viewership, but blog reader polarization is much more extreme. Even though Fox viewers are mostly conservative, they have some moderate and liberal viewers. And the network newscasts, MSNBC, and CNN have many moderate viewers and a few conservatives. Readers of right-wing

blogs are considerably to the right of Fox News viewers, and those readers of left-wing blogs to the left of the rest of the media.[1]

Blogs are another way that individuals can interact with people like themselves. That's true for self-help groups and it is also true of politics. Rather than widening individuals' perspectives, they largely provide a way to reinforce them.

[1] Information about blog readership is drawn from Henry Farrell, Eric Lawrence, and John Sides, "Self Segregation or Deliberation? Blog Readership, Participation, and Polarization in American Politics," paper presented at the Midwest Political Science Association, Chicago, Illinois, April 2008, and linked to the blogsite *Monkey Cage*, a political but nonpartisan blog: www.monkeycage.com.

In 2008, Democrats favoring Obama were the most likely group to be online. More than 80 percent were regular online users, compared to more than 70 percent of Clinton's supporters. Though McCain's supporters were about as likely as those of Obama to use the Internet, they were much less likely to get political news on it or promote their views on it (such as by signing an online petition or forwarding a link to someone else). Democrats are also more likely than Republicans to trust the Internet and to say that the Internet has promoted their political involvement.

The Electoral College

In the United States, we do not have a direct election of the president. So all planning for the campaign has to take into account the peculiar American institution of the **Electoral College**. One wit described the Electoral College as "the exploding cigar of American politics."[130] Most of the time it works fine as "little more than a question on the citizenship test and a subject for political thriller novels…. Then, every so often, "it blows up in our faces, throwing whole elections in doubt and making a mockery of the popular will."[131]

The last time it blew up in our faces was in 2000, when although Al Gore had over 500,000 more votes than George

W. Bush, he lost the election. The Electoral College is another feature of the American constitutional system that limits democracy.[132]

The Way the System Works

What counts is the popular vote in each state, because that vote determines which candidate will receive the state's electoral votes. Each state has as many electors as its total representation in Congress (House plus Senate) (see Figure 4 in Chapter 4). The smallest states (and the District of Columbia) have three, whereas the largest state—California—has fifty-five. Voters choose electors of the Electoral College when they vote for president. Technically, they vote for the electors pledged to the candidate and whose names are on file with the state government. The outcome is not official until these electors gather in each state capital in December after the presidential election to cast their votes for president and vice president.

With the exception of Maine and Nebraska, which divide some of their Electoral College votes according to who wins in each congressional district, all of each state's electoral votes go to the candidate winning the most votes in that state. If one candidate wins a majority (270) of the electors

american diversity | Racism and Sexism in the 2008 Campaign

Will the American presidency continue to be held only by white males? Can an African American or a woman ever be elected? The 2008 campaign provided a definitive answer to these questions.

Other formerly formidable barriers had already fallen: John Kennedy in 1961 became the first Catholic president, and twenty years later Ronald Reagan the first divorced one. Race and gender, however, are much more distinctive barriers than even religion.

In some ways, the 2008 election seemed light-years away from earlier eras where the idea of a woman of any color or an African American man running for president would seem ludicrous. Both Hillary Clinton and Barack Obama had millions of campaign supporters who included men and women and blacks and whites (and, of course, Americans of other ethnicities too) and both their campaigns broke fundraising records. In these ways, their campaigns were much different than **Jesse Jackson**'s 1984 campaign that appealed mostly, though certainly not entirely, to black Americans, or earlier bids for the presidency by **Shirley Chisholm** in 1972 or Elizabeth Dole in 2000, who never had a chance to become mainstream candidates.

But as the campaign unfolded, so too did evidence of the racism and sexism that has historically held African Americans and women back. Sexism was public and needed no code words. John McCain was asked by a supporter how he was going to beat "the bitch," and did not bother to correct her. Several white male cable newscasters seemed to have little compunction about offering a

variety of sexist comments showing their contempt for a woman candidate, such as MSNBC's Mike Barnicle's observation that Clinton "look[ed] like everyone's first wife standing outside a probate court," or MSNBC's Tucker Carlson's comment that "when [Clinton] comes on television, I involuntarily cross my legs." While Chris Matthews of MSNBC was chastised by his network, and made to apologize, for his comments that "Clinton was a front-runner because her husband messed around" (presumably he meant that she mostly was getting sympathy votes), most of the other statements were apparently made without criticism from the newsman's bosses.

The Internet advertised all sorts of campaign-related offensive material slurring both candidates, and others too, but a shop on Chicago's Michigan Avenue (a high-end shopping street) prominently displayed a shirt with the motto "Better a Bro than a Ho." The Clinton "Nutcracker" was advertised widely in mainstream outlets that presumably would not have advertised racially offensive items (imagine Amazon.com selling an Obama jockey doorstop or minstrel figure).

Even by more than this blatant sexism, Clinton defenders were outraged by the presumption, beginning in February, that she should pull out of the race, even though until May it was not clear that Obama had a majority of the convention votes and even though she was winning most of the contests during the chorus of "get outs." These comments were viewed as the male circle of politicians and journalists, including many Obama surrogates though not Obama

himself, telling the "little woman" to leave it to the men. Accurate interpretation or not, and certainly supporters of the candidate in the lead and journalists interested in the next story always pressure the candidate who has fallen behind, this dynamic had a lot to do with the reluctance of many Clinton supporters to join the Obama bandwagon before the convention.

But racism too was alive and well, although sometimes in a more subtle form. Few, if any, commentators made blatantly racist comments analogous to the cable newscasters' sexist ones. Yet race was injected into the campaign in many different ways. A minority of voters, but a significant one, stated in preelection and exit polls that race was a factor in their vote. While some of these were African American voters, presumably positively inclined toward Obama, others were white voters stating they would not vote for a black person. Although Obama was very successful in caucuses in overwhelmingly white states, his support in the larger states with racially diverse populations was more mixed. Though Obama did well among white voters in many states, Clinton won large margins among working-class white men and women in the later primaries in states such as Pennsylvania, Ohio, and West Virginia.

Several Clinton supporters made comments that cast, or seemed to cast, aspersions on Obama as an African American candidate. Geraldine Ferraro, the party's vice presidential candidate in 1984, and the first woman to run as a major party candidate for that position, claimed that Obama would not be the leading candidate if he were white. Obama decried these comments as "divisive," and Clinton removed Ferraro from her fundraising team. Bill Clinton, who during his terms was a strong supporter of African American interests, and they of him, made several statements demeaning Obama in ways that were seen as offensive. Commenting on Obama's South Carolina primary victory, Bill Clinton stated, "Jesse Jackson won South Carolina in '84 and '88. Jackson ran a good campaign. And Obama ran a good campaign here." Neither of these statements is in any obvious way racist, but both comments were seen by Obama supporters as demeaning to him. Obama was trying to run a campaign not focused on race, and Bill Clinton turned the focus to race. (Clinton could have compared Obama's success with other successful white candidates rather than the only African American ever to win the South Carolina primary.) And Hillary Clinton herself questioned Obama's support among "hard working … white Americans."

It is useless to try to argue about whether racism or sexism had a bigger role in the campaign. Only one person has had an opportunity to evaluate that. Shirley Chisholm, an African American woman, declared, "When I ran for the Congress, when I ran for president, I met more discrimination as a woman than for being black. Men are men."[1] However, Chisholm ran more than a quarter century ago and opportunities for both blacks and women have opened up considerably.

Of course, evaluating racism and sexism is difficult in one campaign. Barack Obama and Hillary Clinton are individuals, with individual strengths and weaknesses; they are not representative of all blacks and all women. Obama is inexperienced, though not as much as

his critics charge, and Clinton is polarizing, though more among the pundits and bloggers than the public. These are individual traits and voters well might see other African Americans and other women in a different light.

Moreover, aside from obviously racist or sexist comments, it is often hard to know whether a comment about a policy or personality feature is racist or sexist. Some who called Obama inexperienced mean just that, but others might mean that they think black people don't have the ability and depth to be president. Some who called him an elitist mean that he seems out of touch with common people of any race, a charge made against some white politicians too, but for others it may be a code for calling him an "uppity" black person. Or when people said they were not comfortable with him, did they mean because of his race, or because he is tall and lean and has a Harvard degree?

Commenting on Clinton's polarizing tendencies meant for some people a perception that she vociferously expresses her opinions and may not be able to compromise, but for others it is a sexist comment that would not be made about a man who is expected to be strong and have firm opinions. Some of those people who thought Obama would make a better commander in chief than Clinton meant that women aren't strong enough to lead a nation at war, but others only that they prefer Obama's policies. As long as race and gender remain blockades to advancement to the highest post, we can never be certain what such comments mean.

Racism and charges of racism continued into the general election. McCain accused Obama of playing the race card when Obama declared that McCain was trying to

portray him as "the other," not like other presidents you see on dollar bills. By accusing Obama of playing the race card (though Obama did not mention race and has generally not brought race into the elections), McCain himself was racializing the campaign. Karl Rove and some other advisors who took the low road in the Bush campaigns joined McCain's campaign in mid-2008. However, Americans hardly need to be reminded that this was an historic race, and that Obama was the first African American candidate with a good chance at being president.

In the end, Obama overcame racial barriers. Though he did not win a majority of white votes, he won a higher proportion than any Democrat since Jimmy Carter. In the states that voted Democratic, he did win a majority of white voters. And he won nearly two-thirds of the voters of Asian-American and Hispanic descent. Even for Americans who are prejudiced against black people, for many, their views of their economic interests and positive view of Obama as a steady leader overcame race.

Another "ism" also was obvious in the general election. Our society values youth, health, and fitness, and John McCain is a 71 year old cancer survivor. Both pundits and voters focused on these issues. Many voters said they were worried about his age, and concerned that the vice presidential candidate, Sarah Palin, would not be ready if McCain died in office. McCain's every slip of the tongue, slips made by all candidates in grueling campaigns, were examined as possible evidence that he was too old for the job.

[1] Quoted in her obituary in the *New York Times*, February 3, 2005.
[2] Barry Sussman, "A Black or Woman Does Better Today Than a Catholic in '60," *Washington Post National Weekly Edition*, November 21, 1983, 42.
SOURCE: www.cbsnews.com/htdocs/pdf/ 020306woman .pdf; Gallup Poll data from www.atheists.org/flash.line/ atheism9.htm.

voting across the United States, then the election is decided. If the electoral vote is tied, or if no candidate wins a majority, then the election is decided in the House of Representatives, where each state has one vote and a majority is necessary to win. This has not happened since 1824, when John Quincy Adams was chosen. But it nearly happened in 1976 with the shift of a few vote thousand votes in Delaware and Ohio. If voting in the Electoral College for the vice president does not yield a majority, the Senate chooses the vice president, with each senator having one vote. If it should get to that stage, the largest and smallest states would have equal weight, a very undemocratic procedure.

Strategic Implications

The campaign strategies that candidates use are shaped in part by the Electoral College system. In general, candidates have incentives to spend more time in the large states where the majority of the electoral votes are. A one-vote margin in Pennsylvania, for example, yields twenty-one votes for the winning candidate compared to only three votes in Nebraska. Thus it is more important to get that extra vote in Pennsylvania. Given the need to focus on a small number of swing states, more time is consequently spent in the larger ones than the smaller ones.

However, only some large states get attention. So, in 2008, political activists from California did not spend much time there, but rather headed for Colorado or New Mexico or Oregon where there was competition. The Electoral College system, then, favors "states" over "people." As one

observer pointed out, gun owners or women, for example, live all over the country, but only ones in swing states get wooed.[133]

Smaller states tend to favor the Electoral College system (because their Electoral College votes give them a larger influence on the Electoral College than their population proportion would). But unless they are swing states, they are ignored too. The safe Republican states in the prairies, the South, and the great plains are largely ignored by the candidates.

Rationale and Outcomes of the Electoral College

The Founders neither wanted nor envisioned a popular election of the president; selection of the president was placed in the hands of state elites, the electors. The Founders also agreed to enshrine the influence of small states (at that time, disproportionately Southern, slave-holding states) in the fundamental framework of the Constitution, and the Electoral College was one of the ways of doing that.[134]

The Founders assumed that the Electoral College would have considerable power, with each elector exercising independent judgment and choosing from among a large number of candidates. They did not foresee the development of political parties or the development of a political climate where the popular vote is considered the source of legitimacy for a candidate. In practice, as state parties developed, the electors became part of the party process, pledged to party candi-

| **Figure 3** | **Electoral College Vote** |

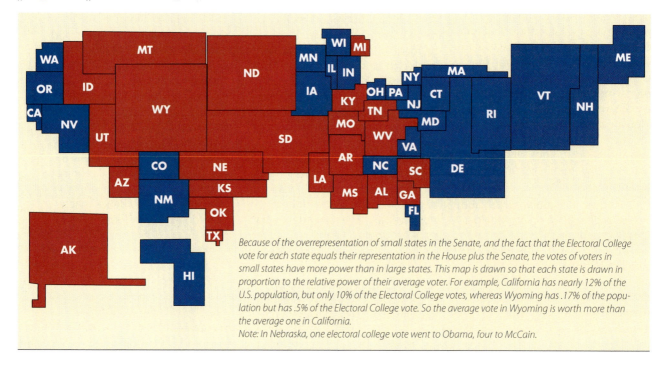

Because of the overrepresentation of small states in the Senate, and the fact that the Electoral College vote for each state equals their representation in the House plus the Senate, the votes of voters in small states have more power than in large states. This map is drawn so that each state is drawn in proportion to the relative power of their average voter. For example, California has nearly 12% of the U.S. population, but only 10% of the Electoral College votes, whereas Wyoming has .17% of the population but has .5% of the Electoral College vote. So the average vote in Wyoming is worth more than the average one in California.
Note: In Nebraska, one electoral college vote went to Obama, four to McCain.

dates. Therefore, electors usually rubber-stamp the choice of voters in each state rather than exercise their own judgment.

A discrepancy between the Electoral College and the popular vote outcome occurred three times in the nineteenth century (1824, 1876, and 1888). However, after more than a century of presidential elections whose outcome was known once the popular vote was tallied, and since the principle of "one person, one vote" has become enshrined in law and political culture, the American public has become used to thinking of elections as an expression of the will of the people.

When the 2000 election yielded an Electoral College winner who had not won the popular vote, there were immediate calls for the elimination or reform of the Electoral College system. However, these calls went nowhere, and the Electoral College remains.

Possible Reforms

The Electoral College was designed both to temper the influence of voters by establishing an intermediate body of electors who actually choose the president and to make sure that the South had a disproportionate influence on the choice of the president.[135] It is a distinctly undemocratic mechanism that institutionalizes in the presidential election process part of the excess weight given to smaller states in the United States Senate (because the number of electors for each state is based on the number of senators and representatives in each state).

Over the years, several proposed reforms have been considered. One reform would be to abolish the Electoral College altogether and leave the choice of president to the popular vote because direct election is a more understandable system. This change would require a constitutional amendment (which requires a two-thirds approval by members of Congress and three-quarters of the states), which is very difficult because the small states that think they benefit from the current system and the swing states that do benefit from the existing system will block it.

Another target of reform is the requirement that if the electoral vote is tied, the presidential choice is to be thrown to the House of Representatives. There is no expectation that each state's House delegation would vote for the presidential candidate that its state's voters chose; rather, states would reflect the majority party in their House delegation. Moreover, each state would have an equal vote. Alaska would carry the same clout as California. This is a very undemocratic feature of the process and would probably cause a crisis if actually used to elect a candidate with a minority of the popular vote.

Another undemocratic feature of the Electoral College is that not all states require their electors to cast their votes for the candidates who won the state vote. The **faithless elector** is one who casts his or her vote for a personal choice, even someone who was not on the ballot. Even though the intent of the Founders was to allow electors to cast their votes any way they desired, modern reformers have proposed that, in our more democratic era, electors should be bound by the wishes of the voters in their states. It is true that no faithless elector has ever made a difference in the outcome of an election, but in the 2000 election, as few as three faithless electors could have made a difference.

A current reform proposal is the National Popular Vote, a movement gaining some ground. The idea, supported by a group of electoral reform advocates, is that each state would pass a law entering into an agreement to award all their electoral votes to the candidate who receives the most popular votes nationally. The proposal, then, could take effect when states whose total electoral votes equal 270, the Electoral College majority, have entered the agreement. Maryland, New Jersey, and Illinois have signed on and other states are considering it. This proposal would make the presidential choice a popular vote choice but without having to amend the Constitution.

Voting Behavior

Voting behavior is shaped by party identification, candidate evaluations, and positions on the issues. We have discussed party identification in Chapter 7. Here we will examine candidate evaluations and issue positions and how the three factors work together.

Candidate Evaluations

Candidates' personalities and styles have had more impact since television has become voters' major source of information about elections. Obama's popularity in 2008 is an example of the influence of a candidate and his personality. The perceived competence and integrity of candidates are other facets of candidate evaluation. Voters are less likely to support candidates who do not seem capable of handling the job, regardless of their issue positions. Jimmy Carter suffered in 1980 because of negative evaluations of his competence and leadership among voters.

Clinton's popularity puzzled some observers. Many voters did not like his evasions and his adulterous behavior, but they voted for him anyway. During the impeachment debates, many journalists expressed amazement that Clinton's popularity remained high. The public, more than journalists, seemed to be able to separate his public and private roles. The public continued to support him because they felt he was doing a good job as president, not because they admired him personally.

Personality was important in the 2004 campaign. John Kerry seemed unable to connect with people and uncomfortable on the campaign trail. At times, he appeared to be going through the motions, playing a role. In answering questions, he often provided lengthy and detailed responses. George Bush, on the other hand, seemed more at ease, comfortable working the crowd. His responses were often truncated and general. Despite his unexpectedly good performance in the debates, Kerry could not shake his image as an effete, somewhat snobbish, Boston patrician who was out of touch with average Americans.

Issues

Issues are a third factor influencing the vote. Although Americans are probably more likely to vote on issues now than they were in the 1950s, issues influence only some of the voters some of the time. In 2000 and 2004, voters saw themselves as much closer to the Democratic candidates than to Bush.[136]

To cast an **issue vote**, voters quite obviously must have a position on an issue. In recent elections, more than 80 percent of the public had a position on issues such as government spending, military spending, and women's rights.[137] An issue vote also requires the candidates to differ with respect to their issue positions and for the voters to recognize this difference. A substantial minority of voters are able to detect some differences among the issue positions of presidential candidates.[138] Lastly, voters must cast their vote for the candidate who reflects their position on the issue or at least the candidate who is closest to their issue position.

In every election since 1972, more than 70 percent of voters who met these conditions cast issue votes.[139] The highest proportion of issue voting was on those issues that typically divided Republicans and Democrats, such as government spending, military spending, and government aid to the unemployed and minorities. However, because many in the electorate were unable to define both their own and the candidates' positions on each issue, the proportion of the total electorate that can be said to cast an "issue vote" is usually less than 40 percent, and for some issues it is much less.[140]

Abortion is another issue on which voters cast issue-related votes. In 2004, for example, about 70 percent of the voters cast issue-related votes on abortion. Of those voters (who had a position and also knew the candidates' position), 32 percent of those who opposed abortion under any conditions voted for Kerry, a supporter of abortion rights, compared with 67 percent of those who believed that abortion should be a matter of personal choice.[141]

Issue voting may be mostly an evaluation of the current incumbents. If voters like the way incumbents, or the incumbent's party, have handled the job in general or in certain areas—the economy or foreign policy, for example—they will vote accordingly, even without much knowledge about the specifics of the issues.

Voting on the basis of past performance is called **retrospective voting**. There is good evidence that many people do this, especially according to economic conditions.[142] Voters support incumbents if national income is growing in the months preceding the election. Since World War II, the incumbent party has won a presidential election only once when the growth rate was less than 3 percent (Eisenhower in 1956) and lost only twice when it was more than 3 percent (Ford in 1976 and Gore in 2000).[143] For example, in 2004, 96 percent of voters who strongly approved of his handling of the economy voted for him; only 3 percent voted for John Kerry. Only 13 percent of those who strongly disapproved his handling voted for him, while 84 percent voted for Kerry.

Parties, Candidates, and Issues

All three factors—parties, candidates, and issues—clearly matter. Party loyalties are especially important because they help shape our views about issues and candidates. However, if issues and candidates did not matter, the Democrats would have won every presidential election between 1932 and 2000. Republican victories suggest that they often have had more attractive candidates (as in 1952, 1956, 1980, and 1984) or issue positions (in 1972 and, in some respects, in 1980). However, the Democrats' partisan advantage shrank throughout the 1980s. Although there are still more registered Democrats than Republicans in the United States, the margin is slight, and the number of independents is large enough to tilt the outcome.

Party loyalty, candidate evaluations, and issues are important factors in congressional elections just as in presidential ones. Chapter 10 discusses voting in congressional elections.

The 2000 Election: A Perfect Storm

The election of 2000 demonstrates the antidemocratic nature of the Electoral College. It was won by George W. Bush, who got fewer votes than his rival, Al Gore. In another antidemocratic twist, the election was decided by the United States Supreme Court, when, by a 5–4 vote, it stopped the recount of votes going on at the order of the Florida Supreme Court. The division in the Electoral College was very close, and the decision rested on the outcome in Florida, where election mismanagement, partisan politics, and unavoidable human error came together to create chaos in a closely divided race.

Election Day exit polls of Florida voters showed Gore winning by a small margin. But after first declaring Gore the winner, the television networks declared Bush the winner, and then in the early morning hours decided it was too close to call. The election hung in the balance. Bush had a tiny lead of several hundred ballots.

Confusion reigned in the days afterward. The press and election observers reported several problems, some of them serious. Thousands of Gore votes were lost because of the strange "butterfly ballot" configuration in Palm Beach County, a heavily Democratic liberal county. The odd format, designed by the supervisor of elections in the county, made it difficult for some voters to determine which punch hole corresponded to which presidential candidate. (It was labeled the "butterfly ballot" because candidate names appeared on both sides of a row of vertical punch holes rather than only on one side, which is the standard, less-confusing format.) Even though the problem was recognized early on Election Day by some distraught voters leaving the polling places, there was no way that local election officials felt they could fix the problem then.

More than 3000 voters punched the hole registering a vote for Patrick Buchanan, listed to the right of Gore's name on the ballot. This is particularly ironic because the areas of Palm Beach County casting the most votes for Buchanan were those inhabited by mostly elderly Jewish voters, the least likely group to support Buchanan, who is thought to be anti-Semitic. As one elderly Jewish woman exclaimed after mistakenly voting for Buchanan, "I would rather have had a colonoscopy than vote for that son-of-a-bitch Buchanan."[144]

Nearly 3000 voted for Gore and the socialist candidate whose punch hole was underneath Gore, apparently thinking they voted for Joseph Lieberman, Gore's vice presidential running mate, whose name was under Gore's. (Bush lost about 1600 votes from those who voted for him and Buchanan.) Although some spoiled ballots are normal in every election, this erratic pattern in one county was a result of the badly designed ballot. But there was nothing the Gore campaign could do. The ballot was designed by a Democratic supervisor of elections who made the candidates' names larger so elderly voters could read them easier. But the larger typeface actually made the format harder to understand. There was no intention to deceive any voters.

There was also a problem with overseas ballots. Americans overseas have the right to vote. They must ask for a ballot before the election and mail it by the day of the election, but the ballot need not be received by local officials until ten days after the election. (This time allows for mail delays.) There are strict rules about how these ballots are to be certified to avoid vote fraud; for example, the ballots have to have legible overseas postmarks showing the ballot was cast on or before Election Day, a witness was present (a Florida requirement), and the voters had to have registered in advance. But hundreds of these ballots came in lacking postmarks (or having U.S. postmarks) or lacking a witness and from voters who were not registered. Many military personnel whose home state was Florida must have decided to vote after the election when the outcome appeared uncertain, and some may have been persuaded to do so by partisan groups. Under law, these ballots shouldn't have been counted, but the Bush campaign, assuming the ballots were mostly Republican, claimed that it would be unpatriotic not to count them. The Gore campaign was put in the untenable position of choosing either to accept the illegal Republican ballots or to appear to deny our overseas military personnel their right to vote.

After the election, Gore pursued a conservative strategy to deal with these problems that likely cost him the election. Nothing could be done about the butterfly ballot problem save a revote, and nothing in Florida law allowed that. To deal with tens of thousands of incompletely punched cards throughout the state, Gore asked for a recount in only four strongly Democratic counties. (Later, after the Bush campaign sued to stop the recount, Gore did challenge Bush to have a recount in every county, but he did not file suit to accomplish it.[145]) Finally, when the Florida Supreme Court mandated a recount in every county, so much time had elapsed that the U.S. Supreme Court threw up its hands and gave the election to Bush.

Gore's biggest mistake was to refrain from challenging the overseas votes, even the hundreds that were patently illegal under Florida laws. Indeed, 680 were flawed, including nearly 200 with U.S. postmarks, indicating that they had been mailed from within the country rather than from overseas; 344 were late, illegible, or missing postmarks; and even 38 reflected double voting by 19 voters.[146] Clearly, the local election judges would have thrown these out had Democratic Party representatives challenged them. But they did not out of a timid concern about not wanting to appear against voting rights of overseas armed forces personnel, even fraudulent ones. As a consequence of the illegal military ballots alone, Gore lost Florida by 537 votes when his Election Day margin—that is, the margin given him by people who voted on Election Day rather than by mail ballot—was a 202-vote victory.[147]

The Bush postelection campaign was more skillful and more aggressive. Republican representatives urged election officials in Democratic-majority counties to follow the law in handling overseas ballots, so illegal ballots would not be counted; in Republican counties, they urged election officials to disregard the law, so illegal ballots would be counted.[148] (There is nothing illegal or even immoral about Republican supporters doing this, but the election officials should not have caved, and the Democratic representatives should have argued that the laws be followed.) At one point the Bush campaign even organized a demonstration to intimidate election officials in Miami-Dade County to stop conducting the recount they were in the middle of. Demonstrators barged into the building, yelling and pounding on doors. Photos from that event showed that many of the "demonstrators" were staffers in conservative congressional Republican offices who had been sent to Florida to do this, though at the time the election officials recounting the ballot did not know that. The demonstration succeeded in getting the officials to halt the recount.

In addition, the Bush campaign had strong political allies in Florida who held the levers of power there. Bush's brother, the governor, and the secretary of state, who oversees the election system, were cochairs of Bush's Florida campaign. At every opportunity she ruled in favor of the Bush campaign and forced the Gore campaign to go to

Damon Winter/The New York Times

Many blue-collar workers, such as these steelworkers in Pennsylvania waiting to hear Barack Obama, were skeptical toward his candidacy.

presidential elections. The election brought into stark relief the problems that shoddy election procedures can create. Former president and Nobel Peace Prize winner Jimmy Carter, who, through his Carter Center, now works for peace and social justice around the world, is often invited to monitor elections in Asia and Africa and to attest to their fairness. He remarked, "I was really taken aback and embarrassed by what happened in Florida. If we were invited to go into a foreign country to monitor the election, and they had similar standards and procedures, we would refuse to participate at all."[153]

court to obtain recounts and redress. Time also worked in favor of the Bush campaign, because it held a narrow lead throughout the post–Election Day period and because it knew that the deadline for certifying Florida's electors would put pressure on the courts to stop the recount. Thus the Bush campaign used delaying tactics to slow and stop the recounts.

The outcome of this election will long be argued. It is likely that a bare majority of Florida voters, in fact, favored Gore.[149] Systematic analyses have proven that the Buchanan vote was inflated by at least 2500 votes intended for Gore in Palm Beach County.[150] As one commentator noted, "No election analyst will say with a straight face that the butterfly design didn't cost Al Gore the presidency."[151]

Of course, the overseas ballots contributed, too, by an unknown amount. That is, we know how many ballots were illegal, but we don't know for sure their distribution between Bush and Gore. Nearly two-thirds of the 2400 overseas ballots counted after November 7 were for Bush. Presumably the illegal overseas ballots also broke for Bush. Two independent scholars argue that the probability is about 99 percent that Gore would have won if the invalid overseas ballots were handled properly and a statewide recount was allowed under any reasonable standard for counting chads.[152]

The confusion surrounding the 2000 election outcome highlights an important aspect of our electoral process: state law and local policies determine the mechanics of

Voting Patterns in Recent Elections

As we discussed in Chapter 4, popular parlance often refers to the solid Republican states as "red" states and the solid Democratic states as "blue" states because TV networks use red and blue to depict them on election night maps. Figure 3 in that chapter illustrates the red states and blue states as well as the results of the 2004 election.

Although the press tends to discuss the red states and blue states as if they were fixed in concrete, of course they are not. There are a core of states that, in recent years, have voted solidly Republican and a core that have voted consistently Democratic, but a few states change their majorities from one election to another.

Analysts of voting in the 2004 election discovered that the crude distinction between red and blue states disguises more telling voting patterns. Most red states are in the poorer half of the states as measured by per capita income. For example, twenty-six of the twenty-eight states with the lowest per capita income voted for Bush. Given that overall the poorer you are the more likely you are to vote Democratic and given that Bush's economic policies have favored the wealthy over the poor, this seems like a paradox.

In fact, in the poorer states, such as Oklahoma and Mississippi, the wealthy are very heavily Republican, voting Republican 80 percent of the time. In these red states, there is significant class voting. In the blue states, such as Maryland, New York, Connecticut, and California, the rich and the poor, on average, vote similarly. In blue states, rich people

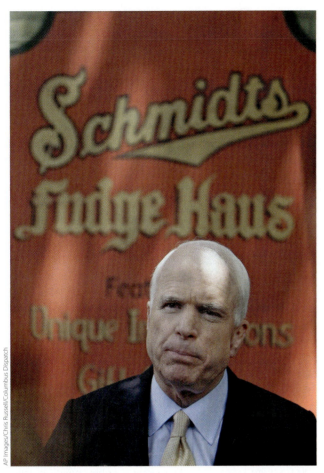

AP Images/Chris Russell/Columbus Dispatch

Until he picked Sarah Palin, John McCain had trouble generating interest in his campaign. While Barack Obama, on a foreign policy trip, spoke before 200,000 in Berlin, Germany, McCain addressed a small crowd in front of a German restaurant in Columbus, Ohio.

are only slightly more likely than poor people to be Republican. Rich people in the blue states are much more likely to be Democrats than they are in the poorer, red states.[154] "Class warfare," as evidenced through the ballot box, is much more prevalent in the red, Republican-voting states.

These patterns are new in American politics. But the 2004 election was also about continuity. Incumbent presidents usually win reelection; that happened fifteen out of the twenty times incumbents ran in the past century. Incumbents, such as Bush, whose party has just captured the White House almost always win; Jimmy Carter was the one exception. Bush's margin compared to that in 2000 was slightly higher across the states, with the exception that in the states most directly affected by the World Trade Center attack (New York, New Jersey, and Connecticut) he gained more, nearly 6 percent.[155]

The Permanent Campaign

The **permanent campaign** is a term coined by political scientists to describe the current state of American electoral politics.[156] During each election cycle, the time between the completion of one election and the beginning of the next gets shorter and shorter. No longer does the election campaign start in the election year; now it is nearly a four-year process, as candidates hire consultants and fundraisers, assemble field operations, and commission polls.

Several factors are responsible for this change, some political and some technological. The political process has changed a great deal during the past thirty years. Primaries have become the chief means by which candidates get nominated, and parties have shrunk in importance in the nominating process. The necessity to win primaries in different regions of the nation means that potential candidates must start early to become known to key political figures, and ultimately to the voting public, in these states. In the "old days," candidates had to woo only party leaders, a process that, though not easy, was much less public and much less expensive than campaigning for primary victories.

Technology has also contributed to the permanent campaign. Certainly, in comparison to the turn of the twentieth century, transportation and communications technology have revolutionized campaigns. Then travel was by rail, ship, or horse, and candidates could not simply dart about the country spending the morning in New York City and the afternoon in Seattle. Telephone communication was primitive, and there were no radios or televisions. The idea of potential candidates spending four years publicly campaigning for office under these conditions would have been ludicrous.

But even in comparison with only thirty years ago, the media and information technology have revolutionized campaigning and thus have contributed to the permanent campaign. Modern computer and telephone technology enables the media and private organizations to take the pulse of the public through opinion polls almost continually. As polls have become more common, they have become a source of fascination to the media (and as pollsters have discovered that the media's appetite for polls is nearly insatiable, polls have proliferated). Whereas in the 1950s polls were rarely done and poll results were rarely discussed in media coverage of elections, by the 1980s hundreds of stories about each election campaign focused on poll results. Indeed, much of the media coverage of the campaign focuses on exactly that. In 2008, there was almost daily polling since the beginning of the primaries, and these are easily accessible at websites such as Rasmussen Polls, Real Clear Politics, and many other sites. Candidates and potential donors and campaign operatives pay considerable attention to these polls, so candidates must begin campaigning early to earn name recognition from the public.

And, more generally, the fact that campaigns have become media events means that candidates must begin early to establish themselves as worthy of media attention. Until candidates have organizations, fundraisers, and pollsters, the media do not take them seriously. Nor would it be very

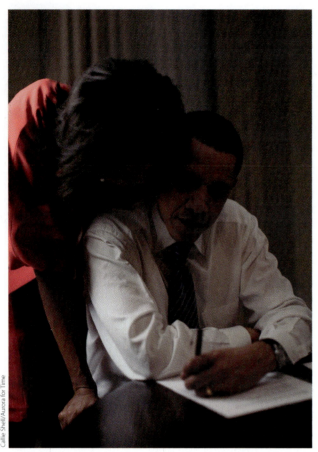

Barack Obama gets suggestions for a speech from wife Michelle.

rational to do otherwise, because a modern campaign cannot succeed without these things.

All of these factors—the decline of the party organizations and the increased importance of primaries, the growth of polling, and the overwhelming role the media now play in campaigns—have contributed to the perpetual motion that modern elections have become. These trends seem irreversible. Only eliminating the primary system would seem to make much difference, and that change is nearly impossible.

Conclusion: Do Elections Make Government Responsive?

Although election campaigns are far less successful in mobilizing voters and ensuring a high turnout today than they were a century ago, in a democracy we expect elections to allow us to control government. Through them we can "throw the rascals out" and bring in new faces with better ideas, or so we think. But other than to change the party that controls government, do elections make a difference?

In the popular press, we hear a lot about "mandates." A president with a **mandate** is one who is clearly directed by the voters to take some particular course of action—reduce taxes or begin arms control talks, for example. George W. Bush won a majority in 2004. Did he have a mandate? If so, what for? The largest proportion of the public, 41 percent, was concerned about national security issues, mainly the war in Iraq and terrorism.[157] Most of those people voted for Bush, but about one-third of Kerry voters thought this was the most important issue, too. So does that mean the president has a mandate to stay in Iraq until we "win," however we define a win, or is there a mandate to withdraw once elections are held? Or just to do what he thinks best?

And how about on domestic issues? More than 25 percent of voters reported that economic issues were the most important to them, and another 11 percent said domestic issues, such as health care and Social Security, were. Most voters concerned about domestic and economic issues favored Kerry, though some of Bush's supporters also thought this was most important. So Bush did not have a mandate on these issues, but as president would, of course, have to deal with them. Only about 10 percent said "cultural" issues were most important to them, and two-thirds of those voted for Bush.[158]

Did Bush have a mandate? Like most things in politics, the answer is not simple. Sometimes elections have an effect on policy, but often their effects are not clear-cut. In close elections, few would argue that there is a mandate. In 2000, voters favored the Democratic policy positions and did so in a time of peace and prosperity. A plurality gave their votes to Gore. Yet Bush became president and acted as though his narrow Electoral College victory was a mandate in support of his foreign policies and conservative domestic policies.

It is primarily political parties that translate the mix of various issues into government action because voters' issue positions influence their party loyalties and their candidate evaluations. Over time, a rough agreement usually develops between public attitudes and policies.[159] A vote for the candidate of one's own party is usually a reflection of agreement on at least some important issues. Once in office, the party in government helps sort out the issues for which there is a broad public mandate from those for which there is not.

Elections that appear to be mandates can become "mandates for disaster." More than one observer has pointed out that every twentieth-century president who won the election by 60 percent or more of the popular vote soon encountered serious political trouble. After his landslide in 1920, Warren Harding had his Teapot Dome scandal involving government corruption. Emboldened by his 1936 triumph, Franklin D. Roosevelt tried to pack the Supreme Court and was rebuffed on that issue. Lyndon Johnson won by a landslide in 1964 and was soon mired in Vietnam. **Richard Nixon** smashed George McGovern in 1972 but then had to resign because of Watergate. Ronald Reagan's resounding victory in 1984 (a shade less than 60 percent) was followed by the blunders of the Iran-Contra affair. Of these presidents, only Roosevelt was able to recover fully from his political misfortune. Reagan regained his personal popularity but seemed to have little influence on policy after Iran-Contra. One recent observer has argued that these disasters come because "the euphoria induced by overwhelming support at the polls evidently loosens the president's grip on reality."[160]

Elections can point out new directions for government and allow citizens to make it responsive to their needs, but the fact that many individuals do not vote means that the new directions may not reflect either the needs or wishes of the public. If election turnout falls too far, the legitimacy of elections may be threatened. People may come to believe that election results do not reflect the wishes of the majority. For this reason, the increase in turnout since 2004, and especially in the 2008 primaries, should hearten all of us. If elections promote government responsiveness to those who participate in them, higher turnouts help increase responsiveness.

On the other hand, if we believe in democracy, we should be concerned about the decline in competitiveness of congressional elections. Essentially, in most states, state legislative majorities have had the capacity to determine election outcomes, including their own seats, for a decade. While the power to redistrict has always been in state legislative hands, the power and precision of new technology makes this power even greater. This is a significant challenge to responsiveness.

Key Terms

Big Sort

suffrage

Reconstruction

literacy tests

grandfather clause

poll tax

white primary

Voting Rights Act (VRA)

gerrymandering

cracking, stacking, and packing

majority-minority districts

split-ticket voting

Progressive reforms

motor voter law

presidential preference primaries

battleground states (swing states)

Electoral College

faithless elector

issue vote

retrospective voting

permanent campaign

mandate

Key Names

Jeannette Rankin

Geraldine Ferraro

Barack Obama

Hillary Clinton

George W. Bush

Bill Clinton

Ronald Reagan

John Kerry

John Edwards

John McCain

Hubert Humphrey

John F. Kennedy

Lyndon Johnson

Al Gore

Jesse Jackson

Shirley Chisholm

Richard Nixon

Please visit our companion website at www.cengage.com/politicalscience/welch/uag12e or use CengageNOW for additional resources dealing with this chapter.

Barack Obama used his popularity to solicit campaign contributions from millions of supporters, such as these folks in Portland, Oregon.

Money and Politics

9

Talking Points

Since 1976, presidential candidates have received public funds for their campaigns. In the general election, according to the law, the candidates cannot themselves raise funds. They must run their campaign on the public funds they receive, which in 2008 would amount to more than $84 million apiece for the major party candidates. Though in 2004, for the first time, some candidates decided not to accept public funds for their primary campaigns, until now, all candidates have relied on public funding for their general election campaign.

In 2007, candidate Barack Obama (D-Il.) indicated that he would accept public funding if his Republican opponent did, indicating in a further comment that "if I am the Democratic nominee, I will aggressively pursue an agreement with the Republican nominee to preserve a publicly financed general election."[1]

Senator Obama shocked even the most informed political professionals with his ability to raise funds during his primary campaign. Energizing hundreds of thousands of voters, he raked in funds from smaller donors through Internet appeals and from political fat cats through his political networks. About 90 percent of his donors gave in amounts less than $100, but a majority of funds were given by those donating more than $200.[2]

By the end of the primary season, he had raised $300 million, by far the most ever raised by a primary candidate (in contrast, in 2004, George Bush raised $258 million). Obama's chief 2008 primary opponent, Hillary Clinton (D-N.Y.), raised $230 million, and John McCain (R-Ariz.) was far behind in his successful quest for the Republican nomination, raising $110 million.

After receiving the nomination, however, Senator Obama announced that he would not be accepting public funding, the first general election candidate to take this position. Arguing that the system was broken, and that Senator McCain's allies would smear him through independent spending, he portrayed his refusal to participate as a reform position because a lot of his support came from the grassroots. (Independent spending, as we will describe later in the chapter, is that done by interest groups that are nominally unattached to any candidate but who in fact are working to elect one candidate, usually by attacks on another.)

Republicans and supporters of campaign finance reform, not surprisingly, had quite a different interpretation. They accused him of hypocrisy and of undermining the part of the system that did allow the average person, not lobbyists, to fund campaigns. There is nothing more grassroots than the public funding donated by millions of taxpayers who can simply check a box on their tax form and have $3 of their tax go to fund the presidential campaigns. Opponents of Obama pointed out that the likely reason for Senator Obama's position is that he was confident he could raise far more than $84 million and far more than Senator McCain.

Though these criticisms of Obama's flip-flopping (changing his mind) on this issue circulated widely, in making his decision, Obama and his campaign staff obviously believed that charges against him for flip-flopping would be outweighed by his ability to raise money and vastly outspend Senator McCain.

Former speaker of the House of Representatives Tip O'Neill (D-Mass.) once said, "There are four parts to any campaign. The candidate, the issues . . . , the campaign organization, and the money. Without money you can forget the other three."[3] Conventional wisdom holds that "money is the mother's milk of politics." But we are not sure whether that milk is tainted or pure. On the one hand, without money, candidates or people with new political ideas would find it hard to become known in our massive and complex society. Television spreads names and ideas almost instantaneously, so having money to buy television time means that your ideas will be heard. In that sense, money contributes to open political debate.

On the other hand, money can be a corrupting influence on politics. At the least, it can buy access to decision makers. At the worst, it can buy decisions. Money allows some points of view to be trumpeted while others are forced to whisper. Some candidates or groups can afford to spend hundreds of thousands of dollars for each prime-time minute of national television or for prestigious Washington law firms to lobby; others can afford only web pages and letters. Money increases inequities in political life.

Although in most cases, we see nothing wrong when individuals of great wealth are able to buy goods and services that others cannot afford, many people feel uneasy when high-income individuals or well-bankrolled groups are able to buy political favors. We feel so uneasy that we have outlawed certain kinds of buying of political favors, such as politicians paying voters for their votes or interest groups paying politicians and bureaucrats for their support.

But we are also uneasy about placing other limits on the influence of money. Many people feel that individuals or groups should be allowed to contribute as much money to candidates as they want and that candidates should be permitted to buy as much media time to get their point of view across as they want and can afford. This view holds that contributing money and buying media time are forms of constitutionally guaranteed freedom of speech.

These issues are growing more important as the cost of political campaigns increases. In 2004, presidential candidates spent slightly over $1 billion, less than half from public funds, an increase of nearly 50 percent from 2000.[4] And various independent groups spent another $1 billion. Costs of congressional and state races are also increasing. So it is not surprising that political candidates scramble for money.

Americans have struggled with these contradictions about money and politics. Periodically, after a series of outrages relating to the impact of money on legislation, regulation, or elections, we pass laws seeking to reduce the impact of money in political life; but then, everyone finds ways around all the rules and a new cycle of outrage and legislation starts again.

In this chapter, we first focus on the development of laws that regulate how money can influence politics, then turn to the role and impact of money in elections, and finally briefly examine conflicts of interest on the part of decision makers in Congress and the executive branch.

Money and Politics in America's Past

Concern about the illegitimate influence of money on politics is older than the Republic. In 1699, after asking how campaign money could be regulated, the Virginia House of Burgesses (the colony's legislature) voted to prohibit the bribing of voters.[5] In his campaign for the Virginia House of Burgesses in 1757, George Washington was accused of vote buying. He had given out twenty-eight gallons of rum, fifty gallons of rum punch, thirty-four gallons of wine, forty-six gallons of beer, and two gallons of cider. Because there were only 391 voters in his district, he had provided more than a quart and a half of beverages per voter![6]

Obviously, Washington survived these charges, and his constituents probably survived the effects of the rum and cider. But most discussions of the impact of money on politics were more sober. In his well-known analysis of controlling factions, James Madison, in *Federalist Paper* 10, recognized that "the most common and durable source of factions has been the various and unequal distribution of property."

The influence of money was evident as the railroads pushed their way across America, pressuring and bribing the government to provide free land for their tracks and additional land along the tracks to make their enterprise "profitable." Here workers toast the completion of the transcontinental railroad line at Promontory Point, Utah, in 1869.

Madison went on to say that although ideally no one should be allowed to make decisions affecting his or her own self-interest, almost any subject of legislation—taxes, tariffs, debts— involves self-interest. For those making laws, "every shilling with which they overburden the inferior number is a shilling saved to their own pockets."

Madison hoped that the design of the new nation, with the power of the government divided among the branches of government and between the nation and the states, would mean that no one interest or faction would overwhelm the others. The interest of one person or group would check the interest of another.

This view of counterbalancing interests is an optimistic one and has not always worked. Over the decades, Americans have found it necessary to make additional rules to restrict the ways that people or groups with money can try to influence policy makers.

Money in Nineteenth-Century American Politics

The influence of money on politics has shaped several epochs of American history. For example, from the earliest westward expansion of the nation, charges of graft and corruption surrounded the government's sale and giveaway of land. Indeed, the West was developed by giving land to speculators and railroads, sometimes in exchange for bribes. When Congress was debating whether to give federal land to the railroads, the lobbyists "camped in brigades around the Capitol building."[7]

The impact of money on political life probably reached its peak in the late nineteenth century, during the so-called Gilded Age after the Civil War. During that time, the United States grew from a small agrarian society to a large industrialized one. This industrialization produced great wealth in such fields as oil exploration and refining, the steel industry, and the railroad companies that were spanning the nation. Major components of the economy came to be controlled by companies that owned most of the country's resources in a particular area, such as steel, oil, and rubber. John D. Rockefeller's Standard Oil sold more than 80 percent of all oil products sold in the United States.[8] This was the era of "robber barons," when the owners of these giant corporations (called *trusts*) amassed huge wealth and openly bought political favors.

Business contributions to campaigns and to politicians were routine. One railroad president justified the bribing of political officials by noting, "If you have to pay money to have the right thing done, it is only just and fair to do so."[9] Mark Hanna, a Republican fundraiser in the presidential election of 1896, assessed banks at a fixed percentage of their capital and also collected substantial sums from most insurance companies and large corporations.[10] However, Cornelius Vanderbilt, one of the wealthiest men of his time, refused to contribute to election campaigns, believing that it was cheaper to buy legislators after they were elected!

Not only did lobbyists bribe politicians, but politicians bribed reporters. In the 1872 presidential campaign, the Republican Party gave money to about three hundred reporters in return for favorable coverage.[11] (See the box "Honest Graft" for more on money's role in nineteenth-century politics.)

U.S. senators bought their own seats (this was before senators were elected by the public) by bribing state legislators to select them. When one member proposed that all of those who had bribed their way into the Senate be expelled, another member observed that "we might lose a quorum" if that were done.[12]

Early Reforms

Around the turn of the twentieth century, the Progressive reformers and their allies in the press, called **muckrakers**, began to attack this overt corruption. They wanted to break up the trusts and break the financial link between business and politicians. In 1907, a law prohibited corporations and banks from making contributions to political campaigns, and a few years later, Congress mandated public reporting of campaign expenditures and set limits on campaign donations. Prohibitions against corporate giving to political campaigns were broadened over time to forbid utilities and labor unions from giving as well.

Teddy Roosevelt is portrayed as the "infant Hercules" wrestling Rockefeller's Standard Oil.

Theodore Roosevelt Collections/Harvard College Library

"HONEST GRAFT"

The influence of money on local politics reached a high point in the late nineteenth century. Urban machines used money to cement a complex network of businesses, voters, and political party organizations. Business payoffs to government and party officials for licenses and contracts and party payoffs to voters for their support were the norm. Graft was tolerated and even expected.

As we saw in Chapter 7, **George Washington Plunkitt** was a famous leader of the New York City machine known as Tammany Hall. Plunkitt, born in 1842, began life as a butcher's helper and ended up a millionaire through deals made in his role as a party leader and public official. He held a number of state and local public offices; at one point, he held four at the same time. He drew a salary for three of them simultaneously.

Plunkitt's view of graft illustrates the casual attitude about the influence of money on politics common among many of his time:

There's all the difference in the world between [honest graft and dishonest graft]. There's an honest graft, and I'm an example of how it works. I might sum up the whole thing by sayin': "I seen my opportunities and I took 'em."

Just let me explain. . . . My party's in power in the city, and it's goin' to undertake a lot of public improvements.

Well, I'm tipped off, say, that they're going to lay out a new park at a certain place. I see my opportunity and take it. I go to that place and I buy up all the land I can in the neighborhood. Then the board of this or that makes its plan public, and there is a rush to get my land, which nobody cared particular for before. Ain't it perfectly honest to charge a good price and make a profit on my investment and foresight? Of course, it is. Well, that's honest graft.

Tammany was beat in 1901 because the people were deceived into believin' that it worked dishonest graft. . . . [They supposed that] Tammany men were robbin' the city treasury or levyin' blackmail on disorderly houses, or workin' in with the gamblers and lawbreakers. . . . Why should the Tammany leaders go into such dirty business when there is so much honest graft lyin' around?

. . . I don't own a dishonest dollar. If my worst enemy was given the job of writin' my epitaph . . . he couldn't do more than write: George W. Plunkitt. He Seen His Opportunities, and He Took 'Em.

SOURCE: William L. Riordon, *Plunkitt of Tammany Hall* (1905; repr., New York: Dutton, 1963), 3–6.

When Republican **Theodore Roosevelt** became president after the assassination of William McKinley, he fought the trusts, forced them to open their books, and filed suits to break them up. Although he accepted campaign contributions from big corporations when he ran for the presidency in 1904, he would not show them any favor. This prompted a major contributor to his campaign to complain, "We bought the son of a bitch, but he did not stay bought."[13]

The 1920s was another era of financial scandal as stock markets rose and banks sold worthless stocks and bonds. The **Teapot Dome scandal** of 1921 stimulated further attempts to limit the influence of money on electoral politics. The secretary of the interior in the Warren Harding administration received almost $400,000 from two corporations that then were allowed to lease oil reserves in California and Wyoming (one of them was called the Teapot Dome). This led to the Federal Corrupt Practices Act (1925), which required the reporting of campaign contributions and expenditures.

Because none of these laws were enforced, each had only a momentary effect. Nevertheless, the reforms did seem to make open graft and bribery less acceptable and less common. Instead of outright bribes, political interests now sought to influence politicians through campaign contributions.

Reforms of the 1970s

A significant period of reform occurred in the early 1970s. Prompted by the increasing use of television in campaigns and the rising cost of buying television time, Congress passed a law regulating spending on advertising in 1971. The law limited the amount that candidates could donate to their own campaigns and required candidates to disclose the names and addresses of donors of more than $100. In the course of the Watergate investigations, it became clear that corporations were not abiding by these restrictions. Several corporations secretly funded President **Richard Nixon**'s reelection campaign. For example, Nixon's Justice Department negotiated a settlement favorable to the ITT Corporation in a pending legal dispute soon after an ITT subsidiary gave the Republican National Committee $400,000.[14] Altogether, twenty-one individuals and fourteen corporations were indicted for illegal campaign contributions, mostly but not entirely to the Nixon reelection campaign.

In response to these scandals, Congress again attempted to regulate campaign financing. New legislation was passed in 1974. The objectives of the 1974 law were to limit campaign spending, to make the campaign finance system more open by disclosing the names of donors, and to force candidates to be less reliant on a few big donors. The act also established the bipartisan **Federal Election Commission** (FEC) to enforce the law. However, within a decade, candidates and parties discovered ways to get around this law, and the Supreme Court had declared parts unconstitutional.

Regulating Money in Modern Campaigns

As the 1974 legislation became ever less effective, new calls for campaign finance reform became more insistent.

McCain-Feingold Act

Calls for further reform were finally answered by Congress when, in 2002, it passed what is called the **McCain-Feingold Act**. The chief aim of this legislation was to eliminate **soft money donations** (funds given to parties and other groups ostensibly for uses other than campaigning). However, by 2004, new ways were found around this law too, as lawyers and political operatives searched for loopholes in the law.

Rather than detail provisions of the act which already have limited effect, the next sections describe the issues that campaign finance laws attempt to address and why it is so difficult to pass meaningful legislation. The laws generally focus on four issues:

1. **Public disclosure**, requiring that the names of donors be on the public record.
2. Public financing of elections.
3. Limitations on candidate spending in political campaigns including so-called independent spending, spending by other groups in support or opposition to candidates.
4. Limiting the overall amount of money that individuals and groups give to candidates, called contribution limits.

Disclosure

Federal law requires candidates to disclose the source of their contributions. The Federal Election Commission provides public reports on who has given money to whom. Through this part of the law, journalists and the public can see what private interests are contributing and who the beneficiaries of their contributions are. In fact, you can find on the Web who in your community has given to what candidates, campaign committees, or PACS (www.fecinfo.com/cgi-win/x_stateguide.exe?DoFn=&sYR=2006. This is one aspect of the legislation that has been relatively effective and uncontroversial. Financers of independent groups must also be disclosed.

Public Funding

Since 1974, presidential candidates have been eligible for public funding for the primary and general elections. The amount increases each year to take account of inflation. The funds come from a voluntary checkoff of $3 that individuals can make on their tax returns. If a candidate accepts

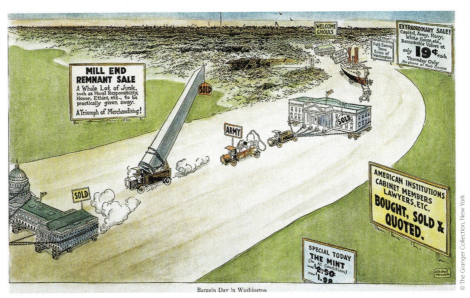

Bargain Day in Washington

Warren G. Harding, one of our least successful presidents, could not say "no" to his friends. This failure led to the Teapot Dome scandal in 1921.

John McCain has pushed for campaign finance reform, though the new law hasn't made much difference.

public funding, he or she must adhere to certain spending limits. Candidates who do not accept public funding can spend as much as they can raise.

Candidates in primaries can receive a significant amount of public funding matched to their own fundraising, by demonstrating their abilities to raise money in at least twenty states (maximum amounts are adjusted each election for inflation).

Once candidates receive their party's nomination, public funding amounts to about $84 million for the general election campaign if the candidate chooses to accept it. Candidates can accept several million more from their party's national committee. At this point, fundraising is supposed to be officially over for the candidates if the public funding is accepted. Accepting public funding does not limit other groups, not under control of the candidate and party, from raising and spending money to sway public opinion and thereby help their favored candidate. If the candidate refuses public funding, he can continue private fundraising under the restrictions described below.

The public financing system is close to death. In 2004, George W. Bush, John Kerry, and Howard Dean decided not to accept public money for their primary campaigns, so they had no spending limits at all at the primary stage.[15] Both Bush and Kerry did accept public funding for the general election, perhaps because each thought he could not raise significantly more money than his opponent (and unless you can do that, it makes sense to avoid the pain, the time and effort, of fund raising).

In 2008, the major Democratic candidates did not accept funding for the primaries either. Then, after winning the nomination, Barack Obama announced that he would not accept public funding for the general election, the first time a general election candidate spurned public funding. Though Obama used the rationale that the campaign finance system was broken, he thought he could raise more money than the $84 million he would receive in public funds. And he did. He raised record breaking amounts in

several months, and had a huge advantage over McCain in campaign spending, both for television ads and for on-the-ground organizations, offices staffed by professionals as well as volunteers. When the final spending is tallied, it will be clear that the 2008 election was the most expensive in history.

Contribution Limits

Federal law also regulates the amount that individuals and groups can give to candidates and campaigns. Individuals can now give $2300 per candidate per election. The law also regulates donations to national party committees, to state or local committees, and overall donations.

Because of the legal restrictions on direct donations to candidates and campaigns, and because of new technology, some candidates have put a lot of effort into raising money through the Internet from people who are big donors. Howard Dean, the Democratic front-runner in the early 2004 primary season, first realized the potential of the Internet to link his supporters with the campaign and with each other. Tens of thousands of his supporters were regularly and successfully solicited for funds. John Kerry responded to Dean's success and, after he won the Super Tuesday primaries, took in $2.6 million in a single day.[16]

In 2008, Barack Obama took the lead in using the Web to raise funds. He mobilized hundreds of thousands of supporters and reaped millions in small contributions, reportedly from 1,500,000 donors. His major primary rival, Hillary Clinton, after an early reliance on bigger donors, also turned to small donors connecting to the Internet, and mention of www.hillaryclinton.com was a staple in her election night speeches. Republican candidates were less reliant on small donors and more on bigger traditional ones, and normally they raise more money than the Democratic candidates. However, in this primary season, McCain and the other leading Republican candidates lagged far behind both Obama and Clinton in their fundraising ability. McCain raised only about $120 million in the primary season, and his closest rival, Mitt Romney, $107 million. This relatively weak fundraising effort was probably partly a function of the candidates themselves and partly the fact that many Republicans were discouraged by the actions and unpopularity of the Bush administration.

Spending Limits

Attempts to limit campaign spending have been ineffective. The Supreme Court knocked huge holes in campaign funding legislation when it struck down spending limits except in publicly funded presidential elections.[17] Because money often goes to buy advertising, the Court argued that spending restrictions violated individuals' First Amendment right of free speech. Spending in a campaign enables candidates to get their message out. Therefore, the Court concluded that giving money is an indirect form of expression pro-

american diversity | Men and Women Target Different Candidates

Hillary Clinton (D-N.Y.) was not the first woman candidate for president. But she was the first who had a realistic chance of winning. Though she did not at first target her candidacy to women, such appeals became a larger part of her campaign as the primaries went on. In most states, women favored her by margins ranging from slim to huge. And, women campaign donors gave disproportionately to her too.

Near-final tallies of primary campaign donations show that women provided about half of the funds that Clinton raised and were 55 percent of all donors to her campaign. Clinton's campaign fundraising was greatly aided by EMILY'S List, a political action group that raises money for pro-choice Democratic women candidates (EMILY stands for Early Money Is Like Yeast), who by bundling individual donations raised more than $500,000 for Clinton.

Among the other major contenders, Barack Obama was next in support from women. He raised 42 percent of his funds from women, and they were about 44 percent of his donors. Female financial support for John McCain, and his chief rival, Mitt Romney, trailed far behind. Romney raised 32 percent and McCain only 23 percent of his funds from women.

Women's Financial Support for Major Primary Candidates

	As % of total funds raised by the candidate	As % of total donors to the candidate
Clinton	50%	55%
Obama	42	44
Romney	32	30
McCain	23	27

SOURCE: Center for Responsive Politics on its web site, Open Secrets opensecrets.org/pres08/index.php?cycle=2008.

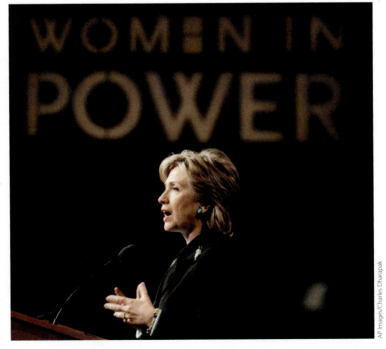

Senator Hillary Clinton speaks at a conference sponsored by EMILY's List, which raises money for female candidates.

tected by the Constitution. (The ruling does not apply to spending limits in presidential races when the candidates accept public funding because they agree to the limits as a condition of accepting the funding.) Consequently, spending limits apply only in presidential races when candidates accept public funds.

Federal law classifies nonparty and candidate spending in different ways. We will discuss political action committees (PACs), independent spending, soft money, and 527 group spending. These alternative methods of spending represent loopholes in the legislation attempting to limit campaign spending.

Political Action Committees   Although federal legislation has limited group contributions to candidates, it does not limit individuals' contributions to groups. As a result, **Political Action Committees** (**PACs**) are a prominent feature of the campaign funding scene (see Figure 1).

PACs are funded from dues and "voluntary" contributions from members in the case of labor unions and "voluntary" contributions from employees in the case of businesses. PACs are one way that individuals can channel more money to their favorite candidates. Individuals could give a limited amount directly to candidates and then give more money to each of several PACs, which in turn gives it to candidates.[18] About 400 of the 4000 or so PACs give more than $100,000 in total. These wealthy PACs represent

corporate interests, trade interests (groups of professionals or industries, such as the National Pork Producers Council), or issue coalitions.

Although PACs differ in the targets of their donations, they show a distinct preference for Republicans in the presidential races and for incumbents—Republicans or Democrats—in congressional races (see Figure 2). PACs usually want to give to the candidate they believe will win, normally the incumbents, so that they will have access to a policy maker. PACs also give money to members in districts where the PACs have a substantial interest, such as a large number of union members for a union PAC or a large factory for a corporate PAC.[19] PACs also target contributions to members of key congressional committees. For example, PACs organized by defense contractors give disproportionately to members who serve on the Armed Services Committees, which have a big role in deciding what weapons to purchase.[20]

Women's PACs, including EMILY's List, one of the biggest-spending PACs, are unusual in focusing most of their money on nonincumbents. Their goal is to get more women elected, which often means supporting nonincumbents with strong chances of winning.

Independent Spending   Spending by nonparty groups is unregulated. In 1985, the Supreme Court ruled that groups, including PACs (discussed later), could spend unlimited amounts working on behalf of issues or candidates, publicly funded or not, as long as they do not give funds directly to parties or candidates.[21]

The Court assumed that this spending would be meaningfully independent. However, **independent spending** is often done by organized groups with indirect links to the candidate. Thus interest groups, through their PACs, can spend as much as they want as long as they are not actually campaigning for a candidate. Instead, they engage in "issues advocacy," usually targeted to promoting a particular candidate or party.[22] Thus anyone not officially part of a campaign or national party can spend as much as he or she wants. However, to be independent, a group cannot be officially linked to a candidate or party nor can it endorse a candidate or party.

Two examples illustrate how tenuous these definitions are. The Media Fund, run by a former Clinton White House adviser, ran television ads throughout the 2004 primary campaign. One featured a shot of a factory with the voice pointing out that "it's true that George W. Bush has created more jobs. Unfortunately, ..." The camera then reveals that the factory is in China, and the voice announces that most of the new jobs were in places like China.[23] The ad did not endorse Kerry but clearly worked in his interest. On the other side, the Swift Boat Veterans for Truth was financed largely by Bush supporters and advised by an attorney who was an official in the Bush campaign (and who resigned when this tie was revealed). Technically, however, the group was "independent" of the Bush campaign.

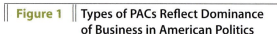

Figure 1 **Types of PACs Reflect Dominance of Business in American Politics**

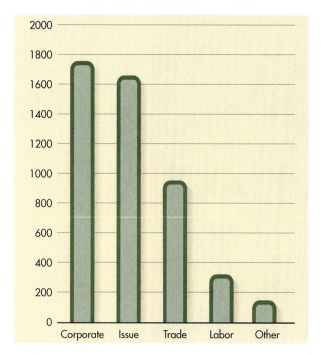

SOURCE: The data are number of PACs of each type. Data from 2004. U.S. Census Bureau, Statistical Abstract of the United States, 2006. (Washington, D.C.: Government Printing Office, 2006), tab. 409.

Figure 2 | Incumbents Receive Most Political Action Committee Donations

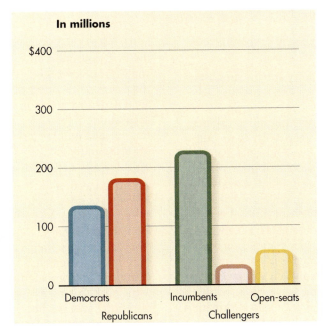

In millions

PACs give overwhelmingly to incumbents. The donations charted here were to House and Senate candidates. Open seats are those races without an incumbent.
SOURCE: U.S. Census Bureau, Statistical Abstract of the United States, 2006. (Washington, D.C.: Government Printing Office, 2006), tab. 414. Data from the 2003-4 election cycle.

Soft Money Some campaign donations are so-called soft money. Soft money is supposed to be used for such "party-building" activities as national party conventions, voter registration drives, direct mailings, polling, issue ads, and advertisements for nonfederal party candidates. Donors who wanted to give more than their legal federal maximum could give soft money to national party committees. Soft money was exempted from limitations of federal legislation because, in theory, it was not to be used for campaigns. In reality, most soft money is spent by independent groups for national television advertisements for the parties' candidates. [24]

527 Groups Big donors can give unlimited funds to so-called **527 organizations**, named after the provision in the tax code authorizing them. These 527 groups also can spend independently. In the 2004 campaign, the most visible were MoveOn.org Voter Fund on the Democratic side and the Swift Boat Veterans for Truth group on the Republican side. These tax-exempt groups, and many others on both sides of the partisan divide, collected unregulated money from supporters of the candidates and then used that money to fund television advertisements. Neither fundraising nor expenditures of groups such as MoveOn.org or

Swift Boat are limited by any federal laws so long as the groups are independent of the campaigns and do not endorse candidates. The organizers of 527 groups were often important party activists and donors. Thus the groups are technically independent, but in reality are closely linked to the candidates.

Overall, then, federal laws regulating campaign finance have been successful in requiring disclosure; somewhat successful in regulating donations to formal candidates, parties, and PACs; but remarkably unsuccessful in limiting the flow of money into the campaign process through soft money and 527 groups. Fat cats can, in fact, give as much as they want to work on behalf of their candidates, just not directly to the candidate or the party.

The Impact of Our Campaign Finance System

There are many potential effects of our campaign finance system. In general, the perception that big money buys influence and access, if not actual votes, has a corrosive impact on public trust in government. Indeed, much of the public believes that most individuals in government are out to feather their own nests and that many are crooks. Some of the reasons for this distrust have nothing to do with money. But public trust was certainly affected by the Watergate scandal in the 1970s, and it is likely that continuous revelations about big-money lobbying activity since then reinforce public cynicism and distrust.

American elections are funded, for the most part, by private money. It is therefore not surprising that candidates turn to people who have money to help with that funding. It is also not surprising that the current system alienates voters. Even if we believe that no votes are actually bought, the appearance of conflicts of interest that permeate the existing system and clearly disturb the public should give pause to those interested in the health of our political system.

Walter Lippmann, a respected journalist, once said that American attitudes about corruption alternate between "fits and starts of unsuspecting complacency and violent suspicion."[25] We think nothing is wrong, and then we think everything is wrong. So it is with our views of campaign money. For several years after major post-Watergate campaign finance reforms in 1974, we thought things were going along pretty well. More recently, many people have become convinced that the nation is in terrible jeopardy because of the influence of money. This fear is compounded because money has helped bring about regulatory lapses, which in turn have been partly responsible for failures to check the dishonesty of many corporations, which in turn has led to eroding confidence in corporate America. So beyond leading Americans to grow cynical about government, the campaign finance system has indirectly helped lead to a loss of confidence in business, too.

BEHIND THE SCENES
HOW THE SWIFT BOAT AD BECAME A NATIONAL NEWS STORY

The original Swift Boat Veterans for Truth ad was run in only a few local spots. However, its metamorphosis from local ad to dominating news story for weeks illustrates how news is disseminated today.

The ad and the charges against John Kerry were first publicized by conservative "bloggers" who wrote news stories on the Web. Bloggers mix fact and opinion and are not subject to the same kinds of standards as regular newspaper reporters. They made no attempt to discern the truth or falsity of any of the charges by seeking official records or interviewing people who were actually there.

Talk radio, mostly dominated by conservatives, picked up the story. Again, they had no interest in looking at the factual basis for the story. Opinions about opinions are the staple of talk radio. Then Fox, the largely Republican television channel, began to publicize the ad and other cable news stations picked it up too. Meanwhile, some major Bush contributors donated more funds so that the ad could be run nationally and frequently.

By this time, the story was everywhere and the mainstream media, the networks and the national press, began to cover it. Although the major media began investigating and presenting the facts about Kerry's war record, the story had already developed a life of its own.

Kerry and his supporters realized that they had made a strategic mistake not countering the story when it first came out. They had looked at the small local ad buys and assumed that everyone would realize that the ad was not truthful, but they did not factor in how stories spread via new modes of communication. This was an incredibly naive view of both the political and information environments.

The story did continue to play among conservative audiences. The men behind the ad published a book, *Unfit for Command*, with Regnery Press, a publisher of popular conservative political books, and it enjoyed huge sales during the election season. The book reprised the points of the original Swift Boat ad and added accusations of treachery, treason, and murder conspiracies to the mix.

What was lost in all the hype was that the primary accusations in the ad were false, according to both the navy's records and the sailors' statements. Despite its falsity, the ad (combined with Kerry's failure to respond to it in an effective way) was one of the primary reasons that he lost the election. The ad was so influential that it spawned a new verb, "to Swiftboat," that journalists have used in subsequent elections.

Although campaign finance is much discussed, it is unlikely that there will be serious reform to curtail its influence. Elected officials appear to be more afraid of being without campaign donations than they are that the campaign finance system will further erode confidence in the whole political system. Ideologically, Democrats are more sympathetic to limiting the influence of big money, but practically, Democratic incumbents are heavily dependent on their PAC "fixes." Thus, neither party has much incentive to support campaign finance reform, despite the fact that the public is repelled by the existing system.

Fundraising in Today's Campaigns

Waging a campaign is expensive. Fundraising for national elections is done by the party committees, candidates themselves, and private groups that support candidates. And because most funding for such campaigns is private, candidates for office must continually look for funding sources. By 2006, potential presidential candidates were appearing on television and flying around the country to woo potential donors and, not less important, potential fundraisers. Without money, even the best candidates with the best ideas will go nowhere.

At least some of those who give money see donations as an opportunity for access and influence, and at least some officeholders see nothing wrong with rewarding large donors with political favors or favorable policy decisions. It is these relationships that prompt continuing calls for campaign finance reform. Yet, as soon as laws are passed, loopholes are opened by the FEC, responsible for overseeing the campaign finance laws, the courts, and candidates themselves, who are very creative in finding ways to get around the limits.

The President as Chief Fundraiser

The chief fundraiser in national politics is likely to be the president. Following the 1996 elections, the Lincoln Bedroom in the White House became a staple of editorial writers and late-night comedians. To raise soft money for the Democratic National Committee and thus for his campaign,

THREE THINGS YOU'LL NEED IF YOU'RE RUNNING FOR PRESIDENT IN AMERICA

CAMPAIGN BUS

CAMPAIGN PLANE

CAMPAIGN BULLDOZER

By permission of Bruce Beattie and Creators Syndicate, Inc.

President Bill Clinton had invited big donors to the White House to have coffee with him and, in some cases, to stay overnight. These and other revelations about fundraising practices prompted new calls for campaign finance reform and cries of outrage from Republicans. Said George W. Bush, "Will we use the White House . . . as a fundraising mechanism—in other words, you give money and you get to sleep in the Lincoln Bedroom? The answer is no."[26]

Once in office, the Bush administration just as blatantly exploited his office for partisan fundraising, as the president invited big donors to dine with diplomats at an embassy and meet with cabinet officials.[27] Indeed, Bush and his organization were by far the biggest fundraisers ever among political candidates. They used their close connections to industry to raise staggering amounts from corporate executives eager to have high-level access to the president and his team.

His top fundraising volunteers are given names of honor: the Pioneers were those who have raised $100,000 for the campaign; the Rangers have raised $200,000; and the Super Rangers have raised $300,000. One fundraising expert provided a lively description: "Carole Bionda darted through the halls of the Capital Hilton, armed with a red-white-and-blue tote bag bulging with checks made out to Bush-Cheney '04. Three hundred executives from the nation's most influential construction firms were meeting at the hotel. . . . As the executives split up into regional caucuses, she ran from room to room, pitting South against East, West against Midwest" in a competition to see who could donate the most.[28]

In three days, Bionda raised $147,000 from the construction executives. This was easy because the Bush administration had gotten rid of regulations that would have improved working and safety conditions at construction sites, which would have cost construction companies more, and other regulations that would have denied government contracts to big polluters.

The Bush-Cheney fundraising organization set as a target $200 million in 2004, most of it expected to come via organized fundraising like this. Each Pioneer, Ranger, or Super Ranger has a number, and all donations through that person are tracked by that number. Results are posted on the Web, and competition between fundraisers is encouraged.

Large donors are given perks, such as photos with the president or the first lady, Laura Bush. After 9/11, capitalizing on the tragedy, Republican donors were given photos of George W. Bush calling Vice President Cheney on September 11, 2001.[29] Some elite donors were offered a chance to "dine with diplomats and embassy officials and discuss international affairs at one of Washington's famous embassies."[30]

More substantively, after the 2000 elections, 104 of the 246 Pioneer fundraisers received government jobs. Four were named cabinet secretaries—Tom Ridge, Don Evans, Elaine Chao, and Alphonso Jackson—and 22 received ambassadorships, including one found guilty of swindling his business partners out of $1 million.[31]

For some, access is more important than jobs. More than half the 2000 Pioneers were heads of companies and another 20 percent were lobbyists.[32] Executives and lobbyists for the financial and real estate world, energy, construction, and transportation were well represented in this elite group.

Did the Bush administration deregulate specifically because it received campaign funds from big construction and other regulated industries? Probably not; conservative Republicans prefer to let business regulate itself and would favor deregulation independent of contributions. Did construction executives give money to the Bush campaign specifically to thank the administration for relaxing regulations and allowing them to make even more money? We do not know. Did they give the funds in the hope and expectation of future policies loosening regulations? Again, no one knows for sure, but that is a reasonable expectation.

It is difficult to point out the exact cause and effect of these close ties between donors and public officials. Even if all that is being bought and sold is access, access is worth something. If access did not influence policy, most people would not be trying to buy it. Even if no favors were exchanged for money and nothing illegal transpired, many Americans find these activities unethical and unbecoming a president. Indeed, the most troubling activities are the ones that are apparently legal. Unless voters elect members of Congress who agree, campaign finance activities will continue to provide material for cartoonists and comedians, embarrassment for public officials, and ultimately loss of public trust in both business and politics.

Members of Congress as Fundraisers

Members of Congress are aggressive in soliciting for donations. They fear defeat in the next election and think that raising a lot of money can protect them. Senators, for

BEHIND THE SCENES

WHERE THE MONEY GOES

On what do candidates spend their money? During the 2008 primaries, the candidates spent nearly $1 billion. The best-funded candidates, Barack Obama and Hillary Clinton, spent more than $1 million a day. The beneficiaries of campaign spending are not just the staff who run and work for the campaigns, but a variety of private firms, consultants, media, telemarketing, pollsters, event planners, and even credit card companies.

Media and consulting comprised more than one-third of all spending. A number of private firms benefit from this, most particularly the consulting and media acquisition firms (firms that plan and execute media buys for the candidates) employed by Obama and Clinton, and to a lesser extent (because they had less money to spend), Mitt Romney, John McCain, and John Edwards.

Salaries and benefits (such as insurance and tax contributions) were the next largest spending category. Although campaigns are largely staffed by volunteers, the top managers and campaign strategists who set the overall directions for the campaign, as well as local operatives who organize the volunteers, are on the payroll.

Direct mail and telemarketing firms together received nearly $150 million of business from the candidates. Travel is another big item, and collectively the candidates spent more than $100 million. In addition to flying the candidate and the staff around the country, the campaigns must also provide for the press. When money is flush, the press may be able to ride on comfortable large planes. When money is tight, they may be riding a bus and staying in cheap motels. The chief beneficiary was one air charter company that both Obama and Clinton used, but one commercial airline also got significant business from a variety of candidates.

Candidates use event planners to stage rallies, election night celebrations, and other events and to make bumper stickers and banners. The candidates collectively spent more than $50 million in this category.

The residual spending includes everything from running local offices, renting space and furniture, obtaining phone service, and paying credit card fees. Obama alone spent $8 million in credit card fees. The Clinton campaign was widely criticized because early on it assumed that the primaries would be over after "Super Tuesday" in early February 2008. Thus, campaign staff stayed at expensive hotels and their election day parties were catered expensively. Even the Dunkin' Donuts bill during one month was $1200. As the primaries moved along, their campaign stretched their dollars much further.[1]

[1] Michael Luo, J Becker, and Patrick Healy, "Donors Worried by Clinton Spending," *New York Times*, February 22, 2008, www.nytimes.com/2008/02/22/us/politics/22clinton.html?ref-opinion.

What Primary Candidates Spent Money on in 2008

Data are for primaries only.

Several fundraisers for George W. Bush's election campaign received important jobs thereafter, including Elaine Chao (clockwise from top left), Don Evans, Alphonso Jackson, and Tom Ridge were given positions as Cabinet secretaries.

example, must raise more than $18,000 each week during all six years of their term to fund an average-cost winning reelection campaign. A senator from a populous, high-cost state needs to raise even more. Many incumbents raise millions even when they face little-known opponents.

Until the 1960s, most fundraising by members of Congress was done in their home districts because members did not want their constituents to think they were influenced by Washington lobbyists. In contrast, today, members of Congress are heavily supported by political action committees (PACs) and the majority of PAC funds are raised in Washington.[33] Members of Congress continually hold fundraisers to which dozens of lobbyists for PACs are invited. Well-known lobbyists get hundreds of invitations to congressional fundraisers every year.[34] Indeed, the number of these events is so large that a private company sells a special monthly newsletter listing all of them.

Raising money for congressional campaigns is becoming nationalized in other ways too. Individual donors from across the country pour money into districts that are considered competitive or otherwise important. Interest groups and political parties may raise the call to their checkbook donors to send contributions to key targeted districts. For example, in 2004, a race in Colorado between a Republican who had won his first term by only 121 votes and was now

running for reelection, and a competitive Democratic challenger drew funds from "virtually every wealthy metropolitan area throughout the country."[35] By the mid 2000s, nearly 70 percent of funding for House races came from outside the district. This interdistrict flow is primarily from the nation's wealthiest areas, often politically noncompetitive themselves, to the nation's most competitive districts. Some areas of the country, indeed, have become "a political A.T.M."[36] These trends tend to strengthen parties and give members of Congress reasons to weigh national interests, as seen by those parties, alongside their local interests.

Reforming Campaign Finance

Campaign finance reform is a perennially vexing topic to both supporters and opponents. It's like weather—everyone talks about it, but few people are in a position to do anything about it. Most Americans find the campaign finance system distasteful and accurately believe that big interests with big money have special access. However, there is no agreement, even among the turned-off public, on what the right solutions are.

Opposition to Reform

There are many reasons why we do not get more serious campaign finance reform. Some individuals, on both sides of the liberal-conservative divide, oppose even trying to get private money out of campaigns. They think prohibitions on private giving are a violation of free speech. Some emphasize that individuals should have the right to spend as much as they wish on the candidate of their choice. Others believe that private groups should be able to run as many advertisements as they want in support of their views.[37] Still others oppose reform because they dislike government regulation.

Some point out that it is largely impossible to regulate campaign finance if we want to allow people to give to campaigns. Campaign finance reform leads to ever more sophisticated searches for loopholes without accomplishing much.[38]

Most elected officials are not big fans of campaign finance reform either. As incumbents, they have an advantage in fundraising. They do not want to tie their own hands by limiting their abilities to raise funds from friendly interest groups. After all, when one party starts spending money in a close race, the impulse is for the other party to match or exceed it, a kind of campaign finance arms race. In a close contest, both sides want to do everything possible to win, and a few extra hundreds of thousands of dollars might indeed make the difference.

Powerful interest groups with money to spend also resist reform. Though reform would save them money in the short run, many big interests believe that their clout with key elected officials in getting favorable legislation is worth what they donate and much more. Major areas of business—including "pharmaceuticals, mining, oil and gas, defense, commercial banking and accounting—have basically made a decision to back the GOP."[39] Democrats, in turn, have the strong support of unions, the entertainment industry, and trial lawyers. These divisions reflect the ideological divisions of the parties,[40] and these groups are not eager to upset the status quo of campaign finance.

Ideas for Reform

Still, the unappetizing spectacle of wealthy donors, both individuals and corporations, receiving political favors from those they supported keeps the idea of reform alive. Large majorities of Americans and of donors favor some change in the current system (see Figure 3). Several ideas have been proposed.

Free Media Time

One proposal might avoid the pitfalls of the attempts to limit soft money by mandating that radio and TV stations grant free time to the candidates. This proposal focuses on reducing the cost of campaigns and hence the need to have so many private donors.

Why should the media be asked to donate time? Radio and television stations have free use of the public airwaves and use that gift to make considerable profit. In what Bob Dole called "a giant corporate welfare program," Congress in 1996 gave away even more airwave space to facilitate the transition to digital technology.[41] Nearly two-thirds of modern democracies do offer free access to the media.[42]

Moreover, a large part of the cost of campaigns is buying media ads. Political ads on television cost nearly $1 billion in the 2000 election and probably topped $1.5 billion in 2004, as the presidential campaigns bought more ads earlier in the race.[43] Nearly 10 percent of TV profit is earned through political ads, which are stations' third-largest advertising category, bigger than, for example, fast-food or movie ads.[44] A New York television station sales manager, contemplating the media ads from the 2000 Hillary Clinton–Rudy Giuliani Senate race exulted, "It's like Santa Claus came."[45]

In light of the fact that the public provides the airwaves free to broadcasters who in turn profit from campaign spending, a panel of broadcasters and reformers are asking stations to donate five minutes of free airtime each day for thirty days before the elections for political discussions among national, state, and local candidates for office. Five minutes a day sounds rather minimal, but currently the major networks broadcast each evening less than one-half minute of candidate dialogue, and local stations offer less.[46] Only 20 of the nation's 1300 commercial television stations agreed to meet this standard in the 2000 election, and the proposal was opposed by the National Association of Broadcasters (NAB), fearing lost revenue.

The NAB lobbied hard and succeeded in defeating another proposal to force stations to offer political candidates

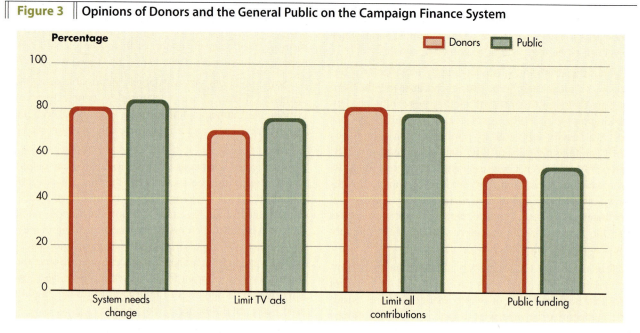

Figure 3 | **Opinions of Donors and the General Public on the Campaign Finance System**

Donors and the public agree that the system needs to be fixed. The bars show the percentage of respondents agreeing with various proposals suggested in a nationwide Washington Post survey.
SOURCE: Ruth Marcus and Charles Babcock, "Feeding the Election Machine," Washington Post National Weekly Edition, February 17, 1997, 10.

their least-expensive advertising rates. This proposal passed the Senate but was killed in the House. We can expect other proposals dealing with media costs to be on the reform agenda because it is unlikely that we can stem the flow of money into campaigns without curbing the costs of the campaigns themselves.

Free or reduced-price media would dramatically reduce the costs of campaigns. Unless it was combined with public financing, however, it would not eliminate private gifts or affect outside groups' playing a role in campaigns.

Public Financing

A second idea is more public financing. Public funding seeks to limit the overall cost of the campaign and eliminate the need for private donations and the special access that comes with them. Currently, the presidential campaigns have such financing, but it does not begin to cover campaign costs. As noted earlier, the presidential candidates together receive $150 million for the general election, and several million more goes to primary candidates who agree not to raise private funds. However, this is a small fraction of the costs of presidential campaigns.

Some people have proposed extending public financing to congressional elections. About half the states have some public financing for their own state legislative or judicial candidates, several in conjunction with spending limits. But it seems unlikely that a major expansion of public funding for national candidates will be adopted anytime soon.[47] Opposition to government spending, public dissatisfaction with political campaigns, and the uncertainty that such a plan would really work to limit private money in politics all militate against it. And even if the official campaigns were funded, public funding does not solve the problem, if it is a problem, of independent organizations' collecting funds and promoting candidates.

Putting Distance between Officeholders and Donors

Many variants of this idea have come to the fore. One is to allow unlimited giving but keep the identity of the givers secret from the recipients. This proposal focuses on the unsavory relationship between money given and favors sought. Thus people would give as much as they want, but it would be channeled to candidates through an organization that would keep the donations anonymous. Some people, who give out of ideological and partisan conviction, would still give, but others might not give if they could not use the fact of their giving as leverage. Of course, anyone could tell a candidate that he or she gave, but the candidate would have no way of knowing who did and who did not.

A more complex idea is to combine raising congressional pay with a provision that members of Congress and the president can accept no gifts at all from anyone, including campaign donations.[48] At the same time, challengers could raise as much money as they wanted from anyone they wanted. Money would have to be immediately reported and disclosed to the public. For every $100,000 the challenger raised, the incumbent would receive a significant portion from public funds. The amount would not be the same, because part of the challenger's campaign costs would be the cost of raising money. The authors of this proposal say that the penalties would be severe (the incumbent would lose his seat if he accepted donations), and if the challenger cheats and doesn't report, she loses her place on the ballot. If the incumbent wishes to spend his own money on the race, the government would pay the challenger an equal amount.

This proposal would combine public funding with the opportunity for challengers to raise whatever they want from whomever they want. It would strengthen public disclosure but deregulate most everything else.

The estimated cost of this proposal, if it had been applied in 2004, would be $800 million. The authors of the proposal argue that this is a lot cheaper than the current system where donors expect to get something in return for their investment: public money for tax breaks, lax regulation, and pork barrel projects.

Constitutional Amendment

Another suggestion for reform is to amend the Constitution, allowing Congress to limit free speech in the area of campaign finance. Proponents of this idea argue that prohibiting donations might limit "speech" in some respects, but the cost to democracy is much greater to allow big money to dictate public policy. This idea seems both impractical, given the difficulty of passing a constitutional amendment, and a threat to traditional free speech values.

Public financing, media donation of time, and separating donors from public officials all may have some merit, but none of the reforms address the fundamental issue of spending by groups who have opinions about candidates and issues. And a constitutional amendment that tried to clamp down on political discussion by independent groups, no matter how seemingly partisan, would surely be further than most Americans would want to go.

Immediate Disclosure

Another idea for reform is to make disclosure of donors more immediate. Currently, while all donations must be disclosed, the process takes weeks until quarterly reports are due. Then, more days elapse while the reports are prepared for public distribution. Donations made in the last half of an election year may not be public until after the election. Some reformers have suggested that moving to a system where donations must immediately be reported and placed on the Web would make the system more accountable.

Enforce Existing Laws

Police have learned that the best way to clean up bad neighborhoods and reduce serious crime is to stringently enforce minor violations. Such a policy reassures the public, who are less likely to be confronted with street graffiti, vandalism, and turnstile jumpers, and who come to believe that the neighborhood has not been left to criminals. It deters potential criminals who come to believe that their crimes will be reported and punished.

Some observers have argued, not wholly in jest, that many ethical issues surrounding Congress could be ameliorated with stricter enforcement of laws that do exist, just like on city streets. Such stricter enforcement might involve not only taking serious complaints to the Ethics Committee and the FEC but FEC investigators actually hanging around congressional and K-Street offices, looking for tips about smelly deals. It might also involve higher penalties for those caught violating the rules. Those convicted of bribery might be sent away for very long terms as an example to others who might be tempted.

Of course, citizens have to demand that laws be enforced, just as they do in neighborhoods being threatened. That is, they say they do, but they reelect their member of Congress 98 percent of the time. As one criminologist noted, local police often are tougher on streetwalkers than on call girls, who commit similar offenses out of the public eye. "Congress is like the call girls," said one observer, "people don't feel the impact directly."[49]

Whatever the problems with the current system, we should be careful not to contrast it with an idealized version of the past. After all, over one hundred years ago, Mark Twain observed, "It could probably be shown by facts and figures that there is no distinctly native American criminal class except Congress."[50] Big interests have always had influence and access in Washington. The ways in which they exercise that influence are different now. In some ways, this influence is more open because the campaign finance reforms have made public the organizations working for special interests and the money they spend doing it. Forty years ago, we would not have known how much each member of Congress received from each lobbying group; today we do.

The Impact of Campaign Money

We have discussed several aspects of money in elections: how much there is, who contributes it, and how they do so. Now we turn to the question of what difference campaign money makes. An obvious question is whether money influences the outcomes of elections. But we will also focus on three other kinds of potential effects of money and the way it is raised: the recruitment of good candidates, the policy decisions of elected leaders, and the cynicism of the public.

Does the Campaign Finance System Deter Good Candidates?

When John Glenn, an unsuccessful Democratic candidate in 1984, was asked whether running for president had been worthwhile despite his defeat, Glenn replied, "My family was humiliated. I got myself whipped. I gained 16 pounds. And I'm more than $2.5 million in debt. Except for that, it was wonderful."[51] In 1998, nearing the end of his career, Glenn remarked in a similar vein, "I'd rather wrestle a gorilla than ask anyone for another 50 cents."[52]

Potential candidates often bow out early, overwhelmed by the magnitude of necessary fundraising. In 2000, George

W. Bush's huge campaign war chest deterred several potential candidates from entering the race. Bush raised more than twice as much as his next-best-financed competitor, **John McCain**. In 2008, the fundraising abilities of **Barack Obama** and Hillary Clinton made it difficult for other Democratic candidates to get much traction, and one by one they dropped out. On the Republican side, Mitt Romney outraised other candidates, but John McCain, better known to voters because of his 2000 run, was able to hang in by holding town hall meetings and getting free publicity. That helped him win New Hampshire, and that win loosened the pockets of Republican donors.

The necessity of raising a lot of money deters congressional candidates, too. As one leading congressional scholar noted, "Raising money is, by consensus, the most unpleasant part of a campaign. Many candidates find it demeaning to ask people for money and are uncomfortable with the implications of accepting it."[53] As one senator commented, "I never imagined how much of my personal time would be spent on fundraising. . . . I do not think a candidate for the U.S. Senate should have to sit in a motel room in Goldendale, Washington, at 6 in the morning and spend three hours on the phone talking to political action committees."[54] And once elected, many new members of Congress are surprised and chagrined to find that they must begin raising funds for their next campaign almost before they are sworn into office.

Does Money Win Elections?

Money helps win elections. It's not the only factor, of course. Many candidates have tried and failed to "buy" elections with their own money. But money certainly aids in getting the candidate's message out.

Looking first at presidential elections, the evidence is mixed as to the impact of money on winning presidential primaries. Primaries are the crucial elections that lead to each party's nomination. Some candidates are never considered serious contenders because they do not have sufficient money to mount a large campaign. In that sense, money is crucial.

In primaries, candidates of each party run against others of their party to achieve the nomination. Most primary candidates start out with little name recognition. Moreover, candidates cannot count on party loyalty to win votes. In primaries, voters choose among candidates of their own party; that is, Republican voters have to choose among Republicans rather than between a Republican and a Democrat. For both those reasons, money is crucial to increase candidate visibility.

Primary candidates who appear to be doing well generally attract money.[55] "Doing well" includes favorable media coverage that suggests the candidate is gaining popularity and momentum. Actual success in early primaries also stimulates giving. Money, in turn, allows further purchases of media ads to become known in the next primaries.

Other things being equal, spending does influence voting in primaries. Money appears to be a necessary condition for primary victory, although it is not sufficient by itself. Money is most important in multicandidate races, as is often typical early in the primary season when candidates are seeking to distinguish themselves from other little-known contenders.[56] Money is less important in two-candidate primary contests, often the situation late in the primary season when one candidate has emerged as a front-runner.

The 2008 primaries did not follow the common wisdom perfectly though. On the Republican side, **Rudy Giuliani**, former mayor of New York City, and **Mitt Romney**, former governor of Massachusetts, outraised John McCain. Giuliani's fundraising success did not, however, translate into votes. He made the strategic mistake of ignoring the early primaries and caucuses, thinking their few votes wouldn't matter. He staked everything on Florida, whose election was a few weeks after Iowa and New Hampshire. By the time attention turned to Florida, Romney and McCain had notched victories and received significant media attention. Giuliani became an "also-ran" before he even got started.

Romney had excellent fundraising success. But questions about what he really stood for dogged him throughout the race. He had been a centrist governor of a liberal state, even going along with gay marriages. But because the Republican primary electorate is conservative, he veered to the right in his primary campaign, opening himself to attacks from both right and center. Some of the Christian Right also found his Mormon religion to be a drawback.

Hillary Clinton was outspent by Obama by margins of three and four in most of the states she won after January. However, Clinton's name recognition gave her some advantages that other candidates would not have. Even so, she was not able to mount as expansive a campaign as Obama did in some states because of her more limited resources. John McCain was also outspent by his rivals early in the primary season, but he survived and racked up enough successes that the money started to flow in.

By the time presidential candidates are nominated, they have already spent a great deal of money. The name recognition achieved during the primaries and at the national conventions carries into the general election campaign. Presidential candidates receive extensive free media coverage in news stories. The amount that they spend after the convention is less likely to be as crucial. This is just as well for the health of the two-party system, because if money determined elections, the Republicans would have won every presidential election since World War II. However, of the presidential elections lost by the Democrats during that time, probably only the election of 1968 between Richard Nixon and Hubert Humphrey and possibly the Gore-Bush 2000 election were close enough that they might have turned out differently had the Democrats been able to spend more.[57] When the elections are close, as in 1968, the Republicans definitely have the advantage by having more money.[58] However, the Democrats are catching up; they have been increasingly aggressive in raising soft money and in 2004 were not significantly behind in fundraising, counting 527 groups.

In 2008, the Democrats were far ahead in fundraising setting new records. Anger at the Bush administration coupled with genuine enthusiasm for several Democratic candidates, especially Obama and Clinton, spurred Democrats to give record amounts in donations small and large. It is this margin that led Obama to spurn public funding and opt to raise funds from private donors.

In congressional races, incumbents usually start with a huge advantage. Some analysts estimate that their advantage is about 5 percent of the vote just by virtue of being incumbents.[59] Their name is recognized by many, if not most, of their constituents. And as incumbents, they are able to raise money early to finance their campaigns. In many cases, the incumbents' huge war chests deter potentially strong challengers from even entering the race.[60] Challengers know that they must raise considerable money to fund media ads even to be competitive. Thus the ability of challengers to raise and spend money is crucial to any chance of success in the election. In 2006, the average amount spent by those running against incumbents was less than $100,000, while incumbents spent about nine times that much.

But incumbent fundraising and spending are also important. Fundraising is important early in the campaign to deter potential opponents. And campaign spending is important, especially for relatively new members of Congress. That is because those who have served only a few terms are less well known than more senior incumbents and thus are considered vulnerable.[61] Of course, incumbents tend to spend the most when they have the toughest opponent. In general, as challengers spend more, so do incumbents.[62]

Most of the time, the person who spends the most to win a congressional seat wins. Most of these winners are incumbents, and the link between spending and victory is also a link between incumbency and victory.

Sometimes the biggest spender loses, but the relative rarity of this occurrence only highlights the general link between spending and victory. In 2006, a number of Democratic challengers to incumbent Republican Senators were outspent by large margins. In the Senate, incumbent Rick Santorum (R-Pa.) outspent his challenger Robert Casey by $6 million, and incumbent George Allen (R-Va.) more than doubled the spending of his rival James Webb (nearly $14 million to $6 million), yet both Santorum and Allen were defeated in an overwhelmingly Democratic year.

Does Money Buy Favorable Policies?

As we have seen, donors are not a random cross section of the public. Money usually buys access, and that access is by the wealthiest segment of the population, whose views on public issues, especially economic issues, are more conservative than those of the larger population.

In recent years, corporate interests have pushed hard to deregulate and to lower taxes and have used substantial gifts to help gain access to rule makers. The accounting industry, for example, in the early 1990s helped fund more than 300 congressional races, including both Democratic and Republican, and spent $2 million for lobbyists. This clout led to Congress passing a law erasing liability for accountants and lawyers aiding and abetting securities fraud. Although President Clinton vetoed the law, his veto was overridden.[63] The law provided a disincentive for auditors to uphold strict accounting standards and removed a tool by which stockholders could hold companies accountable. Enron money bought considerable access (see the box "Buying Energy and Influence.").

If money buys access, does it also buy votes? Both anecdotal and systematic evidence suggest that money does buy votes, although only under some conditions.

Money is not likely to buy votes on issues that are highly publicized, because legislators' constituents usually have strong views on these issues and legislators feel pressured to follow them.[64] For the same reason, money is less likely to buy roll-call votes on the floor of each house than

"It says here that you gave a lot of money to both parties and neither expected nor received anything in return. Very nice, but we'll have to put you in the crazy section."

"No company in America did more to help George W. Bush get elected president than Enron." So reports the *Wall Street Journal*.[1] Enron's CEO, Kenneth Lay, was "the biggest sugar daddy in Bush's political career."[2] During Enron's heyday, its funds helped elect friendly lawmakers, mostly Republicans but also many Democrats; gain access at the highest levels; and buy loosened regulation and favorable tax policies. It made billions of dollars and benefited greatly from government deregulation of the energy industry. In the end, when Enron crashed, though, its substantial influence was not enough to get the government to bail it out.[3]

This seeming contradiction illustrates well the point that money is most influential when the public is not paying attention. They were certainly not paying attention when legislators and regulatory agencies failed to oversee Enron.

What did Enron give, and what did it get in return? Although the full story is unlikely ever to be known, we do know that Enron gave, from 1989 to 2001, nearly $6 million to parties and candidates, three-fourths of it to Republicans.[4] Enron's generosity includes gifts from its executives and other employees, corporate soft money gifts, and gifts from Enron's PAC, funded by contributions by individual Enron employees. Fundraising for the PAC was done by high-level executives who kept track of who gave and who did not.[5] Lay and his wife donated more than $600,000

to the campaigns of George W. Bush, beginning when he first ran for Texas governor and including $325,000 in 2000.[6] Lay also raised millions of dollars for the Bush campaigns. Bush used Enron's planes during the Republican primaries in 2000 to fly staff and even his parents.

But Enron also bought access to top Democrats. When Bill Clinton defeated George H. W. Bush in 1992, Lay began contributing to the Democrats. Enron gave nearly as much in soft money to Democrats as to Republicans in the 2000 election.[7] Enron may have provided funds for nearly half of all members of the House and three-fourth of the senators.[8]

What favors did Enron get from politicians? In 1992, the Democratic-majority Congress approved an energy bill that set the stage for Enron's growth, and later Clinton took an interest in a large Enron project in India. But Enron profited even more consistently from its Republican ties. For example, when Bush was governor, he signed an energy deregulation bill that opened lucrative markets for Enron. He established a panel that acted in secret to grant exemptions allowing power plants to exceed legal pollution limits, and Enron got several of these exemptions.[9] When Bush arrived in Washington, D.C., he rolled back efforts to crack down on American corporations' use of offshore banks (banks set up in the Caribbean, for example, to help U.S. firms—and others such as drug dealers—evade American tax and criminal laws), a

move of great benefit to Enron, which reportedly had 800 offshore accounts. As a consequence of this and other creativity, Enron avoided paying a single penny in U.S. taxes in four of its last five years.[10]

Bush also established an energy policy task force headed by his vice president, Dick Cheney. The task force, meeting in secret and whose membership and agenda have never been released, reportedly included Kenneth Lay and other lobbyists for the utility and energy industries.[11] It is not surprising that the task force recommended a weakening of a major clean-air rule opposed by the utilities and the energy industry. And Lay was also allowed to "interview" candidates for positions on the Federal Energy Regulatory Commission, the government agency that was Enron's regulator.[12]

Enron executives who had advance knowledge of the impending collapse of the firm sold their stock before the announcement that earnings were inflated, and they made millions (Kenneth Lay, the CEO, had made $103 million in the year before the bankruptcy; and the top 100 executives collectively made $300 million). Lower-level Enron employees, many of whose pension plans were invested heavily in Enron, collectively lost millions, many of them their life savings. Enron had forbidden its employees to sell their Enron stock invested in company pension plans, insisting that all was well, until the stock had plummeted to 26 cents a share. Ordinary investors, likewise in the dark about the finan-

cial shenanigans, also found their stock worthless.

Enron's investment in public officials over a dozen years did not, in the end, save the firm from bankruptcy. But as one observer said, "Money allowed the Enron leadership to come to town. . . . Everyone says they didn't get anything. . . . But if you look back over the last five years, what they did get was no oversight."[13] Capitalism depends on a set of institutions, some private and some governmental. As one economist pointed out, "None of the checks and balances that were supposed to prevent insider abuses worked; the supposedly independent players were compromised. Arthur Andersen [Enron's accounting firm] was told of these concerns, but . . . gave Enron a free pass . . . and the regulators were nowhere to be seen, partly because politicians with personal ties to Enron . . . took care to exempt Enron from regulation."[14]

[1] "Enron Lessons: Big Political Giving Wins Firms a Hearing, Doesn't Assure Aid," *Wall Street Journal*, January 15, 2002, 1 ff.
[2] Howard Fineman and Michael Isikoff, "Light's Out: Enron's Failed Power Play," *Newsweek*, January 21, 2002, 15.
[3] Paul Krugman, "A System Corrupted," *New York Times*, January 18, 2002, 15.
[4] Richard Stevenson and Jeff Gerth, "Web of Safeguards Failed as Enron Fell," *New York Times*, January 20, 2002, 1.
[5] Joe Stephens, "Hard Money, Strong Arms, and the 'Matrix,'" *Washington Post National Weekly Edition*, February 18, 2002, 11.
[6] Dan Morgan, "Enron's Cash Was Good for Democrats, Too," *Washington Post National Weekly Edition*, January 21, 2002, 12.
[7] Ibid.
[8] Ibid.
[9] "Enron Lessons"; Bob Port, "Bush, Lay Friendship Is Study of Mutual Benefit," *Lincoln Journal-Star*, February 4, 2002.
[10] Molly Ivins, "Free-Range Markets: How Enron 'Aggressive Accounting' Practiced' the Bank," *Fort Worth Star-Telegram*, January 29, 2002.
[11] Michael Weisskopf and Adam Zagorin, "Getting the Ear of Dick Cheney," *Time*, February 11, 2002, 15.
[12] Jonathan Alter, "Which Boot Will Drop Next?" *Newsweek*, February 4, 2002, 25.
[13] Ibid.
[14] Paul Krugman, "A System Corrupted," *New York Times*, February 18, 2002, A25.

AP Images

Enron CEO Kenneth Lay is led away in handcuffs. In 2006 he died from a heart attack while awaiting sentencing for his financial crimes.

votes in committees. The former are public and recorded; the latter are not as visible to the public. Compared to their activity on the floor, in committees legislators with PAC support are more active in speaking and negotiating on behalf of the PAC's positions and offering amendments that reflect these positions.[65]

Money is also not likely to buy votes on moral issues, because legislators themselves often have firm views on these issues. These sorts of issues (abortion, gay rights, and school prayer, for example) also tend to be publicized.

But most matters that come to a vote are neither highly publicized nor moral issues. Most are relatively technical matters that constituents and legislators do not care as strongly about as PACs do. For these, members are susceptible. The deregulation of the accounting and energy industries was done when the public had no interest. "You can't buy a Congressman for $50,000. But you can buy his vote," a member admitted. "It's done on a regular basis."[66]

One survey of members found that about one-fifth admit that political contributions have affected their votes on occasion, and another one-third are not sure.[67] Analysis of voting has revealed that contributions from the AFL-CIO affected voting on the minimum wage legislation, and contributions from the trucking interests led senators to vote against deregulation of trucking.

Senators facing reelection the year in which the vote was taken were most susceptible.[68] Voting is also related to donations in such disparate areas as minimum wage legislation, gun control, and billboard regulation.[69]

One classic, well-studied example concerns used-car legislation. Auto dealers spent $675,000 in the 1980 congressional elections. This investment seemed to pay off in 1982 when Congress voted against a rule requiring dealers to inform prospective buyers of any known defects in used cars. The senators who opposed the measure received twice as much money from the auto dealers' PAC as those who voted for it. In the House, those who opposed the measure received on average of five times as much money as those who voted for it. Almost 85 percent of the representatives opposing the legislation had received PAC money.[70] The relationship between PAC money and votes still existed even when the party and ideology of the members were taken into account. For conservatives, who might have voted against requiring auto dealers to list defects anyway, PAC contributions made only a marginal difference in their voting; but for liberals, PAC money substantially raised the probability that they would vote with the used-car dealers. "'Of course it was money,' one House member said. . . . 'Why else would they vote for used-car dealers?'"[71]

The relationship between PAC contributions and voting should not be exaggerated, however.[72] Even on these low-visibility votes, a member's party and ideology are important. The constituency interests of members are also key factors explaining votes. For example, members with many union workers in their districts are going to vote for those interests regardless of how much or little they get in PAC contributions.[73] Members without these constituents, though, may be more swayed by PAC contributions.

More recent ties between donors and legislators concern the "buying" of special earmarks in omnibus legislation, legislation that is thousands of pages and contains hundreds of special favors for pet projects of legislators and lobbyists. We discussed earmarking in Chapter 5 and will have more to say about it in Chapter 10.

Money can also buy influence with the executive branch. Presidential candidates tend to have widely publicized views, and their actions as president are subject to intense scrutiny and publicity. Once in office, presidents need donors less than donors need them, thus making the leverage of a campaign donation uncertain. Contributors are sometimes disappointed, as we saw with President Teddy Roosevelt earlier. However, on actions not widely visible to the public, donors can help shape policy. The Bush fundraising success is partly based on support from the oil and gas industries. Their reward has been deregulation of both accounting and financial requirements and environmental standards. The Enron scandal was only the tip of the iceberg. Contractors who received billions of dollars worth of contracts in Iraq and Afghanistan had donated generously to the Bush campaign. The director of the Center for Public Integrity commented that there is a "stench of political favoritism and cronyism surrounding the contracting process in both Iraq and Afghanistan."[74]

Analyses of large donors to and fundraisers for the 1992 George H. Bush campaign reveal that many were given special favors or benefits from the federal government. The Department of Labor reduced a proposed fine by nearly 90 percent against a large sugar farmer who gave $200,000 to the campaign.[75] President Clinton created a furor when on his last day in office, he pardoned the fugitive ex-husband of a major campaign donor, Denise Rich. Rich had contributed generously to the Democratic Party and later to the Clinton presidential library.[76]

Large contributions to presidential campaigns often lead to appointments to public office, especially ambassadorships. The **spoils system**, the practice of rewarding jobs to supporters, has been with us since at least the time of Andrew Jackson, so it cannot be blamed on modern PACs and soft money.

Although it is impossible to prove a cause-and-effect relationship in these cases, clearly large donors who expect favorable treatment have plenty of precedents to lead them to that conclusion. As the leader of a watchdog group noted, "The point is, we're not just electing politicians. . . . We're also electing their patrons and their priorities."[77]

Does Our Campaign Finance System Widen Class Differences?

The influence of big money in presidential campaigns probably makes both parties more conservative. The biggest contributors to the Republicans in the last few presidential elections have been some of the most conservative people in that party. The big-money contributors to the Democrats are, on the whole, less liberal than the mainstream of the party.

Some Democratic House leaders were surprised when members said they could not vote against a capital gains tax cut (which would benefit the wealthy) because it would anger their business contributors. Said one member, "I get elected by voters. I get financed by contributors. Voters don't care about this; contributors do."[78] A former aide to a prominent Democratic senator remarked that he had to remind the senator that a fundraising event was not a focus group. He went on to remark that "it's the rare politician whose perspective is not affected by his or her constant exposure to the wealthy people whose money they need to get elected."[79]

Beyond the specific policies and appointments that reflect the influence of big money, we can step back and look at the bigger picture. Public policy helps shape the distribution of income in our society through taxation, the regulation of corporations and unions, and many other ways. During the past quarter century, the rich have gotten a lot richer, and almost everyone else has struggled to maintain what they have. The wealthiest 1 per cent of Americans now own 47.3 percent of all the country's wealth. In 1980, the richest 5 percent of Americans had 14.6 percent of all income; by 2001, they had 21 percent. The rest of the top 20 percent of wealthiest Americans also gained, but everyone else lost.[80]

Turning from shares of income to income that we actually spend, Table 1 provides an eye-opening look. Between 1970 and 2000, before the Bush administration, the average income of the bottom 90 percent of Americans fell by $25 in real terms (that is, adjusted for inflation), whereas the average income of the top 10 percent grew by tens of thousands, and the top 1 percent by hundreds of thousands. The tax-cut policies of the current Bush administration have increased significantly the inequities since 2000 as higher unemployment and tax cuts directed primarily at the wealthiest Americans further skewed income.[81]

We can look at income and wealth data in different ways, using different years of comparison, but each supports the same general conclusion that the income gap is increasing. In addition, during the past twenty-five years, regulation of corporations has been weakened, health insurance has decreased for millions of Americans, and other holes in our social safety net have been enlarged.

It would be inaccurate to charge the campaign finance system and the policies they have bought with all of these rising inequities. However, it would be shocking if the tens of millions of dollars flowing to the campaign coffers of our elected officials and the consequent increased access and influence of the wealthiest and most powerful interests in society did not have an impact on public policy and the distribution of wealth.

Does Our Campaign Finance System Encourage Extortion?

PAC, corporation, and union contributions to campaigns are products of mutual need. Special interests need access to and votes of members of Congress and the president, and elected officials need (or think they need) large sums of money to win elections. Thus donations are useful to officials and to the donors.

Although special interests try to buy access and sometimes votes, members of Congress are not simply victims of greedy PACs and corporations. Indeed, as one observer remarked, "There may be no question that the money flowing into campaign coffers is a crime. But there is a question

| Table 1 | | The Rich Are Getting Richer | | | | | | |

Year	Bottom 90%	90–95%	95–99%	99–99.5%	99.5–99.9%	99.9–99.99	Top 13,400 Households
1970	$ 27,060	$ 80,148	$ 115,472	$ 202,792	$ 317,582	$ 722,480	$ 3,641,285
2000	$ 27,035	$ 103,860	$ 178,067	$ 384,192	$ 777,450	$ 3,049,226	$ 23,969,767
Percentage Change	−0.1%	29.6%	54.2%	89.5%	144.8%	322.0%	558.3%

Note: Figures are mean individual income in 2000 dollars.
SOURCE: David Cay Johnston, *Perfectly Legal* (New York: Portfolio, 2003). Data from Thomas Piketty and Emmanuel Saez.

whether the crime is bribery of public officials or extortion of private interests."[82]

Pressure on corporations and unions is unrelenting. Some members keep lists of PACs that have given to them on their desks as an implicit indication that it is those groups that will have access. Others play one PAC off against another. **Tom DeLay** (R-Tex.), then the majority leader in the House, was quite open in soliciting funds and promising returns, as we saw in Chapter 6 in the discussion of the K-Street strategy. He offered lobbyists and corporate interests an open quid pro quo: they give, and they get to help develop Republican strategy and interests and shape legislation that Republican leaders will support.[83] (In 2003, he went further and offered a Republican House member an endorsement for his son's race for Congress if the House member would vote with DeLay—an offer that the Ethics Committee deemed a violation of House rules.)

Not all of the fundraisers are for campaign contributions, but all involve putting the arm on lobbyists. A fund-raiser titled "Salute to the President Pro Tempore" was designed to "honor the career and public service" of Ted Stevens (R-Alaska). The funds were to go to Stevens's foundation to benefit Alaska and thus were both tax exempt (campaign contributions are taxable) and not subject to the limitations of campaign finance laws. But Alaskans at the fundraiser were in short supply. The invitation list included most Washington lobbyists who were concerned about the legislation their groups had pending before the Senate Appropriations Committee, of which Stevens is the chair. And the foundation apparently consists of a former staff member in Stevens's office who is his campaign treasurer too.

In recent years, some corporations, including General Motors, Ameritech, and Monsanto, have said that they do not intend to give more political contributions. Companies such as this should favor campaign finance regulation, which could provide a defense to fundraising pressure.[84]

Does Our Campaign Finance System Lead to Public Cynicism?

We have seen repeatedly that public confidence and trust in government have diminished greatly over time. Indeed, most of the public believes that most individuals in government are out to feather their own nests (see Table 2) and that many are crooks. Some of the reasons for this low trust have nothing to do with money. But public trust was certainly affected by the Watergate scandal in the 1970s, and it is likely that revelations about big-money lobbying activity reinforce public cynicism and lack of confidence.

American elections are funded, for the most part, by private money. It is therefore not surprising that candidates turn to people who have money to help with that funding. It is also not surprising that the current system alienates voters. Even if we believe that no votes are actually bought, the appearance of conflicts of interest that permeates the existing system and clearly disturbs the public should give pause to those interested in the health of our political system.

For several years after the 1974 reforms, we thought things were going along pretty well. More recently, many people have become convinced that the nation is in terrible jeopardy because of the influence of money. This fear is

In the 1990s, House Majority Leader Tom DeLay (R-Tex.) told lobbyists that they had "to pay to play."

Ziv Koren/Polaris

Table 2 — Public Opinion Is Cynical about Government

Percentage of People Agreeing That They Have a Great Deal of Confidence in . . .	
The military	36%
The church	26%
The presidency	23%
Congress	11%
Big business	7%
Percentage of People who believe . . .	
Government is run by a few big interests	64%
Government is run for the benefit of all the people	28%

NOTE: 2% had no opinion on the first poll and 8% were unsure on the second poll.
SOURCES: Gallup poll of 1002 adults nationwide, margin of error = 3%, May 21–23, 2004; and CBS News and *New York Times* poll of 955 adults nationwide; margin of error = 3%, July 11–15, 2004; both polls online at www.pollingreport.com/institut.htm.

compounded because money has helped bring about regulatory lapses, which in turn have been partly responsible for failures to check the dishonesty of many corporations, which in turn has led to eroding confidence in corporate America. So beyond leading Americans to grow cynical about government, the campaign finance system has indirectly helped lead to a loss of confidence in business, too.

Elected officials appear to be more afraid of being without campaign donations than they are that the campaign finance system will further erode confidence in the whole political system. Ideologically, Democrats are more sympathetic to limiting the influence of big money, but practically, Democratic incumbents are heavily dependent on their PAC "fixes." Thus neither party has much incentive to support campaign finance reform, despite the fact that the public is repelled by the existing system.

Perhaps the public recognizes that a culture of greed cannot sustain itself forever. The two clearest examples of eras of rampant corruption in the American political and business systems suggest that they end unhappily. In both cases, at the end of the Gilded Age and the Roaring Twenties, they ended with the failure of thousands of banks and companies and with unemployment and despair.

Conflicts of Interest

In addition to money's influence on political campaigns and policy making, it also leads to **conflicts of interest**, situations in which officials face making decisions that directly affect their own personal livelihood or interest. The campaign contribution system we have just described presents a huge conflict of interest. Presidents and members of Congress make decisions about policies affecting people who give them campaign money. But conflicts of interest are not confined to decisions involving campaign money.

As James Madison noted, almost every decision involves potential conflicts of interest. Decisions made by presidents, bureaucrats, and members of Congress can affect their personal financial interests (including stocks, bonds, and other investments).

It is sometimes difficult to untangle the effects of personal financial interests, constituency interests, and party loyalties. For example, most people on the Agriculture Committee have agribusiness interests and represent districts with large agricultural interests. If those members vote in favor of agricultural interests, they are voting both for their own interests and those of their constituents. And they are likely to think that they are advancing the national interest at the same time. It appears that the impact of these personal interests on voting is fairly small once constituency interests are taken into account.[85]

Despite periodic attempts to limit conflicts of interest, violations of ethics codes still occur in Congress and in the executive branch. In 1981, six House members and one senator were convicted in an FBI undercover operation known as Abscam. Five were even videotaped accepting cash bribes. In 2006, Representative William Jefferson (D-La.) was also taped allegedly accepting a bribe, and police found a freezer full of bills in his office refrigerator (at the time of this writing he has been indicted and a federal trial is scheduled for late in 2008). But his alleged misdeeds were overshadowed by those of Randy "Duke" Cunningham (R-Cal.) who resigned after being sentenced to federal prison for accepting more than $2 million in bribes. Cunningham even went so far as to develop a "menu" of his prices (bribes) for giving corporations the contracts they wanted. For example, he would help a business with a federal contract worth $16 million in exchange for a $140,000 gift.[86] Incidents of blatant bribery such as this are rare, but conflicts of interests are very common.

Despite rules against accepting gifts from lobbyists, lawmakers accept millions of dollars worth of gifts, often in the form of free trips to luxury resorts and other vacation areas. A 2006 report found that collectively, over a five-year period, members of Congress had accepted $50 million worth of free trips that involved 23,000 trips. A significant number of trips cost more than $5000 each and some much more. The report concluded that "while some of these trips might qualify as legitimate fact-finding missions, the purpose of others was less clear."[87] Probably in the latter category were the 200 trips to Paris, 150 to Hawaii, and 140 to Italy. Congressional travelers "pondered welfare reform in Scottsdale, Arizona and the future of Social Security at a Colorado ski resort."[88]

The Abramoff Scandal and Concierge Politics

In 2005 to 2006, investigators uncovered one of the largest conflict of interest schemes and other misdeeds in recent memory. **Jack Abramoff**, the former national chairman of the College Republicans, close associate of Tom DeLay, the majority leader of the House of Representatives, was convicted of several felonies and implicated a wide variety of public officials, staffers, and lobbyists in his schemes.[89] A lobbyist who originally represented clients ranging from the apartheid regime in South Africa to Russian energy companies, Abramoff decided he could make money faster through less orthodox means. As one observer remarked, he decided that "the traditional lobbying practice—charging, like law firms, by the hour—was for chumps. Instead he demanded huge commissions that represented a cut of the enormous sums a big government could provide his clients."[90] Abramoff received funds from clients, such as the Indian tribes fighting to prevent casinos from being legalized on non-Indian property, and promised his clients access to the powerful people in Washington, including the White House. He then distributed the money to favored groups and associates in return for access, or to curry favor with powerful officials and old cronies, or as income to be kicked back to himself. Later some of the Indian tribes sued Abramoff and his associates, accusing them of a "blatant, calculated scheme to defraud a client . . . in a series of kickbacks, misappropriated funds, and unauthorized charges."[91]

Abramoff's dealings, and ultimately crimes, can be viewed in the context of the culture that has developed in Washington. Significant conflicts of interests have always existed, but Tom DeLay's K-Street strategy, to make it clear to lobbyists that they pay to play (that is, donate money to Republican candidates in exchange for influencing legislation), has made influence buying more open (see Chapter 4 for more on the K-Street strategy). One scholar, a fellow in a conservative think tank, describes the K-Street Project as a "Tammany Hall operation."[92] Money is kicked into the machine, and favors emerge. Big lobbying firms are expected to hire only Republicans at the top jobs that pay as much as $1 million a year. Once hired, "everyone is expected to contribute some of that money back into Republican campaigns."

Some former colleagues termed DeLay's role as akin to a hotel concierge, calling on favors from these wealthy donors and "arranging corporate jets, private cars, fishing trips and other expense-paid trips during congressional breaks, key votes, and party conventions, all financed by wealthy donors with interests before Congress."[93] Members getting the favors were then expected to come through with appropriate votes on pending legislation.

Abramoff, an early supporter of DeLay's bid for congressional leadership, used the close ties he had developed with DeLay and his key staffers to raise millions of dollars. Potential clients knew that he could use his clout with DeLay to get things done. After all, DeLay had publicly called him one of his "closest and dearest friends."[94]

Only a little of Abramoff's money went to the White House, as when he charged the Indian tribes $25,000 to gain access for two of their representatives to the president.[95] Most went elsewhere. For example, $2.5 million went to the U.S. Family Network, ostensibly a grassroots organization dedicated to moral improvement, but mostly a front organization to pay the organizer of the group, a former DeLay chief of staff. (He in turn hired Tom DeLay's wife at $3200 a month for a job involving little work.) Millions more went to Americans for Tax Reform, founded by Abramoff's old colleague Grover Norquist, who then funneled some of those funds to other operatives. The National Center for Public Policy Research, another Abramoff organization, provided funds to take the House majority leader, Tom Delay, and other officials to Scotland. Yet another organization, Capitol Campaign Strategies, run by another DeLay former staffer, received funds from the Indian tribes and kicked back significant amounts to Abramoff. And the American International Center, supposedly a "think tank," was in reality a house in Rehoboth Beach owned by the same former DeLay staffer. This front organization moved money to Abramoff and also to Ralph Reed. Another front organization, the Capital Athletic Foundation, even funneled funds to a sniper school in Israel and an orthodox Jewish school founded by Abramoff.

High-powered lobbyist Jack Abramoff leaves court during his trial for fraud, conspiracy, and tax evasion.

As of this writing, several people have gone to jail for this scheme, including Abramoff, two former DeLay aides, a member of Congress, and an executive branch employee, the former chief of staff at the General Services Agency (which is the chief purchasing agency of the government) and then the White House's chief procurement officer. Investigations continue and others may be charged; Abramoff himself, from prison, is now cooperating in the investigation. Members of Congress and the White House have hurried to disassociate themselves from Abramoff, of course.

Regulating Ethical Behavior

Congress does have an ethics committee in each house, and there are provisions for registering lobbyists. But the ethics committees are nonfunctional. When in 2004 the House Ethics Committee reprimanded Tom DeLay (R-Tex.) three times, the Speaker of the House, Dennis Hastert (R-Ill.), replaced the chair of the committee and several other Republicans with those less interested in an activist committee and more responsive to the Republican leadership.[96] The Senate committee has not investigated any of the recent scandals.

Although in light of the Abramoff and other 2005 scandals, some members pledged to put new rules in place regulating such travel, nothing was done. In fact, John Boehner (R-Ohio) was elected House majority leader, in part because he opposed any new regulation of such gifts, calling such regulation "childish."[97] Boehner himself took 200 free trips, worth $157,000,[98] during this five-year period.[99]

However, perceived widespread congressional corruption and influence peddling were motivating factors for voters in the 2006 election, and the Republicans lost control of Congress. Whether the Democrats record will be better in their ability to punish sleazy dealings remains to be seen.[100]

In the executive branch, decision makers operate under much less direct public and media scrutiny. Yet they, too, may be acting on matters that affect their personal economic position. Since the Carter administration, all high-level administrative officials have been required to file public financial disclosure statements to allow the public to see when they are making decisions that benefit their own financial interests. But the rules do not require officials to step aside on matters that would affect them financially.

It is also a conflict of interest to use one's government position to line up a job following a public service career. The Ethics in Government Act of 1978 tries to regulate this. The act bars former public servants from lobbying their former agencies for a year and, on matters in which they "personally and substantially" participated as public officials, for life. Current employees also are prohibited from participating in decisions affecting interests with which they are negotiating about future employment. But the act is not very stringently enforced.

Because many companies that regularly deal with government think experience in government is an asset, especially experience in the agency that regulates the company's activities, many officials take well-paying jobs in the industry they came to know while in government. Critics call this the "revolving door," referring to the movement of people from government service to the private sector and sometimes back again. Recently, most of the top executives of the Department of Homeland Security, led by Tom Ridge, its first director, have left government service to become executives, lobbyists, or board members for firms now contracting with the Homeland Security agency.[101]

The term for using access to powerful people to make money is called **influence peddling**. Former high government officials can and do use their access to former colleagues to win jobs representing clients in business or labor and then use that access to lobby for favorable policies and contracts for their new firms. Many of those lobbyists hired by K-Street firms were former Republican members of Congress, now in a position where they could solicit clients on the basis of their close relationship with DeLay and other powerful Republicans.[102]

Democratic and Republican Corruption

Conflicts of interest and influence peddling are bipartisan phenomena. Most of our examples have pinpointed Republicans because they controlled both branches of government from 2001 to 2007, and only since 2007, when they won a majority of both the House and Senate, have Democrats been in control of one branch. When the Republicans controlled both branches, those who wanted to buy influence had to buy it from them. But conflict of interest accusations swirled around the Clinton White House, although no high official was convicted of illegal acts in office. But both President Clinton and First Lady Hillary Clinton were accused of conflicts of interest in the long-running investigation of the Whitewater affair (an investment scheme in which they had participated years earlier), but they were never found guilty of anything. A number of Clinton administration members, including a cabinet secretary, Mike Espy, left office under an ethical cloud relating to conflicts of interest and influence peddling.

George W. Bush came to Washington saying that the ethical standards of his administration would be higher than those of the Clinton White House, but influence peddling seemed to escalate to a whole new level. In some cases, corporate interests have been part of secret policy-making processes inside the White House in ways never seen before. Vice President Cheney's financial interests in one of the major contractors in Iraq, Halliburton, are now the subject of investigation. Halliburton, which Cheney headed from 1995 to 2000, was given advance notice to plan for the postwar period in Iraq and received billions of dollars' worth of contracts without competitive bidding. In 2004, an audit revealed that Halliburton had billed the government for $4.3 billion in reimbursement for work that had cost the company only $1.8 billion (Halliburton's response was that conditions in Iraq made keeping up with paperwork difficult).

Conflicts of interest can never be completely eradicated from government, but presidents can make their expectations clear. George W. Bush's administration has seemed less concerned about conflicts of interest than those of his predecessors, Bill Clinton and George H. W. Bush. His administration seems intent on privatizing many parts of government, including military support operations, and has been unembarrassed about awarding lucrative contracts to top supporters without benefit of competitive bidding.

Some observers have pointed out that although both Democrats and Republicans have ethical lapses, the kinds of ethics problems they have are quite different. Corrupt Democrats steal. They accept bribes and improper campaign donations, divert public funds to their own pocket, and seek personal financial aggrandizement. This style of corruption is reminiscent of the "honest graft" of the big-city political machines (see the box "Honest Graft" earlier in the chapter). Although some Republicans also steal—for example, Abramoff and Cunningham; former Vice President Spiro Agnew, who pleaded no contest to charges of kickbacks, bribery, and extortion; and former representative Joseph McDade (R-Pa.), who was convicted of bribery and racketeering—most of these sorts of scandals have involved Democrats. Examples include Daniel Rostenkowski (D-Ill.), former chair of the House Ways and Means Committee, convicted of corrupt acts involving mail fraud, and Robert Torricelli (D-N.J.), censured by his Senate colleagues for accepting gifts from lobbyists.

Republican ethical failings tend to be related to the use of government for improper means. President Nixon's Watergate scandal involved trying to use the powers of government to punish his personal enemies and then lying about it. He also ordered Cambodia to be bombed and tried to keep it a secret. President Reagan tried to subvert the constitutional powers of Congress by secretly selling arms to Iran and supplying weapons to rebels in Nicaragua, both expressly against the law. The Republicans' K-Street strategy was basically an attempt to get lobbyists to buy influence over government policies and to buy government contracts in a rather overt way.

Although Democratic presidents have also been guilty of misuse of government power (for example, President Johnson lied about alleged attacks by the North Vietnamese on an American ship to justify getting the United States more deeply involved in the Vietnam War, and President Kennedy ordered the FBI to wiretap Martin Luther King, Jr.), subverting government seems more a Republican style of corruption.

Why do these differences exist? They could be coincidental, of course. But one Democrat argued that these differences were tied to the class basis of the parties: "The lower classes steal; the upper classes defraud." A prominent Republican had a different view: "Most Republicans are contemptuous of government; few Democrats are." Whatever the reason, these examples suggest that partisanship extends to more than presidential preferences.

Conclusion: Does the Influence of Money Make Government Less Responsive?

The influence of money in American politics is a perennial source of concern to those who want to live up to the democratic ideals of political equality and popular sovereignty. Our democratic values tell us that government should represent all, the poor as well as the rich, and that everyone should have an equal chance to influence government. We know that in the real world, things do not work this way. We tolerate much inequality in access because that seems to be the way the world works in the private as well as in the public sphere, because everyone is not equally interested in influencing government, and because for most people the effort of changing this pattern would be greater than the benefits gained.

Nevertheless, our reaction to the influence of money seems to be cyclical. We tolerate it; then, when stories of inside deals, influence peddling, and buying access and even votes become too frequent, we act to do something about it. But that happens rarely, and then we slip back into apathy until the next cycle comes along.[103]

In recent history, the low points of the use of money to buy access were probably during the Watergate scandals associated with the 1972 election and then again with the scandals swirling around Jack Abramoff in 2005. After 1972, we reacted strongly by passing new laws and cleaning up our campaign finance system. But as the years went by, we found ways to get around the laws until they became nearly meaningless, with the important exception that we know how much money is being given to candidates. In response to the Abramoff scandals, voters apparently decided that the culture of corruption had gone too far and put the Democrats in control of the Congress. (And Abramoff and several of his colleagues went to jail.) The controversies over the role of lobbyists in the McCain and Obama campaigns also reflect that we continue to be in an era of substantial concern over ethical standards in government.

We should, of course, put the amount of political money into a larger perspective. After all, it is useful to remember, as one columnist points out, that the more than $1 billion spent by the primary candidates in 2008 is about what Americans spend on chocolate each month.[104] Americans spend $5 billion a year on laundry detergent, car companies spend $1 billion a month to sell their wares, and the federal government spends $1 billion every few hours.[105] But it is not the amount of money in politics as much as its possible effects that concern us.

Neither should we think of our times as the low point in government morality. In political campaigns, big money is certainly less influential than it was a century ago. Campaign funding disclosure legislation means that the public can at least know who is buying influence.

Nor should we conclude that ethical standards are lower in government than in the private sector. After all, some public officials are selling favors, but it is members of the private sector who are buying them. Conflicts of interest and influence peddling in government reflect the ethical standards of the larger society. A good part of the news for the last thirty years has focused on stories of Wall Street bankers who bought and sold illegal insider tips, savings and loan officers who looted their institutions of millions of dollars, military contractors who cheated government, and corporate leaders who falsify corporate income and plunder corporate funds for personal gain while shareholders lose their investments. One businessman lamented, "We are all embarrassed by events that make the *Wall Street Journal* read more like the *Police Gazette*,"[106] whereas several years later another remarked, "In my lifetime, American business has never been under such scrutiny, and to be blunt, much of it deserved. You pick up the paper, and you want to cry."[107]

But the effects of money are hard to pin down. It is difficult to measure exactly the influence of money on political outcomes. Money sometimes influences votes and policies. Campaign contributions have some impact on voting in Congress. Money seems to have moved both parties toward more conservative policies. Money in politics is no doubt responsible for the increased inequality between the rich and poor. But sometimes, especially when the public is paying attention, money appears to have little impact.

We do not know exactly how presidential candidates might be influenced by huge campaign donations or whether bureaucrats are using promises of future jobs as trade-offs for current favors. We think that good candidates are hindered or deterred from running by a shortage of money or even just by the knowledge that they need to raise big money, but it is difficult to measure exactly how many. Even though money is very tangible, its influence sometimes is quite intangible.

To the extent that money has an impact, it limits the responsiveness of government to the average citizen. It causes some policy makers to be more responsive to the big interests than to the average person. This does not mean, though, that those with the most money always win. Organization and a sense of the public interest can sometimes defeat even big money.

In designing laws to regulate the use of money in political life, perhaps the best that reformers can reasonably hope for is a system in which public officials who want to be honest will not feel under pressure to be influenced by money. Certainly, there will always be a few "bad apples," and no political system can protect us completely from them. It should be enough to design rules and structures that ensure that people of average honesty who serve in public office are rewarded for putting the public interest, rather than their private interests, first. Our current laws, especially our congressional campaign finance laws, do not always do that. The penalties we suffer are less in politicians stealing from the public till (relatively little of this occurs, certainly in comparison with the stealing that has been revealed in corporate America). They are more in the loss of public trust, an increasing alienation from government, and anger at politicians who seem to be putting their interests before the public interest. Perhaps, then, even a largely symbolic effort by our legislators to limit the influence of money on the political process is important, because it sends the signal that they are aware of and accountable to public concerns.

Any discussion of campaign finance should include a mention of our role as citizens. It is tough to regulate this. John McCain has said, "Money is like water: it finds cracks in the wall."[108] In a democracy, it is hard to find ways of restricting the flow of private resources into political campaigns. We can be appalled by the lies in ads trashing one or the other of the candidates, and independent groups in the process are not really held accountable. That is the public's and media's responsibility. Since the ads would not appear if they were not effective, perhaps it is we, the voters, who need a higher standard for evaluating these ads, a lower tolerance for corruption, and higher expectations for the performance of our elected officials. It is we who keep electing them.

Key Terms

muckrakers

Teapot Dome scandal

Federal Election Commission

McCain-Feingold Act

soft money

political action committees (PACs)

public disclosure

contribution limits

independent spending

527 organizations

spoils system

conflicts of interest

influence peddling

Key Names

Theodore Roosevelt

George Washington Plunkitt

Richard Nixon

Hillary Clinton

John McCain

Barack Obama

Rudolph Giuliani

Mitt Romney

Tom DeLay

Jack Abramoff

Please visit our companion website at www.cengage.com/politicalscience/welch/uag12e or use CengageNOW for additional resources dealing with this chapter.

After the Democrats won a majority of seats in Congress in 2006, Representative Nancy Pelosi (D-Calif.) became the first woman ever elected Speaker of the House.

Congress

10

Talking Points

"He's a Democrat. Waddya' expect?" a Republican member of the congressional staff e-mailed colleagues about the commissioner of the congressional softball league. He has a "long-standing policy of punishing success and rewarding failure." The commissioner, a former congressional staffer on the Democratic side, came back swinging: "Republicans come here and want to bash your head in. And if they don't get their way, they pick up the ball and go home."[1]

The 2006 midterm elections were approaching, partisanship was at fever pitch and Republican teams had just withdrawn from a softball league that for 37 years had been sponsoring games on the Mall between Republican teams like "Fat, Drunk & Awesome" and "Moderately Sober" and Democratic teams like the "Yellow Journalists" and "Mass's Asses." Leading the secession were staff assistants to the Republican House leadership who accused the commissioner of being a "communist" and a "dictator" and of instituting a "socialist" playoff system by adopting rules that favored teams with poor records.[2] One e-mail to the commissioner said the league's top teams were "being screwed by your Softball Welfare Bracketology." But the commissioner countered that the Republicans' proposal for seeding teams for tournament playoffs favored the few

at the top over "the many below them" [in] a plan to get "special rights for your agenda to wage class warfare on the more relaxed teams."[3] The Republicans, he said, "are accustomed to running everything, and they wanted to run playtime, too."[4]

This incident, parodied on *The Daily Show* in a segment called "The Designated Bitter," was one of the more ludicrous manifestations of the partisanship that has hamstrung Congress since the mid-1990s. Members have questioned one another's patriotism, engaged in name-calling, shouting and shoving matches, and even a necktie-pulling confrontation. There was the "brawl in the hall" between Ways and Means committee members caught on C-SPAN, and the time Capitol Hill police had to be called in to break up a pushing match between two House members (both ex-boxers).[5]

Congress has come to be seen as a place where bitter partisan divisions have prevented the negotiation and compromise necessary to carry out the nation's business. "It used to be that softball was one of the few things in Washington that both parties agreed on. Now that is coming to an end too," the league commissioner said.[6] You know partisanship has gone a league too far when even softball has turned into hardball.

Most Americans think the person who represents them in Congress does a very good job. They return them to office at impressively high rates. But most Americans do not think Congress as a whole does a very good job. Its approval ratings are often well below 50 percent; in mid-2008, they were hovering around 10 percent.

The Founders clearly intended Congress to be the dominant branch of government. Their description of Congress and its powers in Article I of the Constitution ⭐ comprises almost half the document. Through its formal powers, Madison believed, Congress would dominate the presidency because it alone had "access to the pockets of the people." But clearly Congress has not always been first in the hearts of the people, nor the most respected or trusted branch of government.

In this chapter, we look at the composition of Congress and ask how representative it is and how its members get elected. We describe how Congress is organized and how it carries out its constitutional responsibilities, then look at how individual members carry out their duties in Washington and their districts and what makes them so popular back home that they usually get reelected. Finally, we look at Congress's relationship to the other branches of government and to the public.

Members and Constituencies

Members

Alexis de Tocqueville was not impressed with the status of members of Congress, noting that they were "almost all obscure individuals, village lawyers, men in trades, or even persons belonging to the lower class." His view was shared by another European visitor, Charles Dickens, who was shocked in 1842 to find Congress full of tobacco spitters who committed "cowardly attacks upon opponents" and seemed to be guilty of "aiding and abetting every bad inclination in the popular mind."[7] However one views their behavior, members of Congress were not then, and are not now, a cross section of the American public. But they are a more diverse group than the membership of Congresses of the eighteenth and nineteenth centuries ever were or thought they should be.

Who Can Serve?

The Constitution places few formal restrictions on membership in Congress. One must

be twenty-five years old to serve in the House and thirty in the Senate. One must have been a citizen for at least seven years to be elected to the House and nine years to be elected to the Senate. Members must reside in the states from which they were elected, but House members need not reside in their own districts. As a practical matter, however, it is highly unlikely that voters will elect a person to represent their district who is not from the district or who does not maintain a residence there. ⭐ Art. 1, Sect. 2

Local identity is not as significant a factor in Senate races; national figures such as Robert Kennedy and Hillary Rodham Clinton, who established in-state residency within weeks or months of the election, both ran successful campaigns in New York. It is, however, difficult to imagine that happening in every state or with relatively unknown transplanted candidates.

Length of Service

Every member of the House stands for election every two years, and senators serve six-year terms, with one-third of the membership standing for election every two years. Although the Articles of Confederation did set a limit on the number of terms a representative could serve, the Constitution placed no cap on how many times an individual can be elected to the House or Senate. Perhaps the Founders thought that no one would want to serve more than a few terms. In the late eighteenth and early nineteenth centuries, leaving one's home to serve in Congress was considered a great sacrifice. Washington was a muddy swamp, with debris-filled streets, farm animals running loose, and transportation so poor almost no one got home during a session. In fact, during Congress's first forty years, 41 percent of House members, on average, dropped out every two years, and in the early 1900s the median length of service for a representative was still only five years.[8]

In its early years, Washington, D.C., was described as "a miserable little swamp." When this photo was taken in 1882, it still retained the look and feel of a small town.

But as Washington became a power center and a much more livable and accessible city, members were more receptive to longer periods of service. In the 1910s and 1920s, power in the House became less centralized, and individuals were able to build personal power bases. And as seats went uncontested in the one-party South, more legislators became career politicians, spending thirty and even forty years in Congress. These long-serving members began to dominate committee work and to control the legislative agenda. Although they by no means comprised a majority of Congress, they were probably foremost in the minds of those Americans who began to see government as increasingly unresponsive to the public.

Term Limits

During the height of public anger with government in the 1990s, there was a nationwide move to limit the number of terms that state and national legislators could serve, and most Americans claimed to favor such limitations in mid-1990s surveys.[9] Although Congress narrowly defeated term-limit legislation, in twenty-three of twenty-four states that allow ballot initiatives, voters adopted term limits for their members of Congress and state legislators.

Some supporters of term limits believed that by not having to worry constantly about getting reelected, legislators would be free to consider the "public interest" and would have no desire to build personal empires. Others also saw term limits as a way to weaken the power of government, by always having inexperienced legislators. Because legislators would be relative novices, opponents thought term limits would weaken Congress at the expense of the special interests and the federal bureaucracy and president.

This debate subsided when in 1995, in a 5–4 vote, the Supreme Court held term limits for members of Congress unconstitutional. The majority argued that permitting individual states to have diverse qualifications for Congress would "result in a patchwork of state qualifications, undermining the uniformity and national character that the framers envisioned and sought to ensure."[10] By adding to the criteria spelled out in the Constitution (age and citizenship), the Court ruled that states were in effect "amending" the Constitution. By definition, then, such laws would be unconstitutional because the Constitution can be amended only through the processes of adoption and ratification it specifies, not by state or congressional laws or ballot initiatives.

By the late 1990s, enthusiasm for term limits in the *state legislatures* had waned. By 2008, only fifteen of the twenty-three states that had adopted term limits still had them.[11]

Constituencies

The district a member of Congress represents is called a **constituency**. The term is used to refer to both the area within the electoral boundaries and its residents. There are two senators from each state, so each senator's constituency is the entire state and all its residents. Most states have multiple House districts, though seven states (Alaska, Delaware, Montana, North Dakota, South Dakota, Vermont, and Wyoming) have populations so small that they are allotted only a single seat in the House of Representatives. For these "at-large districts," the constituency for the House member is also the entire state. Except for those seven states, every House district must have (in accordance with the one-person, one-vote rule) roughly the same number of residents, so the number of districts in each state depends on its total population.

Except in the single-district states, the geographic size of a constituency is determined by the distribution of the population within the state. In states with large urban populations, several districts may exist within a single city. The logistics of campaigning are thus very different for a representative from New York City, whose district may be as small as 12 square miles, and one from Montana, who must cover the entire state (147,042 square miles).

Reapportionment

Initially, the House of Representatives had fifty-nine members, but as the nation grew and more states joined the Union, the size of the House increased too. Since 1910, it has had 435 members, except when seats were added temporarily (while awaiting the 1960 reapportionment) for newly admitted states Alaska and Hawaii. Every ten years, in a process called **reapportionment**, the 435 seats are allocated among the states based on the latest U. S. Census. ⭐ Art. 1, Sect. 2. Since the first Congress, the number of constituents each House member represents has grown from 30,000 to more than 700,000.

Within a constant 435-seat House, states with fast-growing populations gain seats, whereas those with slow-growing or declining populations lose seats. Since World War II, population movement in the United States has been toward the South, West, and Southwest and away from the Midwest and Northeast. This has been reflected in the allocation of House seats. For example, from 1950 through 2000, California gained twenty-three seats and New York lost fourteen. Illinois, Wisconsin, Pennsylvania, and Ohio lost House seats after the 2000 census, whereas Arizona, California, Colorado, Florida, Georgia, Nevada, and Texas gained seats. The same categories of states are on track to continue losing (Eastern and Midwestern states) and gaining (South, West, and Southwest states) seats after 2010.[12]

The census counts all residents, irrespective of legal residency or citizenship, and several of the seat-gaining states are home to millions of undocumented residents. California, for example, had a net loss of native-born population and would have shown population loss after the last census if not for having more undocumented immigrants than any other state.

Redistricting

States that gain or lose seats and states whose population shifts within the state (rural to urban or urban to suburban, for example) must redraw their district boundaries, a process called **redistricting**. This is always a hot political issue. The precise boundaries of a district determine the election prospects of candidates and parties. In most states, the state legislature controls the redistricting process, so districts are normally drawn to benefit the party in control of the legislature. A district whose boundaries are devised to maximize the political advantage of a party or a racial or ethnic group is known as a **gerrymander** (see also Chapter 8). This boundary manipulation can result in bizarrely shaped districts but it also secures political advantage for majority parties in state legislatures. At the same time, boundaries must comply with the Supreme Court ruling that all congressional districts be approximately equal in population.

Before 1960, states were often reluctant to redistrict their state legislative and congressional boundaries to conform to population changes within the state for fear that doing so would endanger incumbents and threaten rural areas whose populations were declining. After decades without reapportioning, some legislative districts in urban areas had nineteen times as many residents as rural districts. When state legislatures, many of which were still dominated by rural representatives, refused to reapportion themselves, the Supreme Court, in *Baker* v. *Carr* (1962), issued the first in a series of rulings forcing states to reapportion their legislative districts.[13] Two years later, the Court required congressional districts to be approximately equal in population, thus mandating the principle of *one person, one vote*.[14] As a result, during the 1960s, most states had to redraw district lines, some more than once. The decisions provoked strong opposition and a constitutional amendment was proposed to overturn them. But over time the principle of one person, one vote has come to be widely accepted.

Because of the important role state legislatures play in the redistricting process, and increasing technological sophistication, relatively few congressional districts are competitive. Software now available can measure voting patterns down to the block level. This allows legislators, using voter registration records that record party preferences, to draw district lines to create "safe" (noncompetitive) legislative districts for either the Republican or Democratic candidate. After the 1990 state legislative elections, which gave Republicans control of the majority of states, many states drew boundaries favoring Republicans, a factor in the Republicans' victories in 1994. If 2010 is a Democratic year, more state legislatures will be controlled by Democrats than Republicans, so a number of states will again become redistricting battlegrounds.

The lack of competitive seats is a serious problem for democratic accountability because fair and competitive elections are the primary way the public exercises authority over government. Due to the number of open seats in the 2008 election and widespread public dissatisfaction with the direction of the country, there were more competitive races than in recent year, but only about 13 percent of the House seats were contested even then.[15]

Many observers are urging states to adopt redistricting systems run by independent commissions, freer of partisan incentives. In that way, voters in many more districts will have a choice between candidates who have good chances of winning rather than have the district outcome largely predetermined. The impetus for independent commissions can also come from partisans. In California, Republican Governor Arnold Schwarzenegger promoted a ballot initiative to create an independent commission to redraw district lines after the 2010 census because he feared that the Democratic legislature would not redraw district lines to reflect growing Republican strength in the center of the state.[16]

Tenure

Given that congressional seats have become ever more safe, congressional tenures have become ever longer.[17] The typical member of the House serves about a decade, and in the Senate about thirteen years. In noncompetitive districts, members are almost certain to be reelected. Thus, there were only sixty newcomers in the 110th Congress (2007–2009) after the 2006 election when Republicans lost seats in both the House and Senate that they had believed were safe. Though that was an increase in newcomers from the previous term, it was small compared to congresses of the previous decade.[18]

Congress as a Representative Body

What Does Representative Mean?

To take the measure of how representative Congress is, we first have to establish what "representation" means. During the Revolutionary War, John Adams said that the legislature

Reps. Tammy Baldwin (D-Wisc) and Barney Frank (D-Mass) appear in support of a bill protecting gays against workplace discrimination. Baldwin was the first openly gay candidate elected to Congress and Frank has been re-elected many times since coming out.

general public was just a romantic notion. Only certain landed, business, or professional white men could even think about running for Congress. It was not until 1920 (with ratification of the Nineteenth Amendment, granting women the right to vote) that a majority of Americans could vote, and most of them, realistically, could not stand for office. Although federal barriers to African American male suffrage had been removed after the Civil War, state laws in the South prevented most from voting until the 1960s. Today, even though adults in all economic categories can meet the minimum requirements needed to stand for office, the demands of the nomination and selection process, especially campaign costs, limit the number of people who are able to run.

to be created under the new government "should be an exact portrait, in miniature, of the people at large, as it should think, feel, reason, and act like them."[19] Benjamin Franklin said simply that Congress should be a mirror of the people. These statements leave unresolved what has priority in representation. Is it more important, for example, for Congress to look like a demographic cross section of the public or to reflect constituents' issue preferences in the policies it advances? And in what situations can elected representatives use their delegated authority to act as their conscience dictates to do what they believe is right or in the national interest, even if not supported by a majority of their constituents?

A Congress that reflects the demographic mix of the country is one where descriptive representation is high. This kind of representation is not rooted in what legislators *do* but rather on their personal characteristics—what they *are,* or *are like.*[20] The rise of identity politics has increased demands for a Congress that better reflects the country's demographic profile, and so today it is more likely than ever that a predominantly Hispanic, white, or African American congressional district will be represented by a member of the corresponding ethnicity or race. But Congress is still far from representative in this sense (see the box,"Congress Is Not a Cross Section of America").

For the first century of the Republic, the possibility of having citizen-legislators who were a cross section of the

"Acting for" Representation

If Congress still has a way to go to *look* like the American public, does it "think, feel, reason, and act" like them? Part of the reason why there has been interest in having Congress look like America is that there is a relationship between a person's sex, race, ethnicity, income, and religious views and that person's position on issues. That is, individuals are not just interested in having someone look like them, but also want representatives "acting for" them.

Women, African Americans, Hispanics, and Asian Americans are seen as *national* constituencies with distinct issue priorities. House members now organize around these identities so as to represent national constituencies as well as their home districts (see "Making Alliances" later in this chapter). But do women, for example, really represent their constituents differently from their male colleagues? There is no guarantee that any one woman (or African American or Mexican American) will represent women (or blacks or Hispanics) collectively better than, say, a white man; there is no rule that a millionaire will not look out for the interests of blue-collar workers or that a Christian or Jew will not care about the civil rights of a Muslim.

There is some evidence that our overly broad categories do not capture similarities of interests. For example, first- and second-generation immigrants are not necessarily supportive of those recently arrived or of illegal immigrants. Do Japanese American, Christian senators from Hawaii really have the same perspective on the world as newly arrived immigrants from China and India or as Muslim Indonesians or Pakistanis? And has Sen. Ken Salazar (D-Col.), a man whose family emigrated from Spain and helped

american diversity | Congress is Not a Cross Section of America

Congress is not now, and never has been, a cross section of the American population. The citizens who serve in Congress are still disproportionately white and male: white non-Hispanic males, who make up about one-third of the total population, held about 62 percent of the seats in the House of Representatives and 78 percent of the seats in the Senate in 2008. Women, who make up 51 percent of the nation's population, are the most underrepresented demographic group. They were just 17 percent of the House membership and 16 percent of the Senate's in the 110th Congress (see Table 10.1). Five states (Delaware, Iowa, Mississippi, New Hampshire, and Vermont) have never elected a woman to Congress.[1] Most states do send at least one female representative, however, and California's delegation had twenty-one women in 2008, including both of its senators (accounting for almost one-quarter of all women in Congress).

Hispanic, Asian, and African Americans are also below parity with their numbers in the population. But thirty-seven of the forty-one congressional districts whose populations are one-third or more African American have elected an African American to represent them.[2]

Congress is also not representative of the range of religious views among the general public. Seventeen percent of the population claims "other" or no religious affiliation, but just one percent of congressional members claim no affiliation and only two percent adhere to religions other than Christianity and Judaism.[3] However, two Buddhists and the first Muslim were elected to the House in 2006.

Members are much better off financially than the average householder; many are millionaires, and a number are multimillionaires.[4] They also tend to rank well above average in education; nearly all have

college degrees and more than 400 have graduate or professional degrees. Although blue-collar workers constitute nearly one-quarter of the working population, only fourteen members of congress claim blue-collar backgrounds.

The most common occupational background of members has been the law. But this pattern is changing, especially in the House, as legislative careers have become more demanding. Today it is difficult for an attorney to maintain a law practice and also serve as a legislator. Ethics laws requiring financial disclosure and information about client relations have also discouraged practicing attorneys from running for congressional office. Although 58 percent of Senators name law as their primary occupation, there are now more House members with backgrounds in public service and business than in law. Nineteen percent list education as their prior occupation, but such fields as engi-

Table 1 | Members of the 110th Congress: Not a Cross Section of the Public (2007–2009)

	Population (%)	House* (%)	Senate (%)
Women	51	17	16
African American	12.3	9.2	1
Hispanic	15	6	3
Asian Pacific	4.3	1.3	2
American Indian	1.3	0.2	0
Lawyer	0.3	41	58
College grad	28	92	98
Millionaires	0.7	27	40
Foreign born	14	2*	1*
Average age	37	56	61.7

Does not include nonvoting members from Puerto Rico, Guam, Samoa, the Virgin Islands, or the District of Columbia.
*Does not include those born abroad of American parents, such as John McCain.
Source: Mildred Amer, "Membership of the 110th Congress: A Profile," Congressional Research Service, Report RS22555, December 15, 2006, 1–6.

neering and science still are barely represented in Congress. Only seven members, excluding medical fields, were trained in the sciences.

Increasingly, Congress is drawing its members from professional politicians; in 2008, over half of all House members and 39 percent of Senators had served in their state legislatures. Others have been mayors, judges, governors, cabinet officials, ambassadors, and law enforcement officials, and over 20 percent had experience as congressional or White House staffers. Another dent in the citizen-legislator ideal has been the presence of "dynasty" families (the Adamses, Harrisons, Lodges, Kennedys, and Bushes). An estimated 5 percent of all members of the 110th Congress came from political families. There were four pairs of siblings (three of them Hispanic) and a father and son. The Udall cousins, who represented House districts in Colorado and Arizona in the 110th and whose fathers served in the House and the Kennedy and Johnson cabinets, both won Senate seats in 2008.

Members of the Senate are even less a cross section of the American population than the House, but the Senate was established to represent the interests of the states, not to be a mirror of the people. Representation in the Senate is based on a one-state, two-vote standard, not one person, one vote. This structure allows for the overrepresentation of the interests of low-population states and the underrepresentation of the interests of the larger, more urban, and more ethnically and racially diverse states. Senators must define and represent state interests in the aggregate, not just those of a specific group or district. This is less complicated for senators from low-population states that are more socially and economically homogeneous, such as Nebraska and Wyoming, than for senators from much larger and more diverse populations and economies such as New York and California.

[1] A list of all women who have served in the House can be found at www.loc/gov/thomas; those who have served in the Senate can be found at www.senate.gov/artandhistory/history/common/briefing/women_senators.htm.
[2] Unless otherwise indicated, data on members of the 110th Congress are taken from Mildred Amer, "Membership of the 110th Congress: A Profile," Congressional Research Service report RS22555, December 15, 2006, 1–6.
[3] The U.S. Census does not collect data on religion, so figures for the general population are estimates from a Pew Research Center survey, published June 24, 2008 (pewresearch.org). Congressional affiliations are by self-declaration and will not add up to 100 percent because ten members specified other denominations and six gave no affiliation.
[4] These are estimates drawn from members' financial disclosure statements, which do not provide exact figures on income. Members need only report income and assets within a broad dollar range. A few members do, however, release their tax statements. Financial disclosure statements are published at several websites including that of the Center for Responsive Politics.

The Sanchez sisters—Loretta (left) and Linda—serve in the House of Representatives as Democrats representing two districts in Southern California.

found Santa Fe in the 1500s (before the Mayflower arrived), really shared the same experiences as those who organize as Hispanic Americans?

There is reason to believe, however, that as women, blacks, Hispanics, and Asians increase their presence in Congress, so will the likelihood that the issues of greatest concern to them will be heard. Imagine a Congress made up not of wealthy males but of blue-collar females. It is hard to imagine that the legislation coming out of that Congress would be the same as it is today. Of course, we cannot test that speculation; but as the proportion of women in Congress has increased, so have the number of bills of special importance to them.[21] This suggests that there is a relationship between *descriptive* and *acting for representation* and that as the Congress begins to look more like a cross section of the population, legislation may become more representative of the wishes of the broadest segment of the electorate.

One simple measure of "acting for" representation is party identification. Although only about 65 percent of the public identifies with one of the two major parties, Republicans and Democrats hold 99.7 percent of the seats.[22] (See Figure 1.) The thirty-five percent of Americans who are independents or identify with a minor party have representation from only two Independents in Congress, who caucus with the Democrats.

Another measure of "acting for" representation is a legislator's voting record. By casting hundreds of votes each year, members try to represent the interests of their constituencies, bring benefits to the district, and in the process win support for reelection. Members must consider what benefits their districts as a whole as well as the needs of subgroups within the district, such as party voters, socioeconomic groups, and personal supporters.[23] Overall, if districts are filled with farmers, the members must represent farmers, whether or not they know anything about farming. Representatives of districts with large universities must be sensitive to the reactions of students and professors even if they personally think academics have pointed heads.

To keep in touch with their home districts so that they can pursue policies their constituents favor and vote as they would on issues, most members do spend about half of each year in their districts. On the whole, the member's issue positions are usually not far from those of his or her party or the majority of the constituency *that votes*. But members are more likely to share the issue position of constituents when the issue is important to constituents and when their opinions are strongly held. Since constituents are often uninformed, divided, or apathetic, and most votes in Congress are on bills the electorate knows little about, members can vote their personal issue preferences, with their party, or with those constituents or donors who most forcibly make their positions known.

Voters can send confusing signals however. At the state level, for example, Iowa, a racially homogenous, conservative agricultural state, sends one Republican and one Democrat to the Senate, where their voting records show an almost seventy-point differential on liberal/conservative positions. Which, if either, is representing the Iowa constituency? South Dakota, New Mexico, and Colorado also elect senators from different parties with a more than fifty-point differential in their liberal/conservative voting records. Sometimes even senators from the same party vary considerably in their policy positions: Arizona Republican John McCain received a 57 composite conservative score for votes cast in the Senate in 2006 compared to his colleague Jon Kyl's 91.[24]

Constituents are becoming more active in communicating with their legislators, flooding them with faxes, e-mails,

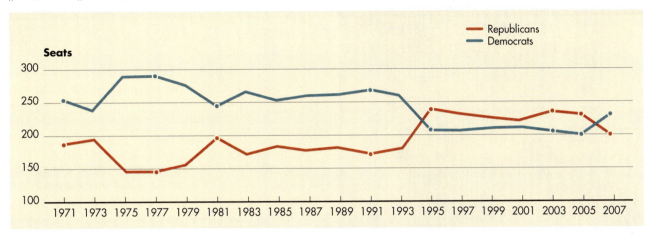

Figure 1 | Makeup of the House of Representatives, by Party, 1971–2007

Representation of the two major parties in the House has been much more equal since 1995 than in earlier decades, but other parties have been shut out. (Note: Figures are for the first day of each Congress and do not include Independents or vacant seats.)
SOURCE: Congressional Quarterly Weekly Review, April 3, 2004, 790; 2008 Statistical Abstract of the United States, tab, 392 p. 244.

poll results, and mailgrams, often at the encouragement of radio or television talk shows or interest groups mobilizing their memberships. These communicative individuals, however, are often not representative of the majority in a member's constituency and tend to hold their positions with greater intensity than the average voter. And Congress itself has become more extreme in its views than the public in general. Republican members have become more conservative and Democrats more liberal. Even though 42 percent of Americans still identify as "moderates," by 2004 only 8 percent of House members were centrists and 9 percent of the Senate.[25]

Electing Members of Congress

Elections determine who gets to represent the rest of us. Because reelection is an important objective for almost all members of Congress and *the* most important objective for many, members work at being reelected throughout their terms.[26] Most are successful, though senators are not as secure as members of the House.

Campaigns

In the nineteenth century, political parties organized congressional and presidential campaigns, and the candidates had relatively little to do. Today, however, congressional as well as presidential campaigns are candidate centered.

Congressional candidates usually hire the staff, raise the money, and organize their own campaigns. They may recruit campaign workers from local political parties; interest groups they belong to; unions, church, civic, or other voluntary organizations; or they may simply turn to friends and acquaintances.[27]

Political parties do have a significant role, however. National and local parties work hard to recruit potential candidates. Presidents make personal appeals to fellow party members who they think can run strong races, and national campaign committees also recruit aggressively. Said one Democratic congressional campaign chair, "I'm not looking for liberals or conservatives. That's not my bag. I'm looking for winners."[28]

Parties redouble their efforts when, as in recent elections, control of Congress is at stake. Besides, if candidates are not closely linked to parties, then, once elected, they are not as indebted to their party nor as obligated to reflect party views. Recognizing this, national parties have increasingly provided services to congressional candidates—helping them manage their campaigns, develop issues, advertise, raise money, and conduct opinion polls. National party organizations give substantial sums of money to congressional candidates.

In 2006, the Democrats worked especially hard to recruit candidates who would be seen as tough on national security. Thus they made a special effort to recruit those who had served in the military, such as Jim Webb (D-Va.), who upset incumbent Republican George Allen in Virginia, or who had moderate records, such as Bob Casey (D-Pa.), who defeated conservative Republican Rick Santorum in Pennsylvania.

Congressional Media Campaigns

To wage a serious campaign, the challenger or a contender for an open seat must wage a media campaign. Candidates hire media consultants and specialists in polling, advertising, and fundraising. The old-style politician who might have been effective in small groups but who cannot appear poised and articulate on television has given way to some-

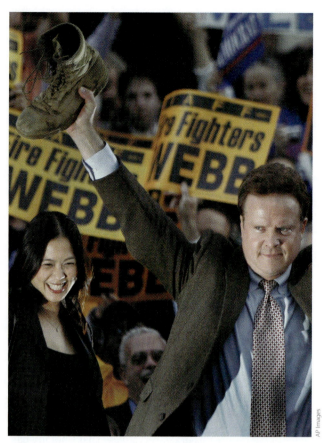

AP Images

Democrat Jim Webb, with his wife, celebrates his election to the Senate from Virginia. During his campaign, Webb criticized the Iraq war and wore the combat boots of his son, a marine serving in the war. Webb was one of six Democratic challengers who unseated Republican incumbents in the 2006 elections, giving the Democrats a majority in the Senate.

one who can project an attractive television image. Candidates are elected on the basis of their media skills, which may not be the same skills as those needed to be a good lawmaker.

Campaign Money

An old adage says, "Half the money spent on campaigns is wasted. The trouble is, we don't know which half." This bromide helps explain why congressional campaigns are expensive. There is a kind of "campaign arms race" as each candidate tries to do what the other candidate does and a little more, escalating costs year by year. We examined congressional fundraising in the previous chapter on money.

The Advantages of Incumbency

Most members are reelected even if they have not done that much for their home districts.[29] Indeed, one Republican member remarked, "Let's face it, you have to be a bozo to lose this job."[30] Still, incumbents believe the best way to

ensure victory is to be so good at serving the home district, so successful in getting money for their districts, and so well known to the voters that no serious rival will want to run. Incumbents hope potential rivals will bide their time and wait for a better year or run for some other office.[31]

Given the advantages of office that incumbents have in name recognition and in favors they can do their constituents, you may wonder why they worry about losing. But worry they do. One political scientist proclaimed that members feel "unsafe at any margin."[32] No matter how big their last victory, they worry that their next campaign will bring defeat. And despite the high reelection rate of incumbents, a few do lose. This fear prompts members to spend even more of their energies preparing for the next campaign.

For the most part, this fear is misplaced. Turnover in Congress comes primarily from those who decide not to run. Even in the anti-incumbent election of 2006, less than 10 percent of House incumbents lost (all of them Republicans). In 2004, a more typical recent election, only 2 percent lost and only about three dozen of the 435 seats were even competitive.

The advantages of incumbency are becoming larger. As we described earlier, most House districts are safe seats. Legislators protect incumbents of their own party, but in doing so create safe seats for the other party, too.

House members really do have to offend their constituencies to lose. Most senators are also reelected, but the probabilities of defeat are higher than for the House. In the late 1970s and early 1980s, it was not uncommon for a third of the senators running to be defeated. Those proportions have decreased, but in 2006 around 20 percent of senators running lost. Even so, the electoral benefit of incumbency still exists for the great majority of candidates who choose to run for reelection.[33]

Before they even take the oath of office, newly elected representatives are given an introduction to the advantages of incumbency. At meetings arranged by the Democratic and Republican leadership and by the House Administrative Committee, new members learn about free mailing privileges, computers and software to help them target letters to specialized groups of constituents, facilities to make videotapes and audiotapes to send to hometown media, and other "perks" designed to keep members in touch with their constituencies and, not coincidentally, to help win reelection (see the box "Pay and Perks of Office").

Incumbents win because they are better known than nonincumbents. Voters have seen their representatives and senators on television or received mail from them, and they can give a general rating of their performance.[34] Although most voters can correctly identify their representatives and senators as liberal or conservative, only a small minority know how these legislators voted on any issue.[35] Therefore, incumbents have the advantage of name recognition without the disadvantage of having voters know how they actually cast their votes on most pieces of legislation.

PAY AND PERKS OF OFFICE

The first members of Congress made $6 a day, which paid for boardinghouse accommodations, firewood, candles, their meals, and a mileage allowance for travel to and from the capital.[1] Today members receive a handsome salary indexed to inflation, a generous benefits package including full medical and dental care, and money for office, staff, mailing, and travel.

Personal Benefits
Salary
Congress has indexed members' pay to inflation so that members no longer have to vote directly each session on increases. Thus, salaries have increased from $90,000 in 1989 to $169,300 in 2008. (The Speaker gets an additional $48,000 and the majority and minority leaders in both chambers an additional $19,000 over the base pay.) Members are among the top 5 percent of American wage earners.[2]

Health Care
For a modest monthly premium, members can opt for a first-class private health care plan or care at one of two military hospitals. Taxpayers spend millions more each year to keep five doctors and fourteen nurses on site at the Capitol's Wellness Center, which also houses a pool and gymnasium, in nearby congressional office buildings.

Pensions
Members of Congress are required to pay Social Security taxes, but they also have 401(k) plans and a generous federal pension program into which they pay just 1.3 percent of their salaries. They can begin collecting pensions as early as age fifty if they have served at least twenty years, but benefits cannot exceed 80 percent of a member's final salary, though this figure is adjusted for inflation over time. A typical payout over the lifetime of a retired member is estimated at between $1 million and $2 million. Members' contributions may account for as little as one-fifth of that amount.[3] If Congress voted to convert its pension system to the same kind of cash balance plan many members have advocated for American workers, the value of their pensions would drop by as much as 60 percent.[4]

And, should members find themselves under criminal investigation, they can be reassured that only certain felony convictions will prevent them from receiving benefits. The law was tightened in 2007 to deny benefits to those convicted of perjury, bribery, or fraud, but as many as twenty members with felony convictions before 2007 have been able to collect retirement benefits, some while in prison.

Benefits That Help Reelection Chances
Office and Clerical Support
Representatives are authorized to hire up to eighteen staff members out of their MRA (member's representational allowance, about $1.3 million per year). In addition, they are given an office allowance to pay for equipment, supplies, and office space and furniture in their home district. Senators' staff budgets vary with the population of their states. There is no limit on the number of aides senators can hire with their MRAs, and average staff size is from thirty to thirty-five full-time workers.[5] Members who serve as committee chairs or in leadership positions have additional staff and larger expense allowances.

Travel, Media, and Mailing Allowances
Members' office allowances also provide funds for travel to and from their districts, the amount set according to distance from Washington. We have already discussed the franking privilege, the free recording facilities, and the website server.

Other Perks
Members of Congress enjoy many other perquisites, including subsidized travel abroad, subsidized meals in the Senate and House dining rooms, free parking in Washington and at airports, free car washes, and a child care center.

A Final Benefit
Taxpayers fund life insurance policies and a death benefit equal to a year's salary for each member of Congress. And if a legislator so desires, the sergeant-at-arms will arrange for an undertaker to plan the member's final journey.

[1] Per diem and travel allowances for the first members were verified in 2002 when Senate custodial staff found an eighteenth-century ledger with payment accounts.
[2] Salary and retirement data are from usgovinfo.about.comlibrary/weekly/aa031200a.htm. The websites of the Center for Public Integrity (www.publicintegrity.org) and the National Taxpayers Union (taxpayersunion.org) are also excellent for tracking congressional pay and benefits.
[3] Data from National Taxpayers Union (www.ntu.org/)
[4] Pension comparison is from *Now with Bill Moyers*, Public Broadcasting System, July 2, 2004, www.pbs.org/now.
[5] Roger H. Davidson, Walter J. Oleszek, and Frances E. Lee, *Congress and Its Members*, 11th ed. (Washington: CQ Press, 2007), 145.

Incumbents' high level of public recognition is not so surprising given that members of Congress spend much of their time and energy looking for and using opportunities to make themselves known to their constituents. Members spend half or more of their days in their district, making an average of thirty-five trips home a year—at taxpayers' expense.[36] Congress is recessed during major holidays, part of the summer, and prior to elections—the House and Senate often do not meet at all in August, a month designated as a "District Work Period."

What are the specific advantages that members have as incumbents?

Casework

Arguably the main advantage of incumbency is the opportunity that being in office gives representatives to perform services and do favors for their constituents. Members send constituents calendars, U.S. flags that have flown over the Capitol, and publications of the federal government. This is one of the best ways members of Congress have to make themselves known in their districts and to create a kind of patron-client relationship. You will not read about this in the Constitution, where the duties of Congress are defined. But in practice, electoral politics has meant that members must spend a great deal of their time serving the specific interests of their districts, which are not necessarily synonymous with the interests of the nation as a whole. Members take this aspect of their representational responsibilities very seriously because it is their own constituents who will reelect them—or not.

Collectively, the House and Senate receive close to 200 million e-mail messages each year and more than 18 million pieces of regular mail.[37] The work of answering questions and doing personal favors for constituents who write or call for help is called **constituency service** or **casework**. More than 30 percent of senators' staffs and almost half of all representatives' staffs are located in their home state or district offices to better serve constituents.[38]

Congressional staff function as red-tape cutters for everyone from elderly citizens having difficulties with Social Security to small-town mayors trying to get federal grants for new sewer systems. They provide information to students working on term papers, people looking for federal jobs, citizens puzzled about which federal agency to ask for assistance, or residents trying to get information about a relative in the military. Typically, responsibility for mediating with federal agencies is divided among the casework staffers by issue area, allowing them to specialize and resolve constituents' problems—passports, immigration, Social Security payments, and the like—more efficiently.

Of course, not all casework is directed toward winning reelection. Some members say they enjoy their casework more than their policy roles, perhaps because the results of casework are more immediate and tangible. Individually, they may have limited power in trying to get important legislation passed, but in dealing with a constituent's problems, their power is much greater because of their clout with bureaucrats. A phone call or letter to a federal agency will bring attention to the constituent's problem. And casework does allow members to build nonpartisan and seemingly nonpolitical ties with their constituents.

Mailing Privileges

For the 110th Congress, taxpayers will provide more than a half billion dollars for office and franking expenses (mailing costs).[39] The franking privilege is a great asset of incumbency because it allows members to write their constituents without paying for postage out of pocket or using campaign funds. (The frank is a facsimile of the member's signature, and it works like metered mail, with the frank appearing where the stamp would be.) It is not free; Congress pays the postal bill at the end of each year. The value of the frank has been estimated as equivalent to $350,000 in campaign contributions.

The frank helps each member increase name recognition (and newly elected members can begin using the frank immediately, even before they are sworn in). Much of the time, the frank is used to send constituents material they have requested, such as government forms or publications, and this too increases a member's name recognition. But members can send out newsletters that inform constituents of their work for the district or to survey constituents' issue positions. These mass mailings cannot be sent out within sixty days of elections, however. Nor can the frank be used to send personal correspondence to constituents or to ask them for their vote or a campaign contribution.

The use of the frank has declined by about two-thirds over the past twenty years. Partly this reflects tighter regulation of its use and partly it reflects the increase in electronic communication.

Examples of letters members send to their constituents using the franking privilege.

AP Images/Gerald Herbert

Media and Technology Advantages

In addition to regular mailings, members use increasingly sophisticated production equipment and technology to make television and radio shows to send home. And Congress provides them a server for their official websites.

Constituents may see or hear stories about their representatives on local television and radio news programs produced in congressional studios by the representatives' own staff and paid for out of campaign or party funds. Members like to tape themselves at committee meetings asking questions or being referred to as "Mr. (or Madam) Chairman" (many members chair at least a subcommittee). The tape then is edited to a thirty-second sound bite and sent to local television stations. Often stations run these productions as news features without telling their viewers that they are essentially self-promotion pieces prepared by the members. Congressional staffers also write press releases about accomplishments of their bosses and fax them to local newspapers, which often print them as written.

Every member of Congress has an official website. Though it focuses on congressional business and cannot be used to solicit funds or do campaigning, it provides voluminous information about the member. Typical websites allow constituents to ask for help, or order American flags that have flown over the Capitol, and they have a section for press releases, information about the member's policy positions, and perhaps headlines about what the member has done for her district or state lately.

Fundraising

As we have discussed in the previous chapter, incumbents have advantages in fundraising. Committee assignments are also extremely important in fundraising. If a member wins a seat on one of the powerful "juice" committees—one that considers legislation important to big-money interests or that appropriates money—the chances of attracting large campaign donations are greatly increased.

Pork-Barrel Funding

Incumbents can gain the attention of or curry favor with constituents by obtaining funds for special projects, new programs, buildings, or other public works that bring jobs, benefits, and business to their districts or states. Such benefits are widely known as **pork-barrel projects**. A pork feature of virtually every annual budget is money for yet another bomber, fighter plane, weapon, or military construction project the Pentagon has not requested. Universities are also perennial winners in the pork sweepstakes, receiving several billion dollars for campus projects.

Because members consider pork-barrel projects crucial to their reelection chances, there is little support in Congress for eliminating projects most know to be unwise

or wasteful. David Stockman, director of the Office of Management and Budget during the Reagan administration, observed, "There's no such thing as a fiscal conservative when it comes to his district."[40] Liberals and conservatives, Democrats and Republicans, protect these kinds of projects.

Voting for Congress

In Chapter 8, we reviewed the impact of parties, issues, and candidates on voting choices. The same factors influence voting choices in congressional races.

Party loyalty, candidate evaluations, and issues are important factors in congressional elections just as in presidential ones.[41] Party loyalty is even more important for congressional than for presidential elections because congressional elections are less visible, so more people base their vote on party identification. Incumbency is also much more important than in presidential races. The result is that increasingly, since about 1960, voters have split their tickets in voting for presidential and congressional candidates. Bill Clinton had to deal with a Republican majority in both houses during most of his presidency, and George W. Bush had to work with a Democratic majority in each house after the 2006 midterm elections.

Normally, the party of a winning presidential candidate gains seats during a presidential election year and loses a number of seats in the midterm election. This maintains a sort of equilibrium in party control of Congress.[42]

To some extent, midterm election results are a referendum on how well citizens think the president is doing. In 1998, Clinton was given credit for the economic good times the country was experiencing, and in 2002, voters rewarded the Republicans for Bush's strong antiterrorist stance. But in 2006, voters delivered a rebuke to the Republicans, who lost twenty-nine House seats and six Senate seats, a majority of voters decided that the Iraq War was not going well and that the president and his party were not doing a competent job of leading the country. This contrasted with the midterm elections of 1998 and 2002, when the president's party actually gained a few seats.

How Congress Is Organized

An institution with 535 voting members that must make thousands of policy decisions every year without benefit of a unified leadership is an institution not likely to work quickly or efficiently. Like all organizations, legislatures need some structure to be able to accomplish their purposes. Congress does have both a leadership system and a committee structure, but each is organized along party lines. Alongside this partisan organization exist many other groups—special interest caucuses, coalitions, work and study groups, and task forces—whose membership cuts

Former Senator Ted Stevens (R-Alk.), called "Uncle Ted" by his constituents because of his ability to obtain federal money for the state, secured $1.5 million to replace this bus stop outside the Anchorage Museum of History and Art.

across party lines or reflects the division of interests within party caucuses. Some of this micro-organizing is a means of bypassing the committee system that dominates Congress's legislative and oversight functions.

The Evolution of Congressional Organization

The Constitution calls for the members of the House of Representatives to select a **Speaker of the House** to act as its presiding officer and for the vice president of the United States to serve as president (or presiding officer) of the Senate. ⭐ Art. I, Sect. 2 & 3. But the Constitution does not say anything about the powers of these officials, nor does it require any further internal organization. So little about the Speaker is specified in the Constitution that there is no requirement the position be held by a member of the House.

The first House, meeting in New York in 1789, had slow and cumbersome procedures. For its first several sessions, Congress's legislative work was accomplished by appointing ad hoc committees. By the Third Congress, there were about 350 committees, and the system had become too unwieldy. Soon permanent committees were created, each with continuing responsibilities in one area, such as taxes or trade.[43]

As parties developed, the selection of the Speaker became a partisan matter, and the Speaker became as much a party leader as a legislative manager. The seventh Speaker, Henry Clay (Whig-Ky.), who served ten of the years between 1811 and 1825, transformed the speakership from a ceremonial office to one of real leadership. To maintain party loyalty and discipline, he used his powers to appoint committee members and chairs. Under Clay's leadership, the House was the dominant branch, but its influence declined when it, like the rest of government, could not cope with the divisiveness of the slavery issue. At the time it was said that "the only people in Congress who are not carrying a revolver are those carrying two revolvers."[44] By 1856, it took 133 ballots to elect a Speaker. Many physical fights broke out on the House floor; duels were held outside.[45]

The Senate, a smaller body than the House, was less tangled in procedures, less rule-bound, and more effective in its operation. Its influence rose as visitors packed the Senate gallery to hear the great debates over slavery waged by Daniel Webster (Mass.), John C. Calhoun (S.C.), and Clay (who had moved from the House). During this era, senators were elected by state legislatures, not directly by the people. ⭐ Art. I, Sect. 3. Thus they had strong local party ties and often used their influence to get presidential appointments for home-state party members. But the Senate, too, became ineffective as the nation moved toward civil war. Senators carried arms to protect themselves as debates over slavery turned to violence.

After the Civil War, with the presidency weakened by the impeachment of Andrew Johnson, strong party leadership reemerged in the House, and a period of congressional government began. Speaker **Thomas Reed** (R-Me.), nicknamed "The Czar" by his colleagues, assumed the authority to name members and chairs of committees and to chair the **Rules Committee**, which decided which bills were to come to the floor for debate. A major consequence of the Speaker's extensive powers was greater party discipline. Members who voted against their party might be punished by a loss of committee assignments or chairmanships.

At the same time, both the House and the Senate became more professional. The emergence of "national" problems and a proactive Congress made a congressional career more prestigious. Prior to the Civil War, membership turnover was high; members of the House served an average of only one term; senators, only four years. After the war, the strengthening of parties and the growth of the one-party South, where Democrats controlled virtually all elective offices, made reelection easier, thus offering the possibility of a congressional career.

Figure 2 │ House Incumbents Have Had Secure Jobs in Recent Years

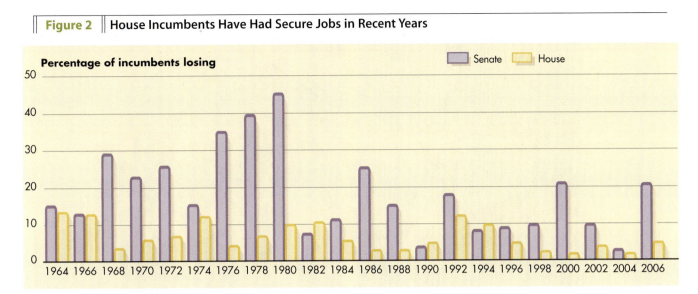

In the 1980s and 1990s, more House incumbents lost in the reapportionment years (1982 and 1991); in the 1970s, most lost in 1974, the Watergate year. In the 1960s, reapportionment occurred both before the 1964 and 1966 election. Senate results do not reflect this cycle because, of course, there is no redistricting of the Senate constituencies. Each senator represents the whole state.
SOURCE: Statistical Abstract of the United States 2004: Center for Responsive Politics (opensecrets.org/bigpicture/reelect.php?cycle=2006)

This desire for permanent careers in the House produced an interest in reform. Members wanted a chance at choice committee seats and did not want to be controlled by the Speaker. Resistance against the dictatorial practices of Reed and his successor, **Joseph Cannon** (R-Ill.), grew. Cannon, more conservative than many of his fellow Republicans, used his powers to block legislation he disliked, to punish those who opposed him, and even to refuse to recognize members who wished to speak. In 1910, there was a revolt against "Cannonism," which had become a synonym for the arbitrary wielding of the Speaker's powers.

The membership voted to remove the Speaker from the Rules Committee and to strip him of his authority to appoint committees and their chairs. The revolt weakened party influence because discipline could no longer be maintained by the Speaker's punishment of members through loss of committee assignments. And it gave committees and their chairs a great deal of independence from leadership influence.

The Senate also was undergoing a major reform. As part of the Progressive movement, pressure began to build for the direct popular election of senators. The election of senators by state legislatures had made many senators pawns of special interests—the big monopolistic corporations (called trusts) and railroads. In a day when millionaires were not as common as now, the Senate was referred to as the "Millionaires' Club" because of whose interests they were thought to represent.

Not surprisingly, the Senate first refused to consider a constitutional amendment providing for its direct election,

although in some states popular balloting on senatorial candidates took place anyway. Finally, under the threat of a call for a constitutional convention, which many members of Congress feared might lead to other changes in the Constitution, a direct-election amendment was passed in the House and Senate in 1912 and ratified by the states a year later. ⭐
Seventeenth Amendment These reforms of the early twentieth century dispersed power in both the House and the Senate and weakened leadership. House members no longer feared the kind of retribution levied by Speaker Cannon on members who deviated from party positions. In the Senate, popular elections made senators responsive to the diverse interests of the electorate rather than to party leaders.

Contemporary Leadership Positions

The Speaker of the House is the only leadership position specified in the Constitution. Other leadership positions came into being with political parties, and the Founders did not anticipate institutionalized national political parties.

House Leadership Positions

The leaders of each party are selected by their respective members sitting in caucus—meeting as a group to conduct party business. **Party caucus** refers both to party meetings and to the party members collectively (alternatively known as the party conference). The House Republican Caucus (or Conference), for example, consists of all Republicans serv-

Vitriolic exchanges are not a new phenomenon in Congress. Shown here is a fight in the House of Representatives in 1798. After Rep. Matthew Lyon (Vt.) spit on Rep. Roger Griswold (Conn.) and the House refused to expel Lyon, Griswold attacked Lyon with a cane. Lyon defended himself with fire tongs as other members of Congress looked on—with some amusement, it seems.

ing in the House, and the Democratic Caucus (or Conference) consists of all Democratic members. When Independents or third-party members are elected to the House, they can ask to caucus with one of the major parties.

The full House must elect the Speaker of the House, as specified in the Constitution, but it is a straight party-line vote, so the real selection is made in the majority party's caucus. Once elected, the Speaker becomes second in line to succeed to the presidency, after the vice president (provided the Speaker is not foreign-born). The Speaker's institutional task is to act as presiding officer and to see that legislation moves through the House.

Party leadership positions in the House, which have evolved through practice, include a majority leader, a minority leader, and majority and minority whips. The **majority leader** is second in command to the Speaker and is officially in charge of the party's legislative agenda (since the Speaker is technically an officer of the House, not of her party). The majority leader, working with the Speaker, also schedules votes on bills. The **minority leader** is, as the name suggests, the leader of the minority party. **Whips** originated in the British House of Commons, where they were named after the "whipper in," the rider who keeps the hounds together in a fox hunt. This aptly describes the whips' role in Congress. Party whips try to maintain contact with party members, determine which way they are leaning on votes, and attempt to gain their support. Assisting the majority and minority whips are a number of deputy

and assistant whips who keep tabs on their assigned state delegations.

Party organization in the House also includes committees that assign party members to standing committees, work out the party's stance on major policy issues, plan legislative and campaign strategies, and allocate funds to party members running for reelection.

Because the Speaker has become more a party than an institutional leader, he or she is expected to use the speakership to maximize partisan advantage in committee and staff appointments and to secure the passage of measures preferred by the party. For this reason, the person selected usually has been someone who has served in the House a long time, is a skilled parliamentarian, and an ideological moderate who can negotiate compromises and put together legislative majorities.

Trying to win partisan support is often difficult, but the Speaker has some rewards and punishments to dispense for loyalty and disloyalty. Speakers have a say in who gets to sit on which committees, which committees will be given jurisdiction over complex bills, what bills will come to the House floor for a vote and under what rules they will be considered, and how their party's congressional campaign funds are allocated. The Speaker also decides who will be recognized to speak on the floor of the House and whether motions are relevant. She has the authority to appoint members to conference and select committees and to control some material benefits, such as the assignment of extra office space. Speakers also have the power to name the chair of the Rules Committee and all of their party's members on the committee. Despite these formal powers, the Speaker must be persuasive to be effective and also attentive to the reelection needs of members of the party caucus. As one veteran legislator has described the Speaker's role, "It's all about your caucus. Never, ever, use your power to twist the results. . . . The Speaker must be empowered at all times to make the call. But you must be sure that your decisions don't cost you and your membership the majority."[46]

In modern times, the only Speaker to attempt the level of control achieved by such strong predecessors as Reed and Cannon was **Newt Gingrich** (R-Ga.). Before his election in 1995, Gingrich had been the intellectual and tactical leader of conservative House Republicans. Like other Speakers who were too controlling, Gingrich met with rebellion in his own party, had to fight back a challenge to his leadership in his third year, and resigned his House seat after his fourth year as Speaker. Gingrich's demands for party discipline in support of a national legislative program (the so-called Contract with America) undercut the power of committee chairs and also left many members with too little flexibility to respond to their constituencies, which risked their chances for reelection. This is one reason why an ideological moderate with a conciliatory manner is often sought for the Speaker's position.

Dennis Hastert (R-Ill.), Gingrich's successor in 1999, came to the leadership more in the mold of a traditional Speaker, even though he had been elected whip as the protégé of Majority Leader **Tom Delay** (R-Tex.), whose nickname "The Hammer" described his methods. Hastert had a friendly, low-key demeanor and was seen as a mediator and persuader in contrast to the agenda-driven disciplinarians Gingrich and Delay.

After the Republicans won the White House and regained control of the Senate in the 2000 elections, Hastert became a much more forceful leader, playing velvet-covered mallet to Delay's hammer in what some saw as a good cop–bad cop ploy. But Hastert was not a strong Speaker in the mold of Gingrich or Cannon, both of whom tried to establish a personal power base within an independent Congress. Instead, Hastert acted as a facilitator for the president's agenda and, in the eyes of his critics, as an "enabler" for Delay's strong-arm tactics.[47]

This worked well for Hastert. But when Bush's poll ratings fell to historic lows in 2006, leading to the Republicans loss of majorities in both houses, and Hastert was relegated to the minority, he announced he was resigning his seat. Shortly thereafter, he became a lobbyist. Hastert had been the longest-serving Republican Speaker, in part because he was, by contrast, such a low-key figure and still little known to the public. A colleague called this "the political advantage of being boring."[48]

Rep. James Clyburn (D-S. Car.), the Democratic Whip, is responsible for counting the heads and persuading—"whipping"—party members to support Democratic proposals.

When **Nancy Pelosi** (D-Ca.) became Speaker, she promised to be a leader of the House not of her party; she promised ethics reform and to open up the legislative process. But Pelosi was born into a political family and had been a party fundraiser and organizer long before she ran for Congress; she almost immediately was seen as a party rather than an institutional leader. But her technique has been as different from Gingrich's rigid ideological approach and insistence on party unity as from the retiring Hastert's, who appeared quite happy to be outshone by his second in command. Unlike Hastert, Pelosi maintains a high profile as party spokesperson and chief headcounter and, unlike Gingrich, is willing to bend to the issue needs of more conservative caucus members, especially new members, in order to get as many reelected as possible. As one of the more conservative members of her caucus said, "She's a very practical, tough strategist who knows what people can and what they can't do."[49] By being attentive to the district needs of all caucus members, she also builds loyalty and increases the chances of achieving consensus on party votes.

Senate Leadership

The Senate has no leader comparable to the Speaker of the House. The vice president of the United States is formally the presiding officer and could attend and preside any time he chooses; part of his expense allowance is designated for Senate work. In reality, the vice president attends infrequently and has relatively little power. However, when sitting as Senate president, he is allowed to cast the tie-breaking vote in those rare instances when the Senate is evenly split. ⭐ Article 1, Sect. 3. Therefore, whenever a head count predicts the chance of a deadlocked vote on an important bill, the vice president shows up to preside. Consistent with the Bush administration's hands-on legislative strategy, Richard Cheney was an active presence on Capitol

Hill during his tenure as vice president, making regular trips to his office just off the Senate floor and holding weekly lunches with Republican Senators.

The Senate has an elected president pro tempore, by tradition the senior member of the majority party. It is an honorific post with few duties except to preside over the Senate in the absence of the vice president. In practice, during the conduct of routine day-to-day business, presiding duties are divided among junior senators. This releases the senior member from boring work while giving the Senate's newest members a chance to learn the rules and procedures.

As in the House, both parties also elect assistant floor leaders and whips to help maintain party discipline. These are important, if not essential, positions for working one's way into the top leadership in both the House and the Senate.

The position of Senate majority leader was not created until 1911 and has often been held by individuals of no particular distinction in their parties. The office has none of the Speakership's potential for control of chamber proceedings. A congressional watcher once said the majority leader "is often more a coat-check attendant than a maitre d' or chef."[50] The instances of powerful majority leaders are few, the most notable being **Lyndon Johnson** (D-Tex.). He assumed office at a time when the Democrats had a slim hold on the Senate, giving him an opportunity to exercise his extraordinary powers of personal persuasion to keep party members in line on key votes. Johnson's reputation was made through a combination of his forceful personality and mastery of the legislative process (he had been a staff aide to the House Speaker and then served in the House before election to the Senate). He made it his business to know everything about his colleagues—"what they drank, where their wives wanted to go on junkets, whether they had a mistress" or were "happy with their parking space [and] what the interests and needs of their constituents were." Acquiring this information and being "ruthless" in using it made him, by one estimation, the "greatest vote counter ever in Congress."[51] There is nothing inherent in the office to give a majority leader the power Johnson had, and no one has had it since.

The Senate majority leader is a spokesperson for his party's legislative agenda and is supposed to help line up members' votes on key issues. But procedurally, the Senate is a free-for-all compared to the House, with "every man and woman for him- or herself."[52] One observer attributes the chamber's resistance to modernization and reform to "its anti-majoritarian and unbounded quality, its free play of antique egos, its cluttered toolbox of little-used procedures."[53] Unlike the Speaker of the House, the Senate majority leader cannot control the terms under which a bill is considered on the floor; instead, rules are assigned by unanimous consent agreements, after negotiations with other Senators and a bill's floor managers.

As Senate majority leader, Lyndon Johnson (left), shown here with Sen. Theodore Green (D-R.I.), "used physical persuasion in addition to intellectual and moral appeals. He was hard on other people's coat lapels." If the man he was trying to persuade was shorter than Johnson, "he was inclined to move up close and lean over the subject of his persuasive efforts." If the man was taller, Johnson "would come at him from below, somewhat like a badger." Quotes are from Eugene McCarthy, *Up 'til Now* (New York: Harcourt, 1987).

The majority leader also has little power to stop a filibuster—a procedural maneuver that allows a minority to block a bill from coming to the floor by monopolizing the session with nonstop speeches. This means that a majority leader needs to do much more than keep his own party in line to keep legislation moving through the Senate. He—there have been no women majority leaders yet—can influence the general atmosphere of deliberation in the Senate by adopting an approach to working with the minority party that is either conciliatory or partisan. But whether he chooses a more traditional conciliatory and clubby approach or a more aggressively partisan approach, the majority leader must be less strident than a Speaker like Gingrich and less of an enforcer than Hastert, because those styles would never be accepted in the more egalitarian atmosphere of the Senate. As Arlen Spector said (R-Pa.), "Senators don't get here to be pushed around."[54] If senators see themselves as less subject to central discipline it is in part because there are only 100 of them, and at any given time, a number of them aspire to or are actively running for the presidency.

The Senate minority leader's job is similar to that of the majority leader in that its effectiveness depends on a limited package of incentives and procedural ploys to enforce party discipline. Historically, the Senate's majority and minority leaders have worked closely together to conduct Senate business. But if either or both are seen as overly partisan, or more interested in personal political ambitions than in running the Senate, it can weaken the collegial relationship and slow the legislative process. One more sign of the deterioration of cross-party cooperation in the Senate is that majority and minority leaders have gone out on the campaign trail to defeat their counterparts in their reelection bids, something unheard of under old rules of collegiality.[55]

Both the majority and minority leaders must articulate their parties' issue positions and try to win support for bills supported by their parties. Fulfilling this duty is tricky if either leader has presidential aspirations because he must carve out issue positions that distinguish him from other senators in his party who are also seeking the nomination.

In representing the party, senate leaders also may undercut their political viability at home if their constituents are more conservative or liberal than the leadership of the national parties. In 2004, Minority Leader Tom Daschle (D-S.D.), a high-profile spokesman for party positions that were more liberal than those held by his constituents, became the first senate party leader in fifty-two years to lose a bid for reelection

Harry Reid (D-Nev.), who succeeded Daschle as minority leader and who became Senate majority leader in 2007, must walk the same fine line. Also a Democrat from a Republican state, Reid is more conservative (an opponent of abortion rights, for example) than the mainstream of his party. As the spokesman for the more liberal Senate Democratic caucus, he risks his own reelection. This contrasts with the situation faced by his counterpart in the House: Speaker Pelosi frequently has to defend Democratic caucus positions that are more conservative than her own or those of her very liberal San Francisco district. The difference is that Pelosi has a safe seat, one she typically wins with 60 to 70 percent majorities.

Committees

Much of the work of Congress is done in committees. Observers of American politics take this for granted, yet the power of legislative committees is rare among Western democracies. In Britain, for example, committees cannot offer amendments that change the substance of a bill. In our Congress, the substance of a bill can be changed in committee *even after its passage* by both chambers.

The division of labor provided by committees and subcommittees enables Congress to consider a vast number of bills each year. If every member had to review every measure in detail, it would be impossible to deal with the current workload. Instead, most bills are killed in committee, leaving many fewer for each member to evaluate before a floor vote. Committees also help members develop specializations. Members who remain on the same committee for some time gain expertise and are less dependent on professional staff and executive agencies for background information.

Standing Committees

In the 110th Congress there were twenty-two **standing committees** in the House and twenty in the Senate. Each deals with a different subject matter, such as finance or education or agriculture. Each has a number of subcommittees, totaling 105 in the House and 72 in the Senate for the 110th Congress.[56] The number of committees and subcommittees fluctuates, declining during years of reform and cost-cutting and increasing during years of government growth. During the Bush administration, as government grew, with a new cabinet department and two new intelligence agencies, so did the number of congressional committees.

The number of seats on any committee also can change from one session to another as party caucuses try to satisfy as many of their members' preferences as possible. Standing committees vary in size from ten to seventy-five members in the House and from six to twenty-nine in the Senate. Party ratios—the number of Democrats relative to Republicans on each committee—are determined by the majority party in the House and negotiated by the leadership of both parties in the Senate. The ratios are generally set in rough proportion to party membership in the particular chamber, but the majority party gives itself a disproportionate number of seats on several key committees to ensure control.

Committee Membership

Committees are essential not only to the legislative process but also for building a power base within Congress, attracting campaign donors, gaining the influence and name recognition needed for reelection, and perhaps even higher office. New members and members seeking committee changes express their preferences to their party's selection committee. The party tries to accommodate members' requests for assignments that will be most beneficial to their constituencies, but there is some self-selection by seniority.

Historically, junior members did not ask for the most prestigious posts, but this tradition has broken down as freshmen have become bolder in their requests and even receive instruction in how to get the assignments they want. And if there are freshmen members whose reelection races are likely to be tough or whom the party leadership believes have the potential to be future leaders, those members will likely be given helpful committee assignments. For example, Barack Obama was given a position on the influential Foreign Relations Committee in his freshman year, just as Hillary Clinton was given a seat on the important Armed Services Committee, her first choice that would help her burnish credentials for a possible future role as commander in chief.

The committees dealing with appropriations, taxes, and finance are always sought after because having a say in the allocation of money and how the tax burden falls on individuals and businesses gives members power and enhances their ability to help their home districts. These are sometime called "juice committees" because of the advantage they give members in squeezing interested parties for campaign contributions. Most members also want committee assignments that let them tell constituents they are working on problems of the district. Members from rural districts, for example, seek seats on committees that deal with agricultural and trade issues.

Media coverage is another criterion important in deciding committee preference. The work of some committees is more likely to be covered by television. Committees scrambled to hold attention-getting hearings on the new Department of Homeland Security and corporate fraud in 2002 and on 9/11 failures and the reorganization of intelligence agencies in 2004. In 2008, the attention-grabbing issue was the investigation of subprime mortgage lenders. Getting on the right committee is important to those who want to become nationally known. When a journalist once asked Senator Joseph Biden (D-Del.) why he was so newsworthy, Biden replied, "It's the committees, of course." Biden served on the three committees with the greatest media exposure, sufficient to make him a credible potential candidate for the presidency in every Democratic primary season for twenty-five years and finally a vice-presidential candidate who could convincingly balance Barack Obama's lack of foreign policy experience.

The practice of filling each committee with representatives whose districts have an especially strong economic interest in its work encourages committees to be rather parochial in their outlook. It also leads to costly and wasteful legislation; if committee members' constituents benefit from programs under their jurisdiction, the members have no incentive to eliminate them or pare them back. This is one of the biggest weaknesses in the committee system.[57]

Committees are also often filled with members who have financial interests in the businesses they make policies for. Most members who sit on the banking committees own bank stock, many on agriculture committees own agribusiness stock, and those on the armed services committees hold stock in defense industries.[58] Former Senate Majority Leader Bill Frist, an ex-surgeon who held stock in a huge hospital management company founded by his family (one that had paid multimillion-dollar fines for overbilling) made it a legislative priority to help rewrite health care and medical malpractice laws. Billy Tauzin, who, as chair of the Ways and Means Committee, shepherded Bush's huge Medicare drug benefit bill through Congress, immediately left Congress to take a two-million-dollar-a-year job as a lobbyist for the pharmaceutical companies who benefit from the legislation.

Committee Chairs

The chair is usually the most influential member of a committee. Chairs have the authority to call meetings, set agendas, and control committee staff and funds. In addition, chairs usually have strong substantive knowledge of the matters that come before their committees, and this, too, is a source of influence.

Historically, the member of the majority party with the longest service on a committee became its chair by the so-called **seniority rule**. The rule was adopted to protect committee members from powerful Speakers of the House, who often used their authority to award committee chairs to friends and allies. But it allowed members who might be senile, alcoholic, or personally disliked by every member of the committee to become chairs if they were the most senior committee member of the majority party. It also led to chairs who were dictatorial and out-of-step with the rest of their party. In response to those complaints, in the early 1970s both parties agreed that the seniority rule no longer had to be followed.

Since then, the Committee on Committees in the Republican caucus and the Steering and Policy Committee in the Democratic caucus have recommended chairs and voted on committee assignments. However, in the House, the Speaker has power to name members to the Rules Committee and to appoint or recommend the chairs of the most powerful committees. Recent Speakers have used this power to build support for their agendas and to curb inde-

ethical dilemmas | Regulating Mortgages

In 2008 Richard Shelby (R-Ala.), the ranking Republican on the House Banking Committee, was negotiating the provisions of a bill that would decide how much help government would provide to homeowners facing foreclosure as a result of the subprime mortgage crisis. He was also one of the biggest landlords in Tuscaloosa, where the mortgages on his rental property were financed by the very industries he helps regulate and whose interests would be affected by the bill he was helping to write. These same businesses were among his largest campaign contributors; since 2000 he had received almost a million dollars in speaking fees and contributions from the banking industry. He has more often than not supported positions advocated by the Mortgage Bankers' Association.

During his years in Congress, Sen. Shelby's wealth, as reported on his financial disclosure statements, had increased from $9 million to $32 million, mostly from rental property. One of the most lucrative was a 124-unit complex near the University of Alabama, where most of the tenants were students. He took out a $5 million mortgage on it from a Virginia bank, which then sold it to Freddie Mac, the quasi-governmental mortgage underwriter that Sen. Shelby's committee oversees.

Two other senators with seats on the Banking and Finance committees had received discounted terms on home mortgages from Countrywide Financial Corp., one of the firms most deeply implicated in the subprime mortgage crisis and under investigation by Congress. In both cases, the sena-

tors said they had no knowledge they had received Countrywide's "V.I.P." discount. Similarly, Sen. Shelby, who received his mortgage in 2002, well before the subprime mortgage crisis and with no evidence of special deals, said his was a "plain-vanilla commercial loan," one he had no way of knowing would be sold to Freddie Mac.[1]

All three senators were in the position of regulating industries that were helping their political careers with campaign contributions and at the same time improving their financial picture. Is this an ethical dilemma? Should senators be trusted to put the public interest first or should they be made to recuse themselves from regulating industries in which they have a personal stake?

[1] Eric Lipton and Eric Lichtblau, "Senator's Ties to Real Estate Draw Criticism," *New York Times*, May 9, 2008, A1.

---

pendent action by committee chairs. In her first year, Speaker Pelosi allowed the seniority system to name most chairs but she did use her powers to bypass several senior members to award the chair of a few important committees to more junior members from whom she could expect less independence. Pelosi also used her power to ensure that women (22 percent of the Democrats) and minority members (28 percent) would hold a percentage of chairs equal to their proportion in the Democratic caucus.[59]

Some members prefer the Speaker appointment system because they believe it can prevent potentially damaging intraparty fights over who will chair important committees, just as the seniority principle did, without producing autocratic chairs, who were common under the seniority rule. Before 1975, committee chairs were less supportive of their party than other party members in roll-call votes.[60] They could go their own way with impunity because their powerful positions were guaranteed. Since 1975, committee chairs in the House have had to be party loyalists if they wanted to keep their jobs. In that sense, the reforms have strengthened party influence in Congress, especially in the

House, where it has led to a greater concentration of power, away from committees and to the leadership.

During the Bush administration the White House rather than the party leadership established policy for the Republican caucus in both houses. When Arlen Specter (R-Pa.), a supporter of abortion rights, made public statements after the 2004 elections that the Bush administration should send the Senate Supreme Court nominees who were moderates if it wanted to ensure confirmation, the White House made it clear that if Specter wanted to serve as chair of the Judiciary Committee he would have to support any and all of the president's court nominees. That Specter backed down is evidence that the power of both House and Senate chairs diminished during the years of the Bush administration when Republicans controlled Congress.

There is now a three-term limit on service as a committee chair. Opponents argue that term limits punish experience and weaken oversight as chairs are forced out just when they have become familiar with the operations of the agencies they oversee.[61] Under Democratic control the term-limit rule for chairs has remained in place. This is another sign that party leadership continues its attempt to dominate the work of committees.

Subcommittees

Each standing committee is divided into subcommittees with jurisdiction over part of the committee's area of responsibility. The House Foreign Affairs Committee, for example, has seven subcommittees—Africa and Global Health; Asia, the Pacific, and the Global Environment; the Western Hemisphere; the Middle East and South Asia; Europe; International Organizations, Human Rights and Oversight; and Terrorism, Nonproliferation, and Trade. These roughly parallel the seven subcommittees of the Senate's Foreign Relations Committee.

In the days of strict seniority rule, standing committee chairs chose the subcommittee chairs and controlled subcommittees' jurisdiction, budget, and staff. For the past three decades, each House and Senate subcommittee operates semi-independently of the parent committee.

These reforms, sometimes called the "subcommittee bill of rights," allowed more members, especially newer members, to share in important decisions. In this way, they made Congress more democratic. But by diffusing power, they also made it less efficient because the very number of subcommittees contributed to government gridlock. Complex legislation might be sent to several subcommittees, each with its own interests and jurisdiction.

In general, there is a tendency toward committee creep, with periods of committee reduction followed by periods of growth, resulting in many overlapping jurisdictions. When President George W. Bush proposed establishing the cabinet-level Department of Homeland Security, for example, twelve House committees were involved in reviewing the bill.

Select, Special, Joint, and Conference Committees

There are a few other types of congressional committees. *Select* or *special committees* are typically organized on a temporary basis to investigate a specific problem or to hold hearings and issue a report on special problems that arise, such as intelligence agency failures prior to 9/11 or government response to Hurricane Katrina. Speaker Pelosi appointed a Select Committee on Energy Independence and Global Warming as a way to move legislation on which the permanent standing committee on Energy had been unwilling to act. Its chair, John Dingell (D-Mich.), is from a state hard hit by the declining auto industry and he consistently resisted measures that might impose new regulations on the industry. Select and special committees are usually disbanded when their work is completed. The exceptions are the House and the Senate Select Committees on Intelligence and the Senate Select Committee on Ethics, which are in effect permanent committees.

Four joint committees include members from both houses, with the chair alternating between a House and Senate member. Conference committees, appointed whenever the Senate and the House pass different versions of the same bill, also have joint membership. Members from the committees that managed the bill in their respective chambers work out a single version for the full membership to vote on. Conference committees are dissolved after the compromise version is agreed on. Their work is discussed in greater detail in the section on lawmaking.

Task Forces

The traffic jams and turf wars around much committee work have led members of Congress with strong interests in particular areas to look for ways to bypass the committee structure. Task forces and ad hoc committees have existed in the House for decades, used by Democratic and Republican leaders alike, to study major issues and draft legislation, sometimes to speed action on a bill when a committee is dragging its feet or producing an outcome not in accord with what the leadership wants.[62] Speaker Pelosi named a bipartisan House task force to write the 2007 ethics reform bill.

Staff and Support Agencies

The legislative branch encompasses not only elected representatives but also a staff of more than 30,000, about 17,000 of whom work directly for the House and Senate.[63] Today, committee staff alone are equal in number to the entire congressional staff in 1947. But Congress cannot serve its proper role as a check on the executive branch if it does not have its own information base.

To this end, staff in support agencies carry out various research functions. The Government Accountability Office (GAO) checks on the efficiency and effectiveness of executive agencies, the Office of Technology Assessment provides long-range analyses of the effects of new and existing technology, and the Congressional Budget Office provides the expertise and support for Congress's budgeting job. To research complex problems, members can call on the 700 full-time staff of the Congressional Research Service (CRS) in the Library of Congress. These researchers have issue specializations and contacts with experts in the academic world, in all the federal agencies, and with the interest groups that lobby on behalf of these issues. No member of Congress would have the time to develop this kind of expertise, yet without it, competent legislation could not be written, and Congress would not have the background it needs to challenge facts and figures presented in communications from the executive branch. The cost of funding the legislative branch as a whole in 2008 was almost $4.5 billion.[64]

What Congress Does

The importance of Congress is reflected in the major, explicit constitutional powers the Founders gave it: to lay and collect taxes, coin money, declare war and raise and support a military, and regulate commerce with foreign governments and among the states. ⭐ Art. I, Sect. 7 & 8. Most of the named powers—including "All legislative Powers herein granted"—the Constitution invests in the national government were given to Congress. ⭐ Art. I, Sect. 1. These and other powers specifically mentioned in the Constitution are called the *enumerated powers* of Congress.

Congress also has *implied powers*; that is, it is permitted to make all the laws "necessary and proper" to carry out its enumerated powers. Although the Founders did not necessarily foresee it, this tremendous grant of power covers almost every area of human activity.

Lawmaking

In each congressional session, thousands of bills and resolutions are introduced but most die in committee. Of those passed, many are noncontroversial, including the so-called sense of the chamber measures, such as resolutions congratulating the winners of the Super Bowl, or very specific bills such as for the naming of a federal courthouse. In recent years, however, even these conventionally nonpolitical resolutions can become victims of partisanship. In the 109th Congress, Senate Majority Leader Bill Frist refused to allow a vote on a congratulatory resolution offered by New Jersey's two Democratic senators on behalf of their constituent, Bruce Springsteen, noting the thirtieth anniversary of his "Born to Run" album. Although Frist had sponsored his own resolutions honoring events in rock and roll and county music history, he blocked the measure honoring Springsteen for no apparent reason other than that the singer had campaigned for the Democratic presidential nominee in 2004.[65]

How does Congress decide which of the thousands of bills it will pass? As we have noted, the Constitution said virtually nothing about the legislative process itself. The way bills work their way through the House and Senate today evolved with the development of party caucuses and the committee system. The procedures can be very arcane, and every several years, or as often as significant procedural changes require, the parliamentarian of the House of Representatives issues a new version of the pamphlet *How Our Laws are Made* (*http://thomas.loc.gov/home/lawsmade.toc .html*), now in its 23rd edition. The Senate publishes its own online description of the legislative process, which it describes, realistically, as "one way" a bill can become a law. We will reduce the complexities by focusing on some general steps in the process: bill introduction and referral, subcommittee hearings and markup, full committee hearing and markup, calendar/rule assignment by leadership, floor

debate, vote, resolution of differences in House/Senate versions, president's signature or veto, vote to override veto when applicable.

A number of the bills passed each year are private; they resolve an issue an individual or private party has with the government, such as citizenship status or a monetary claim. Our concern is with public bills, those that become laws affecting the general public.

Turning a bill into a law is like running an obstacle course. Opponents have an advantage because it is easier to defeat a bill than to pass one. Will Rogers's observation in the 1930s still reflects the difficulty of passing legislation today: "Congress is so strange. A man gets up to speak and says nothing. Nobody listens—and then everyone disagrees."[66]

Because of the need to win a majority at each stage, the end result is almost always a compromise. That does not mean a compromise of all interests, only of the strongest interests that played a role in shaping the bill. The formal steps by which a bill becomes a law are important but do not reveal the bargaining and trade-offs at every step in the process.

Submission and Referral

Bills may be introduced in either the House or the Senate, except for tax measures (which according to the Constitution must be initiated in the House) ⭐ Art. I, Sect. 7. and appropriations bills (which by tradition are introduced in the House). This reflects the Founders' belief that the chamber directly elected by the people should control the purse strings.

Although the White House initiates much of the legislation Congress enacts, only members can introduce bills for consideration. The president, like interest groups or constituents who initiate legislation, must find congressional sponsors for each bill in his legislative agenda. After a bill's introduction, it is referred to a standing committee by the Speaker of the House or the presiding officer in the Senate. The content of the bill largely determines where it will go, although the Speaker has some discretion, particularly over complex bills that cover more than one subject area. Many such bills are referred to more than one committee simultaneously.

Committee Action

Once the bill reaches a committee, it is assigned to the subcommittee that covers the appropriate subject area. One of the main functions of the subcommittees is to screen bills with little chance of passage. (If a committee kills a bill, there are procedures that members can use to try to get the bill to the floor, but these are used infrequently.) If a subcommittee decides to take up a proposed piece of legislation, it may call hearings. Unless otherwise specified, hearings are open to the public, although few people know about them or would have the time or opportunity to sit in. Consequently, lobbyists fill most of the hearing rooms. For critical meetings, lobbyists will hire messengers to stand in line for them, sometimes all night, and then pack the hearing room. Members who receive financial or other support from groups affected by the legislation often face intense and direct pressure to vote a particular way in committee. Sometimes lobbyists mob members as they leave the hearing room.

After the hearings, House subcommittees hold **markup** sessions using the testimony from the hearings and staff research to rewrite a bill or add amendments. Subcommittee markup is more unusual in the Senate, where more work is done outside the committee structure. Following markup in the subcommittee, if the bill is approved, it is sent to the full committee along with a report explaining the subcommittee's action and reasoning. The standing committee may hold additional hearings and markup sessions.

Scheduling and Rules

Once a House committee approves a bill, it is placed on one of five "calendars," depending on the subject matter of the bill. The Senate has just two calendars: one for private and public bills and another for treaties and nominations. Bills from each calendar are generally considered in the order in which they are reported from committee. In the House, the Rules Committee sets the terms of the debate over the bill by issuing a rule on it. The rule either limits or does not limit debate and determines whether amendments will be permitted. A rule forbidding amendments means that members have to vote yes or no on the bill; there is no chance to change it. If the committee refuses to issue a rule, the bill dies.

In earlier years, the Rules Committee was controlled by a coalition of conservative Democrats and Republicans who used their power to block liberal legislative proposals, including, for decades, meaningful civil rights proposals. Under Republican control from 1995 to 2006 the committee was dominated by the Speaker and the majority leadership rather than by coalitions supporting or opposing specific bills. Speaker Pelosi has followed this practice so that in this era the Rules Committee "has become, unambiguously, a tool of the leadership, with its members taking orders from above and hardly ever shaping policy directly."[67]

The powers inherent in the speakership allow the majority leadership to use or bend rules to force measures to the floor, where only a simple majority is necessary for passage. House members have few tactical options against a Speaker who uses full powers to set the rules. Speaker Hastert was willing to use the rules to prevent amendments and other changes in the leadership-agreed-upon wording of bills. (See box "Party Government and Legislative Gridlock.")

When Democrats assumed control, they vowed that bills would "come to the floor under a procedure that allows open, full and fair debate" and an amendment process that would allow "the minority the right to offer its alternatives…." But in the 110th, Democrats used the closed rules that permit no debate on floor amendments about as often as the Republicans did, claiming that Republicans were using the amendment process not to change, but to kill, bills.[68]

Because the Senate is a smaller body, it can operate with fewer rules and formal procedures. It does not have a Rules Committee. A lot of work is accomplished through the use of privately negotiated unanimous consent agreements, which allow the Senate to dispense with standard rules and define terms for debating and amending a specific bill. As the Senate's workload has increased and its sense of collegiality has decreased, it has become more difficult to get opponents to accept a unanimous consent agreement. A single senator can use parliamentary tactics to freeze the agenda. A senator once held up an antibusing bill for eight months with 604 amendments.

Debate and Vote

Debate on a bill is controlled by the bill managers, usually senior members of the committee that sent the bill to the full chamber. The opposition, too, has its managers, who schedule opposition speeches. "Debates" are not a series of fiery speeches of point and counterpoint. They are often boring recitations delivered to a handful of members, some of whom may be reading, conversing, or walking around the floor. In the House after the time allotted (typically five minutes per speaker) for debate is over, often no more than a day, the bill is reported for final action. And if a bill is brought to the floor under a rule allowing no amendments, even a day's debate can lead to no more than an up or down vote on the bill as presented.

In the Senate, the lack of fixed rules on debate, and of the majority leader's power to set them, have made unrestricted debate a principal method of defeating or delaying consideration of a bill. The major mechanism for doing this is the **filibuster**, a continuous speech made by one or more members to prevent a piece of legislation from being brought to the floor for a vote. Before 1917, only a unanimous consent agreement could set limits on debate. Today, an affirmative vote by three-fifths of the members (sixty if there are no vacancies) ends debate on an issue thirty hours after the vote is taken. This is a **cloture** vote, and its success is called invoking cloture, or closing debate. After cloture is invoked, a measure must be brought to a vote.

The filibuster developed in the 1820s when the Senate was divided between slave and free states. Unlimited debate maintained the deadlock.[69] For over a century, the filibuster was used primarily to defeat civil rights legislation. It took a cloture vote to end seventy-three days of debate and get the 1964 Civil Rights Act to the floor for a vote.

government responsiveness

Party Government and Legislative Gridlock

Unified government occurs when one party controls both the White House and Congress. That happened during most of George W. Bush's first six years in office. Simple logic says having one party in control of the White House and Congress should create an environment where a lot gets done. But in fact, it was not: complete control led to overreaching by the Republican majority and that in turn led to obstructionist tactics by the Democratic minority.

Party unity and partisan voting did intensify under unified government; that is, more legislators voted with their own party than had been the case in the past (see Figure 3). But the House and Senate majorities were small and all it took was a handful of crossover votes to keep the Republican majority from pushing through its high-priority bills. Rarely do members of either party give unanimous support to a major piece of legislation, so the narrow split led to a hardening of party discipline to keep members in line.

The Bush White House had little patience with a centrist, compromising approach to the legislative process that might have won support from at least some Democrats. The White House set the legislative agenda and insisted that the congressional leadership enforce it. This attempt to shut down the bipartisan negotiating and compromise common to the legislative process led to Democrats being frozen out of committees and negotiations where traditionally the minority party played a role. This in turn led to another kind of gridlock when Democrats and dissenting (usually centrist) Republicans, frustrated by being marginalized, resorted to obstructionist tactics (filibusters, holds on nominations, denial of unanimous consent agreements) as their only means to affect the process.

The Speaker of the House, Dennis Hastert, used the rules in unprecedented ways, not only by holding open vote counts until the leadership could round up enough votes to win passage but by preventing amendments and other changes in the leadership-agreed-upon wording of bills. Final versions of bills were often written up by the Republican leadership working with a few committee chairs and interest group representatives, rather than marked up in committee. For example, Democrats were shut out of the negotiations on two of the biggest bills considered by the 108th Congress, the prescription drug benefit for seniors and the energy bill. The leadership wrote the prescription drug bill working with representatives of the pharmaceutical companies, HMOs, and other affected interest groups. Hastert personally negotiated terms of the bill with the head of the AARP, as his chosen spokesperson for seniors. But this was not legislative compromise as we have come to understand it; it was not a bill produced through negotiations in committee by elected representatives and deliberation by the full membership.

After Bush's reelection in 2004, Hastert announced he would let no bill come to a vote unless it had the support of "a majority of the majority" (that is, of House Republicans), even if a bill had bipartisan majority support. The practice of advancing bills only when a majority of Republican members favored them meant that the leadership never had to negotiate their passage with the Democrats. Legislation that made it to the floor was the product of a single party and the group interests closest to its political base. This is one way of pushing through the president's legislative agenda, but it does not produce compromise solutions to the nation's problems nor engender buy-in from the minority. It diminishes what was intended to be a delib-

erative process and only makes the minority more obstructionist.

When Congress was created, it was not parties that were meant to make policy; it was the representatives themselves, acting for their constituencies. It is a messy system because of the thousands of interests that have to be brokered in a country this big and diverse. Those who prefer efficiency and party discipline to the more chaotic brokering of local interests are likely to prefer **party government**, a system where the central party leaders recruit those who run for office and all speak with a similar voice (the British system is an example of party government). But the move toward party discipline since the 1990s has led to the lapse of informal norms and civility, gridlock in the Senate, a serious decline in deliberation, and, what many members seemed most concerned about in the Bush years, the forfeiting of legislative initiative and budgetary powers to the White House. A veteran congressional scholar describes it as "the demise of regular order . . . a situation in which producing the party program trumps any institutional concerns. There is no one tending to the institutional maintenance of Congress."[1] This is a concern because Congress is a co-equal branch of government and essential to our democratic system.

After the Democrats assumed control of Congress, the new leadership continued to use restrictive rules and dominate the work of committees. And the Republicans, now the minority party, responded with the same obstructionist tactics they opposed when Democrats used them.[2] If this continues under a new president, , whether Republican or Democrat, the tendency toward party government will strengthen and the committee system will continue to weaken.

[1] Thomas Mann of the Brookings Institution, quoted in Richard E Cohen, Kirk Victor and David Baumann, "The State of Congress," *National Journal*, January 10, 2004, 85.
[2] Edward Epstein, "Her Key to the House," *CQ Weekly*, October 29, 2007, 3165.

Stephen Crowley/The New York Times/Redux

Pizza and chicken dinners were delivered and cots set up in the LBJ room off the Senate floor as the Democratic leadership prepared for a Republican filibuster of their 2007 bill calling for U.S. troops to begin leaving Iraq within 120 days.

Both parties use filibusters (as they do nongermane amendments). During Bill Clinton's first year in office, Republicans frequently used the filibuster to block proposals from the Democratic Senate majority. After a while, only the threat of a filibuster was necessary to block action. That is because the Senate was so evenly divided that the majority party would not have been able to muster sixty votes to override a filibuster if it did occur. So actual filibusters rarely occur, but the threat of a filibuster is used as an almost routine method of blocking a bill. With the breakdown of the deliberative process, threats of filibusters have become an effective way for the minority party to influence legislation other than through amendments.

DEMOCRACY?

Minority rights are a foundational element in our form of democracy, but how far does this principle extend to the legislative process? Should a minority be able to consistently block bills that are supported by a majority of elected officials?

The filibuster impedes the majority's (including a bipartisan majority's) right to legislate and contributes to gridlock but it also can prevent precipitous action or total domination by the majority party. Its use to stop George W. Bush's judicial nominations so infuriated the Republican leadership that they called it "minority tyranny." They threatened to abolish the filibuster by getting a simple majority to support it as a rules change (a threat dubbed "the nuclear option.") However, since the filibuster is one of the most important tools the minority has to check the majority and because majority control does change hands, the threat to abolish it led to a

bipartisan agreement among fourteen Senators (seven Republicans and seven Democrats) to oppose the rules change.

When and if a bill ever makes it to an up-or-down floor vote, the vote may be taken in several different ways—by voice, a standing count, or recording of individual votes—depending on the level of support and the importance of the legislation. At the time members finally cast their votes on major public bills, they are usually voting on the general aim of the bill without knowing its exact provisions. Rarely does any member read a bill in full. The texts of laws like the No Child Left Behind Act, the first PATRIOT Act, NAFTA, and the prescription drug benefit for seniors run from 800 to more than 1000 pages. The very complex USA PATRIOT Act, which had serious implications for civil liberties, was rushed through Congress in just a few weeks with virtually no member having read it.

When a measure passes, it is sent to the other chamber for action.

Conference Committee

The House and Senate must agree on an identical version of a bill before it can become law, and since this rarely happens, the two versions must be reconciled. Sometimes the chamber that passed the bill last will simply send it to the other chamber for minor modifications. But if the differences between the two versions are not minor, a **conference committee** is set up to try to resolve them. The presiding officers of each chamber, in consultation with the chairs of the standing committees that considered the bill, choose the members of the committee. Both parties are represented, but there is neither a set number of conferees nor a rule requiring an equal number of seats for each chamber.

If the leaders of both parties are strongly committed to passing a version of a bill, they may negotiate the compromise themselves and essentially impose it on the committee. They may even negotiate the final version with the president to avoid a veto. These negotiations can also be planned by the White House with the intent of limiting the wiggle room party leaders have to negotiate compromises.

Conference committees, or the individuals in control of them, have tremendous latitude in how they resolve the differences between the House and Senate versions of a bill. Officially, nothing can be added to the bill that is not germane to it and no part of a bill can be amended that had not been amended prior to passage. But sometimes a bill is substantially rewritten, and occasionally a bill is killed. Or, as President Reagan once said, "an apple and an orange could go into a conference committee and come out a pear."[70] A White House aide described these committees as "no-man's land" because there are so few formal rules governing how they operate.[71] The power of conference committees to alter bills after their passage is why they are sometimes called the "Third House" of Congress.[72]

Once the conference committee reaches an agreement, the bill goes back to each chamber, where its approval requires a majority vote. It cannot be amended at that point so is presented to the membership on a take-it-or-leave-it basis. In the Senate, however, any individual member can challenge a provision added in conference that was not related to the original bill. In practice, both House and Senate accept most conference reports because members of both parties in each chamber have participated in working out the compromise version. However, in the years of unified government—in Clinton's first years and during much of the Bush administration—minority parties often felt so blocked out of the negotiations that determined the final wording of a bill that they refused to sign on to conference committee reports.

Clearly, conference committees can be very influential in determining the final provisions in major legislation, yet the work they do happens almost completely out of public view. Knowing how to win a seat on a conference committee, that is, to participate in rewriting an important piece of legislation, is an essential skill for any legislator who wants to wield influence.

As should be clear from this overview of the complex legislation process, to be a successful member of Congress—to get bills passed or to keep them from being passed, to influence other members, or to rise to a position of leadership—a legislator must know how to use the inner workings of the legislative process. The conference committee is an important part of that process, as is the tactical use of a full range of parliamentary rules and procedures within the congressional system.

Presidential Action and Congressional Response

The president may sign a bill, in which case it becomes law. The president may veto it, in which case it returns to Congress with the president's objections. The president also may do nothing, and the bill will become law after ten days unless Congress adjourns during that period. ⭐ Art. I, Sect. 7

Most presidents have not used the veto lightly, but when they do veto a bill, Congress rarely overrides them. A two-thirds vote in each house is required to override a presidential veto. Congress voted to override only nine of former President Reagan's seventy-eight vetoes, only one of President George H. Bush's forty-six, and only two of Clinton's thirty-four. George W. Bush did not exercise his veto power until his sixth year in office, but of the ten he cast in his final two years, two were overridden.

After the bill becomes a law, it is assigned a number (which always begins with the session of Congress that passed it), published, and entered in the United States Code.

Oversight

As part of the checks-and-balances principle, it is Congress's responsibility to make sure that the bureaucracy is administering federal programs as Congress intended. This monitoring function is called **oversight** and has become more important as Congress continues to delegate authority to the executive branch. For a variety of reasons, Congress is not especially well equipped, motivated, or organized to carry out its oversight function. Nevertheless, it does have several tools for this purpose.

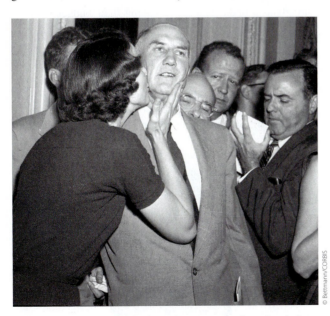

© Bettmann/CORBIS

Senator Strom Thurmond, at the time a Democrat from South Carolina, is congratulated by his wife after setting a record for the longest filibuster. He talked for twenty-four hours and eighteen minutes to prevent a civil rights bill from being voted on in 1957. His effort was in vain, as the bill was adopted.

One tool is the Government Accountability Office, created in 1921 and known as the General Accounting Office until 2004. The GAO functions as Congress's watchdog in oversight and is primarily concerned with making sure that money is used properly. GAO reports have produced most of the information the public has about waste and fraud in military contracts awarded to private firms for logistical support in the Iraq War.

Committee hearings are another method of oversight, albeit not always an effective one. They provide members an opportunity to query executive branch staff on the operation of their agencies, but the level of cooperation and frankness varies with the problem being investigated, and at times with instructions from the White House limiting cooperation. Nevertheless, officials in agencies view hearings as a possible source of embarrassment for their agency and usually spend a great deal of time preparing for them. This is especially true when Congress decides, often for political reasons, to seek maximum media coverage for hearings.

This attempt at publicity points to one of the problems with the use of televised proceedings to carry out the oversight function: hearings are often held after oversight has failed and Congress wants to convince the public that it is doing something to correct a problem. This was painfully clear after the corporate collapses of 2002—of Enron, Global Crossing, and WorldCom, for example—when four Senate and three House committees held hearings in succession, all vying for media time. Prominent members of oversight committees, such as Joseph Lieberman (I-Conn.) and Christopher Dodd (D-Conn.), who represent a state where some of the failed businesses were headquartered and who had received large campaign contributions from them, actively worked to prevent new regulations from being adopted. Then they are seen on an oversight panel questioning regulatory officials and corporate executives about why the crises occurred. But if Congress had exercised oversight and had not weakened the regulatory clout of the Securities and Exchange Commission, these scandals might not have occurred and some of the enormous costs to employees and investors might have been prevented. Occurring after the failures, the hearings were more after-sight than oversight, but they were also a means for Congress to consider remedial measures.

We saw a repeat of this in 2008 when, after the financial crisis caused by lax regulation of mortgages and financial institutions that led to the near collapse of federal mortgage insurers Fannie Mae and Freddie Mac, members of Congress rushed to hold hearings. The barn door was wide open and the horses were loose, but members were eager to exercise "after-sight."

Congress also exercises oversight when it holds hearings on the president's appointees to agencies. These include top officials in a variety of regulatory agencies and cabinet departments. By questioning the experience, training, and perspectives of the nominees, congressional committees are also focusing on what they believe the needs and issues confronting the agencies are.

The incentive of committee members to place constituent protection and the interests of big campaign donors above rule enforcement is one weakness of oversight. The fragmentation of oversight responsibility is also a problem. There were at least seven Senate committees and six House committees with some oversight responsibility for the accounting and financial practices that led to so many industry bankruptcies in 2002. And many more committees were responsible for oversight of the defense and intelligence agencies whose failures were so widely publicized after 9/11.

Congress can also exercise its oversight function through informal means.[73] One way of doing this is to request reports on topics of interest to members or committees. In a given year, the executive branch might prepare 5000 reports for Congress.[74] Moreover, the chair and staff of the committee or subcommittee relevant to the agency's mission are consulted regularly by the agency. But it is hard to find any serious informal oversight. There are few electoral or other incentives for members to become involved in the drudgery of wading through thousands of pages of reports or for doing a really thorough job in any area of oversight, at least until a crisis arises or public confidence in the economy or government institutions is threatened.

The primary means for congressional oversight is its control over the federal budget. Congress can cut or add to agencies' budgets and thereby punish or reward them for their performance. Members with authority over an agency's budget can use that power to get benefits for their constituents, and by going along with the members' wishes, agencies may stand a better chance of having their budget requests approved. There is an incentive in this relationship for congressional committees to exercise oversight, but increasingly they have failed to do so. Congress has allowed authorizing legislation for agencies as important as the Consumer Product Safety Commission, the U.S. Commission on Civil Rights, the Corporation for Public Broadcasting, and the Federal Election and Trade commissions, among others, to

UH, DO YOU MIND? WE'RE TRYING TO CONDUCT SURVEILLANCE ON TERRORISTS HERE.

expire. The agencies continue to function because Congress waives budget rules to provide annual funding for them without oversight by authorization committees.[75]

If Congress has received low marks for gridlock in legislating, it was absent without leave in carrying out much of its oversight function during the first six years of the Bush administration, when compliant Republicans did not want to investigate anything that made the administration look bad. Many members of Congress were critical of the institution's laxity, especially with respect to oversight of intelligence operations and defense policy and appropriations. In the wake of 9/11, the Bush administration encouraged Congress to neglect oversight in these areas by arguing that the president needed a free hand to wage the war on terrorism.

Former Senator Rick Santorum (R-Pa.) explained the weakening of oversight in the Republican-controlled Congress as a party preference: "Republicans don't enjoy oversight—not nearly as much as Democrats—and so . . . we don't do as much."[76] However, as Representative Henry Waxman (D-N.Y.) pointed out, House Republicans' took "more than 140 hours of testimony to investigate whether the Clinton White House misused its holiday card database but less than five hours of testimony regarding how the Bush administration treated Iraqi detainees."[77] In fact, during the years when Republicans had majorities in Congress (1995 to 2006), 99 percent of the 1015 subpoenas issued by Congressional committees to provide testimony or documents for congressional hearings were for investigations of actions by the Clinton administration, and 1 percent for actions of the Bush administration. Not surprisingly, after the Democrats took control of Congress in 2007 the number of oversight hearings doubled and four new oversight committees were created.

In other words, members of Congress would rather exercise oversight on presidents from opposing parties. Members from the president's party fear that negative publicity might weaken not just the president but their party. However, institutional pride in congressional prerogatives and Congress as an equal branch, in most eras, partially overcomes the reluctance to investigate the administration.

Budget Making

The topic of budget making may be dull, but without money government cannot function. Real priorities are reflected not in rhetoric but in the budget. An increasingly large part of the job of Congress is to pass a budget. The Constitution gave Congress the power to appropriate money and to account for its expenditure ⭐ Art. I, Sect. 9, but in the 1920s, Congress delegated its authority to prepare the annual budget to the president (through the Office of Management and Budget, or OMB). In years when the president's party does not control Congress, the congressional majority also produces its own budget, with priorities distinctly different from the president's.

The House and Senate have subcommittee-free budget committees, whose membership includes representatives from the leadership of both parties. The budget committees have existed only since 1974 and were created to work with the Congressional Budget Office (CBO) on big-picture issues such as economic forecasting and fiscal planning, including deficit management and controlling overall spending. The House Budget Committee prepares a budget proposal that sets out spending goals in the context of projected federal revenues. Budget committees are not as powerful as Appropriations and neither the House nor Senate committee can enforce the spending limits they recommend. During the budgetary process, the budget committees hold hearings, but these have become a sideshow to the main event.

Congress is aided in budget review by the CBO, which provides expertise to Congress on matters related to both the budget and the economy. Before the establishment of the CBO, members of Congress felt they were junior partners in budget making because they had to depend on information provided by the president, his budget advisers, and the OMB. Because the CBO is responsible to both parties in Congress, it provides a less politically biased set of forecasts about the budget than the administration or the leadership of either party would.

Characteristics of Budgeting

Historically, congressional budgeting has had two basic characteristics. First, the process is usually incremental; that is, budgets for the next year are usually slightly more than budgets for the current year. Normally, Congress does not radically reallocate money from one year to the next; members assume that agencies should get about what they received the previous year. This simplifies the work of all concerned. Agencies do not have to defend, or members scrutinize, all aspects of the budget. Second, Congress tends to spend more in election years and in times of unemployment.

There are exceptions to these general rules, such as times of war or domestic crisis. The first budget submitted after 9/11, for example, requested a huge increase in defense spending. Thereafter the increases were far larger than the annual budgets show because most of the money for the wars in Afghanistan and Iraq was requested in "supplementals," special appropriations bills that authorize spending not included in the fiscal year budget. There are also instances of ideological budgeting. President Reagan's domestic budget cuts and increased military spending in 1981 were clearly an exception to incrementalism.

Authorizations and Appropriations

Each year, Congress passes a budget resolution that sets a dollar amount of spending for the fiscal year, but money is not appropriated in a single piece of legislation. Since the

1970s, the budget has been divided and reviewed as separate bills, each of which focuses on a different area of expenditure, such as defense. All budget legislation goes through a process similar to but more complicated than other bills.

To grasp the complexity, it is necessary to understand the distinction between budget authorizations and budget appropriations. **Authorizations** are acts that enable agencies and departments to operate, either by creating them or by authorizing their continuance. They also establish the guidelines under which the agencies operate. Although authorization bills might specify funding levels, they do not actually provide the funding. **Appropriations** are acts that give federal agencies the authority to spend the money allocated to them. Both authorization and appropriations bills must pass each house, and differences must be resolved in conference.

Typically, authorizations precede appropriations, although this is not always the case. Budgetary procedures are not defined in the Constitution but are determined by House and Senate rules, which can be, and often have been, changed. The standing committees that oversee the work of the agency or program being funded usually work out the authorizations. The House Interior and Insular Affairs Committee and the Senate Energy and National Resources Committee, for example, review the authorization of the Park Service in the Department of the Interior; the agricultural committees write authorizations for the Department of Agriculture. Close ties often exist between the agency being reviewed and the authorizing committee, which can cause proposed funding levels to be set without consideration of the overall demand on federal revenues. But the real power to limit spending rests with the House and Senate Appropriations committees.

The Appropriations Committee within each house has subcommittees corresponding to the functional areas into which budget allocations are divided (lumped together somewhat differently in the House than the Senate). The chair of the two Appropriations committees and the ranking minority member (and the ranking majority member in the Senate as well) can sit as members of any or all of the subcommittees, adding to their power. The Appropriations Committee assigns a spending limit for each area, and the relevant subcommittee then decides how to apportion it among the agencies in its jurisdiction. The power of those who chair appropriations subcommittees is suggested by their nickname, "The Cardinals." In reviewing an agency's proposed budget, the subcommittee is not bound to fund it at the level requested in the president's budget proposal or the authorization bill. Nor do a subcommittee's funding proposals have to be accepted by the whole committee.

Although appropriations subcommittees may develop close ties with the agencies they review, the committee as a whole does not, and it may not be as generous as its subcommittees. In the bills it sends to the floor for a vote, the Appropriations Committee can increase or cut the previous year's funding levels, or it can recommend the elimination of an agency altogether.

Problems with the Budget Process

Almost everyone is critical of congressional budget making. One reason is that members simply cannot agree on spending for any fiscal year; it is not unusual for the new fiscal year to begin before Congress has passed all the necessary appropriations bills. Then, under time pressure, they will lump spending into several omnibus bills in order to keep government operating. These cumbersome bills are difficult to decipher and make oversight by scrutiny of agency budgets very difficult.

Another problem is that Congress does not honor its own budget resolutions that establish the amount of total spending for each fiscal year. Congress has frequently outspent the dollar limit that it set.[78] As emergencies or unforeseen needs arise, Congress passes supplemental spending bills such as for Iraq and Afghanistan or to deal with a natural disaster like Katrina.

Congress also now consistently violates the pay-as-you-go (paygo) rule that requires all new spending to be offset by a revenue source or spending cuts elsewhere. The paygo rule, established at the end of the first Bush administration and observed throughout Clinton's presidency, was one of several key factors that made it possible to balance the budget in 2000. When George W. Bush took office, the budget was in surplus, and both he and the Congress abandoned paygo. By the end of Bush's first term, all of the supplemental spending on war and emergencies, in addition to much of the budgeted spending, came from borrowing from the Social Security Trust Fund, from private citizens, and increasingly from foreign governments.

Committee government also has disadvantages for the budgeting process. By developing expertise in a few areas, a House member runs the danger of being more responsive to narrow interests and constituencies and less responsive to national priorities when deciding how to spend money. Over time, members of congressional subcommittees develop close relationships both with lobbyists for interest groups whose goals are affected by committee decisions and with the staff in executive branch agencies the subcommittee oversees. Over the years, these three groups—legislators, lobbyists, and bureaucrats, sometimes called an "iron triangle"—get to know each other, often come to like and respect one another, and seek to accommodate each other's interests. The lobbyists likely provide money to help fund the legislators' campaigns. These personal relationships can result in favorable treatment of special-interest groups or reluctance of committee members to alter authorizations for an agency in ways it doesn't approve.

A major problem with budgeting, in fact and in public perception, is the lack of transparency. Few people can imagine what $3 trillion means, and keeping track of how it is spent and how revenues are raised to cover those expenditures is impossible for the average citizen—even though the annual budget is published and available to everyone online. The lack of transparency is due in part to what we might call creative accounting techniques, but certain aspects of the process are deliberately hidden from view (for example, how money is spent gathering intelligence). Paradoxically, the attention paid to lack of transparency has focused on one of the smallest areas of public spending—**earmarks**.

Bringing money and jobs home to the district is nothing new for members of Congress but the earmark method of doing it dates to around 1970. Not surprisingly, the most successful earmarkers have always been the most senior and most powerful members of appropriations and authorization committees, but today all members have the opportunity to include earmarks in the budgets of agencies they oversee. However it is not a level playing field; women and minority members are less successful in winning their earmark requests. The fact that some African American members represent districts gerrymandered to create safe seats has hurt their chances of getting their earmark requests. The corollary is that newer members in highly competitive seats tend to do well because the leadership wants to boost their reelection chances by sending money to their districts.[79]

The argument against earmarking is based primarily on its being a corruption of the budgetary process. Requests are put into appropriations bills or reports to agencies directing them on how to spend their appropriations without any consideration of the merits of the project or program. Second, the requests are often entered unattributed and are seen as violations of what should be an open or transparent process. The public is entitled to know who requests money for these projects. Third, some argue that earmarks are also a kind of pay-for-play arrangement in which members can attract campaign contributions for reelection campaigns by getting funding for a project from which one of the potential donors will benefit.

Earmarking is a beloved bipartisan tradition. It has continued in peacetime and wartime, when the budget is balanced and when it is in deep deficit. The practice is so common and such a necessary legislative skill that a Washington, D.C., firm offers a training seminar in how to get an earmark.[80] Members say they are the people best informed on special problems in their districts and are obligated to get money to deal with them. They also can argue that earmarks comprise little more than 2 percent of the overall budget, and that is not a high price for a road, museum, park, or research center that may mean a great deal to a locality. One member said that taking a share of tax dollars back to the district was his "constitutional obligation."[81]

"Not all earmarks are equal," one House leader argued. A secret earmark for a lobbyist is not the same as earmarking money for a project that will benefit a member's district.

He pointed out that one of his earmarks was for repair of a dangerously unsafe city bridge that was on the exit route Homeland Security designated for emergency evacuations.[82] It is also important to keep in mind that members' constituents are enablers of this behavior. Although collectively we talk as if we want an ethical, high-minded Congress whose members are always responsive first to the national interest, when fragmented into individual constituents, the public often responds quite differently. The average voter does expect his or her representative to deliver for the district.

Although both President Bush and Senator John McCain attributed much of the deficit problem to earmarks, the cost of 2008 earmarks would not pay for two months of the Iraq War. One pundit said trying to balance the budget by eliminating earmarks was like trying to solve global warming by banning bathroom night lights.[83]

When Democrats took control of Congress they vowed to reform earmarks but not to eliminate them. The number of earmarks, and their cost, did decline in 2007 but the following year, an election year, they rose again. So far, the main reform in the earmarking process has been to force every member to publicly identify the projects and amounts they request.

Many members are more troubled by the fact that for decades Congress has been slowly ceding budget-setting power to the executive branch. (And it should not be forgotten that the White House also includes earmarks in its budget proposal—about 500 in 2007.) White House staff typically get involved in negotiating final dollar amounts with congressional leaders, but both the Bush and Clinton administrations superseded the conventional congressional bargaining process by working out final versions of appropriations bills with the congressional leadership before

Senator Olympia Snowe, along with colleague Susan Collins, both from Maine, represent a vanishing breed—moderate Republicans in Congress. As the numbers of moderate Republicans from the Northeast and Midwest and conservative Democrats from the South have declined, Congress has become more polarized.

conference committees ever met. The real budget decisions are made in these kinds of private negotiations among congressional leaders, their staff, administration aides, individual members, and the president. The rest of Congress is often left with a take-it-or-leave-it budget package laid out in separate bills for each of twelve functional areas or in several omnibus bills.

Members on the Job

This section examines how members of Congress go about the day-to-day business of legislating, budget making, oversight, and constituency service, as well as carrying out party caucus- and campaign-related activities.

Negotiating the Informal System

To be successful, representatives and senators must not only serve their constituents and get reelected but must also know how to work with their colleagues and how to maneuver within the intricate system of parliamentary rules, customs, and traditions that govern the House and Senate.

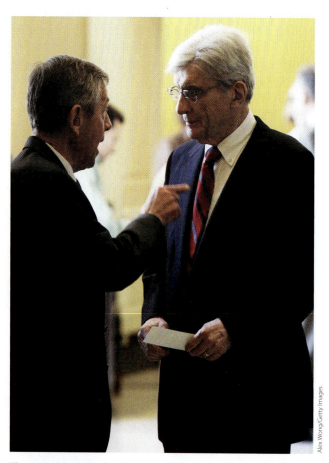

There are ideological splits not only between the two parties but also within each party. Senator George Voinvich (R-Oh.), (left), and former Senator John Warner (R-Va.) argue after a meeting of Senate Republicans.

Alex Wong/Getty Images

Informal Norms

First among the many lessons every new member must learn are the customary ways of interacting with colleagues both on and off the floor of Congress.[84] These **informal norms** help keep the institution running smoothly by attempting to minimize friction and allowing competition to occur within an atmosphere of civility. As in other American institutions, the norms of Congress are changing.

The Founders' velveteen breeches, frock coats, and white wigs symbolized the drawing room gentility of their circle and helped to mask bitter rivalries. It was Thomas Jefferson, the best known of the gentlemen farmers, who in 1801 wrote the foundational rules for in-chamber conduct for members of the new Congress in an effort to contain the inevitable conflict between Federalist and Anti-Federalist, abolitionist and slave owner. His notes laid the groundwork for Congress's system of informal norms.

Throughout much of the twentieth century, the most important norm was institutional loyalty, the expectation that members would respect their fellow members and Congress itself, especially their own chamber. Personal criticism of one's colleagues was to be avoided, and mutual respect was fostered by such conventions as referring to colleagues by title, such as "the distinguished senator from New York," rather than by name.

Although it is still the norm in Great Britain's House of Commons to hear members refer to one another as the "right honorable member" or "my right honorable colleague," never using personal names, today one is apt to hear much more informal and not particularly polite language when members of our Congress talk to and about one another and the institution. And even in the House of Commons, the formal terms of address are a veneer, as Labour and Conservative members sit on opposite sides of a narrow chamber floor hooting and shouting epithets at their fellow honourables. However, this is a long and well-loved tradition in the House of Commons and not a modern manifestation of increased hostility.

In recent years, hostility among members seems as sharp as among those delegates to the First Congress but scholars differ on the origins of this decline in civility. Some say it dates back decades to the time Democrats had a lock on both chambers, leaving Republicans permanently aggrieved. Some say it began with Watergate—that Nixon's enemies list and Congress's impeachment hearings poisoned the atmosphere. Others tie it to the hearings on the nominations of Robert Bork and Clarence Thomas to the Supreme Court, which were notorious for their overheated exchanges and character bashing. Still others trace the decline to Newt Gingrich's strategy as a minority tactician in the 1980s. He attacked not only the Democratic leaders but Congress as an institution, (calling it "sick," a severe departure from the institutional loyalty norm) in an attempt to sour the public on Congress so voters would be inclined to defeat incumbent Democrats. Once the Republicans captured control of the House and Gingrich became their leader, he encouraged an aggressive, combative style on the floor of the House.

The growth in partisan voting, illustrated in Figure 3, gives little support to the Democratic majority or Watergate explanations, though there was a small spike in 1974, the year of those investigations, but then partisanship returned to its formerly low levels. The voting data give more support to the Bork, Thomas, and especially the Gingrich explanations, since there was some increase in partisanship in 1987, at the time of the Bork hearing; in 1992 and 1993, after the Thomas hearings; and dramatically in 1995, after Gingrich became majority leader.

It was in this climate that Republicans launched the impeachment hearings against President Clinton, leaving many Democrats wanting revenge for what they felt was an outrageous diversion of time and energy from crucial business. Under Speaker Hastert's leadership, it seemed at first that there would be a trend toward more conciliation and civility in the conduct of House business. But in 2003, the Republican leadership, reinvigorated by gains in the midterm elections and determined to tighten procedural control over the House, called in the Capitol Police to break up a meeting of Democratic members. Several months later, Hastert broke House rules by holding a vote open for three hours while he rounded up the support needed to pass a Bush administration bill.

The only reassuring aspect of the intense degree of partisanship is that it is neither new nor destined to last. Congress passes through cycles of greater and lesser civility. Although they may be name-calling now, they are not beating up or shooting at one another as members were in the years leading up to the Civil War. And Jefferson's ears were hardly virgin; a frequent target of gossip and character attacks, he could dish with the best and used paid agents to spread slander about his Federalist opponents.

Formal Standards of Conduct

In addition to the informal rules, members of Congress are expected to conform to ethical standards of conduct they have set for themselves. The Constitution gives each chamber the power to establish rules, pass judgment on conduct, and, by a two-thirds vote, expel a member. ⭐ Art. I, Sect. 5. Each chamber has a select committee to hear ethics complaints; it is the only committee where membership is equally split between the parties rather than in proportion to the number of seats they hold. Unethical behavior includes such action as using one's position for personal enrichment, for financial gain of a family member or campaign contributor, misusing campaign funds, violating codes of conduct toward other members, or being found guilty of criminal conduct.

The 109th Congress (2005–2006) was one of the most scandal-ridden in decades, with members of both parties and hundreds of staff members accused of ethics violations for acceptance of gifts, free travel, and questionable campaign contributions from powerful lobbyists. (Refer to Chapter 9 for more on these scandals.)

At the beginning of the 110th Congress, no fewer than eleven members were under federal investigation and several others were being investigated by ethics committees. (Of Alaska's three-member congressional delegation, two were being investigated by federal authorities and the third was the subject of an ethics complaint.[85]) Corruption was

| Figure 3 | Partisan Voting Has Increased Significantly |

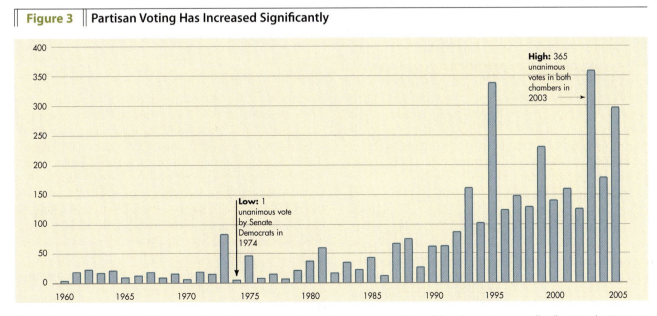

Shown here are the number of times members of one party unanimously opposed a majority of the other party on a roll call vote in the House or Senate. These increasing numbers are a sign of hardened lines and heightened partisanship.
SOURCE: *Congressional Quarterly Weekly Review, January 14, 2008, 143.*

BEHIND THE SCENES
IT ISN'T ALL CONFLICT

With all the attention paid to partisanship, gridlock and the lack of civility in Congress, it may come as a surprise that behind the scenes there are situations in which collegiality is valued. The Congressional Club is one such venue. It was founded in 1908 expressly to provide a place where members could get to know one another by bringing their families together. Club membership is open to spouses and children of members but the families of cabinet members and Supreme Court justices can also join. Reporters cannot enter without permission of the members, which is why most people do not know of its existence. Once dominated by the wives of congressional members, male spouses are joining now too, including Paul

Pelosi, husband of the Speaker of the House. The club's current head (and first African American president) said socializing among the families plays "a vital role in creating friendships between members" of congress.[1] Her husband, a House Democrat, said he had virtually nothing to say to a Republican from Kansas whom he served with on the Appropriations Committee until their wives became friends at the club and the families began socializing.

Then there are the roommate relationships. Because most members spend about half of their time in their home districts and because housing in Washington is very expensive, many families stay at home. To cut costs, and for convenience,

many members room share or become tenants in other members' homes or condos. Rep. George Miller (D-Calif.), whose home has been dubbed "Animal House," has had roomies for twenty years, including two of the Senate's Democratic leaders, Richard Durbin (Ill.) and Charles Schumer (N.Y.). Former *Saturday Night Live* writer and Minnesota Senate candidate Al Franken once tried to sell a sitcom pilot based on the antics in Miller's "crashpad."[2]

Veteran legislator Carolyn Maloney (D-N.Y.) sublets part of her row house to newer members Debbie Wasserman-Schultz (D-Fla.) and Melissa Bean (D-Ill.) on the days Congress is in session. The two younger members are part of a circle of "Mom"

friendships—members who are mothers of school-age children, most of whom have been left at home with their fathers in order not to disrupt their schooling.[3] Bean and Wasserman-Schultz say they have learned a great deal about how things work from living with a veteran legislator while at the same time giving one another much needed moral support. Unlike the Animal House guys, the women do their own cleaning and fix many of their meals, but a male colleague who sublets next door occasionally cooks elaborate dinners and invites them over. He says he is still waiting for the women to reciprocate.[4]

[1] Emily P. Walker, "A Century of Solidarity," *CQ Weekly*, April 28, 2008, 1066.
[2] Richard E. Cohen, "Member Moms," *National Journal*, April 7, 2007, 14.
[3] Ibid., 12–21.
[4] Ibid., 12.

---

one of the issues voters cited as extremely important in how they voted in the 2006 elections, and the Democrats promised to make ethical reform an issue if they won control of either or both houses. The 2007 Honest Leadership and Open Government Act authorized a new Office of Congressional Ethics, which is to be staffed by six nonpartisan outsiders, three chosen by the Speaker and three by the minority leader. The main goal of the reform was to reduce the influence of lobbyists by restricting their ability to make gifts to and do favors for members.[86]

Despite the issuance of new ethics manuals, there is no sign that the reform will actually change the way members and lobbyists interact because both members and lobbyists immediately saw ways to evade the law by passing money previously spent on meals and gifts indirectly to members through their campaign committees. Also, the reforms were mainly a reaction to the lobbying scandals that were in the public eye. Less well known to the public is that thirty-one members of the Senate, including the Senate majority leader, and twenty-four House members have close relatives who lobby Congress. Many members employ family

with campaign funds or use their positions in other ways to financially benefit relatives.[87]

Specialization

By specializing, a member can become an expert, and possibly influential, in a few policy areas. Given the scope of Congress's legislative authority, members cannot be knowledgeable in all areas, so House members especially specialize in subject areas important to their home districts or related to their committees. The leader of one freshman class of legislators advised his new colleagues, "If you've got twenty things you want to do, see where everything is. You'll find that maybe ten of those are already being worked on by people and that while you may be supportive in that role, you don't need to carry the ball. . . . If you try to take the lead on everything, you'll be wasting your time and re-creating the work that's already going on."[88]

The Senate's smaller membership cannot support this degree of specialization. In addition, each senator represents an entire state with interests in a much broader range of issues than those of a single House district. For those

Two foreign policy specialists who worked across the aisle—Senator Richard Lugar (R-Ind.), left, and Senator Joe Biden (D-Del.)—conferred during a hearing by the Foreign Relations Committee about the Iraq War. Biden was elected vice president in 2008.

senators considering a run for the presidency there is also a need to be well versed on a variety of issues.

Reciprocity

Tied to specialization is the norm of reciprocity. Reciprocity, or "logrolling," is summarized in the statement "You support my bill, and I'll support yours." Reciprocity helps each member get the votes needed to pass legislation favored in his or her district. The traditional way in which reciprocity worked was described by the late Sam Ervin, Democratic senator from tobacco-growing North Carolina: "I got to know Milt Young [then a senator from North Dakota] very well. And I told Milt, 'Milt, I would just like you to tell me how to vote about wheat and sugar beets and things like that, if you just help me out on tobacco.'"[89]

Reciprocity is another informal norm that is disappearing. Open meetings, media scrutiny, stronger party leadership, and more partisan voting have made it more difficult for members to "go along" on bills unpopular in their constituency or with the party leadership. However it is still important for winning acceptance of earmark requests (don't oppose the new museum for my district and I won't oppose the road work in your district) and for passing the big Christmas tree bills, such as farm subsidies. Former Sen. Henry Jackson (D-Wash.) explained how he put together enough votes to pass a complex bill this way: "Maggie said he talked to Russell, and Tom promised this if I would back him on Ed's amendment, and Mike owes me one for last year's help on Pete's bill."[90]

Making Alliances

Any member who wants to get legislation passed, move into the party leadership, or run for higher office needs to develop a network of allies among colleagues. Crossing ideological lines to find sponsors or votes for a bill is not uncommon. One of the most unusual alliances of recent years was between Sen. Hillary Clinton (D-N.Y.) and the Christian conservative Sen. Sam Brownback (R-Kans.), who joined forces to promote new measures to stop human trafficking, especially the selling of women and children into prostitution.

An increasingly common venue for cooperation among members, especially in the House, is the **special-interest caucus**. Caucuses are organized by members who share partisan, ideological, issue, regional, or identity interests to pool their strength in promoting shared interests and gaining passage of related legislation. Caucus size ranges from a handful to more than a hundred; almost every member belongs to at least one. The House and Senate have well over 100 caucuses, many organized cross-chamber. Some caucuses have a narrow focus, such as those promoting bikes, ball bearings, boating, the wine industry, or wireless technology. Some are rooted in personal experience, such as the caucuses of Vietnam veterans and cancer survivors.

Among the most significant of the caucuses are those designed to pool the strength of women and minorities. These caucuses develop policy in key issue areas and serve national constituencies. The Caucus for Women's Issues, working across party, racial, and ethnic lines, has managed to recruit almost all women members and many male colleagues as well. With a Republican and a Democrat serving as cochairs, the caucus is regarded as one of the most bipartisan in Congress. Its legislative agenda includes supportive measures for women-owned businesses, pay equity, and women in the military.

Hispanics, East Asians, Native Americans, Asian Indians, and African Americans also have special-interest caucuses. The Black Caucus was organized in 1970 by thirteen House members determined to gain some clout. Today, all forty African Americans in the House are members. Because there are no African American Republicans in Congress, the Black Caucus declined in influence under the Republican majority. With Democrats in the majority, members are back in leadership positions and chairing committees.

Personal Friendships

In some cases, caucuses are the source of a House member's closest political allies. But with the exception of its Centrist Coalition, caucuses are not as important in the much smaller Senate. There, personal friendships might count for more than committee or caucus membership, and strong relationships of trust sometimes develop across party lines. John Kerry (D-Mass.) and John McCain (R-Ariz.), two decorated Vietnam War veterans, became friends while working together on veterans' issues. A more unusual example is the close friendship between the very liberal Senator Edward Kennedy (D-Mass.) and the very conservative Senator Orrin Hatch (R-Utah). Sometimes the chair of a committee develops both a close working relationship and personal friendship with the ranking minority member, as for example between Senators Richard Lugar (R-Ind.) and Joseph Biden (D-Del.) of Foreign Relations, or between Arlen Specter (R-Pa.) and Patrick Leahy (D-Vt.) of the Judiciary. In both houses, much of the work gets hammered out in personal conversations and exchanges away from official venues.

Political Action Committees

The most influential members of Congress now have their own PACs for raising campaign funds to disperse to colleagues. Hillary Rodham Clinton (D-N.Y.), a junior senator and presidential candidate, used her celebrity and connections to raise millions of dollars for her PAC, Friends of Hillary, before running for president. By making donations to the reelection campaigns of colleagues, she has built a network of supporters whose chits she can cash in when looking for a committee chair, a leadership position, or if she makes another run for the presidency. Nancy Pelosi was able to beat out rivals for the minority leader position in 2001 due in large part to her phenomenal ability to get campaign donations for colleagues. By the time she announced that she wanted the position, dozens of fellow House members were in her political debt. Tom DeLay, the very powerful former House majority leader, also built his clout by dispensing funds.

Using the Media

Forty years ago, the workday routine in both House and Senate for resolving most issues involved bargaining with other members, lobbyists, and White House aides. Working privately, one-on-one in small groups or in committees, members and staff discussed and debated issues, exchanged

information, and planned strategies. Even though many issues are still resolved through these private channels, much has changed in the way Congress operates.

For today's members to further their goals, it is often as important to "go public," to reach beyond colleagues and to appeal directly to the larger public, as it is to engage in private negotiation.[91] **Going public** means taking an issue debate to the public through the media, as Congress does when it televises floor debates and important hearings. The most media-oriented members of Congress are experts in providing short and interesting comments for the nightly network news, writing articles for major newspapers, and appearing on talk shows and as commentators on news programs.

With every congressional office wired for Internet access, members not only have a faster way to facilitate casework but a means for self-promotion 24/7. Every district visit, town meeting, and photo-op is put up on the website immediately. Members with larger political ambitions may maintain their own listservs or blogs, but no one in Congress today has to wait for the press to come to them.

In the early days of television, networks broadcast only important congressional proceedings, such as the McCarthy hearings and testimony on investigations into the Watergate scandal and the Iran-Contra affair. In 1979, after considerable controversy and anxiety, the House began televising its proceedings. Fearful of being overshadowed by the House, in 1986 the Senate followed suit. But today exposure comes daily on C-SPAN (the Cable Satellite Public Affairs Network). Two of the three C-SPAN advertisement-free channels are available with almost all basic cable service and have an estimated 52 million viewers each week. Although viewership is small compared with that of commercial networks, the C-SPAN audience has a higher educational level and is better informed and more interested in both local and national government than the general public; nine out of ten viewers voted in the 2000 election.[92]

Local television listings provide times for daily coverage of House and Senate floor proceedings as well as for committee hearings and other official business. In addition, C-SPAN covers members of Congress on the campaign trail, attending fundraisers, giving stump speeches, and chatting with constituents. Besides its unbroken coverage of events, what sets C-SPAN apart from commercial network coverage of Congress is that there is no intermediary between the viewers and the events and people they are watching. C-SPAN does not use reporters, so televised events are free of commentary and on-the-spot analysis. This may be why C-SPAN is only one of three televisions news sources to be named as "most trusted" by Republicans, Democrats, and Independents alike.

The congressional leadership goes public, too. Leaders of both parties regularly call producers of television talk shows to suggest guests. They meet with the press and often have prepared statements. Before important congressional

Representative John Murtha (D-Pa.) provides a sound bite for television news. Members of Congress must become proficient in using the media to reach their constituents.

gress, so it is not surprising that 101 members of the 110th Congress were former congressional staffers.[93]

Congress and the Public

As we have noted, one of the most frustrating things about Congress for the average citizen is the "messiness" of the legislative process. Not only is the process of crafting laws incredibly complex but it provides many places along the way where individual legislators and interest groups, often for seemingly (or truly) selfish motives, can exact concessions from the people who want to pass the bill. Add to that the partisan bickering, with Democrats picking a proposal apart simply because a Republican introduced it or vice versa, and casual observers throw up their hands in exasperation.

It seems that the more media exposure Congress gets, with the processes of democracy exposed for all to see, the less supportive the public is of its work. The conflict and gridlock, if not admirable, are not surprising either, given our complex constituencies with competing interests and worldviews. But members contribute to the poor image by belittling colleagues and the institution itself when they seek reelection by running against "Washington."

Now as never before, every step—or misstep—that members of Congress take is carried to every part of the nation. Or as one observer commented, "A member's every twitch is blared to the world, thanks to C-SPAN, open meetings laws, financial-disclosure reports, and every misstep is logged in a database for the use of some future office seeker."[94] And that was more than a decade ago; today we must add BlackBerries, cell phones, YouTube, and blogs. Members must be aware that every public utterance is almost certainly being monitored by someone and that if it is the least bit newsworthy, it will soon appear in a blog or—worse—YouTube.

Media attention is valuable, because we prize open government in a democracy. But too much is not so good, because in a heterogeneous society we rely on compromise to achieve our public goals, and under the harsh glare of media, there are fewer opportunities to compromise and deliberate without fear of losing votes back home. But the public has little patience for extended partisan debates even when they reflect real policy differences among the people.

Of the three branches of government, the public has been least supportive of Congress. The public generally

votes on key issues, the leadership plans letters to the editors of important newspapers and floor speeches designed for maximum television coverage.

Balancing the Work

Schedules

Multiple committee assignments, in combination with party caucus work, fundraising, and visits to the district, mean that members have impossible schedules. At times, committees cannot obtain quorums because members are tied up with other obligations. Members attend meetings with legislative staff in tow to take notes and to consult with during hearings. If they cannot attend or have to leave for floor business or another meeting, a staffer is there to take notes and brief the member later.

Use of Staff

We have already noted the huge staff available to members. Members of the majority party are at an advantage here because they control two-thirds of the money budgeted for committees and therefore can hire two-thirds of committee staff. Staffers do most of the background work on the complex foreign and domestic issues that cross the members' desks every day, aided when deep expertise is needed by the CRS staff. Through their service, staffers gain a great deal of experience and the opportunity to create a network of contacts who can help them should they decide to run for Con-

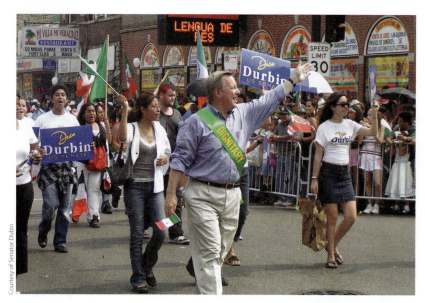

Members frequently return home to maintain their ties to their constituents. Senator Majority Whip Dick Durbin (D-Ill.) participates in the Mexican Independence Day parade in the Little Village neighborhood of Chicago.

gives its highest level of support to the Supreme Court, the institution that is most isolated from the public. Unlike legislative debates, little of the disagreement, negotiation, and compromise of the Court has taken place in public view. When the Court meddles in politics, as it did during the 2000 presidential election vote-counting controversy in Florida, its approval ratings declined for a short time. Confidence in the presidency and approval ratings for individual presidents can fluctuate wildly, as both Bushes discovered when their approval ratings fell from near 90 percent to the high 20s. A president's support can soar when acting as a national leader (chief of state), especially in wartime, then suffer huge losses as a political leader (head of government) when his policies fail.

But the public's attitudes about Congress are also conflicted. In 2007, for example, people's approval of their own representative was about twenty points higher than approval for Congress as a whole, although that gap was substantially less than it has been.[95] Occasionally the public gets so down on Congress that it affects constituents' attitudes toward their own representatives; prior to the 2006 midterm election Congress's approval ratings stood at an historic low of 23 percent.[96] After standoffs between the president and Congress during 2007 and 2008, approval ratings of both fell to historic lows. However, members benefit from local media coverage that is overwhelmingly positive, in part because many of these stories are prepared by the members themselves. But local press stories on Congress as a whole are also far more positive than those written by the national press corps.[97]

A major factor in Congress's low approval ratings is the public's perception that most members care more about

power than about the best interests of the nation and more about pleasing lobbyists who can feed their campaign coffers than serving the interests of the district. It could not be put more plainly than Rep. Michael Capuano (D-Mass.), who wrote the report in support of the 2007 ethics reform, said it: "The public does not trust us on ethics at this point."[98]

The public is not mistaken in its impression of a cozy relationship between Congress and special-interest lobbies. Between 1998 and 2005, 50 percent of the men who left the Senate became registered lobbyists, as did more than 40 percent of the 162 who left the House.[99] Others work as "consultants" and are not required to register as lobbyists, and some members are married to, or have children working as, lobbyists. In addition, many members are in the position of a fox guarding a chicken house as they serve on committees that oversee and legislate in areas where they or their relatives have financial interests; yet they insist they are not compromised in carrying out their duties. One of the factors contributing to low public confidence in government before the 2008 election was the subprime mortgage crisis. It was not lost on the public that antipathy to regulation in both the White House and Congress played some role in the collapse of financial services. It was also not a surprise that some members responsible for legislating to deal with the crisis had ties to the industries under investigation. (See the Ethical Dilemmas box.)

Despite all this, the idea of Congress as a constitutionally mandated "people's house" is esteemed by the public. It is the people in Congress and the way Congress works that the public dislikes. Just over half of all voters turn out for congressional elections (less in years when the president is not being elected), and most of the public is poorly informed about what Congress does. This pattern persists even with C-SPAN coverage and even though many local papers each week print a congressional scorecard with the voting records of local legislators. Constituents are much more likely to know about ethics violations and sexual improprieties of members of Congress than they are about the legislation passed in any session.

The public evaluation of Congress as accomplishing "not much" or "nothing at all" stems in part from the public's lack of awareness of what Congress has actually done. However, in 2006 very little actually was done as members waited to see what the balance of power would be after the 2006 midterm elections. When the Democrats took control of both houses in 2007, the new leadership increased the number of days in session, in large part to pass the main part of their legislative agenda within the first 100 days. The number of votes rose to historic levels and some measures,

| Figure 4 | Public Opinion Toward Congress |

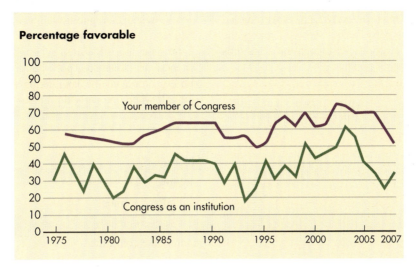

People were asked whether they approve of the way Congress is handling its job and whether they approve of the way the representative from their congressional district is handling his or her job. People consistently voice more approval of their member than of Congress itself.
In 2008, according to Rasmussen polls, congressional approval fell into the single digits.
Source: Combined responses from similar surveys by the Gallup Organization and the Harris Survey. Roger H. Davidson, Walter J. Oleszek, and Frances E. Lee, Congress and Its Members, 11th ed. (Washington, D.C.: CQ Press, 2008), 490.

such as a minimum wage increase and ethics reform, were passed. But because other goals were not accomplished (such as a timetable for troop pullouts in Iraq), the public was unaware of what had been accomplished and Congress gained little in public esteem.[100]

Conclusion: Is Congress Responsive?

Congress is certainly responsive to individual constituents, but is it responsive to the policy demands of the national constituency? The pressures of elections and of constituency service seem to undermine Congress's ability to focus on public policy. Pressure to be in the home district meeting constituents competes with legislators' desires to do a good job at lawmaking and to work more efficiently.

The public wants Congress to be responsive to its individual needs and group interests, but then it looks down on the institution for its pork-barrel politics and big spending. This is the perennial dilemma of representatives and senators: how to meet the demands of the district or state—that is to do the job members are sent to do—in order to get reelected and at the same time serve the national interest.

Pressure to raise money for reelection campaigns incurs obligations to interest groups that may not be consistent with either the members' or the constituents' views. Indeed,

congressional leaders from both parties have problems articulating a clear vision in part because so many of them have become dependent on the contributions of PACs for their campaign funding. This puts them in the position of having to support some interests that are not consistent with voters' views or interests.

The procedures and organization of Congress also give individuals and small groups opportunities to block or redirect action. This is particularly true in the Senate, where procedures allow a minority of senators to engage in unlimited debate unless sixty members vote to stop it. The fragmented committee and subcommittee structure in both houses offers many venues in which bills can be killed. Political parties have been strengthened in recent years, but neither party discipline nor institutional rules and norms, including ethics guidelines, have kept members from bowing to the pressure of lobbyists or outraged constituents. These factors mean that Congress continues to be more responsive to individual and group interests than to national needs.

The increasing partisanship in Congress has been one of the biggest changes since the mid-1990s. During George W. Bush's administration, the White House intervened heavily to press its policy agenda. Partisan voting hit record highs in 2003 under the Republicans and in 2007 under the Democrats as the legislative process was party-dominated.[101] Under Republican control, the Democrats were shut out of many important stages of the process, including the drafting of final versions of legislation in conference committees, and in their first year as the majority party Democrats returned the favor. This heightens partisan divisions and makes the output of Congress less a product of compromise and thus less responsive to the broader public.

Even in the best of times, Congress best represents those voters who identify with one of the two major parties, even though more than a third of the public identify as In-dependents or with a third party. This has complicated what was already a difficult process for the formulation of broadly responsive public policy, namely, the overweening influence of large campaign donors on voting on both sides of the aisle. It is difficult to get consistently good legislation when special interests, pork-hungry legislators, and party rigidity dominate the lawmaking process. It is especially difficult when one party dominates the process.

Key Terms

constituency
reapportionment
redistricting
gerrymander
constituency service
casework
pork barrel
Speaker of the House
earmark
Rules Committee
party caucus
majority leader
minority leader
whips
standing committees
seniority rule
implied powers
markup

filibuster
cloture
unified government
party government
conference committee
oversight
authorizations
appropriations
earmark
informal norms
special-interest caucus
going public

Key Names

Thomas Reed
Joseph Cannon
Newt Gingrich
Dennis Hastert
Tom Delay
Nancy Pelosi
Lyndon Johnson
Harry Reid

The 2008 election was historic, with Barack Obama becoming the first African American—indeed, the first person who isn't a white man—to win the Presidency.

The Presidency

11

Talking Points

In 2008, when former first lady and New York Senator Hillary Clinton seemed likely to become the first woman to secure a major party nomination for president of the United States, opponents of her candidacy asked, "Do we want a plural presidency?" The reference of course was to her husband, Bill Clinton, a man with eight years experience as chief executive, a skilled communicator, and one not known to take a back seat or shy away from the limelight. From the early years of the Republic, people have been worried about first ladies influencing policy making in the White House but the reversal of roles for the Clintons was seen a step beyond, since no first lady had ever brought the experience of being president to a "copresidency."

The question of whether our government should be led by a single or a plural executive was debated at the constitutional convention. There were arguments for a single and a three-person executive, and for a multiple-member executive council to ensure regional representation. The sponsors of both the New Virginia and New Jersey Plans

were open to the idea of a plural executive.[1] But supporters of a single chief executive argued that "to control the executive, you must unite it," that is, with a plural executive it would be very difficult to know who was doing what and to hold them hold accountable.[2] Alexander Hamilton made the case for the presidency in *Federalist* 70. Trying to placate those worried about another King George III, he wrote that a single executive would ensure energy and decisiveness in the office in addition to offering greater assurance of accountability.

While critics of a second Clinton presidency were warning against a plural executive, others were arguing that we already had a de facto copresidency in the Bush-Cheney administration. In a White House that had demanded expansive new powers, the vice president was exercising authority, largely in secret, over a host of delegated policy areas. The paradox: the new unchecked powers jointly exercised by president and vice president were justified using Hamilton's *Federalist* 70 argument (the "Unitary Executive Theory") against a plural executive.[3]

Pharaohs, consuls, kings, queens, emperors, tsars, prime ministers, and councils of varied sizes served as executives in other governments before 1789. But no national government had a president, an elected executive with authority equal to and independent of a national legislature, until **George Washington** was elected president of the United States.

The Founders didn't expect the presidency to be a very powerful office. The office's first occupants were drawn from among the Founders; a few of them, Washington and **Thomas Jefferson** especially, served with some reluctance. Nevertheless, they were willing to lend their reputations and abilities to the cause of stabilizing the new government, and as a result, they had the opportunity to influence the direction of its development.

At its inception, the presidency was a not very powerful office in a fledgling country that had few international ties and virtually no standing army. Today, the president of the United States is among the most powerful people in the world. When he enters a room, everyone stands. When he appears at ceremonial functions, the band plays "Hail to the Chief." Wherever he goes, a military aide carries the nuclear

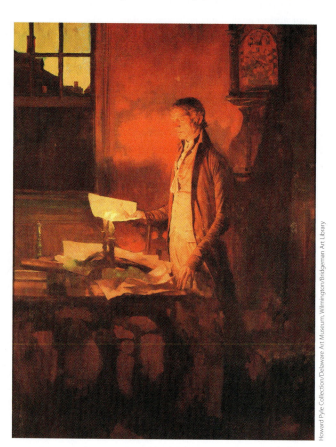

Although political scientists rank Jefferson as a "near great" president, he did not consider the office, or his performance in it, very important. His instructions for an epitaph listed what he thought were his three main accomplishments in life: writing the Declaration of Independence and a Virginia law guaranteeing religious freedom and founding the University of Virginia. He did not include his two terms as president.

"suitcase" containing descriptions of options, protocols, and authentication codes in case he has to launch a nuclear attack. The president is so powerful that some scholars and commentators speak of the "**imperial presidency**."

Nevertheless, all presidents become frustrated with the limits on their power. At times, they feel that they're saddled with an "impossible" or "imperiled" presidency.[4]

Consider the past two presidents. **Bill Clinton** saw his agenda, aside from economic policy and welfare reform, sidetracked by one congressional investigation after another and found himself impeached for lying about a sexual affair. But **George W. Bush**, with a boost from public support after 9/11 and an acquiescent Republican-majority Congress, started two wars, adopted numerous policies restricting civil liberties, and pushed through major tax cuts. The Clinton terms suggested an impossible presidency, whereas the Bush years sparked renewed talk about an imperial presidency.

In this chapter, we'll consider the paradox of presidential power and presidential weakness.

Terms of Service

Eligibility

The Constitution specifies only three conditions to be eligible for the presidency: one must be a "natural-born citizen," at least thirty-five years old, and have resided in the United States for at least fourteen years before taking office. ⭐ Art. II, Sect. 1.

Historically, it has helped to be a white male with roots in small-town America; a Protestant with ancestry from England, Germany, or Scandinavia; a resident of a populous state; and a "good family man." In recent decades, this profile has broadened considerably as society has become more inclusive, the electorate more diverse, and social norms more tolerant of divorce, but sexual, racial, and religious barriers remain.

John Kennedy was the first Roman Catholic elected to the White House (1960) and Ronald Reagan the first divorced man (1980). But no non-Christian has broken the religion barrier. In 2008, Mitt Romney, a Mormon (a member of the Church of the Latter-day Saints, which considers itself a Christian denomination), found his religion a major issue in the race for the Republican nomination, especially among those who do not accept Mormons as Christian. Although the number of religiously unaffiliated Americans is growing, it is improbable that a nonbeliever could get elected to the White House. It is also clear that an openly gay or lesbian candidate cannot yet get elected. And the 2008 primaries revived the debate over whether sexism or racism is the greater barrier to winning the White House. Hillary Clinton outpolled Barack Obama on experience and readiness to be commander in chief but was unable to es-

Figure 1 | Voters' Perceptions of Mitt Romney

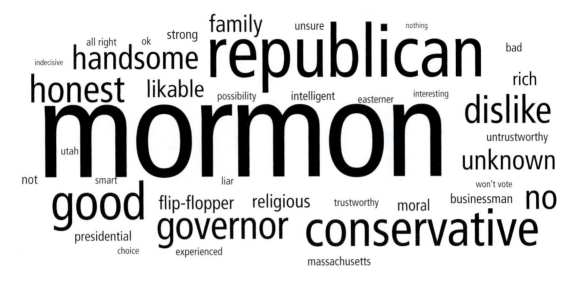

During the presidential primaries in 2008, voters were asked, "What are the first three words that come to mind when you think about [name of candidate]?" The words were assembled in a "tag cloud" according to the frequency with which they were mentioned. The words in largest print were the ones respondents cited most often. Although Republican candidate Mitt Romney had been governor of Massachusetts, his religion was cited far more often than his experience or any other characteristic.
SOURCE: Washington Post poll of a national sample of 1007 adults, November 28–December 2, 2007.

cape her identity as wife of an ex-president. Obama won the Democratic nomination but lost the white working-class vote in the primaries and constantly had to fight attacks on his patriotism and religious convictions because his father was a nonpracticing Muslim from Kenya.

Finally, there is the class issue. Our early presidents were clearly from among the elite, but at least since the election of Andrew Jackson in 1828, most candidates have felt the need to evoke the image of the common man. In 1840, William Henry Harrison used a log cabin as his campaign symbol even though he grew up on a Virginia plantation.[5] Probably no one did more to reinforce the image of the common man as a wise and great leader than Abraham Lincoln, who really did grow up in a log cabin. But Harry Truman, who, like Lincoln, actually had been a plowman, was the only twentieth-century president who profited from playing off that image.

Yet the public continues to expect that candidates should not be too detached from everyday experience. So even though nine of the ten presidential nominees from the major parties since 1988 have had a degree from Harvard or Yale, they have tried to prove they were not far removed from those who live in the heart of the country.[6] George W. Bush played up his Texas rather than his wealthy Maine and Connecticut roots, and John Kerry, another multimillionaire Yale graduate, took the press corps on a hunting photo-op. (Today, when log cabins are no longer in people's memory, nothing says common man like guns and hunting.)

Barack Obama was not born into an elite family—he was abandoned by his father and raised by his mother and,

at times, by his grandparents—but he emphasized his work as a community organizer rather than his degrees from Columbia University and Harvard Law School. He spoke of his Kansas "roots," although he never lived there (his mother had but he grew up in Hawaii and Indonesia), and of his ties to Chicago's tough South Side, although he taught at the elite University of Chicago and lived in an upper-middle-class neighborhood. **John McCain** balanced his background of privilege and wealth by choosing as a running mate a woman from the middle class who hunted and fished and was married to a blue-collar worker and union member.

Experience

In addition to having the right stuff in terms of gender, race, religion, sexual orientation, and a common touch, does it matter if a candidate has experience, and if so, what kind of experience? Evidence suggests there is no neat correlation between experience in government or in the armed services and performance in the White House, or even that experience is that helpful in winning votes. In 2008, the man with least experience among the major candidates led in the polls. Abraham Lincoln had little experience compared to his predecessor James Buchanan, or his successor Andrew Johnson, but he was an incomparably greater president. Neither of the very highly experienced Adamses, John or John Quincy, fared that well in the White House and neither was reelected.

Figure 2 | Experience Does Not Make a President Great

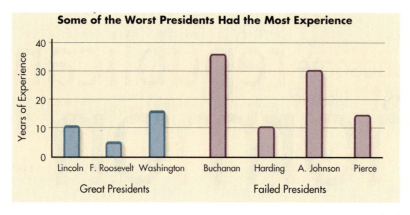

Prior experience includes summed number of years as vice president, U.S. diplomat or cabinet secretary, member of either house of Congress, governor, state legislator, local official, or army general. Ratings based on a 1999 survey of academic historians sponsored by C-SPAN. Lincoln, Roosevelt, and Washington usually rate at the top in any survey of historians. The bottom dwellers are a bit more varied, but these four are usually at or near the bottom, as they were in the C-SPAN survey.

SOURCE: David Von Drehle, "Does Experience Matter in a President?" Time (March 10, 2008): 28-29.

White House staff and cabinet veteran James A. Baker claims "there's no such thing as presidential experience outside of the office itself."[7] Even if this is true, presidents who get reelected usually fare worse in their second than their first term. There is little evidence that experience gained in office builds in a way that makes a president increasingly effective over time.

Pay and Perks

The Constitution authorizes Congress to award the president "a Compensation," which can be neither increased nor decreased during a president's term of office. This was $25,000 a year for our first seventeen presidents, then it jumped in increments to $200,000, where it stayed for many years. It did not reach its current level of $400,000 until 2001. The president continues to receive $50,000 for expenses. In addition, there are *substantial* fringe benefits. Most are obvious—the White House, the rural Camp David retreat, the best health care money can buy, and fleets of cars and aircraft. After leaving office, the president is entitled to a generous pension (about $186,000 per year in 2009), as well as money for travel, an office and staff, and ten years of Secret Service protection.

Tenure and Succession

Presidents serve four-year terms. The Twenty-second Amendment ★ limits them to serving two terms (or ten years if they complete the term of an incumbent who dies or resigns).

Four presidents died in office from illness (Harrison, Taylor, Harding, and Franklin Roosevelt), and four were assassinated (Garfield, McKinley, Lincoln, and Kennedy).

Presidents can be removed from office by impeachment and conviction. The House has the power of **impeachment**, that is, the authority to bring formal charges against a president (similar to an indictment in criminal proceedings) for "Treason, Bribery, or other high Crimes and Misdemeanors" ★ Art. II, Sect. 4. In an impeachment inquiry, the House holds hearings to determine whether there is sufficient evidence to impeach, and if a majority votes yes, the president is impeached and the process moves to the Senate, where a trial is held with the chief justice of the United States presiding. Conviction requires a two-thirds vote of members present in the Senate and results in removal from the presidency.

The Founders established the impeachment option as part of the system of checks and balances, a final weapon against executive abuse of power. They borrowed it from British law as a means to remove a president who had abused his power—for example, violated the Constitution—or committed serious crimes, not as a means for unseating a president for partisan reasons. Thus James Madison objected to the inclusion of the phrase "and other high crimes and misdemeanors" because he thought it was so vague that it *could* be used for political purposes.[8] The phrase was retained, but it was precisely to guard against its partisan use that the Founders divided indictment and removal powers between the House and the Senate. ★ Art. I, Sect. 2 & 3. If trying the charges were left to the popularly elected House, Hamilton wrote in *Federalist Paper* 65, "there will always be the greatest danger that the decision will be regulated more by the comparative strength of parties, than by the real demonstrations of innocence or guilt."

The procedure is cumbersome and meant to be; the Founders did not intend for the president, as head of state and the only nationally elected official in government, to be removed from office easily. Only three presidents have been targets of full impeachment proceedings.[9] Andrew Johnson, who came to office on Lincoln's assassination, was a southerner who was unpopular in his own party; he was impeached by the House in a dispute over Reconstruction policies in the post–Civil War South. The Senate failed to convict by a single vote. A century later, the House Judiciary Committee voted to impeach **Richard Nixon** on obstruction of justice and other charges stemming from the Watergate scandal, whereupon Nixon resigned as president, knowing he would lose the vote if it were brought to the full House. Once out of office, he avoided indictment on criminal charges through a full pardon granted by his successor, Gerald Ford, a move that aroused a storm of controversy at the time. In 1998, Bill Clinton became the third target of the process when the House voted to open an unrestricted inquiry into possible grounds for his impeachment. The House brought two charges against him for obstruction of justice stemming from lies he told about a sexual relationship with a White House intern, but the Senate refused to convict.

Articles of impeachment against George W. Bush were introduced in the House during both of his terms. In 2008, the bill introduced by Rep. Dennis Kucinich (D-Mich.) contained 34 separate counts, including civil rights violations such as suspension of *habeus corpus* for terrorism suspects and the wiretapping of private citizens without court authorization, and also failure to execute legislation as enacted by Congress (see the section on signing statements). The Democratic House leadership refused to let the bill advance.

Should a president be removed, die, resign, or become incapacitated, his replacement is provided for by the Constitution and supplemental laws. ⭐ Art. II, Sect. 1. At the time the Constitution was written, it was assumed that the vice presidency would be occupied by the man who had been the runner-up in the presidential election, and the wording simply said that presidential powers "shall devolve on the Vice President." It was left to Congress to make provisions for filling the vacated vice presidency and dealing with a situation in which both the presidency and the vice presidency were vacated. When Lincoln was assassinated, there still were no provisions for replacing Vice President Andrew Johnson when he succeeded to the presidency. Had Johnson been convicted in his impeachment trial, the presidency would have gone to the president pro tempore of the Senate, who was next in the line of succession according to rules in effect at the time.

Not until 1947, two years after the death of Franklin Roosevelt had put the virtually unknown Harry Truman in the White House, did Congress pass the Presidential Succession Act. It established the order of succession of federal officeholders should both the president and the vice president be unable to serve. The list begins with the Speaker of the House, followed by the president pro tempore of the Senate, and then proceeds through the secretaries of the cabinet departments in the order in which the departments were created. However, if a cabinet member is foreign-born, which is not unusual, he or she would be skipped in the line of succession.

The Succession Act has never been used because we have always had a vice president when something happened to the president. To ensure that this is always the case, the Constitution was amended in 1967. The Twenty-fifth ⭐ Amendment directs the president to name a vice president acceptable to majorities in the House and Senate if the vice presidency falls vacant. These provisions have been used twice. Nixon chose Gerald Ford to replace Spiro Agnew, who resigned after pleading no contest to charges of taking bribes when he was a public official in Maryland. After Nixon resigned and Ford became president, Ford named Nelson Rockefeller, the former governor of New York, as his vice president.

The Twenty-fifth Amendment also charges the vice president and a majority of the cabinet—or some other body named by Congress—to determine, in instances where there is doubt, whether the president is mentally or physically incapable of carrying out his duties. This provision was meant to provide for situations in which it is unclear who is or should be acting as president, such as when James Garfield was shot in July 1881. He did not die until mid-September, and during this period he was unable to fulfill any of his duties. In 1919, Woodrow Wilson had a nervous collapse in the summer and a stroke in the fall and was partially incapacitated for seven months. No one was sure about his condition, however, because his wife restricted access to him.

Under the amendment's provisions, the vice president becomes "acting president" if the president is found mentally or physically unfit to fulfill his duties. As the title suggests, the conferral of power is temporary; the president can resume office by giving Congress written notice of his recovery. If the vice president and other officials who determined the president unfit do not concur in his judgment that he has recovered, they can challenge his return to office by notifying Congress in writing. Then it falls to Congress to decide whether the president is capable of resuming his duties.

Reagan and then George W. Bush followed the spirit of this section. When each was undergoing surgery, they sent their respective vice presidents letters authorizing them to act as president while they were unconscious.

The issue of succession arose again after the terrorist attacks of 2001 when the Bush administration, just hours after the attack, activated an emergency plan established during the Eisenhower administration to provide for continuity of government in case of a nuclear attack. A shadow

Until the twentieth century, Congress was usually the strongest branch of government. Presidents, such as Millard Fillmore (from left), Franklin Pierce, and James Buchanan, were usually ordinary men who did ordinary things.

government of from 75 to 100 senior executive branch officials (serving in a rotation system) were removed to a secret fortified location outside the capital where they lived and worked underground twenty-four hours a day. In the immediate months after the 9/11 attacks, then Vice President Dick Cheney spent much of his time at undisclosed locations that the press referred to collectively as "the Bunker."

Growth of the Presidency

The Founders' Expectations

The American colonists chafed under the strong executives—the British king and the royal governors—who exercised authority over them. When the colonists gained their independence and drafted the Articles of Confederation, they made sure that the new government had no strong executive. In fact, it had no separate executive; the legislature wielded executive, as well as legislative, power. But the new government was too weak, incapable of resolving either domestic or foreign crises. So when the Founders drafted the Constitution, they created a separate executive, and they gave this executive, the president, substantial power. Yet their memories of British rule were still fresh. The Founders rejected proposals for a monarchy or anything akin to a monarchy. They wanted a government with a stronger executive than under the Articles but a weaker executive than under the British. Consequently, the Founders intended the legislature, Congress, to be the dominant branch in that they invested it with all legislative powers.

At its inception, the presidency was a relatively weak office in an infant country with few international ties and no standing army. John Quincy Adams (1825–1829) reflected the relatively low status of the job when he remarked, "No

man who ever held the office would congratulate another on attaining it."

Congressional Government

Throughout the nineteenth century, except during the Civil War, the real power at the national level resided in Congress, so much so that **Woodrow Wilson**, who was a political scientist before becoming president, characterized our national government as a "congressional government."[10]

Consequently, between Andrew Jackson in the 1830s and Franklin Roosevelt in the 1930s, most men who sought the presidency were "ordinary people, with very ordinary reputations."[11] There were powerful exceptions—such as Abraham Lincoln, Theodore Roosevelt, and Woodrow Wilson—and a few with exceptional achievements before their presidencies—such as Ulysses Grant (1869–1877) and Herbert Hoover (1929–1233)—who fared badly in the White House.

Expansion of Executive Power

Over time, the influence and visibility of the presidency has grown to rival and often exceed the powers of Congress. There were critical periods during which the union could have failed—at the birth of the nation, the Civil War, the Great Depression, and World War II—when presidential leadership made the difference. From the beginning, most Americans accepted that we need more government and executive leadership during crises and less at other times. Presidential power was traditionally supposed to return to its "normal" low profile after we resolved special problems.

This expectation may have been realistic early on, but once the nation stretched from Mexico to Canada and from the Atlantic to the Pacific, once it had a standing army, international trade aspirations, and the ambition to dominate the hemisphere, governmental power gravitated to Washington and to the president. The image of Thomas Jefferson sitting at his desk in isolation week after week conducting the presidency by personal correspondence was a quaint memory even twenty years later when **Andrew Jackson** was dubbed the "people's president."[12] Jackson was the first to act assertively to fulfill the popular mandate he saw in his election—the first to veto a bill because *he* did not like it. Thirty years later, **Abraham Lincoln** (1861–1865) assumed extraordinary powers during the Civil War, raising and financing an army while Congress was out of session, blockading southern ports, imposing martial law, suspending *habeas corpus* (which prevents illegal detentions), arresting southern sympathizers, censoring critical newspapers, jailing their editors; and all along interpreting the Constitution to say that the Union was indivisible.

Theodore Roosevelt (1901–1909), who has been called the "preacher militant," used the presidency as a "bully pulpit" in an unprecedented way to challenge corporate power and to argue for labor reform and better living conditions for average Americans. He also saw an imperial role for the United States in world politics, especially through military expansion, and led the country toward those "entangling alliances" that George Washington had warned against. When he desired to send the American fleet around the world, as a display of our military might, Congress balked at the cost. So Roosevelt announced that he had enough money in his budget to send the fleet halfway around the world, and that if Congress wanted the fleet to return home, it could appropriate the rest of the money. Eight years after Roosevelt left office, Wilson became the first twentieth-century president to lead us into a major

foreign involvement, World War I, and he was the first president to travel to Europe while in office.

The Great Depression and Franklin Roosevelt

The Great Depression and World War II led to a large expansion in the role of the national government and tremendous growth in presidential power. **Franklin Delano Roosevelt** (FDR) was elected president in 1932 because people thought he would help them through the crisis. In his first inaugural address, he told Americans that he would ask Congress for "broad executive power" equivalent, he said, to what he might be granted if an enemy had invaded the country, to fight the Depression. The enactment of New Deal programs led to an expansion of the executive branch because new agencies had to be created and new civil servants hired. This increased the president's power by making him more important as a manager and policy maker. And after the United States entered World War II, Roosevelt assumed additional powers as a hands-on commander in chief.

Roosevelt used radio to extend his power. An integral part of national life by the 1930s, radio gave people a way to follow their presidents and presidents a way to sell their policies: as his campaign song promised, "Happy Days Are Here Again." Radio newscasts focused on the president, and his "fireside chats" drew more attention to himself and his policies. Through radio, Roosevelt became a national cheerleader, a one-man band of optimism, persuading the public that solutions were at hand. Roosevelt's experience showed how the broadcast media—radio, and television when it became popular in the 1950s—would enhance

Brown Brothers

Teddy Roosevelt called the presidency a "bully pulpit" from which he could persuade both legislators and the public to support his programs. (In his time, "bully" was slang for "jolly good.")

Teddy Roosevelt's presidency marked the emergence of the United States as a world power. Roosevelt built up the navy, as this illustration from the time portrays. He said the United States should wield "a big stick."

presidential power by making the president the focal point of the government.

Roosevelt was elected for an unprecedented four terms. The country had come a long way from the era of George Washington, who refused to run for a third term because he thought it wouldn't be healthy for democracy if one person accumulated vast power.

After the Depression and the war ended, most Americans gave Roosevelt credit for pulling the country through. Since then, the public has usually expected strong presidents.[13]

The Ebb and Flow of Presidential Power

Roosevelt's successors had little opportunity to shrink the presidency. With the United States emerging from World War II as the preeminent world power and with the Cold War replacing the hot war as the foreign policy challenge, Congress was willing to cede even more authority to presidents to counter the Soviet threat. Responsibilities as the chief diplomat and commander in chief of the world's largest military would make the president a principal actor on the world stage.

The Vietnam War, a small conflict magnified by the Cold War, led to concerns about excessive presidential power. Presidents Kennedy, Johnson, and Nixon all waged war in Vietnam—the use of American troops started during the Kennedy administration, continued through the Johnson and Nixon administrations, and ended during the Ford administration—sometimes in secret and most times without input from Congress.

While waging the war, President Johnson also marshaled his power for a highly ambitious legislative agenda, and President Nixon claimed vast power under a very expansive constitutional interpretation. Nixon said such power was necessary for "national security," even when there was little threat to national security. He also engaged in the illegal activities that collectively would become known as the Watergate scandal—break-ins; phone taps; unauthorized use of government agencies, from the IRS to the FBI and CIA, to retaliate against administration critics; and then obstruction of justice in covering up the evidence of these acts. The back-to-back presidencies of Johnson and Nixon prompted talk about an imperial presidency.

Reaction against the arrogant use of presidential powers led to the modest presidencies of Gerald Ford (1974–1977) and Jimmy Carter (1977–1981). Both men came across as more humble than Johnson or Nixon and less interested in power for its own sake. Ford, who became president when Nixon resigned, was a kind of accidental president and could not get reelected. Nor could Carter; he had ambitious programs, especially in energy and conservation, but his ascetic if not dour, demeanor and demands for American sacrifice put him at a disadvantage against the sunny disposition of his successor, Ronald Reagan (1981–1989). But Reagan, one of our most popular recent presidents, was so frustrated when Congress thwarted his foreign policy initiatives that he condoned illegal activities, producing the Iran-Contra scandal and a tarnished personal reputation. Reagan, George H. W. Bush (1989–1993), and Bill Clinton (1993–2001) all had ambitious agendas, although Reagan and Bush's were directed more toward foreign than domestic policy.

However, under Clinton, the presidency seemed to be imploding. A former employee of Arkansas state government sued him and the Supreme Court ruled that he had no immunity while in office because the conduct occurred before he took office.[14] The judges, in a colossal misjudgment, doubted that the case would take much of his time and attention. In fact, it not only took his time but diverted the attention of the media and Washingtonians from efforts to implement his policies. After that, came the impeachment.

Some historians speculated that Clinton's impeachment would leave a legacy similar to Andrew Johnson's, which weakened the presidency for the next half-century.[15] But when George W. Bush came to office in 2001, he brought with him a retinue of Washington professionals and set out to restore the presidency to its former preeminence. Despite many strong actions and the successes of his first term already mentioned (see the box "From Imperial to Diminished Presidency?" on page 328), Bush also fell prey to the ills that beset second-term presidents. He watched his popularity plummet to historic lows as his once popular wars dragged on at an increasing cost and the economy fell into recession.

Presidential Power versus Congressional Power

Both presidential power and congressional power have grown as the federal government has grown. The presidency has grown through powers delegated by law or voluntarily ceded by Congress (foreign policy making during the Cold War and again in the war against terrorism) or assumed by default through congressional inaction. Crises arose, presidential incumbents responded, and in the process they assumed powers of government never before exercised at the federal level. Although both presidential power and congressional power have grown, presidential power has increased relative to congressional power because the presidency has inherent advantages over Congress.

The president is one person, whereas Congress includes 535 members who are divided into two houses and hundreds of committees and subcommittees. Congressional leaders struggle to develop and articulate policy goals acceptable to their party and their members, and then they struggle to keep the members committed to the goals. While the members of Congress talk and negotiate, the president can decide and act. The president can also attract the attention of the media, which focus on the single president rather than the multiple members of Congress. Hence the White House gets a bigger megaphone.

In addition, the president has more information, collected by the huge bureaucracy of the executive branch. In foreign affairs, the president has a monopoly, or near monopoly, of information from the intelligence agencies. The president can keep this information secret, revealing as much as necessary to persuade the members of Congress and the public. Or he can falsely claim the existence of classified information to make his case. In the run-up to the Iraq War, the administration insisted that Iraq had weapons of mass destruction. Secretary of Defense Donald Rumsfeld said the administration even knew where the weapons were. But no WMD were found there or anywhere.

Despite the advantages, presidential power should not be exaggerated. Most presidents since World War II have seemed at times almost powerless to shape events affecting the national interest. The immensely popular war hero Dwight Eisenhower (1953–1961) was unable to buck Cold War sentiment and prevent the buildup of the military-industrial complex. John Kennedy (1961–1963), who enjoyed an extraordinary success rate in a conservative Congress, was stymied in getting civil rights legislation accepted. The domestic goals of Lyndon Johnson (1963–1968), along with his chances for reelection, were derailed by a war that took Richard Nixon (1969–1974) years to end. And Nixon, for whom the imperial presidency phrase was coined, was forced from office on obstruction of justice charges for covering up criminal activity in the Watergate scandal. Three of their four successors could not get reelected.

The balance of power swings like a pendulum, depending upon major events at the time, the personality of the president, and the composition of Congress. Sometimes the presidency is dominant, sometimes Congress is dominant, and other times the two are evenly matched.[16] The important lesson, as one presidential scholar reminds us, is that "the Presidency is not the government. Ours is not a presidential system."[17] Rather, "the most outstanding feature of the American system is the separation of powers."[18]

Presidential Leadership

Presidents derive their official authority from four sources: explicit powers, which are stated in the Constitution, such as commander in chief, chief executive, or foreign policy leader; implicit (or implied) powers, which are implied in the explicit powers; inherent powers, which are not in the Constitution, explicitly or implicitly, but are considered to be a national executive's prerogatives; and delegated powers, which are granted to Congress by the Constitution but given to the president by various statutes. Collectively, they represent a towering set of responsibilities. With these powers, presidents play various roles, as head of state, chief executive, fiscal leader, legislative leader, diplomatic and military leader, and party leader. ⭐ Art. II, Sect. 2 and 3.

Head of State

The **head of state** is the official representative of a country and its people. He or she symbolizes the identity and the unity of the nation. In the United States, the president is the head of state and as such performs various nonpolitical functions, especially on ceremonial occasions, such as lighting the White House Christmas tree; opening the baseball season; greeting foreign visitors to this country; or attending the swearing in, coronation, or funeral of foreign dignitaries. The president's role as unifier of the nation was acted out by Bill Clinton in leading the national mourning for victims of the bombing of the federal building in Oklahoma City and by George W. Bush participating in a memorial service at Washington's National Cathedral for the victims of 9/11. (See box, "If They Can't Get Back from the Moon….")

The president is also the **head of government**. In this capacity, he is the leader of a political party with a partisan agenda. For these dual roles to be combined in one person is unusual. In most other Western democracies, the state and government are separate entities headed by different people. The government is presided over by politicians and elected officials with partisan interests. The state is the embodiment of the nation itself, the people and their history and traditions, and in most other nations, its representative (a king or queen or elder statesman) is assumed to be above partisan politics. In Great Britain, for example, the queen is head of state and the prime minister is the head of government.

In the United States, the fusion of the two offices gives the president a political advantage that leaders of other Western governments do not have. Members of Congress, the press, or the public who may attack him freely in his partisan role as head of government usually show more—some say too much—deference when the president is acting in his capacity as head of state. When he stands in public behind the Great Seal of the United States of America, he is not just a party leader who was elected to govern, but a nonpartisan representative of all the people, entrusted with the symbols, emblems, and traditions of the country.

Addressing the Nation

As head of state, the president is required by the Constitution to report to Congress "from time to time" about the "State of the Union." ⭐ Art. II, Sect. 3. There is no required form for these reports and Jefferson's practice of submitting it in writing—because in his view a personal address to Congress too closely resembled the monarch's speech that opens each session of the British Parliament—lasted for a hundred years. When Woodrow Wilson revived the practice of reporting in person, one senator labeled it a "cheap and tawdry imitation of English royalty."[19]

Today these addresses are televised and delivered in the House of Representatives before a joint session of Congress within several weeks of the opening of each congressional session. The president notes the successes of the past year, addresses problems, and outlines his policy agenda for the coming year. Part of the report deals with the mood of the country and identifies goals for maintaining or increasing national unity. These addresses are usually written from boilerplate and are rarely memorable; the "state of the union" is pronounced "strong," and Americans are reassured that they live in a great nation. An analysis of all State of the Union addresses concluded that it is impossible for speechwriters to overuse "freedom" or references to the United States as "great" and "good."[20]

BEHIND THE SCENES
IF THEY CAN'T GET BACK FROM THE MOON . . .

When a tragedy strikes, the president is expected to be the "mourner in chief." In the days before American astronauts were sent to the moon in 1969, government officials feared that a malfunction might leave them stranded on the moon, unable to return to Earth. According to documents that surfaced at the National Archives years later, the Nixon administration had prepared for this contingency.

A speechwriter penned a speech for President Nixon to give while the astronauts were still alive but had no hope of returning:

Fate has ordained that the men who went to the moon to explore in peace will stay on the moon to rest in peace.

These brave men . . . know that there is no hope for their recovery. But they also know that there is hope for mankind in their sacrifice.

These . . . men are laying down their lives in mankind's

most noble goal: the search for truth and understanding.

In ancient days, men looked at stars and saw their heroes in the constellations. In modern times, we do much the same, but our heroes are epic men of flesh and blood.

Others will follow, and surely find their way home. Man's search will not be denied. But these men were the first, and they will remain the foremost in our hearts.

Before giving the speech, the president would contact the "widows-to-be." After giving the speech,

he would instruct NASA to cut off all further communications with the astronauts to cut short the public agony over their deaths. Then a clergyman would follow the protocol used for a burial at sea and conclude with "The Lord's Prayer."

Of course, the president didn't have to implement these plans, as the astronauts, after 21 hours on the moon, returned home safely.

Source: "Nixon Had Words Ready for Moon Disaster," *Lincoln Journal Star*, July 10, 1999.

Even when presidents are mired in political controversy at the time of the speech—Nixon during the Watergate investigation or Clinton in 1998, delivering the State of the Union address just weeks after the revelation of personal misconduct—congressional leaders usually caution the membership to show respect to the person who is speaking in his constitutional role as head of state.

Pardon power

As head of state, the president is authorized to grant pardons. Through the **pardon power**, the president can erase the guilt and restore the rights of anyone convicted of a federal crime, except an impeached president. ⭐ Art. II, Sect. 2. One of Lincoln's last acts, signed the day he was assassinated, was to pardon a Union Army deserter. Blanket pardons have been issued to Confederate Army veterans and Vietnam draft evaders, but most presidents have used the power to clear the names of offenders who have served their sentences. This is consistent with Chief Justice Marshall's definition of a pardon as "a private, though official act of grace."[21]

Each year hundreds of people petition the president for pardons, the overwhelming majority of which are vetted by the Office of the United States Pardon Attorney in the Department of Justice and recommended for denial. Presidents usually follow the lawyers' advice but they not required to do so or even to consult government lawyers before granting pardons. In *Federalist* 74 Alexander Hamilton argued that the "benign prerogative of pardoning should be as little as possible fettered or embarrassed." Nevertheless pardons do occasionally embarrass or come back to haunt a president.

Using pardon power to absolve government officials or persons convicted of crimes with political overtones can evoke strong public reactions. George H. W. Bush discovered this when he pardoned Reagan's secretary of defense and five other officials charged with or convicted of crimes related to the Iran-Contra scandal. So did Clinton, with his last-minute pardon of a fugitive commodities trader whose ex-wife was a large donor to the Democratic Party. George W. Bush did not pardon Cheney aide and administration loyalist Lewis "Scooter" Libby, but he did remit, or cancel, the 2½-year prison sentence Libby received after he was convicted of lying and obstructing justice during the investigation into the leak of the identity of CIA agent Valerie Plame.

During his first seven years in office, Bush granted only 142 pardons, fewer than any president since World War II.[22] Near the end of his term, more than 2000 pardon petitions were languishing in the Justice Department and White House counsel's office with insufficient staff to vet them.

Chief Executive

Article II of the Constitution stipulates, "The executive power shall be vested in a president," and it charges him to "take care that the laws be faithfully executed." ⭐ Sect. 1 and 3. The Founders expected Congress to pass laws and the president to implement them and manage the executive branch. Thus the president is the **chief executive**. According to the *Federalist Papers*, with respect to law-making, president's responsibilities would be "mere execution" and "executive details."[23]

The Constitution has few specific provisions describing the president's administrative duties, but it does invest the president with the authority to demand written reports from his "principal officers," assigns him significant appointment and administrative powers, and implies others.

"MADAM SPEAKER, VICE-PRESIDENT CHENEY, MEMBERS OF CONGRESS, MEMBERS OF THE SUPREME COURT AND THE DIPLOMATIC CORPS, DISTINGUISHED GUESTS AND FELLOW CITIZENS, WE REALLY HAVE MADE A MESS OF THINGS, HAVEN'T WE?"

At few times in American history have five presidents been alive at once. This early 1990s photograph shows, from left, Richard Nixon (1969–1974), Gerald Ford (1974–1977), Jimmy Carter (1977–1981), Ronald Reagan (1981–1989), and George H. W. Bush (1989–1993).

Appointment and Removal Powers

Although most of the staff in the executive branch are civil service appointees, the president nominates about 3000 people to civilian positions in the departments and agencies, two-thirds of whom do not require confirmation. Of the remaining one-third who do require formal approval by the Senate, only about 600 of the most important policy-making jobs—heads of regulatory agencies, boards and commissions, cabinet secretaries and ambassadors, and federal judges, for example—receive careful review.[24] For the highest-profile positions, such as the secretaries of state and defense, televised hearings are held prior to a confirmation vote in the Senate.

For decades, it was customary for the Senate, no matter which party controlled it, to approve the president's nominations to policy-making positions on the grounds that having won the election, he is entitled to surround himself with people who can help put his policies in place. But the highly partisan context of the Senate in the last several decades has weakened this tradition somewhat. In practice, the president's freedom to name people to some positions is limited by the custom of **senatorial courtesy**. This gives senators from the president's party a virtual veto over appointments to positions, including judicial appointments, in their states.

As the leader of his party, the president has a political (not governmental) obligation to help senators from his party get reelected. Thus he usually defers to their political needs and wishes when making federal appointments in their home states, even though doing so limits to some extent his freedom to choose.

Presidents have more latitude in nominating people to positions with national jurisdictions, such as cabinet posts and seats on regulatory boards and independent agencies. It has become customary to give preference in some appoint-

ments to people with politically useful backgrounds, such as naming a westerner secretary of the interior, a person with union ties to be labor secretary, or a close associate of the president to be attorney general. But these considerations were never confining and, as traditions, are weakening.

Although the power to remove appointees is not in the Constitution, presidents have it. Their power to name people they trust implies a power to remove those they find wanting, but because the power is not explicit, Congress has not always recognized it. The battle over removal powers was fought and largely won by Grover Cleveland, who on entering office in 1885 insisted on replacing many policy-making officials with his own appointees. He was challenged by the Senate, but he persevered. His persistence is credited with helping revitalize a presidency weakened by Andrew Johnson's impeachment.

In 1935, the Supreme Court refined this removal power by saying that presidents can remove appointees from purely administrative jobs but not from those with quasi-legislative and judicial responsibilities. This ruling protects many appointees, but distinguishing quasi-legislative and judicial positions from those with no policy-making authority can be subjective.[25]

Presidents cannot remove officials appointed to policy-making positions with fixed terms, such as regulatory boards and the Federal Reserve Board. Nor can the president remove federal judges, who serve for life.

Of course, presidents can appoint and remove political aides and advisers on their White House staff at will; none of these appointments require Senate approval. Presidents also have wide latitude in replacing cabinet heads and some agency directors—even though these positions do require Senate confirmation—because they are seen as agents of presidential policy. This does not keep the Senate from trying at times to badger a president into firing one of his appointees, as it did repeatedly and unsuccessfully with Clinton's attorney general, Janet Reno. More widespread pressure was placed on George W. Bush to remove Donald Rumsfeld as his secretary of defense and Alberto Gonzalez as his attorney general. A president may give in for political reasons, as Bush eventually did, but he cannot be compelled to do so. However, Congress does have the power of removal through impeachment and conviction of all "civil Officers of the United States." ⭐ Art. II, Sect. 4.

Reorganizing Agencies

When the president enters office, a huge bureaucracy is already in place. Each new president has to be able to reorganize offices and agencies to fit his administrative and working style and to be consistent with the issue priorities he has set.[26] This can mean reassigning responsibilities, merging or abolishing offices, or creating new ones.

Within the White House Office itself, the president has a fairly free hand to reshuffle staff and offices. But any major reorganization of government departments and agencies requires congressional approval, such as George W. Bush's creation of a new cabinet-level Department of Homeland Security, reorganizing the jurisdictions of dozens of executive branch agencies. The plan called for reassigning almost 200,000 federal employees, transferring funds, and authorizing new spending authority and brought on a classic turf battle, both within the bureaucracy and between the White House and Congress.

Inherent Executive Powers

Because the Constitution charges the president with ensuring that "the laws be faithfully executed," the courts have ruled that the president has inherent power to take actions and issue orders to fulfill that duty.

Executive Orders   One of the president's inherent powers is the authority to issue directives or proclamations, called **executive orders**, that have the force of law as long as they do not contradict the Constitution. Thus executive orders are a form of legislative power for the executive branch.

The rationale for executive orders is that Congress often lacks the expertise and ability to act quickly when technological or other developments require fast action and flexibility.[27] George W. Bush, for example, made heavy use of executive orders in responding to problems created by the 9/11 attacks. Because the numbering and recording of the orders did not start until 1907, it is unclear how many have been issued. Since 1946, Congress has required all executive orders, except those dealing with classified national security issues, to be published in the *Federal Register*.[28]

Many of these executive orders have had a significant impact. Truman, for example, used an executive order to integrate the armed forces, Kennedy to end racial discrimi-

nation in public housing, and Lyndon Johnson to require affirmative action hiring by firms with federal contracts. Presidents more commonly use executive orders to deal with organizational problems and internal procedures, but presidents also use them to implement the provisions of treaties and legislative statutes that are ambiguously stated (perhaps deliberately) by Congress. In fact, presidents have used executive orders to make policies opposed by congressional majorities. Reagan and both Bushes used this power to ban abortion counseling in federally financed clinics and financial aid to United Nations–sponsored family planning programs. Another significant use of executive orders is to manage the controversial system for classifying government documents and withholding information from the public.

Through the exercise of this inherent power of office, the presidency has acquired significant legislative authority. But executive orders are much more easily overridden than congressional acts; a president can rescind or countermand some orders issued by a predecessor, as Clinton did with foreign aid restrictions on family planning and George W. Bush did with several of Clinton's environmental protection orders. Furthermore, the legality of executive orders can be challenged in federal court. Early in his presidency, George W. Bush ordered the posting of signs in union shops informing workers that they were not required to allow union dues to be withheld from their paychecks. A federal court ruled that this was a misuse of an executive order.

DEMOCRACY?

The first sentence of the Constitution assigns "all legislative Powers" to Congress. Is it significant that in a government by the people that the president can, on his own authority, issue directives that have the force of law?

Executive Privilege   To ensure that they receive the full and frank advice of their aides and advisers or of any visitors to the White House, presidents also have **executive privilege**, the right to refuse to make public some internal documents and private conversations.

Presidents since George Washington have asserted executive privilege, usually when Congress has requested information. Since the 1970s, federal court rulings have argued that without such a privilege a president cannot fulfill his administrative duties because he would not be able to get full and frank advice from his aides. The courts have also ruled that the power is limited in scope rather than absolute but have not defined its limits, deferring that task to Congress. Congress has also refused to specify the limits of executive privilege, leaving it to the courts to resolve each invocation of privilege that the president and Congress cannot resolve.

In the landmark ruling **United States v. Nixon**,[29] ordering President Nixon to turn over tape recordings of Oval

Office conversations to the Watergate special prosecutor, the Supreme Court did establish that executive privilege cannot be invoked to withhold evidence material to an investigation of criminal wrongdoing. President Nixon had installed a taping device in the Oval Office, which had secretly recorded conversations between the president and everyone he talked to there. The conversations could confirm or refute the charges of White House complicity in the break-in at the national office of the Democratic Party (in the Watergate Hotel), the attempt to place wiretaps on its phones, and then the cover-up of these actions. The special prosecutor demanded the tapes. When the president, citing executive privilege, refused to hand them over, the special prosecutor filed suit and the justices ruled unanimously that the privilege didn't apply in this situation. After twelve days of weighing his options, Nixon decided to comply with the ruling. Just seventeen days after the ruling, when it became clear that Congress would impeach and remove him, Nixon resigned. Although the tapes didn't indicate that he participated in planning the break-in, they did show that he participated in covering it up. (Years later, however, one aide claimed that the president himself had ordered the break-in).[30]

Similarly, the Supreme Court ruled against President Clinton when he invoked the privilege to prevent an aide from testifying before a grand jury about possible criminal wrongdoing. However, the courts upheld Clinton's extension of executive privilege to his conversations about po-litical strategy with his aides and to those between his aides and the first lady, who served as his political adviser and whom the courts had already recognized as serving in a quasi-official role.

The George W. Bush administration, which has made the strongest case for presidential power since the Nixon administration, has claimed executive privilege many times. In 2002, Congress, in its investigation of Enron's financial collapse, subpoenaed records of Vice President Cheney's meetings with executives from energy industries. The White House, claiming that executive privilege extended to the vice president, refused to turn over most of the documents, even after being ordered to do so by a federal court. Bush also used executive privilege to order active and former aides, including Karl Rove, not to testify before Congress, even when subpoenaed to do so, and even though some of the actions under investigation, such as the alleged Justice Department firing of United States attorneys for political reasons, could have involved criminal wrongdoing. These cases were still being appealed in federal courts in the final months of the Bush administration.

Fiscal Leader

The president has acquired a role as fiscal leader by attaining the power to manage the budget.

For many years, the president had a negligible role in managing the federal budgets because the Founders gave the House of Representatives the power to originate taxing and spending bills and the Senate the power to concur, dissent, or amend. The president's authority was limited to the same signing or vetoing power he has over other legislation. ⭐ Art. I, Sect. 7. Federal agencies sent their budget requests directly to the House, unreviewed and unchanged by the White House. But by the end of World War I, a general awareness had developed that a larger government required better management. In the Budget and Accounting Act of 1921, Congress delegated important priority-setting and managerial responsibilities that have given presidents so inclined the opportunity to dominate budgetary politics.

The president's annual budget message contains recommendations for how much money Congress should appropriate for every program funded by the national government. Formulating the message requires the White House to examine all agency budget requests and to decide which to support or reject. This exercise allows the president and his staff to begin the annual budget debate on their own terms.

Having the Office of Management and Budget within the Executive Office of the President gives the president an edge in dealing with Congress on

". . . to uphold the Constitution and the laws of the United States—as I see them . . ."

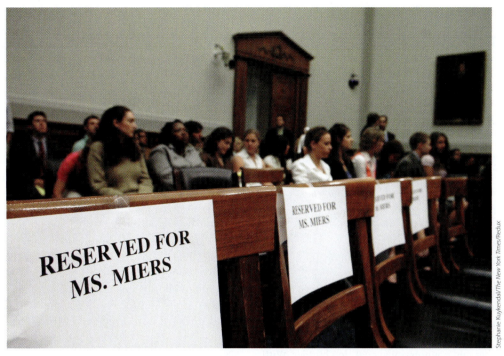

Stephanie Kuykendal/The New York Times/Redux

When the Democrats took control of Congress, they tried unsuccessfully to exercise more oversight of the Bush administration's actions. White House counsel Harriet Miers and adviser Karl Rove were subpoenaed to testify but were no-shows at the hearings, citing the president's claim of executive privilege.

budget issues because its hundreds of experts work only for the president. Thus, the administration understands exactly what's in the budget and shapes the debates over it. Congress's nonpartisan budget office, the Congressional Budget Office (CBO), prepares budget reports that are regarded as substantially more reliable than those of the OMB, but the policy initiative lies with the OMB and the White House because they prepare the first budget draft.

The president's budget-writing power is one of the greatest sources of friction in relations between the executive and legislative branches. Little is possible without funding, so the stakes in the budget process are high. Presidents who are little interested in the details of domestic policy, such as Reagan and both Bushes, do not get maximum political leverage out of the budgetary powers Congress has delegated to them. But a president whose strength lies in the mastery of detail may be able to use those powers, as Clinton did, to dominate budgetary politics and the debate over deficit reduction.

The delegation of budget authority to the president is partly responsible for the growth of presidential power and the engorgement of the Executive Office of the President (EOP)—the OMB alone occupies an eight-story building near the White House. But it carries political liabilities. Although no money can be spent unless authorized by congressionally passed budget resolutions, the president as budget initiator is held responsible for bad fiscal policy and budget deficits.

Legislative Leader

Congress, of course, was expected to dominate the legislative process, but the president has come to play an important role as well. The president is *a* legislative leader, though not necessarily *the* legislative leader. The president sets priorities, proposes solutions, shapes legislation, and vetoes legislation. For some legislation, the president is dominant, for some Congress is dominant, but for the most part the branches share responsibility.[31]

The relationship between president and Congress is a complex one. Ultimately, how persuasive a president is with Congress in getting his legislative agenda passed is an important faction whether he will be judged a successful president.

Our Founders did not think of the president as head of a political party with an issue agenda, but that is what he has become. Whether packaged as the Square Deal (Theodore Roosevelt), the New Deal (Franklin Roosevelt), the Fair Deal (Truman), the New Frontier (Kennedy), or the Great Society (Johnson), or with no snappy title at all, most presidents come to office with a legislative agenda.

Among the ongoing issues of the times, presidents designate their priorities. At any given time, the government's agenda is full to overflowing. If a president is an effective salesman, he can have great influence over which bills are given priority in any session of Congress. But presidents can't dictate what Congress spends its time on or what the media and the public focus on. In the Clinton years, the press and the people found the Lewinsky affair more fascinating than the president's legislative proposals. And the catastrophic failure of the Iraq War made it difficult for Bush to direct public or congressional attention to his legislative program.

Of course, though presidents designate their priorities, members of Congress have their own preferences and initiate their own bills. Even when they take up a president's proposal, they amend it. Virtually all proposals emerge from Congress in very different form from when they were introduced.

But presidents can have considerable influence over the final shape of legislation. It depends on how active a role they want to take and how involved they are in policy detail, as well as their knowledge of congressional operations and powers of persuasion. Franklin Roosevelt was able to impose his agenda during the Great Depression because of the public's desperation and his own great political skills. **Lyndon Johnson**, one of twenty-five presidents who have served in Congress, is the classic example of the president as inside dopester and congressional coalition builder. With service in both chambers and as a former Senate majority leader of legendary persuasiveness, Johnson knew how to put together legislative coalitions and could do it from the White House. As the nation became bogged down in the Vietnam War, however, Johnson's effectiveness with Congress diminished.

Other presidents, too, have had mixed success. Reagan's effectiveness with Congress was greatest in his first year in office, when he got Congress to approve a major tax cut and increase military spending. Economic problems produced

in part by these changes and a growing public awareness that he was uninformed about White House activities led to a drop in his effectiveness with Congress during the remainder of his administration. (See Figure 3.) Congressional support for George H. W. Bush was weak throughout his term. He had fewer congressional Republicans to work with than any GOP president in the twentieth century, and he had low support even among them.

Clinton tried to emulate Reagan's successful first-year strategy of asking Congress to vote on a few high-priority bills. This strategy lets presidents define their positions in relatively simple terms and seek congressional support during the postelection honeymoon period. With both houses of Congress controlled by Democratic majorities at the outset of his administration, Clinton did not have to deal with a divided government. Despite substantial disagreements among congressional Democrats, Clinton succeeded in getting majority support for most of his early economic proposals. His early legislative record was impressive, but it did not give him a reputation for effectiveness. It was overshadowed by the scandals that followed him into his second term and by his failure to articulate larger goals in a way that let the American people know where he wanted to lead them. (See Figure 3.)

George W. Bush's first-year success rate of 87 percent was nearly identical to that of Clinton's first year, partly because Bush took fewer positions and usually took a public stand only after Congress had drafted a bill in a form likely to pass.[32] With this low-risk strategy, Bush equaled Clinton's early success rate. His success rate remained high until his seventh year in office, when it fell to the same level as Clinton's during his seventh year (38 percent).

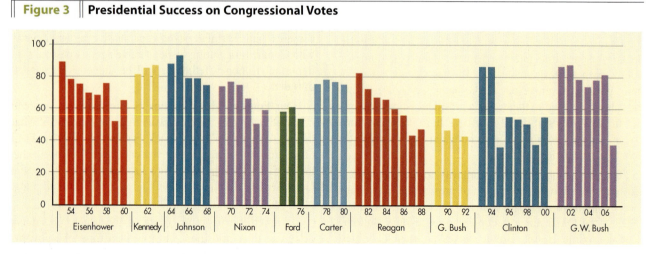

Figure 3 | **Presidential Success on Congressional Votes**

The graph indicates the percentage of the time in which the president got Congress to support his position in roll-call votes. Presidents usually have the most success with Congress early in their first term.
SOURCE: CQ Weekly, January 14, 2008, 133.

Veto Power

The Constitution has given the chief executive **veto power** (Latin for "I forbid") over bills passed by Congress. The veto power is not listed among the president's formal powers in Article II, but rather is included in Article I as a check on Congress's power to legislate. ⭐ Art. I, Sect. 7.

When the president receives a bill passed by Congress, he has three options: he can sign it into law; he can veto it and send it back to Congress along with his objections; or he can take no action, in which case the bill becomes a law after ten congressional working days. An unsigned bill returned by the president can be passed into law if two-thirds of both houses vote to override the veto. But if Congress adjourns within ten working days after sending legislation to the White House and the president chooses to pocket the bill—that is, not to act on it—the legislation dies. This option, called a **pocket veto,** is a means by which the president can kill a bill without facing an override attempt in Congress.

The veto, and the ever-present threat of a veto, helps presidents influence legislation. Given the presence of White House supporters in Congress and the president's ability to go public, mobilizing two-thirds majorities in both houses to override a veto is usually very hard. As a result, presidents can try to influence the content of bills by threatening to veto them if they do not conform to presidential wishes.

George Washington, not surprisingly, cast the first veto, but it was the only veto he cast in his first term. In his second term, he cast one more. In both cases he believed the bills contained provisions that were unconstitutional. He was acting as one who had to execute the law not as one trying to write law. Congress rewrote those provisions rather than trying to override.[33]

Franklin Roosevelt, the longest-serving president, holds the record with 635 vetoes in fourteen years; only 9 were overridden. Only eight presidents never vetoed a bill. George W. Bush didn't use the veto until his sixth year, but then used it ten more times in his last eighteen months in office. It is significant that all of Bush's vetoes on security and intelligence bills were upheld, even though the bills' contents involved controversial interpretations of civil rights and the constitutional powers of the president. The four Bush vetoes Congress overrode were on large spending measures passed in an election year. Presidents who use the veto too often may appear isolated or uncooperative or may seem to be exercising negative leadership. But the fact that presidents are rarely overridden reminds us of their power when they decide that they really want something.

Signing Statements

George W. Bush has tried to establish another presidential power. When a president signs a bill into law he may attach comments when he believes it contains vague language that may hamper implementation or constitutionally ambiguous provisions that may later be contested in federal court. Known as **signing statements,** these written comments are deposited with new laws and recorded in the *Federal Register.*

Historically, presidents made limited use of signing statements, primarily to clarify their understanding of vague language in a bill in case it is later contested. Signing statements have been seen as an administrative act, not as a presidential power. Until the 1980s, just over a dozen signing statements had been issued. But Reagan issued 71 and Clinton 105.[34]

In his attempt to exert executive authority over the legislative branch, George W. Bush interpreted this power very broadly. Bush attached signing statements to 1 out of 10— or more than 750—laws during his first five years in office. These were not limited to foreign and military policy, but included bills on "affirmative action, immigration, whistleblower protections, and safeguards against political interference in federally funded research."[35]

More important than the number of statements is their scope. In some, Bush exempted himself from a president's constitutional obligation to provide information to congressional oversight committees. In others, he exempted himself from a president's constitutional obligation to "faithfully execute" the laws passed by Congress. By use of the signing statement, Bush, for example, signed into law a bill forbidding the use of torture while at the same time attaching a statement—one that no one in the public would read—saying he had no intention of enforcing the legislation when he thought it interfered with his powers as commander in chief.

These and other statements were a de facto declaration of Bush's intention not to enforce, in whole or in part, the laws he was signing, on the grounds that the chief executive has complete authority to instruct executive branch agencies how to implement the laws. For a president to say that he's not obligated to "faithfully execute" the laws was a rare, if not to say bizarre, interpretation of the president's constitutional role to faithfully execute laws passed by Congress. And no president has authority to pass judgment on the constitutionality of a law; that power lies solely with the federal courts.

The only power the Constitution gives a president to block congressional legislation is the veto. But vetoes attract publicity and can be overridden. Signing statements escape public notice and provide no opportunity for congressional challenge. And they mislead the public about the laws the president supports and the ones he opposes. We can expect that Bush's use of the signing statements will be challenged in the federal courts.

Party Leader

The president is the head of his party and chief advocate for its policy agenda. As party leader, the president uses his reputation and his office to push his party's legislative priorities, an important dimension of presidential power.

As party leader, the president is an electoral adversary of members of the House and Senate who do not belong to his party. He can use his reputation and the weight of his office not only to challenge legislative priorities but also to try to unseat those who oppose them.

To improve the electoral chances of their party, presidents try to help recruit good candidates for House and Senate races. They send their political aides to help boost the campaigns of fellow partisans, and sometimes even go themselves. Even unpopular presidents can draw large crowds and media attention because seeing a president in person is exciting, and, for most communities, the visit of a president is a rare event.

In addition, presidents help their congressional candidates raise money by being the headliner at fundraising events and by staying on good terms with major contributors. They invite major donors to the White House and go around the country to help fellow partisans with their campaigns. Presidents also raise money for fellow partisans. Even in 2008, when fewer than 20 percent of the public thought President Bush was doing a good job, he was still popular among many Republican donors and thus was a very successful fundraiser. But the president usually tries to camouflage his role as party leader when trying to persuade people to support him or to vote for his party's candidates, because people are more likely to listen to a president when they see him as head of state.

Playing an active party role has a purpose: the more members of a president's party who sit in Congress, the more support he gets for his policies. However, a president's support, when he chooses to give it, is no guarantee of electoral success for congressional candidates, especially in off-year elections (See Table 1.) Since 1934, the president's party has lost an average of twenty-six House and three Senate seats in off-year elections.

| Table 1 | The President's Tattered Coattails: Congressional Gains and Losses for the President's Party in Off-Year Elections |

Year	President	House	Senate
1934	Roosevelt (D)	+9	+10
1938	Roosevelt (D)	−71	−6
1942	Roosevelt (D)	−55	−9
1946	Truman (D)	−45	−12
1950	Truman (D)	−29	−6
1954	Eisenhower (R)	−18	−1
1958	Eisenhower (R)	−47	−13
1962	Kennedy (D)	−4	+3
1966	Johnson (D)	−47	−3
1970	Nixon (R)	−12	+2
1974	Ford (R)	−48	−3
1978	Carter (D)	−15	−3
1982	Reagan (R)	−26	+1
1986	Reagan (R)	−5	−8
1990	G. H. Bush (R)	−8	−1
1994	Clinton (D)	−52	−8
1998	Clinton (D)	+5	0
2002	G. W. Bush (R)	+6	+2
2006	G. W. Bush	−31	-6
Average, all off-year elections		−26	−3
Average, all presidential election years		+20	+3

SOURCES: *Congressional Quarterly Weekly Review,* various issues; Roger H. Davidson, Walter J. Oleszek, and Frances E. Lee, *Congress and Its Members,* 11th ed. (Washington, D.C.: CQ Press, 2007), 107.

However, this trend no longer prevails, due to the increasing number of safe seats. District lines are drawn to protect incumbents, almost all of whom run for reelection, with a tremendous fundraising advantage. In recent years, these factors have helped make candidates safe even when their presidential candidate loses or is unpopular at midterm. The 1998 election was the first off-year election since 1934 that the president's party had a net gain, and that feat was duplicated in 2002. In the 2006 mid-term elections, the traditional pattern returned with the president's party losing seats in both chambers.

In presidential election years, the average gains for the winning presidential candidate's party in Congress are close to their losses in off-year elections: twenty in the House and three in the Senate. Again, these patterns are changing. In 1988 and 1992, the winning presidential party lost seats in Congress. In 2004, the winning presidential party gained the historical average in the Senate (three) but fell far below the historical average in the House. In 2008 it was the reverse, with the party winning the White House gaining slightly above the historical average of 20 seats in the House but doubling to 7 the number of seats won in the Senate.

Diplomatic and Military Leader

The Constitution includes provisions that make the president the chief diplomat of the country and the commander in chief of the military. Together, these roles enable the president to exercise tremendous power over foreign affairs, greater power than over domestic matters. And most presidents have enjoyed shaping foreign policy more than domestic policy, which Richard Nixon dismissed as having to worry about "outhouses in Peoria."[36]

Chief Diplomat

The Constitution authorizes the president to negotiate treaties, appoint ambassadors, and receive foreign ambassadors. ⭐ Art. II, Sect. 2. These provisions make the president the chief diplomat.

The president has the authority to negotiate treaties with foreign countries, although the Senate must approve them by a two-thirds majority before they can take effect. This requirement is a severe limitation on presidential power. Just as it's difficult to obtain two-thirds majorities to override a veto, it's also difficult to obtain a two-thirds majority to approve a treaty. This fact gives the Senate leverage to bargain with the president. After Jimmy Carter (1977–1981) negotiated a treaty to give the Panama Canal and return the Canal Zone to Panama, the Senate demanded two amendments—that the United States retain the right to intervene militarily against any threats to the canal and get priority passage for U.S. ships during wartime. (Carter renegotiated with Panama and then obtained approval of the amended treaty from the Senate.)

The president evidently can terminate treaties without any involvement by the Senate. The Supreme Court allowed Carter to terminate the 1903 treaty with Panama to make way for the new one.[37] A more striking example of unilateral termination (because no substitution for it was under negotiation) came in 2001 when George W. Bush withdrew the United States from the ABM (anti-ballistic missile) treaty not long after taking office.[38]

The president frequently conducts diplomacy directly with other world leaders, such as at summit conferences where they gather to discuss economic, trade, environmental, or arms issues. In his negotiations with other heads of government, he may reach executive agreements or trade agreements below the treaty level. These aren't mentioned in the Constitution, but are considered implicit in the president's diplomatic authority. Although similar to treaties, they do not require approval by two-thirds of the Senate to be formalized. However some executive agreements and trade deals do require simple majority approval.[39]

The president appoints ambassadors to represent us abroad, although the Senate must confirm them. The president also "receives" ambassadors from other countries. Foreign ambassadors present their credentials upon arriving in the country to begin their posting. What appears to be a ceremonial duty may actually be a significant power. Receiving foreign ambassadors implies recognizing their governments, which means acknowledging the legitimacy of their governments. If a revolution leads to a new government, there may be uncertainty or controversy as to which government is the legitimate government. The authority to "receive" foreign ambassadors thus gives the president the power to decide which government to recognize. The United States didn't recognize the Soviet government until sixteen years after the Bolshevik Revolution or the Communist government of China until twenty-five years after it took power.

From the beginning of the country, officials referred to the president as the "nation's organ for foreign affairs."[40] In 1936, the Supreme Court revised this characterization, calling the president the "sole organ" for foreign affairs.[41] This revision reflected the growth of presidential power by this time. Yet this revision remains controversial, because the Constitution also grants Congress powers over foreign affairs, including treaties and ambassadors, as we've seen here, and over war itself, as we'll see in the next section. Nonetheless, the statement accurately conveys the fact that the president dominates foreign policy making.

To underscore the importance of speaking with one voice in foreign affairs, Congress passed the Logan Act in 1799, after a Philadelphia doctor sailed to France to try his hand at diplomacy when it appeared that France and the United States were heading toward war. The act prohibits unauthorized citizens from negotiating with foreign governments. Such negotiations could undermine official attempts to conduct foreign policy. However, there's no record of any prosecutions for violating the act, although prosecutions were threatened during the Vietnam War when peace advocates traveled to North Vietnam and again when Jesse Jackson traveled to Cuba in violation of U.S. policy.

Commander in Chief

The Constitution designates the president "**Commander in Chief** of the Army and Navy … and of the Militia of the Several States, when called into the Actual service of the United States." ⭐ Art. II, Sect. 2. In doing so, the Founders were designating the president "first general" and "first admiral," as Hamilton wrote in *Federalist Paper* 69. The Founders realized that use of the military is sometimes necessary in the conduct of foreign policy. By making the president the "first general," the Founders made it clear that civilian authority has primacy over military authority; the president can countermand the order of any officer.

National Archives

As commander in chief, the president appoints military officers. During the Civil War, President Lincoln couldn't understand why the Union Army hadn't pressed its advantage over the Confederate army. When he visited the Antietam battlefield, he discovered that his top general, George McClellan, was both pro-Union and proslavery. Hoping for a stalemate in the war, McClellan tried to block Confederate advances but refused to rout Confederate troops. Lincoln replaced him.

Being "first general" and "first admiral" allows the president to determine military strategy. The army could not have dropped hydrogen bombs on Hiroshima and Nagasaki unless it had been authorized by President Truman. The decisions to wage limited wars in Korea and Vietnam and not use tactical nuclear weapons were based on presidential beliefs that victories over North Korea and North Vietnam were not worth risking a nuclear holocaust.

During the Korean War when General Douglas MacArthur tried to expand the conflict into a full-scale war with China against the express orders of President Truman, Truman replaced him, effectively ending his military career. Truman also went against the wishes of the military command by issuing an executive order ending racial segregation in the armed forces. In 2002, prior to the invasion of Iraq, President Bush and his secretary of defense forced the retirement of the chairman of the Joints Chiefs of Staff when he testified before Congress that the war would require far more troops than the civilian leadership was recommending.

But the Founders did not give the president the sole power to make war. In the words of one delegate, they believed "the Executive should be able to repel and not to commence war." The Founders, fearing that presidents, like the British kings from whom they had recently freed themselves, would be too eager to go to war gave Congress the power to declare war.[42] James Madison expressed the view of several of the Founders when he argued that "the executive is the branch of power most interested in war and most prone to it. [The Constitution] has, accordingly, with studied care, vested the question of war in the legislature."[43]

The Founders therefore set up a system of checks and balances in military affairs; the president commands the troops, but Congress has the power to declare war and to decide whether to authorize funds to pay for it. Thomas Jefferson thought this arrangement would be an "effectual check to the dog of war, by transferring the power of letting him loose from the executive to the legislative body, from those who are to spend to those who are to pay."[44]

The War Powers Resolution

The extent of the war-making power exercised by Presidents Johnson and Nixon during the undeclared war in Vietnam inspired the 1970s characterization of the presidency as "imperial" and led Congress to take action to limit the power of the president to take unilateral military action.

In 1973, over Nixon's veto, Congress passed the **War Powers Resolution** to limit the president's ability to commit troops to combat. It says that the president can use troops abroad under three conditions: when Congress has declared war, when Congress has given him specific authority to do so, or when an attack on the United States or its military creates a national crisis. If a president commits troops under the third condition, he is supposed to consult with Congress beforehand, if possible, and notify it within forty-eight hours afterward. Unless Congress approves the

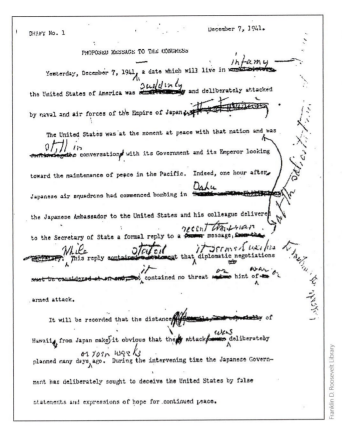

President Franklin Roosevelt edited his own speech to Congress about the Japanese attack on Pearl Harbor. He added the word *infamy* that made memorable the phrase "a date which will live in infamy."

use of troops, the president must withdraw them within sixty days, or ninety days if he needs more time to protect them. Congress can pass a concurrent resolution (not subject to presidential veto) at any time ordering the president to end the use of military force.

Every president since Nixon has believed the resolution violated his constitutional authority to protect the nation from military threats. Although presidents have not questioned Congress's constitutional authority to declare war, all have fought congressional involvement in the use of troops. As a result, enforcement of the act has proved difficult. For example, when George H. W. Bush sent troops to invade Panama in 1989, he did not even refer to the War Powers Resolution in the two-page letter he sent to Congress—sixty hours *after* the invasion began—justifying the invasion. He also ordered 250,000 troops to the Persian Gulf between August and November 1990 on his own authority and delayed announcing his decision to double this number until after the November elections. This kept the decision that changed our mission from defense (Operation Desert Shield) to offense (Operation Desert Storm) from coming to Congress until Bush had mobilized United States and world opinion and gained United Nations support. By the time Congress authorized using force in January 1991, the question of whether it should be used was, practically

speaking, already decided. The same can be said for George W. Bush's decision to invade Iraq in 2003. He reluctantly went to Congress for authorization, but the decision to invade had effectively been taken well before Congress consented.

The act is ineffective because when troops are deployed into combat areas, Congress hesitates to oppose the president because it fears that doing so may be seen as disloyalty to the troops and by other nations as a sign of American weakness or lack of resolve. There is almost always a "rally 'round the flag" effect on the public when the president commits troops to combat. Thus votes against military combat are used against the members of Congress by their political opponents in the next election. However, the presidential advantage can be short-lived, as both George Bushes discovered. Presidents who take military action without a broad consensus need to accomplish their goals quickly or face loss of public support.

The president has also gained an upper hand over Congress in war powers because of the inherent advantages a president has in foreign policy, including a near monopoly on secret intelligence information. The open-ended nature of the Iraq War, its poor execution, and its use to expand presidential powers into the domestic sphere virtually unchecked by Congress led a bipartisan group of constitutional experts and former government officials to conclude, after a year-long study, that the resolution was "ineffective at best and unconstitutional at worst." Former Republican Secretary of State James A. Baker said it was not good for the rule of law to have a statute on such a critical issue be routinely ignored. "No president has complied with it and reports to Congress under it just collect dust. People in Congress say it's just a charade."[45]

DEMOCRACY?

Is it democratic for the president to be able to send troops into combat, with or without the draft, on his own authority?

War and Presidential Powers

By explicitly naming the president as commander in chief of the "Army and Navy," the Constitution leaves no doubt that this role is limited to a relationship with the military. The president is *not* the commander in chief of the nation. His role as chief presiding officer of the government is subject to all the checks and balances enumerated in the Constitution.

Yet some presidents have claimed their commander-in-chief role gave them the authority to impose domestic policies they judged crucial to achieving their national security goals. Historically, these powers have been exercised most extensively during wars endangering our national survival. As discussed earlier, Lincoln assumed extraordinary pow-

government responsiveness

From Imperial to Diminished Presidency?

Presidential historian Arthur Schlesinger coined the term **imperial presidency** for the Nixon administration, but he later wrote that Nixon's expansion of the office, rather than an aberration, was a culmination of the growth of the office since its creation. In fact, their contemporaries wrote similar critiques about other presidents from John Adams to Lyndon Johnson.[1] At some point in George W. Bush's first term, scholars and reporters began attaching the phrase to his administration.

Bush came into office believing that the inherent powers of the office had eroded to "an unsettling degree over the past thirty years." He immediately began exploring how he could use the inherent powers of office, such as executive privilege and executive orders, to bolster the presidency against congressional and public scrutiny.[2]

According to then Senate Minority Leader Tom Daschle (D-S.D.),

the draft resolution Bush sent to Congress three days after 9/11 asking for authority to use "all necessary and appropriate force" against al-Qaeda also asked Congress to endorse the same powers for use *within the United States*, but Congress refused.[3] In search of a legal basis for the power they wanted Congress to endorse, Bush (and Cheney) asked administration lawyers to reinterpret the constitutional and statutory limits on presidential exercise of powers.[4] Their unique reading of the powers assigned the president in Article II held that a president, using his powers as commander in chief, can take any action he deems necessary for national security reasons and take them unilaterally without oversight or restriction by Congress.[5] If practiced, as written, this would make our government closer to a dictatorship than a constitutional democracy.[6]

Under this interpretation, the president was within his rights to resist any congressional oversight he believed interfered with his constitutional responsibilities as he, not the federal courts, interpreted them. Thus, because the Pentagon and all intelligence agencies are in the executive branch, the president has the power to collect any kind of intelligence, open mail and e-mail, look at bank accounts, seize library records, and wiretap phone calls as he sees fit.

Wars and crisis situations are always temptations for a president who believes his office is not as strong as he wants it to be or believes it needs to be to meet a crisis. This tendency has been strengthened by the evolution of a personal presidency and the likelihood that the public will look first to the president to act in a crisis. The ability of the president to command the stage in these situations may in turn tempt Con-

ers during the Civil War, believing the survival of the Union was at stake. Because many in Congress agreed with him, he was able to do what he thought necessary and in some cases receive retroactive congressional approval.

Acting under his expansive definition of commander in chief, Franklin Roosevelt put 100,000 Americans of Japanese descent into camps during World War II. He had the government seize and operate more than sixty industries important to the war effort and vulnerable to union strikes. In addition, he created special agencies to control the consumption and price of gasoline, meat, shoes, and other goods.

Wars that do not threaten our national survival tend not to generate high levels of support for executive actions. When Truman had his secretary of commerce seize most of the nation's steel mills during the Korean War to keep them operating in the face of a possible labor strike, one of the steel companies took him to court. In 1952, the Supreme

Court sided with the company by ruling that Truman had not exhausted other, legal remedies to the problem.[46]

No president ever made more extraordinary claims for the unbounded nature of the commander-in-chief role than did George W. Bush. The national emergency precipitated by the 9/11 attacks gave his administration opportunities to claim more latitude for unilateral action as a "wartime" president. In planning a response immediately after the attacks, Vice President Cheney argued that if there was even a 1 percent chance that a person or a situation was a threat, the government had to act, a position later labeled "The One Percent Doctrine."[47]

Following Cheney's lead, Bush demanded the power to take any action he deemed necessary to protect the American people. He claimed as commander in chief he had unilateral war-making powers that allowed him, on his own authority, to declare any person an enemy combatant, hold them for any length of time without bringing charges or gress to abdicate its constitutional obligations, especially in a unified government. But the Bush administration's interpretation, according to one Republican legal adviser, "staked out powers that are a universe beyond any other administration."[7] In the political climate created by a direct attack on the country and significant loss of lives, the Republican leadership in Congress was reluctant to exercise its oversight of executive branch actions, and it was just as reluctant five years later. Frustrated critics in Congress charged that Bush acted as if the system of checks and balances did not exist.

There is no doubt that the public, after the spectacle of the Clinton impeachment, wanted to see dignity returned to the White House and Congress get back to the real business of governing. But there is no reason to believe the public was looking for more power to gravitate to the presidency or for Congress and the courts to abandon their responsibility to act as checks on executive power. In other words, the move to expand

presidential powers was not necessarily government responding to the people, but rather government officials trying to institutionalize their personal vision of the presidency.

Eventually the Bush-Cheney reach for imperial powers led to the same kind of slap back experienced by other presidents with long arms. Cheney's approval ratings fell to single digits, Bush's to the high twenties, and in 2007 *Time* magazine did not even list the president among the world's most influential people.[8] With a divided government in his last two years, Bush's congressional success rate fell to 38 percent and he began to exercise his previously unused veto power. In his last year in office, *The Daily Show* began referring to him as "Still" President Bush.

This "diminished presidency" was matched by a weak Congress, with approval ratings even lower than the president's. The powerful executive-driven government Bush and Cheney tried to put in place led instead to a stalemated govern-

ment in which no branch was carrying out its role. One evaluation of Bush's presidency concluded that the next president may assume a diminished office and "find it difficult to reclaim powers that have been circumscribed or redistributed."[9]

[1] Arthur Schlesinger Jr. *The Imperial Presidency* (Boston: Houghton Mifflin, 1973), x.
[2] Cheney's paper, "Congressional Overreaching in Foreign Policy," American Enterprise Institute, 1989, is cited in Paul Starobin, "Long Live the King!" *National Journal*, February 18, 2006, 25.
[3] Elizabeth Drew, "Power Grab," *The New York Review of Books* 53 (June 22, 2006), 11.
[4] The two principals were long-time Cheney aide David Addington, who became Cheney's chief of staff when Lewis Libby was indicted on obstruction of justice charges in 2006, and Deputy Assistant Attorney General John Yoo, later a law professor at the University of California-Berkeley, who elaborated on his ideas in *The Powers of War and Peace: The Constitution and Foreign Affairs After 9/11* (University of Chicago Press, 2005). For others involved, see Keith Perine, "Imbalance of Power," *CQ Weekly*, February 27, 2006, 545; and Charlie Savage, *Takeover: The Return of the Imperial Presidency and the Subversion of American Democracy* (New York: Little, Brown & Co., 2007). Savage's book won the Pulitzer Prize.
[5] Jane Mayer, "The Hidden Power," *The New Yorker*, July 3, 2006, 44. Mayer's reporting on the abuses of executive power in the war on terror were published in *The Dark Side: The Inside Story of How the War on Terror Turned into a War on American Ideals* (New York: Doubleday, 2008).
[6] Starobin, "Long Live the King," 26.
[7] Bruce Fein, former associate deputy attorney general in the Reagan administration, quoted in Mayer, "The Hidden Power," 46.
[8] Charles O. Jones and Kathryn Dunn, "Shaping the 44th Presidency," Issues in Governance Studies, Paper #9, Brookings Institution, August 2007, 5.
[9] Ibid., 6–8.

allowing access to lawyers or courts, have them interrogated under rules he set independently of international laws and treaties the United States has signed, and establish tribunals outside the military justice system to try detainees. The president could do this, his legal advisers argued, without court or congressional oversight—except when the president chose to brief members of Congress on whatever aspects of a program he chose to reveal. We will discuss these issues further in Chapter 14.

Historically, when presidents have used war or other national crises to justify expansion of their powers, the separation of powers reasserted itself when the crises eased. But the powers that Bush claimed for his office presented a greater threat to maintaining three coequal branches than those made by presidents in earlier wars because the "war on terrorism," as Bush defined it, would last into the indefinite future. (See box, "From Imperial to Diminished Presidency?")

Presidential Staff

To perform all of the above functions, modern presidents have a large staff, especially compared to their early predecessors. George Washington paid a nephew out of his own pocket to be his only full-time aide, and Jefferson had only four cabinet officers to advise him. Congress did not appropriate funds for a presidential clerk until 1857, and even then Lincoln, with a staff of four, opened and answered much of the daily mail himself. The telephone was introduced in the White House in 1879, and in the 1880s Grover Cleveland was still answering it himself. Even in the early twentieth century, Woodrow Wilson typed many of his own speeches.[48]

As the work of the president has expanded, staff size has exploded. Today, as presiding officer of the executive branch, the president heads, in addition to the military, a civilian bureaucracy of fifteen cabinet departments and

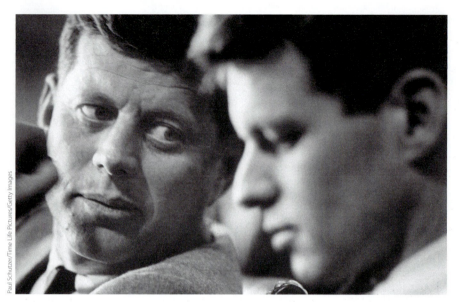

President John Kennedy confers with his brother Bobby, the attorney general.

2.7 million civil servants (their work is described in Chapter 12). To carry out the day-to-day duties of his office, he has a large staff of policy specialists and liaisons to Congress and federal agencies.

Executive Office of the President

The bureaucracy that surrounds the modern president had its origins in the administration of Franklin Roosevelt. Because his small staff was overwhelmed by the workload of administering New Deal agencies and programs, FDR called in a team of public administration experts to help restructure his office. Congress in 1939 finally passed the statute creating the **Executive Office of the President (EOP)**, and with it the White House Office.[49]

The EOP is essentially the president's personal bureaucracy, sitting atop the executive branch and monitoring the work done in cabinet departments and agencies to see that the president's policies are carried out. Many EOP staffers are career civil servants, but the president appoints those who fill the top policy-making positions. Some presidential scholars see this act as codifying changes that established "the president, rather than the parties and Congress," as "the principal agent of popular government in the United States."[50]

Since FDR's administration, the EOP has been reorganized many times to reflect changing national problems and the issue priorities of individual presidents. It is not a single office but a group of offices, councils, and boards devoted to specific functional or issue areas such as national security, trade, the budget, drug abuse, the economy, and the environment.

The EOP continued to grow in size from the 1930s to more than 1700 people in George H. W. Bush's administra-

tion. The powerful OMB accounts for a large part of the growth. The influence of other EOP heads varies with the president's issue priorities, but the head of OMB is almost always influential.[51]

White House Office

The EOP also includes the White House Office, which employs the president's closest advisers. Members of the White House staff have greater influence than most advisers because the president appoints all of them, works daily with them, and tends to trust them more than others. They are often people who helped him get elected or worked for him when he held other offices. Many presidents have counted their wives among their closest advisers, and every first lady has her own office and staff within the Office of the White House. (See the box "The First Lady: A Twofer?")

Jimmy Carter and Bill Clinton are notable among recent presidents for their degree of reliance on their wives and other longtime associates. Unlike Kennedy, Nixon, Johnson, and the first George Bush, neither Carter nor Clinton had experience in Washington, and they filled their top staff positions with old friends and political operatives from their respective home states, Georgia and Arkansas. George H. W. Bush was a consummate Washington insider but relied heavily on his fellow Texan and longtime friend James Baker to serve on the White House staff, in the cabinet, and as his campaign manager. Of recent presidents, Ronald Reagan, who had no close personal friends in politics, was the only one not to fill his top staff positions with long-time friends and close associates.

George W. Bush's initial appointments were notable for their insider backgrounds; three-quarters had previous Washington experience, and nearly half had served in his father's administration. His closest advisers, Karl Rove and Karen Hughes, had worked for him in Texas, and his first chief of staff, Andrew Card, and national security adviser, Condoleezza Rice, worked in his father's administration.[52] Bush was said to be so close to Karen Hughes that she could finish his sentences.

Management of the White House staff varies with the president's personal style. Franklin Roosevelt and John Kennedy cared little for rigid lines of responsibility. They were more concerned with who could serve the president best; they gave staffers different jobs over time and fostered a competitive spirit. Lyndon Johnson's style was the archetype of aggressive, hands-on management. Known for his commitment to using all resources at his disposal to find

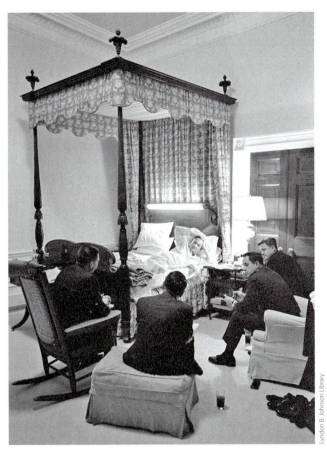

President Johnson worked continuously. When he awoke, he read newspapers, ate breakfast, and met with his staff all before getting out of bed.

government solutions to virtually every problem, Johnson was often accused of overworking and bullying his staff.[53]

Richard Nixon valued formal lines of authority. Nixon's chief of staff, H. R. Haldeman, saw his job this way: "Every president needs a son of a bitch, and I'm Nixon's. I'm his buffer and his bastard. I get done what he wants done and I take the heat instead of him."[54] Part of Nixon's approach was to be reclusive and keep his cards close to his vest. He demanded at least two days a week when he would see no one so he could work in seclusion; even his closest staff often did not know what he was working on.[55]

The Watergate scandal led Presidents Ford and Carter to avoid the appearance of strong staff chiefs. Reagan prided himself on delegating authority to the best people and letting them do their work without interference.[56] Serious problems developed, however, because no one had authority to make final decisions on more important matters, and Reagan was too removed from daily affairs to do so. This detached management style had its costs, most noticeably the Iran-Contra scandal.[57] After that, he appointed a series of strong staff chiefs whose coordination of White House operations helped restore his image.

Clinton's appointment of many staffers with little Washington experience and diverse policy positions showed his determination to immerse himself in policy details and to be the final arbiter of many competing views. He directed his first staff chief to channel all paperwork to him. However, running the White House this way made it difficult for Clinton to keep his and the nation's focus on important issues. He got so bogged down in details that his wife complained that he had become the "mechanic-in-chief."[58]

Clinton also rejected a hierarchical organizational structure. In fact, White House meetings resembled college bull sessions. A young, unruly staff and Clinton's penchant for sitting up all night with them talking issues and policy without fixed agendas were taken by some as symptomatic of a chaotic and disorganized management style.[59] Under Clinton's second and third staff chiefs, lines of authority and communication were tightened.

George W. Bush employed a near-opposite approach to management. With experience as an enforcer of political loyalties on his father's staff, and as the only president to hold a master of business administration degree, Bush set out to run his White House along corporate lines. He tried to delegate work along crisp lines of authority, kept to a tight schedule, and demanded complete team loyalty with no public dissent from administration policy.[60] But the deeper the president got into his term, as his policies played out, he found what most presidents find: that it is impossible to keep rivalries and dissident policy positions from emerging, even among close advisers. The most noted negative relationship among Bush's appointees was that between his Secretary of Defense Donald Rumsfeld and his first Secretary of State Colin Powell, who had disagreements over the use of intelligence and the conduct of the war in Iraq.

But this top-down style, though efficient, insulated the president, preventing him from receiving essential information. Aides were discouraged from correcting his misconceptions or challenging his policy ideas. "The first time I told him he was wrong," a young aide said, "he started yelling at me. Then I showed him where he was wrong, and he said, 'All right, I understand. Good job.' He patted me on the shoulder. I went and had dry heaves in the bathroom."[61] Stifling dissent discourages aides from challenging common wisdom and bringing new facts and perspectives to the discussion. Perhaps consequently, Bush's first secretary of the treasury said that in cabinet and private meetings, he seemed disengaged and uninformed on issues.[62]

An unusual, perhaps unique, aspect of Bush's organizational structure was the central role played by his political strategist, Karl Rove (until he left in late 2007). Today, all presidents have political strategists, of course, but Bush fully integrated Rove (nicknamed "Boy Genius" by the president and "Bush's Brain" by the press) into the policy process in the White House. Rove assessed the political implications of competing policy options and had a commanding voice in every major decision.[63] Rove's goal was to engineer a permanent Republican majority, so he shaped the

Lyndon B. Johnson Library

THE FIRST LADY: A TWOFER?

There is no mention of a presidential spouse in the Constitution, and she has no official duties and no salary. Yet a president's wife is expected to serve as what Martha Washington called "the hostess of the nation."[1] Concern over the influence and public impact of presidential spouses is as old as the republic. George Washington expected his wife "to set a tone both dignified and democratic." Long before there were cameras, radio, or television, the savvy Martha Washington knew that on her first visit to the capital she should wear a homespun gown in keeping with the plain brown suit her husband wore to his inauguration.[2] The first lady has always had to walk a fine line, being supportive of her husband without looking as though she is politically out in front of him. Louisa Adams, wife of John Quincy Adams, feeling hemmed in by the limits of acceptable behavior, titled her autobiography *The Adventures of a Nobody*.[3]

In addition to an intense schedule of state social functions, the first lady must oversee the White House domestic staff. (Whether a first husband would do this remains to be seen.) And it has become the custom for them to identify causes, usually nonpartisan, on which they will focus special effort. Jacqueline Kennedy devoted herself to historic preservation, Claudia (Lady Bird) Johnson to environmental

issues, Barbara and Laura Bush to literacy, and Hillary Rodham Clinton to child welfare. But it was not until 1978 that Congress made formal budgetary provisions for the Office of the First Lady as an official unit within the EOP's White House office.[4] Although still without salary, she is entitled to a small annual pension.

The visibility of the first lady increased enormously after the arrival of photography in the mid-nineteenth century; mass-circulation newspapers and magazines provided new means for satisfying public curiosity about the president's private life. Early in the twentieth century, first ladies began accompanying their husbands at official functions, and with the advent of television the candidates' wives began to figure much more prominently in campaign strategy. But wives had long been involved in promoting their husbands' careers. Even first ladies not interested in electoral politics were used to great effect in getting votes. For example, Dwight Eisenhower considered his wife a better campaigner than he was, and Jacqueline Kennedy attained a level of popularity and celebrity that surpassed her husband's. Laura Bush's approval ratings were at least double her husband's during his second term.

First ladies have been loved (Dolley Madison),

feared (Abigail Adams, Edith Wilson), and both loved and feared (Eleanor Roosevelt). When John Adams's opponents referred to his wife, Abigail, as "Mrs. President," they meant something more than her marital status. **Abigail Adams** was an accomplished writer with strong political opinions and not afraid to express them (for example, that women would "foment a Rebellion" if made subject to laws without representation). Her views on women's rights and other issues, coupled with the fact that her long and happy marriage to John Adams made her his principal adviser, led both supporters and opponents of the president to believe that she might have "undue" influence on policy decisions. Edith Wilson served what she called a "stewardship" (but what others called "bedside government") during a seven-month period when her husband was disabled by a stroke.[5] She decoded classified diplomatic and military messages, encoded presidential responses, controlled access to her husband, and kept information about his condition from the public.

Although many first ladies have been political advisers to their husbands, no one did it quite so publicly, or from such an independent platform, as **Eleanor Roosevelt**. She held press conferences for women journalists shut out of

the president's briefings and wrote a syndicated newspaper column read by millions. She also made regular radio broadcasts and was the first person from the administration to address the country after the Japanese attack on Pearl harbor.[6] She discussed policy with her husband, peppered him with memos, and brought supporters of the causes she advocated into the White House. (It was reportedly common for FDR, at cabinet meetings, to begin sentences with "My Missus tells me."[7]) She served on countless committees and traveled around the world promoting racial equality, women's and social justice issues, and the war effort. After her husband's death, she served as a delegate to the United Nations, where her efforts in support of human rights and international cooperation earned her the title "First Lady of the World."

Mrs. Roosevelt's stature was attained under the exceptional circumstances of her husband's long tenure in the White House during a prolonged period of national crisis. Although some thought her too powerful, Mrs. Roosevelt always deferred to her husband in joint appearances, saying it was the job of a wife to offer no personal opinions, limit her appearances, and "lean back in an open car so voters always see *him*."[8]

Most first ladies have not been traditional wives who limited themselves to the domestic sphere. And since the 1960s, strong-willed women have been the norm. Lady Bird Johnson, whose husband pronounced her "the brains and money of this family," is said to have greeted him in the evenings with the query, "Well, what did you do for women today?" Although she exercised her influence mainly out of public view, her stamp was said to have been on each of the 200 environmental laws passed during her husband's administration.[9]

Betty Ford was an outspoken supporter of the Equal Rights Amendment and abortion rights in defiance of her husband's party's position, and she argued for a salary for her successors as first lady. Her popularity often surpassed that of her husband. Nancy Reagan, most often seen in public gazing adoringly at her husband, controlled access to the Oval Office and weighed in on the hiring and firing of key advisers.

The term *copresident* was revived for **Hillary Clinton,** a lawyer and lobbyist for child welfare causes, who was one of her husband's closest advisers and strategists throughout his career in elective office while also serving as the family's principal wage earner. Shortly after her husband's inauguration she moved the first lady's office into the West Wing to be among the policy makers. She prompted greater opposition to first-lady activism than anyone since Eleanor Roosevelt.[10] Nevertheless, in 2000, Mrs. Clinton became the first presidential wife to run for and win elective office. However, in her failed run for the presidential nomination in 2008 it became apparent that the career-for-two she had shared with her husband for so many years made it difficult for her to move out of his shadow—or for him to lean back in the car so the people could see *her*. Michelle Obama, a former corporate lawyer with young children, said after her husband's election that she intended to be "Chief Mom" and had no interest in a policy role or being co-president.

When wives have played active roles in getting their husbands nominated and elected, it is likely that their advice will be sought after the election. And in most long and close marriages, it is natural for husbands and wives to become confidants and to rely on one another's judgment. The first lady is not subject to congressional approval, but neither are the members of the White House staff or the president's close advisers outside government. Yet worry persists that the special nature of a marital relationship provides opportunities for influence—of the kind Betty Ford called "pillow talk"—unavailable to others. We frequently refer to lobbyists as "getting into bed" with politicians, but wives do not have to pay to get there, and if they are successful in changing their husband's views, it is not likely that money will have had anything to do with it.

[1] Edith P. Mayo, ed. *Smithsonian Book of First Ladies* (Washington, D.C.: Smithsonian Institution, 1996) 11. Much of the material in this box is drawn from Carol Chandler Waldrop, *Presidents' Wives: The Lives of 44 American Women of Strength* (Jefferson, N.C.: McFarland, 1989); Lewis L. Gould, ed., *American First Ladies* (New York: Garland, 1996); and Kati Marton, *Hidden Power: The Impact of Presidential Marriages on Our Recent History* (New York: Pantheon, 2001).

[2] Cokie Roberts, *Founding Mothers* (New York: William Morrow, 2004), 230–231.

[3] Mayo, *The Smithsonian Book of First Ladies*, 11, 43.

[4] Gil Troy, *Affairs of State: The Rise and Rejection of the First Couple since World War II* (New York: Free Press, 1997), 250. Troy also discusses attempts at reorganizing the first lady's office. See especially 178–188 and 248–258.

[5] Phyllis Lee Levin, *Edith and Woodrow* (New York: Scribner, 2001).

[6] You can listen to Mrs. Roosevelt's Pearl Harbor broadcast by going to www.c-span.org/PresidentialLibraries and linking to the Franklin D. Roosevelt Library.

[7] Jonathan Alter, *The Defining Moment* (New York: Simon and Schuster, 2006), 261.

[8] Carl Sferrazza Anthony, "The First Ladies: They've Come a Long Way, Martha," *Smithsonian*, October 1992, 150.

[9] Lawrence Wright, "Lady Bird's Lost Legacy," *New York Times*, July 20, 2007; and Lady Bird Johnson, *A White House Diary* (New York, Holt, Rinehart and Winston, 1970), 518. Mrs. Johnson kept a daily record—an estimated 1 million words—during her years in the White House. This book is drawn from that diary and is an excellent account of what the first lady's job looks like from the inside.

[10] Henry Louis Gates Jr., "Hating Hillary," *The New Yorker*, February 26, 1996, 121.

Betty Ford, in her last day in the White House, couldn't resist the urge to step out of the expected role for a first lady.

administration's domestic and foreign policies toward that end. The result was that partisan calculation influenced government policies to an unprecedented degree. This strategy had short-term successes but engendered a pro-Democratic reaction in the last quarter of Bush's time in office.

With the parallel power base established by his vice president (see the next section) and Rove's reputation as the key political strategist, Bush sometimes appeared to be a secondary figure in his own administration. Bush's press staff had to work hard to convince the public that the president was in charge of the White House, and the president himself frequently reminded the press corps that he was "the decider."

Office of the Vice President

The EOP also includes the Office of the Vice President. The vice president has his own budget for office and staff (housed adjacent to the White House), an official airplane (*Air Force Two*), and his own white mansion (the former home of the chief of naval operations).[64]

The vice president has few formal duties—to preside over the Senate, which he rarely does (junior senators are assigned to do so); cast tie-breaking votes, which he rarely needs to; and succeed to the presidency if necessary. That vice presidents have succeeded to office unexpectedly nine times (following eight presidential deaths and one resignation) may be responsible for the growing importance of the office.

Benjamin Franklin suggested a title for the vice president—"His Superfluous Excellency." For many years, vice presidents had little to do, other than to serve as "standby equipment," in the words of Nelson Rockefeller. Woodrow Wilson's vice president, Thomas R. Marshall, said that holding the job was like being "a man in a cataleptic fit. He cannot speak, he cannot move. He suffers no pain. He is perfectly conscious of all that goes on. But he has no part in it." Franklin Roosevelt's first vice president, John

BEHIND THE SCENES
THE VICE PRESIDENT WHO WASN'T

The vice presidency of William Rufus DeVane King, the running mate of Franklin Pierce in 1852, was one of the most exceptional in American history—exceptional because he was the only vice president ever to be sworn into office on foreign soil and because behind the scenes, for years prior to his nomination, he had been the target of rumors that he was homosexual.

King was a man of substantial political experience, having served in his state legislature and the U.S. House, and almost thirty years in the Senate, where he became president pro tem. In between terms, he had been an envoy to several European countries. He was regarded as "courtly," generous, and a fastidious dresser.[1] His refine-

ment contrasted with the heavy-drinking Pierce, who was said to be "the hero of many a well-fought bottle."[2] Pierce also brought inexperience and no particular reputation or policy positions to the top of the ticket, except that like King he was committed to the Union, which the Democratic party valued at a time when all the major players were lining up for and against slavery and turning the capital into a battleground. On the surface, it was a conventional ticket with King, a Southerner, balancing Pierce, the Northerner (campaign slogan: "We Polked you in 1844, we shall Pierce you in 1852.")

While drink was the subject of gossip about Pierce, it was King's friendship with James Buchanan that inspired

the rumormongers. Buchanan, our only never-married president, was both friend and political ally to King—a long-time aspirant to the vice presidency—and for some years the two men shared a Washington apartment. Some of the catty remarks about their relationship were undoubtedly inspired by political rivalry within the party . . . President Polk's law partner called King "Mrs. Buchanan" and referred to him with the feminine pronoun. The warrior militant and former president Andrew Jackson (1829–1837) called King "Miss Nancy."[3] This did not stop Buchanan and Pierce from being favored for a short time to head the Democratic ticket in 1844.[4] Instead, King was named U.S. ambassador to France, from where he

wrote letters to Buchanan about the pain of being parted from him.[5]

The country never got a chance to see how Vice President King would have fared presiding over the Senate as the civil war approached. He was so ill in the last months of the 1852 campaign that after his election victory he sailed for Cuba seeking a warm-climate cure for his tuberculosis. It took an act of Congress to allow him to take the oath as vice president on foreign soil. Soon after, he was taken home to Alabama, where he died the month after the inauguration, never making it to Washington. His friend went on to win the White House in 1856.

[1] L. Edward Purcell, *The Vice-Presidents: A Biographical Dictionary* (New Haven: Facts on File, 1998), 124.
[2] Diana Dixon Healy, *America's Vice-Presidents* (New York: Atheneum, 1984), 71.
[3] Purcell, 124–125; Healy, 74.
[4] Purcell, op. cit., 125.
[5] Ibid.

Nance Garner, was less elegant in observing that his job was not worth a "pitcher of warm piss."

Historically, presidents gave their vice presidents little information and few opportunities to prepare for succession. They were usually chosen to balance the ticket geographically or ideologically not because they were men who presidents wanted to work with. In 1960, the youthful New Englander, John Kennedy, chose the experienced Texan, Lyndon Johnson. The two had a chilly relationship. Kennedy was wary of the less polished Johnson, and the self-made Johnson bristled at the privileged background and Harvard degrees of the Kennedy clan.

Sometimes presidents have been reluctant to delegate important responsibilities to their vice presidents because they were planning their own runs for the office and working to build an independent political base. This may make them more loyal to their own ambitions than to the president's agenda. Historically, vice presidents were assigned ceremonial duties or partisan activities (such as being the attack dog during the campaign, leaving his running mate free to appear more presidential).

How much work and authority vice presidents are given depends on the personal relationship with the president, how needy the president is for assistance, or how generous he is about sharing power. Jimmy Carter was the first president to delegate to his vice president responsibilities for day-to-day White House operations.[65] Walter Mondale had the Washington experience Carter lacked. Carter gave him a White House office, scheduled weekly lunches with him, included him in all White House advisory groups and all important meetings, and asked him to lobby Congress and read the paperwork that crossed the president's desk. Ronald Reagan, Bill Clinton, and both George Bushes added to this new tradition.

Prior to the Bush-Cheney administration, the closest working relationship between a president and vice president was undoubtedly that between Bill Clinton and Al Gore. Gore became so influential in the Clinton White House that he was referred to as a "shadow president" and his staff as a "shadow cabinet." Divisions did not surface until Gore was running his own presidential campaign and trying to distance himself in order to establish his own identity.

Richard Cheney, Bush's vice president, was already well known to George W. Bush from service in his father's administration, and he had far more administrative and Washington experience than the new president. Cheney ran Bush's transition team and chose many members of the White House staff. He came to office with the goal of "merging" the vice president's office with the president's to create a "single Executive Office" in which the vice president would serve as the president's "executive and implementer."[66] He headed the most important policy-making groups in the White House and was the author of its energy policy. He also created his own national security staff,

Vice President John Nance Garner, here in retirement, complained to President Franklin Roosevelt that he didn't have much to do.

placed his own people in key defense and state department offices, and worked closely on military policy with his old friend Donald Rumsfeld, secretary of defense (a position Cheney had once held).

Cheney had unprecedented access to the Oval Office, meeting the president every morning and sometimes several times more during the day. He was also deeply involved in the president's legislative strategy, went to Capitol Hill at least once a week to meet with the Republican caucus, and kept an office in the House of Representatives. Bush told members, "When you're talking to Dick Cheney, you're talking to me."[67] All vice presidents have an office in the Senate, but Cheney was the only vice president in history to have had an office in the House as well.

At the end of Bush's first term one political scientist said Cheney had accrued so much power that it was an "insult" to call him "vice" president. "He's got this weird combination of roles and responsibilities that make him a ... legitimizer, mentor, grim reaper, tutor, and grandfather."[68] Well into Bush's second term, many observers continued to believe that the far more experienced and policy-savvy Cheney was running a large part of the White House operation, especially because it was consistent with Bush's preference for delegating work. A White House lawyer said that Bush "thinks that the Reagan style of leadership is best—guiding the ship of state from high up on the mast.... the vice president is more willing to get down in the wheelhouse below the decks."[69]

By virtually everyone's judgment Cheney was the most powerful vice president in U.S. history. But outperforming the president, setting policy directions, and serving as attack dog had consequences for the vice president's political standing. Midway into Bush's second term, Cheney's approval ratings stood at 18 percent.[70] It is unlikely that taking the office to this entirely new level was precedent setting; it was an exceptional situation of a much more experienced

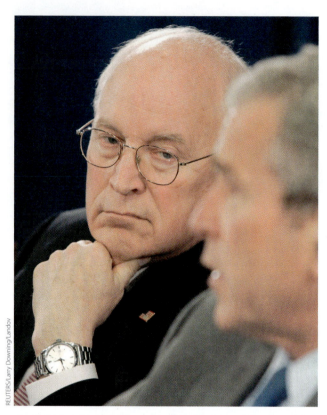

Vice President Dick Cheney was the driving force behind some Bush administration policies.

man in the second rather than the top spot, with both men believing deeply in the expansion of executive over legislative power. Few people who reach the White House are as willing as Bush was to gamble their professional reputations on their second in command.

Presidential Persuasion

Although presidents have significant constitutional authority, this alone doesn't allow them to exercise great power, because the system of separation of powers gives significant authority to the other branches. Members of Congress have their own priorities and views, as do the career bureaucrats in the executive branch. And, of course, so do interest groups, political parties, the media, and the public, who influence what Congress does. Consequently, presidents can't simply order other officials to adopt and implement the policies they advocate. Instead, presidents must persuade them.

Persuading Officials

In a discouraged mood, Harry Truman said, "I sit here all day, trying to persuade people to do the things they ought to have sense enough to do, without my persuading

them. . . . They talk about the power of the president, how I can just push a button to get things done. Why, I spend most of my time kissing somebody's ass."[71]

Presidents must discuss, cajole, negotiate, bargain, and then, at the right moment, compromise to get as much as they can. *Politics* is a dirty word to many Americans, but the presidency, after all, is a political job requiring political skills. Dwight Eisenhower (1953–1961), before entering politics, was a general in the army and used to issuing orders down the chain of command and having them obeyed by underlings. This approach didn't work in the government. Along the way, his orders got modified or ignored or disobeyed and Eisenhower had to be a more hands-on president than perhaps he intended.[72]

Every president develops a reputation for his persuasiveness among the Washingtonians, who include the members of Congress, professionals in the bureaucracy, leaders and lobbyists of interest groups, and reporters and commentators in the media.[73] A strong reputation contributes to a president's continuing ability to persuade them.

To persuade members of Congress, presidents may simply give them a call. Former Speaker of the House Tip O'Neill (D-Mass.) remarked, "The men and women in Congress love nothing better than to hear from the head guy, so they can go back to their districts and say, 'I was talking to the president the other day.' The constituents love it too."[74] After a call from President Reagan, a Democrat exclaimed, "I was so thrilled, I thought I was talking to the pope."[75]

Social invitations, such as to receptions or dinners at the White House, are prized. These lavish occasions can be nights to remember, as when Lyndon Johnson invited Delbert Latta, the ranking Republican on an important committee, and his wife to a fancy White House dinner. After the dinner a band played and the couples danced. At one point, the president asked Mrs. Latta to dance. When the couple got home, they were so excited that they awoke their children and Latta announced, "Your mother danced with the president of the United States!" (Their son, less impressed, remarked "But, Dad, the president is a Democrat.")

Whether in phone calls, casual conversations at social events, or formal meetings, presidents can ask for lawmakers' support. Presidents can point out the advantages of their position and, for foreign policy, reveal classified information that bolsters their position

As the chief executive—the one who provides choice jobs to many people and the one who prepares the budget for the country—and as the party's leader, presidents have various favors and penalties to dispense to enhance their persuasiveness. They can wheel and deal. They might promise to back a bill sponsored by the legislator or appoint an official or judge recommended by the legislator. They might direct government projects to the district or state of the legislator. Or presidents might call in their "chits," re-

ethical dilemmas | Trading Favors

In 1962 President John Kennedy received a call from Senate Minority Leader Everett Dirksen (R-Ill.) requesting a favor. An aide to former president Dwight Eisenhower was under investigation for income tax evasion and expected to be formally charged the next day. Eisenhower's wife, Mamie, was a close friend of the aide's wife, and she worried that the aide might commit suicide if indicted. Eisenhower did not know Kennedy, so he asked his fellow Republican, Dirksen, to approach the president and ask, "as a personal favor to me, to put the . . . indictment in the deep freeze. . . . [A]dvise him he'll have a blank check in my bank if he will grant me this favor."

Kennedy had no knowledge of the matter but said he would do what Eisenhower asked. He called his brother Robert, the attorney general, and told him not to sign the indictment. His brother objected on the grounds that granting a special favor to a tax evader would be politically disastrous. But the president told him to do it or submit his resignation.

Weeks later, the nuclear test ban treaty with the Soviet Union was pending in the Senate, where ratification required a two-thirds vote. This was especially difficult to obtain at the height of the Cold War. Americans didn't trust the Soviets, and conservatives claimed a treaty banning the testing of nuclear weapons would give the Soviets the upper hand. A head count showed the treaty falling short of a two-thirds majority. Kennedy rang Dirksen and called in his chits. He asked the senator to change his vote and to get Ike to endorse the treaty too, saying the treaty was important to him, the country, and all mankind. If both men lent their support, Kennedy would consider his favor repaid. With public support from the minority leader and the popular former president, enough Republicans joined the Democrats to ratify the treaty.

Was Kennedy right to order the attorney general not to follow the law so he could do a favor for an ex-president and bank the chits for later use? Was the attorney general wrong to do the political bidding of his brother rather than to implement the law? The test ban treaty was far more important than a tax cheat, but when Kennedy made the deal he did not know support for the treaty is what he would ask in return.

Source: The account of this deal appeared in Bobby Baker (with Larry L. King), *Wheeling and Dealing: Confessions of a Capitol Hill Operator* (New York: W.W. Norton, 1978), 97–99.

---

minding the legislator about the time they backed a bill or appointed an official or judge pushed by the legislator or the time they campaigned for the legislator back home. The message? "Now it's your turn to help me."

If the legislator still refuses to heed their request, presidents can threaten retaliation. They might block a bill sponsored by the legislator or refuse to appoint an official or judge recommended by the legislator. They can play hardball, vowing to reduce the party's funding for the legislator in the next election or, as a last resort, even to campaign for the legislator's opponent in the primary election.

Presidents also use the trappings of their office. Johnson employed his "taxi" when a member was going to the same event as the president. Johnson would offer the member a ride in his limousine, with its motorcycle escort and Secret Service tail and with the lights flashing and sirens wailing. During the exciting ride, Johnson would press his case for a pending bill. Sometimes presidents offer members rides in *Air Force One* when they are traveling to the same part of the country. The lawmakers' awe, and the experience they get from the ride and the story they can tell about it, can make them more favorably disposed to a president's request.

Thus, presidents have numerous means at their disposal, but they can't use all of them or even many of them on a single issue, because these tactics, when multiplied by many members of Congress, take considerable time and they lose their effect if used too often.

No president was more effective in persuading members of Congress than **Lyndon Johnson**. Having been in both houses of Congress and majority leader in the Senate, he knew how the institution worked and what made its members tick. He knew their views, their favorite programs and least favorite programs, their strengths and weaknesses, their health, their quirks—which ones had "a nagging wife" and which ones liked a 5 o'clock scotch. A congressional leader said LBJ "could talk a bone away from a dog." But his efforts to persuade weren't just sweet talk. One senator remembered, "You needed a bridge built on some highway, and, by God, he got your vote or you didn't get the bridge."[76] When he wanted the vote of Sen. Harry Byrd (D-Va.), who was resisting a civil rights bill, Johnson summoned him to the White House and said, "You know, Harry, [Defense Secretary Robert] McNamara says we got to close that Norfolk naval base down there, and I don't much want to do it," but, Johnson added, he needed Byrd's vote. The

Norfolk naval base was the largest in the country, so its closure would have devastated Virginia's economy and undermined Bryd's reputation among his constituents. Byrd rushed back to the Senate and announced his support for the bill.[77]

Johnson also knew where the skeletons were buried. When necessary, he quoted FBI reports about a member having a mistress or IRS reports about a member submitting inaccurate tax returns. His unspoken threat was that he would leak the incriminating information to the media or ask the IRS to conduct an audit. These efforts were all-consuming. When asked how a president should deal with Congress, Johnson replied: "continuously, incessantly, and without interruption."[78]

As a result of Johnson's tremendous drive and consummate skills working with Congress, he left a legacy of legislative accomplishments. One presidential scholar expressed a common view: "He did more for racial justice than any president since Abraham Lincoln. He built more social protections than anyone since Franklin Roosevelt. He was probably the greatest legislative politician in American history." Unfortunately, he was also "largely responsible for one of the greatest disasters in American history"—the Vietnam War, which he inherited but sharply escalated.[79] The failure of the war, and the divisions in our society it fostered, caused him to not seek reelection.

In contrast, George W. Bush was not an effective persuader, especially during the period of divided government. Although he had strong support after 9/11, enabling him to get much of what he wanted from Congress, he lost support as the Iraq War dragged on and Congress changed hands. He was unable to get his domestic legislative agenda passed, in part because he lacked the skills and the interest in the legislative process that many of his predecessors had.

Bush did not have close relationships with members of Congress and did not engage in "Washington schmoozing."[80] His early-to-bed, early-to-rise habits kept him from the capital's social scene, where the politicians become comfortable with and trusting of each other. Presidents chat up the Washingtonians whose support they need. But Bush shied away from these events. He demonstrated "thinly veiled contempt" for Congress, even when Republicans controlled both chambers.[81] He treated the Republicans "as if they were his valets," according to one observer, and the Democrats "as if they were infected with tuberculosis."[82] When he met with lawmakers about funding for Iraq, he simply demanded their support. As one senator tried to ask a question, the president interrupted him, saying, "I'm not here to debate you."[83] A presidential and congressional scholar concluded, "If you had to evaluate presidents, 1 to 10, and Johnson is a 10, this president [Bush] is a 1" in his ability to work with Congress.[84]

Persuading the Public

In addition to persuading officials directly, presidents try to persuade the American public in the hope that citizens will pressure officials to follow the president's lead.

The Founders didn't anticipate that one day the president would be the leader of a national party with a political agenda and accountable to the people. They envisioned a president chosen by the Electoral College and removed from the people. Our earliest presidents had little contact with the general public. George Washington and Thomas

The public didn't always agree with President Reagan's views or policies, but he remained popular partly because of his image as a rugged individualist.

Richard Nixon Presidential Library and Museum (NLRNS)

A presidential photo-op gone awry. In 1968, an issue of *Life* magazine featured a cover of Bobby Kennedy running on the beach with his shoes off and his pants rolled up. The image became an iconic photo. As he prepared to run for reelection in 1972, President Nixon tried to emulate the Kennedy photo, but instead he appeared forlorn and awkward wading in the surf with his dress pants and dress shoes.

Jefferson averaged only three speeches a year to the public; John Adams averaged one. Adams spent eight months of his presidency at home in Massachusetts, avoiding Congress and procrastinating on a decision whether to get involved in a war between England and France.[85] Abraham Lincoln thought it prudent to make few speeches. He told people gathered at Gettysburg the night before his famous address, "I have no speech to make. In my position it is somewhat important that I should not say foolish things. It very often happens that the only way to help it is to say nothing at all."[86]

But now presidents are dependent on a national electorate, and they must have a media strategy. They try to persuade the public directly, and also indirectly by persuading opinion leaders, such as the executives, reporters, columnists, and commentators of the media, and the leaders and lobbyists of interest groups, including the executives of big businesses. These people have the ability to influence the public (and interest groups have the money to provide campaign contributions).

Going Public

The strategy of appealing to the people to gain cooperation from Congress and Washington power brokers is known as **going public**.[87] The strategy entails giving television and radio addresses, holding press conferences, making speeches at various events around the country, and giving interviews, through satellite technology, to local media, big conventions, or other audiences. These techniques have become so important that the president sometimes is referred to as the "salesman in chief."

Franklin Roosevelt pioneered this strategy with his **fireside chats**, which were the first attempt to use the media to speak directly and regularly to the people in their homes. The talks made the president the focal point and public face of the government. In a personalized style and conversational tone, FDR began, "My friends," and even talked about his dog. People gathered around their radios whenever he was on, and many felt as though he was talking directly to them. Whereas predecessor Herbert Hoover (1929–1933) had received an average of 40 letters a day, Roosevelt, after initiating his chats, received 4000 a day.[88] He even received some addressed not to himself, by name or position, but simply to "My Friend, Washington, D.C." Whereas Hoover needed one clerk to handle his mail, Roosevelt needed fifty.

Roosevelt also pioneered the use of public opinion polls to gauge the public's views. Thus he created a communications loop—to the people and from the people—which helped him sell his policies.

Christopher Morris/VII

George W. Bush cultivated an image as a tough cowboy. This image proved quite popular with many people. However, as his administration's foreign policy failures mounted, the image became a liability.

Now when a president is not heard from frequently, the media complain because they count on presidential communications to fill their newscasts and news columns. George W. Bush took heat from the press for giving few press conferences and for spending 535 days at Camp David, his ranch in Texas, and his parents' home in Maine during his first three years in office.[89]

Ronald Reagan, often called the "Great Communicator," spoke in public an average of 200 times a year. When he spoke, he didn't discuss the details of his proposals. Rather, he dwelled on anecdotes about people he knew earlier in life or people who had written letters to the White House. Like FDR, he personalized his speeches. As Roosevelt was the most effective president on radio, Reagan was the most effective on television. Bill Clinton spoke in public an amazing 550 times a year.[90] Perhaps the most effective extemporaneous speaker ever to serve in the White House, Clinton also partially wrote or revised his formal speeches, sometimes in the back of the limousine on the way to the event.

Today presidents have a large communications staff, led by a media adviser and a press secretary, to get their message out. Following Reagan's practice, they determine a message for every day and every week, and they direct everyone in the administration to stay "on message"—to repeat the message and to avoid other topics that could deflect attention from the message. Inevitably, other topics will pop up, prompting the administration to regain control of the agenda.

The George W. Bush administration was very disciplined in staying on message, especially during the first four years. On any day, viewers of newscasts or listeners of talk radio heard administration officials delivering the same message in virtually the same words. Running such an operation is a high-pressure job, and press secretaries usually do not last long. When Bush's first press secretary resigned after two years, he said he wanted to do "something more relaxing, like dismantling live nuclear weapons."[91] After his second press secretary resigned, he wrote a book describing how the White House staff manipulated intelligence information to convince the public an invasion of Iraq was necessary.[92]

Of course, going public, even when staying on message, is no guarantee of success. After winning reelection, Bush identified Social Security privatization as his major domestic goal. For six months, he made one public appearance after another on behalf of this goal, but he couldn't convince the public. In fact, the public was less supportive of privatization after his efforts than it had been before them.[93]

Spectacle Presidency

An important part of going public is being seen as well as heard. And the important reason for being seen is projecting an image that conveys what presidents want their character and style to appear to be. Presidents "make fully realized dramatic characters out of themselves. . . . The character has to bear some relation to the real person . . . but it is still a genuine act of creation."[94] The observation that "politics is theater" is intended as ridicule, but images do matter in presidents' drive for popular support.

Presidents' attempts to shape public perceptions and gain public support by presenting symbolic spectacles—gestures designed to influence the public rather than actions that achieve a goal—led to what some political scientists call the **spectacle presidency**.[95] Through history, many presidents have tried to shape their image. Teddy Roosevelt cast himself as a manly man—a big-game hunter and a Rough Rider who led a charge in the Spanish-American War. But the television screen was the modern impetus to the spectacle presidency.

Although television became popular in the 1950s, politicians didn't recognize its potential. Dwight Eisenhower shunned televised speeches because "I can think of nothing more boring, for the American public, than to have to sit in their living rooms for a whole half hour looking at my face on their television screens."[96] But the young medium became a powerful presence in politics in the 1960s. John

Kennedy was the first president to recognize its utility for presidential spectacles. To overcome public concerns about his youth and inexperience, he initiated live television coverage of presidential press conferences. The idea was to court the viewers rather than the reporters asking the questions. He would demonstrate his intelligence and command of the issues and, in the process, leaven it with his wit.

In other ways, Kennedy tried to make a virtue of his youth and inexperience by conveying a sense of athleticism, with photo-ops of sailing and playing touch football and by exhorting Americans to take long hikes. And always Kennedy promised "vigor," which became his signature word. In fact, Kennedy had been ill for most of his life, with many hospitalizations and daily drug treatment for Addison's disease, a fact he kept from the public.

Another image of his administration, largely created by his wife after his death, was that of the King Arthur's mythical "Camelot," with the royal couple bringing glamour and sophistication to the White House and their acolytes (like King Arthur's "Knights of the Round Table") carrying social justice and democratic ideals to the world. The administration left a lasting image of a tuxedoed president and his beautiful wife hosting galas for classical musicians and great intellects. Although the first lady may have favored these activities, the president himself preferred listening to Frank Sinatra and reading Ian Fleming's James Bond books.

Ronald Reagan and George W. Bush portrayed themselves as dramatic characters who evoked masculine toughness. A Reagan aide proposed that the president reflect "America's idealized image of itself."[97] An actor, Reagan had little difficulty projecting himself as a rugged individualist, riding horses and clearing brush at his California ranch, even though he had spent most of his life in Hollywood's studio system.

Bush's persona as a Texas cowboy—he wore cowboy boots to his inaugural and made sure the press photographed him wearing them—was mostly invented. His packaging as a war leader was even more intentional. The staging of the flight-suited commander in chief landing by fighter jet on an aircraft carrier and speaking in front of a *MISSION ACCOMPLISHED* banner was one of the most dramatic image-creating photo opportunities in the history of the presidency. The advantage of such bold efforts is that the visual image lingers. But for Bush that was also the disadvantage. He had announced the end of the war in Iraq far too soon and the photo-op came back to haunt him.

If a president fails to manage his image, the press or his opponents will do it for him—and in ways he won't like. Bill Clinton intended to convey an image of a knowledgeable leader whose gaze was directed toward the future but who, with his own humble origins, understood the problems of average people and knew how to deal with them. Instead, his image for many people became that of a womanizer who hung out with Hollywood celebrities and paid for a $200 haircut. Although he was one of our most knowledgeable presidents, he allowed his intellect to be overshadowed by his personal indiscretions.

Personal Presidency

As the presidency has grown since the Depression, and as the media have become pervasive, we have developed what political scientists call a **personal presidency**.[98] The president is the most powerful and visible figure in the government. The media cover not only presidents' official acts but their private lives as well, so the public learns that Gerald Ford toasted his own English muffins and Bill Clinton wore boxers rather than briefs. Consequently, the people come to feel that they have a personal relationship with their presidents. This relationship prompts the people to entrust them with greater power. In return, however, the people expect them to achieve greater results. "Everybody now expects the man inside the White House to do something about everything."[99] Thus the people have an unwritten contract with the president.

Presidents themselves fuel the personal presidency by their willingness to reveal private matters—Clinton didn't have to answer the MTV reporter's question about boxers or briefs—and by their efforts to reach out to the people. One example, among many, is the number of Christmas cards sent by the presidents. Eisenhower, who started the custom, sent 1100; Clinton, in his last year, sent 400,000; and George W. Bush, in 2002, sent 1 million.[100]

When President Franklin Roosevelt died, most Americans, reflecting the personal presidency, felt a personal loss. Here Chief Petty Officer Graham Jackson plays "Nearer My God to Thee" as the president's body is carried to the train that returned him to Washington for burial.

Time Life Pictures/Getty Images

The personal presidency reached a new level during the Clinton years. The continuous investigations of Clinton by Congress, special prosecutors, the lawyers representing Paula Jones, and conservative groups looking for dirt resulted in media saturation of the most private and intimate details of a president's life ever revealed. At one point, the lawyers representing Paula Jones promised titillating information about the "distinguishing characteristics" of the president's genitals if her suit ever came to trial. "It is entirely possible," one reporter observed, "that the Clinton era will be remembered by historians primarily as the moment when the distance between the President and the public evaporated forever."[101]

The personal presidency has both advantages and disadvantages for the country. The relationship enables presidents to marshal public support for important goals and thus overcome the inertia of a system with fragmented power. On the other hand, the relationship fosters unrealistic assumptions about what presidents can achieve. Many citizens who don't understand our system assume that presidents are all-powerful. They assign presidents too much blame when things go wrong and give them too much credit when things go right, such as when the economy sags or surges.

Because they have unrealistic expectations, citizens encourage, actually pressure, candidates for president to make unrealistic promises. The candidates oblige in order to garner more contributions for their campaign or votes for their election. Jimmy Carter, who was one of our most honest presidents, nonetheless told campaign audiences, "If you ever have any questions or advice for me, please write. . . . I open every letter myself, and read them all."[102] George H. W. Bush promised to send astronauts to Mars, be the "education president," the "environmental president," and do many other things while cutting the budget deficit yet promising "no new taxes."

Despite these examples, most presidents deliver, or at least try to deliver, on a majority of their promises.[103] Inevitably, however, they neglect some and Congress blocks others, prompting the presidents to seek more power. They get caught in a cycle in which they try to grasp more power to honor past promises, then make new promises for which they need even more power. Thus the rise of the personal presidency has fed the expansion of the office. After 9/11, George W. Bush, boosted by sky-high public support, perceived a mandate from the people to prevent further terrorist attacks. He declared a war on terrorism and presented himself as a wartime president. He used this status to make extraordinary claims of presidential power.

Figure 4 || **Presidential Popularity**

Since the end of World War II, presidential popularity has usually declined over time. Only three presidents—Eisenhower, Reagan, and Clinton—left office with ratings at a level comparable to that when they entered.

SOURCE: Gallup polls, reported in Public Opinion *and updated at www.presidency.ucsb.edu/data/popularity.php. The question asked is, "Do you approve or disapprove of the way [name of president] is handling his job as president?"*

As the people experience one personal presidency after another, they can become disillusioned. Their unrealistic assumptions about presidential power, which prod the presidential candidates to make unrealistic promises, set the presidents up for failure in the eyes of the people. When the presidents can't deliver, the people lose faith. And, all along, the media exposure and scrutiny take a toll. Presidents' novelty wears off and their flaws appear. Few presidents can withstand the media microscope without losing their public esteem. Most presidents suffer a decline in popularity as they continue in office. (See Figure 4.)

Despite presidents' constant concerns about their public support, as measured by their approval ratings, there's no strong correlation between presidents' popularity and their clout in Congress.[104] High approval ratings don't guarantee passage of their legislative proposals, because most constituents never learn whether their representative or senators voted for a president's proposals.

Conclusion: Is the Presidency Responsive?

The presidency has become the most consistently visible office in government as well as one of the most personalized and responsive. Americans expect leadership from the president even in times of "less" government. The presidency is responsive in that whoever holds that office has an almost direct relationship with the public. Using the media, a skillful president can tell us what he wants and attempt to shape our opinion. Through public opinion polls and the ballot box, we tell the president what we think.

The Founders did not intend the president to have this close relationship to the people. After all, the president was to be chosen by an Electoral College, not a popular constituency. But as the president became the head of a political party with a political agenda, and as the Electoral College evolved to embrace voters' participation, the president developed a popular constituency. Having a direct and personal relationship with the people, the president is highly responsive to the people.

In this relationship, there is a danger of overresponsiveness. To remain popular, a president may seek short-term solutions to the nation's problems and neglect long-term needs. And short-term responsiveness that caters to public opinion can siphon off the attention and resources a president should be devoting to the real needs of the nation.

Most recent presidents gradually came to understand the limits of presidential power, sometimes the hard way. Indeed, the moral of the personal presidency suggests that presidents who become popular by making exaggerated promises have trouble keeping both the promises and their popularity in this system of fragmented power. The Clinton years illustrated another danger of exercising the personal presidency in the age of tabloid media: the risk of diminishing the office when scrutiny of the occupant's private life overtakes evaluation of his public role.

One of the most interesting aspects of this unusual office is its resilience and elasticity. It can be stretched and shrunk from one administration to another or even within a single administration. Each occupant is likely to make something quite different of it than his predecessor, either by the attitude and skills he brings to it or because the times force him to do so.

Key Terms

imperial presidency
impeachment
head of state
head of government
pardon power
chief executive
senatorial courtesy
executive orders
executive privilege
United States v. *Nixon*
veto power
pocket veto
signing statements
commander in chief
War Powers Resolution
Executive Office of the President (EOP)
going public
fireside chats
spectacle presidency
personal presidency

Key Names

George Washington
Thomas Jefferson
Bill Clinton
George W. Bush
Barack Obama
John McCain
Richard Nixon
Woodrow Wilson
Andrew Jackson
Abraham Lincoln
Theodore Roosevelt
Franklin Delano Roosevelt
Abigail Adams
Eleanor Roosevelt
Hillary Clinton
Richard Cheney
Lyndon Johnson
Ronald Reagan

Please visit our companion website at www.cengage.com/politicalscience/welch/uag12e or use CengageNOW for additional resources dealing with this chapter.

At the IRS, a bureaucrat is surrounded by her file boxes.

The Bureaucracy

12

Talking Points

A frustrated George W. Bush, meeting in Prague in 2007 with political dissidents from around the world, told a leading opponent of Egypt's military dictatorship, "I too am a dissident in Washington. Bureaucracy in the United States does not help change." Bush was alluding to American diplomats he believed were not committed to his vision of "ending tyranny in our world." Egypt's president, he said, had "brainwashed" State Department personnel posted there. He told the dissidents that he would order his ambassadors to meet with opposition leaders in all non-democratic countries. But, as if to prove his point, the State Department waited two months before sending out that directive to U.S. embassies.[1]

This is why presidents often feel as thwarted as Bush did with "permanent Washington." George W. Bush set out not just to lead, but to gain control over and transform the bureaucracy. But as his administration wore on he saw that many career civil servants—the permanent bureaucracy—were opposed to both his domestic and foreign policies. A White House official, trying to clarify to a State Department bureaucrat the administration's position on spreading democracy, reminded him, "It's our policy.... Read the president's speech." Unimpressed, the bureaucrat replied, "Policy is not what the president says in speeches. Policy is what emerges from interagency meetings."[2]

Presidents who believe they alone issue orders to the federal bureaucracy are bound to be frustrated. The bureaucracy is responsible for implementing congressional legislation and judicial rulings as well as following presidential directives. Those career civil servants who are in positions to resist or stymie presidential policies are usually highly trained career professionals—lawyers, scientists, diplomats, high-ranking military officers—who gained their positions through merit appointment and advancement through the ranks. Their job is to bring their professional competence to the performance of their duties and to give presidents the benefit of their expertise.

As the undisputed chief foreign policy maker, Bush may have had some justification in being angry at foreign service officers who did not carry out his policy to the full. But like those in other professions, people in the State Department and Pentagon, find it hard to act against their own professional judgment.

When George Wallace ran as a third-party candidate for president in 1968, he campaigned against "pointy-headed bureaucrats" in Washington making decisions that regulated good people's lives. Bureaucrats, according to Wallace, were out of touch with everyday citizens and their concerns. Wallace did not invent bureaucracy bashing, but he helped make it popular among candidates for federal office.

President Reagan never tired of talking about his dissatisfaction with big government and liked to say he preferred flying over Washington to being on the ground because from the air, government looked smaller. Presidential candidates Patrick Buchanan and Ross Perot ran for office by disparaging the people who ran the government they wanted to lead. And not long after taking office, George W. Bush discounted a report on global warming "put out by the bureaucracy," implying that, given its source, it need not be taken seriously.

When most politicians refer to "Washington" they mean big government using too much money to do unnecessary things. Government critics imply that bureaucrats are not like ordinary citizens. Rather, they are busybodies committed to expanding government's size, spending taxpayers' money, and designing regulations to make life more difficult for individuals and businesses.

Bureaucratic decision making is involved in so much of our lives because government has come to serve many different purposes and interests. The federal government employs butchers, truck drivers, engineers, mathematicians, physicists, chemists, and accountants. In all, it employs 2.7 million civilians who work in 100 agencies at more than 800 different occupations. (The armed forces put another 2.3 million on the federal payroll.) Federal bureaucrats do crop research and soil analysis, run hospitals and utilities, fight drug trafficking, check manufacturers' claims about their products, inspect mines, develop high-tech weapons systems, send out Social Security checks, authorize Medicare payments, administer student loan programs, and regulate air traffic, to mention only a few responsibilities.

To some people, the federal bureaucracy has become the symbol of big government and the embodiment of everything they dislike about it. It is seen as equivalent to a fourth branch of government—powerful, uncontrollable, and with a life of its own. In fact, the federal bureaucracy has no *independent* legislative authority, only that delegated by Congress, and it has no budgetary powers. The bureaucracy's official role is to implement and enforce policies made by elected officials—that is, by Congress and the president. In doing this, bureaucrats do, in some instances, make new law. But departments and agencies exist at the pleasure of Congress, which can eliminate them or trim their budgets if it does not approve of their behavior. If an agency within the bureaucracy consistently supersedes its authority, it is because Congress is intentionally letting it do so or is failing to fulfill its oversight duties.

As we shall see, government bureaucrats are a lot like everyone else. They are ordinary citizens with attitudes that mirror those of their fellow citizens. Very few of these civil servants, about 16 percent, work in the Washington, D.C., metropolitan area. It may not fit your image of people pushing paper in buildings the size of the Pentagon, but the great majority of federal bureaucrats serve in offices near you; check the U.S. government listing in your telephone book and see how many branch offices of federal agencies are located in or near your hometown.

In this chapter, we look at the evolution of the federal bureaucracy—its growth in size, function, and lawmaking powers. We describe the people who staff the bureaucracy, how they are recruited, what rules govern their work, and how Congress and the president set guidelines for the executive branch and oversee its activities. Finally, we describe ways in which the public can join in the work of monitoring the bureaucracy and have a say in the rules it makes.

The Nature of Bureaucracies

Many people automatically associate the word *bureaucracy* with the federal government. They may visualize rows of cubicles with nameless clerical workers doing monotonous work very inefficiently. Trying to cash in on this stereotype, a Virginia company once sold a "Bureaucrat" doll as "a product of no redeeming social value. Place the Bureaucrat on a stack of papers on your desk, and he will just sit on them."[3] The problem with this joke is that the parodied traits are not necessarily common among government bureaucrats, nor are they unique to bureaucrats. All organizations except the very smallest have bureaucracies: your college or university has one, as did your local school dis-

"I'm sorry, dear, but you knew I was a bureaucrat when you married me."

trict; every corporation, most religious denominations, and large philanthropic foundations have them, too, not to mention the Olympics, your favorite sports league, and the unions that represent the players in that league.

All these bureaucracies, public and private, share some common features. For example, all have hierarchies of authority; that is, everyone in a bureaucracy has a place in a pyramidal network of jobs, with fewer near the top and more near the bottom. Almost everyone in a bureaucracy has a boss, and except for those in the bottom tier, most have some subordinates. People advance up the hierarchy on the basis of performance or seniority, so those with more authority tend to be those with more experience and expertise.

Because of the hierarchical structure, bureaucratic behavior is not always consistent with democratic principles. Most bureaucrats are not elected, and as in any hierarchical organization, higher-level authorities can restrict the opportunity of someone lower in the pyramid to express an opinion or share expertise in the decision-making process. In their relative lack of openness, bureaucracies have the potential to restrict consumer and client access to information about their products and services and how they operate and to limit citizens' access to information about their own government. In effect, organizational tendencies, if unrestrained in a government bureaucracy, could transform "citizens" into "subordinates."[4] But our constitutional system provides checks on the power of federal bureaucrats and ways for the public to participate in decision making that few people know about or take advantage of.

Not only are government bureaucracies structurally similar to private ones, but they do the same types of work. Employees in both private and public bureaucracies perform a lot of routine tasks. Auditing expense vouchers, managing employee travel, and creating personnel systems, for example, are as routine in business firms as in public agencies. And both also have workers who are productive, honest, and efficient and others who are not. But there are some distinctions between private and public bureaucracies. Here we look at several.[5]

Goals

Businesses are supposed to make a profit; if they do not, they fail. Public agencies are supposed to promote the "public interest"; if they do not, they fail to serve the people who pay their salaries. Although people disagree over what the public interest is, it is not the same thing as making a profit, just as a government is not a business. This is why we have different words for these two kinds of organizations: they exist for completely different reasons.

The goals of a public bureaucracy are defined by elected officials, who collectively determine what is in the public interest. They are sometimes accused of setting goals as if they were in a private bureaucracy— that is, making policies that will help them at the polls rather than policies that best serve the public. But in general, the goals set by these officials are supposed to accomplish tasks and provide services that private bureaucracies cannot. In some cases, such as providing for national security during wartime, they must do so irrespective of cost.

Some part of the public's varying perception of how well the bureaucracy does its job stems from a lack of agreement on the work it is given to do. One person's lazy, red-tape-ridden, uncaring bureaucracy is another's responsive agency. But even when unhappy with its performance, Americans still expect government to provide a vast array of services costing billions of dollars annually, from highways that accommodate high-speed cars to Social Security payments that arrive on time, from clean tap water to safe neighborhoods, from protection from foreign enemies to a cure for cancer.

Performance Standards

It is relatively easy to judge if a private organization is meeting its goals (ignoring for the moment fraudulent accounting) by asking if it profitable. We might dislike the chocolate-covered raisins that a candy company produces but would still consider the company successful if it made a profit selling them. We would not typically denigrate the

To save lives, federal regulations mandate setting standards and testing autos for safety. These dummies allow simulations of the impact of crashes.

BEHIND THE SCENES

PRIVATIZING WAR

Government has increasingly outsourced government jobs to private industry. The process has been underway for at least thirty years as one president after another has been convinced that privatization is one way to make government more efficient and less costly by downsizing the permanent bureaucracy and the armed forces. Under George W. Bush, the process accelerated with few new measures introduced to ensure accountability.

The most publicized aspect of this process has been in the military: in the first Gulf war about 10 percent of the personnel were hired by private contractors, the same was true of the Clinton-ordered military involvement in Bosnia in the 1990s. But in the occupation of Iraq during the current war, there are more private contractors than military personnel.

There is no proof that outsourcing has brought greater efficiencies and cost savings for taxpayers. But for certain there has been far less accountability than required of a federal agency. In 2008, 60,000 federal contractors, over half of them defense contractors, owed almost $8 billion in back taxes.[1] The top 50 contractors have paid $12 billion in fines for 350 counts of misconduct since 1995 and yet continue to receive additional federal contracts.[2]

More than $102 billion in contracts were awarded for work in Iraq and Afghanistan in the first six years after the wars began. Most of the early contracts were no-bid, with contractors essentially naming their own price. Contractors have been paid for work done well or badly or not done at all.[3] KBR, the former Halliburton subsidiary, had received $24 billion in military contracts by 2007 but attempts to audit its accounts were stymied because the military felt it was too dependent on its services. Faulty electrical work by KBR caused almost 300 fires that damaged or destroyed military facilities. It led to at least 18 deaths and to many other soldiers being severely shocked while taking showers.[4] Yet the Pentagon's contract manager, a career civil servant, who tried to hold up payments and threaten KBR with penalties, was fired and an outside auditor (nongovernmental) brought in to approve the payments.

Despite paying out $4 billion to private contractors in 2007, the State Department still had only 17 contract compliance officers.[5] And the civilian body guards it hired to protect U.S. diplomats in Iraq created a diplomatic furor when they claimed to be unaccountable to the Iraqi government for alleged murder of civilians. Congress did pass a law making contractors subject to Iraqi criminal laws, but a full accounting of what privatization is costing taxpayers awaits another administration.

[1] GAO figures quoted in Editorial, "Tracking the Spoils of the Private Sector," New York Times, April 27, 2008, Wk 11.
[2] Project on Government Oversight figures quoted in ibid., Wk 11.
[3] Department of Defense, "Internal Controls Over Payments in Iraq, Kuwait, and Egpyt, May, 2008. Auditing and oversight reports can be found at the website of the Department of Defense's Inspector General, www.dodig.osd.mil.
[4] James Risen, "Electrical Risks at Iraqi Bases Are Worse Than Said," New York Times, July 18, 2008.
[5] John M. Broder and David Rohde, "Use of Contractors by State Department Has Soared," New York Times, October 24, 2007.

---

company because it makes something we do not approve of. We rightly use a different standard in judging government. But what is the appropriate standard for evaluating the performance of government if making a profit is not the goal?

One obvious method is to determine whether a public agency is efficient and cost-effective. That sounds logical, but any method of assigning dollar values to bureaucratic output must be partly subjective. It is usually easier to place a value on a commodity than on a government service. We can estimate what price to place on a chair or a house by computing the cost of constructing it. But placing a dollar value on such public goals as education or consumer safety is much harder. How many children have to die from swallowing pills and medications before government requires pharmaceutical manufacturers to use childproof caps on bottles? How many lives saved makes it worthwhile for government to require auto manufacturers to install air bags? How much was the life of each person killed in the World Trade Center on 9/11 worth (a calculation made in order to provide compensation to their families)?

These are questions bureaucrats must answer. To determine whether it is cost-effective to adopt a safety rule, for example, bureaucrats in regulatory agencies put a dollar value on human life by calculating how productive an individual will be during his or her lifetime. Then they estimate the cost of putting the policy in place, as well as of monitoring and enforcing it.

Private bureaucracies ask the same questions before their leaders decide whether it is profitable to install safer fuel tanks in cars or to remove a low-risk flaw from a child's toy. Although the federal bureaucrat, too, is always weighing costs against benefits, many people believe that the government should not use cost as the primary standard when lives are at risk.

Another way to evaluate performance is to measure waste that stems from inefficiency and corruption. It is not particularly difficult to calculate how much more an agency paid out because it failed to get competitive bids for equipment and supplies, hired more employees than necessary to do a job, contracted consultants to do imaginary work, or erred in calculating welfare payments or farm subsidies. Two spectacular cases of waste in government spending resulted from the Pentagon's awarding five-year, no-bid contracts to Haliburton and its subsidiary KBR to provide housing, food, laundry, and security services in Iraq that, prior to the 1980s, would have been provided by military personnel, and from the Department of Homeland Security's (DHS's) mismanagement of rescue and recovery after Hurricane Katrina. Millions in housing support was paid out to ineligible applicants and millions more wasted in purchases made on no-bid contracts.

Some kinds of government waste are harder to measure because no matter how well a program may be run, part of the public will always be opposed to its goals. Perhaps the program is providing services a taxpayer thinks inappropriate for government, or maybe it serves relatively few people at a large cost. These were the criteria many Americans used to evaluate welfare programs. Accusations of waste and fraud were common, but as a percentage of overall expenditures, there was little client fraud in the welfare program. Most criticism stemmed from opposition to the program itself and services provided at great cost to a small clientele without appropriate results.

Similar criticism comes from opponents of government health care and social insurance programs; some argue that private health insurance and pension programs are by definition more efficiently run because private businesses exist to make a profit. But in fact the administrative costs of Medicare are well below those of private health care insurers, and many private pension programs have been catastrophically underfunded and either terminated or placed in government receivership.

In a less-publicized example, a government commission called it wasteful to keep open hundreds of very small post offices that served rural communities. The commission was not alleging fraud or mismanagement, but believed that the post offices cost too much for the small number of people served. To the residents of these communities, however, their post offices were a good return on their tax dollars, and paying to keep them open was more efficient than having to drive miles to a distant office.

Citizens have rarely applied this standard of waste to corporate behavior, at least not prior to our more environmentally conscious era. Historically, private corporations have been able to waste more than a government agency of comparable size without the public ever taking notice. If a business or industry makes a profit, most people think it is a job well done, without asking whether the product or service offered is in itself wasteful. Marketing a hundred different kinds of breakfast cereal in packaging twice the size of the contents may not be an efficient use of resources, but if they sell, consumers are inclined to say, "Why not?" We may not like lime-green sofas with pink stripes, but we do not consider their manufacturer wasteful for making them as long as the product is profitable. In 2001, when senior managers in the federal bureaucracy got bonuses averaging $11,000, it prompted public scrutiny of their agencies' performances.[6] But when CEOs of corporations that lost billions got multimillion-dollar bonuses, much of the public simply said, "Whatever the market will allow." (That thinking began to change with growing income inequality and the criminal convictions of some CEOs.)

We see government expenditures as *our* money (it is!), and we feel entitled to complain, especially since payment of that money (taxes) is not voluntary. Only recently has such a large percentage of the public invested in stock that they have begun paying attention to how private bureaucracies manage *investors'* money. Yet private investments are often made through public bureaucracies, such as a university's or a school district's pension fund, and when losses occur because of corruption or poor performance by the corporate bureaucracy, it may still be the public bureaucracy that takes much of the heat.

Openness

The openness of public bureaucracy is another feature distinguishing it from a private bureaucracy. Private firms operate with much more secrecy than public agencies do, even when private actions have a significant impact on the public. For example, tobacco companies' lack of openness—long assumed to be their right—cost the lives of many people. The courts ordered tobacco companies to open their files only after much scientific evidence on the dangers of tobacco had accumulated.

In contrast, the greater visibility, or openness, of public agencies helps make them more responsive. Only by having

"Are you sure this is the correct way to declassify documents?"

knowledge of both the process and the content of public decisions can interested groups and individuals express their preferences effectively. No one articulated this better than James Madison when he wrote, "A popular Government without popular information or the means of acquiring it, is but a Prologue to a Farce or a Tragedy or perhaps both. Knowledge will forever govern ignorance, and a people who mean to be their own Governors, must arm themselves with the power knowledge gives."[7]

To this end, Congress in 1813 established the federal depository library program "to guarantee public access to government information by making it available free of charge" in local libraries around the country. Today there are 1250 depository libraries. But as government grew and agencies and paper proliferated, it became harder for the public to keep track of what government was doing. In 1934, Congress passed the Federal Register Act, requiring that all government rules, regulations, and laws be published in the *Federal Register* and that all rules in their final version appear in the *Code of Federal Regulations.* (Today both are available online at www.gpoaccess.gov/fr/index .html.)

Congress went further in 1946 by passing the **Administrative Procedure Act (APA)**, which provides for public participation in the rule-making process. All federal agencies must disclose their rule-making procedures and publish all regulations at least thirty days in advance of their effective date to allow time for public comment. Today citizens can often post comments on proposed rules at an agency's website, but it is common for public hearings to be held on controversial rules or those with wide impact. Environmental rules frequently provoke citizen reactions, with comments sometimes numbering in the tens of thousands.

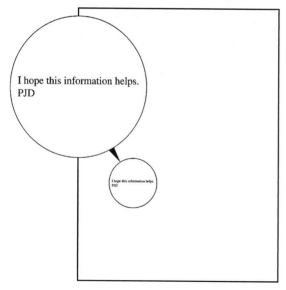

FOIA requires the release of documents, but sometimes the government will censor information within them. This comment was all that remained of an e-mail that the Bush administration censored before releasing it.

Congress increased public access to the bureaucracy in another way by passing the Freedom of Information Act in 1966. As amended in 1974, **FOIA** (pronounced "foy-ya") lets any person (corporate or individual) apply to an agency for access to unclassified documents in its archives. The act has been amended several times since, including in 1996 to provide for access to electronic records.[8]

FOIA requests must be made according to a formal procedure, and they must cite specific documents. The government puts out a handbook telling how to take advantage of access rights, and every government website is required to have a link to its FOIA office. Agencies are not obligated to give "information," only to provide copies of the documents requested, if they have them and if they are not in an exempt category. Intelligence agencies cannot make any record available to a foreign government and FOIA cannot be used to gain access to trade secrets, internal records such as personnel files, or sensitive documents on a living person.[9] But it can be used to get your FBI file, should you have one, or the file of a person no longer living.

Federal agencies receive hundreds of thousands of FOIA requests annually and each agency is required to make public the number of requests it receives.[10] Efforts to make government agencies more open often run up against a desire to limit the distribution of critical or embarrassing information. It is the rare public or private bureaucracy that wants to reveal its failures. Thus an evaluation of FOIA found that agencies used many tactics to discourage people from seeking information, such as delaying responses to requests, charging high fees for copies of records, and requiring detailed descriptions of documents requested.[11] The FBI once refused to expedite the release of information to a prisoner on death row who was afraid he would be executed before the information was available. The FBI's judgment that his situation did not show "exceptional need or urgency" was overruled by a federal court.[12]

As the chief executive, a president's views on the openness of agencies are also important. The president's policy on FOIA implementation is communicated to federal agencies by the attorney general at the beginning of each administration. Under Presidents Reagan and Bush Sr., federal agencies adopted a narrow reading of the act, making it more difficult to get information.[13] In contrast, President Carter banned classification of documents unless they were clearly related to national security, and President Clinton issued an executive order authorizing the declassification of most documents twenty-five years old or older. A FOIA request was to be met unless there was "foreseeable harm" in the document's release.[14] Clinton also put a ten-year limit on the classified status of new documents unless a review had determined that they must remain secret.[15]

George W. Bush began tightening access to government documents virtually upon taking office, as part of his broader goals of strengthening the presidency and reducing both congressional and public oversight of the executive branch.[16] For the same reasons, Vice President Cheney had been a long-standing opponent of FOIA.[17] By executive order, Bush immediately established new rules for access to presidential papers, including his father's, which were due to be opened to the public. He extended the right to review and withhold sensitive papers to the vice president and to presidents' heirs and descendants. (The American Political Science Association was among the plaintiffs who sued to reverse the order.) Midway in Bush's second term there was a five-year backlog of requests for access to presidential records, compared to an eighteen-month delay when he entered office.[18]

After 9/11, Bush also used national security as grounds for restricting access to government records. Under the Bush standard, any FOIA request denied by an agency on any "sound legal basis" could expect Justice Department backing. The administration ordered thousands of scientific and technical documents removed from public release, some from libraries, and many from government websites, such as an Environmental Protection Agency (EPA) database on chemicals used at industrial sites.[19] Information of interest to potential terrorists is not all that the Bush administration had removed from public view. Documents on World War II, the Korean War, relations with China, and other foreign policy papers that had been declassified decades ago were reclassified and removed from public view. (See the Ethical Dilemmas box below.)

The government also asked scientists' professional associations to restrict what they publish.[20] Some of this censorship just created confusion. For example, the Federal Aviation Administration warned pilots they were not to fly in the vicinity of nuclear power plants but at the same time told them it could not say where the plants were located because that was "sensitive security information."[21]

By executive order, Bush also reversed a Clinton policy that had prohibited thousands of department and agency heads from stamping documents "secret" on their own authority. Whereas during Clinton's presidency four times as

ethical dilemmas | To Declassify or Not

Alerted by an historian working in the National Archives in 2006, the new head of the Archives discovered that 55,000 pages of material formerly open to the public had been reclassified as secret. Some of it had been in the public domain for fifty years, copied by researchers, and even published by government agencies in some cases. One item reclassified as "secret" was a CIA assessment that the Chinese would not enter the Korean War, made just two weeks before China sent 300,000 troops into Korea in 1950. The fact that we fought against the Chinese army in the Korean war is hardly a secret, so why remove such material from public access?

The director of the Archives discovered that each day thirty bureaucrats from intelligence agencies were reviewing Archive materials with the aim of taking anything they thought should be secret out of circulation.

In cases like this, an archivist finds his professional ethics and his obligations as a federal bureaucrat in possible conflict. The head of the National Archives (NARA) is a presidential appointee and must take presidential directives. But the NARA director is also almost always an historian or a librarian/archivist. The principles of openness and public access to research records are foundational to a librarian's and an historian's professional ethics. Historians in particular are dependent on access to archival records to carry out their research. Certainly, the National Archives is committed to ensuring that all material that could present a threat to national security be classified for an appropriate period of time, but it was hard to see how reclassifying historical materials that had been open for decades was preserving national security.

The Archivist had to decide whether to accept the decisions of bureaucrats who were reclassifying once-public material or countermand a subordinate who had agreed to let the intelligence officials close the papers. By that arrangement NARA would not disclose the reason for the presence of intelligence personnel in the Archives, what material they removed, or why they removed it.

In this case, facing a cascade of public rebuke, much of it from historians and librarians, the NARA director suspended the reclassification process until his own oversight agency could audit the process. He called on the agencies that had withdrawn the material to "restore to the public shelves as quickly as possible the maximum amount of information consistent with the obligation to protect truly sensitive national security information."[1]

[1] Scott Shane, "Archivist Urges U. S. to Reopen Classified Files," *New York Times*, March 3, 2006. A list of materials withdrawn was posted at www.gwu.edu/nsarchiv.

much material had been declassified as in the previous fifteen years, during Bush's first term the number of classified documents doubled and declassification dwindled to about 10 percent of what it had been at the end of the nineties.[22] By 2004, the Bush administration was classifying an historic high of 125 documents per minute, in large part by creating vague new security classifications—at an estimated cost of $7.2 billion.[23]

Another step the Bush administration took to limit access to executive branch communications was to restrict use of e-mail on government servers. He came into office after the 1996 FOIA amendment that expanded public access to many electronic records and had learned from rulings that went against the two previous administrations. The first George Bush took his aides' e-mail tapes with him when he left office and argued that they were not public property. A federal appeals court ruled that these tapes were public records and must be preserved, and they applied the same ruling to Clinton administration requests for exemption.

Because of these rulings, George W. Bush was very cautious about exchanges of views by e-mail, and Bush himself stopped sending personal e-mail. In Bush's second term a congressional investigation into alleged political firings of U.S. attorneys demanded access to e-mails between Bush aides relevant to the investigation only to find that thousands had "gone missing" and many others had apparently been sent on Republican party e-mail accounts rather than from the government accounts that are public property.

Bush's narrow definition of public access rights and his penchant for secrecy drew criticism from both conservatives and liberals. In 2007–2008, many new laws were introduced in Congress to expedite FOIA requests, keep costs reasonable, and open federal contracts (such as with military contractors in Iraq) to public scrutiny.[24]

Despite the limitations placed on FOIA, it has enabled individuals and groups to gain important and useful information. Citizens have used it to gather injury and fatality information on defective cars, to assess dangerous infant formulas, to reveal a link between aspirin and a disease known as Reye's syndrome, to learn that J. Edgar Hoover authorized the FBI to carry out a four-year investigation of women's rights groups, and to force the Internal Revenue Service (IRS) to release a 40,000-page manual on its

auditing procedures.[25] Scholars have used FOIA to retrieve thousands of documents on Cold War diplomacy, to get records of medical experiments on the effect of radioactivity conducted on unwitting subjects, and to retrieve the FBI files of anthropologists kept under surveillance during the Cold War and the McCarthy era.

Another significant law mandating openness in government is the aptly named **Sunshine Act**. Adopted in 1976, it requires that most government meetings be conducted in public and that notice of such meetings must be posted in advance. Regulatory agencies, for example, must give notice of the date, time, place, and agenda of their meetings and follow certain rules to prevent unwarranted secrecy. State governments have adopted their own sunshine laws, and today it is difficult for any public body—city council or planning commission or any of their subgroups—to meet in secret to conduct official business. Results of meetings conducted in closed, unannounced sessions are open to citizen challenge.

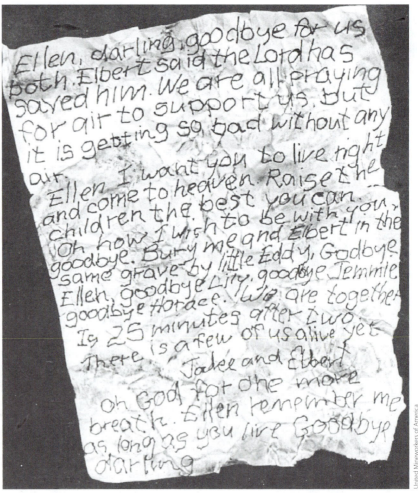

Jacob Vowell wrote this letter shortly before suffocating after a mine collapse in Fraterville, Tennessee, in 1902. Such disasters prompted government regulation of mining, which has since saved many lives. However, mining companies resist some regulations, and occasional disasters, such as the one in West Virginia in 2006, still occur.

Growth of the Federal Bureaucracy

Readers will note almost no Constitution icons in this chapter. That is because the Founders made few formal provisions for the federal "bureaucracy." Of course they recognized the need for administrators and clerical workers to carry out laws and programs passed by Congress, and in Article II they refer to "executive Departments" and "Heads of Departments." ⭐ Art. II, Sect. 2. By authorizing the raising of an army and navy, levying of taxes, creation of a diplomatic corps and a judiciary, they anticipated all of the early growth of the bureaucracy, if not how the growing size and complexity of the country would engorge it.

George Washington's first cabinet included only three departments and the offices of attorney general and postmaster general, and all combined employed just a few hundred people. More people worked at Mount Vernon, Washington's plantation, than in the executive branch in the 1790s.[26] The Department of State had just nine employees. By 1800, the bureaucracy was still small, with only 3000 civil servants. Only the Treasury Department had much to do, collecting import and excise taxes and purchasing military supplies for an army of a few thousand. From then until 1990, the bureaucracy grew continuously, though at an uneven rate.

Why the Bureaucracy Has Grown

As we saw in Chapter 3, government, over time, responded to public wishes by creating federal agencies to assist and promote emerging economic interests of business, agriculture, and labor and more recently to provide health and economic protections for workers, consumers, retirees, and other groups.[27] One scholar explained the bureaucracy's growth by pointing to Americans' discovery that "government can protect and assist as well as punish and repress."[28] Thus at the same time we criticize government's growth, we demand education, irrigation projects, roads, airports, job training, effective policing, consumer protection, agricultural subsidies, student loans, and many other services. Each of us might be willing to cut benefits for someone else, but most of us want to keep the benefits *we* have.

National crises also contribute to the growth of bureaucracy. The Great Depression prompted President **Franklin Roosevelt** to propose numerous programs to put the unemployed to work and pull the country out of the hard times. These programs required more bureaucratic agencies and personnel to administer them. As a result, the size of the bureaucracy nearly doubled during the 1930s.

World War II created additional demands for health care and other services for veterans. The Administrative Procedure Act was passed in 1946 partly because the bureaucracy had grown so much in size and power during the Depression and World War II that Congress believed it needed to increase its oversight.[29] After the Cold War, when thoughts turned to downsizing the Defense Department, supporters of military spending found new justifications for expansion in the threat of global terrorism. Forty-five days after 9/11, Congress rushed to pass the USA PATRIOT Act (officially, the Uniting and Strengthening America by Providing Appropriate Tools Required to Intercept and Obstruct Terrorism Act), which increased both the power and the size of the federal bureaucracy. Implementation of government's extraordinary new power to wiretap, search e-mail, and gain access to library borrowing records and many business records, both paper and electronic, required more personnel and increased spending.

Bureaucrats cannot produce growth on their own. Every agency and its budget is authorized and approved by Congress and the president and continues to exist because it is valuable to enough people with enough influence to sustain it. Sometimes government grows because the president and Congress want it to be more accountable. This often results in hiring more managers, producing greater inefficiency, and, ironically, more difficulty in holding agencies accountable.[30]

A federal inspector examines poultry in 1910.

National Archives #87 Photo #88-GN-C-156

During the Depression, government agencies hired the unemployed for numerous projects. Out-of-work artists were paid to paint murals in government buildings, post offices, and public monuments such as Coit Tower in San Francisco.

The growth of the bureaucracy should be seen in the perspective of the overall growth of our economy and population. For example, the number of federal bureaucrats for every 1000 people in the United States decreased from sixteen in 1953 to nine in 2006. We saw in Chapter 3 that the major growth in public employment in recent decades has been at the state and local levels. Over 37 percent of all government workers were federal employees in 1953; in 2006, fewer than 13 percent were.[31]

Controlling Growth

When new bureaucracies are created, the intent is to hold them to their original size, but most grow over time because once they are in place, additional responsibilities are assigned to them. Consolidation or elimination is rare. More commonly, departments become so large that they must subdivide (for example, the Department of Commerce and Labor was divided into separate departments of Labor and Commerce) or for offices and agencies to become so big or their work so important they are made into cabinet departments (Veterans Affairs, DHS), where they become even larger.

Almost every president since Lyndon Johnson (1963–1968) has tried to streamline or downsize the bureaucracy on the general assumption that size and performance are linked. Presidents often think they can establish more effi-cient management plans and then cut personnel. Richard Nixon tried to merge seven departments into four but could not gain approval, and despite many attempts to ax the Department of Education, it is stronger than it ever has been. **Jimmy Carter** (1977–1981) was a committed deregulator and a micromanager who oversaw the elimination of thousands of rules and some regulators.

For all **Ronald Reagan**'s (1981–1989) talk against big government, it grew by over 200,000 employees during his administration. Although many agencies lost personnel (the biggest loser was the Department of Housing and Urban Development), others, such as Defense, Justice, and the Treasury, gained. In addition, Reagan created a new cabinet office, the Department of Veterans Affairs, from what had been an independent agency. He had entered office with a plan to wage a "war on waste," but he left office with the country another trillion dollars in debt and the Defense Department buying $600 toilet seats.

Bill Clinton's administration (1993–2001) had its "reinventing government" initiative, a brainchild of Vice President **Al Gore**. It did have limited success; the number of government employees decreased by 1.5 percent during their years in office.

Despite George W. Bush's (2001–2009) stated admiration for smaller, more efficient government, the federal bureaucracy grew by 5 percent (79,000 jobs) during his first three years in office.[32] Some of the growth was due to the war on terrorism—adding a new cabinet department and increasing defense appointments. But there was also some padding—or thickening—of the bureaucracy through the creation of new positions at the senior level in cabinet departments that have nothing to do with national security.[33] The number of people at the highest pay level more than tripled during Bush's first three years. Layers of administration were added to cabinet departments at a time when the efficient upward and downward flow of information within the bureaucracy has become a major issue, even a life-and-death issue, as it was in the intelligence bureaucracy in 2001. The new Department of Homeland Security (DHS) developed twenty-one layers of administration and had 146 senior administrative positions two years after its creation.[34]

Career civil servants are skeptical about the attempt of every administration to take on the bureaucracy and cut it down to size. One explanation of the perception gap is that there is a "natural antipathy" between presidents and career civil servants because the president is elected on his ability to articulate basic human values, whereas "civil service is about enforcing rules and procedures and treating all citizens and issues equally." Bureaucrats are not about values in the sense that politicians use that term.[35] Reform is difficult when presidents fill political leadership positions in agencies with individuals who do not stay around long enough to learn their jobs and have little chance of really reshaping their agencies. Presidents and their appointees find that reality does not always match political slogans. And presidents find that reforming the bureaucracy is much tougher than they anticipated and soon turn to other activities with more immediate payoffs. Thus in the view of a former OMB official, reform is mostly "three yards and a cloud of dust."[36]

Agencies within the Federal Bureaucracy

The Constitution says little about the organization of the executive branch other than indicating a need for the president to have a cabinet. As government's role expanded, it became clear that a single type of organization would not be appropriate for every task assigned to the bureaucracy. Cabinet departments, for example, are headed by people who serve at the president's pleasure and who are there to help carry out his policies. But other agencies must implement law without reference to an individual president's preferences. These agencies require protection from political interference, as do those established to carry out highly technical work. In this section, we review the major types of agencies in the executive branch.

Departments

Departments are organizations within the executive branch that form the president's cabinet. Their heads, called secretaries (except for the head of the Justice Department who is called the attorney general), are appointed by the president with the consent of the Senate, and they are directly responsible to the president. There are fifteen departments; the newest is DHS. (See Figure 1.) These departments constitute the lion's share of the federal bureaucracy; the largest employer is the Defense Department, with close to 30 percent of all civil servants.

Cabinet departments exist to carry out the president's policy in specific functional areas: national security, federal law enforcement, fiscal policy, health and welfare, foreign relations, and so forth. They are staffed by career civil servants, but all top policy-making positions in each division of a department are held by presidential appointees. The fifteen cabinet departments have more than 350 such positions. Permanent staff believe that the increase in the number of appointive senior positions makes their work more difficult.

Independent Agencies

Independent agencies differ from departments in that they are usually smaller and their heads do not sit in the cabinet. Agency heads are, however, appointed by and responsible to the president. And occasionally a president does extend cabinet status to the head of an independent agency, most notably the director of the EPA. Some agencies, such as the EPA, the CIA, the Social Security Administration, the Peace Corps, and the National Aeronautics and Space Administration (NASA), are well known to the public. Others, such as the Office of Government Ethics, are relatively unknown.

Some independent agencies are responsible for highly specialized areas of policy such as space exploration (NASA) or law enforcement (FBI). The people appointed to head them usually have an appropriate professional background, not just a political profile acceptable to the president. However, if the agency deals with policy that has widespread impact, as the EPA and CIA do, political credentials are likely to be the president's first consideration in naming a director.

Independent Regulatory Boards and Commissions

Although unfamiliar to most Americans, independent agencies affect almost every aspect of our daily lives—the air we breathe, the water we drink, the interest on a bank loan, the fee at an ATM, the terms under which we buy or sell stock, labeling on food and manufactured goods and conditions in the plants where they were made, phone and mail service, and the construction of every car, train, plane, or bus we ride on.

Each independent regulatory board and commission regulates a specific area of business or the economy. Examples include the Federal Communications Commission

Figure 1 | The Development and Relative Size of Cabinet Departments

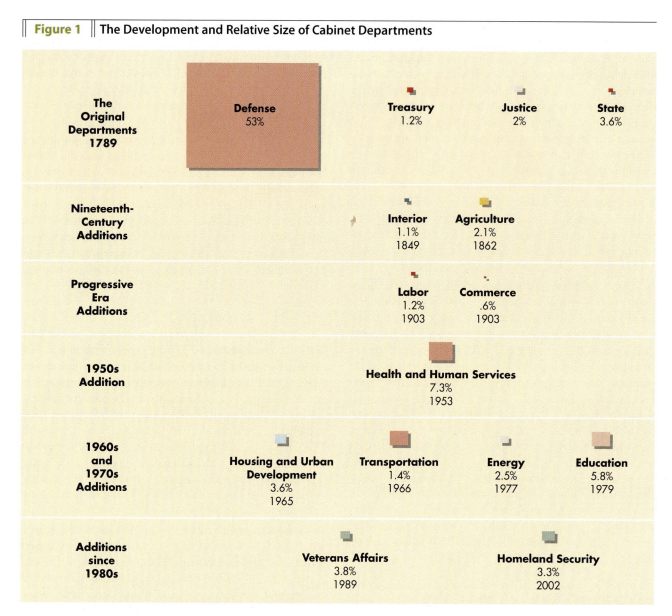

Percentages are each department's share of the **discretionary** budget authority for fiscal 2007. The figures add to less than 100 percent because of noncabinet agencies that are allocated funds (the judicial branch, the independent agencies, etc.). The modern Department of Defense (1949) replaced the Departments of War (1789) and the Navy (1798); the Justice Department (1870) replaced the Department of the Attorney General (1789); the Commerce and Labor Departments were first established in 1903 as a joint enterprise; and the Department of Health, Education and Welfare (1953) was divided in 1979 into the Department of Health and Human Services and the Department of Education.
SOURCE: United States Budget for Fiscal Year 2008, Historical Tables (Washington, D.C.: Government Printing Office, 2007), tabls. 5-3, 153.

(FCC), which regulates the electronic media; the Securities and Exchange Commission (SEC), which makes and enforces rules regarding stocks, bonds, and securities; and the Federal Reserve System (the Fed), which sets prime interest rates and controls the amount of money in circulation. These and other regulatory agencies are designated "independent" because the work they do is supposed to be removed from politics as much as possible. Congress created the first such commission, the Interstate Commerce Commission, in 1887 to decide such things as interstate

freight rates, railroad ticket prices, routes, and conditions of service.

Each of these independent regulatory boards and commissions is directed by five to ten presidential appointees. By law, each board and commission must be balanced with members of both major political parties. Appointees serve staggered terms and cannot be removed by presidents who dislike their decisions. Because of the technical knowledge needed for decision making, appointments are supposed to be based on expertise rather than partisan considerations.

Of course, it is almost impossible for politics, in the sense of an individual's values, not to have some impact on decision making. Presidents who want less government regulation appoint commissioners who share that value. Commissioners, in turn, can then make it difficult for the professionals in the agency to carry out their regulatory mission. However, the goal of having these independent commissions is to make politics secondary to professional expertise.

Government Corporations

Government corporations are businesses run by government to provide services the public needs but that no private company will provide because they are not profitable— or were not profitable at the time government began providing the service. The first government corporation, the Tennessee Valley Authority (TVA), was created during the Franklin Roosevelt administration when no utility company was willing to invest in the infrastructure necessary to bring electricity to what was then a very poor, undeveloped region of the country. The TVA still supplies electricity to its part of the country.

The United States Postal Service, which was originally a cabinet department, was converted to a business operation in 1971. Formerly a government monopoly, it now has competition from UPS and FedEx, for example, for some of the services it provides. In the 1960s, when railroads were no longer willing to provide passenger service, the government created the National Railroad Passenger Corporation (Amtrak). And because no private insurance company would ever bear the risk of insuring private bank deposits, the government established a corporation to protect your savings account (the Federal Deposit Insurance Corporation).

Similarly, the government is now the main purveyor of terrorism insurance. After 9/11, private firms were no longer willing to assume the risk, just as after Hurricane Katrina, private insurers wanted government to take even greater responsibility for insuring homeowners in coastal areas against flood damage.

Government corporations charge for their services or products but their primary objective is to provide a needed service, not to make a profit. Of course, the government is quite happy if they do or if they at least break even. When a government corporation does become profitable, its assets may be sold to private businesses and the corporation closed. This is what happened with CONRAIL, the government corporation that took over rail freight and turned it back into a profitable enterprise. The U.S. Postal Service, after decades of needing government subsidies to balance its budget, also has shown a profit during some of the years since its conversion. Opponents of government corporations would like to see both the Postal Service and the unprofitable Amtrak completely privatized. But the services provided are so important to the national economy that without the certainty that private businesses would guarantee their continuation, government would have difficulty justifying the sale of their assets.

What Bureaucracies Do

After elected officials make a law, someone must implement it. **Policy implementation** is the primary job of the bureaucracy. Bureaucrats convert laws passed by Congress and signed by the president into rules and actions that make it possible to realize the intent of the law. The general process of policy implementation has two major components: administering policies and making them.

But before looking at the specifics of administering and making policies, it is important to remember that the bureaucracy provides continuity in governing. Presidents and members of Congress come and go, and political appointees in the bureaucracy stay an average of two years, many barely learn their jobs by the time they leave. Career civil servants have a much deeper knowledge of their agencies' work, which makes them better at it and more productive than short-term political appointees. They keep government agencies functioning day in and day out so that all essential work continues even as elected and appointed officials come and go from office.

We now look in greater detail at the sources of the bureaucracy's authority and the policy-administering and policy-making responsibilities assigned to it.

Administering Policy

Public bureaucracy's oldest job is to administer the law. To "administer" is to execute, enforce, and apply the rules that have been made either by Congress or the bureaucracy itself. Thus if policy makers decide to go to war, they must empower agencies to acquire weapons, recruit and train soldiers, and devise a winning strategy. Policy making without administration is tantamount to no policy at all.

Administration includes thousands of different kinds of activities. It involves writing checks to farmers who receive payments for growing—or not growing— crops, providing direct services to the public, evaluating how well programs are working, prosecuting those who try to defraud the government, and maintaining buildings and offices. For forest rangers, administration involves helping backpackers in the Grand Canyon or putting out a forest fire in northern Minnesota.

Making Policy

Responsibility for administering policy inevitably confers lawmaking powers on the bureaucracy. This can be illustrated with the example of the Americans with Disabilities

american diversity | Women and Minorities in the Civil Service

Americans expect their public bureaucracies to be open and responsive. Andrew Jackson recognized this when he opened the civil service to people of "common" origins. By putting his frontier supporters in office, he hoped to make the bureaucracy more responsive by making it more representative. In the twentieth century, the expectation that public agencies should be open to all qualified applicants gave some groups, such as Irish, Jewish, and African Americans, more job opportunities than were open to them in the private sector because of segregation and quotas.

In the past two decades, significant progress has been made in making the federal bureaucracy more reflective of American diversity. Thirty-one percent of Americans were identified as minorities in the 2000 census, and they were 31.5 percent of the civilian federal workforce in 2004. African Americans are particularly well represented, being a substantially larger portion of the federal workforce (17 percent) than of the general population. American Indians and Asian Americans have a percentage of federal jobs close to their population share, whereas Hispanics remain significantly underrepresented

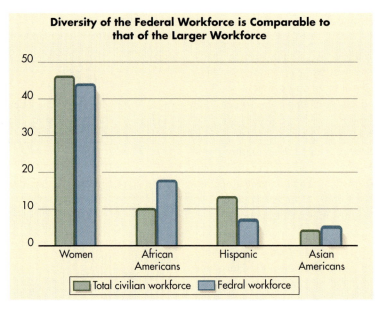

Diversity of the Federal Workforce is Comparable to that of the Larger Workforce

Legend: Total civilian workforce, Fedral workforce

SOURCE: *Office of Personnel Management, 2005 Fact Book, 48*

Act (ADA). The ADA directs employers to make a "reasonable accommodation" for a competent worker with a disability that "substantially limits" a major life activity such as seeing or walking, except when this causes "undue hardship."[37]

This seemingly straightforward law is in fact extremely complex and its impact far-reaching. Although the act went into effect in 1992, the Equal Employment Opportunity Commission (EEOC), which has responsibility for its implementation, was still clarifying what specific provisions in the act meant when Congress revised and strengthened it in 2008. Some of the ambiguities in wording that the EEOC had to help clarify were what Congress meant by a "reasonable accommodation" and an "undue hardship." When voters want local governments to spend less, is the $2 million that Des Plaines, Illinois, had to shell out for sidewalks and curb cuts an "undue hardship" or not?[38] Would colleges and universities be allowed to make only some classrooms and offices accessible to students and staff in wheelchairs, or would they have to make every classroom and faculty office accessible to people with disabilities? When do the costs of such changes become unsustainable?

in the federal workforce, despite an aggressive Hispanic recruitment program. However, the census does not distinguish between legal and illegal residency, and millions of Hispanics included in the population count would not be eligible for federal jobs. Women are represented almost in exact proportion as in the private sector labor force, though still not at parity with their 51 percent share of the population.[1]

The relatively good news about the overall profile of the bureaucracy fades at the top of the pay scale. Women and minority men have not yet broken completely through the "glass ceiling" that has kept them out of top management positions. There is progress, however. In 2004 (latest OPM data available) women filled almost 26 percent of senior-grade pay positions (about one-fifth of whom were minority women), more than twice the share held in 1990. And, collectively, minorities held 14 percent of all senior positions. Federal court rulings and out-of-court settlements in discrimination cases, as well as changing generations in leadership positions, account for some of the improvement in upward mobility.

[1] Office of Personnel Management, *The Fact Book*, 2005 Edition, 47.

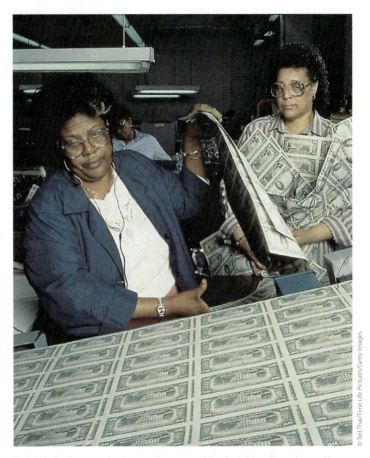

Federal employment has opened opportunities for African Americans. Shown here are two Bureau of Engraving and Printing employees checking the quality of $20 bills. The woman at right is holding $8000 in printing mistakes.

© Ted Thai/Time Life Pictures/Getty Images

Answering such questions and formulating rules to implement them is de facto policy making. Implementation requires disseminating the rules and negotiating interpretations with the parties who have to put them in place and enforce them. State and local counterparts of the EEOC and their clients must be informed of the rules, assisted in their attempts to use the rules, and monitored in their progress. Bills must be paid, disputes resolved, and information collected as to how successful the program is. If affected parties reject the EEOC's interpretation or the officials' implementation, the rules can be challenged in

federal court. This is where almost all disputed provisions of the ADA are being decided. Bureaucrats very often do not have the last word in determining how a policy is implemented.

The passage of thousands of complex bills like the ADA accounts for the growth in policy-making functions of public bureaucracies. Industrialization, population growth, urbanization, and profound changes in science, transportation, and communications have put problems of a more complex nature on government's agenda. The large number and technical nature of these problems—think about writing environmental protection rules, for example—as well as policy differences among its members, have often limited Congress's ability to draft specific policy responses.

Congress often responds to this situation by enacting a general statement of goals and identifying actions that would help achieve them. Congress then delegates the power to an agency with the relevant expertise to draft specific rules that will achieve these goals. This **delegated legislative authority** empowers executive branch agencies to draft, as well as execute, specific policies. Just as the ADA left rule making to the EEOC, any tax-reform legislation requires thousands of rules to be written by the IRS and the Treasury Department. Agency-made policy is just as binding as acts of Congress because agencies *make it at the direction of Congress*. In strictly numerical terms, agencies make much more policy than Congress because agencies issue many new rules and regulations for the implementation of each new law Congress passes.

Many political scientists believe that Congress abdicates its authority and acts in an irresponsible manner by refusing, because of political pressures and its heavy workload, to develop specific guidelines for agencies.[39] This leaves agencies to implement policies without much guidance from Congress beyond the wording of each bill. Sometimes, however, agency complaints about the ambiguities or lack of specificity in legislation are just excuses not to implement disliked policies. Differences in interpretation can lead to partisan conflicts, especially over regulatory policy. Congress can send more detailed directives to agencies. But this does not prevent the political appointees who head executive branch agencies from resisting congressional directives they dislike on the grounds that they are too complex or unrealistic to follow.

In effect, the competition between the White House and Congress was extended to the bureaucracy when Congress delegated legislative authority to agencies. This competition can intensify or subside, depending on whether the president is of the same party as congressional majorities. However, the competition has continued even under unified governments.

Sometimes agencies are in the difficult position of having to satisfy competing demands. To figure out what Congress, the president, and others want, agency officials read congressional debates and testimony and talk to members of Congress, committee staffers, White House aides, lobbyists, and others. Although agencies also try to determine what the public wants, they are more likely to respond to well-organized and well-funded groups that closely monitor their actions. As a result, agency-made policy is often less responsive to the general public than to particular interests.

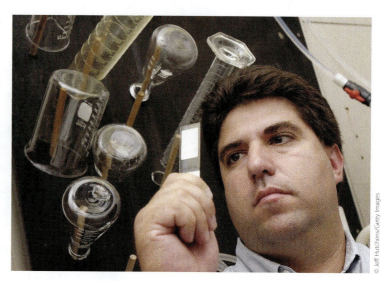

Not all bureaucrats push paper. This scientist with the Food and Drug Administration (FDA) examines breast cancer protein in his lab in Bethesda, Maryland.

© Jeff Hutchens/Getty Images

DEMOCRACY?

In practice, bureaucracies make policy. What features of our constitutional system make this consistent with democracy? Under what circumstances can it be undemocratic?

Regulation

A special kind of policy making called **regulation** produces rules, standards, or guidelines conferring benefits and imposing restrictions on business conduct and economic activity. Regulations have the force of law and are made by agencies whose directors and board members are appointed by the president and whose operating procedures are generally governed by the Administrative Procedure Act. Regulatory agencies include not only independent regulatory boards and commissions but also some independent agencies, such as the EPA, and some agencies within cabinet departments, such as the Food and Drug Administration (FDA) in Health and Human Services and the Office of Safety and Health Administration (OSHA) in the Labor Department.

Regulatory actions include two steps: making rules and adjudicating their enforcement. Rule making is the establishment of standards that apply to a class of individuals or businesses. Adjudication is the process of trying individuals or firms charged with violating standards. To do this, they use procedures that are very similar to those of courts.

Most regulations derive from laws passed by Congress that direct agencies to take actions to accomplish the goals established in the legislation. Environmental legislation, for example, requires regulatory agencies to set standards for clean air, safe disposal of toxic wastes, or safe workplaces that businesses must meet. Businesses are often allowed some flexibility in the methods used to meet the standard, but failure to comply can result in fines or other legal penalties.

Consumer protection legislation directs federal regulators to set quality or safety standards for certain types of products, such as cars, toys, food, and medical equipment. This is why there are seat belts, air bags, and shatterproof windows in cars and why materials used to make children's toys or clothing cannot be flammable or toxic. Regulations may also require businesses to provide information through labeling, such as the cancer warnings on cigarette packages and lists of ingredients noting trans fats, sugar, salt, and vitamin content on packaged food.

Another form of regulation is licensing the right to own or use public properties. For example, the FCC licenses the publicly owned airwaves to people who own and operate radio and television stations.

Data Collection and Analysis

In the course of policy making and administration, the bureaucracy performs other functions. It collects data, as in the decennial census, and it makes information available to the public. Much of what we know about ourselves as a people comes from the government's collection of data on births and deaths, occupations and income, housing and health, crime, and many other things. A cursory glance at the annual *Statistical Abstract of the United States* shows that the government reports on everything from the incidence of abortions to the export of zinc and in between informs us how much celery we eat and how many DVDs we own.

Bureaucracy also keeps us informed about what government is doing, and the Internet is a valuable tool to assist in this function. Every federal agency has a website with information about its policies and programs and an e-mail link for feedback from the public. If we want to know the rules governing camping in national parks, we can call the National Park Service or go to its website. If we want to know the fate of a bill in Congress or how our representatives voted on it, we can find it posted on the Internet.

The bureaucracy engages in research, too. A prime example is the Department of Agriculture, which for nearly 150 years has conducted research on how to grow bigger and better crops, raise healthier animals, and transport and market products more effectively. Government researchers, such as those at the National Institutes of Health and the Centers for Disease Control and Prevention, do much of the country's medical research, especially research related to mental health and epidemiology. Many vaccines and prescription drugs are also developed in government labs, and the Internet was invented by military bureaucrats. Every cabinet department has career civil servants—geologists, chemists, physicists, engineers, social scientists—carrying out research relevant to its area of policy making, be it rocketry, soil erosion, climate change, space travel, weapons development, high-tech communications and surveillance, or housing issues.

Politics and Professional Standards

As the part of government that implements policies made by elected officials, the bureaucracy cannot escape politics. It is subject to constant lobbying. That does not mean that civil servants have the green light to implement policy in a partisan manner. Today's civil servants are governed by laws that give priority to professional competence over political loyalty. Most Americans want fair, apolitical performance such that the quantity and quality of any government service they receive is not dependent on whether they belong to the same party as the president or their member of Congress. And most of us would prefer to have a civil engineer rather than a political crony in charge of building the dam near our town. The chances that the engineer will get the job over the crony have improved significantly since patronage was outlawed in the federal bureaucracy.

The Merit System

For decades, American public bureaucracies were staffed under the **patronage** system, which allowed elected officials to fill administrative jobs on the basis of political loyalty rather than merit. By providing their supporters with jobs, elected officials could strengthen their political base, and many people regarded this as simply a means for government agencies to provide employment to citizens. Patronage hiring was usually referred to as the spoils sys-

When a disappointed office seeker assassinated President Garfield, that violent act alerted federal officials to the level of public anger over the use of patronage to staff the bureaucracy and led to adoption of the Pendleton Act, which required that federal employees be hired and retained on the basis of competence rather than political consideration.

tem because it operated in rough accordance with the principle "to the victor belong the spoils," as the newly elected filled jobs with their own supporters.

At the federal level, **Andrew Jackson**'s presidential election in 1828 was a watershed in using the patronage system. Jackson believed that any white male citizen of average intelligence and goodwill could do a government job well. So he reversed the existing practice of naming mostly well-off people from the East Coast by appointing less well-off supporters from frontier areas.

The most obvious problem with staffing the bureaucracy with political supporters rather than by competitive recruitment is that jobs will go to people who are not competent to perform their duties. This became a major problem as government work became more technical and specialized. Furthermore, patronage could and frequently did lead to corruption, in particular to deal making between candidates and voters or individuals who controlled blocs of voters. Voters supported candidates who promised them jobs or other favors. Such corruption increasingly sullied city councils, state legislatures, and Congress during the 1800s.

Although patronage was affecting government performance, the influence wielded by the political machines that had grown powerful through its use kept Congress from acting until an unsuccessful job seeker assassinated President James Garfield in 1881. The Pendleton Act of 1883 established the **Civil Service Commission** to fill designated positions within the bureaucracy with people who had proved their competence in competitive examinations. Jobs under the commission's jurisdiction were part of the **merit system**. The new law also protected people holding merit positions from pressure to support or oppose particular candidates and from dismissal for political reasons.

Neutral Competence

The merit system established **neutral competence** as the professional standard for civil service employees. It requires that individuals filling merit positions be chosen for their expertise in executing policy and that they carry out their work in a nonpartisan or neutral manner. This standard assumes that there is no Republican or Democratic way to build a sewer, collect customs duties, or fight a war. In effect, it says that partisan politics has no place in bureaucracy. It also implies that bureaucrats should not profit personally from the decisions they make.

Theodore Roosevelt (1901–1909) is considered the "father" of the modern civil service for his championing of merit hiring and neutral competence. "The government is us," he said. "Government jobs belong to the American people, not to politicians, and should be filled only with regard to public service."[40]

Woodrow Wilson (1913–1921), another strong advocate of neutral competence, believed that bureaucrats could learn to execute policy both expertly and responsively.[41] He saw government jobs as either political or administrative in nature and felt that by knowing which was which, we could create a bureaucracy that elected officials could control. Most current observers are less sanguine about the possibility of completely separating politics from administration.[42]

The Pendleton Act authorized the president to extend merit system coverage to additional federal jobs by executive order. In 1884, the merit system covered about 10 percent of the jobs in the federal bureaucracy, and by the middle of the twentieth century the figure rose to 90 percent. This created a rather rigid system of job classifications, pay, and rank known as the *general schedule*. It limited the president's appointment powers and also made it difficult to remove people for cause.

Improving the Merit System

Reforming the system was a central issue in Jimmy Carter's 1976 run for the presidency. The Civil Service Reform Act of 1978 was an attempt to modernize the personnel system and make it more competitive with the private sector. It was also a response to complaints from interest groups such as Ralph Nader's Public Interest that the Civil Service Commission was concentrating on management at the expense of merit hiring, equal opportunity, and regulation.

The act got rid of the Civil Service Commission and divided its functions among several agencies. The Office of Personnel Management (OPM) today is responsible for managing a merit system for all federal employees nationwide and for working with the president to ensure that appointments to positions in exempt categories also adhere to basic standards of merit and political neutrality. Grievances and discrimination complaints are now handled by separate agencies—the Merit Systems Protection Board and the Equal Employment Opportunity Commission. The act also created a Whistleblowers Protection Agency (WBA) and an Office of Special Counsel to defend whistleblowers against retaliatory action by their agencies.

The act gave managers more opportunity to fire incompetent subordinates, and it established a more flexible classification of civil service positions. It also created the Senior Executive Service (SES) to fill the top management positions in the executive branch in the civil service. Those in the SES may be career civil servants or political appointees; they are not locked into a position but can move from agency to agency, carrying rank with them. They are also paid on the basis of performance and may receive bonuses. A number of other alternate personnel systems have been created, such as the State Department's Foreign Service and the personnel systems for the Pentagon and DHS.

At least one-quarter of all positions in the federal bureaucracy are now in categories exempt from the hiring and compensation rules that govern the general schedule of civil service appointments, although all are supposed to be governed by the basic rules of merit and neutral competence. In fact, there are many more political appointments in the upper levels of bureaucracy today than there were thirty years ago.

ethical dilemmas | Neutral Competence in Intelligence Gathering

The day after the 9/11 attacks, President Bush made clear to the head of his counterterrorism unit and to others in his administration his interest in establishing a connection between Iraq and al-Qaeda.[1] The evidence of a connection was weak, but Bush thought an invasion of Iraq could be justified on the grounds that Saddam Hussein's arsenal of weapons of mass destruction presented an imminent threat.

He asked CIA Director George Tenet whether the evidence was strong enough to make his case to Congress and the public. Tenet had been a Clinton appointee whom Bush had retained but his reappointment was dependent on Bush's judgment of his work. Because Bush's policy preferences on Iraq were well known inside and outside the administration, Tenet had to decide whether to tell the president, a man he genuinely liked and had a good working relationship with, what he wanted to hear or to exercise neutral competence and give him the much less simple view of intelligence experts working on Iraq. He may also have been weighing how not telling the president what he wanted to hear would affect his reappointment.

When Bush asked the CIA head directly if he would be able to make a convincing case to the public, Tenet told him it was a "slam dunk."[2] After postwar investigators failed to find evidence that Iraq possessed stockpiles of weapons of mass destruction or even active programs to develop them,[3] some intelligence experts revealed that the findings in the reports they wrote for the CIA did not match what the director had told the president.

To many it appeared that Tenet had violated his neutral competence mandate and simply told the president what he wanted to hear. Having lost credibility in Congress and with the public, Tenet was forced to resign in 2004. A number of the agency's highest-level, longest-serving agents resigned or were forced out when Bush appointed a member of the House Intelligence Committee to replace Tenet. Some became sources (leaks) for new books on the politicization of intelligence gathering and analysis.[4]

[1] This was revealed by the head of the Clinton and Bush counterterrorism unit, Richard A. Clarke, who spoke with Bush on September 12, 2001, in the war room and recounted the event in *Against All Enemies* (New York: Free Press, 2004) and in public testimony before the televised 9/11 Commission hearings in 2004.
[2] Public testimony before the televised 9/11 Commission hearings, 2004.
[3] Report issued by the chief U.S. arms inspector, Charles A. Duelfer, October 2004.
[4] See, for example, James Risen, *State of War: The Secret History of the CIA and the Bush Administration* (New York: The Free Press, 2006); and Ron Suskind, *The One Percent Doctrine* (New York: Simon and Schuster, 2006). George Tenet himself was a major source for Suskind's book and later wrote his side of the story in *At the Center of the Storm* (New York: HarperCollins, 2007).

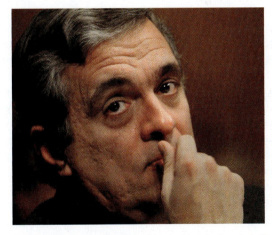

CIA Director George Tenet had to decide whether to tell President Bush what the president wanted to hear about Iraq's WMDs or what the intelligence indicated about these weapons.

Even within the regular civil service, merit is not all that counts. The system favors veterans by adding a 5-point bonus to their test scores (disabled veterans get 10 points). And positioning counts as well: people already in the system are favored because they know about job openings first and may have skills identical to those in the job listing. As in the private sector, sometimes job descriptions are written to fit particular individuals.

Civil Service Employees and Political Activity

Banning patronage from federal hiring did not end partisan political activity by federal employees, so Congress passed another law expressly defining the limits on such activities.

The **Hatch Act** of 1939 prohibited federal employees from active participation in partisan campaigns, even at the state and local levels. Political activities were restricted to voting, attending rallies, and having private conversations. Under the 1939 act, federal employees were not allowed to participate in party-sponsored voter registration drives, endorse party candidates, or work for or against them in any way. These prohibitions also applied to employees of state and local government who were supported by federal funds.

The Hatch Act was controversial from the beginning. Supporters argued that it protected the neutral competence of civil servants from partisan influences. Critics said it made civil servants second-class citizens by denying them the First Amendment guarantees of freedom of speech and association. In 1993, Congress changed the law to allow most federal employees to hold office within a political party, to participate in political campaigns, and to raise funds for political action committees when they are not on duty. However, all employees of law enforcement and national security agencies remain under the earlier, more stringent prohibitions.[43]

Politicizing the Merit System

No president has challenged the basic principles of merit hiring or neutral competence in theory or rhetoric, but some have challenged them in practice. White House and Justice Department staff in the George W. Bush administration were charged with multiple violations of both principles. Bush's chief aide, Karl Rove, organized White House liaisons to cabinet agencies into an "asset deployment team" that tried to coordinate the travel of cabinet secretaries and the awarding of grants and policy decisions by federal agencies with the needs of White House–backed candidates in the 2004 election campaign. During Bush's first seven years in office Rove held more then 100 political briefings for political appointees in executive branch agencies to offer advice on how the assets of the agency could be used to make Republican candidates more competitive in battleground states. Rove claimed such briefings were within the law because they were directed only at political appointees, not the permanent bureaucracy. But federal agency decisions on the use public money and other assets cannot be made on the basis of the political needs in election campaigns and the Office of Special Counsel found at least one of the briefings in violation of the Hatch Act.[44] Congressional oversight committees launched investigations into other actions of Rove's asset deployment teams.

Bush appointees were also found guilty of multiple violations of merit hiring standards. A 2005 directive from the White House to its executive branch liaisons recommended that Internet searches be conducted on applicants for federal jobs to look for evidence of their political views and activities and their attitudes toward the president. Novice Justice Department lawyer Monica M. Goodling took this to heart, searching the Internet for applicant views on "guns, god + gays" and asking interviewees, "Why are you a Republican."[45] The Department of Justice's inspector general found that the department had broken the law and violated departmental practices in using political criteria for the hiring of federal prosecutors, immigration judges, and other nonpolitical offices. Goodling admitted to a congressional committee she had "crossed the line."[46]

Science is another area where neutral competence often conflicts with political agendas. The thousands of government scientists, mathematicians, engineers, investigators, and data analyzers who provide the information that informs policy making and implementation were hired specifically for their professional expertise, and it is their mandate as civil servants to provide that information with neutral competence. It is up to elected officials whether they choose to act on the information provided.

All administrations vet scientific reports, and on many issues there is no clear consensus in the findings. There are many examples of this, such as whether it is the right or wrong time to raise taxes or cut taxes, to raise the prime interest rate or hold it steady, or whether there is enough evidence to approve or ban a new medical procedure. Even when there is consensus among experts, presidents are not obligated to act on it and they may even cherry-pick reports for the evidence that supports their own policy preferences. Government researchers whose findings are not followed may not be happy with the policy results, but if they are not pressured to change their data or their conclusions, their neutral competence has not been challenged.

For example, President Reagan did not try to alter scientific findings about HIV/AIDS, but he did refuse to act on them. However, **C. Everett Koop**, his surgeon general, undertook a mass education campaign on AIDS, against administration wishes but in accordance with his own understanding of his public responsibility. The mailing of information to every American household helped reduce panic and fear about the disease, change behavior, and undoubtedly contributed to saving many lives. And, even by going against the man who appointed him, Koop managed to keep his job.

The threat to neutral competence comes when a president, or his political appointees in federal agencies, suppress data or actually edit the content of research reports to fit policy. These attempts are most egregious when there is a consensus among experts. For example, George W. Bush did not deny that global warming was occurring, but he did not accept the international scientific consensus, nor the findings of government scientists, that human behavior was a major contributing factor. In 2002 and 2003, a White House lawyer who had worked for the oil industry's largest lobby, the American Petroleum Institute, and who had no science training, edited reports on global warming by government scientists to make their conclusions seem far less certain.[47]

The many examples of the Bush administration's attempts to edit scientific reports to distort their meaning (see the Government Responsiveness box, "Science and Politics in the Bush Administration") led to a charge by the Union of Concerned Scientists that the president ordered politically motivated changes in the evidence and conclusions of reports prepared by government scientists on mercury pollution, drug safety, and the effectiveness of sex education in disease prevention, in addition to climate change.[48]

government responsiveness

Science and Politics in the Bush Administration

In 2006, **Jim Hansen**, an expert on climate change and the long-time head of NASA's Goddard Institute for Space Studies, complained that the administration had ordered him to stop giving speeches on global warming and not to talk about how his findings differed from administration policy.[1] One of his reports had been edited to bring the conclusions nearer the president's position. The wording changes were made by a twenty-four-year-old political appointee at NASA, previously a public relations aide in Bush's presidential campaign, who had no scientific training and in fact no college degree.[2]

Hansen's case is but one of many attempts by the Bush administration to put policy preferences above neutral competence.[3] The former surgeon general, Richard Carmona, testified in 2007 that high officials in the Bush administration prohibited him for speaking about or reporting on a range of health issues, from stem cell research to contraception. Administration officials "delayed for years and tried to 'water down' a landmark report on secondhand smoke" that when eventually released documented the dangers of even brief exposure to cigarette smoke. He was also asked to mention the president three times on every page of his speeches.[4]

Bush appointees have also ordered changes in scientific papers that are unrelated to policy but illustrate micromanaging of scientific wording to conform to a political sensibility. A discussion of the Big Bang explanation of the origins of the universe, for example, was altered to magnify its uncertainty,

presumably to leave room for a biblical interpretation. In another paper a reference by NASA scientists to the death of the sun in the far distant future was expunged. A spokeswoman for the agency said, "NASA is not in the habit of frightening the public with doom and gloom scenarios."[5]

It is probably easier for political appointees to accept presidential policy directives than it is for career professionals. A NASA public affairs officer, for example—a political appointee—said his job was "to make the president look good." However, his counterpart at the Goddard Institute said it was not *her* job nor that of the Institute's. "I'm a career civil servant and Jim Hansen is a scientist."[6]

Falsifying or suppressing scientific research in the interest of political goals can work in the short run. In the long run, however, it undermines the public's faith in government and in science, too, and it can delay government action on issues crucial to public welfare and national security. As a retiring chair of the House Committee on Science remarked, "This is a town where everyone says

they are for science-based decision making—until the science leads to a politically inconvenient conclusion."[7]

[1] Andrew C. Revkin, "Climate Expert Says NASA Tried to Silence Him," *New York Times*, January 29, 2006, 1; Juliet Eilperin, "Censorship Is Alleged at NOAA: Scientists Afraid to Speak Out," *Washington Post*, February 11, 2006, A7. For an overview of findings on climate change, go to www.realclimate.org.
[2] Andrew Revkin, "Bush Aide Softened Greenhouse Gas Links to Global Warming," *New York Times*, June 8, 2005, 1.
[3] For reports on these issues, go to the website of the Union of Concerned Scientists (www.ucsusa.org) and that of the Federation of American Scientists (www.usfas.org)
[4] Gardiner Harris, "Surgeon General Sees Five Year Term as Compromised," *Washington Post*, July 11, 2006, www.nytimes.com/2007/07/11/washington/11surgeon.html?_r=1&oref=slogin.
[5] Dennis Overbye, "Someday the Sun Will Go Out and the World Will End (but Don't Tell Anyone)," *New York Times*, February 14, 2006, F3.
[6] Revkin, "Climate Expert Says NASA Tried to Silence Him."
[7] Claudia Dreifus, "A Conversation with Sherwood Boehlert: A Science Advocate and 'An Endangered Species,' He Bids Farewell," *New York Times*, May 9, 2006, pF2.

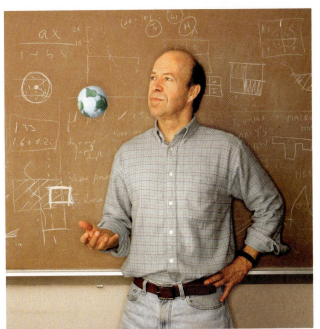

Jim Hansen, a government expert on climate change, was ordered by the Bush administration to stop giving speeches about global warming and explanations about how scientific findings differed from administration policy.

Ethics

The neutral competence standard prohibits bureaucrats from gaining materially from their decisions. Civil servants are supposed to make decisions based on their professional judgment and not to advance the cause of something in which they have a financial stake. For example, bureaucrats who are stockholders in chemical companies are not supposed to be making policy about chemical waste. Even if it were possible for policy makers to put self-interest aside, holding stakes in firms they regulate automatically takes on the appearance of a conflict of interest. This in turn would allow critics of a decision to challenge the regulation in court. Furthermore, the appearance of a conflict of interest undermines public confidence in government.

To better define what constitutes a conflict of interest, Congress passed the Ethics in Government Act in 1978. The act sought to prevent former public officials with inside information from using it and their contacts to give their new employers an unfair competitive advantage. The act barred former public servants from lobbying their agencies for one year and prohibited for life lobbying on matters in which they "personally and substantially" participated as public officials. In 1989, news that former Reagan administration officials had used their government service for substantial financial gain led to the passage of a law designed to strengthen the 1978 act. These new rules had little more impact than the old ones.

President Clinton issued an executive order requiring many of his political appointees to sign a pledge that they would not lobby the agencies in which they worked for five years after leaving government and would never lobby for foreign political parties and governments. But in 2002, four of Clinton's former cabinet members and other high-level political appointees, including his trade representative and the heads of the FCC and the SEC, each held multiple seats on corporate boards. It is not unthinkable that they were hired for their government contacts, although holding such positions in itself does not violate any ethics rule.

George W. Bush appointed more corporate executives to head government agencies than any other president. Some were responsible for regulating industries whose payrolls they had just left or in which they had held stock.

Sometimes the range within which bureaucrats can exercise neutral competence is severely restricted by their superiors. Agencies and department heads are political, not merit, appointees, and many are specifically charged with carrying out the programs of the president who appointed them. In addition, some of the policy that bureaucrats are implementing was made by presidential directive or executive order. EPA bureaucrats gearing up to implement Clinton's executive orders on clean water and clean air in December 2000 were required to write very different rules several months later when Bush rescinded Clinton's orders and substituted radically different policies. When an agency appears to be partisan in the way it implements, or fails to implement, congressional acts, it may be because of presidential directives or orders issued by the short-term political appointee temporarily heading the agency.

Overseeing the Bureaucracy

The principal overseers of the bureaucracy are, of course, the president, who heads it and appoints its top policy makers; the Senate, which holds confirmation powers; Congress as a whole, which has authority to create, monitor, and fund agencies; and the federal courts, which often have to interpret the meaning of regulations or rule on their constitutionality. Congress has also given the public a significant, if vastly underused, role through legislation that mandates openness in government.

President

The president, constitutionally the chief executive, has primary responsibility for directing executive branch agencies and monitoring their responsiveness. He has several significant means for providing executive leadership, including budgeting, appointment and removal powers, the authority to initiate executive branch reorganizations, and, of course, his power to issue executive orders.

Congress decidedly enhanced the president's administrative powers in 1921 by delegating authority to write the annual budget. In 1937, when Congress approved Franklin Roosevelt's executive branch reorganization, it moved the Bureau of the Budget (BOB) into the new Executive Office of the President (EOP) to help the president manage the bureaucracy. During Nixon's reorganization of the EOP, the newly created Office of Management and Budget (OMB) absorbed BOB and was given specific responsibility for overseeing executive agency performance. (It reports its findings to the public as well as the president by posting them on its website.) This constant monitoring of agencies from within the EOP gives the president more administrative control than does budget writing itself. Presidents can try to cut agency appropriations to limit agencies' range of actions or they can tie conditions to appropriations to make them take specific actions, but Congress does not have to approve White House requests. And because it has power to approve appropriations Congress has more opportunity than the president to attach strings to funding.

Reagan established the practice of using OMB to review all regulations proposed by executive branch agencies, giving the White House the opportunity to reject or modify them before the rules were issued. Both Reagan and Clinton used this process to reduce the number of new rules and the cost to businesses of enforcing them. The Bush administration continued the practice with a stronger ideological focus, trying to eliminate regulations opposed by industry. Many of the new rules rejected by Bush's OMB were based on findings of government scientists, leading to additional charges of politically charged decision making in what is supposed to be a neutrally competent bureaucracy.

A president's best chance to direct the work of an agency is to put a surrogate in charge of it, that is, to appoint someone who shares his views. It is easiest to do this with cabinet departments because it is accepted that a president is entitled to appoint politically like-minded people to his own cabinet. Thus, Reagan and both Bushes filled health care–related positions in the Department of Health and Human Services with people who were against keeping abortion legal, whereas Clinton filled them with people who were pro-choice. Appointments to independent and regulatory agencies receive more scrutiny because neutral competence plays a greater role, but presidents do get most of their choices confirmed. Republican presidents tend to appoint people who favor business and Democratic presidents appoint those who lean toward the interests of consumers and organized labor. Reagan chose heads for regulatory agencies such as OSHA, the Consumer Product Safety Commission, and the EPA who agreed with his goal of reducing government regulation, whereas Clinton named a lifelong environmental activist to head the EPA.

Of course, sometimes presidential appointees, despite their being screened for issue positions, may end up, especially if they stay in a position long enough, representing long-standing agency policies and norms rather than the president's interests. Most appointees have less expertise and experience in agency operations than career civil servants, and some come to rely on career officials for information about agency history, procedures, and policy questions. But much depends on the president's leadership, how high a priority change in the agency is for him, and how closely he monitors a particular agency's activities and directives.

Administrative reform is a third means a president can use to increase his control over the bureaucracy. Generally, the more sweeping a president's recommendation for change, the more he must anticipate congressional and interest group resistance. For example, Reagan wanted to abolish the Departments of Education and Energy and merge the Commerce and Labor Departments, but Congress would not support him. When George W. Bush reorganized twenty-two executive branch agencies with 220,000 employees to create the new cabinet-level Department of Homeland Security (DHS), he found Congress resistant to his request that it cede substantial budgetary and oversight powers over the agency to the White House. After the DHS's organizational problems led to its disastrous response to Hurricane Katrina, Congress reorganized the chain of command, giving FEMA primary responsibility for responding to such natural disasters. The secretary of DHS, presumably with the president's approval, immediately tried to override this congressional directive by re-claiming for his own office the responsibility Congress had just given FEMA.

The White House can also try to influence independent agencies and commissions by lobbying and mobilizing public opinion. Attempts by presidents of both parties to influence Federal Reserve Board decisions on interest rates, for example, are legion.

Despite these powers, there are many limits on the president's executive leadership. Given the size and complexity of the federal bureaucracy, the president cannot possibly influence every important decision. Moreover, as the civil service expanded, presidents found it increasingly difficult to lead an executive branch with 90 percent of its positions filled by merit system employees deliberately insulated from presidential control. The creation of the SES and alternative personnel systems allows for short-term and emergency appointments and easier movement within the bureaucracy. In addition, the 1978 law gave managers more opportunity to fire incompetent subordinates and it authorized bonuses and a new pay scale for managers to encourage better performance.

Despite the changes, presidents often still feel thwarted by the constraints on removing civil servants for poor performance or because they will not do a president's bidding. Although job security is not meant to shield public servants who do poor work, it does make firing incompetent workers difficult and time-consuming. The organization of public employees into unions contributes to this, although unions also protect workers from being dismissed without grounds. The government's rate of discharging people for inefficiency, 0.01 percent a year, did not increase after the 1978 reforms, though no doubt some employees left after being threatened with dismissal or demotion. As one public employee said, "We're all like headless nails down here—once you get us in you can't get us out."[49] This attitude captures what some say is the civil service's built-in bias toward job survival rather than innovation.[50]

Agencies that have strong allies in Congress, in powerful interest groups, or in the public provide another limit to presidential leadership. Presidents have more success controlling agencies that lack strong congressional allies and domestic clientele groups, such as the Treasury and State departments, than agencies that have such allies, such as the Social Security Administration and the Agriculture and Health and Human Services departments. However, the increasing number of political appointees in senior positions gives the president many more opportunities to exercise his influence over agency operations, even in agencies like the EPA, which has strong bipartisan support in Congress and powerful interest groups monitoring its work.

Not all presidents have the same interest in exercising executive leadership over the bureaucracy. Some are preoccupied with foreign policy, some not interested in administration, and most realize that a president' ability to manipulate bureaucratic decision making will run up against the constraints of civil service law. Although all want to appoint people to policy-making positions who are committed to a similar set of goals, the will to pressure these individuals after they have been appointed varies. As discussed in Chapter 11, **George W. Bush** arguably has interpreted the president's role as chief executive more absolutely than any of his predecessors. He maintained that a president's powers as chief executive as stated in Article II are exclusive and that as a **unitary executive** his orders to executive branch agencies trump any directions from Congress or the courts. (We have discussed some of these claims in the previous chapter.) Bush used the interpretation that he had absolute control of the executive branch to try to staff even positions in the permanent bureaucracy, which are subject to the neutral competence standard of performance, using political criteria and to justify overriding congressional mandates to executive branch agencies as well.

Congress

Although the president has the edge in leadership through his appointment powers, Congress has greater scope for oversight and control. Much of the bureaucracy's power is delegated authority from Congress, and much of its work is implementing laws passed by Congress. Congress has the power to create, reorganize, or eliminate agencies and the ultimate instrument of control—the power of the purse strings. Congress not only has the power to increase or decrease the amount of money the president requests to fund an agency, it can tell an agency how it has to spend the money it allocates. Often, a congressional committee tells an agency that it must spend x number of dollars from its budget to pay for a project earmarked by one or more members of Congress, even when the project was not named in the budget and even when the president opposes the spending or the project itself.

Congress also has dozens of committees (supported by a staff of thousands) to which executive agencies must report. But just as an agency's outside allies can work to thwart presidential control, they can also limit congressional oversight. Agencies frequently work closely with certain congressional committees and interest groups for mutual support and outcomes favorable to all. (These relationships are sometimes called "iron triangles" or issue networks.) Agencies may adjust their actions to suit the preferences of the congressional committees that authorize their programs and appropriate their funds. For example, decisions by members of independent regulatory commissions are sensitive to the views of members of their congressional oversight committees. When the membership of the committees becomes more liberal or more conservative, so do the decisions regulators make.[51]

Iron triangles make oversight look less like monitoring the bureaucracy and more like collusion. Constituent service, by contrast, provides a motive for members of Congress to try to shape bureaucratic decision making. Members often try to influence agencies to take some action on behalf of constituents or in the interest of their districts. In fact, congressional staff who do casework often have their duties assigned according to the agencies they are responsible for contacting about constituent complaints. This can lead members to pressure bureaucrats to help satisfy constituent demands rather than using neutral competence as their standard of decision making. It is this kind of pressure that keeps military bases open years beyond their usefulness simply because they are good for the economy of a member's district.

Courts

Federal courts act as another check on the bureaucracy. Judicial decisions shape agency actions by directing agencies to follow legally correct procedures. Of course, the courts cannot intercede in an agency's decision making unless some aggrieved person or corporation files a suit against the agency. Nevertheless, in almost any controversial agency action, there will be aggrieved parties and possibly some with sufficient resources to bring a court action.

The courts interpret lawmakers' intentions by deciding what congressional majorities and the president had in mind when they made a law. This can be difficult. Sometimes, in their haste, lawmakers fail to specify crucial elements of a law, or they may be unable to reach agreement on a provision and leave it ambiguous in order to get the bill passed. Lawmakers may also write a certain amount of vagueness into a law so that agencies will be able to adapt it to unknown future conditions. How the courts read a law may

Former Surgeons General C. Everett Koop (left), Richard Carmona, and David Sachter testified before a congressional committee that they all had felt political pressure. Carmona, who served in the George W. Bush administration, said he had experienced more pressure than the others, as he was instructed not to discuss the medical implications of global warming, second-hand smoke, stem cells, sex education, or emergency contraception.

© UPI Photo/Kevin Dietsch

augment or reduce the ability of Congress and the president to influence its implementation. In the current Supreme Court, the conservative majority has increasingly used its authority to interpret the intent of congressional acts in ways that expand the Court's own powers. We discuss these issues in Chapter 13.

Regulators and other agency policy makers appear to be quite sensitive to federal court decisions. For example, when the courts overturn the National Labor Relations Board's decisions in a prolabor direction, the board's decisions soon become more prolabor. Similarly, decisions drift the other way when courts overturn agency decisions in a probusiness direction.[52]

Interest Groups and Individuals

The public has numerous opportunities to oversee and to influence bureaucratic decision making. Most of these rights stem from laws designed to ensure openness in government.

Openness laws also extend to media access and thus provide another important check on bureaucratic abuses. But the media can also make the bureaucracy's work more difficult. Reporters like to cover conflict and bad news and are therefore usually on the lookout for stories about internal policy disputes. Newspapers and other media outlets make frequent use of FOIA to obtain documents from government agencies.

Businesses and interest groups also use FOIA to gain access to agency information or government data that help them develop strategies to better influence future agency decisions that will affect them. Businesses want information that will help them avoid new regulations. Interest groups want to make sure bureaucracies adopt rules and enforcement practices they favor. An environmental group cannot rest on its laurels just because Congress has passed a law placing new safeguards on toxic waste disposal. The group's job is not over until it makes sure the EPA writes strict rules to enforce the law. Consequently, the group must lobby the regulators as well as Congress.

Interest groups and their lobbyists are also part of the public. Lobbyists tend to take much greater advantage of their rights of access than the general public does, and they are the source of many of the public comments on proposed rules received by agencies. But it is not unusual for the EPA or other regulatory agencies to get thousands of responses when they post new rules on their websites for public comment.

If an agency seems to be sabotaging the intent of Congress, interest groups can work with friendly congressional committees to put pressure on the agency to mend its ways. And interest groups can also try to rally public opinion to their side to pressure Congress or the president to do something about the agency. Environmental groups are especially skilled at this. Sometimes interest groups pressure an agency so ef-

fectively that the agency is said to be "captured."[53] This term is used most frequently for regulatory agencies thought to be controlled by the groups they are supposed to be regulating.

We know that interest groups can influence the bureaucracy, but can individual citizens affect policy too? It is difficult for an individual to influence public agencies when acting alone, but that does not mean there are no opportunities to do so. Perhaps one person posting a comment on a website will not change agency policy, but if all residents opposed to a decision on cleaning up a hazardous waste site in their neighborhood file comments, it can make a difference. Rules have been reversed or amended.

An individual who uses FOIA to retrieve documents that expose agency corruption or abuse can also make a difference by going public with the story. And members of the general public are increasingly taking advantage of openness laws even though the process is not easy for those who try. A lot of paperwork is involved, some costs, and often a long wait, even though government agencies employ over 5000 administrators to process the requests.

Ordinary citizens could have a greater impact if they used all the tools that Congress has given them to oversee and to influence the bureaucracy. They can even be whistleblowers by suing companies with government contracts that defraud the government (and if successful, share in the money recovered).[54] But individual **whistleblower**s within the bureaucracy often have the best opportunity to monitor agency practices. Some whistleblowing is unsuccessful, but some makes a real difference. One of the most famous whistleblowers was Pentagon employee Daniel Ellsberg, who in 1968 leaked thousands of documents on the conduct of the Vietnam War to the *New York Times*. Henry Kissinger claimed that Ellsberg was the most dangerous man in the world, but Ellsberg's acts helped the public understand that the Johnson and Nixon administrations' private rationale for fighting the war was not the same as the reasons they stated in public.

Bunny Greenhouse, chief contracting officer in the United States Army Corps of Engineers, blew the whistle on a no-bid, five-year, $7-billion offer to Halliburton and its subsidiaries to get Iraqi oilfields running. (Halliburton was the company of which Vice President Cheney was CEO before becoming vice president). After being pressured by superiors to approve that and other contracts that would allow the company essentially to set costs and add a service fee, and without competitive bidding or appropriate controls, she signed the contracts because of the needs of those trying to get Iraq stabilized, but with a note saying she was doing it under pressure and in spite of irregularities. A FOIA request uncovered the documents and her comments. She later testified at a 2005 forum organized by the Democrats looking into charges of overbilling and fraud in Iraq War contracts (the Republican-dominated Congress refused to hold such hearings). She indicated that these agreements were "the worst activity in contracting that I'd ever seen in all my contracting career."[55] Three weeks later, Greenhouse was demoted to a lower civil service grade despite years of exemplary reviews. Although she asked for a full investigation, she is still waiting for her case to be resolved.

Bureaucrats who blow the whistle on mismanagement, sexual or political harassment, or other abuses of power in their agencies are supposed to be protected from arbitrary firing. But rarely does an agency publicly thank an employee for blowing the whistle, as FBI Director Robert Mueller did when Coleen Rowley went public with that agency's mishandling of a 9/11–related investigation. Rowley, a Minneapolis-based agent involved in the case of Zacarias Moussaoui, an Algerian later indicted and tried as the so-called twentieth hijacker, had complained to Director Mueller that a midlevel manager had thwarted her attempt to get a search warrant to go through Moussaoui's personal belongings and the contents of his computer.[56] Rowley testified before the Senate Judiciary Committee, but even if her complaints had not become public, they would have been hard for the agency to ignore given her record. Mueller went public to commend her for her actions, but his praise was not so much an indication of changing attitudes toward whistleblowers as a measure of the trouble the agency was in with Congress and also of the media attention to Rowley's case.

Disclosure of bureaucratic failures increased after 9/11 because many individuals saw that neglected shortcomings could have serious consequences. But retaliation continued. In recent years, airport baggage screeners, border patrol agents, and the chief of the United States Park Police were disciplined or fired for reporting problems in their agencies. The most publicized case was that of Medicare's chief actuary, who was threatened with dismissal by the political appointee who headed his agency if he provided Congress with accurate numbers on the cost of the Bush administration's proposed prescription drug benefit for seniors.

In 2004, Congress responded by writing a new law with stronger protections for whistleblowers, including freedom from reprisal for those, like the Medicare actuary, who provide information to Congress. But the bill was strongly opposed by the Bush administration, which contended that it "unconstitutionally interferes with the president's ability to control and manage the government."[57] Protections for whistleblowers hit a new low in 2008 when the Office of Special Counsel, which is charged with providing legal protection to whistleblowers, was raided by the FBI. The director of the office had been under investigation for three years for abuse of office, retaliating against whistleblowers in his own office, and destroying evidence on his office computer.[58]

Despite the legal protections, it is the rare person who will set aside cordial relations with colleagues and ambition for promotion in order to challenge the status quo. Most people, whether working in the private or the public sector, find it difficult to expose their employer's dirty laundry. And even if the law does protect their jobs, their careers may be effectively ruined. About half of all whistleblowers lose their jobs, half of those lose their homes, and half of those lose their families.[59]

Conclusion: Is the Bureaucracy Responsive?

In 2002, Congress oversaw the biggest reorganization of the federal bureaucracy in a half century when it created the DHS. The changes were prompted by failures in performance that helped make possible the terrorist attacks of September 11, 2001. Particular targets of the reform were intelligence and law enforcement agencies and customs and immigration services. The bureaucratic morass in the former Immigration and Naturalization Service was encapsulated in the title of the official put in charge of the reorganization: the "assistant deputy executive associate commissioner for immigration services."[60]

The failure of the reorganization either to streamline communications, as revealed in DHS's response to Hurricane Katrina, or consolidate preparedness for future terrorist attacks was more evidence of the limits of reform. In fact, many observers believe that the reorganization diminished rather than enhanced the functions of agencies (for example, FEMA and Immigration) that were incorporated into the DHS.

Is the federal bureaucracy an impenetrable forest or an uncontrollable fourth branch of government, as some portray it? The turf wars, miscommunication, and fragmented authority that surfaced after 9/11 certainly indicate that at least part of the federal bureaucracy is an impenetrable forest. It is not surprising that most of the agencies that failed so badly at that time (for example, the CIA and the FBI) were among the least open to citizens or the media and even to congressional oversight. Those agencies continued to oppose reform even as Congress was implementing the recommendations of the 9/11 Commission to reorganize our fifteen different intelligence agencies under a sixteenth—a single directorate to improve communication, gain more central control, and limit interagency rivalries. Seven years after 9/11 the problems of interagency information sharing had still not been resolved.

But the bureaucracy as a whole is not an errant fourth branch of government. With the exception of supersecret agencies like the National Security Agency (a.k.a. No Such Agency), for which Congress has forfeited much of its oversight responsibility in the interests of national security, most of the bureaucracy is subject to presidential and congressional control, providing they are willing to exercise their powers. Indeed, one of the by-products of the Bush administration's attempts to increase presidential control of executive branch agencies at the expense of Congress is that it has reawakened some members of Congress to their oversight lapses.

Nothing brought the lapses in oversight and regulation more sharply to public attention than the subprime mortgage crisis of 2008. Had regulatory agencies been doing their jobs and Congress monitoring them to see that they were doing their jobs, the risky and sometimes fraudulent lending practices that led to the crisis may have been terminated before they became pervasive. But the permanent bureaucracy cannot do its job or exercise neutral competence if their political minders will not let them do so. As investigations subsequent to 9/11 revealed, part of the reason for the failures of intelligence agencies was that their experts were overridden by their politically appointed superiors and not allowed to exercise neutral competence. As a consequence, a number of our most experienced intelligence professionals left the government.

Our fragmented political system means that our public agencies operate in an environment of uncertainty and competition. Bureaucrats have many bosses: a president, his appointees, Congress and its many committees and subcommittees, and the federal courts. In addition, numerous interest groups try to influence the work of federal agencies. The often contradictory demands for responsiveness and neutral competence contribute to an uncertainty of expectations. As a result, agencies try to protect themselves by cultivating the support of congressional committees and interest groups. Even presidents can have trouble influencing agencies because of these alliances.

There is a vaguely defined but frequently articulated public suspicion that any bureaucracy is destined to be intransigent and inefficient. We have tried to show that some of that attitude stems from lack of consensus on what the work of government should be. If you do not like the work that Congress and the president have assigned to the bureaucracy, there is not much chance you will view the bureaucracy as responsive to your needs. If the dissatisfaction is more over how the bureaucracy does its work, there is hope that at least some areas of performance will meet with your approval. The public does have tools to influence how bureaucrats do their work, but it has many more ways to lobby Congress and the president to change the work they give the bureaucracy to do.

Despite people's negative feelings about the bureaucracy, the mail is delivered, Social Security paid, and passports issued. The bureaucracy usually does what it is supposed to do. Some public agencies, such as Social Security and Medicare, operate far more efficiently than their private counterparts When government fails badly, such as before 9/11, or in the response to Hurricane Katrina, or in the refusal to regulate financial markets or to enforce the most basic standards for bidding, auditing, and accountability in the awarding of military contracts for work in Iraq, the human cost can be enormous. But these failures are not caused by the public's view of or trust in government. These failures are most likely to happen when those in charge of overseeing the bureaucracy have a negative view of government, the bureaucracy in particular, and refuse to let it function according to professional standards.

Today there is a more serious concern for and greater awareness of the costs of poorly functioning government agencies. The head of one government watchdog group summarized the feeling this way: "Before September 11 there was a bit of a blasé attitude of 'OK, the government screwed up again.' Now people see the consequences on their lives and see the necessity of government functioning well."[61]

Key Terms

Administrative Procedure Act (APA)
FOIA
Sunshine Act
independent agencies
policy implementation
delegated legislative authority
regulation
patronage
Civil Service Commission
merit system
neutral competence
Hatch Act
unitary executive
whistleblowers

Key Names

Theodore Roosevelt
Jimmy Carter
Ronald Reagan
Bill Clinton
Al Gore
Andrew Jackson
Franklin Roosevelt
Woodrow Wilson
C. Everett Koop
Jim Hansen
George W. Bush

Please visit our companion website at www.cengage.com/politicalscience/welch/uag12e or use CengageNOW for additional resources dealing with this chapter.

Lily Ledbetter lobbies Congress to overturn the Supreme Court ruling limiting pay discrimination lawsuits.

The Judiciary

13

Talking Points

When Did the Clock Start? After Lilly Ledbetter had worked at the Goodyear Tire and Rubber Company plant in Gadsden, Alabama, as a manager for nineteen years, she received an anonymous memo from a coworker, which indicated that she was being paid less than her male counterparts. In fact, she was being paid $6,700 to $18,000 less per year than the fifteen men who were performing the same job.

This disparity appeared to violate the Civil Rights Act of 1964, which prohibits discrimination on the basis of gender, as well as race,[1] so Ledbetter sued. She convinced a jury and the judge, who awarded her $300,000 in compensation, but Goodyear appealed the decision.[2]

The legal dispute revolved around the act's provision that an employee file a complaint within 180 days "after the alleged unlawful employment practice occurred." The question was, When did the 180-day clock start? Goodyear claimed that the clock started when the discrimination first occurred years ago. Under this interpretation, the clock ran out years before she filed her complaint. Therefore, the courts should not allow her to sue. Ledbetter claimed that the clock started—restarted—every time she received a lower paycheck reflecting the pay discrimination. Under this interpretation, she filed her complaint in time. Therefore, the courts should allow her to sue.

The Equal Employment Opportunity Commission (EEOC), which enforces the act, and most federal appellate courts had interpreted that provision as Ledbetter urged the courts to. Otherwise, the statute wouldn't help most victims of pay discrimination.

The justices had discretion. Given the wording of the statute, they could plausibly interpret the provision either way. In *Ledbetter* v. *Goodyear Tire and Rubber* in 2007, a narrow majority of the Supreme Court interpreted it in favor of Goodyear.[3] Thus they interpreted it to favor employers over employees, even those who could prove discrimination in court. The majority acknowledged that Ledbetter was a victim of sex discrimination, but their interpretation prevented her from bringing a suit and courts from hearing such suits or doing anything about such discrimination.

Justice **Ruth Bader Ginsburg**, the only woman on the Supreme Court, wrote a dissenting opinion. Always conscious of proper etiquette and reluctant to give offense, Ginsburg was so upset by the decision that she took an unusual action—she read her opinion aloud—to call attention to the majority's position. She emphasized the realities of the workplace for many women—pay disparities often occur in small increments; such disparities often aren't recognized for some time; and in fact the salaries or wages usually are kept hidden by employers or kept private by employees. A victim normally is unaware of any discrimination at first—indeed, for far longer than 180 days. Thus the Court's ruling will prevent most victims from using this act in the future.[4]

After the justices wiped out Ledbetter's $300,000 award, Goodyear sent her a $3,165 bill for its "court costs."[5]

The public expresses more support for the Supreme Court than for the president or Congress.[6] The public dislikes the disagreements and debates and the negotiations and compromises among governmental officials, and it deplores the efforts of interest groups to influence governmental policies. These messy features of democratic government, which are visible in the executive and legislative branches, aren't visible in the judicial branch. Many people conclude that they don't occur.

Indeed, many people assume that courts *are* nonpolitical and that judges *are* objective. These people say we *have* "a government of laws, not of men." Other people, who criticize their decisions, assume that courts *could be* nonpolitical and that judges *could be* objective. These people say we *could have* "a government of laws, not of men." But both views are myths. At any time in our history, "it is individuals who make, enforce, and interpret the law."[7] When judges interpret the law, they are political actors and courts are political institutions. And we'll see it's inevitable that judges interpret the law.

Thus public support for the Supreme Court and the lower courts rests partly on false assumptions about the absence of politics in this branch. There is a lot of politics, as will be seen in each of the topics covered in this chapter.

Courts

Due to federalism, the United States has a complete system of national courts side by side with complete systems of state courts, for a total of fifty-one separate systems.[8]

Structure of the Courts

The Constitution mentions only one court—a supreme court—although it allows Congress to set up additional lower courts ⭐ Art. III, Sec. 1, which it did in 1789 and again in 1891, completing the basic structure of the federal judiciary.

The **federal district courts** are trial courts. There are ninety-four, based on population, but with at least one in each state. They have multiple judges, although a single judge or a jury decides each case.

The **federal courts of appeals** are intermediate appellate courts. They hear cases that have been decided by the district courts and then appealed by the losers. There are twelve, based on regions of the country known as "circuits."[9] They have numerous judges, from six to twenty-eight, although a panel of three judges decides each case.[10]

The Supreme Court is the ultimate appellate court. It hears cases that have been decided by the courts of appeals, district courts, or state supreme courts. (Although it can hear some cases—those involving a state or a diplomat—that have not been heard by the lower courts first, in practice it hears nearly all of its cases on appeal.) The group of nine justices decides its cases.

The district courts conduct trials. The courts of appeals and Supreme Court don't; they don't have juries or witnesses to testify and present evidence—just lawyers for the opposing litigants. Rather than determine guilt or innocence, these courts evaluate arguments about legal questions arising in the cases.

The state judiciaries have a structure similar to the federal judiciary. In most states, though, there are two tiers of trial courts. Normally, the lower tier is for criminal cases involving minor crimes, and the upper tier is for criminal cases involving major crimes and for civil cases. In about three-fourths of the states, there are intermediate appellate courts, and in all of the states there is a supreme court (although in a few it is known by another name).

Since 1978, the federal system has also had an unusual secret court, which few Americans are aware of (see the box "Surveillance Court").

Jurisdiction of the Courts

Jurisdiction is the authority to hear and decide cases. The federal courts can exercise jurisdiction over cases in which the subject involves the U.S. Constitution, statutes, or treaties; maritime law; or cases in which the litigants include the U.S. government, more than one state government, one state government and a citizen of another state, citizens of more than one state,[11] or a foreign government or citizen ⭐ Art. I, Sec. 2. The state courts exercise jurisdiction over the remaining cases. These include most criminal cases because the states have authority over most criminal matters and pass most criminal laws. Consequently, the state courts hear far more cases than the federal courts.

Despite this dividing line, some cases begin in the state courts and end in the federal courts. These involve state law and federal law, frequently a state statute and a federal constitutional right—for example, a criminal law and a legal question about the search and seizure (Fourth Amendment) or interrogation (Fifth Amendment) conducted by the police. For these cases, there are two paths from the state judiciary to the federal judiciary. One is for the litigant who lost at the state supreme court to appeal to the U.S. Supreme Court.

The other path, available only in a criminal case, is for the defendant who has exhausted all possible appeals in the state courts to appeal to the local federal district court through a writ of **habeas corpus** ("Bring the body!" in Latin). This order demands that the state produce the defendant and justify his or her incarceration. If the district court decides that the state courts violated the defendant's constitutional rights, it will reverse the conviction. After the district court's decision, the losing side can try to appeal to the courts of appeals and the Supreme Court (see Figure 1).

BEHIND THE SCENES
SURVEILLANCE COURT

Behind closed doors in a windowless room in the Justice Department, a highly secretive court meets. The court hears requests from the FBI for electronic surveillance of possible spies and terrorists and sometimes for physical searches of their homes and computers.

The **Foreign Intelligence Surveillance Court** operates like no other court in the United States. It consists of eleven district court judges handpicked by the chief justice of the Supreme Court. The members sit in panels of three judges and serve for seven years. Lawyers for the government, acting on behalf of the FBI, seek approval for electronic surveillance, much as law enforcement officers seek search warrants for routine searches from regular courts. To protect the secrecy of the surveillance, lawyers for the defense—the targets of the surveillance—do not appear in court. In fact, they are not informed, and not aware, that a case involving the defendants is being heard at all.

Congress established the court in 1978 after abuses by the Nixon administration, which itself authorized the FBI to engage in wiretapping, bugging, and other forms of electronic surveillance. The administration spied on American citizens active in the antiwar and civil rights movements, claiming that these protesters were threats to "national security," and then tried to disrupt their organizations and harass their leaders. Yet Congress recognized that the government might need to use electronic surveillance when national security actually was at stake—from foreign agents or American citizens spying for foreign countries. Congress established the court to approve the surveillance when it was justified and to check the government when it was overzealous.

However, the court has been little more than a rubber stamp for the government. Through 2005, the court approved almost 19,000 requests and denied just 4.[1] In 2007, it approved 2,370 and denied 3.[2] Because of the need for strict secrecy, the court's decisions are shielded from virtually all scrutiny.

If the government loses, it can appeal the court's decision to the Foreign Intelligence Surveillance Court of Review, which consists of three appellate court judges, also handpicked by the chief justice. (And if the government loses here, it can appeal to the Supreme Court.) But the Court of Review has heard just one pair of cases during its existence, and it thwarted a rare attempt by the Surveillance Court to check the government.

The Surveillance Court had turned down the government's request in one pair of cases when the judges realized that the FBI had been misleading the court. When the FBI had lacked sufficient evidence to obtain approval for surveillance in ordinary criminal cases—not spying or terrorism cases—from regular courts, it had tried to circumvent the law by going to the Surveillance Court, which requires less evidence to grant surveillance because of the seriousness of spying and terrorism.[3] The furious judges admonished the FBI to discontinue this practice. But the Bush administration appealed, and the Court of Review overturned the decision, concluding that the USA PATRIOT Act had broadened the law to allow the FBI to continue this practice after all. Thus it appears that the secret Surveillance Court will be hearing many requests for surveillance, whether for spying and terrorism cases or for ordinary criminal cases, in the future as a result of 9/11.

[1] "Foreign Intelligence Surveillance Act Orders, 1979–2005," Electronic Privacy Information Center, May 2, 2006, www.epic.org/privacy/wiretap/stats/fisa_stats.html.
[2] "Numbers," *Time*, May 19, 2008, 16.
[3] John Podesta and Peter Swire, "Speaking Out about Wiretaps," *Washington Post National Weekly Edition*, September 9, 2002, 27; Seymour M. Hersh, "The Twentieth Man," *New Yorker*, September 30, 2002, 56–76.

DEMOCRACY?

Consider the implications of *habeas corpus* for our democracy. It gives criminal defendants several opportunities (by the district court, the court of appeals, and the Supreme Court) to get the constitutional rights they are supposed to get. Thus *habeas corpus* helps protect minority rights, which is one aspect of democratic government. (Although we often think of racial minorities when we speak of minority rights, criminal defendants also are a minority who have their rights.) Toward this end, *habeas corpus* enables the federal courts to oversee the state courts, forcing state judges to provide these rights.

Judges

Selection of Judges

Benjamin Franklin proposed that judges be selected by lawyers because lawyers would pick "the ablest of the profession in order to get rid of him, and share his practice among themselves."[12] The Founders rejected this unique idea, instead deciding that the president and the Senate should share the appointment power. The Constitution stipulates that the president shall nominate judges and the Senate shall provide "advice and consent"—that is, recom-

Figure 1 | **Federal and State Court Systems**

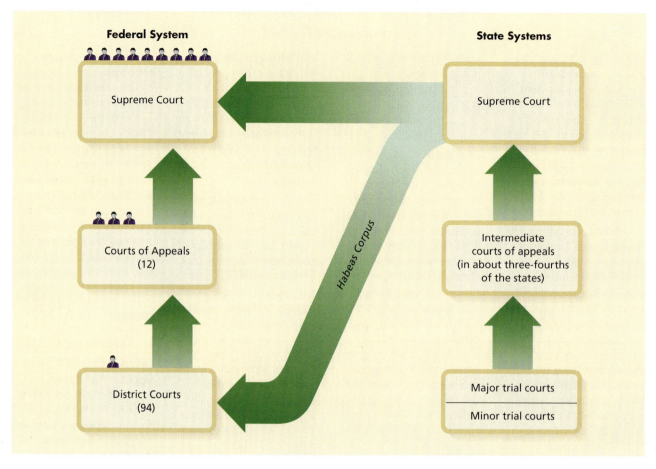

The arrows indicate the primary avenues of appeal, and the heads indicate the usual number of judges who hear cases in the federal system.

mend judges and then confirm or reject them ⭐ Art. II, Sec. 2.[13] There are no other requirements in the Constitution, although there is an unwritten requirement that judges be trained as lawyers.

DEMOCRACY?

Does the appointment of federal judges contradict the essence of democracy by denying our citizens the opportunity to choose their judges through elections?

The Founders expected these appointments to be based on merit rather than on politics. However, as soon as political parties developed, presidents and senators used politics as well as merit in making the appointments.

Mechanics of Selection

For the lower courts, lawyers who want to become judges get politically active in their party and make financial contributions to it. When vacancies arise, they lobby political officials, bar association leaders, or interest group leaders in

the hope that these elites will recommend them to the administration.

They especially focus on their senators, who play a role through the practice of **senatorial courtesy**. This tradition allows senators in the president's party to recommend, or veto, candidates for judgeships in their state. This practice applies not only to district courts, which lie within individual states, but also to courts of appeals, which span several states. For courts of appeals, senators informally divide the seats among the states within the circuit. (This practice doesn't apply to the Supreme Court because it has too few seats to divide among the states.)

Senatorial courtesy can limit the president's choices. During President Kennedy's term, the practice was ironclad. In deference to southern senators, the president, who advocated civil rights, was forced to appoint southern judges who favored segregation. One of them characterized the Supreme Court's desegregation ruling as "one of the truly regrettable decisions of all time," and another even called black litigants "niggers" and "chimpanzees" from the bench.[14] However, senatorial courtesy is not as ironclad now as it was then. Since the 1970s, most administrations have sought certain candidates for their ideology or diversity, so they have pressured senators to cooperate. Consequently, there is more give-and-take between the senators and the president than there used to be. Nevertheless, in 1999 Senator Orin Hatch (R-Utah), chair of the Judiciary Committee, blocked all of President Clinton's nominees for six months until the president agreed to nominate one of Hatch's allies for a judgeship in Utah.

For the Supreme Court, lawyers who want to become justices also try to become prominent in the legal profession. They write articles or give speeches designed to attract officials' attention. When vacancies arise, political officials, bar association leaders, and interest group leaders urge consideration of certain candidates. The administration also conducts a search for acceptable candidates. Sometimes even sitting justices make a recommendation. Chief Justice Warren Burger, who discouraged President Nixon from choosing a woman, claiming that not one was qualified, recommended Harry Blackmun, a childhood pal and the best man at his wedding. Justice William Rehnquist recommended Sandra Day O'Connor, a law school classmate whom he had dated occasionally.

Once the president has chosen a candidate, he submits the nomination to the Senate, where it goes to the Judiciary Committee for hearings. Senators question the nominee about his or her judicial philosophy, and interest groups voice their concerns. If a majority of the committee consents, the nomination goes to the whole Senate. If a majority of the Senate consents, the nomination is confirmed.

The Judiciary Committee is the battleground for controversial nominations. The committee is controlled by the party that has a majority in the Senate, so the committee reflects the views of that party. If the committee confirms the nominee, usually the whole Senate will confirm the nominee. If the committee rejects the nominee, usually the president will have to submit another one.

The mechanics of selection for all federal courts are similar, but the process of selection for the Supreme Court is more politicized at every stage because the Court is more powerful and visible, so its seats are fought over more intensely.

Criteria Used by Presidents

Although presidents want judges who demonstrate merit, they choose judges who meet various political criteria. Presidents normally nominate members of their party. In fact, they normally nominate active members who have served in public office or contributed to party candidates. In the twentieth century, presidents selected members of their party from 82 percent of the time (William Howard Taft) to 99 percent of the time (Woodrow Wilson).[15] This practice has become so established that senators of the opposition party usually confirm the nominees of the president's party.

Some presidents want judges who hold certain ideological views. President Theodore Roosevelt sought judges who opposed business monopolies and supported labor unions, and President Franklin Roosevelt sought judges who favored his New Deal policies. President Nixon sought conservatives who would reverse the direction of the Supreme Court and prompt southern whites to join the Republican Party.[16]

The Reagan administration was the first to establish systematic procedures for choosing lower court judges as well as Supreme Court justices according to ideology. The George H. W. Bush administration did the same. These two administrations sought conservatives who would roll back the rulings of previous courts. They had candidates fill out lengthy questionnaires and then submit to daylong interviews probing their positions. They expected candidates, for example, to oppose the right to abortion, the Supreme Court's ruling establishing the right, and the Supreme Court's reasoning in the case.[17]

The George W. Bush administration followed a similar process. The unusual feature, however, was the role of Vice President Dick Cheney, who took the lead within the administration. He sought conservative judges, especially those who had a broad interpretation of presidential power and a narrow interpretation of congressional authority, so they would uphold the administration's sweeping claims of presidential power in the war on terror. After rigorous screening and interviewing of the candidates, Cheney submitted a list of five names for Bush to choose from. In this way, Cheney steered Bush toward his conservative nominees for the Supreme Court—John Roberts and Samuel Alito.[18]

These three Republican administrations—Reagan's, George H. W. Bush's, and George W. Bush's—made the most concerted efforts to select judges according to ideology.

Some presidents want judges who provide more diversity on the courts. In the past, presidents chose westerners to balance the easterners who dominated the bench and Catholics and Jews to balance the Protestants who dominated the bench. In 1967, President Johnson chose the first black justice, **Thurgood Marshall**; in 1981, President Reagan chose the first woman justice, **Sandra Day O'Connor**. Presidents bowed to the pressure from various groups to solidify their support from these groups. Reagan, who wasn't an advocate of women's rights, pledged to appoint a woman to the Court to shore up his support among female voters. (After fulfilling this pledge, he felt no need to appoint many women to the lower courts.)

Now Hispanics want a seat on the Supreme Court. Both parties, who see support from this growing group as crucial to future electoral success, would welcome the opportunity to appoint the first Hispanic justice.

Presidents Carter and Clinton appointed numerous women and minorities to the lower courts. Before Carter took office, only eight women had ever served on the federal bench.[19] Sixteen percent of Carter's appointees were women,

BEHIND THE SCENES
THE STRATEGY FOR CONFIRMATION HEARINGS

During the confirmation process for Supreme Court justices, the **Senate Judiciary Committee** holds hearings in which the senators question the nominee about his or her views. Nominees aren't asked how they would decide any pending cases, but they are asked how they view current legal issues.

When President Reagan nominated **Robert Bork** to the Supreme Court in 1987, the hearings were especially contentious. Bork had been a law school professor and a federal court judge. In articles and speeches, he had rejected a right to privacy, which is the basis of judicial decisions allowing birth control and abortion, and he had criticized Court rulings and congressional laws advancing racial equality and

sexual equality. Although Bork had legal reasons for these positions—he had not advocated that whites *should* discriminate against blacks, for example, only that they shouldn't be forbidden from doing so by the Court or Congress—he seemed oblivious to the practical consequences of his positions. The confirmation hearings revolved around these positions, with the senators challenging his conclusions.

Bork's positions struck many Americans as extreme. A political cartoonist captured the feeling with a cartoon, which appeared when daylight saving time ended in the fall, and which depicted Bork admonishing people, "Now, this fall remember to turn your clocks back thirty years."

A coalition of interest groups mounted the first grassroots campaign against a judicial nomination. The Senate denied his confirmation.

When President George H. W. Bush had his first vacancy, he chose a man who had left no trail of controversial writings and speeches. David Souter, though formerly the New Hampshire attorney general and then a state supreme court justice, was called the "stealth candidate" (after the bomber designed to elude radar). A private person who lived alone in a house at the end of a dirt road, Souter had expressed few positions and made few decisions reflecting his views on constitutional doctrine. In the hearings, he refused to reveal his views. Nevertheless, senators confirmed him.

"No footprints, no fight," an administration official observed.

The success of the Souter nomination, in contrast with the failure of the Bork nomination, persuaded administration officials to counsel their nominees to reveal as little as possible about their views. Administration officials fashioned a two-pronged strategy for the hearings. First, they instructed nominees, talk as little as possible. Let the senators talk— pontificate—to their constituents in the process of questioning you. A consultant, hired to guide Republican nominees through the hearings, advised them that "your role in this process is that of a bridegroom at a wedding: stay out of the way, be on time, and keep your mouth shut." Therefore, "the most important rule is

---

and 21 percent were racial minorities.[20] Twenty-nine percent of Clinton's appointees were women, and 25 percent were racial minorities.[21] These two Democratic administrations, which were not as driven by ideology, made the most concerted efforts to select judges for diversity.

President George W. Bush also made an effort, greater than previous Republican administrations, to appoint women and minorities to the lower federal courts.[22] However, he passed over most female and all minority candidates for Supreme Court vacancies because those under consideration either were not conservative enough for the interest groups that wield power within the Republican Party or too conservative for more moderate senators and voters to accept.

Demands for diversity can reduce presidents' choices, but presidents can acquiesce to these demands and still find candidates with the desired party affiliation and ideological views. When Thurgood Marshall retired in 1991, President George H. W. Bush felt obligated to nominate another African American for this seat, but he wanted to nominate a conserva-

tive. He chose **Clarence Thomas**, a court of appeals judge. Whereas Marshall had been an ardent champion of civil rights, Thomas opposes affirmative action and other policies favored by many black leaders. Whereas Marshall had been one of the most liberal justices on the Warren Court, Thomas is the most conservative justice in many years, espousing a return to some positions abandoned by the Court in the 1930s.[23] Occasionally, groups have to satisfy themselves with the symbolic benefits from having "one of their own" on the Court. Thus many blacks get the psychological lift from having an African American on the bench but not the additional satisfaction from having one who reflects their policy views.

Criteria Used by Senators

Although the Senate played a vigorous role in the appointment process in the nineteenth century, rejecting twenty-two of eighty-one presidential nominations to the Supreme Court between 1789 and 1894, it routinely accepted the

the 80–20 rule, which is if the senators are talking 80 percent of the time and you're talking 20 percent of the time, you're winning, and if it's 60–40 you've got a problem, and if it's 50–50, you've lost and you might as well go home."[1] Second, they instructed nominees, when you must talk, be as general, as vague, as possible so you offer as small a target as possible.

When President George W. Bush nominated **John Roberts** to be chief justice, senators pressed the candidate for his views. Roberts deflected their questions, saying, "Judges are like umpires. Umpires don't make the rules; they apply them." He was confirmed (though on the bench he has been willing to make the rules as well as apply them).

When President George W. Bush had his second vacancy, he chose **Samuel Alito**, who had been a federal court judge for fifteen years and a Reagan administration lawyer before that. Alito was quite conservative. As a lawyer in the Reagan administration, he wrote that "the Constitution does not protect a right to an abortion."[2] He argued for more presidential power than courts allow and less congressional power than Congress exercises. He maintained, for example, that Congress didn't have the power to pass the Truth in Mileage Act, which forbids car dealers from misleading the buyers by turning back the odometers in used cars.

Because his views might have alienated many Americans, Alito was coached to downplay them. Administration officials held mock hearings, known as "murder boards," in which administration lawyers, acting as various senators, asked Alito the questions they expected the senators to ask. They devised answers, and Alito rehearsed them.

At the hearings, Alito talked no more than necessary, resisting all attempts to engage in a dialogue. "He was like a chauffeur who speaks only when spoken to, and doesn't presume to converse."[3] When asked about his past statements, he soft-pedaled them, saying that he was an advocate in the Reagan administration. As a justice, he insisted, he would have no political agenda. Like Roberts, he was confirmed easily (though, like Roberts, on the bench he has revealed a political agenda).[4]

After Alito's confirmation, the chair of the Judiciary Committee observed, "The hearings are really... a subtle minuet, with the nominee answering as many questions as he thinks necessary in order to be confirmed."[5]

A media consultant observed, judicial nominees today are "filtered through a machine that covers them in vanilla topping.... It's hard to organize against vanilla."[6]

[1]Tom Korologos, "Roberts Rx: Speak Up, but Shut Up," *New York Times,* September 4, 2005, WK122.
[2]"Judging Samuel Alito," *New York Times,* January 8, 2006, WK13.
[3]Janet Malcolm, "The Art of Testifying," *New Yorker,* March 13, 2006, 74.
[4]See, for example, Erwin Chemerinsky, "Conservative Justice," *Los Angeles Times,* June 29, 2007, www.latimes.com/news/opinion/la-oe-chemerinsky29jun29,0,504056,print.story?col.
[5]Arlen Specter (R-Pa.), quoted in Jeffrey Toobin, "Comment: Unanswered Questions," *New Yorker,* January 23 and 30, 2006, 30.
[6]David Axelrod, quoted in James A. Barnes, "Confirming Their Furstration," *National Journal,* January 21, 2006, 54.

president's nominations in the first half of the twentieth century, rejecting only one nomination until 1968.[24] Then it rejected two by President Johnson, two by President Nixon, and two by President Reagan.[25]

Of these six nominees, most were qualified in an objective sense.[26] Although some were accused of ethical lapses, most were rejected for ideological reasons.[27] Johnson's were deemed too liberal, while Nixon's and Reagan's were deemed too conservative.

Nominations to the Supreme Court have been contentious since the 1960s partly because of the Court's activism—both liberals and conservatives have seen what the Court can do—and partly because of the divisions that have characterized our government for most years since the late 1960s. Often Republicans dominated the presidency while Democrats dominated Congress (although in the 1990s, the situation was the reverse), so both have fought over the judiciary to tip the balance. Nominations have also become contentious because of the culture wars between reformers and traditionalists, of which the abortion debate is the most obvious manifestation, and the corresponding rise of interest groups on the left and the right that scrutinize the appointments, pressuring presidents and senators on their side to nominate and vote their way.

DEMOCRACY?

What are the implications for our democracy when judicial nominees refuse to reveal their views on legal controversies, yet senators confirm them anyway? Consider the implications for presidential power and congressional power, and the implications for the role of the people in this process. Are the American people entitled to know the nominees' views so the people can register their approval or disapproval before the Senate confirms the nominees for lifetime appointments? Or are the American people entitled to know the views only of the candidates for president and Congress?

Stephen Voss/WPN

The newest justices on the Supreme Court, Samuel Alito (left) and John Roberts, are appointees of President George W. Bush.

Even nominations to the lower courts, especially to the courts of appeals, which serve as "farm teams" for future justices, have become contentious in recent decades.[28] This reflects the polarization of American politics and the role of interest groups today. "You go out on the streets of Raleigh," Sen. Jesse Helms of North Carolina said, "and ask one hundred people: 'Do you give a damn who is on the Fourth Circuit Court of Appeals?' They'll say: 'What's that?'"[29] But political activists representing interest groups on the left and the right do know and do care, deeply, because they see the connection between the lower court judges and the interest groups' goals. In elections, these political activists mobilize their party's base of voters. Thus they have influence on their party, which needs their help. They can persuade, sometimes demand, that their party's senators fight a nomination by the other party's president.[30]

Results of Selection

Judges are drawn from large law firms or the federal government, and higher court judges are often drawn from the lower courts. These established legal circles are dominated by white men, so most judges have been white men. Although recent presidents have appointed more minorities and women, the bench's composition changes slowly because of judges' life tenure. (See the box "Do Women Judges Make a Difference? on page 384)

Despite the efforts to provide racial and sexual diversity, no effort has been made to reflect socioeconomic diversity. Throughout history, judges have come from a narrow, elite slice of society. Most have come from upper-middle-class or upper-class families with prestige and connections as well as expectations for achievement.[31]

No Supreme Court justice since Warren Burger in 1969 has attended a public university or graduate school. Every justice since then has had a degree from one of four prestigious, private schools—Chicago, Harvard, Stanford, or Yale.[32] Many justices—at least six on the current Court—have been millionaires.[33] Many lower court judges have been millionaires, too. Forty percent of Clinton's appointees were and 58 percent of Bush's appointees are.[34]

DEMOCRACY?

What implications might the class background, prestigious education, and wealth of most Supreme Court justices and many lower court judges have on court decisions? On judicial interpretations of the Constitution?

With the power to nominate judges, presidents have a tremendous opportunity to shape the courts and their decisions (see Figure 2).

Tenure of Judges

Once appointed, judges can serve for "good behavior" Art. III, Sec. 1., which means for life, unless they commit "high crimes and misdemeanors." These are not defined in the Constitution but are considered to be serious crimes or, possibly, political abuses. Congress can impeach and remove judges as it can presidents, but it has impeached only thirteen and removed only six. The standard of guilt—"high crimes and misdemeanors"—is vague, the punishment drastic, and the process time-consuming, so Congress has been reluctant to impeach judges.[35]

Qualifications of Judges

Given the use of political criteria in selecting judges, are judges well qualified?

Political scientists who study the judiciary consider federal judges generally well qualified. This is especially true of Supreme Court justices. Presidents realize that they will be held responsible for their appointees. Moreover, presidents have so few vacancies to fill that they can confine themselves to persons of their party and political views and even to persons of a particular region, religion, race, and sex and still locate good candidates. This is less true of lower court judges. Presidents and senators (through senatorial courtesy) jointly appoint them, so both can avoid taking responsibility for them. These judges are also less visible, so a lack of merit is not as noticeable.

Presidents do appoint some losers. President Truman put a longtime supporter on a court of appeals who was

John Roberts (left) is sworn in for his confirmation hearing with the Senate Judiciary Committee.

american diversity | Do Women Judges Make a Difference?

Some people believe that there should be more women judges because women are entitled to their "fair share" of all governmental offices, including judgeships. Others believe that there should be more so women will feel that the courts represent them too. Still others believe that there should be more because women hold different views than men and therefore would make different decisions.

A study of Justice Sandra Day O'Connor, the first woman on the Supreme Court, shows that although she generally voted as a conservative, she usually voted as a liberal in sex discrimination cases. Moreover, her presence on the Court apparently sensitized her male colleagues to gender issues. Most of them voted against sex discrimination more frequently after she joined the Court.[1]

Some studies find similar results for women justices on state supreme courts. Even women justices from opposite political parties support a broad array of women's rights in cases ranging from sex discrimination to child support and property settlement.[2]

But studies that compare voting patterns on issues less directly related to gender have less clear findings. Women judges appear more liberal than men in cases involving employment discrimination and racial discrimination. Perhaps the treatment they have experienced as women has made them more sympathetic to the discrimination others have faced. They're also more liberal than men in cases involving asylum for immigrants.[3] On the other hand, women judges don't appear more liberal or conservative than men in cases involving obscenity or criminal rights.[4]

Studies that compare the sentencing of criminal defendants in state courts find scant differences between men and women judges.[5] However, women judges do tend to sentence convicted defendants somewhat more harshly.[6]

"drunk half the time" and "no damn good." When asked why he appointed the man, Truman candidly replied, "I . . . felt I owed him a favor; that's why, and I thought as a judge he couldn't do too much harm, and he didn't."[36]

Sometimes presidents appoint qualified persons who later become incompetent. After serving for many years, they incur the illnesses and infirmities of old age, and perhaps one-tenth become unable to perform their job well.[37] Yet they hang on because they are allowed to serve for "good behavior," and they prevent other lawyers from filling their seats on the bench.

This problem has prompted proposals for a constitutional amendment setting a term limit of eighteen years[38] or a mandatory retirement age of seventy. Either of these changes would have a substantial impact because over one-third of all Supreme Court justices have served longer than twenty years and past seventy-five years old. But constitutional amendments are difficult to pass, and mandatory retirement ages are out of favor now. Furthermore, some of the best judges have done some of their finest work late in their career.

Independence of Judges

Given the use of political criteria in selecting judges, can judges be independent on the bench? Can they decide cases as they think the law requires? Or do they feel pressure to decide cases as presidents or senators want them to?

Because judges are not dependent on presidents for renomination or senators for reconfirmation, they can be independent to a great extent. When President Nixon claimed executive privilege to keep the Watergate tapes secret, three of his appointees joined the other justices in ruling against him.[39] When President Clinton asserted presidential immunity from Paula Jones's lawsuit charging sexual harassment, both of his appointees joined the Republican justices in deciding against him.[40]

After surveying the Warren and Burger Court decisions involving desegregation, obscenity, abortion, and criminal defendants' rights, one scholar observed, "Few American politicians even today would care to run on a platform of desegregation, pornography, abortion, and the 'coddling' of criminals."[41]

Presidents have scoffed at the notion that their appointees become their pawns. A study concluded that one-fourth of the justices deviated from their president's expectations.[42] Theodore Roosevelt placed Oliver Wendell Holmes on the Court, believing that Holmes shared his views on trusts. But Holmes voted against Roosevelt's position in an antitrust case, prompting Roosevelt to declare, "I could carve out of a banana a judge with more backbone than that!"[43] Holmes had ample backbone; he just didn't agree

Women judges in Harris County, Texas, which includes Houston, have applied the death penalty with "greater ferocity" than their male predecessors. This *county*, a majority of whose judges are female, has given the death penalty to more defendants than all other *states* but one.[7]

But the studies comparing men and women judges find more similarities than differences. This should not be surprising, because the two sexes were subject to the same training in law school and the same socialization in the legal profession, and they became judges in the same ways as others in their jurisdiction.

Perhaps the greatest difference women judges have made is to protect the credibility of women lawyers and witnesses. In court, some men judges and lawyers made disparaging remarks about women lawyers, suggesting that they should not be in the profession—for example, calling them "lawyerettes." Many male judges and lawyers made paternalistic or personal remarks to female lawyers and witnesses, referring to them by their first name or by such terms as "young lady," "sweetie," or "honey." Or the men, in the midst of the proceedings, commented about their perfume, clothing, or appearance. "How does an attorney establish her authority when the judge has just described her to the entire courtroom as 'a pretty little thing'?"[8] Even if the men considered their remarks harmless compliments rather than intentional tactics, their effect was to undermine the credibility of women lawyers and witnesses in the eyes of jurors. Women judges have squelched such remarks.

[1] Karen O'Connor and Jeffrey A. Segal, "Justice Sandra Day O'Connor and the Supreme Court's Reaction to Its First Female Member," in *Women, Politics, and the Constitution*, ed. Naomi B. Lynn (New York: Haworth Press, 1990), 95–104.
[2] David W. Allen and Diane E. Wall, "Role Orientations and Women State Supreme Court Justices," *Judicature* 77 (1993), 156–165.
[3] Julia Preston, "Big Disparities in Judging of Asylum Cases," *New York Times*, May 31, 2007.
[4] Sue Davis, Susan Haire, and Donald R. Songer, "Voting Behavior and Gender on the U.S. Courts of Appeals," *Judicature* 77 (1993), 129–133; Thomas G. Walker and Deborah J. Barrow, "The Diversification of the Federal Bench," *Journal of Politics* 47 (1985), 596–617.
[5] John Gruhl, Cassia Spohn, and Susan Welch, "Women as Policymakers: The Case of Trial Judges," *American Journal of Political Science* 25 (1981), 308–322.
[6] Darrell Steffensmeier and Chris Hebert, "Women and Men Policymakers: Does the Judge's Gender Affect the Sentencing of Criminal Defendants?" *Social Forces* 77 (1999), 1163–1196.
[7] Jeffrey Toobin, "Women in Black," *New Yorker*, October 30, 2000, 48.
[8] William Eich, "Gender Bias in the Courtroom: Some Participants Are More Equal than Others," *Judicature* 69 (1986), 339–343.

with Roosevelt's position in this case. Likewise, President Eisenhower placed Earl Warren on the Court, assuming that Warren was a moderate. But Warren turned out to be a liberal. Later Eisenhower said his appointment of Warren was "the biggest damn fool thing I ever did"[44] (although many legal scholars rank Warren as a great justice). President Truman concluded that "packing the Supreme Court simply can't be done. . . . I've tried it and it won't work. . . . Whenever you put a man on the Supreme Court he ceases to be your friend."[45]

Truman exaggerated, although some presidents have had trouble "packing" the courts. They have not been able to foresee the issues their appointees would face or the ways their appointees would change on the bench. (During Harry Blackmun's confirmation hearings, no senators asked about his views on abortion law, yet within six months *Roe* v. *Wade* would reach the Court, and Blackmun would author the controversial opinion.[46]) Nevertheless, presidents who have made a serious effort to find candidates with similar views usually have been able to.[47]

Access to the Courts

In our litigation-prone society, many individuals and groups want courts to resolve their disputes. Whether these individuals and groups get their "day in court" depends on their case, their wealth, and the court involved.

Courts hear two kinds of cases. **Criminal cases** are those in which governments prosecute persons for violating laws. **Civil cases** are those in which persons sue others for denying their rights and causing them harm. Criminal defendants, of course, must appear in court. Potential civil litigants, however, often cannot get access to court.

Wealth Discrimination in Access

Although the courts are supposed to be open to all, most individuals don't have enough money to hire an attorney and pay the costs necessary to pursue a case. Only corporations, wealthy individuals, or seriously injured victims suing corporations or wealthy individuals do. (Seriously injured victims with a strong case can obtain an attorney by agreeing to pay the attorney a sizable portion of what they win.) In addition, a small number of poor people supported by legal aid programs can pursue a case.

The primary expense is paying an attorney. New lawyers in law firms charge approximately $100 an hour; established partners may charge several times that.[48] Other expenses include various fees for filing the case, summoning the jurors, paying the witnesses, and also lost income from missed work due to numerous meetings with the attorney and hearings in court.

Even if individuals have enough money to initiate a suit, the disparity continues in court. Those with more money

Figure 2

Figure 2 | **Percentage of Liberal Decisions Handed Down by District Court Appointees of Presidents Woodrow Wilson through George W. Bush**

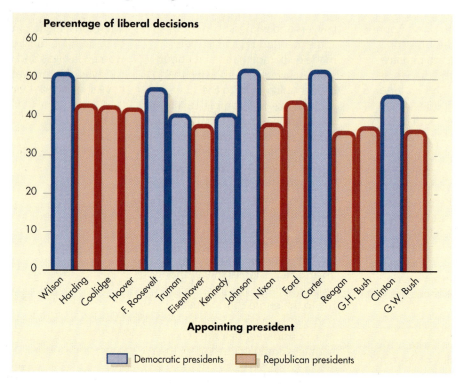

Appointees of Democratic and Republican presidents tend to decide cases somewhat differently.
SOURCE: Robert A. Carp, Ronald Stidham, and Kenneth L. Manning, Judicial Process in America, 6th ed. (Washington, D.C.: CQ Press, 2004), fig. 7-1.

can develop a full case, whereas others must proceed with a skeletal case that is far less likely to persuade judges or jurors. Our legal system, according to one judge, "is divided into two separate and unequal systems of justice: one for the rich, in which the courts take limitless time to examine, ponder, consider, and deliberate over hundreds of thousands of bits of evidence and days of testimony, and hear elaborate, endless appeals and write countless learned opinions" and one for the nonrich, in which the courts provide "turnstile justice."[49] (During the week that one judge spent conducting the preliminary hearing to determine whether there was sufficient evidence to require O. J. Simpson to stand trial for murdering his ex-wife and her friend, other judges in Los Angeles disposed of 474 preliminary hearings for less wealthy defendants.) Consequently, many individuals are discouraged from pursuing a case in the first place.

Interest Group Help in Access

Interest groups, with greater resources than most individuals, help some individuals gain access to the courts. The groups sponsor and finance the individuals' cases. Of course, the groups don't act out of altruism. They choose the cases that will advance their goals. An attorney for the **American Civil Liberties Union (ACLU)**, which takes criminal cases to

prod judges to protect constitutional rights, admitted that the defendants the ACLU represents "sometimes are pretty scurvy little creatures, but what they are doesn't matter a whole hell of a lot. It's the principle that we're going to be able to use these people for that's important."[50]

Some liberal groups—especially civil liberties organizations such as the ACLU, civil rights organizations such as the National Association for the Advancement of Colored People (NAACP), environmental groups such as the Sierra Club, and consumer and safety groups such as Ralph Nader's organizations—use litigation as a primary tactic. Other groups use it as an occasional tactic. In the 1980s and 1990s, some conservative groups began to use litigation as aggressively as these liberal groups. The Rutherford Institute arose to help persons who claimed that their religious rights were infringed, representing children who were forbidden from reading the Bible on the school bus or praying in the school cafeteria. The institute also funded Paula Jones's suit against President Clinton. Today, the Alliance Defense Fund, which sponsors eighty to one hundred cases at a time, prods the courts to reflect conservative Christian values in disputes involving education, homosexuality, and embryonic stem cell research.[51]

Interest groups have become ubiquitous in the judicial process. About half of all Supreme Court cases involve a liberal or conservative interest group[52] and many lower court cases do as well. Even so, interest groups can help only a handful of the individuals who lack the resources to finance their cases.

Proceeding through the Courts

Cases normally start in a district court. Individuals who lose have a right to have their case decided by one higher court to determine whether there was a miscarriage of justice. They normally appeal to a court of appeals. Individuals who lose at this level have no further right to have their case decided by another court, but they can appeal to the Supreme Court. However, the Court can exercise almost unlimited discretion in choosing cases to review. No matter how important or urgent an issue seems, the Court doesn't have to hear it.

When the husband of Terri Schiavo, who was brain dead but physically alive in a persistent vegetative state, sought to have her feeding tube removed, her parents, with the help of pro-life groups, sued to take custody from her husband, then to maintain the feeding tube, and, once taken out, to reinsert it. They appealed to the Supreme Court six times. Although congressional leaders, thundering about federal judges, made her situation a political cause, the Supreme Court refused to hear the case each time it was appealed. Sen. Tom Coburn (R-Okla.) responded, "I don't want to impeach judges; I want to impale them."[53] Still, the Court refused to hear the case.

Litigants who appeal to the Supreme Court normally file a petition for a **writ of *certiorari*** ("made more certain" in Latin). The Court grants the writ—agrees to hear the case—if four of the nine justices vote to do so. The rationale for this "rule of four" is that a substantial number, though not necessarily a majority, of the justices should deem the case important enough to review. Generally, the Court agrees to review a case when the justices think an issue hasn't been resolved satisfactorily or consistently by the lower courts.

From about ten thousand petitions each year, the Court selects about eighty to hear (only seventy in 2007–2008), thus exercising considerable discretion.[54] The oft-spoken threat "We're going to appeal all the way to the Supreme Court" is usually just bluster. Likewise, the notion that the Court is "the court of last resort" is misleading. Most cases never get beyond the district courts or courts of appeals.

That the Supreme Court grants so few writs means that the Court has tremendous power to determine which policies to review. It also means that the lower courts have considerable power because they serve as the court of last resort for most cases.

Deciding Cases

In deciding cases, judges need to interpret statutes and the Constitution and determine whether to follow precedents. In the process, they exercise discretion and make law.

Interpreting Statutes

In deciding cases, judges start with **statutes**—laws passed by legislatures. Often statutes are ambiguous. Then judges need to interpret them in order to apply them to their cases.

For example, Congress passed the **Americans with Disabilities Act** to protect people from discrimination in employment and public accommodations (businesses open to the public, such as stores, restaurants, hotels, and health care facilities). The act applies to people who have a "physical impairment" that "substantially limits" any of their "major life activities." The statute does not define these terms. Thus the courts have to do so, and in the process they determine the scope of the act.

When a dentist refused to fill a cavity for a woman with HIV, she sued, claiming discrimination under this act. The Supreme Court agreed by a 5–4 vote.[55] The majority concluded that HIV was a "physical impairment," although the woman was in the early stages and the disease didn't prevent her from performing any activity yet. The majority acknowledged that HIV would limit the "major life activity" of reproduction, because the disease could infect her fetus if she got pregnant. (Of course, HIV would also affect other important life activities as well.) The dissenters interpreted the statute to mean repetitive activities that are essential for daily existence rather than important activities that rarely occur in a person's life. Therefore, they denied that reproduction is a "major life activity."

Ruth Bader Ginsburg, appointed by President Clinton, was the second female justice and is the only one now. Although she tied for first place in her graduating class from Columbia Law School in 1959, she was turned down for a clerkship by Justice Felix Frankfurter and for law jobs with New York City firms. As a Jew, a woman, and a mother with young children, she had three liabilities at that time. Instead, she taught law and served as an attorney with the ACLU. In the 1970s, she argued six sex discrimination cases before the Supreme Court, winning five.

When a woman developed carpal tunnel syndrome on the assembly line at a manufacturing plant, she sued, claiming that the company didn't make the reasonable accommodation—give her a different job that didn't require repetitive manual labor—that was required under the act. She said her condition limited her "major life activities" of performing manual tasks at work and at home, including lifting, sweeping, and gardening; playing with her children; and driving long distances. The Court ruled that these aren't "major life activities,"[56] because they aren't of central importance to daily life, as seeing, hearing, and walking are.

Thus the Court had discretion. It interpreted the act broadly when it covered persons with HIV but narrowly when it refused to cover workers with less serious ailments.

Interpreting the Constitution

After interpreting statutes, judges determine whether the statutes are constitutional. Or if the cases involve actions of government officials rather than statutes, judges determine whether the actions are constitutional. For either, they need to interpret the Constitution.

Compared to constitutions of other countries, our Constitution is short and therefore ambiguous. It speaks in broad principles rather than in narrow details. The Fifth Amendment states that persons shall not be "deprived of life, liberty, or property without due process of law." The Fourteenth Amendment states that persons shall not be denied "the equal protection of the laws." What is "due pro-

cess of law"? "Equal protection of the laws"? Generally, the former means that people should be treated fairly and the latter means that they should be treated equally. But what is fairly? Equally? These are broad principles that need to be interpreted in specific cases.

Sometimes the Constitution uses relative terms. The Fourth Amendment provides that persons shall be "secure . . . against unreasonable searches and seizures." What are "unreasonable" searches and seizures? Other times, the Constitution uses absolute terms, which appear more clear-cut but aren't. ⭐ The First Amendment provides that there shall be "no law . . . abridging the freedom of speech." Does "no law" mean literally no law? Then what about a law that punishes someone for falsely shouting "Fire!" in a crowded theater and causing a stampede that injures some patrons? Whether relative or absolute, the language needs to be interpreted in specific cases.

Occasionally, politicians, following the lead of Richard Nixon, assert that judges ought to be "strict constructionists," that they ought to interpret the Constitution "strictly." This is nonsense. Judges can't interpret ambiguous language strictly. When politicians or commentators use this phrase, they're trying to persuade voters that judges from the other party are deciding cases incorrectly, as though they are departing from some clear and fixed standard.

When judges interpret the Constitution, they exercise discretion. As former Chief Justice Charles Evans Hughes candidly acknowledged, "We are under a constitution, but the Constitution is what the Supreme Court says it is."[57]

Restraint and Activism

All judges exercise discretion, but not all engage in policy making to the same extent. Some, classified as restrained, are less willing to declare laws or actions of government officials unconstitutional, whereas others, classified as activist, are more willing to do so.

Restrained judges believe that the judiciary is the least democratic branch because federal judges are appointed for life rather than elected and reelected. Consequently, they should defer to the other branches, whose officials are elected. That is, they should accept the laws or actions of the other branches rather than substitute their own views. They should be wary of "government by judiciary." They should recognize, Justice Harlan Stone said, that "courts are not the only agency of government that must be presumed to have the capacity to govern. For the removal of unwise laws from the statute books, appeal lies not to the courts, but to the ballot and the processes of democratic government."[58]

Restrained judges also maintain that the power to declare laws unconstitutional is more effective if it is used sparingly. Justice Louis Brandeis concluded that "the most important thing we do is not doing."[59] That is, the most important thing judges do is declare laws constitutional and

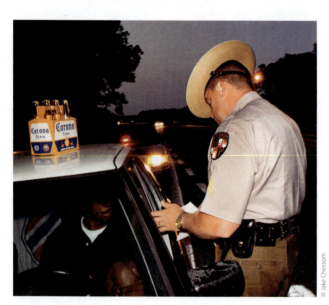

The Fourth Amendment prohibits "unreasonable" searches and seizures, but the courts have to define which ones are reasonable and which ones are unreasonable. The Supreme Court has established guidelines for stops and searches of automobiles, such as this one in Maryland.

© Jake Chessom

BEHIND THE SCENES
DO PERSONAL PREFERENCES MATTER?

The Supreme Court ruled that Michigan and New York can't prohibit out-of-state wineries from shipping wine to customers in their states while allowing in-state wineries to ship wine to residents in their states.[1] That is, the states can't discriminate against out-of-state wineries, which some states did to boost the business of their in-state wineries. The ruling means that wine connoisseurs can order fine wine from wineries throughout the United States.

The question was whether the commerce clause (Art. I, Sec. 8), which prohibits states from interfering with interstate commerce, or the Twenty-first Amendment, which repealed Prohibition and which allows states to regulate liquor, should prevail. A plausible argument could be made either way.

The majority emphasized the commerce clause rather than the Twenty-first Amendment. One insider observed that the five justices in the majority (Breyer, Ginsburg, Kennedy, Scalia, and Souter) happened to be the wine aficionados on the Court. Justice Breyer called the majority "the rosy-cheeked caucus."[2]

[1] *Granholm v. Heald*, 161 L.Ed.2d 796 (2005).
[2] Jeffrey Toobin, *The Nine: Inside the Secret World of the Supreme Court* (New York: Doubleday, 2007), 306.

thereby build up political capital for the occasional times that they declare laws unconstitutional.

Ultimately, restrained judges contend that showing appropriate deference and following proper procedures are more important than reaching desired results. When a friend taking leave of Justice Oliver Wendell Holmes one morning said, "Well, Mr. Justice, I hope you do justice today," Holmes replied, "My job is not to do justice but to follow the law."

Justice Harry Blackmun reflected this view in a capital punishment case:

> I yield to no one in the depth of my distaste, antipathy, and, indeed, abhorrence for the death penalty, with all its aspects of physical distress and fear and of moral judgment exercised by finite minds. That distaste is buttressed by a belief that capital punishment serves no useful purpose that can be demonstrated. For me, it violates childhood's training and life's experiences, and is not compatible with the philosophical convictions I have been able to develop. It is antagonistic to any sense of "reverence for life." Were I a legislator, I would vote against the death penalty.

But as a judge, he voted for it in 1972.[60]

Activist judges are less concerned with showing appropriate deference and following proper procedures. Some are more concerned with the results; others are more outraged at injustice. Chief Justice Earl Warren said that the courts' responsibility was "to see if justice truly has been done." He asked lawyers who emphasized technical procedures during oral arguments, "Yes, yes, yes, but is it right? Is it good?"[61]

Activist judges don't believe that the judiciary is the least democratic branch. Warren, who had served as governor of California, saw that the legislators, though elected, were often the captives of special interests. As a result of these attitudes, activist judges have a flexible view of separation of powers. District court judge Frank Johnson, who issued sweeping orders for Alabama's prisons and mental hospitals, replied to critics, "I didn't ask for any of these cases. In an ideal society, all of these . . . decisions should be made by those to whom we have entrusted these responsibilities. But when governmental institutions fail to make these . . . decisions in a manner which comports with the Constitution, the federal courts have a duty to remedy the violation."[62]

Activist judges don't believe that the power to declare laws unconstitutional is more effective if it is used sparingly. Rather, they claim that the power is enhanced if it is used frequently—essentially, they urge their colleagues to "use it or lose it"—because the public gets accustomed to it.

Thus judicial restraint and judicial activism are belief systems and role concepts that people think judges should follow when they decide cases. Some judges tend to be restrained, whereas others tend to be activist; most fall somewhere in between.

Both conservatives and liberals have practiced both restraint and activism depending on the political climate at the time. In the late nineteenth and early twentieth centuries, the Court was conservative and activist, striking down regulations on business. After its switch in the 1930s, the Court was liberal and restrained, upholding regulations on business. Then in the 1950s and 1960s, the Court was liberal and activist, striking down restrictions on individual rights. (See the box "Who Are the Activists?")

Although restraint and activism are useful concepts, we shouldn't make too much of them. It's usually more important to know whether a judge is conservative or liberal than whether the judge purports to be restrained or activist. Political science research shows that justices' votes reflect their ideology: conservative justices vote for the conserva-

WHO ARE THE ACTIVISTS?

Ever since the 1950s and 1960s, when the Supreme Court under Chief Justice Earl Warren was a liberal court and an activist court, many people have assumed that liberals are activist judges and conservatives are restrained judges. This is not necessarily true. Liberals may be activist or restrained, just as conservatives may be restrained or activist.

A study of the last eleven terms, from 1994 through 2005, of the Supreme Court under Chief Justice William Rehnquist confirms this conclusion.[1]

The study shows that the conservative justices (Thomas, Kennedy, Scalia, Rehnquist, and O'Connor) voted to declare congressional statutes unconstitutional far more often than the liberal justices (Breyer, Stevens, Ginsburg, and Souter) did.[2] Thus the conservative justices were the most activist toward federal laws. But the liberal justices were the most activist toward state laws. The liberal justices (Stevens, Souter, Breyer, and Ginsburg) voted to declare state statutes unconstitutional far more

often than the conservative justices (Rehnquist, Scalia, Thomas, Kennedy, and O'Connor) did.

The study also incorporates votes to overturn precedents as a measure of judicial activism. Examining these votes shows that the conservatives (Thomas, Scalia, Kennedy, O'Connor, and Rehnquist) were more activist than the liberals (Souter, Ginsburg, Stevens, and Breyer) were.

When all three measures are totaled, the study reveals that Jus-

tice Thomas—the most conservative member of the Court—was the most activist justice. Other conservatives (Kennedy, Scalia, and O'Connor) were among the most activist justices. The liberals (Souter, Stevens, Breyer, and Ginsburg) were among the most restrained justices. Only Chief Justice Rehnquist, who was both conservative and restrained, fit the (inaccurate) stereotype that most people hold. (All but Rehnquist and O'Connor are on the current Supreme Court.)

Justice	Votes to Declare a Congressional Statute Unconstitutional	Votes to Declare a State Statute Unconstitutional	Votes to Overturn a Precedent	Total
Thomas	34	27	23	84
Kennedy	31	36	16	83
Scalia	30	27	19	76
O'Connor	24	39	12	75
Souter	21	45	7	73
Stevens	17	46	9	72
Breyer	14	44	10	68
Ginsburg	17	41	8	66
Rehnquist	25	21	12	58

Source: Lori A. Ringhand, "Judicial Activism: an Empirical Examination of Voting Behavior on the Rehnquist Natural Court," *Constitutional Commentary,* 24 (2007), 43–67.
[1] The membership of the Court during these years remained unchanged, so these justices heard the same cases.
[2] This group of conservatives includes justices who are moderately conservative and others who are very conservative. This group of "liberals" includes justices who are more liberal than the conservatives but who are considered moderate or moderately liberal. The most liberal, Justice Stevens, insists that he's simply moderate, as he was when appointed by President Ford in 1975.

tive position, and liberal justices vote for the liberal position in most cases. When justices claim to be restrained, their decision, allowing a particular law or policy to continue, produces the conservative or liberal outcome they prefer.[63] Thus some political scientists conclude that "judicial restraint" is little more than "a cloak for the justices' policy preferences."[64] It enables them to proclaim their "restraint" while actually voting on the basis of their ideology—without ever admitting this to the public.

We should be skeptical when we hear judges or politicians using these terms, whether touting their "restraint" to pacify the public or deriding opponents' "activism" to inflame the public.

Following Precedents

In interpreting statutes and the Constitution, judges are expected to follow precedents established by their court or higher courts in previous cases. This is the rule of **stare decisis** ("stand by what has been decided" in Latin).

Stare decisis provides stability in the law. If different judges decided similar cases in different ways, the law would be unpredictable, even chaotic. "*Stare decisis,*" Justice Brandeis said, "is usually the wise policy; because in most matters it is more important that the applicable rule of law be settled than that it be settled right."[65] *Stare decisis* also promotes equality in the law. If different judges de-

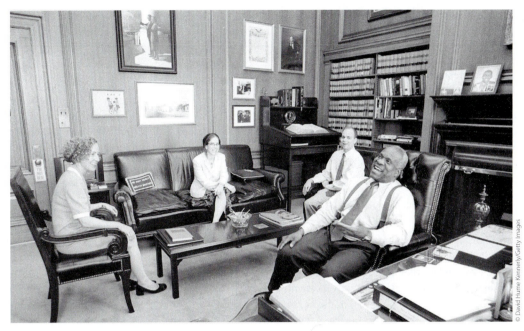

Justice Clarence Thomas shares a laugh with his clerks in his chambers.

cided similar cases in different ways, the courts would appear discriminatory toward some litigants.

In 1962, the Supreme Court held unconstitutional a New York law requiring public school students to recite a nondenominational prayer every day. This ruling became a precedent.[66] The following year, the Court held unconstitutional a Baltimore school policy requiring students to recite Bible verses.[67] The Court followed the precedent it had set the year before. In 1980, the Court held unconstitutional a Tennessee law forcing public schools to post the Ten Commandments in all classrooms.[68] Although this law differed from the previous ones in that it did not require recitation, the majority concluded that it reflected the same goal—to use the public schools to promote the Christian religion—so it violated the same principle—separation of church and state. In 1992, the Court ruled that clergy cannot offer prayers at graduation ceremonies for public schools.[69] Although this situation, too, differed from the previous ones in that it did not occur every day at school, the majority reasoned that it, too, reflected the same goal and violated the same principle. Finally, in 2000, the Court ruled that schools cannot use, or allow clergy or students to use, the public address system to offer prayers before high school football games.[70] For almost four decades, the Court followed the precedent it originally set when it initially addressed this issue.

Stare decisis is considered so important that judges sometimes follow precedents that they wouldn't have agreed to establish originally, even precedents that they don't agree with still. In *Roe* v. *Wade* in 1973, the Supreme Court established a right to abortion.[71] After five straight Republican appointments to the Court since the ruling, it appeared that a majority on the Court might be willing to reverse the ruling. Pennsylvania passed a law denying a right to abortion—essentially inviting the justices to reverse the ruling. In 1992, the law reached the Court. A bare majority overturned the state law and upheld the Court's precedent.[72] Three justices in the majority said they disagreed with the precedent but felt obligated to follow it. One of these, Justice Souter, wrote,

> For two decades of economic and social developments, people have organized intimate relationships and made choices…in reliance on the availability of abortion in the event that contraception should fail. The ability of women to participate equally in the economic and social life of the nation has been facilitated by their ability to control their reproductive lives….[O]nly the most convincing justification… could suffice to demonstrate that a later decision overruling the first was anything but a surrender to political pressure…. So to overrule under fire in the absence of the most compelling reason to re-examine a watershed decision would subvert the Court's legitimacy beyond any serious question.

Thus the right to abortion remained only because three justices who disagreed with it decided to follow the precedent rather than their preference. (Of course, not all justices feel equally obligated to follow precedents. See the box "Who Are the Activists?")

Making Law

Many judges deny that they make law. They say that it is already there, that they merely "find" it or, with their education and experience, "interpret" it. They imply that they use a mechanical process. Justice Owen Roberts wrote for the majority that struck down a New Deal act in 1936:

> It is sometimes said that the Court assumes a power to over-rule . . . the people's representatives. This is a misconception. The Constitution is the supreme law of the land. . . . All legislation must conform to the principles it lays down. When an act of Congress is appropriately challenged in the courts as not conforming to the constitutional mandate, the judicial branch of government has only one duty—to lay . . . the Constitution . . . beside the statute . . . and to decide whether the latter squares with the former.[73]

In other words, the Constitution itself dictates the decision.

However, by now it should be apparent that judges do not use a mechanical process. They *do* exercise discretion, and they *do* make law—when they interpret statutes, when they interpret the Constitution, and when they determine which precedents to follow or disregard.[74] In doing so, they reflect their own political preferences. As Justice Benjamin Cardozo said, "We may try to see things as objectively as we please. Nonetheless, we can never see them with any eyes except our own."[75] They do not shed their attitudes, even their prejudices, when they don their robes.

But to say that judges make law is not to say that they make law as legislators do. Judges make law less directly. They make it in the process of resolving disputes brought to them. They usually make it by telling governments what they cannot do, rather than what they must do and how they must do it. And judges make law less freely. They start not with clean slates, but with established principles embodied in statutes, the Constitution, and precedents. They are expected to follow these principles. If they deviate from them, they are expected to explain their reasons, and they are subjected to scrutiny by the legal profession.

DEMOCRACY?

Once we realize that judges make law as they decide cases, do we have to alter our conception of democratic government?

Deciding Cases at the Supreme Court

The Supreme Court's term runs from October through June. Early in the term, the justices decide which cases to hear, and by the end of the term, they decide how to resolve those cases.

After the Court agrees to hear a case, litigants submit written arguments. These "briefs" identify the issues and marshal the evidence—statutes, constitutional provisions, and precedents—for their side. (The word *briefs* is a misnomer, as some run to more than one hundred pages.)

Often interest groups and governments, whether federal, state, or local, submit briefs to support one side. These

friend of the court briefs present additional evidence or perspectives not included in the litigants' briefs. Major cases can prompt many briefs. A pair of affirmative action cases from the University of Michigan in 2003 had a record 102 briefs.[76]

Several weeks after receiving the briefs, the Court holds oral arguments. The justices gather in the robing room, put on their black robes, and file into the courtroom, taking their places at the half-hexagon bench. The chief justice sits in the center, with the associate justices extending out in order of seniority. The crier gavels the courtroom to attention and announces:

> The Honorable, the Chief Justice and Associate Justices of the Supreme Court of the United States! Oyez, oyez, oyez! [Give ear, give ear, give ear!] All persons having business before the Honorable, the Supreme Court of the United States are admonished to draw near and give attention, for the Court is now sitting. God save the United States and this Honorable Court.

The chief justice calls the case. The lawyers present their arguments, although the justices interrupt with questions whenever they want. When Thurgood Marshall, as the counsel for the NAACP before becoming a justice, argued one school desegregation case, he was interrupted 127 times. The justices ask about the facts of the case: "What happened when the defendant . . . ?" They ask about relevant precedents that appear to support or rebut the lawyers' arguments: "Can you distinguish this case from . . . ?" They ask about hypothetical scenarios: "What if the police officer . . . ?" These questions help the justices determine what is at stake, how a ruling would relate to existing doctrine, and how a ruling might govern future situations. They are experienced at pinning lawyers down. Chief Justice Rehnquist, who was affable toward his colleagues, was tough on the lawyers appearing before him. When asked whether the lawyers were nervous, he replied, "I assume they're all nervous—they should be."[77] Occasionally, one faints on the spot.

In the process of questioning the lawyers, the justices are also trying to persuade each other. Their questions, while directed at the lawyers, are designed to reveal the weakness of the position they oppose and to convey this weakness to their colleagues.[78]

The chief justice allots a half hour per side. When time expires, a red light flashes on the lectern, and the chief justice halts any lawyer who continues. Rehnquist, who valued efficiency and punctuality, cut lawyers off in mid-sentence when their time was up.

The oral arguments identify and clarify the major points of the case for any justices who did not read the briefs, and they assess the potential impact of the possible rulings. The oral arguments also serve as a symbol: they give the litigants a chance to be heard in open court, which encourages the litigants to feel that the eventual ruling is legitimate.

However, the oral arguments rarely sway the justices, except occasionally when a lawyer for one side is especially effective or ineffective.

As a lawyer before becoming chief justice, John Roberts argued thirty-nine cases at the Court. He was considered especially effective.[79]

The Court holds Friday conferences to make tentative decisions and assign the opinions. The decision affirms or reverses the lower court's decision. The opinion explains why. It expresses principles of law and establishes precedents for the future. Thus it tells lower courts how to resolve similar cases.

A portrait of Chief Justice John Marshall presides over the conference. To ensure secrecy, no one is present but the justices. They begin with handshakes. (During his tenure, Chief Justice Marshall suggested that they begin with a drink whenever it was rainy. But even when it was sunny, Marshall sometimes announced, "Our jurisdiction extends over so large a territory that the doctrine of chances makes it certain that it must be raining somewhere."[80] Perhaps this accounts for his extraordinary success in persuading his colleagues to adopt his views.) Then the justices get down to business. The chief justice initiates the discussion of the case. He indicates what the issues are and how they ought to be decided, and he casts a vote. The associate justices follow in order of seniority. Although the conference traditionally featured give-and-take among the justices, discussion became perfunctory under Rehnquist, and the conference became a series of quick votes.[81]

The Court reaches a tentative decision based on these votes. If the chief justice is in the majority, he assigns the writing of the opinion to himself or another justice. If he is not in the majority, the most senior associate justice in the majority assigns it. This custom reveals the chief justice's power. Although his vote counts the same as each associate justice's vote, his authority to assign the opinion can determine what the opinion says. He knows that certain colleagues will use strong language and lay down broad principles, whereas others will use guarded language and hew closely to specific facts in the case.

Before Marshall became chief justice, each justice wrote his own opinion. But Marshall realized that one opinion from the Court would carry more weight. He often convinced the other justices to forsake their opinions for his. As a result, he wrote almost half of the more than eleven hundred opinions the Court handed down during his thirty-four years. Recent chief justices have assigned most opinions—82 to 86 percent—but have written just slightly more than their share—12 to 14 percent.[82] Some Court watchers believe that Rehnquist downplayed his conservative views after he became chief justice to stay in the majority and retain control of the opinion.[83]

After the conference, the Court produces the opinion. This is the most time-consuming stage in the process. After Justice Brandeis died, researchers found in his files the thirty-seventh draft of an opinion he had written but still had not been satisfied with.

Because the justices are free to change their vote anytime until the decision is announced, the justice assigned the opinion tries to write it to command support of the justices in the original majority and possibly even some in the original minority. The writer circulates the draft among the others, who suggest revisions. The writer circulates more drafts. These go back and forth as the justices attempt to persuade or nudge their colleagues toward their position.

Unlike legislators, however, the justices don't engage in horse-trading—if you join me on this, I'll join you on that. According to one justice, there's "[n]one of that, zero. The coalitions float. Each . . . case is a new day."[84]

Sometimes the outcome changes between the tentative vote in the conference and the final vote in the decision. According to Justice Blackmun's notes, eleven times during his last three years on the Rehnquist Court, one or more justices switched sides to fashion a new majority from the original minority. In the case involving graduation prayers, Justice Anthony Kennedy was writing the **majority opinion** to allow such prayers, but he was unable to persuade himself. He abandoned the majority and joined the minority, thus making it the eventual majority.[85]

These inner workings underscore the politicking among the justices. **Justice William Brennan**, a liberal activist on the Warren and Burger Courts, was a gregarious and charming Irish American who was well liked by his colleagues. After drafting an opinion, he sent his clerks to other justices' clerks to learn whether their justices had any objections. Then he tried to redraft it to satisfy them. If they still had qualms, he went to their offices and tried to persuade

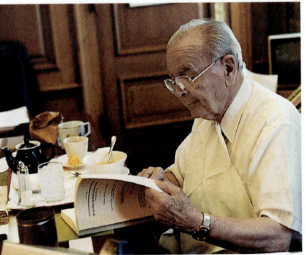

The job of a justice is unlike that of other political officials. Even after three decades of experience, Justice William Brennan often ate at his desk so he could finish his work. He was one of the most influential members of the Warren and Burger Courts.

them. If necessary, he compromised. He didn't want "to be 100 percent principled and lose by one vote," a law professor observed.[86] Brennan was so adept at persuasion that some scholars consider him "the best coalition builder ever to sit on the Supreme Court."[87] In fact, some say the Warren and Burger Courts should have been called the Brennan Court.

Justice Antonin Scalia, a conservative activist on the Rehnquist and Roberts Courts, is a brilliant and gregarious Italian American who, when appointed by President Reagan, was expected to dominate his colleagues and become the leader of the Court. Yet he has not fulfilled this expectation. He has been brash and imprudent, appearing to take more pleasure in insulting his colleagues than in persuading them.[88] In a case in which Justice O'Connor, who also was conservative but more cautious, did not want to go as far in limiting abortion rights as he did, Scalia wrote that her arguments "cannot be taken seriously."[89] In another case in which Chief Justice Rehnquist, who usually voted with Scalia, voted opposite him, Scalia wrote that his arguments were "implausible" and suggested that any lawyer who advised his client as Rehnquist urged should be "disbarred."[90] As a result, Scalia has not been as effective in forging a consensus among conservatives as Brennan was among liberals.

Justice Scalia, with a characteristic gesture in 2006.

© Peter A. Smith

Leadership, by someone, is necessary with nine strong-willed individuals, each of whom has risen to the top of the legal profession and each of whom is essentially operating a one-person law firm. (See the box "Anti-Semitism on the Bench.") Sometimes the chief justice becomes the informal leader. Marshall set the standard; Warren and Rehnquist were also effective leaders. Burger, however, possessed neither the interpersonal skills nor the intellectual firepower to earn the respect of his colleagues. Some observers think Roberts has the potential to become an effective leader.

If the opinion does not command the support of some justices in the original majority, they write a **concurring opinion**, which indicates that they agree with the decision but not the reasons for it. Meanwhile, the justices in the minority write a **dissenting opinion**, which indicates that they do not agree even with the decision. Both concurring and dissenting opinions weaken the force of the majority opinion. They question its validity, and they suggest that at a different time with different justices, there might be a different ruling. Chief Justice Hughes used to say that a dissenting opinion is "an appeal to the brooding spirit of the law, to the intelligence of a future day."[91]

Unlike the high courts of many other countries, which don't report any dissents, the Supreme Court of the United States routinely does, and the American people usually accept the existence of such disagreements.[92] In recent terms, about 60 percent of the Court's cases have had dissents.[93] But too many dissents indicate a fractious Court. One-third of the Rehnquist Court's cases were decided by a 5–4 vote in 2001, possibly the highest proportion ever.[94]

Finally, the print shop in the Court's basement prints the opinions, thus preventing the leaks that might occur if the opinions were printed elsewhere, and the Court announces its decisions and distributes the opinions in public session.

Exercising Power

The Founders expected the judiciary to be the weakest branch of government. In the *Federalist Papers,* Alexander Hamilton wrote that Congress would have power to pass the laws and appropriate the money; the president would have power to execute the laws; but the courts would have "merely judgment"—that is, only power to resolve disputes in cases brought to them. In doing so, they would exercise "neither force nor will." They would not have any means to enforce decisions, and they would not use their own values to decide cases. They would simply apply the Constitution and laws as written. Consequently, the judiciary would be the "least dangerous" branch.[95]

This prediction was accurate for the early years of the Republic. The federal courts seemed inconsequential. The Supreme Court was held in such low esteem that some distinguished men refused to accept appointment to it; others accepted appointment but refused to attend sessions. The first chief justice thought the Court was "inauspicious,"[96]

american diversity | Anti-Semitism on the Bench

President Woodrow Wilson admired James McReynolds' zeal as a trust-busting attorney, so Wilson chose McReynolds as his attorney general. But after brief service as attorney general, McReynolds' "violent temper and abusive nature" made Wilson anxious to get rid of him, so Wilson appointed him to the Supreme Court in 1914,[1] where McReynolds exercised his violent temper and abusive nature for twenty-seven years. He was called "the rudest man in Washington."[2]

The product of a severe upbringing along the Kentucky-Tennessee border, McReynolds was especially prejudiced toward Jews. When Louis Brandeis, the first Jew on the Supreme Court, was appointed, McReynolds refused to speak to him for three years. And McReynolds refused to sit next to him, where he was assigned according to seniority, for the annual photograph of the justices one year, forcing the chief justice to cancel the photo shoot. McReynolds also refused to join the other justices at a ceremonial event in Philadelphia because, he wrote the chief justice, "I am not

always to be found when there is a Hebrew abroad." For the same reason, the chief justice had to divide the justices into two groups when he invited them to dinner. Years later, when Benjamin Cardozo, the second Jew, was sworn in, McReynolds conspicuously read a newspaper while muttering, "another one." When Felix Frankfurter, the third Jew, was appointed, McReynolds exclaimed, "My God, another Jew on the Court!" and refused to attend Frankfurter's robing ceremony.[3] His clerk commented about his anti-Semitism as well. McReynolds didn't want Jews to visit his Washington apartment, and he didn't want his aides to fraternize with the aides of the Jewish justices.[4]

McReynolds was so cantankerous and intemperate that Justice William Douglas named a card game after him. It was called "Son of a Bitch."[5]

It wasn't only McReynolds' sour personality that dismayed Washingtonians, but his evident shift from a progressive attorney for the government to a reactionary

member of the Court. McReynolds became one of the "Four Horsemen" who, when they were able to obtain the vote of another justice, struck down government regulations on businesses and stymied President Franklin Roosevelt's New Deal program for years.[6]

Yet, after McReynolds retired from the Court, European newspapers reported that this life-long bachelor was financially supporting thirty-three English children left homeless by the German blitz during World War II. And when he died, he willed most of his estate to charities for needy children.

Nonetheless, McReynolds has gone down in history as perhaps the worst justice, based on his jurisprudence and his personality, ever to sit on the Supreme Court.[7]

[1] Henry J. Abraham, *Justices and Presidents: A Political History of Appointments to the Supreme Court*, 2nd ed. (New York: Oxford University, 1985), 175.
[2] Dennis J. Hutchinson and David J. Garrow, eds., *The Forgotten Memoir of John Knox: A Year in the Life of a Supreme Court Clerk in FDR's Washington* (Chicago: University of Chicago, 2002), xix.
[3] Abraham, *Justices and Presidents*, 176.
[4] Hutchinson and Garrow, *Forgotten Memoir*, 36–37.
[5] Ibid., 177.
[6] The other three "Horsemen" were Justices Butler, Sutherland, and Van Devanter.
[7] Abraham, *Justices and Presidents*, 178, 377–379.

without enough "weight and dignity" to play an important role.[97] So he resigned to be governor of New York. The second chief justice resigned to be envoy to France.

When the nation's capital was moved to Washington, D.C., in 1801, new homes were built for Congress and the president but not for the Supreme Court. Planners considered the Court too insignificant for more than a small room in the Capitol. But the Court couldn't even keep this room. For decades, it would be shunted from one location to another, from the marshal's office to the clerk's office, from the clerk's home to the Capitol's cellar—a dark and damp chamber in which visitors joked that Lady Justice wouldn't need to wear a blindfold because she couldn't see

anyway—and from one committee room to another.[98] It wouldn't get its own building until 1935.

However, the status of the Court began to change after the appointment of the fourth chief justice, **John Marshall**. Under his leadership, the Court began to develop "weight and dignity" and to play an important role in government.

The use of judicial review by the courts and the exercise of political checks against the courts show the extent of their power.

Use of Judicial Review

We'll examine two eras—the Founding era and the modern era—to see how the Court has used judicial review.

Chief Justice John Marshall (right) swears in President Andrew Jackson in 1829. Although Marshall's party, the Federalists, had dissolved, Marshall remained as chief justice, serving for thirty-four years.

The Founding Era

In the Founding era, the Supreme Court established judicial review and national supremacy.

Establishing judicial review   **Judicial review** is the authority to declare laws or actions of government officials unconstitutional. The Constitution doesn't mention judicial review. Although the idea was proposed at the Constitutional Convention, it was strongly opposed by some delegates who feared that it would strengthen the federal courts too much and, ultimately, weaken the state governments. The delegates who favored judicial review didn't press for its inclusion because they worried that doing so might jeopardize the Constitution's ratification.[99]

Nevertheless, the Supreme Court claimed the authority of judicial review in the case of **Marbury v. Madison** in 1803.[100] The dispute originated in 1800, when the Federalist president, John Adams, was defeated in his bid for re-election by Thomas Jefferson and many Federalist members of Congress were defeated by Jeffersonians. With both the presidency and Congress lost, the Federalists tried to maintain control of the judiciary. The lame-duck president and lame-duck Congress added more judgeships, most of which were unnecessary. (Forty-two were for justices of the peace for the District of Columbia, which was a sparsely populated swamp.) They hoped to fill these positions with loyal Federalists before the new president and new Congress took over.

In addition, Adams named his secretary of state, John Marshall, to be chief justice. At the time, though, Marshall

was still secretary of state and responsible for delivering the commissions to the new appointees. But he ran out of time, failing to deliver four commissions for District of Columbia justices of the peace. He assumed that his successor would deliver them. But Jefferson, angry at the Federalists' efforts to pack the judiciary, told his secretary of state, James Madison, not to deliver the commissions.[101] Without the signed commissions, the appointees could not prove that they had in fact been appointed.[102]

William Marbury and the three other appointees petitioned the Supreme Court for a writ of *mandamus* ("we command" in Latin), an order that forces government officials to do something they have a duty to do. In this case, it would force Madison to deliver the commissions.

As chief justice, Marshall was in a position to rule on his administration's efforts to appoint these judges. Today this would be considered a conflict of interest, and he would be expected to disqualify himself. But at the time, people were not as troubled by such conflicts.

Marshall could issue the writ, but Jefferson would tell Madison to disobey it, and the Court would be powerless to enforce it. Or Marshall could decline to issue the writ, and the Court would appear powerless to issue it. Either way, the Court would reflect weakness rather than project strength.

This portrait of William Marbury is the only portrait of a litigant owned by the Supreme Court Historical Society, testifying to the importance of the case of *Marbury* v. *Madison*.

Marshall shrewdly found a way out of the dilemma. He interpreted a provision of a congressional statute in a questionable way and then a provision of the Constitution in a questionable way as well.[103] As a result, he could claim that the statute violated the Constitution. Therefore, the statute was unconstitutional, and the Court couldn't order the administration to give the commissions. Thus Marshall exercised judicial review. He wrote, in a statement that would be repeated by courts for years to come, "It is emphatically the province and duty of the judicial department to say what the law is."

Marshall sacrificed the commissions—he couldn't have gotten them anyway—and established the power of judicial review instead. In doing so, with one hand he gave the Jeffersonians what they wanted—permission not to deliver the commissions—while with the other he gave the Federalists something much greater—judicial review. And all along he claimed he did what the Constitution required him to do.

Jefferson saw through this. He said the Constitution, in Marshall's hands, was "a thing of putty,"[104] adding that Marshall's arguments were "twistifications." But the decision didn't require Jefferson to do anything, so he couldn't do anything but protest. Most of Jefferson's followers were satisfied with the result. They weren't upset that the Court had invalidated a Federalist law, even though it had established judicial review to do so.

Of course, they were shortsighted because this decision laid the cornerstone for a strong judiciary. A case that began as a "trivial squabble over a few petty political plums"[105] became perhaps the most important case the Court has ever decided.

Establishing national supremacy After *Marbury,* the Marshall Court declared numerous state laws unconstitutional.[106] These decisions solidified the authority of judicial review, and they symbolized the supremacy of the national government over the state governments.

The Court also advanced the supremacy of the national government by broadly construing congressional power. In **McCulloch v. Maryland**, discussed in Chapter 2, the Court interpreted the **"necessary and proper clause"** to allow Congress to legislate in many matters not mentioned in the Constitution and not anticipated by the Founders.[107]

In the Founding era, the Court laid the foundation for judicial review and national supremacy. Of course, it would take the Civil War to resolve the conflict between the nation and the states and to enable the Court to build upon this foundation.

Now let's leap forward to the modern era, where we'll see how the Court has used judicial review and national supremacy to grant civil liberties and civil rights.

The Modern Era

The modern era for the Supreme Court began when President Dwight Eisenhower, fulfilling a campaign pledge to a presidential rival, **Earl Warren**, appointed him chief justice. In the 1950s and 1960s, the **Warren Court** decided many cases involving civil liberties and civil rights. These cases pitted individuals against the government. Often they pitted minority individuals—whether a racial minority, a political minority, or a religious minority—against the majority of the public, whose views were reflected in government policy.

Historically, the courts had paid little attention to civil liberties and civil rights, allowing the government to ignore these constitutional rights. But the Warren Court reversed this lax attitude. It replaced traditional legal doctrine involving racial segregation, legislative reapportionment, criminal defendants' rights, libel, obscenity, and religion. It also modified traditional legal doctrine involving political speech. In the process, it held many laws, especially state laws, unconstitutional. The Warren Court was more activist in civil liberties and civil rights cases than any Supreme Court had ever been (see Figure 3).

The Warren Court sympathized with powerless groups and unpopular individuals when they challenged government policies. Thus the most elite institution in our government used its power to benefit many nonelites in our society. In its sympathies, the Warren Court differed sharply from previous Courts, which typically favored the haves over the have-nots and the efforts to preserve the status quo over the struggles to change it.

Chief Justice Earl Warren, flanked by Justices Hugo Black *(left)* and William O. Douglas.

Figure 3 **Laws Regulating Economic Activity and Restricting Civil Liberties and Rights Declared Unconstitutional by the Supreme Court since 1900**

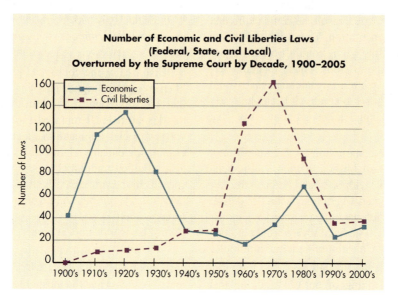

The Supreme Court was nearly as activist in striking down laws in the 1910s, 1920s, and 1930s, as it was in the 1950s, 1960s, and 1970s. But in the former years, it was activist in economic cases (usually those involving government regulation of business), whereas in the latter years, it was activist in civil liberties and rights cases.
SOURCE: Lawrence Baum, The Supreme Court, 9th ed. (Washington, D.C.: CQ Press, 2007), 176.

The Warren Court's decisions brought about a conservative backlash.[108] President Richard Nixon vowed to change the Court's direction, and after Earl Warren retired he appointed **Warren Burger** to be chief justice. Then Nixon and his former vice president, President Gerald Ford, appointed four more justices as vacancies occurred. They sought to slow, halt, or even reverse the Court's liberal doctrine. They expected the **Burger Court** to bring about a "constitutional counterrevolution."

But the Burger Court in the 1970s and 1980s did not. Although it eroded some liberal doctrine,[109] it left most intact. And it initiated new liberal doctrine in two areas where the Warren Court had been silent—sexual discrimination and abortion. Although it was not as committed to civil liberties and civil rights as the Warren Court, the Burger Court was more committed to them than any earlier Court.

President Ronald Reagan and his former vice president, George H. W. Bush, also sought to reverse the Court's liberal doctrine. When Burger retired, Reagan elevated **William Rehnquist**, the most conservative associate justice, to be chief justice. Then Reagan and Bush appointed five more conservatives as vacancies occurred. By this time, Republican presidents had named ten justices in a row.

President Bill Clinton's election led to the first Democratic justices since 1967. Although these two moderate liberals slowed any further swing to the right, the conservative justices controlled the **Rehnquist Court** in the 1980s, 1990s, and

early 2000s. But conflicts among the conservatives splintered their bloc. Some were bold, eager to sweep away liberal precedents and substitute conservative principles. Others were cautious, willing to uphold liberal precedents they would not have agreed to set in the first place and inclined to decide cases on narrow bases rather than on broad principles. In some terms, the former group dominated, but in other terms, the latter group dominated.[110] Overall, the Rehnquist Court, though markedly more conservative than the Burger Court,[111] did not bring about a "constitutional counterrevolution" either.

The Rehnquist Court also practiced judicial activism, though from the right rather than from the left. For example, it struck down laws implementing gun registration, affirmative action, legislative districts that help racial minorities elect their candidates, and governmental policies that help religious minorities practice their religion. It also invalidated a series of congressional laws regulating the states. In eight of the last years of the Rehnquist Court, the justices invalidated thirty-three federal laws, the highest annual average ever.[112]

In **Bush v. Gore**, which arose from the disputed presidential election of 2000, the conservative majority deliberately intervened—essentially, picked the president—although the Constitution lays out the procedures to resolve electoral deadlocks.[113] These procedures give Congress, not the courts, primary authority to choose the president. The Court's ruling was pure judicial activism.

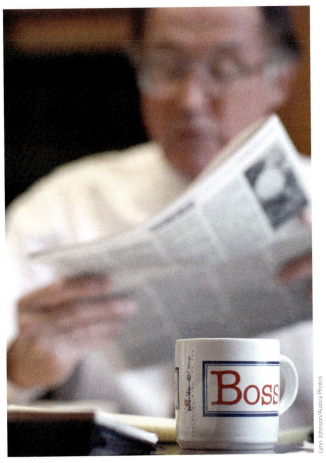

Chief Justice William Rehnquist

President George W. Bush, like recent Republican presidents, tried to fashion a more conservative Court. When William Rehnquist died in 2005, he appointed John Roberts to be chief justice. He then appointed another conservative, Samuel Alito. The **Roberts Court** is emerging as a more conservative court than the Rehnquist Court.

Since the Warren Court, there has been a steady trend toward more conservative justices. Justice John Paul Stevens, who was appointed by President Ford in 1975, has observed that every justice appointed since 1971, except perhaps one, has been more conservative than the justice he or she replaced. Stevens himself was a moderate Republican, and he's now the most liberal justice. He insists that he's not moved left but that the Court has moved that far right.[114]

Table 1	Modern Supreme Courts
Warren Court	1953–1969
Burger Court	1969–1986
Rehnquist Court	1986–2005
Roberts Court	2005–present

In the modern era, the Court has used judicial review to be a policy maker. In general, the Warren Court was a liberal policy maker, the Burger Court a moderate policy maker, and the Rehnquist Court a conservative policy maker. All three courts were activist rather than restrained.

The Role of Judicial Review

Judicial review is the most powerful tool courts use to wield power. When the courts declare a law or action unconstitutional, they not only void that law or action but also might put the issue on the public agenda, and they might speed up or slow down the pace of change in the government's policy.

When the Supreme Court declared Texas's abortion law unconstitutional in *Roe* v. *Wade* in 1973, the Court put the abortion issue on the public agenda. Abortion hadn't been a raging controversy before the Court's ruling.

The Court used judicial review as a catalyst to speed up change in the desegregation cases in the 1950s. At the time, President Eisenhower wasn't inclined to act, and Congress wasn't able to act because both houses were dominated by senior southerners who, as committee chairs, blocked civil rights legislation. The Court broke the logjam.

The Court used judicial review as a brake to slow down change in the business cases in the first third of the twentieth century. After the Industrial Revolution swept the United States, powerful corporations abused their employees, their customers, and their competitors. Although Congress and state legislatures passed laws to regulate these abuses, the Court, dominated by justices who had been lawyers for corporations, often struck down the laws. The Court delayed some policies for several decades.

Judicial review, an American contribution to government, was for years unique to this country. It is now used in numerous other countries, but not as extensively or as effectively as in the United States.

The Supreme Court alone has struck down over 150 provisions of federal laws and over 1200 provisions of state and local laws.[115] The number of laws struck down, however, isn't a true measure of the importance of judicial review. Instead, the ever-present threat of review has prevented the legislatures from enacting many laws they feared would be struck down.

By using judicial review to play a strong role in government, the Court has contradicted the Founders' expectation that the judiciary would always be the weakest branch. Usually it has been the weakest branch, but occasionally it has been stronger. Arguably, these times include some years during the early nineteenth century, when the Court established national supremacy; the late nineteenth century and early twentieth century, when the Court thwarted efforts to regulate business; and the 1950s and 1960s, when the Court extended civil liberties and civil rights.

Nevertheless, the extent to which the Court has played a strong role in government shouldn't be exaggerated. At

Utah State Historical Society

Although many children worked long days in unsafe conditions, for years the Supreme Court interpreted the Constitution to bar laws prohibiting child labor. This boy worked in the coal mines in the early 1900s.

any given time, the Court has focused on one broad area of the law—in the modern era, civil liberties and civil rights—and has paid little attention to other areas. Moreover, this area has always involved domestic policy. Traditionally, the Court has been reluctant to intervene in foreign policy.[116]

Use of Political Checks against the Courts

The courts have exercised judicial review cautiously because they're subject to various political checks by the other branches.

Checks by the Executive

Presidents can impose the most effective check. If they dislike courts' rulings, they can appoint new judges when vacancies occur. Many appointees remain on the bench two decades after their president has left the White House.[117] President Nixon resigned in disgrace in 1974, but his appointee William Rehnquist stayed on the Court until he died in 2005.

Presidents and state and local executives, such as governors and mayors and even school officials and police officers, can refuse to enforce courts' rulings. School officials have disobeyed decisions requiring desegregation and in-

validating class prayers. Police officers have ignored decisions invalidating some kinds of searches and interrogations. Yet executives who refuse to enforce courts' rulings risk losing public support, unless the public also opposes the rulings. Even President Nixon complied when the Court ordered him to turn over the incriminating Watergate tapes.

Checks by the Legislature

Congress and state legislatures can overturn courts' rulings by adopting constitutional amendments. They have done so four times (with the Eleventh, Fourteenth, Sixteenth, and Twenty-sixth Amendments).[118]

They can also overturn courts' rulings by passing new statutes. When courts base decisions on their interpretations of statutes, or when they make decisions in the absence of statutes, legislatures can pass new statutes, with clear language, that negate the decisions. From 1967 through 1990, Congress passed statutes to negate 121 Supreme Court rulings.[119] In 1986, the Court ruled that the Air Force didn't have to allow an ordained rabbi to wear his yarmulke with his uniform.[120] The next year, Congress passed a statute permitting military personnel to wear some religious apparel while in uniform.

Legislatures can refuse to implement courts' rulings, especially when money is necessary to implement them. The legislators simply don't appropriate the money.

Although these checks are the most common, Congress has invoked others, though only rarely. It can alter the structure of the lower federal courts, it can limit the appellate jurisdiction of the Supreme Court, and it can impeach and remove judges.

It can also limit the use of *habeas corpus* if there's a rebellion or an invasion of the country. After prodding by the Bush administration, Congress twice tried to eliminate the use of *habeas corpus* by alien detainees at Guantanamo Bay, Cuba. This would have prevented the detainees from challenging their detention in any court. However, the Supreme Court invalidated the congressional acts, ruling that the constitutional provisions for suspending the writ must be interpreted narrowly because the writ serves as a check on the legislative and executive branches.[121]

As a result of occasional checks or threatened checks, the courts have developed a strong sense of self-restraint to ensure self-preservation. This caution, more than the checks themselves, limits their use of judicial review.

DEMOCRACY?

Is judicial review compatible or incompatible with democratic government? In what ways is it compatible? Incompatible? Does the existence of political checks against the courts make judicial review more compatible with democratic government than it would be without them?

Conclusion: Are the Courts Responsive?

The courts tend to reflect the views of the public. Studies comparing 185 Supreme Court rulings from the mid-1930s through the mid-1990s with public opinion polls on the same issues found that the rulings mirrored the polls in approximately 60 percent of the cases.[122] The justices reflected the views of the public about as often as elected officials did. Thus the justices either responded to the public or, having been appointed by political officials chosen by the public, simply reflected the views of the public as political officials did.

Research shows that citizens know almost nothing about the judges; more adults can identify the character names of the Three Stooges than a single justice on the Supreme Court.[123] They also know little about the cases, but they do remember controversial decisions and they do recognize broad trends.[124] If they dislike these decisions or trends, their opinions pressure presidents and members of Congress to appoint justices with different views.

Although the courts are directly or indirectly responsive to the public, the Founders did not intend for them to be very responsive. The Founders gave judges life tenure so the courts would be relatively independent of both officials and the public. Indeed, the courts are more independent of political pressures than the other branches are. This enables them, in the words of appellate court judge Learned Hand, to stand as a bulwark against the "pressure of public panic." They can provide a "sober second thought."[125]

The courts can even protect the rights of various minorities—racial minorities, religious minorities, political dissidents, and criminal defendants—against the demands and the wrath of the majority. Chapters 14 and 15 will show how the courts extended civil liberties and civil rights to unpopular groups and individuals who lacked clout with the other branches and support from the public. Yet protecting the rights of these groups and individuals has historically been the exception rather than the rule. It was typical of the Warren Court and to some extent the Burger Court, but it was not typical of Supreme Courts before and has not been typical of Supreme Courts since.

The courts are part of the political process and are sensitive to others in the process, especially to the president, Congress, and the public. Although they enjoy relative independence, they aren't immune to political pressure. They have therefore "learned to be a political institution and to behave accordingly" and have "seldom lagged far behind or forged far ahead" of public opinion.[126]

Key Terms

Foreign Intelligence Surveillance Court
federal district courts
federal courts of appeals
jurisdiction
habeas corpus
senatorial courtesy
Senate Judiciary Committee
criminal cases
civil cases
American Civil Liberties Union (ACLU)
writ of *certiorari*
statutes
Americans with Disabilities Act
restrained judges
activist judges
stare decisis
friend of the court briefs
majority opinion
concurring opinion
dissenting opinion
judicial review
Marbury v. *Madison*

McCulloch v. *Maryland*
"necessary and proper clause"
Warren Court
Burger Court
Rehnquist Court
Bush v. *Gore*
Roberts Court

Key Names

Justice Ruth Bader Ginsburg
Justice Thurgood Marshall
Justice Sandra Day O'Connor
Justice Clarence Thomas
Robert Bork
Chief Justice John Roberts
Justice Samuel Alito
Justice William Brennan
Justice Antonin Scalia
Chief Justice John Marshall
Chief Justice Earl Warren
Chief Justice Warren Burger
Chief Justice William Rehnquist

Please visit our companion website at www.cengage.com/politicalscience/welch/uag12e or use CengageNOW for additional resources dealing with this chapter.

An American soldier poses with the body of an Iraqi prisoner who died during his interrogation at Abu Ghraib prison.

Getty Images

Civil Liberties

14

Talking Points

Sabrina Harman loved taking pictures. Flashing a big smile and giving a thumbs-up, she also loved having her picture taken. She wanted to be a police officer who serves as a forensic photographer. Although friends said she "would not let you step on an ant," she was fascinated by wounded and dead animals and people.[1] "Even if somebody is hurt," she said, "the first thing I think about is taking photos of that injury."[2]

Harman joined the Army Reserves to get money to help pay for college. She never expected to go to war, but her unit of military police was sent to Iraq and stationed at Saddam Hussein's old prison at **Abu Ghraib,** near Baghdad, where Americans were holding thousands of Iraqis. Soon after arriving in Iraq, she wrote her father, "On June 23 I saw my first dead body. I took pictures!"[3]

Harman's unit of M.P.s wasn't trained as prison guards or educated about military procedures for, or legal constraints on, prisoner interrogations. (Their company commander sold window blinds in civilian life.) Yet these reservists were used by the CIA agents who conducted the interrogations. The reservists were instructed to prepare the prisoners for the interrogations through sleep deprivation, sensory disorientation, sexual humiliation, and physical punishment. Harman was taken aback. "In the beginning," she said, "you see somebody naked and you see underwear on their head and you're like, 'Oh, that's pretty bad—I can't believe I just saw that.' And then you go to bed and you come back the next day and you see something worse."[4]

The women soldiers were used to humiliate the prisoners, to demonstrate their powerlessness. The women could look at them, even laugh at them, and the prisoners couldn't do anything about it.

Over the months, Harman experienced a transformation in her feelings, from mockery of the prisoners to sympathy for them, and from acceptance of the treatment to doubt and outrage about it.[5] So she took photos to record what she saw and, psychologically, to position herself as an observer rather than a participant in the degradation.

One night when she reported for duty, their commanding officer told them that a prisoner had died from a heart attack. His body was packed in ice and zipped into a rubber body bag. When Harman and her immediate superior entered the room where the body lay, she took a picture. Then they unzipped the bag. "We...realized right away that there was no way he died of a heart attack because of all the cuts and blood coming out of his nose."[6] She took more photos. Then her superior took a picture of her posing with the body. Later that night she and another soldier returned to examine the body more closely. They looked under the bags of ice and the bandages. They saw more injuries—big bruises, a split lip, a chipped tooth, and more blood. "Hey, I was just lied to. This guy did not die of a heart attack," she concluded.[7] Indeed, the official autopsy would show that he was killed by the CIA agent interrogating him.[8] Her grisly photos would become stark public evidence that he was killed.

The interrogator was never charged with any crime, but Harman was charged with multiple crimes stemming from her photographs. Ultimately, these charges were dropped, but she was court-martialed for maltreatment of prisoners and dereliction of duty, as were other reservists in her unit, and she was sentenced to six months in prison and given a bad-conduct discharge. But no higher-up was ever convicted, although the reservists were implementing the administration's policy of harsh treatment toward the Iraqi prisoners.[9]

Americans value their "rights." Eighteenth-century Americans believed that people had **"natural rights"** by virtue of being human. Given by God, not by government, the rights could not be taken away by government. Contemporary Americans do not normally use this term, but they do think about their rights much as their forebears did.

Yet Americans have a split personality when assessing their rights. Most people tell pollsters they believe in constitutional rights, but many don't accept these rights in concrete situations. During the Cold War, for example, most people said they believe in free speech, but many said communists, socialists, or atheists shouldn't be allowed to speak in public or teach in schools.

Surveys show that Americans remain divided over their support for civil liberties. Many would ban expression that might upset others.[10] One-third said they wouldn't allow a rally that might offend community members. Two-thirds said they wouldn't allow people to say things in public that might offend racial groups, and over one-half said they wouldn't allow people to say things in public that might offend religious groups. One-fifth said they wouldn't allow newspapers to publish without government approval of the articles.[11]

Conflicts over civil liberties and rights have dominated the courts since the 1950s. This chapter, covering civil liberties, and the next, covering civil rights, explain how the courts have interpreted these rights and tried to resolve these conflicts. The chapters show how judges have acted as referees between the litigants, brokers among competing groups, and policy makers in the process of deciding these cases.

The Constitution and the Bill of Rights

Individual Rights in the Constitution

Although the term **civil liberties** usually refers to the rights in the Bill of Rights, a few rights are granted in the body of the Constitution. The Constitution bans religious qualifica-

tions for federal office ⭐ Art. VI. (England had required its citizens who sought public office to profess their allegiance to the Church of England, which kept Catholics and religious dissenters on the sidelines.) The Constitution guarantees jury trials in federal criminal cases ⭐ Art. III, Sec. 2. It bans bills of attainder, which are legislative acts rather than judicial trials pronouncing specific persons guilty of crimes, and *ex post facto* ("after the fact") laws, which are legislative acts making some behavior illegal that wasn't illegal when it was done ⭐ Art. I, Secs. 9 and 10. The Constitution also prohibits suspension of the writ of *habeas corpus,* except during rebellion or invasion of the country ⭐ Art. I, Sec. 9.

The Bill of Rights

Origin and Meaning

The Constitution originally didn't include a bill of rights; the Founders didn't think traditional liberties needed specific protections because federalism, separation of powers, and checks and balances would prevent the national government from becoming too powerful. But to win support for ratification, the Founders promised to adopt constitutional amendments to provide such rights. James Madison proposed twelve, Congress passed them, and in 1791 the states ratified ten of them, which came to be known as the **Bill of Rights**.[12]

The first eight grant specific rights. (See the box "Civil Liberties in the Bill of Rights.") The Ninth Amendment says that the listing of these rights does not mean they are the only ones the people have, and the Tenth says that any powers not granted to the federal government are reserved for the state governments.

The Bill of Rights provides rights against the government. According to Justice Hugo Black, it is a list of "Thou shalt nots" directed at the government.[13] In practice, it provides rights for political, religious, or racial minorities

---

CIVIL LIBERTIES IN THE BILL OF RIGHTS

-First Amendment grants freedom of religion, freedom of speech, assembly, and association, freedom of the press.

-Second Amendment grants right to keep and bear arms.

-Third Amendment forbids quartering soldiers in houses during peacetime.

-Fourth Amendment forbids unreasonable searches and seizures.

-Fifth Amendment grants right to a grand jury in criminal cases and right to due process.

- Fifth Amendment forbids double jeopardy (more than one trial for the same offense),

compulsory self-incrimination, taking private property without just compensation.

-Sixth Amendment grants right to speedy trial, right to public trial, right to jury trial in criminal cases, right to cross-examine adverse witnesses, right to present favorable

witnesses, right to counsel.

-Seventh Amendment grants right to jury trial in civil cases.

-Eighth Amendment forbids excessive bail and fines and cruel and unusual punishment.

against the majority, because government policy toward civil liberties tends to reflect the views of the majority.

As explained in Chapter 2, the Founders set up a government to protect property rights for the well-to-do minority against a jealous majority. The Constitution's fragmentation of power and some specific provisions (see box "Constitutional Provisions Protecting Property" in that chapter) were designed to prevent the masses from curtailing the rights of the elites. However, as Americans became more egalitarian and as the masses gained more opportunity to participate in politics in the nineteenth and twentieth centuries, the relative importance of property rights declined while the relative importance of other rights increased. Thus the Bill of Rights became the means to protect the fundamental rights of political, religious, and racial minorities and of criminal defendants—people who are out of the mainstream and often unpopular and powerless—when they come in conflict with the majority.

Responsibility for interpreting the Bill of Rights lies with the federal courts. Because federal judges are appointed for life, they are more independent of majority pressure than elected officials are.

DEMOCRACY?

Does the emphasis upon minority rights in the Bill of Rights contradict democracy or enhance democracy? What implications does this emphasis have for a conception of democracy that is based on majority rule?

Application

For many years, the Supreme Court applied the Bill of Rights only to the federal government, not to the state governments (or to the local governments, which are under the authority of the state governments). That is, the Bill of Rights restricted the actions only of the federal government.[14]

In ruling this way, the Court followed the intentions of the Founders, who assumed that the states, with their capitals closer to their people, would be less likely to violate the liberties of their people.[15] The Founders didn't realize that the states would in fact be more likely to violate the liberties of their people. Because the state governments represent smaller, more homogeneous populations, they tend to reflect majority sentiment more closely than the federal government, so they often ignored—and sometimes obliterated—the rights of political, religious, or racial minorities or of criminal defendants.

However, in the twentieth century there was a growing sense that individual rights are important and that the state governments, as well as the federal government, should accord them. Starting in 1925[16] and continuing through 1972,[17] the Supreme Court gradually applied most provisions of the Bill of Rights to the states.[18] In addition, the

Court established some rights not in the Bill of Rights, and it applied these to the states, too—presumption of innocence in criminal cases, right to travel within the country, and right to privacy. Thus most provisions in the Bill of Rights, and even some not in it, now restrict the actions of both the federal and the state governments.

By forcing the states to grant national constitutional rights, the Supreme Court strengthened national governmental authority. This development was one factor that contributed to the evolution from the state-centered federalism favored by some Founders to the nation-centered federalism evident today. (Recall the discussion of these concepts in Chapter 3.)

To see how the Court has interpreted these provisions, we'll look at four major areas—freedom of expression, freedom of religion, rights of criminal defendants, and right to privacy—and also look at implications for civil liberties from the war on terrorism. We'll put the major rulings of the Supreme Court in italics because the Court's doctrine is complex.

Freedom of Expression

The **First Amendment** guarantees freedom of expression, which includes freedom of speech, assembly, and association, and freedom of the press.[19] The amendment also guarantees freedom of religion, which will be addressed in the next section. (Take note, in case you're asked. In 2006, Americans could name more members of *The Simpsons* cartoon family and more judges on *American Idol* than they could rights in the First Amendment.)[20]

The amendment states that "Congress shall make no law" abridging these liberties. The language is absolute, but no justices interpret it literally.[21] They cite the example of the person who falsely shouts "Fire!" in a crowded theater and causes a stampede that injures someone. Surely, they say, the amendment doesn't protect this expression. So the Court needs to draw a line between expression the amendment protects and that which it doesn't.

Freedom of Speech

Freedom of speech, Justice Black asserted, is "the heart of our government."[22] There are important theoretical justifications for freedom of speech. By creating an open atmosphere, it promotes individual autonomy and self-fulfillment. By encouraging a wide variety of opinions, it furthers the advancement of knowledge and the discovery of truth. The English philosopher **John Stuart Mill**, who championed freedom of speech, observed that individuals decide what is correct by comparing different views. Unpopular opinions might be true or partly true. Even if completely false, they might prompt a reevaluation of accepted opinions. By permitting citizens to form opinions and express them to others, freedom of speech helps them participate in government. It especially helps them check inefficient or corrupt government. Finally, by channeling conflict toward persuasion, freedom of speech promotes a stable society. Governments that deny freedom of speech become inflexible. Eventually, their inflexibility fosters rebellion among their people. [23]

DEMOCRACY?

Why would philosopher John Dewey say that "democracy begins in conversation"?[24]

Because of our tradition and constitutional guarantee, almost all speech is allowed. However, there are some restrictions on the content of speech—what is said—and other restrictions on the manner of speech—how it is said. We'll first examine the restrictions on the content of speech, focusing on seditious speech, offensive speech, hate speech, and sexual speech. We'll then examine the restrictions on the manner of speech.

Seditious Speech

Seditious speech is speech that encourages opposition to or rebellion against the government.[25] The public becomes most hostile to seditious speech, and the government becomes most likely to prosecute people for such speech, during or shortly after war, when society is most sensitive about patriotism and loyalty. Criminal prosecution for seditious speech strikes at the heart of our principle of freedom of speech, which is supposed to protect individuals and groups who criticize the government and its officials.

World War I era Numerous prosecutions came with World War I and the Russian Revolution, which brought the Communists to power in the Soviet Union in 1917. The Russian Revolution prompted the **Red Scare**, in which people feared conspiracies to overthrow the U.S. government. Congress passed laws that prohibited "disloyal, profane, scurrilous, or abusive language about the form of government, Constitution, soldiers and sailors, flag or uniform of the armed forces."[26] State legislatures passed similar laws.

The federal government prosecuted almost two thousand and convicted almost nine hundred persons under these acts, and the state governments prosecuted and convicted many others. They prosecuted individuals for saying that war is contrary to the teachings of Jesus, that World War I should not have been declared until after a referendum was held, and that the draft was unconstitutional. Officials even prosecuted an individual for remarking to women knitting clothes for the troops, "No soldier ever sees those socks."[27]

These cases gave the Supreme Court numerous opportunities to rule on seditious speech. In six major cases, the Court upheld the governments' laws and affirmed the defendants' convictions.[28] The Court concluded that *these defendants' speech constituted a "clear and present danger"* to the government. Justice Edward Sanford wrote, "A single revolutionary spark may kindle a fire that, smoldering for a time, may burst into a sweeping and destructive conflagration."[29] In reality, there was nothing clear or present about the danger; the defendants' speech had little effect. The Court, reflecting our society at the time, was simply intolerant of dissent.

When a Harvard Law professor criticized the Court's rulings, the university's administration, prompted by the Justice Department, charged him "unfit" to be a professor. He was narrowly acquitted.[30]

Cold War era More prosecutions came after World War II, as the uneasy alliance between the United States and the Soviet Union during the war gave way to the Cold War between the two countries in the 1950s. Politicians, especially Sen. **Joseph McCarthy** (R-Wisc.), exploited the tensions. McCarthy claimed that many government officials were Communists. He said he had a list of 205 "known Communists" in the State Department alone. He had little evidence—and provided no list.[31] Other Republicans also accused the Democratic Truman administration of covering for Communists in government. They goaded it into prosecuting Communists outside government so it would not appear "soft on communism."

Congress passed an act that prohibited advocating overthrow of the government by force and organizing or joining individuals who advocated overthrow.[32] The government used the act against the Communists. The Court upheld the act and affirmed the convictions of eleven upper-echelon leaders of the American Communist Party.[33] These leaders organized the party, and the party advocated overthrowing

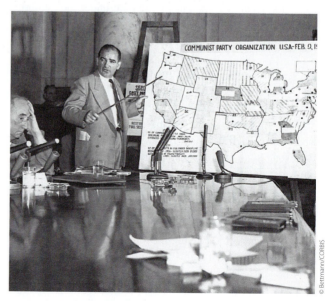

At congressional hearings, Sen. Joseph McCarthy identified the supposed locations of alleged Communists and "fellow travelers."

During the Cold War, Americans feared communism so much that some built bomb shelters in their yards, believing that taking refuge would protect their family in a nuclear attack.

to individuals who had never been Communists but who were lumped together as "Commie dupes" or "comsymps" (Communist sympathizers).

The federal government and some state governments required government employees to take "loyalty oaths" and then fired those who refused, even on principle, and those who (purportedly) lied. Some state governments banned Communists, former Communists, and alleged subversives from public jobs such as teaching or private jobs such as practicing law or serving as union officers. Federal and state legislative committees held hearings to expose and humiliate them. These actions cost an estimated ten thousand Americans their jobs.

Eventually, the Cold War thawed somewhat, and the Senate condemned McCarthy after he tried to bully the Army. His method was likened to witch hunts, and the tactic of making political accusations or name-calling based on little or no evidence came to be known as **McCarthyism**. (However, McCarthyism began before and continued after McCarthy's tenure in the 1950s, as other politicians and the Senate's Internal Security Committee and the House's Un-American Activities Committee used similar tactics.)[34]

Although McCarthy and others were bullies who hurt many innocent or harmless people, there actually were Communist spies in the federal government, from the atomic labs at Los Alamos, New Mexico, to the State Department and the White House, according to records revealed after the collapse of the Soviet Union. Apparently most spies were discovered before the 1950s, but some were never uncovered.[35]

In the meantime, two new members, including Chief Justice **Earl Warren**, joined the Supreme Court. In a series of cases in the mid- to late 1950s and early 1960s, the **Warren Court** made it more difficult to convict the Communists.[36] (See box "The President Summons the Chief Justice.")

Ultimately, the Warren Court created new doctrine for seditious speech.[37] The justices drew a distinction between advocacy and incitement. *People can advocate, enthusiastically, even heatedly, as long as they don't incite illegal action—that is, urge immediate action to violate any laws.*

the government by force, but the leaders had not attempted to overthrow the government. (If they had, they clearly would have been guilty of crimes.) Even so, the Court concluded that *they were a clear and present danger.* After the Court's decision, the government prosecuted and convicted almost one hundred lower-level Communists as well.

The public's fear was so consuming that the government's actions extended beyond criminal prosecutions to other measures, and beyond active Communists to former Communists—some Americans had dabbled with communism during the Great Depression in the 1930s—and even

BEHIND THE SCENES
THE PRESIDENT SUMMONS THE CHIEF JUSTICE

When the Supreme Court made it more difficult to convict American Communists in the 1950s and 1960s, the justices incurred the wrath of the public, Congress, and President Dwight Eisenhower, who summoned Chief Justice Warren to the White House. In a private conversation, the president criticized the rulings. Warren asked Eisenhower what he thought the Court should have done with the Communists.

Eisenhower replied, "I would kill the S.O.B.s."[1] Warren ignored the remark.

[1] Earl Warren, *The Memoirs of Earl Warren* (Garden City, New York: Doubleday, 1977), 6.

This doctrine protects most criticism of the government, whether at a rally, from a pulpit, or through the media, and it remains in effect today.

Thus after many years and many cases, the Court concluded that the First Amendment protects seditious speech as much as other speech. Justice William Douglas noted that "the threats were often loud but always puny."[38] Even the attorney general who prosecuted the major Communist cases later admitted that the cases were "squeezed oranges. I didn't think there was much to them."[39] Nevertheless, the Court had permitted public fear to overwhelm the First Amendment for a long time.

The Vietnam War didn't prompt the same concerns as did the Red Scare during World War I or the Cold War following World War II. Congress didn't pass any comparable laws. Nonetheless, the federal government took some actions against individuals and groups. Antiwar groups were harassed by federal grand juries, and their leaders were spied on by the U.S. Army. Some prominent opponents were prosecuted for conspiring against the draft.[40] However, opposition to this war was so widespread that the government's actions didn't silence the protesters' speech.

The collapse of the Soviet Union and the demise of the Cold War made communism less threatening, but this doctrine remains important. After the Oklahoma City bombing in 1995, government surveillance of right-wing militia groups increased, but prosecution of the members, under terrorism laws, was limited because most of the evidence was fiery rhetoric, which is protected speech (unless it urges immediate action to violate any laws).

After the terrorist attacks in 2001, pressure to conform—to temper criticism and to support the government's policies—mounted. An organization identified forty college professors with "un-American" agendas, in an effort to prod the schools to discipline and restrain their professors. (Negative reaction prompted the organization to remove the names from its website.)[41] A tenured professor at the University of New Mexico who cracked, "Anyone who can

blow up the Pentagon gets my vote," was reprimanded, and a lawsuit demanding his termination was filed.[42] During the Iraq War, pressure to conform was linked to support for our troops. Critics were branded as "unpatriotic" and "disloyal" by conservative commentators who stoked their listeners' anger.[43] Pressure to conform was muted only when the initial victory unraveled in the invasion's aftermath and the public's criticism increased.

Although the government didn't adopt laws during the war on terrorism or the war in Iraq comparable to those adopted during the twentieth century, it did take other actions that have important implications for civil liberties. These measures will be covered later in this chapter.

The state and federal governments have also limited offensive speech, hate speech, and sexual speech, which we will turn to now.

Offensive Speech

Arrests for swearing, especially at police officers or in the presence of police officers, were common. In the District of Columbia, for example, about ten thousand people per year were arrested for swearing (and charged with "disorderly conduct").[44] As swearing became more common in the 1960s and 1970s, and as it became a clear manifestation of the poor relations between inner-city residents and the officers who patrolled their neighborhoods, the justices decided that *swearing in many situations is protected speech* (though not on radio or television, as we'll see). They expect police, who are trained to face emotionally charged situations, to tolerate swearing.[45]

During the Vietnam War, a man on his way to observe a trial walked through the corridors of the Los Angeles County courthouse wearing a jacket with the words "Fuck the Draft" emblazoned on the back. A cop arrested him, and a judge convicted him. The Supreme Court reversed the young man's conviction, as seventy-two-year-old Justice John Harlan remarked that "one man's vulgarity is another's lyric."[46] Harlan recognized that "much linguistic expression serves a dual communicative function: it conveys not only ideas capable of relatively precise, detached explication, but otherwise inexpressible emotions as well. In fact, words are often chosen as much for their emotive as their cognitive force. . . . [The former] may often be the more important element of the overall message."

Hate Speech

Hate speech is derogatory speech—racial, ethnic, sexual, or religious slurs—usually aimed at a group rather than at an individual. When aimed at an individual, the speech impugns a characteristic the individual shares with the group. Hate speech demeans people for characteristics that are innate, such as race, ethnicity, or sexuality, or characteristics that are deeply held, such as religious faith. Such speech can cause emotional or psychological harm.

Opposition to the Vietnam War was so widespread that there were few prosecutions for seditious speech.

their race, national origin, or religion." These ordinances were an attempt to bar the demonstration, and the courts threw them out. One court quoted Justice Oliver Wendell Holmes's statement that "if there is any principle of the Constitution that more imperatively calls for attachment than any other it is the principle of free thought—not free thought for those who agree with us but freedom for the thought we hate."[49]

DEMOCRACY?

Does the outcome of this case suggest another theoretical justification for freedom of speech? Does freedom of speech make people more tolerant, because they can't silence those they disagree with? Tolerance is essential in a multiracial, multiethnic, multicultural nation like the United States. If we can tolerate the Nazis' venomous speech, we should be able to tolerate the less hateful speech of other groups.

Cross-burning by the Ku Klux Klan presents a more difficult question. In the Klan's heyday, a cross-burning was a clear threat to the black families it was directed toward, and even today it might be used this way. But in other circumstances, a cross-burning *might* be intended only as a rallying symbol to the Klan's members. The Supreme Court ruled that persons who burn a cross to intimidate or to threaten—for example, to frighten their black neighbors—can be prosecuted, but those who burn a cross at a KKK rally in a private field hidden from other people and passing cars cannot be prosecuted.[50]

Despite the First Amendment, many colleges and universities adopted hate speech codes in the 1980s and 1990s. They worried that such speech created a hostile and intimidating environment for the victims.[51] A student who was jeered nightly by taunts of "Faggot!" said, "When you are

The First Amendment prevents governments—not businesses—from restricting your speech. When Lorrie Heasley boarded a Southwest Airlines plane, she wore a T-shirt featuring President Bush, Vice President Cheney, Secretary of State Rice, and the title of the movie *Meet the Fockers*—except an expletive was substituted. The flight crew removed her from the plane. Although the government could not restrict this expression, the airline could.

Even so, it can be difficult to distinguish hate speech from other speech. What one person considers hate speech another may consider a simple observation or a valid criticism. And because of the First Amendment, *hate speech normally can't be prohibited by governments.*[47]

Lower federal courts required the Chicago suburb of Skokie to permit the American Nazi Party to demonstrate in 1978.[48] The Nazis intentionally chose Skokie as the site for their demonstration because many Jews lived there—forty thousand of the seventy thousand residents. Hundreds were survivors of German concentration camps during World War II, and thousands were relatives of people who had died in the camps. The city, in anticipation of the demonstration, passed ordinances that prohibited wearing "military-style" uniforms and distributing material that "promotes and incites hatred against persons by reason of

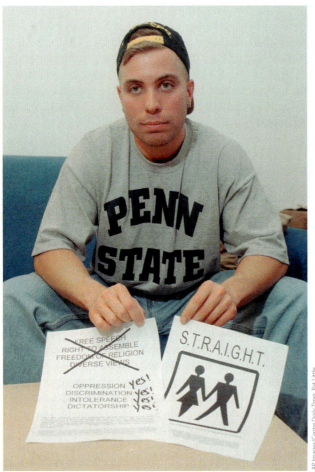

Some conservative Christian students object to school policies promoting tolerance of homosexuals. This student heads a campus group called S.T.R.A.I.G.H.T.—Students Reinforcing Adherence in General Heterosexual Tradition. The presence and activities of such groups pit the guarantee of free speech against the goal of social tolerance.

told you are not worth anything, it is difficult to function."[52] Some students were disciplined under the codes. But colleges and universities, more than other institutions in our society, have traditionally fostered free expression and debate. And the codes, which were inherently difficult to write, were often too broad or too vague. Some were struck down by lower courts, and others were abandoned by the schools. Some were rewritten to focus on harassment and threats, which can be prohibited, and to apply to computers. George Mason University forbade students from using computers "to harass, threaten, or abuse others." Virginia Tech disciplined a student for posting a message on the home page of a gay men's group calling for gays to be castrated and to "die a slow death."[53]

Some conservative Christians, funded by evangelical ministries and interest groups, have launched an attack on tolerance policies toward gays and lesbians. They demand that schools and workplaces revoke their policies, including speech codes and, in lower grades, dress codes prohibiting antigay T-shirts. A Georgia Tech student who was repri-

manded for sending a letter that berated students who came out as gay filed suit, claiming that her faith compelled her to speak out against homosexuality.[54]

These disputes highlight the fine line between harassment and free speech. So far, the Supreme Court hasn't addressed college and university speech codes or school tolerance policies.

In contrast to the United States, most western countries, including Canada, England, France, and Germany, and other countries such as India and South Africa, ban hate speech. It is a crime to provoke racial or religious hatred. French actress Brigitte Bardot, an animal rights activist, was fined $23,000 for criticizing a Muslim ceremony that entails the slaughter of sheep.

Sexual Speech

In some contexts, sexual speech—that is, language or situations that fall short of obscenity—has been prohibited. (Obscenity, whether in print or film or on radio or television, is never allowed. But its legal definition and judicial doctrine are complex and beyond the scope of this text.)

Governments can forbid nude dancing,[55] although it may be expression. Through zoning, *governments can restrict pornographic theaters or sex shops* from most (though not all) parts of their cities.[56]

The Federal Communications Commission (FCC) can forbid radio and television stations from broadcasting some sexual language and situations. A California radio station broadcast a monologue by comedian George Carlin. Titled "Filthy Words," it lampooned society's sensitivity to seven words that "you couldn't say on the public airwaves . . . the ones you definitely wouldn't say, ever." The seven words, according to the FCC report, included "a four-letter word for excrement" repeated seventy times in twelve minutes. A majority of the Court ruled that although the monologue was part of a serious program on contemporary attitudes toward language, it was not protected under the First Amendment because people, including children, tuning the radio could be subjected to the language in their homes.[57] Now the FCC forbids indecent material, except "fleeting" profanities, on radio and noncable television between 6 A.M. and 10 P.M. and fines any media that violate the ban.[58] (Large fines were levied on the *Howard Stern Show,* before it moved to satellite radio, and on a New York City radio station that broadcast a tape of a couple having sex in Saint Patrick's Cathedral.)[59] Yet the Court struck down a Utah law restricting indecent material on cable television. By subscribing to and paying for cable television, its customers are accepting exposure to its programming.[60]

In each of these areas we have covered—seditious speech, offensive speech, hate speech, and sexual speech—courts allow more freedom for individuals today because the Supreme Court broadened its interpretation of the First Amendment during the second half of the twentieth century.

We'll now examine the restrictions on the manner of speech, focusing on demonstrations and symbolic speech.

Demonstrations

Protesters want people to see or hear their demonstrations, so they seek locations where people congregate and provide an audience. Although some people won't like their message or their use of public places to disseminate the message, protesters have a right to demonstrate.

Individuals are allowed to use public places, such as streets, sidewalks, parks, theaters,[61] and the grounds around public buildings,[62] *to express their views on public issues.* These places constitute the **public forum** and serve as "the poor person's printing press."

Private property is not part of the public forum, so *individuals have no right to demonstrate on private property* without the owner's permission.[63] Shopping malls usually forbid demonstrations. During the run-up to the Iraq War, a sixty-year-old man wore a T-shirt with the slogan "Give Peace a Chance" at a mall in Albany, New York. Security guards ordered him to take off the shirt or leave the mall. When he refused, he was arrested.[64] Although his shirt was not what we think of as a demonstration, it did express his views, and the mall could forbid such expression.

Even in the public forum, individuals can't demonstrate whenever or however they want. The streets, sidewalks, parks, and theaters in the public forum are used for purposes other than demonstrations—especially for transporta-tion and recreation—so individuals can't disrupt these activities. They can't, Justice Arthur Goldberg remarked, hold "a street meeting in the middle of Times Square at the rush hour."[65]

Therefore, abortion protesters can demonstrate on public streets and public sidewalks near abortion clinics, and they can approach staffers and patients who come and go. But *protesters cannot block access* (and to ensure this, judges can order them not to come within a certain distance—for example, fifteen feet—of driveways and doorways).[66] Moreover, they cannot demonstrate at the doctor's house even if they stand on a public sidewalk. After protesters repeatedly picketed at a doctor's residence in a Milwaukee suburb, the town passed an ordinance forbidding such picketing. The Court ruled that protesters can march through residential neighborhoods but *cannot focus on particular houses,* because such picketing interferes with the privacy of the home.[67]

To ensure that potential demonstrations don't disrupt the normal activities of the places in the public forum, *governments can require groups to obtain a permit, which can specify the place, time, and manner of the demonstration. Officials can establish restrictions to avoid disruptions. However, officials cannot use these restrictions to censor speech.* They cannot allow one group to demonstrate but forbid another, no matter how much they dislike the group or its message. They cannot forbid the group even if they say they fear violence (unless the group actually threatens violence).

When young men illegally burned their draft cards to protest the Vietnam War, the Supreme Court refused to protect their action as symbolic speech.

Symbolic Speech

Some demonstrations feature **symbolic speech**, which is the use of symbols rather than words to convey ideas. Sometimes symbolic speech has been prohibited when actual speech, with the same message, would have been permitted.

During the Vietnam War, some young men burned their draft cards to protest the war and the draft. Their action was powerful expression—symbolic speech was a novelty in the 1960s—and Congress tried to stifle it by passing a law prohibiting the destruction of draft cards. The justices upheld the law and expressed their discomfort with the concept of symbolic speech.[68]

But the Court came to accept symbolic speech in the late 1960s and early 1970s.[69] To protest the war, a Massachusetts man wore a flag patch on the seat of his pants and was arrested and sentenced to six months in jail. A Washington student taped a peace symbol on a flag and then hung the flag upside down outside his apartment. The Court reversed both convictions.[70]

When a member of the Revolutionary Communist Youth Brigade burned an American flag outside the Republican convention in 1984, the justices faced the issue of *flag desecration*—the ultimate symbolic speech. A bare majority of the **Rehnquist Court** *permitted* this symbolic speech.[71] Justice William Brennan wrote that the First Amendment can't be limited just because this expression offends most people. "We do not consecrate the flag by punishing its desecration, for in doing so we dilute the freedom that this cherished emblem represents." The ruling invalidated the laws of forty-eight states and the federal government.

In a dissent, Chief Justice **William Rehnquist** emotionally criticized the decision. He said the First Amendment shouldn't apply because the flag is a unique national symbol. He recounted the history of "The Star-Spangled Banner" and the music of John Philip Sousa's "Stars and Stripes Forever," he quoted poems by Ralph Waldo Emerson and John Greenleaf Whittier that refer to the flag, and he discussed the role of the Pledge of Allegiance.

Civil liberties advocates praised the decision, but veterans' groups were outraged and many Americans were upset. President George H. W. Bush proposed a constitutional amendment to override the decision. Members of Congress, always eager to appear patriotic, lined up in support. But others, mostly Democrats, criticized the proposal for creating an unprecedented exception to the First Amendment. Eventually, instead of an amendment, Congress passed a statute prohibiting flag desecration. A majority felt that a statute, not as permanent and not a part of the Constitution, would be an acceptable compromise between the Court's doctrine and the public's anger. Yet the justices, dividing the same way, declared the new statute unconstitutional for the same reasons they reversed the prior conviction.[72] By then, the public's anger had ebbed.[73] Even so, congressional Republican leaders periodically propose an amendment to overturn the ruling as a way to rally their conservative base.

Student speech that celebrates or condones drug use can be prohibited by school administrators.

BEHIND THE SCENES
THE INTERNET AND FREE SPEECH IN CHINA

China doesn't grant free speech to its citizens, but many people have predicted that the Internet will force the regime to open up and allow more freedom. Yet American computer companies, in an effort to land lucrative business deals in the communist country, have been complicit in the government's crackdown on dissidents and censorship of speech. Cisco Systems provided the hardware China uses to monitor and censor Internet communications among its people. At the behest of the government, Google, Microsoft, and Yahoo censor Internet searches in the country. Microsoft shut down a blogger who antagonized Chinese officials. Yahoo identified two journalists who disseminated prodemocracy writings. This information led to their arrest and conviction and their sentence of ten years in prison.

Although top executives at these companies speak about the Internet's liberating power, their drive for profits may exceed their commitment to free speech and transparent government. However, the companies respond that they must follow the laws of the countries they operate in and that a censored Internet is better than no Internet.

Source: Editorial, "Yahoo Betrays Free Speech," *New York Times*, December 2, 2007, WK 9.

In 2006, they fell just one vote short in the Senate. With one vote more, the amendment would have been sent to the states for ratification.

In this chapter so far, we've focused on adult speech. Now we'll turn to student speech. Students below the college level are considered children rather than adults, so they aren't afforded full First Amendment rights.

Student Speech

During the Vietnam War, junior and senior high school students in Des Moines, Iowa, wore black armbands to protest the war. When they were suspended, their families sued school officials. The Warren Court ruled that the schools must allow the students freedom of speech, as long as the students don't disrupt the schools.[74] Public schools, Justice Abe Fortas said, "may not be enclaves of totalitarianism."

However, this case, which involved political speech, has proven to be the exception to the rule. According to the **Burger Court** and the Rehnquist Court, *administrators in public or private schools can restrict student speech for educational purposes.* They can restrict speech or clothing that is lewd or vulgar[75] or that promotes sex, drugs, or violence.

When the Olympic Torch Relay passed through Juneau, Alaska, for the 2002 Winter Games, high school students were dismissed early to watch. As the relay approached and television cameras filmed the scene, some students unfurled a banner that said, "BONG HiTS 4 JESUS." The principal was not amused and suspended the student who initiated the prank. Although the student said the phrase was "meaningless and funny, in order to get on television," the **Roberts Court**, by a 5–4 vote, upheld the suspension because the phrase might have been understood to celebrate or condone drug use.[76]

Administrators restrict hate speech as well. Conflicts over hate speech arise in public schools because many administrators and teachers believe they should encourage tolerance. Disputes over antigay speech have been especially controversial, but the Supreme Court hasn't ruled on this issue.

Administrators can also censor student publications, even serious articles that don't promote sex, drugs, or violence or contain hate speech. The Rehnquist Court allowed censorship of student newspaper articles about the impact of pregnancy and of parents' divorce on teenagers.[77]

After the ruling, a Colorado principal blocked an editorial criticizing his study hall policy while allowing another editorial praising it. A Texas principal banned an article about the class valedictorian who succeeded despite the death of her mother, the desertion of her father, and her own pregnancy. North Carolina administrators shut down a high school newspaper and fired its adviser because of three articles, including a satirical story about the "death" of the writer after eating a cheeseburger from the school cafeteria.

Some principals have tried to restrict their students from using the Internet to criticize school officials or policies. But like the underground newspapers of the 1960s and 1970s, web pages created off campus (rather than in class) can't be censored and their creators can't be disciplined by administrators, unless the pages urge illegal action or make terrorist threats. A Georgia student was arrested for suggesting that the principal be shot, his daughter kidnapped, his car keyed, and its locks clogged with Superglue. (Also see the box, "The Internet and Free Speech in China.")

Freedom of Association

Although the First Amendment does not mention *association*, the Supreme Court has interpreted the right to speak, assemble, and petition the government for a redress of grievances, all of which the amendment does list, to encompass a **freedom of association** for individuals to join with others to do these things.

This freedom implicitly entails a right not to associate as well. Therefore, groups can exclude individuals.

The right is strongest when the organization forms for "expressive association"—that is, when it speaks, assembles, and petitions the government for a redress of grievances. The right is also strong when the organization forms for "intimate association"—that is, when it is relatively personal, selective, and small, such as a social club or a country club.

Organizations formed for expressive or intimate association can exclude others. The Supreme Court allowed organizers of Boston's Saint Patrick's Day parade to exclude a group of gays, lesbians, and bisexuals.[78] Because the organizers were private individuals—the parade wasn't sponsored by the city—and because a parade is an expressive activity, the organizers didn't have to allow any views contrary to their views. The Supreme Court also allowed the Boy Scouts of America to expel an assistant scoutmaster who was openly gay.[79] The Court concluded that the Boy Scouts is an expressive organization, which espouses various values, including an opposition to homosexuality.

The right is weakest when the organization forms for "commercial association"—that is, when it is designed to enhance business interests of its members and is relatively large, unselective, and impersonal. *Organizations formed for commercial association, such as civic clubs, can't exclude others* (in states or cities that adopt nondiscrimination laws). Their right to associate can be overridden by the individual's right to be free from discrimination.[80] Therefore, the Jaycees (the Junior Chamber of Commerce), which was a business organization of young men, and the Rotary Club, which was a civic organization of men, can't discriminate against women in states that have laws forbidding sex discrimination.[81]

Freedom of the Press

Freedom of the press is measured by freedom from prior restraint and from restrictions on gathering news.

Prior Restraint

The core of **freedom of the press** is freedom from prior restraint—censorship. If the press violates laws prohibiting, for example, libelous or obscene material, it can be punished after publishing such materials. But freedom from prior restraint means the press can disseminate the information it considers appropriate and the public can see this information.

Yet freedom from prior restraint isn't absolute. During the Vietnam War, the secretary of defense in the Johnson administration, Robert McNamara, ordered a thorough study of our engagement. The study, known as the **Pentagon Papers**, laid bare the reasons the country was embroiled—

reasons not as honorable as ones the officials had fed the public—and it questioned the effectiveness of military policy. The study was so revealing that McNamara confided to a friend, "They could hang people for what's in there."[82] He classified the papers "top secret" so few persons could see them. One of the authors, Daniel Ellsberg, who was a planner in the war, originally supported the war but later turned against it. Haunted by his involvement, he photocopied the papers and passed them to the *New York Times* and *Washington Post* in the hope that their publication would sway public opinion and force the government to halt the war. (He also passed them to the television networks—ABC, CBS, and NBC—but they were afraid to use them.)[83]

The newspapers began to publish excerpts of the papers. Although the information implicated the Kennedy and Johnson administrations, the Nixon administration, which was still fighting the war, sought injunctions to restrain the newspapers from publishing more excerpts. In the *Pentagon Papers Case*, the Supreme Court refused to grant the injunctions.[84] Most justices said they would grant the injunctions if publishing the papers clearly jeopardized national security. But the information in the papers was historical; its disclosure didn't hinder the current war effort.[85] Thus *the rule—no prior restraint—remained, but some exceptions could be made.* (See box "The Road to Watergate.")

One exception occurred in 1979 when *The Progressive,* a monthly political magazine, planned to publish technical material about the design of hydrogen bombs. The article, "The H-Bomb Secret: How We Got It, Why We're Telling It," argued against secret classification of this material. Although the article wasn't a "do-it-yourself guide," it might have helped a medium-size nation develop a bomb sooner than the nation could otherwise. At the government's request, a federal judge granted an injunction prohibiting the magazine from publishing the article.[86]

The press in the United States is freer than that in Great Britain, where freedom from prior restraint began. Britain has no First Amendment and tolerates more secrecy. The government banned radio and television interviews with all members of the outlawed Irish Republican Army and its political party, including its sole representative in Parliament.[87] The French government banned the sale of a song critical of the West during the Persian Gulf War, and it blocked the broadcasting of anti-Semitic programming by an Arab channel in 2005. The German government, which has prohibited the display of the Nazi swastika since World War II, banned the sale of music by skinhead groups after neo-Nazi violence in recent years. The Austrian government imprisoned a British historian for publicizing his book denying the Holocaust. (Austria is the birthplace of Hitler.)

Restrictions on Gathering News

Although prior restraint is an obvious limitation on freedom of the press, restrictions on gathering news are less obvious but no less serious. They also keep the news from the public.

BEHIND THE SCENES

THE ROAD TO WATERGATE

When the *New York Times* and *Washington Post* began to publish excerpts of the Pentagon Papers, President Richard Nixon was furious. He hated the press, especially the Eastern press, and he feared the groups on the left who were criticizing—undermining, he believed—his Vietnam policies and his entire administration as well.

He summoned his chief of staff and his national security adviser and demanded:

I have a project I want somebody to take. . . . This takes eighteen hours a day. It takes devotion and loyalty and diligence such as you've never seen. . . . I really need a son of a bitch . . . who will work his butt off and do it dishonorably. . . . And

I'll direct him myself. I know how to play this game and we're going to start playing it. . . . I want somebody just as tough as I am for a change. . . . We're up against an enemy, a conspiracy. They're using any means. We're going to use any means.[1]

This tirade set in motion the developments that would culminate in the Watergate scandal. The president and his under-

lings initiated a series of actions challenging the rule of law. Among these actions was a directive to party operatives to break in and steal Daniel Ellsberg's records from his psychiatrist's office and then leak the records to the press in an effort to tarnish his reputation.

[1] Erwin N. Griswold, "No Harm Was Done," *New York Times*, June 30, 1991, E15.

The Burger Court *denied reporters the right to keep the names of their sources confidential.* In investigative reporting, reporters frequently rely on sources who demand anonymity in exchange for information. The sources might have sensitive positions in government or relations with criminals that would place them in jeopardy if their names were publicized. A Louisville reporter was allowed to watch persons make hashish from marijuana if he kept their names confidential. But after publication of his story, a grand jury demanded their names. When the reporter re-

The press chief of the *Washington Post* hails the Court's decision allowing publication of the Pentagon Papers.

fused to reveal them, he was cited for contempt of court, and his conviction was upheld by the Supreme Court.[88] The majority said reporters' need for confidentiality isn't as great as courts' need for information about crimes. So reporters face a difficult choice: either do not guarantee anonymity to a potential source, which means they might not obtain information for an important story; or do guarantee anonymity, which means, if the courts demand their source, they might be cited for contempt and jailed for months. Grand juries have demanded reporters' sources increasingly in recent years.[89]

Invasion of Privacy

The right to a free press can conflict with an individual's desire for privacy when the press publishes personal information. The Supreme Court has *permitted the press to publish factual information.* For example, although Georgia law prohibited the press from releasing the names of crime victims, to spare them embarrassment, an Atlanta television station announced the name of a high school girl who was raped by six classmates and left unconscious on the lawn to die. When her father sued the station, the Court said the press needs freedom to publish factual information from the public record so that citizens can scrutinize the workings of the judicial system.[90]

When a man in a crowd watching President Gerald Ford noticed a woman, close by, pull out a gun, he grabbed the gun and prevented an assassination. Reporters wrote stories about this hero, including the fact that he was a homosexual. This coverage caused him considerable embarrassment and practical problems as well, so he sued. The courts sided with the press again. The man's good deed made him newsworthy, whether he wanted to be or not.[91] Persons who become newsworthy are granted little privacy. Justice Brennan said this is a necessary evil "in a society which places a primary value on freedom of speech and of press."[92]

However, the Court has prohibited the press from sending reporters and photographers with law enforcement officers when they conduct a search or make an arrest at someone's home.[93] The Court decided that the police department's desire for good publicity and the local media's desire for interesting stories didn't justify the invasion of a defendant's or a resident's privacy.

DEMOCRACY?

Recall the assertion earlier in the chapter that freedom of speech is "the heart of our government." Some commentators claim that freedom of the press is just as important, or more important, for a democracy in modern society. Why would they claim this?

Libel

Libel consists of printed or broadcast statements that are false and that tarnish someone's reputation. Victims are entitled to sue for money to compensate them for the harm done.

Historically, the justices considered libelous material irrelevant to the exposition of ideas and search for truth envisioned by the framers of the First Amendment. The minimal benefit such material might have had was outweighed by the greater need to protect persons' reputations. For many years, the Court allowed the states to adopt libel laws as they saw fit.

However, the Warren Court recognized that state libel laws could be used to stifle legitimate political criticism; they could be used to thwart freedom of the press. The justices forced radical changes in these laws in the landmark case *New York Times* v. *Sullivan* in 1964.[94]

The *Times* ran an ad by black clergymen criticizing Montgomery, Alabama, officials for their response to racial protests. The ad contained trivial inaccuracies. Although the ad didn't name any officials, the commissioner of police claimed that it implicitly referred to him, and he sued. A local jury ordered the *Times* to pay him a half-million dollars. Meanwhile, another local jury ordered the *Times* to pay another commissioner another half-million dollars for the same ad. It was apparent that traditional libel laws could be used to wreak vengeance on a critical press—in this case, on a detested northern newspaper for its coverage of controversial civil rights protests.

The Court, ruling against the commissioner, made it more difficult for public officials to win libel suits. It held that *officials must show not only that the statements made about them were false, but also that the statements were made with "reckless disregard for the truth."* This standard gives the press some leeway to make mistakes—to print inaccurate statements—as long as the press is not careless to the point of recklessness.

This protection for the press is necessary, according to Justice Brennan, because the "central meaning of the First Amendment" is that citizens should have the right to criticize officials. This statement prompted one legal scholar to herald the decision "an occasion for dancing in the streets."[95]

In later cases, the Court *extended this ruling to public figures*—other persons who have public prominence or who thrust themselves into public controversies. These included candidates for public office[96] and activists for various causes.[97] The Court reasoned that it should be more difficult for public figures, as for public officials, to win libel suits because they also influence public policy and also are newsworthy enough to get media attention to rebut false accusations against them.[98]

In sum, the Warren Court's doctrine shifted the emphasis from protection of personal reputation to protection of press freedom.

This shift in emphasis has helped the press report the news—and helped the public learn about the government—during a time when media coverage of controversial events has angered many people. Since the 1960s, individuals and groups have sued the press not primarily to gain compensation for damage to their reputation, but to punish the press for its coverage. For example, a lawyer for a conservative organization that sued CBS for its depiction of the army general who commanded the U.S. military in Vietnam admitted that the organization sought the "dismantling" of the network through libel suits.[99]

Freedom of Religion

Some people came to America for religious liberty, but once they arrived, many didn't want to grant this liberty to others. Some communities became as intolerant as those in the Old World from which the people had fled.[100] But the colonists came with so many religious views that the diversity gradually led to grudging tolerance. By the time the Constitution and the Bill of Rights were adopted, support for religious liberty was fairly widespread.

Both the diversity and the tolerance are reflected in the two documents. Unlike the Declaration of Independence, the Constitution is a secular document, as noted in Chapter 2. It doesn't mention "God," "Creator," "Providence," or "divine."[101] It doesn't claim to be a compact between the people and God (or, like some monarchies, between the rulers and God); rather, it's a compact among the people, as the Preamble underscores—"We the people . . . ."

The Bill of Rights grants freedom of religion in the First Amendment, which states, "Congress shall make no law respecting an establishment of religion, or prohibiting the free exercise thereof." These two clauses—the establishment clause and the free exercise clause—were intended to work in tandem to provide freedom for people's religions and, by implication, freedom from others' religions.

The Founders recoiled from Europeans' experience of continuous conflict and long wars fought over religious schisms. Consequently, **Thomas Jefferson** explained, the clauses were designed to build "a wall of separation between church and state."[102] Each would stay on its own side of the wall and not interfere or even interact with the other. **Separation of church and state** was a novel idea; according to one historian, although the phrase isn't in the Constitution, it's the "most revolutionary" aspect of the Constitution.[103]

When the District of Columbia was designed, a triangular configuration popular at the time was adopted. In one corner was the Capitol building for Congress, and in another was the White House for the president. In the third corner in many other nations, a large church representing the state religion reflected the spiritual power. Due to separation of church and state, the Founders didn't want a church in that corner. (They could have put the Supreme Court there, but the Court wasn't considered important then and wouldn't get its own building until 1935.) Instead, they located the Patent Office in that corner to represent the spirit of innovation. They anticipated many inventions.[104] (Now the building houses the National Portrait Gallery and the Museum of American Art.)

Today some deeply religious people scorn the idea of separation of church and state. They think it devalues the importance of religion. But the Founders saw it as a means to preserve the peace that had eluded European states. In addition, they saw it as a way to protect religion itself. Without interference by government officials, whether to hinder or to help, churches would be free to determine their dogma and establish their practices as they saw fit. They would be free to flourish. Indeed, religion is stronger in the United States than in western Europe, where the churches endorsed and supported by the government sit mostly empty and most people are not believers. Some scholars think that religion is stronger in the United States *because of* separation of church and state.[105]

Despite the Founders' intention to separate church and state, as society became more complex and government became more pervasive, church and state came to interact, sometimes to interfere, with each other. Inevitably, the wall began to crumble, and the courts had to devise new doctrine to keep church and state as separate as possible while still accommodating the needs of each as we'll see.

Free Exercise of Religion

The **free exercise clause** allows individuals to practice their religion without government coercion.

Amish children head for the cornfields to avoid school officials in Iowa.

© Tom Defoe, 1965, Des Moines Register and Tribune Co.

Direct Restrictions

Government has occasionally restricted free exercise of religion directly. Early in the country's history, some states prohibited Catholics or Jews from voting or holding office, and as late as 1961, Maryland prohibited nonbelievers from holding office.[106] In the 1920s, Oregon prohibited students from attending parochial schools.[107] More recently, prisons in Illinois and Texas prohibited Black Muslims and Buddhists from receiving religious publications and using prison chapels.[108] The Supreme Court *invalidated each of these restrictions.*

A suburb of Miami tried to ban the Santeria religion in 1987. Santeria blends ancient African rites and Roman Catholic rituals, but its distinguishing feature is animal sacrifice. Adherents believe that animal sacrifice is necessary to win the favor of the gods, and they practice it at initiations of new members and at births, marriages, and deaths. They kill chickens, ducks, doves, pigeons, sheep, goats, and turtles. When adherents, who had practiced their religion underground since refugees from Cuba brought it to Florida in the 1950s and 1960s, announced plans to construct a church building, cultural center, museum, and school, the city passed ordinances against ritualistic animal sacrifice, essentially forbidding adherents from practicing their religion. The Court struck down the ordinances.[109] "Although the practice of animal sacrifice may seem abhorrent to some," Justice Anthony Kennedy wrote, "religious beliefs need not be acceptable, logical, consistent, or comprehensible to others in order to merit First Amendment protection."

Indirect Restrictions

Government has also restricted free exercise of religion indirectly. As society has become more complex, some laws have interfered with religion, even when not designed to do so. The laws have usually interfered with minority religions, which don't have many members who serve as legislators and look out for their interests.

At first the Court distinguished between belief and action: individuals could believe what they wanted, but they could not act accordingly if such action was against the law. In 1878, male Mormons who believed their religion required polygamy could not marry more than one woman.[110] The Court rhetorically asked, "Suppose one believed that human sacrifices were a necessary part of religious worship?" Of course, belief without action gave little protection and scant satisfaction to the individuals involved.

In the 1960s, the Warren Court recognized this problem and broadened the protection by *granting exemptions to laws.* A Seventh-Day Adventist who worked in a textile mill in South Carolina quit when the mill shifted from a five-day to a six-day workweek that included Saturday—her Sabbath. Unable to find another job, she applied for unemployment benefits, but the state refused to provide them. To receive them, she had to be "available" for work, but the state said she wasn't available because she wouldn't accept any jobs that required Saturday work. The Court ordered the state to grant an exemption to its law.[111] The Burger Court, which followed the Warren Court's doctrine, ruled that employers need to make a reasonable effort to accommodate employees' requests to fit work schedules around their Sabbath.[112]

Congress, too, has granted some exemptions. It excused the Amish from participating in the Social Security program because the Amish support their own elderly. And in every draft law, it excused conscientious objectors from participating in war.

The Court has been most reluctant to exempt individuals from paying taxes. It didn't excuse either the Amish[113] or the Quakers, who as pacifists tried to withhold the portion of their income taxes that funded the military.[114] The Court worried that many other persons would try to avoid paying taxes, too.

The Rehnquist Court, which was less sensitive to minority rights, *refused to grant such exemptions.*[115] The Native American church uses peyote, a hallucinogen derived from a cactus, in worship ceremonies. Church members believe that the plant embodies their deity and that ingesting the plant is an act of communion. Although peyote is a controlled substance, Congress has authorized its use on

Alfred Smith, fired for using peyote in religious ceremonies, challenged Oregon's law prohibiting use of the drug.

Indian reservations, and many states have authorized its use off the reservations by church members. But when two members in Oregon, a state that didn't allow its use off the reservations, were fired from their jobs and denied unemployment benefits for using the drug, the Court refused to grant an exemption.[116] A five-justice majority rejected the doctrine and precedents of the Warren and Burger Courts. Justice Antonin Scalia, a Catholic, admitted that denying such exemptions will put minority religions at a disadvantage but insisted that this is an "unavoidable consequence of democratic government."

DEMOCRACY?

Compare the implications for democracy of (a) the Warren and Burger Courts' doctrine granting exemptions to religious minorities with (b) the Rehnquist Court's doctrine denying exemptions to these groups. Is one more democratic? Or do they emphasize different facets of democracy? Assume that the Rehnquist Court's doctrine is extended to other provisions of the Bill of Rights. What would be the consequences?

As a result of the decision, some adherents of minority religions weren't allowed to practice the tenets of their religions. Families of deceased Jews and Laotians, whose religions reject autopsies, were overruled. Muslim prisoners, whose religion forbids them to eat pork, were denied other meat as a substitute. Sikh construction workers, whose religion requires them to wear turbans, had been exempted from the law mandating hard hats at construction sites; after the decision, this exemption was rescinded.[117]

Even mainstream churches worried about the ruling's implications, and a coalition of religious groups lobbied Congress to overturn it. Congress passed an act reversing the ruling and substituting the previous doctrine from the Warren and Burger Courts. But the Rehnquist Court invalidated the act because it challenged the justices' authority and altered their interpretation of the First Amendment without going through the process required to amend the Constitution.[118]

Establishment of Religion

Two competing traditions reflecting the role of government toward religion have led to intense conflict over the **establishment clause**. Many settlers were Christians who wanted the governments to reinforce their religion, yet the framers of the Constitution were products of the Enlightenment, which emphasized the importance of reason and deemphasized the role of religion. Many Founders, including the most important ones, were Deists rather than Christians. They believed in a Supreme Being but rejected much religious dogma, as explained in Chapter 2.

The two considered most responsible for the religious guarantees in the First Amendment, Thomas Jefferson and

The country's religious diversity has led to demands for some exotic exemptions. Inspired by the Bible's statement that Jesus's followers "shall take up serpents" and "if they drink any deadly thing, it shall not hurt them," members of the Holiness Church of God in Jesus's Name handle snakes and drink strychnine. Some become enraptured and entranced to the point of hysteria, and occasionally some die. The Tennessee Supreme Court forbade such practices, saying that the state has "the right to guard against the unnecessary creation of widows and orphans." However, these practices continue in some places.

James Madison, especially feared the divisiveness of religion. They wanted separation of church and state, advocating not only freedom *of* religion for believers but freedom *from* religion for others.[119]

Even some religious groups wanted separation of church and state. The Baptists and the evangelicals had been harassed and persecuted by the Anglicans (Episcopalians) and Congregationalists, and they feared that these larger groups would use the power of the state to promote their views and practices.[120]

The Supreme Court initially reflected the first of these traditions. In 1892, Justice David Brewer proclaimed that "this is a Christian nation."[121] But as the country became more pluralistic, the Court moved toward the second of these traditions. Since the 1960s, the Court has *generally interpreted the establishment clause to forbid government not only from designating an official church,* like the Church of England, which receives tax money and special privileges, *but also from aiding one religion over another or even from aiding religion over nonreligion.*

School Prayers

Courts have used the establishment clause to resolve disputes about public school prayers. In 1962 and 1963, the Warren Court initiated its prayer rulings. At the start of each day, New York had students recite a nondenominational prayer, and Pennsylvania and Baltimore had students recite the Lord's Prayer or Bible verses. The Court, with only one justice dissenting, ruled that *these practices violated the establishment clause*.[122] Although the prayers officially were voluntary—students could leave the room—the Court doubted that the prayers really were voluntary. The justices noted that nonconforming students would face tremendous pressure from teachers and peers. The Court therefore concluded that the prayers fostered religion. According to Justice Black, "Government in this country should stay out of the business of writing and sanctioning official prayers and leave that purely religious function to the people themselves and to those the people . . . look to for religious guidance." Although schools could teach religion as a subject, they could not promote religion. For similar reasons, the Court ruled that Kentucky *could not require public schools to post the Ten Commandments* in classrooms.[123]

Many people sharply criticized the rulings. A representative from Alabama lamented, "They put the Negroes in the schools, and now they've driven God out."[124] Yet students, of course, can still pray on their own at any time.

Empirical studies in the years after the rulings found that prayers and Bible readings decreased but by no means disappeared, especially in the South.[125] A Tennessee school official asserted, "I am of the opinion that 99 percent of the people in the United States feel as I do about the Supreme Court's decision—that it was an outrage . . . . The remaining 1 percent do not belong in this free world."[126]

News reports in recent years indicate that some schools, especially in the rural South, still use prayers or Bible readings in violation of the Court's rulings. These practices are reinforced by social pressure. A woman whose family had moved to Pontotoc, Mississippi, discovered that Christian prayers were being broadcast on the intercom and the Bible was being taught in a class. When she objected, rumors circulated that she was an outside agitator paid by the ACLU to force the town to change. One of her children had a teacher who told the class that the child didn't believe in God, while another of her children kept "getting jumped" in the bathroom. Then the woman lost her job in a convenience store after customers threatened to boycott the store.[127] News reports also indicate that officials in Kentucky and Ohio allowed volunteers to put the Ten Commandments inside or outside public schools in violation of the Court's ruling.[128]

Although many people wanted a constitutional amendment to allow official prayers in public schools, Congress never passed one. Some people supported the rulings. Other people, who supported the Court, didn't want to challenge its authority and set a precedent for other groups on other matters. Some religious leaders doubted that the religious groups would ever agree on specific prayers. America's religious diversity means that any prayers would offend some students or parents. Prayers that suit Christians might offend Jews; those that suit Jews might offend adherents of other faiths. Recent immigrants from Asia and the Middle East, practicing Buddhism, Shintoism, Taoism, and Islam, have made the country even more pluralistic. Now, according to one researcher, America's religious diversity is greater than that of any country in recorded history.[129] Asking the students in this country to say a prayer would be like "asking the members of the United Nations to stand and sing the national anthem of one country."[130]

However, many small communities don't reflect this nationwide diversity, and their residents often assume that everyone, or at least "normal" people, share their views toward religion.

In lieu of an amendment, about half of the states have passed laws providing for a "moment of silence" to begin each school day. A majority of justices indicated that they *would approve a moment of silence if students were not urged to pray*.[131]

Muslim students in Dearborn, Michigan, reflect our religious pluralism. The Detroit area has the second-largest concentration of Arabs outside the Middle East.

The Rehnquist Court reaffirmed and extended the prayer rulings of the Warren Court. It held that *clergy can't offer prayers at graduation ceremonies* for public elementary, middle, and high schools.[132] The prayers in question were brief and nonsectarian, but the majority concluded, "What to most believers may seem nothing more than a reasonable request that the nonbeliever respect their religious practices, in a school context may appear to the nonbeliever or dissenter to be an attempt to employ the machinery of the state to enforce a religious orthodoxy." Although attendance at the ceremony was voluntary, like participation in school prayers, the majority didn't consider it truly voluntary. Justice Kennedy wrote, "Everyone knows that in our society and in our culture high school graduation is one of life's most significant occasions. . . . Graduation is a time for family and those closest to the student to celebrate success and express mutual wishes of gratitude and respect."

Although the Court's language here was emphatic, its stance on student-led prayers has been ambiguous. In 1992, the Court refused to review a federal court of appeals ruling that allowed student-led prayers at graduation ceremonies.[133] A Texas school board permitted the senior class to decide whether to have a prayer and, if so, which student to give it. The appellate court held that this policy wasn't precluded by the Supreme Court's ruling because the decision wasn't made by officials and the prayer wasn't offered by a clergy member, so official coercion wasn't present. But in 1996, the Court also refused to review a federal court of appeals ruling from a different circuit that prohibited student-led prayers.[134] The Court's reluctance to resolve this controversy means that the ruling of each court of appeals remains but applies only to the schools in its circuit.

The first appellate court's holding encouraged opponents of the Supreme Court's rulings to use the same approach to circumvent these rulings as well. Several southern states passed laws allowing student-led prayers to start each school day. Some school officials, who selected the students, let them give the prayers over the intercom. Federal courts in Alabama and Mississippi invalidated these laws because school officials were involved and because all students were required or at least pressured to listen to the prayers.

The Rehnquist Court did invalidate the use of schools' public address systems by clergy or students to give prayers at high school football games.[135] Although student attendance is voluntary, the games are official school events.

The public desire for official school prayers is fueled by nostalgia for the less troubling times before the 1960s. As one writer perceived, the desire "doesn't have much to do with prayer anyway, but with a time, a place, an ethos that praying and pledging allegiance at the beginning of school each day represent."[136] For some people, buffeted by the upheavals and dislocations of our times, the reinstitutionalization of school prayers would symbolize that our society still stands for appropriate values.

The public desire for official school prayers is also fueled by occasional reports of school officials who mistakenly believe that court rulings require them to forbid all forms of religious expression. Some confused administrators have prohibited a few students from wearing religious jewelry, reading the Bible while riding the bus, and praying before eating their lunch.[137]

In another case, the Supreme Court held that the University of Missouri at Kansas City had to make its meeting rooms available to students' religious organizations on an equal basis with other organizations, even if the religious organizations use the rooms for prayer or worship.[138] Otherwise, the university would be discriminating against religion.

After this decision, Congress passed a law that *requires public high schools as well as colleges and universities to allow meetings of students' religious, philosophical, or political groups outside class hours.* The Court accepted this law in 1990.[139] Justice Sandra Day O'Connor said that high school students "are likely to understand that a school does not endorse or support student speech that it merely permits on a nondiscriminatory basis." Students have established Bible clubs in one-quarter of public high schools, according to one estimate.[140] (As a result of this act, students have also established gay-straight clubs—organizations of gay and straight students who support the rights of gays, lesbians, and bisexuals—in more than seven hundred high schools.)[141] The Rehnquist Court also held that the University of Virginia had to provide funding, from students' fees, to students' religious organizations on an equal basis with other campus organizations, even if a religious organization sought the money to print a religious newspaper.[142] Following this precedent, a federal court of appeals ruled that the University of South Alabama had to provide funding to a gay organization.

Religious Symbols

Despite its prayer rulings, the Court has been *reluctant to invalidate traditional religious symbols.* It has not questioned the motto "In God We Trust," on our coins since 1865 and paper money since 1955, or the phrase "one nation under God," in the Pledge of Allegiance since 1954.[143]

In 2002, a federal court of appeals held the phrase "under God" in the Pledge unconstitutional when recited in the public schools. The court said it promotes religion as much as if it professed that we are a nation "under Jesus" or "under Vishnu" or "under Zeus" or "under no god." It promotes Christianity and leaves out not only atheists and agnostics but believers of other deities, such as Buddhists and many Native Americans. Although the ruling was a logical extension of the prayer rulings, it was a lightning rod for the public's anger, and the Supreme Court sidestepped the issue (deciding that the student's father, an atheist, lacked authority to bring suit on the student's behalf because the student's mother, a born-again Christian, had custody of the child after their divorce).[144]

The Burger Court upheld the display of a nativity scene on government property, at least when it is part of a broader display for the holiday season.[145] Pawtucket, Rhode Island, had a crèche, Christmas tree, Santa Claus, sleigh with reindeer, and talking wishing well. The Court said that Christmas had become a secular as well as a religious holiday and that the secular decorations diluted any religious impact the nativity scene would have. A crèche by itself, however, would be impermissible.[146]

The chief justice of Alabama's supreme court had a granite marker bearing the Ten Commandments installed in Alabama's Judicial Building in the middle of the night. Lower federal courts ruled this display, which stood by itself, a violation of the establishment clause. When the chief justice defied a federal court order to remove the 5300-pound marker, he was suspended by his own court.

The Rehnquist Court addressed Ten Commandments displays and ruled much like the Burger Court did for Christmas nativity scenes. A Ten Commandments monument on the Texas capitol grounds could remain because it was just one of sixteen other monuments and twenty-one historical markers, which were secular, and because it had been there for forty years.[147] But copies of the Ten Commandments in two Kentucky courthouses could not remain because they were not part of historical displays[148] and they were posted recently for religious purposes.[149]

Evolution

Courts have also used the establishment clause to resolve disputes about teaching evolution in schools. In 1968, the Supreme Court invalidated Arkansas' forty-year-old law forbidding schools from teaching evolution.[150] Arkansas and Louisiana then passed laws requiring schools that teach evolution to also teach "creationism"—the biblical version of creation.[151] In 1987, the Court *invalidated these laws because their purpose was to advance the fundamentalist Christian view.*[152]

Evolution remains controversial. In 2005, at least twenty states considered antievolution proposals. A suburban Atlanta school district pasted disclaimers onto ninth-grade biology textbooks stating "Evolution is a theory, not a fact" and it should be "critically considered." A federal court ordered the disclaimers removed because their denigration of evolution reflected a religious view.

Critics of evolution also promoted "intelligent design"—the notion that some life is so complex that it must have been designed by an intelligent creator rather than have evolved through random chance, as the theory of evolution posits.[153] In 2005, the Dover, Pennsylvania, school district required teachers to discuss intelligent design. A federal court invalidated the policy because intelligent design isn't a science. Its proponents invoke a supernatural designer—that is, God[154]—whereas science deals with natural phe-

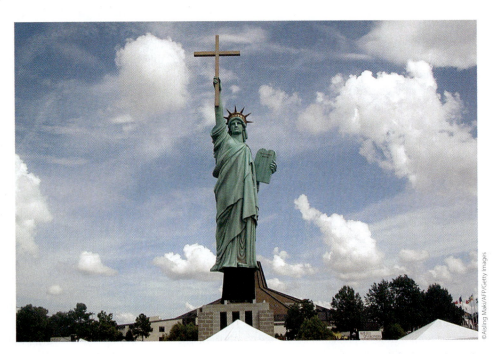

A megachurch with 12,000 members in Memphis, Tennessee, unveiled its "Statue of Liberation Through Christ" in 2006. In contrast to the Statue of Liberty, this monument holds a cross rather than a torch and, with the other arm, the Ten Commandments. She also has a tear running down her cheek because of modern secularism, legal abortions, and the absence of school prayers. According to the pastor, the purpose of the monument is to let people know that "God is in the foundation of our nation." Hence the merger of church and state.

nomena. Although intelligent design proponents make scientific critiques of evolution, intelligent design itself isn't based on empirical evidence and doesn't offer testable hypotheses.

Other Policies

Conservative Christians have pushed Republican officials to adopt policies and programs reflecting their beliefs. Despite the establishment clause, the Bush administration limited scientific research with stem cells, withheld federal money from family planning organizations and programs in the United States and abroad, gave federal money to abstinence education programs, and gave federal money to hundreds of church-run marriage, child care, and drug treatment programs. As a result, for example, the government gave federal money to Louisiana, which funneled it to Protestant groups to teach abstinence through Bible lessons and to Catholic groups to hold prayer sessions at abortion clinics.[155] So far, the courts haven't ruled that these policies and programs violate the establishment clause.

Despite ever-present tensions and very frequent conflicts, the effort to separate church and state has enabled the United States to manage, even nourish, its religious pluralism. The effort has kept potential religious fights out of the political arena. But today this practical arrangement is opposed by those religious conservatives who most fear the changes in modern society. They consider their religion a shield protecting their family against these changes, and they want the authority of the government to reinforce their religion. In one of her last opinions, Justice O'Connor, a moderate conservative, addressed these religious conservatives: "At a time when we see around the world the violent consequences of the assumption of religious authority by the government, Americans may count themselves fortunate.... [Those] who would renegotiate the boundaries between church and state must therefore answer a difficult question: Why would we trade a system that has served us so well for one that has served others so poorly?"[156]

Rights of Criminal Defendants

The Fourth, Fifth, Sixth, and Eighth Amendments provide numerous **due process** rights for criminal defendants. When the government prosecutes defendants, it must give them the process—that is, the procedures—they are due; it must be fair and "respect certain decencies of civilized conduct,"[157] even toward uncivilized people.

One defense attorney said that many of his clients "had been monsters—nothing less—who had done monstrous things. Although occasionally not guilty of the crime charged, nearly all my clients have been guilty of something."[158] Then why do we give them rights? We give criminal defendants rights because we give all individuals

rights in court. As Justice Douglas observed, "respecting the dignity even of the least worthy . . . citizen raises the stature of all of us."[159]

But why do we give all individuals rights in court? We do so because we have established the **presumption of innocence**. This presumption is "not . . . a naive belief that most or even many defendants are innocent, or a cavalier attitude toward crime." It reflects a mistrust of the state, as it recognizes the possibility of an overzealous prosecutor or an unfair judge. It requires the state to prove the defendant's guilt, essentially saying, "We won't take your word for it."[160] Of course, when the crime rate is high or a particular crime is heinous, many people fear the state less than the criminals. Then they want to give officials more authority and defendants fewer rights. But this is the way all people eventually lose their rights.

Search and Seizure

England fostered the notion that a family's home is its castle, but Parliament made exceptions for the American colonies. It authorized writs of assistance, which allowed customs officials to conduct general searches for goods imported by the colonists without paying taxes to the crown. The English tradition of home privacy combined with the colonists' resentment of these writs led to adoption of the Fourth Amendment, which forbids **unreasonable searches and seizures**.

In these cases, the Supreme Court has tried to walk a fine line between acknowledging officials' need for evidence and individuals' desire for privacy. This judicial doctrine is so complex that we will note just its basic principles here.

One type of seizure is the arrest of a person. *Police must have evidence to believe that a person committed a crime.*

Another type of seizure is the confiscation of illegal contraband. *The general requirement is that police must get a search warrant from a judge by showing evidence that a particular thing is in a particular place.*

However, *the Court has made numerous exceptions to this requirement* that complicate the law. These exceptions account for most searches. If persons consent to a search, police can conduct a search without a warrant. If police see contraband in plain view, they can seize it; they don't have to close their eyes to it. If police have evidence to arrest someone, they can search the person and the area within the person's control. If police have reason to suspect that someone is committing a crime but lack evidence to arrest the person, they can "stop and frisk" the person—conduct a pat-down search. If police have reason to believe that a person's life is in jeopardy, they can search for weapons. In some situations, if police want to search a motor vehicle, they can do so because vehicles are mobile and could be gone by the time police get a warrant.

WHEN A COURT REVERSES A CONVICTION . . .

... the defendant does not necessarily go free. An appellate court only evaluates the legality of the procedures used by officials; it does not determine guilt or innocence. Therefore, when it reverses a conviction, it only indicates that officials used some illegal procedure in convicting the defendant—for example, evidence from an improper search and seizure. Then the prosecutor can retry the defendant, without this evidence, if the prosecutor thinks there is enough other evidence. Often prosecutors do retry the defendants, and frequently judges or juries reconvict them.

Customs and border patrol officials can search persons and things coming into the country to enforce customs and immigration laws. Airport guards can search passengers and luggage to prevent hijackings and terrorism. And prison guards can search prisoners to ensure security. (See the box "When a Court Reverses a Conviction. . . .")

Exclusionary Rule

To enforce search and seizure law, the Supreme Court has *established the* **exclusionary rule***, which bars from the courts any evidence obtained in violation of the Fourth Amendment.* The purpose is to deter illegal conduct by police officers.

Although the Court created this rule for federal courts in 1914,[161] it didn't impose the rule on state courts until 1961 in *Mapp* v. *Ohio.*[162] Until this time, police in many states had ignored search and seizure law. *Mapp* was one of the Warren Court's most controversial rulings. Many people didn't think that evidence of guilt should be barred from court, even if search and seizure law had been violated by police.

The decision still hasn't been widely accepted. The Burger Court created an exception to it. In a pair of cases, the justices allowed evidence obtained illegally to be used in court because the police had acted "in good faith."[163] The Roberts Court has also created an exception to it.[164]

Electronic Surveillance

The Fourth Amendment traditionally applied to searches involving a physical trespass and seizures producing a tangible object. Electronic surveillance, however, does not require a physical trespass or involve a tangible object.

This posed a problem for the Supreme Court when it heard its first wiretapping case in 1928. Federal prohibition agents tapped a bootlegger's telephone by installing equipment on wires in the basement of the bootlegger's apartment building. The Court's majority rigidly adhered to its traditional doctrine, saying that this was not a search and seizure, so the agents did not need a warrant.[165]

In a classic example of keeping the Constitution up-to-date with the times, the Warren Court overruled this precedent in 1967.[166] Because electronic eavesdropping might threaten privacy as much as traditional searching, *officials must get judicial authorization,* similar to a warrant, *to engage in such eavesdropping.*

Self-Incrimination

The Fifth Amendment stipulates that persons shall not be compelled to be witnesses against themselves—that is, to incriminate themselves. Because defendants are presumed innocent, the government must prove their guilt.

This right means that *defendants on trial don't have to take the witness stand and answer the prosecutor's questions,* and neither the prosecutor nor the judge can call attention to their decision to exercise this right. Neither can suggest or imply that the defendants must have something to hide and must therefore be guilty. (But if the defendants do take the stand, they thereby waive their right, so the prosecutor can cross-examine them and they must answer.)

This right also means that *prosecutors can't introduce into evidence statements or confessions from defendants that weren't voluntary.* The meaning of *voluntary* has evolved over time.

For years, police used physical brutality—"the third degree"—to get confessions. After 1936, when the Supreme Court ruled that confessions obtained in this manner were invalid,[167] police used psychological techniques. They held suspects incommunicado, preventing them from contacting relatives or lawyers and delaying them from going to court, to pressure them to confess.[168] They interrogated suspects for long periods of time without food or rest, in one case with alternating teams of interrogators for thirty-six hours straight,[169] to wear them down and break their will. The Court ruled that confessions obtained by these techniques were also invalid.

The Warren Court still worried that many confessions weren't truly voluntary, so it issued a landmark decision in 1966. Arizona police arrested a poor, mentally disturbed

Ernesto Miranda

man, Ernesto Miranda, for kidnapping and raping a woman. After the woman identified him in a lineup, police interrogated him, prompting him to confess. He hadn't been told that he could remain silent or be represented by an attorney. In *Miranda* v. *Arizona,* the Court concluded that his confession wasn't truly voluntary.[170] Chief Justice Warren, as a former district attorney, knew the advantage that police officers have in an interrogation and thought the suspects needed more protection. The Court ruled that *officials must advise suspects of their rights before their interrogation.* These came to be known as the **Miranda rights**:

You have the right to remain silent.
If you talk, anything you say can be used against you.
You have the right to be represented by an attorney.
If you can't afford an attorney, one will be appointed for you.

The Burger and Rehnquist Courts didn't require police and prosecutors to follow *Miranda* as strictly as the Warren Court did but, contrary to expectations, didn't abandon it. In 2000, the Rehnquist Court reaffirmed *Miranda* by a 7–2 vote.[171]

Even with the warnings, most suspects talk anyway. Some don't understand the warnings. Others think the police, who may rattle off the warnings very fast or in a monotone, give them as a formality but wouldn't follow them. Also, suspects being interrogated face a coercive atmosphere and law enforcement tactics designed to exploit their weaknesses. Detectives are trained to persuade suspects to talk despite the warnings. One said, "Before you ever get in there, the first thing an investigator usually thinks about is . . . how can I breeze through this *Miranda* thing so I don't set the guy off and tell him not to talk to me, song and dance it, sugarcoat it, whatever."[172] So detectives frequently lie and trick suspects.

Counsel

The Sixth Amendment provides the **right to counsel** in criminal cases. Initially, it meant that defendants could hire an attorney to help them prepare a defense, and later it meant that defendants could also have the attorney represent them at the trial. But it was no help to most defendants because they were too poor to hire an attorney for either. Consequently, the Supreme Court required federal trial courts to furnish an attorney to all indigent defendants in 1938.[173] But most criminal cases are state cases, and the Court was reluctant to require state trial courts also to furnish an attorney.[174]

However, the Warren Court was willing to do so in 1963. It heard the case of Clarence Earl Gideon, who was charged with breaking into a pool hall and stealing beer, wine, and change from a vending machine. At trial, Gideon asked the judge for a lawyer. The judge wouldn't appoint one, leaving Gideon to defend himself. The prosecutor didn't have a strong case, but Gideon wasn't able to point out its weaknesses. He was convicted and sentenced to five years. On appeal, the Warren Court unanimously declared that Gideon was entitled to be represented by counsel.[175] Justice Black explained that "lawyers in criminal courts are necessities, not luxuries." The Court finally established a broad rule: state courts must provide an attorney to indigent defendants in felony cases.

When he was tried again, Gideon was given a lawyer, who proved the Court's point. The lawyer did an effective job defending him, which Gideon hadn't been able to do himself. Gideon wasn't convicted this time.

The Burger and Rehnquist Courts expanded the rule: state courts must provide an attorney to indigent defendants in misdemeanor cases, too, except those that result in no incarceration (or probation),[176] because misdemeanor cases as well as felony cases are too complex for the defendants to defend themselves. Thus *all courts must offer an attorney to indigent defendants in all cases except the most minor ones, such as traffic violations.* The Supreme Court also decided that in addition to an attorney for the trial, *the courts must provide an attorney for one appeal.*[177]

Receiving counsel doesn't necessarily mean receiving effective counsel, however. Some assigned attorneys are inexperienced, some are incompetent, and most are overworked and have little time to prepare the best possible defense.

Some jurisdictions make little effort to provide effective counsel, even in murder cases where capital punishment looms. In Illinois, at least thirty-three convicts on death row had been represented at trial by attorneys who were later disbarred or suspended.[178] In Louisiana, a defendant was represented by an attorney who was living with the prosecutor in the case. In Florida, a defendant was represented by a part-time attorney who was a deputy sheriff. In Georgia, a black defendant was represented by a white attorney who

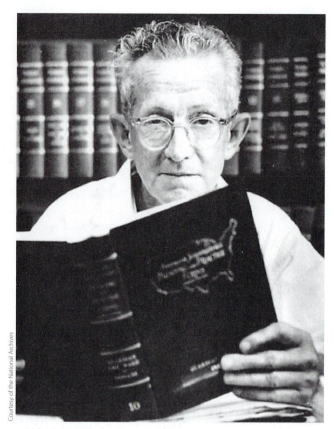

Courtesy of the National Archives

National Archives #01073

Clarence Earl Gideon, convinced that he was denied a fair trial because he was not given an attorney, read law books in prison so he could petition the Supreme Court for a writ of *certiorari*. He wrote his petition by hand. Although he had spent much of his life in prison, he was optimistic. "I believe that each era finds an improvement in law [and] each year brings something new for the benefit of mankind. Maybe this will be one of those small steps forward."

had been the Imperial Wizard of the local Ku Klux Klan for fifty years.[179] Also in Georgia, an attorney was so unversed in criminal law that when he was asked to name criminal rulings he was familiar with, he could think of only one (*Miranda*).[180] In three murder cases in one recent year in Texas, defense attorneys slept through the trials. When one of these defendants appealed his conviction on the ground that he didn't receive his constitutional right to counsel, the appellate court announced that "the Constitution doesn't say the lawyer has to be awake."[181] (Stung by criticism, the appellate court sat *en banc*—that is, the entire court, rather than a three-judge panel, reheard the case—and overruled itself.) At least these attorneys were present. In Alabama, a defendant was represented by an attorney who failed to appear when his case was argued before the state supreme court. The defendant lost and was executed.[182]

In recent years, the issue of legal counsel for the defendants subject to capital punishment has received more scrutiny because new investigations and technologies, involving DNA analysis, have demonstrated that dozens of inmates on death row didn't commit the murder they were convicted of and sentenced for. Nonetheless, there is little effort to provide effective counsel for criminal defendants because few groups, other than lawyers' associations, urge adequate representation. Criminal defendants have no po-

litical power in our system, and the public has limited sympathy for their rights.[183]

Jury Trial

The Sixth Amendment also provides the **right to a jury trial** in "serious" criminal cases. The Supreme Court has defined "serious" cases as those that could result in more than six months' incarceration.[184]

The right was adopted to prevent oppression by a "corrupt or overzealous prosecutor" or a "biased . . . or eccentric judge."[185] It has also served to limit governmental use of unpopular laws or enforcement practices. Regardless of the evidence against a defendant, a jury can refuse to convict if it feels that the government overstepped its bounds.

The jury is supposed to be impartial, so persons who have made up their minds before trial should be dismissed. It is also supposed to be "a fair cross section" of the community, so no group should be systematically excluded.[186] But the jury need not be a perfect cross section and in fact need not have a single member of a particular group.[187] Most courts use voter registration lists to obtain the names of potential jurors. These lists aren't closely representative because poor people don't register at the same rate as others, but the courts have decided that the lists are sufficiently representative. And the "motor voter law," which requires drivers' license and welfare offices to offer voter registration forms, has prompted more people to register to vote and thus to make themselves available to serve on juries.

Cruel and Unusual Punishment

The Eighth Amendment forbids **cruel and unusual punishment** but doesn't define such punishment. The Supreme Court had interpreted the phrase to prohibit torture or punishment grossly disproportionate to the offense. The death penalty was used at the time the amendment was adopted, so for many years it was assumed to be constitutional.[188]

But in 1972 the Burger Court narrowly ruled that *the death penalty, as it was then being administered, was cruel and unusual punishment*.[189] The laws and procedures allowed too much discretion by those who administered the punishment and resulted in too much arbitrariness and discrimination for those who received it. The death penalty was imposed so seldom, according to Justice Potter Stewart, that it was "cruel and unusual in the same way that being struck by lightning is cruel and unusual." Yet when it was imposed, it was imposed on black defendants more often than on white defendants.

The decision invalidated the laws of forty states and commuted the death sentences of 629 inmates. But because the Court didn't hold capital punishment cruel and unusual in principle, about three-fourths of the states adopted revised laws that permitted less discretion in an attempt to achieve less arbitrariness and discrimination.

These changes satisfied a majority of the Burger Court, which ruled that *capital punishment isn't cruel and unusual for murder if administered fairly*.[190] But it can't be imposed automatically for everyone convicted of murder, because the judge or jury must consider any mitigating factors that would justify a lesser punishment.[191] Also, it can't be imposed for rape, as some states legislated, because it's disproportionate to that offense.[192]

The revised laws have reduced but not eliminated discrimination. Where past studies showed discrimination against black defendants, recent studies show discrimination against black or white defendants who murder white victims. People who affect the decision to impose the death penalty—prosecutors, defense attorneys, judges, and jurors—appear to value white lives more. Despite evidence from Georgia that those who killed whites were more than four times as likely to be given the death penalty as those who killed blacks, the Rehnquist Court, by a 5–4 vote, upheld capital punishment in the state.[193]

The revised laws have not addressed an equally serious problem—inadequate representation given to poor defendants who face the death penalty—which we discussed in conjunction with the right to counsel.

For years, most people dismissed any suggestions that innocent defendants might be put to death. They assumed that the criminal justice system used careful procedures and made no mistakes in these cases at least. However, since capital punishment was reinstated and stricter procedures were mandated in the 1970s, at least 124 inmates awaiting execution have been released because new evidence, including DNA tests, revealed their innocence.[194] This number represents one exoneration for every seven to eight executions—a disturbing frequency for the ultimate punishment.[195] Some defendants were the victims of sloppy or biased police or overzealous prosecutors; some were the victims of mistaken witnesses; others were the victims of emotional or prejudiced jurors. Many were the victims of inadequate representation.

Due to the patterns of racial discrimination and inadequate representation, the American Bar Association and some state governors have called for a moratorium on the use of capital punishment. Although a majority of the public still supports capital punishment, that support is declining as more inmates are being found innocent.[196] Juries are becoming more reluctant to impose it, instead opting for life in prison.[197]

Even the Rehnquist Court, long a staunch supporter of the death penalty, reflected the public's mood. In 2002, it ruled that states can't execute the mentally retarded.[198] Previously, it had allowed execution of the retarded, including a man who had the mental capacity of a seven-year-old and still believed in Santa Claus.[199] Now, the six-justice majority observed, there is a new "national consensus" against such executions. In 2005, it ruled that states can't execute juveniles who were younger than eighteen when they killed.[200] Previously, it had allowed execution of juveniles as young as sixteen. Now, Justice Kennedy noted, there are "evolving standards of decency" in society. Nonetheless, most states retain the death penalty for adults even though nearly all other developed countries (except Japan) have abolished it.[201] (See Figure 1.)

Despite the Burger Court's ruling that states can't execute rapists, a half dozen states passed laws providing for capital punishment for those who rape children, even when the crime doesn't result in a death. In 2008, the Roberts Court invalidated these laws.[201(a)]

Rights in Theory and in Practice

Overall, the Supreme Court has interpreted the Bill of Rights to provide an impressive list of rights for criminal defendants (although a significant change from the Warren Court to the Burger and Rehnquist Courts was a narrowing of the rights for criminal defendants). Yet not all rights are available for all defendants in all places. Some police, prosecutors, and judges don't comply with Supreme Court rulings.

When the rights are available, most defendants don't take advantage of them. About 90 percent of criminal de-

| Figure 1 | Capital Punishment Declines |

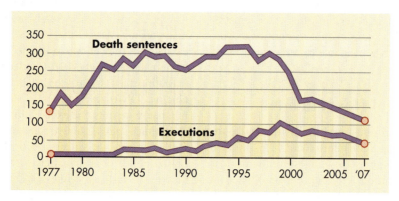

This figure displays the number of death sentences and executions since the Supreme Court reauthorized the death penalty.

fendants plead guilty, and many of them do so through a **plea bargain**. This is an agreement among the prosecutor, the defense attorney, and the defendant, with the explicit or implicit approval of the judge, to reduce the charge or the sentence in exchange for a guilty plea. A plea bargain is a compromise. For officials, it saves the time, trouble, and uncertainty of a trial. For defendants, it eliminates the fear of a harsher sentence. However, it also reduces due process rights. A guilty plea waives the defendants' right to a jury trial, at which the defendants can present their own witnesses and cross-examine the government's witnesses and at which they can't be forced to incriminate themselves. A guilty plea also reduces the defendants' right to counsel because it reduces their lawyers' need to prepare a defense. Most attorneys pressure their clients to forgo a trial so that the attorneys don't have to spend the time to investigate and try the case. Despite these drawbacks for due process rights, the Supreme Court allows plea bargaining, and the trial courts encourage the practice because it enables judges and attorneys to dispose of their cases quickly.[202]

Right to Privacy

Neither the Constitution nor the Bill of Rights mentions privacy. Nevertheless, the right to privacy, Justice Douglas noted, is "older than the Bill of Rights,"[203] and the framers undoubtedly assumed that the people would have such a right. In fact, the framers did include several amendments that reflect their concern for privacy: the First Amendment protects privacy of association; the Third, privacy of homes from quartering soldiers; the Fourth, privacy of persons and places where they live from searches and seizures; and the Fifth, privacy of knowledge and thoughts from compulsory self-incrimination. The Supreme Court would use these to establish an explicit **right to privacy**.

So far, the Court's right-to-privacy doctrine reflects a right to autonomy—what Justice Louis Brandeis called "the right to be left alone"—more than a right to keep things confidential. As noted earlier in the chapter, the Court has been reluctant to punish the press for invading people's privacy.[204]

Birth Control

The Warren Court explicitly *established a right to privacy* in *Griswold* v. *Connecticut* in 1965. In violation of an 1879 law, which prohibited distributing or using contraceptives or even disseminating information about them, Planned Parenthood and a professor at Yale University Medical School established a birth control clinic in New Haven. After authorities shut it down, the founders challenged the law, and the Court struck it down.[205] To enforce the law, the state would have had to police people's bedrooms, and the Court said the very idea of policing married couples' bedrooms was absurd. Then the Court struck down Massachusetts and New York laws that prohibited distributing contraceptives to unmarried persons.[206] "If the right of privacy means anything," Justice Brennan said, "it is the right of the individual, married or single, to be free from unwarranted governmental intrusion into matters so fundamentally affecting a person as the decision whether to bear or beget a child."[207]

Abortion

When twenty-two-year-old Norma McCorvey became pregnant in 1969, she was distraught. She had one young daughter, she had relinquished custody of two previous children, and she was divorced. She sought an abortion, but Texas prohibited abortions unless the mother's life was in danger. "No legitimate doctor in Dallas would touch me," she discovered. "I found one doctor who offered to abort me for $500. Only he didn't have a license, and I was scared to turn my body over to him. So there I was—

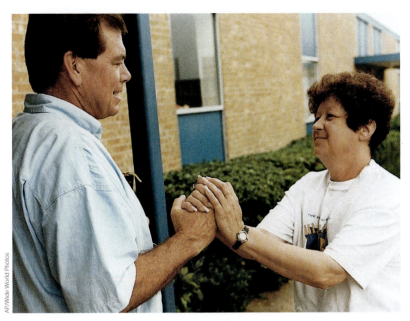

Norma McCorvey—"Jane Roe" of *Roe v. Wade*—switched sides and joined forces with Operation Rescue's Flip Benham in 1995.

pregnant, unmarried, unemployed, alone, and stuck."[208] Unaware of states that permitted abortions, McCorvey put her baby up for adoption. But the state law rankled her. When she met two women attorneys who recently graduated from law school and also disliked the law, they offered to take her case to challenge the law. She adopted the name Jane Roe to conceal her identity.

In *Roe* v. *Wade* in 1973, the Burger Court *extended the right to privacy from birth control to abortion.*[209] Justice Harry Blackmun surveyed the writings of doctors, theologians, and philosophers over the years and found that these thinkers didn't agree when life begins. Therefore, the majority on the Court concluded that judges shouldn't assert that life begins at any particular time, whether at conception, which would make a fetus a person and abortion murder, or at birth. Without this factor in the equation, a woman's privacy, or control, of her body became paramount.

The Court ruled that *women have a* **right to abortion** *during the first six months of pregnancy.* States can prohibit an abortion during the last three months because the fetus becomes viable—it can live outside the womb—at this point. (However, states must allow an abortion for a woman whose life is endangered by continuing her pregnancy.) Thus the right is broad but not absolute. The justices, as revealed in memos discovered years later, acknowledged that their division of the nine-month term was "legislative," but they saw this as a way to balance the rights of the mother in the early stages of pregnancy with the rights of the fetus in the later stage.[210]

The case has had an enormous impact on American politics. The Court's ruling invalidated the abortion laws of forty-nine states[211] and increased the number of abortions

performed in the country (see Figure 2). It put abortion on the public agenda, and it galvanized conservative groups who saw the ruling as a symbol of loosening social restraints at a time of rampaging social problems. Disparate groups, such as Roman Catholics and evangelical Protestants (and some Orthodox Jews), rural residents and urban ethnics, who rarely saw eye to eye, coalesced around this issue and exercised leverage within the Republican Party.

In hindsight, some observers believe that the Court's ruling may have been imprudent or at least premature. Before the ruling, some states began liberalizing their laws, but there wasn't time for others to follow or for the citizens to ponder the issue. There was little public debate, let alone the extended debate necessary to develop a broad consensus. The Court's ruling short-circuited the normal political process and prompted opponents to mobilize and supporters to countermobilize. Both sides scorned the compromises that typify political solutions to most issues.[212]

The right-to-life movement pressured presidents and senators to appoint justices and lower court judges who opposed the ruling. The movement also lobbied members of Congress and state legislatures to overturn or circumvent the ruling. Although Congress refused to pass constitutional amendments banning abortions or allowing states to regulate them, Congress and state legislatures did pass statutes limiting abortions in various ways.

The Burger Court invalidated most of these statutes,[213] but it upheld a major limitation. The Medicaid program, financed jointly by the federal and state governments, had paid for abortions for poor women. As a result, the program had paid for a third of the abortions in the country each year.[214] But Congress eliminated federal funding (except when pregnancy threatens the life of the mother or is the result of rape or incest), and thirty-three state legislatures eliminated state funding. In these states, poor women need to pay the entire cost. The Court upheld these laws, ruling that

The pro-choice movement uses this symbol, referring to the history of coat-hanger abortions in the back alleys before *Roe*. Sarah Weddington, an attorney who challenged Texas' law in *Roe*, often wears this pin while traveling. Not long ago a young flight attendant asked, "What do you have against coat hangers?"

| Figure 2 | Abortion Rate since *Roe* |

The abortion rate climbed after Roe *and peaked in the 1980s. Since then it has declined steadily.*
SOURCE: *New York Times, November 6, 2005.*

governments have no obligation to finance abortions, even if this means that some women cannot take advantage of their right to have them.[215] For some women, these laws delay abortions while the women search for the money. For an estimated 20 percent of the women, these laws deny abortions because the women can't obtain the money.[216]

Many people, including pro-choice advocates, support these bans because they dislike welfare spending. Yet according to an analysis of the states that do provide abortion funding for poor women, the states save money. For every $1 they spend on abortions, they save $4 in welfare and medical expenses in what would have been the first two years of the child's life.[217] They save much more over a longer period. Ironically, public distaste for welfare spending actually leads to more welfare spending here.

Presidents Reagan and George H. W. Bush sought justices who opposed *Roe,* and after they filled their fifth vacancy on the Court, pro-life advocates expected the Court to overturn it. Yet the Rehnquist Court didn't overturn it.[218] In 1992, a bare majority reaffirmed the right to abortion.[219] At the same time, the majority *allowed more restrictions on the right—as long as the restrictions don't place an "undue burden" on the women seeking abortions.* In other words, states must permit abortions but can discourage them.[220]

Therefore, the majority upheld Pennsylvania's twenty-four-hour waiting period between the time a woman indicates her desire to have an abortion and the time a doctor can perform one. Although a twenty-four-hour waiting period is not a burden for many women, it can be for poor women who live in rural areas and must travel to cities for abortions. One Mississippi woman hitchhiked to the city and planned to sleep on outdoor furniture in the Kmart parking lot until the clinic offered to pay for her motel room.[221]

A waiting period can also affect teenagers. Some pro-life groups note the license numbers of cars driven to clinics by teenagers. After looking up the name and address of the family, they inform the parents in the hope that the parents will persuade or pressure their daughter to change her mind during the waiting period.

The majority struck down Pennsylvania's requirement that a married woman notify her husband before having an abortion.[222] This was an undue burden because a woman who fears physical abuse from her husband would be deterred from seeking an abortion. Justice O'Connor wrote that a state "may not give to a man the kind of dominion over his wife that parents exercise over their children."

The Court upheld thirteen states' requirement that unmarried minors notify their parents and twenty-one states' requirement that unmarried minors obtain their parents' consent before having an abortion.[223] For either requirement, if a daughter doesn't want to tell her parents, she can seek permission from a judge. She must convince the judge that an abortion would be in her best interest or that she is mature enough to make the decision herself. If she isn't mature enough, she must become a mother.

Pro-life groups advocated these laws with the expectation that they would result in fewer abortions. They believed that many teenagers would go to their parents rather than face the forbidding atmosphere of a court hearing with an unknown judge and that their parents would persuade or pressure them not to have the abortion. Some evidence indicates that the laws have had this effect.[224]

When teenagers do go to court, they routinely get waivers in some states but not in others.

After the Rehnquist Court reaffirmed the right to abortion, pro-life groups tried to prohibit one abortion procedure known as "intact dilation and extraction" in medicine but referred to as "partial-birth abortion" in politics—a rhetorical success of antiabortion supporters. In this procedure, a doctor delivers the fetus except for the head, punctures the skull and drains the contents, and then removes the fetus from the woman.[225] Because the procedure seems gruesome, pro-life groups used it to sway undecided people in the abortion debate. Numerous states passed laws banning the procedure. A bare majority of the Rehnquist Court struck down the laws in 2000.[226] But Justice Sandra Day O'Connor, who supported abortion rights, retired, and Justice Samuel Alito, who opposes abortion rights, replaced her. Congress passed a similar law for the whole country. A bare majority of the Roberts Court upheld the law in 2007.[227] For the majority, Justice Kennedy said the law protects women from themselves. "While we find no reliable data to measure the phenomenon," he concluded that some women "regret their choice to abort," so the law prevents other women from making that choice.

For the time being, a five-justice majority, including Kennedy, supports the basic right to abortion.

The pro-life movement is divided over its current tactics. Some factions prefer an incremental strategy, passing numerous restrictions that might go unnoticed by most people, rather than a frontal attack that might prompt a backlash by the majority. When South Dakota, which had no doctors who performed abortions—Minnesota doctors flew in to the state's sole facility—banned all abortions in 2005, abortion supporters petitioned to put the issue on the ballot in 2006. Voters repealed the law.

In some states, pro-life groups have quietly pressed the legislatures to enact extra-stringent building codes for abortion clinics. These codes specify such things as the heights of ceilings, widths of hallways and doorways, dimensions of counseling rooms and recovery rooms, rates of air circulation, and the types and angles of jets in drinking fountains. (Although all states have construction codes for their buildings, these new laws apply only to abortion clinics.) Some codes require equipment or levels of staffing, such as a registered nurse rather than a licensed practical nurse, beyond what is normal in these clinics. Although the stated goal is health and safety, the real purpose is to drive up the clinics' expenses so they have to increase their patients' fees to the point where many women can no longer afford to have an abortion.[228] When South Carolina's law, which mandates twenty-seven pages of requirements just for abortion clinics, was challenged, a lower court upheld the law and the Supreme Court refused to hear the case, thus allowing the law to stand.

Despite dissatisfaction by activists on both sides of this controversy—pro-life groups are disappointed that the conservative Supreme Court has upheld the right to abortion, whereas pro-choice groups are critical that it has upheld some restrictions on abortion—it is worth noting that the nonelected, nonmajoritarian Supreme Court has come closer to forging a policy reflective of public opinion than most politicians have. Polls show that the public is ambivalent. A majority believes that abortion is murder, but a two-thirds majority opposes banning it. This two-thirds majority favors letting women choose. (The apparent contradiction occurs because over half of those who believe that abortion is murder nonetheless favor letting women choose.[229] See

Figure 3.) Thus many people support the right to abortion but are uncomfortable with it and willing to allow restrictions on it. The Court's doctrine articulates this position.[230]

But the Court's rulings aren't necessarily the final word in this controversy, as they haven't been the final word in some other controversies. Frustrated by the Court's refusal to overturn *Roe*, activists in the pro-life movement (not most of the pro-life supporters) adopted more militant tactics. First they targeted abortion clinics. Organizations such as Operation Rescue engaged in civil disobedience, blockading clinics and harassing workers and patients as they came and went. Some activists sprayed chemicals inside clinics, ruining carpets and fabrics and leaving a stench that made the clinics unusable. Such incidents occurred fifty times in one year alone.[231]

Then activists targeted doctors, nurses, and other workers at the clinics. Operation Rescue ran a training camp in Florida that instructed members how to use public records to locate personal information about clinic employees, how to tail them to their homes, and how to organize demonstrations at their homes. Activists put up "Wanted" posters, with a doctor's picture, name, address, and phone number, and then encouraged people to harass the doctor, the doctor's spouse, and even their children. (One thirteen-year-old was confronted in a restaurant and told that he was going to burn in hell.)[232] Letters containing powder and threatening death by anthrax were sent to over one hundred doctors and clinics.[233] Some extremists even advocated killing the doctors. One minister wrote a book—*A Time to Kill*—and marketed a bumper sticker reading "execute abortionists–murderers."[234]

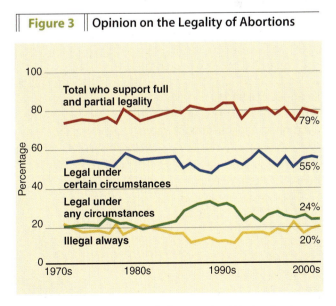

Figure 3   Opinion on the Legality of Abortions

People were asked, "Do you think abortions should be legal under any circumstances, legal only under certain circumstances, or illegal in all circumstances?"
SOURCE: New York Times, November 6, 2005.

In this climate, three doctors, two clinic receptionists, and one clinic volunteer were killed, and seven other doctors, employees, and volunteers were wounded.[235] Numerous clinics were firebombed.

The tactics have had their intended effect on doctors.[236] They have made the practice of providing abortions seem dangerous and undesirable. Fewer medical schools offer abortion classes, fewer hospitals provide abortion training, fewer doctors study abortion procedures, and fewer gynecologists and obstetricians, despite most being pro-choice, perform abortion operations.[237] As a result, the number of abortion providers has dropped significantly.[238]

One pro-life leader proclaimed, "We've found the weak link is the doctor."[239] Another observed, "When you get the doctors out, you can have all the laws on the books you want and it doesn't mean a thing."[240]

Abortions remain available in most metropolitan centers but not in most rural areas. Eighty-seven percent of U.S. counties, containing 32 percent of the American women aged fifteen to forty-four, have no doctor who performs abortions. Some states have only one and others have only two cities where women can obtain abortions.[241]

Nevertheless, an abortion is still one of the most common surgical procedures for American women. Moreover, the French abortion pill—RU-486, whose brand name is Mifeprex—offers a nonsurgical procedure (if used by the seventh week of pregnancy), allowing women to take one pill in the doctor's office and another at home. This procedure is increasingly common.[242] (See the box "Who Has an Abortion?")

Birth Control, Revisited

Although the pro-life movement has been frustrated by its inability to overturn *Roe*, it was stimulated by the conservatism of the Bush administration and the appointment of new justices to the Supreme Court. Now the movement has trained its sights on contraception in addition to abortion.[243] Initially the pro-life movement was dominated by Catholics, whose church opposes contraceptives. The movement's leaders muted their views to avoid scaring off potential supporters. (Ninety-three percent of all Americans, and 90 percent of Catholics, supported contraceptives in 2005.)[244] The pro-life movement was joined by conservative Protestants who didn't oppose birth control. Recently, however, more movement leaders, Protestants as well as Catholics, have voiced opposition to contraception. The president of the American Life League declared, "We oppose all forms of contraception."[245] Now religious interest groups, such as the Christian Coalition and Focus on the Family, address birth control. Increasing numbers of evangelical theologians oppose it and evangelical churches discuss it. A cluster of representatives and senators spearheads congressional efforts against some forms of birth control. Members have spoken out against condoms, charging that they don't prevent pregnancy or disease to the extent people believe.

The Bush administration has shifted federal family planning policy from contraception to abstinence—from sex education, including information about birth control, to abstinence education—at least for individuals who aren't married. For 2007, the administration budgeted more than $200 million for abstinence education. The administration

---

BEHIND THE SCENES
WHO HAS AN ABORTION?

More than a third of American women have an abortion sometime during their life.

Half of all pregnancies in American women are unintended, and four in ten of these result in an abortion. Ninety-two percent of the abortions are performed on women who said they used birth control, but they didn't use it that month or they didn't use it properly.

Despite the perception, fueled by movies such as *Juno,* that most abortions are performed on minors, only 7 percent occur in girls younger than eighteen. A disproportionate number—45 percent—occur in women from eighteen through twenty-four, because they are more sexually active than the younger females. The rest—48 percent—occur in women older than twenty-four. Among

those over twenty who have an abortion, the majority have attended (though not necessarily graduated from) college.

Most women—more than eight in ten—who have an abortion are unmarried. About six in ten have at least one child; about three in ten have two or more. A disproportionate number are poor. The abortion rate for those below the poverty level is four times greater than

for those who are middle income or affluent. Thus most women who have an abortion do so because of their family or economic situation.

Black women have a disproportionate number of abortions. Blacks are 13 percent of our population but have 35 percent of the abortions.

Sources: David Crary, "Abortion Stats Differ from Perceptions," *Lincoln Journal Star,* January 20, 2008, 11A; Atul Gawande, "Let's Talk About Sex," *New York Times,* May 19, 2007, select .nytimes.com/2007/05/19/opinion/19gawand .html?_r=1&hp=&oref=slogin&pa…

also shifted federal aid to foreign countries for AIDS prevention from contraception to abstinence.[246] Thus it stopped sending condoms to many countries, including those with high rates of AIDS.[247]

President Bush, when asked whether he supports *the right* to use contraceptives, refused to answer.[248] (His father, as a member of Congress, was so insistent that foreign aid include contraceptives that he was nicknamed "Rubbers" by other members of the committee.)[249]

Current opposition to contraception makes it difficult for the two sides in the abortion controversy to find common ground. Some on each side had called for greater availability of contraceptives so there would be less need for abortions. But this common ground is giving way as more who oppose abortion also oppose contraception.

What this indicates is that for some in the pro-life movement it's not so much about abortion as it is about sex. One leader said, "We see a direct connection between the practice of contraception and the practice of abortion." They both reflect "an anti-child mindset."[250] Both serve "the selfish demands of the individual."[251] The president of the Southern Baptist Theological Seminary stated, "The effective separation of sex from procreation may be one of the most important defining marks of our age—and one of the most ominous."[252] Their goal is to reverse the sexual revolution of the 1960s, when "the pill" became commonplace, and instead to confine sex to marriage.

This debate reflects sharp cultural differences between European countries and the United States. In those countries, contraceptives are readily available and unintended pregnancies and abortions are less frequent. There, "these things are in the open, and the only issue is to be careful. Here in the U.S., people are still arguing about whether it's O.K. to have sex."[253]

Homosexuality

For years, states prohibited adultery, fornication, and sodomy. Reflecting Christian doctrine, the statutes targeted various forms of nonmarital sex and nonprocreative sex (including masturbation and withdrawal prior to ejaculation).[254] After the "sexual revolution" of the 1960s, many states repealed these statutes. However, most states retained their sodomy statutes, which prohibited oral or anal sex (performed by heterosexuals or homosexuals) because of legislators' disgust at homosexual practices and their opposition to the emerging gay rights movement.[255] Although these statutes were primarily symbolic, they were occasionally enforced against homosexuals.

The Supreme Court refused to extend the right to privacy to protect homosexual practices in 1986,[256] but the Rehnquist Court reversed itself in 2003. When a neighbor phoned a false report of an armed intruder, police responded and discovered two men violating Texas's law. The men were arrested, jailed, and fined. The Texas courts affirmed their conviction, but in *Lawrence* v. *Texas,* the Supreme Court overturned it and *invalidated the sodomy laws* of the thirteen states that still had them.[257] In a broad opinion, Justice Kennedy wrote, "Liberty presumes an autonomy of self that includes freedom of thought, belief, expression, and certain intimate conduct." Therefore, homosexuals are entitled to "dignity" and "respect for their private lives."

A sizable shift in public opinion had occurred in the seventeen years between the two rulings.[258] As more homosexuals "came out," they gained greater acceptance from straights. Most Americans say they know someone who is gay or lesbian, and a majority says they are sympathetic to the gay and lesbian communities. Numerous states repealed their sodomy statutes after the 1986 ruling (even though the ruling allowed the states to keep the statutes). Thus in the *Lawrence* case, according to one law professor, "The Court legitimized and endorsed a cultural consensus."[259] (See Table 1.)

Although the majority in *Lawrence* said the ruling would not necessarily extend to same-sex marriages, the dissenters feared that establishing a right to privacy for homosexual practices would indeed lead to a right to marry for homosexual couples. Congress adopted the Defense of Marriage Act, which allows states to disregard same-sex marriages performed in other states. (About forty states have passed laws to do so.) The act also forbids federal recognition of same-sex marriages and thus denies federal benefits, such as Social Security, to same-sex couples.[260]

Although marriage was a fantasy for most homosexuals, their lack of legal rights was both a cause for concern and a source of anger. In the 1980s and 1990s, the AIDS epidemic

Table 1	Coming Out

The largest percentage increases in same-sex couples willing to identify themselves as homosexual in government surveys between 2000 and 2005.

New Hampshire	106%
Wisconsin	81
Minnesota	76
Nebraska	71
Kansas	68
Ohio	62
Colorado	58
Iowa	58
Missouri	56
Indiana	54

Source: Gary J. Gates, "Same-Sex Couples and the Gay, Lesbian, Bisexual Population: New Estimates from the American Community Survey" (Williams Institute on Sexual Orientation Law and Public Policy, n.d.), as reported in "Leaving the Closet," *Atlantic Monthly,* January–February, 2007, 44.

By permission of Mike Luckovich and Creators Syndicate, Inc.

swept gay communities across the United States. "Lovers, friends, and AIDS 'buddies' were spooning food, emptying bedpans, holding wracked bodies through the night. They were assuming the burdens of marriage at its hardest."[261] Yet gay partners had no legal rights. They encountered problems involving health insurance, hospital visitation, disability benefits, funeral planning, and estate settling. Gays were often unable to participate fully in these life-and-death matters due to legal impediments that didn't exist for married couples. In the same decades, lesbians gave birth using donated sperm, and gays got children through adoption and surrogate mothers, yet homosexual couples realized that they didn't have legal protections for their families. These developments increased the calls for legal rights commensurate with the rights of heterosexual couples.[262]

In 1999, the Vermont supreme court ruled that the state must either legalize same-sex marriages or equalize the rights and benefits received by same-sex couples and traditional married couples. The legislature decided to equalize the rights and benefits. To implement this policy, the legislature established "civil unions," with procedures for couples to become official partners (similar to marriage) and procedures for them to dissolve their relationship (similar to divorce).

Although these civil unions provide most of what regular marriages provide, the unions don't apply when couples move from Vermont to other states. And they don't apply

to federal benefits. By one count, 1138 federal laws apply to married couples that don't apply to unmarried couples. Some impose responsibilities; most provide rights and benefits, such as tax breaks.[263] Also, of course, the unions don't provide the symbolism that regular marriages do.

So the pressure for same-sex marriages continued. In 2004, the Massachusetts Supreme Judicial Court, hearing a suit brought by seven couples, ruled that same-sex marriages were allowed under the state's constitution. Otherwise, same-sex couples are relegated to "a different status. . . . The history of our nation has demonstrated that separate is seldom, if ever, equal."[264]

Holding their twin daughters, this couple exchanges marriage vows in San Francisco before same-sex marriages were invalidated there.

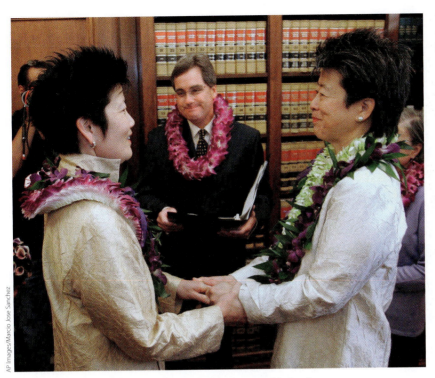

This couple says "I do" in San Francisco, but the courts said "Adieu."

In quick succession, officials in San Francisco; Portland, Oregon; and smaller cities in New York, New Jersey, and New Mexico were inspired to issue marriage licenses to same-sex couples. State courts halted the licenses but not until thousands of beaming couples had married and posed for news photos. Although the marriages were pronounced invalid, the head of the Lambda Legal Defense and Education Fund observed, "You can't put the toothpaste back in the tube."[265]

There was an immediate backlash. Polls showed that a majority of the public opposed same-sex marriages. President Bush proposed a constitutional amendment. One congressional sponsor claimed, "There is a master plan out there from those who want to destroy the institution of marriage." Another senator, comparing the threat of gay marriage to that of terrorism, called the amendment "the ultimate homeland security." An evangelist predicted that "the family as it has been known for five millennia will crumble, presaging the fall of Western civilization itself."[266] Yet there was more fire from the pulpits than there was in the pews. Evangelical leaders expressed puzzlement and frustration that there was no loud outcry from their faithful.[267] But many people who oppose gay marriage don't feel threatened by it. Consequently, the amendment failed to pass. Nevertheless, voters in over half of the states adopted such amendments to their state constitution, most by a wide margin.

Despite many people's objections, gay rights leaders predict that once homosexuals begin to marry and straights see that "the sky doesn't fall," people will stop opposing their marriages.[268] Indeed, the initial backlash against Mas-

sachusetts' same-sex marriages dissipated. Then Connecticut also allowed same-sex marriages. Other northeastern states—Maine, New Hampshire, and New Jersey—and California passed domestic-partnership laws that formally recognize same-sex partnerships and provide them some or all rights associated with marriage. In 2008, the California Supreme Court ruled that the state's domestic-partnership law wasn't sufficient, that same-sex marriages must be allowed in that state too. Yet this ruling was negated by voters, especially by blacks who turned out in record numbers to support Barack Obama, in 2008. The legal status of couples who married between the judicial ruling and the election outcome will have to be determined by the California courts.

Some states that don't allow same-sex couples the right to marry, however, do allow them to adopt children. These states grant such couples parental rights.

Some states and cities have passed laws barring discrimination in employment, housing, credit, insurance, and public accommodations, (And thirteen states have also passed laws barring discrimination against transgendered persons—those who are born as one gender but live as the opposite gender.)[269]

Yet homosexuals remain vulnerable at other workplaces. Congress rejected a bill barring discrimination in employment at the same time it passed the Defense of Marriage Act.[270] In most states, employees can be fired merely for being homosexual.

Even so, homosexuals have gained equal benefits at more workplaces. Some states and cities and many large corporations have offered health care packages to same-sex couples as a way to attract and retain good workers.

Right to Die

The Court has broadened the right to privacy to provide a limited right to die. When Nancy Cruzan's car skidded off an icy road and flipped into a ditch in 1983, doctors were able to save her life but not her brain. She never regained consciousness. She lived in a vegetative state, similar to a coma, and was fed through a tube. Twenty-five at the time of the accident, she was expected to live another thirty years. When her parents asked the doctors to remove the tube, the hospital objected, and the state of Missouri, despite paying $130,000 a year to maintain her, also objected. This issue became entangled in other issues. Pro-life groups contended that denying life support was analogous to abortion; disability groups, claiming that her condition was merely a disability, argued that withholding food and water from her would lead to withholding treatment from others with disabilities.[271]

When Cruzan's parents filed suit, the Rehnquist Court established a limited **right to die**.[272] The justices ruled that *individuals can refuse medical treatment, including food and water, even if this means they will die.* But individuals must make their decision while competent and alert. They can also act in advance, preparing a "living will" or designating another person as a proxy to make the decision if they're unable to.

Cruzan's parents presented evidence to a Missouri court that their daughter would prefer death to being kept alive by machines. Three of Cruzan's coworkers testified that they recalled conversations in which she said she'd never want to live "like a vegetable." The Missouri court granted her parents' request to remove the feeding tube. She died twelve days later.

Although the legal doctrine is clear, various practical problems and emotional issues limit its use. Many people don't make their desires known in advance. Approximately ten thousand people in irreversible comas now didn't indicate their decision beforehand.[273] Some people who do indicate their decision beforehand waver when they face death. Some doctors, who are in the habit of prolonging life even when their patients have no chance of enjoying life, resist their patients' decision.[274]

The Rehnquist Court *refused* patients' pleas *to expand the limited right into a broader right to obtain assistance in committing suicide.*[275] The Court drew a distinction between stopping treatment and assisting suicide; individuals have a right to demand the former but not the latter. The justices seemed tentative, as is typical with an issue new to the courts. Chief Justice Rehnquist emphasized, "Our holding permits this debate to continue, as it should in a democratic society."

Oregon decided to allow assisted suicide. The law provides some safeguards. The patient must submit written requests in the presence of two witnesses, get two doctors to concur that he or she has less than six months to live, and wait fifteen days. The Bush administration challenged Oregon's law, claiming that individual states can't allow assisted suicide. But the Supreme Court rebuffed the Bush administration and *allowed the state law to stand.*[276] So far, a modest number of terminally ill patients—about thirty a year—have taken advantage of the law.[277]

In Ashland, Oregon, Steve Mason suffered from terminal lung cancer and waited until he could no longer eat or sleep. Then he took the lethal drugs (on the table) prescribed by his doctor. He said, "I've lived my life with dignity. I want to go out the same way."

A majority of the public favors a right to assisted suicide,[278] but conservative religious groups oppose one. They insist that people, even when facing extreme pain and no hope of recovery, shouldn't take their life. In addition, ethicists worry that patients will be pressured to give up their life because of the costs, to their family or health care provider, of continuing it. The ethicists fear that a right will become a duty.

Meanwhile, the practice, even where officially illegal, is widely condoned, much as abortion was before *Roe*. Almost a fifth of the doctors who treat cancer patients in Michigan admitted in a survey that they have assisted suicide, and over half of two thousand doctors who treat AIDS patients in San Francisco also admitted that they have done so.[279]

Implications for Civil Liberties from the War on Terrorism

Although the **George W. Bush administration** was lax about the terrorist threat before September 11, 2001, after the terrorist attacks it was aggressive in investigating and pursuing possible terrorists around the world. The administration's policies were devised by Vice President **Dick Cheney** and the legal team working under him.[280] These policies have serious implications for civil liberties.

This section will address detention of suspects, interrogation of detainees, surveillance of Americans and foreigners, and provisions of the USA PATRIOT Act. These issues all pose the question, Can we wage an effective war against the radical Islamists and still maintain our civil liberties?

Detentions

Suspected terrorists have been detained at the United States Naval Base at Guantanamo Bay, Cuba, and in secret prisons around the world.

Guantanamo Bay

The naval base consists of forty-five square miles of land and water along the southeastern coast of Cuba. The United States acquired the base after the Spanish-American War in 1898.[281] It has complete control of the territory.

Almost 800 men from forty-four countries have been rounded up and flown to "Gitmo." Most were captured in Afghanistan or Pakistan. Vice President Cheney called them "the worst of a very bad lot." Secretary of Defense Donald Rumsfeld called them "the most dangerous, best-trained, vicious killers on the face of the earth."[282] Officials said they would be detained indefinitely.

Detainees at Guantanamo Bay, Cuba.

Their detention has led to a legal and political battle over **habeas corpus**. Some families filed lawsuits, petitioning federal courts for a writ of *habeas corpus* on behalf of the detainees. *Habeas corpus* is a traditional and integral component of English and American law, mandating that the government justify a defendant's incarceration. As explained in Chapter 13, criminal defendants use *habeas corpus* to challenge the legality of their confinement. *Habeas corpus* was considered so important that it was included in the body of the Constitution before the Bill of Rights was adopted. The Constitution stipulates that *habeas corpus* can't be suspended unless there is a rebellion or foreign invasion. A congressional statute grants federal courts jurisdiction to hear petitions for *habeas corpus* from anyone claiming to be held in violation of the Constitution, laws, or treaties of the United States. The statute doesn't distinguish between American citizens and aliens, and it doesn't distinguish between peacetime and wartime.[283]

The Bush administration claimed that these provisions shouldn't apply to the prisoners at Guantanamo Bay because the naval base isn't part of the United States. The administration also claimed that international law shouldn't apply because the naval base is our military base. In other words, the administration, reflecting Cheney's views, maintained that no laws applied to the base and no rights protected the prisoners (not even the minimal rights for prisoners of war).[284] Essentially, the detainees were in a legal black hole.[285] This may be the first time that the United States officially held anyone outside of all legal processes.[286]

The Bush administration made another sweeping claim. It insisted that the president, as commander in chief, has expanded power during wartime, so the courts can't review or question his policies.[287]

The Supreme Court, however, rejected these contentions and rebuffed the president, telling him that he, too, must follow the law. The justices decided that federal courts do have the authority to review the detentions and that the detainees do have the right to challenge their designation as "enemy combatants."[288]

The Court's ruling was a tentative step. Its opinion didn't specify what procedures should be used or what rights, such as a right to an attorney, should be accorded the detainees.[289] The Bush administration interpreted the ruling as narrowly as possible. The Pentagon began military hearings before military officers, rather than before federal judges, and denied the detainees an actual lawyer (although it allowed them a "personal representative" chosen by the military). Even so, numerous detainees were released.

Other detainees, who weren't released, sought a review by federal courts. Their appeals prompted Congress, at the urging of the administration, to pass a law stripping the Guantanamo detainees of *habeas corpus* rights (at least until a military tribunal issues a final ruling in their case).[290] The Supreme Court rebuffed Congress, invalidating the law and holding that the Guantanamo detainees do have *habeas corpus* rights.[291]

The files of many detainees, including those who were released and others who were not released, were opened to the media. The files show that many innocent or at least harmless people have been housed at Gitmo.

The president and vice president said that the prisoners were "picked up off the battlefield," but according to the files only 5 percent were. Eighty-six percent were apprehended by Afghani or Pakistani warlords or tribesmen and turned over to the United States. Some were captured because they were rivals or enemies of the warlords or tribesmen; others were captured because, as purported "terrorists," they would bring a bounty from the United States (reportedly $1000 a head).[292] Others were foreigners who worked for Muslim organizations operating charities, clinics, and schools.[293] At least ten wore the wrong watch—a Casio model used by al-Qaeda bombers because of its timer, but also worn by many Arabs because of its compass, which enables them to point toward Mecca for prayer.[294]

A thorough review of the government's files concluded, "Most, when captured, were innocent of any terrorist activity, were Taliban foot soldiers at worst, and were often far less than that. And some, perhaps many, were guilty only of being foreigners in Afghanistan or Pakistan at the wrong time."[295] The former head of the CIA's bin Laden unit concluded that many were "absolutely . . . the wrong people."[296] The U.S. military was under so much pressure to find al-Qaeda members that it accepted any persons who were de-

livered by the warlords and tribesmen. With too few experienced interpreters and interrogators, it couldn't separate the terrorists from the others.

The problems continued at Gitmo. The interrogators were under tremendous pressure from Washington to identify terrorists and, knowing that al-Qaeda trained its agents to lie, were reluctant to conclude that the prisoners were innocent. During his interrogation, one Yemeni who was asked whether he knew bin Laden said, "I saw bin Laden five times: three times on al Jazeera [TV] and twice on Yemeni news." In his file, the interrogator noted, "Detainee admitted to knowing Osama bin Laden," so he was held as a terrorist.[297]

The indefinite detentions put the detainees under great stress. A hundred went on a hunger strike. They were force-fed through a tube up their nose. Over a hundred tried to commit suicide; four succeeded.[298] The human rights group Amnesty International, referring to the notorious Soviet prison for dissidents, called Guantanamo the "gulag of our times."[299] European leaders and a United Nations committee, in addition to American politicians, urged the administration to shut down the prison. President Bush expressed a desire "to close Guantanamo," but Vice President Cheney resisted.[300]

The administration planned to try the detainees through military commissions, which would have resembled civilian trials but would not have given the detainees some crucial rights given to our criminal defendants. A slim majority of the Supreme Court ruled that the administration's plan violated both U.S. law and international law because the commissions weren't established courts and wouldn't afford adequate rights to the detainees.[301]

As a result of the ruling, the administration revised the procedures for military commissions and persuaded Congress to authorize the commissions. Then the administration tried one detainee—Osama bin Laden's driver—and obtained a conviction on a relatively minor charge (though not on a more serious charge). The sentence was just five months longer than the detainee had already served, though it was unclear whether the administration would release him when he completed his sentence in 2008. It was also unclear (as of fall 2008) whether the proceeding by the commission, which used secret testimony by secret witnesses, was legal. The administration planned to try other detainees, though not most detainees, fearing acquittals. So these detainees were left in legal limbo, with no date for a trial or their release.

The Court's rulings on detentions and military commissions reflect the justices' beliefs that at least some constitutional standards must be followed even during wartime. And the Court's rulings challenge the president's assertion that he alone can determine how to fight terrorism. The lawyer for the detainee who filed one suit exclaimed, "There are not many countries where a noncitizen with a fourth-grade education can sue the president. That is our great gift to the world. We're strong enough to say our system can handle it."[302] (See box "A Valentine from Guantanamo Bay.")

ethical dilemmas | A Valentine from Guantanamo Bay

In his family, Matthew Diaz was the one who tried to do the right thing. He helped the others, and he kept the peace. But after his parents were divorced and his father was charged with murder, he left home at sixteen. He dropped out of high school and enlisted in the army at seventeen. There he found himself. In the army, he got a college degree, and after the army, intrigued by his father's case, he got a law degree. Then he joined the navy, this time as an officer and a lawyer.[1]

After ten years as a lawyer in the navy, Lt. Commander Diaz was assigned to the base at Guantanamo Bay, where he was responsible for various matters involving the detainees and their lawyers, and the prosecutors and defense attorneys, for upcoming trials of the detainees. Diaz became disillusioned by what he saw. Although some detainees were dangerous, he believed, many others were not, yet they were treated badly. He became angry especially after the Supreme Court ruled that the detainees had a right to challenge their detention in federal court. He saw that the Bush administration was throwing up roadblocks to circumvent the ruling. In particular, the administration was refusing to release the names of the detainees to the lawyers and groups that were volunteering to represent them. Without the names, the lawyers and groups couldn't represent them. And without legal representation, the detainees couldn't challenge their detention in federal court. "No matter what the courts said, [the administration] would just keep stonewalling," he concluded. "I knew that if I didn't do anything, nobody else was going to."[2]

One night, near the end of his tour at the base, Diaz printed the names of the 551 men being held at the time. He trimmed the pages to the size of index cards, and he enclosed the pages in a large Valentine card. He thought the large red envelope would pass through the base's mail system with little scrutiny as Valentine's Day approached. He mailed the card to the Center for Constitutional Rights, a left-wing advocacy group opposed to the administration's Guantanamo policies. The Center had been asking the navy for the detainees' names and had been suing the government over its Guantanamo policies.

When the card reached the Center, its lawyers, unaware of Diaz or anyone who might be sending this information, suspected a government trick. Uncertain what to do, they asked the judge overseeing their suit to accept the information for safe-keeping. Instead, the judge instructed them to turn it over to the Justice Department, which no-

Lt. Commander Matthew Diaz

ticed that the list included alphanumeric codes, one of which indicated the detainees who provided information to their interrogators. (Diaz didn't know what the codes indicated.) The FBI also discovered Diaz's fingerprints.

Close to a promotion and then to his retirement with a pension, Diaz was convicted of disclosing secret information and sentenced to six months' imprisonment. He was stripped of his license to practice military law, and he faces the prospect of losing his license to practice civilian law as well.

Still, he wasn't contrite. "I could have gone up the chain [of command]. But nothing I said would have ever left the island."[3] After his release from prison, he sent the Center donations of $25 a month.

Do you think Diaz did the right thing? Do you think he did it in the right way?

If he didn't do the right thing, what should he have done? If he didn't do it in the right way, how should he have done it? Should he have deleted the codes and sent the names alone?

Or was his problem his naivete? What if he had first hired a lawyer to approach the Center (and to retype the list on clean paper without his fingerprints)? The lawyer could have explained the list, so the Center wouldn't have contacted the judge, and the lawyer could have kept Diaz's identity secret because of the attorney-client privilege. But would this have changed the ethics of Diaz's act?

[1]This box is drawn from Tim Golden, "Naming Names at Gitmo," *New York Times Magazine*, October 21, 2007, 78–83.
[2]Ibid., 83.
[3]Ibid.

Secret Prisons

For its most important prisoners, the Bush administration established a covert prison system run by the CIA. These "black sites," as they were known, were located in at least six countries in Eastern Europe and Asia. They were so secret that President Bush agreed with intelligence officials that even he shouldn't be told of their locations.[303] Until the *Washington Post* broke this story, these prisons were unknown to all but a handful of government officials.[304] And, of course, they were unknown to the International Red Cross, which monitors prisoners' treatment. In 2006, the administration announced that these prisons would be shut down.[305]

Interrogations

The restrictions on police interrogations of criminal suspects, explained earlier in the chapter, don't apply outside the United States or to enemy combatants captured in a war. Nevertheless, these restrictions create norms of behavior, reflecting standards of civility and decency that we have come to expect. Do no-holds-barred methods of interrogation of suspected terrorists violate these norms and standards? Might they undermine our methods of interrogation of criminal defendants?

Methods

For interrogations at the secret prisons, Guantanamo Bay, and Abu Ghraib, the Bush administration, again reflecting Vice President Cheney's views, authorized procedures borrowed from the Chinese during the Korean War and the Soviets during the Cold War. The administration called these procedures **"stress and duress."** Some observers called them "torture lite," to distinguish them from actual torture,[306] but many critics called them simply "torture." The techniques varied from place to place and from prisoner to prisoner, but they included the following.

Prisoners were stripped—interrogators were instructed how to tear clothing off detainees—and left naked, or photographed naked, and their body cavities were searched or implanted with suppositories, all to demoralize and debilitate them.[307] They were subjected to cold and water. "You put the people in garbage cans," a soldier at Abu Ghraib described, "and you'd put ice in it, and water. Or stick them underneath the shower spigot naked…. Open a window while it was, like, forty degrees outside and watch them disappear into themselves…before they go into shock."[308]

They were forced into "stress positions" for hours. Some were put in a cubicle in which they couldn't stand, sit, or lie; they had to kneel or squat. Others were suspended from the ceiling by their arms, with their toes barely touching the floor, or they were chained to the floor.[309] Some were shackled for twenty-four hours and left in their own excrement.

Many were sleep-deprived, subjected to bright lights, perhaps strobe lights, and loud noise—cacophonous sounds such as babies' cries, cats' meows, and heavy metal music. (Interrogators also experimented with children's songs, such as "Barney's" song, to drive them crazy.) If prisoners dozed, they were awakened. One suspect was sleep-deprived for twenty hours a day for seven weeks.[310] A CIA officer explained, "Your electrolyte balance changes. You lose all balance and ability to think rationally."[311] To disorient them further, they were fed irregular amounts of food at irregular times of the day, and some were drugged.[312]

They were slapped and beaten. This "stress and duress" process, according to one government official, is "not pulling out fingernails, but it's pretty brutal."[313] A few key prisoners were subjected to waterboarding, which simulates drowning. The suspect is bound to a board, which is inclined so his head is lower than his feet. Then water is poured up his nose.[314] Although the United States had prosecuted military personnel for using this tactic since 1901, Vice President Cheney approved it. (The only tactic that the CIA requested approval for that was denied was threatening to bury a prisoner alive.)[315]

Other prisoners were subjected to sexual humiliation. Some were forced to wear a bra or to dance with other men. Female interrogators rubbed their breasts against detainees and squeezed their genitals.[316] One wiped red ink, which she said was her menstrual blood, on a detainee. By violating sexual taboos, the interrogators tried to make the men feel unclean and unable to pray to their god for strength.[317]

International law forbids torture, which is generally defined as acts that intentionally inflict "severe pain or suffering, whether physical or mental."[318] International law also forbids "outrages upon personal dignity, in particular humiliating and degrading treatment."[319] Domestic law prohibits torture as well, and the Uniform Code of Military Justice commands military personnel not to engage in "cruelty" or "maltreatment" toward prisoners or to threaten or assault them.

The Bush administration claimed that its tactics didn't amount to torture.[320] After 9/11, however, it secretly redefined *torture* to encompass only such pain that produces the impairment of a function, the failure of an organ, or death. Under this definition, the "stress and duress" procedures, including most beatings, wouldn't constitute torture. Of course, the administration couldn't unilaterally alter the definition of torture. But by secretly redefining the term, the administration could insist that the government didn't engage in torture.

After the photos of the horrors at Abu Ghraib, Congress adopted a law that prohibits cruel treatment of our prisoners.[321] The law was proposed by Sen. John McCain (R-Ariz.), who was tortured during the Vietnam War. The administration opposed McCain's proposal, but the president was forced to sign it into law by strong congressional support for it. Yet the president issued a signing statement indicating that he wouldn't feel bound by the law.[322]

Many Americans would countenance torture, and certainly "torture lite," against terrorists in the event of a "ticking time bomb." But such scenarios, though common on television, are rare in reality. (Military officers and veteran interrogators have urged television producers of shows such as "24" to offer more realistic scenarios.)[323] And once rough treatment is used, it tends to be extended to other enemies and other situations that are less urgent.

When the insurgency in Iraq proved difficult to control, American officials became frustrated. A general who had overseen the interrogations at Guantanamo Bay was sent to Baghdad to introduce similar tactics there.[324] But many arrestees in Iraq were neither terrorists nor insurgents. When attacks occurred, the American military, adopting a tactic used by the Israeli military for suicide bombings, conducted a sweep of the area, rounding up all men, roughly interrogating them, and weeding out those who seemed innocent.[325] Intelligence officers estimated that 70 to 90 percent of the men who were arrested and interrogated in Iraq were innocent.[326] Yet they were subjected to harsh treatment.

Another problem with rough treatment is that interrogators have trouble restraining themselves when their approach isn't producing any results.[327] We know that severe beatings were administered to some detainees, and burning cigarettes were put in their ears.[328] We also know that at least one was sodomized with a broomstick, and several were subjected to electric shocks.[328(a)] As many as thirty-four prisoners may have been killed during interrogations in Afghanistan and Iraq.[329] (See the box "Insurance for Interrogators.")

Renditions

For some important prisoners, the government arranged with other countries to perform the interrogations for us. In a procedure called **rendition**, the CIA seized suspects in foreign countries and whisked them away to other countries whose intelligence services had ties with the CIA. Islamic extremists were seized not only from the Middle East but also from countries in Africa, Asia, and Europe and taken to Egypt, Jordan, Morocco, Saudi Arabia, Syria, and Uzbekistan, all of which are known to use torture.[330] "We don't kick the [expletive] out of them," an American official

---

BEHIND THE SCENES

INSURANCE FOR INTERROGATORS

The Bush administration protected CIA agents and also civilian employees who interrogated terrorist suspects. Even when the Defense Department referred cases of detainee abuse to the Justice Department for prosecution, the administration dropped most cases (twenty-two out of twenty-four).[1] With a new administration taking office in 2009, the CIA feared that its interrogation methods might be the subject of presidential or congressional investigations. Both presidential candidates opposed some techniques used by the agency, so the new administration might not shield the agency like the Bush administration did. In fact, there was a "high level of anxiety about political retribution," one CIA officer said. "[S]everal guys expect to be thrown under the bus."[2]

If CIA interrogators are subpoenaed to testify before congressional committees, they will need a lawyer. So, before the election, the CIA offered to reimburse its employees who were involved in covert activities the cost of liability insurance for any actions, such as the interrogations, they conducted.

A company in Arlington, Virginia, sells the insurance for $300 each year. This plan covers legal bills for the interrogator up to $100,000 in a criminal case and $200,000 in a noncriminal case. The plan also pays court judgments or settlements against the interrogator up to $1 million.

[1]Dan Eggen and Josh White, "A Secret Memo after 9/11," *Washington Post National Weekly Edition*, April 14–20, 2008, 33.
[2]Jane Mayer, "The Black Sites," *New Yorker*, August 13, 2007, 49.
Source: Adam Zagorin, "Washington Memo," *Time*, March 31, 2008, 20.

said. "We send them to other countries so *they* can kick the [expletive] out of them."[331]

The transfers were made in secret, using unmarked airplanes in remote corners of airports at night. The transfers ignored legal formalities, such as extradition procedures, and have defied national laws. Six suspects were taken from Bosnia even though the Bosnian supreme court had ordered them released. The secrecy reduced court battles and minimized the publicity that could tip off suspects' comrades or inflame public opinion. An official in Indonesia, which has the world's largest Muslim population, said, "We can't be seen cooperating too closely with the United States."[332]

People in Germany, Italy, and Sweden expressed outrage when they learned that the CIA had snatched suspects from their countries. Prosecutors in Germany and Italy have issued arrest warrants for the CIA agents involved. Renditions do appear to violate international agreements signed by the United States.[333]

Surveillance

Soon after 9/11, the government began to intercept international calls and domestic calls of American citizens without judicial approval.[334] The **National Security Agency**, which is our largest intelligence agency, conducts this program. The NSA was established in secret in 1952 to obtain intelligence of our adversaries' communications. Located at Fort Meade in Maryland, the agency was so secretive that for years the government refused to acknowledge its existence. (Washingtonians joked that "NSA" stood for No Such Agency.) Today its existence is acknowledged, and the huge agency has its own off-ramp from the Baltimore-Washington Parkway, marked "NSA Employees Only."

The agency operates two programs relevant here, one wiretapping international calls and e-mails and another analyzing domestic calls.

Wiretapping International Calls and E-mails

The NSA eavesdrops on phone calls and e-mails between people in the United States and people in foreign countries. It gains access through American telecommunications companies, which have created a robust network of fiber-optic cables that carry most worldwide communications that travel on wires. Then it uses computer searches to look for telltale words and phrases that might be used by terrorists.

When the revelations about this program broke, President Bush said, "[I]f you're talking to a member of al-Qaeda, we want to know why."[335] Vice President Cheney downplayed the revelations. "If you're calling Aunt Sadie in Paris, we're probably not really interested." A White House representative emphasized that the NSA was recording calls "from very bad people to very bad people."[336] Apparently, however, the program has been more extensive than the administration admitted. Thousands of ordinary Americans have had their conversations recorded.[337]

The snooping occurs without judicial authorization. For electronic eavesdropping, the Foreign Intelligence Surveillance Act (FISA) required the government to obtain authorization from the Foreign Intelligence Surveillance Court (explained in Chapter 13).[338] To obtain authorization, the government had to present some evidence against the targets of the search. But the administration didn't have any evidence—it was conducting "a fishing expedition"—so it didn't seek authorization.[339]

This program, according to legal experts, was a clear violation of the FISA law. At the administration's request, Congress amended the FISA law to allow this program to continue in 2007.[340] (See also the box, "War on Terrorism or War on Drugs?")

BEHIND THE SCENES
WAR ON TERRORISM OR WAR ON DRUGS?

The NSA program to eavesdrop on phone calls between people in the United States and those in foreign countries was assumed to have begun after the terrorist attacks. But investigative reporters discovered that the program began far earlier. Its roots extend at least to the 1990s, when the Clinton administration approved a program for the NSA to eavesdrop on phone calls between people in the United States and those in drug-producing countries in Latin America. The goal was to help the Drug Enforcement Administration interdict drug shipments and break up drug cartels.

Shortly after taking office, the Bush administration expanded the program, and after 9/11 expanded it further to target the terrorist threat as well as the drug trade. The portion of the program directed at possible terrorists has received public scrutiny, but the portion directed at drug producers, which remains classified, has escaped much attention.

Source: Eric Lichtblau, James Risen, and Scott Shane, "Wide Monitoring Fuels Plan to Aid Phone Industry," *New York Times*, December 16, 2007, YTI.

Analyzing Domestic Calls

The NSA also analyzes calls between people within the United States. From the telecommunications companies, the NSA obtains the callers' and receivers' numbers; the date, time, and duration of the calls; and even the content of the calls as well. The goal is to uncover hidden terrorists through social network analysis. Al-Qaeda is so amorphous and diffuse that it's difficult for outsiders to identify its members. By correlating calls, computers map patterns of interactions among people. If the government knows that one person is a member of al-Qaeda, social network analysis might identify other members too.

It's not clear how extensive this program is; evidently, the government has examined the calls of "tens of thousands" of Americans without seeking judicial authorization.[341]

It's also not clear whether either the international program or the domestic program has identified any terrorists.

USA PATRIOT Act

The **USA PATRIOT Act** also expands surveillance of people within the United States. (The title is an acronym for Uniting and Strengthening America by Providing Appropriate Tools Required to Intercept and Obstruct Terrorism.) This act, which was passed in a rush after 9/11, with limited congressional consideration and little public debate,[342] also has important implications for civil liberties.

The Patriot Act expands domestic intelligence gathering. It shifts the FBI's primary function from solving crimes to gathering intelligence within the country. (The CIA, NSA, and other agencies gather intelligence outside the country.) The act allows the FBI and CIA to share intelligence, which had been prohibited after abuses by both agencies in the 1960s and 1970s. The goal is to coordinate their efforts and pool their information.

The act loosens some restrictions on searches and seizures and on wiretaps. It enables the FBI to obtain various papers and records, including the records of books bought from bookstores or checked out from libraries and the records of websites visited on library computers. For other computers, including personal computers, the act allows surveillance of the websites visited and key words used in search engines, and header information (to, from, and subject lines) of e-mail messages. (A later act encourages Internet service providers to turn over the *contents* of their customers' e-mail messages.)[343] The act extends surveillance to financial data—where people make and spend money, including what they buy online and what they borrow and invest.

Because some 9/11 terrorists entered the country on student visas, the act establishes a database to monitor foreign students in American colleges. When foreign students apply for a visa, their data is logged into the database. Each semester the schools are required to forward information about the students' classes and activities on campus. When government officials investigate particular students, the schools are forbidden from telling the students that their records were checked.

Because most 9/11 terrorists lived in the United States for some time before the attacks, the act authorizes the government to monitor foreign visitors in the country. The U.S. Citizenship and Immigration Services (USCIS) requires nonresident aliens who are male and over sixteen and who come from an Arab or Muslim country to report to its offices to be fingerprinted, photographed, and interrogated. The men must notify the agency of any new address within ten days, and they must reappear annually.

The PATRIOT Act puts in place a surveillance state more extensive than Americans have ever experienced.[344] Yet the act is difficult to evaluate—how it is implemented and what impact it has had—because the Bush administration was unusually secretive, shielding its policies and their effects from congressional oversight, judicial review, and public scrutiny.

DEMOCRACY?

What are the implications for democratic government when the executive branch deemphasizes or ignores civil liberties? When the executive branch unilaterally reinterprets—essentially, overrides—national and international laws addressing civil liberties, and when the legislative branch looks the other way? Or are these concerns irrelevant when there's a risk to national security? These questions point toward a bigger question: can democratic government function as it's supposed to in the face of a serious threat or an actual crisis?

During other crises in our history, well-meaning political leaders, responding to peoples' fears, took bold action that affected civil liberties. During the Civil War, President Lincoln suspended the writ of *habeas corpus*. During World War II, President Roosevelt ordered the internment of Japanese Americans. In response to the Russian Revolution, the executive and legislative branches launched the Red Scare. In response to the Cold War, history repeated itself as Congress pursued efforts that led to McCarthyism. In hindsight, all of these actions have been condemned as overreactions. All of them have been criticized as unnecessary infringements of civil liberties and rights.[345] Might some of today's efforts to identify potential terrorists be seen this way by later generations? Or will these efforts be considered prudent behavior under the circumstances?

Conclusion: Are the Courts Responsive in Interpreting Civil Liberties?

The Supreme Court has interpreted the Constitution to provide invaluable civil liberties. The Warren Court in the 1950s and 1960s, which included four of the most committed and forceful advocates of the Bill of Rights ever to sit on the High Court—Chief Justice Warren and Justices Black, Brennan, and Douglas—expanded civil liberties more than any other Court in history. It applied many provisions of the Bill of Rights to the states. It greatly broadened First Amendment rights and criminal defendants' rights. It also established a right to privacy.

Observers predicted that the Burger Court would lead a constitutional counterrevolution. However, it didn't. The Burger Court in the 1970s and 1980s narrowed some rights, especially for criminal defendants. But the Court accepted the core of the Warren Court's doctrine and even extended the right to privacy to encompass abortions.

Nor did the Rehnquist Court in the 1980s, 1990s, and 2000s produce a constitutional counterrevolution. It, too, narrowed some rights, but it also accepted most of the Warren Court's doctrine and even extended the right to privacy to encompass homosexual practices.

The decisions by these Courts show the extent to which the Supreme Court is responsive to the people in civil liberties cases. The majority of the people support civil liberties in general but not necessarily in specific situations. The majority supports civil liberties less than the elites. As the Court expanded civil liberties, it was more responsive to various minorities—political and religious minorities and unpopular groups such as criminal defendants—and to the elites rather than to the majority.

When the Supreme Court has upheld civil liberties, it has fulfilled what many legal scholars consider the quintessential role of the highest court in a democracy—"to vindicate the constitutional rights of minorities, of dissidents, of the unrepresented, of the disenfranchised, of the unpopular." The other branches of government, whose officials are elected every two, four, or six years, are sensitive to the needs of "the majority, the politically powerful, the economically influential, and the socially popular."[346] According to this view, the judicial branch should be sensitive to the needs of the others.

Because the Founders didn't intend the Court to be very responsive to the majority, they gave it substantial independence. Therefore, it doesn't have to mirror public opinion, although it can't ignore this opinion either. The Warren Court went too far too fast for too many people. It produced a backlash that led to the Burger and Rehnquist Courts, which were somewhat more responsive to majority opinion—and somewhat less vigilant in protecting civil liberties.

Key Terms

Abu Ghraib prison

natural rights

civil liberties

Bill of Rights

First Amendment

freedom of speech

seditious speech

Red Scare

McCarthyism

Warren Court

hate speech

public forum

symbolic speech

Rehnquist Court

Burger Court

Roberts Court

freedom of association

freedom of the press

Pentagon Papers

libel

separation of church and state

free exercise clause

establishment clause

due process

presumption of innocence

unreasonable searches and seizures

exclusionary rule

Miranda rights

right to counsel

right to a jury trial

cruel and unusual punishment

plea bargain

right to privacy

right to abortion

right to die

George W. Bush administration

habeas corpus

"stress and duress"

rendition
National Security Agency
USA PATRIOT Act

William Rehnquist
Thomas Jefferson
James Madison
George W. Bush
Dick Cheney

Key Names

John Stuart Mill
Joseph McCarthy
Earl Warren

Please visit our companion website at www.cengage.com/politicalscience/welch/uag12e or use CengageNOW for additional resources dealing with this chapter.

In recent years, interracial dating and marriage have increased.

Civil Rights

15

Talking Points

In the tiny town of Central Point, Virginia, Mildred Jeter and Richard Loving fell in love, and they decided to marry in 1958. Mildred was black; Richard was white. Virginia, like fifteen other states at the time, prohibited miscegenation—interracial marriage—to preserve "racial integrity" and prevent "a mongrel breed."[1] Whites considered blacks so inferior that they thought the races should have no contact except in a master-slave or a master-servant relationship. Romantic attractions were especially threatening to official segregation. Interracial couples represented the clearest breach, and their offspring the greatest threat, to the established order. So, the sheriff arrested Mildred and Richard, and the court convicted them, sentencing them to leave the state and not return, as a couple, for twenty-five years.

The Lovings didn't intend to be civil rights pioneers. In Virginia and Central Point, there were two standards. While the state banned miscegenation, the town condoned it. Interracial relationships were so common in the town that many residents who were legally defined as black, due to their ancestry, appeared almost white. Some who moved away passed for white and married into families that were white. Mildred and Richard simply did what

others before them had done. But state officials tried to enforce the law, and the local sheriff, for some unknown reason, arrested this one couple.[2]

The Lovings appealed to the Supreme Court, which overturned their conviction and struck down the antimiscegenation laws in Virginia and the other states.[3] The couple returned to Central Point and shunned media attention. But their case and the Court's decision would presage societal changes in attitudes and behavior toward interracial relationships.

Since the 1960s, whites and blacks both report more social contact with members of the other race and more approval of interracial dating and marriage, which is especially significant because these practices were the ultimate taboos. According to one survey, four of every ten Americans say they have dated someone of another race, and almost three of every ten say it has been a "serious" relationship.[4] According to the 2000 census, 6.7 percent of all marriages—up from 4.4 percent in the 1990 census—are interracial. (And many cohabitations, which aren't included in the census, are interracial as well.) Thirteen percent of marriages involving blacks are interracial, and a third of marriages involving Hispanics and Asians are as well.[5]

The term *civil rights* means equal rights for persons regardless of their race, sex, or ethnic background. The **Declaration of Independence** proclaimed that "all men are created equal." The author, **Thomas Jefferson**, knew that all men were not created equal in many respects, but he meant that they should be considered equal in their rights and equal before the law. This notion represented a break with Great Britain, where rigid classes with unequal rights existed; nobles enjoyed more rights than commoners.

The Declaration's promise didn't include nonwhites or women, however. So although colonial Americans advocated equality, they envisioned it only for white men. Other groups eventually gained more equality, but the Declaration's promise remains unfulfilled for some.

This engraving depicts a woman who jumped from a window after being sold.

Race Discrimination

African Americans, Hispanics, and American Indians all have endured and continue to experience discrimination. This chapter recounts the struggle for equal rights by these groups.

Discrimination against African Americans

Slavery

The first Africans came to America in 1619, just twelve years after the first whites. Like many whites, the Africans initially came as indentured servants. In exchange for their passage across the ocean, they were bound to an employer, usually for four to seven years, and then freed. Later in the century, however, the colonies passed laws making the Africans and their children slaves for life.

Once slavery was established, the slave trade flourished. In the South, slavery provided the foundation for an agricultural economy with huge and prosperous plantations. (See the box "Preventing Escapes.")

In the North, slavery also was common. Large plantations in Connecticut, Massachusetts, and Rhode Island shipped agricultural products to the West Indies in exchange for molasses used to make rum. Tradesmen and households in the cities also used slaves. In the mid-1700s, New York City had more slaves than any city in the colonies except Charleston, and in the early 1800s, it had more slaves than any city, including Charleston. About 40 percent of its households owned slaves (though, unlike southern plantations, an average of only two slaves per household).[6]

At the outbreak of the Revolutionary War in 1776, one-fifth of the American population was enslaved. The British, in an attempt to disrupt American society, promised freedom for the slaves. (The promise was a tactical maneuver rather than an ethical stand, as British generals themselves had slaves.) Perhaps as many as 80,000 escaped and fought alongside the Redcoats.[7] After the war, some fled to Canada with the Loyalists, some sailed to Caribbean islands, where they would be enslaved again, and others shipped out to Sierra Leone. Most remained in America.

Before and after the war, abolitionist sentiment grew in the North. Most slaves were freed by the time of the war, though other slaves were kept for several decades. The

BEHIND THE SCENES
PREVENTING ESCAPES

After some slaves ran away, slave owners began to cut off the toes or fingers of other slaves. This practice became widespread, and

local doctors were enlisted to perform the surgery. The practice was legalized by the Virginia Assembly in 1705. Then, in 1723, the

owners and the doctors were absolved of liability for manslaughter if the dismembering led to a slave's death.

Source: Henry Wiencek, *An Imperfect God: George Washington, His Slaves, and the Creation of America* (New York: Farrar, Straus, and Giroux, 2003), 46.

1820 census recorded 30,000 slaves in these states.[8] And these states, with their prominent merchants and bankers, served as the hub of the international trade in the commodities produced by slave labor—cotton, sugar, and tobacco.[9]

Nevertheless, abolitionist sentiment among the populace in the North was strong enough that by the Constitutional Convention there were sharp differences between northern and southern attitudes toward slavery. In most parts of the North, slavery was condemned,[10] but in the South it was accepted and ingrained.

As a result of the compromises between northern and southern states, the Constitution protected slavery. It allowed the importation of slaves until 1808, when Congress could bar further importation, and it required the return of escaped slaves to their owners.

In 1808, Congress barred the importation of slaves but not the practice of slavery. Yet Thomas Jefferson, a Virginia slave owner, foresaw its demise, "whether brought on by the generous energy of our own minds" or by a "bloody process."[11]

DEMOCRACY?

Democratic government began in ancient Greece, which held prisoners captured in wars as slaves. Because slavery and democracy coexisted in ancient Greece, we might ask, Is slavery incompatible with democracy?

Abolitionists called for an end to slavery. In response, southerners began to question the Declaration of Independence and to repudiate its notion of natural rights, attributing this idea to Jefferson's "radicalism."[12]

The Supreme Court tried to quell the antislavery sentiment in the **Dred Scott case** in 1857.[13] Dred Scott, a slave who lived in Missouri, was taken by his owner to the free state of Illinois and the free territory of Wisconsin and, after five years, was returned to Missouri. The owner died and passed title to his wife, who moved and left Scott in the care of people who opposed slavery. They arranged for Scott to sue his owner for his freedom. They argued that Scott's time in a free state and a free territory made him a free man

even though he was returned to a slave state. The owner also opposed slavery, so she could have simply freed Scott, but they all sought a major court decision to keep slavery out of the territories.

In this infamous case, Chief Justice Roger Taney, from Tennessee, stated that blacks, whether slave or free, were not citizens and were, in fact, "so far inferior that they had no rights which the white man was bound to respect." Taney could have stopped here—if Scott wasn't a citizen, he couldn't sue in federal court at the time—but Taney continued. He declared that Congress had no power to control slavery in the territories. This meant that slavery could extend into the territories that Congress had declared free. It also raised the possibility that slavery might extend into the states that had prohibited it.

By this time, slavery had become the hottest controversy in American politics, and this decision fanned the flames. It provoked vehement opposition in the North and produced bitter polarization in the country, leading to the Civil War. Today it is cited among the worst decisions ever made by the Supreme Court. (Yet three decades earlier, Taney had freed his own slaves, whom he had inherited

Slavery became a polarizing issue years before the Civil War. The *Anti-Slavery Alphabet*, a children's book, was first published in 1847.

american diversity | Black Masters

Although most slave owners were white, some were black. In the South, as many as 3,700 were black.[1] William Ellison of South Carolina was one. Born a slave, he bought his freedom and then his family's by building and repairing cotton gins. Over time, he earned enough money to buy slaves himself and operate a plantation. With sixty-three slaves, Ellison ranked in the top 3 percent of all slaveholders, black or white. Ellison was unusual, but he was not unique. In Charleston, South Carolina, alone, more than one hundred African Americans owned slaves in 1860. Most, however, owned fewer than four.[2]

As a member of the slave-owning class, Ellison was allowed to sue a white man who didn't pay his bills (and even to win the case). Ellison's family was granted a pew on the main floor of the Episcopal church. Yet in most respects the black owners weren't seen as equals by whites. They were expected to maintain the norms of black-white relations, especially to act deferentially toward whites.

And as the Civil War approached, whites increasingly viewed free blacks, even slaveholders, as a threat to the established order. State legislatures passed harsh legislation to regulate free blacks. For example, they had to

have a white "guardian" to vouch for their moral character, and they had to carry special papers to prove their free status. Without these papers, they could be sold back into slavery.

Some black slaveholders showed little sign that they shared the concerns of black slaves. Indeed, Ellison freed none of his slaves.

Source: Michael Johnson and James L. Roark, *Black Masters* (New York: Norton, 1984).
[1]Loren Schweninger, *Black Property Owners in the South, 1790–1915* (Urbana, Illinois: University of Illinois Press, 1990), cited in David Brion Davis, *Inhuman Bondage: The Rise and Fall of Slavery in the New World* (New York: Oxford University Press, 2006), 373, n. 17.
[2]For an acclaimed novel exploring the moral intricacies for black slave owners, read Edward P. Jones, *The Known World* (New York: Amistad, 2003).

from his parents, and he remained with the Union when the war broke out.)[14]

Although Scott received his freedom from his owner, most slaves weren't so lucky (see the box "Black Masters"). When the Civil War began, one of every nine black people in America was free; the other eight were slaves. The slaves were so integral to the southern economy that the paper money of some Confederate states depicted slaves harvesting cotton.[15]

The North's victory in the Civil War gave force to President Lincoln's Emancipation Proclamation ending slavery.[16] But blacks would find short-lived solace.

Reconstruction

After the war, Congress passed and the states ratified three constitutional amendments. The Thirteenth Amendment prohibited slavery. (In 1995, Mississippi became the last state to ratify the amendment, but of course the state's ratification was merely a symbolic act by then.) The Fourteenth Amendment granted citizenship to blacks, thus overruling the Dred Scott decision, and also granted "equal protection of the laws" and "due process of law." The **equal protection clause** would eventually become the primary guarantee that government would treat people equally. The Fifteenth Amendment gave black men the right to vote.

These amendments not only granted specific rights for African Americans but also transformed the relationship between the federal and state governments. Each amendment included the stipulation that "Congress shall have power to enforce" the provisions of the amendment. (In the wake of the war, Congress didn't trust the southern states to enforce the constitutional provisions.) This stipulation granted the federal government new power—whatever power was necessary to guarantee these rights. This power was in marked contrast to the Founders' original understanding that the federal government would have limited power. The Civil War and these amendments together thus constituted a constitutional revolution, as explained in Chapter 2.[17]

Congress also passed a series of Civil Rights Acts, which allowed blacks to buy, own, and sell property; to make contracts; to sue; and to serve as witnesses and jurors in court. The acts also allowed blacks to use public transportation, such as railroads and steamboats, and to patronize hotels and theaters.[18]

During Reconstruction, the Union Army, which occupied the South, enforced the new amendments and acts. Military commanders established procedures to register voters and hold elections. The commanders also started schools for the children of former slaves. But the army didn't have enough troops in the region to maintain Reconstruction policies (just as our military didn't have enough troops in Iraq to maintain order). And in state after state, the South resisted.[19]

Eventually, the North capitulated. The 1876 presidential election between Republican Rutherford Hayes and Democrat Samuel Tilden was disputed in some states. To resolve the dispute, Republicans, most of whom were northerners, and Democrats, many of whom were southerners, agreed to a compromise: Hayes would be named president, and the remaining Union troops would be removed from the South. Without the Union troops, there was no way to enforce the Reconstruction policies.

The collapse of Reconstruction limited the impact of the Civil War. In effect, the South was allowed to nullify one result of the war—granting legal and political rights to blacks—in exchange for accepting two other results—preserving the Union and abolishing slavery.

In hindsight, it isn't surprising that Reconstruction didn't accomplish more. It was difficult, if not impossible, to integrate 4 million former slaves into a society that was bitter in its defeat and weak economically. Northerners who expected progress to come smoothly were naive. When it didn't come quickly, they grew weary. At the same time, there was a desire for healing between the regions and lingering feelings for continuity with the past.

Public attitudes during Reconstruction thus began a recurring cycle that continues to this day: periodically the public gets upset about the treatment of African Americans and is determined to improve the conditions. But the public is naive and impatient, and when the efforts don't produce the results it expects as soon as it expects, the public becomes disillusioned with the efforts and dissatisfied with their costs. Then the public forces the government to put the race problem on the back burner until some future generation picks it up again.[20]

Neoslavery

Despite the outcome of the Civil War and the passage of the Thirteenth Amendment, many southern blacks were subjected to **neoslavery**, which was new forms of slavery or near slavery.

One type of neoslavery was **sharecropping**. After the war, Congress had rejected proposals to break up the plantations and give former slaves "forty acres and a mule" or to provide aid to establish schools. Without land or education,

Black men and boys were arrested and used like slave laborers for local landowners and factory owners. This boy is being punished in a forced labor camp in Georgia in the 1930s.

the former slaves had to work for their former masters as hired hands. As sharecroppers, they were dependent on the landowners, who had designed a system to bind the workers to the plantations. A landowner contracted with former slaves to work on his fields and live at his plantation. The sharecroppers were allowed to sell half of their crop to the landowner and keep the proceeds, but they were paid so little, regardless of how hard they worked, that the families had to borrow to tide themselves over the winter. The next year, they had to work for the same landowner to pay off their debts. The cycle continued, year after year. And lacking education, most sharecroppers didn't keep any records, so they didn't know how much they were owed, and many were cheated.

Another type of neoslavery was even harsher. Landowners or factory owners who needed more workers conspired with local officials to charge black men with minor crimes, such as vagrancy, gambling, "selling cotton after sunset," or changing employers without permission.[21] The men would be tried, convicted, and fined more than they could afford, so they would be jailed. Then they would be leased to local plantations, mines, mills, lumber camps, turpentine camps, brick companies, or steel factories to work off their fines. The arrest rates seemed to fluctuate according to the labor needs of the local businesses. (Some factories owned by northern corporations also benefited from this scheme.)[22]

The prisoners were guarded—some were shackled to their bed at night—and many were worked to their death. One, convicted of "gaming" in 1903, was leased to a mine. His fine could be worked off in 10 days, but his "fees" to the sheriff, court clerk, and the witnesses at his trial required 104 more days. He didn't survive long enough to be released.

This industrial servitude was pervasive in rural Alabama and common in other southern states. It continued until the mid-1940s.

Segregation

In both the South and the North, blacks came to be segregated from whites.

Segregation in the South   The reconciliation between Republicans and Democrats—northerners and southerners—was effected at the expense of blacks. Removing the troops enabled the South to govern itself again, and this enabled the South to reduce blacks to near-slave status.

Before the Civil War, there was no segregation in rural areas, where slaves' shacks sat near plantation mansions, or in urban areas, where few blocks were solidly black. Segregation would have been inconvenient, with blacks and whites working in proximity, and it would have been unnecessary—slavery itself kept blacks at the bottom of society. But after slavery was abolished, southerners established segregation as a new way to keep blacks "in their place."

The southern states established a pervasive pattern of **Jim Crow laws** by the turn of the century.[23] These laws segregated residential areas—city blocks or whole neighborhoods. Some small towns excluded blacks altogether, either by passing explicit laws or by adopting **sundown laws**, which required blacks to be off the streets by 10 P.M.

Other Jim Crow laws segregated schools, which blacks had been allowed to attend during Reconstruction, and even textbooks (black schools' texts had to be stored separately from white schools' books).

Many laws segregated public accommodations, such as hotels, restaurants, bars, theaters, and streetcars. Other laws segregated sporting events, circuses, and parks. They separated black and white checkers players in Birmingham and districts for black and white prostitutes in New Orleans.

The laws were pervasive, segregating entrances, exits, ticket windows, waiting rooms, restrooms, and drinking fountains. They segregated the races in prisons, hospitals, and homes for the blind. They even segregated the races in death—in morgues, funeral homes, and cemeteries.

Although blacks were denied access to better locations or facilities, the greatest damage from segregation was that they were degraded. The system of Jim Crow laws was "an officially organized degradation ceremony, repeated day after day." Segregation told blacks that they were inferior and did not belong in the communities in which they lived.[24]

In addition to the laws, blacks were forced to defer to whites in informal settings as well—for instance, to move off the sidewalk when a white pedestrian approached. Failure to defer could bring punishment for being "uppity." Blacks were "humiliated by a thousand daily reminders of their subordination."[25]

Meanwhile, northern leaders, who had championed the cause of the slaves before and during the Civil War, abandoned African Americans a decade after the war. Congress declined to pass new laws, presidents refused to enforce existing laws, and the Supreme Court gutted the constitutional amendments and Civil Rights Acts.[26]

Then the Court upheld segregation itself. Louisiana passed "an Act to promote the comfort of passengers," which mandated separate accommodations in trains. New Orleans black leaders sponsored a test case challenging the act's constitutionality. Homer Adolph Plessy, who was seventh-eighths white—an "octoroon" in the parlance of the time—nonetheless was considered black, and he sat in the white car. When the conductor ordered him to move to the black car, Plessy refused. He maintained that the act was unconstitutional under the Fourteenth Amendment. In **Plessy v. Ferguson** in 1896, the Court disagreed, claiming that the act was not a denial of equal protection because it provided equal accommodations.[27] The Court established the **separate-but-equal doctrine**, which allowed separate facilities if they were "equal." Of course, government required separate facilities only because people thought the races

Library of Congress #LC-DIG-fsa-8a17588

Some restaurants in the North, such as this one in Lancaster, Ohio, in the 1930s, maintained segregation by refusing to serve blacks.

were not equal, but the Court brazenly commented that the act did not stamp "the colored race with a badge of inferiority" unless "the colored race chooses to put that construction on it." Only Justice John Harlan, a former Kentucky slaveholder, dissented: "Our Constitution is color-blind, and neither knows nor tolerates classes among citizens."

Three years later, the Court accepted segregation in schools.[28] A Georgia school board turned a black high school into a black elementary school without establishing a new high school for blacks or allowing them to attend the existing high schools for whites. Nevertheless, the Court said this action was not a denial of equal protection. Its ruling set a pattern in which separate but equal meant separation but not equality.

Segregation in the North   Although Jim Crow laws were not as pervasive in the North as in the South, they were quite common. In fact, sundown laws were more prevalent in the North, especially in the Midwest. In the 1930s, Hawthorne, California, posted a sign at its city limits: "Nigger, Don't Let The Sun Set On YOU In Hawthorne."[29] Jim Crow laws in the northern states prompted one writer to proclaim, "The North has surrendered!"[30]

Yet job opportunities were better in the North. While southern blacks were sharecropping—as late as 1930, 80 percent of those who farmed were working somebody else's land[31]—northern factories were offering jobs. Between 1915 and 1940, more than a million southern blacks headed north in the **Great Migration**. Although they got decent jobs, they were forced to live in black ghettos because they couldn't afford better housing and they weren't allowed to live in some areas.

Denial of the Right to Vote

With the adoption of the Fifteenth Amendment, many African Americans voted and elected fellow African Americans to office during Reconstruction, but southern states began to disfranchise them in the 1890s (as explained in Chapter 7).

Violence

To solidify their control, whites engaged in violence against blacks. In the 1880s and 1890s, whites lynched about 100 blacks a year. In the 1900s, vigilante "justice" continued (see Table 1). For example, a mob in Livermore, Kentucky, dragged a black man accused of murdering a white man into a theater. The ringleaders charged admission and hanged the man. Then they allowed the audience to shoot at the swinging body—those in the balcony could fire once; those in the better seats could empty their revolvers.[32]

Lynchings often began with a false report of a white woman being sexually assaulted by a black man. An irate mob would gather and, after locating the man, would subject him to an excruciating ordeal. Usually, they castrated him before they killed him. Frequently, they hacked off his fingers and ears as well.[33]

Lynchings were not the result of a few troublemakers; rather, they were a social institution in the South. The ritualized spectacles were a desperate attempt to cling to the antebellum order upset by the Civil War. At the same time, lynchings were an outgrowth of the increase in white

Table 1	Why Whites Lynched Blacks in 1907

Whites gave the following reasons for lynching blacks, who may or may not have committed the acts cited.

Reason	Number of Lynchings
Murder	5
Attempted murder	5
Manslaughter	10
Rape	9
Attempted rape	11
Burglary	3
Harboring a fugitive	1
Theft of 75 cents	1
Having a debt of $3	2
Winning a fight with a white man	1
Insulting a white man	1
Talking to white girls on the telephone	1
Being the wife or son of a rapist	2
Being the father of a boy who "jostled" white women	1
Expressing sympathy for the victim of mob violence	3

SOURCE: Adapted from Ray Stannard Baker, *Following the Color Line* (New York: Harper & Row, 1964), 176–177.

© Bettmann/CORBIS

Lynching occurred not only in the South but also in northern cities such as Marion, Indiana, in 1930. The girls on the left hold pieces of the victims' clothing, torn off as "souvenirs."

women who worked outside the home at the turn of the century. As these women experienced greater independence, insecure men feared that the women would become too independent, perhaps even leave them for black men. Hence the ritual of castration.[34] Through lynchings, then, white men could remain in charge—at home and in the community—while appearing to defend women's honor.

Lynchings were considered entertaining as well as essential to maintain order. They would be photographed and, later, postcards would be sold (though after 1907, postal regulations banned them from the mail).

In 1919, twenty-five race riots erupted in six months. White mobs took over cities in the North and South, burning black neighborhoods and terrorizing black residents for days on end.[35] In 1921, 10,000 whites burned down thirty-five blocks of Tulsa's black neighborhood. The incident that precipitated the riot was typical—a report of an assault by a black man on a white woman. The report was false, fabricated by the woman (and later retracted), but residents were inflamed by a racist newspaper and encouraged by the city's officials. Almost 300 people were shot, burned alive, or tied to cars and dragged to death. Survivors reported corpses stacked like firewood on street corners and piled high in dump trucks.[36]

The white-supremacist **Ku Klux Klan**, which began during Reconstruction and started up again in 1915, played a major role in inflaming prejudice and terrorizing blacks. It was strong enough to dominate many southern towns and even the state governments of Oklahoma and Texas. It also made inroads into some northern states, such as Indiana.

In addition, bands of white farmers known as "White-caps" nailed notes, with a drawing of a coffin and a warning

Tulsa Historical Society

Tulsa's black neighborhood after whites burned it down in 1921.

to leave or die, on the doors of black farmers. Their goal was to drive black farmers off the land. Then the local governments put the land up for auction or simply gave it to the white families who owned the adjacent land.[37] The impact of this intimidation continued for many generations and, in fact, continues to this day. The black families lost wealth for themselves and their descendants, and the white families gained wealth that is appreciating in value for their descendants today, many of whom may be unaware of how "their" land changed hands.

Federal officials contended that racial violence was a state problem—presidents refused to speak out, and Congress refused to pass legislation making lynching a federal offense—yet state officials did nothing.

For at least the first third of the twentieth century, white supremacy reigned, not just in the southern states but also in the border states and in many northern states. It also pervaded the nation's capital, where President Woodrow Wilson instituted segregation in the federal government.[38]

Overcoming Discrimination against African Americans

African Americans fought white supremacy primarily in three arenas: the courts, the streets, and Congress. In general, they fought in the courts first and Congress last, although as they gained momentum they increasingly fought in all three arenas at once.

The Movement in the Courts

The first goal was to convince the Supreme Court to overturn the separate-but-equal doctrine of *Plessy* v. *Ferguson.*

The NAACP   In response to racial violence, a group of blacks and whites founded the National Association for the Advancement of Colored People, or **NAACP**, in 1909. In its first two decades, it was led by **W. E. B. Du Bois**, a black sociologist. In time, it became the major organization fighting for blacks' civil rights.

Frustrated by presidential and congressional inaction, the NAACP decided to appeal to the courts, which are less subject to political pressure from the majority. The association assembled a cadre of lawyers, mainly from Howard University Law School, a historically black school in Washington, D.C., to bring lawsuits attacking segregation and the denial of the right to vote. In 1915, they persuaded the Supreme Court to strike down the grandfather clause (which exempted persons whose ancestors could vote from the literacy test);[39] two years later, they convinced the Court to invalidate residential segregation laws.[40] But the Court continued to allow most devices to disfranchise blacks and most efforts to segregate.

In 1938, the NAACP chose a thirty-year-old attorney, **Thurgood Marshall**, to head its litigation arm.[41] Marshall—

whose mother had to pawn her engagement and wedding rings so he could go to an out-of-state law school because his in-state school, the University of Maryland, didn't admit blacks—would become a tireless and courageous advocate for equal rights. (In 1946, after defending four blacks charged with attempted murder during a riot in rural Tennessee, he would narrowly escape a lynch mob.)[42]

Desegregation of schools   Seventeen states and the District of Columbia segregated their schools (and four other states allowed cities to segregate their schools). The states gave white students better facilities and white teachers larger salaries. Overall, they spent from two to ten times more on white schools than on black ones.[43] Few of these states had graduate schools for blacks: as late as 1950, they had fifteen engineering schools, fourteen medical schools, and five dental schools for whites and none for blacks; they had sixteen law schools for whites and five for blacks.

The NAACP's tactics were first to show that "separate but equal" actually resulted in unequal schools and then, attacking the concept head-on, to argue that "separate but equal" led to unequal status in general.

The NAACP challenged segregation in graduate schools. Missouri provided no black law school but offered to reimburse blacks who went to out-of-state law schools. In 1938, the Supreme Court said the state had to provide black students a law school or admit them to the white school.[44] Texas established a black law school, but it was clearly inferior to the white law school at the University of Texas. In 1950, the Court said the black school had to be substantially equal to the white school.[45] Oklahoma allowed a black student to attend the white graduate school at the University of Oklahoma but designated a separate section of the classroom, library, and cafeteria for the student. The Court said this, too, was inadequate because it deprived the student of the exchange of views with fellow students necessary for education.[46] The Court didn't invalidate the separate-but-equal doctrine in these decisions, but it made segregation almost impossible to implement in graduate schools.

The NAACP turned its attention to the lower levels of the school system. Marshall filed suits in two southern states, one border state, one northern state, and the District of Columbia. The suit in the northern state was brought against Topeka, Kansas, where Linda Brown could not attend the school just four blocks from her home because it was a white school. Instead, she had to go to a school twenty-one blocks away.[47]

When the cases reached the Supreme Court, the justices were split. Although Chief Justice Fred Vinson might have had a majority to uphold the separate-but-equal doctrine, the Court put off a decision and rescheduled oral arguments for its next term. Between the Court's terms, Vinson suffered a heart attack, and President **Dwight Eisenhower** appointed **Earl Warren** to take his place. When the Court reheard the case, the president pressured his appointee to rule in favor of segregation. Eisenhower invited Warren and the attorney for the states to the White House for dinner. When the conversation turned to the segregationists, Eisenhower said, "These are not bad people. All they are concerned about is to see that their sweet little girls are not required to sit in schools alongside some big overgrown Negroes."[48] However, Warren not only voted against segregation but used his considerable determination and charm to persuade the other justices, some of whom had supported segregation, to vote against it too. Justice Felix Frankfurter later said Vinson's heart attack was "the first indication I have ever had that there is a God."[49]

In the landmark case of **Brown v. Board of Education** in 1954, the **Warren Court** ruled unanimously that school segregation violated the Fourteenth Amendment's equal protection clause.[50] In the opinion, Warren asserted that separate but equal not only resulted in unequal schools but was inherently unequal because it made black children feel inferior. (See box "Passing the 'Brown Bag Test.'")

In overruling the *Plessy* doctrine, the Court showed how revolutionary the equal protection clause was—or could be interpreted to be. The Court required the segregated states to change their way of life to a degree unprecedented in American history. (See box "The Social Code.")

After overturning laws requiring segregation in schools, the Court overruled laws mandating segregation in other places, such as public parks, golf courses, swimming pools, auditoriums, courtrooms, and jails.[51]

BEHIND THE SCENES

PASSING THE "BROWN BAG TEST"

Whites' preoccupation with skin color affected blacks even in their relationships with other blacks. In the early twentieth century, African Americans who wanted to join certain African American clubs and churches had to pass the **brown bag test**. They had to put their hand into a brown paper bag; if their skin was a lighter color than the bag, they were eligible for membership. A social club in Nashville had a similar test. Aspiring members had to demonstrate that their blue veins could be seen through their pale skin on the underside of their wrists.

This concern for lighter skin stemmed from the slavery era, when light-skinned blacks often brought higher prices and got better jobs as household workers and skilled craftsmen than as field hands. Light-skinned blacks also were more likely to be free. In 1860, the census classified fully 30 percent of free blacks as "mulatto" (having some white ancestry), compared with only 10 percent of the slaves.

After emancipation, lighter skin continued to be a social and economic advantage. Those who, as slaves, were able to learn crafts had a head start. Many blacks with darker skin used bleach, lye, or other products to lighten their color.

Although black colleges did not restrict admission to African Americans with lighter skin, in the 1930s most of their students did have lighter skin. They were the children of doctors, dentists, lawyers, and morticians, who themselves had lighter skin and were more successful in their communities. They were predominant among African Americans who could afford to send their children to college in those years.

At college, their children took up whites' pastimes, such as cotillions and tennis, in an attempt to distinguish themselves from poor blacks and to gain acceptance from whites. (But acceptance was not granted.)

As late as the 1960s, when the slogan "Black is beautiful" became popular, the homecoming queen at Howard University usually had a light complexion.

This concern for lighter skin persists. Fashion models on *Ebony*'s covers often have pale skin, and the sales of bleaching products still continue. Lighter-skinned African Americans have higher socioeconomic status, and many African Americans prefer lighter-skinned mates.

Source: "For Black College Students in the 1930s, Respectability and Prestige Depended on Passing the Brown Bag Test," *Journal of Blacks in Higher Education*, January 31, 1999, 119–120; Louie E. Ross, "Mate Selection Preferences Among African American College Students," *Journal of Black Studies* 27 (1997), 554–569; St. Clair Drake and Horace R. Clayton, *Black Metropolis* (New York: Harcourt, Brace, 1945); Mark Hill, "Color Differences in the Socioeconomic Statuses of African American Men," *Social Forces* 78 (2000), 1437–1460.

Sorority sisters at Fisk University, a historically black college, in 1936.

National Archives/Harmon Collection, 200(S)-HS-1-92

In *Brown*, the Court had ordered the schools to desegregate "with all deliberate speed."[52] This standard was a compromise between justices who thought schools should do so immediately and those who thought communities would need to do so gradually.[53] The ambiguity of the phrase, however, allowed the communities to do so slowly, even imperceptibly. The ruling prompted much deliberation but little speed.

The South engaged in massive resistance. The Court needed help from the other branches, but Congress was controlled by southerners and President Eisenhower was reluctant to tell the states to change. In fact, the president criticized the decision. With his power and immense popularity, he could have speeded implementation by speaking out in support of the ruling, yet he offered no help for three years. When nine black students tried to attend a white high school under a desegregation plan in Little Rock, Arkansas, the governor's and state legislature's inflammatory rhetoric against desegregation encouraged local citizens to take the law into their own hands. Finally, Eisenhower acted, sending federal troops and federalizing the state's national guard to quell the riot.

President Kennedy also used federal marshals and paratroopers to stop the violence after the governor of Mississippi blocked the door to keep James Meredith from registering at the University of Mississippi. Kennedy again sent troops when the governor of Alabama, **George Wallace**, proclaiming "segregation now, segregation tomorrow, segregation forever," blocked the door to keep blacks from enrolling at the University of Alabama.

After outright defiance, some states attempted to circumvent the ruling by shutting down their public schools and providing tuition grants, textbooks, and recreation facilities for students to use at new private schools, which at the time could segregate.

The states also tried less blatant schemes, such as "freedom of choice" plans that allowed the students to choose the school they wanted to attend. Of course, virtually no whites chose a black school, and due to social pressure very few blacks chose a white school. The idea was to achieve desegregation on paper, or token desegregation in practice, in order to avoid actual desegregation. But the Court rebuffed these schemes and even forbade private schools from discriminating.[54]

To black southerners, the Court's persistence raised hopes. Chief Justice Warren, according to Thurgood Marshall, "allowed the poor Negro sharecropper to say, 'Kick me around Mr. Sheriff, kick me around Mr. County Judge, kick me around Supreme Court of my state, but there's one person I can rely on.'"[55]

To white southerners, however, the Court's rulings reflected a federal government, a distant authority, that was exercising too much control over their traditional practices. The rulings engendered much bitterness. Justice Hugo Black, who was from Alabama, was shunned by former friends from the state, and his son was driven from his legal practice in the state. The justice wasn't even sent an invitation to his fiftieth reunion at his alma mater, the University of Alabama.[56]

Despite the Court's rulings, progress was excruciatingly slow. If a school district was segregated, a group like the NAACP had to run the risks and spend the money to bring a suit in a federal district court. Judges in these courts reflected the views of the state or local political establishment, so the suit might not be successful. If it was, the school board would prepare a desegregation plan. Members of the school board reflected the views of the community and the pressures from the segregationists, so the plan might not be adequate. If it was, the segregationists would challenge it in a federal district court. If the plan was upheld, the segregationists would appeal to a federal court of appeals. Judges in these courts, based in Richmond and New Orleans, came from the South, but they were not as tied to the state or local political establishment, and they usually ruled against the segregationists. But then the segregationists could appeal to the Supreme Court. The segregationists knew they would lose sooner or later, but the process took several years, so they could delay the inevitable.

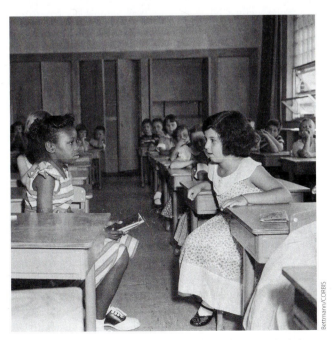

The first day for desegregated schools in Fort Myer, Virginia, brings apprehension and curiosity.

DEMOCRACY?

Does the role of the Supreme Court in the civil rights era reflect or contradict the concept of democracy? That is, was it democratic for the nonelected justices to mandate equality to the elected officials of the southern states and cities? (Consider the tension between popular sovereignty and political equality and that between majority rule and minority rights.)

BEHIND THE SCENES
THE SOCIAL CODE

At the time the Supreme Court was deciding *Brown* v. *Board of Education,* a strict social code governed interactions between blacks and whites in the South. The code, which differed from place to place, was barely visible yet clearly understood by residents and

very effective in keeping blacks "in their place."

A white woman, who had moved from the North to Alabama in the 1950s, accidentally bumped into a black woman while shopping, causing the black woman to drop her packages. The white woman

picked up the packages and handed them to her. After this courtesy, the store clerks, while making no comments, refused to wait on the white woman.

In another store on another day, the white woman and her daughter were shopping when

a black child offered her daughter a piece of candy. After her daughter accepted the candy, these clerks also refused to wait on the woman.

Source: Tinsley E. Yarbrough, *Race and Redistricting: The Shaw-Cromartie Cases* (Lawrence, Kansas: University Press of Kansas, 2003), 30.

Thus the segregationists tried to resist, then to evade, and finally to delay. In this they succeeded. In 1964, a decade after *Brown,* 98 percent of all black children in the South still attended all-black schools.[57]

By this time, the mood in Congress had changed. Congress passed the Civil Rights Act of 1964, which, among other things, cut off federal aid to school districts that continued to segregate. The following year, it passed the first major program providing federal aid to education. This was the carrot at the end of the stick; school districts complied to get the money.

Finally, by 1970, only 14 percent of all black children in the South still attended all-black schools. Of course, many others went to mostly black schools. Even so, the change was dramatic.

Busing

Brown and related rulings addressed **de jure segregation**—segregation enforced by law. This segregation can be attacked by striking down the law. *Brown* didn't address **de facto segregation**—segregation based on residential patterns—typical of northern cities and large southern cities, where most blacks live in black neighborhoods and most whites live in white neighborhoods. Students attend their neighborhood schools, which are mostly black or mostly white. This segregation is more intractable because it doesn't stem primarily from a law, so it can't be eliminated by striking down a law.

Civil rights groups proposed busing some black children to schools in white neighborhoods and some white children to schools in black neighborhoods. They hoped to improve black children's education, their self-confidence, and eventually, their college and career opportunities. They also hoped to improve black and white children's ability to get along together.

The **Burger Court** authorized busing within school districts—ordinarily cities. These included southern cities where there was a history of de jure segregation, and northern cities where there was a pattern of de facto segregation and evidence that school officials had located schools or assigned students in ways that perpetuated this segregation.[58]

However, busing for desegregation was never extensive. In one typical year, only 4 percent of students were bused for desegregation. Far more students were bused, at public expense, to segregated public and private schools.[59]

Even so, court orders for mandatory busing ran into a wall of hostile public opinion. White parents criticized the courts sharply. Their reaction stemmed from a mixture of prejudice against black people, bias against poor persons, fear of the crime in inner-city schools, worry about the quality of inner-city schools, and desire for the convenience of neighborhood schools.[60]

Due to the opposition of white parents, busing—and publicity about it—prompted an increase in "white flight" as white families moved from public schools to private schools and from the cities to the suburbs to avoid the busing in the cities.[61] This trend overlapped other trends, especially a reduction in the white birthrate and an increase in the nonwhite immigration rate, which altered the racial and economic composition of our big cities. As a result, there were fewer white students to balance enrollments and fewer middle-class students to provide stability in the cities' schools.

Therefore, even extensive busing couldn't desegregate the school systems of most big cities, where blacks and other minorities together were more numerous than whites. Consequently, civil rights groups proposed busing some white children from the suburbs to the cities and some black children from the cities to the suburbs. This approach would provide enough of both races to achieve balance in both places.

The Burger Court rejected this proposal by a 5–4 vote in 1974.[62] It ruled that busing isn't appropriate between school districts unless there is evidence of intentional segregation in both the city and its suburbs. Otherwise, such extensive busing would require too long a ride for students and too much coordination by administrators.

Although there was intentional segregation by many cities and their suburbs,[63] the evidence is not as clear-cut as that of the de jure segregation by the southern states, so it was difficult to satisfy the requirements laid down by the Court. The ruling made busing between the cities and their suburbs very rare.

Thurgood Marshall, by then a Supreme Court justice, dissented and predicted that the ruling would allow "our great metropolitan areas to be divided up each into two cities—one white, the other black." Indeed, the ruling was the beginning of the end of the push to desegregate public schools in urban areas.

In 1991, the **Rehnquist Court** ruled that school districts have no obligation to reduce de facto segregation, and the Court also diminished their obligation to reduce the vestiges of de jure segregation.[64] This ruling relieved the pressure on school districts, and most stopped busing.[65] The result was increasing resegregation.

Some districts tried other ways to balance enrollments. The county that includes Louisville, Kentucky, voluntarily adopted a "managed choice" program in which parents indicated their preference for the schools their children would attend, but the school district kept the black enrollment in each school between 15 and 50 percent. To do this, the district used extensive busing. Yet the plan was popular with most parents, including white parents, almost all of whom got their first or second choice of schools.[66] Louisville became one of the most desegregated cities in the nation.

In 2007, however, the **Roberts Court** invalidated the Louisville program and a limited program in Seattle.[67] The five-justice majority ruled that school districts can't use race as a basis for assigning students. The ruling may jeopardize the programs in a thousand school districts across the country.[68]

The Court's decisions in the 1990s and 2000s reflect none of "the moral urgency of *Brown.*"[69] Instead, they reflect hostility toward government efforts, even school districts' voluntary efforts, to achieve desegregation. For most justices, desegregation is relatively unimportant, certainly less important than allowing white parents unfettered choice where they send their children. In this way, the Court's majority mirrors the views of the Republican presidents who appointed them.

Some districts have tried to integrate the races by integrating social classes. Because black students disproportionately come from the lower classes, assigning a percentage of poor students to middle-class schools would also integrate the races to a degree. This may require students to attend schools far from home and ride buses for long distances. But Raleigh, North Carolina, which uses this approach, has seen

Dorothy Counts, the first black student to attend one white high school in Charlotte, North Carolina, is escorted by her father in 1957.

Firefighters turn their hoses on demonstrators in Birmingham, Alabama, in 1963.

a dramatic improvement in poor students' performance.[70] Such economic integration isn't likely to be overruled by the courts because it isn't based directly on race.

The Movement in the Streets

After the NAACP's early successes in the courts, other blacks, and some whites, took the fight to the streets. Their bold efforts gave birth to the modern civil rights movement.

The movement came to public attention in Montgomery, Alabama, in 1955, when **Rosa Parks** refused to move to the back of the bus. Her courage, and her arrest, roused others to boycott city buses. For their leader they chose a young Baptist minister, Dr. **Martin Luther King Jr.** The boycott catapulted the movement and King to national attention (as explained in Chapter 6).

King was the first charismatic leader of the movement. He formed the Southern Christian Leadership Conference (SCLC) of black clergy and adopted the tactics of Mahatma Gandhi, who had led the movement to free India from Britain. The tactics included direct action, such as demonstrations and marches, and civil disobedience—intentional and public disobedience of unjust laws. The tactics were based on nonviolence, even when confronted with violence. This strategy was designed to draw support from whites by contrasting the morality of the movement's position with the immorality of the opponents' discrimination and violence toward blacks.

For a long time, some southern whites, focusing on movement leaders and college students from other states, and fearing even infiltration by foreign communists, deluded themselves into thinking that "outside agitators" were responsible for the turmoil in their communities.[71] But the movement grew from the grass roots, and it eventually shattered this delusion.

The movement spread among black students. In 1960, four students of North Carolina A&T College sat at the lunch counter in Woolworth's, a chain of dime stores, and asked for a cup of coffee. The waitress refused to serve them, but they remained until they were arrested. On successive days, as whites waved the Confederate flag and jeered, more students sat at the lunch counter.[72] Within a year, such sit-ins occurred in more than 100 cities.

When blacks asserted their rights, whites often reacted with violence. In 1963, King led demonstrators in Birmingham, Alabama, seeking desegregation of public facilities. Police unleashed dogs to attack the marchers. In 1964, King led demonstrators in Selma, Alabama, for voting rights. State troopers clubbed some marchers, and vigilantes beat and shot others.

In the summer of 1964, black and white college students mounted a voter registration drive in Mississippi. By the end of the summer, 1000 had been arrested, 80 beaten, 35 shot, and 6 killed.[73] When a black cotton farmer, who had tried to register to vote, was shot in the head in broad daylight by a white state legislator, the act wasn't even treated as a crime.[74]

Indeed, perpetrators of the violence usually were not apprehended or prosecuted. When they were, they usually were not convicted. Law enforcement was frequently in the hands of bigots, and juries were normally all white.[75]

During these years, whites told pollsters they disliked the civil rights movement's speed and tactics: "They're pushing too fast and too hard." At the same time, most said they favored integration more than ever. And they seemed repelled by the violence. The brutality against black demonstrators generated more support for black Americans and their cause.

The media, especially national organizations based in northern cities such as the *New York Times,* the Associated Press, and the major television networks, played a role simply by covering the conflict. The leaders of the civil rights movement staged events that captured attention, and violent racists played into their hands. As northern reporters and photographers relayed the events and violence to the nation, the movement gained public sympathy in the North. Yet the national press became as vilified as the federal government in the South. (This anger would fuel southerners' distrust of the media for many years.)[76]

Although the movement's tactics worked well against southern de jure segregation, they didn't work as well

When three civil rights workers were murdered in Neshoba County, Mississippi, no one was indicted by the state. Later, eighteen persons, including the sheriff (right) and deputy sheriff (left), were indicted by the federal government for the lesser charge of conspiracy. (There was no applicable federal law for murder.) Ultimately, seven persons, including the deputy, were convicted by the federal court.

against northern de facto segregation or against job discrimination in either region. By the mid-1960s, progress had stalled and dissatisfaction had grown. Young blacks from the inner city, who hadn't been involved in the movement, questioned two of its principles: interracialism and nonviolence. As James Farmer, head of the Congress of Racial Equality (CORE), explained, they asked, "What is this we-shall-overcome, black-and-white-together stuff? I don't know of any white folks except the guy who runs that store on 125th Street in Harlem and garnishes wages and repossesses things you buy. I'd like to go upside his head. [Or] the rent collector, who bangs on the door demanding rent that we ain't got. I'd like to go upside his head."[77] These blacks criticized King and his tactics.

In place of the integration advocated by King, some leaders began to call for "black power." This phrase, which implied black pride and self-reliance, meant different things to different people. To some it meant political power through the ballot box, and to others it meant economic power through business ownership. To a few it meant violence in retaliation for violence by whites. The movement splintered further.

The Movement in Congress

As the civil rights movement expanded, it pressured presidents and members of Congress to act. President **John Kennedy**, who was most concerned about the Cold War, considered civil rights a distraction. President **Lyndon Johnson**, who was a champion of "the poor and the downtrodden and the oppressed"—a biographer calls him our second most compassionate president, after Abraham Lincoln[78]—supported civil rights but felt hamstrung by southerners in Congress who, through the seniority system, chaired key committees and dominated both houses. As a result, the presidents considered the civil rights leaders unreasonable, because their movement alienated the southerners on whom the presidents had to rely for other legislation.

But once the movement demonstrated real strength, it convinced the officials to act. After 200,000 blacks and whites marched in Washington in 1963, President Kennedy introduced civil rights legislation. His successor, President Johnson, with consummate legislative skill, forged a coalition of northern Democrats and northern Republicans to overcome southern Democrats and pass the Civil Rights Act of 1964. After 1000 blacks and whites had been attacked and arrested in Selma, Johnson introduced and Congress passed the Voting Rights Act of 1965. Three years later, Johnson introduced and Congress passed the Civil Rights Act of 1968. Within a span of four years, Congress passed legislation prohibiting discrimination in public accommodations, employment, housing, and voting. These would become the most significant civil rights acts in history.

It is impossible to exaggerate how controversial these laws were. In 1964, the Republican nominee for president, Sen. Barry Goldwater of Arizona, opposed the Civil Rights Act. He had been assured by two advisers—Phoenix attorney William Rehnquist and Yale professor Robert Bork—that it was unconstitutional.[79] The conservative Republican Ronald Reagan, preparing to run for California governor, also strongly opposed the act.[80] (Years later, as president, Reagan would appoint Rehnquist as chief justice and nominate Bork to serve as an associate justice on the Supreme Court. Bork wasn't confirmed, in part due to his views toward civil rights laws and rulings.)

Although President Johnson believed he was doing the right thing, he realized the political ramifications. He said he was handing the South to the Republican Party "for the next fifty years."[81] And that's exactly what happened. In less than a decade, the South went from the most Democratic region to one of the most Republican regions in the country.[82]

After the 1966 congressional elections, when it was evident that the party was losing southern voters, Democratic governors in southern and border states demanded a meeting with Johnson. They criticized administration efforts to desegregate the schools and even suggested that the president was a traitor to his heritage. The next day Johnson was still fuming. To an aide he vented, "'Niggah! Niggah! Niggah!' That's all they said to me all day. Hell, there's one thing they'd better know. If I don't achieve anything else while I'm president, I intend to wipe that word out of the English language and make it impossible for people to come here and shout 'Niggah! Niggah! Niggah!' to me and the American people."[83]

Desegregation of public accommodations The **Civil Rights Act of 1964** prohibits discrimination on the basis of race, color, religion, or national origin in public accommodations.[84] The act doesn't cover private clubs, such as country clubs, social clubs, or fraternities and sororities, on the principle that the government shouldn't tell people who they may or may not associate with in private. (The Court has made private schools an exception to this principle to help enforce *Brown,* so they can't discriminate.)

Desegregation of employment The Civil Rights Act of 1964 also prohibits employment discrimination on the basis of race, color, religion, national origin, or sex and (as amended) physical disability, age, or Vietnam-era veteran status. The act covers employers with fifteen or more employees and unions.[85]

In addition to practicing blatant discrimination, some employers practiced more subtle discrimination. They required applicants to meet standards unnecessary for the jobs, a practice that hindered blacks more than whites. A high school diploma for a manual job was a common example. The Court held that the standards must relate to the jobs.[86]

Desegregation of housing Although the Supreme Court had struck down laws that prescribed segregation in residential areas, whites maintained segregation by making **restrictive covenants**—agreements among neighbors not to sell their houses to blacks. In 1948, the Court ruled that courts could not enforce these covenants because doing so would involve the government in discrimination.[87]

Real estate agents also played a role in segregation by practicing **steering**—showing blacks houses in black neighborhoods and whites houses in white neighborhoods. Unscrupulous real estate agents practiced **blockbusting**. After a black family bought a house in a white neighborhood, the agents would warn the white neighbors that more black families would move in. Because of prejudice and fear that their house values would decline, the whites would panic and sell to the agents at low prices. Then the agents would resell to black families at higher prices. In this way, neighborhoods that might have been desegregated were instead resegregated—from all white to all black.

Bank and savings and loan officers also played a role. They were reluctant to lend money to blacks who wanted to buy houses in white neighborhoods. Some engaged in **redlining**—refusing to lend money to people who wanted to buy houses in racially changing neighborhoods. The lenders worried that if the buyers couldn't keep up with the payments, the lenders would be left with houses whose value had declined.

The government also played an important role. The Veterans Administration and the Federal Housing Authority, which guaranteed loans to some buyers, were reluctant to authorize loans to blacks who tried to buy houses in white neighborhoods (but they did provide loans to whites who fled from the cities to buy houses in all-white suburbs). And the federal government, which funded low-income housing, allowed local governments to locate such housing in ghettos. In these ways, the governments fostered and

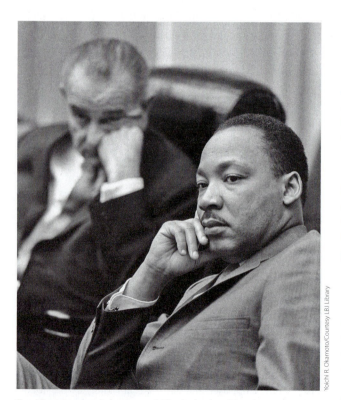

President Lyndon Johnson and Martin Luther King Jr., compatriots with a tense relationship.

Yoichi R. Okamoto/Courtesy LBJ Library

extended residential segregation (which is at the heart of the segregation of the schools and other activities such as neighborhood sports and businesses). [88]

The **Civil Rights Act of 1968** bans discrimination in the sale or rental of housing on the basis of race, color, religion, or national origin and (as amended) on the basis of sex, having children, or having a disability. The act covers 80 percent of the housing and prohibits steering, blockbusting, and redlining.

Restoration of the right to vote The Voting Rights Act of 1965, which implemented the Fifteenth Amendment, includes measures that enable blacks to vote (as explained in Chapter 8).

DEMOCRACY?

Consider the actions of the people who participated in the civil rights movement and the efforts by Congress during these years. In what ways do each of these reflect democracy?

Continuing Discrimination against African Americans

African Americans have overcome much discrimination but still face lingering prejudice. Overt laws and blatant practices have been struck down, but subtle manifestations of old attitudes persist—and in ways far more numerous and with effects far more serious than this one chapter can convey.[89] Moreover, African Americans must cope with the legacy of generations of slavery, segregation, discrimination, and for many, the effects of poverty.

They also must cope with the attitudes of whites. Although few people say they want to return to the days of legal segregation, about half reject the dream of an integrated society.[90]

Discrimination in Education

Segregated schools Some black children, mostly those who have affluent parents who pay for private schools or live in well-off neighborhoods with good public schools, go to integrated schools. However, most black children, especially those who live in big cities or areas where private schools predominate, go to segregated schools.

Although de jure segregation of schools has been eliminated, de facto segregation remains. In fact, this segregation is getting worse. After progress in the 1960s, 1970s, and 1980s, the trend toward desegregation reversed itself in the 1990s. "For the first time since the *Brown* v. *Board* decision," one study concluded, "we are going backwards"[91] (see Figure 1). A smaller proportion of black and Latino students attend schools that have a majority of white stu-

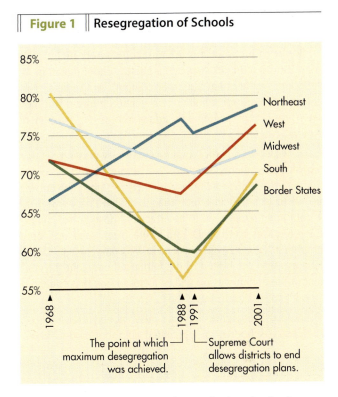

Figure 1 **Resegregation of Schools**

The point at which maximum desegregation was achieved.

Supreme Court allows districts to end desegregation plans.

Percentage of black students attending predominantly minority schools (schools in which 50%–100% of students are nonwhite) SOURCE: The Civil Rights Project, Harvard University. Chart by L. Eckstein.

dents than at any time since 1968.[92] One-third of black students attend schools that are 90 to 100 percent minority.[93]

The segregation is worse in the North, where it has been de facto, than in the South, where it had been de jure.[94] In the Northeast and Midwest, more than one-fourth of black and Latino students attend schools that are 99 to 100 percent nonwhite.[95]

The resegregation is due to white flight to private schools and to the suburbs, leaving fewer white children, and due to higher nonwhite birthrates and immigration rates, bringing more nonwhite children to the public schools. These changes affect the decisions of white parents who look for schools with low numbers of racial minorities.[96] Although many say they move for "better schools," few ever visit the schools or check the schools' test scores before moving. They use racial composition as a proxy for school quality. The more racial minorities, the poorer the quality, they assume.[97]

To an extent, the resegregation is also due to a shift in government policies and court decisions, which sent the message to school districts that desegregation is no longer an important national goal.[98]

The persistence of de facto segregation and the waning of society's commitment to integration have led national, state, and local officials to adopt a resigned attitude: "We still agree with the goal of school desegregation, but it's too hard, and we're tired of it, and we give up."[99]

Reforms proposed for urban schools rarely include desegregation. Officials speak of a ghetto school that is more "efficient" or one that gets more "input" from ghetto parents or offers more "choices" for ghetto children. But they seem to accept segregated education as "a permanent American reality."[100]

A writer who visited many central-city classrooms and talked with students, teachers, and administrators observed that Martin Luther King was treated as "an icon, but his vision of a nation in which black and white kids went to school together seemed to be effaced almost entirely. Dutiful references to 'The Dream' were often seen in school brochures and on wall posters in February, when 'Black History' was celebrated in the public schools, but the content of the dream was treated as a closed box that could not be opened without ruining the celebration."[101]

Indeed, many cities have a school named after King—a segregated school in a segregated neighborhood—"like a terrible joke on history," a fourteen-year-old, wise beyond her years, remarked.[102] In fact, if you want to find a school that's really segregated, look for schools named after champions of integration—Jackie Robinson, Rosa Parks, and Thurgood Marshall.[103]

Some minorities have gotten so frustrated that they themselves have questioned the goal of school desegregation. Instead, they have voiced greater concern about improving the quality and safety of their schools and neighborhoods.[104] However, one education analyst observes, "For African Americans to have equal opportunity, higher test scores will not suffice. It is foolhardy to think black children can be taught, no matter how well, in isolation and then have the skills and confidence as adults to succeed in a white world where they have no experience."[105]

Unequal schools   In areas where the schools are segregated, their quality varies enormously—from "the golden to the godawful," in the words of a Missouri judge.[106] And of course, blacks and Latinos are more likely to be in the "godawful" ones. By virtually every measure of school

---

Figure 2 || **Shortcomings among Schools in Los Angeles County**

In Los Angeles County, schools in black and Hispanic neighborhoods have far more shortcomings than schools in white and Asian neighborhoods. A light dot represents a high school with no significant shortcomings. A darker dot represents a high school that has a significant shortcoming involving its teachers (less than 80 percent are certified), its curriculum (less than two-thirds of the courses prepare students for a four-year college), or its facilities (the students attend school in shifts because the buildings are too crowded, so they have a shorter school year). The more shortcomings, the darker the dot. Not a single school that is 90 percent or more white and Asian has a significant shortcoming.
SOURCE: Atlantic Monthly, July–August 2004, 64.

quality—school funding, class size, teacher credentials, teacher salaries, breadth of curriculum, number of computers, opportunities for gifted students—these black and Latino children attend worse schools.[107]

Public schools are financed largely by property taxes paid by homeowners and businesses. Wealthy cities, where property costs more to buy and is assessed more in taxes, collect more in taxes than poor ones. In modern America, this means that suburban school districts have more to spend per pupil than central-city school districts.[108]

In about three-fourths of the states, school districts with the highest percentages of black and Latino children receive less funding than the districts with the fewest.[109] Nationwide, the difference amounts to $25,000 less per *classroom* per year for school districts with the most black and Latino children. In Illinois, the difference totals $47,000 less per classroom, and in New York, it totals $50,000 less.[110] And these official figures don't count the extra money that affluent parents, on their own or through PTAs, contribute to hire additional teachers to reduce class sizes or to provide art and music instruction, or to buy books for the library or equipment for the gym and playground.

Spending-per-pupil figures also don't take into account the fact that the needs of poor children, after years of neglect and with scores of problems in their homes and neighborhoods, are greater than the needs of other children. Schools for poor children would require *more* funding to provide their students an *equal* education.[111]

So, many inner-city schools are bleak institutions, filthy and in disrepair. A 30-year veteran of seven District of Columbia schools said all should be condemned. Of her current school, she said, "I have to cover books, computers, and student work stations with plastic to catch the falling plaster and water from the leaking roof. In the school cafeteria, 55-gallon garbage cans are strategically placed to catch the water from gaping holes in the ceiling."[112] Teachers in some Los Angeles schools said the children count the rats.[113]

Most inner-city schools are overcrowded. They lack up-to-date texts and paper and pencils. They lack books for literature classes, chemicals for chemistry classes, and computers for computer classes. (Teachers *talk* about using computers.)[114]

Most inner-city schools can't attract enough good teachers. A New York City principal said he is forced to take the "tenth-best" teachers. "I thank God they're still breathing."[115] In Illinois, which measures the quality of its teachers, just 11 percent of the teachers in majority-white schools are in the lowest quartile of the teachers in the state, but 88 percent of the teachers in almost-all-minority schools are in the lowest quartile.[116]

Despite the pattern of unequal funding, cash alone wouldn't solve the problems of inner-city schools. Cultural and economic factors in these communities also restrict the quality of education available. For example, black and Latino students see their school as a more rowdy, disrespectful, and dangerous place, with more drugs, weapons, and fights, than white students report in their school.[117] Nevertheless, cash would help.

Some states have equalized funding for public schools, but the attempts to do so in other states have encountered fierce opposition. Some states have considered supplementary funding for inner-city schools, as an alternative to equalized funding, but people's priorities run in other directions. In 1999, the Pennsylvania legislature approved $160 million of public financing for new stadiums for the Eagles and Phillies and another $160 million of public financing for new stadiums for the Steelers and Pirates, while the schools in Philadelphia and Pittsburgh languished.[118]

Discrimination in Employment

Although the Civil Rights Act of 1964 and affirmative action (discussed later in the chapter) have prompted more employers to hire and promote African Americans, discrimination remains.

For example, researchers used pairs of white and black high school graduates, matched according to their job histories and demeanors, to apply for low-skilled positions in Milwaukee. The white male applicants had a fictional record that included eighteen months in prison for possession of cocaine with intent to sell, while the black male applicants had no criminal record. Nonetheless, the whites received slightly more callbacks than the blacks.[119]

A teacher tries to teach in the hallway of an overcrowded school in the underfunded system of Philadelphia.

© David Fields Photography

Many blacks who are hired encounter negative stereotypes that question their competence on the job. These workers are passed over when they could be promoted.[120] Other blacks who are hired face racial slurs in comments, notes, and graffiti from coworkers. They endure an unfriendly or hostile environment.[121] Although most upper-level executives realize that it is economically advantageous to have a diverse workforce, some middle-level white managers and lower-level white workers interact poorly with the black employees.

Discrimination in Housing

The Civil Rights Act of 1968, which prohibits discrimination in housing, has fostered some desegregation of housing, but extensive segregation persists.

One reason is economic. Many blacks don't have enough money to buy homes in white neighborhoods. But another reason is discrimination. Social pressure and occasional violence discourage blacks who try to move into white neighborhoods. Continuing discrimination by homeowners, real estate agents, lenders, and insurers also stymies them. A study of twenty metropolitan areas, using white and minority testers responding to house and apartment ads, found that blacks who try to buy a house face discrimination 17 percent of the time, and those who try to rent an apartment do so 22 percent of the time.[122] If callers sound black, landlords may claim that the apartment has already been rented.[123]

Although residential segregation remains pervasive in metropolitan areas, it is declining. The 2000 census shows that the fast-growing suburban areas in the West and South are much more likely to have integrated neighborhoods than a decade earlier, though the stagnant "rust belt" cities in the East and Midwest are integrating too, but more slowly.[124] Middle-class blacks who escape the ghetto often end up in black neighborhoods in the suburbs of these cities.[125]

Segregation doesn't continue because black people "want to live among their own kind," as some whites insist. Surveys show that only about 15 percent want to live in segregated neighborhoods, and most of them cite their fear of white hostility as the reason. Eighty-five percent would prefer mixed neighborhoods. Many say the optimal level would be half black and half white. But whites tend to move out when the concentration of blacks reaches 8 to 10 percent.[126] These contrasting attitudes make integration an elusive goal. Blacks constitute 13 percent of the population in the country but a much larger percentage in some cities.

These patterns and attitudes are all the more troublesome because residential segregation, of course, is at the heart of school segregation.

Discrimination in Other Ways

Law enforcement African Americans face discrimination from police officers. The practice of **racial profiling**, which is based on the assumption that minorities, especially males, are more likely to commit crimes, especially those involving drugs, targets minorities for stops and searches. Without evidence, officers stop minority drivers and search them and their vehicles.[127] Sometimes officers stop minority pedestrians as well. Although police departments deny profiling, statistics show clear evidence of the practice.

Nationwide, black, Latino, and white drivers are equally likely to be stopped, though black and Latino drivers are twice as likely to be searched. Black and Latino drivers are also more likely to be given a ticket—and less likely to be given a warning—when stopped than white drivers.[128] In some places, profiling is more pronounced. In Los Angeles, blacks are two times as likely to be stopped and four times as likely to be searched as other drivers. Yet they are less likely to be found with illegal substances.[129] Therefore, the higher rates of stops and searches aren't because police have more evidence, or better hunches, of illegal substances in the cars of black drivers.

African Americans speak of the moving violation "DWB"— *driving while black.* A Chicago

African American communities often have tense relationships with local police departments. After Hurricane Katrina, Leonard Thomas's family was living in its flooded home when a SWAT team burst in, believing that the family was squatting in another family's house.

AP Images/Rick Bowmer

journalist who was stopped at least every other time he traveled through the Midwest learned not to rent flashy Mustangs or wear his beret. Others avoid tinted windshields or expensive sunglasses—any flamboyance—to avoid the cops.[130] Former Rep. J. C. Watts (R-Okla.) was pulled over by police six times in one day in his home state.[131]

Profiling might be justified if it led to the apprehension of dangerous criminals, but apparently it does not. Although African American young men evidently do commit a larger percentage of certain crimes,[132] profiling does not lead the police to many criminals. When police stop motorists, they find no greater evidence of crimes by blacks and Hispanics than by whites.[133] Meanwhile, the encounters often humiliate those who are stopped and spark animosity toward the police in these communities (as the movie *Crash* so clearly depicted).

Some states and many counties and cities have taken steps to reduce profiling, such as recording data on every stop to see whether the police, or individual officers, are prone to profile. Yet the cops on the beat, who feel that profiling is useful, are reluctant to change their habits.

Other discrimination from police officers is less common but more serious. Sometimes officers arrest black citizens without legal cause, and occasionally they use excessive force against them. Numerous examples attest to improper beatings.[134] Sometimes officers lie while testifying against black suspects in court. As a result, even prominent African Americans say their "worst fear" is to go before the criminal justice system.[135] It is little wonder that black jurors hearing the O. J. Simpson trial and black citizens following it put less faith in the police testimony than white observers did (even though legal experts believe Simpson was guilty).

Cautious parents teach their children how to avoid sending the wrong signals to police. Some parents urge their children not to wear street fashions and not to use cell phones, which from a distance might be mistaken as weapons. Some schools offer survival workshops for police encounters. Minority officers instruct the students what to do when they get stopped: Don't reach for an ID unless the officer asks for one; don't mumble or talk loudly; don't antagonize by asking for a badge number or threatening to file a complaint.[136]

Insults   Most blacks, even professionals, face insults because of their race. Black women tell of being mistaken for hotel chambermaids by white guests at the hotels.[137] They tell of being mistaken for prostitutes, while waiting in hotel lobbies, by white men and police officers. A distinguished black political scientist was mistaken for a butler in his own home. Black doctors tell of dressing up to go shopping to avoid being regarded as shoplifters. But dressing up is no guarantee. A black lawyer, a senior partner in a large law firm, arrived at work early one morning, before the doors were unlocked. As he reached for his key, a young white

lawyer, a junior associate in the firm, arrived at the same time, blocked his entrance, and asked, repeatedly and demandingly, "May I help you?" The white associate had taken the black partner for an intruder.[138] Although in these encounters the insults were unintentional, the stings hurt just the same. The accumulation of such incidents, which more than eight in ten blacks say they occasionally experience, has created a "black middle-class rage" among many.[139]

Overall, discrimination against African Americans continues. Whites speak of "past discrimination"—sometimes referring to slavery, sometimes to official segregation—but this phrase is misleading. Of course, there is a lot less discrimination now due to the civil rights movement, Supreme Court decisions, and congressional acts. However, there is nothing "past" about much "past discrimination."[140] The effects linger, and the discrimination itself persists. As a black journalist observes, "[M]odern bigotry usually isn't some nitwit screaming the N-word. It is jobs you don't get and loans you don't get and health care you don't get and justice you don't get, for reasons you get all too clearly, even though no one ever quite speaks them."[141]

Even when blacks point out the discrimination, some whites insist that little discrimination is left. These whites apparently assume that they know more than blacks do about what it is like to be black. Indeed, the perceptual gap between blacks and whites about the existence of discrimination is a real barrier to improved race relations. Whites who believe nothing is wrong don't favor actions to fix what they see as a nonexistent problem.

Improving Conditions for African Americans?

Despite continuing discrimination, African Americans have taken long strides toward achieving equal rights. These strides have led to much better living conditions for them and to a healthier racial climate in society. But serious problems remain.

Progress

As a result of the civil rights movement, Supreme Court decisions, and congressional laws, the United States has undergone a racial transformation in just one generation. As a black law professor observed, racism has become "unlawful, immoral, and, perhaps more important, déclassé" (out of style).[142] Antiracism has replaced racism as the dominant ideology toward race relations in our major institutions, such as the schools, the military, the media, big corporations, and labor unions. And the civil rights movement has become "as much a part of American nationalist lore as the Boston Tea Party or Paul Revere's midnight ride."[143]

Consequently, blacks' lives have improved in most ways that can be measured.[144] Blacks have a lower poverty rate and a longer life expectancy than before. They have completed more years of education, with larger numbers attending college and graduate school. They have attained higher occupational levels—for example, tripling their proportion of the country's professionals[145]—and higher income levels. Many—well over half—have reached the middle class.[146] Almost half own their own homes,[147] and a third have moved to the suburbs.[148]

During the years that blacks' lives have improved, whites' racial attitudes have also improved. Although answers to pollsters' questions cannot be accepted as perfect reflections of people's views, especially on sensitive matters such as racial attitudes, the answers can be considered general indicators of these views. The polls show that whites' views have changed significantly (even assuming that some whites gave socially acceptable answers rather than expressed their real feelings).[149]

Some whites, of course, remain blatant racists. Due to socioeconomic reasons, these whites are more likely to have contacts with blacks—to live near and work with them—than are tolerant whites, who are more educated and more prosperous. Even so, overt racist behavior occurs less frequently and is condemned more quickly than before. In some circles today, a blatant racist is considered not only a "fossil," but a "moral pervert" as well.[152] Yet covert racist attitudes persist in the minds of many whites, resulting in more subtle distrust and disapproval, rather than outright

antipathy, toward blacks and toward policies that involve, or are perceived to involve, race, such as affirmative action and welfare spending.[153]

Problems

Although the push for civil rights has opened many doors, some blacks aren't in a position to pass through. About a quarter of the black population lives in poverty—two and one-half times the rate among the white population—and about a tenth, the poorest of the poor, exists in a state of economic and social "disintegration."[154] This "underclass" is trapped in a cycle of self-perpetuating problems from which it is extremely difficult to escape.

The problems of the lower class and the underclass were exacerbated by economic changes that intensified in the 1970s and have continued since then. These changes hit the poor the hardest. Good-paying manufacturing jobs in the cities—the traditional path out of poverty for immigrant groups—disappeared. Chicago lost over 300,000 jobs, New York over 500,000.[155] Many jobs were eliminated by automation, while many others were moved to foreign countries or to the suburbs. Although service jobs increased, most were outside the cities and required more education or paid lower wages than the manufacturing jobs had.

As black men lost their jobs, they lost their ability to support a family. This led to a decrease in the number of "marriageable" black men and an increase in the number of households headed by black women.[156] The percentage of such households rose from 20 percent of all black families in 1960 to 45 percent in 2000.[157] And 60 percent of black children live in such households. These families are among the poorest in the country.

Meanwhile, much of the black middle class fled the inner cities to the suburbs. Their migration left the ghettos with fewer healthy businesses and strong schools to provide stability and fewer role models to portray mainstream behavior.[158] By 1996, one Chicago ghetto with 66,000 people had just one supermarket and one bank but forty-eight state-licensed lottery agents and ninety-nine state-licensed liquor stores and bars.[159]

The combination of chronic unemployment in the inner cities and middle-class migration from the inner cities created an environment that offers ample opportunity and some incentive to use drugs, commit crimes, and engage in other types of antisocial behavior. The development of crack, a cheap form of cocaine, in the mid-1980s aggravated these conditions. Crack led to more drug use and drug trafficking and, because of steady demand by users and huge profits for dealers, much more violence. As a result, crack overwhelmed whole neighborhoods.[160] The spread of AIDS, rampant among intravenous drug users, further aggravated these conditions.

Now, about 11 percent of black men between 20 and 34 are in jail or prison.[161] Consequently, about 41 percent of

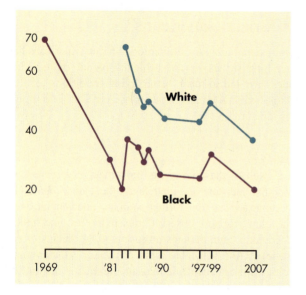

Figure 3   **Fewer Blacks and Whites See Black Progress**

Blacks and whites were asked whether they believe blacks are better off now than five years ago. After Barack Obama's election, however, related surveys have indicated that both blacks and whites expect to see more racial progress in coming years. SOURCE: pewsocialtrends.org/pubs/700/black-public-opinion.

federal and state prisoners are black, though only 13 percent of the U.S. population is black. Therefore, three times as many black people live in prison cells as live in college dorms.[162]

It is commonly recognized that the plight of young black men is worse than that of any other group in society. More black men receive their GED (high school equivalence degree) in prison than graduate from college.[163] About half as many black men as black women attend college. A black man in Harlem has less chance of living past forty than a man in Bangladesh.[164]

These problems affect even middle-class blacks who escaped to the suburbs. While returning from the city to see their relatives or old friends or to get a haircut, they may be in the wrong place at the wrong time. They may wear the wrong color shirt, wrong logo hat, or wrong brand of shoes and get caught up in gang violence. A father asks, "How many cultures can you say that when a guy turns twenty-five, he actually celebrates because he didn't think he would make it?"[165]

After widespread riots in the 1960s, the Kerner Commission, appointed by President Johnson to examine the cause of the riots, concluded, "What white Americans have never fully understood—but what the Negro can never forget—is that white society is deeply implicated in the ghetto. White institutions created it, white institutions maintain it, and white society condones it." After the riots, however, governments did little to improve the conditions that precipitated the riots.

After the riots in Los Angeles following the trial of police officers who beat Rodney King in 1992, there was more talk about improving the conditions in the ghetto. But a columnist who had heard such talk before commented, "My guess is that when all is said and done, a great deal more will be said than done. The truth is we don't know any quick fixes for our urban ills and we lack the patience and resources for slow fixes."[166]

And we lack the will to make the effort. A national focus on our big cities and their impoverished residents dissipated in the furious backlash against government and taxes that arose in the late 1970s and has continued for the three decades since then.[167] This backlash has starved governments of the revenue and sapped them of the desire necessary to act.

During these decades, the cities have lost political power as they have lost population due to white flight and black migration. Since 1992, more voters have lived in the suburbs than in the cities. (More than 40 percent of blacks live in the suburbs too.) Suburban voters don't urge action on urban problems. Sometimes they resist action if it means an increase in their taxes or a decrease in their services.

For the black lower class, and especially for the black underclass, it is apparent that civil rights aren't enough. As one black leader said, "What good is a seat in the front of the bus if you don't have the money for the fare?"[168]

But most blacks don't fall in the lower class or underclass, and most don't dwell in the inner cities. It would be a serious mistake to hold the stereotypical view that the majority resides in the inner cities and that most of them live in dysfunctional families filled with crackheads and prone to violence. Although black men lag behind, black women especially have vastly improved lives—academically, professionally, and financially—over the span of one generation.[169]

Black women are making great progress. They are more likely than black men to graduate from college and professional schools. At Tuskegee University, they dominate the veterinary school.

© Paul D'Amato

The hostility of many Anglos to Hispanic immigration, both legal and illegal, can make a family picnic in a public park, such as this birthday party in Carpentersville, Illinois, seem like a provocative act to some Anglos.

Even so, many professional black women can relate to Michelle Obama's experience in the presidential campaign. An accomplished lawyer, she was quickly portrayed as someone who isn't "one of us"—not patriotic, because of an offhand remark; too radical, because of a writing 20 years earlier; and, in general, an "angry black woman." Professional black women often face the same stereotypes at work.

Discrimination against Hispanics

Hispanics, also called Latinos, are people in the United States who have a Spanish-speaking background. Although sometimes they are considered a separate race, in fact they can be of any race. Some are brown skinned, others black skinned, and still others white skinned. Many are an amalgam of European, African, and American Indian ancestry that makes it impossible to classify them by race. Thus Hispanics should be regarded as an ethnic group rather than a distinct race. (But Hispanics are so diverse, as we will see, that some scholars are reluctant to consider them even an ethnic group, preferring to consider them simply a statistical category for the convenience of government reports, academic research, and media coverage.)

About 60 percent of America's Hispanics trace their ancestry to Mexico.[170] They are heavily concentrated in the Southwest but are increasingly spreading throughout the United States, including the Midwest and the South. About 10 percent are from Puerto Rico, which is a

commonwealth—a self-governing territory—of the United States. As members of the commonwealth, they are U.S. citizens. Most live in New York, Boston, Chicago, and other cities in the North. Another 4 percent are from Cuba. Following the establishment of a Communist government in Cuba in 1959, many fled to the United States and settled in South Florida. A significant number are from various islands in the Caribbean and countries in Central America, where emigrants left turmoil and oppression. A smaller number are from countries in South America or from Spain.

Despite the diversity of their origins, Hispanics are especially concentrated in six states. More than half live in California and Texas, where they make up one-third of the population. Already they outnumber Anglos in Los Angeles and Houston.[171] Many of the rest live in Florida, New Jersey, New York, and Illinois, but there are growing pockets in the South, rural Midwest, and elsewhere.

Latinos have overtaken blacks as the largest minority in the United States. They represent 15 percent of our population. (This number includes legal and illegal residents.) Fueled by high immigration rates and birthrates, this group is the fastest-growing minority (slightly faster growing than Asians) in the United States.

Hispanics never endured slavery in this country,[172] but some have faced severe discrimination. Although some Hispanics are Caucasian, many Puerto Ricans and Cubans have African ancestry, and many Mexicans have Indian ancestry, so they have darker skin than non-Hispanic whites.[173] Like blacks, Hispanics, especially Mexicans and Puerto Ricans,[174] have faced discrimination in education, employment, housing, and voting.[175]

Discrimination Due to Immigration

Latinos also endure discrimination due to immigration. The flood of illegal immigrants pouring in from Latin America, especially from Mexico, has produced a wave of anti-immigration sentiment throughout the United States, even in the states and cities with few immigrants.[176] This sentiment affects not only illegal immigrants but the Latinos who are legal residents and U.S. citizens; it even affects those who are native-born Americans, because the average person or law enforcement officer often can't tell, simply by watching or listening to them, which Latinos are legal and which ones are illegal.

Border patrol agents and local police officers often stop Latinos for questioning. Because illegal immigrants can't get driver's licenses and most don't get driver's insurance, the officers expect to identify illegal immigrants by demanding these documents. Border patrol agents stopped the mayor of Pomona, California, a hundred miles from the Mexican border, and ordered him to produce papers proving that he's a legal resident. Local police officers also assume that many Latinos are involved in drug trafficking, so they practice profiling, as they do toward blacks.[177] Even when the officers are well intentioned, their conduct—the stopping and questioning and demanding of documents—seems like harassment to law-abiding residents and citizens.

But more pervasive than occasional stops by border patrol or police officers is the hostility from ordinary Americans who are opposed to the influx of illegal immigrants. In their looks and comments, some Americans send a message that these immigrants, especially the Latinos, aren't welcome here.

Actually, the controversy over illegal immigrants may be less about illegal immigration than about immigration in general, though it may be less about immigration in general than about assimilation to the American culture and adoption of the English language.[178] Among Anglos, there is widespread unease about the Latino culture and real anxiety about whether, and how fast, these recent arrivals will discard their culture in favor of our culture. There are fears that immigrants will change us more than we will change them.

These fears are aggravated by the fact that 40 percent of Latinos are first-generation immigrants, meaning that they themselves came from other countries.[179] In general, these immigrants haven't assimilated or learned English, just as the first generation of previous immigrant groups didn't assimilate or learn English.[180] With so many new immigrants in recent decades, Anglo Americans often encounter first-generation immigrants, and the Anglos draw conclusions about all Latinos from these immigrants.

Yet clear patterns of cultural assimilation and language acquisition are emerging. Many immigrants are illegal aliens, so they live in the shadows, in fear of deportation. They're not in position to assimilate. Many immigrants who are le-gal residents came to the United States to work for a few years and then to return to their home country, so they haven't been interested in assimilating. But most immigrants do remain here, and their children do assimilate.[181]

In fact, immigrants in the past quarter century have been assimilating at a faster rate than previous immigrants. They are assimilating economically, by holding jobs and earning money and by buying homes; culturally, by learning English and intermarrying with U.S. citizens; and in civic ways, by becoming citizens and voting and by serving in the military. (See Figures 4 and 5. For further evidence of assimilation, see the box "Latinos Choose Anglo Names.") A study concluded that "the nation's capacity to assimilate new immigrants is strong."[182] However, immigrants from Mexico, while following the historical pattern, are assimilating at a slower rate than those from other countries (though in some ways faster than those from India and China), due to the facts that many are illegal and many plan to return home.

Immigrants in the past quarter century have also been learning English. Cuban Americans are learning English as fast or faster than any group in history.[183] As with assimilation, Mexican Americans are learning English slower than other groups, but they are learning it as they reside longer in the United States. Although many who come for work and plan to return to Mexico don't speak English, most who remain in the United States learn to speak some English, and almost all of their children learn to speak fluent English.[184] Most of these second-generation Americans are bilingual, speaking Spanish at home with their parents and relatives and English outside of home. But many of *their* children—the third-generation Americans—are monolingual, speaking only English. The drive to learn English is

Cuban Americans are more likely than other Latinos to be middle class.

Figure 4 ‖ Assimilation of Immigrants, by Country of Origin

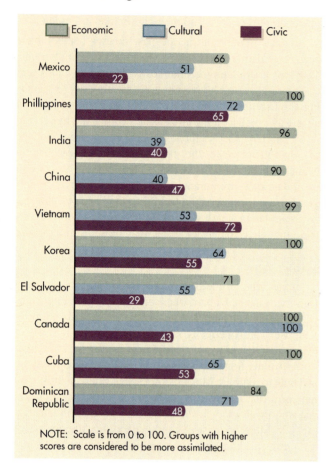

NOTE: Scale is from 0 to 100. Groups with higher scores are considered to be more assimilated.

Researchers created indices reflecting the economic, cultural, and civic assimilation of immigrants, and they assessed immigrants from the ten countries that provide the most immigrants to the United States (listed in order). The figure shows the extent of each nationality's assimilation, based on data from 2006.
SOURCE: Manhattan Institute.

Figure 5 ‖ Most Hispanics Accept Assimilation

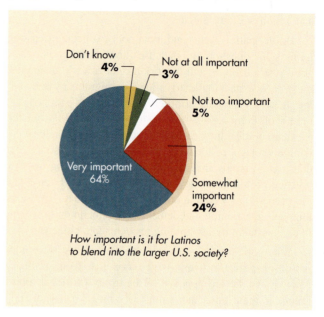

How important is it for Latinos to blend into the larger U.S. society?

SOURCE: Time, August 22, 2005, 56. Poll conducted by phone, with interviews in English and Spanish. N = 503. Margin of error = ±5 percentage points.

border bear a disproportionate share of the burden from this immigration. Their education costs rise as children fill the schools; their health costs increase when immigrants without health insurance need health care; and their law enforcement costs rise too. Because the federal government has failed to act on the issue of illegal immigration, residents of these communities and states feel overwhelmed by problems largely not of their making.

Discrimination in Education

In some places, Hispanic children were not allowed to attend any schools. In other places, they were segregated into "Mexican" schools that were inferior to Anglo schools.[188] When the Supreme Court declared segregation illegal, many school districts achieved "integration" by combining Hispanics with blacks, leaving non-Hispanic whites in their own schools.[189]

Although de jure segregation has been struck down,[190] de facto segregation exists in cities where Latinos are concentrated. Many Latinos attend schools with more than 90 percent minorities, and most attend schools with more than 50 percent minorities.[191]

Predominantly Latino schools, like predominantly black schools, aren't as well funded as other schools because they're located in poor communities that don't get as much revenue from property taxes. In San Antonio, wealthy families, who were concentrated in one section of the city, got their section incorporated as a separate school district, though it was surrounded by the rest of the city. As a sepa-

so strong that just a third of Latinos born in the United States are bilingual. Most can't speak Spanish.[185]

It is true that some immigrant communities, especially Cubans in South Florida and Mexicans in some parts of the Southwest, are so large that they can survive without learning English. But most feel pressure to learn English to function in society and for their children to succeed in school. Indeed, 89 percent of Latinos believe that those who immigrate must learn English to succeed in the United States.[186] Children do learn English in schools, though it is harder for adults to find English classes that fit with their work schedules, especially given the long hours and multiple jobs that many immigrants have.[187]

While illegal immigration doesn't result in all of the harms that its opponents charge, it certainly leads to some problems. The communities and states near the Mexican

LATINOS CHOOSE ANGLO NAMES

Despite Anglos' concern that Latinos are not assimilating, Latinos are favoring Anglo names for their children.

For Hispanic children born in Texas in a recent year, the most popular names

for boys:	for girls:
Jose	Ashley
Daniel	Jennifer
Jonathan	Emily
David	Samantha
Christopher	Maria

For Hispanic children born in New York City, the most popular names for

boys :	for girls:
Justin	Ashley
Christopher	Jennifer
Kevin	Emily
Anthony	Brianna
Brandon	Samantha

Source: Sam Roberts, "In a Changing Nation, Smith Is Still King," *New York Times*, July 11, 2004.

---

rate district, its property taxes financed its schools only. When Mexican American parents sued, the Burger Court ruled that the Fourteenth Amendment's equal protection clause doesn't require states to equalize funding among school districts, even where artificial districts have been carved out of a city.[192] Despite the Court's ruling, this case highlighted the problem of unequal funding, prompting some states to equalize funding, though allowing other states to maintain the status quo.

Latinos' primary problem in education, however, is the language barrier. Many are unable to speak English, causing them to fail in school and drop out of school at higher rates than other students, even African Americans. One-third of Latinos drop out before graduating from high school.[193]

Bilingual education was created to help such students. Bilingual classes used the students' native language to teach the students English and their other subjects. The goal was to transition them from their native language to English rather than to immerse them in a foreign language—English—that they didn't understand.[194] Around the country, more than 150 languages were offered; Spanish was the most common.[195]

Bilingual programs faced numerous problems. They were expensive because they required more teachers and smaller classes. They were impractical because schools couldn't find enough teachers in various languages. Schools in California, where half of all students in bilingual programs lived, fell 21,000 teachers short in one year.[196] The schools couldn't offer bilingual education to most students who were eligible for it.[197]

Bilingual programs were controversial as well. Although Latino groups advocated for these programs as a way to preserve Latino culture, Latino parents worried that these programs would delay their children's mastery of English.[198] Many Anglos also opposed these programs for the same reason that Latino groups favored them. For all of these reasons, California citizens voted to abolish bilingual programs in 1998.

Discrimination against Farmworkers

Latino farmworkers have encountered particular problems. Agribusinesses have long avoided regulations imposed on other businesses. For decades, the minimum wage law didn't apply to farmworkers. Even today, the laws providing overtime pay and the right to organize don't apply. In many states, the laws establishing workers' compensation and unemployment benefits programs don't apply. Farmworkers' lack of governmental protection, coupled with their economic desperation, makes them vulnerable to unscrupulous employers. The Department of Justice has investigated more than 100 cases of involuntary servitude—slavery—and has prosecuted a half dozen from South Florida in recent years.[199]

Combating Discrimination against Hispanics

In the 1960s, Hispanic advocacy groups tried to imitate African American groups by using protests and other forms of direct action. The Chicano movement attempted to forge a powerful bloc from the diverse population of Hispanics. **César Chávez** successfully led a coalition of labor, civil rights, and religious groups to obtain better working conditions for migrant farmworkers in California. But few other visible national leaders or organizations emerged.

Latinos remain more diverse and less cohesive than blacks. Most don't even consider themselves part of a common group.[200] They identify strongly with their national origin and have little contact with Latinos of other national origins. And they lack a shared, defining experience in their background, such as slavery for blacks, to unite them.

Where Latinos are highly concentrated, they are increasingly powerful at the local and state levels of government. Yet Latino politicians haven't shaped a common agenda, perhaps because Latino people don't share a common agenda.[201]

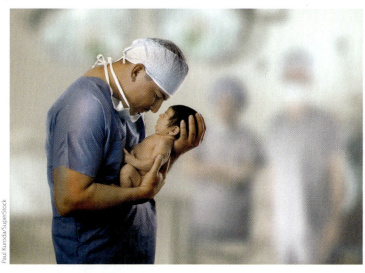

Latinos are gradually improving their status as more go to college and graduate school and become professionals, such as this doctor.

They are potentially powerful at the national level as well. When Congress considered harsh measures toward illegal immigrants in 2006, hundreds of thousands of Latinos rallied against the measures. Many families include legal and illegal residents—children who were born here living with parents who are illegal, or nuclear families who are legal residents living with grandparents or aunts and uncles who are illegal—so congressional threats of deportation sparked real concern in these families. Politicians' comments that immigrants are taking jobs from citizens and not contributing anything to society ignited their anger. In their passion, some observers saw the stirrings of political activism among young Latinos especially.

With their huge numbers, Latinos are a coveted bloc of voters. Yet many aren't citizens, and many of those who are citizens don't register and vote. Although the Latino population is slightly larger than the African American population, 6 million fewer Latinos are registered to vote.[202] Nonetheless, in several swing states, such as Texas and New Mexico, they are a large bloc of voters that political candidates pay attention to.

Meanwhile, Latino individuals are moving up society's ladder. More attend college and become managers and professionals. At least those who speak educated English appear to be following the pattern of earlier generations of immigrants from Southern and Eastern Europe—arriving poor, facing discrimination, but eventually working their way up. Along the way, they are also assimilating through high rates of marriage to non-Latinos.

Discrimination against American Indians

More than 2 million American Indians live in the United States. Most live in the West, and half live on reservations. Although some native Americans are Eskimos and Aleuts

from Alaska, most are Indians, representing more than 550 tribes with different histories, customs, and languages. Proud of their tribal heritage, they prefer to be known by their tribal name, such as Cheyenne or Sioux, than by the collective terms *Indians* or *Native Americans*.[203] (Of the collective terms, they prefer to be called *Indians*, so our text will follow their preference.)

American Indians have endured treatment quite different from what African Americans or Hispanics have experienced.

Government Policy toward American Indians

Government policy toward Indians has ranged from forced separation at one extreme to forced assimilation at the other.

Separation   Initially, the policy was separation. People believed that the North American continent was so vast that most of its interior would remain wilderness populated by Indians who would have ample room to live and hunt. The Constitution reflects this belief. It grants Congress authority to "regulate commerce with foreign nations, and among the several states, and with the Indian tribes." In early cases, Chief Justice John Marshall described the tribes as "dependent domestic nations."[204] They were within U.S. borders but outside its political process.

Early treaties reinforced separation by establishing boundaries between Indians and non-Indians. The boundaries were intended to minimize conflict. White hunters or settlers who ventured across the boundaries could be punished by the Indians. But as the country grew, it became increasingly difficult to contain the settlers within the boundaries. Mounting pressure to push the Indians farther

"I love the way you make those yams. You'll have to give me the recipe before your culture is obliterated from the face of the earth."

west led to the Indian Removal Act of 1830, which mandated removal of tribes east of the Mississippi River and relocation on reservations west of the river. At the time, people considered the Great Plains as a great desert, unfit for habitation by whites but suitable for Indians.

Assimilation   As more settlers moved west, the vision of a separate Indian country far beyond white civilization faded. In the 1880s, the government switched its policy to assimilation. Prompted by Christian churches, government officials sought to "civilize" the Indians—to integrate them into American society, whether they wanted to be integrated or not. In place of their traditional means of subsistence, rendered useless once the tribes were removed from their historical homelands, the government subdivided reservation land into small tracts and allotted these tracts to tribe members in the hope that they would turn to farming as white and black settlers had.

Bureau of Indian Affairs (BIA) agents, who supervised the reservations, tried to root out Indian ways and replace them with white dress and hairstyles, the English language, and the Christian religion. Government boarding schools separated Indian children from their families to instill these new practices.

Since the adoption of the Constitution, Native Americans were not considered citizens but members of separate nations.[205] In 1890, after government policy had switched to assimilation, Congress permitted Indians who remained on reservations to become citizens. In a formal ceremony marking his new citizenship, the Indian shot his last arrow and then took hold of the handles of a plow to demonstrate his assimilation.[206] After World War I, Congress granted citizenship to those who served in the military during the war, and finally, in 1924, Congress extended it to all who were born in the United States.

Citizenship enabled Indians to vote and hold office, though some states effectively barred them from the polls for decades. Arizona denied them the right to vote until 1948, Utah until 1956.[207]

Tribal restoration   By the 1930s, the government recognized the consequences of coerced assimilation. Most Indians, though able to speak English, were poorly educated. And with their traditional means of earning a living gone, most were poverty-stricken. The policy had led to the destruction of native culture without much assimilation into white society. Consequently, in 1934 Congress implemented a new policy of tribal restoration that recognized Indians as distinct persons, and tribes as autonomous entities encouraged to govern themselves once again. Traditional cultural and religious practices were accepted, and Indian children, no longer forced to attend boarding schools, were taught some Indian languages.

Reflecting the policy of tribal restoration and the efforts of other minorities in the 1960s and 1970s, Indian interest groups became active. Indian law firms filed lawsuits, seeking to protect not only tribal independence and traditional ways but also land, mineral, and water resources.

The diversity and the dispersion of the tribes—they are divided by culture and by geography, often located in the remotest and poorest parts of the country—make it difficult for them to present a united front. Nevertheless, they have been able to wrest some autonomy from the government. In particular, they have gained more authority over the educational and social programs administered by the BIA for the tribes.[208]

In recent years, Indians have fought for the return of some tribal land and for an accounting of the money owed them for the use of their individual land held in trust by the government. In the early nineteenth century, the government took tribal land and put it in trust for the Indians. But then the government divided the land, classified large tracts as "surplus," and offered the tracts to white settlers. In return, it paid individual Indians a pittance. In this way, the Indians lost two-thirds of their territory. The government held the remaining land in trust for the Indians, leasing it to ranchers, loggers, and miners. The government collected the rents and royalties for the Indians. But the BIA didn't bother to keep accurate records or even to preserve its records. A class-action lawsuit, dubbed "the Indian Enron case," seeks a reckoning of the accounts and a payment to the Indians who are owed money.[209]

Denver Public Library, Western History Collection, J. N. Choate (X-32984)

Denver Public Library, Western History Collection, J. N. Choate (X-32985)

Dilos Lonewolf became Tom Torlino during his transformation at a boarding school in Carlisle, Pennsylvania. Indians were shorn of their hair and clothes and trained to adopt white ways.

After a Supreme Court ruling and a congressional law in the 1980s underscored tribal sovereignty on tribal land, tribes could establish gambling casinos on reservations, even if their state didn't allow any casinos.[210] Almost three hundred tribes have done so, although less than a dozen have found a bonanza—mostly small tribes in populous states where the casinos attract numerous customers.[211] And many of the casinos are bankrolled by unknown investors who keep most of the profits. A Malaysian businessman owns one, a South African developer another. From these casinos, little money trickles down to tribal members.[212]

With their casino businesses, some tribes have begun to buy into the political process, as other groups have done. Threatened by gambling interests in Las Vegas and Atlantic City, which fear that tribal casinos will lure away their customers, the tribes have formed a lobby, the National Indian Gaming Association, and made political contributions. These contributions reportedly total more than the contributions by individual corporations such as AT&T, Boeing, or General Motors.[213]

Now more Indians share the views of one activist who says, "You have a federal government, state governments, and tribal governments—three sovereigns in one country. This is the civil rights movement of Native Americans."[214] Indeed, Indians enjoy renewed pride, which has led tribes to establish programs to preserve their language and culture.[215]

DEMOCRACY?

Do you think that any one of the government's policies toward Indians—separation, assimilation, or tribal restoration—is more democratic than the others?

Nevertheless, Indians remain at the bottom of America's racial and ethnic ladder. They are the least educated and most unemployed group, the poorest and sickest group, with the highest alcoholism rates and lowest life expectancy, of any people in the country.

Indians feel renewed cultural pride in ancient traditions but also the lure of modern technology.

Sex Discrimination

Most sex discrimination has been directed at women, though some has been directed at men.

Discrimination against Women

The Traditional View

People used to believe that natural differences between the sexes required men and women to occupy separate spheres of life. Men would dominate the public domain of work and government, and women would dominate the private domain of the home. Both domains were important, and men were considered superior in one and women were considered superior in the other.

Thomas Jefferson, the most egalitarian of the male Founders, reflected this view when he said, "Were our state a pure democracy there would still be excluded from our deliberations women, who, to prevent deprivation of morals and ambiguity of issues, should not mix promiscuously in gatherings of men."[216] That is, women are more moral than men, so they would be corrupted by politics, and they are more irrational, so they would confuse the issues. For both reasons, they should not participate in politics.

So, women were denied the right to vote, and married women were denied other rights—to manage property they acquired before marriage, to manage income they received from jobs, to enter into contracts, and to sue. Some states eventually granted these rights, but when disputes arose within families, male judges hesitated to tell other men how to treat their wives.

Even women's citizenship was tied to their husbands' citizenship. If a foreign woman married an American man, she automatically became a United States citizen. But if an American woman married a foreign man, she automatically lost her United States citizenship. (Women's citizenship wouldn't become independent of their husbands' citizenship until 1922.)

Women were barred from schools and jobs. Before the Civil War, they weren't admitted to public high schools. Because they were being prepared for motherhood, education was considered unnecessary, even dangerous. According to the *Encyclopaedia Britannica* in 1800, women had smaller brains than men.[217] Education would fatigue them and possibly ruin their reproductive organs. For the same reasons, women weren't encouraged to hold jobs. Those who did were shunted into jobs that were seen as extensions of the domestic domain, such as producing textiles, clothes, and shoes in sex-segregated factories.[218]

This traditional conception of gender roles created problems for women who didn't fit the standard mold. After the Civil War, Myra Bradwell ran a private school, founded a weekly newspaper, and worked for various civic organizations. She was active in the women's suffrage movement and instrumental in persuading the Illinois legislature to expand women's legal rights. After learning the law, however, she was denied a license to practice it solely because she was a woman. The Supreme Court upheld the Illinois policy in 1873.[219] Justice Joseph Bradley declared:

> Law, as well as nature itself, has always recognized a wide difference in the respective spheres and destinies of man and woman. Man is, or should be, the woman's protector and defender. The natural and proper timidity and delicacy which belongs to the female sex evidently unfits it for many of the occupations of civil life. . . .The constitution of the family organization . . . indicates the domestic sphere as that which properly belongs to the domain and functions of woman-hood. The harmony . . . of interests and views which belong, or should belong, to the family institution is repugnant to the idea of a woman adopting a distinct and independent career from that of her husband. . . . The paramount destiny and mission of woman are to fulfill the noble and benign offices of wife and mother. This is the law of the Creator. And the rules of civil society must be adapted to the general constitution of things, and cannot be based upon exceptional cases.

Sometimes this separate-but-equal view gave way to even more clear-cut discrimination. In the 1860s and 1870s, the doctors who practiced scientific medicine formed the American Medical Association (AMA) to drive out other people who offered medical services. These people included not only hucksters and quacks but also women who served as midwives or abortionists. Although abortions had been widely available, the AMA, drawing on popular fears about the women's suffrage movement, convinced state legislatures that abortions were "a threat to social order and to male authority." The woman who seeks an abortion, the AMA explained, is "unmindful of the course marked out for her by Providence, she overlooks the duties imposed on her by the marriage contract. She yields to the pleasure—but shrinks from the pains and responsibilities of maternity. . . . Let not the husband of such a wife flatter himself that he possesses her affection."[220]

Occasionally the discrimination even allowed physical brutality. The Mississippi Supreme Court acknowledged a husband's right to beat his wife.[221] Using the "rule of thumb," the court held that a husband could not beat his wife with a weapon thicker than his thumb.

The Women's Movement

Early feminists were determined to remedy these inequities. Many had gained political and organizational experience in the abolitionist movement. It wasn't considered "unladylike" for women to campaign for abolition of slavery because that movement was associated with religious groups. Yet the women weren't allowed to participate fully in antislavery societies.

When Abigail Kelley was nominated as an official of the American Anti-Slavery Society, almost three hundred men left the meeting to form another antislavery society in which women couldn't vote or hold office. Later, when Kelley rose to speak at a meeting of the Connecticut Anti-Slavery Society, the chair insisted,

> No woman will speak or vote where I am moderator. It is enough for women to rule at home. It is woman's business to take care of the children in the nursery; she has no business to come into this meeting and by speaking and voting lord it over men. Where women's enticing eloquence is heard, men are incapable of right and efficient action. She beguiles and blinds men by her smiles and her bland winning voice…. I will not submit to PETTICOAT GOVERNMENT.[222]

Angry at such treatment, the women held a meeting to discuss the "social, civil, and religious rights of women." In 1848, this Women's Rights Convention adopted a declaration of rights based on the Declaration of Independence, proclaiming, "We hold these truths to be self-evident: that all men and women are created equal." The convention also passed a resolution calling for women's suffrage.

After the Civil War, the women who had worked in the abolitionist movement expected that women, as well as blacks, would get legal rights and voting rights. When the Fourteenth and Fifteenth Amendments did not include women, they felt betrayed, and they disassociated themselves from the black movement.

The women formed their own organizations to campaign for women's suffrage. This movement, led by **Susan B. Anthony** and **Elizabeth Cady Stanton**, succeeded in 1920, when the Nineteenth Amendment gave women the right to vote.

Then dissension developed within the movement. Many groups felt that the Nineteenth Amendment was just the first step in the struggle for equal rights. They proposed the Equal Rights Amendment to remedy remaining inequities. Other groups felt that the battle had been won. They opposed the Equal Rights Amendment, arguing that it would overturn labor laws recently enacted to protect women. Due to this dissension and the conservatism in the country at the time, the movement became dormant.[223]

The movement reemerged in the 1960s. As a result of the civil rights movement, many women recognized their own inferior status. Female writers sensitized other women. **Betty Friedan** published *The Feminine Mystique*, which grew out of a questionnaire she circulated at her fifteenth college reunion. The book addressed the malaise that afflicted college-educated women who were socialized into the feminine role but found it unsatisfying.[224] Friedan observed that women reared the children, shopped for groceries, cooked the meals, and cleaned the house, while secretly wondering, "Is this all?" Friedan's manifesto became the best-selling nonfiction paperback in 1964. Its popularity spurred Friedan and other upper-middle-class, professional women to form the **National Organization for Women (NOW)** in 1966. They resolved "to bring women into full participation in the mainstream of American society *now*."

Other women, also middle class but veterans of the civil rights and antiwar movements, had developed a taste for political action. They formed other organizations. Where NOW fought primarily for women's political and economic rights, the other organizations fought broadly for women's liberation in all spheres of life. Together these organizations pushed the issue of women's rights back onto the public agenda.

Nevertheless, they weren't taken seriously for years. In 1970, *Time* magazine reported, "No one knows how many shirts lay wrinkling in laundry baskets last week as thousands of women across the country turned out for the first big demonstration of the women's liberation movement. They took over [New York City's Fifth Avenue], providing not only protest but some of the best sidewalk ogling in years."[225]

Although the movement tried to broaden its base beyond upper-middle-class and college-educated women, it was unable to do so. The movement fostered an image of privileged women who looked on other women with disdain. *Housewife* became a derisive term. Traditional women viewed the movement as antimotherhood and antifamily and, when it became more radical in the 1970s, prolesbian. This image gave "women's liberation" a bad name, even though most women agreed with most goals of the move-ment.[226] This image persists. More Americans believe that extraterrestrials have visited the earth than think that the word *feminist* is a compliment.[227] (It is unclear, however, whether this says more about Americans' attitudes toward gender equality or their penchant for paranoid conspiracy theories.)

The Movement in Congress and the Courts

Congress initially didn't take the women's movement seriously either. When the House debated a bill forbidding racial discrimination in employment, eighty-one-year-old Rep. Howard Smith (D-Va.) proposed an amendment to add sex discrimination to the bill. A staunch foe of equal rights for blacks, Smith thought his proposal so ludicrous and so radical that it would help defeat the entire bill. Indeed, during their debate on the amendment, members of Congress laughed so hard that they could barely hear each other speak.[228] But the joke was on these members, because the amendment, and then the bill—the Civil Rights Act of 1964—passed.

Equal Rights Amendment Congress also passed the **Equal Rights Amendment (ERA)**. The amendment simply declared, "Equality of rights under the law shall not be denied or abridged by the United States or by any state on

During World War II, women were urged into the labor force to replace men called to war. "Rosie the Riveter" became the symbol of the women who were contributing to the war effort. Following the war, they were told that it was patriotic to give their jobs to returning veterans. The 1955 magazine cover depicts the stereotypical women's role in the postwar era before the modern women's movement.

In addition to "Rosie the Riveter," there was "Rosalita." During World War II, when aircraft factories needed more workers, the government overlooked the influx of illegal aliens.

account of sex." Introduced in 1923 and every year thereafter, Congress passed the amendment in 1972.

It looked like the amendment would zip through the states. Both parties endorsed it, and a majority of the public supported it. But the amendment stalled. Observers speculated that it could make women subject to the draft for the military (if there was another draft). Opponents charged, falsely, that it would result in unisex restrooms and homosexual rights.

The main problem, however, was the amendment's symbolism. For many women, the ERA represented an attack on the traditional values of motherhood, the family, and the home. Early feminists had emphasized equal employment so much that they gave some women the impression that they opposed these values. Traditional women sensed implicit criticism for becoming housewives.[229] To underscore the symbolism, the women in anti-ERA groups baked bread for state legislators scheduled to vote on ratification.

Consequently, numerous women, even some who favored equality, opposed the amendment. Although many young women supported it, fewer middle-age and elderly women did; and although many working women supported it, fewer housewives did. Women's organizations hadn't created an effective grassroots campaign to sway traditional women. Their disaffection allowed male legislators to vote according to their male attitudes. They didn't need to worry about a backlash from their female constituents.[230]

In 1980, the Republican Party became the first party not to endorse the ERA since 1940, and President Reagan became the first president not to support the amendment since Truman.

When the deadline for ratification set by Congress expired in 1982, the ERA fell three states short of the three-fourths necessary. As with the Nineteenth Amendment, it was opposed primarily by the southern states.

Supreme Court Rulings   But women would assert their rights in court.

Historically courts upheld laws that limited women's participation in the public domain and occasionally even laws that diminished their standing in the private domain. As late as 1970, the Ohio supreme court ruled that a wife is a husband's servant with "no legally recognized feelings or rights."[231]

The Burger Court finally reversed this pattern. In 1971, for the first time, the Court struck down a law that discriminated against women,[232] heralding a long series of rulings that invalidated a variety of such laws. ⭐ The Court used the congressional statutes and broadened the Fourteenth Amendment's equal protection clause to apply to women as well as to racial minorities.

The change was especially apparent in a pair of cases involving the selection of jurors. For the pool of potential jurors, some states drew the names of men, but not women, from voter registration or other lists. These states allowed women to serve only if they voluntarily signed up at the courthouse. Consequently, few women served. In 1961, the Court let Florida use these procedures because the "woman is still regarded as the center of home and family life."[233] In 1975, however, the Court forbade Louisiana from using similar procedures,[234] thus overturning a precedent only fourteen years old.

The Court's rulings rejected the traditional stereotypes that men are the breadwinners and women the child rearers in society. The Court invalidated Utah's law that required divorced fathers to support their daughters until eighteen but their sons until twenty-one.[235] The state assumed that the daughters would get married and be supported by their husbands, whereas the sons would need to get educated for their careers. But the Court noted, "No longer is the female destined solely for the home." (See Figure 6.)

Congressional laws   Congress adopted legislation to forbid sex discrimination in employment and education.

The Civil Rights Act of 1964 forbids discrimination on the basis of both sex and race in hiring, promoting, and firing. It prohibits discrimination on the basis of sex, except where sex is a "bona fide occupational qualification" for the job. Sex is considered a legitimate qualification for very few jobs, such as restroom attendants, lingerie salesclerks, models, or actors. It is not considered a legitimate qualification for jobs men traditionally held, such as those that entail heavy physical labor, unpleasant working conditions, late-night hours, overtime, or travel. Employers can no longer reserve these jobs for male applicants.

Figure 6 | Acceptance of Women in the Workplace

Generally speaking, do you prefer a male or female boss?

Male boss — 34%

Female boss — 9%

No preference — 55%

I would feel comfortable dating a woman who earns significantly more than me

Strongly agree — 55%

Somewhat agree — 24%

Somewhat disagree — 8%

Strongly disagree — 7%

A majority of men don't care whether their boss is a woman or a man or whether the woman they date has a higher salary than they do. Shown here are the responses of 1302 men asked the above questions in 2004.
SOURCE: Time, August 23, 2004, 38.

However, discrimination in hiring, promoting, and firing persists, even forty years after the act. A major study examined the records in lawsuits alleging sex discrimination in one recent year. A surprising and staggering number, they required employers to pay $263 million to the female plaintiffs in that year alone.[236] Testimony by mid-level managers revealed that higher executives instructed them, "We do not employ women," or, "The day I hire a woman will be a cold day in hell." In dozens of cases, the managers were told to throw women's applications into the trash.[237]

The same result occurs when male managers decide according to their "gut instinct" that a man is more qualified. Their "gut instinct" may be biased without them realizing it.

The discrimination occurs up and down the ladder. Huge lawsuits have been brought against both Merrill Lynch and Wal-Mart in recent years. But the discrimination appears most prevalent for traditional male, blue-collar jobs. Some men don't want to work with women; they don't want to break up the "good-ol'-boys' clubhouse."[238] Mysteriously, a woman's application disappears; or the letter telling her when to come for the interview gets lost in the mail; or her examination is invalidated for some reason.[239]

Some companies that fill their positions through hiring agencies instruct the agencies to send them only men for traditional male jobs and only women for traditional female jobs.[240]

Discrimination in firing, especially for pregnancy, continues as well, despite the **Pregnancy Discrimination Act** of 1978, which forbids firing or demoting women when they become pregnant or after they return from maternity leave.[241] Some women have been fired as soon as they men-

tioned being pregnant; others as soon as their body showed it. Many have seen their performance evaluations drop as their bellies swelled, even though their actual performance did not decline.[242] Others have been demoted after giving birth. "When I returned from maternity leave," a lawyer recounted, "I was given the work of a paralegal and I wanted to say, 'Look, I had a baby, not a lobotomy.'"[243]

The cases examined in these studies probably represent the tip of the iceberg. To sue an employer for sex discrimination is to embark on an expensive and exhausting legal battle that will take several years of one's life. It requires a strong-willed woman who has experienced discriminatory behavior egregious enough for her to persuade a lawyer to take the case and then a company to settle or a judge or jury to find for her. Although there are some frivolous lawsuits in our legal system, there is more discriminatory behavior in our workplaces than is ever brought to court.

The **Equal Pay Act** of 1963 requires that women and men receive equal pay for equal work. The act makes exceptions for merit, productivity, and seniority. As a result of the act, the gap between what women and men earn has slowly shrunk. In the 1960s, working women earned just 59 cents for every dollar men earned.[244] Today, working women earn 80 cents for every dollar men earn—an improvement but far short of real equality.[245]

One reason for the gap is old-fashioned sex discrimination. Despite the Equal Pay Act, some male employers with ingrained attitudes are reluctant to pay women equally. The act allows exceptions for merit and productivity, which usually are determined subjectively. The employer may insist, whether sincerely or not, that the man is more meritorious or productive. Legions of women believe that they need to perform better to be paid equally.[246]

Now the Roberts Court has made it more difficult for women to bring lawsuits for pay discrimination (as explained in the "Talking Points" in Chapter 13).[247] To bring a suit, the law requires victims to file a complaint within 180 days of the discrimination. The Equal Employment Opportunity Commission (EEOC), which administers the law, had interpreted the law to require victims to file a complaint within 180 days of their *last* paycheck reflecting the discriminatory salary or wages. Thus the180-day clock reset after each paycheck. In 2007, a five-justice majority of the Roberts Court, however, interpreted the provision to require victims to file a complaint within 180 days of their *first* paycheck. At this time, few employees would be aware of any pay differential and new employees would be leery of filing a formal complaint anyway. The Court's decision, unless overturned by Congress, means that few suits will be brought, even when clear discrimination exists.

Another reason for the gap between what women and men earn is because women and men have different jobs, whether due to discrimination or to choice. Despite the Civil Rights Act of 1964 and the societal changes—the blurring of lines between genders—many women have traditional women's jobs and most men have traditional men's jobs. And traditional women's jobs pay less.

Historically, women were shunted into a small number of jobs. Even by 2000, two-thirds of working women were crowded into just twenty-one of the occupations identified by the Department of Labor.[248] These "pink-collar" jobs include secretaries (98 percent are women), household workers (97 percent), child care workers (97 percent), nurses (93 percent), bank tellers (90 percent), librarians (83 percent), elementary school teachers (83 percent), and health technicians (81 percent). In contrast, few women are carpenters (1 percent), firefighters (2 percent), mechanics (4 percent), or truck drivers (5 percent).[249]

Although the Equal Pay Act mandates equal pay for equal work, it does not require equal pay for comparable work—usually called **comparable worth**. According to a study in Washington state, maintenance carpenters and secretaries performed comparable jobs in terms of the education, the skill, or other qualifications required, but the carpenters, mostly men, made about $600 a month more than the secretaries, mostly women. In general, "men's jobs" paid about 20 percent more than comparable "women's jobs." Yet courts rejected demands by public employees that government employers boost the pay for "women's jobs." Nonetheless, some state and city governments implemented comparable worth for their employees after prodding by labor unions and women's groups. Private companies, however, did not, because doing so would require them to pay many female employees more.

Although the push for comparable worth has stalled, in recent years grassroots campaigns organized by labor unions and church groups have called for laws mandating a **living wage**.[250] These laws would require employers to pay

"I feel like a man trapped in a woman's salary."

more than the federal minimum wage, to pay whatever is necessary so a full-time worker doesn't fall below the poverty line.

Some proposals would apply only to government employees and to the employees of the companies that do business with the government. Other proposals would apply to all employees within a city or state. Still other proposals would apply just to the employees of "big-box stores," such as Wal-Mart and Home Depot, because these companies drive down the wages for workers throughout society. Most proposals would exempt small businesses with fewer than twenty-five workers.

So far, some cities (Baltimore, San Francisco, and Santa Fe) and one state (Nevada) have adopted such laws.[251] If many cities and states did, living wage laws would have a significant impact on women and minorities, because women and minorities hold a disproportionate number of the lowest-paying jobs. In addition, living wage laws would have a ripple effect, prompting employers to raise the wages of the workers just above the lowest level.

Another reason for the gap between what women and men earn is that women have children. The gap is mostly between married women and married men. Single women and single men between the ages of twenty-one and thirty-five receive nearly equal pay. But when the women get married and have children, their pay lags. Some interrupt their career until their children start school. Others continue to work but shift from the fast track to the so-called "mommy track," working fewer hours due to child care and household responsibilities.[252] Still others fall victim to stereotypes—that mothers aren't serious about their careers, that mothers aren't dependable because they won't show up when their children get sick, or that mothers will quit sooner or later anyway.[253] Through such stereotypes, managers move mothers to the "mommy track" in their own minds, whether the mothers want that track or not.

For whichever reasons, the difference in pay makes a difference in life. Early in her career, it means that a woman might not be able to pay off her credit card debts or college loans as quickly. She might not be able to have as nice a car or an apartment as her male counterpart. Later in her career, she might not be able to have as nice a house or as exotic vacations. Then, if her husband divorces her or dies before her, she might not be able to have as comfortable a retirement. The accumulated shortfall in her retirement savings means that she might struggle in her old age.[254]

Mothers with young children confront more obstacles than unequal pay. Male employers do little to accommodate the demands of child rearing. Most companies don't provide paid maternity leave, paid sick days, on-site day care, or flexible schedules. The United States lags far behind most other countries, including all wealthy countries, in creating family-friendly policies. Of 173 countries, all but the United States, Papua New Guinea, and three African countries guarantee paid maternity leaves. Sixty-five countries even provide paid paternity leaves. (In the United States, only California provides partly paid family leaves.) One hundred forty-five countries provide paid sick days.[255]

Congress passed and President Clinton signed a bill requiring employers to grant unpaid maternity and paternity leaves. Companies must allow unpaid leaves for up to three months for workers with newborn or recently adopted children or with seriously ill family members. The act applies to companies that have fifty employees and to workers who work twenty-five hours a week for a year.[256] This covers about half of American workers.

But relatively few workers take advantage of these leaves. Most workers can't afford to take unpaid leaves. Moreover, many managers don't support such measures, and some coworkers resent the additional burdens, so employees are reluctant to ask for leaves. When companies are laying off workers to cut costs, "If you look like you are not career oriented, you can lose your job."[257]

Due to the influx of women workers, "the workforce has changed enormously in the last thirty years, but the workplace has not kept pace."[258] The workplace is "stuck in a time warp, modeled for [*Leave It to Beaver's*] Ward and June Cleaver when the reality feels more like . . . 'Survivor.'"[259]

Workers in the United States put in longer hours than those in other industrialized countries, and these hours, for both sexes, have increased since the 1970s.[260] The result is that mothers and fathers with young children often face unreasonable demands on their time. Neither spouse has the time to do what the housewife once did. (It's not really a joke when someone quips, "Both spouses need a housewife.") In many families, the woman tries to do these tasks at night and on weekends. Where both spouses work full-time, the woman does twice as much of the housework and four times as much of the child care as the man,[261] but both spouses frequently feel stretched thin and stressed out. Two-thirds of parents say they don't have enough time with their children, and nearly two-thirds of married workers say they don't have enough time with their spouse.[262]

So even though women have gained greater acceptance in the workplace, they—and their spouses—have not overcome the expectations that developed long before they were ever allowed in the workplace. And these expectations are exacerbated by Americans' glorification of work and, with new communications technology, a perverse celebration of a "24/7 workweek." "We glorify an all-work, all-the-time lifestyle," notes one commentator, "and then weep crocodile tears for kids whose parents are never home."[265]

In addition to their difficulties in getting hired, promoted, and paid equally, some women also face sexual harassment (see the box "Sexual Harassment at Work").

The Education Amendments of 1972 (to the Civil Rights Act of 1964) forbade discrimination on the basis of sex in schools and colleges that receive federal aid. The amendments were prompted by discrimination against women by undergraduate and graduate colleges, especially in admissions and financial aid.

The language of the amendments, often referred to as **Title IX**, is very broad, and the Department of Education, which administers the provisions, has established extensive rules that cover more aspects of education than Congress expected.[266] The department has used Title IX to prod institutions into employing and promoting more female teachers and administrators, opening vocational training classes to girls and home economics classes to boys, and offering equal athletic programs to girls and women. If institutions don't comply, the government can cut off their federal aid. (See Table 2.)

Title IX has affected athletic programs especially. Before, schools provided far fewer sports for females than for males, and they spent far fewer dollars—for scholarships, coaches, and facilities—on women's sports. Now the department interprets Title IX to require a school either to have approximately the same percentage of female athletes as female undergraduates, to continually expand opportunities for female athletes, or to fully accommodate the interests and abilities of female students. (The latter would occur if female students at a school were satisfied that there were sufficient opportunities for them, given their interests and abilities, even if the opportunities were unequal to those for men.)

Very few colleges meet the first requirement. To comply, most are trying to meet the second requirement by expanding the number of women's sports. But they worry that they will have to fulfill the first requirement eventually. And they fear that they will have to cap the squad size of their

SEXUAL HARASSMENT AT WORK

The Supreme Court has ruled that sexual harassment is a form of job discrimination prohibited by the Civil Rights Act of 1964,[1] and Congress has passed a law allowing victims to sue employers and collect money for distress, illness, or loss of their job due to such behavior. Although sexual harassment can be directed toward either sex,[2] it is usually directed toward women.

Courts recognize two types of **sexual harassment**. The most obvious is quid pro quo, in which a supervisor makes unwanted sexual advances and either promises good consequences (for example, a promotion or pay raise) if the employee goes along or threatens bad consequences (for example, an undesirable reassignment) if the employee refuses. The less obvious type is creating a hostile environment that interferes with the employee's ability to perform the job. To prove that a hostile environment existed, the employee must demonstrate that the offensive conduct was severe or persistent.

Paula Jones's suit against President Clinton, who as Arkansas governor allegedly asked her for oral sex, was dismissed because the sexual advance was considered neither severe enough nor, as a single incident, persistent enough to constitute a hostile environment. If it happened, the judge said, it was "boorish and offensive" but not technically harassment.

Despite many men's fears, occasional innocuous comments, jokes, or requests for dates would not be classified as harassment. Justice Antonin Scalia emphasized that the law did not create "a general civility code."[3]

Yet confusion persists because several outlandish examples have received widespread publicity. A library employee filed a complaint against a coworker who had posted a *New Yorker* cartoon in his cubicle.[4] A graduate teaching assistant filed a complaint against another who had placed a photograph of his wife, wearing a bikini, on his desk in their office at the University of Nebraska. If sexual harassment were defined this broadly, it would interfere with freedom of speech. (Anyone can file a complaint, as anyone can bring a lawsuit, but of course this doesn't mean that a bureaucratic agency or court agrees with the person filing the complaint or bringing the lawsuit. Yet the publicity gives many people this impression.)

Confusion also persists because some employers, who can be held responsible for sexual harassment by their employees,[5] have adopted "zero-tolerance" policies to insulate them from potential lawsuits. These policies are stricter than the law, and they have led to the firing of a few men who would not have been convicted under the law. For example, a male executive told a female coworker about the

plot of the *Seinfeld* show the night before. Seinfeld had told his friends about a woman he met but whose name he could not remember except that it rhymed with a female body part. The coworker complained of sexual harassment, and Miller Brewing Company fired the executive, despite his nineteen years with the company. (When the executive sued the company, however, a mostly female jury awarded him millions of dollars for being wrongfully dismissed.)

Women in traditional female jobs, such as secretaries, are more likely to be subjected to quid pro quo harassment from supervisors, whereas women in traditional male jobs, especially blue-collar jobs, are more likely to be subjected to hostile-environment harassment from coworkers. Examples abound of male laborers posting sexual pictures or writing sexual messages in women's lockers or restrooms or leaving plastic penises in their toolboxes; taunting the women with sexual questions and comments or addressing them as "Bitch," "Slut," or "Whore" instead of by name; and grabbing their breasts, buttocks, or genitals. Worse for new workers, however, is having supervisors or coworkers who will not train them or help them, or coworkers who will sabotage their work, making them appear slow and shoddy, to drive them off the job. Some coworkers have even sabotaged the women's machinery or

equipment—for example, male firefighters have disabled their female colleagues' life-saving equipment—and thus endangered the women's lives.

The dynamics of sexual harassment don't revolve around sex as much as they reflect abuse of power. (In fact, the law doesn't forbid sex between workers, even if one supervises another.) A supervisor or coworker makes a woman feel vulnerable and thus exercises psychological dominance over her. He wants her to leave the workplace or, at least, to suffer inferior status if she remains there.

Consultants have found that a very small percentage of men harass women, but these men do it a lot. Perhaps three to five men out of one hundred create problems, but these men might affect fifty women. They typically feel bitter toward women or threatened by them. Some also have been bullies toward men as well.[6]

Surveys and stories from women indicate that many more have been sexually harassed than have sued. Relatively few have filed formal complaints, let alone brought lawsuits, because they need their jobs.

[1] *Mentor Savings Bank v. Vinson*, 91 L.Ed.2d 49 (1986).
[2] *Oncale v. Sundowner Offshore Services*, 140 L.Ed.2d 201 (1998).
[3] *Oncale v. Sundowner Offshore Services*.
[4] Henry Louis Gates Jr., "Men Behaving Badly," *New Yorker*, August 18, 1997, 5.
[5] *Faragher v. Boca Raton*, 141 L.Ed.2d 662 (1998); *Burlington Industries v. Ellerth*, 141 L.Ed.2d 633 (1998).
[6] Kirsten Downey Grimsley, "Confronting Hard-Core Harassers," *Washington Post National Weekly Edition*, January 27, 1997, 6.

Table 2   Taking Strides

Since 1970, women have made dramatic gains in higher education.

Women are graduating from college at a higher rate than men.

percentage of bachelor's degrees earned by women:

1970:	40%
1980:	47
1990:	54
2004:	57

Women are graduating from law and medical school at nearly the rate of men.

percentage of law degrees earned by women:

1970:	5%
1980:	28
1990:	42
2000:	46
2004:	49

percentage of medical degrees earned by women:

1970:	8%
1980:	23
1990:	34
2000:	43
2004:	46

SOURCES: National Center for Education Statistics; *Statistical Abstract of the U.S.* 1999, tab. 333 and 329; 2007, tab. 293.

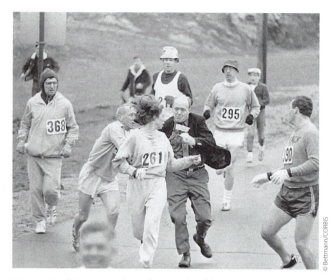

Men resisted the expansion of women's athletics. The Boston Marathon was traditionally for men only. When the first woman tried to participate in 1967, a marathon official assaulted her.

football team, which has the most players and costs the most money, to do so. This would lessen the imbalance in the numbers of male and female athletes, and it would free more money for women's teams.

Some colleges have resisted the enforcement of Title IX, partly because athletic departments are struggling to balance their budget and partly because the act threatens deeply ingrained cultural values reflected in men's athletics. Administrators and boosters fear that women's sports will take money from men's sports and thereby weaken the primacy of men's athletics.

Already Title IX has had a major impact. Colleges have increased their women's teams—more than three times as many as in the early 1970s—and their female athletes—more than ten times as many as before.[267] Women now make up 42 percent of all college athletes and receive 42 percent of the scholarship money, though their teams have lower coaches' salaries and operating expenses than men's teams, and their teams have a smaller proportion of women coaches than they used to.[268] (See box "The Strange Case of Women Coaches.")

Colleges with successful football or basketball programs have increased their women's teams the most because these sports generate revenue that funds women's sports. Colleges with no football program have also increased their women's teams. Colleges with football programs that don't generate a profit (as most don't) lag behind. They pour money into football but lack revenue from television or bowl contracts to fund women's sports.[269]

To reduce the gender imbalance, many colleges have eliminated low-profile men's teams, especially wrestling, gymnastics, tennis, and track. Marquette University eliminated men's wrestling even though the team was financed mostly by private donations.[270]

Title IX has also had a major impact on high schools, which have increased their girls' teams. Before Title IX, 1 of every 27 girls played on a high school team; now 1 of every 2.5 girls does.[271]

But supporters have a broader goal in mind as well. "If girls are socialized the way boys are to take part in sports," the editor of a women's sports magazine says, and "if boys and girls grow up with the idea that girls are strong and capable, it will change the way girls and women are viewed—by themselves and by society."[272]

Overall, Congress and the courts have moved steadily toward legal equality for the sexes. Women have accomplished through congressional and judicial action much of what they would have accomplished with the ERA. It is an indication of the success of the movement that young women today take their equality for granted and focus on their personal lives rather than on the need for further progress.

However, challenges remain. Besides the noncompliance with congressional laws, as noted above, the demands on working parents are overwhelming. "The failure of the

THE STRANGE CASE OF WOMEN COACHES

Although women are becoming more numerous in most traditional male occupations, since Title IX the proportion of women coaching women's intercollegiate athletic teams has shrunk from over 90 percent to barely over 40 percent. As the numbers of female teams and female athletes have expanded dramatically, the number of female coaches has failed to keep pace. Why?

Before Title IX, there were relatively few women's intercollegiate teams. Typically, they were coached by a gym teacher and outfitted with hand-me-down uniforms and equipment. Their schedule featured a few games with nearby schools, and they traveled on a bus. After Title IX, the number of women's teams skyrocketed, and their institutional support increased. The NCAA, which had previously spurned women's athletics, now was eager to make them a part of its organization, establishing national championships in most women's sports. The top conferences also gained television contracts and revenue.

With this dramatic increase in the number of women' teams, not enough women were initially available to lead them. As women's sports rose from nearly invisible campus activities to big-time college and university operations, their coaching jobs paid more money and provided more prestige, and they became more attractive to men. And as the coaching jobs became more demanding, requiring full-time work, extensive travel, and unpredictable schedules, they became less attractive to some women.

However, unlike business, where discrimination prevents many women from reaching the top rungs, in Division I women's basketball, which is the most visible women's sport, women disproportionately occupy the coaching positions of the premier teams.

Source: Susan Welch and Lee Sigelman, "Who's Calling the Shots: Women Coaches in Division I Women's Sports," *Social Science Quarterly* 88 (December, 2007) :1414–1435.

---

workplace to make accommodations for working parents is one of the biggest unmet demands of American voters."[273] Increasingly, the battle over "family values" is becoming a battle over workplace expectations that undermine family life.[274]

Discrimination against Men

The traditional conception of gender roles has also created problems for men who don't fit the standard mold.

When the Burger Court rejected stereotypes that led to discrimination against women, it also rejected some that led to discrimination against men. It invalidated Mississippi's law barring men from a state university's nursing school.[275] It also invalidated Alabama's law allowing only women to seek alimony upon divorce.[276] Thus the Court rejected stereotypes that only women become nurses and only women are dependent on their spouses.

On the other hand, the Burger Court upheld some laws that were designed to protect women but that discriminate against men. It affirmed laws prohibiting statutory rape—intercourse with a minor, with consent—by males but not by females.[277] It also affirmed a law mandating draft registration for males but not for females.[278] It rationalized that registration eventually could lead to the draft and the draft eventually could lead to combat, and it insisted that most women aren't capable of combat. Thus the Court accepted the stereotypes that only men initiate sex with underage partners and only men can fight in war.

In the absence of a draft, the most significant discrimination against men may occur in divorce cases, where the norm is to grant custody of children to mothers and require payment of support by fathers. Although courts give fathers visitation rights, they permit mothers to move miles away, making visitation difficult and sporadic. And although governments have taken steps to enforce support payments, they have done little to enforce visitation rights. This practice reflects the stereotype that fathers are capable of funding their children but not of raising them. The Supreme Court has ignored this problem.

Other discrimination against men may occur in cases of unintended pregnancy. Women may choose abortion, adoption, or raising the child. Men have no choice. The Supreme Court invalidated laws requiring a husband's consent before his wife's abortion, because the woman carries the fetus so she is most affected by the decision.[279] (See the box "Choice for Men?")

Affirmative Action

Assume that a black runner and a white runner compete at a track meet. But the officials force the black runner to carry heavy weights, and he falls behind. Eventually, the officials realize that this is unfair, and they take the weights off. Of course, the black runner is still behind. Would this be fair? Assume instead that the officials not only take the weights off but also allow him to catch up. Would this be fairer?[280]

ethical dilemmas | Choice for Men?

A twenty-five-year-old man repeatedly told his girlfriend that he didn't want to have a child, but she assured him—falsely—that she couldn't get pregnant, due to a physical condition. Then, after unprotected sex, she got pregnant. She did want to have the child, and a Michigan court ordered the man, now her ex-boyfriend, to pay $500 a month in child support. With help from the National Center for Men, he filed a lawsuit, nicknamed *Roe* v. *Wade for Men*.[1]

According to traditional notions of morality, fashioned before the right to abortion, if you engage in intercourse, you risk becoming a parent and shouldering financial responsibilities. But the right to abortion changes the calculus. It frees women from the unintended consequences of pregnancy. Should a comparable right free men from the unintended consequences of pregnancy? Assuming men have no say over the decision to continue pregnancy and give

birth, should a comparable right allow men to opt out of financial obligations at least? Should this man, who evidently was deceived, be saddled with eighteen years of child support? Or is the unfairness to him overridden by the child's need for financial support from two parents?

[1] David Crary, "Man Sues for Right to Decline Fatherhood," *Lincoln Journal Star*, March 9, 2006, 7A.

This scenario captures the dilemma of civil rights policy today. Although most discrimination has been repudiated by the courts and legislatures, the effects of past discrimination persist. Now the question is whether civil rights policy should ignore race and sex or take race and sex into account to compensate for the effects of past discrimination. That is, should the policy require nondiscrimination only or **affirmative action** as well?

Affirmative action applies to employers when hiring and promoting minorities and women, colleges and universities when admitting minorities and women, and governments when reserving a portion of their contracts for businesses owned by minorities and women. We'll examine the first two of these issues.

In Employment

The Civil Rights Act of 1964, which bars discrimination in employment, does not mention affirmative action, but it does authorize the bureaucracy to make rules to end discrimination. In 1969, the Department of Labor called for affirmative action by companies doing business with the federal government. Later, the Equal Employment Opportunities Commission called for affirmative action by governments themselves, and the Office of Education called for affirmative action by colleges as well. Presidents from Nixon through Carter supported it with executive orders, and the Supreme Court sanctioned it in a series of cases.[281]

Affirmative action requires positive steps to ensure that qualified minorities and women receive a fair share of the jobs at each level. What the positive steps and the fair share should be are the subjects of considerable controversy.

If the number of minorities or women who work in a government agency or in a private company that has government contracts is less than the number in the local labor force, the agency or company must agree to recruit more minorities or women or, in serious cases, draw up an affirmative action plan. The plan must include goals to hire or promote more minorities or women. If the agency or com-

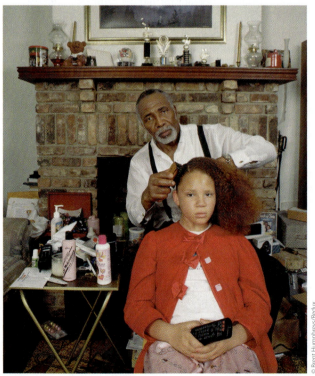

Although most single parents are women, an increasing number are men, such as this father of an eleven-year-old in Dallas.

pany does not reach the goals, it must show that it made an effort to do so. If the company does not satisfy the government, it can be denied future contracts (though in reality a company rarely is penalized).

Although affirmative action plans speak of "goals," critics charge that they mandate quotas and that quotas amount to "reverse discrimination" and result in lower standards.[282] The terms do blur; if employers are pressured to meet goals, they might interpret *goals* to mean *quotas*. But only after a finding of deliberate and systematic discrimination does affirmative action entail actual quotas.[283]

Furthermore, the courts scrutinize the plans to make sure that they allow white men, as well as minorities and women, to be hired and promoted and that they are temporary (usually until the percentage of minority or female employees reaches the percentage of minority or female workers in the community).

Affirmative action applies to hiring and promoting but not to laying off workers. Because of a belief that affirmative action shouldn't impose much burden on innocent individuals, the Court has struck down the use of affirmative action—any protection for minorities and women—when employers pare their workforce for economic reasons. Instead, the Court has accepted the traditional practice, based on seniority, that the last hired can be the first fired, even if the last hired were minorities and women.[284]

In addition to these long-standing limits on affirmative action, the Rehnquist Court made it more difficult for the government to mandate affirmative action for government agencies or private companies.[285] The government must show clear evidence of some particular past discrimination by a government agency or a private company (or by the entire industry in which the company is a part), rather than simply point to the pervasive historical discrimination in society as the justification for affirmative action in employment.

Affirmative action has definitely helped minorities and women. White men dominate public and private institutions, and as the personnel director of a Fortune 500 company observed, "People tend to hire people like themselves."[286] Thus affirmative action has prodded employers to hire more minorities and women.[287] It has also prodded managers to promote more minorities and women who had been stuck in low-level positions.[288]

Although affirmative action is controversial among the public, it is routinely used and even championed, under the name of "diversity," by big businesses. It enables the businesses to locate untapped talent in overlooked groups and to gain new insights for selling their products to minority and female consumers.[289] Corporations' use of "diversity" also provides a competitive advantage in the global economy.[290]

Whether affirmative action is mandated by the government or practiced by big businesses, it has helped some blacks move up a rung—from the lower middle class to the

middle class or from the middle class to the upper middle class.[291] But affirmative action has not pulled many blacks out of the underclass. In families mired in poverty, these individuals often lack the education and skills necessary to compete for available jobs.[292] And, of course, affirmative action has not created new jobs or better jobs, so it has not helped minorities or women as much as a flourishing economy would.

In short, affirmative action should not be given more credit or saddled with more blame than it deserves. It has boosted some minorities and women but has not helped many others. It has displaced some white men but has not affected most others.

Yet 13 percent of white men think they have lost a job or promotion because of their race, and 10 percent think they have because of their sex.[293] Many others claim they have "heard about" another white man who did. Yet affirmative action is not as pervasive as most people assume.[294] Many people view affirmative action as they do handicapped parking. When looking for a parking space in a crowded lot, many drivers see an empty handicapped space and think, "If it weren't for that, I could park here." Of course, if the space weren't reserved for handicapped drivers, only one other driver could park there.[295] So it is with affirmative action. Many white men think they would get a particular job if it weren't for affirmative action, but only one would. Meanwhile, the rest feel victimized by the policy.

For both sides in the controversy, affirmative action has become a symbol. For civil rights leaders, it represents fairness and a step toward equality and progress. For critics, it represents unfairness and an attack on individuality and merit. It's important to debate these values, but it's also important to recognize that affirmative action is neither the key public policy for racial and sexual equality, as some supporters portray it, nor a big stumbling block for individual achievement, as some detractors characterize it. Indeed, affirmative action reaches so few individuals that in the eyes of some observers the policy is an attempt to achieve "racial justice on the cheap," without adopting the more extensive programs that would be necessary to address the much greater problem of the underclass.[296]

In College Admissions

Affirmative action also applies to college and university admissions. Colleges and universities began to use affirmative action in the 1970s. Some schools used limited programs that gave a boost to minority applicants, while other schools used extensive programs that reserved seats—essentially, set quotas—for minority applicants. The medical school of the University of California at Davis reserved sixteen seats in its class of one hundred students for minorities. In *University of California* v. *Bakke,* the Burger Court upheld the use of race as a factor in admissions, emphasizing the value of diversity, but struck down the use of quotas (unless the school had a history of intentional discrimination).

The Supreme Court would not rule on this issue again until 2003. In the meantime, voters in California and Washington, the governor of Florida, and federal courts in two circuits mandated an end to the use of race in admissions to public universities in those states. (The federal courts ignored the *Bakke* precedent of the Supreme Court.)

The moves against affirmative action prompted concerns that minority enrollments would plunge.[297] Some state legislatures and universities decided not to let this happen. The Texas legislature passed a law guaranteeing admission to its state universities for all high school graduates in the top 10 percent of their class. The University of California Board of Regents guaranteed admission to at least one of the UC campuses for those in the top 4 percent.[298]

These programs use geography instead of race; in particular, they use residential segregation, which has stymied the efforts to desegregate grade schools through high schools, as a way to diversify the universities. Minority students who perform well in their schools can get admitted to the universities, even if their segregated schools provide a lower-quality education than the white schools offer.

Although the programs in both states have increased the numbers of minorities above the numbers there would be without the programs, the numbers are lower than they had been with affirmative action.[299] Asians—not whites—have been the prime beneficiaries of the demise of affirmative action in these states, as they would be with the end of affirmative action throughout the country.[300]

The Rehnquist Court revisited the *Bakke* ruling in 2003. In a pair of cases from the University of Michigan, one directed at undergraduate admissions and one directed at law school admissions, five justices upheld affirmative action, though only as part of a "holistic review" that gives "individualized consideration" to each application. Schools can't use formulas that add points for minority status; they must use a more labor-intensive review.[301] The decision to uphold affirmative action came as a surprise, because the Rehnquist Court had limited affirmative action in employment cases. (See box "Marshalling Support for Affirmative Action.")

The future of affirmative action is in doubt, however, because Justice O'Connor, the swing justice on affirmative action, has retired and been replaced by the more conservative Justice Alito. Now at least four, if not five, justices on the Roberts Court are hostile to any use of race to ameliorate past discrimination.[302] And voters in more states (including Michigan) have adopted ballot measures outlawing the use of race or "preferential treatment" in education.

Just as some white men believe that affirmative action has cost them a job or promotion, some white students believe that it has cost them, or will cost them, a seat in the college or university of their choice. But 60 percent of colleges admit nearly all students who apply; only 20 percent are selective enough to use affirmative action.[303]

Students who apply to elite schools that do use affirmative action are more likely to be rejected because these schools give preferential treatment to their "legacies"— the sons and daughters of their alumni—than because these schools practice affirmative action. (Giving preferential treatment to their legacies encourages their alums to donate to the school.) Typically, a fifth of Harvard's students receive preferential treatment because their parents attended the school. Harvard's "legacies" are more than twice as likely to be admitted as blacks or Latinos. A similar advantage exists at other selective schools, including public schools such as the Universities of California and Virginia.[304]

Affirmative action may be more widespread in graduate and professional schools.[305] For some beneficiaries of affirmative action in law schools, recent social science research has found a mismatch between these students' abilities and the schools' demands. These students attended law schools that were too difficult for them, making it harder for them to graduate, pass the bar exam, and join the legal profession.[306] These findings are controversial, but, if confirmed, suggest that some schools may need to adjust the scope of their affirmative action programs.

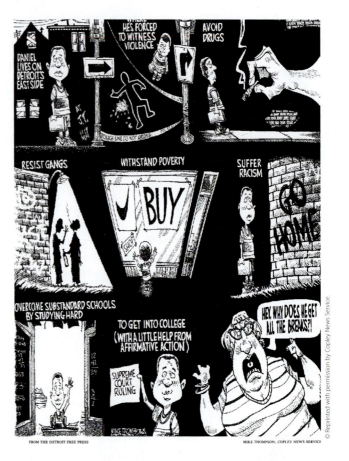

FROM THE DETROIT FREE PRESS   MIKE THOMPSON, COPLEY NEWS SERVICE

BEHIND THE SCENES
MARSHALLING SUPPORT FOR AFFIRMATIVE ACTION

Former President Gerald Ford kept a low profile toward most political controversies after leaving the White House. Yet he remained interested in his alma mater, the University of Michigan, where he was a football star, and he worried about the impact of the affirmative action lawsuits against the university. He encouraged a former aide, James Cannon, to help the university.

Cannon contacted university administrators, and they crafted a strategy to persuade the justices that "the establishment"—not just civil rights groups—favored affirmative action. They recruited sixty-five Fortune 500 companies, including Boeing, Coca-Cola, General Electric, General Motors, and Microsoft, to sponsor a friend-of-the-court brief supporting affirmative action. The brief concluded,

"Today's global marketplace and the increasing diversity in the American population demand the cross-cultural experience and understanding gained from [an education where students] are exposed to diverse people, ideas, perspectives, and interactions."

Cannon, as a member of the board of visitors of the U.S. Naval Academy, knew that the navy considered affirmative action important for effective leadership and morale. So, the team that Ford set in motion also recruited former generals and admirals and former service academy superintendents (current officers and superintendents couldn't get involved) to sign another friend-of-the-court brief. Noting that 22 percent of the enlisted personnel were African American while just 8 percent of the officer corps were, the

brief stated, "Based on decades of experience, [we] have concluded that a highly qualified, racially diverse officer corps educated and trained to command our nation's racially diverse enlisted ranks is essential to the military's ability… to provide national security." The brief recalled the Vietnam War, when there were fewer minority officers and there was greater tension between the officers, who were overwhelmingly white, and enlisted men, who were disproportionately minority. This brief also explained that the three major service academies—at West Point, Annapolis, and Colorado Springs—and the ROTC program all practiced affirmative action in their admissions.

By recruiting these supporters, the university was adopting a political strategy to supplement

the legal strategy that would be reflected in its own brief. The point was that "the establishment" supports affirmative action. The implication was that if affirmative action is appropriate for major corporations and the military, it is also appropriate for colleges and universities.

The strategy apparently persuaded Justice Sandra Day O'Connor, who had not been a consistent supporter of affirmative action, to provide the crucial fifth vote for affirmative action in these cases. She acknowledged that selective universities—the ones that use affirmative action—train the leaders of our society and that an integrated leadership helps govern a diverse people.

Source: Jeffrey Toobin, *The Nine: Inside the Secret World of the Supreme Court* (New York: Doubleday, 2007), 212–214.

DEMOCRACY?

How does the debate over the pros and cons of affirmative action highlight the contradictions among the core values of democracy (discussed in Chapter 1)?

Conclusion: Is Government Responsive in Granting Civil Rights?

When summarizing civil rights progress for minorities and women, an apt analogy is a glass that is half full. The same idea is expressed in a website's title—the Half Changed World.

Blacks and women have taken long strides toward equality since the time when people would say, "A Negro's place is in the cotton field" or "A woman's place is in the home." The civil rights movement and the women's movement initiated the changes. They protested inequality, and they put that issue on the public agenda. As the movements grew and garnered support, they pressured the government. Eventually, a century after the movements began, the government responded.

Within the government, the Supreme Court exercised decisive leadership. In the 1950s and 1960s, the Warren Court was activist in striking down racial segregation, and in the 1970s and 1980s, the Burger Court was activist in striking down sexual discrimination. These Courts' efforts may go down in history as their major achievements. But the Courts' rulings themselves weren't sufficient. Because the Supreme Court lacks the means to enforce its decisions, the president and Congress had to help overcome public resistance.

Thus the areas of racial and sexual discrimination show the power, and the limits of the power, of the courts. The Supreme Court exercised power because it articulated society's emerging views that racial segregation and sexual discrimination by law are wrong and because it forced the government to address this discrimination. But the Court could not bring about the changes by itself. And the Court could not bring about further changes to overcome residential segregation, which leads to school segregation and school inequality, or to ameliorate the poverty that renders many blacks unable to take advantage of their rights. These intractable conditions will require concerted action by the other branches and levels of government as well.

The changes in racial and sexual policies over the years illustrate the responsiveness of the government. In its subjugation of blacks until the 1950s and its treatment of women until the 1970s, the government was responding to majority opinion. When blacks and women organized to protest their status, the government began responding to them and to the shifts in majority opinion that their protests prompted.

In pressuring the government to respond, African Americans have benefited from being numerous, visible, and—with their common legacy of slavery, segregation, and discrimination—cohesive. Their concentration in large northern cities and some southern states has helped them exercise political power. Their legacy, though, has fostered the ghetto, with its debilitating conditions, and denied them the resources to make faster progress.

Thus there are two black Americas—a middle class that has benefited tremendously from the civil rights movement and the changes in our society—and a lower class, especially the underclass, that has been left behind to fend for itself.[307]

Latinos, whose movement is younger, have also taken strides toward equality. With increased immigration, they have become more numerous, and in coming years they will become even more numerous, giving them a large voting bloc. Their concentration in some states and cities has enabled them to influence these state and local governments. Their diversity and lack of cohesiveness, however, have hindered their ability to influence the national government.

American Indians are the smallest, most isolated, and least organized minority, so they have had the poorest success in pressuring the government.

As minority groups grow—together they are expected to make up half of the U.S. population by 2050—they will be able to exert pressure on government more effectively. But they will increasingly come into conflict with each other, especially when economic conditions are stagnant and government jobs and services are scarce. Already there are tensions (as the Academy-Award-winning movie *Crash* poignantly and powerfully depicts). Some blacks resent the faster progress of Latinos and Asians. These blacks say African Americans were here before most Hispanics and all Asians, they suffered more and struggled longer, and so they should reap the rewards sooner. On the other hand, Latino leaders resent the reluctance of black groups to help them with their issues.[308] There have been conflicts, even riots. Blacks have rioted in Miami from frustration with the Cuban-dominated leadership. Latinos have rioted in Washington, D.C., out of anger with the black power structure. Continuing illegal immigration could exacerbate the tensions by pitting new immigrants against poor blacks in competition for jobs.

Nonminority women were never subjugated as much as minority men and women, so they have had less to overcome. Moreover, women are a majority, they vote as frequently as men, and they have well-organized and well-funded interest groups. Consequently, they have made the greatest strides toward equality.

Key Terms

civil rights

Declaration of Independence

Dred Scott case

equal protection clause

neoslavery

sharecropping

Jim Crow laws

sundown laws

Plessy v. *Ferguson*

separate-but-equal doctrine

Great Migration

Ku Klux Klan

NAACP

Brown v. *Board of Education*

Warren Court

brown bag test

de jure segregation

de facto segregation

Burger Court

Rehnquist Court

Roberts Court

Civil Rights Act of 1964

restrictive covenants

steering

blockbusting

redlining

Civil Rights Act of 1968

racial profiling

National Organization for Women (NOW)

Equal Rights Amendment (ERA)

Pregnancy Discrimination Act

Equal Pay Act

comparable worth

living wage

Title IX

sexual harassment

affirmative action

Key Names

Thomas Jefferson

W. E. B. Du Bois

Thurgood Marshall

Dwight Eisenhower

Earl Warren

George Wallace

Rosa Parks

Martin Luther King, Jr.

John Kennedy

Lyndon Johnson

César Chávez

Susan B. Anthony

Elizabeth Cady Stanton

Betty Friedan

Please visit our companion website at www.cengage.com/politicalscience/welch/uag12e or use CengageNOW for additional resources dealing with this chapter.

The Declaration of Independence*

In Congress, July 4, 1776.

A Declaration by the Representatives of the United States of America, in General Congress assembled.

When in the Course of human Events, it becomes necessary for one People to dissolve the Political Bonds which have connected them with another, and to assume among the Powers of the Earth, the separate and equal Station to which the Laws of Nature and of Nature's God entitle them, a decent Respect to the Opinions of Mankind requires that they should declare the causes which impel them to the Separation.

We hold these Truths to be self-evident, that all Men are created equal, that they are endowed by their Creator with certain unalienable Rights, that among these are Life, Liberty, and the Pursuit of Happiness—That to secure these Rights, Governments are instituted among Men, deriving their just Powers from the Consent of the Governed, that whenever any Form of Government becomes destructive of these Ends, it is the Right of the People to alter or to abolish it, and to institute new Government, laying its Foundation on such Principles, and organizing its Powers in such Forms, as to them shall seem most likely to effect their Safety and Happiness. Prudence, indeed, will dictate that Governments long established should not be changed for light and transient Causes; and accordingly all Experience hath shewn, that Mankind are more disposed to suffer, while Evils are sufferable, than to right themselves by abolishing the Forms to which they are accustomed. But when a long Train of Abuses and Usurpations, pursuing invariably the same Object, evinces a Design to reduce them under absolute Despotism, it is their Right, it is their Duty, to throw off such Government, and to provide new Guards for their future Security. Such has been the patient Sufferance of these Colonies; and such is now the Necessity which constrains them to alter their former Systems of Government. The History of the present King of Great Britain is a History of repeated Injuries and Usurpations, all having in direct Object the Establishment of an absolute Tyranny over these States. To prove this, let facts be submitted to a candid World.

He has refused his Assent to Laws, the most wholesome and necessary for the public Good.

He has forbidden his Governors to pass Laws of immediate and pressing Importance, unless suspended in their Operation till his Assent should be obtained; and when so suspended, he has utterly neglected to attend to them.

He has refused to pass other Laws for the Accommodation of large Districts of People, unless those People would relinquish the Right of Representation in the Legislature, a Right inestimable to them, and formidable to Tyrants only.

He has called together Legislative Bodies at Places unusual, uncomfortable, and distant from the Depository of their Public Records, for the sole Purpose of fatiguing them into Compliance with his Measures.

He has dissolved Representative Houses repeatedly, for opposing with manly Firmness his Invasions on the Rights of the People.

He has refused for a long Time, after such Dissolutions, to cause others to be elected; whereby the Legislative Powers, incapable of Annihilation, have returned to the People at large for their exercise; the State remaining in the mean time exposed to all the Dangers of Invasion from without, and Convulsions within.

He has endeavoured to prevent the Population of these States; for that Purpose obstructing the Laws for Naturalization of Foreigners; refusing to pass others to encourage their Migration hither, and raising the Conditions of new Appropriations of Lands.

*The spelling, capitalization, and punctuation of the original have been retained here.

He has obstructed the Administration of Justice, by refusing his Assent to Laws for establishing Judiciary Powers.

He has made Judges dependent on his Will alone, for the Tenure of their offices, and the Amount and payments of their Salaries.

He has erected a Multitude of new Offices, and sent hither Swarms of Officers to harass our People, and eat out their Substance.

He has kept among us, in times of Peace, Standing Armies, without the consent of our Legislatures.

He has affected to render the Military independent of, and superior to the Civil Power.

He has combined with others to subject us to a Jurisdiction foreign to our Constitution, and unacknowledged by our Laws; giving his Assent to their Acts of pretended Legislation:

For quartering large Bodies of Armed Troops among us:

For protecting them, by a mock Trial, from Punishment for any Murders which they should commit on the Inhabitants of these States:

For cutting off our Trade with all Parts of the World:

For imposing Taxes on us without our Consent:

For depriving us, in many cases, of the Benefits of Trial by Jury:

For transporting us beyond Seas to be tried for pretended Offences:

For abolishing the free System of English Laws in a neighbouring Province, establishing therein an arbitrary Government, and enlarging its Boundaries, so as to render it at once an Example and fit Instrument for introducing the same absolute Rule into these Colonies:

For taking away our Charters, abolishing our most valuable Laws, and altering fundamentally the Forms of our Governments:

For suspending our own Legislatures, and declaring themselves invested with Power to legislate for us in all Cases whatsoever.

He has abdicated Government here, by declaring us out of his Protection and waging War against us.

He has plundered our Seas, ravaged our Coasts, burnt our towns, and destroyed the Lives of our People.

He is, at this Time, transporting large Armies of foreign Mercenaries to compleat the works of Death, Desolation, and Tyranny, already begun with circumstances of Cruelty and Perfidy, scarcely paralleled in the most barbarous Ages, and totally unworthy the Head of a civilized Nation.

He has constrained our fellow Citizens taken Captive on the high Seas to bear Arms against their Country, to become the Executioners of their Friends and Brethren, or to fall themselves by their Hands.

He has excited domestic Insurrections amongst us, and has endeavoured to bring on the Inhabitants of our Frontiers, the merciless Indian Savages, whose known Rule of Warfare is an undistinguished Destruction, of all Ages, Sexes and Conditions.

In every state of these Oppressions we have Petitioned for Redress in the most humble Terms: Our repeated Petitions have been answered only by repeated Injury. A Prince, whose Character is thus marked by every act which may define a Tyrant, is unfit to be the Ruler of a free People.

Nor have we been wanting in Attentions to our British Brethren. We have warned them from Time to Time of Attempts by their Legislature to extend an unwarrantable Jurisdiction over us. We have reminded them of the Circumstances of our Emigration and Settlement here. We have appealed to their native Justice and Magnanimity, and we have conjured them by the Ties of our common Kindred to disavow these Usurpations, which would inevitably interrupt our Connections and Correspondence. They too have been deaf to the Voice of Justice and of Consanguinity. We must, therefore, acquiesce in the Necessity, which denounces our Separation, and hold them, as we hold the rest of Mankind, Enemies in War, in Peace Friends.

We, therefore, the Representatives of the UNITED STATES OF AMERICA, in General Congress Assembled, appealing to the Supreme Judge of the World for the Rectitude of our Intentions, do, in the Name, and by Authority of the good People of these Colonies, solemnly Publish and Declare, That these United Colonies are, and of Right ought to be, Free and Independent States; that they are absolved from all Allegiance to the British Crown, and that all political Connection between them and the State of Great Britain, is and ought to be totally dissolved; and that as Free and Independent States, they have full Power to levy War, conclude Peace, contract Alliances, establish Commerce, and to do all other Acts and Things which Independent States may of right do. And for the support of this declaration, with a firm Reliance on the Protection of divine Providence, we mutually pledge to each other our Lives, our Fortunes, and our sacred Honor.

Constitution of the United States of America*

We the people of the United States, in Order to form a more perfect Union, establish Justice, insure domestic Tranquility, provide for the common defence, promote the general Welfare, and secure the Blessings of Liberty to ourselves and our posterity, do ordain and establish this Constitution for the United States of America.

Article I

Section 1. All legislative Powers herein granted shall be vested in a Congress of the United States, which shall consist of a Senate and House of Representatives.

Section 2. The House of Representatives shall be composed of Members chosen every second Year by the People of the several States, and the Electors in each State shall have the Qualifications requisite for Electors of the most numerous Branch of the State Legislature.

No person shall be a Representative who shall not have attained to the Age of twenty-five Years, and been seven Years a Citizen of the United States, and who shall not, when elected, be an Inhabitant of that State in which he shall be chosen.

Representatives and direct [Taxes][1] shall be apportioned among the several States which may be included within this Union, according to their respective Numbers [which shall be determined by adding to the whole Number of free Persons, including those bound to Service for a Term of Years, and excluding Indians not taxed, three fifths of all other Persons].[2] The actual Enumeration shall be made within three Years after the first Meeting of the Congress of the United States, and within every subsequent Term of ten Years, in such Manner as they shall by Law direct. The Number of Representatives shall not exceed one for every thirty Thousand, but each State shall have at Least one Representative; and until such enumeration shall be made, the State of New Hampshire shall be entitled to chuse three, Massachusetts eight, Rhode Island and Providence Plantations one, Connecticut five, New-York six, New Jersy four, Pennsylvania eight, Delaware one, Maryland six, Virginia ten, North Carolina five, South Carolina five, and Georgia three.

When vacancies happen in the Representation from any State, the Executive Authority thereof shall issue Writs of Election to fill such Vacancies.

The House of Representatives shall chuse their Speaker and other Officers; and shall have the sole Power of Impeachment.

Section 3. The Senate of the United States shall be composed of two Senators from each State [chosen by the Legislature thereof],[3] for six Years; and each Senator shall have one Vote.

Immediately after they shall be assembled in Consequence of the first Election, they shall be divided as equally as may be into three Classes. The Seats of the Senators of the first Class shall be vacated at the Expiration of the second year, of the second Class at the Expiration of the fourth Year, and of the third Class at the Expiration of the sixth Year, so that one third may be chosen every second Year [and if Vacancies happen by Resignation, or otherwise, during the Recess of the Legislature of any State, the Executive thereof may make temporary Appointments until the next Meeting of the Legislature, which shall then fill such Vacancies.][4]

---

*The spelling, capitalization, and punctuation of the original have been retained here. Brackets indicate passages that have been altered by amendments to the Constitution.
1. Modified by the Sixteenth Amendment.
2. Modified by the Fourteenth Amendment.
3. Repealed by the Seventeenth Amendment.
4. Modified by the Seventeenth Amendment.

No Person shall be a Senator who shall not have attained to the Age of thirty Years, and been nine Years a Citizen of the United States, and who shall not, when elected, be an Inhabitant of that State for which he shall be chosen.

The Vice President of the United States shall be President of the Senate, but shall have no Vote, unless they be equally divided.

The Senate shall chuse their other Officers, and also a President pro tempore, in the Absence of the Vice President, or when he shall exercise the Office of President of the United States.

The Senate shall have the sole Power to try all Impeachments. When sitting for that Purpose, they shall be on Oath or Affirmation. When the President of the United States is tried, the Chief Justice shall preside: And no Person shall be convicted without the Concurrence of two thirds of the Members present.

Judgment in Cases of Impeachment shall not extend further than to removal from Office, and disqualification to hold and enjoy any Office of honor, Trust or Profit under the United States; but the Party convicted shall nevertheless be liable and subject to Indictment, Trial, Judgment and Punishment, according to Law.

Section 4. The Times, Places and Manner of holding Elections for Senators and Representatives, shall be prescribed in each State by the Legislature thereof; but the Congress may at any time by Law make or alter such Regulations, except as to the Places of chusing Senators.

[The Congress shall assemble at least once in every Year, and such Meeting shall be on the first Monday in December, unless they shall by Law appoint a different Day.]⁵

Section 5. Each House shall be the Judge of the Elections, Returns and Qualifications of its own Members, and a Majority of each shall constitute a Quorum to do Business; but a smaller Number may adjourn from day to day, and may be authorized to compel the Attendance of absent Members, in such Manner, and under such Penalties as each House may provide.

Each House may determine the Rules of its Proceedings, punish its Members for disorderly Behaviour, and, with the Concurrence of two thirds, expel a Member.

Each House shall keep a Journal of its Proceedings, and from time to time publish the same, excepting such Parts as may in their Judgment require Secrecy; and the Yeas and Nays of the Members of either House on any question shall, at the Desire of one fifth of those present, be entered on the Journal.

Neither House, during the Session of Congress, shall, without the Consent of the other, adjourn for more than

5. Changed by the Twentieth Amendment.

three days, nor to any other Place than that in which the two Houses shall be sitting.

Section 6. The Senators and Representatives shall receive a Compensation for their Services, to be ascertained by Law, and paid out of the Treasury of the United States. They shall in all Cases, except Treason, Felony and Breach of the Peace, be privileged from Arrest during their Attendance at the Session of their respective Houses, and in going to and returning from the same; and for any Speech or Debate in either House, they shall not be questioned in any other Place.

No Senator or Representative shall, during the Time for which he was elected, be appointed to any civil Office under the Authority of the United States, which shall have been created, or the Emoluments whereof shall have been encreased during such time; and no Person holding any Office under the United States, shall be a Member of either House during his Continuance in Office.

Section 7. All Bills for raising Revenue shall originate in the House of Representatives; but the Senate may propose or concur with Amendments as on other Bills.

Every Bill which shall have passed the House of Representatives and the Senate, shall, before it become a Law, be presented to the President of the United States; If he approves he shall sign it, but if not he shall return it, with his objections to that House in which it shall have originated, who shall enter the Objections at large on their Journal, and proceed to reconsider it. If after such Reconsideration two thirds of that House shall agree to pass the Bill, it shall be sent, together with the Objections, to the other House, by which it shall likewise be reconsidered, and if approved by two thirds of that House, it shall become a Law. But in all such Cases the Votes of both Houses shall be determined by yeas and Nays, and the Names of the Persons voting for and against the Bill shall be entered on the Journal of each House respectively. If any Bill shall not be returned by the President within ten Days (Sundays excepted) after it shall have been presented to him, the Same shall be a Law, in like Manner as if he had signed it, unless the Congress by their Adjournment prevent its Return, in which Case it shall not be a Law.

Every Order, Resolution, or Vote to which the Concurrence of the Senate and House of Representatives may be necessary (except on a question of Adjournment) shall be presented to the President of the United States; and before the Same shall take Effect, shall be approved by him, or being disapproved by him, shall be repassed by two thirds of the Senate and House of Representatives, according to the Rules and Limitations prescribed in the Case of a Bill.

Section 8. The Congress shall have Power To lay and collect Taxes, Duties, Imposts and Excises, to pay the Debts and provide for the common Defence and general Welfare of the United States; but all Duties, Imposts and Excises shall be uniform throughout the United States;

To borrow Money on the credit of the United States;

To regulate Commerce with foreign Nations, and among the several States, and with the Indian Tribes;

To establish a uniform Rule of Naturalization, and uniform Laws on the subject of Bankruptcies throughout the United States;

To coin Money, regulate the Value thereof, and of foreign Coin, and fix the Standard of Weights and Measures;

To provide for the Punishment of counterfeiting the Securities and current Coin of the United States.

To establish Post Offices and post Roads;

To promote the Progress of Science and useful Arts, by securing for limited Times to Authors and Inventors the exclusive Right to their respective Writings and Discoveries;

To constitute Tribunals inferior to the supreme Court;

To define and punish Piracies and Felonies committed on the high Seas, and Offences against the Law of Nations;

To declare War, grant Letters of Marque and Reprisal, and make Rules concerning Captures on Land and Water;

To raise and support Armies, but no Appropriation of Money to that Use shall be for a longer Term than two Years;

To provide and maintain a Navy;

To make Rules for the Government and Regulation of the land and naval Forces;

To provide for calling forth the Militia to execute the Laws of the Union, suppress Insurrections and repel Invasions;

To provide for organizing, arming, and disciplining the Militia, and for governing such Part of them as may be employed in the Service of the United States, reserving to the States respectively, the Appointment of the Officers, and the Authority of training the Militia according to the discipline prescribed by Congress;

To exercise exclusive Legislation in all Cases whatsoever, over such District (not exceeding ten Miles square) as may, by Cession of particular States, and the Acceptance of Congress, become the Seat of the Government of the United States, and to exercise like Authority over all Places purchased by the Consent of the Legislature of the State in which the Same shall be, for the Erection of forts, Magazines, Arsenals, dockYards, and other needful Buildings;—And

To make all Laws which shall be necessary and proper for carrying into Execution the foregoing Powers, and all other Powers vested by this Constitution in the Government of the United States, or in any Department or Officer thereof.

Section 9.   The Migration or Importation of such Persons as any of the States now existing shall think proper to admit, shall not be prohibited by the Congress prior to the Year one thousand eight hundred and eight, but a Tax or duty may be imposed on such Importation, not exceeding ten dollars for each Person.

The Privilege of the Writ of Habeas Corpus shall not be suspended, unless when in Cases of Rebellion or Invasion the public Safety may require it.

No Bill of Attainder or ex post facto Law shall be passed.

[No Capitation, or other direct, Tax shall be laid, unless in Proportion to the Census or Enumeration herein before directed to be taken.][6]

No Tax or Duty shall be laid on Articles exported from any State.

No Preference shall be given by any Regulation of Commerce or Revenue to the Ports of one State over those of another; nor shall Vessels bound to, or from, one State, be obliged to enter, clear, or pay Duties in another.

No Money shall be drawn from the Treasury, but in Consequence of Appropriations made by Law; and a regular Statement and Account of the Receipts and Expenditures of all public Money shall be published from time to time.

No Title of Nobility shall be granted by the United States; and no Person holding any Office or Profit or Trust under them, shall, without the Consent of the Congress, accept of any present, Emolument, Office, or Title, of any kind whatever, from any King, Prince, or foreign State.

Section 10.   No state shall enter into any Treaty, Alliance, or Confederation; grant Letters of Marque and Reprisal; coin Money; emit Bills of Credit; make any Thing but gold and silver Coin a Tender in Payment of Debts; pass any Bill of Attainder, ex post facto Law, or Law impairing the Obligation of Contracts, or grant any Title of Nobility.

No State shall, without the Consent of the Congress, lay any Imposts or Duties on Imports or Exports, except what may be absolutely necessary for executing its inspection Laws; and the net Produce of all Duties and Imposts, laid by any State on Imports or Exports, shall be for the Use of the Treasury of the United States; and all such Laws shall be subject to the Revision and Controul of the Congress.

No State shall, without the Consent of Congress, lay any duty of Tonnage, keep Troops, or Ships of War in time of Peace, enter into any Agreement or Compact with another State, or with a foreign Power or engage in War, unless actually invaded, or in such imminent Danger as will not admit of delay.

Article II

Section 1.   The executive Power shall be vested in a President of the United States of America. He shall hold his Office during the Term of four Years, and, together with the

6. Modified by the Sixteenth Amendment.

Vice President, chosen for the Same Term, be elected, as follows.

Each State shall appoint, in such Manner as the Legislature thereof may direct, a Number of Electors, equal to the whole Number of Senators and Representatives to which the State may be entitled in the Congress; but no Senator or Representative, or Person holding an Office of Trust or Profit under the United States, shall be appointed an Elector.

[The Electors shall meet in their respective States, and vote by Ballot for two Persons of whom one at least shall not be an Inhabitant of the same State with themselves. And they shall make a List of all the Persons voted for, and of the Number of Votes for each; which List they shall sign and certify, and transmit sealed to the Seat of the Government of the United States, directed to the President of the Senate. The President of the Senate shall, in the Presence of the Senate and House of Representatives, open all the Certificates, and the Votes shall then be counted. The Person having the greatest Number of Votes shall be the President, if such Number be a Majority of the whole Number of Electors appointed; and if there be more than one who have such Majority, and have an equal Number of Votes, then the House of Representatives shall immediately chuse by Ballot one of them for President; and if no Person have a Majority, then from the five highest on the List the said House shall in like Manner chuse the President. But in chusing the President, the Votes shall be taken by States, the Representation from each State having one Vote; A quorum for this Purpose shall consist of a Member or Members from two thirds of the States, and a Majority of all the states shall be necessary to a Choice. In every Case, after the Choice of the President, the Person having the greatest Number of Votes of the Electors shall be the Vice President. But if there should remain two or more who have equal Votes, the Senate shall chuse from them by Ballot the Vice President.][7]

The Congress may determine the Time of chusing the Electors, and the Day on which they shall give their Votes; which Day shall be the same throughout the United States.

No person except a natural born Citizen, or a Citizen of the United States, at the time of the Adoption of this Constitution, shall be eligible to the Office of President; neither shall any Person be eligible to that Office who shall not have attained to the Age of thirty five Years, and been fourteen Years a Resident within the United States.

[In Case of the Removal of the President from Office, or of his Death, Resignation, or Inability to discharge the Powers and Duties of the said Office, the same shall devolve on the Vice President, and the Congress may by Law provide for the Case of Removal, Death, Resignation or Inability, both of the President and Vice President, declaring what Officer shall then act as President, and such Offi-

cer shall act accordingly, until the Disability be removed, or a President shall be elected.][8]

The President shall, at stated Times, receive for his Services, a Compensation, which shall neither be increased nor diminished during the Period for which he shall have been elected, and he shall not receive within that Period any other Emolument from the United States, or any of them.

Before he enter on the Execution of his Office, he shall take the following Oath or Affirmation:—"I do solemnly swear (or affirm) that I will faithfully execute the Office of President of the United States, and will to the best of my Ability, preserve, protect and defend the constitution of the United States."

Section 2.   The President shall be Commander in Chief of the Army and Navy of the United States, and of the Militia of the several States, when called into the actual Service of the United States; he may require the Opinion, in writing, of the principal Officer in each of the executive Departments, upon any Subject relating to the Duties of their respective Offices, and he shall have Power to grant Reprieves and Pardons for Offences against the United States, except in Cases of Impeachment.

He shall have Power, by and with the Advice and Consent of the Senate, to make Treaties, provided two thirds of the Senators present concur; and he shall nominate, and by and with the Advice and Consent of the Senate, shall appoint Ambassadors, other public Ministers and Consuls, Judges of the supreme Court, and all other Officers of the United States, whose Appointments are not herein otherwise provided for, and which shall be established by Law; but the Congress may by Law vest the Appointment of such inferior Officers, as they think proper, in the President alone, in the Courts of Law, or in the Heads of Departments.

The President shall have Power to fill up all Vacancies that may happen during the Recess of the Senate, by granting Commissions which shall expire at the end of their next Session.

Section 3.   He shall from time to time give to the Congress Information of the State of the Union, and recommend to their Consideration such Measures as he shall judge necessary and expedient; he may, on extraordinary Occasions, convene both Houses, or either of them, and in Case of Disagreement between them, with Respect to the Time of Adjournment, he may adjourn them to such Time as he shall think proper; he shall receive Ambassadors and other public Ministers; he shall take Care that the Laws be faithfully executed, and shall Commission all the Officers of the United States.

Section 4.   The President, Vice President and all civil Officers of the United States, shall be removed from Office on

---

7. Changed by the Twelfth Amendment.

8. Modified by the Twenty-fifth Amendment.

Impeachment for, and Conviction of, Treason, Bribery, or other high Crimes and Misdemeanors.

Article III

Section 1. The judicial Power of the United States, shall be vested in one supreme Court, and in such inferior Courts as the Congress may from time to time ordain and establish. The Judges, both of the supreme and inferior Courts, shall hold their Offices during good Behaviour, and shall, at stated Times, receive for their Services, a Compensation, which shall not be diminished during their Continuance in Office.

Section 2. The judicial Power shall extend to all Cases, in Law and Equity, arising under this Constitution, the Laws of the United States, and Treaties made, or which shall be made, under their Authority;—to all Cases affecting Ambassadors, other public Ministers and Consuls;—to all Cases of admiralty and maritime Jurisdiction;—to Controversies to which the United States shall be a Party;—to Controversies between two or more States;—[between a State and Citizens of another State;][9]—between Citizens of different States,—between Citizens of the same State claiming Lands under Grants of different States, [and between a state, or the Citizens thereof, and foreign States, Citizens or Subjects.][10]

In all cases affecting Ambassadors, other public Ministers and Consuls, and those in which a State shall be Party, the supreme Court shall have original Jurisdiction. In all the other Cases before mentioned, the supreme Court shall have appellate Jurisdiction, both as to Law and Fact, with such Exceptions, and under such Regulations as the Congress shall make.

The Trial of all Crimes, except in Cases of Impeachment, shall be by Jury; and such Trial shall be held in the State where the said Crimes shall have been committed; but when not committed within any State, the Trial shall be at such Place or Places as the Congress may by Law have directed.

Section 3. Treason against the United States, shall consist only in levying War against them, or in adhering to their Enemies, giving them Aid and Comfort. No Person shall be convicted of Treason unless on the Testimony of two Witnesses to the same overt Act, or on Confession in open Court.

The Congress shall have Power to declare the Punishment of Treason, but no Attainder of Treason shall work Corruption of Blood, or Forfeiture except during the Life of the Person attainted.

Article IV

Section 1. Full Faith and Credit shall be given in each State to the public Acts, Records, and judicial Proceedings of every other State. And the Congress may by general Laws prescribe the Manner in which such Acts, Records and Proceedings shall be proved, and the Effect thereof.

Section 2. The Citizens of each State shall be entitled to all Privileges and Immunities of Citizens in the several States.

A Person charged in any State with Treason, Felony, or other Crime, who shall flee from Justice, and be found in another State, shall on Demand of the executive Authority of the State from which he fled, be delivered up, to be removed to the State having Jurisdiction of the Crime.

[No Person held to Service or Labour in one State under the Laws thereof, escaping into another, shall, in Consequence of any Law or Regulation therein, be discharged from such Service or Labour, but shall be delivered up on Claim of the Party to whom such Service or Labour may be due.][11]

Section 3. New States may be admitted by the Congress into this Union; but no new State shall be formed or erected within the Jurisdiction of any other State; nor any State be formed by the Junction of two or more States, or Parts of States, without the Consent of the Legislatures of the States concerned as well as of the Congress.

The Congress shall have Power to dispose of and make all needful Rules and Regulations respecting the Territory or other Property belonging to the United States; and nothing in this Constitution shall be so construed as to Prejudice any Claims of the United States, or of any particular State.

Section 4. The United States shall guarantee to every State in this Union a Republican Form of Government, and shall protect each of them against Invasion, and on Application of the Legislature, or of the Executive (when the Legislature cannot be convened) against domestic Violence.

Article V

The Congress, whenever two thirds of both Houses shall deem it necessary, shall propose Amendments to this Constitution, or on the Application of the Legislatures of two thirds of the several States, shall call a Convention for proposing Amendments, which, in either Case, shall be valid to all Intents and Purposes, as Part of this Constitution, when ratified by the Legislatures of three fourths of the several States, or by Conventions in three fourths thereof, as the one or the other Mode of Ratification may be proposed by the Congress; Provided that no Amendment which may be

9. Modified by the Eleventh Amendment.
10. Modified by the Eleventh Amendment.

11. Repealed by the Thirteenth Amendment.

made prior to the Year One thousand eight hundred and eight shall in any Manner affect the first and fourth Clauses in the Ninth Section of the first Article; and that no State, without its Consent, shall be deprived of its equal Suffrage in the Senate.

Article VI

All Debts contracted and Engagements entered into, before the Adoption of this Constitution, shall be as valid against the United States under this Constitution, as under the Confederation.

This Constitution, and the laws of the United States which shall be made in Pursuance thereof; and all Treaties made, or which shall be made, under the Authority of the United States, shall be the supreme Law of the Land; and the Judges in every State shall be bound thereby, any Thing in the Constitution or Laws of any State to the Contrary notwithstanding.

The Senators and Representatives before mentioned, and the Members of the several State Legislatures, and all executive and judicial Officers, both of the United States and of the several States, shall be bound by Oath or Affirmation, to support this Constitution; but no religious Test shall ever be required as a Qualification to any Office or public Trust under the United States.

Article VII

The Ratification of the Conventions of nine States, shall be sufficient for the Establishment of this constitution between the States so ratifying the Same.

Done in Convention by the Unanimous Consent of the States present the Seventeenth Day of September in the Year of our Lord one thousand seven hundred and Eighty seven and of the Independence of the United States of America the Twelfth. In Witness whereof we have hereunto subscribed our Names.

Go. WASHINGTON

Presid't. and deputy from Virginia

Attest

William Jackson

Secretary

Delaware

Geo. Read

Gunning Bedford jun

John Dickinson

Richard Basset

Jaco. Broon

Massachusetts

Nathaniel Gorham

Rufus King

Connecticut

Wm. Saml. Johnson

Roger Sherman

New York

Alexander Hamilton

New Jersey

Wh. Livingston

David Brearley

Wm. Paterson

Jona. Dayton

Pennsylvania

B. Franklin

Thomas Mifflin

Robt. Morris

Geo. Clymer

Thos. FitzSimons

Jared Ingersoll

James Wilson

Gouv Morris

Virginia

John Blair

James Madison Jr.

North Carolina

Wm. Blount

Richd. Dobbs Spaight

Hu Williamson

South Carolina

J. Rutledge

Charles Cotesworth Pinckney

Charles Pinckney

Pierce Butler

Georgia

William Few

Abr. Baldwin

New Hampshire

John Langdon

Nicholas Gilman

Maryland

James McHenry

Dan of St Thos. Jenifer

Danl. Carroll

Amendment I[12]

Congress shall make no law respecting an establishment of religion, or prohibiting the free exercise thereof; or abridging the freedom of speech, or of the press; or the right of the people peaceably to assemble, and to petition the Government for a redress of grievances.

Amendment II

A well regulated militia, being necessary to the security of a free State, the right of the people to keep and bear arms, shall not be infringed.

Amendment III

No Soldier shall, in time of peace be quartered in any house, without the consent of the owner, nor in time of war, but in a manner to be prescribed by law.

12. The first ten amendments were passed by Congress on September 25, 1789, and were ratified on December 15, 1791.

Amendment IV

The right of the people to be secure in their persons, houses, papers, and effects, against unreasonable searches and seizures, shall not be violated, and no warrants shall issue, but upon probable cause, supported by oath or affirmation, and particularly describing the place to be searched, and the persons or things to be seized.

Amendment V

No person shall be held to answer for a capital, or otherwise infamous crime, unless on a presentment or indictment of a Grand Jury, except in cases arising in the land or naval forces, or in the militia, when in actual service in time of war or public danger; nor shall any person be subject for the same offence to be twice put in jeopardy of life or limb; nor shall be compelled in any criminal case to be a witness against himself, nor be deprived of life, liberty, or property, without due process of law; nor shall private property be taken for public use, without just compensation.

Amendment VI

In all criminal prosecutions, the accused shall enjoy the right to a speedy and public trial, by an impartial jury of the State and district wherein the crime shall have been committed, which district shall have been previously ascertained by law, and to be informed of the nature and cause of the accusation; to be confronted with the witnesses against him; to have compulsory process for obtaining witnesses in his favor, and to have the assistance of counsel for his defence.

Amendment VII

In Suits at common law, where the value in controversy shall exceed twenty dollars, the right of trial by jury shall be preserved, and no fact tried by a jury, shall be otherwise reexamined in any Court of the United States, than according to the rules of the common law.

Amendment VIII

Excessive bail shall not be required, nor excessive fines imposed, nor cruel and unusual punishments inflicted.

Amendment IX

The enumeration in the Constitution, of certain rights, shall not be construed to deny or disparage others retained by the people.

Amendment X

The powers not delegated to the United States by the Constitution, nor prohibited by it to the States, are reserved to the States respectively, or to the people.

Amendment XI
(Ratified February 7, 1795)

The Judicial power of the United States shall not be construed to extend to any suit in law or equity, commenced or prosecuted against one of the United States by Citizens of another State, or by Citizens or Subjects of any Foreign State.

Amendment XII
(Ratified June 15, 1804)

The Electors shall meet in their respective states, and vote by ballot for President and Vice-President, one of whom, at least, shall not be an inhabitant of the same state with themselves; they shall name in their ballots the person voted for as President, and in distinct ballots the person voted for as Vice President, and they shall make distinct lists of all persons voted for as President, and of all persons voted for as Vice-President, and of the number of votes for each, which lists they shall sign and certify, and transmit sealed to the seat of the government of the United States, directed to the President of the Senate;—The President of the Senate shall, in the presence of the Senate and House of Representatives, open all the certificates and the votes shall then be counted;—The person having the greatest number of votes for President, shall be the President, if such number be a majority of the whole number of Electors appointed; and if no person have such majority, then from the persons having the highest numbers not exceeding three on the list of those voted for as President, the House of Representatives shall choose immediately, by ballot, the President. But in choosing the President, the votes shall be taken by states, the representation from each state having one vote; a quorum for this purpose shall consist of a member or members from two-thirds of the states, and a majority of all the states shall be necessary to a choice. [And if the House of Representatives shall not choose a President whenever the right of choice shall devolve upon them, before the fourth day of March next following, then the Vice-President shall act as President, as in the case of the death or other constitutional disability of the President.][13]—The person having the greatest number of votes as Vice-President, shall be the Vice-President, if such number be a majority of the whole number of Electors appointed, and if no person have a majority,

13. Changed by the Twentieth Amendment.

then from the two highest numbers on the list, the Senate shall choose the Vice-President; a quorum for the purpose shall consist of two-thirds of the whole number of Senators, and a majority of the whole number shall be necessary to a choice. But no person constitutionally ineligible to the office of President shall be eligible to that of Vice-President of the United States.

Amendment XIII (Ratified on December 6, 1865)

Section 1.   Neither slavery nor involuntary servitude, except as a punishment for crime whereof the party shall have been duly convicted, shall exist within the United States, or any place subject to their jurisdiction.

Section 2.   Congress shall have power to enforce this article by appropriate legislation.

Amendment XIV (Ratified on July 9, 1868)

Section 1.   All persons born or naturalized in the United States, and subject to the jurisdiction thereof, are citizens of the United States and of the State wherein they reside. No State shall make or enforce any law which shall abridge the privileges or immunities of citizens of the United States; nor shall any State deprive any person of life, liberty, or property, without due process of law; nor deny to any person within its jurisdiction the equal protection of the laws.

Section 2.   Representatives shall be apportioned among the several States according to their respective numbers, counting the whole number of persons in each State, excluding Indians not taxed. But when the right to vote at any election for the choice of electors for President and Vice President of the United States, Representatives in Congress, the Executive and Judicial officers of a State, or the members of the Legislature thereof, is denied to any of the male inhabitants of such State, being [twenty-one]^{14} years of age, and citizens of the United States, or in any way abridged, except for participation in rebellion, or other crime, the basis of representation therein shall be reduced in the proportion which the number of such male citizens shall bear to the whole number of male citizens twenty-one years of age in such State.

Section 3.   No person shall be a Senator or Representative in Congress, or elector of President and Vice President, or hold any office, civil or military, under the United States, or under any State, who having previously taken an oath, as a member of Congress, or as an officer of the United States, or as a member of any State legislature, or as an executive or judicial officer of any State, to support the Constitution of the United States, shall have engaged in insurrection or rebellion against the same, or given aid or comfort to the enemies thereof. But Congress may by a vote of two-thirds of each House, remove such disability.

Section 4.   The validity of the public debt of the United States, authorized by law, including debts incurred for payment of pensions and bounties for services in suppressing insurrection or rebellion, shall not be questioned. But neither the United States nor any State shall assume or pay any debt or obligation incurred in aid of insurrection or rebellion against the United States, or any claim for the loss or emancipation of any slave, but all such debts, obligations and claims shall be held illegal and void.

Section 5.   The Congress shall have power to enforce, by appropriate legislation, the provisions of this article.

Amendment XV (Ratified on February 3, 1870)

Section 1.   The right of citizens of the United States to vote shall not be denied or abridged by the United States or by any State on account of race, color, or previous condition of servitude.

Section 2.   The Congress shall have power to enforce this article by appropriate legislation.

Amendment XVI (Ratified on February 3, 1913)

The Congress shall have power to lay and collect taxes on incomes, from whatever source derived, without apportionment among the several States, and without regard to any census or enumeration.

Amendment XVII (Ratified on April 8, 1913)

The Senate of the United States shall be composed of two Senators from each State, elected by the people thereof, for six years; and each Senator shall have one vote. The electors in each State shall have the qualifications requisite for electors of the most numerous branch of the State legislatures.

When vacancies happen in the representation of any State in the Senate, the executive authority of such State shall issue writs of election to fill such vacancies: *Provided,* That the legislature of any State may empower the executive thereof to make temporary appointments until the people fill the vacancies by election as the legislature may direct.

14. Changed by the Twenty-sixth Amendment.

This amendment shall not be so construed as to affect the election or term of any Senator chosen before it becomes valid as part of the Constitution.

Amendment XVIII
(Ratified on January 16, 1919)

Section 1. After one year from the ratification of this article the manufacture, sale, or transportation of intoxicating liquors within, the importation thereof into, or the exportation thereof from the United States and all territory subject to the jurisdiction thereof for beverage purposes is hereby prohibited.

Section 2. The Congress and the several States shall have concurrent power to enforce this article by appropriate legislation.

Section 3. This article shall be inoperative unless it shall have been ratified as an amendment to the Constitution by the legislatures of the several States, as provided in the Constitution, within seven years from the date of the submission hereof to the States by the Congress.[15]

Amendment XIX
(Ratified on August 18, 1920)

The right of citizens of the United States to vote shall not be denied or abridged by the United States or by any State on account of sex.

Congress shall have power to enforce this article by appropriate legislation.

Amendment XX
(Ratified on January 23, 1933)

Section 1. The terms of the President and Vice President shall end at noon on the 20th day of January, and the terms of Senators and Representatives at noon on the 3rd day of January, of the years in which such terms would have ended if this article had not been ratified, and the terms of their successors shall then begin.

Section 2. The Congress shall assemble at least once in every year, and such meeting shall begin at noon on the 3rd day of January, unless they shall by law appoint a different day.

Section 3. If, at the time fixed for the beginning of the term of the President, the President elect shall have died, the Vice President elect shall become President. If a President shall not have been chosen before the time fixed for the beginning of his term, or if the President elect shall have failed to qualify, then the Vice President elect shall act as President until a President shall have qualified; and the Congress may by law provide for the case wherein neither a President elect nor a Vice President elect shall have qualified, declaring who shall then act as President, or the manner in which one who is to act shall be selected, and such person shall act accordingly until a President or Vice President shall have qualified.

Section 4. The Congress may by law provide for the case of the death of any of the persons from whom the House of Representatives may choose a President whenever the rights of choice shall have devolved upon them, and for the case of the death of any of the persons from whom the Senate may choose a Vice President whenever the right of choice shall have devolved upon them.

Section 5. Sections 1 and 2 shall take effect on the 15th day of October following the ratification of this article.

Section 6. This article shall be inoperative unless it shall have been ratified as an amendment to the Constitution by the legislatures of three-fourths of the several States within seven years from the date of its submission.

Amendment XXI
(Ratified on December 5, 1933)

Section 1. The eighteenth article of amendment to the Constitution of the United States is hereby repealed.

Section 2. The transportation or importation into any State, Territory, or possession of the United States for delivery or use therein of intoxicating liquors, in violation of the laws thereof, is hereby prohibited.

Section 3. This article shall be inoperative unless it shall have been ratified as an amendment to the Constitution by conventions in the several States, as provided in the Constitution, within seven years from the date of the submission hereof to the States by the Congress.

Amendment XXII
(Ratified on February 27, 1951)

No person shall be elected to the office of the President more than twice, and no person who has held the office of President, or acted as President, for more than two years of a term to which some other person was elected President shall be elected to the office of the President more than once. But this Article shall not apply to any person holding

---

15. The Eighteenth Amendment was repealed by the Twenty-first Amendment.

the office of President when this Article was proposed by the Congress, and shall not prevent any person who may be holding the office of President, or acting as President, during the term within which this Article becomes operative from holding the office of President or acting as President during the remainder of such term.

Amendment XXIII
(Ratified on March 29, 1961)

Section 1.   The District constituting the seat of Government of the United States shall appoint in such manner as the Congress may direct:

A number of electors of President and Vice President equal to the whole number of Senators and Representatives in Congress to which the District would be entitled if it were a State, but in no event more than the least populous State; they shall be in addition to those appointed by the States, but they shall be considered, for the purposes of the election of President and Vice President, to be electors appointed by a State; and they shall meet in the District and perform such duties as provided by the twelfth article of amendment.

Section 2.   The Congress shall have power to enforce this article by appropriate legislation.

Amendment XXIV
(Ratified on January 23, 1964)

Section 1.   The right of citizens of the United States to vote in any primary or other election for President or Vice President, for electors for President or Vice President, or for Senator or Representative in Congress, shall not be denied or abridged by the United States or any State by reason of failure to pay any poll tax or other tax.

Section 2.   The Congress shall have power to enforce this article by appropriate legislation.

Amendment XXV
(Ratified on February 10, 1967)

Section 1.   In case of the removal of the President from office or of his death or resignation, the Vice President shall become President.

Section 2.   Whenever there is a vacancy in the office of the Vice President, the President shall nominate a Vice President who shall take office upon confirmation by a majority vote of both Houses of Congress.

Section 3.   Whenever the President transmits to the President pro tempore of the Senate and the Speaker of the House of Representatives his written declaration that he is unable to discharge the powers and duties of his office, and until he transmits to them a written declaration to the contrary, such powers and duties shall be discharged by the Vice President as Acting President.

Section 4.   Whenever the Vice President and a majority of either the principal officers of the executive departments or of such other body as Congress may by law provide, transmit to the President pro tempore of the Senate and the Speaker of the House of Representatives their written declaration that the President is unable to discharge the powers and duties of his office, the Vice President shall immediately assume the powers and duties of the offices as Acting President.

Thereafter, when the President transmits to the President pro tempore of the Senate and the Speaker of the House of Representatives his written declaration that no inability exists, he shall resume the powers and duties of his office unless the Vice President and a majority of either the principal officers of the executive department or of such other body as Congress may by law provide, transmit within four days to the President pro tempore of the Senate and the Speaker of the House of Representatives their written declaration that the President is unable to discharge the powers and duties of his office. Thereupon Congress shall decide the issue, assembling within forty-eight hours for that purpose if not in session. If the Congress, within twenty-one days after receipt of the latter written declaration, or, if Congress is not in session, within twenty-one days after Congress is required to assemble, determines by two-thirds vote of both Houses that the President is unable to discharge the powers and duties of his office, the Vice President shall continue to discharge the same as Acting President; otherwise; the President shall resume the powers and duties of his office.

Amendment XXVI
(Ratified on July 1, 1971)

Section 1.   The right of citizens of the United States, who are eighteen years of age or older, to vote shall not be denied or abridged by the United States or by any State on account of age.

Section 2.   The Congress shall have the power to enforce this article by appropriate legislation.

Amendment XXVII
(Ratified on May 7, 1992)

No law, varying the compensation for the services of the Senators and Representatives, shall take effect, until an election of Representatives shall have intervened.

Federalist Paper 10

Among the numerous advantages promised by a well-constructed Union, none deserves to be more accurately developed than its tendency to break and control the violence of faction. The friend of popular governments never finds himself so much alarmed for their character and fate as when he contemplates their propensity to this dangerous vice. He will not fail, therefore, to set a due value on any plan which, without violating the principles to which he is attached, provides a proper cure for it. The instability, injustice, and confusion introduced into the public councils have, in truth, been the mortal diseases under which popular governments have everywhere perished, as they continue to be the favorite and fruitful topics from which the adversaries to liberty derive their most specious declamations. The valuable improvements made by the American constitutions on the popular models, both ancient and modern, cannot certainly be too much admired; but it would be an unwarrantable partiality to contend that they have as effectually obviated the danger on this side, as was wished and expected. Complaints are everywhere heard from our most considerate and virtuous citizens, equally the friends of public and private faith and of public and personal liberty, that our governments are too unstable, that the public good is disregarded in the conflicts of rival parties, and that measures are too often decided, not according to the rules of justice and the rights of the minor party, but by the superior force of an interested and overbearing majority. However anxiously we may wish that these complaints had no foundation, the evidence of known facts will not permit us to deny that they are in some degree true. It will be found, indeed, on a candid review of our situation, that some of the distresses under which we labor have been erroneously charged on the operation of our governments; but it will be found, at the same time, that other causes will not alone account for many of our heaviest misfortunes; and, particularly, for that prevailing and increasing distrust of public engagements and alarm for private rights which are echoed from one end of the continent to the other. These must be chiefly, if not wholly, effects of the unsteadiness and injustice with which a factious spirit has tainted our public administration.

By a faction I understand a number of citizens, whether amounting to a majority or minority of the whole, who are united and actuated by some common impulse of passion, or of interest, adverse to the rights of other citizens, or the permanent and aggregate interests of the community.

There are two methods of curing the mischiefs of faction: the one, by removing its causes; the other, by controlling its effects.

There are again two methods of removing the causes of faction: the one, by destroying the liberty which is essential to its existence; the other, by giving to every citizen the same opinions, the same passions, and the same interests.

It could never be more truly said than of the first remedy that it was worse than the disease. Liberty is to faction what air is to fire, an aliment without which it instantly expires. But it could not be a less folly to abolish liberty, which is essential to political life, because it nourishes faction than it would be to wish the annihilation of air, which is essential to animal life, because it imparts to fire its destructive agency.

The second expedient is as impracticable as the first would be unwise. As long as the reason of man continues fallible, and his is at liberty to exercise it, different opinions will be formed. As long as the connection subsists between his reason and his self-love, his opinions and his passions will have a reciprocal influence on each other; and the former will be objects to which the latter will attach themselves. The diversity in the faculties of men, from which the rights of property originate, is not less an insuperable obstacle to a uniformity of interests. The protection of these faculties is the first object of government. From the protection of different and unequal faculties of acquiring property, the possession of different degrees and kinds of property immediately results; and from the influence of these on the sentiments and views of the respective proprietors ensues a division of the society into different interests and parties.

The latent causes of faction are thus sown in the nature of man; and we see them everywhere brought into different degrees of activity, according to the different circumstances of civil society. A zeal for different opinions concerning religion, concerning government, and many other points, as well of speculation as of practice; an attachment to different leaders ambitiously contending for pre-eminence and power; or to persons of other descriptions whose fortunes have been interesting to the human passions, have, in turn, divided mankind into parties, inflamed them with mutual animosity, and rendered them much more disposed to vex and oppress each other than to cooperate for their common good. So strong is this propensity of mankind to fall into mutual animosities that where no substantial occasion presents itself the most frivolous and fanciful distinctions have been sufficient to kindle their unfriendly passions and excite their most violent conflicts. But the most common and durable source of factions has been the various and unequal distribution of property. Those who hold and those who are without property have ever formed distinct interests in society. Those who are creditors, and those who are debtors, fall under a like discrimination. A landed interest, a manufacturing interest, a mercantile interest, a moneyed interest, with many lesser interests, grow up of necessity in civilized nations, and divide them into different classes, actuated by different sentiments and views. The regulation of these various and interfering interests forms the principal task of modern legislation and involves the spirit of party and faction in the necessary and ordinary operations of government.

No man is allowed to be a judge in his own cause, because his interest would certainly bias his judgment, and, not improbably, corrupt his integrity. With equal, nay with greater reason, a body of men are unfit to be both judges and parties at the same time; yet what are many of the most important acts of legislation but so many judicial determinations, not indeed concerning the rights of single persons, but concerning the rights of large bodies of citizens? And what are the different classes of legislators but advocates and parties to the causes which they determine? Is a law proposed concerning private debts? It is a question to which the creditors are parties on one side and the debtors on the other. Justice ought to hold the balance between them. Yet the parties are, and must be, themselves the judges; and the most numerous party, or in other words, the most powerful faction must be expected to prevail. Shall domestic manufacturers be encouraged, and in what degree, by restrictions on foreign manufacturers? are questions which would be differently decided by the landed and the manufacturing classes, and probably by neither with a sole regard to justice

and the public good. The apportionment of taxes on the various descriptions of property is an act which seems to require the most exact impartiality; yet there is, perhaps, no legislative act in which greater opportunity and temptation are given to a predominant party to trample on the rules of justice. Every shilling with which they overburden the inferior number is a shilling saved to their own pockets. It is in vain to say that enlightened statesmen will be able to adjust these clashing interests and render them all subservient to the public good. Enlightened statesmen will not always be at the helm. Nor, in many cases, can such an adjustment be made at all without taking into view indirect and remote considerations, which will rarely prevail over the immediate interest which one party may find in disregarding the rights of another or the good of the whole.

The inference to which we are brought is that the *causes* of faction cannot be removed and that relief is only to be sought in the means of controlling its *effects*.

If a faction consists of less than a majority, relief is supplied by the republican principle, which enables the majority to defeat its sinister views by regular vote. It may clog the administration, it may convulse the society; but it will be unable to execute and mask its violence under the forms of the Constitution. When a majority is included in a faction, the form of popular government, on the other hand, enables it to sacrifice to its ruling passion or interest both the public good and the rights of other citizens. To secure the public good and private rights against the danger of such a faction, and at the same time to preserve the spirit and the form of popular government, is then the great object to which our inquiries are directed. Let me add that it is the great desideratum by which alone this form of government can be rescued from the opprobrium under which it has so long labored and be recommended to the esteem and adoption of mankind.

By what means is this object attainable? Evidently by one of two only. Either the existence of the same passion or interest in a majority at the same time must be prevented, or the majority, having such coexistent passion or interest, must be rendered, by their number and local situation, unable to concert and carry into effect schemes of oppression. If the impulse and the opportunity be suffered to coincide, we well know that neither moral nor religious motives can be relied on as an adequate control. They are not found to be such on the injustice and violence of individuals, and lose their efficacy in proportion to the number combined together, that is, in proportion as their efficacy becomes needful.

From this view of the subject it may be concluded that a pure democracy, by which I mean a society consisting of a small number of citizens, who assemble and administer the government in person, can admit of no cure for the mischiefs of faction. A common passion or interest will, in almost every case, be felt by a majority of the whole; a communication and concert results from the form of government itself; and there is nothing to check the inducements to sacrifice the weaker party or an obnoxious individual. Hence it is that such democracies have ever been spectacles of turbulence and contention; have ever been found incompatible with personal security or the rights of property; and have in general been as short in their lives as they have been violent in their deaths. Theoretic politicians, who have patronized this species of government, have erroneously supposed that by reducing mankind to a perfect equality in their political rights, they would at the same time be perfectly equalized and assimilated in their possessions, their opinions, and their passions.

A republic, by which I mean a government in which the scheme of representation takes place, opens a different prospect and promises the cure for which we are seeking. Let us examine the points in which it varies from pure democracy, and we shall comprehend both the nature of the cure and the efficacy which it must derive from the Union.

The two great points of difference between a democracy and a republic are: first, the delegation of the government, in the latter, to a small number of citizens elected by the rest; secondly, the greater number of citizens and greater sphere of country over which the latter may be extended.

The effect of the first difference is, on the one hand, to refine and enlarge the public views by passing them through the medium of a chosen body of citizens, whose wisdom may best discern the true interest of their country and whose patriotism and love of justice will be least likely to sacrifice it to temporary or partial considerations. Under such a regulation it may well happen that the public voice, pronounced by the representatives of the people, will be more consonant to the public good than if pronounced by the people themselves, convened for the purpose. On the other hand, the effect may be inverted. Men of factious tempers, of local prejudices, or of sinister designs, may, by intrigue, by corruption, or by other means, first obtain the suffrages, and then betray the interests of the people. The question resulting is, whether small or extensive republics are most favorable to the election of proper guardians of the public weal; and it is clearly decided in favor of the latter by two obvious considerations.

In the first place it is to be remarked that however small the republic may be the representatives must be raised to a certain number in order to guard against the cabals of a few; and that however large it may be they must be limited to a certain number in order to guard against the confusion of a multitude. Hence, the number of representatives in the two cases not being in proportion to that of the constituents, and being proportionally greatest in the small republic, it follows that if the proportion of fit characters be not less in the large than in the small republic, the former will present a greater option, and consequently a greater probability of a fit choice.

In the next place, as each representative will be chosen by a greater number of citizens in the large than in the small republic, it will be more difficult for unworthy candidates to practice with success the vicious arts by which elections are too often carried; and the suffrages of the people being more free, will be more likely to center on men who possess the most attractive merit and the most diffusive and established characters.

It must be confessed that in this, as in most other cases, there is a mean, on both sides of which inconveniencies will be found to lie. By enlarging too much the number of electors, you render the representative too little acquainted with all their local circumstances and lesser interests; as by reducing it too much, you render him unduly attached to these, and too little fit to comprehend and pursue great and national objects. The federal Constitution forms a happy combination in this respect; the great and aggregate interests being referred to the national, the local and particular to the State legislatures.

The other point of difference is the greater number of citizens and extent of territory which may be brought within the compass of republican than of democratic government; and it is this circumstance principally which renders factious combinations less to be dreaded in the former than in the latter. The smaller the society, the fewer probably will be the distinct parties and interests composing it; the fewer the distinct parties and interests, the more frequently will a majority be found of the same party; and the smaller the number of individuals composing a majority, and the smaller the compass within which they are placed, the more easily will they concert and execute their plans of oppression. Extend the sphere and you take in a greater variety of parties and interests; you make it less probable that a majority of the whole will have a common motive to invade the rights of other citizens; or if such a common motive exists, it will be more difficult for all who feel it to discover their own strength and to act in unison with each other. Besides other impediments, it may be remarked that, where there is a consciousness of unjust or dishonorable purposes, communication is always checked by distrust in proportion to the number whose concurrence is necessary.

Hence, it clearly appears that the same advantage which a republic has over a democracy in controlling the effects of faction is enjoyed by a large over a small republic—is enjoyed by the Union over the States composing it. Does this advantage consist in the substitution of representatives whose enlightened views and virtuous sentiments render them superior to local prejudices and to schemes of injustice? It will not be denied that the representation of the Union will be most likely to possess these requisite endowments. Does it consist in the greater security afforded by a greater variety of parties, against the event of any one party being able to outnumber and oppress the rest? In an equal degree does the increased variety of parties comprised within the Union increase this security. Does it, in fine, consist in the greater obstacles opposed to the concert and accomplishment of the secret wishes of an unjust and interested majority? Here again the extent of the Union gives it the most palpable advantage.

The influence of factious leaders may kindle a flame within their particular States but will be unable to spread a general conflagration through the other States. A religious sect may degenerate into a political faction in a part of the Confederacy; but the variety of sects dispersed over the entire face of it must secure the national councils against any danger from that source. A rage for paper money, for an abolition of debts, for an equal division of property, or for any other improper or wicked project, will be less apt to pervade the whole body of the Union than a particular member of it, in the same proportion as such a malady is more likely to taint a particular county or district than an entire State.

In the extent and proper structure of the Union, therefore, we behold a republican remedy for the diseases most incident to republican government. And according to the degree of pleasure and pride we feel in being republicans ought to be our zeal in cherishing the spirit and supporting the character of federalists.

Federalist Paper 51

To what expedient, then, shall we finally resort, for maintaining in practice the necessary partition of power among the several departments as laid down in the Constitution? The only answer that can be given is that as all these exterior provisions are found to be inadequate the defect must be supplied, by so contriving the interior structure of the government as that its several constituent parts may, by their mutual relations, be the means of keeping each other in their proper places. Without presuming to undertake a full development of this important idea I will hazard a few general observations which may perhaps place it in a clearer light, and enable us to form a more correct judgment of the principles and structure of the government planned by the convention.

In order to lay a due foundation for that separate and distinct exercise of the different powers of government, which to a certain extent is admitted on all hands to be essential to the preservation of liberty, it is evident that each department should have a will of its own; and consequently should be so constituted that the members of each should have as little agency as possible in the appointment of the members of the others. Were this principle rigorously adhered to, it would require that all the appointments for the supreme executive, legislative, and judiciary magistracies should be drawn from the same fountain of authority, the people, through channels having no communication whatever with one another. Perhaps such a plan of constructing the several departments would be less difficult in practice than it may in contemplation appear. Some difficulties, however, and some additional expense would attend the execution of it. Some deviations, therefore, from the principle must be admitted. In the constitution of the judiciary department in particular, it might be inexpedient to insist rigorously on the principle: first, because peculiar qualifications being essential in the members, the primary consideration ought to be to select that mode of choice which best secures these qualifications; second, because the permanent tenure by which the appointments are held in that department must soon destroy all sense of dependence on the authority conferring them.

It is equally evident that the members of each department should be as little dependent as possible on those of the others for the emoluments annexed to their offices. Were the executive magistrate, or the judges, not independent of the legislature in this particular, their independence in every other would be merely nominal.

But the great security against a gradual concentration of the several powers in the same department consists in giving to those who administer each department the necessary constitutional means and personal motives to resist encroachments of the others. The provision for defense must in this, as in all other cases, be made commensurate to the danger of attack. Ambition must be made to counteract ambition. The interest of the man must be connected with the constitutional rights of the place. It may be a reflection on human nature that such devices should be necessary to control the abuses of government. But what is government itself but the greatest of all reflections on human nature? If men were angels, no government would be necessary. If angels were to govern men, neither external nor internal controls on government would be necessary. In framing a government which is to be administered by men over men, the great difficulty lies in this: you must first enable the government to control the governed; and in the next place oblige it to control itself. A dependence on the people is, no doubt, the primary control on the government; but experience has taught mankind the necessity of auxiliary precautions.

This policy of supplying, by opposite and rival interests, the defect of better motives, might be traced through the whole system of human affairs, private as well as public. We see it particularly displayed in all the subordinate distributions of power, where the constant aim is to divide and arrange the several offices in such a manner as that each may be a check on the other—that the private interest of every individual may be a sentinel over the public rights. These inventions of prudence cannot be less requisite in the distribution of the supreme powers of the State.

But it is not possible to give to each department an equal power of self-defense. In republican government, the legislative authority necessarily predominates. The remedy for this inconveniency is to divide the legislature into different branches; and to render them, by different modes of election and different principles of action, as little connected with each other as the nature of their common functions and their common dependence on the society will admit. It may even be necessary to guard against dangerous encroachments by still further precautions. As the weight of the legislative authority requires that it should be thus divided, the weakness of the executive may require, on the other hand, that it should be fortified. An absolute negative on the legislature appears, at first view, to be the natural defense with which the executive magistrate should be armed. But perhaps it would be neither altogether safe nor alone sufficient. On ordinary occasions it might not be exerted with the requisite firmness, and on extraordinary occasions it might be perfidiously abused. May not this defect of an absolute negative be supplied by some qualified connection between this weaker department and the weaker branch of the stronger department, by which the latter may be led to support the constitutional rights of the former, without being too much detached from the rights of its own department?

If the principles on which these observations are found be just, as I persuade myself they are, and they be applied as a criterion to the several State constitutions, and the federal Constitution, it will be found that if the latter does not perfectly correspond with them, the former are infinitely less able to bear such a test.

There are, moreover, two considerations particularly applicable to the federal system of America, which place that system in a very interesting point of view.

First. In a single republic, all the power surrendered by the people is submitted to the administration of a single government; and the usurpations are guarded against by a division of the government into distinct and separate departments. In the compound republic of America, the power surrendered by the people is first divided between two distinct governments, and then the portion allotted to each subdivided among distinct and separate departments. Hence a double security arises to the rights of the people. The different governments will control each other, at the same time that each will be controlled by itself.

Second. It is of great importance in a republic not only to guard the society against the oppression of its rulers, but to guard one part of the society against the injustice of the other part. Different interests necessarily exist in different classes of citizens. If a majority be united by a common interest, the rights of the minority will be insecure. There are but two methods of providing against this evil: the one by creating a will in the community independent of the majority—that is, of the society itself; the other, by comprehending in the society so many separate descriptions of citizens as will render an unjust combination of a majority of the whole very improbable, if not impracticable. The first method prevails in all governments possessing an hereditary or self-appointed authority. This, at best, is but a precarious security; because a power independent of the society may as well espouse the unjust views of the major as the rightful interests of the minor party, and may possibly be turned against both parties. The second method will be exemplified in the federal republic of the United States. Whilst all authority in it will be derived from and dependent on the society, the society itself will be broken into so many parts, interests and classes of citizens, that the rights of individuals, or of the minority, will be in little danger from interested combinations of the majority. In a free government the security for civil rights must be the same as that for religious rights. It consists in the one case in the multiplicity of interests, and in the other in the multiplicity of sects. The degree of security in both cases will depend on the number of interests and sects; and this may be presumed to depend on the extent of country and number of people comprehended under the same government. This view of the subject must particularly recommend a proper federal system to all the sincere and considerate friends of republican government, since it shows that in exact proportion as the territory of the Union may be formed into more circumscribed Confederacies, or States, oppressive combinations of a majority will be facilitated; the best security, under the republican forms, for the rights of every class of citizen, will be diminished; and consequently the stability and independence of some member of the government, the only other security, must be proportionally increased. Justice is the end of government. It is the end of civil society. It ever has been and ever will be pursued until it be obtained, or until liberty be lost in the pursuit. In a society under the forms of which the stronger faction can readily unite and oppress the weaker, anarchy may as truly be said to reign as in a state of nature, where the weaker individual is not secured against the violence of the stronger; and as, in the latter state, even the stronger individuals are prompted, by the uncertainty of their condition, to submit to a government which may protect the weak as well as themselves; so, in the former state, will the more powerful factions or parties be gradually induced, by a like motive, to wish for a government which will protect all parties, the weaker as well as the more powerful. It can be little doubted that if the State of Rhode Island was separated from the Confederacy and left to itself, the insecurity of rights under the popular form of government within such narrow limits would be displayed by such reiterated oppressions of factious majorities that some power altogether independent of the people would soon be called for by the voice of the very factions whose misrule had proved the necessity of it. In the extended republic of the United States, and among the great variety of interests, parties, and sects which it embraces, a coalition of a majority of the whole society could seldom take place on any other principles than those of justice and the general good; whilst there being thus less danger to a minor from the will of a major party, there must be less pretext, also, to provide for the security of the former, by introducing into the government a will not dependent on the latter, or, in other words, a will independent of the society itself. It is no less certain than it is important, notwithstanding the contrary opinions which have been entertained, that the larger the society, provided it lie within a practicable sphere, the more duly capable it will be of self-government. And happily for the *republican cause,* the practicable sphere may be carried to a very great extent by a judicious modification and mixture of the *federal principle.*

Abraham Lincoln's Gettysburg Address

Four score and seven years ago our fathers brought forth on this continent a new nation, conceived in liberty and dedicated to the proposition that all men are created equal. Now we are engaged in a great Civil War, testing whether that nation or any nation so conceived and so dedicated can long endure. We are met on a great battlefield of that war. We have come to dedicate a portion of that field as a final resting place for those who here gave their lives that that nation might live. It is altogether fitting and proper that we should do this. But in a larger sense, we cannot dedicate—we cannot consecrate—we cannot hallow this ground. The brave men, living and dead, who struggled here have consecrated it far above our poor power to add or detract. The world will little note nor long remember what we say here, but it can never forget what they did here. It is for us the living, rather, to be dedicated here to the unfinished work which they who fought here have thus far so nobly advanced. It is rather for us to be here dedicated to the great task remaining before us—that from these honored dead we take increased devotion to that cause for which they gave the last full measure of devotion—that we here highly resolve that these dead shall not have died in vain, that this nation, under God, shall have a new birth of freedom, and that government of the people, by the people, for the people shall not perish from the earth.

Endnotes

Chapter 1

[1] Roosevelt quotations in this section are from Theodore Roosevelt, "True Americanism," in *American Ideals and Other Essays* (New York: Putnam's Knickerbocker Press, 1901, 15-34.

[2] In a copy of his 1915 book, *America and the World War*, presented to the great American novelist, Roosevelt wrote "To Edith Wharton from an American-American." Quoted in Alan Cowell, "After a Century, an American Writer's Library Will Go to America," *New York Times*, December 15, 2005, E1.

[3] John R. Hibbing and Beth Theiss-Morse, *Congress. As Public Enemy: Public Attitude toward American Political Institutions* (Cambridge: Cambridge University Press,1995; John R. Hibbing and Beth Theiss-Morse, "Civics is not Enough: Teaching Barbarics in K-12," *PS*, March 1996, 57-62.

[4] Hibbing and Morse, *Congress*.

[5] Michael Kinsley, "In Defense of Partisan Bickering," *Time* (February 5, 2007): 41.

[6] Gore Vidal, "Coached by Camelot," *New Yorker*, December 1, 1997, 88.

[7] Walt Whitman, Preface to *Leaves of Grass* (1855), in *Leaves of Grass and Selected Prose*, ed. Lawrence Buell (New York: Random House, 1981), 449.

[8] Edward Countryman, *Americans: A Collision of Histories* (New York: Hill & Wang, 1996).

[9] As noted by historian Carl Wittke, John Elson, "The Great Migration," *Time*, Fall, 1983, 28.

[10] John Sugden, *Tecumseh: A Life* (New York: Holt, 1998).

[11] U.S. Immigration and Naturalization Service, *2000 Statistical Yearbook of the Immigration and Naturalization Service* (Washington, D.C.: Government Printing Office, 2000). These are estimates; the government collects detention and return figures but has not collected emigration data since 1957.

[12] *Year Book of Immigration Statistics*, 2007, tab 10. (www.usins.gov)

[13] Pew Research Center, "U.S. Population Projections, 2005-2050," February 11, 2008. 9.

[14] Kenneth C. Davis, "The Founding Immigrants," *New York Times*, July 3, 2007, A17.

[15] Patrick McGee, "They Don't Belong Here," *Champaign-Urbana News-Gazette*, October 28, 2007, B1.

[16] For many years, the flag was not flown in battle or over government buildings or public schools.

[17] The Spanish-American War and World War I also gave a boost to efforts to use the flag as a symbol.

[18] James Q. Wilson, "The History and Future of Democracy," lecture delivered at the Ronald Reagan Presidential Library, November 15, 1999.

[19] "Religion and the Founding of the American Republic. Part I: America as a Religious Refuge: The Seventeenth Century," Library of Congress exhibit (lcweb.loc.gov/exhibits/religion).

[20] Nicholas von Hoffman, "God Was Present at the Founding," *Civilization* (April-May 1998), 39B42.

[21] Michael J. Sandel, *Democracy's Discontent: America in Search of a Public Philosophy* (Cambridge, Mass.: Belknap Press, 1997), 56-57.

[22] Sarah Mondale and Sarah B. Patton, eds., *School: The Story of American Public Education* (Boston: Beacon Press, 2001), 36.

[23] Elizabeth Becker, "All White, All Christian, and Divided by Diversity," *New York Times*, June 10, 2001, sec. 4, 7. Becker was writing about her hometown.

[24] "Summary of Findings: U.S. Religious Landscape Survey," Pew Forum on Religion and Public Life, February 26, 2008, 1.The findings are the results of two 2007 surveys for which 36,000 adults were interviewed.

[25] See for example the discussion in Larry M Bartels: *Unequal Democracy:The Political Economy of the New Gilded Age* (Princeton: N. J.: Princeton University Press, 2008).

[26] On identity politics, see Walter Benn Michaels, *Our America: Nativism, Modernism, and Pluralism* (Durham, N.C.: Duke University Press, 1997).

[27] U. S. Census Bureau, Census 2000 Special Reports, "We the People: American Indians and Alaska Natives in the United States," February 2006, 2-4.

[28] Jack Hitt, "The Newest Indians," *New York Times Magazine*. August 21, 2005: 38.

[29] Rachel L. Swarns, "Hispanics Resist Racial Grouping by Census," *New York Times*, October 24, 2004, 1.

[30] ABC Evening News with Peter Jennings, February 21, 2005.

[31] "Black Americans: One Race, or More?" *New York Times*, November, 18, 2007, Wk2. Based on survey data from the Pew Research Center.

[32] "Muslim Americans: Middle Class and Mostly Mainstream," Pew Research Center, November 28, 2007, 1.

[33] U.S. Census Bureau, *General Social and Economic Characteristics: U.S. Summary* (Washington, D.C.: Government Printing Office, 1990), pt. 1, tab. 12.

[34] "Guess Who's Coming to Dinner: 22% of Americans Have Relative in a Mixed-Race Marriage," Pew Research Center, May 14, 2008, 1.

[35] The origins of governmental systems are discussed by John Jay in *Federalist Paper 2*.

[36] Garry Wills, *Lincoln at Gettysburg: The Words That Remade America* (New York: Simon & Schuster, 1992), 145.

[37] Carl F. Kaestle, "Introduction," in *School*, ed. Mondale and Patton, 13.

[38] Ibid., 16.

[39] Brian Friel, "Don't Know Much about History," *National Journal*, August 2, 2003, 2500-2501.

[40] "The Educated Citizen," in *School*, ed. Mondale and Patton, 22.

[41] Ibid.

42 Adam Cohen, "According to Webster: One Man's Attempt to Define 'America,'" *New York Times*, February 12, 2006, Sec. 4, 13.

43 Noah Webster quoted in Jack Lynch, "Dr. Johnson's Revolution," *New York Times*, July 2, 2005, sec. 4, A15.

44 Robert Reinhold, "Resentment against New Immigrants," *New York Times*, October 26, 1986, 6E.

45 For a discussion of the Declaration of Independence's origins in pragmatism versus the political philosophy of the Founders, see Pauline Maier, *American Scripture: Making the Declaration of Independence* (New York: Knopf, 1997).

46 Thomas Hobbes, *Leviathan*, any edition. Originally published London, 1651.

47 John Locke, *Two Treatises of Government* (New York: Hafner,1947), 184ff. For a comparison of Hobbes' and Locke's influence on the Founders see Donald S. Lutz and Jack Warren, *A Covenanted People* (Providence, R.I.: The John Carter Brown Library, 1987, 51-53.

48 The writings of Thomas Hobbes also shaped this belief. Hobbes wrote that individuals give up some rights they would have in "a state of nature" to governnment in exchange for government protection of their remaining rights.

49 Survey conducted by Peter D. Hart and Robert Teeter for the Council for Excellence in Government, 1999, and cited in David S. Broder, "Where Did Our Government Go?" *Washington Post National Weekly Edition* (July 19-26, 1999), 37.

50 For the parallels between a country's emphasis on individual liberty and its deemphasis on government help for less fortunate or successful citizens see John W. Kingdon, *America the Unusual* (New York: St. Marin's/Worth, 1999).

51 Wilfred M. McClay, "Communitarianism and the Federal Idea," in *Community and Political Thought Today*, ed. Peter Augustine Lawler and Dale McConkey (Westport, Conn.: Praeger, 1998), 102.

52 President Johnson quoted in Tim Funk, "Civil Rights Act of 1964 Paved Way for Prosperity," *Champaign-Urbana News Gazette*, July 11, 2004, B1.

53 Alexis de Tocqueville, *Democracy in America* (New York: Knopf, 1945; originally published 1835).

54 See Michael Parenti, *Democracy for the Few*, 7th ed. (Belmont, California: Wadsworth, 2001) on "permanent losers."

55 For elaboration, see Thomas G. West, *Vindicating the Founders: Race, Sex, Class, and Justice in the Origins of America*. (Lanham, Maryland: Rowman & Littlefield, 1997): 43-54.

56 Quoted in Anthony Lewis, "Hail and Farewell," *New York Times*, December 15, 2001, A31.

57 This discussion draws on Sidney Verba and Norman Nie, *Participation in America* (New York: Harper & Row, 1972), and Stephen Earl Bennett and Linda L. M. Bennett, "Political Participation," in *Annual Review of Political Science*, ed. Samuel Long (Norwood, N.J.: Ablex, 1986).

58 Alan Wolfe, "Couch Potato Politics," *New York Times*, March 15, 1998, sec. 4, 17.

59 League of Conservative Voters poll, March 2002.

Chapter 2

1 This vignette is drawn from Brooke Allen, *Moral Minority: Our Skeptical Founding Fathers* (Chicago: Ivan R. Dee, 2006). For similar conclusions, see Forrest Church, *So Help Me God: The Founding Fathers and the First Great Battle Over Church and State* (Orlando, Fla.: Harcourt, 2007); David L. Holmes, *The Faiths of the Founding Fathers* (New York: Oxford University Press, 2006); Martha Nussbaum, *Liberty of Conscience: In Defense of America's Tradition of Religious Equality* (New York: Basic Books, 2008); Steven Waldman, *Founding Faith: Providence, Politics, and the Birth of Religious Freedom in America* (New York: Random House, 2008); and Garry Wills, *Head and Heart: American Christianities* (New York: Penguin, 2007). James Monroe, our fifth president, wasn't a Christian either.

2 Today deism is most closely reflected in the Unitarian church. Allen, *Moral Minority*, 173.

3 Ibid., 74.

4 In particular, the Roman Stoics and the Roman general Cincinnatus.

5 Allen, *Moral Minority*, 31.

6 Ibid., 72.

7 Ibid., 105.

8 Hamilton did not become a practicing Christian until late in life after his son was killed in a duel.

9 The only religious reference in the Constitution, besides the ban on religious tests for public office, is the date when the document was written: "Year of our Lord one thousand seven hundred and eighty-seven." This was the conventional way to express A.D.

10 The Indians, of course, had their own governments, and the Spanish may have established Saint Augustine, Florida, and Santa Fe, New Mexico, before the English established Jamestown. The Spanish settlements were extensions of Spanish colonization of Mexico and were governed by Spanish officials in Mexico City.

11 This is not to suggest that the Pilgrims believed in democracy. Apparently, they were motivated to draft the compact by threats from some on the *Mayflower* that when the ship landed they would "use their owne libertie; for none had power to command them." Thus the compact was designed to bind them to the laws of the colony. Richard Shenkman, *"I Love Paul Revere, Whether He Rode or Not"* (New York: HarperCollins, 1991), 141–142.

12 David Hawke, *A Transaction of Free Men* (New York: Scribner, 1964), 209.

13 For an account of the foreign affairs problems under the Articles of Confederation, see Frederick W. Marks III, *Independence on Trial: Foreign Affairs and the Making of the Constitution* (Baton Rouge: Louisiana State University Press, 1973).

14 Louis Fisher, *President and Congress* (New York: Free Press, 1972), 14.

15 The government under the Articles, however, could boast one major accomplishment: the Northwest Ordinance, adopted in 1787, provided for the government and future statehood of the land west of Pennsylvania (land that would become most of the Great Lakes states). The law also banned slavery in this territory.

16 Gordon S. Wood, "The Origins of the Constitution," *This Constitution: A Bicentennial Chronicle* (Summer 1987), 10–11.

17 Eric Black, *Our Constitution* (Boulder, Colo.: Westview Press, 1988), 6.

18 For development of this idea, see Kenneth M. Dolbeare and Linda J. Medcalf, "The Political Economy of the Constitution," *This Constitution: A Bicentennial Chronicle* (Spring 1987), 4–10.

19 Black, *Our Constitution*, 59.

20 The Constitution would, however, retain numerous positive aspects of the Articles. See Donald S. Lutz, "The Articles of Confederation as the Background to the Federal Republic," *Publius* 20 (Winter 1990), 55–70.

21 Robert McCloskey, *The American Supreme Court* (Chicago: University of Chicago Press, 1960), 29.

22 Robert A. Dahl, *A Preface to Democratic Theory* (Chicago: University of Chicago Press, 1956), 5.

23 Yet according to a poll in 1987, the bicentennial of the Constitution, only 1 percent of the public identified Madison as the one who played the biggest role in creating the Constitution. Most—31 percent—said Thomas Jefferson, who was a diplomat in France during the convention. Black, *Our Constitution*, 15.

Some argue that Hamilton, rather than Madison, was the driving force behind the Constitution, especially if his efforts after ratification— as an influential member of Washington's cabinet and later—are taken into account. Kenneth M. Dolbeare and Linda Medcalf, "The Dark Side of the Constitution," in *The Case Against the Constitution: From the Antifederalists to the Present*, eds. Kenneth M. Dolbeare and John F. Manley (Armonk, N.Y.: Sharpe, 1987), 120–141.

24 Only Hamilton suggested a monarchy, and only one delegate—Gouverneur Morris of Pennsylvania—suggested an aristocracy.

25 Robert A. Dahl, *How Democratic is the American Constitution?* (New Haven, Conn.: Yale University Press, 2001), 11–12.

26 Ibid., 14.

27 The large states did extract a concession that all taxing and spending bills must originate in the house in which representation is based on population. This provision would allow the large states to take the initiative on these important measures.

28 Paul Finkelman, "Slavery at the Philadelphia Convention," *This Constitution: A Bicentennial Chronicle* (1987), 25–30.

29 Ibid., 29.

30 Ibid., 18.

31 Quoted in Thomas G. West, *Vindicating the Founders: Race, Sex, Class, and Justice in the*

Origins of America (Lanham, Md.: Rowman & Littlefield, 1997), 15.

[32] Theodore J. Lowi, *American Government* (Hinsdale, Ill.: Dryden, 1976), 97.

[33] William Gladstone, quoted in C. Herman Pritchett, *Constitutional Law of the Federal System* (Englewood Cliffs, N.J.: Prentice Hall, 1984), xi.

[34] Quoted in Richard Hofstadter, *The American Political Tradition* (New York: Vintage, 1948), 6–7.

[35] Under some state constitutions.

[36] *Federalist Paper* 51.

[37] Although we use this term today, neither it nor the word *federal* appears in the Constitution.

[38] In the United States, each state government is unitary with respect to its local governments. The state government can alter or eliminate cities, counties, townships, or school districts.

[39] James Madison, *Federalist Paper* 10.

[40] Madison also saw our vast territory as a way to limit factions, because it would be difficult for a group to extend its influence throughout the entire country.

[41] Creating a separate executive branch and making the selection of president independent of Congress also strengthened the national government, because it gave the president a political base from which to exercise national leadership.

[42] However, the amendment's checkered history indicates that the amendment hasn't always played a significant role in limiting the national government.

[43] Max Farrand, *The Framing of the Constitution of the United States* (New Haven, Conn.: Yale University Press, 1913).

[44] Charles O. Jones, *The Presidency in a Separated System* (Washington, D.C.: Brookings Institution, 1994), 14.

[45] Charles O. Jones, *Separate but Equal Branches* (Chatham, N.J.: Chatham House, 1995), 12.

[46] *Federalist Paper* 51.

[47] Jones, *Presidency in a Separated System,* 16, thus modifying Neustadt's classic definition of "a government of separated institutions sharing powers." Richard E. Neustadt, *Presidential Power and the Modern Presidents* (New York: Macmillan, 1990), 29.

[48] For elaboration, see Dahl, *How Democratic Is the American Constitution?* 24–25.

[49] Ibid.

[50] Locke called for majority rule but never resolved the conflict between majority rule and natural rights—in particular, the rights of the minority.

[51] Donald S. Lutz, "The Relative Influence of European Writers on Later Eighteenth-Century American Political Thought," *American Political Science Review* 78 (1984), 139–197.

[52] Alpheus T. Mason and Richard H. Leach, *In Quest of Freedom: American Political Thought and Practice,* 2nd ed. (Englewood Cliffs, N.J.: Prentice Hall, 1973), 51.

[53] For development of this idea, see Martin Landau, "A Self-Correcting System: The Constitution of the United States," *This Constitution: A Bicentennial Chronicle* (Summer, 1986), 4–10.

[54] John P. Roche, "The Founding Fathers: A Reform Caucus in Action," *American Political Science Review* 55 (1961), 799–816.

[55] Benjamin F. Wright Jr., "The Origins of the Separation of Powers in America," in *Origins of American Political Thought,* ed. John P. Roche (New York: Harper & Row, 1967), 139–162.

[56] Roche, op. cit., 805.

[57] James MacGregor Burns, *The Vineyard of Liberty* (New York: Knopf, 1982), 33.

[58] Bernard Bailyn, *Voyagers to the West* (New York: Knopf, 1982), 20.

[59] The Boston Tea Party, contrary to myth, was not prompted by higher taxes on British tea. Parliament lowered the taxes to give the British East India Company, facing bankruptcy, an advantage in the colonial market. This threatened American shippers who smuggled tea from Holland and controlled about three-fourths of the market. The shippers resented Parliament's attempt to manipulate the economy from thousands of miles away. Shenkman, *"I Love Paul Revere,"* 155.

[60] *Federalist Paper* 10.

[61] Of the fifty-five delegates, forty were owners of government bonds that had depreciated under the Articles, and twenty-four were moneylenders. Black, *Our Constitution,* 21.

[62] For elaboration, see Dolbeare and Medcalf, "Dark Side of the Constitution."

[63] Calvin C. Jillson and Cecil L. Eubanks, "The Political Structure of Constitution Making," *American Journal of Political Science* 29 (1984), 435–458.

[64] Jonathan Elliot, *The Debates in the Several State Conventions on the Adoption of the Federal Constitution as Recommended by the General Convention at Philadelphia, in 1787,* 2nd ed., 5 vols. (Philadelphia, 1896), 2: 102.

[65] On Anti-Federalist thinking, see William B. Allen and Gordon Lloyd, eds., *The Essential Antifederalist,* 2nd ed. (Lanham, Md.: University Press of America, 2002); John F. Manley and Kenneth M. Dolbeare, *The Case against the Constitution* (Armonk, N.Y.: Sharpe, 1987).

[66] Richard S. Randall, *American Constitutional Development,* vol. 1, *The Powers of Government* (New York: Longman, 2002), 54.

[67] "A Fundamental Contentment," *This Constitution: A Bicentennial Chronicle* (Fall 1984), 44.

[68] Quoted in Charles Warren, *The Making of the Constitution* (Boston: Little, Brown, 1928), xiv. Jefferson made this observation from afar, as he was serving as ambassador to France at the time of the Constitutional Convention.

[69] Keith Perine, "Congress Shows Little Enthusiasm for Bush's Marriage Amendment," *CQ Weekly* (February 28, 2004), 533.

[70] Alan P. Grimes, *Democracy and the Amendments to the Constitution* (Lexington, Mass.: Lexington Books, 1978). Grimes also shows how the adoption of new amendments reflects the rise of new power blocs in society.

[71] 4 Wheaton 316 (1819).

[72] Historian James McPherson, quoted in George P. Fletcher, *Our Secret Constitution: How Lincoln Redefined American Democracy* (New York: Oxford University Press, 2001), 57. For a similar view, see Bruce Ackerman, *We the People,* vol. 2, *Transformations* (Cambridge, Mass.: Belknap Press, 1998), 10. This discussion borrows heavily from Fletcher and Ackerman and also from Garry Wills, *Lincoln at Gettysburg* (New York: Simon & Schuster, 1992). For a complementary view, see Charles Black, *A New Birth of Freedom: Human Rights, Named and Unnamed* (New York: Grosset/Putnam, 1997).

[73] Many of Lincoln's prejudicial comments came in response to more blatant racist remarks by his opponents. Lincoln abandoned his support for black emigration before he was elected to a second term as president. For a critical perspective on Lincoln's racial views, see Lerone Bennett Jr., *Forced into Glory: Abraham Lincoln's White Dream* (Chicago: Johnson, 2000). For a positive perspective, see William Lee Miller, *Lincoln's Virtues: An Ethical Biography* (New York: Knopf, 2002).

[74] Fletcher, *Our Secret Constitution,* 24.

[75] For examination of the role of abolitionist sentiment on Lincoln's decisions, see James Oakes, *The Radical and the Republican: Frederick Douglass, Abraham Lincoln, and the Triumph of Antislavery Politics* (New York: W. W. Norton, 2007).

[76] These paragraphs rely on the interpretations of Wills, *Lincoln at Gettysburg,* and Fletcher, *Our Secret Constitution.*

[77] Fletcher, *Our Secret Constitution,* 53.

[78] A precursor of this view was the era of Jacksonian democracy in the 1830s.

[79] A contemporary celebration of the nation as an entity can be seen in the poetry of Walt Whitman.

[80] Wills, *Lincoln at Gettysburg,* 38. Wills insists that this was not a coincidence, and he debunks the notion that Lincoln hastily dashed off his remarks while on his way to the town or to the speech itself (27–31).

[81] Fletcher, *Our Secret Constitution,* 35, 4. Others might nominate Lincoln's second inaugural address, in which he offered reconciliation to the South, or Martin Luther King Jr.'s "I Have a Dream" speech.

[82] The *Dred Scott* case is explained in Chapter 15.

[83] The equal protection clause is covered fully in Chapter 13, and the due process clause is covered fully in Chapter 12.

[84] Fletcher, *Our Secret Constitution,* 25.

[85] In this vein, Congress first experimented with an income tax during the war. It would return to this tax in the decades after the war.

[86] For example, the abolitionist movement and the Fifteenth Amendment would fuel the drive for women's suffrage, as explained in Chapter 15.

[87] E. J. Dionne Jr., "Culture Wars," *Washington Post National Weekly Edition,* March 17–23, 2008, 25.

[88] This section borrows heavily from Ackerman, *We the People,* and Theodore J. Lowi, *The Personal President* (Ithaca, N.Y.: Cornell University Press, 1985). For a different view about the impact of the New Deal, see G. Edward White, *The Constitution and the New Deal* (Cambridge, Mass.: Harvard University Press, 2001).

[89] We never had a pure laissez-faire approach—there always was some governmental regulation—but this is the term most associated with the attitudes of the time.

[90] At least one legal scholar dismisses the notion that the Court's "old men" were reactionaries or fools. Although today people consider them mistaken, at the time they were following established doctrine. Ackerman, *We the People.*

[91] Lowi, *Personal President,* 49. Writers during the Depression and in the decades after it also recognized this as a revolution. Ernest K. Lindley, *The Roosevelt Revolution, First Phase* (New York: Viking, 1933); Mario Einaudi, *The Roosevelt Revolution* (New York: Harcourt, Brace & World, 1959).

[92] Karl Vick, "A President Who Woke Up Washington," *Washington Post National Weekly Edition,* April 28, 1997, 8.

[93] Ibid., 9.

[94] Lowi, *Personal President,* 44.

[95] Ibid., xi.

[96] This era also saw a shift to a more presidency-centered government that persists to a significant degree today. Lowi, *Personal President.*

[97] President Ronald Reagan in the 1980s and congressional Republicans in the early 1990s mounted major challenges to the changes initiated by the Depression and the New Deal. President George W. Bush has also mounted significant challenges. These will be addressed in later chapters. In addition, some conservative judges and legal scholars support the "Constitution in exile" movement, which claims that the changes in legal doctrine during and after the 1930s have been illegitimate.

[98] Of course, the process was evolutionary; the changes did not spring solely from these two crises. Moreover, some might maintain that the Supreme Court under the leadership of Chief Justice Earl Warren in the 1950s and 1960s also remade the Constitution because of its rulings expanding the Bill of Rights. Yet the changes brought about by the Warren Court probably had less impact overall than those wrought by Reconstruction or the New Deal.

[99] For a discussion of the role played by the philosophy of pragmatism in resolving these conflicts, see Fletcher, *Our Secret Constitution,* ch. 11.

[100] Henry Steele Commager, *Living Ideas in America* (New York: Harper & Row, 1951), 109.

[101] West, *Vindicating the Founders,* xi.

[102] Parts of the Constitution have been copied by some Latin America countries, Liberia (founded by Americans), and the Philippines (formerly an American territory).

[103] "South Africa Looks at U.S. Constitution," *Lincoln Journal Star,* October 7, 1990; David Remnick, "'We, the People,' from the Russian," *Washington Post National Weekly Edition,* September 10, 1990, 11.

[104] European countries, Australia, Canada, Costa Rica, Israel, Japan, and New Zealand.

[105] Dahl, *How Democratic . . . ?* tabs. 1 and 2, 164–165. Dahl counts only countries that have "strong" federalism, bicameralism, and judicial review.

[106] Jones, *Presidency in a Separated System,* xiii.

[107] Dahl, *How Democratic . . . ?* 115.

[108] Jones, *Presidency in a Separated System,* 3.

[109] John W. Kingdon, *America the Unusual* (Boston: Bedford/St. Martin's, 1999), 7–22. Exceptions include education and regulation of civil rights and the environment. They also include a massive national defense establishment and an extensive criminal justice system. In these aspects, our government is bigger than in many other advanced industrialized countries.

[110] Richard Morin, "Happy Days Are Here Again," *Washington Post National Weekly Edition,* August 25, 1997, 35.

[111] About 25 percent split their ticket between candidates for president and representative. In addition, others split their vote between candidates for president and senator or between candidates for representative and senator. For an examination of the research about divided government, see Morris Fiorina, *Divided Government,* 2nd ed. (Boston: Allyn & Bacon, 1996), 153.

[112] Lewis Lapham, "Get Me Rewrite!" *New York Times Book Review,* February 4, 1996, 11.

Chapter 3

[1] "Confessions on Climate," (Editorial), *New York Times,* March 4, 2008, A24.

[2] The delegate was George Read of Delaware. See William H. Riker, *Democracy in America,* 2nd ed. (New York: Macmillan, 1965).

[3] William H. Riker, *The Development of American Federalism* (Boston: Kluwer Academic, 1987), 6.

[4] *Federalist Paper* 39.

[5] Riker, 17.

[6] Bernard Bailyn, *The Federalist Papers* (Washington, D.C.: Library of Congress, 1998), 14. This is the text of a lecture Bailyn gave in the Bradley Lecture series.

[7] Part of this discussion is drawn from Richard Leach, *American Federalism* (New York: Norton, 1970), ch. 1. See also Christopher Hamilton and Donald Wells, *Federalism, Power and Political Economy: A New Theory of Federalism's Impact on American Life* (Englewood Cliffs, N.J.: Prentice Hall, 1990).

[8] See Madison's discussion of this in *Federalist Paper* 39.

[9] Vernon L. Parrington, *Main Currents in American Thought* (New York: Harcourt, Brace, 1927).

[10] David Truman, "Federalism and the Party System," in *Federalism: Mature and Emergent,* ed. Arthur W. MacMahon (New York: Russell & Russell, 1962), 123.

[11] Richard Neustadt, *The American Presidency,* episode 5, PBS, April 2000.

[12] Daniel J. Elazar, *The American Partnership* (Chicago: University of Chicago Press, 1962).

[13] Timothy Conlan, *From Federalism to Devolution: Twenty-Five Years of Intergovernmental Reform* (Washington, D.C.: Brookings Institution, 1998), 6.

[14] Alfred Kelly and Winfred Harbeson, *The American Constitution: Its Origins and Development* (New York: Norton, 1976).

[15] Linda Greenhouse, "In Roberts Hearing, Specter Assails Court," *New York Times,* September 15, 2005, 1.

[16] Dan Carney, "Latest Supreme Court Rulings Reinforce the Federalist Trend," *Congressional Quarterly,* June 26, 1999, 1528; Linda Greenhouse, "High Court Faces Moment of Truth in Federalism Cases," *New York Times,* March 28, 1999, 20.

[17] David Broder, "Take Back the Initiative," *Washington Post National Weekly Edition,* April 10, 2000, 6.

[18] James W. Brosnan, "Not Taxing Internet Sales Hurts," *Champaign-Urbana News-Gazette,* February 21, 2000, A6.

[19] Rep. Barney Frank (D-Mass.), quoted in Michael Grunwald, "Everybody Talks about States' Rights," *Washington Post National Weekly Edition,* November 1, 1999, 29. Frank was referring to Republicans only, but the quote fits Democrats as well.

[20] Alice Rivlin, *Reviving the American Dream: The Economy, the States, and the Federal Government* (Washington, D.C.: Brookings Institution, 1992).

[21] Jia Lynn Yang, "States: Battling Cleanup," *National Journal,* August 9, 2003, 2544.

[22] *2008 Statistical Abstract of the United States* (Washington D.C.: Government Printing Office, 2008), tab. 418, p. 265.

[23] On Nixon's managerial approach to federalism, see Lawrence D. Brown, *New Policies, New Politics: Government's Response to Government's Growth* (Washington, D.C.: Brookings Institution, 1983). The comparative discussion of Lyndon Johnson's, Richard Nixon's, and Ronald Reagan's federalism policies draws on Conlon, *From New Federalism to Devolution* chs. 1, 6, and 13.

[24] Conlon, *From New Federalism to Devolution,* 109.

[25] See, for example, William J. Clinton, "Federalism," Executive Order 13132, *Federal Register* 54, no. 163 (August 10, 1999): 43255–43259. Clinton discussed his views on state activism and federalism in general with the historian Gary Wills in "The War between the States and Washington." July 5, 1998, 26.

[26] Grover Norquist, arguably the most powerful lobbyist in Washington, quoted in Philip Gourevitch, "Fight on the Right," *The New Yorker,* April 12, 2004, 37.

[27] For a review of the politics surrounding the law, its provisions, and limitations, see Conlon, *From New Federalism to Devolution,* ch. 13.

[28] The Mandate Monitor page is at www.ncsl.org/standcomm/scbudg/manmom.htm.

29 "2006 State Homeland Security Directors Survey" (Issue Brief of the NGA Center for Best Practices), April 3, 2006, www.nga.org/center.

30 Pam Belluck, "Mandate for ID Meets Resistance from States," *New York Times,* May 6, 2006, A1; "Real ID Law: States, Feds Working Out Issues," *Champaign-Urbana News Gazette,* March 22, 2008, A4.

31 *U.S. Budget for Fiscal Year 2007, Historical Tables* 15.1 (Washington, D.C.: U.S. Government Printing Office, 2006), 309.

32 Ibid., 15.2, 311.

33 David Dagan, "Personal Politics" (Special Report), Center for Public Integrity Special Report, September 24, 2004, www. publicintegrity.org, 1.

34 Garry Wills, "War between the States and Washington," *New York Times Magazine*

35 Stephen Labaton, "Washington's Deregulatory Mood Finds Its Opposite in Vexed States," *New York Times,* January 13, 2002, 1.

36 Two advocates of using the states as test laboratories are Tammy Baldwin (D-Wisc) and Tom Price (R-Ga.). Guy Boulton, "Health Care Reform: Test Laboratories," *Champaign-Urbana News Gazette,* December 2, 2006, B1.

37 Gar Alperovitz, "California Split," *New York Times,* February 10, 2007, A15. Alperovitz is a professor of political economy. For a related argument see Pietro S. Nivola, "Rediscovering Federalism," Issues on Governance Studies, Paper #8 (Brookings Institution, July 2007), 1–18.

38 Quoted in Alperovitz, A15.

39 Neela Banerjee, "Christian Conservatives Turn to Statehouses," *New York Times,* December 13, 2004. 1.

40 John D. Donahue, "The Disunited States," *Atlantic Monthly,* May 1997, 20.

41 "Lobbyists, Yes. The People, Maybe" (Editorial), *New York Times,* July 10, 2006, A16.

42 Letter from the National Governors' Association to President George W. Bush, February 3, 2006, www.nga.org.

43 John M. Broder, "Governors Join in Creating Regional Climate Pacts on Climate Change," *New York Times,* November 15, 2007, A20.

44 Enid F. Beaumont and Harold Hovey, "State, Local, and Federal Development Policies: New Federalism Patterns, Chaos, or What?" *Public Administration Review* 45 (1985), 327–332; Barry Rubin and C. Kurt Zorn, "Sensible State and Local Development," *Public Administration Review* 45 (1985), 333–339.

45 Shaila Dewan, "Cities Compete in Hipness Battle to Attract Young," *New York Times,* November 25, 2006, A1.

46 Robert Pear, "U.S. Report Criticizes States' Use of Medicaid Consultants," *New York Times,* June 28, 2005, A20.

47 John Tierney, "New York Wants Its Money Back, or at Least Some of It," *New York Times,* June 27, 2004, sect. 4, 4.

48 A discussion of current issues in state-tribal relations can be found at the National Conference of State Legislatures' website, www.ncsl.org.

49 Dagan, "Personal Politics," 1, www.publicintegrity.org.

50 "Hot-Button Vox Pop," (Editorial) *New York Times,* November 10, 2006, A30.

51 "That Flurry of Ballot Questions" (Editorial), *New York Times,* November 5, 2005, A16.

52 Wills, "War between the States and Washington," 27.

53 Jennifer Steinhauer, "In California, Coastal Commission Wields Vast Power," *New York Times,* February 23, 2008, A10.

54 Katherine Sullivan, "In Defense of Federal Power," *New York Times Magazine,* August 18, 1996, 36.

55 NBC News/*Wall Street Journal* poll, December 2001; both CBS and Gallup polls in June 2002 showed declining approval levels for Congress and the Supreme Court. Data for 2006 from Pew Research Center survey cited by David Brooks, "The Age of Skepticism," *New York Times,* December 1, 2005, A33.

56 "Federal Government's Favorable Ratings Slump," Pew Research Center, May 14, 2008. (people-press.org/reports)

Chapter 4

1 Scott Keeter, "Young Voters in the 2008 Presidential Primaries." Pew Research Center Publications, February 11, 2008, pewresearch.org/pubs/730/young-voters.

2 Ibid.

3 Conducted by the National Constitution Center.

4 Ibid., March 2008.

5 Timothy E. Cook, "The Bear Market in Political Socialization and the Costs of Misunderstood Psychological Theories," *American Political Science Review* 79 (1985), 1079–1093.

6 S. W. Moore et al., "The Civic Awareness of Five- and Six-Year-Olds," *Western Political Quarterly* 29 (1976), 418.

7 R. W. Connell, *The Child's Construction of Politics* (Carlton, Australia: Melbourne University Press, 1971).

8 Fred I. Greenstein, *Children and Politics* (New Haven, Conn.: Yale University Press, 1965), 122; see also Fred I. Greenstein, "The Benevolent Leader Re-visited: Children's Images of Political Leaders in Three Democracies," *American Political Science Review* 69 (1975), 1317–1398; Robert D. Hess and Judith V. Torney, *The Development of Political Attitudes in Children* (Chicago: Aldine, 1967).

9 Amy Carter and Ryan Teten, "Assessing Changing Views of the President: Ravishing Greenstein's Children and Politics," *Presidential Studies Quarterly* 32 (2002), 453–462.

10 Greenstein, *Children and Politics.*

11 Hess and Torney, *The Development of Political Attitudes in Children*; Connell, *The Child's Construction of Politics.*

12 Greenstein, *Children and Politics*; Greenstein, "The Benevolent Leader Revisited: Children's Images of Political Leaders in Three Democra-

cies"; and Hess and Torney, *The Development of Political Attitudes in Children.*

13 Connell, *The Child's Construction of Politics.*

14 Carter, "Assessing Changing Views."

15 F. Christopher Arterton, "The Impact of Watergate on Children's Attitudes toward the President," *Political Science Quarterly* 89 (1974), 269–288; see also P. Frederick Hartwig and Charles Tidmarch, "Children and Political Reality: Changing Images of the President," paper presented at the 1974 Annual Meeting of the Southern Political Science Association; J. Dennis and C. Webster, "Children's Images of the President and Government in 1962 and 1974," *American Politics Quarterly* 4 (1975), 386–405; Robert Hawkins, Suzanne Pingree, and D. Roberts, "Watergate and Political Socialization," *American Politics Quarterly* 4 (1975), 406–436.

16 Gallup Organization, "Public Trust in Federal Government Remains High," January 8, 1999.

17 Michael Delli Carpini, *Stability and Change in American Politics: The Coming of Age of the Generation of the 1960s* (New York: New York University Press, 1986), 86–89.

18 Richard M. Merelman, *Political Socialization and Educational Climates* (New York: Holt, Rinehart and Winston, 1971), 54; more recently, the percentage of liberals among college freshmen and the public is about the same.

19 Roberta Sigel and Marilyn Hoskin, *The Political Involvement of Adolescents* (New Brunswick, N.J.: Rutgers University Press, 1981).

20 John R. Hibbing and Elizabeth Theiss-Morse, *Congress as Public Enemy: Public Attitudes toward American Political Institutions* (Cambridge, England: Cambridge University Press, 1995). It is plausible to assume that the content of early political socialization influences what is learned later, but the assumption has not been adequately tested. Thus we might expect the positive opinions toward government and politics developed early in childhood to condition the impact of traumatic events later in life; David Easton and Jack Dennis, *Children in the Political System: Origins of Regime Legitimacy* (New York: McGraw-Hill, 1969); Robert Weissberg, *Political Learning, Political Choice, and Democratic Citizenship* (Englewood Cliffs, N.J.: Prentice Hall, 1974). See also Donald Searing, Joel Schwartz, and Alden Line, "The Structuring Principle: Political Socialization and Belief System," *American Political Science Review* 67 (1973), 414–432.

21 Jack Citrin, "Comment: The Political Relevance of Trust in Government," *Washington Post National Weekly Edition* 68, September 1974, 973–1001; Jack Citrin and Donald Green, "Presidential Leadership and the Resurgence of Trust in Government," *British Journal of Political Science* 16 (1986), 431–453.

22 John Alford, Carolyn Funk, and John Hibbing, "Are Political Orientations Genetically Transmitted," *American Political Science Review* 99 (May, 2005), 153–168. How do scientists determine hereditary traits from those environmentally determined? Much of this research looks at identical twins, who share the exact same genetic traits, and compares them with nonidentical twins, who do not.

23 Christopher Achen, "Parental Socialization and Rational Party Identification," *Political Behavior* 24 (June, 2002), 151–170.

24 Dean Jaros, Herbert Hirsch, and Frederic J. Fleron Jr., "The Malevolent Leader: Political Socialization in an American Subculture," *American Political Science Review* 62 (1968), 564–575.

25 Kent Tedin, "The Influence of Parents on the Political Attitudes of Adolescents," *American Political Science Review* 68 (1974), 1579–1592.

26 M. Kent Jennings, *Generations and Politics* (Princeton, N.J.: Princeton University Press, 1981).

27 Kathleen Dolan, "Attitudes, Behaviors, and the Influence of the Family: A Re-examination of the Role of Family Structure," *Political Behavior* 17 (1995), 251–264.

28 On the impact of the public schools and teachers on political socialization, particularly with respect to loyalty and patriotism, see Hess and Torney, *The Development of Political Attitudes in Children*.

29 Gabriel A. Almond and Sidney Verba, *The Civic Culture: Political Attitudes and Democracy in Five Nations, an Analytic Study* (Boston: Little, Brown, 1965); John R. Hibbing and Elizabeth Theiss-Morse, "Civics Is Not Enough: Teaching Barbarics in K–12," *PS: Political Science and Politics* (1996), 12; Norman H. Nie, Jane Junn, and Kenneth Stehlik-Barry, *Education and Democratic Citizenship in America* (Chicago: University of Chicago Press, 1996).

30 Nie et al., *Education and Democratic Citizenship in America*.

31 Hibbing and Theiss-Morse, *Congress as Public Enemy: Public Attitudes toward American Political Institutions*.

32 Richard G. Niemi and Jane Junn, *Civil Education: What Makes Students Learn* (New Haven, Conn.: Yale University Press, 1998). See also Richard G. Niemi and Julia Smith, "Enrollments in High School Government Classes: Are We Shortchanging Both Citizenship and Political Science Training?" *PS: Political Science and Politics* 34 (2001), 281–288. Honors and advanced placement (AP) programs, along with active learning, can improve student understanding and achievement in American history.

33 Stephen Bennett, Staci Rhine, and Richard Flickinger, "Reading's Impact on Democratic Citizenship in America," *Political Behavior* 22 (2000), 167–195.

34 Nie et al., *Education and Democratic Citizenship in America*.

35 Alfonso Damico, M. Margaret Conway, and Sandra Bowman Damico, "Patterns of Political Trust and Mistrust: Three Moments in the Lives of Democratic Citizens," *Polity* 32 (2000), 377–400.

36 Joel Westheimer and Joseph Kahne, "Educating the 'Good' Citizen: Political Choices and Pedagogical Goals," *PS: Political Science and Politics* 2 (2004), 241–247.

37 Richard M. Merelman, "Democratic Politics and the Culture of American Education," *American Political Science Review* 74 (1980), 319–332; Hibbing and Theiss-Morse, "Civics Is Not Enough: Teaching Barbarics in K–12"; Nie et

al., *Education and Democratic Citizenship in America*.

38 Material for this section is drawn from Everett C. Ladd and Seymour M. Lipset, *The Divided Academy: Professors and Politics* (New York: McGraw-Hill, 1975); Charles Kesler, "The Movement of Student Opinion," *National Review*, November 23, 1979, 29; Ernest L. Boyer, *College: The Undergraduate Experience in America* (New York: Harper & Row, 1987); "Fact File: Attitudes and Characteristics of This Year's Freshman," *Chronicle of Higher Education*, January 11, 1989, A33–A34; General Social Survey, *National Opinion Research Center*, 1984, 87. During the early 1970s, more college freshmen identified themselves as liberal compared with the public at large.

39 David Horowitz, *The Professors: The 101 Most Dangerous Academics in America* (Regnery Publishing, 2006).

40 Cathy Young, "The Impact of Academic Bias," *Reason Magazine*, March 8, 2007 at www.reason.com.

41 Ibid.

42 Rebecca Trounson, "Poll Says College Freshmen Lean Left," www.commondreams.org/headlines02/0128-01.htm.

43 Young, op. cit.

44 Alexander W. Astin, William S. Korn, and Linda Sax, *The American Freshman: Thirty Year Trends* (Los Angeles: Higher Education Research Institute, Graduate School of Education and Information, 1997).

45 "College Freshman More Politically Liberal Than in the Past, UCLA Survey Reveals," 2001 CIRP Press Release: CIRP Freshman Survey, January 28, 2001.

46 Linda Sax, Alexander W. Astin, William S. Korn, and Kathryn M. Mahoney, *The American Freshman: National Norms for Fall 1999* (Los Angeles: Higher Education Research Institute, Graduate School of Education and Information Studies, 1999).

47 "Attitudes and Characteristics of Freshmen," *Chronicle of Higher Education*, August 27, 2004, 19; John H. Pryor, Sylvia Hurtado, Jessica Sharkness, and William Korn, *American Freshman: National Norms For Fall 2007* (Los Angeles, Calif.: Higher Education Research Institute, 2007), pp. 37–38, February 3, 2006.

48 Maxwell McCombs and Donald Shaw, "The Agenda Setting Function of the Media," *Public Opinion Quarterly* 36 (1972), 176–187.

49 Benjamin I. Page, Robert Y. Shapiro, and Glenn R. Dempsey, "What Moves Public Opinion?" *American Political Science Review* 81 (1987), 23–44.

50 Herbert F. Weisberg, "Marital Differences in American Voting," *Public Opinion Quarterly* 51 (1987), 335–343.

51 Michael A. Fletcher, "On Campus, a Patriotic Surge," *Washington Post National Weekly Edition*, December 10, 2001, 31.

52 Philip E. Converse, Aage R. Clausen, and Warren E. Miller, "Electoral Myth and Reality: The 1964 Election," *American Political Science Review* 59 (1965), 321–326.

53 John P. Robinson, "The Press as Kingmaker: What Surveys Show from the Last Five Campaigns," *Journalism Quarterly* 49 (1974), 592.

54 See jacob@jacbian.org; also Nick Anderson, "Kerry Wins the Paper Endorsement Derby, for What It's Worth," *Los Angeles Times*, October 29, 2004, A5. Two hundred twelve newspapers endorsed Kerry; 199 recommended Bush. Newspapers endorsing Kerry had a circulation of twenty-two million; Bush, sixteen million.

55 For a review of the history of polling, see Bernard Hennessy, *Public Opinion*, 4th ed. (Monterey, Calif.: Brooks/Cole, 1983), 42–44, 46–50. See also Charles W. Roll and Albert H. Cantril, *Polls: Their Use and Misuse in Politics* (New York: Basic Books, 1972), 3–6.

56 Peverill Squire, "Why the 1936 Literary Digest Poll Failed," *Public Opinion Quarterly* 52 (1988), 125–133; see also Don Cahalan, "The Digest Poll Rides Again," *Public Opinion Quarterly* 53 (1989), 107–113.

57 Jack Rosenthal, "Precisely False vs. Approximately Right: A Reader's Guide to Polls," *New York Times*, August 27, 2006, Week in Review, p. 10.

58 Hennessy, *Public Opinion*, 4th ed., 46.

59 "Consulting the Oracle," *U.S. News and World Report*, December 4, 1995, 52–55; Joshua Green, "The Other War Room," *Washington Monthly*, April 2002, 11–16.

60 Green, "The Other War Room."

61 Joe Klien, *The Natural* (New York: Doubleday, 2002), 7.

62 Green, "The Other War Room."

63 Harris, "Presidency by Poll."

64 Steven Mufson and John E. Harris, "Clinton's Global Growth," *Washington Post National Weekly Edition*, January 22, 2001, 8–9.

65 Ibid., 11.

66 Lawrence R. Jacobs and Robert Y. Shapiro, *Politicians Don't Pander: Political Manipulation and the Loss of Democratic Responsiveness* (Chicago: University of Chicago Press, 2000).

67 Ibid., 12.

68 Richard Morin, "Surveying the Surveyors," *Washington Post National Weekly Edition*, March 2, 1992, 37.

69 David Broder, "Push Polls Plunge Politics to a New Low," *Lincoln Journal Star*, October 9, 1994, 5E.

70 Jonathan Martin, "Apparent Pro-Huckabee Third Party Group Flooded Iowa with Negative Calls," *Politico.com*, Dec. 3, 2007.

71 Bill Kovack and Tom Rosensteil, "Campaign Lite," *Washington Monthly*, January-February 2001, 31–38.

72 "All Things Considered," National Public Radio, October 30, 1992.

73 Richard Morin, "Voters Are Hung Up on Polling," *Washington Post National Weekly Edition*, November 1–7, 2004, 12.

74 Ibid.

75 Ibid.

76 Claudia Deane, "And Why Haven't You Been Polled?" *Washington Post National Weekly Edition*, January 18, 1999, 34; Richard Morin, "The Election Post Mortem," *Washington Post*

National Weekly Edition, September 30, 1996, 37.

77 Real Clear Politics, www.realclearpolitics .com/ polls.html; see also "Pre-Election Polls Largely Accurate," *The Pew Research Center for the People and the Press,* November 23, 2004, www.peoplepress.org/commentary/ display.php3?AnalysisID5 102.

78 Larry Sabato, "The Lash of Unfair Criticism," *Crystalball'08* (Larry Sabato and the University of Virginia Center for Politics, 2008).

79 Richard Morin and Claudia Deane, "Why the Florida Exit Polls Were Wrong," *Washington Post,* November 8, 2000.

80 Diana Owen, "Media Mayhem: Performance of the Press in Election 2000," in *Overtime! The Election 2000 Thriller,* ed. Larry J. Sabato (New York: Longman, 2002), 144.

81 *New York Times Magazine,* December 31, 2006, p. 28.

82 Steve Freeman, *Polling Bias or Corrupted Count* (Philadelphia: American Statistical Association, Philadelphia Chapter, October 14, 2005). (Freeman is a faculty member at the University of Pennsylvania).

83 *The New Yorker,* March 20, 1999, 18.

84 A study by the Pew Foundation, http://people-press.org/reports/display.php3?ReportID=319.

85 Richard Morin, "Tuned Out, Tuned Off," *Washington Post National Weekly Edition,* February 5, 1996, 6–8.

86 Ibid., 8.

87 Pew Foundation study, 2007, people-press .org/reports/display.php3?ReportID=319.

88 Reference omitted

89 Center for Political Studies, 1986 National Election Study, University of Michigan, "Wapner Top Judge in Recognition Poll," *Lincoln Journal Star,* June 23, 1989, 1.

90 "Public Knowledge" op. cit.

91 Morin, "They Know Only What They Don't Like," 35.

92 Ibid.

93 Richard Morin, "Foreign Aid: Mired in Misunderstanding," *Washington Post National Weekly Edition,* March 20, 1995, 37.

94 Richard Morin, "What Informed Public Opinion?" *Washington Post National Weekly Edition,* April 10, 1995, 36.

95 Richard Morin, "We Love It—What We Know of It," *Washington Post National Weekly Edition,* September 22, 1997, 35.

96 Michael Delli Carpini and Scott Keeter, "Stability and Change in the U.S. Public's Knowledge of Politics," *Public Opinion Quarterly* (1991), 583–612.

97 Vladimer Orlando Key, *The Responsible Electorate* (Cambridge, Mass.: Harvard University Press, 1966); Norman H. Nie, Sidney Verba, and John R. Petrocik, *The Changing American Voter* (Cambridge, Mass.: Harvard University Press, 1976), ch. 18; Samuel L. Popkin, *The Reasoning Voter: Communication and Persuasion in Presidential Campaigns* (Chicago: University of Chicago Press, 1994).

98 Gallup Organization, poll conducted April 6, 2004.

99 Popkin, *The Reasoning Voter.*

100 Morin, "Tuned Out, Turned Off," 8.

101 Gallup Organization, poll conducted June 16, 2003.

102 *Newsweek,* poll conducted September 2–3, 2004.

103 Harold Meyerson, "Fact-Free News," *Washington Post National Weekly,* October 10–26, 2003, 26.

104 Lloyd Free and Hadley Cantril, *The Political Beliefs of Americans* (New Brunswick, N.J.: Rutgers University Press, 1967).

105 Andrew Sullivan, article found on www .andrewsullivan.com/main_article.php? artnum520040126.

106 General Social Survey, 2002.

107 Jonathan Rauch, "Bipolar Disorder," *Atlantic Monthly* (January–February 2005), 102.

108 Ibid., 165, 178, 192.

109 E. J. Dionne Jr., "One Nation Deeply Divided," *Washington Post,* November 7, 2004, A31, quoted in Morris P. Fiorina with Samuel J. Abrams and Jeremy C. Pope, *Culture War? The Myth of the Polarized America* (New York: Pearson Longman, 2005), 6.

110 Matthew Dowd, quoted in Fiorina, ibid., 6.

111 Conducted by the Gallup Organization for the online dating service Match.com during July 2004. Cited in Jonathan Rauch, "Bipolar Disorder," *Atlantic Monthly,* January–February, 2005, 105.

112 Various studies are summarized in Rauch, "Bipolar Disorder," 102–110.

113 Editorial, "A Polarized Nation?" *Washington Post,* November 14, 2004, 6. Several of these ideas were summarized nicely in this article.

114 This section draws heavily on Howard Schuman, Charlotte Steeh, and Lawrence Bobo, *Racial Attitudes in America* (Cambridge, Mass.: Harvard University Press, 1985); Howard Schuman, Charlotte Steeh, Lawrence Bobo, and Maria Krysan, *Racial Attitudes in America,* rev. ed. (1997); data summaries are drawn from the General Social Surveys of the National Opinion Research Center, University of Chicago, and National Elections Studies of CPS, University of Michigan; see also Lee Sigelman and Susan Welch, *Black Americans' Views of Racial Inequality* (Cambridge, Mass.: Cambridge University Press, 1991).

115 General Social Survey, 1996; Richard Morin, "Polling in Black and White: Sometimes the Answers Depend on Who's Asking the Questions," *Washington Post National Weekly Edition,* October 30, 1989, 37.

116 General Social Survey, 1996; "Whites Retain Negative Views of Minorities, a Survey Finds," *New York Times,* January 10, 1991, C19; Mary R. Jackman, "General and Applied Tolerance: Does Education Increase Commitment to Racial Inequality?" *American Journal of Political Science* 25 (1981), 256–269; Donald Kinder and David Sears, "Prejudice and Politics: Symbolic Racism versus Racial Threats to the Good Life," *Journal of Personality and Social Psychology* 40 (1981), 414–431.

117 Richard Morin, "We've Moved Forward, but We Haven't," *Washington Post National Weekly Edition,* October 5, 1998, 34.

118 "Whites Retain Negative Views of Minorities, a Survey Finds," C19.

119 General Social Survey, 1998; see also Donald Kinder and Lynn Saunders, *Divided by Color: Racial Politics and Democratic Ideals* (Chicago: University of Chicago Press, 1996); Howard Schuman and Lawrence Bobo, "Survey-Based Experiments on White Attitudes toward Residential Integration." *American Journal of Sociology* 94 (1988), 519–526; see also Schuman et al., *Racial Attitudes in America,* rev. ed.

120 General Social Survey, 1998.

121 Richard Morin, "It's Not as It Seems," *Washington Post National Weekly Edition,* July 16, 2001, 34.

122 Ibid.

123 Morin, "It's Not as It Seems"; ABC/ *Washington Post* poll, 1981 and 1986.

124 Steven A. Holmes and Richard Morin, "Poll Reveals Shades of Promise and Doubt," *Washington Post National Weekly Edition* (June 12–18, 200), 9–11.

125 Ibid.

126 Benjamin I. Page and Robert Y. Shapiro, "Effects of Public Opinion on Policy," *American Political Science Review* 77 (1983), 175–190.

127 Morin, "Voters Are Hung Up on Polling."

128 Lawrence Jacobs and Robert Y. Shapiro, *Politicians Don't Pander* (Chicago: University of Chicago Press, 2000).

129 Ibid.

Chapter 5

1 Lydia Saad, "Local TV is No. 1 Source of News for Americans," The Gallup Poll, www. galluppoll.com/content/Default.aspx?ci=26053 &VERSION=p.

2 Linda Hirshman, "16 Ways of Looking at a Female Voter," *New York Times Magazine,* February 3, 2008, 41.

3 Ibid.; "Numbers," *Time,* February 25, 2008, 16.

4 Hirshman, "16 Ways of Looking at a Female Voter," 41.

5 "Numbers," *Time,* 16.

6 Hirshman, "16 Ways of Looking at a Female Voter, 41.

7 Sidney Verba, Nancy Burns, Kay Lehman Schlozman, "Knowing and Caring about Politics: Gender and Political Engagement," *Journal of Politics,* 59 (November, 1997), 1051–1072.

8 For examination of some explanations, see Verba et al. and Kira Sanbonmatsu, "Gender Related Political Knowledge and Descriptive Representation," *Political Behavior,* 25 (December, 2003), 367–388.

9 James David Barber, *The Pulse of Politics* (New York: Norton, 1980), 9.

[10] Kevin Phillips, "A Matter of Privilege," *Harper's*, January 1977, 95.

[11] Media time overlaps with work time per day, because many people listen to music, watch TV, or surf the Web while working. Richard Harwood, "So Many Media, So Little Time," *Washington Post National Weekly Edition*, September 7, 1992, 28.

[12] Edwin Diamond, *The Tin Kazoo* (Cambridge, Mass.: MIT Press, 1975), 13.

[13] Study by Kaiser Family Foundation, cited in Lauran Neergaard, "Parents Encouraging TV Use among Young Kids, Study Says," *Lincoln Journal Star*, May 25, 2006, 4A, and in Ruth Marcus, "Is Decency Going Down the Tubes?" *Washington Post National Weekly Edition*, June 26–July 9, 2006, 26.

[14] Lindsey Tanner, "Studies Suggest Watching TV Harms Children Academically," *Lincoln Journal Star*, July 5, 2005, 6A.

[15] Doris A. Graber, *Mass Media and American Politics* (Washington, D.C.: Congressional Quarterly Press, 1980), 2.

[16] William Lutz, *Doublespeak* (New York: Harper & Row, 1989), 73–74.

[17] Robert W. McChesney and John Nichols, "It's the Media, Stupid," in *Voices of Dissent*, 5th ed., eds. William F. Grover and Joseph G. Peschek (New York: Longman, 2004), 116–120.

[18] According to the Kaiser Family Foundation. Claudia Wallis, "The Multitasking Generation," *Time*, March 27, 2006, 50–51.

[19] Brian Stelter, "Finding Political News Online, the Young Pass It On," *New York Times*, March 27, 2008, www.nytimes.com/2008/03/27/us/politics/27voters.html?ref5todayspaper&pagewant.

[20] Rob McGann, "Internet Edges Out Family Time More than TV Time," *ClickZ*, January 5, 2005, www.clickz.com/stats/sectors/demographics/article.php/3455061.

[21] Shanto Iyengar, *Is Anyone Responsible? How Television Frames Political Issues* (Chicago: University of Chicago Press, 1991), 1.

[22] Elizabeth Gleick, "Read All about It," *Time*, October 21, 1998, 66; Dana Millbank, "A Bias for Mainstream News," *Washington Post National Weekly Edition*, March 28–April 3, 2005, 23. See also Tom Rosenstiel, *The State of the News Media, 2004* (Washington, D.C.: Project for Excellence in Journalism, 2004).

[23] Eric Alterman, "Out of Print," *New Yorker*, March 31, 2008, 49.

[24] Since 1960. James Rainey, "More News Outlets, Fewer Stories: New Media 'Paradox,'" *Los Angeles Times*, March 13, 2006, www.latimes.com/news/nationworld/nation/la-nanews-13mar13,0,2018145.story?

[25] Project for Excellence in Journalism, "The Changing Newsroom," July 21, 2008, http://journalism.org/node/11963.

[26] Millbank, "A Bias for Mainstream News."

[27] Michael J. Wolf and Geoffrey Sands, "Fearless Predictions," *Brill's Content*, July–August 1999, 110. For a discussion of the future impact of the Internet on media concentration and diversity, see Robert W. McChesney, *The Problem of the Media* (New York: Monthly Review Press, 2004), 211–217.

[28] Eve Gerber, "Divided We Watch," *Brill's Content*, February 2001, 110–111.

[29] Donald Kaul, "Effects of Merger between AOL, Time Warner Will Be Inescapable," *Lincoln Journal Star*, January 18, 2000; Ken Auletta, "Leviathan," *New Yorker*, October 29, 2001, 50.

[30] McChesney, *Problem of the Media*, 182–183.

[31] McChesney and Nichols, "It's the Media," 120. Antitrust laws impose few restrictions on these activities. McChesney, *Problem of the Media*, 235–240.

[32] For examination of this development, see Lawrence Lessing, *The Future of Ideas* (New York: Random House, 2001). For an alternative view, see McChesney, *Problem of the Media*, 205–209.

[33] Benjamin M. Compaine, *Who Owns the Media?* (White Plains, N.Y.: Knowledge Industry Publications, 1979), 11, 76–77; Michael Parenti, *Inventing Reality* (New York: St. Martin's Press, 1986), 27; Paul Farhi, "You Can't Tell a Book by Its Cover," *Washington Post National Weekly Edition*, December 5, 1988, 21; Edmund L. Andrews, "A New Tune for Radio: Hard Times," *New York Times*, March, 1992. "A New Tune for Radio."

[34] Robert McChesney, "AOL–Time Warner Merger Is Dangerous and Undemocratic," *Lincoln Journal Star*, January 17, 2000.

[35] Rosenstiel, *State of the News Media*, 9.

[36] Daren Fonda, "National Prosperous Radio," *Time*, March 24, 2003, 50; Marc Fisher, "Sounds All Too Familiar," *Washington Post National Weekly Edition*, May 26, 2003, 23.

[37] McChesney, *Problem of the Media*, 178.

[38] Ibid., 188.

[39] Mary Lynn F. Jones, "No News Is Good News," *American Prospect*, May 2003, 39. For a history of the development of Clear Channel, see Alec Foege, *Right of the Dial: the Rise of Clear Channel and the Fall of Commercial Radio* (Faber & Faber, 2008).

[40] "Clear Channel Growth the Result of 1996 Deregulation," *Lincoln Journal Star*, October 5, 2003.

[41] David Gram, "Opponents of War Have Trouble Getting Message Out," *Lincoln Journal Star*, February 25, 2003.

[42] "Broadcaster: *Nightline* Won't Air on Its Stations," *Lincoln Journal Star*, April 30, 2004.

[43] money.cnn.com/2004/10/11/news/newsmakers/sinclair_kerry/index.htm?cnn5yes

[44] Elizabeth Lesly Stevens, "Mouse.Ke.Fear," *Brill's Content*, December 1998–January 1999, 95. For other examples, see Jane Mayer, "Bad News," *New Yorker*, August 14, 2000, 30–36.

[45] Jim Hightower, *There's Nothing in the Middle of the Road but Yellow Stripes and Dead Armadillos* (New York: HarperCollins, 1997), 121.

[46] The Project for Excellence in Journalism, affiliated with Columbia University's Graduate School of Journalism, concluded after a five-year study that newscasts by stations owned by smaller companies were significantly higher in quality than newscasts by stations owned by larger companies. "Does Ownership Matter in Local Television News?" February 17, 2003. www.journalism.org.

[47] Neil Hickey, "Money Lust," *Columbia Journalism Review*, July–August 1998, 28.

[48] David Simon, "Does Anyone Care?" *Washington Post National Weekly Edition*, January 28–February 3, 2008, 27.

[49] *Now, with Bill Moyers*, PBS, April 11, 2003. Clear Channel uses "voice tracking" to give the illusion that the programming is originating locally. The company's disc jockey tapes short segments with local references and integrates these into the program feed to the local station.

[50] Ted Turner, "Break Up This Band!" *Washington Monthly*, July–August, 2004, 35.

[51] In response, ABC made all of its prime-time programming available in Spanish in 2005.

[52] Joe Mathews, "Smart News, en Espanol," *Washington Post National Weekly Edition*, May 9-15, 2008, 27.

[53] Howard Kurtz, "Welcome to Spin City," *Washington Post National Weekly Edition*, March 16, 1998, 6. See also Roger Parloff, "If This Ain't Libel . . . ," *Brill's Content*, Fall 2001, 95–113.

[54] Times Mirror Center for the People and the Press, *The Vocal Minority in American Politics* (Washington, D.C.: Times Mirror Center for the People and the Press, 1993).

[55] In addition, she received $50,000 for a book elaborating on her story, $250,000 for posing nude for *Penthouse* magazine, and about $20,000 for appearing on German and Spanish television shows. "Flowers Says She Made Half Million from Story," *Lincoln Journal Star*, March 21, 1998.

[56] Ernest Tollerson, "Politicians Try to Balance Risk against Rewards of Reaching Talk-Radio Audiences," *New York Times*, March 31, 1996, 12.

[57] McChesney, *Problem of the Media*, 96; Paul Taylor, "The New Political Theater," *Mother Jones*, November–December 2000, 30–33.

[58] David Halberstam, "Preface," in Bill Kovach and Tom Rosenstiel, *Warp Speed: America in the Age of Mixed Media* (New York: Century Foundation Press, 1999), x.

[59] During the Vietnam War, some of the vets in the "Swift Boat" ads had lauded Kerry for bravery in incidents that the ad claimed never occurred. One of the vets had received an award for heroism in a battle—the same battle in which Kerry had received his third Purple Heart—that the ad claimed never occurred. Kate Zernike, "Veterans Rebut 'Swift Boat' Charges Against Kerry in Answer to Challenge," *New York Times*, June 22, 2008, Y17.

[60] None of the "Swift Boat Veterans for Truth" served with Kerry on his boat. The charges were disputed by Kerry's crewmates and contradicted by Navy records. Evidently, the "Swift Boat Veterans for Truth" were motivated by their anger toward Kerry's antiwar stance after he returned from Vietnam, which became the subject of the group's second commercial. Todd Gitlin, "Swifter Than Truth," *American Prospect*, November, 2004, 29–30.

[61] Quoted in Richard Corliss, "Look Who's Talking," *Time*, January 23, 1995, 25.

[62] Scott Shane, "For Liberal Bloggers, Libby Trial is Fun and Fodder," *New York Times,* February 15, 2007, wwwnytimes.com/2007/02/15/washington/15bloggers.html?hp&ex=1171602000&en=5afe9e7498071C7f&ei=50948partner=homepage.

[63] Matt Bai, "Can Bloggers Get Real?" *New York Times Magazine,* May 28, 2006, 13.

[64] Elizabeth LeBel, "Life in This Girl's Army," www.sgtlizzie.blogspot.com, cited in Jonathan Finer, "The New Ernie Pyles: Sgtlizzie and 67cshdocs," www.washingtonpost.com/wp-dyn/content/article/2005/08/11/AR2005081102168.

[65] Ibid.

[66] Garance Franke-Ruta, "Blog Rolled," *American Prospect,* April, 2005, 40.

[67] Farhad Manjoo, "Rumor's Reasons," *New York Times Magazine,* March 16, 2008, 22; "Weekend Edition Sunday," NPR April 20, 2008.

[68] Eli Saslow, "In Findlay, Ohio, False Rumors Fly," *Washington Post National Weekly Edition,* July 7-13, 2008, 16.

[69] Charles Peters, "Tilting at Windmills," *Washington Monthly,* September, 2007, 8.

[70] Bill Keller, quoted in Eric Alterman, "Out of Print," *New Yorker,* March 31, 2008, 56.

[71] Richard A. Posner, "Bad News," *New York Times Book Review,* July 31, 2005, 10–11.

[72] Dom Bonafede, "Press Paying More Heed to Substance in Covering 1984 Presidential Election," *National Journal,* October 13, 1984, 1923.

[73] Seth Mnookin, "Advice to Ari," *Brill's Content,* March 2001, 97.

[74] Ken Auletta, "Fortress Bush," *New Yorker,* January 19, 2004, 53.

[75] Charles Peters, *How Washington Really Works* (Reading, Mass.: Addison-Wesley, 1980), 18.

[76] Matthew Brzezinski, *Fortress America: On the Front Lines of Homeland Security—an Inside Look at the Coming Surveillance State* (New York: Bantam, 2004).

[77] William Greider, "Reporters and Their Sources," *Washington Monthly,* October 1982, 13–15.

[78] Rajiv Chandrasekaran, *Imperial Life in the Emerald City: Inside Iraq's Green Zone* (New York: Vintage, 2006), 146.

[79] See, for example, Jeffrey Toobin, *A Vast Conspiracy: The Real Story of the Sex Scandal That Nearly Brought Down a President* (New York: Simon & Schuster, 1999), 310.

[80] Murray Waas, "Why Novak Called Rove," *National Journal,* December 17, 2005, 3874–3878.

[81] There is some uncertainty whether the initial leak, by State Department official Richard Armitage, was intended as retaliation, but at least the subsequent leaks, by White House officials, were. For examination of this incident and the practice of leaking, see Max Frankel, "The Washington Back Channel," *New York Times Magazine,* March 25, 2007, 40.

[82] When a spy's identity becomes public, foreign governments try to retrace the spy's movements and determine his or her contacts to see how the CIA operated in their country.

[83] Howard Kurtz, "Lying Down on This Job Was Just Fine," *Washington Post National Weekly Edition,* April 19, 1999, 13.

[84] Ann Devroy, "The Republicans, It Turns Out, Are a Veritable Fount of Leaks," *Washington Post National Weekly Edition,* November 18, 1991, 23.

[85] Daniel Schorr, "A Fact of Political Life," *Washington Post National Weekly Edition,* October 28, 1991, 32.

[86] Howard Kurtz, "How Sources and Reporters Play the Game of Leaks," *Washington Post National Weekly Edition,* March 15, 1993, 25.

[87] Dan Eggen, "Bush's Plumbers," *Washington Post National Weekly Edition,* March 13–19, 2006, 11.

[88] Nancy Franklin, "Rather Knot," *New Yorker,* October 4, 2004, 108–109.

[89] Samuel Kernell, *Going Public: New Strategies of Presidential Leadership* (Washington, D.C.: Congressional Quarterly Press, 1986), 59. Woodrow Wilson also tried to cultivate correspondents and host frequent sessions, but he did not have the knack for this activity and so scaled back the sessions. Kernell, *Going Public,* 60–61. He did perceive that "some men of brilliant ability were in the group, but I soon discovered that the interest of the majority was in the personal and the trivial rather than in principles and policies." James Bennet, "The Flack Pack," *Washington Monthly,* November 1991, 27.

[90] Dwight Eisenhower was actually the first president to let the networks televise his press conferences, but he did not do so to reach the public. When he wanted to reach the public, he made a formal speech. The networks found his conferences so untelegenic that they stopped covering the entire session each time. Kernell, *Going Public,* 68.

[91] Bennet, "The Flack Pack," 19.

[92] Frank Rich, "The Armstrong Williams NewsHour," *New York Times,* June 26, 2005, WK13.

[93] Dom Bonafede, " 'Mr. President,' " *National Journal,* October 29, 1988, 2756.

[94] Charles Hagen, "The Photo Op: Making Icons or Playing Politics?" *New York Times,* February 9, 1992, H28.

[95] Frank Rich, "Operation Iraqi Infoganda," *New York Times,* March 28, 2004, AR21.

[96] "The Man behind the Curtain Award," *Mother Jones,* September–October 2002, 67.

[97] Molly Ivins, "It's Up to Us to Stop This War, and Now," *Lincoln Journal Star,* January 7, 2007, 8C. This incident is also shown and discussed in the documentary *Control Room.*

[98] Maureen Dowd, "This Bud's For You," *New York Times,* May 4, 2008, WK13.

[99] Kiku Adatto, cited in Howard Kurtz, "Networks Adapt to Changed Campaign Role," *Washington Post,* June 21, 1992, A-19. See also Diana Owen, "Media Mayhem: Performance of the Press in Election 2000," in *Overtime! The Election 2000 Thriller,* ed. Larry J. Sabato (New York: Longman, 2002), 123–156.

[100] Lance Morrow, "The Decline and Fall of Oratory," *Time,* August 18, 1980, 78.

[101] George E. Reedy, *The Twilight of the Presidency* (New York: New American Library, 1970), 112.

[102] Sam Donaldson, quoted in Thomas Griffith, "Winging It on Television," *Time,* March 14, 1983, 71.

[103] Auletta, "Fortress Bush," 61–62.

[104] W. Lance Bennett, *News: The Politics of Illusion,* 2nd ed. (White Plains, N.Y.: Longman, 1988).

[105] Larry J. Sabato, *Feeding Frenzy: How Attack Journalism Has Transformed American Politics* (New York: Free Press, 1991).

[106] Deborah Tannen, *The Argument Culture* (New York: Ballantine, 1998), 81.

[107] Ibid., 55.

[108] Orville Schell, "Preface" to Michael Massing, *Now They Tell Us: the American Press and Iraq* (New York: New York Review of Books, 2004), xiv.

[109] James Fallows, *Breaking the News,* (New York: Vintage, 1997), 62–63.

[110] Joan Konner, "Diane 'Got' Gore. But What Did We Get?" *Brill's Content,* September 1999, 59–60.

[111] See Sabato, *Feeding Frenzy,* for additional reasons for this increase.

[112] "Ticker," *Brill's Content,* July–August 1998, 152, citing the Project for Excellence in Journalism, "Changing Definitions of News: A Look at the Mainstream Press over 20 Years," March 6, 1998.

[113] Fallows, *Breaking the News,* 196.

[114] An examination of 224 incidents of criminal or unethical behavior by Reagan administration appointees found that only 13 percent were uncovered by reporters. Most were discovered through investigations by executive agencies or congressional committees, which then released the information to the press. Only incidents reflecting personal peccadilloes of government officials, such as sexual offenses, were exposed first by reporters. John David Rausch Jr., "The Pathology of Politics: Government, Press, and Scandal," *Extensions* (University of Oklahoma), Fall 1990, 11–12. For the Whitewater scandal, reporters got most of their tips from a Republican Party operation run by officials from Republican presidential campaigns. Regarding sexual matters, reporters got most of their tips from prosecutors for the independent counsel, lawyers for Paula Jones, or a book agent for Linda Tripp. See Steven Brill, "Pressgate," *Brill's Content,* July/August, 1998, 134.

[115] These are only a few of the key questions that have gone largely unexplored by the media. For an examination of these and others, see the documentary, *9/11: Press for Truth.*

[116] Except for a reporter at a small paper in North Carolina. Charles Peters, "Tilting at Windmills," *Washington Monthly,* October/November, 2005, 15.

[117] William Rivers, "The Correspondents after 25 Years," *Columbia Journalism Review* 1 (Spring 1962), 5.

118 Coolidge, in his reelection campaign, was actually the first president to use radio as a means of addressing the public directly.

119 James David Barber, *Presidential Character* (Englewood Cliffs, N.J.: Prentice Hall, 1992), 238.

120 Reagan got his start in show business as a radio sportscaster in Des Moines, Iowa, announcing major league baseball games "live." Of course, he was not actually at the games: he got the barest details—who was at bat, whether the pitch was a strike or a ball or a hit—from the wireless and made up the rest to create a commentary that convinced listeners that he was watching in person.

121 Timothy J. Russert, "For '92, the Networks Have to Do Better," *New York Times,* March 4, 1990, E23.

122 Hedrick Smith, *The Power Game* (New York: Random House, 1988) , 420.

123 Steven K. Weisman, "The President and the Press," *New York Times Magazine,* October 14, 1984, 71–72; Dick Kirschten, "Communications Reshuffling Intended to Help Reagan Do What He Does Best," *National Journal,* January 28, 1984, 154.

124 Auletta, "Fortress Bush," 60.

125 Ibid., 54, 57, 64.

126 *All Things Considered,* NPR, March 21, 2006.

127 Ibid., 55.

128 David Barstow and Robin Stein, "Is it News or Public Relations? Under Bush, Lines Are Blurry," *New York Times,* March 13, 2005, YT1. The Clinton administration also used these, though less extensively.

129 According to a report by the Government Accountability Office (GAO). Christopher Lee, "Report: White House Spent $1.6 Billion on PR," *Lincoln Journal Star,* February 19, 2006, 3A.

130 John F. Harris, "On the World Stage, Bush Shuns the Spotlight," *Washington Post National Weekly Edition,* April 23, 2001, 11; Ronald Brownstein, "Bush Forced into Role He May Not Want: Communicator," *Lincoln Journal Star,* September 15, 2001.

131 John F. Harris and Dan Balz, "A Well-Oiled Machine," *Washington Post National Weekly Edition,* May 14, 2001, 6.

132 James Carville, quoted in John F. Harris, "Bush's Lucky Break," *Washington Post National Weekly Edition,* May 14, 2001, 23.

133 Aides claimed that *Air Force One* was a target, but it was revealed that this claim was an exaggeration to parry the criticism that Bush received. Eric Pooley and Karen Tumulty, "Bush in the Crucible," *Time,* September 24, 2001, 49.

134 Calvin Woodward, "Warrior Bush: It Doesn't Come Naturally," *Lincoln Journal Star,* October 6, 2002.

135 Michael Duffy, "Marching Alone," *Time,* September 9, 2002, 42.

136 Presidential historian Henry Graff, cited in Ron Fourier, "President Stumbles with Mideast Rhetoric," *Lincoln Journal Star,* April 20, 2002.

137 Joe Klein, "Why the 'War President' Is Under Fire," *Time,* February 23, 2004, 17.

138 For an empirical examination, see David Domke, *God Willing? Political Fundamentalism in the White House, the War on Terror, and the Echoing Press* (Ann Arbor, Mich.: Pluto, 2004). Domke also examines the intolerance of dissent reflected in speeches and remarks issued by the administration.

139 David Greenberg, "Fathers and Sons," *New Yorker,* July 12 and 19, 2004, 97.

140 David L. Greene, "Bush Often Great Miscommunicator," *Lincoln Journal Star,* October 6, 2002.

141 Philip Gourevitch, "Bushspeak," *New Yorker,* September 13, 2004, 38.

142 Stephen Hess, *Live from Capitol Hill!* (Washington, D.C.: Brookings Institution, 1991), 62; Timothy E. Cook, *Making Laws and Making News: Media Strategies in the U.S. House of Representatives* (Washington, D.C.: Brookings Institution, 1989), 2.

143 Hess, *Live from Capitol Hill!* 102.

144 Joe Klein, *The Natural* (New York: Doubleday, 2002), 109.

145 Robert Schmidt, "May It Please the Court," *Brill's Content,* October 1999, 74.

146 For analysis, see Rorie L. Spill and Zoe M. Oxley, "Philosopher Kings or Political Actors? How the Media Portray the Supreme Court," *Judicature,* July–August 2003, 22–29.

147 Ibid.

148 During the invasion of Grenada in 1983, the military excluded all journalists, even turning away at gunpoint those who reached the island on their own. During the invasion of Panama in 1989 and the Persian Gulf War in 1990, the military created press pools with some journalists escorted to selective sites, who reported the news for news organizations in the pools.

149 Michael Tomasky, "Breaking the Code: Or, Can the Press Be Saved from Itself?" in Cynthia Brown, ed., *Lost Liberties* (New York: New Press, 2003), 151–152.

150 Auletta, "Fortress Bush," 62.

151 Andrew M. Lindner, "Controlling the Media in Iraq," *Contexts* 7, Spring, 2008, 32-38.

152 And President Bush tried to use Tillman for his reelection campaign, proposing to tape a memorial for a Cardinals game just before Election Day. (The family refused.) Frank Rich, "The Mysterious Death of Pat Tillman," *New York Times,* November 6, 2005, WK12. Tillman was killed in Afghanistan during the war in Iraq.

153 Edward Jay Epstein, *News from Nowhere* (New York: Random House, 1973), 13.

154 Graber, *Mass Media and American Politics,* 62.

155 Milton Coleman, "When the Candidate Is Black Like Me," *Washington Post National Weekly Edition,* April 23, 1984, 9.

156 Roper Organization, "A Big Concern about the Media: Intruding on Grieving Families," *Washington Post National Weekly Edition,* June 6, 1984. See also Joseph N. Cappella and Kathleen Hall Jamieson, *Spiral of Cynicism* (New York: Oxford University Press, 1997), 210.

157 Herbert J. Gans, *Democracy and the News* (New York: Oxford University, 2003), 87.

158 For further examination of this phenomenon, see Neal Gabler, "Cannibal Liberals," *Los Angeles Times,* June 29, 2008, www.latimes.com/ news/opinion/la-op-gabler29-2008jun29,0 ,2574530,print.story.

159 In 1987 Reagan appointees to the Federal Communications Commission (FCC) abandoned the Fairness Doctrine, which had required broadcasters to maintain editorial balance. When Congress reinstated the doctrine, President Reagan vetoed the bill, thus allowing broadcasters to cater to any audience.

160 McChesney, *Problem of the Media,* 116.

161 Karen Tumulty, "I Want My Al TV," *Time,* June 30, 2003, 59. A new liberal network, Air America Radio, which reaches some of these cities, began in 2004. Even the Sunday talk shows of the major television networks lean right. Significantly more guests are conservative or Republican than liberal or Democrat, and the journalists who question them are more conservative than liberal, according to a study of the shows from 1997 through 2005. Paul Waldman, "John Fund Again? It's Not Your Imagination— the Sunday Shows Really Do Lean Right," *Washington Monthly,* March, 2006, 9–13.

162 Liddy, who was convicted in the Watergate scandal, instructed listeners where to aim when shooting agents of the Bureau of Alcohol, Tobacco, and Firearms to kill them.

163 McChesney, *Problem of the Media,* 117.

164 "The Structural Imbalance of Political Talk Radio," Center for American Progress and Free Press, June 22, 2007. Report available from www.themonkeycage.org/2008/02/post_54.html.

165 Julia Preston, "As Immigration Plan Folded, Grass Roots Roared," *New York Times,* June 10, 2007, YT1.

166 For a history of the origins of Fox News, see David Carr, *Crazy Like a Fox* (New York: Portfolio, 2004).

167 For analysis, see Ken Auletta, "Vox Fox," *New Yorker,* May 26, 2003, 58.

168 Geneva Overholser, "It's Time for News Networks to Take Sides," *Lincoln Journal Star,* August 26, 2001.

169 Robert S. Boynton, "How to Make a Guerrilla Documentary," *New York Times Magazine,* July 11, 2004, 22. See also the documentary *Outfoxed* (2004) and Chandrasekaran, *Imperial Life in the Emerald City, 147.*

170 According to the Project for Excellence in Journalism. David Bauder, "Study: Fox Spends Less Time on Iraq War than MSNBC, CNN," *Lincoln Journal Star,* June 14, 2007. In the first three months of 2007, Fox devoted half as much airtime to the war as MSNBC did and considerably less than CNN did.

171 Nicholas D. Kristof, "A Challenge for Bill O'Reilly," *New York Times,* December 18, 2005, WK13. The crusade coincided with publication of a book on this subject by a Fox broadcaster.

172 Joe Klein, "Above the Fray," *Time,* April 28, 2008, 27.

173 Auletta, "Vox Fox," 63–64.

174 Overholser, "It's Time"; David Plotz, "Fox News Channel," *Slate,* November 22, 2000 (slate.msn.com).

175 Jeff Cohen and Jonah Goldberg, "Face-Off: Beyond Belief," *Brill's Content,* December 1999–January 2000, 54.

176 For examination, see Tommy Nguyen, "The Reel Liberal Majority," *Washington Post National Weekly Edition,* August 2–8, 2004, 14.

177 Edith Efron, *The News Twisters* (Los Angeles: Nash, 1971); L. B. Bozell and B. H. Baker, "And That's the Way It Isn't," *Journalism Quarterly* 67 (1990), 1139; Bernard Goldberg, *Bias* (New York: Regnery, 2002); Eric Alterman, *What Liberal Media?* (New York: Basic Books, 2003).

178 S. Robert Lichter, Stanley Rothman, and Linda S. Lichter, *The Media Elite* (Bethesda, Md.: Adler & Adler, 1986), 21–25. See also Hess, *Live from Capitol Hill!* app. A, 110–130.

179 John Johnstone, Edward Slawski, and William Bowman, *The Newspeople* (Urbana: University of Illinois Press, 1976), 225–226.

180 Stanley Rothman and S. Robert Lichter, "Media and Business Elites: Two Classes in Conflict?" *Public Interest* 69 (1982), 111–125; S. Robert Lichter and Stanley Rothman, "Media and Business Elites," *Public Opinion,* October-November 1981, 44.

181 Alterman, "Out of Print," 49.

182 Stephen Hess, *The Washington Reporters* (Washington, D.C.: Brookings Institution, 1981), 89; see also Lichter et al., *Media Elite,* 127–128.

183 James Fallows, "The Stoning of Donald Regan," *Washington Monthly,* June 1984, 57.

184 Sometimes media executives or editors pressure reporters because they have contrary views. Kimberly Conniff, "All the Views Fit to Print," *Brill's Content,* March 2001, 105.

185 Howard Kurtz, *Media Circus* (New York: Random House, 1994), 48.

186 Russell J. Dalton, Paul A. Beck, and Robert Huckfeldt, "Partisan Cues and the Media Information Flows in the 1992 Presidential Election," *American Political Science Review* 92 (March 1998), 118.

187 C. Richard Hofstetter, *Bias in the News* (Columbus: Ohio State University Press, 1976); Graber, *Mass Media and Politics,* 167–168; Michael J. Robinson, "Just How Liberal Is the News?" *Public Opinion,* February-March 1983, 55–60; Maura Clancy and Michael J. Robinson, "General Election Coverage: Part I," *Public Opinion,* December 1984-January 1985, 49–54, 59; Michael J. Robinson, "The Media Campaign, '84: Part II," *Public Opinion,* February–March 1985, 43–48.

188 Dave D'Alessio and Mike Allen, "Media Bias in Presidential Elections: A Meta-Analysis," *Journal of Communication* 50 (2000), 133–156. Some studies did find some bias against incumbents, front-runners, and emerging challengers. For these candidates, the media apparently took their watchdog role seriously. Clancy and Robinson, "General Election Coverage"; Robinson, "Media Campaign, '84"; Michael J. Robinson, "Where's the Beef? Media and Media Elites in 1984," in *The American Elections of 1984,* ed. Austin Ranney (Durham, N.C.: Duke University

Press, 1985), 184; Michael J. Robinson, "News Media Myths and Realities: What Network News Did and Didn't Do in the 1984 General Campaign," in *Elections in America,* ed. Kay Lehman Schlozman (Boston: Allen & Unwin, 1987), 143–170; Kim Fridkin Kahn and Patrick J. Kenney, *The Spectacle of U.S. Senate Campaigns* (Princeton, N.J.: Princeton University, 1999), 126–129.

189 Robert Shogan, *Bad News: Where the Press Goes Wrong in the Making of the President* (Chicago: Dee, 2001), 231.

190 It helped the Democrat Carter in 1976 but hurt him in 1980. It helped the Republican Bush in 1988 but hurt him in 1992. Thomas E. Patterson, *Out of Order* (New York: Vintage, 1994), 131. It helped the Democrat Clinton in 1996, and at different stages of the campaign, it helped the Republican Bush or the Democrat Gore in 2000.

191 Shogan, *Bad News,* 204–245;

192 Fewer than one in ten stories on the 2000 debates focused on policy differences; seven in ten focused on candidates' performance or strategy. Bill Kovach and Tom Rosenstiel, "Campaign Lite," *Washington Monthly,* January–February 2001, 31–32. For a perceptive analysis, see Clymer, "Better Campaign Reporting."

193 The media, however, did pay a lot of attention to Ross Perot's presidential bid in 1992 because he said he would spend $100 million on his campaign and because polls showed he could compete with Bush and Clinton.

194 For a recounting of his 2000 campaign, see Ralph Nader, "My Untold Story," *Brill's Content,* February 2001, 100.

195 "Clinton Gains More Support from Big Papers," *Lincoln Journal Star,* October 25, 1992. Newspapers insist that there is little relationship between their editorial endorsements and their news coverage or even their political columns. An endorsement for one candidate does not mean more positive coverage or columns for that candidate because American media have established a tradition of autonomy in the newsroom. Dalton et al., "Partisan Cues," 118. However, some research shows that when papers endorse candidates, the papers show a small bias toward the candidates in their news stories (if the candidates are incumbents). Kim Fridkin Kahn and Patrick J. Kenney, "The Slant of the News: How Editorial Endorsements Influence Campaign Coverage and Citizen's Views of Candidates," *American Political Science Review* 96 (June 2002), 381–394.

196 By Media Matters for America, cited in David Bauder, "Study Finds Conservatives Dominate Editorial Pages," *Lincoln Journal Star,* September 16, 2007, F5.

197 Hofstetter, *Bias in the News;* Hess, *Live from Capitol Hill!* 12–13.

198 Robinson, "Just How Liberal . . . ?" 58; Arthur H. Miller, Edie N. Goldenberg, and Lutz Erbring, "Type-Set Politics," *American Political Science Review* 73 (January 1979), 69; Patterson, *Out of Order,* 6; Charles M. Tidmarch and John J. Pitney Jr., "Covering Congress," *Polity* 17 (Spring 1985), 463–483.

199 Richard Morin, "The Big Picture Is out of Focus," *Washington Post National Weekly Edition,* March 6, 2000, 21.

200 Steven Brill, "Quality Control," *Brill's Content,* July–August 1998, 19–20.

201 Patterson, *Out of Order,* 25, 245.

202 Stanley Rothman and S. Robert Lichter, "The Nuclear Energy Debate," *Public Opinion,* August–September 1982, 47–48; Stanley Rothman and S. Robert Lichter, "Elite Ideology and Risk Perception in Nuclear Energy Policy," *American Political Science Review* 81 (June 1987), 383–404; Lichter et al., *Media Elite,* ch. 7; Sabato, *Feeding Frenzy,* 87, and sources cited therein. But a study examining twenty years' coverage of governors and their states' unemployment and murder rates shows no bias toward Democratic or Republican governors. David Niven, "Partisan Bias in the Media?" *Social Science Quarterly* 80 (December 1999), 847–857.

203 Goldberg, *Bias,* ch. 5; Alterman, *What Liberal Media?* ch. 7.

204 Alterman, *What Liberal Media?* 104–117.

205 For examination of "24," see Jane Mayer, "Whatever It Takes," *New Yorker,* February 19 and 26, 2007, 66.

206 Mireya Navarro, "On Abortion, Hollywood Is No Choice," *New York Times,* June 10, 2007, ST1.

207 Ibid., 118–138. For an analysis of the coverage of the economy in the booming 1990s, see John Cassidy, "Striking It Rich: The Rise and Fall of Popular Capitalism," *New Yorker,* January 14, 2002, 63–73.

208 Bruce Nussbaum, "The Myth of the Liberal Media," *Business Week,* November 11, 1996; Fallows, *Breaking the News,* 49.

209 Further, the media give scant attention to labor matters, except when strikes inconvenience commuters. Mark Crispin Miller, "The Media and the Bush Dyslexicon," in Grover and Peschek, *Voices of Dissent,* 137–146. In 2001, the three main television networks used representatives of corporations as sources thirty times more often than representatives of unions. McChesney, *Problem of the Media,* 70–71.

210 McChesney, *Problem of the Media,* 106.

211 Hightower, op. cit., 137.

212 This tendency is reflected even in the nature of the reporters' questions at presidential press conferences. For foreign issues, their questions are less aggressive than for domestic issues. Steven E. Claymans, John Heritage, Marc N. Elliott, and Laurie L. McDonald, "When Does the Watchdog Bark? Conditions of Aggressive Questioning in Presidential Press Conferences," *American Sociological Review,* 72 (February, 2007), 23–41. The researchers examined the period from 1953 to 2000.

213 Robinson, "Just How Liberal . . . ?" 59.

214 Parenti, *Inventing Reality,* ch. 7–11; Charles E. Lindblom, *Politics and Markets* (New York: Basic Books, 1977); J. Fred MacDonald, *One Nation under Television: The Rise and Decline of Network TV* (New York: Pantheon Books, 1990); Dan Nimmo and James E. Combs, *Mediated Political Realities* (White Plains, N.Y.: Longman, 1983), 135; Benjamin I. Page and R. Y. Shapiro, *The Rational Public* (Chicago: University of Chicago Press, 1992); John R. Zaller and Dennis Chiu, "Government's Little Helper: U.S. Press Coverage of Foreign Policy

Crises, 1945–1991," *Political Communication* 13 (1996), 385–405.

[215] John R. MacArthur, *Second Front: Censorship and Propaganda in the Gulf War* (New York: Hill & Wang, 1992); James Bennet, "How They Missed That Story," *Washington Monthly*, December 1990, 8–16; Christopher Dickey, "Not Their Finest Hour," *Newsweek*, June 8, 1992, 66.

[216] In the 1950s and early 1960s, newspapers, magazines, and television networks sent few correspondents to Vietnam, so most accepted the government's account of the conflict. Susan Welch, "The American Press and Indochina, 1950–1956," in *Communication in International Politics*, ed. Richard L. Merritt (Urbana: University of Illinois Press, 1972), 207–231; Edward J. Epstein, "The Selection of Reality," in *What's News?*, ed. Elie Abel (San Francisco: Institute for Contemporary Studies, 1981), 124. When they did dispatch correspondents, many filed pessimistic reports, but their editors believed the government rather than the correspondents and refused to print these reports. Instead, they ran articles quoting optimistic statements by government officials. See David Halberstam, *The Powers That Be* (New York: Dell, 1980), 642–647. In 1968, the media did turn against the war, but rather than sharply criticize it, they conveyed the impression that it was futile. Daniel C. Hallin, *The "Uncensored War": The Media and Vietnam* (New York: Oxford University Press, 1986).

[217] David Domke, *God Willing? Political Fundamentalism in the White House, the "War on Terror," and the Echoing Press* (London: Pluto, 2004).

[218] "Return of Talk Show Is Healthy Sign," *Lincoln Journal Star*, October 6, 2001.

[219] Alterman, *What Liberal Media?* 202.

[220] Anthony Collings, "The BBC: How to Be Impartial in Wartime," *Chronicle of Higher Education*, December 21, 2001, B14.

[221] *Weapons of Mass Deception*, a documentary film by Danny Schechter (Cinema Libre Distribution, 2005).

[222] Alterman, *What Liberal Media?* 29; Todd Gitlin, "Showtime Iraq," *American Prospect*, November 4, 2002, 34–35.

[223] *Weapons of Mass Deception*.

[224] Bill Moyers, "Our Democracy Is in Danger of Being Paralyzed," Keynote address to the National Conference on Media Reform, November 8, 2003, www.truthout.org/docs_03/printer_111403E.shtml.

[225] James Poniewozik, "What You See vs. What They See," *Time*, April 7, 2003, 68–69. For example, that U.S. searches caused considerable damage to Iraqi homes and that these raids swept up many innocent family members, *Morning Edition*, National Public Radio, May 4, 2004. Also, that in the run-up to the war, U.S. agents had bugged the homes and offices of United Nations Security Council members who had not proclaimed support for the war, Camille T. Taiara, "Spoon-Feeding the Press," *San Francisco Bay Guardian*, March 12, 2003, www.sfbg.com/37/24/x_mediabeat.html.

[226] Frank Rich, "The Spoils of War," *New York Times*, April 13, 2003, AR1; Paul Janensch,

"Whether to Show Images of War Dead Is Media Dilemma," *Lincoln Journal Star*, March 31, 2003.

[227] Terry McCarthy, "Whatever Happened to the Republican Guard?" *Time*, May 12, 2003, 38.

[228] Frank Rich, *The Greatest Story Ever Told* (New York: Penguin Press, 2006), 155.

[229] Todd Gitlin, "Embed or in Bed?" *American Prospect*, June 2003, 43.

[230] Schell, "Preface," vi.

[231] Massing, *Now They Tell Us*, 7.

[232] For an examination, see Massing, *Now They Tell Us*.

[233] "Buying the War," PBS, April 25, 2007.

[234] Howard Kurtz, quoted in Todd Gitlin, "The Great Media Breakdown," *Mother Jones*, November–December, 2004, 58.

[235] Rich, *The Greatest Story Ever Sold*, 87.

[236] "The *Times* and Iraq," *New York Times*, May 26, 2004, A10; Daniel Okrent, "Weapons of Mass Destruction? Or Mass Distraction?" *New York Times*, May 30, 2004, WK1.

[237] Jim Thompson, "Letters to the Public Editor," *New York Times*, June 6, 2004, WK2.

[238] Reporters turn to officials because it is easy and because, ironically, they want to avoid charges of bias. They believe that their superiors and the public consider officials to be reliable, so ignoring or downplaying them might be construed as showing bias against them. Cook, *Making Laws and Making News*, 8. See also Leon V. Sigal, *Reporters and Officials* (Lexington, Mass.: Heath, 1973), 120–121; Lucy Howard, "Slanted 'Line'?" *Newsweek*, February 13, 1989, 6; Hess, *Live from Capitol Hill!* 50. Trivia buffs might wonder who has been the subject of the most cover articles in *Time* magazine—the answer is Richard Nixon (fifty-five). "Numbers," *Time*, March 9, 1998, 189.

[239] W. Lance Bennett, "Toward a Theory of Press-State Relations in the United States," *Journal of Communication* 40 (1990), 103–125.

[240] Three times as many people believe the media are "too liberal" than believe they are "too conservative" (45 percent to 15 percent). McChesney, *Problem of the Media*, 114.

[241] M. D. Watts, D. Domke, D. V. Shah, and D. P. Fan, "Elite Cues and Media Bias in Presidential Campaigns: Explaining Public Perceptions of a Liberal Press," *Communication Research* 26 (1999), 144–175.

[242] William Kristol, quoted in Alterman, *What Liberal Media?* 2–3.

[243] Elizabeth Wilner, "On the Road Again," *Washington Post National Weekly Edition*, June 6–12, 2005, 22.

[244] For further examination of this conclusion, see Alterman, "Out of Print," 55.

[245] Robert Vallone, Lee Ross, and Mark R. Lepper, "The Hostile Media Phenomenon," *Journal of Personality and Social Psychology* 49 (1985), 577–585; Roger Giner-Sorolla and Shelly Chaiken, "The Causes of Hostile Media Judgments," *Journal of Experimental Social Psychology* 30 (1994), 165–180.

[246] Dalton et al., "Partisan Cues and the Media."

[247] W. Phillips Davison, "The Third-Person Effect in Communication," *Public Opinion Quarterly* 47 (1983), 1–15.

[248] Dave D'Alessio, "An Experimental Examination of Readers' Perceptions of Media Bias," unpublished manuscript, University of Connecticut, n.d.; Mark Peffley, James M. Avery, and Jason E. Glass, "Public Perceptions of Bias in the News Media," paper presented at the annual meeting of the Midwest Political Science Association, Chicago, April 19–22, 2001.

[249] According to a statement by a CNN producer in the documentary *Outfoxed*.

[250] And HBO postponed a documentary film, *Last Letters Home*, based on excerpts of letters from soldiers later killed in Iraq, because this powerful film might have turned viewers against the war. *All Things Considered*, NPR, November 11, 2004.

[251] Ted Koppel, "And Now, a Word for Our Demographic," *New York Times*, January 29, 2006, WK16.

[252] Goldberg, *Bias*, 92

[253] Theodore H. White, *America in Search of Itself* (New York: Harper & Row, 1982), 186.

[254] Goldberg, *Bias*, 92

[255] "Anchorwoman Verdict Raises Mixed Opinions," *Lincoln Journal Star*, August 9, 1983.

[256] Kovach and Rosenstiel, *Warp Speed*, 64

[257] Hess, *Live from Capitol Hill!* 34; Rosenstiel, *State of the News Media*, 21.

[258] Molly Ivins, "Media Conglomerates Profit at Expense of News, Public," *Lincoln Journal Star*, October 26, 2001.

[259] James Fallows, "On That Chart," *Nation*, June 3, 1996, 15

[260] Maureen Dowd, "Flintstone Futurama," *New York Times*, August 19, 2001, WK 13

[261] A poll of reporters and executives found that a third admitted to avoiding stories that would embarrass an advertiser or harm the financial interests of their own organization. "Poll: Reporters Avoid, Soften Stories," *Lincoln Journal Star*, May 1, 2000; David Owen, "The Cigarette Companies: How They Get Away with Murder, Part II," *Washington Monthly*, March 1985, 48–54. See also Daniel Hellinger and Dennis R. Judd, *The Democratic Facade*, 2nd ed. (Belmont, Calif.: Wadsworth, 1994), 59. Through the 1920s, newspapers refrained from pointing out that popular "patent medicines" were usually useless and occasionally dangerous because the purveyors bought more advertising than any other business. Mark Crispin Miller, "Free the Media," *Nation*, June 3, 1996, 10.

[262] Roger Mudd, quoted in *Television and the Presidential Elections*, ed. Martin A. Linsky (Lexington, Mass.: Heath, 1983), 48.

[263] "Q&A: Dan Rather on Fear, Money, and the News," *Brill's Content*, October 1998, 117.

[264] Barry Sussman, "News on TV: Mixed Reviews," *Washington Post National Weekly Edition*, September 3, 1984, 37.

[265] Bill Carter, "Networks Fight Public's Shrinking Attention Span," *Lincoln Journal Star*, September 30, 1990.

[266] Epstein, *News from Nowhere*, 4.

267 William A. Henry III, "Requiem for TV's Gender Gap," *Time,* August 22, 1983, 57.

268 Richard Morin, "The Nation's Mood? Calm," *Washington Post National Weekly Edition,* November 5, 2001, 35.

269 According to the Tyndall Report, cited in Nicholas Kristof, "Please, Readers, Help Bill O'Reilly!" *New York Times,* February 7, 2006, A21.

270 Charles Peters, "Tilting at Windmills," *Washington Monthly,* September, 2006, 7.

271 John Mecklin, "Over the Horizon," *Miller-McCune,* June/July, 2008, 6.

272 For an examination of how the media exaggerated the Whitewater scandal, see Gene Lyons, *Fools for Scandal* (New York: Franklin Square Press, 1996).

273 The third and final special prosecutor concluded that there might be some evidence of wrongdoing in the law firm records of Hillary Clinton but that there was not enough evidence to justify prosecution.

274 The pope was making a historic visit to Cuba. The networks had considered this so important that they had sent their anchors to Havana. At the same time, renewed violence in Northern Ireland threatened to scuttle the peace talks between Catholics and Protestants, and continued refusal from Iraq to cooperate with United Nations biological and chemical weapons inspectors threatened to escalate to military conflict.

275 Eric Pooley, "Monica's World," *Time,* March 2, 1998, 40.

276 Quoted in Fallows, *Breaking the News,* 201.

277 Samuel G. Freedman, "Fighting to Balance Honor and Profit on the Local News," *New York Times,* September 30, 2001, sec. 2, 26.

278 Lawrie Mifflin, "Crime Falls, but Not on TV," *New York Times,* July 6, 1997, E3. According to one researcher, crime coverage is also "the easiest, cheapest, laziest news to cover" because stations just listen to the police radio and then send a camera crew to shoot the story.

279 Heather Maher, "Eleven O'Clock Blues," *Brill's Content,* February 2001, 99.

280 Molly Ivins, "Don't Moan about the Media, Do Something," *Lincoln Journal Star,* November 1999.

281 David S. Broder, "Can We Govern?" *Washington Post National Weekly Edition,* January 31, 1994, 23.

282 Newspaper ads were placed in college papers by Holocaust deniers, claiming that there is no proof that gas chambers actually existed. The editor of one paper justified accepting the ad by saying, "There are two sides to every issue and both have a place on the pages of any open-minded paper's editorial page." Tannen, *Argument Culture,* 38. For examination of this phenomenon, see Deborah E. Lipstadt, *Denying the Holocaust: The Growing Assault on Truth and Memory* (New York: Plume, 1993).

283 Howard Kurtz, quoted in Tannen, *Argument Culture,* 29.

284 Patterson, *Out of Order,* 53–59.

285 Lee Sigelman and David Bullock, "Candidates, Issues, Horse Races, and Hoopla: Presidential Campaign Coverage, 1888–1988," *American Politics Quarterly* 19 (January 1991), 5–32. So was emphasis on human interest. In 1846, the *New York Tribune* described the culinary habits of Representative William "Sausage" Sawyer (D-Ohio), who ate a sausage on the floor of the House every afternoon: "What little grease is left on his hands he wipes on his almost bald head which saves any outlay for Pomatum. His mouth sometimes serves as a finger glass, his shirtsleeves and pantaloons being called into requisition as a napkin. He uses a jackknife for a toothpick, and then he goes on the floor again to abuse the Whigs as the British party." Cook, *Making Laws and Making News,* 18–19.

286 Patterson, *Out of Order,* 74; Marion R. Just, Ann N. Crigler, Dean E. Alger, Timothy E. Cook, Montague Kern, and Darrell M. West, *Crosstalk: Citizens, Candidates, and the Media in a Presidential Campaign* (Chicago: University of Chicago Press, 1996); Mathew Robert Kerbel, *Remote and Controlled* (Boulder, Colo.: Westview Press, 1995); Bruce Buchanan, *Electing a President* (Austin: University of Texas Press, 1991).

287 Owen, "Media Mayhem," 127.

288 Richard Morin, "Toward the Millennium, by the Numbers," *Washington Post National Weekly Edition,* July 7, 1997, 35.

289 Patterson, *Out of Order,* 81–82.

290 Fallows, *Breaking the News,* 162, 27.

291 Epstein, *News from Nowhere,* 179, 195.

292 Rosenstiel, *State of the News Media,* 18.

293 John Horn, "Campaign Coverage Avoids Issues," *Lincoln Journal Star,* September 25, 1988. Another survey found that 28 percent of women and 40 percent of men change channels every time during commercial breaks. "Ticker," *Brill's Content,* September 1999, 128.

294 John Eisendrath, "An Eyewitness Account of Local TV News," *Washington Monthly,* September 1986, 21.

295 Michael Deaver, "Sound-Bite Campaigning: TV Made Us Do It," *Washington Post National Weekly Edition,* November 7, 1988, 34.

296 Fred Friendly, quoted on *All Things Considered,* National Public Radio, March 4, 1998.

297 Thomas E. Patterson, *The Vanishing Voter* (New York: Knopf, 2002), 92.

298 Project for Excellence in Journalism, "Changing Newsroom."

299 Lara Logan, quoted in Brian Stelter, "Reporters Say Networks Put Wars on Back Burner," *New York Times,* June 23, 2008, nytimes.com/2008/06/23/business/media/23logan.html?dpc.

300 Graber, *Mass Media,* 244; Doris Graber, *Processing News: How People Tame the Information Tide* (White Plains, N.Y.: Longman, 1984). A 1993 survey concluded that almost half of Americans over sixteen have such limited reading and math skills that they are unfit for most jobs. One task the survey included was to paraphrase a newspaper story. Many people could scan the story but not paraphrase it when they finished it. Paul Gray, "Adding Up the Under-Skilled," *Time,* September 20, 1993, 75. For a critique, claiming that the oligopolistic structure of the media makes it impossible to know if people are getting what they actually want, see McChesney, *Problem of the Media,* 198–202.

301 Reuven Frank, quoted in Neil Hickey, "Money Lust," *Columbia Journalism Review,* July–August 1998, 35.

302 James Poniewozik, "Don't Blame It on Jayson Blair," *Time,* June 9, 2003, 90.

303 Kathleen Hall Jamieson, quoted in Howard Kurtz, "Tuning Out the News," *Washington Post National Weekly Edition,* May 29, 1995, 6; William Raspberry, "Blow-by-Blow Coverage," *Washington Post National Weekly Edition,* November 6, 1995, 29.

304 Michael J. Robinson, "Public Affairs Television and the Growth of Political Malaise," *American Political Science Review* 70 (1976), 409–432; Miller et al., "Type-Set Politics."

305 "Study: Public More Cynical than Media," *Champaign-Urbana News-Gazette,* May 22, 1995.

306 Fallows, *Breaking the News,* 202–203.

307 Cappella and Jamieson, *Spiral of Cynicism.*

308 Fallows, *Breaking the News,* 247.

309 Stephen Earl Bennett, "Trends in Americans' Political Information," *American Politics Quarterly* 17 (October 1989), 422–435; Richard Zoglin, "The Tuned-Out Generation," *Time,* July 9, 1990, 64.

310 Robert N. Entman, *Democracy without Citizens: Media and the Decay of American Politics* (New York: Oxford University Press, 1989), 17.

311 See McChesney, *Problem of the Media,* 96–97.

312 Peters, *How Washington Really Works,* 32.

Chapter 6

1 Andrew S. Natsios, "Race Against Time," *Washington Post National Weekly Edition* (March 3–9, 2008), 27; Kristin Nwazota, "China-Sudan Trade Relations Complicate Darfur Crisis," *News Hour,* April 25, 2006.

2 China is the largest arms supplier to Sudan. In addition, China apparently worries that international intervention in other countries may lead to calls for such intervention in Tibet.

3 Natsios, op. cit., 27.

4 Natsios, op. cit., 55.

5 Natsios, op cit., 56

6 Jeffrey H. Birnbaum, *The Lobbyists: How Influence Peddlers Get Their Way in Washington* (New York: Times Books, 1993), 32.

7 Mark A. Peterson and Jack L. Walker, Jr., "Interest Group Responses to Partisan Change: The Impact of the Reagan Administration upon the National Interest Group System," in *Interest Group Politics,* 2nd ed., eds. Allan J. Cigler and Burdett A. Loomis (Washington, D.C.: CQ Press, 1987), 162.

8 Alexis de Tocqueville, *Democracy in America* (New York: Knopf, 1945), 191. (Originally published 1835.)

9 Gabriel Almond and Sidney Verba, *Civil Culture* (Boston: Little, Brown, 1965), 266–306.

10 David Truman, *The Governmental Process* (New York: Knopf, 1964), 25–26.

11 Ibid., 59.

12 James Q. Wilson, *Political Organizations* (New York: Basic Books, 1973), 198.

13 Graham K. Wilson, *Interest Groups in America* (Oxford: Oxford University Press, 1981), ch. 5; see also Graham K. Wilson, "American Business and Politics," in *Interest Group Politics,* 2nd ed., eds. Cigler and Loomis, 221–235.

14 Kay Lehman Schlozman and John T. Tierney, "More of the State: Washington Pressure Group Activity in a Decade of Change," *Journal of Politics* 45 (1983), 335–356.

15 Christopher H. Foreman Jr., "Grassroots Victim Organizations: Mobilizing for Personal and Public Health," in *Interest Group Politics,* 4th ed., eds. Allan J. Cigler and Burdett A. Loomis (Washington, D.C.: CQ Press, 1994), 33–53.

16 William Brown, "Exchange Theory and the Institutional Impetus for Interest Group Formation," in *Interest Group Politics,* 6th ed., eds. Allan J. Cigler and Burdett A. Loomis (Washington, D.C.: CQ Press, 2002), 313–329; William Brown, "Benefits and Membership: A Reappraisal of Interest Group Activity," *Western Political Quarterly* 29 (1976), 258–273; Terry M. Moe, *The Organization of Interests: Incentives and the Internal Dynamics of Political Interest Groups* (Chicago: University of Chicago Press, 1980).

17 This applies to public, or collective, goods, rather than to private goods available only to the members.

18 Mancur Olson, *The Logic of Collective Action* (Cambridge, Mass.: Harvard University, 1971).

19 Nicholas Babchuk and Ralph V. Thompson, "The Voluntary Associations of Negroes," *American Sociological Review* 27 (1962), 662–665; see also Patricia Klobus-Edwards, John N. Edwards, and David L. Klemmack, "Differences in Social Participation of Blacks and Whites," *Social Forces* 56 (1978), 1035–1052.

20 Robert D. Putnam, *Bowling Alone* (New York: Simon & Schuster, 2000).

21 Richard Stengel, "Bowling Together," *Time,* July 22, 1996, 35.

22 Theda Skocpol, "Associations without Members," *American Prospect,* July–August 1999, 66–73.

23 Mark T. Hayes, "The New Group Universe," in *Interest Group Politics,* 2nd ed., eds. Cigler and Loomis, 133–145.

24 Jack L. Walker, "The Origins and Maintenance of Interest Groups," *American Political Science Review* 77 (June, 1983), pp. 390–406; E. E. Schattschneider, *Semi-Sovereign People* (New York: Holt, Rinehart and Winston, 1960), 118.

25 David S. Broder and Michael Weisskopf, "Finding New Friends on the Hill," *Washington Post National Weekly Edition,* October 3, 1994, 11.

26 Charles E. Lindblom, "The Market as Prison," *Journal of Politics* 44 (1982), 324–336; Michael Genovese, *The Presidential Dilemma: Leadership in the American System* (New York: HarperCollins, 1995).

27 M. Asif Ismail, "Drug Lobby Second to None," The Center for Public Integrity, www.publicintegrity.org/rx/report.aspx?a id=723.

28 Ibid.

29 Jeffrey H. Birnbaum, "Working Both Sides of the Aisle," *Washington Post National Weekly Edition* (March 17–23, 2008), 24.

30 Ibid.

31 *Democracy on Drugs: The Medicare Prescription Drug Bill: A Study in How Government Shouldn't Work.* Common Cause, May 18, 2004, www.commoncause.org/atf/cf/%7BFB3C17E2 CDD1-4DF6-92BE-BD4429893665%7D/ democracy_on_drugs.pdf.

32 "Pharmaceutical Industry Ranks as Most Profitable Industry—Again," *Public Citizen,* April 18, 2002, www.citizen.org/pressroom/release.cfm?ID51088.

33 Unions contributed to their decline by becoming complacent toward the recruitment of new members. Instead, they focused on achieving greater gains for existing members. Harold Myerson, "Organize or Die," *American Prospect,* September 2003, 39–42.

34 Steven Greenhouse, "Union Membership Rose in '98, but Unions' Percentage of Workforce Fell," *New York Times,* January 20, 1999, A22; Paul E. Johnson, "Organized Labor in an Era of Blue-Collar Decline," in *Interest Group Politics,* 3rd ed., eds. Allan J. Cigler and Burdett A. Loomis (Washington, D.C.: CQ Press, 1991), 33–62.

35 Thomas B. Edsall, "Working With the Union You Have," *Washington Post National Weekly Edition,* March 14–20, 2005, 15.

36 Steven Greenhouse, "Report Faults Laws for Slowing Growth of Unions," *New York Times,* October 24, 2000, A14.

37 Jeffrey Goldberg, "Selling Wal-Mart," *New Yorker,* April 2, 2007, 33.

38 Harold Meyerson, "Wal-Mart Comes North," *American Prospect,* April 2007, 28–29.

39 Joshua Green, "The New War Over Wal-Mart," *Atlantic Monthly,* June 2006, 38–44.

40 Steven Greenhouse, "The Most Innovative Figure in Silicon Valley? Maybe This Labor Organizer," *New York Times,* November 14, 1999, 26.

41 Steven Greenhouse, "Graduate Students Push for Union Membership," *New York Times,* May 15, 2001, A18.

42 Information on annual expenditures is found in U.S. Census Bureau, *Statistical Abstract of the United States, 2003* (Washington, D.C.: Government Printing Office, 2003), tab. 812.

43 Andrew S. McFarland, *Common Cause: Lobbying in the Public Interest* (Chatham, N.J.: Chatham House, 1984); see also Andrew S. McFarland, *Public Interest Lobbies: Decision Making on Energy* (Washington, D.C.: American Enterprise Institute, 1976).

44 Ronald G. Shaiko, "More Bang for the Buck: The New Era of Full-Service Public Interest Groups," in *Interest Group Politics,* 3rd ed., eds. Cigler and Loomis, 109.

45 For a discussion of the evolution of NOW and its success in lobbying Congress, see Anne N. Costain and W. Douglas Costain, "The Women's Lobby: Impact of a Movement on Congress," in *Interest Group Politics,* eds. Cigler and Loomis.

46 Richard Morin and Claudia Deane, "The Administration's Right-Hand Women," *Washington Post National Weekly Edition,* May 7, 2001, 12.

47 Eric M. Uslaner, "A Tower of Babel on Foreign Policy," in *Interest Group Politics,* 3rd ed., eds. Cigler and Loomis, 309.

48 Kenneth D. Wald, *Religion and Politics* (New York: St. Martin's Press, 1985), 182–212.

49 Randall Balmer, *God and the White House* (New York: Harper One, 2008), 95–96.

50 Sidney Blumenthal, "Christian Soldiers," *New Yorker,* July 18, 1994, 36.

51 James L. Guth, John C. Green, Lyman A. Jellstedt, and Corwin E. Struck, "Onward Christian Soldiers: Religious Activist Groups in American Politics," in *Interest Group Politics,* 3rd ed., eds. Cigler and Loomis, 57; Charles Levendosky, "Alternative Religious Voice Finally Being Raised," *Lincoln Journal Star,* March 3, 1996, 7B.

52 Michael Lind, "The Right Still Has Religion," *New York Times,* December 9, 2001, sec. 4, 13; Blumenthal, "Christian Soldiers."

53 "Citing 'Moral Crisis,' a Call to Oust Clinton," *New York Times,* October 23, 1998, A1, A8.

54 Richard Parker, "On God and Democrats," *American Prospect,* March 2004, 40.

55 Frank Rich, "The Reverend Falwell's Heavenly Timing," *New York Times,* May 20, 2007, WK13.

56 Sam Tanenhaus, "Down, But Maybe Not Out," *New York Times,* May 20, 2007, WK14.

57 Harold Meyerson, "Target of Opportunism," *Washington Post National Weekly Edition,* March 28–April 3, 2005, 26.

58 David Kuo, *Tempting Faith: An Inside Story of Political Seduction* (New York: Free Press, 2006).

59 Ibid.

60 Levendosky, "Alternative Religious Voice."

61 Lynette Clemetson, "Clergy Group to Counter Conservatives," *New York Times,* November 17, 2003, A15.

62 Christopher J. Bosso, "Adaptation and Change in the Environmental Movement," in *Interest Group Politics,* 3rd ed., eds. Cigler and Loomis, 155–156.

63 Ibid., 162.

64 Katharine Q. Seelye, "Bush Team Still Reversing Environmental Policies," *New York Times,* November 18, 2001, A20.

65 Brent Kendall, "License to Kill," *Washington Monthly,* January–February, 2003, 11–14.

66 John Mintz, "Would Bush Be the NRA's Point Man in the White House?" *Washington Post National Weekly Edition,* May 8, 2000, 14; Mike Doming, "NRA Promises an All-Out Assault on Al Gore's Presidential Campaign," *Lincoln Journal Star,* May 21, 2000, 2A; Thomas B. Edsall, "Targeting Al Gore with $10 Mil-

lion," *Washington Post National Weekly Edition,* May 29, 2000, 11.

[67] Linda Greenhouse, "U.S., in a Shift, Tells Justices Citizens Have a Right to Guns," *New York Times,* May 8, 2002, A1.

[68] Linda Greenhouse, "Justices Rule for Individual Gun Rights," *New York Times,* June 27, 2008, http://www.nytimes.com/2008/06/27/ washington/27scotuscnd.html?_r=1&scp= 2&sq=supreme%20courts%20gun%20rights% 20decision&st=cse&oref=slogin.

[69] Blaine Harden, "The NRA Moves Away from Bush," *Washington Post National Weekly Edition,* January 15–21, 2007, 12.

[70] Robin Toner, "Abortion's Opponents Claim the Middle Ground," *New York Times,* April 25, 2004, sec. 4, 1.

[71] David S. Broder, "Let 100 Single-Issue Groups Bloom," *Washington Post,* January 7, 1979, C1–C2; see also David S. Broder, *The Party's Over: The Failure of Politics in America* (New York: Harper & Row, 1972).

[72] Wilson, *Interest Groups in America,* ch. 4.

[73] Robert Pear, "Lobbyists Seek Special Spin on Federal Bioterrorism Bill," *New York Times,* December 11, 2001, A1, A18.

[74] The president usually has to get congressional approval for budgetary shifts and occasionally for bureaucratic reorganizations.

[75] Lowell Bergman and Jeff Gerth, "Power Trader Tied to Bush Finds Washington All Ears," *New York Times,* May 25, 2001, A1.

[76] Charles Peters, "Tilting at Windmills, " *Washington Monthly,* July–August, 2004, 4.

[77] Sheryl Gay Stolberg, "Bush in Political Hot Spot in Picking an FDA Chief," *New York Times,* February 8, 2002, A17; Sheryl Gay Stolberg, "Deputy Is Appointed to Direct Food and Drug Agency as Impasse Continues," *New York Times,* February 26, 2002, A22.

[78] "Some Funny Facts About D.C.," *Parade Magazine,* March 19, 2006, 25.

[79] And this was in 1986! This admission was reported only because it surfaced during a divorce. Charles Peters, "Tilting at Windmills," *Washington Monthly,* May, 1986, 6, quoting *Washingtonian* magazine, April 1986.

[80] As revealed in the documentary *Sicko.*

[81] Todd S. Purdum, "Go Ahead, Try to Stop K Street," *New York Times,* January 8, 2006, WK 4.

[82] David Segal, "Bob Dole Leads the Cast of Rainmakers," *Washington Post National Weekly Edition,* September 27, 1997, 20.

[83] For an examination of Enron's influence in this process, see Lowell Bergman and Jeff Gerth, "Power Trader Tied to Bush Finds Washington All Ears," *New York Times,* May 25, 2001, A1.

[84] Quote attributed to Lord Acton, a nineteenth-century historian.

[85] Jeffrey H. Birnbaum, "Seeking Influence," *Washington Post National Weekly Edition,* April 30–May 6, 2007, 17.

[86] Diana M. Evans, "Lobbying the Committee: Interest Groups and the House Public Works and Transportation Committee in the Post-

Webster Era," in *Interest Group Polities,* 3rd ed., eds. Cigler and Loomis, 257–276.

[87] Birnbaum, *Lobbyists,* 40.

[88] Purdum, op. cit.

[89] Elizabeth Drew, *Politics and Money: The New Road to Corruption* (New York: Macmillan, 1983), 78.

[90] Ibid.

[91] Tina Daunt, "Hollywood Leans Right, Too," *Los Angeles Times,* November 3, 2006, www.calendarlive.com/printedition/calendar/cl-et-cause3nov03,0,498316,print.story. However, individual contributions, rather than company contributions, went mostly to Democratic candidates.

[92] Samuel Kernell, *Going Public: New Strategies of Presidential Leadership* (Washington, D.C.: CQ Press, 1986), 34.

[93] William P. Browne, *Groups, Interests, and U.S. Public Policy* (Washington, D.C.: Georgetown University Press, 1998), 23.

[94] Richard Harris, "If You Love Your Grass," *New Yorker,* April 20, 1968, 57.

[95] Ibid.

[96] "MoveOn's Big Moment," *Time,* November 24, 2003, 32.

[97] Stephanie Mencimer, *Blocking the Courthouse Door* (New York: Free Press, 2007).

[98] Birnbaum, *Lobbyists,* 40.

[99] The Union of Concerned Scientists. Britain's leading scientific academy drew similar conclusions. "Scientists: ExxonMobil Misleads the Public," *Lincoln Journal Star,* January 4, 2007, 3A.

[100] There have also been charges that ExxonMobil funded scientists who aren't experts in climatology and whose research wasn't reviewed by scholars in the field. Greenpeace, *Denial and Deception: A Chronicle of ExxonMobil's Efforts to Corrupt the Debate on Global Warming* (Washington, D.C.: Greenpeace, 2002).

[101] "Lobbyist Blitzkrieg Criticized," *Lincoln Journal Star,* September 23, 1994.

[102] For many examples, see David Cay Johnston, *Perfectly Legal* (New York: Portfolio/ Penguin, 2003).

[103] Dan Clawson, Alan Neustadt, and Denise Scott, *Money Talks* (New York: Basic Books, 1992), 91.

[104] John Christensen (R-Neb.), from Omaha. [no author] "It Takes Only One Cook to Spoil the Batter," *Time,* July 7, 1997, 18.

[105] E. E. Schattshneider, *Semi-Sovereign People* (New York: Holt, Rinehart and Winston, 1960), 35.

[106] David S. Broder, "Can We Govern?" *Washington Post National Weekly Edition,* January 31, 1994, 23.

[107] Robert Wright, "Hyper Democracy," *Time,* January 23, 1995, 18.

[108] Comment "Reckless Driver," *New Yorker Magazine,* March 8, 2004, 25. Nader may also be the person most responsible for the election of George W. Bush to the presidency, but that's another story.

Chapter 7

[1] Based on information from Peter Nicholas, "In Philadelphia, Its Get out the Money," *Los Angeles Times,* April 11, 2008, online at articles.latimes.com/2008/apr/11/nation/an-street,money11, and Tom Ferrick, "Cash and Carry (the City)," *New York Times,* April 22, 2008, online at www.nytimes.com/2008/04/22/ opinion/22ferrick.html?_r=1&oref=slogin.

[2] E. E. Schattschneider, *Party Government* (New York: Holt, Rinehart and Winston, 1960), 1.

[3] Frank J. Sorauf, *Political Parties in the American System,* 4th ed. (Boston: Little, Brown, 1980).

[4] Maurice Duverger, *Political Parties* (New York: Wiley, 1963). See also Edward R. Tufte, "The Relationship between Seats and Votes in Two-Party Systems," *American Political Science Review* 67 (1973), 540–554.

[5] In a few PR systems, citizens vote for multiple candidates rather than for a party slate.

[6] Robert G. Kaiser, "Hindsight Is 20/20," *Washington Post National Weekly Edition,* February 19, 2001, 11. Similar dynamics cost Gore a victory in New Hampshire.

[7] "Republicans Helping Nader," NewsMax.com, July 12, 2004, www.newsmax.com/archives/ articles/2004/7/11/160540.shtml. This amounted to about $50,000 of the $1 million Nader had raised at the time.

[8] Ralph Nader, "My Untold Story," *Brill's Content,* February 2001.

[9] *CQ Weekly,* January 12, 2002, 136; *CQ Weekly,* January 2, 2004, 53.

[10] Frank J. Sorauf, *Money in American Elections* (Glenview, Ill.: Scott, Foresman, 1988), 121–153; Paul Herrnson, *Party Campaigning in the 1980s* (Cambridge, Mass.: Harvard University Press, 1988).

[11] Janet Hook, "Meet the Powers Behind the Democrats' Strategy," *Los Angeles Times,* July 5, 2006, www.latimes.com/news/nationworld/ nation/la-na-dems5jul05,0,1314589,print.story?c.

[12] Ibid.

[13] Richard Hofstadter, *The Idea of the Party System: The Rise of Legitimate Opposition in the United States, 1780–1840* (Berkeley: University of California Press, 1969).

[14] Theodore Lowi, *The Personal President* (Ithaca, N.Y.: Cornell University Press, 1985), 35.

[15] James MacGregor Burns, *The Vineyard of Liberty* (New York: Knopf, 1982).

[16] Property requirements continued to exist in a few places until the 1850s.

[17] Instead of the party's members in Congress.

[18] In 1820, there had been around 1.2 million free white men over twenty-five years of age; by 1840, there were 3.2 million white men of over the age of twenty.

[19] When Harvard students established a charity for poor people in the city, they got few takers because the machine was already providing welfare for these people, so they shut down the charity.

20 William L. Riordon, *Plunkitt of Tammany Hall* (New York: E.P. Dutton, 1963), 28.

21 They also were allowed to dispense jobs with private companies, such as streetcar, gas, electric, and phone companies, that wanted to curry favor with local officials.

22 Milton L. Rakove, *Don't Make No Waves, Don't Back No Losers* (Bloomington: Indiana University Press, 1975), 112.

23 Benjamin Ginsberg and Martin Shefter, *Politics by Other Means* (New York: Viking, 1999), 19.

24 Ibid.

25 When independent newspapers emerged as profit-making businesses, the party papers declined. But the independent papers tended to favor one side or the other for many years as a way to attract and retain readers used to the advocacy of party papers.

26 Walter Dean Burnham, *Critical Elections and the Mainstream of American Politics* (New York: Norton, 1970); Helmut Norpoth and Jerrold Rusk, "Partisan Dealignment in the American Electorate," *American Political Science Review,* 76 (1982), 522–537; David W. Rhode, "The Fall Elections: Realignment and Dealignment," *Chronicle of Higher Education,* December 14, 1994, 131–132.

27 National Election Studies, Center for Political Studies, University of Michigan, 1952–2000 (www.umich.edu/nes). Although many people who claim to be independent regularly vote for candidates of the same party, their unwillingness to identify themselves as party members indicates some detachment from the party.

28 Larry M. Bartels, "Partisanship and Voting, 1952–1996," *American Journal of Political Science* 44 (January 2000), 35–50.

29 Everett Carill Ladd, *Where Have All the Voters Gone?* (New York: Norton, 1982).

30 Martin P. Wallenberg, *The Rise of Candidate-Centered Politics* (Cambridge, Mass.: Harvard University Press, 1991).

31 Thomas E. Patterson, *The Vanishing Voter* (New York: Knopf, 2002).

32 For a discussion of party influence on voting in Congress, see William R. Shaffer, *Party and Ideology in the United States Congress* (Lanham, Md.: University Press of America, 1980).

33 Bruce I. Oppenheimer, "The Importance of Elections in a Strong Congressional Era," in *Do Elections Matter?* eds. Benjamin Ginsberg and Alan Stone (Armonk, N.Y.: Sharpe, 1996), 120–138.

34 Mary Lunn F. Jones, "Rock and a Hard Place," *American Prospect,* June 2003, 18–19.

35 Dan Carney, "As Hostilities Rage on the Hill, Partisan-Vote Rate Soars," *Congressional Quarterly Weekly Report,* January 27, 1996, 199–200.

36 In this realignment, the Republicans went from a bare majority to an overwhelming majority, so they remained the dominant party.

37 James L. Sundquist, *Dynamics of the Party System: Alignment and Realignment of Political Parties in the United States* (Washington, D.C.: Brookings Institution, 1973).

38 Kevin Phillips, *The Emerging Republican Majority* (New York: Doubleday, 1969).

39 Patrick Reddy, "Why It's Got to Be All or Nothing," *Washington Post National Weekly Edition,* October 18, 1999, 23.

40 Tali Mendelberg, *The Race Card* (Princeton, N.J.: Princeton University Press, 2001).

41 Ibid., 97.

42 Ibid., 3.

43 Thomas F. Shaller, "Forget the South," *Washington Post National Weekly Edition,* November 24, 2003, 21.

44 Thomas B. Edsall, "The Fissure Running through the Democratic Party," *Washington Post National Weekly Edition,* June 6, 1994, 11.

45 John R. Petrocik and Frederick T. Steeper, "The Political Landscape in 1988," *Public Opinion,* September–October 1987, 41–44; Helmut Norpoth, "Party Realignment in the 1980s," *Public Opinion Quarterly,* 51 (1987), 376–390.

46 Edsall, "Fissure," 11.

47 Thomas B. Edsall, "The Shifting Sands of America's Political Parties," *Washington Post National Weekly Edition,* April 9, 2001, 11.

48 Ibid.

49 According to Pew Research Center surveys. Ross Douthat, "Crises of Faith," *The Atlantic,* July–August, 2007, 38.

50 Quoted in Robert B. Reich, "Deepening the Religious Divide," *American Prospect,* May, 2005, 40.

51 Kevin Phillips, "All Eyes on Dixie," *American Prospect,* February, 2004, 24.

52 Gallup Poll, May 12, 2006.

53 Gebe Martinez and Mary Agnes Carey, "Erasing the Gender Gap Tops Republican Playbook," *CQ Weekly,* March 6, 2004, 565.

54 Mary Agnes Carey, "Democrats Want Women: Party Targets Single Female Voters," *CQ Weekly,* March 6, 2004, 567.

55 Robert A. Dahl, *How Democratic Is the American Constitution?* (New Haven, Conn.: Yale University Press, 2003), 30.

Chapter 8

1 Bill Bishop, *The Big Sort* (Boston: Houghton Mifflin, 2008).

2 William H. Flanigan, *Political Behavior of the American Electorate,* 2nd ed. (Boston: Allyn and Bacon, 1972), 13. See also Chilton Williamson, *American Suffrage from Property to Democracy 1760–1860* (Princeton, N.J.: Princeton University Press, 1960).

3 James MacGregor Burns, *Vineyard of Liberty* (New York: Knopf, 1982), 363.

4 August Meier and Elliot M. Rudwick, *From Plantation to Ghetto: An Interpretive History of American Negroes* (New York: Hill & Wang, 1966), 69.

5 Robert Darcy, Susan Welch, and Janet Clark, *Women, Elections, and Representation* (Lincoln: University of Nebraska Press, 1994).

6 Ralph G. Neas, "The Long Shadow of Jim Crow: Voter Intimidation and Suppression in America Today," *People for the American Way Foundation,* August 2004, or online at www .naacp.org/inc/pdf/jimcrow.pdf.

7 Grandfather clause: *Guinn* v. *United States,* 238 U.S. 347 (1915); white primary: *Smith* v. *Allwright,* 321 U.S. 649 (1944).

8 Data on black and white voter registration in the southern states are from the *Statistical Abstract of the United States* (Washington, D.C.: U.S. Bureau of the Census, various years).

9 California, Florida, Michigan, New Hampshire, New York, and South Dakota.

10 Richard J. Timpone, "Mass Mobilization or Government Intervention? The Growth of Black Registration in the South," *Journal of Politics* 57 (1995), 425–442.

11 *City of Mobile* v. *Bolden,* 446 U.S. 55 (1980).

12 *Thornburg* v. *Gingles,* 478 U.S. 301 (1986).

13 Bob Benenson, "Arduous Ritual of Redistricting Ensures More Racial Diversity," *Congressional Quarterly Weekly Report,* October 24, 1992, 3385. For a very thorough review of the legal and behavioral impact of the Voting Rights Act, see Joseph Viteritti, "Unapportioned Justice: Local Elections, Social Science, and the Evolution of the Voting Rights Act," *Cornell Journal of Law and Public Policy* (1994), 210–270.

14 *Shaw* v. *Reno,* 125 L.Ed.2d 511, 113 S.Ct. 2816 (1993); *Miller* v. *Johnson,* 132 L.Ed.2d 762, 115 S.Ct. 2475 (1995); *Bush* v. *Vera,* 135 L.Ed.2d 248, 116 S.Ct. 1941 (1996).

15 Darcy et al., *Women, Elections, and Representation.*

16 Speech in 1867 by George Williams cited in Peter Pappas's "Re-defining the Role of Women in Industrial America" at www.peterpappas.com /journals/industry/women3.pdf.

17 The discussion in this paragraph is drawn largely from Lois W. Banner, *Women in Modern America: A Brief History* (New York: Harcourt Brace Jovanovich, 1974), 88–90; Glenn Firebaugh and Kevin Chen, "Vote Turnout of Nineteenth Amendment Women," *American Journal of Sociology* 100 (1995), 972–996.

18 See Pamela Paxton, *Women, Politcs, and Power.* (Los Angeles: Pine Forge Press, 2007), especially pp. 38–43.

19 Alabama, Florida, Virginia, and Kentucky.

20 Nicholas Thompson, "Locking up the Vote: Disenfranchisement of Former Felons was the Real Crime in Florida," *Washington Monthly* (January–February 2001), 18.

21 "Groups Report Progress against Laws Banning Felons from Voting," *Lincoln Journal Star,* June 22, 2005, 4a.

22 Thompson, ibid., 20.

23 Tom Fiedler, "The Perfect Storm," in *Overtime!: The Election 2000 Thriller,* ed. Larry J. Sabato (New York: Longman, 2002), 11.

24 Liz Krueger, "Budgeting for Another Florida," *New York Times,* February 8, 2004, 14.

25 Dale Keiger, "E-lective Alarm," *Johns Hopkins Magazine,* February 2004, 50.

26 See an up-to-date list of state laws on www .verifiedvotingfoundation.org/article.php?id=6430.

The website www.votersunite.org/electionproblems .asp contains a tally of problems reported with electronic machines.

27 Sasha Abramsky, *Conned: How Millions Went to Prison, Lost the Vote, and Helped Send George W. Bush to the White House* (New York: New Press, 2006). This book is partly anecdotal but does point out the huge numbers of people disfranchised by both laws and intimidation.

28 See www.Tallahassee.com/mld/tallahassee/ news/9202503.htm.

29 Richard Jensen, "American Election Campaigns: A Theoretical and Historical Typology," paper delivered at the 1968 Midwest Political Science Association Meeting, quoted in Walter Dean Burnham, *Critical Elections and the Mainsprings of American Politics* (New York: Norton, 1970), 73.

30 Frances Fox Piven and Richard A. Cloward, *Why Americans Don't Vote* (New York: Pantheon Books, 1988), 30.

31 These examples are from the editorial, "Barriers to Student Voting," *New York Times,* September 28, 2004, 26.

32 Part of the explanation for declining voting rates is that the number of citizens who are ineligible to vote has increased, which depresses voter-turnout statistics. Immigrants, other noncitizens, and, in some states, convicted felons are not eligible to vote. When those individuals are removed from the calculation of proportion voting, the proportion voting is increased by about 5 points; and most of the turnout decline occurred in the 1960s. See Michael P. McDonald and Samuel Popkin, "The Myth of the Vanishing Voter," *American Political Science Review* 95 (2001), 963–974.

33 Alan Wolfe, "The Race's Real Winner: Democracy," *Washington Post National Weekly Edition,* May 19–25, 2008, 25.

34 *Statistical Abstract of the United States 2006,* tab. 406.

35 Daniel J. Elazar, *American Federalism: A View from the States* (New York: Crowell, 1972); *Statistical Abstract of the United States 2006,* tab. 406.

36 Norman H. Nie, Sidney Verba, Henry Brady, Kay Lehman Schlozman, and Jane Junn, "Participation in America: Continuity and Change," paper presented at the Midwest Political Science Association, April 1988. The standard work, though now dated, on American political participation is Sidney Verba and Norman H. Nie, *Participation in America: Political Democracy and Social Equality* (New York: Harper & Row, 1972).

37 Piven and Cloward, *Why Americans Don't Vote,* 162; *Statistical Abstract of the United States 2001,* tab.401; Frances Fox Piven and Richard A. Cloward, *Why Americans Still Don't Vote: And Why Politicians Want It That Way* (Boston: Beacon Press, 2001).

38 G. Bingham Powell, "American Voter Turnout in Comparative Perspective," *American Political Science Review* 80 (1986), 30; Piven and Cloward, *Why Americans Don't Vote,* 119; Arend Lijphart, "Unequal Participation: Democracy's Unresolved Dilemma," *American Political Science Review* 91 (1997), 1–14.

39 Henry Brady,Sidney Verba, and Kay Lehman Schlozman, "Beyond SES: A Resource Model of Political Participation,"*American Political Science Review* 89 (June 1995), 271–294.

40 Nie et al., "Participation in America: Continuity and Change"; Verba and Nie, *Participation in America: Political Democracy and Social Equality.*

41 Steven Hill and Rashad Robinson, "Demography vs. Democracy: Young People Feel Left Out of the Political Process," *Los Angeles Times,* November 5, 2002, 2. Posted by the Youth Vote Coalition, www.youthvote.org/news/ newsdetail. cfm?newsid56. The survey cited was conducted by Harvard University.

42 Eric Plutzer, "Becoming a Habitual Voter: Inertia, Resources, and Growth in Young Adulthood," *American Political Science Review* 96 (2002), 41–56.

43 Anna Greenberg, "New Generation, New Politics," *American Prospect,* October 1, 2003, A3.

44 *Time Magazine,* February 11, 2008, p. 36.

45 Paul Allen Beck and M. Kent Jennings, "Political Periods and Political Participation," *American Political Science Review* 73 (1979), 737–750; Nie et al., "Participation in America: Continuity and Change."

46 George F. Will, "In Defense of Nonvoting," *Newsweek,* October 10, 1983, 96.

47 Richard Morin, "The Dog Ate My Forms, and, Well, I Couldn't Find a Pen," *Washington Post National Weekly Edition,* November 5, 1990, 38.

48 Lawrence R. Jacobs and Robert Y. Shapiro, *Politicians Don't Pander: Political Manipulation and the Loss of Democratic Responsiveness* (Chicago: University of Chicago Press, 2000).

49 Emmett H. Buell Jr. and Lee Sigelman, *Attack Politics: Negativity in Presidential Campaigns Since 1960.* (Lawrence: University of Kansas Press, 2008), especially 246ff. But see John Geer, *In Defense of Negativity: Attack Ads in Presidential Campaigns.* (Chicago: University of Chicago Press, 2006), who found increased negativity in television ads.

50 Richard Lau, Lee Sigelman, Caroline Heldman, and Paul Babbitt, "The Effects of Negative Political Advertisements," *American Political Science Review* 93 (1999), 851–875; Steven E. Finkel and John Geer, "A Spot Check: Casting Doubt on the Demobilizing Effect of Attack Advertising," *American Journal of Political Science* 42 (1998), 573–595. Research on turnout is found in Stephen Ansolabehere and Shanto Iyengar, *Going Negative* (New York: Free Press, 1996). In her book *Packaging the Presidency: A History and Criticism of Presidential Campaign Advertising* (New York: Oxford University Press, 1984), Kathleen Jamieson also argues that there are checks on misleading advertising, but later ("Is the Truth Now Irrelevant in Presidential Campaigns?"), she notes that these checks do not always work well. See Jamieson, *Dirty Politics: Deception, Distraction, and Democracy* (New York: Oxford University Press, 1992).

51 Thomas E. Patterson, *The Vanishing Voter* (New York: Knopf, 2002); Curtis B. Gans; "The Empty Ballot Box," *Public Opinion* 1 (September–October 1978), 54–57; Curtis Gans, quoted in

Jack Germond and Jules Witcover, "Listen to the Voters—and Nonvoters," *Minneapolis Star Tribune,* November 26, 1988. This effect was foreshadowed by Michael J. Robinson, "American Political Legitimacy in an Era of Electronic Journalism," in *Television as a Social Force: New Approaches to TV Criticism,* eds. Douglass Cater and Richard Adler (New York: Praeger, 1975). See also Austin Ranney, *Channels of Power: The Impact of Television on American Politics* (New York: Basic Books, 1983); and Richard Boyd, "The Effect of Election Calendars on Voter Turnout," paper presented at the Annual Meeting of the Midwest Political Science Association, April 1987, Chicago.

52 Boyd, "The Effect of Election Calendars on Voter Turnout," 43. See Piven and Cloward, *Why Americans Don't Vote,* 196–197, for illustrations of these kinds of informal barriers, and Piven and Cloward, *Why Americans Still Don't Vote: And Why Politicians Want It That Way,* for further examples.

53 Ibid.

54 "Numbers," *Time* (May 15, 2006), 17.

55 Anthony Downs, *An Economic Theory of Democracy* (New York: Harper, 1957).

56 Morin, "The Dog Ate My Forms, and, Well, I Couldn't Find a Pen."

57 Kay Lehman Schlozman, Sidney Verba, and Henry Brady, "Participation's Not a Paradox: The View from American Activists," *British Journal of Political Science* 25 (1995), 1–36.

58 Ruy Texeira, *Why Americans Don't Vote: Turnout Decline in the United States 1960– 1984* (Boulder, Colo.: Greenwood, 1987); Ruy Texeira, *The Disappearing American Voter* (Washington, D.C.: Brookings Institute, 1992); and Peverill Squire, Raymond Wolfinger, and David Glass, "Residential Mobility and Voter Turnout," *American Political Science Review* 81 (1987), 45–66.

59 Jennifer Joan Lee, "Pentagon Blocks Site for Voters Outside U.S.," *International Herald Tribune,* September 20, 2004. The site was run by the Pentagon for both military and civilian overseas citizens.

60 More recent studies of turnout include Richard J. Timpone, "Structure, Behavior and Voter Turnout in the United States," *American Political Science Review* 92 (1998), 145–158; Henry Brady, Sidney Verba, and Kay Lehman Schlozman, "Beyond SES: A Resource Model of Political Participation," *American Political Science Review* 89 (1995), 271–294.

61 Bill Winders, "The Roller Coaster of Class Conflict: Class Segments, Mass Mobilization, and Voter Turnout in the United States, 1840– 1996," *Social Forces* (March 1999), 833–862. For a review of this literature, see John Petrocik, "Voter Turnout and Electoral Preference," in *Elections in America,* ed. Kay Lehman Schlozman (Boston: Allen & Unwin, 1987). See also Bernard Grofman, Guillermo Owen, and Christian Collet, "Rethinking the Partisan Effects of Higher Turnout," *Public Choice* 99 (1999), 357–376.

62 Tom Hamburger and Peter Wallsten, "Parties Are Tracking Your Habits," *Los Angeles Times,* July 24, 2005: www.latimes.com/news/ nationworld/nation/lanarncdnc24jul24,0,535024 ,full.story

63 Kim Quaile Hill, Jan Leighley, and Angela Hinton-Anderson, "Lower-Class Mobilization and Policy Linkage in the U.S. States," *American Journal of Political Science* 39 (1995), 75–86.

64 Mark Gray and Miki Caul, "Declining Voter Turnout in Advanced Industrial Democracies, 1950 to 1997," *Comparative Political Studies* 33 (November 2000), 1091–1122.

65 Piven and Cloward, *Why Americans Don't Vote,* 17.

66 Ibid.

67 Raymond E. Wolfinger and Steven J. Rosenstone, *Who Votes?* (New Haven, Conn.: Yale University Press, 1980), tab. 6-1.

68 Steven J. Rosenstone and Raymond E. Wolfinger, "The Effect of Registration Laws on Voter Turnout," *American Political Science Review* 72 (1978), 22–45; Glenn Mitchell and Christopher Wlezien, "Voter Registration Laws and Turnout, 1972–1982," paper presented at the Annual Meeting of the Midwest Political Science Association, April 1989, Chicago; Mark J. Fenster, "The Impact of Allowing Day of Registration Voting on Turnout in U.S. Elections from 1960 to 1992," *American Politics Quarterly* 22 (1994), 74–87.

69 Kim Quaile Hill and Jan E. Leighley, "Racial Diversity, Voter Turnout, and Mobilizing Institutions in the United States," *American Politics Quarterly* 27 (1999), 275–295.

70 Editorial, "Block the Vote," *New York Times,* May 30, 2006.

71 Piven and Cloward, *Why Americans Don't Vote,* 230–231.

72 Stephen Knack, "Does 'Motor Voter' Work?" *Journal of Politics* 57 (1995), 796–811.

73 Michael Martinez and David Hill, "Did Motor Voter Work?" *American Political Quarterly* 27 (1999), 296–315; Piven and Cloward, *Why Americans Still Don't Vote: And Why Politicians Want It That Way.*

74 Jo Becker, "Voters May Have Their Say before Election Day," *Washington Post,* August 26, 2004, A01.

75 Texas, Minnesota, Louisiana, and Missouri are the only states west of the Mississippi not allowing unrestricted absentee voting; Florida, North Carolina, Vermont, and Maine are the only states east of the Mississippi who do. See Michael Moss, "Parties See New Promise When Ballot Is in the Mail," *New York Times,* August 22, 2004, 12; R. W. Apple Jr., "Kerry Pins Hopes in Iowa on Big Vote from Absentees," *New York Times,* September 28, 2004, 18.

76 These examples are drawn from Raymond Wolfinger, Benjamin Highton, and Megan Mullin, "How Postregistration Laws Affect the Turnout of Blacks and Latinos," paper presented at the 2003 Annual Meeting of the American Political Science Association, Philadelphia, Pennsylvania, August 28–31.

77 Diane Feldman and Cornell Belcher, "Democracy at Risk, the 2004 Election in Ohio," report for the Democratic National Committee found online at a9.g.akamai.net/7/9/8082/v001/www.democrats.org/pdfs/ohvrireport/fullreport.pdf.

78 Miles Rapoport, "The Democracy We Deserve," *Prospect,* January 2005, A7.

79 David S. Broder, "Voting's Neglected Scandal," *Washington Post,* June 26, 2008, A19.

80 The following discussion draws heavily upon John H. Aldrich, *Before the Convention: Strategies and Choices in Presidential Nomination Campaigns* (Chicago: University of Chicago Press, 1980).

81 Ibid. See also David W. Rohde, "Risk Bearing and Progressive Ambition: The Case of Members of the United States House of Representatives," *American Journal of Political Science* 23 (1979), 1–26.

82 Quoted in Audrey A. Haynes, Paul-Henri Gurian, and Stephen M. Nichols, "The Role of Candidate Spending in Presidential Nomination Campaigns," *Journal of Politics* 59 (February 1997), 213–225.

83 "The Fall Campaign," *Newsweek Election Extra,* November–December 1984, 88.

84 Hendrick Hertzberg, "This Must Be the Place," *New Yorker,* January 31, 2000, 36–39.

85 B. Drummond Ayres Jr., "It's Taking Care of Political Business," *New York Times,* July 18, 1999, 22.

86 Katharine Q. Seelye and Marjorie Connelly, "Republican Delegates Leaning to Right of G.O.P. and the Nation," *New York Times,* August 29, 2004, 13.

87 Gerald M. Pomper and Susan S. Lederman, *Elections in America: Control and Influence in Democratic Politics* (New York: Longman, 1980), ch. 7.

88 Quote from Gerald M. Pomper in Adam Nagourney, "What Boston Can Do for Kerry," *New York Times,* July 18, 2004, 5.

89 David Carr, "Whose Convention Is It? Reporters Outnumber Delegates 6 to 1" *New York Times,* July 27, 2004, E1.

90 As told by Gail Collins, "Vice is Nice," *New York Times* June 21, 2008.

91 Lee Sigelman and Paul Wahlbeck, "The 'Veep-stakes': Strategic Choice in Presidential Running Mate Selection," *American Political Science Review* 94 (1997), 855–864.

92 Ibid.

93 Ibid.

94 Robert L. Dudley and Ronald B. Rapaport, "Vice-Presidential Candidates and the Home State Advantage: Playing Second Banana at Home and on the Road," *American Journal of Political Science* 33 (1989), 537–540.

95 *New York Times,* July 11, 2004, 16.

96 Collins, "Vice is Nice."

97 Daron Shaw, "A Study of Presidential Campaign Event Effects from 1952 to 1992," *Journal of Politics* 61 (1999), 387–422.

98 See *Congressional Quarterly,* July 23, 1988, 2015; Thomas M. Holbrook, "Campaigns, National Conditions and U.S. Presidential Elections," *American Journal of Political Science* 38 (1994), 973–998.

99 From a report by FairVote and quoted in Michael Waldman, "Majority Rule at Last," *The Washington Monthly,* April 2008, 20.

100 www.fivethirtyeight.com

101 Benjamin I. Page and Richard A. Brody, "Policy Voting and the Electoral Process: The Vietnam War Issue," *American Political Science Review* 66 (1972), 979–995.

102 The discussion of the functions of the media relies heavily on the excellent summary found in Stephen Ansolabehere, Roy Behr, and Shanto Iyengar, "Mass Media and Elections," *American Politics Quarterly* 19 (1991), 109–139.

103 Kathleen Hall Jamieson, "Ad Wars," *Washington Post National Weekly Edition,* October 4, 2004, 22.

104 L. Marvin Overby and Jay Barth," Radio Advertising in American Political Campaigns," *American Politics Research* 34 (July, 2006): 451–478.

105 Robert MacNeil, *People Machine: The Influence of Television on American Politics* (New York: Harper & Row, 1968), 182.

106 Elisabeth Bumiller, "Selling Soup, Wine and Reagan," *Washington Post National Weekly Edition,* November 5, 1984, 6–8.

107 Jim Rutenberg, "Seeking Voters through Habits in TV Viewing," *New York Times,* July 18, 2004, 1.

108 Data are drawn from Rutenberg, ibid. See Thomas E. Mann, "Elections and Change in Congress," in *The New Congress,* eds. Thomas E. Mann and Norman J. Ornstein (Washington, D.C.: American Enterprise Institute for Public Policy Research, 1981), 32–54; David Mayhew, *Congress: The Electoral Connection* (New Haven, Conn.: Yale University Press, 1974); Glenn R. Parker and Roger H. Davidson, "Why Do Americans Love Their Congressmen So Much More Than Their Congress?" *Legislative Studies Quarterly* 4 (1979), 53–62.

109 Daron Shaw, "The Methods behind the Madness: Presidential Electoral College Strategies, 1988–1996," *Journal of Politics* 61 (1999), 893–913, shows the evolution of advertising focus during these three elections.

110 Through early summer, about three-fourths of Bush's were negative, whereas only one-fourth of Kerry's were. As election day drew nearer, the proportion of negative ads increased. Dana Milbank and Jim VandeHei, "The Mean Season Is in Full Bloom," *Washington Post National Weekly Edition,* June 7, 2004, 13. Both campaigns agreed the figures were accurate.

111 John Theilmann and Allen Wilhite, "Campaign Tactics and the Decision to Attack," *Journal of Politics* 60 (1998), 1050–1062.

112 The study of negative advertising research was done by Richard Lau, Lee Sigelman, Caroline Heldman, and Paul Babbitt, "The Effects of Negative Political Advertisements," *American Political Science Review* 93 (1999), 851–875.

113 Democratic consultants are more likely to find negative advertising distasteful than Republican consultants. However, this does not necessarily translate into partisan differences in use.

114 Paul Taylor, "Pigsty Politics," *Washington Post National Weekly Edition,* February 13, 1989, 6.

115 See Seth Borenstein, "Negative Political Ads Produce 'Shocking' Reactions on Brains," *Lincoln Journal Star,* November 4, 2006, p. 6a. The article reported research of Shanto Iyengar,

Going Negative: How Political Advertisements Shrink and Polarize the Electorate.

116 Howard Kurtz, "The Ad-Slingers in the TV Corral," *Washington Post,* October 10, 2004, A06.

117 Ansolabehere and Iyengar, *Going Negative.*

118 Jamieson, *Packaging the Presidency.*

119 Eileen Shields West, "Give 'Em Hell These Days Is a Figure of Speech," *Smithsonian* (October 1988), 149–151. The editorial was from the *Connecticut Courant.*

120 Charles Paul Freund, "But Then, Truth Has Never Been Important," *Washington Post National Weekly Edition,* November 7, 1988, 29.

121 Ibid., 29.

122 Thomas E. Patterson, *The Mass Media Election: How Americans Choose Their President* (New York: Praeger, 1980), 3.

123 Martin Schram, *The Great American Video Game: Presidential Politics in the Television Age* (New York: Morrow, 1987).

124 Mike Allen, "Bush's Isolation from Reporters Could Be a Hindrance," *Washington Post,* October 8, 2004, A09.

125 Daron Shaw, "A Study of Presidential Campaign Event Effects from 1952 to 1992," *Journal of Politics* 61 (May, 1999), 387–422, reports on a systematic study of campaign events and their impact on the elections.

126 Adam Nagourney, "Internet Injects Sweeping Change into U.S. Politics," *New York Times,* April 2, 2006, 1ff.

127 Brian Stelter, "Finding Political News Online, the Young Pass It On," *New York Times,* March 27, 2008, www.nytimes.com/2008/03/27/us/politics/27voters.html.

128 David Perlmutter, "Political Blogs: The New Iowa?" *Chronicle of Higher Education,* May 26, 2006, B6.

129 These data on Internet use are from the Pew Foundation's Internet and American Life Project, "The Internet and the 2008 Election," June 15, 2008, and found on their website, www.pewinternet.org.

130 Waldman, "Majority Rule at Last," 18.

131 Ibid.

132 Robert Dahl, *How Democratic Is the American Constitution?* (New Haven, Conn.: Yale University Press, 2001).

133 Waldman, op. cit.

134 Akhil Reed Amar, *America's Constitution: A Biography* (New York: Random House, 2005).

135 Ibid.

136 Paul Abramson, John H. Aldrich, and David Rohde, *Change and Continuity in the 2000 Elections* (Washington, D.C.: CQ Press, 2003); Paul Abramson, John H. Aldrich, and David Rohde, *Change and Continuity in the 2004 and 2006 Elections* (Washington, D.C.: CQ Press, 2007).

137 Ibid.

138 In recent elections, the percentages able to identify correctly general differences between the major party candidates varied between 26 and 55 percent.

139 Abramson, Aldrich, and Rohde, *Change and Continuity, 2004 and 2006.*

140 Ibid.

141 Abramson, Aldrich, and Rohde, *Change and Continuity in the 2004 and 2006 Elections.* However, of those who knew where the candidates stood on abortion, 19 percent of those who would not allow abortion under any conditions still voted for Kerry, and 26 percent of those who thought abortion should be a matter of personal choice voted for Bush, who wants to outlaw abortion.

142 Morris Fiorina, *Retrospective Voting in American National Elections* (New Haven, Conn.: Yale University Press, 1981).

143 Edward R. Tufte, *Political Control of the Economy* (Princeton, N.J.: Princeton University Press, 1978); Douglas Hibbs, "The Mass Public and Macroeconomic Performance," *American Journal of Political Science* 23 (1979), 705–731; John Hibbing and John Alford, "The Electoral Impact of Economic Conditions: Who Is Held Responsible," *American Journal of Political Science* 25 (1981), 423–439.

144 Quoted in Alan M. Dershowitz, *Supreme Injustice: How the High Court Hijacked Election 2000* (New York: Oxford University Press, 2001), 25.

145 Hendrik Hertzberg, "Up for the Count," *New Yorker,* December 18, 2000, 41.

146 Kosuke Imai and Gary King, "Did Illegally Counted Overseas Absentee Ballots Decide the 2000 U.S. Presidential Election?" available at gking.Harvard.edu.

147 Ibid.

148 David Barstow and Don Van Natta Jr., "How Bush Took Florida: Mining the Overseas Absentee Vote," *New York Times,* July 15, 2001, available at www.nytimes.com/2001/07/15/www.national/15ball.

149 Ibid.

150 Jonathan Wand, Kenneth Shotts, Jasjeet Sekhon, Walter R. Mebane Jr., Michael Herron, and Henry Brady, "The Butterfly Did It: The Aberrant Vote for Buchanan in Palm Beach," *American Political Science Review* 95 (2001), 793–809. They examined the Palm Beach Buchanan vote in relation to all other counties in the United States compared to the absentee ballots (which did not use the butterfly format) in Palm Beach County, precinct-level data, and individual ballots.

151 Tom Fiedler, "The Perfect Storm," in *Overtime! The Election 2000 Thriller,* ed. Larry J. Sabato (New York: Longman, 2002), 8.

152 Imai and King, 3.

153 Jimmy Carter, quoted from *NPR* in Kéllia Ramares's special report "House Strikes Truth from the Record," *Online Journal,* July 23, 2004. You can find the full Ramares article at www.onlinejournal.com/Special_Reports/072304Ramares/072304ramares.html.

154 Andrew Gelman, Boris Shor, Joseph Bafumi, and David Park, "Rich State, Poor State, Red State, Blue State: What's the Matter with Connecticut?" abstract and slides can be found at home.uchicago.edu/~bshor/papers. A summary can be found at harrisschool.uchicago.edu/

about/publications/HarrisView/ spring06/shor.asp.

155 Alan Abramowitz, "Terrorism, Gay Marriage, and Incumbency: Explaining the Republican Victory in the 2004 Presidential Election," *The Forum* 2 (4), 2004. Found online at the Berkeley Electronic Press, www.bepress.com/forum.

156 For example, see Norman J. Ornstein and Thomas E. Mann, eds., *The Permanent Campaign and Its Future* (Washington, D.C.: American Enterprise Institute and the Brookings Institution, 2000).

157 Data on voters' issue preferences on Election Day can be found in the article "41% Said National Security Issues Most Important," *Rasmussen Reports,* November 2, 2004 at www.rasmussenreports.com/Issue%20Clusters_Election%20Night.htm.

158 Editorial, "A Polarized Nation?" *Washington Post,* November 14, 2004, 6. Several of these ideas were summarized nicely in this article.

159 Benjamin I. Page and Robert Y. Shapiro, "Effects of Public Opinion on Policy," *American Political Science Review* 77 (1983), 175–190.

160 Arthur Schlesinger Jr., *Wall Street Journal,* December 5, 1986. But see also Jacobs and Shapiro, *Politicians Don't Pander.*

Chapter 9

1 Adam Nagourney and Jeff Zeleny, "Obama Foregoes Public Funds in a First for Major Candidate," *New York Times* (June 20, 2008), www.nytimes.com/2008/06/20/us/politics/20obamacnd.html?_r=1&hp&oref=slogin.

2 Matt Bai, "Promises to Keep," *New York Times Sunday Magazine,* July 13, 2008, 12.

3 Jimmy Breslin, *How the Good Guys Finally Won: Notes from an Impeachment Summer* (New York: Ballantine, 1974), 14.

4 Federal Election Commission Report, www.fec.gov/press/press2005/20050203pressum/20050203pressum.html.

5 Robert E. Mutch, "Three Centuries of Campaign Finance Law," in *A User's Guide to Campaign Finance Reform,* ed. Gerald C. Lubenow (Lanham, Md.: Rowman & Littlefield, 2001).

6 Congressional Quarterly, *Dollar Politics,* 3rd ed. (Washington, D.C.: CQ Press, 1982), 3.

7 Haynes Johnson, "Turning Government Jobs into Gold," *Washington Post National Weekly Edition,* May 12, 1986, 6–7.

8 Richard Lacayo, "Fighting the Fat Cats," *Time* July 3, 2006, 71.

9 Quoted in Richard Hofstadter, *The American Political Tradition* (New York: Vintage, 1958), 165.

10 Congressional Quarterly, *Dollar Politics,* 3.

11 Larry J. Sabato, *Feeding Frenzy* (New York: Free Press, 1991).

12 Kevin Phillips, "How Wealth Defines Power," *American Prospect,* Summer 2003, A9. The U.S. Constitution defines a quorum as a majority of senators currently in office.

[13] Digital History, *Hypertext History*, "The Progressive Era," October 30, 2004, www.digitalhistory.uh.edu/database/hyper_titles.cfm. The history was made by steel baron Henry Frick.

[14] Elizabeth Drew, *Politics and Money* (New York: Collier, 1983), 9.

[15] Glen Justice, "Irrelevance Stalks a Post-Watergate Invention," *New York Times*, November 16, 2003, 3.

[16] Glen Justice, "Kerry's Campaign Finances Soar," *International Herald Tribune*, June 28, 2004, 7.

[17] *Buckley* v. *Valeo*, 424 U.S. 1 (1976); the Vermont case is *Randall* v. *Sorrell* 548 U.S. (2006).

[18] See Larry J. Sabato and Glenn Simpson, *Dirty Little Secrets: The Persistence of Corruption in American Politics* (New York: Times Books, 1996); Marick Masters and Gerald Keim, "Determinants of PAC Participation among Large Corporations," *Journal of Politics* 47 (1985), 1158–1173; and J. David Gopoian, "What Makes PACs Tick?" *American Journal of Political Science* 28 (1984), 259–281.

[19] See Kevin Grier and Michael Mangy, "Comparing Interest Group PAC Contributions to House and Senate Incumbents," *Journal of Politics* 55 (1993), 615–643.

[20] J. David Gopoian, "Change and Continuity in Defense PAC Behavior," *American Politics Quarterly* 13 (1985), 297–322; Richard Morin and Charles Babcock, "Off Year, Schmoff Year," *Washington Post National Weekly Edition*, May 14, 1990, 15.

[21] *Federal Election Commission* v. *National Conservative PAC*, 470 U.S. 480 (1985).

[22] To judge whether an ad is a campaign ad, rather than an issue ad, the Court's rule is whether the ad uses language such as "vote for" or "vote against." However, this is a meaningless criterion because only 4 percent of the ads sponsored by the candidates themselves use these phrases. David S. Broder, "Both Major Parties Abuse Soft Money Loophole," *State College* (Pa.) *Centre Daily Times*, May 30, 2000, 6A.

[23] Pauol Farhi, "A Team Effort," *Washington Post National Weekly Edition*, March 29, 2004, 12.

[24] Recent legislation has attempted to close part of the soft money loophole by banning soft money contributions to national political parties. However, it left a huge loophole allowing soft money contributions to various independent groups and, to a lesser extent, to state and local parties.

[25] Walter Lippmann, "A Theory about Corruption," in Arnold J. Heidenheimer, ed., *Political Corruption* (New York: Holt, Rinehart and Winston, 1970), 294–297.

[26] Mike Allen, "Does an Embassy Trump the Lincoln Bedroom?" *Washington Post National Weekly Edition*, May 7, 2001, 14.

[27] Ibid.

[28] Barry Yeoman, "Bush's Bagmen," *Rolling Stone*, March 10, 2004, www.rollingstone.com/politics/story/_/id/5940033. See also Thomas Byrne Edsall, Sarah Cohen, and James Grimaldi,

"Pioneers Fill War Chest, Then Capitalize," *Washington Post*, May 16, 2004, A1.

[29] Mike Allen, "The Mother of All Fundraisers," *Washington Post National Weekly Edition*, May 20, 2002, 13.

[30] Mike Allen, "Does an Embassy Trump the Lincoln Bedroom?" *Washington Post National Weekly Edition*, May 7, 2001, 14.

[31] Edsall, Cohen, and Grimaldi, "Pioneers Fill War Chest," A1.

[32] Ibid.

[33] Larry Makinson and Joshua Goldstein, *Open Secrets: The Cash Constituents of Congress*, 2nd ed. (Washington, D.C.: CQ Press, 1994), 23.

[34] Amy Dockser, "Nice PAC You've Got There . . . A Pity If Anything Should Happen to It," *Washington Monthly*, January 1984, 21.

[35] James Gimpel, Frances Lee, Shanna Pearson-Merkowitz, "The Check is in the Mail: Interdistrict Funding Flows in Congressional Elections," *American Journal of Political Science* 52 (April 2008): 373–394.

[36] Ibid, p. 390, quoting Patrick Healy.

[37] Bradley Smith, *Free Speech: The Folly of Campaign Finance Reform* (Princeton, N.J.: Princeton University Press, 2001); Russ Lewis, "Foreign to the First Amendment," *Washington Post*, July 2, 2002, A15.

[38] George Will, "Corrupt Campaign 'Reform,'" *Washington Post*, June 29, 2006, A27.

[39] Thomas Byrne Edsall, "Campaign Reform Boomerang," *American Prospect*, September 2003, 61.

[40] Ibid.

[41] Paul Taylor, "TV's Political Profits," *Mother Jones*, May–June 2000, 32.

[42] Robert Pastor, "America Observed," *Prospect* (January 2005), A3. An earlier study of 146 countries found that the U.S. was the only country without free media, *Washington Post*, February 24, 2002, B7.

[43] David S. Broder, "Where the Money Goes," *Washington Post National Weekly Edition*, March 26, 2001, 4.

[44] Jeff Leeds, "TV Stations Balk at Free Air Time for Candidates," *Lincoln Journal Star*, May 14, 2000, 3A.

[45] Ibid.

[46] Ibid.

[47] "Public Order in the Courts," *American Prospect*, November 18, 2002, 8. See also Harold Stanley and Richard Niemi, *Vital Statistics on American Politics, 2001–02* (Washington, D.C.: CQ Press, 2002), tab. 2-3.

[48] James Carville and Paul Begala," Not One Dime," *Washington Monthly* (March 2006), 14–15.

[49] Jack Levin in Michael Grunwald, "Neighborhood Watch," *Washington Post National Weekly Edition* (February 20–26, 2006), p. 22.

[50] Mark Twain, *Pudd'nhead Wilson's New Calendar*.

[51] Quoted in *New York Times*, June 13, 1998, A7.

[52] Ibid.

[53] Quoted in Gary Jacobson, *Money in Congressional Elections* (New Haven, Conn.: Yale University Press, 1980), 61.

[54] David S. Broder, "The High Road to Lower Finance?" *Washington Post National Weekly Edition*, June 29, 1987, 4; see also Diane Granat, "Parties' Schools for Politicians or Grooming Troops for Election," *Congressional Quarterly Weekly Report*, May 5, 1984, 1036.

[55] Diana C. Mutz, "Effects of Horse-Race Coverage on Campaign Coffers: Strategic Contributing in Presidential Primaries," *Journal of Politics* 57 (1995), 1015–1042.

[56] Haynes, Gurian, and Nichols, "Role of Candidate Spending," 223.

[57] Nelson Polsby and Aaron Wildavsky, *Presidential Elections* (New York: Scribner, 1984), 56.

[58] David Nice, "Campaign Spending and Presidential Election Results," *Polity* 19 (1987), 464–476, shows that presidential campaign spending is more productive for Republicans than for Democrats.

[59] John Alford and David Brady, "Person and Partisan Advantages in U.S. Congressional Elections, 1846–1990," in *Congress Reconsidered*, ed. Larry Dodd and Bruce Oppenheimer, 5th ed. (Washington, D.C.: Congressional Quarterly, 1993).

[60] David Epstein and Peter Zemsky, "Money Talks: Deterring Quality Challengers in Congressional Elections," *American Political Science Review* 89 (1995), 295–308.

[61] Robert S. Erickson and Thomas R. Palfrey, "Campaign Spending and Incumbency: An Alternative Simultaneous Equations Approach," *Journal of Politics* 60 (1998), 355–373; Alan Gerber, "Estimating the Effect of Campaign Spending on Senate Election Outcomes Using Instrumental Variables," *American Political Science Review* 92 (1998), 401–411.

[62] Jacobson, *Money in Congressional Elections*; Gary Jacobson, "The Effects of Campaign Spending in House Elections," *American Journal of Political Science* 34 (1990), 334–362; Christopher Kenny and Michael McBurnett, "A Dynamic Model of the Effect of Campaign Spending on Congressional Vote Choice," *American Journal of Political Science* 36 (1992), 923–937; Donald Green and Jonathan Krasno, "Salvation for the Spendthrift Incumbent," *American Journal of Political Science* 32 (1988), 884–907; Gary Jacobson, *The Politics of Congressional Elections*, 2nd ed. (Boston: Little, Brown, 1987), ch. 4; Stephen Ansolabehere and Alan Gerber, "The Mismeasure of Campaign Spending," *Journal of Politics* 56 (1994), 1106–1118; Alan Gerber, "Estimating the Effect of Campaign Spending."

[63] "Scandal Shocks Even Those Who Helped It Along," *New York Times*, February 3, 2002, 7.

[64] See Woodrow Jones and K. Robert Keiser, "Issue Visibility and the Effects of PAC Money," *Social Science Quarterly* 68 (1987), 170–176. Janet Grenzke, "PACs and the Congressional Supermarket," *American Journal of Political Science* 33 (1989), 1–24, found little effect of PAC money on a series of votes that were not obscure. Laura Langbein, "Money and

Access," *Journal of Politics* 48 (1986), 1052–1064, shows that those who received more PAC money spend more time with interest group representatives.

65 Jean Reith Schroedel, "Campaign Contributions and Legislative Outcomes," *Western Political Quarterly* 39 (1986), 371–389; Richard L. Hall and Frank Wayman, "Buying Time: Moneyed Interests and the Mobilization of Bias in Congressional Committees," *American Political Science Review* 84 (1990), 797–820.

66 Thomas Downey (D-N.Y.), quoted in "Running with the PACs," *Time,* October 25, 1982, 20.

67 "Congress Study Links Funds and Votes," *New York Times,* December 30, 1987, 7.

68 John Frendreis and Richard Waterman, "PAC Contributions and Legislative Behavior: Senate Voting on Trucking Deregulation," *Social Science Quarterly* 66 (1985), 401–412. See also W. P. Welch, "Campaign Contributions and Legislative Voting," *Western Political Quarterly* 25 (1982), 478–495.

69 Diana Evans, "Policy and Pork: The Use of Pork Barrel Projects to Build Policy Coalitions in the House of Representatives," *American Journal of Political Science* 38 (1994), 894–917; Laura Langbein, "PACs, Lobbies, and Political Conflict: The Case of Gun Control," *Public Choice* 75 (1993), 254–271; Laura Langbein and Mark Lotwis, "The Political Efficacy of Lobbying and Money: Gun Control in the House, 1986," *Legislative Studies Quarterly* 15 (1990), 413–440; Schroedel, "Campaign Contributions and Legislative Outcomes."

70 Adam Clymer, "84 PACs Gave More to Senate Winners," *New York Times,* January 6, 1985, 13.

71 Quoted in Drew, *Politics and Money,* 79.

72 See Grenzke, "PACs and the Congressional Supermarket"; also see Frank Sorauf, *Money in American Elections* (Glenview, Ill.: Scott, Foresman, 1988).

73 Grenzke, "PACs and the Congressional Supermarket"; John Wright, "Contributions, Lobbying, and Committee Voting in the U.S. House of Representatives," *American Political Science Review* 84 (1990), 417–438; Henry Chappel Jr., "Campaign Contributions and Voting on the Cargo Preference Bill," *Public Choice* 36 (1981), 301–312.

74 John Alford and David Brady, "Person and Partisan Advantages in U.S. Congressional Elections, 1846–1990," in *Congress Reconsidered,* ed. Larry Dodd and Bruce Oppenheimer, 5th ed. (Washington, D.C.: CQ Press, 1993); Peter Slevin, "Postwar Contracting Called Uncoordinated," *Washington Post,* October 31, 2003, A23.

75 "Study: Bush Donors Get Government Favors," *Lincoln Journal Star,* May 28, 1992.

76 "Clinton Regrets Rich Pardon," March 31, 2002, CBSNEWS.com/stories/2002/03/31/politics/main505042.shtml; BBC News World Edition, "Rich's '$450,000' for Clinton Library," news.bbc.co.uk/hi/English/world/Americas/newid_1163000/1163917.stm. George H. W. Bush's last-minute pardon of a convicted $1.5 million heroin trafficker got much less publicity; John Monk and Gary Wright, "Why Did Bush

Free Smuggler? Mystery Lingers in Charlotte Case," *Charlotte Observer,* March 27, 1993, 1A.

77 Charles Lewis, quoted in "Book Details Candidates' Extensive Financial Alignments," *Lincoln Journal Star,* January 12, 1996, 5A.

78 Tom Kenworthy, "The Color of Money," *Washington Post National Weekly Edition,* November 6, 1989, 13.

79 Quoted in Daniel Franklin," Heiristrocracy," *The Washington Monthly* (May, 2005), 60.

80 Kevin Phillips, "How Wealth Defines Power," *American Prospect,* Summer 2003, A9; U.S. Census Bureau, *Statistical Abstract of the United States, 2003* (Washington, D.C.: Government Printing Office, 2003), tab. 688.

81 Aviva Aron-Dean and Isaac Shapiro, "New Data Show Extraordinary Jump in Income Concentration in 2004," Center on Budget and Policy Priorities, July 10, 2006; www.cbpp.org/7-10-06inc.htm.

82 Gary Wasserman, "The Uses of Influence," *Washington Post National Weekly Edition,* January 11, 1993, 35.

83 Juliet Eilperin, "The 'Hammer' DeLay Whips Lobbyists into Shape," *Washington Post National Weekly Edition,* October 25, 1999, 8.

84 Jeff Leeds, "TV Stations Balk at Free Air Time for Candidates," *Lincoln Journal Star,* May 14, 2000, 3A.

85 Susan Welch and John Peters, "Private Interests in the U.S. Congress," *Legislative Studies Quarterly* 7 (1982), 547–555; see also John Peters and Susan Welch, "Private Interests and Public Interests," *Journal of Politics* 45 (1983), 378–396.

86 "Congress for Sale," *USA Today,* March 7, 2006, 17A.

87 Jeffrey Birnbaum, "Privately Funded Trips Add up on Capitol Hill," *Washington Post,* June 6, 2006, A1.

88 Ibid.

89 Many news media covered this scandal and the complicated interrelationships within it extensively. See for example, Karen Tumulty, "The Man Who Bought Washington," *Time,* January 16, 2006, 31–39.

90 Norman Ornstein, "The House that Jack Built," *The New York Times Book Review,* January 14, 2007, 25. See also Peter H. Stone, *Heist* (New York: Farrar, Straus, and Giroux, 2007).

91 Ibid. See also indianz.com/News/2006/014803.asp; Philip Shenon, "Senate Report Lists Lobbyists' Payments to Ex-Head of Christian Coalition," *New York Times,* June 23, 2006, 22.

92 Norman Ornstein, a fellow at the American Enterprise Institution, as quoted in Lou DuBose, "Broken Hammer," *Salon,* http://dir.salon.com/story/news/feature/2005/04/08/scandals/index1.html.

93 R. Jeffrey Smith and Juliet Eilperin, "Caught in an Ethical Snare," *Washington Post National Weekly Edition,* January 16–22, 2006, 14.

94 Lou DuBose, "K Street Croupiers," *Texas Observer,* observer.bryhost.com/article.php?aid=2138.

95 For a rundown of these confusing front organizations see Tumulty, op. cit.; DeBose, ibid.

96 Eliza Newlin Carney,"Cleaning House (and Senate)," *National Journal,* January 28, 2006, 33.

97 "Congress for Sale," ibid.

98 Ibid.

99 Birnbaum, ibid.

100 Mike McIntire, "New House Majority Leader Keeps Old Ties to Lobbyists," *New York Times,* July 15, 2006.

101 Frank Rich, "The Road from K Street to Yusafiya," *New York Times,* June 25, 2006, WK13.

102 "Having It All, Then Throwing It Away," *Time,* May 25, 1987, 22.

103 Elizabeth Drew, "Letter from Washington," *New Yorker,* May 1, 1989, 99–108; see also Dan Balz, "Tales of Power and Money," *Washington Post National Weekly Edition,* May 1, 1989, 11–12.

104 George Will, "Conservatives Have Plenty of Reasons to Hold Onto Hope," *Lincoln Journal-Star,* November 9, 2006, 7B.

105 Keith Bradsher, "How to Pooh-Pooh $70 Million War Chests," *New York Times,* April 30, 2000, 6.

106 Quoted in Drew, "Having It All," 22.

107 Hank Paulson, CEO of Goldman Sachs, quoted in Joseph Nocera, "System Failure," *Fortune,* June 24, 2002, 62ff.

108 Quoted in Nancy Gibbs and Karen Tumulty, "A New Day Dawning," *Time,* April 9, 2001, 50.

Chapter 10

1 Brody Mullins, "Congressional Softball League is Hit by Secession," *Wall Street Journal,* April 24, 2006, A1.

2 Bob Cohn, "For Hill Teams, It's a Whole new Ballgame; Partisans Split League," *Washington Times,* July 189, 2006, A01.

3 Mullins, "Congressional Softball League," A1.

4 Cohn, "For Hill Teams," A01.

5 "C-span's Capitol Questions: the House," www.c-span.org/questions/weekly39.asp.

6 Mullins, "Congressional Softball League," A1.

7 James R. Chiles, "Congress Couldn't Have Been This Bad, or Could It?" *Smithsonian,* November 1995, 70–80.

8 Susan Webb Hammond, "Life and Work on the Hill: Careers, Norms, Staff, and Informal Caucuses," in *Congress Responds to the Twentieth Century,* eds. Sunil Ahuja and Robert Dewhirst (Columbus: Ohio State University Press, 2003), 74.

9 David S. Broder, "Dumbing Down Democracy," *Lincoln Journal Star,* April 5, 1995, 18.

10 Quoted in Kenneth J. Cooper and Helen Dewar, "No Limits on the Term Limits Crusade," *Washington Post National Weekly Edition,* May 29, 1995, 14.

11 A list of states that have term limits can be found at www.termlimits.org.

[12] Michael Barone and Richard E. Cohen, *The Almanac of American Politics 2008* (Washington: National Journal Group, 2007), 33–37.

[13] *Baker* v. *Carr,* 369 U.S. 186 (1962).

[14] *Wesberry* v. *Sanders,* 376 U.S. 1 (1964).

[15] Bob Benenson, "With Enemies Like These," *CQ Weekly,* April 28, 2008, 1086–1097.

[16] Barone and Cohen, *The Almanac of American Politics,* 36–37.

[17] "Congress of Relative Newcomers Poses Challenge to Bush, Leadership," *Congressional Quarterly Weekly Review,* January 20, 2001, 179–181.

[18] "Datafile," *Congressional Quarterly Weekly Review,* February 21, 2004, 456. "For the Record," *CQ Monthly Report,* November 13, 2006, 3068–3075.

[19] Hanna F. Pitkin, *The Concept of Representation* (Berkeley: University of California, 1967), 60.

[20] Ibid., 60–61.

[21] Leslie Laurence, "Congress Makes Up for Neglect," *Lincoln Journal Star,* December 5, 1994, 8.

[22] "Fewer Voters Identify as Republicans," Pew Research Center Publications, March 20, 2008, 1.

[23] Roger H. Davidson and Walter J. Oleszek, *Congress and Its Members,* 9th ed. (Washington, D.C.: CQ Press, 2004), 132–134; Richard Fenno, *Home Style: House Members in Their Districts,* 2nd ed. (New York: Longman, 2003), 232–247.

[24] "Senate Odd Couples," *National Journal,* March 3, 2007, 37.

[25] Carl M. Cannon, "State of Our Disunion," *National Journal,* January 21, 2006, 23; Norman Ornstein and Barry McMillion, "One Nation, Divisible," *New York Times,* June 23, 2005.

[26] See Thomas E. Mann, "Elections and Change in Congress," in *The New Congress*; Mayhew, *Congress: The Electoral Connection*; Parker and Davidson, "Why Do Americans Love Their Congressmen So Much More Than Their Congress?"

[27] Edie N. Goldenberg and Michael W. Traugott, *Campaigning for Congress* (Washington, D.C.: CQ Press, 1984); Gary C. Jacobson and Samuel Kernell, *Strategy and Choice in Congressional Elections.* (New Haven, Conn.: Yale University Press, 1981).

[28] Edward Walsh, "Wanted: Candidates for Congress," *Washington Post National Weekly Edition,* November 25, 1985, 9.

[29] See Paul Feldman and James Jondrow, "Congressional Elections and Local Federal Spending," *American Journal of Political Science* 28 (1984), 152; Glenn R. Parker and Suzanne Parker, "The Correlates and Effects of Attention to District by U.S. House Members," *Legislative Studies Quarterly* 10 (1985), 239.

[30] Christopher Buckley, "Hangin' with the Houseboyz," *Washington Monthly* (June 1992), 44.

[31] Linda L. Fowler and Robert D. McClure, *Political Ambition: Who Decides to Run for Congress?* (New Haven, Conn.: Yale University Press, 1989), 47; John Hibbing and Sara

Brandes, "State Population and the Electoral Success of U.S. Senators," *American Journal of Political Science* 27 (1983), 808–819. See also Glenn R. Parker, "Stylistic Change in the U.S. Senate, 1959–1980," *Journal of Politics* 47 (1985), 1190–1202.

[32] Thomas E. Mann, *Unsafe at Any Margin: Interpreting Congressional Elections* (Washington, D.C.: American Enterprise Institute for Public Policy Research, 1978).

[33] "Women, Minorities Join Senate," *CQ Almanac* (1992), 8A–14A;"Wave of Diversity Spared Many Incumbents," *CQ Almanac* (1992), 15A–21A, 24A;"The Elections," *Congressional Quarterly,* November 12, 1994, 3237.

[34] Davidson and Oleszek, *Congress and Its Members,* 9th ed. 114.

[35] John Alford and John Hibbing, "The Disparate Electoral Security of House and Senate Incumbents," paper presented at the annual meeting of the American Political Science Association, Atlanta, Georgia, September 1989.

[36] Fenno, *Home Style.*

[37] John Cochran, "A New Medium for the Message," *Congressional Quarterly Weekly Review,* March 13, 2006, 657.

[38] Ibid., 145.

[39] *Budget of the United States, Fiscal 2007: Appendix* (Washington, D.C.: Government Printing Office, 2006), 15–18.

[40] Quoted in Kenneth Shepsle, "The Failures of Congressional Budgeting," *Social Science and Modern Society* 20 (1983), 4–10. See also Howard Kurtz, "Pork Barrel Politics," *Washington Post,* January 25, 1982.

[41] See Gerald C. Wright Jr. and Michael B. Berkman, "Candidates and Policy in United States Senate Elections," *American Political Science Review* 80 (1986), 567–588; Robert S. Erikson and Gerald C. Wright, "Voters, Candidates, and Issues in Congressional Elections," in *Congress Reconsidered,* 7th ed., eds. Lawrence C. Dodd and Bruce I. Oppenheimer (Washington, D.C.: CQ Press, 2001), 67–95.

[42] See James Campbell, "Explaining Presidential Losses in Midterm Elections," *Journal of Politics* 47 (1985), 1140–1157. See also Barbara Hinckley, "Interpreting House Midterm Elections," *American Political Science Review* 61 (1967), 694–700; Samuel Kernell, "Presidential Popularity and Negative Voting," *American Political Science Review* 71 (1977), 44–66; Edward Tufte, "Determinants of the Outcomes of Midterm Congressional Elections," *American Political Science Review* 69 (1975), 812–826; Alan Abramowitz, "Economic Conditions, Presidential Popularity and Voting Behavior in Midterm Elections," *Journal of Politics* 47 (1985), 31–43.

[43] Congressional Quarterly, *The Origins and Development of Congress* (Washington, D.C.: CQ Press, 1976).

[44] Historian David S. Reynolds quoting a newspaper reporter of the time in Sheryl Gay Stolberg, "What Happened to Compromise," *New York Times,* May 29, 2005, sec. 4, 4.

[45] Neil McNeil, *Forge of Democracy* (New York: McKay, 1963), 306–309.

[46] Willie Brown, long-time speaker of the California state house, quoted in Edward Epstein, "Her Key to the House," *CQ Weekly,* October 29, 2007, 3161.

[47] Rep. Barney Frank (D-Mass.), quoted in David D. Kirkpatrick, "As Dust Settles, The Speaker of the House Emerges, Still Standing," *New York Times,* February 5, 2006, 24.

[48] Ibid.

[49] Epstein, "Her Key to the House," quoting Rep. Alan Boyd (D-Fla.), 3159.

[50] Michael Barone, Richard E. Cohen, and Charles E. Cook Jr., *Almanac of American Politics, 2002* (Washington, D.C.: National Journal, 2002), 46.

[51] Historian Robert Dallek quoted in John M. Broder, "Let Them Persuade You," *New York Times,* November 19, 2006, WK2.

[52] Ibid.

[53] Mark Schmitt, "Our Senate Problem," *The American Prospect,* March 2008, 9.

[54] Quoted by Carl Hulse, "Breakdown in Relations in the Senate Hobbles Its Ability to Get Things Done," *New York Times,* July 20, 2007.

[55] Kathleen Hunter, "Safe Seat is No Job Perk for Today's Senate Leaders," *CQ Weekly,* May 5, 2008, 1157–1158.

[56] For a review of all congressional committees and subcommittees in the 110th Congress, see the special report, "CQ Guide to the Committees," *CQ Weekly,* April 16, 2007, 1084–1117.

[57] Davidson and Oleszek, *Congress and Its Members,* 9th ed. 198.

[58] See Roger Davidson, "Subcommittee Government," in *The New Congress,* eds. Thomas E. Mann and Norman J. Ornstein (Washington, D.C.: American Enterprise Institute for Public Policy Research, 1981), 110–111. Some of this occurs because members of Congress tend to be wealthy, and the wealthy make investments in corporations. It also occurs because members' financial interests are often similar to the interests in their districts (for example, representatives from farm districts are likely to be involved in farming or agribusiness).

[59] Rebecca Kimitch, "CQ Guide to the Committees: Democrats Opt to Spread the Power," *CQ Weekly,* April 16, 2007, 1080.

[60] Sara Brandes Crook and John Hibbing, "Congressional Reform and Party Discipline: The Effects of Changes in the Seniority System on Party Loyalty in the U.S. House of Representatives," *British Journal of Political Science* 15 (1985), 207–226.

[61] Richard E. Cohen, "Best Seats in the House," *National Journal,* March 4, 2000, 682; Karen Foerstel, "House Offers Mixed Reviews for Committee Term Limits," *Congressional Quarterly Weekly Review,* June 22, 2002, 1653–1655.

[62] For a review of how the task force has been used, see Walter J. Oleszek, "The Use of Task Forces in the House," Congressional Research Service Report No. 96-8, 3-GOV, 1996, www.house.gov/rules/96-843.htm.

[63] Ida A. Brudnick, "The Congressional Research Service and the American Legislative Process," CRS report RL33471, March 19, 2008, 2.

64 *Budget of the United States, Fiscal 2008: Appendix* (Washington, D.C.: Government Printing Office, 2007), 13–16.

65 Harlan Coben, "Rock and a Hard Place," *New York Times,* November 25, 2005.

66 www.willrogerstoday.com/will_rogers_quotes/quotes.cfm?w_ID=4.

67 Kimitch, "CQ Guide to the Committees", 1080.

68 Edward Epstein, "Her Key to the House," *CQ Weekly,* October 29, 2007, 3164-3165.

69 Thomas Geoghegan, "Bust the Filibuster," *Washington Post National Weekly Edition,* July 12, 1994, 25.

70 Paul C. Light, "Filibusters Are Only Half the Problem," *New York Times,* June 3, 2005.

71 Clinton aide Chuck Brain, quoted in Richard E. Cohen, "The Third House Rises," *National Journal,* July 28, 2001, 2395.

72 David J. Vogler, *The Third House: Conference Committees in the United States Congress* (Evanston, Ill.: Northwestern University Press, 1971); see also Lawrence D. Longley and Walter J. Oleszek, *Bicameral Politics* (New Haven, Conn.: Yale University Press, 1989).

73 Morris Ogul, "Congressional Oversight: Structures and Incentives," in *Congress Reconsidered,* eds. Dodd and Oppenheimer; see also Loch Johnson, "The U.S. Congress and the CIA: Monitoring the Dark Side of Government," *Legislative Studies Quarterly* 5 (1980), 477–501.

74 Joseph Califano, "Imperial Congress," *New York Times Magazine,* January 23, 1994, 41.

75 Richard E. Cohen, Kirk Victor, and David Bauman, "The State of Congress," *National Journal,* January 10, 2004, 104–105.

76 Quoted in ibid., 105.

77 Henry A. Waxman, "Free Pass from Congress," *Washington Post,* July 6, 2004, A19.

78 Cohen, Victor, and Bauman, "State of Congress," 96.

79 Jonathan Allen, "Manifest Disparity," *CQ Weekly,* 2836–2841.

80 David Baumann, "Tempest in a Barrel," *National Journal,* February 11, 2006, 58.

81 Sheryl Gay Stolberg, "What's Wrong With a Healthy Helping of Pork?" *New York Times,* May 28, 2006, wk 4.

82 Rahm Emanuel, "Don't Get Rid of Earmarks, *New York Times,* August 24, 2007. Emanuel, now White House chief of staff, was a member of the House Democratic leadership when he wrote this.

83 Gail Collins, "George Speaks, Badly," *New York Times,* March 15, 2008, 19.

84 Herbert Asher, "Learning of Legislative Norms," *American Political Science Review* 67 (1973), 499–513. Michael Berkman points out that freshmen who have had state legislative experience adapt to the job faster than other members. See "Former State Legislators in the U.S. House of Representatives: Institutional and Policy Mastery," *Legislative Studies Quarterly* 18 (1993), 77–104.

85 Citizens for Responsibility and Ethics in Washington, "Beyond Delay: The 22 Most Corrupt Members of Congress," www.beyonddelay.org/report.

86 Molly Hooper and Alan K. Ota, "House Votes for Outside Ethics Review," *CQ Weekly,* March 17, 2008, 726.

87 Citizens for Responsibility and Ethics in Washington, "Family Affair," June 2007.

88 Rep. Jim DeMint (R-S.C.), quoted in Davidson and Oleszek, *Congress and Its Members,* 9th ed. 264.

89 *Minot* (N.D.) *Daily News,* June 17, 1976.

90 Roger H. Davidson, Walter H. Oleszek, and Frances E. Lee, *Congress and Its Members,* 11th ed. (Washington, D.C.: CQ Press, 2008), 299. 299.

91 Samuel Kernell, *Going Public* (Washington, D.C.: CQ Press,1986).

92 C-Span does not collect ratings information but the results of other surveys are available at its website, www.c-span.org. The most recent data are from the 2006 News Consumption and Believability Study conducted by the Pew Research Center for the People & the Press.

93 Mildred Amer, "Membership of the 110th Congress: A Profile," Congressional Research Service Report RS22555, December 15, 2006, 3.

94 Michael Wines, "Washington Really Is in Touch. We're the Problem," *New York Times,* October 16, 1994, sec. 4: 2.

95 Davidson, Oleszek, and Lee, *Congress and Its Members,* 11th ed., 299.

96 *New York Times/*CBS poll, May, 2006.

97 Davidson, Oleszek, and Lee, 11th ed., 150.

98 Hooper and Ota, 727.

99 Editorial, "A Richer Life Beckons Congress," *New York Times,* August 8, 2005.

100 Paul Kane, "110th Congress Eclipses Voting Pace, *Washington Post,* October 25, 2007, A23.

101 Catherine Richert, "CQ Vote Studies—Party Unity: United We Stand Opposed," *CQ Weekly,* June 14, 2008, 143.

Chapter 11

1 Garry Wills, "Two Presidents Are Worse Than One," *New York Times,* January 26, 2008.

2 Ibid.

3 Charlie Savage, *Takeover: the Return of the Imperial Presidency* (New York: Little, Brown & Co, 2007), 48.

4 Harold M. Barger, *The Impossible Presidency* (Glenview, Ill.: Scott, Foresman, 1984).

5 Carl M. Cannon, "Untruth and Consequences," *The Atlantic* (January–February, 2007), 59.

6 Bob Dole, a Republican who ran in 1996, was the exception. David Leonhardt, "Who's in the Corner Office?" *New York Times,* November 27, 2005, BU 1.

7 Quoted in David von Drehle, "Does Experience Matter in a President?" *Time,* March 10, 2008, 30.

8 "George Mason: Forgotten Founder," *Smithsonian,* May 2000, 145.

9 Information on all three impeachment proceedings can be found at www.historyplace.com.

10 Woodrow Wilson, *Congressional Government: A Study in American Politics* (New Brunswick, N.J.: Transaction, 2002). Originally published in 1885.

11 Theodore Lowi, *The Personal President: Power Invested, Promise Unfulfilled* (Ithaca, N.Y.: Cornell University Press, 1985).

12 Jefferson's management of the presidency is described in Joseph J. Ellis, *American Sphinx: The Character of Thomas Jefferson* (New York: Knopf, 1997), 186–228.

13 With the possible exception of the 1950s, when people who had lived through the Depression, World War II, and the Korean War, were tired of government activity and ready to focus on their private lives. Even so, President Dwight Eisenhower (1953–1961) was expected to make sure the country was protected during the Cold War.

14 Harold M. Barger, *The Impossible Presidency*).

15 See, for example, the comments of Arthur M. Schlesinger Jr. in Cannon, "Judging Clinton," 22; Steven A. Holmes, "Losers in Clinton-Starr Bouts May Be Future U.S. Presidents," *New York Times,* August 23, 1998, 18; and Adam Clymer, "The Presidency Is Still There, Not Quite the Same," *New York Times,* February 14, 1999, 4: 1.

16 Jones found that evenly matched was more common in his study. Charles O. Jones, *Presidency in a Separated System* (Washington, D.C.: Brookings, 1994), 293.

17 Ibid., 1.

18 Charles O. Jones, *Separate But Equal Branches* (Chatham, N.J.: Chatham House, 1995), 107.

19 Francis Wilkinson, "Song of Myself," *New York Times,* January 31, 2006.

20 Ted Widmer, "The State of the Union Is Unreal," *New York Times,* January 31, 2006.

21 Quoted in George Lardner Jr., "A High Price for Freedom," *New York Times,* March 26, 2007.

22 George Lardner Jr., "Begging Bush's Pardon, *New York Times,* February 4, 2008.

23 *Federalist Paper* 69, by Alexander Hamilton.

24 Michael Nelson, ed., *Presidency A to Z* (Washington, D.C.: CQ Press, 1998), 12.

25 For discussion of the president's removal powers in light of a 1988 Supreme Court decision regarding independent counsels, see John A. Rohr, "Public Administration, Executive Power, and Constitutional Confusion," and Rosemary O'Leary, "Response to John Rohr," *Public Administrative Review* 49 (1989), 108–115.

26 Jones, *Presidency in a Separated System,* 53.

27 Nelson, *Presidency A to Z,* 169.

28 Ibid., 170.

29 For elaboration, see Lee Epstein and Jeffrey A. Segal, *Advice and Consent.* (New York: Oxford University Press, 2005), chap. 5.

30 Jeb Stuart Magruder, "Ex-aide: Nixon Ordered Watergate Break-in," *Lincoln Journal Star,* July 27, 2003.

31 Jones, *The Presidency in a Separated System,* 209.

32 "Bush Starts a Strong Record of Success with the Hill," *Congressional Quarterly Weekly Review,* January 12, 2002, 112.

33 Carl M. Cannon, "Veto This!" *National Journal,* October 13, 2007, 32.

34 Andrew Sullivan, "We Don't Need a New King George," *Time,* January 23, 2006 74.

35 Reference omitted

36 Richard J. Barnet, "Reflections: The Disorders of Peace," *The New Yorker,* January 20, 1992, 64.

37 Rather than expressly authorizing the president to abrogate a treaty by himself, the majority ruled that the dispute was a "political question," which avoided a ruling on the merits of Carter's claim. Thus the Court allows, but doesn't authorize, the president to take this action. *Goldwater* v. *Carter,* 444 U.S. 996 (1979).

38 He also "unsigned" the treaty creating the International Criminal Court, which Clinton had signed but never submitted for Senate approval. Thus the United States wasn't a party to the treaty, but because Clinton had signed it, the United States was a participant in discussions of rules for the court. Bush's "unsigning," for symbolic reasons, pulled the United States out of these discussions.

39 For some trade deals, Congress delegates power to the president in advance.

40 John Marshall, as a member of the House of Representatives. Later, Marshall would become chief justice of the United States.

41 *United States* v. *Curtiss-Wright Export Corporation,* 299 U.S. 304 (1936).

42 See the discussion in *Federalist Paper* 69, written by Alexander Hamilton.

43 Quoted in "Notes and Comment," *The New Yorker,* June 1, 1987, 23.

44 Ibid.

45 John M. Broder, "Report Urges of Overhaul of War Powers Law," *New York Times,* July 9, 2008.

46 *Youngstown Sheet and Tube Co.* v. *Sawyer,* 343 U.S. 579 (1952).

47 Ron Suskind, *The One Percent Doctrine: Deep Inside America's Pursuit of Its Enemies Since 9/11* (New York: Simon & Schuster, 2006), 65.

48 Thomas F. Cronin, *The State of the Presidency* (Boston: Little, Brown, 1975), 118.

49 Congress's anger at Roosevelt's court-packing scheme held up the reorganization for two years; see Chapter 13.

50 Sidney M. Milkis, "George W. Bush and the 'New' Party System," *Clio: Newsletter of Politics and History* 16 (1, Fall/Winter 2005–2006), 44.

51 Jones, *The Presidency in a Separated System,* 56–57.

52 For more on Bush's White House staff and method of making appointments, see G. Calvin Mackenzie, "The Real Invisible Hand: Presidential Appointees in the Administration of George W. Bush," and Martha Joynt Kumar, "Recruiting and Organizing the White House Staff," *PS: Political Science and Politics* 1 (2002), 27–40.

53 "Hell from the Chief: Hot Tempers and Presidential Timber," *New York Times,* November 7, 1999, 4: 7.

54 Quoted in Richard Pious, *The American Presidency* (New York: Basic Books, 1979), 244.

55 Public Broadcasting System, *The American President,* episode 10.

56 Ann Reilly Dowd, "What Managers Can Learn from Manager Reagan," *Fortune,* September 15, 1986, 32–41.

57 See John H. Kessel, "The Structures of the Reagan White House," *American Journal of Political Science* 28 (1984), 231–258.

58 Hillary Rodham Clinton, quoted in Carol Gelderman, *All the Presidents' Words: The Bully Pulpit and the Creation of the Virtual Presidency* (New York: Walker, 1997), 160.

59 A good description of Clinton's relationship to his White House staff can be found in Joe Klein, *The Natural: The Misunderstood Presidency of Bill Clinton* (New York: Doubleday, 2002).

60 For more on Bush's management style, see the several articles in the special section "C.E.O. U.S.A.," *New York Times Magazine,* January 14, 2001, 24–58.

61 Mike Allen, "Living too Much in the Bubble," *Time,* September 19, 2005, 44.

62 Ron Suskind, *The Price of Loyalty: George W. Bush, the White House, and the Education of Paul O'Neill* (New York: Simon & Schuster, 2004).

63 James C. Moore, " Karl Rove: Counting Votes While Bombs Drop," *Lincoln Journal Star,* May 11, 2003, 5E.

64 Nelson, *The Presidency A to Z,* 487–488.

65 For a review of the backgrounds of men who have served in the vice presidency and the roles they have played, see L. Edward Purcell, *Vice Presidents* (New York: Facts on File, 2001); Michael Nelson, *A Heartbeat Away* (New York: Priority, 1988); Paul C. Light, *Vice-Presidential Power: Advice and Influence in the White House* (Baltimore: Johns Hopkins University Press, 1984); and George Sirgiovanni, "The 'Van Buren Jinx': Vice Presidents Need Not Beware," *Presidential Studies Quarterly* 18 (1988), 61–76.

66 Jane Mayer, "The Hidden Power," *New Yorker,* July 3, 2006, 50.

67 Nicholas Lemann, "The Quiet Man," *New Yorker,* May 7, 2001, 68.

68 Paul Light quoted in Daniel Radosh, "No. 1 Authority," *The New Yorker,* July 26, 2004, 30.

69 Former White House counsel Bradford A. Berenson, quoted in Jo Becker and Barton Gellman, "A Strong Push from Backstage," *Washington Post,* June 26, 2007, A01. This article is from a series by Becker and Gellman that ran in the *Post* June 24–27, 2007, under the title "Angler: the Cheney Vice Presidency."

70 CBS News poll, March 2006.

71 Barger, *Impossible Presidency,* 145.

72 Fortunately, in the 1950s, the public, worn out from government activity during the Great Depression and World War II, didn't expect the president to accomplish much. People focused on their private lives. Eisenhower does receive high marks for a steady hand during the Cold War. For an examination of presidential persuasion, particularly the Truman and Eisenhower presidencies, see Richard E. Neustadt, *Presidential Power: The Politics of Leadership from FDR to Carter* (New York: Wiley, 1980).

73 These ideas come especially from Neustadt, *Presidential Power.*

74 Thomas P. O'Neill Jr., with William Novak, *Man of the House* (New York: Random House, 1987), 341–342.

75 The representative wasn't identified. "Contra Proposal Heads for Showdown in House," *Lincoln Journal,* June 25, 1986, A1.

76 Sen. Barry Goldwater (R-Ariz.), who was referring to Johnson's tenure as majority leader, although the same could have been said about his tenure as president. Burton Bernstein, "Profiles—AuH_2O," *The New Yorker,* April 28, 1988, 64.

77 According to former Sen. Dale Bumpers (D-Ark.), quoted in Lloyd Grove, "Replacing the Carrot with a Stick," *Washington Post National Weekly Edition,* April 12–18, 1993, 12.

78 Doris Kearns Goodwin, *Lyndon Johnson and the American Dream* (New York: Harper & Row, 1976), 226.

79 Presidential historian Alan Brinkley in "The Making of a War President," *New York Times Book Review,* August 20, 2006, 10.

80 Sheryl Gay Stolberg, "As Agenda Falters, Bush Tries a More Personal Approach in Dealing with Congress," *New York Times,* June 11, 2006, YT26.

81 According to congressional scholar, Thomas Mann, quoted in Janet Hook, "Bush Gets Personal on Social Security, *Los Angeles Times,* April 25, 2005, www.latimes.com/news /nationalworld/la=ha=bushlobby25apr25 .story."

82 E.J. Dionne Jr., "The System at Work," *Washington Post National Weekly Edition,* June 18–24, 2007, 31.

83 Hook, "Bush Gets Personal on Social Security." However, when the president pushed his proposal for Social Security in 2006, he did make an effort to meet with and listen to lawmakers, once he realized that his proposal was in trouble.

84 James A. Thurber, quoted in Stolberg, "As Agenda Falters, Bush Tries a More Personal Approach in Dealing with Congress."

85 Jeffrey K. Tulis, *The Rhetorical Presidency* (Princeton, N.J.: Princeton University Press, 1987).

86 Quoted in Garry Wills, *Lincoln at Gettysburg* (New York: Simon & Schuster, 1992), 31.

87 Samuel Kernell, *Going Public: New Strategies of Presidential Leadership* (Washington, D.C.: CQ Press, 1986), 15.

88 David Halberstam, *The Powers That Be* (New York: Dell, 1980), 30.

89 "Travels of the President," *New York Times,* August 8, 2004, 18.

90 Michael Waldman, Clinton's former chief speechwriter, interviewed on *Morning Edition,* National Public Radio, January 1, 2002.

91 Ari Fleischer, quoted in *Congressional Quarterly Today News,* May 19, 2003, www.cq.com.

92 Scott McClellan, *What Happened: Inside the Bush White House and Washington's Culture of Deception* (New York: Public Affairs, 2008).

93 Janet Hook, "Social Security Plan Hits Shoals," *Los Angeles Times,* June 27, 2005, www.latimes.com/news/nationworld/nation/la-na-social27jun27,0,7154171,full.story.

94 Nicholas Lemann, "Remember the Alamo," *The New Yorker,* October 18, 2004, 153.

95 Bruce Miroff, "The Presidency and the Public: Leadership and Spectacle," in *The Presidency and the Political System,* 5th ed., ed. Michael Nelson (Washington: CQ Press, 1998), 320. This section draws heavily from Miroff's observations.

96 James David Barber, *The Presidential Character,* 2nd ed. (Englewood Cliffs, N.J.: Prentice Hall, 1977), 157.

97 Ibid.

98 Theodore Lowi coined this term and our discussion will draw from Lowi, *The Personal President.*

99 Richard E. Neustadt, *Presidential Power* (New York: Wiley, 1960), 5–6.

100 Malcolm Gladwell, "Comment: The Politics of Politesse," *The New Yorker,* December 23 and 30, 2002, 57.

101 Klein, *The Natural,* 208.

102 Benjamin C. Bradlee, "When They Made George Washington, They Broke the Mold," *Washington Post National Weekly Edition,* November 25–December 1, 1991, 23.

103 Thomas E. Patterson, *The Vanishing Voter* (New York: Knopf, 2002), 54.

104 Jones, *The Presidency in a Separated System,* chap. 4.

Chapter 12

1 Peter Baker, "As Democracy Push Falters, Bush Feels Like a 'Dissident'," *Washington Post,* August 20, 2007, A9.

2 Ibid., 1.

3 Bruce Adams, "The Frustrations of Government Service," *Public Administration Review* 44 (1984), 5. For more discussion of public attitudes about the civil service, see Herbert Kaufman, "Fear of Bureaucracy: A Raging Pandemic," *Public Administration Review* 41 (1981), 1.

4 The classic early work on western bureaucracy is Max Weber's. See H. H. Gerth and C. Wright Mills, trans., from Max Weber, *Essays on Sociology* (New York: Oxford University Press, 1946), 196–239.

5 On distinctions between public and private bureaucracies, see Barry Bozeman, *All Organizations Are Public: Bridging Public and Private Organizational Theories* (San Francisco: Jossey-Bass, 1987).

6 "Federal Executives' Bonuses Scrutinized," *Champaign-Urbana News-Gazette,* January 23, 2002, A4.

7 From a letter to W. T. Barry, quoted in "A Citizen's Guide on Using the Freedom of Information Act and the Privacy Act of 1974 to Request Government Records," report to the U.S. House of Representatives 50 (1999), 2.

8 Harold C. Relyea and Michael W. Kolakowski, "Access to Government Information in the United States," Congressional Research Service Report 97-71 GOV, December 5, 2007, 2–3.

9 For a description of the nine exempt categories of information, see Harold C. Relyea, "Freedom of Information Act (FOIA) Amendments: 110th Congress, Congressional Research Service Report RL32780, January 7, 2008, 3. A link to CRS reports on openness in government can be found at www.fas.org.

10 This information is posted by the Justice Department at www.usdoj.gov/04foia/04_6html.

11 Reported in Sam Archibald, "The Early Years of the Freedom of Information Act, 1955–1974," *PS: Political Science and Politics,* December 1993, 730.

12 Debra Gersh Hernandez, "Many Promises, Little Action," *Editor and Publisher,* March 26, 1994, 15.

13 Government Accounting Office, *Freedom of Information Act: State Department Request Processing* (Washington, D.C.: Government Printing Office, 1989).

14 Clinton administration policy on compliance with FOIA can be found in Federation of American Scientists, Project on Government Secrecy, "Clinton Administration Documents on Classification Policy," 2003, www.fas.org/sgp/clinton/index.html.

15 "President Declassifies Old Papers," *Omaha World-Herald,* April 18, 1995, 1.

16 Linda Greenhouse, "A Penchant for Secrecy," *New York Times,* May 5, 2002, WK1.

17 As a presidential aide in the Ford administration, Cheney encouraged President Ford to veto the 1974 bill that strengthened FOIA rights. Congress ultimately passed the bill over Ford's veto.

18 Editorial, "Sunshine on History," *New York Times,* March 12, 2007, A22.

19 Useful websites for tracking data removed from government websites include: www.ombwatch.org, openthegovernment.org and www.fas.org.

20 William S. Broad, "U.S. Is Tightening Rules on Keeping Scientific Secrets," *New York Times,* February 17, 2002, 1, 13.

21 David Nather, "Pilots Need-to-Know Conundrum," *CQ Weekly,* July 18, 2005, 1966.

22 Ellen Nakashima, "Frustration on the Left—and the Right," *Washington Post National Weekly Edition,* March 11, 2002, 29; Scott Shane, "Increase in the Number of Documents Classified by the Government," *New York Times,* July 3, 2005, 12.

23 Shane, "Increase in the Number of Documents Classified by the Government,"12; David Nather, "Classified: A Rise in State Secrets," *CQ Weekly,* July 18, 2005, 1960.

24 For a review of legislation introduced in the 110th congress see Relyea, CRS Report RL32780, 2-15.

25 Evan Hendricks, *Former Secrets: Government Records Made Public through the Freedom of Information Act* (Washington, D.C.: Campaign for Political Rights, 1982);"Behind the Freedom of Information Act," *Now with Bill Moyers,* PBS, April 5, 2002.

26 Joyce Appleby, "That's General Washington to You," *New York Times Book Review,* February 14, 1993, 11, a review of Richard Norton Smith, *Patriarch* (Boston: Houghton Mifflin, 1993). See also James Q. Wilson, "The Rise of the Bureaucratic State," *Public Interest* 41 (1975), 77–103.

27 Wilson, "Rise of the Bureaucratic State."

28 Leonard D. White, *Introduction to the Study of Public Administration,* 4th ed. (New York: Macmillan, 1955), 4.

29 David H. Rosenbloom, "'Whose Bureaucracy Is This Anyway?' Congress's 1946 Answer," *PS: Political Science and Politics,* December 2001, 773.

30 Paul C. Light, *Thickening Government: Federal Hierarchy and the Diffusion of Accountability* (Washington, D.C.: Brookings Institution, 1995).

31 U.S. Census Bureau, *Statistical Abstract of the United States,* 2006 (Washington, D.C.: Government Printing Office, 2005), tab. 451.

32 "Federal Government Found to Have Gotten Bigger," *Champaign-Urbana News-Gazette,* January 23, 2004, A3.

33 Paul C. Light, "Fact Sheet on the Continued Thickening of Government," Brookings Institution, July 23, 2004, www.brookings.edu/views/papers/light/20040723.htm.

34 Ibid. Light does an "inventory" of senior positions in cabinet departments every six years.

35 Jim Hoagland, "Dissing Government," *Washington Post National Weekly Edition,* December 8, 2003, 5.

36 Paul C. Light, "What Federal Employees Want from Reform: Reform Watch Brief No. 5," Brookings Institution, March 2002, www.brookings.edu/comm/reformwatch/rw05.htm.

37 For a discussion of these issues, see Peter T. Kilborn, "Big Change Likely as Law Bans Bias toward Disabled," *New York Times,* July 19, 1992, 1, 16.

38 Jill Smolows, "Noble Aims, Mixed Results," *Time,* July 31, 1995, 54.

39 Theodore Lowi, *The End of Liberalism* (New York: Norton, 1969).

40 This quote from Roosevelt and others about the merit system can be found at www.opm.gov/about_opm/tr/quotes/asp.

41 Woodrow Wilson, "The Study of Administration," *Political Science Quarterly* 56 (1941), 481–506. Originally published in 1887.

42 See David H. Rosenbloom, "Have an Administrative Rx? Don't Forget the Politics!" *Public Administration Review* 53 (1993), 503–507.

43 The changes in allowable political activities made possible by the Hatch Act Reform Amendments are outlined by the Office of Personnel Management in its online history, "Biography of an Ideal." See the section "Hatch Act Revisited and Transformed," www.opm.gov.

44 John Solomon, Alec MacGillis and Sarah Cohen, "How Rove Harnessed Government for GOP Gains," *Washington Post,* August 19, 2007, 1, A6. The Hatch Act violation came in a briefing to the General Services Administration where it was recommended that GSA contracts be awarded with an eye to helping Republican candidates. The head of the GAO was later forced to resign.

45 Charlie Savage, "For White House, Hiring is Political," *New York Times,* July 31, 2008, 17.

46 The 146-page report is available at the Department of Justice website, www.justice.gov.

47 Andre Revkin, "Bush Aide Softened Greenhouse Gas Link to Global Warming," *New York Times,* June 8, 2005, 1.

48 For reports on these issues, see www.ucsusa.org, the website of the Union of Concerned Scientists; and that of the Federation of American Scientists, www.usfas.org.

49 Charles Peters, *How Washington Really Works* (Reading, Mass.: Addison-Wesley, 1980), 46–47.

50 Nicolas Thompson, "Finding the Civil Service's Hidden Sex Appeal," *Washington Monthly,* November 2000, 31.

51 Terry More, "Regulators' Performance and Presidential Administrations," *American Journal of Political Science* 26 (1982), 197–224; Terry More, "Control and Feedback in Economic Regulation," *American Political Science Review* 79 (1985), 1094–1116.

52 More, "Control and Feedback."

53 Use of the term *capture* by political scientists studying regulation seems to have originated with Samuel Huntington, "The Marasmus of the ICC," *Yale Law Journal* 61 (1952), 467–509; it was later popularized by Marver Bernstein, *Regulating Business by Independent Commission* (Princeton, N.J.: Princeton University Press, 1955).

54 W. John Moore, "Citizen Prosecutors," *National Journal,* August 18, 1990, 2006–2010.

55 Interview with David Brancaccio, *NOW* (PBS), October 14, 2005.

56 Steve Fainaru and Dan Eggen, "Chief among the Charges," *Washington Post National Weekly Edition,* June 10, 2002, 30.

57 Robert Pear, "Congress Moves to Protect Federal Whistleblowers," *New York Times,* October 3, 2004, 21.

58 Philip Shenon, "F.B.I. Raids Office of Special Counsel," *New York Times,* May 7, 2008, 18.

59 Fred Alford, quoted in Barbara Ehrenreich, "All Together Now," *New York Times,* July 15, 2004, A23.

60 Eric Schmitt, "The Rube Goldberg Agency," *New York Times,* March 24, 2002, WK5.

61 Schmitt, "Is This Any Way to Run a Nation?", *New York Times,* April 14, 2002, WK4.

Chapter 13

1 This act is discussed in more detail in Chapter 15.

2 The jury awarded her $3.8 million, to punish Goodyear as well as to compensate her, but the judge reduced the award to $300,000.

3 167 L.Ed.2d 982 (2007).

4 A bill was introduced in Congress to allow such suits, but it was blocked by a Republican filibuster in 2008. In some circumstances, the Equal Pay Act could be used instead, but Ledbetter's lawyers decided that it wouldn't work for her. This act is also discussed in Chapter 15.

5 Lisa Takeuchi Cullen, "Show Us Our Money," *Time,* May 12, 2008, 137.

6 John Hibbing and Elizabeth Theiss-Morse, *Congress as Public Enemy: Public Attitudes toward American Political Institutions* (New York: Cambridge University Press, 1995), chs. 2 and 3.

7 John R. Schmidhauser, *Justices and Judges* (Boston: Little, Brown, 1979), 11.

8 However, federalism doesn't require this exact arrangement. Most federal countries have one national court over a system of regional courts.

9 In addition, there is the Court of Appeals for the Federal Circuit, which handles customs and patents cases.

10 Occasionally, for important cases, the entire group of judges in one circuit will sit together, "en banc." (In the large Ninth Circuit, eleven judges will sit.)

11 If at least $75,000 is at stake, according to congressional law.

12 Quoted in Henry J. Abraham, "A Bench Happily Filled," *Judicature* 66 (1983), 284.

13 For elaboration on the Senate's role, see Stephen B. Burbank, "Politics, Privilege, and Power: The Senate's Role in the Appointment of Federal Judges," *Judicature* 86 (2002), 24.

14 Victor Navasky, *Kennedy Justice* (New York: Atheneum, 1971), 245–246.

15 Harry P. Stumpf, *American Judicial Politics,* 2nd ed. (Upper Saddle River, N.J.: Prentice Hall, 1998), 175. After Taft nominated a Catholic to be chief justice, the Speaker of the House cracked, "If Taft were Pope, he'd want to appoint some Protestants to the College of Cardinals." Henry J. Abraham, *Justices and Presidents: A Political History of Appointments to the Supreme Court,* 2nd ed. (New York: Oxford University Press, 1985), 168.

16 The Nixon administration was the first to recognize that it could accomplish some policy goals by selecting lower court judges on the basis of ideology. Elliot E. Slotnick, "A Historical Perspective on Federal Judicial Selection," *Judicature* 86 (2002), 13.

17 For an analysis of internal documents that established this process in the Reagan administration, see Dawn Johnsen, "Tipping the Scale," *Washington Monthly,* July–August 2002, 1–18.

18 Jo Becker and Barton Gellman, "The Veep Steered While Vetting Conservatives for the Court," *Washington Post National Weekly Edition,* July 16–22, 2007, 9. For Bush's second nomination to the Court, the president departed from Cheney's list, selecting White House Counsel Harriet Miers. The vice president was miffed, commenting, "Didn't have the nerve to tell me himself," and conservative groups were concerned that Miers wasn't reliably conservative. After these groups torpedoed her nomination, Bush selected a name—Alito's—from Cheney's list.

19 Marilyn Nejelski, *Women in the Judiciary: A Status Report* (Washington, D.C.: National Women's Political Caucus, 1984).

20 Sheldon Goldman, "Reagan's Second-Term Judicial Appointments," *Judicature* 70 (1987), 324–339.

21 Sheldon Goldman, Elliott E. Slotnick, Gerard Gryski, Gary Zuk, and Sara Schiavoni, "W. Bush Remaking the Judiciary: Like Father Like Son?" *Judicature* 86 (2003), 304, 308. For further examination, see Rorie L. Spill and Kathleen A. Bratton, "Clinton and Diversification of the Federal Judiciary," *Judicature,* March–April, 2001, 256.

22 Ibid.

23 Especially congressional power under the commerce clause.

24 David Greenberg, "Actually, It Is Political," *Washington Post National Weekly Edition,* July 26-August 1, 2004, 23.

25 One of President Reagan's nominees, Douglas Ginsburg, withdrew his nomination due to widespread opposition in the Senate, so officially his nomination was not denied.

26 Nixon's nomination of G. Harold Carswell was a notable exception. At his confirmation hearing, a parade of legal scholars called him undistinguished. Even his supporters acknowledged that he was mediocre. Nixon's floor manager for the nomination, Senator Roman Hruska (R-Neb.), blurted out in exasperation, "Even if he is mediocre, there are a lot of mediocre judges and people and lawyers. They are entitled to a little representation, aren't they, and a little chance? We can't have all Brandeises, Cardozos, and Frankfurters, and stuff like that there." Abraham, *Justices and Presidents,* 6–7.

27 For an examination of the relationship between ethical lapses and ideological reasons, see Charles M. Cameron, Albert D. Cover, and Jeffrey A. Segal, "Senate Voting on Supreme Court Nominees: A Neoinstitutional Model," *American Political Science Review* 84 (1990), 525–534.

28 For some time, the Senate confirmed fewer nominees to the lower courts in the fourth year of a president's term when the Senate's majority was from the other party. The senators hoped their candidate would capture the White House in the next election. They delayed confirmation so there would be numerous vacancies for their president and, through senatorial courtesy, for themselves to fill as well. Jeffrey A. Segal and Harold Spaeth, "If a Supreme Court Vacancy Occurs, Will the Senate Confirm a Reagan Nominee?" *Judicature* 69 (1986), 188–189.

29 Quoted in Savage, "Clinton Losing Fight for Black Judge," *Los Angeles Times,* July 7, 2000, A1.

30 Scherer, "Judicial Confirmation Process," 240–250.

31 Schmidhauser, *Justice and Judges,* 55–57.

32 David Leonhardt, "Who Has a Corner Office?" *New York Times,* November 27, 2005, BU4.

33 All except Kennedy, Thomas, and possibly Alito.

34 Goldman et al., "W. Bush Remaking the Judiciary," 304, 308.

[35] As an alternative, Congress in 1980 established other procedures to discipline lower court judges. Councils made up of district and appellate court judges can ask their fellow judges to resign or can prevent them from hearing cases, but they cannot actually remove them. The procedures have been used infrequently, although their existence has prompted some judges to resign before being disciplined.

[36] Merle Miller, *Plain Speaking* (New York: Berkeley Putnam, 1974), 121.

[37] Harold W. Chase, *Federal Judges* (Minneapolis: University of Minnesota Press, 1972), 189.

[38] John Gruhl, "The Impact of Term Limits for Supreme Court Justices," *Judicature* 81 (1997), 66–72.

[39] The fourth, Rehnquist, disqualified himself because he had worked on the administration's policy toward executive privilege.

[40] *Jones* v. *Clinton,* 137 L.Ed.2d 945, 117 S. Ct. 1636 (1997).

[41] Martin Shapiro, "The Supreme Court: From Warren to Burger," in *The New American Political System,* ed. Anthony King (Washington, D.C.: American Enterprise Institute, 1978), 180–181.

[42] Robert Scigliano, *The Supreme Court and the Presidency* (New York: Free Press, 1971), 147–148.

[43] Quoted in Abraham, *Justices and Presidents,* 62.

[44] Earl Warren, *The Memoirs of Earl Warren* (Garden City, N.Y.: Doubleday, 1977), 5.

[45] Quoted in Abraham, *Justices and Presidents,* 63.

[46] Linda Greenhouse, "In the Confirmation Dance, the Past but Rarely the Prologue," *New York Times,* July 24, 2005, WK5.

[47] For elaboration, see Lee Epstein and Jeffrey A. Segal, *Advice and Consent* (New York: Oxford University Press, 2005), ch. 5.

[48] "How Much Do Lawyers Charge?" *Parade,* March 23, 1997, 14.

[49] Lois G. Forer, *Money and Justice* (New York: Norton, 1984), 9, 15, 102.

[50] Jonathan Casper, "Lawyers Before the Supreme Court: Civil Liberties and Civil Rights, 1957–1966," *Stanford Law Review,* February, 1970, 509.

[51] Peter Slevin, "Courting Christianity," *Washington Post National Weekly Edition,* July 17–23, 2006, 29.

[52] Karen O'Connor and Lee Epstein, "The Rise of Conservative Interest Group Litigation," *Journal of Politics* 45 (1983), 481. See also Richard C. Cortner, *The Supreme Court and the Second Bill of Rights* (Madison: University of Wisconsin Press, 1981), 282.

[53] Rick Perlstein, "Christian Empire," *New York Times Book Review,* January 7, 2007, 15.

[54] Jeffrey Rosen, "Supreme Court Inc.," *New York Times Magazine,* March 16, 2008, 44. The Court also takes about this many to decide summarily—without oral arguments and full written opinions. Dahlia Lithwick, "Realignment?" *Washington Post National Weekly Edition,* June 23–July 6, 2008, 25.

[55] The dentist agreed to fill the cavity only in a hospital, where the procedure would be far more expensive. *Bragdon* v. *Abbott,* 141 L. Ed.2d 540 (1998).

[56] *Toyota Motor Manufacturing* v. *Williams,* 151 L.Ed.2d 615 (2001).

[57] Abraham, *Judicial Process,* 324.

[58] *United States* v. *Butler,* 297 U.S. 1, at 94.

[59] Murphy and Pritchett, *Courts, Judges, and Politics,* 586.

[60] *Furman* v. *Georgia,* 408 U.S. 238 (1972). Blackmun did vote against the death penalty later in his career.

[61] Quoted in Alexander Bickel, *The Morality of Consent* (New Haven, Conn.: Yale University Press, 1975), 120.

[62] "Judicial Authority Moves Growing Issue," *Lincoln Journal,* April 24, 1977.

[63] Jeffrey A. Segal and Albert D. Cover, "Ideological Values and the Votes of U.S. Supreme Court Justices," *American Political Science Review* 83 (1989), 557–564. For different findings for state supreme court justices, see John M. Scheb II, Terry Bowen, and Gary Anderson, "Ideology, Role Orientations, and Behavior in the State Courts of Last Resort," *American Politics Quarterly* 19 (1991), 324–335.

[64] Harold Spaeth and Stuart Teger, "Activism and Restraint: A Cloak for the Justices' Policy Preferences," in *Supreme Court Activism and Restraint,* eds. Stephen P. Halpern and Clark M. Lamb (Lexington, Mass.: Lexington Books, 1982), 277.

[65] *Burnet* v. *Coronado Oil and Gas,* 285 U.S. 293 (1932), at 406.

[66] *Engel* v. *Vitale,* 370 U.S. 421 (1962).

[67] *Abington School District* v. *Schempp,* 374 U.S. 203 (1963).

[68] *Stone* v. *Graham,* 449 U.S. 39 (1980).

[69] *Lee* v. *Weisman,* 120 L.Ed.2d 467 (1992).

[70] *Santa Fe Independent School District* v. *Doe,* 147 L.Ed.2d 295 (2000).

[71] *Roe* v. *Wade,* 410 U.S. 113 (1973).

[72] *Planned Parenthood of Southeastern Pennsylvania* v. *Casey,* 120 L.Ed.2d 674 (1992).

[73] *United States* v. *Butler,* 297 U. S. 1 (1936), at 79.

[74] Some might say that judges, rather than make law, mediate among various ideas that rise to the surface, killing off some and allowing others to survive. Robert Cover, "Nomos and Narrative," *Harvard Law Review* 97 (1983), 4.

[75] Quoted in Murphy and Pritchett, *Courts, Judges, and Politics,* 25.

[76] *Gratz* v. *Bollinger,* 156 L.Ed.2d 257 (2003); *Grutter* v. *Bollinger,* 156 L.Ed.2d 304 (2003).

[77] Quoted in David J. Garrow, "The Rehnquist Reins," *New York Times Magazine,* October 6, 1996, 70.

[78] Jeffrey Toobin, *The Nine: Inside the Secret World of the Supreme Court* (New York: Doubleday, 2007), 129, 195.

[79] Ibid., 263.

[80] Quoted in Robert Wernick, "Chief Justice Marshall Takes the Law in Hand," *Smithsonian,* November 1998, 162.

[81] Joan Biskupic, "Here Comes the Judge? Maybe Not," *Washington Post National Weekly Edition,* February 14, 2000, 30.

[82] Jeffrey A. Segal and Harold J. Spaeth, *The Supreme Court and the Attitudinal Model* (New York: Cambridge University Press, 1993), 262–264.

[83] Jeffrey Rosen, "Rehnquist's Choice," *New Yorker,* January 11, 1999, 31.

[84] Justice Breyer, quoted by Jeffrey Toobin, "Breyer's Big Idea," *New Yorker,* October 31, 2005, 43.

[85] *Morning Edition,* National Public Radio, March 5, 2004.

[86] Michael S. Serrill, "The Power of William Brennan," *Time,* July 22, 1985, 62.

[87] Ibid.

[88] David J. Garrow, "One Angry Man," *New York Times Magazine,* October 6, 1996, 68–69.

[89] *Webster* v. *Reproductive Health Services,* 492 U.S. 490 (1989).

[90] *United States* v. *Virginia,* 135 L.Ed.2d 735, 787–789 (1996).

[91] Charles Evans Hughes, *The Supreme Court of the United States* (New York: Columbia University Press, 1928), 68.

[92] Interview with Justice Ruth Bader Ginsburg, *Morning Edition,* National Public Radio, May 2, 2002. Ginsburg said that foreign jurists admit they disagree with each other but do not make it public.

[93] Craig R. Ducat, *2005 Supplement for Constitutional Interpretation,* 8th ed. (Belmont, Calif.: Wadsworth, 2006), 3.

[94] Linda Greenhouse, "The High Court and the Triumph of Discord," *New York Times,* July 15, 2001, sec. 4, 1. Perhaps this calls into question Rehnquist's reputation as an effective leader.

[95] *Federalist Paper* 78.

[96] Henry J. Abraham, *Justices and Presidents* (New York: Oxford University Press, 1974), 74.

[97] Henry J. Abraham, *The Judicial Process,* 3rd ed. (New York: Oxford University Press, 1975), 309.

[98] Drew Pearson and Robert S. Allen, *The Nine Old Men* (New York: Doubleday/Doren, 1937), 7; Barbara A. Perry, *The Priestly Tribe: The Supreme Court's Image in the American Mind* (Westport, Conn.: Praeger, 1999), 8–9.

[99] There's evidence that many Founders expected the federal courts to use judicial review eventually. Some state courts already used judicial review, and in *Federalist Paper* 78 Hamilton said that the federal courts would have authority to void laws contrary to the Constitution.

[100] 5 U.S. 137 (1803). Technically, *Marbury* was not the first use of judicial review, but it was the first clear articulation of judicial review by the Court.

[101] Jefferson was also angry at the nature of the appointees. One had led troops loyal to England during the Revolutionary War. Eric Black, *Our Constitution: The Myth That Binds Us* (Boulder, Colo.: Westview Press, 1988), 66.

[102] Debate arose over whether the four should be considered appointed. Their commissions had been signed by the president, and the seal

of the United States had been affixed by Marshall, as secretary of state. Yet it was customary to require commissions to be delivered, perhaps because of less reliable record keeping by government or less reliable communications at the time.

103 Marbury had petitioned the Court for a writ of *mandamus* under the authority of a provision of the Judiciary Act of 1789 that permitted the Court to issue such a writ. Marshall maintained that this provision broadened the Court's original jurisdiction and thus violated the Constitution. (The Constitution allows the Court to hear cases that have not been heard by any other court before—if they involve a state or a foreign ambassador. Marbury's involved neither.) Yet it was quite clear that the provision did not broaden the Court's original jurisdiction—so clear, in fact, that Marshall did not even quote the language he was declaring unconstitutional. Furthermore, even if the provision did broaden the Court's original jurisdiction, it is not certain that the provision would violate the Constitution. (The Constitution does not say that the Court shall have original jurisdiction only in cases involving a state or a foreign ambassador.) Many members of Congress who had drafted and voted for the Judiciary Act had been delegates to the Constitutional Convention, and it is unlikely that they would have initiated a law that contradicted the Constitution. And Oliver Ellsworth, who had been a coauthor of the bill, then served as chief justice of the Supreme Court before Marshall. But these interpretations allowed Marshall a way out of the dilemma.

104 Quoted in Walter F. Murphy and C. Herman Pritchett, *Courts, Judges, and Politics,* 3rd ed. (New York: Random House, 1979), 4.

105 John A. Garraty, "The Case of the Missing Commissions," in *Quarrels That Have Shaped the Constitution,* ed. John A. Garraty (New York: Harper & Row, 1962), 13.

106 *Fletcher* v. *Peck,* 10 U.S. 87 (1810); *Martin* v. *Hunter's Lessee,* 14 U.S. 304 (1816); *Cohens* v. *Virginia,* 19 U.S. 264 (1821).

107 In other cases, the Court narrowly construed state power, especially to regulate commerce. *Gibbons* v. *Ogden,* 22 U.S. 1 (1824).

108 However, the Warren Court may not have been as out of step with the political branches as is often believed. See Lucas A. Powe, *The Warren Court and American Politics* (Cambridge, Mass.: Harvard University Press, 2000), 160–178.

109 Particularly regarding criminal defendants' rights.

110 One legal scholar says the most striking feature about Supreme Court decision making in the 1990s was the effort by five justices to resolve most issues as narrowly as possible, shunning sweeping pronouncements for case-by-case examination. Cass R. Sunstein, *One Case at a Time: Judicial Minimalism on the Supreme Court* (Cambridge, Mass.: Harvard University Press, 2001).

111 The Rehnquist Court reduced the scope of criminal defendants' rights, racial minorities' rights, and affirmative action. It also tightened access to the courts for individuals and groups trying to challenge government policies, and it limited efforts by Congress to impose new regu-

lations on the states. However, the Court did take the first step toward homosexuals' legal rights.

112 Thomas M. Keck, *The Most Activist Supreme Court in History* (Chicago: University of Chicago Press, 2004).

113 531 U.S. 98 (2000).

114 The possible exception is Justice Ginsburg, who replaced Justice Byron White. Jeffrey Rosen, "The Dissenter," *New York Times Magazine,* September 23, 2007, 52.

115 Baum, *Supreme Court,* 170, 173.

116 Craig R. Ducat and Robert L. Dudley, "Federal Appellate Judges and Presidential Power," paper presented at the Midwest Political Science Association meeting, April 1987.

117 Sheldon Goldman, "How Long the Legacy?" *Judicature* 76 (1993), 295.

118 The Eleventh Amendment overturned *Chisholm* v. *Georgia* (1793), which had permitted the federal courts to hear suits against a state by citizens of another state. The Fourteenth overturned the Dred Scott case, *Scott* v. *Sandford* (1857), which had held that blacks were not citizens. The Sixteenth overturned *Pollock* v. *Farmers' Loan and Trust* (1895), which had negated a congressional law authorizing a federal income tax. The Twenty-Sixth overturned *Oregon* v. *Mitchell* (1970), which had negated a congressional law allowing eighteen-year-olds to vote in state elections.

119 William N. Eskridge Jr., "Overriding Supreme Court Statutory Interpretation Decisions," *Yale Law Journal* 101 (1991), 338.

120 *Goldman* v. *Weinberger,* 475 U.S. 503 (1986).

121 Detainee Treatment Act of 2005 and Military Commissions Act of 2006. *Hamdan* v. *Rumsfeld,* 548 U.S. 557 (2006); *Boumediene* v. *Bush* (2008)

122 Thomas R. Marshall, "Public Opinion and the Rehnquist Court," in *Readings in American Government and Politics,* 3rd ed. (Boston, Mass.: Allyn & Bacon, 1999), 115–121.

123 Richard Morin, "A Nation of Stooges," *Washington Post,* October 8, 1995, C5.

124 Gregory A. Caldeira, "Neither the Purse nor the Sword," paper presented at the American Political Science Association meeting, August 1987.

125 Quoted in Abraham, *Justices and Presidents,* 342–343.

126 Robert G. McCloskey, *The American Supreme Court* (Chicago: University of Chicago Press, 1960), 225.

Chapter 14

1 This "Talking Points" is drawn from Philip Gourevitch and Errol Morris, "Exposure," *New Yorker,* March 24, 2008, 44–57. Quotation is from p. 47.

2 Ibid., 47.

3 Ibid.

4 Ibid., 51.

5 Ibid., 52.

6 Ibid., 56.

7 Ibid.

8 The death was officially classified as a homicide. Ibid.

9 Only one above the rank of staff sergeant was ever charged, and he was cleared. Ample evidence shows that such harsh treatment was the de facto, if not official, policy. Ibid., 49. See also the sources cited later in the chapter.

10 Richard Morin, "The High Price of Free Speech," *Washington Post National Weekly Edition,* January 8, 2001, 34.

11 After 9/11, support for civil liberties dropped, reflecting people's fears. By 2005, however, support returned to pre–9/11 levels. First Amendment Center, in cooperation with the *American Journalism Review.* Survey conducted May 13–23, 2005. (N = 1003; sampling error = 3%).

12 The states didn't ratify a proposed amendment that would have required at least one representative in Congress for every fifty thousand people. That amendment would have put about five thousand members in today's Congress. The states also didn't ratify, until 1992, another proposed amendment that would have prohibited a salary raise for members of Congress from taking effect until after the next election to Congress.

13 *Reid* v. *Covert,* 354 U.S. 1 (1957).

14 *Barron* v. *Baltimore,* 32 U.S. 243 (1833).

15 Also, many states had their own bill of rights at the time, and other states were expected to follow.

16 *Gitlow* v. *New York,* 268 U.S. 652 (1925). Gitlow is usually cited as the first because it initiated the twentieth-century trend. However, Chicago, *Burlington and Quincy R. Co.* v. *Chicago,* 166 U.S. 266 (1897), was actually the first. It applied the Fifth Amendment's just compensation clause, requiring government to pay owners "just compensation" for taking their property.

17 *Argersinger* v. *Hamlin,* 407 U.S. 25 (1972).

18 It hasn't applied the Fifth Amendment's guarantee of a grand jury in criminal cases or the Seventh Amendment's guarantee of a jury trial in civil cases. The grand jury no longer serves as a protective shield for potential criminal defendants; rather, it's become a prosecutorial tool. The Seventh Amendment guarantees a jury trial in civil cases when $20 or more is at stake, so that would require a commitment of scarce resources even for trivial cases.

19 The amendment also includes a right "to petition the government for a redress of grievances," which is incorporated in freedom of speech and assembly. The language doesn't explicitly include freedom of association, but the Court has interpreted the amendment to encompass this right.

20 Anna Johnson, "Know Your First Amendment Rights? Poll Shows Many Don't," *Lincoln Journal Star,* March 1, 2006, 10A.

21 Even Justice Black, who claimed that he interpreted it literally. To do so, he had to define some speech as "action" so that it wouldn't be protected.

22 *Milk Wagon Drivers Union* v. *Meadowmoor Dairies*, 312 U.S. 287 (1941).

23 Thomas I. Emerson, *The System of Freedom of Expression* (New York: Random House/Vintage, 1971), 6–8.

24 Quoted in Deborah Tannen, *The Argument Culture* (New York: Ballantine, 1998), 25.

25 For a history of speech cases between the Civil War and World War I, see David M. Rabban, *Free Speech in Its Forgotten Years* (New York: Cambridge University Press, 1997).

26 The Sedition Act of 1918. In addition, the Espionage Act of 1917 prohibited interfering with military recruitment, inciting insubordination in military forces, and mailing material advocating rebellion.

27 Zechariah Chafee Jr., *Free Speech in the United States* (Cambridge, Mass.: Harvard University Press, 1941), 51–52.

28 *Schenk* v. *United States*, 249 U.S. 47 (1919); *Frohwerk* v. *United States*, 249 U.S. 204 (1919); *Debs* v. *United States*, 249 U.S. 211 (1919); *Abrams* v. *United States*, 250 U.S. 616 (1919); *Gitlow* v. *New York*, 268 U.S. 652 (1925); *Whitney* v. *California*, 274 U.S. 357 (1927).

29 *Gitlow* v. *New York*.

30 David Cole, "The Course of Least Resistance: Repeating History in the War on Terrorism," in *Lost Liberties*, ed. Cynthia Brown (New York: New Press, 2003), 15.

31 Novelist Philip Roth observes, "McCarthy understood better than any American politician before him that people whose job was to legislate could do far better for themselves by performing; McCarthy understood the entertainment value of disgrace and how to feed the pleasures of paranoia. He took us back to our origins, back to the seventeenth century and the stocks. That's how the country began: moral disgrace as public entertainment." *I Married a Communist* (New York: Vintage, 1999), 284.

32 The Smith Act (1940). This act wasn't as broad as the World War I acts because it didn't forbid criticizing the government.

33 *Dennis* v. *United States*, 341 U.S. 494 (1951).

34 For the role of the Senate's Internal Security Committee, see Michael J. Ybarra, *Washington Gone Crazy: Senator Pat McCarran and the Great American Communist Hunt* (Hanover, N. H.: Steerforth, 2004).

35 The records included some code names that haven't been linked to real people. Charles Peters,"Tilting at Windmills," *Washington Monthly*, May, 2006, 8. See also Ted Morgan, *Reds: McCarthyism in Twentieth-Century America* (New York: Random House, 2003).

36 In the cases of *Yates* v. *United States*, 354 U. S. 298 (1957), and *Scales* v. *United States*, 367 U.S. 203 (1961), among others.

37 The doctrine was created in a case in which a Ku Klux Klan leader said at a rally that the Klan might take "revengeance" against the president, Congress, and the Supreme Court if they continued "to suppress the white, Caucasian race." *Brandenburg* v. *Ohio*, 395 U.S. 444 (1969).

38 *Brandenburg* v. *Ohio*.

39 Attorney General Tom Clark quoted in *Esquire*, November 1974.

40 Cole, "Course of Least Resistance," 1.

41 Jean E. Jackson, "ACTA Report Criticizes Professors," *Anthropology News*, March 2002, 7.

42 Gia Fenoglio, "Is It 'Blacklisting' or Mere Criticism?" *National Journal*, January 19, 2002, 188.

43 For some examples, see Michael Tomasky, "Dissent in America," *American Prospect*, April 2003, 22. See also Ann Coulter, *Treason: Liberal Treachery from the Cold War to the War on Terrorism* (New York: Crown Forum, 2003), and Sean Hannity, *Deliver Us from Evil* (New York: Regan Books/HarperCollins, 2004).

44 C. Herman Pritchett, *The American Constitution*, 2nd ed. (New York: McGraw-Hill, 1968), 476, n. 2. However, police in some places continue to arrest for swearing. Judy Lin, "ACLU Fights Police on Profanity Arrests in Pittsburgh Area," *Lincoln Journal Star*, July 11, 2002.

45 *Gooding* v. *Wilson*, 405 U.S. 518 (1972); *Lewis* v. *New Orleans*, 408 U.S. 913 (1972).

46 *Cohen* v. *California*, 403 U.S. 15 (1971).

47 However, businesses can restrict the speech of their employees at work because they're private entities.

48 *Collin* v. *Smith*, 447 F.Supp. 676 (N.D. Ill., 1978); *Collin* v. *Smith*, 578 F.2d 1197 (7th Cir, 1978).

49 *United States* v. *Schwimmer*, 279 U.S. 644 (1929).

50 *Virginia* v. *Black*, 155 L.Ed.2d 535 (2003). Previously, the Court invalidated a St. Paul, Minnesota, ordinance prohibiting the display of a Nazi swastika or a cross-burning on public or private land. *R.A.V.* v. *St. Paul*, 120 L.Ed.2d 305 (1992).

51 For a legal analysis supporting these codes, see Richard Delgado and David H. Yun, "Pressure Valves and Bloodied Chickens: An Analysis of Paternalistic Objections to Hate Speech Regulation," *University of California Law Review*, 82 (1994), 716.

52 Mary Jordan, "Free Speech Starts to Have Its Say," *Washington Post National Weekly Edition*, September 21–27, 1992, 31.

53 Michael D. Shear, "A Tangled World Wide Web," *Washington Post National Weekly Edition*, October 30–November 5, 1995, 36.

54 Stephanie Simon, "Christians Sue for Right Not to Tolerate Policies," *Los Angeles Times*, April 10, 2006, www.latimes.com/news/ nationworld/nation/la-nachristians10apr10,0, 6204444. story?

55 *Barnes* v. *Glenn Theater*, 501 U.S. 560 (1991).

56 *Young* v. *American Mini Theatres*, 427 U.S. 50 (1976); *Renton* v. *Playtime Theatres*, 475 U.S. 41 (1986).

57 *FCC* v. *Pacifica Foundation*, 438 U.S. 726 (1968).

58 By "fleeting" profanities, the FCC evidently means brief and spontaneous profanities that the networks couldn't foresee and bleep.

59 Jonathan D. Salant, "FCC Wants to Up Fine for Cursing," *Lincoln Journal Star*, January 15, 2004.

60 *Wilkinson* v. *Jones*, 480 U.S. 926 (1987).

61 *Southeastern Promotions* v. *Conrad*, 420 U.S. 546 (1975).

62 *Jeannette Rankin Brigade* v. *Chief of Capital Police*, 409 U.S. 972 (1972); *Edwards* v. *South Carolina*, 372 U.S. 229 (1963); *United States* v. *Grace*, 75 L.Ed.2d 736 (1983). The grounds around jails and military bases are off-limits due to the need for security. *Adderley* v. *Florida*, 385 U.S. 39 (1966); *Greer* v. *Spock*, 424 U. S. 828 (1976).

63 According to the Burger Court, which emphasized property rights over First Amendment rights. *Lloyd* v. *Tanner*, 407 U.S. 551 (1972); *Hudgens* v. *NLRB*, 424 U.S. 507 (1976).

64 Leonard Pitts Jr., "Intolerance Meets Its Nemesis at an Albany Mall," *Lincoln Journal Star*, March 10, 2003.

65 *Cox* v. *Louisiana*, 379 U.S. 536 (1965).

66 *Schenk* v. *Pro-Choice Network*, 137 L.Ed.2d 1 (1997).

67 *Frisby* v. *Schultz*, 101 L.Ed.2d 420 (1988).

68 *United States* v. *O'Brien*, 391 U.S. 367 (1968).

69 *Tinker* v. *Des Moines School District* (1969).

70 *Smith* v. *Goguen*, 415 U.S. 566 (1974); *Spence* v. *Washington*, 418 U.S. 405 (1974).

71 *Texas* v. *Johnson*, 105 L.Ed.2d 342 (1989).

72 *United States* v. *Eichman*, 110 L.Ed.2d 287 (1990).

73 However, in 1995, after Republicans became the majority in Congress, they renewed efforts to adopt a constitutional amendment but fell just three votes short in one house.

74 *Tinker* v. *Des Moines School District*, 393 U. S. 503 (1969)..

75 *Bethel School District* v. *Fraser*, 478 U.S. 675 (1986).

76 *Morse* v. *Frederick*, 168 L.Ed.2d 290 (2007).

77 *Hazelwood School District* v. *Kuhlmeier*, 98 L.Ed.2d 592 (1988).

78 *Hurley* v. *Irish-American Gay, Lesbian and Bisexual Group of Boston*, 515 U.S. 557 (1995).

79 *Boy Scouts of America* v. *Dale*, 147 L.Ed.2d 554 (2000).

80 The Court invalidated racial discrimination in labor unions and private schools and sexual discrimination in law firms, despite claims of freedom of association. *Railway Mail Association* v. *Corsi*, 326 U.S. 88 (1945); *Runyon* v. *McCrary*, 427 U.S. 160 (1976); *Hison* v. *King & Spalding*, 467 U.S. 69 (1984) 6957.

81 *Roberts* v. *U.S. Jaycees*, 468 U.S. 609 (1984); *Board of Directors of Rotary International* v. *Rotary Club of Duarte*, 481 U.S. 537 (1987).

82 Quoted in David Halbertstam, *The Best and the Brightest* (Greenwich, Conn.: Fawcett, 1969), 769.

83 Bill Moyers, "Our Democracy Is in Danger of Being Paralyzed," *Keynote Address to the National Conference on Media Reform*, November 8, 2003, www.truthout.org/docs_03/printer_ 111403E.shtml.

84 *New York Times* v. *United States*, 403 U.S. 713 (1971). In addition to seeking injunctions, the Nixon administration sent a telegram to the New York Times demanding that it cease publication of the excerpts, but the FBI had the wrong telex number for the newspaper, so the telegram went first to a fish company in Brooklyn. R. W. Apple, "Lessons from the Pentagon Papers," *New York Times*, June 23, 1996, E5.

85 Actually, the Pentagon Papers did include some current information regarding ongoing negotiations and the names of CIA agents in Vietnam, but Ellsberg had not passed this information to the newspapers. However, the government and the Court were unaware of this, so the government argued that publication could affect national security, and the Court decided the case with this prospect in mind. Thus the Court's ruling was stronger than legal analysts realized at the time. Erwin N. Griswold, "No Harm Was Done," *New York Times*, June 30, 1991, E15.

86 *United States* v. *Progressive*, 467 F.Supp. 990 (W.D., Wisc., 1979).

87 Then radio and television stations used actors with Irish accents to dub the comments made by IRA members. In 1994, the government lifted the ban.

88 *Branzburg* v. *Hayes*, 408 U.S. 665 (1972).

89 Jeffrey Toobin, "Name That Source," *New Yorker*, January 16, 2006, 30.

90 *Cox Broadcasting* v. *Cohn*, 420 U.S. 469 (1975).

91 This was not a Supreme Court case.

92 *Time* v. *Hill*, 385 U.S. 374 (1967).

93 *Wilson* v. *Layne*, 143 L.Ed.2d 818 (1999); *Hanlon* v. *Berger*, 143 L.Ed.2d 978 (1999).

94 *New York Times* v. *Sullivan*, 376 U.S. 254.

95 Harry Kalven, "The New York Times Case: A Note on 'the Central Meaning of the First Amendment,'" *Supreme Court Review* (1964), 221.

96 *Monitor Patriot* v. *Roy*, 401 U.S. 265 (1971).

97 *Associated Press* v. *Walker*, 388 U.S. 130 (1967); *Greenbelt Cooperative* v. *Bresler*, 398 U.S. 6 (1970). This set of rulings began with *Curtis Publishing* v. *Butts*, 388 U.S. 130 (1967).

98 *Gertz* v. *Robert Welch*, 418 U.S. 323 (1974), and *Time* v. *Firestone*, 424 U.S. 448 (1976).

99 Eric Press, "Westmoreland Takes on CBS," *Newsweek*, October 22, 1984, 62.

100 The Pilgrims, who had experienced religious toleration in Holland (after persecution in England), left because they wanted a place of their own, not because they could not worship as they pleased. The Dutch were so tolerant that the Pilgrims' children had begun to adopt Dutch manners and ideas. Richard Shenkman, *I Love Paul Revere, Whether He Rode or Not* (New York: HarperCollins, 1991), 20–21.

101 The only religious reference in the Constitution occurs in the date when the document was written: "Year of our Lord one thousand seven hundred and eighty-seven." And that may have been mere convention; "year of our Lord" is the English equivalent of A.D.

102 Apparently Roger Williams, a clergyman and the founder of Rhode Island, was the first to use this metaphor. Lloyd Burton, "The Church in America," *New Yorker*, September 29, 2003, 10. James Madison was another of the Founders who pioneered our religious freedom. For an analysis of his views, see Vincent Phillip Munoz, "James Madison's Principle of Religious Liberty," *American Political Science Review*, 97 (2003), 17–32.

103 Gary Wills, quoted on *Thomas Jefferson*, PBS, February 18, 1997.

104 According to Mark Pachter, Curator of the National Portrait Gallery, *Morning Edition*, NPR, June 25, 2006.

105 See, for example, Forrest Church, *So Help Me God: The Founding Fathers and the First Great Battle Over Church and State* (Orlando, FL: Harcourt, 2007); David L. Holmes, *The Faiths of the Founders* (New York: Oxford University, 2006); Martha Nussbaum, *Liberty of Conscience: In Defense of America's Tradition of Religious Equality* (New York: Basic Books, 2008); Steven Waldman, *Founding Faith: Providence, Politics, and the Birth of Religious Freedom in America* (New York: Random House, 2008); and Garry Wills, *Head and Heart: American Christianities* (New York: Penguin, 2007).

106 *Torcaso* v. *Watkins*, 367 U.S. 488 (1961).

107 *Pierce* v. *Society of Sisters*, 268 U.S. 510 (1925).

108 *Cooper* v. *Pate*, 378 U.S. 546 (1963); *Cruz* v. *Beto*, 405 U.S. 319 (1972).

109 *Church of the Lukumi Babalu Aye* v. *Hialeah*, 124 L.Ed.2d 472 (1993).

110 *Reynolds* v. *United States*, 98 U.S. 145 (1879). Most Mormons, however, didn't approve of polygamy. Even when polygamy was most popular, perhaps only 10 percent of Mormons practiced it. Shenkman, *I Love Paul Revere*, 31. Yet today reports indicate that polygamy is still flourishing among Mormons, perhaps more than ever. Lawrence Wright, "Lives of the Saints," *New Yorker*, January 21, 2002, 43.

111 *Sherbert* v. *Verner*, 374 U.S. 398 (1963).

112 Although a congressional statute mandates "reasonable accommodation," the Court interpreted it so narrowly that it essentially requires only minimal accommodation. *Trans World Airlines* v. *Hardison*, 432 U.S. 63 (1977). For analysis, see Gloria T. Beckley and Paul Burstein, "Religious Pluralism, Equal Opportunity, and the State," *Western Political Quarterly* 44 (1991), 185–208. For a related case, see *Thornton* v. *Caldor*, 86 L.Ed.2d 557 (1985).

113 *United States* v. *Lee*, 455 U.S. 252 (1982).

114 *United States* v. *American Friends Service Committee*, 419 U.S. 7 (1974).

115 *Goldman* v. *Weinberger*, 475 U.S. 503 (1986); *O'Lone* v. *Shabazz*, 482 U.S. 342 (1986).

116 *Employment Division* v. *Smith*, 108 L.Ed.2d 876 (1990).

117 Congress did pass the American Indian Religious Freedom Act of 1994 to allow Indians to use peyote, but this law did not address the broader implications of the ruling. Ruth Marcus, "One Nation, under Court Rulings," *Washington Post National Weekly Edition*, March 18, 1991, 33.

118 *Boerne* v. *Flores*, 138 L.Ed.2d 624 (1997). Congress then passed another law that addressed just two kinds of government action—zoning and the rights of inmates at public correctional and mental institutions. The law required state and local governments to consider exceptions for religious practices. Although this was another attempt to override the Court's ruling, the Court upheld the law. *Cutter* v. *Wilkinson*, 125 S.Ct. 2113 (2005).

119 William Lee Miller, "The Ghost of Freedoms Past," *Washington Post National Weekly Edition*, October 13, 1986, 23–24.

120 Steven Waldman, "The Framers and the Faithful," *Washington Monthly*, April, 2006, 33–38.

121 *Church of Holy Trinity* v. *United States*, 143 U.S. 457 (1892).

122 *Engel* v. *Vitale*, 370 U.S. 421 (1962); *Abington School District* v. *Schempp*, 374 U.S. 203 (1963).

123 *Stone* v. *Graham*, 449 U.S. 39 (1980). The Ten Commandments themselves have been divisive. In 1844, six people were killed in a riot in Philadelphia over which version of the Ten Commandments to post in the public schools. E. J. Dionne Jr., "Bridging the Church-State Divide," *Washington Post National Weekly Edition*, October 11, 1999, 21.

124 George W. Andrews (D-Ala.), quoted in C. Herman Pritchett, *The American Constitution*, 3rd ed. (New York: McGraw-Hill, 1977), 406.

125 Kenneth M. Dolbeare and Phillip E. Hammond, *The School Prayer Decisions* (Chicago: University of Chicago Press, 1971).

126 Robert H. Birkby, "The Supreme Court and the Bible Belt," *Midwest Journal of Political Science*, 10 (1966), 304–315.

127 Julia Lieblich and Richard N. Ostling, "Despite Rulings, Prayer in School Still Sparks Debate, Still Practiced," *Lincoln Journal Star*, January 16, 2000.

128 "Five Schools Get Ten Commandments," *Lincoln Journal Star*, August 12, 1999.

129 J. Gordon Melton, quoted in Jon D. Hull, "The State of the Union," *Time*, January 30, 1995, 55.

130 Peter Cushnie, "Letters," *Time*, October 15, 1984, 21.

131 The Supreme Court invalidated Alabama's law that authorized a moment of silence "for meditation or voluntary prayer" because the wording of the law endorsed and promoted prayer. But most justices signaled approval of a moment of silence without such wording. *Wallace* v. *Jaffree*, 86 L.Ed.2d 29 (1985).

132 *Lee* v. *Weisman*, 120 L.Ed.2d 467 (1992).

133 *Jones* v. *Clear Creek*, 977 F.2d 965 (5th Cir., 1992).

134 *Moore* v. *Ingebretsen*, 88 F.3d 274 (1996).

135 *Santa Fe Independent School District* v. *Doe*, 530 U.S. 290 (2000).

136 Anna Quindlen, "School Prayer: Substitutes for Substance," *Lincoln Journal Star*, December 8, 1994.

137 A current guide for public school teachers, addressing practices that are permissible and those that are advisable in various situations, is

Charles C. Haynes and Oliver Thomas, *Finding Common Ground* (Nashville, Tenn.: First Amendment Center, 2002).

[138] *Widmar* v. *Vincent*, 454 U.S. 263 (1981). The law requires high schools that receive federal funds to allow meetings of students' religious, philosophical, or political groups if the schools permit meetings of any "noncurriculum" groups. Schools could prohibit meetings of all noncurriculum groups. A Salt Lake City high school banned all nonacademic clubs rather than let students form an organization for homosexuals in 1996. Interviews with teachers and students two years later indicated that as a result of the ban on clubs, school spirit declined and class and racial rifts expanded. Clubs no longer brought students together, and clubs such as Polynesian Pride and the Aztec Club, for Latinos, no longer provided a link between these students and their school. "Club Ban Aimed at Gays Backfires," *Lincoln Journal Star*, December 6, 1998.

[139] *Board of Education of the Westside Community Schools* v. *Mergens*, 496 U.S. 226 (1990).

[140] David Van Biema, "Spiriting Prayer into School," *Time*, April 27, 1998, 28–31.

[141] Harriet Barovick, "Fear of a Gay School," *Time*, February 21, 2000, 52.

[142] *Rosenberger* v. *University of Virginia*, 132 L.Ed.2d 700 (1995). Yet the Rehnquist Court later ruled that states that provide scholarships for students at colleges and universities don't have to provide them for students preparing for the ministry. *Locke* v. *Davey*, 158 L.Ed.2d 21 (2004).

[143] For the nation's first celebration of Columbus Day in 1892, Francis Bellamy wrote, "I pledge allegiance to my flag and the republic for which it stands, one nation indivisible, with liberty and justice for all." For Bellamy, the key words were indivisible, which referred to the Civil War and emphasized the Union over the states, and liberty and justice for all, which emphasized a balance between freedom for individuals and equality between them. During the Cold War in the 1950s, Americans feared "godless communism." Some objected to communism as much because of the Soviet Union's official policy of atheism as because of its totalitarianism. A religious revival swept the United States as preachers such as Billy Graham warned that Americans would perish in a nuclear holocaust unless they opened their arms to Jesus Christ. Congress replaced the traditional national motto—"E Pluribus Unum" ("Out of Many, One")—with "In God We Trust," and it added this new motto to our paper money. Fraternal organizations, especially the Catholic Knights of Columbus, and religious leaders campaigned to add "under God" to the Pledge of Allegiance. The Presbyterian pastor of President Eisenhower's church in Washington urged the addition in a sermon as the president sat in a pew. With little dissent, Congress passed and the president signed a bill to do so in 1954. The legislative history of the act stated that the intent was to "acknowledge the dependence of our people and our government upon . . . the Creator . . . [and] deny the atheistic and materialistic concept of communism." The president stated that "millions of our school children will daily proclaim in every city and town . . .

. . the dedication of our nation and our people to the Almighty." Thus the phrase was adopted expressly to endorse religion. David Greenberg, "The Pledge of Allegiance: Why We're Not One Nation 'under God,'" *Slate*, June 28, 2002, slate.msn.com/?id_2067499 S.

[144] *Elk Grove Unified School District* v. *Newdow*, 159 L.Ed.2d 98 (2004).

[145] *Lynch* v. *Donnelly*, 79 L.Ed.2d 604 (1984).

[146] *Allegheny County* v. *ACLU*, 106 L.Ed.2d 472 (1989). *Allegheny County* v. *ACLU*, 106 L.Ed.2d 472 (1989).

[147] *Van Orden* v. *Perry*, 162 L.Ed. 2d 607 (2005).

[148] Initially they stood alone. As the cases proceeded through the lower courts, officials added other historical documents but never made a sincere effort to integrate them.

[149] *McCreary County* v. *ACLU*, 162 L.Ed.2d 729 (2005).

[150] *Epperson* v. *Arkansas*, 393 U.S. 97 (1968).

[151] Some groups use the more sophisticated-sounding term creation science. Although these groups do address the science of evolution, courts consider creationism and creation science as interchangeable.

[152] *Edwards* v. *Aguillard*, 482 U.S. 578 (1987).

[153] They do acknowledge that some, limited evolution has occurred.

[154] However, to avoid court rulings similar to those against creationism—that it reflects a religious view—they try to avoid mention of God.

[155] Wendy Kaminer, "The God Bullies," *American Prospect*, November 18, 2002, 9.

[156] *McCreary County* v. *ACLU*, 162 L.Ed.2d 729 (2005).

[157] *Rochin* v. *California*, 342 U.S. 165 (1952).

[158] Seymour Wishman, *Confessions of a Criminal Lawyer* (New York: Penguin, 1981), 16.

[159] *Stein* v. *New York*, 346 U.S. 156 (1953).

[160] Wendy Kaminer, *It's All the Rage* (Reading, Mass.: Addison-Wesley, 1995), 78.

[161] *Weeks* v. *United States*, 232 U.S. 383 (1914).

[162] *Mapp* v. *Ohio*, 367 U.S. 643 (1961).

[163] This exception applies when police use a search warrant that they did not know was invalid. *United States* v. *Leon*, 82 L.Ed.2d 677 (1984); *Massachusetts* v. *Sheppard*, 82 L.Ed.2d 737 (1984). The Roberts Court has also created an exception to the exclusionary rule. When police have a search warrant but fail to knock and announce their presence before entering, as they have traditionally been required to do, any evidence seized may be used against the suspect despite the violation of the Fourth Amendment. *Hudson* v. *Michigan*, 165 L.Ed.2d 56 (2006).

[164] In situations in which police are required by law to knock and identify themselves before entering a residence, they can still use any evidence they find inside, even though the search is illegal because of their failure to knock and identify themselves. *Hudson* v. *Michigan*, 165 L.Ed.2d 56 (2006).

[165] *Olmstead* v. *United States*, 277 U.S. 438 (1928).

[166] *Katz* v. *United States*, 389 U.S. 347 (1967).

[167] *Brown* v. *Mississippi*, 297 U.S. 278 (1936).

[168] *McNabb* v. *United States*, 318 U.S. 332 (1943); *Mallory* v. *United States*, 354 U.S. 449 (1957); *Spano* v. *New York*, 360 U.S. 315 (1959).

[169] *Ashcraft* v. *Tennessee*, 322 U.S. 143 (1944).

[170] *Miranda* v. *Arizona*, 384 U.S. 436 (1966).

[171] *Dickerson* v. *United States*, 530 U.S. 428 (2000).

[172] Jan Hoffman, "Police Tactics Chipping Away at Suspects' Rights," *New York Times*, March 29, 1998, 35.

[173] *Johnson* v. *Zerbst*, 304 U.S. 458 (1938).

[174] The Court did require state courts to furnish an attorney when there were "special circumstances" involved. *Powell* v. *Alabama*, 287 U.S. 45 (1932).

[175] *Gideon* v. *Wainwright*, 372 U.S. 335 (1963).

[176] *Argersinger* v. *Hamlin*, 407 U.S. 25 (1972); *Scott* v. *Illinois*, 440 U.S. 367 (1974); *Alabama* v. *Shelton*, 152 L.Ed.2d 888(2002).

[177] *Douglas* v. *California*, 372 U.S. 353 (1953).

[178] Wendy Cole, "Death Takes a Holiday," *Time*, February 14, 2000, 68.

[179] Jill Smolowe, "Race and the Death Penalty," *Time*, April 29, 1991, 69.

[180] Peter Applebome, "Indigent Defendants, Overworked Lawyers," *New York Times*, May 17, 1992, E18.

[181] Alan Berlow, "Texas, Take Heed," *Washington Post National Weekly Edition*, February 21, 2000, 22.

[182] Richard Carelli, "Death Rows Grow, Legal Help Shrinks," *Lincoln Journal Star*, October 7, 1995.

[183] The Burger Court did rule that the right to counsel entails the right to "effective" counsel, but the Court set such stringent standards for establishing the existence of ineffective counsel that few defendants can take advantage of this right. See *Strickland* v. *Washington*, 466 U.S. 668 (1984), and *United States* v. *Cronic*, 466 U.S. 640 (1984).

[184] *Baldwin* v. *New York*, 339 U.S. 66 (1970); *Blanton* v. *North Las Vegas*, 489 U.S. 538 (1989).

[185] *Duncan* v. *Louisiana*, 391 U.S. 145 (1968).

[186] *Taylor* v. *Louisiana*, 419 U.S. 522 (1975).

[187] *Swain* v. *Alabama*, 380 U.S. 202 (1965).

[188] The Court implicitly upheld the death penalty in *Wilkerson* v. *Utah*, 99 U.S. 130 (1878), and In re *Kemmler*, 136 U.S. 436 (1890).

[189] *Furman* v. *Georgia*, 408 U.S. 238 (1972).

[190] *Gregg* v. *Georgia*, 428 U.S. 153 (1976).

[191] *Woodson* v. *North Carolina*, 428 U.S. 289 (1976).

[192] *Coker* v. *Georgia*, 433 U.S. 584 (1977).

[193] *McCleskey* v. *Kemp*, 95 L.Ed.2d 262 (1987). Studies of Florida, Illinois, Mississippi, and North Carolina have found similar results. Fox Butterfield, "Blacks More Likely to Get Death Penalty, Study Says," *New York Times*, June 7, 1998, 16.

[194] Jeffrey Toobin, "Killer Instincts," *New Yorker*, January 17, 2005, 54.

195 As of October, 2007.

196 Frank R. Baumgartner, Suzanna De Boef, Amber E. Boydstun, *The Decline of the Death Penalty and the Discovery of Innocence* (Cambridge, England: Cambridge University Press, 2008).

197 Adam Liptak, "Juries Reject Death Penalty in Nearly All Federal Trials," *New York Times*, June 15, 2003, 12; Alex Kotlowitz, "In the Face of Death," *New York Times Magazine*, June 6, 2003, 34.

198 *Atkins* v. *Virginia*, 153 L.Ed. 2d 335 (2002).

199 *Penry* v. *Lynaugh*, 106 L.Ed.2d 256 (1989).

200 *Roper* v. *Simmons*, 161 L.Ed.2d 1 (2005).

201 Some Asian countries (notably China) and many Middle Eastern countries also retain it.

201(a) *Kennedy* v. *La.*, 171 L.Ed 2d 525 (2008).

202 *Brady* v. *United States*, 397 U.S. 742 (1970).

203 *Griswold* v. *Connecticut*, 38 U.S. 479 (1965).

204 For a rare exception, see *Time* v. *Hill*, 385 U.S. 374 (1967).

205 *Griswold* v. *Connecticut*.

206 *Eisenstadt* v. *Baird*, 405 U.S. 438 (1972); *Carey* v. *Population Services International*, 431 U.S. 678 (1977).

207 *Eisenstadt* v. *Baird*.

208 Lloyd Shearer, "This Woman and This Man Made History," *Parade*, 1983.

209 *Roe* v. *Wade*, 410 U.S. 113 (1973).

210 Bob Woodward, "The Abortion Papers," *Washington Post National Weekly Edition*, January 30, 1989, 24–25.

211 All but New York's. Three other states allowed abortion on demand, though not quite as extensively as Roe, so the ruling also invalidated their laws. Jeffrey A. Segal and Harold J. Spaeth, *The Supreme Court and the Attitudinal Model* (New York: Cambridge University Press, 1993), 333.

212 For example, Alan Dershowitz, *Supreme Injustice* (New York: Oxford University, 2001), 191–196. For a contrast with same-sex marriage, see Jonathan Rauch, "A Separate Peace," *Atlantic Monthly*, April, 2007, 21.

213 *Akron* v. *Akron Center for Reproductive Health*, 76 L.Ed.2d 687 (1983).

214 "The Supreme Court Ignites a Fiery Abortion Debate," *Time*, July 4, 1977, 6–8.

215 *Beal* v. *Doe*, 432 U.S. 438 (1977); *Maher* v. *Roe*, 432 U.S. 464 (1977); *Poelker* v. *Doe*, 432 U.S. 519 (1977); *Harris* v. *McRae* 448 U.S. 297 (1980).

216 "The Abortion Dilemma Come to Life," *Washington Post National Weekly Edition*, December 25, 1989, 10–11.

217 Alan Guttmacher Institute, *Facts in Brief: Abortion in the United States* (New York: Alan Guttmacher Institute, 1992); Stephanie Mencimer, "Ending Illegitimacy as We Know It," *Washington Post National Weekly Edition*, January 17, 1994, 24.

218 *Webster* v. *Reproductive Health Services*, 106 L.Ed.2d 410 (1989).

219 *Planned Parenthood of Southeastern Pennsylvania* v. *Casey*, 120 L.Ed.2d 674 (1992). Justice Anthony Kennedy changed his mind after the justices' conference, from essentially overturning Roe to reaffirming it. His was the fifth vote to reaffirm, as it would have been to overturn.

220 Kathleen Sullivan, cited in Robin Toner and Adam Liptak, "In New Court, Roe May Stand, So Foes Look to Limit Its Scope," *New York Times*, July 10, 2005, YT16.

221 William Booth, "The Difference a Day Makes," *Washington Post National Weekly Edition*, November 23, 1992, 31.

222 *Planned Parenthood of Southeastern Pennsylvania* v. *Casey*, 120 L.Ed.2d 674 (1992).

223 *Hodgson* v. *Minnesota*, 111 L.Ed.2d 344 (1990); *Ohio* v. *Akron Center for Reproductive Health*, 111 L.Ed.2d 405 (1990); *Planned Parenthood Association of Kansas City* v. *Ashcroft*, 462 U.S. 476 (1983). Number of states from Holly Ramer, "Never-Enforced Abortion Law to Go before Supreme Court," *Lincoln Journal Star*, November 27, 2005, 4A.

224 Margaret Carlson, "Abortion's Hardest Cases," *Time*, July 9, 1990, 24.

225 Before this procedure was adopted for late-term abortions, doctors removed the fetus in pieces. Jeffrey Toobin, *The Nine: Inside the Secret World of the Supreme Court* (New York: Doubleday, 2007), 132.

226 *Stenberg* v. *Carhart*, 530 U.S. 914 (2000).

227 *Gonzales* v. *Carhart*, 167 L.Ed.2d 480 (2007).The Court didn't overrule the 2000 decision, because that Nebraska law, unlike this congressional law, was too broad.

228 Barry Yeoman, "The Quiet War on Abortion," *Mother Jones*, September-October 2001, 46–51.

229 "Survey Reveals U. S. Views on Abortion to Be Contradictory," *Lincoln Journal Star*, June 19, 2000.

230 For an analysis of the political dynamics that produced this moderate result, see William Saleton, *Bearing Right: How Conservatives Won the Abortion War* (Berkeley: University of California Press, 2003). The title is an exaggeration.

231 Alissa Rubin, "The Abortion Wars Are Far from Over," *Washington Post National Weekly Edition*, December 21, 1992, 25.

232 Richard Lacayo, "One Doctor Down, How Many More?" *Time*, March 22, 1993, 47.

233 Rebecca Mead, "Return to Sender the Usual Hate Mail," *New Yorker*, October 29, 2001, 34.

234 Douglas Frantz, "The Rhetoric of Terror," *Time*, March 27, 1995, 48–51.

235 Dan Sewell, "Abortion War Requires Guns, Bulletproof Vests," *Lincoln Journal Star*, January 8, 1995.

236 "Blasts Reawaken Fear of Domestic Terrorism," *Lincoln Journal Star*, January 17, 1997.

237 Richard Lacayo, "Abortion: The Future Is Already Here," *Time*, May 4, 1992, 29; Jack Hitt, "Who Will Do Abortions Here?" *New York Times Magazine*, January 18, 1998, 20.

238 Jodi Enda, "The Women's View," *American Prospect*, April, 2005, 26.

239 Randall Terry, quoted in Anthony Lewis, "Pro-Life Zealots 'Outside the Bargain,'" *Lincoln Journal Star*, March 14, 1993.

240 Joseph Scheidler, quoted in Sandra G. Boodman, "Bringing Abortion Home," *Washington Post National Weekly Edition*, April 15, 1993, 6.

241 Stanley K. Henshaw, "Abortion Incidence and Services in the United States, 1995–1996," *Family Planning Perspectives*, November–December 1998; Stephanie Simon, "Abortions Down 25% From Peak," *Los Angeles Times*, January 17, 2008, www.latimes.com/news/nationworld/nation/la-na-abort17jan17,0,1592814.

242 Rob Stein, "As Clinical Abortions Decline, an Alternative Rises," *Washington Post National Weekly Edition*, January 28–February 3, 2008, 33.

243 Much of this section is taken from Russell Shorto, "Contra-Contraception," *New York Times Magazine*, May 7, 2006, 48–55, 68.

244 Ibid., Harris Poll, 54.

245 Judie Brown, quoted in ibid., 50.

246 Ibid., 50, 68.

247 Editorial, "Misguided Faith on AIDS," *New York Times*, October 10, 2003.

248 Ibid., 51, 53.

249 Nicholas D. Kristof, "Abortion, Condoms and Bush," *New York Times*, November 5, 2006, WK13.

250 Judie Brown, quoted in Ibid., 50.

251 As the author concludes from the leaders' statements. Ibid., 54.

252 R. Albert Mohler, Jr., quoted in Ibid., 50.

253 Sarah Brown of the National Campaign to Prevent Teen Pregnancy, quoted in ibid., 83.

254 For an elaboration of this history, see "In Changing the Law of the Land, Six Justices Turned to Its History," *New York Times*, July 20, 2003, WK7.

255 Four states at this time revised their statutes to bar sodomy only between homosexuals: Kansas, Missouri, Oklahoma, and Texas.

256 *Bowers* v. *Hardwick*, 92 L.Ed.2d 140 (1986); see also *Doe* v. *Commonwealth's Attorney*, 425 U.S. 901 (1976).

257 *Lawrence and Garner* v. *Texas*, 539 U.S. 558 (2003).

258 "Gays Getting More Acceptance as They're More Open, Poll Says," *Lincoln Journal Star*, April 11, 2004.

259 Paul Gewirtz, quoted in Joe Klein, "How the Supremes Redeemed Bush," *Time*, July 7, 2003, 27.

260 The House sponsor of the act, Robert Barr (R-Ga.), said the act was necessary because "the flames of hedonism, the flames of narcissism, the flames of self-centered morality are licking at the very foundation of our society, the family unit." At the time he was protecting the family unit, he was in his third marriage. Margaret Carlson, "The Marrying Kind," *Time*, September 16, 1996, 26.

261 Jonathan Rauch, "Families Forged by Illness," *New York Times*, June 11, 2006, WK15.

262 For elaboration, see David Von Drehle, "Same-Sex Unions Take Center Stage," *Wash-*

ington Post National Weekly Edition, December 1, 2003, 29.

263 John Cloud, "1,138 Reasons Marriage Is Cool," *Time*, March 8, 2004, 32. A few go in the opposite direction, such as eligibility for Medicaid, which takes into account a spouse's income.

264 Advisory Opinion on Senate No. 2175, Supreme Judicial Court of Massachusetts, February 3, 2004.

265 David J. Garrow, "Toward a More Perfect Union," *New York Times Magazine*, May 9, 2004, 54.

266 Senator Wayne Allard (R-Colo.); Senator Rick Santorum (R-Pa.); James Dobson. Andrew Sullivan, "If at First You Don't Succeed . . . ," *Time*, July 26, 2004, 78.

267 Alan Cooperman, "Anger without Action," *Washington Post National Weekly Edition*, June 28, 2004, 30.

268 Garrow, "Toward a More Perfect Union," 57.

269 Geoff Mulvihill, "Transgender Protection Law Begins in New Jersey," *Lincoln Journal Star*, June 13, 2007, 7A.

270 The Supreme Court did invalidate a Colorado constitutional amendment prohibiting laws barring discrimination against homosexuals, saying that the amendment singled out homosexuals and denied them the opportunity enjoyed by others to seek protection from discrimination. This put the brakes on a drive to adopt similar provisions in other states. *Roemer* v. *Evans*, 134 L.Ed.2d 855 (1996).

271 Al Kamen, "When Exactly Does Life End?" *Washington Post National Weekly Edition*, September 18, 1989, 31; Alain L. Sanders, "Whose Right to Die?" *Time*, December 11, 1989, 80.

272 *Cruzan* v. *Missouri Health Department*, 111 L.Ed.2d 224 (1990).

273 Otto Friedrich, "A Limited Right to Die," *Time*, July 9, 1990, 59.

274 Tamar Lewin, "Ignoring 'Right to Die' Directives, Medical Community Is Being Sued," *New York Times*, June 2, 1996, 1.

275 *Washington* v. *Glucksberg*, 138 L.Ed.2d 772 (1997); *Vacco* v. *Quill*, 138 L.Ed.2d 834 (1997).

276 *Gonzales* v. *Oregon*, 163 L.Ed.2d 748 (2006).

277 Kathy Barks Hoffman, "On Eve of Kevorkian Release from Prison, Little Has Changed," *Lincoln Journal Star*, May 29, 2007, 6A.

278 David E. Rosenbaum, "Americans Want a Right to Die—or So They Think," *New York Times*, June 8, 1997, E3.

279 Ibid.

280 Barton Gellman and Jo Becker, "A 'Surrogate Chief of Staff,'" *Washington Post National Weekly Edition*, July 9–15, 2007, 6–12.

281 When the United States granted Cuba independence four years later, it retained the right to lease the base as a refueling station. In 1934, it renegotiated the treaty to remain in effect as long as the United States wants it to. The terms specify that the United States has complete control and jurisdiction.

282 Ian James, "Importance of Gitmo Questioned," *Lincoln Journal Star*, June 26, 2004.

283 The Supreme Court did rule that habeas corpus does not apply to aliens who are outside of U.S. territory. *Johnson* v. *Eisentrager*, 339 U.S. 763 (1950).

284 The administration also claims that international law doesn't apply because the detainees, as (alleged) members of al-Qaeda, don't represent an official army of an actual country, so they are "unlawful combatants."

285 This wasn't a coincidence. Administration officials talked among themselves of finding the legal equivalent of outer space. Michael Isikoff and Stuart Taylor Jr., "The Gitmo Fallout," *Newsweek*, July 17, 2006, 23.

286 Joseph Margulies, "At Guantanamo Bay, a Year in Limbo," *Washington Post National Weekly Edition*, January 6, 2003, 22.

287 A related argument is that the military has discretion on the battlefield, and in the war on terrorism, all American territory, including foreign bases, is part of the battlefield.

288 *Rasul* v. *Bush*, 159 L.Ed.2d 548 (2004). On the same day, the Court decided a similar case involving an American citizen who had been raised in Afghanistan and captured during the war against the Taliban. The Court ruled similarly, although the fact that he was an American citizen prompted eight justices (all but Thomas) to declare that he was entitled to contest his detention and four justices to conclude that his detention was unlawful. *Hamdi* v. *Rumsfeld*, 159 L.Ed.2d 578 (2004).

289 The Court gave the government a distinct advantage in this process, stipulating that the government merely has to present credible evidence against the detainees. Then they have to prove that they aren't enemy combatants; that is, they have to prove their innocence. If they are determined to be enemy combatants, they can be held for the duration of the conflict.

290 The Detainee Treatment Act of 2005. Petitions for a writ of habeas corpus were filed for all detainees before this law was passed, so the courts might conclude that the law doesn't apply to these cases already in progress.

291 *Boumediene* v. *Bush* (2008). In April 2007, the Court refused to hear this case, but in June 2007, it changed its mind. In the intervening months, military officers and lawyers asserted that the panels were biased and the procedures made it impossible for detainees to defend themselves.

292 *This American Life*, NPR, March 12, 2006.

293 Corine Hegland, "Guantanamo's Grip," *National Journal*, February 1, 2006, 20–34.

294 Ibid., 29.

295 Ibid., 28.

296 Michael Scheuer, quoted in ibid., 31.

297 Ibid., 30–31.

298 "Military: Detainees Attempted Mass Hanging Protest in 2003," *Lincoln Journal Star*, January 25, 2005, 6A. By this date, the guards had logged 120 instances in which prisoners had tried to hang themselves, although the military says the majority were done in protest rather than in an attempt to commit suicide. Also see Jeffrey Toobin, "Camp Justice," *New Yorker*, April 14, 2008, 32-38.

299 Hegland, "Guantanamo's Grip," 23.

300 Gellman and Becker, "A 'Surrogate Chief of Staff,'" 12.

301 *Hamden* v. *Rumsfeld*, 165 L.Ed.2d 723 (2006).

302 Neal Katyal, quoted in Jonathan Mahler, "A Check Against Fear," *New York Times Magazine*, July 7, 2006, 14.

303 Scott Shane and Mark Mazzetti, "Tapes by C.I.A. Lived and Died to Save Image," *New York Times*, December 30, 2007, YT1.

304 Dana Priest, "The CIA's Secret Prisons," *Washington Post National Weekly Edition*, November 7–13, 2005, 10–11. For a later, fuller summary, see Jane Mayer, "The Black Sites," *New Yorker*, August 13, 2007, 46-57.

305 Warren P. Strobel, "Report: U.S. Has 39 Secret Detainees," *Lincoln Journal Star*, June 7, 2007, 3A.

306 For the vice president's role, see Gellman and Becker, "A 'Surrogate Chief of Staff.'" For a very useful article on the concept of torture, see Mark Bowden, "The Dark Art of Interrogation," *Atlantic Monthly*, October, 2003, 51–76.

307 Mayer, "Black Sites," 54.

308 Gourevitch and Morris, "Exposure," 50.

309 Mayer, "Black Sites," 54.

310 Adam Zagorin, "One Life Inside Gitmo," *Time*, March 13, 2006, 22.

311 Mayer, "Black Sites," 54.

312 Although the administration denied this, a persuasive article is Joby Warrick, "Ways of Making Them Talk," *Washington Post National Weekly Edition*, April 28–May 4, 2008, 34.

313 Anonymous official, quoted in Jodie Morse, "How Do We Make Him Talk?" *Time*, April 15, 2002, 92.

314 For more information, including the role of medical personnel in devising the tactics, see Jane Mayer, "The Experiment," *New Yorker*, July 11 and 18, 2005, 60–71.

315 Gellman and Becker, "A 'Surrogate Chief of Staff,'" 10.

316 Neil A. Lewis and Eric Schmitt, "Inquiry Finds Abuses at Guantanamo Bay," *New York Times*, May 1, 2005, YT23.

317 Paisley Dodds, "Guantanamo Translator Tells of Sexual Tactics Used on Detainees," *Lincoln Journal Star*, January 28, 2005, 5A.

318 According to the Geneva Conventions and the United Nations Convention Against Torture and also under treaty law, to which the United States is a party, and customary law, which is binding on all nations.

319 From the Geneva Conventions.

320 The administration also claims that al-Qaeda members aren't entitled to the protection of international law because as stateless fighters they are "unlawful enemy combatants" and because neither al-Qaeda nor the Taliban regime of Afghanistan were a party to the Geneva Conventions.

321 The law is essentially a statement of our policy. It doesn't authorize prisoners to bring lawsuits to stop such treatment or to penalize the interrogators.

322 In a signing statement, he said that he would interpret the law "in a manner consistent with

the constitutional authority of the President to supervise the unitary executive branch and as Commander in Chief and consistent with the constitutional limitations on the judicial power." In President Bush's second term, the U.S. military branches insisted on following the army field manual, which adheres to the Geneva Conventions and prohibits most aggressive methods described above. Congress passed a bill that would have extended these standards to the CIA as well, but the president vetoed the bill.

[323] Martin Miller, "'24' Gets a Lesson in Torture from the Experts," *Los Angeles Times*, February 13, 2007, www.calendarlive.com/printedition/calendar/cl-et-torture13feb13,0,2384998; Jane Mayer, "Whatever It Takes," *New Yorker*, February 19 and 26, 2007, 66.

[324] Mayer, "The Experiment," 70.

[325] *Marketplace*, NPR, May 5, 2004.

[326] Rajiv Chandrasekaran and Scott Wilson, "Many in Prison in Error," *Lincoln Journal Star*, May 11, 2004. These conclusions were confirmed by General Antonio Taguba, who prepared the army's official report on Abu Ghraib. Seymour M. Hersh, "The General's Report," *New Yorker*, June 25, 2007, 64.

[327] The phenomenon is known as "force drift." Mayer, "The Experiment," 70.

[328] According to the government's own documents. For more incidents and documents, see Mark Danner, *Torture and Truth* (New York: New York Review of Books, 2004).

[328(a)]Bob Herbert, "All Too Human," *New York Times*, June 28, 2008, www.nytimes.com/2008/06/28/opinion/28herbert.html?_r51&pagewanted5print&or.

[329] Ninety-eight have died, and thirty-four of these have been suspected or confirmed homicides, according to Human Rights First, a human rights group. Drew Brown, "Report: 98 Died in U.S. Custody," *Lincoln Journal Star*, February 23, 2006, 3A.

[330] Don Van Natta Jr., "How Ally with Abuse Record Became a Surrogate U.S. Jailer," *New York Times*, May 1, 2005, YT1.

[331] Dana Priest and Barton Gellman, "U.S. Decries Abuse but Defends Interrogations; 'Stress and Duress' Tactics Used on Terrorism Suspects Held in Secret Overseas Facilities," *Washington Post*, December 26, 2002, A1.

[332] Rajiv Chandrasekaran and Peter Finn, "Interrogating Terrorist Suspects 'in a Way We Can't Do on U.S. Soil,'" *Washington Post*, March 12, 2002, A1.

[333] U.N. Convention against Torture and Other Cruel, Inhuman, or Degrading Treatment or Punishment of 1984, signed in 1994.

[334] There are assertions that the administration notified two judges on the FISA court, but it did not seek official approval.

[335] Barton Gellman, Dafna Linzer, and Carol D. Leonnig, "Spying That Yields Little," *Washington Post National Weekly Edition*, February 13–19, 2006, 6.

[336] Zev Borow, "Very Bad People," *New Yorker*, February 6, 2006, 44.

[337] Ibid.

[338] The law allows warrantless wiretapping for just three days. The administration sought congressional authority for warrantless wiretapping for long periods, but Congress refused to grant this authority.

[339] After its initial eavesdropping, the government did seek authorization to continue spying on about a hundred persons.

[340] The legislation was prompted by two judges on the FISA Court who challenged the program, maintaining that the NSA needed judicial authorization as the law required. The Protect America Act allows the government to monitor these phone calls and emails, usually without obtaining any warrants and without going through any courts, including the FISA Court. Warrants are required only if the government targets specific American citizens. The act was slated to expire six months after it took effect. Congress renewed and expanded it in 2008, providing immunity for telecommunications companies that are sued for invasion of privacy by furnishing the information to the government.

[341] Seymour M. Hersh, "National Security Dept.: Listening In," *New Yorker*, May 29, 2006, 25.

[342] In just forty-five days after the 9/11 attacks. There were few hearings, and there was no committee report, and during this time senators were evacuated from their offices because of the anthrax attacks. In 2005, the act, with minor revisions, was made permanent.

[343] The Homeland Security Act.

[344] Although the act focuses on intelligence gathering, it contains other important provisions that enhance the government's ability to detain and prosecute aliens. Those suspected of committing a crime related to terrorism can be detained, without trial, longer than before. And those accused of providing "material support" to organizations involved in terrorism can be prosecuted more easily than before.

[345] Joseph J. Ellis, "Finding a Place for 9/11 in American History," *New York Times*, January 28, 2006. Available online at www.select.nytimes.com/ search/restricted/article?res5FB0A1 3F93A5B0C. .7B8EDDA8089.

[346] Alan M. Dershowitz, *Supreme Injustice: How the High Court Hijacked Election 2000* (New York: Oxford University Press, 2001), 189.

Chapter 15

[1] According to the Virginia Supreme Court, cited in *Loving v. Virginia*, 388 U.S. 1 (1967).

[2] Brent Staples, "*Loving v. Virginia* and the Secret History of Race," *New York Times*, May 14, 2008, A22.

[3] *Loving v. Virginia*.

[4] Francine Russo, "When Love Is Mixing It Up," *Time*, November, 2001, Bonus Section, F5.

[5] Benedict Carey, "In-laws In the Age of the Outsider," *New York Times*, December 18, 2005, WK1.

[6] Exhibition "Slavery in New York," New York Historical Society, November, 2005. For more details, see Ira Berlin and Leslie M. Harris, eds., *Slavery in New York* (New York: New York Historical Society/New Press, 2006). Also see

Anne Farrow, Joel Lang, and Jenifer Frank, *Complicity: How the North Promoted, Prolonged, and Profited from Slavery* (New York: Ballantine, 2006).

[7] Gary B. Nash, *The Forgotten Fifth* (Cambridge, Mass.: Harvard University Press, 2006). See also Simon Schama, *Rough Crossings: Britain, the Slaves, and the American Revolution* (New York: Ecco, 2006).

[8] New York didn't abolish slavery until 1827, and New Jersey didn't until 1865.

[9] Farrow, Lang, and Frank, *Complicity*.

[10] In most of the North, slavery was officially abolished shortly after ratification of the Constitution.

[11] Adam Goodheart, "Setting Them Free," *New York Times Book Review*, August 7, 2005, 1.

[12] Russell Nye, *Fettered Freedom* (Lansing: Michigan State University Press, 1963), 187, 227–229.

[13] *Scott* v. *Sandford*, 60 U.S. 393 (1857).

[14] Taney considered slavery "a blot on our national character." Richard Shenkman, *I Love Paul Revere, Whether He Rode or Not* (New York: HarperCollins, 1991), 168.

[15] *Fresh Air Weekend*, NPR, August 18, 2002.

[16] The Emancipation Proclamation, issued during the Civil War in 1863, was apparently a tactical move to discourage European countries from aiding the Confederacy. It gave the Civil War a moral purpose, making foreign intervention less likely. The proclamation couldn't free southern slaves at the time because the Union didn't control the southern states, which had seceded.

[17] Bruce Ackerman, *We the People: Transformations* (Cambridge, Mass.: Harvard University Press, 1998); George Fletcher, "Unsound Constitution: Oklahoma City and the Founding Fathers," *New Republic*, June 23, 1997, 14–18. These conclusions make dubious the arguments that judges should be guided only by the intentions of the original Founders as they resolve contemporary cases. Ignoring the transformation that occurred as a result of the Civil War and these amendments amounts to using a highly selective and self-serving version of history.

[18] Civil Rights Act of 1866; Civil Rights Act of 1871; Civil Rights Act of 1875. These acts reversed the "Black Codes" that southern states passed to deny rights to former slaves.

[19] See Nicholas Lemann, *Redemption: the Last Battle of the Civil War* (New York: Farrar, Straus and Giroux, 2006).

[20] See Eric Foner, *Reconstruction: America's Unfinished Revolution* (New York: Harper & Row, 1988).

[21] Employers included this provision in the contract with their workers, so their workers could be charged with a crime if they quit their job.

[22] This and the following paragraphs are drawn from Douglas A. Blackmon, *Slavery by Another Name: the Re-Enslavement of Black Americans from the Civil War to World War II* (New York: Doubleday, 2008).

[23] The name Jim Crow came from a white performer in the 1820s who had a vaudeville routine in which he blackened his face with burnt

cork and mimicked black men. He sang "Wheel About and Turn About and Jump, Jim Crow." This routine led to minstrel shows in high schools and colleges, with students portraying and satirizing blacks. The shows were popular into the 1960s.

24 Kenneth Karst, "Equality, Law, and Belonging: An Introduction," in *Before the Law,* 5th ed., ed. John J. Bonsignore et al. (Boston: Houghton Mifflin, 1994), 429.

25 C. Vann Woodward, *The Strange Career of Jim Crow,* 2nd ed. (London: Oxford University Press, 1966), 44.

26 *Civil Rights Cases,* 109 U.S. 3 (1883).

27 *Plessy* v. *Ferguson,* 163 U.S. 537 (1896). The Court's ruling prompted states to expand their Jim Crow laws. Before *Plessy,* states segregated just trains and schools.

28 *Cumming* v. *Richmond County Board of Education,* 175 U.S. 528 (1899). Then the Court enforced segregation in colleges. It upheld a criminal conviction against a private college for teaching blacks together with whites. *Berea College* v. *Kentucky,* 211 U.S. 45 (1908).

29 See, generally, James W. Loewen, *Sundown Towns: A Hidden Dimension of American Racism* (New York: New Press, 2005).

30 Woodward, *The Strange Career of Jim Crow,* 113. Before the Civil War, northern states had passed some Jim Crow laws, which foreshadowed the more pervasive laws in southern states after the war. Leon F. Litwack, *Trouble in Mind: Black Southerners in the Age of Jim Crow* (New York: Knopf, 1998).

31 Jacqueline Jones, *The Dispossessed: America's Underclasses from the Civil War to the Present* (New York: Basic Books, 1992), 83. And they were still being cheated. One sharecropper went to the landowner at the end of the season to settle up but was told he would not receive any money that year because the landowner needed it to send his son to college. The sharecropper moved to the North. Interview with the sharecropper's son on *The Best of Discovery,* Discovery television channel, June 11, 1995.

32 Richard Kluger, *Simple Justice* (New York: Knopf, 1976), 89–90.

33 Philip Dray, *At the Hands of Persons Unknown* (New York: Random House, 2002).

34 Ibid.

35 Woodward, *The Strange Career of Jim Crow,* 114.

36 Yet talk of the riot was banished from newspapers, textbooks, and everyday conversations. After some years, most Oklahomans were unaware of it, except those who lived through it. In the 1990s, newspaper articles prompted the state to establish a commission to investigate the riot, leading to more awareness. Jonathan Z. Larsen, "Tulsa Burning," *Civilization,* February–March 1997, 46–55; Brent Staples, "Unearthing a Riot," *New York Times Magazine,* December 19, 1999, 64–69. For an examination, see James S. Hirsch, *Riot and Remembrance: The Tulsa Race War and Its Legacy* (New York: Houghton Mifflin, 2002).

37 "Torn from the Land," Associated Press, wire .ap.org. The website offers an investigative report with numerous stories. For an illuminating

look at the lives and status of black people in the Deep South in the 1920s, see Nan Woodruff, *American Congo: The African American Freedom Struggle in the Delta* (Cambridge, Mass.: Harvard University Press, 2003).

38 Wilson apparently opposed segregation in government but still allowed it to appease southerners who were a major portion of his Democratic Party and whose support was essential for his economic reforms.

39 *Guinn* v. *United States,* 238 U.S. 347 (1915). This clause had been written into election laws to make it more difficult for freed blacks and their children to qualify to vote (their grandfathers having been illiterate slaves) while effectively exempting whites from having to submit to literacy testing.

40 *Buchanan* v. *Warley,* 245 U.S. 60 (1917).

41 In 1939, the NAACP established the NAACP Legal Defense and Educational Fund as its litigation arm. In 1957, the Internal Revenue Service, pressured by southern members of Congress, ordered the two branches of the NAACP to break their connection or lose their tax-exempt status. Since then, they have been separate organizations, and further references in this chapter to the NAACP are in fact to the NAACP Legal Defense and Educational Fund.

42 Juan Williams, "The Case for Thurgood Marshall," *Washington Post,* February 14, 1999, W16.

43 Kluger, *Simple Justice,* 134.

44 *Missouri ex rel. Gaines* v. *Canada,* 305 U.S. 337 (1938).

45 *Sweatt* v. *Painter,* 339 U.S. 629 (1950).

46 *McLaurin* v. *Oklahoma State Regents,* 339 U.S. 637 (1950).

47 Esther Brown, a white woman from a Kansas City suburb, had a black maid who lived in nearby South Park. In 1948, when Brown saw the decrepit school for black students in South Park, she complained to the board of education in the town. At a meeting, she said, "Look, I don't represent these people. One of them works for me, and I've seen the conditions of their school. I know none of you would want your children educated under such circumstances. They're not asking for integration, just a fair shake." From the audience, Brown received catcalls and demands to go back where she came from. A woman behind her tried to hit her. The school board responded by gerrymandering the black neighborhood out of the South Park school district. Kluger, *Simple Justice,* 388–389.

48 Earl Warren, *The Memoirs of Earl Warren* (Garden City, N.Y.: Doubleday, 1977), 291. However, Eisenhower later advocated the Civil Rights Act of 1957, which created a civil rights commission to investigate voting irregularities and a civil rights division in the Justice Department to prosecute law violations, and he persuaded reluctant Republicans to drop their opposition to civil rights. David A. Nichols, "Ike Liked Civil Rights," *New York Times,* September 12, 2007.

49 Kluger, *Simple Justice,* 656.

50 *Brown* v. *Board of Education of Topeka,* 347 U.S. 483 (1954).

51 *Holmes* v. *Atlanta,* 350 U.S. 879 (1955); *Baltimore* v. *Dawson,* 350 U.S. 877 (1955); *Schiro* v. *Bynum,* 375 U.S. 395 (1964); *Johnson* v. *Virginia,* 373 U.S. 61 (1963); *Lee* v. *Washington,* 390 U.S. 333 (1968).

52 *Brown* v. *Board of Education II,* 349 U.S. 294 (1955).

53 Justice Tom Clark later told a political science conference that one justice had proposed desegregating one grade a year, beginning with kindergarten or first grade, but this concrete standard was rejected because the other justices felt it would take too long. In retrospect, it might have been quicker, and easier, than the vague standard used.

54 *Griffin* v. *Prince Edward County School Board,* 377 U.S. 218 (1964); *Norwood* v. *Harrison,* 413 U.S. 455 (1973); *Gilmore* v. *Montgomery,* 417 U.S. 556 (1974); *Green* v. *New Kent County School Board,* 391 U.S. 430 (1968).

55 Quoted in James F. Simon, *In His Own Image* (New York: McKay, 1974), 70.

56 *All Things Considered,* NPR, December 10, 2003.

57 William Cohen and John Kaplan, *Bill of Rights* (Mineola, N.Y.: Foundation Press, 1976), 622.

58 *Swann* v. *Charlotte-Mecklenburg Board of Education,* 402 U.S. 1 (1971); *Columbus Board of Education* v. *Penick,* 443 U.S. 449 (1979); *Dayton Board of Education* v. *Brinkman,* 443 U.S. 526 (1979); *Keyes* v. *School District 1, Denver,* 413 U.S. 921 (1973).

59 Lee A. Daniels, "In Defense of Busing," *New York Times Magazine,* April 17, 1983, 36–37.

60 Some black parents opposed busing because it disrupted their children's lives and because it implied that their children could learn only by sitting beside white children. But other black parents favored busing because it offered their children an opportunity to go to better schools.

61 White flight began after World War II as affluent families moved to the suburbs. Although white flight continued for economic reasons, it increased because of busing as well.

62 *Milliken* v. *Bradley,* 418 U.S. 717 (1974).

63 For example, some suburbs of Kansas City, Missouri, didn't allow black students to attend high schools. Some black families, then, moved back to the city, aggravating both school segregation and residential segregation. James S. Kunen, "The End of Integration," *Time,* April 29, 1996, 41.

64 *Board of Education of Oklahoma City* v. *Dowell,* 112 L.Ed.2d 715 (1991). The Court said that school districts could stop busing when "the vestiges of past discrimination had been eliminated to the extent practicable." See also *Freeman* v. *Pitts,* 118 L.Ed.2d 108 (1992).

65 *Missouri* v. *Jenkins,* 132 L.Ed.2d 63 (1995).

66 Julie Rawe, "When Public Schools Aren't Color-blind," *Time,* December 4, 2006, 54–56.

67 *Parents Involved in Community Schools* v. *Seattle School District,* (2007).

68 These districts use race in some way, although most don't use it as extensively as Louisville did. David G. Savage, "Justices Reject School Integration Efforts," *Los Angeles Times,* June 29, 2007, www.latimes.com/news/la-na

-scotus29jun29,0,2236400,print.story?coll=la-tot-topst. Unlike most justices in the majority, Justice Kennedy indicated that he may be willing to allow some efforts to promote desegregation.

[69] Anjetta McQueen, "Desegregation Waning," *Lincoln Journal Star,* May 16, 1999.

[70] Alan Finder, "Integrating Schools by Income Is Cited as a Success in Raleigh," *New York Times,* September 25, 2005, YT1. Also see Emily Bazelon, "The Next Kind of Integration," *New York Times Magazine,* July 20, 2008, 37.

[71] FBI director J. Edgar Hoover ordered wiretaps that he hoped would link King with communists. When the taps failed to reveal any connection, Hoover had agents bug a hotel room, where they heard King having extramarital sex. Taylor Branch, *Pillar of Fire: America in the King Years, 1963–65* (New York: Simon & Schuster, 1998).

[72] Although this sit-in usually is cited as the first, a sit-in at a lunch counter in a drugstore in Wichita, Kansas, actually was the first—in 1958. But the Greensboro sit-in prompted the wave of sit-ins through the South.

[73] Woodward, *The Strange Career of Jim Crow,* 186.

[74] This incident occurred in 1961. Nicholas Lemann, "The Long March," *New Yorker,* February 10, 2003, 88.

[75] The Supreme Court had struck down discrimination in choosing juries, but discrimination continued through informal means. *Norris* v. *Alabama,* 294 U.S. 587 (1935); *Smith* v. *Texas,* 311 U.S. 128 (1940); *Avery* v. *Georgia,* 345 U.S. 559 (1952).

[76] An excellent collection of articles is presented in *Reporting Civil Rights: American Journalism, 1941–1973* (New York: Library of America, 2003).

[77] Henry Louis Gates Jr., "After the Revolution," *New Yorker,* April 29 and May 6, 1996.

[78] Robert A. Caro, "The Compassion of Lyndon Johnson," *New Yorker,* April 1, 2002, 56.

[79] Louis Menand, "He Knew He Was Right," *New Yorker,* March 26, 2001, 95.

[80] Lemann, "Long March," 86.

[81] Patrick Reddy, "Why It's Got to Be All or Nothing," *Washington Post National Weekly Edition,* October 18, 1999, 23.

[82] This was true for national elections. The transformation took longer for state and local elections.

[83] Joseph A. Califano, Jr., *The Triumph and Tragedy of Lyndon Johnson* (New York: Simon & Schuster, 1991), 177–178.

[84] The Supreme Court unanimously upheld the law. *Heart of Atlanta Motel* v. *United States,* 379 U.S. 421 (1964).

[85] For discussion of organized labor's ambivalence toward enactment and enforcement of the employment provisions of the act, see Herbert Hill, "Black Workers, Organized Labor, and Title VII of the 1964 Civil Rights Act: Legislative History and Litigation Record," in *Race in America,* eds. Herbert Hill and James E. Jones (Madison: University of Wisconsin Press, 1993), 263–341.

[86] *Griggs* v. *Duke Power,* 401 U.S. 424 (1971). However, standards that hinder blacks more than whites aren't necessarily unlawful. Washington, D.C. required police applicants to pass an exam. Although a higher percentage of blacks failed to pass, the Court said the exam related to the job. *Washington* v. *Davis,* 426 U.S. 229 (1976).

[87] *Shelley* v. *Kraemer,* 334 U.S. 1 (1948).

[88] Less directly, the numerous national and state policies that encouraged urban sprawl—e.g., road building—provided the opportunity for middle-class whites to flock to the suburbs, leaving the cities disproportionately black.

[89] For more extensive examination, see Andrew Hacker, *Two Nations: Black and White, Separate, Hostile, Unequal* (New York: Scribner, 1992).

[90] Richard Morin, "Southern Discomfort," *Washington Post National Weekly Edition,* July 15, 1996, 35.

[91] Gary Orfield, quoted in Mary Jordan, "Separating the Country from the *Brown* Decision," *Washington Post National Weekly Edition,* December 20, 1993, 33. See also Maia Davis, "Harvard Study Finds New Segregation," *Lincoln Journal Star,* January 20, 2003.

[92] Jonathan Kozol, *The Shame of the Nation: the Restoration of Apartheid Schooling in America* (New York: Crown, 2005), 19.

[93] Adam Cohen, "The Supreme Struggle," *New York Times,* January 18, 2004, E22.

[94] Kozol, *The Shame of the Nation,* 226–227.

[95] Ibid., 19.

[96] Consequently, magnet schools in minority neighborhoods often don't attract many white students. Sandy Banks, "Mixed Results for L. A.'s Magnet Schools," *Los Angeles Times,* January 20, 2006, www.latimes.com/news/local/ la-me-magnet20jan20,0,6132919,fullstory?coll= la-home-headlines.

[97] Thomas M. Shapiro, *The Hidden Cost of Being African American* (New York: Oxford University, 2004), 170–179.

[98] Jordan, "Separating the Country from the *Brown* Decision."

[99] Kunen, "End of Integration," 39.

[100] Jonathan Kozol, *Savage Inequalities: Children in America's Schools* (New York: Harper-Perennial, 1992), 4.

[101] Ibid., 3.

[102] Ibid., 35. However, only three public schools in Alabama are named after King, a native of the state. "Numbers," *Time,* January 24, 2000, 23.

[103] Kozol, *The Shame of the Nation,* 24–25.

[104] Rob Gurwitt, "Getting off the Bus," *Governing,* May 1992, 30–36; Jervis Anderson, "Black and Blue," *New Yorker,* April 29 and May 6, 1996.

[105] Richard Rothstein, quoted in Kozol, *The Shame of the Nation,* 230.

[106] "That's Quite a Range," *Lincoln Journal,* January 21, 1993.

[107] Shapiro, *Hidden Cost,* 144–145.

[108] In addition, cities have numerous nonprofit institutions—colleges, museums, hospitals—that benefit the entire urban area but don't pay property taxes. According to one estimate, 30 percent of the cities' potential tax base is tax-exempt, compared with 3 percent of the suburbs'. There are a few exceptions.

[109] Kozol, *The Shame of the Nation,* 245.

[110] Ibid., 60.

[111] For an examination of just what it would take, see Paul Tough, "Can Teaching Poor Children to Act More Like Middle-Class Children Help Close the Education Gap?" *New York Times Magazine,* November 26, 2006, 44.

[112] Charles Peters, "Tilting at Windmills," *Washington Monthly,* March, 2006, 6.

[113] Kozol, *The Shame of the Nation,* 172

[114] Ibid., 171

[115] Ibid., 53, 84.

[116] Tough, "Can Teaching Poor Children to Act More Like Middle–Class Children Help Close the Education Gap?" 71.

[117] Ben Feller, "Minorities See School as Rougher, Tougher Place," *Lincoln Journal Star,* May 31, 2006, 10A.

[118] Steve Lopez, "Money for Stadiums but Not for Schools," *Time,* June 14, 1999, 54.

[119] David Wessel, "Studies Suggest Potent Race Bias in Hiring," *Wall Street Journal,* September 4, 2003, A2.

[120] Earl G. Graves, *How to Succeed in Business without Being White* (New York: Harper Business, 1997).

[121] Reed Abelson, "Anti-Bias Agency Is Short of Will and Cash," *New York Times,* July 1, 2001, BU1.

[122] These figures from 2002 are about 25 percent lower than the results from 1989, which was the last time the government had conducted this research. "Hispanics Face More Bias in Housing," *Lincoln Journal Star,* November 8, 2002. Another study found similar discrimination in fairly progressive northern cities. "Professional Should Address Discrimination," *Lincoln Journal Star,* April 24, 2002.

[123] Most Americans can identify a telephone caller as white or black. *All Things Considered,* NPR, August 5, 2001.

[124] John Iceland and Daniel Weinberg with Erika Steinmetz, *Racial and Ethnic Residential Segregation in the United States, 1980–2000.* (Washington, D.C.: United States Census, 2002), ch. 5. Available on the web at www.census.gov/hhes/www/ housing/housing_patterns/ pdf/censr-3.pdf.

[125] James Traub, "The Year in Ideas," *New York Times Magazine,* December 9, 2001, 94.

[126] Hacker, *Two Nations,* 35–38. For information on why blacks do not want to live in white neighborhoods, see Maria Krysan and Reynolds Farley, "The Residential Preferences of Blacks: Do They Explain Persistent Segregation?" *Social Forces* 80 (2002), 937–980.

[127] According to the Supreme Court's interpretation of Fourth Amendment search and seizure law, police can stop and frisk individuals who officers have a "reasonable suspicion" to believe are committing a crime. But officers must have more than a hunch to meet the standard of "reasonable suspicion" (though less than the "prob-

able cause" required to obtain a search warrant). A person's race is not a valid criterion, except when the person's race and physical description match those of a particular suspect being sought.

128 Eugene Robinson, "Pulling Over for Prejudice," *Washington Post National Weekly Edition,* May 5–13, 2007, 31.

129 Sandy Banks, "Growing Up on a Tightrope," *Los Angeles Times,* March 3, 2006, www.latimes.com/ news/local/la-me boys-3mar03,0,2282338.full.story.

130 Michael A. Fletcher, "May the Driver Beware," *Washington Post National Weekly Edition,* April 8, 1996, 29.

131 Jake Tapper, "And Then There Were None," *Washington Post National Weekly Edition,* January 13, 2003, 9.

132 Jeffrey Goldberg, "The Color of Suspicion," *New York Times Magazine,* June 20, 1999, 53.

133 David Cole and John Lamberth, "The Fallacy of Racial Profiling," *New York Times,* May 13, 2001, sec. 4, 13.

134 Pierre Thomas, "Bias and the Badge," *Washington Post National Weekly Edition,* December 18, 1995, 6–9.

135 Henry Louis Gates Jr., "Thirteen Ways of Looking at a Black Man," *New Yorker,* October 23, 1995, 59; Anderson, "Black and Blue," 64.

136 Tammerlin Drummond, "Coping with Cops," *Time,* April 3, 2000, 72–73.

137 Laura M. Markowitz, "Walking the Walk," *Networker,* July–August 1993, 22.

138 William Raspberry, "The Little Things That Hurt," *Washington Post National Weekly Edition,* April 18, 1994, 29. See also Ellis Cose, *The Rage of a Privileged Class* (New York: HarperCollins, 1993).

139 Richard Morin and Michael H. Cottman, "The Invisible Slap," W*ashington Post National Weekly Edition,* July 2, 2001, 6.

140 Kozol, *Savage Inequalities,* 179–180.

141 Leonard Pitts, Jr., "Kramer's Meltdown: If Not Racism, Then What Was It?" *Lincoln Journal Star,* November 26, 2006, 9D.

142 Richard Thompson Ford, *The Race Card: How Bluffing about Bias Makes Race Relations Worse* (New York: Farrar, Straus and Giroux, 2008), 26.

143 Ibid., 27.

144 Stephan Thernstrom and Abigail Thernstrom, *America in Black and White: One Nation, Indivisible* (New York: Simon & Schuster, 1997), especially part 3. Some improvement began before the civil rights movement, when southern blacks migrated to northern cities in the 1940s.

145 Andrew Tobias, "Now the Good News about Your Money," *Parade,* April 4, 1993, 5.

146 James Smith and Finis Welch, "Race and Poverty: A 40-Year Record," *American Economic Review* 77 (1987), 152–158.

147 However, their rate of home ownership—48 percent—is the same as the national rate was in the 1940s. Whites' rate is 74 percent now. Deborah Kong, "Strides Made, but Still Much Disparity between Blacks, Whites," *Lincoln Journal Star,* July 22, 2002.

148 Joel Garreau, "Candidates Take Note: It's a Mall World after All," *Washington Post National Weekly Edition,* August 10, 1992, 25.

149 Thernstrom and Thernstrom, *America in Black and White,* 500.

150 Reference omitted

151 Reference omitted

152 Ford, *The Race Card,* 30.

153 This is not to say that opposition to affirmative action or welfare spending is necessarily racist. For a review of this research, and also for a creative and sophisticated example of such research, see Charles S. Taber, "Principles of Color: Race, Ideology, and Political Cognition" (Working Draft, 2008, Stony Brook University)

154 Orlando Patterson, quoted in Anderson, "Black and Blue," 62.

155 From 1967 to 1987, according to calculations by William Julius Wilson. David Remnick, "Dr. Wilson's Neighborhood," *New Yorker,* April 29 and May 6, 1996.

156 Sociologist William Julius Wilson develops this idea extensively in *The Truly Disadvantaged* (Chicago: University of Chicago Press, 1987).

157 U.S. Census Bureau, *Statistical Abstract of the United States, 2001* (Washington, D.C.: Government Printing Office, 2001), tab. 38.

158 Wilson, *The Truly Disadvantaged.*

159 Remnick, "Dr. Wilson's Neighborhood," 98.

160 Samuel Walker, *Sense and Nonsense about Crime and Drugs,* 3rd ed. (Belmont, Calif.: Wadsworth, 1994), xviii, 3.

161 According to the Pew Center on the States, cited in Clarence Page, "Quiet Riots and the Other Kind," *Lincoln Journal Star,* March 6, 2008, 7B.

162 "More Hispanics, Blacks in Cells than Dorms," *Champaign-Urbana News-Gazette,* September 27, 2007, B2.

163 Rosa A. Smith, "Saving Black Boys," *American Prospect,* February 2004, 49.

164 "Doctor: Harlem's Death Rate Worse than Bangladesh's," *Lincoln Journal,* January 18, 1990.

165 Banks, "Growing Up on a Tightrope."

166 Donald Kaul, "Only Surprise Is That Riots Didn't Happen Sooner," *Lincoln Journal,* May 19, 1992.

167 Kevin Boyle, "The Fire This Time," *Washington Post National Weekly Edition,* August 6–12, 2007, 25.

168 Drummond Ayres Jr., "Decade of Black Struggle: Gains and Unmet Goals," *New York Times,* April 2, 1978, sec. 1, 1.

169 See Veronica Chambers, *Having It All?* (New York: Doubleday, 2003).

170 "Inside America's Largest Minority," *Time,* August 22, 2005, 56.

171 Harold Meyerson, "A Tale of Two Cities," *American Prospect,* June, 2004, A8.

172 Except for some immigrant farmworkers, whose situation will be addressed.

173 And among immigrants, skin color makes a difference. Those with lighter skin earn an average of 8 percent to 15 percent more than similar immigrants with darker skin. Each shade lighter has the same effect as one year more education. Study by Joni Hersch, cited in "Study Finds Higher Income for Lighter-Skinned Immigrants," *New York Times,* January 28, 2007, YT14.

174 Cubans have experienced less discrimination, because they were admitted to this country under preferential treatment, and with financial support, due to the Cold War.

175 According to the most recent research, in 2002, Hispanics might face somewhat more discrimination in housing than blacks. Hispanics who tried to buy a house faced discrimination 20 percent of the time, and those who tried to rent an apartment did so 25 percent of the time. "Hispanics Face More Bias in Housing," *Lincoln Journal Star,* November 8, 2002.

176 Fifty-nine percent of voters in counties in which immigrants are less than 5 percent of the population say that all illegals should be deported. Joe Klein, "Bush Is Smart on the Border—and the G.O.P. Isn't," *Time,* May 29, 2006, 25.

177 Tammerlin Drummond, "It's Not Just in New Jersey," *Time,* June 14, 1999, 61.

178 Alex Kotlowitz, "Our Town," *New York Times Magazine,* August 5, 2007, 31.

179 Ibid., 37.

180 Karin Brulliard, "At Odds Over Assimilation," *Washington Post National Weekly Edition,* August 20–26, 2007, 35.

181 Kotlowitz, "Our Town," 52.

182 Jacob L. Vigdor, quoted in N. C. Aizenman, "Newcomers to the U.S. Assimilate Rapidly," *Washington Post National Weekly Edition,* May 19–25, 2008, 33.

183 Thomas Boswell and James Curtis, *The Cuban American Experience* (Totowa, N.J.: Rowman & Allanheld, 1983), 191.

184 Kevin F. McCarthy and R. Burciaga Valdez, *Current and Future Effects of Mexican Immigration in California—Executive Summary* (Santa Monica, Calif.: RAND Corp., 1985), 27; Nancy Landale and R. S. Oropesa, "Schooling, Work, and Idleness among Mexican and Non-Latino White Adolescents," working paper, Pennsylvania State University, Population Research Institute, 1997; Pew Hispanic Center, cited in Frank Greve, "English Grows Each Generation," *Lincoln Journal Star,* November 30, 2007, A1.

185 Ruben Navarrette Jr., "Hispanics See Themselves as Part of United States," *Lincoln Journal Star,* December 23, 2002.

186 Ibid.

187 NPR, September 11, 2007.

188 Guadalupe San Miguel, "Mexican American Organizations and the Changing Politics of School Desegregation in Texas, 1945–1980," *Social Science Quarterly* 63 (1982), 701–715.

189 Ibid., 710.

190 Even children of illegal aliens have been given the right to attend public schools by the Supreme Court. The majority assumed that most of these children, although subject to deportation, would remain in the United States, given the large number of illegal aliens who do remain here. Denying them an education would

deprive them of the opportunity to fulfill their potential and would deprive society of the benefit of their contribution. *Plyler* v. *Doe,* 457 U.S. 202 (1982).

191 Luis Ricardo Fraga, Kenneth J. Meier, and Robert E. England, "Hispanic Americans and Educational Policy: Structural Limits to Equal Access and Opportunities for Upward Mobility," unpublished paper, University of Oklahoma, 1985, 6.

192 *San Antonio Independent School District* v. *Rodriguez,* 411 U.S. 1 (1973).

193 Anjetta McQueen, "Dual-Language Schools Sought," *Lincoln Journal Star,* March 16, 2000.

194 In 1968 Congress encouraged bilingual education by providing funding, and in 1974 the Supreme Court, in a case brought by Chinese parents, held that schools must teach students in a language they can understand. *Lau* v. *Nichols,* 414 U.S. 563 (1974). This can be their native language, or it can be English if they have been taught English. These federal actions prompted states to establish bilingual education programs.

195 McQueen, "Dual-Language Schools Sought."

196 "Bilingualism's End Means a Different Kind of Change," *Champaign-Urbana News-Gazette,* June 7, 1998.

197 Margot Hornblower, "No Habla Español," *Time,* January 26, 1998, 63.

198 James Traub, "The Bilingual Barrier," *New York Times Magazine,* January 31, 1999, 34–35.

199 John Bowe, "Nobodies," *New Yorker,* April 21, 2003, 106.

200 "Survey: Hispanics Reject Cohesive Group Identity," *Lincoln Journal,* December 15, 1992.

201 Gregory Rodriguez, "Finding a Political Voice," *Washington Post National Weekly Edition,* February 1, 1999, 22–23.

202 Karen Tumulty, "Courting a Sleeping Giant," *Time,* June 11, 2001, 74.

203 A 1995 Census Bureau Survey indicated that 49% of Native people preferred being called *American Indian,* 37% preferred *Native American,* 3.6% preferred "some other term," and 5% had no preference. Bureau of Labor Statistics, U.S. Census Bureau Survey, May 1995. www.census.gov/ prod/2/gen/96arc/ivatuck.pdf.

204 *Cherokee Nation* v. *Georgia,* 30 U.S. 1 (1831); *Worcester* v. *Georgia,* 31 U.S. 515 (1832).

205 Treaties made exceptions for those who married whites and those who left their tribes and abandoned tribal customs.

206 Vine Deloria Jr. and Clifford M. Lytle, *American Indians, American Justice* (Austin: University of Texas Press, 1983), 221.

207 Ibid., 222–225.

208 Indian Self-Determination Act (1975).

209 Ellen Nakashima and Neely Tucker, "A Fight over Lost Lands, Money Owed," *Washington Post National Weekly Edition,* April 29, 2002, 30.

210 According to the Indian Gaming Regulatory Act (1988), tribes can establish casinos if their reservation lies in a state that allows virtually any gambling, including charitable "Las Vegas nights."

211 Kathleen Schmidt, "Gambling a Bonanza for Indians," *Lincoln Journal Star,* March 23, 1998.

212 Donald L. Bartlett and James B. Steele, "Wheel of Misfortune," *Time,* December 16, 2002, 44–48.

213 Ibid., 47.

214 W. John Moore, "Tribal Imperatives," *National Journal,* June 9, 1990, 1396.

215 Jack Hitt, "The Newest Indian," *New York Times Magazine,* August 21, 2005, 40–41.

216 Quoted in Ruth B. Ginsburg, *Constitutional Aspects of Sex-Based Discrimination* (Saint Paul, Minn.: West, 1974), 2.

217 Karen De Crow, *Sexist Justice* (New York: Vintage, 1975), 72.

218 Nadine Taub and Elizabeth M. Schneider, "Women's Subordination and the Role of Law," in *The Politics of Law: A Progressive Critique,* rev. ed., ed. David Kairys (New York: Pantheon, 1990), 160–162.

219 *Bradwell* v. *Illinois,* 83 U.S. 130 (1873).

220 From an *amicus curiae* ("friend of the court") brief by 281 historians filed in the Supreme Court case, *Webster* v. *Reproductive Health Services,* 106 L.Ed.2d 410 (1989).

221 Donna M. Moore, "Editor's Introduction" in *Battered Women,* ed. Donna M. Moore (Beverly Hills, Calif.: Sage, 1979), 8.

222 Jill Lepore, "Vast Designs," *New Yorker,* October 29, 2007, 92.

223 Barbara Sinclair Deckard, *The Women's Movement,* 2nd ed. (New York: Harper & Row, 1979), 303.

224 In the early 1960s, a board game for girls— *What Shall I Be?*—offered these options: teacher, nurse, stewardess, actress, ballerina, and beauty queen. David Owen, "The Sultan of Stuff," *New Yorker,* July 19, 1999, 60.

225 Reprinted in "Regrets, We Have a Few," *Time Special Issue: 75 Years of* Time, 1998, 192.

226 For an examination of Betty Friedan's role in the movement and the political dynamics among the various factions in the movement, see Judith Hennessee, *Betty Friedan: Her Life* (New York: Random House, 1999). For an examination of women's views toward feminism, see Elinor Burkett, *The Right Women* (New York: Scribner, 1998).

227 Robert Alan Goldberg, *Enemies Within* (New Haven, Conn.: Yale University Press, 2002).

228 De Crow, *Sexist Justice,* 119.

229 This is why Betty Friedan later felt compelled to write a book espousing the concept of motherhood: *The Second Stage* (New York: Summit, 1981).

230 For a discussion of these points, see Jane Mansbridge, *Why We Lost the ERA* (Chicago: University of Chicago Press, 1986); Mary Frances Berry, *Why ERA Failed* (Bloomington: Indiana University Press, 1986); Janet Boles, "Building Support for the ERA: A Case of 'Too Much, Too Late,'" *PS: Political Science and Politics* 15 (1982), 575–592.

231 Shenkman, *I Love Paul Revere,* 136–137.

232 *Reed* v. *Reed,* 404 U.S. 71 (1971).

233 *Hoyt* v. *Florida,* 368 U.S. 57 (1961).

234 *Taylor* v. *Louisiana,* 419 U.S. 522 (1975).

235 *Stanton* v. *Stanton,* 421 U.S. 7 (1975).

236 Cases were from 2002. They were compiled by The WAGE Project (www.wageproject.org) and examined and reported in Evelyn F. Murphy, with E. J. Graff, *Getting Even: Why Women Don't Get Paid Like Men—and What to Do about It* (New York: Simon & Schuster, 2005), 40–48. This total also includes sexual harassment suits, which, of course, reflect a type of sexual discrimination.

237 Ibid., 56.

238 Ibid., 157.

239 Ibid., 153

240 Ibid., 60–61.

241 Ibid., 84–85.

242 Ibid., 200.

243 Ibid., 199.

244 Ibid., 4.

245 David Leonhardt, "Gender Pay Gap, Once Narrowing, Is Stuck in Place," *New York Times,* December 24, 2006, YT18.

246 Murphy, *Getting Even,* 185.

247 *Ledbetter* v. *Goodyear Tire and Rubber,* 167 L.Ed.2d 982 (2007).

248 Ibid., 146.

249 U.S. Census Bureau, *Statistical Abstract of the United States, 1997* (Washington, D.C.: Government Printing Office, 1997), tab. 645.

250 The phrase itself is not new. It was used by workers in the nineteenth century and as the title of a book by a Catholic priest in 1906. Jon Gertner, "What Is a Living Wage?" *New York Times Magazine,* January 15, 2006, 42.

251 For discussion, see ibid., 38.

252 Lisa McLaughlin, "In Brief," *Time,* October 9, 2000, G12.

253 For discussion, see Murphy, *Getting Even,* 194–213.

254 See Murphy, *Getting Even,* for numerous examples.

255 David Crary, "U.S. Among Worst in Family vs. Work Policies," *Lincoln Journal Star,* February 1, 2007, 5A. There's no federal law requiring employers to provide paid sick days. Most do provide them for salaried employees but not for hourly employees.

256 The Family and Medical Leave Act. The act also requires employers to continue health insurance coverage during the leave and to give the employee the same job or a comparable one upon her or his return.

257 Lisa Genasci, "Many Workers Resist Family Benefit Offers," *Lincoln Journal Star,* June 28, 1995.

258 Ellen Bravo, "The Architecture of Work and Family," *American Prospect,* March, 2007, A5.

259 Jodie Levin-Epstein, "Responsive Workplaces," *American Prospect,* March, 2007, A16.

260 Joan C. Williams, "The Opt-Out Revolution Revisited," *American Prospect,* March, 2007, A14.

261 This pattern appears in all social classes. From the National Survey of Families and Households, University of Wisconsin, cited in

Lisa Belkin, "When Mom and Dad Share It All," *New York Times Magazine,* June 15, 2008, 44.

262 Heather Boushey, "Values Begin at Home, but Who's Home?" *American Prospect,* March, 2007, A2.

263 Ann Crittenden, "Parents Fighting Back," *American Prospect,* June 2003, 22.

264 Reference omitted

265 Reference omitted

266 Joyce Gelb and Marian Lief Palley, *Women and Public Policies* (Princeton, N.J.: Princeton University Press, 1982), 102. The author of Title IX, Rep. Patsy Mink (D.-Hawaii), had applied to medical schools but was not considered because she was a woman. Mink intended Title IX to open the doors. She said it was "never intended to mean equal numbers or equal money" in athletics. Susan Reimer, "Title IX Has Unintended Consequences," *Lincoln Journal Star,* April 9, 2000.

267 R. Vivian Acosta and Linda Jean Carpenter, *Women in Intercollegiate Sport: A Longitudinal, National Study. Twenty-nine Year Update,* 2006, www.womenssportsfoundation.org/cgi-bin/iowa/issues/part/article.html?record=1107.

268 Welch Suggs, "Uneven Progress for Women's Sports," *Chronicle of Higher Education,* April 7, 2000, A52–A56; Bill Pennington, "More Men's Teams Benched as Colleges Level the Field," *New York Times,* May 9, 2002, A1; Susan Welch and Lee Sigelman,"Who Calls the Shots: Women Coaches in Division I Women's Sports," forthcoming *Social Science Quarterly,* 2008.

269 Suggs, "Uneven Progress for Women's Sports," A52.

270 Michele Orecklin, "Now She's Got Game," *Time,* March 3, 2003, 57.

271 "Title IX Facts Everyone Should Know," www.womensportsfoundation.org/cgibin/iowa/issues/geena/record,html?record=862.

272 Mary Duffy, quoted in E. J. Dionne Jr., "Nothing Wacky about Title IX," *Washington Post National Weekly Edition,* May 19, 1997, 26.

273 Karen Kornbluh, "The Joy of Flex," *Washington Monthly,* December 2005, 30.

274 For elaboration, see Eyal Press, "Do Workers Have a Fundamental Right to Care for Their Families? The Latest Front in the Job-Discrimination Battle," *New York Times Magazine,* July 29, 2007, 37.

275 *Mississippi University for Women* v. *Hogan,* 458 U.S. 718 (1982).

276 *Orr* v. *Orr,* 440 U.S. 268 (1979).

277 *Michael M.* v. *Sonoma County,* 450 U.S. 464 (1981).

278 *Rostker* v. *Goldberg,* 453 U.S. 57 (1981).

279 *Planned Parenthood of Southeastern Pennsylvania* v. *Casey,* 120 L.Ed.2d 674 (1992).

280 This scenario was used by President Johnson in support of affirmative action.

281 Early decisions include *University of California Regents* v. *Bakke,* 438 U.S. 265 (1978); *United Steelworkers* v. *Weber,* 443 U.S. 193 (1979); and *Fullilove* v. *Klutznick,* 448 U.S. 448 (1980).

282 Two critics include Thomas Sowell, *Preferential Policies: An International Perspective* (New York: Morrow, 1990), and Dinesh D'Souza, *Illiberal Education* (New York: Free Press, 1991).

283 *United Steelworkers* v. *Weber; Sheet Metal Workers* v. *EEOC,* 92 L.Ed.2d 344 (1986); *Firefighters* v. *Cleveland,* 92 L.Ed.2d 405 (1986); *United States* v. *Paradise Local Union,* 94 L. Ed.2d 203 (1987).

284 *Firefighters* v. *Stotts,* 467 U.S. 561 (1985); *Wygant* v. *Jackson Board of Education,* 90 L.Ed.2d 260 (1986).

285 *Richmond* v. *Croson,* 102 L.Ed.2d 854 (1989); *Adarand Constructors* v. *Pena,* 132 L. Ed.2d 158 (1995). The perception that minorities are taking over is also reflected in a peculiar poll finding: The average American estimated that 32 percent of the U.S. population was black and 21 percent was Hispanic at a time when they were just 12 percent and 9 percent. Richard Nadeau, Richard G. Niemi, and Jeffrey Levine, "Innumeracy about Minority Populations," *Public Opinion Quarterly* 57 (1993), 332–347.

286 Quoted in Robert J. Samuelson, "End Affirmative Action," *Washington Post National Weekly Edition,* March 6, 1995, 5.

287 Private companies that have government contracts, and therefore are subject to affirmative action, have shown more improvement in hiring minorities and women than other companies have. State and local governments, also subject to affirmative action, have shown more improvement in hiring than private companies have.

288 James E. Jones, "The Genesis and Present Status of Affirmative Action in Employment," paper presented at the annual meeting of the American Political Science Association, Washington, D.C., September, 1984; Nelson C. Dometrius and Lee Sigelman, "Assessing Progress toward Affirmative Action Goals in State and Local Government," *Public Administration Review* 44 (1984), 241–247; Peter Eisinger, *Black Employment in City Government* (Washington, D.C.: Joint Center for Political Studies, 1983); Milton Coleman, "Uncle Sam Has Stopped Running Interference for Blacks," *Washington Post National Weekly Edition,* December 19, 1983.

289 This "is one of the better kept secrets of the debate." Alan Wolfe, "Affirmative Action, Inc.," *New Yorker,* November 25, 1996, 107. See also the numerous sources cited there.

290 Joe Klein, "There's More Than One Way to Diversify," *Time,* December 18, 2006, 29.

291 Gertrude Ezorsky, *Racism and Justice: The Case for Affirmative Action* (Ithaca, N.Y.: Cornell University Press, 1991), 48–49, 63–65.

292 Wilson, *The Truly Disadvantaged.*

293 Donald Kaul, "Privilege in Workplace Invisible to White Men Who Enjoy It," *Lincoln Journal-Star,* April 9, 1995; Richard Morin and Lynne Duke, "A Look at the Bigger Picture," *Washington Post National Weekly Edition,* March 16, 1992, 9.

294 Eisinger, *Black Employment in City Government.*

295 Thomas J. Kane, "Racial and Ethnic Preference in College Admissions," paper presented at the Ohio State University College of Law Conference, "Twenty Years after *Bakke,*" Columbus, April 1998.

296 Stephen Carter, quoted in David Owen, "From Race to Chase," *New Yorker,* June 3, 2002, 54.

297 This has happened in Florida. "Fewer Black Students Enrolled in Florida," *Lincoln Journal Star,* September 11, 2005, 3A.

298 And the UC campuses at Berkeley and Los Angeles began to take into account "disadvantage" more than they used to. That is, they began to use "disadvantage" as a proxy for race. David Leonhardt, "The New Affirmative Action," *New York Times Magazine,* September 30, 2007, 76.

299 Jeffrey Rosen, "How I Learned to Love Quotas," *New York Times Magazine,* June 1, 2003, 54; Lee Hockstader, "The Texas 10 Percent Solution," *Washington Post National Weekly Edition,* November 11, 2002, 30. A major effect on the University of California system has been "cascading," with minority enrollments dropping at the most competitive UC campuses but increasing at the less competitive ones. Minorities have been cascading from the top tier to the next tiers, where their academic records more closely match those of the other students. James Traub, "The Class of Prop. 209," *New York Times Magazine,* May 2, 1999, 51.

300 Jacques Steinberg, "The New Calculus of Diversity on Campus," *New York Times,* February 2, 2003, WK3; Timothy Egan, "Little Asia on the Hill," *New York Times,* January 7, 2007, Education Life, 26.

301 *Gratz* v. *Bollinger,* 156 L.Ed.2d 257; *Grutter* v. *Bollinger,* 156 L.Ed.2d 304.

302 Chief Justice Roberts and Justices Alito, Scalia, and Thomas. The question mark is Justice Kennedy.

303 Traub, "Class of Prop. 209."

304 John Larew, "Why Are Droves of Unqualified, Unprepared Kids Getting into Our Top Colleges?" *Washington Monthly,* June 1991, 10–14; Theodore Cross, "Suppose There Was No Affirmative Action at the Most Prestigious Colleges and Graduate Schools," *Journal of Blacks in Higher Education,* March 31, 1994, 47, 50; Joe Klein, "There's More Than One Way to Diversify," *Time,* December 18, 2006, 29.

305 For an examination of the *Bakke* ruling and its impact on graduate schools, see Susan Welch and John Gruhl, *Affirmative Action and Minority Enrollments in Medical and Law Schools* (Ann Arbor: University of Michigan Press, 1998).

306 Richard H. Sander, "House of Cards for Black Law Students," *Los Angeles Times,* December 20, 2004, www.latimes.com/news/opinion/la-oe-sander20dec20,0,436015,print.story; Adam Liptak, "For Blacks in Law School, Can Less Be More?" *New York Times,* February 13, 2005, WK3.

307 For further discussion, see David T. Canon, *Race, Redistricting, and Representation* (Chicago: University of Chicago Press, 1999), 23–25. Of course, there's also a small upper class

of wealthy business people, entertainers, and athletes.

[308] Dick Kirschten, "Not Black-and-White," *National Journal,* March 2, 1991, 496–500.

Chapter 16

[1] Starting with Plato.

[2] Joseph Schumpeter, *Theory of Economic Development,* Redvers Opie, trans., (New York: Oxford University Press, 1961). Originally published in 1934.

[3] J. Bradford Delong, "Creative Destruction's Reconstruction: Joseph Schumpeter Revisited," *Chronicle of Higher Education,* December 7, 2007, 2.

[4] Adam Smith, *Inquiry into the Nature and Causes of the Wealth of Nations* (1776; reprinted in several editions, including Indianapolis: Bobbs-Merrill, 1961).

[5] James K. Galbraith, *Balancing Acts: Technology, Finance, and the American Future* (New York: Basic Books, 1989); Robert L. Heilbroner and Lester C. Thurow, *Five Economic Challenges* (Englewood Cliffs, N.J.: Prentice Hall, 1981), 62.

[6] Quoted in John Greenwald, "Knitting New Notions," *Time,* January 30, 1989, 46.

[7] John Maynard Keynes, *The General Theory of Employment, Interest and Money* (New York: Harcourt, Brace, 1935).

[8] Ibid., 1496.

[9] The FOMC is made up of a board of governors including five Federal Reserve Bank heads.

[10] For a brief review of the Fed's work, see James L. Rowe Jr., "Holding the Purse Strings," *Washington Post National Weekly Edition,* June 28, 1999, 6–8.

[11] William Greider, *Secrets of the Temple: How the Federal Reserve Runs the Country* (New York: Simon & Schuster, 1987), 461. Grieder's analyses of the Reserve Board's anti-inflation policies in the early 1980s are revealing and compelling.

[12] Ben Wildavsky, "Atlas Schmoozes," *National Journal,* May 17, 1997, 974–977.

[13] Paul Krugman, "The Maestro Slips Out of Tune," *New York Times Magazine,* June 6, 2004, 80.

[14] See, for example, Greenspan's criticism of Bush's fiscal policies in the book he wrote after leaving the Fed, *Age of Turbulence: Adventures in a New World* (New York: Penguin, 2007).

[15] Gardiner Harris, "F.D.A. Approves Broader Access to Next-Day Pill," *New York Times,* August 25, 2006.

[16] See discussion in William Ophuls, *Ecology and the Politics of Scarcity; Prologue to a Political Theory of the Steady State* (San Francisco: W. H. Freeman, 1977), 145–147.

[17] NBC News Special Report on the 20th Anniversary of Earth Day, April 22, 1991.

[18] William P. Cunningham, et al., eds., *Environmental Encyclopedia,* 2nd ed.(Detroit: Gale Research, 1998), 395; Ruth A. Eblen and William R. Eblen, eds., *The Encyclopedia of the Environment* (Boston: Houghton Mifflin, 1994), 243.

[19] Victor Allred, "PAYGO Goes by the Wayside," *Congressional Quarterly Weekly Report,* January 13, 2001, 96.

[20] Andrew Taylor, "Deal on Pay-As-You-Go Rules a Must for Budget Resolution," *Congressional Quarterly Weekly Report,* April 17, 2004, 897–900.

[21] John Maggs, "Winners and Losers in the Bush Economy," *National Journal,* May 15, 2004, 1495.

[22] For a worst-case scenario, see Laurence J. Kotlikoff and Scott Burns, *The Coming Generational Storm: What You Need to Know about America's Economic Future* (Cambridge, Mass.: MIT Press, 2004). Kotlikoff estimated the government would have a gap of $51 trillion between revenues and obligations over the coming decade, and that was before the borrowing for the Wall Street rescue plan.

[23] Gretchen Morgenson, "Another Day Older and Deeper in Debt," *New York Times,* July 20, 2008, 1.

[24] Rep. Jim Cooper, "Why This Report Matters to You," commentary on the Financial Report of the United States, 2005, xv (transcript is at www.pbs.org/now).

[25] Roger Lowenstein, "Tax Break: Who Needs the Mortgage-Interest Deduction?" *New York Times Magazine,* March 5, 2006, 78.

[26] Jill Barshay, "Rich vs. Poor," *CQ Weekly,* February 7, 2005, 297.

[27] "Problems Cited at IRS Help Centers," *Champaign-Urbana News-Gazette,* September 4, 2003, 1.

[28] Ibid.

[29] N. Gregory Mankiw, "Fair Taxes? Depends What You Mean by 'Fair.'" *New York Times,* July 15, 2007, BU4.

[30] Jill Barshay, "Business Lobby Storms Senate to Shape Corporate Tax Bill," *CQ Weekly,* May 8, 2004, 1073.

[31] Jill Barshay, "Rich vs. Poor," *CQ Weekly,* February 7, 2005, 295.

[32] Edmund L. Andrews, "Senate Approves 2-Year Extension of Bush Tax Cuts," *New York Times,* May 12, 2006, citing data from the Tax Policy Center.

[33] Joseph J. Schatz, "National Sales Tax: The Pros and Cons," *CQ Weekly,* June 13, 2005, 1558.

[34] David Alan Stockman, *Triumph of Politics: How the Reagan Revolution Failed* (New York: Harper & Row, 1986).

[35] Citizens for Tax Justice, "Bush Still on Track to Borrow $10 Trillion by 2014 According to Latest Official Estimates," Paper issued January 30, 2004, 1 (www.ctj.org).

[36] Robert Greenstein, "President's Budget Uses Accounting Devices and Implausible Assumptions to Hide Hundreds of Billions of Dollars in Costs," Center for Budget and Policy Priorities, February 5, 2002, 2, www.cbpp.org.

[37] Mark Murray, John Maggs, et al., quoting Brookings' analyst William G. Gale in "The Deficit Difference," National Journal, February 9, 2002, 384.

[38] U.S. Treasury Department, The Federal Government's Financial Health: A Citizen's Guide to the 2007 Financial Report of the United States Government, www.ustreas.gov.

[39] John Crawford, "Code Words: Tax Neutrality," *CQ Weekly,* February 7, 2005, 289. The economist quoted is Alice Rivlin, former director of the CBO and the OMB, and former vice-chair of the Fed.

[40] Joseph L. Schatz, "The Power of the Status Quo," *CQ Weekly,* February 6, 2006, 322.

[41] This is a proposal made by Yale law professor Michael J. Graetz, "To the Point of No Returns," *New York Times,* November 15, 2004, A23.

[42] Former chair of the Senate Finance Committee, Bob Packwood (R-Ore.) quoted in ibid., 323.

[43] Joseph J. Schatz, "IRS Set to Lean Harder on Wayward Taxpayers," *CQ Weekly,* April 25, 2005, 1055.

[44] The study was done by Irwin Kellner, senior economist for MarketWatch, cited in Marhsall Loeb, "Where Will the Economy Go From Here?" *Lincoln Journal Star,* July 6, 2008 H1.

[45] Larry M. Bartels, *Unequal Democracy: The Political Economy of the New Gilded Age* (Princeton, N.J.: Princeton University Press, 2008).

[46] "Family Wealth Down for 1st Time in 55 Years," *Champaign-Urbana News-Gazette,* March 14, 2001, A8.

[47] "Family Wealth Down for 1st Time in 55 Years," *Champaign-Urbana News-Gazette,* March 14, 2001, A8.

[48] Isabel V.Sawhill, "Overview," in Ron Haskins, Julia B. Isaacs and Isabel Sawhill, *Getting Ahead or Losing Ground in America* (Washington D.C.: Brookings Institution, 2008), 3.

[49] Based on latest (2007) census data available at this writing, released August 26, 2008 (www.cenus.gov) .

[50] Gretchen Morgenson, "Another Day Older and Deeper in Debt," *New York Times,* July 20, 2008, 1,18–19.

[51] Ellen Simon, "Way More Pay," *Champaign-Urbana News-Gazette,* June 10, 2007, B1.

[52] *For a New Thrift: An Appeal to Prospective Colleagues (*New York: Institute for American Values January, 2008), 4.

[53] Haskins, Isaacs, and Sawhill, *Getting Ahead or Losing Ground,* 4, 7.

[54] Economic Mobility Project (2008), Pew Charitable Trusts, www.pewresearch.org.

[55] Ibid., 8. The comparative mobility data is based on the work of Miles Corak.

[56] Michael Lind, *The Next American Nation: The New Nationalism and the Fourth American Revolution* (New York: Free Press, 1995), 139–216.

[57] Haskins, Isaacs, and Sawhill, *Getting Ahead or Losing Ground,* 9.

[58] Edward R. Tufte, *Political Control of the Economy* (Princeton, N.J.: Princeton University Press, 1978).

[59] Spoils to GOP Victors," *Champaign-Urbana News-Gazette,* August 6, 2002, 1.

[60] Paul Krugman, "Dynamo and Microchip," *New York Times,* February 20, 2000, sec. 4, 13.

[61] CBS/*New York Times* Poll, August 2006.

[62] Joseph A. Schumpeter, *Business Cycles: A Theoretical, Historical, and Statistical Analysis of the Capitalist Process* (New York: McGraw-Hill) 1939.

[63] David E. Sanger, "Look Who's Carping Most about Capitalism," *New York Times,* April 6, 1997, E5. This estimate has been accepted by the former chair of the Council of Economic Advisers, Laura D. Tyson.

[64] Lael Brainard and Robert E. Litan, "'Offshoring' Service Jobs: Ban or Boon and What to Do?" *Brookings Policy Brief #132,* April 2004, 2.

[65] Louis Uchitelle, "It's Not New Jobs. It's All the Jobs." *New York Times,* August 29, 2004, 3, 6.

[66] Louis Uchitelle and David Leonhardt, "Men Not Working, and Not Wanting Just Any," *New York Times,* July 31, 2006, 1.

[67] Louis Uchitelle, "Women Are Now Equal As Victims of Poor Economy," *New York Times,* July 22, 2008, A1.

[68] Peter S. Goodman, "When Foreigners Buy The Factory, Two Towns, Opposite Paths" *New York Times,* April 7, 2008, A1.

[69] Micheline Maynard and Jeremy W. Peters, "2 Asian Automakers Plan Ventures in 2 States Left by U.S. Carmakers," *New York Times,* March 14, 2006, C1.

[70] Peter S. Goodman and Louise Story, "Foreigners Buy Stakes in the U.S. at a Record Pace," *New York Times,* January 20, 2008, 1.

[71] Thomas L. Friedman, *"The World Is Flat: A Brief History of the Twenty-first Century"* (New York: Farrar, Straus and Giroux, 2005).

[72] Richard Florida, *Who's Your Ciy? How the Creative Economy is Making Where You Live the Most Important Decision of Your Life* (New York: Basic Books, 2008), 48–49.

[73] One proponent of protectionist policies is Sen. Byron Dorgan (D-ND). He makes his argument in *Take This Job and Ship It: How Corporate Greed and Brain-dead Politics Are Selling Out America* (New York: Thomas Dunne Books/St. Martin's Press, 2006).

[74] This is the view of Richard W. Fisher, president of the Federal Reserve Bank of Dallas.

[75] Friedman, *The World Is Flat, 259.,*

[76] Diana Jean Schemo, "2-Year Colleges, Students Eager but Unready," *New York Times,* September 2, 2006.

[77] William Greider, "America's Truth Deficit," *New York Times,* July 18, 2005. A more complete statement of Greider's view in his *One World, Ready or Not.* (New York: Simon & Schuster, 1997)

Chapter 17

[1] Julia B. Isaacs, "Economic Mobility of Families Across Generations," in Ron Haskins, Julia B. Isaacs, and Isabel Sawhill, *Getting Ahead or Losing Ground in America* (Washington, D.C.: Brookings Institution, 2008), 5.

[2] For comparative information on government spending in industrial countries, see www.oecd.org.

[3] All of the statistics on Social Security recipients are from Social Security Administration, "Social Security Basic Facts," www.socialsecurity.gov/ pressoffice/basicfact.htm.

[4] Social Security Administration, "Social Security Information for Women," www.ssa.gov/pressoffice/factsheets/women.htm.

[5] U.S. Census Bureau press release, "Household Income Rises, Poverty Rate Unchanged, Number of Uninsured Down," August 2, 2008, www.census.gov/.

[6] Rachel L. Swarns, "Bipartisan Calls for New Federal Poverty Measure," *New York Times,* September 2, 2008, A14.

[7] "Supplemental Security Income (SSI)," www.ssa.gov/ssi/text-general-ussi.htm.

[8] Greg J. Duncan, *Years of Poverty, Years of Plenty: The Changing Economic Fortunes of American Workers and Families* (Ann Arbor: Survey Research Center, Institute for Social Research, University of Michigan, 1984); Spencer Rich, "Who Gets Help and How," *Washington Post National Weekly Edition,* May 15, 1989, 37.

[9] Department of Health and Human Services, Temporary Assistance for Needy Families (TANF) Program, Administration for Children and Families, final rule summary, www.acf.dhhs. gov/programs/ofa/exsumcl.htm; Liz Schott, Ed Lazere, Heidi Goldberg, and Eileen Sweeney, "Highlights of the Final TANF Regulations," Center on Budget and Policy Priorities, April 29, 1999, www.cbpp.org/4-29-99wel.htm.

[10] Ibid.

[11] Stephen D. Holt, "Periodic Payment of the Earned Income Tax Credit," Brookings Institution Metropolitan Policy Project paper, June 2008, 4–6, www.brookings.edu.

[12] USDA, "Food Stamp Program: A Short History," www.fns.usda.gov/fsp/rules/Legislation/about_fsp.htm.

[13] Aliya Sternstein, " 'Hunger' Not in UDSA Lexicon," *CQ Weekly,* May 12, 2008, 1240.

[14] Jay Mathews, "Study Shows Early Head Start Gains," *State College* (Pa.) *Centre Daily Times,* June 5, 2002, 1.

[15] U.S. Census Bureau, *Statistical Abstract of the United States, 2001* (Washington, D.C.: Government Printing Office, 2001), tab. 801.

[16] Nicholas Kristof, "Farm Subsidies That Kill," *New York Times,* July 5, 2002, A21.

[17] John Kelly, "Lion's Share of Farm Subsidies Going to a Select Few," *State College* (Pa.) *Centre Daily Times,* September 10, 2001, 1.

[18] John Lancaster, "Our Farm-Friendly Lawmakers," *Washington Post National Weekly Edition,* September 10, 2001, 11.

[19] Quoted in ibid.

[20] Gebe Martinez, "Free-Spending Farm Bill a Triumph of Politics," *Congressional Quarterly Weekly Review,* May 4, 2002, 114. The first quote is from John Boehner (R-Ohio) and Cal Dooley (D-Calif.), the second from Patrick Toomey (R-Pa.).

[21] Elizabeth Becker, "As House Prepares Farm Bill, Questions of Who Needs Help and How Much," *New York Times,* September 9, 2001, 22.

[22] Timothy Egan, "Big Farms Reap Two Harvests with Aid as Bumper Crop," *New York Times,* December 26, 2004, sec. 1, 36.

[23] Press release from the office of former Senator Tim Hutchinson, May 13, 2002.

[24] Dan Barber, "Stuck in the Middle," *New York Times,* November 23, 2005.

[25] Kristof, "Farm Subsidies That Kill."

[26] "VA Benefits and Health Care Utilization, July 2008, www.va.gov.

[27] Richard B. Freeman, "Labor Market Institutions and Earnings Inequality," *New England Economic Review,* May–June 1996, 158; U.S. Census Bureau, "Current Population Survey," March 1960 to 2001, www.census.gov.

[28] U.S. Census Bureau, "Income, Poverty in 2007" www.census.gov; Center on Budget and Policy Priorities, "Poverty and Share of Americans Without Health Insurance were Higher in 2007," August 26, 2008, 3, www.cbpp.org/8-26-08pov.htm.

[29] Ron Haskins, "The Rise of the Bottom Fifth: How to Build on the Gains of Welfare Reform," Brookings Institution paper, September 3, 2008, 2, www.brookings.edu/articles/2007/0529useconomics_haskins.aspx.

[30] Mark Murray, Marilyn Werber Serafini, and Megan Twohey, "Untested Safety Net," *National Journal,* March 10, 2001, 691.

[31] Clarke E. Cochran et al., *American Public Policy,* 6th ed. (New York: St. Martin's/Worth, 1999), 282.

[32] Centers for Medicaid and Medicare, Medicaid Program—General Information, www.cms.hhs.gov; Robert Pear, "Nursing Home Inspections Miss Violations, Report Says," *New York Times,* January 16, 2006, A9.

[33] Erin Heath, "Medicaid: The Pendulum Swings," *National Journal,* August 9, 2003, 2546.

[34] Paul Krugman, "Our Sick Society," *New York Times,* May 5, 2006, A23.

[35] Editorial, "Hospital-Caused Deaths" *New York Times,* July 5, 2006, A16; Gardiner Harris, "Report Finds a Heavy Toll From Medication Errors," *New York Times* July 21, 2006, A12.

[36] Institute of Medicine study, cited in Hillary Rodham Clinton, "Now Can We Talk About Health Care?" *New York Times Magazine,* April 18, 2004, 20.

[37] Kevin Sack, "Health Plan from Obama Spurs Debate," *New York Times,* July 23, 2008, A1.

[38] Reed Abelson and Milt Freudenheim, "Even the Insured Feel the Strain of Health Costs," *New York Times,* May 4, 2008, 1.

[39] "Europe Mulls Private Medical Care," *Champaign-Urbana News-Gazette,* November 29, 2003, A3.

[40] Robert Fitch, "Big Labor's Big Secret," *New York Times,* December 28, 2005, A19.

[41] Lawrence J. Schweinhart et al., *Lifetime Effects: The High/Scope Perry Preschool Study through Age 40* (Ypsilanti, Mich.: High/Scope Press, 2004).

[42] "Greenspan Warns about Mortgage Giants' Debt," *Champaign-Urbana News-Gazette,* February 24, 2004, C8.

[43] Timothy L. O'Brien and Jennifer Lee, "Seismic Shift under the House of Fannie Mae," *New York Times,* October 3, 2004, sec. 3, 1, 9.

[44] "Nature Humbles a State of Mind," *New York Times,* February 10, 1991, E3; Marc Reisner, "The Emerald Desert," *Greenpeace,* July–August 1989, 7.

[45] Donald L. Barlett and James B. Steele, "Corporate Welfare," *Time,* November 23, 1998, 38.

[46] Ibid., 87.

[47] See Donald L. Barlett and James B. Steele, "Paying a Price for Polluters," *Time,* November 23, 1998, 77, and "Corporate Welfare," 39.

[48] For some sample costs of industrial waste cleanup, see Barlett and Steele, "Paying a Price for Polluters," 72–80.

[49] Kevin Sack, "The Short End of the Longer Life," *New York Times,* April 27, 2008, WK 1.

[50] The findings of a study on this subject can be found in "Trends in Quality of Care and Racial Disparities in Medicare Managed Care," *New England Journal of Medicine,* August 18, 2005, 692–700.

[51] Anna Bernasek, "Health Care Problem? Check the American Pysche," *New York Times,* December 3, 2006, BU3.

[52] Donald L. Barlett and James B. Steele, "The Health of Nations," *New York Times,* October 24, 2004, WK11.

[53] (Dr.) Arthur Garson, *Health Care Half-Truths: Too Many Myths, Not Enough Reality* (Lanham: Rowman & Littlefield, 2007).

[54] Clinton, "Now Can We Talk?" 30

[55] Steve Lohr, "Health Care Costs Are a Killer but Maybe That's a Plus," *New York Times,* September 26, 2004, W5; Malcolm Caldwell, "High Prices," *New Yorker,* October 25, 2004, 88.

[56] Caldwell, "High Prices," 88; see also John Abramson, *Overdosed America* (New York: Harper-Collins, 2004).

[57] Gina Kolata, "More May Not Mean Better in Health Care, Studies Find," *New York Times,* July 21, 2002, sec. 1, 20.

[58] Erik Eckholm, "Those Who Pay Health Costs Think of Drawing Lines," *New York Times,* March 28, 1993, 1.

[59] Kolata, "Research Suggests More Health Care May Not Be Better," 20.

[60] Mark Sherman, "Doctors Call for National Coverage," *Lincoln Journal Star,* August 13, 2003, 1.

[61] Robin Toner and Janet Elder, "Most Support U.S. Guarantee of Health Care," *New York Times,* March 2, 2007, 1.

[62] www.taxpolicycenter.org/publications/url.cfm?ID=411749; Thomas Buchmueller, Sherry A. Glied, Anne Royalty, and Katherine Swartz, "Cost and Coverage Implications of the McCain Plan to Restructure Health Insurance," *Health Affairs* 27 (2008). Published online September 16, 2008.

[63] Ibid.; Joseph Antos, Gail Wilensky, and Hanns Kuttner, "More Regulation, Unsustainable Spending," *Health Affairs* 27 (2008). Published online September 16, 2008.content.healthaffairs.org/cgi/content/abstract/hlthaff.27.6.w462.

[64] Social Security Administration, "Social Security Basic Facts 2008," 2, www.ssa.gov/ pressoffice/basicfact.htm.

[65] Robert Pear, "AARP Opposes Bush Plan to Replace Social Security with Private Accounts," *New York Times,* November 12, 2004, A19.

[66] Richard W. Stevenson, "Bush's Social Security Plan Is Said to Require Vast Borrowing," *New York Times,* November 28, 2004, 1, 22.

[67] "Social Security Basic Facts, 2008," 2.

[68] Clea Barton, "Saving Us From Ourselves," *CQ Weekly,* June 23, 2008, 1691.

[69] Department of Health and Human Services, "Reauthorization of the Temporary Assistance for Needy Families Program," 4, www.aphsa.org. Program renewal was part of the Deficit Reduction Act of 2005.

[70] Douglas J. Besharov, "End Welfare Lite as We Know It," *New York Times,* August 15, 2006, A19.

[71] Ibid.

[72] Eileen P. Sweeney, "Recent Studies Indicate That Many Parents Who Are Current or Former Welfare Recipients Have Disabilities," Center on Budget and Policy Priorities, February 29, 2000, www.cbpp.org/2-29-00wel.pdf; Erica Goode, "Childhood Abuse and Adult Stress," *New York Times,* August 2, 2000, A22.

[73] Kevin Freking, "Many States Facing Welfare Dilemma," *Champaign-Urbana News-Gazette,* September 10, 2006, C-3.

[74] *Budget of the United States 2007,* 116.

[75] On Bush's marriage initiative and work requirements, see Bill Swindell, "Welfare Reauthorization Becomes Another Casualty in Congress's Partisan Crossfire," *Congressional Quarterly Weekly,* April 3, 2004, 805–806.

[76] Gardiner Harris, "Teenage Birth Rate Rises for First Time Since '91," *New York Times,* December 6, 2007, A26.

[77] Pietro S. Nivola, Jennifer L. Noyes, and Isabel V. Sawhill, "Welfare and Beyond," Policy Brief No. 29, Brookings Institution, March 2004, 2.

[78] Ibid., 3–6.

[79] Report of Congress's Joint Economic Committee, July 2008.

[80] Gordon Berlin, vice president of MDRC, a nonpartisan research group, quoted in Corine Hegland, "What Works for Welfare?" *National Journal,* January 10, 2004, 108.

Chapter 18

[1] Joseph S. Nye, Jr., *Soft Power: the Means to Success in World Politics* (New York: Public Affairs, 2004), x. Nye is a professor of political science and a former assistant secretary of defense.

[2] Francis Fukuyama, *The End of History and the Last Man* (New York: Free Press, 1992).

[3] Walter LaFeber, "Making Revolution, Opposing Revolution," *New York Times,* July 3, 1983, sec. 4, 13.

[4] The group was known as the Project for the New Century (PNAC); it circulated its call for the overthrow of Saddam Hussein in 1995.

[5] This was Michael Scheurer. For a discussion of his differences with the Bush administration, see *Imperial Hubris* (Washington, D.C.: Brassey's, 2004), originally published anonymously because of Scheurer's position in the intelligence community.

[6] Philip Bobbitt, "Why We Listen," *New York Times,* January 30, 2006, A23.

[7] The findings of the congressional investigation into intelligence failures prior to and after 9/11 can be read at the website for the Senate Select Intelligence Committee (intelligence.senate.gov). See transcripts of the testimony of Eleanor Hill, director of the Joint Inquiry staff.

[8] Madison's notes from *Documents Illustrative of the Formation of the Union of the American States,* quoted in Joan Biskupic, "Constitution's Conflicting Clauses Underscored by Iraqi Crisis," *Congressional Quarterly Weekly Report,* January 5, 1991, 34.

[9] Ronald D. Elving, "America's Most Frequent Fight Has Been the Undeclared War," *Congressional Quarterly Weekly Report,* January 5, 1991, 37.

[10] Representative Toby Roth (R-Wis.), quoted in Katharine Q. Seelye, "House Defeats Bid to Repeal 'War Powers,'" *New York Times,* June 11, 1995, A7.

[11] David Rieff, "Will Little Havana Go Blue?" *New York Times Magazine,* July 13, 2008, 46–51

[12] On Mia Farrow's skillful use of the Beijing Olympics to pressure the Chinese government to change its policy toward the Sudan and Darfur, see Ilan Greenberg, "Changing the Rules of the Game," *New York Times Magazine,* March 30, 2008, 52–57.

[13] For a discussion of the foreign policy establishment, see Walter Isaacson and Evan Thomas, *The Wise Men: Six Friends and the World They Made* (New York: Simon & Schuster, 1986).

[14] Tom Zeller, "The Iraq-al-Qaeda Link: A Short History," *New York Times,* June 20, 2004, WK4.

[15] Andrew Kohut, "Speak Softly and Carry a Smaller Stick," *New York Times,* March 24, 2006, A19. Kohut is a pollster for the Pew Foundation.

[16] Carl M. Cannon, "Judging Clinton," *National Journal,* January 1, 2000, 21.

[17] Robert Wright, "Private Eyes," *New York Times Magazine,* September 5, 1999, 50–54; William J. Broad, "North Korea's Nuclear Intentions, Out There for All to See," *New York Times,* October 8, 2006, WK5; and www.earth.google.com.

[18] Historian Michael Hogan, quoted in John M. Broder, "Gentler Look at the U.S. World Role," *New York Times,* October 31, 1999, 14.

[19] Paul Johnson, "The Myth of American Isolationism," *Foreign Affairs,* May–June 1995, 162.

[20] Quoted in Robert Dallek, *Lyndon B. Johnson, Portrait of a President* (New York: Oxford University Press, 2004), 179.

[21] See James Nathan and James Oliver, *United States Foreign Policy and World Order*, 2nd ed. (Boston: Little, Brown, 1981), 359–361.

[22] For one view of the impact of Vietnam on the thinking of today's high-ranking officers, see H. R. McMaster, *Dereliction of Duty* (New York: Harper-Collins, 1997).

[23] Robert S. McNamara, *In Retrospect: The Tragedy and Lessons of Vietnam* (New York: Times Books, 1995).

[24] Michael Beschloss, *Reaching for Glory: Lyndon Johnson's Secret White House Tapes, 1964–1965* (New York: Simon & Schuster, 2001), 166.

[25] Robert Weissberg, *Public Opinion and Popular Government* (Englewood Cliffs, N.J.: Prentice Hall, 1976), 144–148.

[26] Ole Holsti, "The Three-Headed Eagle," *International Studies Quarterly* 23 (1979), 339–359; Michael Mandelbaum and William Schneider, "The New Internationalisms," in *The Eagle Entangled: U.S. Foreign Policy in a Complex World*, eds. Kenneth Oye, Donald Rothchild, and Robert J. Lieber (New York: Longman, 1979), 34–88.

[27] For an analysis of U.S.-Soviet relations in the Reagan era, see Alexander Dallin and Gail Lapidus, "Reagan and the Russians," and Kenneth Oye, "Constrained Confidence and the Evolution of Reagan Foreign Policy," in *Eagle Resurgent?* eds. Kenneth Oye, Robert Lieber, and Donald Rothchild (Boston: Little, Brown, 1987); and John Newhouse, "The Abolitionist" (pts. 1 and 2), *The New Yorker*, January 2 and 9, 1989.

[28] See George F. Kennan, "After the Cold War," *New York Times Magazine*, February 5, 1989, 32ff.

[29] Bill Clinton, "A Democrat Lays Out His Plan," *Harvard International Review*, Summer 1992, 26.

[30] For a concise summary of the advantages and disadvantages of protectionism and free trade, see Paul Krugman, *The Age of Diminished Expectations* (Cambridge, Mass.: MIT Press, 1992), 101–113.

[31] Bill Clinton, quoted in Jane Perlez, "At Conference on Trade, Clinton Makes Pitch for Poor," *New York Times*, January 30, 2000, 6.

[32] Thomas Friedman, "What Big Stick? Just Sell," *New York Times*, October 2, 1995, E3.

[33] Elaine Sciolino, "Monroe's Doctrine Takes Another Knock," *New York Times*, August 7, 1994, E6. For a discussion of the U.S. turn to multilateralism, see Stanley Hoffmann, "The Crisis of Liberal Internationalism," *Foreign Policy* 98 (1995), 159–177.

[34] "National Security Strategy of the United States," September 2002. This is an annual report the president makes to Congress and during Bush's time in office was posted at www.whitehouse.gov.

[35] "Bush Plans 'Strike First' Military Policy," *Champaign-Urbana News-Gazette*, June 10, 2002, A-3.

[36] Fred Kaplan, "JFK's First-Strike Plan," *Atlantic Monthly*, October 2001, 81–86.

[37] Michael Wines and Sharon LaFraniere, "Hut by Hut, AIDS Steals Life in a Southern Africa Town," *New York Times*, November 28, 2004, 1.

[38] "AIDS Threatens Global Security," *NewsHour with Jim Lehrer*, PBS, October 1, 2002.

[39] William J. Broad and David E. Sanger published a series of articles on this topic in the *New York Times*, "Fraying Old Restraints Risks a Second Nuclear Age," October 15, 2006, 1; "With Eyes on Iran Rivals Pursuing Nuclear Power; April 15, 2007,1; "U.S. Secretly Aids Pakistan in Guarding Nuclear Arms," November 8, 2007, 1; and "In Nuclear Net's Undoing, a Web of Shadowy Deals," August 25, 2008, 1. Also see Wiliam Langewiesche, *The Atomic Bazaar* (New York: Farrar, Straus & Giroux, 2007), and Jonathan Schell, *The Seventh Decade: The New Shape of Nuclear Danger* (New York: Henry Holt & Co, 2007).

[40] "What Does It Take to Make a Bomb?" *Frontline*, PBS, 1998, www.pbs.org/wgbh/pages/ frontline/shows/nukes/stuff/faqs.html.

[41] Leslie Wayne, "America's For-Profit Secret Army," *New York Times*, October 13, 2002, sec. 3, 10.

[42] Interview for the documentary *Why We Fight*, 2005. President Eisenhower's military-industrial speech can also be heard in *Why We Fight*.

[43] Joan Spero, an undersecretary of state, quoted in David E. Sanger, "How Washington Inc. Makes a Sale," *New York Times*, February 19, 1995, sec. 3, 1.

[44] Estimate by Clyde Prestowitz, former Reagan official and president of the Economic Strategy Institute, cited in Eduardo Porter, "DP World and U.S. Trade: A Zero-Sum Game," *New York Times*, March 10, 2006, C1.

[45] James Fallows, "The $1.4 Trillion Question," *Atlantic Monthly*, January/February 2008, 46-48.

[46] Keith Bradsher, "China Leans Less on U.S. Trade," *New York Times*, April 18, 2007, C1. The trade figures are from Goldman-Sachs.

[47] "Diplomacy's New Hit Man: The Free-Market Dollar," *New York Times*, May 24, 1998, sec. 4, 5.

[48] Roger Lowenstein citing work of Harvard economist Dani Rodrik in "Tariff to Nowhere," *New York Times Magazine*, June 15, 2008,16.

[49] Steven R. Weisman, "Trade Bills Now Face Tough Odds," *New York Times*, November 16, 2006, C1.

[50] "National Security Strategy of the United States," 18.

[51] U.S. Department of State, "FY 2004–2009 Department of State and USAID Strategic Plan," 1, www.state.gov.

[52] *Congressional Quarterly Daily Monitor*, August 28, 2002.

[53] Quoted in David E. Sanger, "Strategies in a Market Era," *New York Times*, January 4, 1998, sec. 4, 4.

[54] U.S. Department of State, Bureau of Public Affairs, "Diplomacy: The State Department at Work," May 25, 2005, 2, www.state.gov. On the subject of revamping our approach to aid, see Paul Collier, *The Bottom Billion: Why the Poor Countries Are Failing and What We Can Do About It* (New York: Oxford University Press, 2007).

Glossary

527 groups Tax-exempt groups, named after the provision in the tax code, that are organized to provide politically relevant advertising, usually with the aim of helping particular candidates or parties. Technically they are supposed to be independent but in reality are often closely linked to the candidates.

Abu Ghraib Prison A prison near Baghdad, Iraq, where Americans held thousands of Iraqis and tortured some of them.

Activist judges Judges who are not reluctant to overrule the other branches of government by declaring laws or actions of government officials unconstitutional.

Administrative Procedure Act (APA) Legislation passed in 1946 that provides for public participation in the rule-making process. All federal agencies must disclose their rule-making procedures and publish all regulations at least thirty days in advance of their effective date to allow time for public comment.

Adversarial relationship A relationship where two parties or groups are often in opposition, such as public officials and the media.

Affirmative action A policy in job hiring or university admissions that gives special consideration to members of historically disadvantaged groups.

Agents of political socialization Sources of information about politics; include parents, peers, schools, the media, political leaders, and the community.

Aid to Families with Dependent Children (AFDC) A program that provides income support for the poor. Replaced by TANF.

American Civil Liberties Union (ACLU) A nonpartisan organization that seeks to protect the civil liberties of all Americans.

Americans with Disabilities Act Passed to protect those with disabilities from discrimination in employment and public accommodations, such as stores, restaurants, hotels, and health care facilities.

Antifederalists Those who opposed the ratification of the U.S. Constitution.

Antitrust law Laws that prohibit **monopolies.**

Appropriations Budget legislation that specifies the amount of authorized funds that will actually be allocated for agencies and departments to spend.

Articles of Confederation The first constitution of the United States; in effect from 1781 to 1789.

Asymmetrical warfare Conflict between combatants of very unequal military strength.

Authorizations Budget legislation that provides agencies and departments with the legal authority to operate; may specify funding levels but do not actually provide the funding (the funding is provided by **appropriations**).

Baker v. Carr A 1962 Supreme Court decision giving voters the right to use the courts to rectify the malapportionment of legislative districts.

Balanced budget amendment A proposed constitutional amendment that would require balancing the federal budget.

Ballot initiative A means for placing policy questions on state ballots and having them decided directly by voters.

Bandwagon effect The tendency of voters to follow the lead of the media, which declare some candidates winners and others losers, and vote for the perceived winner. The extent of this effect is unknown.

Battleground states Also known as "swing states." During a presidential election, these are states whose Electoral College votes are not safely in one candidate's pocket; candidates will spend time and more money there to try to win the state.

Bible Belt A term used to describe portions of the South and Midwest that were strongly influenced by Protestant fundamentalists.

Big sort A term coined to describe how Americans tend to live among others of similar economic statuses and cultural beliefs.

Bilingual education Programs where students whose native language is not English receive instruction in substantive subjects such as math in their native language.

Bill of Rights The first 10 amendments to the U.S. Constitution.

Bills of attainder Legislative acts that pronounce specific persons guilty of crimes.

Black budget The part of the U.S. budget, unknown to the public and to much of Congress, that funds certain intelligence activities.

Black Codes Laws passed by Southern states following the **Civil War** that denied most legal rights to the newly freed slaves.

Blockbusting The practice in which realtors would frighten whites in a neighborhood where a black family had moved by telling the whites that their houses would decline in value. The whites in panic would then sell their houses to the realtors at low prices, and the realtors would resell the houses to blacks, thereby resegregating the area from white to black.

Block grants A system of giving federal funds to states and localities under which the federal government designates the purpose for which the funds are to be used but allows the states some discretion in spending.

Blog Common term for independent web log, which is an independent website created by an individual or group to disseminate opinions or information.

Blue states These are the states that voted Democratic in 2000 and 2004 and in general more liberal in outlook. They include New England, Middle Atlantic, Upper Midwest, and Pacific Coast states.

Bradley effect A discrepancy in polls and actual voting, that overestimates white vote for black candidates because some white voters might falsely report that they intend to vote for an African-American candidate. Named after the 1982 California gubernatorial candidate Tom Bradley.

Broadcasting An attempt by a network to appeal to most of the television or radio audience.

Brown bag test An informal requirement of some African American clubs and churches in the first half of the twentieth century that prospective members have enough "white blood" so that their skin color was lighter than the color of a brown paper bag.

Brown v. Board of Education The 1954 case in which the U.S. Supreme Court overturned the **separate-but-equal doctrine** and ruled unanimously that segregated schools violated the Fourteenth Amendment.

Budget and Accounting Act of 1921 This act gives the president the power to propose a budget and led to presidential dominance in the budget process. It also created the **Bureau of the Budget,** changed to the **Office of Management and Budget** in 1970.

Budget deficit Occurs when federal spending exceeds federal revenues.

Bureau of the Budget Established in 1921 and later changed to the **Office of Management and Budget,** the BOB was designed as the president's primary means of developing federal budget policy.

Burger Court The U.S. Supreme Court under Chief Justice Warren Burger (1969–1986). Though not as activist as the **Warren Court,** the Burger Court maintained most of the rights expanded by its predecessor and issued important rulings on abortion and sexual discrimination.

Bush v. Gore U.S. Supreme Court case in 2000 where the Supreme Court set aside the Florida Supreme Court's order for a manual recount of the presidential votes cast in the state. The Court's decision meant that Bush got Florida's electoral votes, giving him a majority of all electoral votes and, thus, the election.

Capitalist economy An economic system in which the means of production are privately owned and prices, wages, working conditions, and profits are determined solely by the market.

Captured agencies Refers to the theory that regulatory agencies often end up working on behalf of the interests they are supposed to regulate.

Casework The assistance members of Congress provide to their constituents; includes answering questions and doing personal favors for those who ask for help. Also called **constituency service.**

Caucus Today, a meeting of local residents who select delegates to attend county, state, and national conventions where the delegates nominate candidates for public office. Originally, caucuses were limited to party leaders and officeholders who selected the candidates.

Central Intelligence Agency (CIA) Created after World War II, the CIA is a federal agency charged with coordinating overseas intelligence activities gathering and analysis.

Checkbook members People who "join" interest groups by donating money.

Checks and balances The principle of government that holds that the powers of the various branches should overlap to avoid power becoming overly concentrated in one branch.

Chief Executive In the U.S. government, the President of the United States.

Christian right Evangelical Protestant denominations which came together as a political movement to forward their conservative agenda, usually through the Republican party.

Civil case A case in which individuals sue others for denying their rights and causing them harm.

Civil disobedience Peaceful but illegal protest activity in which those involved allow themselves to be arrested and charged.

Civil liberties Individual rights outlined in the Constitution and the Bill of Rights.

Civil rights The principle of equal rights for persons regardless of their race, sex, or ethnic background.

Civil Rights Act of 1964 Major civil rights legislation that prohibits discrimination on the basis of race, color, religion, or national origin in public accommodations.

Civil Rights Act of 1968 Civil rights legislation that prohibits discrimination in the sale or rental of housing on the basis of race, color, religion, or national origin; also prohibits **blockbusting, steering,** and **redlining.**

Civil Service Commission An agency established by the **Pendleton Act of 1883** to curb **patronage** in the federal bureaucracy and replace it with a merit system.

Civil War The war between the Union and the Confederacy (1861–1865), fought mainly over the question of whether the national or state governments were to exercise ultimate political power. Secession and slavery were the issues that precipitated this great conflict.

Classical democracy A system of government that emphasizes citizen participation through debating, voting, and holding office.

Closed primary A primary election where participation is limited to those who are registered with a party or declare a preference for a party.

Cloture A method of stopping a **filibuster** by limiting debate to only 20 more hours; requires a vote of three-fifths of the members of the Senate.

Coalition A network of **interest groups** with similar concerns that combine forces to pursue a common goal; may be short-lived or permanent.

Coalition building The union of **pressure groups** that share similar concerns.

Cold War The era of hostility between the United States and the Soviet Union that existed between the end of World War II and the collapse of the Soviet Union.

Commander in Chief The president's constitutional role as head of the armed forces with power to direct their use

Commercial bias A slant in news coverage to please or avoid offending advertisers.

Committee of the Whole Refers to the informal entity the House of Representatives makes itself into to debate a bill.

Commodity interest groups Associations that represent producers of specific products, such as cattle, tobacco, or milk producers.

Comparable worth The principle that comparable jobs should pay comparable wages.

Concurring opinion The opinion by one or more judges in a court case who agree with the decision but not with the reasons given by the majority for it. The concurring opinion offers an alternate legal argument for the ruling.

Confederal system A system in which the central government has only the powers given to it by the subnational governments.

Conference committee A committee composed of members of both houses of Congress that is formed to try to resolve the differences when the two houses pass different versions of the same bill.

Conflict of interest The situation when government officials make decisions that directly affect their own personal livelihoods or interests.

Conscientious objectors Persons who oppose all wars and refuse military service on the basis of religious or moral principles.

Conservative A person who believes that the domestic role of government should be minimized and that individuals are responsible for their own well-being.

Constituency Both the geographic area and the people a member of Congress represents. For a senator, the state and all its residents; for a member of the House, a congressional district and all its residents.

Constituency service The assistance members of Congress provide to residents in their districts (states, if senators); includes answering questions and doing personal favors for those who ask for help. Also called **casework.**

Constitution The body of basic rules and principles that establish the functions, limits, and nature of a government.

Constitutional Convention The gathering in Philadelphia in 1787 that wrote the U.S. Constitution; met initially to revise the **Articles of Confederation** but produced a new national **constitution** instead.

Containment A policy formulated by the Truman administration to limit the spread of communism by meeting any action taken by the Soviet Union with a countermove; led U.S. decision makers to see most conflicts in terms of U.S.- Soviet rivalry.

Contribution limits Ceilings set on the overall amount of money that individuals and groups give to candidates.

Cooperative federalism The day-to-day cooperation among federal, state, and local officials in carrying out the business of government.

Cooperative internationalism The belief that problems of global poverty, inequitable distribution of wealth, abuse of human rights, and regional competitiveness are substantial threats to world order, and that the United States should work with other nations to solve these problems.

Corporate welfare Tax breaks or financial subsidies given by government to corporations.

Court-packing plan President Franklin D. Roosevelt's attempt to expand the size of the U.S. Supreme Court in an effort to obtain a Court more likely to uphold his New Deal legislation.

Courts of appeals Intermediate courts between trial courts (**district courts** in the federal system) and the supreme court (the U.S. Supreme Court in the federal system).

Cracking, stacking, and packing Methods of drawing district boundaries that minimize black representation. With cracking, a large concentrated black population is divided among two or more districts so that blacks will not have a majority anywhere; with stacking, a large black population is combined with an even larger white population; with packing, a large black population is put into one district rather than two so that blacks will have a majority in only one district.

Crafted talk A way of packaging policies that caters to a specific base while appearing to remain mainstream.

Creative destruction The belief that American capitalism works because entrepreneurs and innovators are constantly introducing new products, forms of organization, marketing, and new technologies and thus destroying old and less efficient ways.

Criminal case A case in which a government (national or state) prosecutes a person for violating its laws.

Cruel and unusual punishment Torture or any punishment that is grossly disproportionate to the offense; prohibited by the Eighth Amendment.

Cumulative voting A proposed reform to increase minority representation; calls for members of Congress to be elected from at-large districts that would elect several members at once. Each voter would have as many votes as the district had seats and could apportion the votes among the candidates as he or she wished, such as giving all votes to a single candidate.

Dealignment Term used to refer to the diminished relevance of political parties.

Declaration of Independence A founding document that proclaimed "all men are created equal" and outlined the unalienable rights given to the American people.

De facto **segregation** Segregation that is based on residential patterns and is not imposed by law; because it cannot be eliminated by striking down a law, it is more intractable than **de jure segregation.**

Deficit A budgetary condition in which government expenditures exceed revenues.

Deism Belief in a Supreme Being who created the world but who didn't play an active role in day-to-day life.

De jure **segregation** Segregation imposed by law; outlawed by *Brown* v. *Board of Education* and subsequent court cases.

Delegated legislative authority The power to draft, as well as execute, specific policies; granted by Congress to executive branch agencies when a problem requires technical expertise.

Democracy A system of government in which sovereignty resides in the people.

Depression A period of prolonged high unemployment.

Deregulation Ending **regulation** in a particular area.

Detente A policy designed to deescalate **Cold War** rhetoric and promote the notion that relations with the Soviet Union could be conducted in ways other than confrontation; developed by President Richard M. Nixon and Secretary of State Henry Kissinger.

Devolution The delegation of authority by the national government to lower units of government (such as at the state and local level) to make and implement policy.

Direct democracy A system of government in which citizens govern themselves directly and vote on most issues; e.g., a New England town meeting.

Direct lobbying Direct personal encounters between lobbyists and the public officials they are attempting to influence.

Direct primary An election in which voters select a party's candidates for office.

Discretionary spending Spending levels set by the federal government in annual **appropriations** bills passed by Congress; includes government operating expenses and salaries of many federal employees.

Dissenting opinion The opinion by one or more judges in a court case who do not agree with the decision of the majority. The dissenting opinion urges a different outcome.

District courts The trial courts (lower-level courts) in the federal system.

Divided government The situation when one political party controls the presidency and the other party controls one or both houses of Congress.

Dixiecrat A member of a group of southern segregationist Democrats who formed the States' Rights Party in 1948.

Domino theory The idea that if one country fell under communist rule, its neighbors would also fall to communism; contributed to the U.S. decision to intervene in Vietnam.

Dred Scott case An 1857 case in which the U.S. Supreme Court held that blacks, whether slave or free, were not citizens and that Congress had no power to restrict slavery in the territories; contributed to the polarization between North and South and ultimately to the **Civil War.**

Dual federalism The idea that the Constitution created a system in which the national government and the states have separate grants of power with each supreme in its own sphere.

Due process The 14th Amendment guarantee that the government will follow fair and just procedures when prosecuting a criminal defendant.

Earmark A specific amount of money designated—or set aside—at the request of a member of Congress, for a favored project, usually in his or her district. The dollar amount may be included in one of the budget authorization bills, but more commonly is in the committee report attached to the bill that instructs the relevant executive branch agency how to spend the money authorized for its operations.

Earned income tax credit (EITC) A negative income tax. On filing income tax reports, persons with low incomes receive a payment from the government or a credit toward their taxes owed.

Electoral College A group of electors selected by the voters in each state and the District of Columbia; the electors officially elect the president and vice president.

Emancipation Proclamation Abraham Lincoln's 1863 proclamation that the slaves "shall be . . . forever free." At the time, applied only in the Confederate states, so had little practical impact, because the Union did not control them. However, it had an immense political impact, making clear that the Civil War was not just to preserve the Union but to abolish slavery.

Enlightenment An intellectual force throughout Europe in the 1600s and 1700s. Also called the "Age of Reason" because enlightenment beliefs were that humans could improve themselves and their world through their reason. America's Founders were greatly influenced by Enlightenment principles.

Environmental Protection Agency (EPA) The regulatory agency with responsibility for pollution control; created in 1970 by President Richard M. Nixon.

Equal Credit Opportunity Act This act forbids discrimination on the basis of sex or marital status in credit transactions.

Equal Employment Opportunity Commission (EEOC) The EEOC enforces the **Civil Rights Act of 1964,** which forbids discrimination on the basis of sex or race in hiring, promotion, and firing.

Equal Pay Act A statute enacted by Congress in 1963 that mandates that women and men should receive equal pay for equal work.

Equal protection clause The Fourteenth Amendment clause that is the Constitution's primary guarantee that everyone is equal before the law.

Equal Rights Amendment (ERA) A proposed amendment to the Constitution that would prohibit government from denying equal rights on the basis of sex; passed by Congress in 1972 but failed to be ratified by a sufficient number of states.

Establishment clause The First Amendment clause that prohibits the establishment of a state religion.

European Union (EU) A union of European nations formed in 1957 to foster political and economic integration in Europe; formerly called the European Economic Community or Common Market.

Exclusionary rule A rule that prevents evidence obtained in violation of the Fourth Amendment from being used in court against the defendant.

Executive leadership The president's control over the bureaucracy in his capacity as chief executive; achieved through budgeting, appointments, administrative reform, lobbying, and mobilizing public opinion.

Executive Office of the President (EOP) The president's personal bureaucracy that monitors the work done in cabinet departments and agencies.

Executive orders Rules or regulations issued by the president that have the force of law; issued to implement constitutional provisions or statutes.

Executive privilege The authority of the president to withhold specific types of information from the courts and Congress.

Exit polls Election-day poll of voters leaving the polling places, conducted mainly by television networks and major newspapers.

Ex post facto **law** A statute that makes some behavior illegal that was not illegal when it was done.

Externality A cost or benefit of production that is not reflected in the product's market price. **Regulation** attempts to eliminate negative externalities.

Faithless elector A member of the **Electoral College** who votes on the basis of personal preference rather than the way the majority of voters in his or her state voted.

Farm subsidies Government payments to farmers for withholding land from production or to guarantee set prices for certain crops.

Federal Communication Commission (FCC) A regulatory agency that controls interstate and foreign communication via radio, television, telegraph, telephone, and cable. The FCC licenses radio and television stations.

Federal Court of Appeals Intermediate appellate courts that hear appeals from cases that have been decided by the district courts. There are twelve, based on regions of the country.

Federal District Courts The courts that try cases based on federal law. There are ninety-four in the United States.

Federal Election Campaign Act A 1974 statute that regulates campaign finance; provided for public financing of presidential campaigns, limited contributions to campaigns for federal offices, and established the **Federal Election Commission,** among other things.

Federal Election Commission Created in 1975, the commission enforces federal laws on campaign financing.

Federalism A system in which power is constitutionally divided between a central government and subnational or local governments.

Federalist Papers A series of essays in support of ratification of the U.S. Constitution; written for New York newspapers by Alexander Hamilton, James Madison, and John Jay during the debate over ratification.

Federalists Originally, those who supported the U.S. Constitution and favored its ratification; in the early years of the Republic, those who advocated a strong national government.

Federal Register A government publication that provides official notification of executive orders, agency rulings and federal statutes.

Federal Reserve Board Created by Congress in 1913, the board regulates the lending practices of banks and plays a major role in determining **monetary policy.**

Felonies Crimes considered more serious than **misdemeanors** and carrying more stringent punishment.

Fifteenth Amendment An amendment to the Constitution, ratified in 1870, that prohibits denying voting rights on the basis of race, color, or previous condition of servitude.

Fighting words Words which are so inflammatory that when spoken face to face prompt even reasonable listeners to retaliate.

Filibuster A mechanism for delay in the Senate in which one or more members engage in a continuous speech to prevent the Senate from voting on a bill.

Fireside chats Short radio addresses given by Presi- dent Franklin D. Roosevelt to win support for his policies and reassure the public during the Great Depression.

First Amendment The first amendment to the United States constitution, guaranteeing freedom of expression, which includes freedom of speech, religion, assembly, association, and freedom of the press.

Fiscal policy Government's actions to regulate the economy through taxing and spending policies.

Flat tax A tax structured so that all income groups pay the same rate.

Focus groups A group of a dozen or so average men and women brought together by political consultants and pollsters to share their feelings and reactions to different things in an effort to develop a campaign strategy that will attract voters to or away from a particular candidate.

FOIA The Freedom of Information Act, passed in 1966 and amended in 1974, lets any member of the public apply to an agency for access to unclassified documents in its archives.

Food stamp program A poverty program that gives poor people electronic credits redeemable in grocery stores for food.

Foreign Intelligence Surveillance Court Created by the Foreign Intelligence Surveillance Act of 1978, this secretive court hears requests from the U.S. government to conduct electronic surveillance, or physical searches of the home and computer, of suspected spies or terrorists.

Franking The privilege of members of Congress that allows them to send free mail to their constituents at government expense.

Freedom of association Guarantees the right of an individual to join with others to speak, assemble, and petition the government for a redress of grievances. This right allows a minority to pursue interests without being prevented from doing so by the majority.

Freedom of speech The First Amendment guarantee of a right of free expression.

Freedom of the press Freedom from censorship, so the press can disseminate the news, information, and opinion that it deems appropriate.

Free exercise clause The First Amendment clause that guarantees individuals the right to practice their religion without government intervention.

Free Rider problem Individuals who benefit from actions of groups they are not a part of, such as workers whose raises are influenced by union pressure but who are not members of unions.

Free trade A policy of minimum intervention by government in trade relations.

Friend of the court briefs Legal arguments filed in court cases by individuals or groups who aren't litigants in the cases. These briefs often provide new information to the court and usually urge the judges to rule one way.

Frontrunners Candidates whom political pros and the media have portrayed as likely winners.

Full faith and credit A clause in the U.S. Constitution that requires the states to recognize contracts that are valid in other states.

Fundraiser An event, such as a luncheon or cocktail party, hosted by a legislator or candidate for which participants pay an entrance fee.

Gaining access The ability of lobbyists to reach policy makers to make their case.

Game orientation The assumption in political reporting that politics is a game and that politicians are the players; leads to an emphasis on strategy at the expense of substance in news stories.

Gender gap An observable pattern of modest but consistent differences in opinion between men and women on various public policy issues.

General revenue sharing A Reagan administration policy of giving states and cities federal money to spend as they wished, subject to only a few conditions.

George W. Bush Administration The president and his subordinates within the executive branch of government.

Gerrymander A congressional district whose boundaries are drawn so as to maximize the political advantage of a party or racial group; often such a district has a bizarre shape.

Gettysburg Address Famous 1863 speech by President Lincoln to dedicate the battlefield where many had fallen during the Civil War. Lincoln used the occasion to advance his ideal of equality and to promote the Union.

Glasnost Mikhail Gorbachev's policy of opening the Soviet Union to the outside world by encouraging foreign investment, allowing more Soviet citizens to emigrate, and permitting multiparty elections in eastern Europe.

Globalization The international dispersion of economic activity through the networking of companies across national borders.

Going public The process in which Congress or its members carry an issue debate to the public via the media; e.g., televising floor debates or media appearances by individual members.

GOP Grand Old Party or Republican Party, which formed in 1856 after the Whig Party split. The GOP was abolitionist and a supporter of the Union.

Government contracts Agreements to provide goods or services to government.

Grandfather clause A device used in the South to prevent blacks from voting; such clauses exempted those whose grandfathers had the right to vote before 1867 from having to fulfill various requirements that some people could not meet. Since no blacks could vote before 1867, they could not qualify for the exemption.

Grand jury A jury of citizens who meet in private session to evaluate accusations in a given **criminal case** and to determine if there is enough evidence to warrant a trial.

Grants-in-aid Federal money provided to state and, occasionally, local governments for community development and to establish programs to help people such as the aged poor or the unemployed; began during the New Deal.

Grassroots lobbying The mass mobilization of members of an **interest group** to apply pressure to public officials, usually in the form of a mass mailing.

Great Compromise The decision of the **Constitutional Convention** to have a bicameral legislature in which representation in one house would be by population and in the other house, by states; also called the Connecticut Compromise.

Great Migration The period during World War I and until World War II when more than a million southern blacks headed north to look for better jobs and housing.

Habeas corpus Latin for "have ye the body." A writ of habeas corpus is a means for criminal defendants who have exhausted appeals in state courts to appeal to a federal **district court.**

Hatch Act A statute enacted in 1939 that limits the political activities of federal employees in partisan campaigns.

Hate speech Racial, ethnic, sexual, or religious slurs which demean people for characteristics that are innate or beliefs that are deeply held.

Head of government The president's partisan, policy-making role as head of the executive branch and as head of his party in government, in contrast to his nonpartisan duties as head of state and representative of the country.

Head of state The president's role as a symbolic leader of the nation and representative of all the people.

Health maintenance organization (HMO) A group of doctors who agree to provide full health care for a fixed monthly charge.

Home rule The grant of considerable autonomy to a local government.

Honoraria Legal payments made to legislators who speak before **interest groups** or other groups of citizens.

Horse race coverage The way in which the media reports on the candidates' polling status and strategies, rather than covering their positions on relevant issues.

House of Representatives One house of Congress, where states are represented in proportion to their population size.

Hyperpluralism The idea that it is difficult for government to arrive at a solution to problems because **interest groups** have become so numerous and so many groups have a "veto" on issues affecting them.

ICBM Intercontinental ballistic missiles, or land-based missiles.

Identity politics The practice of organizing on the basis of sex, ethnic or racial identity, or sexual orientation to compete for public resources and influence public policy.

Ideology A highly organized and coherent set of opinions.

Impeachment The process provided for in the Constitution by which the House of Representatives can indict (impeach) a president for "Treason, Bribery, or other High Crimes and Misdemeanors." If the House votes to lodge formal charges against the president he is impeached. But a president cannot be removed from office unless two-thirds of the Senate finds him guilty of the charges.

Imperial presidency A term that came into use at the end of the 1960s to describe the growing power of the presidency.

Implied powers clause The clause in the U.S. Constitution that gives Congress the power to make all laws "necessary and proper" for carrying out its specific powers.

Independent A voter who is not aligned with any political party.

Independent agencies Government bureaus that are not parts of **departments.** Their heads are appointed by and responsible to the president.

Independent counsel See **Special prosecutor.**

Independent expenditures Campaign contributions made on behalf of issues or candidates, but not made directly to candidates or political parties.

Independent spending Spending on political campaigns by groups not under the control of the candidates.

Indirect democracy A system of government in which citizens elect representatives to make decisions for them.

Indirect lobbying Attempts to influence legislators through such nontraditional means as letter-writing campaigns.

Individualistic political culture One in which politics is seen as a way of getting ahead, of obtaining benefits for oneself or one's group, and in which corruption is tolerated. See also **moralistic** and **traditionalistic political cultures.**

Inflation The situation in which prices increase but wages and salaries fail to keep pace with the prices of goods.

Influence peddling Using one's access to powerful people to make money, as when former government officials use access to former colleagues to win high-paying jobs in the private sector.

Informal norms Unwritten rules designed to help keep Congress running smoothly by attempting to diminish friction and competition among the members.

Infotainment A word for television newscasts that attempt to entertain as they provide information.

Initiative A process that allows citizens and interest groups to collect signatures on petitions and place a proposal on the ballot.

Injunction A court order demanding that a person or group perform a specific act or refrain from performing a specific act.

Institutional loyalty An **informal norm** of Congress that calls for members to avoid criticizing their colleagues and to treat each other with mutual respect; this norm has eroded in recent decades.

Interest groups Organizations that try to achieve at least some of their goals with government assistance.

Investigative reporting In-depth news reporting, particularly that which exposes corruption and wrongdoing on the part of government officials and big institutions.

Isolationism A policy of noninvolvement with other nations outside the Americas; generally followed by the United States during the nineteenth and early twentieth centuries.

Issue consistency The extent to which individuals who identify themselves as "**liberal**" or "**conservative**" take issue positions that reflect their professed leanings.

Issue voting Refers to citizens who vote for candidates whose stands on specific issues are consistent with their own.

Jacksonian democracy Democracy where participation is open to common people. Named for Andrew Jackson, who first mobilized common people to participate in government.

Jeffersonian Republicans (Jeffersonians) Opponents of a strong national government. They challenged the **Federalists** in the early years of the Republic.

Jim Crow laws Laws enacted in southern states that segregated schools, public accommodations, and almost all other aspects of life.

Joint resolutions Measures approved by both houses of Congress and signed by the president that have the force of law.

Judicial review The authority of the courts to declare laws or actions of government officials unconstitutional.

Junkets Trips by members of Congress to desirable locations with expenses paid by lobbyists; the trips are ostensibly made to fulfill a "speaking engagement" or conduct a "fact-finding tour."

Jurisdiction The authority of a court to hear and decide cases.

Justices of the peace Magistrates at the lowest level of some state court systems, responsible mainly for acting on minor offenses and committing cases to higher courts for trial.

Keynesian economics The argument by John Maynard Keynes that government should stimulate the economy during periods of high unemployment by increasing spending even if it must run **deficits** to do so.

Kitchen cabinet A group of informal advisers, usually longtime associates, who assist the president on public policy questions.

Know-Nothing Party An extreme right-wing party in mid-nineteenth-century America that opposed Catholics and immigrants.

Korematsu v. *United States* After the attack on Pearl Harbor during World War II, Fred Korematsu and many other Japanese Americans were relocated (by presidential order) to detention camps in inland states. Korematsu claimed that the order discriminated against him on the basis of his race and thereby violated his Fifth Amendment right to due process of law. On appeal, the U.S. Supreme Court upheld the order removing 120,000 Japanese Americans from the West Coast. The majority held that the government could take precautions to prevent espionage and sabotage during wartime.

Ku Klux Klan A white supremacy group aimed at inflaming prejudice and terrorizing blacks during and after Reconstruction.

Labor unions A group that seeks agreements with business and policies from the government that protect workers' jobs, wages, and benefits and ensure the safety of workplaces.

Lame duck An officeholder who has diminished authority because he or she has lost an election or is near the end of the term in office.

Landslide An election won by a candidate who receives an overwhelming majority of the votes, such as more than a 10-point gap.

Leaks Disclosures of information that some government officials want kept secret.

Legislative calendar An agenda or calendar containing the names of all bills or resolutions of a particular type to be considered by committees or either legislative chamber.

Libel Printed or broadcast statements that are false and meant to tarnish someone's reputation.

Liberal A person who believes in government activism to help individuals and communities in such areas as health, education, and welfare.

Limited government A government that is strong enough to protect the people's rights but not so strong as to threaten those rights; in the view of John Locke, such a government was established through a **social contract.**

Line-Item veto A proposal that would give a president the power to veto one or more provisions of a bill while allowing the remainder of the bill to become law.

Literacy tests Examinations ostensibly carried out to ensure that voters could read and write but actually a device used in the South to disqualify blacks from voting.

Litigation Legal action.

Living wage A wage that is high enough to allow full-time workers' to mee the basic cost of living, something the minimum wage does not do.

Lobbying The efforts of **interest groups** to influence government.

Lobbyist A representative of a group or interest who attempts to influence government decisions generally through personal contact.

Majority leader The title of both the leader of the Senate, who is chosen by the majority party and the head of the majority party in the House of Representatives who is second in command to the **Speaker.**

Majority-minority district A congressional district whose boundaries are drawn to give a minority group a majority in the district.

Majority opinion The joint opinion by a majority of the judges in a federal court case which explains why the judges ruled as they did.

Managed competition An aspect of the Clinton health care plan that involved joining employers and individuals into large groups or cooperatives to purchase health insurance.

Mandamus, writ of A court order demanding government officials or a lower court to perform a specified duty.

Mandate A term used in the media to refer to a president having clear directions from the voters to take a certain course of action; in practice, it is not always clear that a president, even one elected by a large majority, has a mandate or, if so, for what.

Mandatory spending Spending by the federal government that is required by permanent laws; e.g., payments for **Medicare.**

Marbury v. *Madison* The 1803 case in which the U.S. Supreme Court enunciated the doctrine of **judicial review.**

Market share The number of members of an **interest group** compared to its potential membership; having a large market share is an advantage.

Markup The process in which a congressional subcommittee rewrites a bill after holding hearings on it.

Marshall Plan A plan which provided economic relief to the nations of Western Europe in 1947, following World War II.

McCain-Feingold Act Also known as the Bipartisan Campaign Finance Reform Act of 2001, this legislation was created to regulate campaign financing. It limited the amount of gifts and banned soft money contributions to the national parties but not to certain types of private groups.

McCarthyism Methods of combating communism characterized by irresponsible accusations made on the basis of little or no evidence; named after Senator Joseph McCarthy of Wisconsin who used such tactics in the 1950s.

McCulloch v. *Maryland* An 1819 U.S. Supreme Court decision that broadly interpreted Congress's powers under the **implied powers clause.**

Means test An eligibility requirement for poverty programs under which participants must demonstrate that they have low income and few assets.

Media event An event, usually consisting of a speech and a photo opportunity, that is staged for television and is intended to con-vey a particular impression of a politician's position on an issue.

Media malaise A feeling of cynicism and distrust toward government and officials that is fostered by media coverage of politics.

Medicaid A federal-state medical assistance program for the poor.

Medicare A public health insurance program that pays many medical expenses of the elderly and the disabled; funded through **Social Security** taxes, general revenues, and premiums paid by recipients.

Merit system A system of filling bureaucratic jobs on the basis of competence instead of **patronage.**

Minority leader The leader of the minority party in either the House of Representatives or the Senate.

Minority rights The individual rights of those not in the political or religious majority.

Miranda rights A means of protecting a criminal suspect's **rights against self-incrimination** during police interrogation. Before interrogation, suspects must be told that they have a right to remain silent; that anything they say can be used against them; that they have a right to an attorney; and that if they cannot afford an attorney, one will be provided for them. The rights are named after the case *Miranda* v. *Arizona.*

"Mischiefs of faction" A phrase used by James Madison in the *Federalist Papers* to refer to the threat to the nation's stability that factions could pose.

Misdemeanors Crimes of less seriousness than **felonies,** ordinarily punishable by fine or imprisonment in a local rather than a state institution.

Missouri Compromise of 1820 A set of laws by which Congress attempted to control slavery in the territories, maintaining the balance between slave and nonslave states.

Mixed economies Countries that incorporate elements of both capitalist and socialist practices in the workings of their economies.

Moderates Also referred to as "middle of the roaders," these are persons with centrist positions on issues that distinguish them from liberals and conservatives.

Monetary policy Actions taken by the **Federal Reserve Board** to regulate the economy through changes in short-term interest rates and the money supply.

Monopoly One or a few firms that control a large share of the market for certain goods and can therefore fix prices.

Monroe Doctrine A doctrine articulated by President James Monroe in 1823 that warned European powers not already involved in Latin America to stay out of that region.

Moralistic political culture One in which people feel obligated to take part in politics to bring about change for the better, and in which corruption is not tolerated. See also **individualistic** and **traditionalistic political cultures.**

Motor voter law A statute that allows people to register to vote at public offices such as welfare offices and drivers' license bureaus.

Muckrakers Reform-minded journalists in the early twentieth century who exposed corruption in politics and worked to break the financial link between business and politicians.

Multiparty system A type of political party system where more than two groups have a chance at winning an election.

Mutual assured destruction (MAD) The capability to absorb a nuclear attack and retaliate against the attacker with such force that it would also suffer enormous damage; believed to deter nuclear war during the **Cold War** because both sides would be so devastated that neither would risk striking first.

NAACP (National Association for the Advancement of Colored People) An organization founded in 1909 to fight for black rights; its attorneys challenged segregation in the courts and won many important court cases, most notably, *Brown* v. *Board of Education.*

Nader's Raiders The name given to people who work in any of the "public interest" organizations founded by consumer advocate and regulatory watchdog Ralph Nader.

Narrowcasting An attempt by a network to appeal to a small segment of the television or radio audience rather than to most of the audience.

Nation-centered federalism The view that the Constitution was written by representatives of the people and and ratified by the people. Nation-centered federalists believe that the national government is the supreme power in the federal relationship. (Hamilton articulated this view in the *Federalist Papers.*) Nation-centered federalism was the view used by northerners to justify a war to prevent the southern states from seceding in 1861. The alternative view, state-centered federalism, holds that the Constitution is a creation of the states.

National chair The head of a political **party organization,** appointed by the **national committee** of that party, usually at the direction of the party's presidential nominee.

National committee The highest level of **party organization;** chooses the site of the national convention and the formula for determining the number of delegates from each state.

National debt The total amount of money owed by the federal government; the sum of all budget **deficits** over the years.

National Organization for Women (NOW) A group formed in 1966 to fight primarily for political and economic rights for women.

National Security Agency (NSA) The U.S. government's largest intelligence service, which uses electronic surveillance to obtain the communications of possible adversaries.

NATO (North Atlantic Treaty Organization) A mutual defense pact established by the United States, Canada, and their western European allies in 1949 to protect against Soviet aggression in Europe; later expanded to include other European nations.

Natural rights Inalienable and inherent rights such as the right to own property (in the view of John Locke).

"Necessary and proper" A phrase in the **implied powers clause** of the U.S. Constitution that gives Congress the power to make all laws needed to carry out its specific powers.

Neoslavery After slavery was declared unconstitutional, the practice of depriving southern blacks of their rights, casting them back to subordinate positions .

"netroots" Grass roots organizations mobilized by political websites.

Neutral competence The concept that bureaucrats should make decisions in a politically neutral manner in policymaking and should be chosen only for their expertise—not their political affiliation.

New Deal A program of President Franklin D. Roosevelt's administration in the 1930s aimed at stimulating economic recovery and aiding victims of the Great Depression; led to expansion of the national government's role.

New Deal coalition The broadly based coalition of southern conservatives, northern liberals, and ethnic and religious minorities that sustained the Democratic Party for some 40 years.

New federalism During the Nixon administration, the policy under which unrestricted or minimally restricted federal funds were provided to states and localities; during the Reagan administration, a policy of reducing federal support for the states.

News release A printed handout given by public relations workers to members of the media, offering ideas or information for new stories.

Nineteenth Amendment An amendment to the Constitution, ratified in 1920, guaranteeing women the vote.

Nullification A doctrine advocated by supporters of state-centered federalism, holding that a state could nullify laws of Congress.

Obscenity Sexual material that is patently offensive to the average person in the community and that lacks any serious literary, artistic, or scientific value.

Obstruction of justice A deliberate attempt to impede the progress of a criminal investigation or trial.

Occupational Safety and Health Administration (OSHA) An agency formed in 1970 and charged with ensuring safe and healthful working conditions for all American workers.

Office of Management and Budget (OMB) A White House agency with primary responsibility for preparing the federal budget.

Open primary A primary election that is not limited to members of a particular party; a voter may vote in either party's primary.

Outsourcing (offshoring) Companies' transfer of jobs abroad in order to increase their profit (because they pay foreign workers less).

Overlapping membership The term refers to the tendency of individuals to join more than one group. This tends to moderate a group's appeals, since its members also belong to other groups with different interests.

Oversight Congress's responsibility to make sure the bureaucracy is administering federal programs in accordance with congressional intent.

Pardon power Authority given to the president to erase the guilt and restore the rights of anyone convicted of a federal crime, except an impeached president.

Parliamentary government A system in which voters elect only their representatives in parliament; the chief executive is chosen by parliament, as in Britain.

Partisan Affiliated with, believing in, or acting on behalf of a political party.

Party boss The head of a **political "machine,"** a highly disciplined state or local **party organization** that controls power in its area.

Party caucus Meetings of members of political parties, often designed to select party nominees for office, or of all members of a party in the House or Senate to set policy and select their leaders.

Party convention A gathering of party delegates, on the local, state, or national level, to set policy and strategy and to select candidates for elective office.

Party government A system where the central party leaders recruit candidates for office, and when elected, the candidates vote with party leaders.

Party identification A psychological link between individuals and a political party that leads those persons to regard themselves as members of that party.

Party in government Those who are appointed or elected to office as members of a political party.

Party in the electorate Those who identify with a political party.

Party organization The "professionals" who run a political party at the national, state, and local levels.

Party system The configuration of parties in a political system. Usually noted in conjunction with the number of parties in the system—one party system, two party system, or multiparty system.

Patronage A system in which elected officials appoint their supporters to administrative jobs; used by **political machines** to maintain themselves in power.

Paygo ("pay-as-you-go") Budgetary rules adopted by Congress that set caps on spending and bars legislation to increase spending without offsetting cuts in spending or increases in revenue.

Pendleton Act of 1883 This act created the **Civil Service Commission,** designed to protect civil servants from arbitrary dismissal for political reasons and to staff bureaucracies with people who have proven their competence by taking competitive examinations.

Pentagon Papers A top-secret study, eventually made public, of how and why the United States became embroiled in the Vietnam War; the study was commissioned by Secretary of Defense Robert McNamara during the Johnson administration.

Permanent campaign The situation in which elected officials are constantly engaged in a campaign; fund-raising for the next election begins as soon as one election is concluded.

Personal presidency A concept proposed by Theodore Lowi that holds that presidents since the 1930s have amassed tremendous personal power directly from the people and, in return, are expected to make sure the people get what they want from government.

Photo op A "photo opportunity" that frames the politician against a backdrop that symbolizes the points the politician is trying to make.

Platform committee The group that drafts the policy statement of a political party's convention.

Plea bargain An agreement between the prosecutor, defense attorney, and defendant in which the prosecutor agrees to reduce the charge or sentence in exchange for the defendant's guilty plea.

Plebiscite A direct vote by all the people on a certain public measure. Theodore Lowi has spoken of the "Plebiscitary" presidency, whereby the president makes himself the focus of national government through use of the mass media.

Plessy v. Ferguson The 1896 case in which the U.S. Supreme Court upheld segregation by enunciating the **separate-but-equal doctrine.**

Pluralism The theory that American government is responsive to groups of citizens working together to promote their common interests and that enough people belong to **interest groups** to ensure that government ultimately hears everyone, even though most people do not participate actively in politics.

Pocket veto A legislative bill dies by pocket veto if a president refuses to sign it and Congress adjourns within 10 working days.

Policy implementation The process by which bureaucrats convert laws into rules and activities that have an actual impact on people and things.

Political action committee (PAC) A committee established by corporation, labor union, or **interest group** that raises money and contributes it to a political campaign.

Political bias A preference for candidates of particular parties or for certain stands on issues that affects a journalist's reporting.

Political culture A shared body of values and beliefs that shapes perceptions and attitudes toward politics and government and, in turn, influences political behavior.

Political efficacy The belief that a person can make a difference in government.

Political equality The principle that every citizen of a democracy has an equal opportunity to try to influence government.

Political machines Political organizations based on **patronage** that flourished in big cities in the late nineteenth and early twentieth centuries. The machine relied on the votes of the lower classes and, in exchange, provided jobs and other services.

Political parties A group that seeks to gain and maintain political power though elections.

Political patronage Party leaders who, once in office, openly award government jobs and other benefits to their supporters.

Political socialization The process of learning about politics by being exposed to information from parents, peers, schools, the media, political leaders, and the community.

Political trust The extent to which citizens place trust in their government, its institutions, and its officials.

Politics A means by which individuals and **interest groups** compete, via political parties and other extragovernmental organizations, to shape government's impact on society's problems and goals.

Poll tax A tax that must be paid before a person can vote; used in the South to prevent blacks from voting. The Twenty-fourth Amendment prohibits poll taxes in federal elections.

Popular sovereignty Rule by the people.

Pork barrel Funding for special projects, buildings, and other public works in the district or state of a member of Congress. Members support such projects because they provide jobs for constituents and enhance the members' reelection chances, rather than because the projects are necessarily wise.

Power to persuade The president's informal power to gain support by dispensing favors and penalties and by using the prestige of the office.

Practice of objectivity Newspapers and other mainstream media try to present the facts in their news stories, not opinions.

Precedents In law, judicial decisions that may be used subsequently as standards in similar cases.

Precinct The basic unit of the American electoral process—in a large city perhaps only a few blocks—designed for the administration of elections. Citizens vote in precinct polling places.

Preemption Military strategy of "striking first." Endorsed by the Bush national security team after the September 11, 2001 terrorist attacks.

Preemptive war The strategy of striking a country first without knowing whether it is going to attack the United States.

Pregnancy Discrimination Act A congressional act from 1978 that forbids firing or demoting employees for becoming pregnant.

Presidential preference primary A **direct primary** where voters select delegates to presidential nominating conventions; voters indicate a preference for a presidential candidate, delegates committed to a candidate, or both.

Presidential press conference A meeting at which the president answers questions from reporters.

Pressure group An organization representing specific interests that seeks some sort of government assistance or attempts to influence public policy. Also known as an **interest group.**

Presumption of innocence A fundamental principle of the U.S. criminal justice system in which the government is required to prove the defendant's guilt. The defendant is not required to establish his innocence.

Pretrial hearings Preliminary examinations of the cases of persons accused of a crime.

Primary elections Elections held several weeks or months before the general election that allow voters to select the nominees of their political party.

Prior restraint Censorship by restraining an action before it has actually occurred; e.g., forbidding publication rather than punishing the publisher after publication has occurred.

Private interest groups Interest groups that chiefly pursue economic interests that benefit their members; e.g., business organizations and labor unions.

Probable cause In law, reasonable grounds for belief that a particular person has committed a particular crime.

Pro-choice groups Groups that work to maintain women's right to choose abortion.

Productivity The ratio of total hours worked by the labor force to total goods and services produced.

Professional association A **pressure group** that promotes the interests of a professional occupation, such as medicine, law, or teaching.

Progressive Movement Reform movement designed to wrest control from political machines and the lower-class immigrants they served. These reforms reduced corruption in politics, but they also seriously weakened the power of political parties.

Progressive reforms Election reforms introduced in the early twentieth century as part of the Progressive movement; included the secret ballot, primary elections, and voter registration laws.

Progressive tax A tax structured so that those with higher incomes pay a higher percentage of their income in taxes than do those with lower incomes.

Prohibition Party A political party founded in 1869 that sought to ban the sale of liquor in the United States.

Pro-life groups Groups that work to outlaw abortion.

Proportional representation An election system based on election from multimember districts. The number of seats awarded to each party in each district is equal to the percentage of the total the party receives in the district. Proportional representation favors the multiparty system.

Protectionism Government intervention to protect domestic producers from foreign competition; can take the form of **tariffs,** quotas on imports, or a ban on certain imports altogether.

Public disclosure The requirement that names of campaign donors be made public.

Public forum A public place such as a street, sidewalk, or park where people have a First Amendment right to express their views on public issues.

Public interest A term generally denoting a policy goal, designed to serve the interests of society as a whole, or the largest number of people. Defining the public interest is the subject of intense debate on most issues.

Public interest groups Interest groups that chiefly pursue benefits that cannot be limited or restricted to their members.

Public opinion The collection of individual opinions toward issues or objects of general interest.

Push poll A public opinion poll presenting the respondent with biased information favoring or opposing a particular candidate. The idea is to see whether certain "information" can "push" voters away from a candidate or a neutral opinion toward the candidate favored by those doing the poll. Push polls seek to manipulate opinion.

Quorum calls A roll call of members of a legislative body to determine if enough members are present to conduct business; often used as a delaying tactic.

Racial profiling Practice that targets a particular group for attention from law enforcement based on racial stereotypes, A common occurrence is black drivers being stopped by police disproportionately.

Realignment The transition from one stable party system to another, as occurred when the **New Deal coalition** was formed.

Reapportionment The process of redistributing the 435 seats in the House of Representatives among the states based on population changes; occurs every 10 years based on the most recent census.

Recall elections A process that enables voters to remove officials from office before their terms expire.

Recession Two or more consecutive three-month quarters of falling production.

Reciprocity An **informal norm** of Congress in which members agree to support each other's bills; also called logrolling.

Reconstruction The period after the **Civil War** when black rights were ensured by a northern military presence in the South and by close monitoring of southern politics; ended in 1877.

Reconstruction Amendments Three amendments (13th, 14th, and 15th), adopted after the Civil War from 1865 through 1870, that eliminated slavery (13), gave blacks the right to vote (15), and guaranteed due process rights for all (14)

Redistricting The process of redrawing the boundaries of congressional districts within a state after a census to take account of population shifts.

Redlining The practice in which bankers and other lenders refused to lend money to persons who wanted to buy a house in a racially changing neighborhood.

"Red Scare" Prompted by the Russian Revolution in 1917, this was a large-scale crackdown on so-called seditious activities in the United States.

Red states These are the states that voted for George Bush in 2000 and 2004 and in general more conservative in outlook. They include the states of the South, Great Plains, and Rocky Mountain West.

Reelection constituency Those individuals a member of Congress believes will vote for him or her. Differs from a geographical, loyalist, or personal constituency.

Referendum A process that allows the legislature to place a proposal on the ballot.

Regressive tax A tax structured so that those with lower incomes pay a larger percentage of their income in tax than do those with higher incomes.

Regulation The actions of regulatory agencies in establishing standards or guidelines conferring benefits or imposing restrictions on business conduct.

Rehnquist Court The U.S. Supreme Court under Chief Justice William Rehnquist (1986–2005); a conservative Court, but one that did not overturn most previous rulings.

Religious tests Tests once used in some states to limit the right to vote or hold office to members of the "established church."

Rendition The process in which the CIA seizes terrorist suspects in foreign countries and takes them to other countries for interrogation. The purpose is to have other countries use methods of interrogation, often torture, that the U.S. would not use.

Republic A system of government in which citizens elect representatives to make decisions for them; an **indirect democracy.**

Republican party One of the major political parties in the U.S. since the era of the Civil War. Republicans tend to be more conservative than Democrats.

Responsible party government A governing system in which political parties have real issue differences, voters align according to those issue differences, and elected officials are expected to vote with their party leadership or lose their chance to run for office.

Responsiveness The extent to which government conforms to the wishes of individuals, groups, or institutions.

Restrained judges Judges who are reluctant to overrule the other branches of government by declaring laws or actions of government officials unconstitutional.

Restrictive covenants Agreements among neighbors in white residential areas not to sell their houses to blacks.

Retrospective voting Voting for or against incumbents on the basis of their past performance.

Right against self-incrimination A right granted by the Fifth Amendment, providing that persons accused of a crime shall not be compelled to be witnesses against themselves.

Right to abortion U.S. Supreme Court ruling in *Roe* v. *Wade* (1973) established that women have a right to terminate a pregnancy during the first six months. States can prohibit an abortion during the last three months because at that time the fetus becomes viable—it can live outside the womb.

Right to a jury trial The Sixth Amendment's guarantee of a trial by jury in any **criminal case** that could result in more than six months' incarceration.

Right to counsel The Sixth Amendment's guarantee of the right of a criminal defendant to have an attorney in any **felony or misdemeanor** case that might result in incarceration; if defendants are indigent, the court must appoint an attorney for them.

Right to die Rehnquist court ruling that individuals can refuse medical treatment, including food and water, even if this means they will die. Individuals must make their decision while competent and alert. They can also act in advance, preparing a "living will" or designating another person as a proxy to make the decision if they are unable to.

Right-to-own property The rights of individuals to own and work their private property.

Right to privacy A right to autonomy—to be left alone—that is not specifically mentioned in the U.S. Constitution, but has been found by the U.S. Supreme Court to be implied through several amendments.

Roberts Court The current Supreme Court under the leadership of Chief Justice John Roberts (2005–).

Rules Committee The committee in the House of Representatives that sets the terms of debate on a bill.

Sample A group of people who are surveyed. If the selection of the sample is random and large enough, their opinions should reflect those of the larger group from which they are drawn.

Scientific polls Systematic, probability-based sampling techniques that attempt to gauge public sentiment based on the responses of a small, selected group of individuals.

Scoops Leaks in information that enable reporters to break their stories before their competitors can report them.

Second Amendment "The right of the people to keep and bear arms." Some interpret this as an absolute right to own and use guns, others as only an indication that guns can be owned if one is part of a state militia.

Secret ballot A system of voting which protects the privacy of an individual's vote choice.

Seditious speech Speech that encourages rebellion against the government.

Selective perception The tendency to screen out information that contradicts one's beliefs.

Senate One house of Congress, where each state is represented by two members.

Senate Judiciary committee A Senate committee, charged, among other things, with recommending for or against presidential appointees to the federal courts.

Senatorial courtesy The custom of giving senators of the president's party a virtual veto over appointments to jobs, including judicial appointments, in their states.

Senior Executive Service The SES was created in 1978 to attract high-ranking civil servants by offering them challenging jobs and monetary rewards for exceptional achievement.

Seniority rule The custom that the member of the majority party with the longest service on a particular congressional committee becomes its chair; applies most of the time but is occasionally violated.

Separate-but-equal doctrine The principle, enunciated by the U.S. Supreme Court in *Plessy* v. *Ferguson* in 1896, that allowed separate facilities for blacks and whites as long as the facilities were equal.

Separation of church and state Constitutional principle that is supposed to keep church and state from interfering with each other. In practice it restricts government from major efforts either to inhibit or advance religion.

Separation of powers The principle of government under which the power to make, administer, and judge the laws is split among three branches—legislative, executive, and judicial.

Setting the agenda Influencing the process by which problems are deemed important and alternative policies are proposed.

Sexual harassment A form of job discrimination prohibited by the Civil Rights Act of 1964. Sexual harassment can consist of either 1) a supervisor's demands for sexual favors in exchange for a raise or promotion or in exchange for not imposing negative consequences; or 2) the creation of a hostile environment which prevents workers from doing their job.

Sharecroppers Tenant farmers who lease land and equipment from landowners, turning over a share of their crops in lieu of rent.

Shays's Rebellion A revolt of farmers in western Massachusetts in 1786 and 1787 to protest the state legislature's refusal to grant them relief from debt; helped lead to calls for a new national **constitution.**

Shield laws Laws that protect news reporters from having to identify their sources of information.

Signing Statements Written comments a president may attach to a law after signing it and sending it to the Federal Register for publication. Historically they have been used to indicate provisions in a law the president believes the federal courts may find unconstitutional. George W. Bush used them frequently to indicate sections of laws he would refuse to implement, thus setting up a conflict between the executive and legislative branches.

Single-issue groups Interest groups that pursue a single public interest goal and are characteristically reluctant to compromise.

Single-member districts Where only one individual is elected from a particular electoral district.

Sixteenth Amendment A Constitutional amendment giving Congress power to levy taxes on personal income.

Social choice An approach to political science based on the assumption that political behavior is determined by costs and benefits.

Social contract An implied agreement between the people and their government in which the people give up part of their liberty to the government in exchange for the government protecting the remainder of their liberty.

Social insurance A social welfare program such as **Social Security** that provides benefits only to those who have contributed to the program and their survivors.

Socialism An economic system in which the government owns the country's productive capacity—industrial plants and farms—and controls wages and the supply of and

demand for goods; in theory, the people, rather than the government, collectively own the country's productive capacity.

Social issue An important, noneconomic issue affecting significant numbers of the populace, such as crime, racial conflict, or changing values.

Social Security A social insurance program for the elderly and the disabled.

Soft money Contributions to national party committees that do not have to be reported to the federal government (and sometimes not to the states) because they are used for voter registration drives, educating voters on the issues, and the like, rather than for a particular candidate; the national committees send the funds to the state parties, which operate under less stringent reporting regulations than the federal laws provide.

Soft power The ability of a country to get what it wants through the attractiveness of a country's culture, political ideals, and policies rather than military or economic coercion.

Sound bite A few key words or phrase included in a speech with the intent that television editors will use the phrase in a brief clip on the news.

Southern strategy The strategy followed by the Republicans in the latter part of the twentieth century to capture the votes of southern whites.

Speaker of the House The leader and presiding officer of the House of Representatives; chosen by the majority party.

Special interest caucuses Groups of members of the House of Representatives and Senate who are united by some personal interest or characteristic; e.g., the Black Caucus.

Specialization An **informal norm** of Congress that holds that since members cannot be experts in every area, some deference should be given to those who are most knowledgeable about a given subject related to their committee work.

Special prosecutor A prosecutor charged with investigating and prosecuting alleged violations of federal criminal laws by the president, vice president, senior government officials, members of Congress, or the judiciary.

Spectacle presidency Term used to describe presidents who are mostly seen by the public as actors in public spectacles, stage-managed photo ops, featuring the president in a dramatically staged event or setting.

Spin What politicians do to portray themselves and their programs in the most favorable light, regardless of the facts, often shading the truth.

Split-ticket voting Voting a for a member of one party for one office and another party for a different office, such as for a Republican presidential candidate but a Democratic House candidate.

Spoils system The practice of giving political supporters government jobs or other benefits.

Stagflation The combination of high inflation and economic stagnation with high unemployment that troubled the United States in the 1970s.

Standing committees Permanent congressional committees.

Stare decisis Latin for "stand by what has been decided." The rule that judges should follow **precedents** established in previous cases by their court or higher courts.

"Star Wars" The popular name for former President Reagan's proposed space-based nuclear defense system, known officially as the Strategic Defense Initiative.

State-centered federalism The view that our Constitutional system should give precedence to state sovereignty over that of the national government. State centered federalists argue that that the states created the national government and the states are superior to the federal government.

States as laboratories The idea of states as places for policy experimentation.

States' rights The belief that the power of the federal government should not be increased at the expense of the states' power.

Statutes Laws passed by the legislative body of a representative government.

Steering The practice in which realtors promoted segregation by showing blacks houses in black neighborhoods and whites houses in white neighborhoods.

Straw polls Unscientific polls.

Stress and duress Also called "torture lite," this term refers to a wide variety of measures that constitute rough interrogation just short of serious physical injury.

Subcommittee bill of rights Measures introduced by Democrats in the House of Representatives in 1973 and 1974 that allowed members of a committee to choose subcommittee chairs and established a fixed jurisdiction and adequate budget and staff for each subcommittee.

Subgovernment A mutually supportive group comprising an **interest group,** an executive agency, and a congressional committee or subcommittee with common policy interests that makes public policy decisions with little interference from the president or Congress as a whole and little awareness by the public. Also known as an iron triangle.

Subpoena A court order requiring someone to appear in court to give testimony under penalty of punishment.

Suffrage The right to vote.

Sundown laws During the Jim Crow period in the South, laws adopted to require blacks to be off the streets by 10 P.M. as a way to maintain white supremacy.

Sunshine Act Adopted in 1977, this act requires that most government meetings be conducted in public and that notice of such meetings must be posted in advance.

Superdelegates Democratic delegates, one-fifth of the total sent to the national convention who are appointed by Democratic Party organizations, in order to retain some party control over the convention. Most are public officials, such as members of Congress.

Super Tuesday The day when most southern states hold **presidential preference primaries** simultaneously.

Superwaiver Blanket exemptions that free states from federal program standards and requirements and give them greater latitude to set standards and eligibility requirements. Has been applied to welfare programs.

Supplemental Security Income (SSI) A program that provides supplemental income for those who are blind, elderly, or disabled and living in poverty.

Supply-side economics The argument that tax revenues will increase if tax rates are reduced; on the assumption that more money will be available for business expansion and modernization. This in turn would stimulate employment and economic growth and result in higher tax revenues.

Supremacy clause A clause in the U.S. Constitution stating that treaties and laws made by the national government take precedence over state laws in cases of conflict.

Symbiotic relationship A relationship in which the parties use each other for mutual advantage.

Symbolic speech The use of symbols, rather than words, to convey ideas; e.g., wearing black armbands or burning the U.S. flag to protest government policy.

Tariff A special tax or "duty" imposed on imported or exported goods.

Tax deductions Certain expenses or payments that may be deducted from one's taxable income.

Tax exemptions Certain amounts deductible from one's annual income in calculating income tax.

Tax neutrality A tax policy that does not favor certain kinds of economic activity over others.

Teapot Dome scandal A 1921 scandal in which President Warren Harding's secretary of the interior received large contributions from corporations that were then allowed to lease oil reserves (called the Teapot Dome); led to the Federal Corrupt Practices Act of 1925, which required reporting of campaign contributions and expenditures.

Temporary Assistance for Needy Families (TANF) A program that provides income support for the poor; successor to Aid to Families with Dependent Children (AFDC).

Tenth Amendment Constitutional amendment stating that powers not delegated to the federal government nor prohibited to the states are reserved to the states and to the people. This amendment has generally not had much impact, though a few recent Supreme Court cases have referred to it.

Third party A political party established in opposition to two dominant parties, often advocating radical change or pushing single issues.

Three-fifths Compromise The decision of the **Constitutional Convention** that each slave would count as three-fifths of a person in apportioning seats in the House of Representatives.

Ticket splitting Voting for a member of one party for a high-level office and a member of another party for a different high-level office.

Title IX Equal Opportunity in Education Act that forbids discrimination on the basis of sex in schools and colleges that receive federal aid. The amendment was prompted by discrimination against women by colleges, especially in admissions, sports programs, and financial aid.

Tracking polls Polls in which a small number of people are polled on successive evenings throughout a campaign in order to assess changes in the level of voter support.

Trade association An **interest** or **pressure group** that represents a single industry, such as builders.

Traditionalistic political culture One in which politics is left to a small elite and is viewed as a way to maintain the status quo. See **individualistic** and **moralistic political cultures.**

Tragedy of the commons The concept that although individuals benefit when they exploit goods that are common to all such as air and water, the community as a whole suffers from the resulting pollution and depletion of resources; a reason for **regulation.**

Treason The betrayal of one's country by knowingly aiding its enemies.

Truth in labeling The requirement that manufacturers, lenders, and other business entities provide certain kinds of information to consumers or employees.

Turnout The proportion of eligible citizens who vote in an election.

Two-party system A political system like that in the U.S. in which only two parties have a realistic chance of winning most government offices. This system is rare among the world's other democracies.

Unanimous consent agreements Procedures by which the Senate may dispense with standard rules and limit debate and amendments.

Underdogs Candidates for public office who are thought to have little chance of being elected.

Unfunded mandates Federal laws that require the states to do something without providing full funding for the required activity.

Unified government One party controls both the White House and Congress.

Unitary executive A minority interpretation of Article II of the Constitution made by lawyers in the Bush administration that claims the president has sole power to direct the work of executive branch agencies, without interference from Congress or the federal courts. This interpretation is considered at odds with the conventional understanding of the checks and balances built into our system of three branches of government.

Unitary system A system in which the national government is supreme; subnational governments are created by the national government and have only the power it allocates to them.

United States Census A Census is a count, and a census of all U.S. inhabitants is done every ten years in years divisible by ten.

United States v. Nixon The landmark ruling which forced President Nixon to turn over tape recordings of Oval Office conversations to the Watergate special prosecutor. It established the principle that executive privilege cannot be used to withhold evidence of a crime.

Unreasonable searches and seizures Searches and arrests that are conducted without a warrant or that do not fall into one of the exceptions to the warrant requirement; prohibited by the Fourth Amendment.

Unscientific polls Unsystematic samplings of popular sentiments; also known as **straw polls.**

USA PATRIOT Act An act that expands surveillance of people within the United States passed after 9/11. (The title is an acronym for Uniting and Strengthening America by Providing Appropriate Tools Required to Intercept and Obstruct Terrorism.)

Veto power The president's constitutional authority to refuse to sign a law passed by Congress. Vetoes may be overridden by a two-thirds vote in each house of Congress.

Vietnam syndrome An attitude of uncertainty about U.S. foreign policy goals and our ability to achieve them by military means; engendered among the public and officials as a result of the U.S. failure in Vietnam.

Voter registration A process which requires voters to register their name and address before an election.

Voting Rights Act (VRA) A law passed by Congress in 1965 that made it illegal to interfere with anyone's right to vote. The act and its subsequent amendments have been the main vehicles for expanding and protecting minority voting rights.

War Powers Resolution A 1973 statute enacted by Congress to limit the president's ability to commit troops to combat without congressional approval.

Warren Court The U.S. Supreme Court under Chief Justice Earl Warren (1953–1969); an activist Court that expanded the rights of criminal defendants and racial and religious minorities.

Watergate scandal The attempt to break into Democratic National Committee headquarters in 1972 that ultimately led to President Richard M. Nixon's resignation for his role in attempting to cover up the break-in and other criminal and unethical actions.

Weber, Max German social scientist, author of pioneering studies on the nature of bureaucracies.

Whigs Members of the Whig Party, founded in 1834 by National Republicans and several other factions who opposed Jacksonian Democrats.

Whips Members of the House of Representatives who work to maintain party unity by keeping in contact with party members trying to ensure they vote for party-backed bills. Both the majority and the minority party have a whip and several assistant whips.

Whistleblower An individual employee who exposes mismanagement and abuse of office by government officials.

White primary A device for preventing blacks from voting in the South. Under the pretense that political parties were private clubs, blacks were barred from voting in Democratic primaries, which were the real elections because Democrats always won the general elections.

Whitewater investigation An investigation conducted by a **special prosecutor** into the activities of President Bill Clinton and Hillary Rodham Clinton in connection with an Arkansas land deal and other alleged wrongdoings.

Winner-take-all The outcome of an election where only one individual is elected from a district or state, the individual who receives the most votes. It is contrasted with multi member systems where more than one person wins seats in an election.

Wire services News-gathering organizations such as the Associated Press and United Press International that provide news stories and other editorial features to the media organizations that are their members.

World Trade Organization (WTO) Founded in 1995 to remove barriers to free trade and to mediate trade disputes between member countries. WTO policies are set primarily by consensus of its member countries, represented by their trade ministers. Its general council, to which all members belong, is empowered to resolve trade disputes.

Writ of *certiorari* An order issued by a higher court to a lower court to send up the record of a case for review; granting the writ is the usual means by which the U.S. Supreme Court agrees to hear a case.

Index